ANNUAL REVIEW OF PSYCHOLOGY

ANNUAL REVIEW OF PSYCHOLOGY

VOLUME 36, 1985

MARK R. ROSENZWEIG, *Editor*

University of California, Berkeley

LYMAN W. PORTER, *Editor*

University of California, Irvine

ANNUAL REVIEWS INC.   4139 EL CAMINO WAY   PALO ALTO, CALIFORNIA 94306 USA

ANNUAL REVIEWS INC.
Palo Alto, California, USA

International Standard Serial Number: 0066-4309
International Standard Book Number: 0-8243-0236-2
Library of Congress Catalog Card Number: 50-13143

Typesetting by Kachina Typesetting Inc., Tempe, Arizona; John Olson, President
Typesetting coordinator, Dennis Phillips

PRINTED AND BOUND IN THE UNITED STATES OF AMERICA

PREFACE

As our readers know, the fine contributions of our able, dedicated, and carefully selected authors determine the quality and value of this series. This proposition gained added force recently when we considered the prefatory chapters that were inaugurated in the *Annual Review of Psychology* (*ARP*) in 1979 and that will by next year have included seven such chapters—by Jean Piaget, Ernest R. Hilgard, Leona E. Tyler, Neal E. Miller, Paul Fraisse, Harriet L. Rheingold, and Anne Anastasi. We were intrigued to find that all five of the American authors of prefatory chapters had previously been authors of *ARP* reviews, although this had not been a criterion for their selection as authors of the prefatory chapters. In fact, these five authors have eight *ARP* reviews to their credit, in addition to their prefatory chapters. We probably should not have been surprised, because this small sample supports a generalization that the career of a productive American psychological investigator typically includes the contribution of an *ARP* review chapter.

Invitations to write a prefatory chapter go to distinguished senior scientists who have long been occupied with major themes of research. The invitations to these eminent psychologists encourage them to write about a topic of their own choice. Thus these prefatory chapters provide a depth of historical analysis that differentiates them from our typical review chapters. Most of the *Annual Reviews* in other disciplines also carry prefatory chapters, but they tend to be autobiographical in nature. Since there are other publications that provide autobiographical chapters by eminent psychologists, the Editorial Committee of *ARP* decided to seek thematic prefatory chapters instead.

It is good to welcome back Dr. Rheingold as author of the prefatory chapter for this volume. She and W. C. Stanley had coauthored the chapter on developmental psychology in Vol. 14 (1963). In her current chapter, Dr. Rheingold returns to a developmental theme, offering thoughtful and penetrating insights into the topic of development as acquisition of familiarity; in this discussion, novelty appears not to be the polar opposite of familiarity but as a separate variable.

The authors of our prefatory chapters are so well known and have received so many honors that it would be needless and invidious to offer detailed lists of examples of such recognition. We will make a single exception, however, to mention a recent award that is intimately related to the topic of reviewing. Since 1979 the National Academy of Sciences USA has given an annual James Murray Luck Award for Excellence in Scientific Reviewing. The award is named for Dr. Murray Luck, who founded the first *Annual Review* (of Biochemistry) in 1932 and who was for many years Editor-in-Chief of Annual Reviews Inc. The winner of the Award in 1984 was psychologist Ernest R.

(continued)   v

Hilgard. His citation praised his outstanding series of reviews in two quite different fields of research: (*a*) learning and conditioning, and (*b*) hypnosis. Two of his reviews of research on hypnosis appeared ten years apart in *ARP*, in Vol. 16 (1965) and in Vol. 26 (1975). (Now, after another ten years, the present volume contains a further review of research in hypnosis, this time by John Kihlstrom.) Professor Hilgard was also an active member of the Board of Directors of Annual Reviews Inc. for a long period, serving as Vice President from 1953 through 1955 and as President from 1956 through 1972.

In addition to the prefatory chapters, one other set of chapters stands somewhat apart from the main review chapters. These are the "Timely Topic" reviews of subjects that are not treated on a regular basis. These chapters are often written under a shorter deadline than the usual chapters so that they can reflect recent developments. In the present volume there are two special topic chapters: "Sex and Gender" by Kay Deaux, and "Health Psychology" by David Krantz, Neil Grunberg, and Andrew Baum.

Special mention of the prefatory and timely topic chapters is not meant to slight the review chapters on the Master List that form the core of each volume. As participation in the 1984 International Congress of Psychology again confirmed, psychologists around the world are grateful to *ARP* authors for their skillful and conscientious presentation and evaluation of research in psychology and related disciplines.

The wise choice of these authors is the task of the Editorial Committee at its annual meeetings. We regret that the 1984 meeting marked the end of the five-year term of Frances Graham. Her service to *ARP* was characterized by wide knowledge of psychology and psychologists, emphasis on the highest standards, and good humor.

M.R.R.
L.W.P.

Annual Review of Psychology
Volume 36, 1985

CONTENTS

(continued)

SOME ARTICLES IN OTHER *ANNUAL REVIEWS* OF INTEREST TO PSYCHOLOGISTS

From the *Annual Review of Anthropology,* Volume 13 (1984)

From the *Annual Review of Sociology,* Volume 10 (1984)

From the *Annual Review of Medicine,* Volume 36 (1985)

From the *Annual Review of Neuroscience,* Volume 8 (1985)

(continued) ix

Coming for 1986 . . .

CHAPTERS PLANNED FOR THE NEXT
ANNUAL REVIEW OF PSYCHOLOGY, Volume 37

ANNUAL REVIEWS OF		SPECIAL PUBLICATIONS
Anthropology	Medicine	Annual Reviews Reprints:
Astronomy and Astrophysics	Microbiology	Cell Membranes, 1975–1977
Biochemistry	Neuroscience	Cell Membranes, 1978–1980
Biophysics and Biophysical Chemistry	Nuclear and Particle Science	Immunology, 1977–1979
Cell Biology	Nutrition	
Earth and Planetary Sciences	Pharmacology and Toxicology	Excitement and Fascination
Ecology and Systematics	Physical Chemistry	of Science, Vols. 1 and 2
Energy	Physiology	
Entomology	Phytopathology	History of Entomology
Fluid Mechanics	Plant Physiology	
Genetics	Psychology	Intelligence and Affectivity,
Immunology	Public Health	by Jean Piaget
Materials Science	Sociology	Telescopes for the 1980s

For the convenience of readers, a detachable order form/envelope is bound into the back of this volume.

Harriet L. Rheingold

Ann. Rev. Psychol. 1985. 36:1–17

DEVELOPMENT AS THE ACQUISITION OF FAMILIARITY[1]

Harriet L. Rheingold

Department of Psychology, University of North Carolina, Chapel Hill,
North Carolina 27514

CONTENTS

In this paper I examine the development of behavior in terms of the increasing familiarity with objects, events, and skills that an individual acquires in the course of living. At first glance, no simpler attribute of experience than familiarity can be imagined. For like experience, familiarity is so pervasive and unremarkable as to seem simple. Yet what is now familiar was once novel, so that to define the one is to define the other, and the attribute of familiarity is then seen to be only deceptively simple. Familiarity, furthermore, like similarity, escapes notice, while novelty, like difference, arouses attention. That this is true is revealed by the much more common entry of novelty than of familiarity in the indexes of textbooks; reasonably so, on second thought, because so many entries could be subsumed under the heading of familiarity, especially in

[1]This is the sixth in a series of prefatory chapters written by eminent senior psychologists. For more information about this series, see the Preface to this volume.

1

developmental textbooks. In one book (Cofer & Appley 1967), however, the entry of familiarity said only "see also experience" (p. 944), showing an awareness on the part of the indexer of the usually obscured role of familiarity.

FAMILIARITY AND NOVELTY IN THE SERVICE OF DEVELOPMENT

The development of behavior, including mental processes, may be conceptualized as our becoming familiar with the world, the world inside us and outside. In development, the acquisition of knowledge and skills is a gradual process dependent on learning and remembering, and beginning with life—at birth, and even before—knowledge and skills continue to increase with living.

What is known, what is familiar, provides the basis for recognizing something as different, new, that is as novel. Learning is itself a process of the new becoming familiar for, in acquiring familiarity, novelty is being dissipated and rendered familiar. Every effort to gauge the effect of novelty, then, presupposes a condition of familiarity; indeed, familiarity may be conceived as the substratum. Thus, the familiarity and novelty of stimuli, events, experiences, together constitute a psychological variable by virtue of their relativity to the individual's past experience. These considerations lift familiarity from its obscurity, and emphasize its importance in delineating novelty.

Familiarity and novelty as attributes of experience, furthermore, transcend species and ages, and apply to all areas of behavior, whether motor, cognitive, or social and, for the human species, to all cultures. As they apply to all species of animals, they qualify as comparative in the psychologist's terminology, and as they apply at every age in their lives, they qualify as developmental. Their generality also warrants invoking the additional principle of biological adaptiveness because they bear on how organisms learn the dimensions of their environment and how they may survive in it.

Some Explanatory Notes

Here I treat two matters: the source of my interest in the topic and, second, some definitional problems.

In a study I conducted in 1954, I expected, on the basis of the literature, that infants in an institution who received a major part of their care from one person (the experimental group) would, following an increase in social responsiveness to that person, show discomfort and withdrawal at the appearance of a stranger; and that, in contrast, infants cared for by many different persons (the control group) would show no awareness of a stranger. The results were quite otherwise: The experimental children were more rather than less socially responsive to the stranger than were the control children, and furthermore they did not withdraw or show distress (Rheingold 1956). From that time until the present, in many of my studies and those of my students and colleagues, we have found infants and young children to be ready accepters of unfamiliar persons, both adults and peers, as well as active explorers of unfamiliar environments and objects (Rheingold & Eckerman 1969, 1970, 1973; Eckerman & Rheingold 1974; Ross et al 1972; Ross 1974; Ross & Goldman 1977a,b; Hay 1977). We also saw them during the second year of life sharing their toys with unfamiliar persons and helping those persons to complete household chores (Rheingold et al 1976; Rheingold 1982). Although the effect of the novel would thus appear to have been a continuing interest of mine over a span of many years, it was never clearly in focus, while the role of the familiar was only half seen. In time, however, I became aware of its generality past infancy in humans, of its applicability to other species, and of its power to order behavior by some simple and elementary principles.

But definitional problems abound. Shall we call the adjectives *familiar* and *novel* and their nouns *familiarity* and *novelty* dimensions, attributes, character-istics, or variables? According to English & English (1958) the terms *attribute* and *dimension* are synonyms, but dimension is "broader and is largely super-seding" attribute (p. 153); yet dimension implies some position in a quantitative series, and I doubt that we shall be able to estimate quantity. The term *variable* comes closer to my use: "any distinct function, aspect, attribute, or property that can change" (p. 578). Although I shall use all these terms, *variable* is preferred to bring the account into line with Berlyne's (1960) usage of novelty as a "collative" variable. (His other collative variables—complexity, conflict, uncertainty, and surprisingness—are related to novelty in many ways, but are not separately considered here.)

Then the variable of novelty, and familiarity, must apply to something, and in this paper that something includes a great many entities. The most general term would seem to be *stimulus,* but the entities encompassed include visual and auditory stimulus patterns, objects, persons, events, experiences, concepts and ideas, and skills of many kinds.

The terms *novel* and *familiar* also deserve scrutiny. For my purposes, the most appropriate of familiar's many meanings is "frequently seen or experi-enced" and of novel's is "new and not resembling something formerly known or used" (Webster 1983). However, under the entry *new* we find, of several synonyms, that novel applies to what is not only new but strange or unprece-dented. And the adjective *strange* includes, along with singular and unique, such other synonyms as peculiar, queer, and outlandish. Because of these latter connotations of the term strange, I prefer the terms *unfamiliar* and *unfamiliarity* to *novel* and *novelty,* but shall often use the terms novel and novelty for concordance with the psychological literature.

Dictionary definitions notwithstanding, I take familiar to apply to what has been seen or experienced without regard to its frequency. As for novel, in

Berlyne's (1960) words, here "we face a whole succession of snares and dilemmas" (p. 18). A year earlier, Bindra (1959) wrote, "What constitutes novelty? The answer to this question is not known. However, it is known that any stimulus pattern is novel only with respect to, and by virtue of, other stimuli to which the animal has been exposed in the past" (p. 233). Thus, a precise definition of novelty in terms of the stimulus characteristics of a situation is not sufficient without knowledge of the individual's past experience. Furthermore, any new stimulus must be similar in some respects to other things. "However bizarre a nonsense figure may be that is shown to a human adult, it must consist of lines, angles, and curves, such as he has seen on countless occasions. . . . When we come to new ideas or facts, which are expressed in familiar words arranged according to familiar grammatical form, the point is too plain to be worth laboring" (Berlyne 1960, p. 20).

Clearly, then, the variable of familiarity and novelty (assuming for the present that it does in fact constitute only a single variable) resides not in the object but in the observing individual's perception, which is always based on past experience. Its very relativity thwarts precise definition. The outside observer, the experimenter, is seldom if ever able to predict whether the individual will view a stimulus as novel or familiar, or how novel or familiar. Furthermore, even the perceiving subject is often scarcely aware, unless challenged, of whether an object or experience is familiar or novel. We have recourse, then, only to the behavior of the individual, and of course to the verbal report of older human subjects. The problem is further complicated because probably every experience coming our way is already an intermingling of the familiar and the novel.

These many considerations ought to persuade me that it is foolhardy to proceed beyond this point. Still, the difficulties provide the incentive. As I proceed, I shall draw the argument more often for the human subject than for the nonhuman, although the similarities are great.

THE ACQUIRING OF FAMILIARITY

From birth on, and even before, individuals in the course of daily living are becoming familiar with the world, the world outside the body and the world inside it. Although the process is most patent in the growing child, it continues throughout life. As each experience, once experienced, acquires a measure of familiarity, so all we come to know and all the skills we come to acquire have become familiar. The natural concomitant of living is the acquisition of familiarity.

Infants learn the sights and sounds of their environment. From the moment of birth, they hear the language they will gradually learn to understand and speak (Rheingold & Adams 1980). They learn that day follows night, and day comes again. They become familiar with the states of hunger, satiety, and fatigue, of distress and ease. They learn that blankets are soft and rattles are hard, that people come when they cry and speak when they vocalize, and in time they come to distinguish among these various persons. They begin to acquire and perfect their skills of ingesting food, of reaching, grasping, and releasing, and of interacting effectively with people. Even before they can locomote efficiently, they are learning the physical dimensions of their environment. They acquire expectancies, living to be sure in a changing but not entirely capricious world.

As children grow older, they learn the days of the week, the months of the year, their telephone numbers and addresses. They learn to count, to add, subtract, multiply, and divide, and to read and write. They learn what is expected of them at home, in school, and on the playground. They learn their gender roles and the roles assigned to mothers and fathers, big and little children, and babies.

And thus the process of acquiring familiarity continues, as portrayed through all the chapters of the textbooks in developmental psychology. To name only a few examples: Adolescents become accustomed to new physical changes in their bodies, as for their part do the elderly; parents adjust to the changing needs of their offspring, and of each other; we learn to play musical instruments and to read foreign languages; we solve crossword puzzles and prepare our income taxes; we find our way on land, sea, and now in space; we drive automobiles at great speeds on superhighways; and we build houses, bridges, skyscrapers, and lethal weapons. We learn appropriate social behavior for our culture and for the historical times in which we live, with their religious and ethical codes. We become William James's bundles of habits, unaware of them, once learned.

An additional note here calls attention to how what is now familiar was built up step by familiar step—whether by slow and small increments or by apparently large leaps. Piaget (1952) has set out in exquisite detail how through many successive stages the infant and child acquire knowledge about the world of things and their relationships in space, time, and causality. What is already known enables us to learn more and more, and so step by step we can trace the progression of skills required to write a letter, shoot a basket, cook a meal, or build a boat—to say nothing of social skills—each step an acquiring of familiarity, each now submerged in consciousness.

Let no one take offense at my labeling such dearly won knowledge, concepts, insights, and skills as *just* familiar; yet once won, the effort is forgotten, and they have become familiar. "No matter what the activity may be—learning the multiplication table, or how to drive a car, to speak intelligibly, or to sew—learning is a process of thinking and deliberation and trial and decision, but the *state of having learned* is the state in which one need think no longer" (Medawar 1957, p. 138).

Although the case has been drawn for human beings, the process of acquiring familiarity obtains for all other living creatures. In what follows, allowance must be made for the wide variations among organisms in the rest of the animal kingdom, and for variations even down to the level of species. In general, then, animals become familiar with their environment, themselves, their kin, and other organisms of their own or different species. They learn to walk, run, swim, or fly. They learn what to eat and what to avoid. They find a place to live and establish routes within their living space. They learn to evade predators, when to cooperate and when to compete in finding a mate, and remember where they stored food. At least birds and mammals learn who are their parents and in turn nurture their own young. And all acquire systems of communication.

The psychological processes of acquiring knowledge and skills I here equate with those of learnining. Despite many debates and schools of thought on the exact nature of the processes of learning, we deal with individuals who can pay attention and perceive; who can remember; who can associate events by contiguity and by the law of effect; who can discriminate and generalize; and many of whom can imitate. As psychologists continue their efforts to understand the processes of learning, less and less is mysterious about how both human beings and other animals become increasingly familiar with the physical and social world and with how they adapt themselves to its demands.

In summary, development, and more generally, living, is conceived as becoming familiar with the physical and social environment and with one's interactions with these worlds. What is already known, the accustomed, the stable, the bounds of living, provides not only the standard from which the new is perceived but also the basis for further learning.

THE UBIQUITY OF THE NOVEL

In the course of daily living, the novel comes willy-nilly; it awaits us around every corner. As each bit of knowledge is acquired, the ability to discern the novel is simultaneously acquired (see Bateson 1973 for a theoretical model). In George Eliot's words, "The beginning of an acquaintance whether with persons or things is to get a definite outline of our ignorance." It follows, then, that as more and more of the world becomes familiar, more and more can be recognized as unfamiliar. Familiarity supplies the ground, and the novel becomes figure against ground.

For many years I entertained the notion that everything must be novel to newborns. Now I see that newborns are new only to us who behold them for the first time, but for them, for whom so little is yet familiar, not much can be novel. Peter Stratton (personal communication) clarified this insight for me, but Piaget saw this long before either of us when he wrote, "It is a remarkable thing that the younger the child, the less novelties seem new to him" (1952, p. 196).

In classical studies to determine infants' perceptual and memorial abilities, the procedure of first habituating them to an oft-repeated stimulus pattern and then recording their response to a different one has a long history (Olson & Sherman 1983). Universally in these studies, the novel stimulus pattern, whether visual or auditory, restores the response to its initial level.

Studies aside, new sights, sounds, smells, and tastes assail the infant on all sides. As mothers and fathers lean over the crib, a wealth of different expressions pass over their faces, a multitude of different sounds issue from their mouths. These novel changes rung on familiar objects, arousing interest, expand the infant's knowledge. In fact, at the basis of all knowledge about the world lie the attempts of infants to incorporate new objects and new activities into what they already know, as Piaget (1952) has shown through all the stages of sensorimotor development. So far, this account makes explicit only a few of a myriad of new stimulus patterns, objects, and experiences to arise in the days, weeks, and months to come. I mention only new bodily sensations, new foods, new routines as the seasons change, and new toys. As important as anything that can be catalogued are the changing connections between the infants' behavior and the responses of familiar persons, parents, and siblings, as well as of unfamiliar persons entering their ken.

I turn now from infants to the parents who, for their part, are also daily faced by new behaviors of their offspring. As the parents adapt to the changes wrought by development, the infants' new behaviors—as well as the parents' own adjustments to them—become so familiar as to escape attention and thus merge into the ground, from which now new behaviors of their offspring become figure against ground. In the process, now the parent, now the child, becomes something of an enigma for the other.

Thereafter, and throughout life, daily living brings new experiences for the growing child, the adolescent, and for adults at all ages. The child enters school, the adolescent becomes a member of a peer group, the young adult enters the world of work, marries, has a baby, and moves to a new community. But all these major sources of novelty only override the countless minor sources of novelty, so numerous as to defy cataloguing. To leave aside the changes in the world of things and to attend to the world of people, consider only how one's behavior brings forth a different response from different persons and from the same person at different times. Then, living brings chance encounters, often of great consequence (Bandura 1982). As we live, we move with the times, with political changes and social movements. We acquire new ideas and theories, master new skills, hear new music, and appreciate new art forms. We learn new words and forever compose them in new arrangements. We invent, construct, and create.

To this brief sketch of the novelty that living brings must now be added the novel experiences brought about by just the absence of the familiar. Once accustomed to the persons and things in one's environment, and their positions in space, their absence also constitutes novelty. The very young child's response to the absence of the mother under certain circumstances has been movingly portrayed by Bowlby (1973), but at any age the absence of a privileged person disrupts behavior—absence by death, a disruption scarcely imaginable. And our behavior is also disrupted by the removal of far less consequential objects, such as the toaster's being in the shop for repairs. How perplexed were the shoppers when my supermarket saw fit to rearrange its wares!

Although so far I have written only of human beings, all other animals also encounter novelty in the daily round of their activities, both the appearance of novel objects and stimulus patterns and the absence or disappearance of familiar ones. They encounter novelty in forays from the mother, in foraging for food, in patrolling their routes, in making a home, finding a mate, and having offspring. The rains come for them, too. They have "a place system," that is, a memory of spatial relations within their environment, and "a misplace system" that signals the presence of a new object or the absence of an old one (O'Keefe & Nadel 1978). Laboratory studies document, for example, that the absence of familiar home cues disrupts learning in young rats (Smith & Spear 1978), that kittens are more distressed by the absence of their mother and siblings than of their home environment (Rheingold & Eckerman 1971), and that young monkeys, like human children, are upset by being separated from their mothers (Seay et al 1962).

What Is to Be Feared?

At this juncture I must examine the claim so often made that the novel is to be feared (e.g. Bowlby 1969, 1973). If the novel were in fact feared, we would still be lolling in our natal cribs. We would not have been able to proceed through Piaget's (1952) elementary stages of sensorimotor intelligence, for on every page of his account, it is the new that furthers development—with nowhere any mention of fear. Too, were the novel feared, the classical infant studies of habituation would have foundered. More generally, given the ubiquity of the novel, fear would disrupt our behavior at every turn.

Fear of the strange, and neophobia, the term attributed to rats, although simple and even dramatic concepts, gloss over too much. Here indeed is discrimination called for. First, careful inspection and slow approach, sometimes characteristic of a response to the novel, scarcely deserves the label of fear; in fact, Barnett (1963), in indexing neophobia in the rat, refers the reader to "avoidance behaviour," and consistently puts the term *fear* in quotation marks. Then, the novel comes in all sizes and shapes, and the common denominator for arousing fear would seem to be how the novel makes its appearance, especially in relation to the organism's past experience and present state. Abrupt and sudden appearances startle, whether the objects are familiar or strange. Of course I know how I could frighten a baby, but infants do not flee from unfamiliar persons who behave normally. Animals tend to avoid an unfamiliar object in a familiar setting, but only for a time. In general, given freedom to encounter the new, people—even infants—and animals eventually do; forced to encounter the new, they hold back, but even then not for long.

Counterbalancing the proposed fear of the unfamiliar is the very real fear that may be evoked by the familiar; indeed, some familiar objects, persons, animals, and events may be *known* to be harmful, or potentially so (I owe this observation to H. S. Ross). As everyday examples, I mention the hot stove, painful medical procedures, and the dog down the street who nips at one's heels. Furthermore, with increasing knowledge of the world, we come to fear the possibility of earthquakes and tornadoes, of war, famine, and pestilence, and of nuclear explosions. Once we accept that the familiar, the known, may also make us wary, the categorical statement that the novel is to be feared loses its special status. And when the word *strange* is used, as in "fear of the strange" or "fear of the stranger," we are in danger of prejudging the outcome or we are using the term to mean something more than new, novel, or unfamiliar (a point I made earlier), opening the door to such other synonyms of strange as peculiar, erratic, odd, queer, and outlandish.

In summary, living brings the new to us and all other animals. To cope with the new, we fall back on the familiar, on what is known. But the new experience "always causes the old framework to crack" (Piaget 1952, p. 265), and thus does development proceed.

Some Related Concepts

A number of concepts bear on the topic of familiarity and novelty, each of them related to one or more of the others. The concept of arousal (Hebb 1955), often based on physiological measures, has been invoked to underlie the response to novel events, but of course under certain circumstances the concept could as well be applied to the appearance of the familiar. The concept of arousal is related to Helson's (1964) level of adaptation, defined as a weighted mean of all past and present stimuli against which new stimulation is gauged, with stimuli below as well as above that level exerting positive effects on behavior. Then, the concept of varied stimulation (Fiske & Maddi 1961) deals with an organism's propensity to seek fresh stimulation, which could include the seeking of novel stimuli but does not rule out changes in already familiar stimuli. Related to this concept is Leuba's (1955) of optimal stimulation, specifying that organisms respond in such a manner as to increase stimulation when overall stimulation is low, and conversely to decrease stimulation when overall stimulation is high. I note that here, too, the increase in stimulation may be only changes in the amount of already familiar stimulation, although novel stimulation is not ruled out.

These concepts are closely related to the older and oft-invoked discrepancy hypothesis (Hebb 1949), an inverted U-shaped function specifying that such behaviors as attention, learning, pleasure, and fear are maximal at some intermediate level of stimulation. Piaget (1952) provides an example in describing the one-month-old infant who "looks neither at what is too familiar, because he is in a way surfeited with it, nor at what is too new because this does not correspond to anything in his schemata . . ." (p. 68). Given the difficulty of empirically specifying the dimensions of the variables (here, stimulation), the hypothesis is more descriptive than explanatory (Thomas 1971).

I come at last to the concept of exploratory and related behavior now generally acknowledged, but for many years a puzzle to theories of drives. Harlow (1953) stated that the key to human learning was motivation aroused by external stimulation, and then proposed a curiosity-investigatory motive to explain his infant daughter's behavior, as well as a curiosity-manipulative motive to account for his monkeys' persistent solving of puzzles. White (1959) argued effectively for competence as a powerful motive, which he recognized as similar to Woodworth's (1958) behavior-primacy theory. Curiosity, a term needing no definition, finds a place in more than Harlow's (1953) proposal, and its relation to these concepts requires only mention.

All these concepts are related not only to each other but also to the topic here of interest, the roles of familiarity and novelty in development. My brief treatment scants their importance, but although they run parallel to my argument at many points, at others they veer away from it.

THE PULL OF THE FAMILIAR

The familiar exerts a great attraction. We need consider only the concept of attachment most vividly described for infants' responses to the persons who nurture them—seeking to be near them, greeting their appearance with pleasure, and being disturbed by their absence (Bowlby 1958, 1973; Ainsworth 1973). Similar responses are very soon accorded other familiar persons, such as their siblings, relatives, and friends (Schaffer & Emerson 1964; Hartup 1983). This process by no means ends with infancy or childhood but continues throughout life, to include spouses, one's children, colleagues, and all persons with whom we share memories. We visit our parents and friends, and find the job made pleasant by associates in work. We telephone these people, write letters to those at distances (or used to), remember their birthdays, send them Christmas cards and enjoy the notes they include with theirs. In part, we go to conventions to see our friends. We become attached to places as well as to people. We establish routes from home to school or to work, and these seem the right and best ways to go.

The sights and sounds of childhood last a lifetime. The country is too quiet for the city-bred person; the city, too noisy, busy, and strange-smelling for the country-bred. The summer traveler to the land of the midnight sun rejoices in the accustomed darkness of night on his return home. Who cannot sympathize with Beret, fresh from the wooded mountains of Norway, who saw the plains of South Dakota as "a nameless, blue-green solitude, flat, endless, still, with nothing to hide behind" (Rölvaag 1927, p. 101)? The sound of anything like a foghorn never fails to transport me to my childhood bed as I lay awake listening to the ships in the New York harbor finding their way on a foggy night. More vividly expressed is Thomas Wolfe's (1934) account when he returned home as a grown man of how "Down by the river's edge . . . he heard the bell, the whistle, and the pounding wheel of the night express coming into town . . . and it brought him once more, as it had done forever in his childhood, its wild and secret exultation, its pain of going, and its triumphant promise of morning, new lands, and a shining city" (p. 146).

Familiar things, too, exert their appeal. Children become attached to blankets, dolls, and teddy bears. We harbor throughout life trinkets of no value except their early associations. When the British Railways Board decided to give electronic watches to its locomotive engineers, the rail workers union, "approaching this brave new world of timekeeping cautiously, opted for a traditional analog watch, the kind with hands, rather than a digital model" (*Wall Street Journal* 6 January 1984, p. 25). The tastes of childhood also persist. Religious taboos, learned early, often have lasting effects, and long after immigrants have learned the language and customs of the new country they continue to use the flavorings of their original cuisine (Rozin 1977).

I have only skirted the full panoply of evidence to show how great is the attraction of the familiar in our lives. Yet I cannot leave the topic without including the tenacity of beliefs, acquired early and indeed privileged and cherished, despite the efforts of teachers and scientific discoveries to modify them (e.g. McCloskey et al 1980). Against odds, the familiar is defended as right. How strong was the opposition to baby carriages because everyone knew that babies belonged in their mothers' arms! Dire indeed were the predictions of the harmful effects of trains on cattle and horses. Even more zealously guarded is our own familiar self-image, the centrality of one's own self, with its inner experiences and unique memories—a Proustian retrieval of the past melding with the present.

As great as the attraction of the familiar is among human beings, so it is among other animals. The phenomenon of imprinting in some young precocial birds provides one striking example (Lorenz 1937, Hess 1959, Bateson 1966). Many birds and mammals yearly travel long migration routes between feeding and reproductive sites. Salmon after traversing the vast reaches of the ocean return to spawn in their natal stream, based on their remembering over the many years of their travels the unique odor of that home stream, swimming "over barriers and waterfalls with rejection of tributary after tributary until the stream of origin is reached" (Hasler 1966, p. 142).

Laboratory studies show that rats acquired the food preferences of their mothers (Galef & Henderson 1972), and that kittens, raised with rats, protected them from strange kittens (Kuo 1930). Lambs came to prefer, and were disturbed by the absence of, dogs with whom they had been raised (Cairns 1966), and monkeys raised with different amounts of contact with peers preferred peers raised as they were, even if they were completely unfamiliar (Pratt & Sackett 1967).

Mere exposure has been proposed as the mechanism responsible for attractions between organisms and objects, and between organisms and organisms (Maslow 1937; Zajonc 1968, 1971). Indeed, just familiarity has been invoked to account for friendships. Yet even in mere exposure, and especially in repeated exposures, objects appear in certain settings and living creatures behave, and these accompanying events enrich the attractiveness of the association.

THE ATTRACTION OF THE NOVEL

It is not only that we encounter novel objects, stimulus patterns, and experiences at every turn, but that we also often behave to increase the likelihood of such encounters. We not only solve the problems brought to us by the novel but we set ourselves new problems to solve. Much of the psychological literature on human beings as well as on other animals supports these statements.

The literature on early infancy abounds with examples. Infants work to make interesting spectacles last and reappear (Piaget 1952). As soon as infants can locomote by any means they move away from their mothers, we say to explore the environment. Nothing could be more instructive than to watch a nine-month-old infant creep from its mother's side, cross a threshold, and enter an empty room, devoid of even pictures or mobiles, all in a never-before-encountered set of rooms in a university laboratory (Rheingold & Eckerman 1970). A favorite anecdote illustrating this proclivity of the very young child stems from the common observation of parents running after their children in crowded airports, a situation usually daunting to adults. In many years of studying now hundreds of infants and very young children, of course accompanied by their parents, I have yet to see one distressed by entry into our laboratory playrooms.

Since the relatively recent interest in exploratory behavior, and its concomitant behavioral state labeled curiosity (here defined simply as the desire to know), the topic has received a fair amount of interest in the psychological and ethological literature, in studies of infants, children, and animals, even though its status as a drive presents theoretical problems (see Some Related Concepts). Although any peregrination and a great deal of ordinary behavior could be conceived of as exploratory behavior, and we cannot tell by just looking at the actor, nevertheless there are now enough studies (reviewed by Archer & Birke 1983) and enough everyday observations to give credence to the behavior.

Infants look longer at novel stimuli and persons than at familiar ones. They, as well as older children, choose to play with new toys more often than with old ones (see review by Voss & Keller 1983), and in our laboratory Dale Hay (1977) saw infants follow a toy rather than their mothers, and an unfamiliar person as often as their mothers.

A casual scrutiny of everyday behavior would reveal the strong tendency of persons at all ages to seek new experiences, as though life itself did not bring sufficient novelty at every turn. We turn on the TV for new sights and sounds and our students tread the campus with Walkman earphones. We ski, scuba dive, and fly planes. We ride roller-coasters, seeking excitement while enjoying the imagined risks. Adults travel the far reaches of the world. Although Kant was reported never to have gone more than ten miles from his home and Thoreau declared that he had traveled much in Concord, we can assume that the attraction of new thoughts occupied them sufficiently. Just so, artists, philosophers, poets, and scientists set themselves new problems to solve, with no coercion but their own genius.

Does the familiar bore us? Even infants seem to fret if kept too long in one place and become all smiles when held to the window. The familiar is often not enough, and Berlyne writes of the torments of boredom. A recent advertisement in a local newspaper reads, "Do you sit home nights wishing you had somewhere to go, something to do . . . ? Well, here's how to turn boring nights into hours of pleasure. . . . Come join our club of adult men and women, all with a similar purpose, to enjoy life more through dancing. . . . Don't sit home another minute. . . ."

Animals, too, seek out the novel, although I cannot do as well in conjuring up their motives. How many infant hamsters, kittens, and puppies I have seen elude their mothers' compulsive attempts to carry them back to the nest! How else account for my observation in Caya Santiago of juvenile monkeys climbing tall trees to fling themselves into the pool below, or slyly sneaking up behind me to pull off my hat? Many years ago, at a pier in Bar Harbor I watched a young seal, enclosed in a crib, catch a feather on its nose, release it, watch it float down in the water, catch the feather on its nose just before it touched bottom, bring it to the surface, and repeat the process again and again. This observation provides the occasion to introduce the concept of play, which in all its human and animal manifestations deserves mention for its role in pursuing novelty for its own sake. Furthermore, in laboratory studies, rats try new routes in mazes (W. Dennis's "spontaneous alternation" 1939); monkeys work and rework mechanical puzzles (Harlow 1953), and open windows to view a toy train in motion or just another monkey (Butler 1954). For all animals in their native habitat, exploring their environment can be proposed as of adaptive significance, but it will be more difficult to propose categorically that they seek novelty for its own sake, apparent examples notwithstanding.

THE BLENDING OF THE FAMILIAR AND THE NOVEL

In our lives the familiarity and novelty of physical, social, and cognitive events are intricately interwoven. To consider familiarity I resort to considering novelty, and I cannot treat novelty without resorting to familiarity. To write of novelty I use our same familiar words, as Berlyne (1960) pointed out. To invent a metaphor I use only a novel connection between two known objects, events, or ideas. So, too, is the literature of imaginary, utopian, and anti-utopian worlds woven out of familiar elements; Polyphemus was a giant with one eye; Lemuel Gulliver encountered tiny people in Lilliput, in their small stature like Tolkein's hobbits; and Ursula LeGuin (1969) envisioned human beings who from time to time assumed the biological functions of either men or women. All are constrained by the familiar, as are a culture's myths, legends, and fables. It could not be otherwise, for the new is fabricated out of the old and there may be nothing new under the sun (although perhaps beyond it). As for our sciences and philosophies, there too we see that new theories are built on familiar knowledge; they are but conceptual leaps of reorganizing the old.

Now I turn to considering the affective properties of the variables of interest. Let us imagine a two-dimensional space containing an horizontal axis running from the familiar at the left to the novel at the right, and a perpendicular axis bisecting the first axis at midpoint that runs from pleasure at the top to distress at the bottom. Then, within the four quadrants of this space, each object, event, experience, or bit of knowledge is to be assigned a position. For example, this object is very familiar but gives little pleasure; that object, in contrast, just as familiar, gives much pleasure; and so on through a host of combinations. But psychological and physiological states come and go—fatigue, illness, boredom, and loneliness—and each powerfully alters the object's, event's, experience's, or idea's position in this hypothetical space. Weary of work, a person seeks novelty; weary in body, the familiar gives relief. In illness, the familiar foods of childhood soothe. The lonely American traveler in Paris or Rome goes just to sit in the American Express office. The child happy at camp cries when his parents come on visitor's day. No, we cannot place anything once and for all time on a fixed point in what has now become a hyperspace.

When a new, more spacious and modern library was recently opened on my campus, the students suddenly discovered an affection for the old library with its imposing columns, marble stairs, its dome and elegant chandeliers; they wrote nostalgically in the student newspaper of missing its traditional and formal air, never noticed until faced by the new. Similarly, Freeman Dyson wrote movingly in the *New Yorker* (13 February 1984) of the warmth and friendliness that Londoners experienced in the shelters of the underground stations during the Second World War, who today are left "with a persistent nostalgia, which sometimes hits them unexpectedly when they travel by underground and contemplate the platforms now stripped of bunks and of friendliness" (p. 116). Just so, the imaginative reconstruction of memories (Bartlett 1932) is jolted, when among a commingling of emotions people return after many years to their childhood homes; they seize with joy on recognizing the garden they played in (although shrunk by half from their childhood memory), while they are dismayed and confused by seeing changes or what they had forgotten.

Not two axes, nor ten or twenty, may be sufficient to fix our experiences or to contain the flux and tension of the familiar and novel in our lives.

CONCLUSION

The simple idea that motivated me to write this chapter, that the development of behavior could be conceived as the acquiring of familiarity, on analysis proved to be more complex than I had envisioned. The related idea that the novel is not necessarily to be feared, an idea based on my studies of infants and young children as well as on those of my colleagues, also proved to be too simple as I came to see its larger import for learning, and hence for development. Without the appearance of new stimulus patterns and experiences there can be no learning, and without knowledge acquired by familiarity, the new cannot be discerned. Not only then does the development of behavior require the functioning of both processes but preferences for the one or the other are also acquired simultaneously.

I came finally to question the oft-held proposition that familiarity and novelty define the ends of a single dimension or variable. In the first place, as familiarity—that is knowledge, including motor, social, and cognitive skills—increases, the possibility of recognizing the novel also increases, so that the farther point of that variable recedes indefinitely. The more we know, the more we know we do not know, a condition that obtains for more than scientists or writers of prefatory chapters. Then, the possibility exists that we are dealing not with one variable but with two, a variable of familiarity and another of novelty, because so many encounters contain an admixture of both. Consider only the effect of context—a familiar object in an unfamiliar setting, or the effect of psychological state—the appearance of a familiar person when one is distressed. The easy and taken-for-granted opposition of these terms in our language does not withstand examination. Familiarity and novelty each in its own way, and at times in combination, may therefore be conceived as important, if not powerful, determiners of behavior, and thus as fundamental for the processes of its development.

ACKNOWLEDGMENTS

I would like to dedicate this chapter to the late Dan Berlyne for his pioneering work in this field. I am grateful to Dale F. Hay, Don W. Hayne, and Hildy S. Ross for critical comments, and to Karen A. Donovan for bibliographic assistance.

Literature Cited

Ainsworth, M. D. S. 1973. The development of infant-mother attachment. In *Review of Child Development Research,* Vol. 3, ed. B. M. Caldwell, H. N. Ricciuti. Chicago: Univ. Chicago Press

Archer, J., Birke, L. I. A. 1983. *Exploration in Animals and Humans.* Berkshire, England: Van Nostrand Reinhold

Bandura, A. 1982. The psychology of chance encounters and life paths. *Am. Psychol.* 37:747–55

Barnett, S. A. 1963. *The Rat: A Study in Behaviour.* Chicago: Aldine

Bartlett, F. C. 1932. *Remembering, a Study in Experimental and Social Psychology.* Cambridge: Univ. Press

Bateson, P. P. G. 1966. The characteristics and context of imprinting. *Biol. Rev.* 41:177–220

Bateson, P. P. G. 1973. Preferences for familiarity and novelty: A model for the simultaneous development of both. *J. Theor. Biol.* 41:249–59

Berlyne, D. E. 1960. *Conflict, Arousal, and Curiosity.* New York: McGraw-Hill

Bindra, D. 1959. *Motivation, a Systematic Reinterpretation.* New York: Ronald

Bowlby, J. 1958. The nature of the child's tie to his mother. *Int. J. Psycho-Anal.* 39:350–73

Bowlby, J. 1969. *Attachment and Loss, Vol. I, Attachment.* London: Hogarth

Bowlby, J. 1973. *Attachment and Loss, Vol. II, Separation: Anxiety and Anger.* New York: Basic Books

Butler, R. A. 1954. Incentive conditions which influence visual exploration. *J. Exp. Psychol.* 48:19–23

Cairns, R. B. 1966. Development, maintenance, and extinction of social attachment behavior in sheep. *J. Comp. Physiol. Psychol.* 62:298–306

Cofer, C. N., Appley, M. H. 1967. *Motivation: Theory and Research.* New York: Wiley

Dennis, W. 1939. Spontaneous alternation in rats as an indicator of the persistence of stimulus effects. *J. Comp. Psychol.* 28:305–12

Eckerman, C. O., Rheingold, H. L. 1974. Infants' exploratory responses to toys and people. *Dev. Psychol.* 10:255–59

English, H. B., English, A. C. 1958. *A Comprehensive Dictionary of Psychological and Psychoanalytical Terms.* New York: Longmans, Green

Fiske, D. W., Maddi, S. R., eds. 1961. *Functions of Varied Experience.* Homewood, Ill: Dorsey

Galef, B. G. Jr., Henderson, P. W. 1972. Mother's milk: A determinant of the feeding preferences of weaning rat pups. *J. Comp. Physiol. Psychol.* 78:213–19

Harlow, H. F. 1953. Mice, monkeys, men, and motives. *Psychol. Rev.* 60:23–32

Hartup, W. W. 1983. Peer relations. In *Handbook of Child Psychology, Vol. 4: Socialization, Personality, and Social Development,* ed. E. M. Hetherington. New York: Wiley

Hasler, A. D. 1966. *Underwater Guideposts: Homing of Salmon.* Madison: Univ. Wis. Press

Hay, D. F. 1977. Following their companions as a form of exploration for human infants. *Child Dev.* 48:1624–32

Hebb, D. O. 1949. *The Organization of Behavior.* New York: Wiley

Hebb, D. O. 1955. Drives and the C.N.S. (Conceptual Nervous System). *Psychol. Rev.* 62:243–54

Helson, H. 1964. *Adaptation-Level Theory.* New York: Harper & Row

Hess, E. H. 1959. Imprinting. *Science* 130:133–41

Kuo, Z. Y. 1930. The genesis of the cat's responses to the rat. *Comp. Psychol.* 11:1–35

LeGuin, U. K. 1969. *The Left Hand of Darkness.* New York: Walker

Leuba, C. 1955. Toward some integration of learning theories: The concept of optimal stimulation. *Psychol. Rep.* 1:27–33

Lorenz, K. Z. 1937. The companion in the bird's world. *Auk* 54:245–73

Maslow, A. H. 1937. The influence of familiarization on preference. *J. Exp. Psychol.* 21:162–80

McCloskey, M., Caramazza, A., Green, B. 1980. Curvilinear motion in the absence of external forces: Naive beliefs about the motion of objects. *Science* 210:1139–41

Medawar, P. B. 1957. *The Uniqueness of the Individual.* New York: Basic Books

O'Keefe, J., Nadel, L. 1978. *The Hippocampus as a Cognitive Map.* Oxford: Clarendon

Olson, G. M., Sherman, T. 1983. Attention, learning and memory in infants. In *Handbook of Child Psychology, Vol. 2: Infancy and the Biology of Development,* ed. M. Haith, J. Campos. New York: Wiley

Piaget, J. 1952. *The Origins of Intelligence in Children,* transl. M. Cook. New York: Int. Univ. Press

Pratt, C. L., Sackett, G. P. 1967. Selection of social partners as a function of peer contact during rearing. *Science* 155:1133–35

Rheingold, H. L. 1956. The modification of social responsiveness in institutional babies. *Monogr. Soc. Res. Child Dev.* 21(2), Serial No. 63

Rheingold, H. L. 1982. Little children's participation in the work of adults, a nascent prosocial behavior. *Child Dev.* 53:114–25

Rheingold, H. L., Adams, J. L. 1980. The significance of speech to newborns. *Dev. Psychol.* 16:397–403

Rheingold, H. L., Eckerman, C. O. 1969. The infant's free entry into a new environment. *J. Exp. Child Psychol.* 8:271–83

Rheingold, H. L., Eckerman, C. O. 1970. The infant separates himself from his mother. *Science* 168:78–83

Rheingold, H. L., Eckerman, C. O. 1971. Familiar social and nonsocial stimuli and the kitten's response to a strange environment. *Dev. Psychobiol.* 4(1):71–89

Rheingold, H. L., Eckerman, C. O. 1973. Fear of the stranger: A critical examination. In *Advances in Child Development and Behavior,* ed. H. W. Reese, 8:185–222. New York: Academic

Rheingold, H. L., Hay, D. F., West, M. J. 1976. Sharing in the second year of life. *Child Dev.* 47:1148–58

Rölvaag, O. E. 1927. *Giants in the Earth.* New York: Harper

Ross, H. S. 1974. The influence of novelty and complexity on exploratory behavior in 12-month-old infants. *J. Exp. Child Psychol.* 17:436–51

Ross, H. S., Goldman, B. D. 1977a. Establishing new social relations in infancy. In *Attachment Behavior,* ed. T. Alloway, P. Pliner, L. Krames, pp. 61–79. New York: Plenum

Ross, H. S., Goldman, B. D. 1977b. Infants' sociability toward strangers. *Child Dev.* 48:638–42

Ross, H. S., Rheingold, H. L., Eckerman, C. O. 1972. Approach and exploration of a novel alternative by 12-month-old infants. *J. Exp. Child Psychol.* 13:85–93

Rozin, P. 1977. The significance of learning mechanisms in food selection: Some biology, psychology and sociology of science. In *Learning Mechanisms in Food Selection,* ed. L. M. Barker, M. R. Best, M. Domjan. Waco: Baylor Univ. Press

Schaffer, H. R., Emerson, P. E. 1964. The development of social attachments in infancy. *Monogr. Soc. Res. Child Dev.* 29(3), Serial No. 94

Seay, B., Hansen, E., Harlow, H. F. 1962. Mother-infant separation in monkeys. *J. Child Psychol. Psychiatry* 3:123–32

Smith, G. J., Spear, N. E. 1978. Effects of the home environment on withholding behaviors and conditioning in infant and neonatal rats. *Science* 202:327–29

Thomas, H. 1971. Discrepancy hypotheses: Methodological and theoretical considerations. *Psychol. Rev.* 78:249–59

Voss, H.-G., Keller, H. 1983. *Curiosity and Exploration, Theories and Results.* New York: Academic

Webster's Ninth New Collegiate Dictionary. 1983. Springfield, Mass: Merriam-Webster

White, R. W. 1959. Motivation reconsidered: The concept of competence. *Psychol. Rev.* 66:297–333

Wolfe, T. 1934. *You Can't Go Home Again.* New York: Harper

Woodworth, R. S. 1958. *Dynamics of Behavior.* New York: Holt

Zajonc, R. B. 1968. Attitudinal effects of mere exposure. *J. Pers. Soc. Psychol. Monogr. Suppl.* 9(2):1–27

Zajonc, R. B. 1971. Attraction, affiliation, and attachment. In *Man and Beast: Comparative Social Behavior,* ed. J. F. Eisenberg, W. S. Dillon, pp. 143–79. Washington DC: Smithsonian Inst.

Ann. Rev. Psychol. 1985. 36:19–48
Copyright © 1985 by Annual Reviews Inc. All rights reserved

LATENT STRUCTURE AND ITEM SAMPLING MODELS FOR TESTING

Ross E. Traub and Y. Raymond Lam

Department of Measurement, Evaluation and Computer Applications, The Ontario Institute for Studies in Education, Toronto, Ontario M5R 1V6, Canada

CONTENTS

Test theory is the branch of psychometrics devoted to the quantitative analysis of test responses and test scores. In preparing this review of recent work on test theory, we surveyed the literature published in English during the three years from January 1980 to December 1982. From this we discerned that a trend apparent through the 1970s has continued into the 1980s. Fifteen and more years ago, research was focussed primarily on classical reliability theory and its near relative, generalizability theory. During the past decade, however, research has concentrated to an ever increasing extent on latent structure and item sampling models. We devote the whole of this review to these models and related applications.

    The models considered here have been developed principally for use with tests composed of dichotomously scored items. Moreover, these models have typically been applied in situations where ability or achievement is tested. In

19

this we reflect the dominant interests of persons currently working on test theory and of their clients.

The order of material is as follows: First, latent structure analysis is introduced. Then, the most important subclass of latent structure models, that referred to as item response theory, is considered. Latent class models, which also come under the umbrella of latent structure analysis, are covered next, but more briefly. Finally, we consider recent work on item sampling models.

LATENT STRUCTURE ANALYSIS

Latent structure analysis is a theoretical framework for modelling categorical variables, such as those defined by typical ability and achievement test items. It is addressed to tests composed of a number of items, say n in total. The responses given by an examinee to the test items comprise the examinee's response pattern. There are 2^n different possible response patterns for a test composed of n dichotomously scored items.

The basic assumption of latent structure analysis is that each examinee in a population may be characterized by his or her score on one unobserved latent variable or more, such that in a subpopulation of examinees, each with the same score on each latent variable, responses to the items in the test are mutually statistically independent. This states in words the assumption of local independence; it can be expressed mathematically as follows:

$$p(\mathbf{u}|\boldsymbol{\theta}) = p(u_1|\boldsymbol{\theta} \cdot p(u_2|\boldsymbol{\theta}) \cdot \ldots \cdot p(u_n|\boldsymbol{\theta}), \tag{1.}$$

where $\mathbf{u}$ is the response pattern of an examinee, u_i is the dichotomously scored response of the examinee to the ith item, $\boldsymbol{\theta}$ is the vector of the examinee's scores on the latent variables, $p(\mathbf{u}|\boldsymbol{\theta})$ is the conditional probability of the response pattern, and $p(u_i|\boldsymbol{\theta})$ is the probability of the response, either zero or one, to item i given the examinee's scores on the latent variables. Equation 1 expresses the probability of an examinee's response pattern in terms of separate probabilities for the items in the test.

The objective of latent structure analysis is to obtain from the observed response patterns of a sample of examinees (*a*) estimates of quantities that characterize the items in the test or (*b*) estimates of quantities that characterize the examinees or (*c*) estimates of both. These quantities are the parameters of the conditional probabilities, $p(u_i|\boldsymbol{\theta})$.

A distinction is drawn between two types of latent structure models, those for item response theory (IRT) and those for latent class analysis (LCA). The basis of this distinction lies in the presumed nature of the distribution of $\boldsymbol{\theta}$ in the population of examinees. This distribution is taken to be continuous for IRT and discrete for LCA. Thus, IRT is appropriately considered for psychological tests of ability or attitude, in which examinees in a population are viewed as being distributed continuously over the underlying latent variables. Latent class analysis, on the other hand, is appropriate for those situations in which examinees are viewed as falling into only two, or at most a very few distinct groups. This might be the case, for example, in testing for mastery.

Item Response Theory

Our consideration of developments in IRT is organized under four main subheadings—models, estimation, assessment of misfit, and applications.

MODELS   A particular item response model is defined by an assumption as to the mathematical form of the conditional probability function, $p_i (\theta) = p(u_i = 1|\theta)$. Thus, $p_i (\theta)$ defines the probability of a correct response to an item (indexed by i), given a set of latent ability scores (denoted by θ). When there is only one latent trait and items are dichotomously scored, this function is known as the item characteristic curve (icc). The icc defines the regression of the observed scores for an item on the single latent trait θ.

The popular models for unidimensional IRT are the one-, two-, and three-parameter logistic models. The two-parameter logistic icc can be written as follows:

$$p_i (\theta) = 1/\{1 + \exp[-a_i (\theta - b_i)]\}, \qquad\qquad 2.$$

where a_i and b_i are parameters associated with item i. Under certain assumptions, these item parameters can be related to the conventional indices of item discriminating power and item difficulty (Lord & Novick 1968, Chap. 16). It is common practice to refer to a_i as the item discrimination parameter and b_i as the item difficulty parameter.

What is known as the one-parameter or Rasch model can be derived from Equation 2 by setting the discrimination parameter, a_i, equal to one. Thus, items suited to the Rasch model should all possess the same discrimination parameter.

The third of the popular IRT models is the three-parameter logistic model. In addition to parameters for discrimination and difficulty, it includes a parameter that limits the probability of answering an item correctly to a value greater than zero for examinees of low ability. This model can be stated as follows:

$$p_i^t(\theta) = c_i + (1 - c_i)p_i(\theta), \qquad\qquad 3.$$

where $p_i(\theta)$ is defined by Equation 2. The third item parameter, c_i, is loosely referred to as the guessing parameter, although it is more accurately described as the lower-asymptote parameter. This model has obvious a priori validity for multiple-choice items.

The one- and two-parameter IRT models have been extended by expressing item difficulty or person ability as a linear combination of parameters associated with item or person characteristics other than the trait of the IRT model. To see how this might work for item difficulty, suppose that matrix items are cross-classified according to features of physical appearance and solution rule. Then a question that can be addressed is whether or not the difficulty parameter for an item can be reproduced, hence explained, as the sum of parameters associated with the item's features. Fischer has extended the Rasch model in this way (e.g. Fischer 1983). Practical applications are reviewed by Fischer & Formann (1982). An extension of the two-parameter model was described by Reiser (1983), who worked with data from a survey of educational achievement. Reiser expressed IRT ability as a combination of parameters associated with the demographic and personal characteristics of the examinees in a cell of the survey sampling frame. An application of this model to data collected in the U.S. National Assessment of Educational Progress was reported by Mislevy et al (1981).

Our discussion of models has so far applied only to dichotomous items. Another class of unidimensional models, in which item responses are recorded on a Likert scale, was developed by Andersen (1980), Andrich (1982), Masters (1982), and Wright & Masters (1982).

The assumption of unidimensionality seems inappropriate for many kinds of test data, especially those pertaining to tests of educational achievement (Traub 1983, Traub & Wolfe 1981). Models that can include more than one latent trait are needed to investigate the dimensionality of a set of items.

It is a straightforward matter to write a multidimensional version of Equation 2:

$$p_i = F[a_i'(\theta - b_i)], \qquad 4.$$

where F is the cumulative normal or logistic function, and a_i, b_i, and θ are vectors of order k, with k being the number of underlying traits or dimensions.

In practice, it is computationally impossible to estimate all the item and person parameters of a multidimensional model. One way to make the model tractable is to add simplifying assumptions about the item parameters. Stegelmann (1983) took this approach with a multidimensional version of the Rasch model. Stegelmann required that the investigator specify a priori which of the latent traits in the set of k traits are measured by an item. (This can be done by setting the elements of vector a_i in Equation 4 equal to one—trait measured—or zero—trait not measured.) Also, he assumed that each trait contributes the same amount to the difficulty of an item, in which case items differ in difficulty only if they involve a different number of traits. Stegelmann's restrictions preclude exploratory analysis for the purpose of deciding whether or not a set of items measures more than one trait.

Developments suggestive of a multidimensional Rasch model have been reported by Whitely (1980, 1981). She analyzed complex tasks (e.g. verbal analogies) into subordinate tasks, and constructed items to measure each subtask. Separate Rasch models were then fit to the items for each subtask. Whitely's objective was to see whether or not the probability of a correct response to an item of the complex task could be reproduced by multiplying together the Rasch iccs for the items of the corresponding subtasks. A drawback to this approach is that it does not include a test of whether the latent abilities defined by the subtasks are different from one another and from the ability measured by the complex task.

Work on multidimensional models extends beyond the framework of the Rasch model. Bock & Aitkin (1981) have reported successful implementation of a multidimensional version of the two-parameter model. Also promising are adaptations of (linear) factor analysis for use with dichotomously scored items. Developments of this kind were reported by Bartholomew (1980), Christoffersson (1975), McDonald (1967, 1980), and Muthén (1978, 1982). (Note that the multidimensional models described in this paragraph do not contain the separate components of difficulty defined in Equation 4. Instead, an overall indicator of difficulty, which may be viewed as the vector product $\mathbf{a}'_i\mathbf{b}_i$, is included in the model.)

All the work on multidimensional models noted thus far has been directed at the analysis of responses to dichotomously scored items. Thissen et al (1983) redressed this imbalance to the extent of showing how to use restricted linear factor analysis to fit an IRT model to attitude or personality items for which responses are recorded on a Likert scale.

ESTIMATION   In IRT models the probability that an examinee answers an item correctly depends on characteristics (parameters) of both the item and the person. It is these parameters that are to be estimated from item responses. A standard estimation strategy is to work with the likelihood function for a set of item responses. For dichotomously scored items, this function is the product over examinees of the probabilities defined in Equation 1, when these probabilities are considered functions of the parameters. The desired parameter estimates are those that make the likelihood function a maximum. An implementation of this approach is found in BICAL (Wright & Mead 1976), a program for fitting the Rasch model; another implementation, this in modified form so that omitted responses are treated differently from incorrect responses, is found in LOGIST, a program for fitting the one-, two-, or three-parameter model (Wingersky 1983).

An important fact about the popular IRT models is that as the number of observations increases, through increases in the number of examinees or the number of items or both, the number of parameters to be estimated also increases. A problem with the method of maximum likelihood estimation under this condition is that there is no guarantee that as the number of examinees is increased the estimates of an item's parameters converge to their true values. (For discussion, see, for example, Andersen 1973a, 1980; Haberman 1977; Lord & Wingersky 1982.)

Another problem arises in estimating the parameters of the three-parameter model. The results of Monte Carlo work by Thissen & Wainer (1982) indicate that the guessing parameters of easy items cannot be estimated accurately. Furthermore, Lord & Wingersky (1982) found that the errors incurred in estimating item parameters are correlated. Together, these findings imply that any imprecision in the estimation of the guessing parameter will affect the estimates of discrimination and difficulty.

An alternative to a maximum likelihood estimation procedure is the Bayesian estimation procedure of Lindley & Smith (1972). Swaminathan (1983) has described how to use this procedure to estimate the parameters of the popular one-, two-, and three-parameter models. Before estimation begins, the analyst must supply so-called prior information about the distributions of the item and person parameters. Provision of this prior information yields the following benefits: (a) The Bayesian approach gives estimates of ability for examinees who answered all the items either correctly or incorrectly, and it provides estimates of difficulty for items that were answered either correctly or incorrectly by all examinees; and (b) the Bayesian approach keeps the estimates of parameters within reasonable bounds without the need for fix-up procedures. (Fix-up procedures are required in estimating the item parameters of the two- and three-parameter model using the method of maximum likelihood.) A limitation of this Bayesian approach is that the analyst is unable to include any prior information he/she may possess about differences in the relative difficulty of the items. Swaminathan & Gifford (1982) were successful in using this method to estimate the parameters of the Rasch model.

Instead of estimating item and examinee parameters jointly, as in the foregoing procedures, we can estimate only the item parameters. A partial likelihood function is used for this, a function that contains only the item parameters. The estimates of the item parameters are those that maximize the partial likelihood function. A well-known method of this kind is conditional maximum likelihood (Andersen 1973b) for the Rasch model. Although computationally demanding, conditional maximum likelihood estimation has now been implemented in a program that will handle perhaps as many as 100 items (Gustafsson 1980a, Wainer et al 1980).

What is known to statisticians as integrated maximum likelihood (Fraser 1979) offers a way of forming a partial likelihood function for any of the popular unidimensional IRT models. If a weighting function (e.g. a standard normal distribution) for each examinee's ability parameter is introduced into the likelihood, then it is possible to integrate over ability and obtain a function that contains only item parameters. Bock & Lieberman (1970) and more recently Bock & Aitkin (1981) and Thissen (1982) applied partial likelihood procedures to the one- and two-parameter IRT models. This method is programmed in BILOG (Mislevy & Bock 1982b), which will estimate the parameters of any of the popular unidimensional models.

A factor-analytic approach can be used to fit both unidimensional and multidimensional versions of the one- and two-parameter IRT models. Here it is assumed that underlying the observed dichotomous variable for an item is an unobservable continuous variable, and that the joint probability distribution of these unobservable variables is multivariate normal. The unobservable item variables are expressed in the factor model as linear functions of the latent trait(s) underlying the items. The problem is to estimate the parameters of the factor model given only the manifest item response data, which is dichotomous. One solution to this problem is described by Lord & Novick (1968, Chap. 16). It involves fitting the factor model to estimates of the tetrachoric intercorrelations among the unobservable (continuous) item variables. A well-known problem with this approach is that the matrix of tetrachoric correlation coefficients for a sample of examinees is not necessarily positive definite. Christoffersson (1975) used tetrachoric functions directly, and thus did not have this problem. McDonald (1982) used his (1967) orthogonal polynomial analysis to the same effect.

A disadvantage of the factor-analytic approach is that it effectively constrains the icc to have a zero lower asymptote. In other words, it is not possible to estimate a lower-asymptote parameter even when it would be appropriate to do so, as in the analysis of responses to multiple-choice items. Carroll (1945) showed that tetrachoric coefficients may give misleading factor-analytic results when items can be answered correctly by guessing. The application in this case of an ad hoc suggestion due to Samejima for correcting the tetrachoric correlation coefficients is recommended by Green et al (1982). Estimates of the lower-asymptote parameter are needed to implement this procedure, hence the adequacy of the correction would seem to depend on the accuracy of the estimates.

The use of robust methods to estimate ability parameters when the item parameters are known has been considered by Jones (1982a,b), Mislevy & Bock (1982a), and Wainer & Wright (1980). The essential idea of robust ability estimation is that the greater the difference between an observation and its expected value under the model, the less weight that observation is given in the estimate of ability. Robust estimates of ability should be better than maximum likelihood estimates because they are less subject to the influence of a few extreme responses. (An example of an extreme response would be an incorrect answer to an easy item by an examinee who had answered many difficult items correctly.) Not surprisingly, however, results presented by Wainer & Wright suggest that, when a model correct for the data is used, the correlation between known ability parameters and robust estimates of those parameters is no higher than the correlation between the known ability parameters and maximum likelihood estimates of the parameters.

It is clear from the foregoing review that several techniques are available for fitting the popular unidimensional IRT models and that factor-analytic approaches are available for fitting a (possibly) multidimensional IRT model. There is as yet no convincing evidence that one method is generally preferrable to another. Indeed, when a model has been fit to a set of data by different methods, any difference in estimates associated with a difference in methods has been too small to be of practical consequence (see, for example, Bock & Aitken 1981).

ASSESSMENT OF MISFIT   One of the advantages of IRT models is that they are falsifiable. This means, according to Lord (1980a), that ". . . it is possible to make various tangible predictions from the model and then to check with observed data to see if these predictions are approximately correct. One substitutes estimated parameters for true parameters and hopes to obtain an approximate fit to observed data" (p. 15).

The most elementary indicator of misfit is the residual difference between the observed item score for an examinee and his/her expected item score under the model. This is an example of what we will refer to as a first-order indicator of misfit. Second- and higher-order indicators can also be defined. A second-order indicator would be based on the difference between observed and expected performance on items taken in pairs. Third- or higher-order indicators would involve residuals for combinations of three items or more.

The most widely used measures of misfit for the popular IRT models are first-order indicators. Some of these resemble Pearsonian chi-square statistics. Indicators of this kind have been proposed by Martin-Löf (cited in Gustafsson 1980b, p. 213) and Wright & Panchapakesan (1969) for the Rasch model, and by Bock (1972) for the two-parameter model. To this armamentarium has been added an index, Q_1, by van den Wollenberg (1982a,b) for the Rasch model, and another by Yen (1981) for either the one-, two-, or three-parameter model.

Other first-order indicators of misfit are likelihood-ratio statistics. Best known of these is Andersen's (1973b) conditional likelihood-ratio statistic for the Rasch model. Waller (1981) proposed another such statistic, one that can be used with either the one-, two-, or three-parameter model. This ratio measures the extent to which the likelihood under the restricted hypothesis (that the proportion of correct answers in a subgroup all of the same ability is given by the model) is different from the likelihood under the unrestricted hypothesis (that it is any proportion, including the one observed).

The importance of considering the dimensionality of a set of test items in assessing the fit of an IRT model is widely recognized, but the question of what to take as evidence of multidimensionality has yet to be answered in a way that is widely accepted by IRT analysts of different theoretical persuasions. McDonald (1981) supplied a compelling answer that starts from Spearman's conception of the unidimensional linear factor model for quantitative variables. McDonald reminds us that this conception extends to nonlinear IRT models for dichotomous item variables and that the dimensionality of a set of items is the number of components needed in θ to satisfy the assumption of local independence. (See Equation 1 and related discussion.) An implication of this definition of dimensionality is that, when a unidimensional model has been fit to item response data, variation in the size of the item discrimination parameters—these are analogous to factor loadings in linear latent trait theory (factor analysis)—is not indicative of multidimensionality. Thus, the fact that a Rasch model fails to fit the items in a test due to variation in slopes of the iccs—first-order indicators of misfit are sensitive to this kind of variation—is an inappropriate basis for concluding that a set of items is multidimensional.

Another implication that flows from McDonald's (1981) analysis is that evidence of multidimensionality should be sought in a second- or higher-order indicator of misfit. Hattie (1981), Smith (1980), and van den Wollenberg (1982a,b) demonstrated that first-order indicators of misfit are insensitive to multidimensionality as McDonald defined it. Use of a second-order indicator makes it possible in principle to determine whether or not a one-dimensional model satisfies the weak form of the principle of local independence, that responses to pairs of items, conditional on the latent trait, are uncorrelated. This fact has been recognized in recent work on the Rasch model. Van den Wollenberg (1982a,b) has proposed the use of Q_2, a second-order analogue of Q_1. The results of a Monte Carlo study indicated that Q_2 was sensitive to multidimensionality when Q_1 was not.

Second-order misfit statistics have yet to be devised for the two- and three-parameter IRT models. It is worth noting, however, the ingenious application of a first-order indicator of misfit in which the investigator divides the items into subgroups hypothesized to measure different latent abilities, computes the value of the indicator for each item subgroup, and compares the sum of these values over item subgroups to the value of the indicator for the total group of items. This application has been made to reveal multidimensionality; see Goldstein (1980) for a demonstration. Also, McDonald (1981) noted that it is possible, and easy, to compute the residual inter-item covariance matrix after a fixed effects model has been fit to a set of item responses. This matrix would seem to offer a rational basis for a decision as to dimensionality.

An alternative route to assessing the dimensionality of a set of item responses is to take a factor-analytic approach to the fitting of an IRT model. Available procedures for this yield residual joint-proportions or residual tetrachoric correlation coefficients; these are second-order indicators of misfit. The generalized least-squares approach to estimation used by Christofferson (1975) and

Muthén (1978) also provides an overall measure of second-order misfit in the form of a chi-square statistic. Whether it is residuals or chi-square statistics that are inspected, these procedures make it possible to compare the fit of a model with, say, one dimension to the fit of a model with one dimension more. This comparison provides a basis for judging whether the added dimension substantially improves the fit.

Ideally, the assessment of misfit should not stop at the use of first- and second-order indicators. Just as a first-order indicator can suggest that a model fits when a second-order indicator reveals that it does not, so a second-order indicator can suggest that a model fits when a third- or higher-order indicator would not. As is the case in factor analysis, however, we may be willing to rest content if the second-order requirement is satisfied. A challenge of the times is to obtain second-order misfit statistics for use with the two- and three-parameter IRT models, and then to elevate the standard of practice in IRT analysis to the point where second-order evidence of misfit is obtained routinely.

The discussion thus far has presumed that our objective is to falsify an IRT model for the responses to a set of items. Another objective is frequently pursued, the identification of items that do not fit the model. For what seems an obvious reason, this is an important issue for analysts committed to the Rasch model. The assumptions of the Rasch model are more stringent than those of the two- and three-parameter models, hence it is more difficult to produce items fitting the Rasch model than to produce items fitting a less restricted model. The indices of item misfit that have been proposed for the Rasch model include the Pearsonian chi-square statistics mentioned previously; the index for an item is the contribution that the item would make to the index for the complete test. Other first-order indices of item misfit are described by Gustafsson (1980b), van den Wollenberg (1982a,b), and Wright & Stone (1979).

Quantitative measures of item misfit, such as item chi-square statistics, may fail to reveal the way in which the data for a misfitting item depart from the theoretical icc. This information is important for understanding why an item misfits and for deciding whether to discard the item or revise it in an effort to make it conform to the model. Gustafsson (1980b) showed for the Rasch model how supplementary plots of observed versus expected proportions of correct answers for subgroups of examinees can reveal (a) when an item is more or less discriminating than the theoretical icc, and (b) when the empirical icc approaches a nonzero lower asymptote, contrary to expectation. In addition, it would be nice to have a misfit statistic that could be used in comparing the fit of the Rasch model to an item with the fit of the two- or three-parameter model. This would provide an empirical basis for choosing among the one-, two-, and three-parameter models, and supplement such logical considerations as that the Rasch and two-parameter models are inappropriate for multiple-choice items because they do not provide a lower-asymptote parameter. It seems that Yen's (1981) fit statistic could be used in this way.

An argument can also be advanced for trying to identify misfitting examinees. In the context of responses from many examinees, those of a particular examinee may be poorly modelled. For example, the examinee may respond incorrectly to a number of easy items, but, unexpectedly, respond correctly to some difficult items.

Two interesting approaches to the detection of aberrant examinee response patterns have been reported in the recent literature. One of them, dubbed appropriateness measurement by Levine & Rubin (1979), involves the use of IRT. The notion, not the label, is well established in the literature on the Rasch model (Wright & Stone 1979). Levine & Rubin (1979) defined appropriateness measures that can be used with the one-, two-, or three-parameter IRT model. The easiest of their indices to describe is l_0, the natural logarithm of the contribution made by the response pattern of a given examinee to the likelihood of all the data. This index should be small for aberrant patterns. The performance of this and two other indices was investigated by Drasgow (1982), Levine & Drasgow (1982), and Levine & Rubin (1979). It appears (a) that these indices are "robust to errors in estimation of item parameters, to inclusion of unidentified [aberrant response patterns] in the test norming (calibration) sample and to violations of the three-parameter logistic model" (Levine & Drasgow 1982, p. 53); (b) that indices based on the three-parameter logistic model work better than corresponding indices based on the Rasch model; and (c) that the indices are better at detecting examinees with spuriously high total test scores than at detecting examinees with spuriously low total scores.

The second approach to the detection of aberrant examinee response patterns is to compute what are known as caution indices. This approach does not require that an IRT model be fit to the data. Instead, caution indices are based on the sequence of correct and incorrect answers in a response pattern. When items are arranged in sequence according to some criterion, these indices measure the extent to which a response pattern with a given number of zero item scores departs from the ideal answer pattern (Walker 1931); an ideal pattern has the same number of zero item scores, but all the item scores of one precede all the item scores of zero. The question arises as to how the criterion sequence of items should be determined. Sato (see, for example Harnisch & Linn 1981) established it from the average performance of the group of examinees who were tested. When an examinee has been assessed repeatedly by the same test or by tests that are parallel item for item, the criterion order can be based on the examinee's average performance (Tatsuoka & Tatsuoka 1982).

The potential utility of caution indices for detecting examinees who have employed wrong response rules in answering arithmetic questions was demonstrated by Tatsuoka & Linn (1983) and Tatsuoka & Tatsuoka (1982). Other empirical work, in which a number of diagnostic indices have been computed on the same data and compared, was reported by Drasgow (1982), Harnisch & Linn (1981), and Harnisch & Tatsuoka (1983). Research on this topic is still too sparse, however, to form an adequate basis for conclusions as to which index, or indeed which type of index, should be preferred for specified kinds of item response data.

We cannot leave the matter of assessing misfit without mentioning two well-known problems with all statistical measures of IRT misfit: (a) Their sampling distributions for samples of realistic size are unknown, and (b) statistical tests of misfit increase in power as the amount of data collected increases. In view of these problems, can any comfort be derived from the fact that IRT models are falsifiable? We answer this question affirmatively provided it is possible to work with nested models. Then there exists a rational basis for comparing the fit of a basic model (e.g. the Rasch model) against the fit of a more complex model (e.g. the two-parameter model or a two-dimensional model).

The foregoing emphasis on indicators of misfit is not to deny the important role that can and should be played by substantive theory in deciding whether or not a model is appropriate for the data. In this connection, it is appropriate to call attention to the work of Birenbaum & Tatsuoka (1982, 1983). They found that the conclusion that would be drawn about the latent structure underlying a set of item responses changed substantially when adjustments were made to examinee responses for which there was evidence, based on a substantive theory of the response process, that correct answers had been obtained through the application of incorrect response rules. A change in less than 6% of the item scores (from correct to incorrect) affected several statistics, including the inter-item correlation coefficients; these tended to increase in value, and those that had been negative became positive. Thus, the adjustments changed the data set from one that did not satisfy Holland's (1981) second-order requirement for the fit of a unidimensional IRT model for abilities (that all inter-item correlation coefficients are positive) to one that did.

APPLICATIONS OF IRT   Several practical applications of IRT have been made or suggested. Limited by space, we consider only three—the equating of tests, the assessment of item bias, and the method of computerized adaptive testing.

Test equating   The purpose of test equating is to define a table of equivalent scores such that an examinee's observed score on one test can be reported in terms of the score he/she would be expected to earn on a second (equated) test of the same characteristic(s). Equating is a necessary part of any testing program in which different tests of the same ability or domain of achievement are constructed from time to time.

An important contribution to the literature on equating during the period under review is the volume edited by Holland & Rubin (1982). Useful in the present context is a paper from that volume by Morris (1982) in which the concepts of strong and weak equating are defined. According to Morris, *"Two tests are* strongly equated *if every individual in the test population has the same probability distribution for [his/her test] score on both tests. . . . Two tests are* weakly equated *if each individual in the population has the same expected score on both tests"* (p. 171, emphasis in the original). The first of these accords with Lord's (1980a) definition, and implies that tests have been equated when it is a matter of indifference to the examinee which is administered. This is not an easy condition to satisfy. The tests must measure identically the same attributes, otherwise an examinee should prefer the test that measures his/her best qualities. Moreover, the tests should measure with equal reliability; otherwise, as Werts et al (1980) noted, the able examinee should prefer the most reliable test on the grounds that it is most likely to yield an observed score near his/her true score, and the weak examinee should prefer the least reliable test on the grounds that it is most likely to yield an observed score very much different from and, if luck would have it, very much higher than his/her true score.

In general, as Lord (1980a) and Morris (1982) have shown, tests cannot be equated in the sense of Morris' strong definition. The alternative is to equate in the sense of Morris' weak definition, a sense that is satisfied by true score equating. Conventionally, this is accomplished by equating standard scores of the estimated true score distributions. When IRT is used, the equating is done either on the scale of the latent trait, as recommended by Wright & Stone (1979), or on the estimated true score scale of each test (Lord 1980a). Estimated true score equating provides a basis for IRT pre-equating, which involves equating a new test, i.e. a collection of items not yet administered as a test, to an old test (Bejar & Wingersky 1982, Marco 1977). Estimates of the IRT parameters of the items in the new test are required, and must be obtained in pretesting experiments.

Tests that do not measure the same attributes cannot be equated meaningfully any more than instruments measuring height and weight can be equated meaningfully. Until recently, however, the practitioner has lacked an easily implemented technology for testing the null hypothesis that true scores on two tests are perfectly (linearly) correlated. Rock (1982) and Werts et al (1980) have shown how to test this hypothesis using available computer programs for the analysis of covariance structures. If one of the models of congeneric test theory (Jöreskog 1971) can be shown to fit test data, then this kind of analysis yields the parameters needed for linear true score equating. As yet, few practitioners have exploited this technology. (See Bejar & Wingersky 1982 for an exception.)

A question of continuing interest is whether one method of equating is generally better than another. Cook & Eignor (1983) reviewed much of the recent research on this question. It appears that linear equating methods work well when tests are approximately equal in difficulty; when they are not, curvilinear equating methods, including IRT methods, are required (Petersen et al 1982). We have been reminded by Goldstein (1982), however, that the question of which equating method is best is impossible to answer because there exists no true equating against which to judge different methods. Thus, when different methods are compared, considerations based on theory or common sense must serve to establish reasonable expectations for an accept-able equating. Investigators who have brought relevant considerations to light include Jaeger (1981), who defined and evaluated five indices that should indicate when a linear equating has successfully adjusted ". . . for differences between score distributions of two approximately parallel test forms" (p. 25), and Divgi (1981), who showed us how to look systematically and hard for biases in an equating, however it has been done. Divgi's work is especially important in that it appears to have resolved an issue that occupied a lot of journal space in recent years—whether or not the Rasch model can provide an acceptable equating of tests composed of multiple-choice items when the tests differ in difficulty. It cannot.

The question arises of what to do if tests measure more than one attribute and the attributes are represented to different extents in different tests. (If the attributes were represented equally in each test, then a covariance structure analysis would not necessarily reveal that the tests were multidimensional because each examinee would have the same true score on each test.) Morris (1982) demonstrated that tests like this can be weakly equated provided attribute subscores are equated separately before they are combined into a total test score.

Recent advances have been made on two technical matters that bear on equating. One is the matter of choosing a metric for the latent ability scale when a set of items has been administered to independent groups of examinees; this occurs in the anchor-test design for equating studies. If the IRT model is correct, then the ability scales in independent calibrations of the same items should be linearly related, except for the effects of estimation errors; also, the means and standard deviations of the estimated difficulty parameters of the common items can then be used to estimate the parameters of the linear transformation needed to take the metric of the scale for one group into the metric of the scale for the other group. Robust methods for doing this, methods that weight the difficulty estimates of items inversely according to their dis-tance from the transformation line, have been proposed by Bejar & Wingersky (1982), Cook et al (1979), Linn et al (1981) and Stocking & Lord (1983). All these methods are deficient, however, in that they ignore information contained in the parameters for discrimination and guessing, if one or both of these are needed in the IRT model. Procedures not subject to this deficiency have been proposed by Divgi (1980), Haebara (1980), and Stocking & Lord (1983). These procedures employ the icc, which is defined by all the item parameters in the model.

The second technical matter is that of estimating the standard error of an equating. Lord (1982a,b) provided estimates for the standard errors of equipercentile and IRT equating, and compared them with the standard error of linear equating. An important conclusion supported by Lord's comparison studies is that the standard error of an equating, however done, is small relative to the standard error of measurement of the test.

Item bias   To begin, we need a definition of item bias. Shepard et al (1981) are especially clear: "an item is biased if two individuals with equal ability but from different groups do not have the same probability of success on an item" (p. 319). In other words, what we are seeking in a study of bias is evidence of an interaction between item performance and group membership when ability differences between the groups have been controlled.

Three general approaches to the assessment of item bias can be distinguished. They differ in the way examinee ability is controlled. In one approach, bias is defined in terms of the extent to which proportion correct statistics (p-values) or transformed p-values for an item differ by more than would be expected, this expectation being based on the major axis of the plot of the p-values or transformed p-values for one group against those for the other group. (See, for example, Angoff & Ford 1973, Plake & Hoover 1979, Sinnott 1982.) Note that examinee ability is not directly controlled in this approach. In another approach, total test score is used as the measure of ability. Marascuilo & Slaughter (1981), Mellenbergh (1982), and Scheuneman (1979) propose contingency table analysis with intervals on the scale of the total test score defining one dimension of the table. Also in this category is Stricker's (1982) index, the partial correlation between score on an item and group membership, with total test score serving as the control for examinee ability. The third approach is based on IRT. These measures of item bias reflect an aspect of the difference between an item's iccs for different groups. Ironson (1983) has prepared an extensive review of indices based on IRT. A limitation of all three approaches is that ability is defined by the items being investigated for bias, hence there is an element of circularity in the logic of bias assessment by these means.

Ortiz & Searls (1982) were critical of item bias indices for another reason, that they do not rest on sound statistical theory. Ortiz & Searls pointed out that the approach based on item p-values or transformed p-values does not include distributional theory for the distance measure used as the indicator of bias. This criticism also applies to most IRT measures of bias. The contingency table approach was criticized on the grounds that the classification of examinees according to total test score is done a posteriori, which results in a violation of ". . . the assumption of random sampling, since factors other than chance are influencing the results" (p. 2).

Despite their limitations, there is reason to think that IRT indices and those based on the analysis of a contingency table are sensitive to bias. Rudner et al (1980) simulated data in accordance with the three-parameter IRT model, and introduced several kinds of bias. Not surprisingly, indices based on the three-parameter IRT model gave best results, with a contingency table method about as good. Application of various indices to real data (Ironson & Subkoviak 1979, Shepard et al 1981) also suggests that an index based on the three-parameter IRT model performs well. In this context the study by Subkoviak et al (1984) is noteworthy. These investigators included items that had been so constructed as to be biased in a test of vocabulary, and found that an index of bias based on the three-parameter model was highly correlated with whether or not the item was biased by construction.

Despite all this good news about bias detection, there is reason to temper optimism with caution. As Novick (1980) points out, indices based on unidimensional IRT models can be expected to work only when the assumption of unidimensionality is satisfied. If the test is multidimensional, then IRT bias indices should not be expected to distinguish traits that the test is intended to measure from those that are irrelevant and indicative of bias.

Computerized adaptive testing   If the measure of an examinee's ability is an estimated IRT parameter, then it is neither necessary nor efficient to have each examinee respond to the same items. Instead, each examinee should respond to only those items in a pool of calibrated items that are both matched in difficulty to the examinee's ability and most highly discriminating. Computerized adaptive testing is an implementation of this idea. The first step in a computerized adaptive testing program is to estimate the parameters of the items in a pool. Assume this is done using the three-parameter model. Examinees are then tested as follows: An arbitrarily chosen small set of items (e.g. two) is administered to obtain a provisional estimate of an examinee's ability. This estimate is used to select from those items remaining in the pool the one that will provide the most information about the examinee's ability. This will be the item that has the highest discrimination parameter of those with difficulty equal or near to the examinee's provisional estimate of ability. This item is administered and the ability estimate is updated. The procedure of choosing an item, administering it, and updating the ability estimate is continued until either a predefined number of items has been given or a prespecified minimum for the standard error of the estimate of ability has been reached.

Simulation studies (Lord 1980b) show that computerized adaptive tests can provide equally precise measurement across the range of ability, something that conventional tests cannot do. Moreover, these studies show that computerized adaptive tests can provide measurement as precise as that provided by conventional tests for any level of ability, and do so with fewer items.

The alternate-forms coefficient of reliability has been used in empirical work to compare the measurements provided by a computerized adaptive test with those provided by a conventional test. Kreitzberg & Jones (1980) and Martin et al (1983) found that a computerized adaptive test requires fewer items than a conventional test to achieve the same alternate-forms coefficient of reliability. But this coefficient does not reflect the average over the sample of examinees of the error variances associated with the ability estimates. (This average should be lower for a computerized adaptive test than a conventional test.) The marginal reliability coefficient suggested by Green et al (1982) does reflect this average. (The marginal reliability index is obtained by computing the average over examinees of the squared standard error of the IRT estimate of ability for each examinee, dividing this average by the variance of the IRT estimates of ability, and subtracting the result from one. Note that there is no guarantee that the marginal reliability index will lie in the range zero to one inclusive.)

It is important in computerized adaptive testing to have accurate estimates of the item parameters; the statistical rules for selecting items, for deciding when to stop testing, and for estimating the examinee's ability depend on these parameters. Only recently, however, have there appeared reports about the bias and precision of maximum likelihood estimates of the item parameters of the three-parameter model. Lord (1983) found that estimates of discrimination are biased positively and those of difficulty are biased negatively, although the size of the bias in each case is small. Thissen & Wainer (1982) studied the precision of item parameter estimates. They found that for any of the popular IRT models the standard errors associated with the parameter estimates are large for items with low difficulty parameters or low discrimination parameters or large guessing parameters; they also found that the size of a standard error increases with the complexity of the model. These results imply that if items with extreme parameter estimates are included in the pool, then the ability estimates of examinees who are administered these items will also have large standard errors.

Perhaps a focus on the accuracy of item parameter estimates is misplaced, at least for some intended uses of computerized adaptive testing. Ree (1981) obtained a correlation coefficient of 0.927 between estimated and true ability parameters, even though the correlations between estimated and true item parameters were approximately 0.2 for guessing, 0.7 for discrimination, and 0.9 for difficulty, and the standard errors of the item parameter estimates were large. Despite inaccuracies in the estimates of the item parameters, it seems that computerized adaptive testing can very successfully rank order examinees according to ability.

Wainer (1981) suggested an interesting departure from the strategy of computerized adaptive testing as it has been described. He distinguished between the item screening and the operational phases of such a testing program, and suggested use of the three-parameter model in the screening phase and the Rasch model in the operational phase. During the screening phase, items would be eliminated if they had small discrimination parameters or large guessing parameters or both. Since the items that remained after screening would vary relatively little in the value of their discrimination parameters, Wainer would arbitrarily set these parameters to the same value for the operational phase of testing. This would eliminate any tendency during the operational phase to select items for which the discrimination parameter had been overestimated. (Such a tendency would result in premature termination of testing, especially for examinees of extremely high or low ability.) Wainer argued that the guessing parameter should be ignored during the operational phase for the reason that most of the items administered to an examinee would be neither too difficult nor too easy. Under this condition, guessing would be of less concern than if the items were much too difficult for the examinee. To guard against the effect of departures in the item pool from the one-parameter Rasch model, Wainer advocated the use of a robust estimator of ability. A Monte Carlo study seems needed to evaluate Wainer's suggestion.

Latent Class Analysis

In LCA, it is assumed that the distribution of examinees on the latent variables is discrete, in other words, that the population of examinees can be sorted into two or more mutually exclusive and exhaustive latent classes. Recently, psychometricians with an interest in education have paid considerable attention to LCA for the reason that it seems an attractive model by which to try to account for student achievement of an imaginable kind. A student in possession of this kind of achievement would be able to answer correctly any member of a well-defined universe or domain of test items, whereas a student not in possession of this achievement would be unable to answer correctly any items in the domain. This is the kind of achievement that could be described appropriately as mastery of the domain of items.

The basic equations of latent class analysis define the probabilities of a correct and an incorrect response to an item given the examinee's class membership. Consider, for example, the mastery learning case, which involves only two classes, that for masters with $\theta = M$ and that for nonmasters with $\theta = \bar{M}$. For a randomly chosen examinee who responds to a dichotomously scored item, the probability that the observed item score, u_i, is 1 or 0 given that the examinee's latent class is M or $\bar{M}$, may be specified as follows:

$$p(u_i = 1 \,|\, \theta = M) = 1 - \beta_i,$$
$$p(u_i = 0 \,|\, \theta = M) = \beta_i,$$
$$p(u_i = 1 \,|\, \theta = \tilde{M}) = \alpha_i,$$
$$p(u_i = 0 \,|\, \theta = \tilde{M}) = 1 - \alpha,$$

5.

where the item parameters α_i and β_i are probabilities. Interpreted for the mastery testing case, the number α_i is the probability that someone from the latent class of nonmasters responds correctly in any event, as by guessing the answer to a multiple-choice item. The number β_i is the probability that an examinee from the class of masters responds incorrectly, perhaps through carelessness.

The objective of LCA is two-fold: to use the response patterns of a sample of examinees (a) to obtain estimates of the item parameters α_i and β_i, and (b) to assign each examinee to one of the latent classes, and in the process to estimate the proportion of examinees in the population who are masters. The latter objective can be accomplished either to minimize the probability that an error of classification is made or to minimize the cost of such errors (Macready & Dayton 1977).

The model as presented will not be identified if examinees respond to only two items. Then it is necessary to restrict the item parameters α_i and β_i in order to produce an identified model. Emrick (1971) suggested making $\alpha_i = \alpha$ and $\beta_i = \beta$ for all items. These restrictions imply that the probabilities of the two kinds of response errors, that for answering correctly when the examinee is not a master and that for answering incorrectly when the examinee is a master, are the same for all items. Other restrictions that might be imposed include making $\alpha_i = \beta_i$ for each item or setting $\beta_i = 1$ for all items (Macready & Dayton 1980a). A computer program that provides maximum likelihood estimates of the parameters of identified latent class models has been prepared by Dayton & Macready (1977).

More complicated versions of LCA have been suggested for the validation of learning hierarchies (Gagné & Paradise 1961) or of any hypothesized arrangement of two or more domains of items. To take the simplest possible case, suppose that two domains of items have been defined. It might be hypothesized that domain I precedes domain II in the sense that persons who can answer items from domain II correctly are necessarily able to answer items from domain I correctly, whereas persons who can answer items from domain I correctly are not necessarily able to answer items from domain II correctly. This hypothesis leads to the prediction that persons tested on items representing both domains should fall into one of three groups: (a) those who can perform none of the items, (b) those who can perform only items representing domain I, and (c) those who can perform items representing both domains.

White & Clark (1973) apparently were first to devise a method for fitting this hierarchical model and testing the null hypothesis that the proportion of examinees who can correctly answer items from domain II and not from domain I is zero. Owston (1979) recently offered an improved method, one that avoids the need to impose such restrictions as that examinees who have mastered domain I invariably will respond correctly when asked to answer an item from this domain. (White & Clark imposed this restriction when examinees had been tested with only two items from each domain.)

LCA theory for hierarchies of more than two item domains was presented by Dayton & Macready (1976). When the hypothesized hierarchy is complex, the associated model may not be identified. To circumvent this problem, should it arise, Macready & Dayton (1980b) devised a two-stage estimation procedure. When following this procedure it is necessary to have each examinee respond to more than one item per domain. Sufficient information then exists to calculate, in the first stage of the procedure, the parameter estimates needed in the second stage.

Most prospective users of hierarchical LCA will have a hierarchy in mind when they begin their data analyses. In the event, however, that an investigator is engaged in exploratory work, Price et al (1980) described forward and backward selection procedures for choosing, for the domains of items under consideration, those hierarchical arrangements of latent classes of masters and nonmasters that are consonant with the data.

Van der Linden (1978, 1979) has expressed dissatisfaction with LCA. He argued that, at least in educational applications, an IRT approach is more appropriate than an LCA approach for the reason that school learning involves the gradual (continuous) acquisition of knowledge. A sufficient response to van der Linden would be a list of references to research in which the LCA model has been shown to apply. We are in no better position to provide such a list than was McDonald (1967), who asked "How often will a latent class case be discovered in empirical data, which is nontrivial theoretically?" (pp. 108–9). The empirical answer to McDonald's question is that the discovery of a latent class case has not been reported very often. Perhaps the problem is that we have not been precise enough in defining item domains; items drawn from a mixture of several domains would likely yield response data indistinguishable from data commensurate with an IRT model. (The IRT model might have to be multidimensional.) It may also be the case that too little effort has been expended on LCA. In this connection, we note the success that Haertel (1984) reported recently in applying LCA to reading comprehension items.

ITEM SAMPLING MODELS

One approach to the task of describing an item sampling model is to compare its main purpose with that of latent class analysis. As applied to testing for mastery, a purpose of LCA is to estimate the proportion of examinees in a population who are masters of the items in a specified universe or domain. The main purpose of an item sampling model is to estimate the proportion of items in a universe or domain that an examinee can answer correctly from knowledge.

There is a duality to the latent class and item sampling models. Thus, a theoretical framework for item sampling can be formed by interchanging persons and items in the framework for LCA. When this is done in Equations 5, we obtain expressions for four conditional probabilities. Two of these define the probabilities that an examinee answers an item correctly on the one hand, incorrectly on the other, given that it is from the latent category of items that the examinee "knows." The other two conditional probabilities pertain to answers to items from the latent category of items that the examinee "does not know." Given these basic conditional probability statements and independence of item responses, it is possible to write conditional probability statements for a fixed examinee's responses to a sequence of randomly chosen items. As described, the model includes three parameters: (*a*) the probability, say α, that the examinee correctly answers an item from the latent category of items not known, (*b*) the probability, say ß, that the examinee incorrectly answers an item from the category of known items, and (*c*) the proportion, say ζ, of items in the domain that the examinee knows. It is not possible to estimate all three parameters from only the information contained in an examinee's response pattern (of zero and one item scores). Other steps must be taken to produce an identified model.

One way to achieve an identified model is to deny the possibility that the examinee answers an unknown item correctly or a known item incorrectly, that is, to assume that $\alpha = ß = 0$. This assumption might be appropriate for constructed response items. The estimator of ζ is then the proportion of items answered correctly. This model was considered by Lord & Novick (1968, Chap. 11).

Setting α, the probability of correctly answering items in the unknown category, to zero seems unreasonable for multiple-choice items. Several investigators, including, during the period under review, van den Brink & Koele (1980) and Wilmink & Nevels (1982), have relaxed this restriction and assumed instead that $\alpha = 1/R$, where R is the number of response options to each multiple-choice item. It is improbable, however, that α should be the same for all examinees, and at that exactly equal to $1/R$.

Wilcox (1979a, 1981b) proposed two other ways of restricting the item sampling model, both of which allow for individual differences in the probability of correctly answering items from the category of unknown items. The first of these rests on the supposition that every item in the domain can be cloned to produce at least one equivalent item, such that if the item is a member of the latent category of known (or unknown) items, its clone or equivalent item is also a member of that category. Assume now that when an item is selected at random from the domain, its equivalent is also selected. Administration of a pair of eqivalent items will yield one of four response patterns: both items correct, the first correct and the second incorrect, the first incorrect and the second correct, and both incorrect. The observed relative frequency of each response pattern can be computed from an examinee's responses to a sample of item pairs. With parameter ß set to zero, these relative frequencies contain sufficient information for estimating α and ζ (Wilcox 1979a); ß can be estimated too if it is possible to produce equivalent items in sets of three or more.

The idea that an element of knowledge or ability can be represented in a pair or a triplet of items that are different in some sense but that have the same level of difficulty seems dubious, at least for many domains of content (Molenaar 1981). Fortunately, equivalent items are not required in the second of Wilcox's ways of restricting the item sampling model. He discovered (1981b) how to use the answer-until-correct (A-U-C) technique for this purpose. According to this technique, if the examinee's first response to a multiple-choice item is incorrect, then he/she makes a second response to the same item. Moreover, the examinee continues responding until the correct response has been chosen. The underlying response model that Wilcox offers for this is similar to that proposed by Horst (1933). Specifically, if we define $\zeta \equiv \zeta_{R-1}$ to be the proportion of items in the domain that fall into the examinee's category of known items and for which the first response is correct, and if ζ_t is the proportion of items for which the examinee (correctly) sets aside t distractors, $t = 0, \ldots, R-1$, then p_k, the probability that the examinee's response is correct on the kth response to item i, is defined by

$$p_k = \Sigma_{t=0}^{R-k} \zeta_t / (R-t), \ k = 1, \ldots, R.$$

If y_k is the number of items that the examinee answered correctly on the kth attempt, then it follows that an estimate of ζ is the proportion of items answered correctly on the first attempt (y_1/n) less the proportion answered correctly on the second attempt (y_2/n). This estimate, which to be reasonable requires at least that y_1/n should be no less than y_2/n, is corrected for what may be loosely described as partial information (i.e. the information that enables an examinee to eliminate one or more of the distractors to an item); unfortunately, it is not corrected for misinformation (i.e. the "information" that causes an examinee to eliminate the correct answer as wrong).

Item sampling models have provided the foundation for an attack on the problem of classifying examinees into two groups. It is common practice to refer to these groups as masters and nonmasters, but these labels seem inappropriate here whereas they were acceptable for the two-group LCA model. In LCA the examinees are presumed either to know how to answer correctly all the items in the domain or not to know how to answer correctly any of them. In item sampling, however, it is presumed that each examinee knows how to answer correctly only a fraction of the items in the domain. In other words, it is presumed in item sampling that examinees are distributed more or less continuously across the scale of proportion correct true scores for a domain. An implication is that the domains for LCA and item sampling may differ in character; those for LCA are necessarily homogeneous in a sense that is obvious, but those for item sampling models are not necessarily so.

A large literature has developed on the subject of classifying examinees into high and low scoring groups. Care must be taken in reading this literature to distinguish papers based on an item sampling model from those based on some other model. For example, Hambleton (1983a) considered the classification problem from the perspective of IRT. Our focus, however, is on applications of item sampling models.

In order to divide examinees into high and low scoring groups within the context of item sampling models, it is necessary to establish a cutoff or passing score on the scale of the estimated domain score, $\hat{\zeta}$. This estimated score can also be referred to as the observed domain score. Most methods for setting the cutoff score require that the investigator specify a priori either one cutting score or two on the scale of the true domain score ζ. When one such score is given, it separates those domain scores to be designated as high from those to be designated as low. When two cutting scores are specified, the higher of the two is sufficiently low that no examinee with a smaller true score would be placed in the high scoring group and the lower of the two cutting scores is sufficiently high that no examinee with a larger true score would be placed in the low scoring group. Between the higher and lower cutting scores is a zone of scores about which the investigator is indifferent as to whether examinees possessing them are included in the high or low scoring groups. Note that even when an indifference zone is specified on the scale of the true domain score, only one cutting score is defined on the scale for estimated (observed) domain scores. Thus, in practice each examinee is uniquely classified into one or the other group. (In the literature on item sampling models, true cutting scores are usually assumed to be known from the outset, and no attention is paid to their origin. We note in passing that there is a large literature, not reviewed here, on the subject of setting standards or cutoff scores. For a review, see Shepard 1980.)

The cutting score on the scale of estimated domain scores is set with reference to the probability of making an error in classifying an examinee. Two kinds of errors need to be considered. An examinee whose true domain score is above the true cutting point may be assigned erroneously to the low scoring group on the basis of his/her observed domain score. This is a false negative error. A complementary error is the false positive error. Under an assumption as to the form of the distribution of observed domain scores given the true domain score, a cutoff can be located on the observed score scale in such a way that the (possibly weighted) sum of the probabilities of false positive and false negative errors is as small as possible for a person whose true domain score is located anywhere in the range of true high or true low scores.

A problem related to that of setting the cutting score on the observed score scale is that of determining the number of items to be administered so that the probability of an error in classification is no larger than an acceptable minimum level. Most solutions to this problem and that of setting a cutting score have been based on the assumption that the conditional distribution of observed scores given the true domain score is binomial. Early attempts at solving these problems incorporated the additional assumption that the parameters α and β of the item sampling model are zero. (For a review of these studies, see Wilcox 1980.) Recently, van den Brink & Koele (1980) investigated the effect of errors due to the fact that items from the category of unknown items may be answered correctly. When these investigators set the parameter α to 1/2 (as for true-false items) or 1/3 or 1/4 (as for three- or four-option multiple-choice questions), they found, not unexpectedly, that the required number of items has to be substantially larger to achieve the same consistency of classification as when α is 0 (as for constructed response items).

Thus far, our development of the item sampling model has been with reference to a single examinee who responds to a randomly chosen series of items. The model has been expanded to encompass a group of examinees by marrying a Beta distribution for true domain scores ζ to the binomial distribution of observed domain scores given ζ. The resulting Beta-binomial model defines the joint bivariate distribution of true and observed domain scores. In an interesting application of this model, Huynh (1976, 1979) assessed the consistency with which examinees are classified into the high and low scoring groups. He did so given only one observed score for each examinee. Under the assumption that there exists for each examinee an observed score on a (hypothetical) second random sampling of items from the domain and that the same Beta distribution for ζ underlies the observed scores on the actual and hypothetical samplings of items, Huynh derived a formula for the joint distribution of the actual and hypothetical domain scores, and used this distribution for calculating a measure of consistency.

The Beta-binomial model may not be easy to apply in practice (Wilcox 1979b) and, when applied, it may not yield satisfactory results (Wilcox 1981a). But the problem may not reside with the model; instead, the fault may lie with the test data to which the model is applied. In a true implementation of item sampling, each examinee responds to his/her own random sample of items from the domain. In practice, however, the Beta-binomial model has been applied to data obtained by administering the same set of items to every examinee. A necessary but not sufficient condition for this application to work is that all the items in the domain are equally difficult for every examinee (van der Linden 1979). This condition will not be satisfied by real domains of items.

Wilcox (1981b) reported the development of a model analogous to the Beta-binomial model for the A-U-C approach to fitting the item sampling model. He has also used this model to estimate (*a*) the consistency of high-group/low-group classification decisions (Wilcox 1982b), and (*b*) the length of test needed to achieve a desired probability of correct classifications (Wilcox 1982a). It remains to be seen, however, whether this model suffers the same problem as the Beta-binomial model in applications where all examinees respond to the same set of items.

CONCLUDING REMARKS

As our allocation of space in this review will have suggested, item response theory has attracted most attention in recent years. Consequently, considerable progress has been made on several fronts, most particularly that of estimation. There are now several methods implemented in operational computer programs for estimating the item and person parameters of the popular one-, two-, and three-parameter models. Progress has also been made in applying these models to practical testing problems. For example, they are now being used to develop and standardize commercially available tests (Yen 1983). Still, as we have tried to show, much remains to be learned about IRT. Little is yet known about the statistical properties of IRT parameter estimates. And there is need for indicators of model misfit due to multidimensionality. There is also need to learn more about the effect of misfit due to multidimensionality on practical applications of a unidimensional IRT model. Studies that build on the knowledge provided by, for example, Drasgow & Parsons (1983), are needed.

Of latent class analysis and item sampling models, the latter strike us as most promising. They are attractive in relation to unidimensional IRT models for the reason that item sampling models do not invoke an assumption as to dimensionality. Moreover, they seem ideal for any application where there exists a large pool or domain of items, and there is interest in obtaining a direct estimate of the proportion of the items in the domain that an examinee can answer from knowledge. The rapidly increasing availability of inexpensive and powerful computers makes computerized administration an obvious and attractive means by which to implement a testing program based on an item sampling model; computerized administration would make even the answer-until-correct approach feasible. This is not to deny the limitations of item sampling models. Like all models, they are oversimplifications of reality. The fact, for example, that the A-U-C model does not correct an examinee's estimated domain score for misinformation is a serious limitation. It must be noted too that with item sampling we do not obtain the information that IRT provides about the difficulty of each item and its quality as reflected in a measure of its relationship to a latent trait—the IRT discrimination index provides this measure. Also, we need to know more than we now do about examinee and public acceptance of an item sampling approach to testing, an approach in which each examinee responds to a (different) random sample of items from the domain. It is to be hoped that during the next few years descriptions and evaluations of the use of item sampling models will appear in the literature.

ACKNOWLEDGMENTS

We are grateful to H. Goldstein, B. F. Green Jr., R. K. Hambleton, R. P. McDonald, and R. R. Wilcox for their helpful comments on an earlier draft of this chapter. All remaining errors of fact and interpretation remain our responsibility, of course. Partial support for this work was provided the senior author by the Educational Research Institute of British Columbia and Macquarie University.

Literature Cited

Andersen, E. B. 1973a. Conditional inference for multiple-choice questionnaires. *Br. J. Math. Stat. Psychol.* 26:31–44

Andersen, E. B. 1973b. A goodness of fit test for the Rasch model. *Psychometrika* 38:123–40

Andersen, E. B. 1980. *Discrete Statistical Models with Social Science Applications.* Amsterdam: North Holland. 383 pp.

Andrich, D. 1982. An extension of the Rasch model for ratings providing both location and dispersion parameters. *Psychometrika* 47:105–13

Angoff, W. H., Ford, S. F. 1973. Item-race interaction on a test of scholastic aptitude. *J. Educ. Meas.* 10:95–105

Bartholomew, D. J. 1980. Factor analysis for categorical data. *J. R. Stat. Soc. Ser. B* 42:293–321

Bejar, I. I., Wingersky, M. S. 1982. A study of pre-equating based on item response theory. *Appl. Psychol. Meas.* 6:309–25

Birenbaum, M., Tatsuoka, K. K. 1982. On the dimensionality of achievement test data. *J. Educ. Meas.* 19:259–66

Birenbaum, M., Tatsuoka, K. K. 1983. The effect of a scoring system on the algorithm underlying the students' response patterns on the dimensionality of achievement test data of the problem solving type. *J. Educ. Meas.* 20:17–26

Bock, R. D. 1972. Estimating item parameters and latent ability when responses are scored in two or more nominal categories. *Psychometrika* 37:29–51

Bock, R. D., Aitkin, M. 1981. Marginal maximum likelihood estimation of item parameters: Application of an EM algorithm. *Psychometrika* 46:443–59

Bock, R. D., Lieberman, M. 1970. Fitting a response model for *n* dichotomously scored items. *Psychometrika* 35:179–97

Carroll, J. B. 1945. The effect of difficulty and chance success on correlations between items or between tests. *Psychometrika* 10:1–19

Christoffersson, A. 1975. Factor analysis of dichotomized variables. *Psychometrika* 40:5–32

Cook, L. L., Eignor, D. R., Hutton, L. R. 1979. *Considerations in the application of latent trait theory to objectives-based criterion-referenced tests.* Presented at Ann. Meet. Am. Educ. Res. Assoc., San Francisco

Cook, L. L., Eignor, D. R. 1983. Practical considerations regarding the use of item response theory to equate tests. See Hambleton 1983b, pp. 175–95

Dayton, C. M., Macready, G. B. 1976. A probabilistic model for validation of behavioral hierarchies. *Psychometrika* 41:189–204

Dayton, C. M., Macready, G. B. 1977. Model3G and Model5: Programs for the analysis of dichotomous, hierarchic structures. *Appl. Psychol. Meas.* 1:412

Divgi, D. R. 1980. *Evaluation of scales for multilevel test batteries.* Presented at Ann. Meet. Am. Educ. Res. Assoc., Boston

Divgi, D. R. 1981. Model-free evaluation of equating and scaling. *Appl. Psychol. Meas.* 5:203–8

Drasgow, F. 1982. Choice of test model for appropriateness measurement. *Appl. Psychol. Meas.* 6:297–308

Drasgow, F., Parsons, C. K. 1983. Applications of unidimensional item response theory models to multidimensional data. *Appl. Psychol. Meas.* 7:189–99

Emrick, J. A. 1971. An evaluation model for mastery testing. *J. Educ. Meas.* 8:321–26

Fischer, G. H. 1983. Logistic latent trait models with linear constraints. *Psychometrika* 48:3–26

Fischer, G. H., Formann, A. K. 1982. Some applications of logistic latent trait models with linear constraints on the parameters. *Appl. Psychol. Meas.* 6:397–416

Fraser, D. A. S. 1979. *Inference and Linear Models.* London: McGraw-Hill. 297 pp.

Gagné, R. M., Paradise, N. E. 1961. Abilities and learning sets in knowledge acquisition. *Psychol. Monogr.* 75:1–23

Goldstein, H. 1980. Dimensionality, bias, independence and measurement scale problems in latent trait test score models. *Br. J. Math. Stat. Psychol.* 33:234–46

Goldstein, H. 1982. Models for equating test scores and for studying the comparability of public examinations. *Educ. Anal.* 4:107–18

Green, B. F. Jr., Bock, R. D., Humphreys, L. G., Linn, R. L., Reckase, M. D. 1982. *Evaluation plan for the computerized adaptive vocational aptitude battery.* Res. Rep. 82–1, Dept. Psychol., The Johns Hopkins Univ., Baltimore, MD

Gustafsson, J. E. 1980a. A solution of the conditional estimation problem for long tests in the Rasch model for dichotomous items. *Educ. Psychol. Meas.* 40:377–85

Gustafsson, J. E. 1980b. Testing and obtaining fit of data to the Rasch model. *Br. J. Math. Stat. Psychol.* 33:205–33

Haberman, S. 1977. Maximum likelihood estimates in exponential response models. *Ann. Stat.* 5:815–41

Haebara, T. 1980. Equating logistic ability scales by a weighted least squares method. *Jpn. Psychol. Res.* 22:144–49

Haertel, E. H. 1984. Detection of a skill dichotomy using norm-referenced achievement test items. *J. Educ. Meas.* 21:59–72

Hambleton, R. K. 1983a. Application of item response models to criterion-referenced assessment. *Appl. Psychol. Meas.* 7:33–44

Hambleton, R. K., ed. 1983b. *Applications of Item Response Theory.* Vancouver, BC: Educ. Res. Inst. B. C. 233 pp.

Harnisch, D. L., Linn, R. L. 1981. Analysis of item response patterns: Questionnable test data and dissimilar curriculum practices. *J. Educ. Meas.* 18:133–46

Harnisch, D. L., Tatsuoka, K. K. 1983. A comparison of appropriateness indices based on item response theory. See Hambleton 1983b, pp. 104–22

Hattie, J. A. 1981. *Decision criteria for determining unidimensionality.* PhD thesis, Univ. Toronto. 154 pp.

Holland, P. W. 1981. When are item response models consistent with observed data? *Psychometrika* 46:79–92

Holland, P. W., Rubin, D. B., eds. 1982. *Test Equating.* New York: Academic. 365 pp.

Horst, P. 1933. The difficulty of a multiple-choice test item. *J. Educ. Psychol.* 24:229–32

Huynh, H. 1976. Statistical consideration of mastery scores. *Psychometrika* 41:65–78

Huynh, H. 1979. Statistical inference for two reliability indices in mastery testing based on the beta-binomial model. *J. Educ. Stat.* 4:231–46

Ironson, G. H. 1983. Using item response theory to measure bias. See Hambleton 1983b, pp. 155–74

Ironson, G. H., Subkoviak, M. J. 1979. A comparison of several methods of assessing item bias. *J. Educ. Meas.* 16:209–25

Jaeger, R. M. 1981. Some exploratory indices for selection of a test equating method. *J. Educ. Meas.* 18:23–38

Jones, D. H. 1982a. *Redescending M-type estimators of latent ability.* Res. Rep. 82–15, Educ. Test. Serv., Princeton, NJ

Jones, D. H. 1982b. *Tools of robustness for item response theory.* Res. Rep. 82–41, Educ. Test. Serv., Princeton, NJ

Jöreskog, K. G. 1971. Statistical analysis of sets of congeneric tests. *Psychometrika* 36:109–33

Kreitzberg, C. B., Jones, D. H. 1980. *An empirical study of the broad range tailored test of verbal ability.* Res. Rep. 80–5, Educ. Test. Serv., Princeton, NJ

Levine, M. V., Drasgow, F. 1982. Appropriateness measurement: Review, critique and validating studies. *Br. J. Math. Stat. Psychol.* 35:42–56

Levine, M. V., Rubin, D. F. 1979. Measuring the appropriateness of multiple-choice test scores. *J. Educ. Stat.* 4:269–90

Lindley, D. V., Smith, A. F. M. 1972. Bayesian estimates for the linear model. *J. R. Stat. Soc. Ser. B* 34:1–41

Linn, R. L., Levine, M. V., Hastings, C. N., Wardrop, J. L. 1981. Item bias in a test of reading comprehension. *Appl. Psychol. Meas.* 5:159–73

Lord, F. M. 1980a. *Applications of Item Response Theory to Practical Testing Problems.* Hillsdale, NJ: Lawrence Erlbaum. 274 pp.

Lord, F. M. 1980b. Some how and which for practical tailored testing. See van der Kamp et al 1982, pp. 189–205

Lord, F. M. 1982a. Standard error of an equating by item response theory. *Appl. Psychol. Meas.* 6:463–72

Lord, F. M. 1982b. The standard error of equipercentile equating. *J. Educ. Stat.* 7:165–74

Lord, F. M. 1983. Statistical bias in maximum likelihood estimators of item parameters. *Psychometrika* 48:425–36

Lord, F. M., Novick, M. R. 1968. *Statistical Theories of Mental Test Scores.* Reading, Mass: Addison-Wesley. 568 pp.

Lord, F. M., Wingersky, M. S. 1982. *Sampling variances and covariances of parameter estimates in item response theory.* Res. Rep. 82–33, Educ. Test. Serv., Princeton, NJ

Macready, G. B., Dayton, C. M. 1977. The use of probabilistic models in the assessment of mastery. *J. Educ. Stat.* 2:99–120

Macready, G. B., Dayton, C. M. 1980a. The nature and use of state mastery models. *Appl. Psychol. Meas.* 4:493–516

Macready, G. B., Dayton, C. M. 1980b. A two-stage conditional estimation procedure for unrestricted latent class models. *J. Educ. Stat.* 5:129–56

Marascuilo, L. A., Slaughter, R. E. 1981. Statistical procedures for identifying possible sources of item bias based on chi-square statistics. *J. Educ. Meas.* 18:229–48

Marco, G. L. 1977. Item characteristic curve solutions to three intractable testing problems. *J. Educ. Meas.* 14:139–60

Martin, J. T., McBride, J. R., Weiss, D. J. 1983. *Reliability and validity of adaptive and conventional tests in a military recruit population.* Res. Rep. 83–1, Dept. Psychol., Univ. Minnesota, Minneapolis

Masters, G. N. 1982. A Rasch model for partial credit scoring. *Psychometrika* 47:149–74

McDonald, R. P. 1967. Nonlinear factor analysis. *Psychom. Monogr,* No. 15. 167 pp.

McDonald, R. P. 1980. A simple comprehensive model for the analysis of covariance structures: Some remarks on applications. *Br. J. Math. Stat. Psychol.* 33:161–83

McDonald, R. P. 1981. The dimensionality of tests and items. *Br. J. Math. Stat. Psychol.* 34:100–17

McDonald, R. P. 1982. Some alternative approaches to the improvement of measurement in education and psychology: Fitting latent trait models. In *The Improvement of Measurement in Education and Psychology,* ed. D. Spearritt, pp. 213–37. Hawthorn, Australia: Aust. Counc. Educ. Res. 262 pp.

Mellenbergh, G. J. 1982. Contingency table models for assessing item bias. *J. Educ. Stat.* 7:105–18

Mislevy, R., Bock, R. D. 1982a. Biweight estimates of latent ability. *Educ. Psychol. Meas.* 42:725–37

Mislevy, R., Bock, R. D. 1982b. *BILOG: Maximum likelihood item analysis and test scoring with logistic models.* Mooresville, Indiana: Scientific Software, Inc.

Mislevy, R., Reiser, M. R., Zimowski, M. 1981. *Scale score reporting of national assessment data.* Chicago: International Educational Services

Molenaar, I. W. 1981. On Wilcox's latent structure model for guessing. *Br. J. Math. Stat. Psychol.* 34:224–28

Morris, C. 1982. On the foundations of test equating. See Holland & Rubin 1982, pp. 169–92

Muthén, B. 1978. Contributions to factor analysis of dichotomous variables. *Psychometrika* 43:551–60

Muthén, B. 1982. Some categorical response models with continuous latent variables. In *Systems Under Indirect Observation: Causality, Structure, Prediction,* ed. K. G. Jöreskog, H. Wold, pp. 65–79. Amsterdam: North Holland. 292 pp.

Novick, M. R. 1980. Policy issues of fairness in testing. See van der Kamp et al. 1982,pp. 123–27

Ortiz, E. A., Searls, D. T. 1982. *Statistical identification of biased items.* Presented at Joint Meet. Am. Stat. Assoc., Cincinnati

Owston, R. D. 1979. A maximum likelihood approach to the "test of inclusion." *Psychometrika* 44:421–25

Petersen, N. S., Marco, G. L., Stewart, E. E. 1982. A test of the adequacy of linear score equating models. See Holland & Rubin 1982, pp. 71–135

Plake, B. S., Hoover, H. D. 1979. An analytical method of identifying biased test items. *J. Exp. Educ.* 48:153–54

Price, L. C., Dayton, C. M., Macready, G. B. 1980. Discovery algorithms for hierarchical relations. *Psychometrika* 45:449–65

Ree, M. J. 1981. The effects of item calibration sample size and item pool size on adaptive testing. *Appl. Psychol. Meas.* 5:11–19

Reiser, M. 1983. An item response model for the estimation of demographic effects. *J. Educ. Stat.* 8:165–86

Rock, D. A. 1982. Equating using the confirmatory factor analysis model. See Holland & Rubin 1982, pp. 247–57

Rudner, L. M., Getson, P. R., Knight, D. L. 1980. A Monte Carlo comparison of seven biased item detection techniques. *J. Educ. Stat.* 5:213–33

Scheuneman, J. 1979. A method of assessing bias in test items. *J. Educ. Meas.* 16:143–52

Shepard, L. 1980. Standard setting issues and methods. *Appl. Psychol. Meas.* 4:447–67

Shepard, L., Camilli, G., Averill, M. 1981. Comparison of procedures for detecting test-item bias with both internal and external ability criteria. *J. Educ. Stat.* 6:317–75

Sinnott, L. T. 1982. *The identification of biased items.* Res. Rep. 82–3, Educ. Test. Serv., Princeton, NJ

Smith, J. K. 1980. On the examination of test unidimensionality. *Educ. Psychol. Meas.* 40:885–89

Stegelmann, W. 1983. Expanding the Rasch model to a general model having more than one dimension. *Psychometrika* 48:259–67

Stocking, M. L., Lord, F. M. 1983. Developing a common metric in item response theory. *Appl. Psychol. Meas.* 7:201–10

Stricker, L. J. 1982. Identifying test items that perform differentially in population subgroups: A partial correlation index. *Appl. Psychol. Meas.* 6:261–73

Subkoviak, M. J., Mack, J. S., Ironson, G. H.,

Craig, R. 1984. Empirical comparison of selected item bias detection procedures with bias manipulation. *J. Educ. Meas.* 21:49–58

Swaminathan, H. 1983. Parameter estimation in item response models. See Hambleton 1983b, pp. 24–44

Swaminathan, H., Gifford, J. A. 1982. Bayesian estimation in the Rasch model. *J. Educ. Stat.* 7:175–91

Tatsuoka, K. K., Linn, R. L. 1983. Indices for detecting unusual patterns: Links between two general approaches and potential applications. *Appl. Psychol. Meas.* 7:81–96

Tatsuoka, K. K., Tatsuoka, M. M. 1982. Detection of aberrant response patterns and their effect on dimensionality. *J. Educ. Stat.* 7:215–31

Thissen, D. 1982. Marginal maximum likelihood estimation for the one-parameter logistic model. *Psychometrika* 47:175–86

Thissen, D., Steinberg, L., Pyszczynski, T., Greenberg, J. 1983. An item response theory for personality and attitude scales: Item analysis using restricted factor analysis. *Appl. Psychol. Meas.* 7:211–26

Thissen, D., Wainer, H. 1982. Some standard errors in item response theory. *Psychometrika* 47:397–412

Traub, R. E. 1983. A priori considerations in choosing an item response model. See Hambleton 1983b, pp. 57–70

Traub, R. E., Wolfe, R. G. 1981. Latent trait theories and the assessment of educational achievement. In *Review of Research in Education*, ed. D. C. Berliner, 9:377–435. Washington, DC: Am. Educ. Res. Assoc. 450 pp.

van den Brink, W. P., Koele, P. 1980. Item sampling, guessing and decision-making in achievement testing. *Br. J. Math. Stat. Psychol.* 33:104–8

van den Wollenberg, A. L. 1982a. A simple and effective method to test the dimensionality axiom of the Rasch model. *Appl. Psychol. Meas.* 6:83–91

van den Wollenberg, A. L. 1982b. Two new test statistics for the Rasch model. *Psychometrika* 47:123–40

van der Kamp, L. J. Th., Langerak, W. F., de Gruijter, D. N. M., eds. 1982. *Psychometrics for Education Debates.* London: Wiley. 337 pp.

van der Linden, W. J. 1978. Forgetting, guessing, and mastery: The Macready and Dayton models revisited and compared with a latent trait approach. *J. Educ. Stat.* 3:305–18

van der Linden, W. J. 1979. Binomial test models and item difficulty. *Appl. Psychol. Meas.* 3:401–11

Wainer, H. 1981. *Are we correcting for guessing in the wrong direction?* Res. Rep. 81–59, Educ. Test. Serv., Princeton, NJ

Wainer, H., Morgan, A., Gustafsson, J. E. 1980. A review of estimation procedures for the Rasch model with an eye toward longish tests. *J. Educ. Stat.* 5:35–64

Wainer, H., Wright, B. D. 1980. Robust estimation of ability in the Rasch model. *Psychometrika* 45:373–91

Walker, D. A. 1931. Answer pattern and score scatter in tests and examinations. *Br. J. Psychol.* 22:73–86

Waller, M. I. 1981. A procedure for comparing logistic latent trait models. *J. Educ. Meas.* 18:119–25

Werts, C. E., Grandy, J., Schabacker, W. H. 1980. A confirmatory approach to calibrating congeneric measures. *Mult. Behav. Res.* 15:109–22

White, R. T., Clark, R. M. 1973. A test of inclusion which allows for errors of measurement. *Psychometrika* 38:77–86

Whitely, S. E. 1980. Multicomponent latent trait models for ability tests. *Psychometrika* 45:479–94

Whitely, S. E. 1981. Measuring aptitude processes with multicomponent latent trait models. *J. Educ. Meas.* 18:67–84

Wilcox, R. R. 1979a. Achievement tests and latent structure models. *Br. J. Math. Stat. Psychol.* 32:61–71

Wilcox, R. R. 1979b. Estimating the parameters of the beta binomial distribution. *Educ. Psychol. Meas.* 39:527–35

Wilcox, R. R. 1980. Determining the length of a criterion-referenced test. *Appl. Psychol. Meas.* 4:425–46

Wilcox, R. R. 1981a. A cautionary note on estimating the reliability of a mastery test with the beta-binomial model. *Appl. Psychol. Meas.* 5:531–37

Wilcox, R. R. 1981b. Solving measurement problems with an answer-until-correct scoring procedure. *Appl. Psychol. Meas.* 5:399–414

Wilcox, R. R. 1982a. Determining the length of multiple-choice criterion-referenced tests when an answer-until-correct scoring procedure is used. *Educ. Psychol. Meas.* 42:789–94

Wilcox, R. R. 1982b. Some empirical and theoretical results on an answer-until-correct scoring procedure. *Br. J. Math. Stat. Psychol.* 35:57–70

Wilmink, F. W., Nevels, K. 1982. A Bayesian approach for estimating the knowledge of the item pool in multiple choice tests. *Br. J. Math. Stat. Psychol.* 35:90–101

Wingersky, M. S. 1983. LOGIST: A program for computing maximum likelihood procedures for logistic test models. See Hambleton 1983b, pp. 45–56

Wright, B. D., Masters, G. 1982. *Rating Scale Analysis.* Chicago: MESA. 206 pp.

Wright, B. D., Mead, R. J. 1976. *BICAL:*

Calibrating items with the Rasch model. Res. Mem. 23, Dept. of Educ., Univ. Chicago, Chicago, Ill.

Wright, B. D., Panchapakesan, N. 1969. A procedure for sample-free item analysis. *Educ. Psychol. Meas.* 29:23–48

Wright, B. D., Stone, M. H. 1979. *Best Test Design.* Chicago: MESA. 222 pp.

Yen, W. M. 1981. Using simulation results to choose a latent trait model. *Appl. Psychol. Meas.* 5:245–62

Yen, W. M. 1983. Use of the three-parameter logistic model in the development of a standardized achievement test. See Hambleton 1983b, pp. 123–41

Ann. Rev. Psychol. 1985. 36:49–81

SEX AND GENDER

Kay Deaux

Department of Psychological Sciences, Purdue University, West Lafayette, Indiana 47907

CONTENTS

0066-4308/85/0201-0049$02.00

INTRODUCTION

A chapter entitled "Sex and Gender" has never before appeared in the *Annual Review of Psychology;* nonetheless, there are important predecessors to this piece. In 1975, Mednick and Weissman authored a review of selected topics in the psychology of women. Volumes in other *Annual Review* series have included chapters on sex roles (Lipman-Blumen & Tickamyer 1975, Miller & Garrison 1982), sex differences and language (Philips 1980), women's status (Quinn 1977), and family structure (Yanagisako 1979). The most recent edition of the *Handbook of Social Psychology* includes a chapter on sex roles (Spence et al 1985), the first such chapter since Catherine Cox Miles (1935) contributed to the original Murchison volumes. The dates of these reviews provide some indication of the resurgence of this topic area, a currency that can be further documented in a variety of ways.

Restricting consideration to the psychological literature for the moment, one finds two journals that have been established within the past 10 years: *Sex Roles* and *Psychology of Women Quarterly,* first published in 1975 and 1976 respectively. Virtually all other psychology journals have shown an increase in the number of articles dealing with sex and gender during the same period. The extent of this activity is evidenced by the number of articles included in *Psychological Abstracts* between 1967 and 1982 that are indexed under human sex differences (N=12,689), sex role attitudes (N=1765), and sex roles (N=3621). Supplementing the flow of empirical articles are a number of influential books, including those by Maccoby & Jacklin (1974), Spence & Helmreich (1978), and Gilligan (1982). Edited collections such as those by Lloyd & Archer (1976), Mayo & Henley (1981), and O'Leary et al (1984) further stock the field.

Although this quantity certainly prompts the most dedicated reviewer to cry "Enough!", analysis of sex and gender cannot in good conscience be restricted to the psychological literature. The interdisciplinary women's studies journal *Signs* has been a rich source of material related to gender, including periodic reviews of the state of the art in psychology (Henley 1984; Parlee 1975, 1979; Vaughter 1976) and other fields. Disciplinary journals in fields such as sociology, anthropology, and history have also included many articles pertinent for the psychologist interested in gender. Similarly, a wide variety of books by sociologists, anthropologists, and other social scientists have informed the analysis, including those by Bernard (1981), Chodorow (1978), and Sanday (1981). This magnitude mandates selectivity—a selectivity that is inevitably biased by the viewpoint of the author. To render that viewpoint something less than opaque, let me draw with rough strokes some of the themes that will be developed in this chapter: first, general terminology; second, a brief but critical overview of the field; and third, the specific issues that will be addressed.

Terminology

To avoid later confusion, I should stipulate how I will use some terms. Terminology in this area has provided a continuing forum for debate (cf M. Gould 1980, Unger 1979), and my attempt to define terms here is intended less as an ultimate resolution of controversy than as a clarification for the reader. By sex, I will be referring to the biologically based categories of male and female. In the use of gender, I refer to the psychological features frequently associated with these biological states, assigned either by an observer or by the individual subject. Thus studies that select two groups of subjects based on their biological characteristics will be considered appropriate for use of the word sex. In this context, one is studying sex differences rather than gender differences. In contrast, if judgments are made about nonbiological characteristics or social categories, then gender will be used as a referent; hence the appearance of such terms as gender identity, gender stereotypes, and gender roles.

In avoiding use of the term "sex role," I concur with the contention of the late Carolyn Sherif: the term "has become a boxcar carrying an assortment of sociological and psychological data along with an explosive mixture of myth and untested assumptions" (1982, p. 392). Too frequently this label is used as explanation, deflecting more careful consideration of the behaviors of interest.

In general, more consistent use of terms would clarify many of the discussions in this area. The confusion, however, is not merely an issue of semantics. Frequently underlying the debate on the use of sex versus gender, for example, are assumptions about the determinants of differences between men and women, whereby sex often implies biological causes while gender invokes explanations based on socialization. Resolution of these controversies is probably not imminent, although recognition of some of the sources may hasten the process.

Overview of the Area

To characterize research and theory in the area of sex and gender, recognizing both the breadth of topics and the numerosity of reports, is a difficult task and the reader must be willing to accept some generalizations that undoubtedly have their exceptions. With that caveat in mind, let me offer a brief analysis of the area in terms of empirical work, theoretical contributions, methodological concerns, and problem-oriented efforts.

EMPIRICAL RESEARCH   Empirical studies have certainly dominated the activity within psychology. After years of relative neglect, questions related to sex and gender have become "hot topics," and many previous vacuums have been filled. The scope of this empirical work is broad. Comparisons of the sexes in virtually every form of behavior imaginable have been reported, and an increasing number of meta-analytic studies have taken advantage of this abundance to make more conclusive statements about the significance of obtained differences. Numerous other studies have demonstrated various manifestations of sexism, ranging from the evaluation of performance to representations in the media. Previously ignored phenomena as diverse as rape, sexual harassment, menstruation, and dual career marriages have been subjected to empirical scrutiny. Still other studies have investigated the nature of the research process itself, documenting many ways in which past investigations have been insensitive or biased on issues of sex and gender.

THEORY   While empirical work has grown and multiplied, theoretical advances have been much more sluggish. When assessing the more theoretically oriented efforts within psychology, one thinks immediately of fear of success, postulated by Horner (1972), and androgyny, introduced by Sandra Bem (1974). Both of these concepts were heralded on their arrival but have suffered serious criticism as more empirical data became available. Perhaps the initial appeal of each of these efforts was their reliance on single variables to explain a broad range of behavior. In the case of fear of success, the responses of people to a relatively simple projective test were presumed to illuminate the "intellectual, professional, and personal lives of men and women in our society" (Horner 1972, p. 173). Bem postulated equally broad ramifications for her measures of masculinity and femininity. A further appeal of each of these theoretical models may have been the convenience with which simple categorization systems could be put forward: those who did or did not fear success in the Horner model, and a four-category system highlighting androgyny in the subsequent development of Bem's work. Although such simple typologies and single-variable predictors have generally fallen from favor among the personality psychologists most traditionally associated with their development, it is perhaps indicative of the impoverished state of theory that these models were so readily adopted in the area of sex and gender. Notable, too, is the fact that both theories relied primarily on internal personal factors, giving relatively little attention to structural and situational influences.

Gilligan's (1982) postulation of sex-differentiated patterns of moral development has been the most recent contender in the theory arena, and although its basic thesis has been widely acclaimed by many (e.g. Lifton 1982, Benjamin 1983, Douvan 1983), empirical supports for the full theoretical network have yet to be firmly established. (Moreover, some dissenting voices have already been heard, e.g. Benton et al 1983). Chodorow's (1978) work could certainly be considered theoretical, but its reliance on a psychoanalytic framework rather than empirical studies make it less relevant to the present review. The only theoretical paper dealing with sex and gender to be published in *Psychological Review* during the past 10 years is Bem's (1981) introduction of gender schema theory. [Two additional review papers that could be considered relevant to the broadly defined topic, but which are outside the range of the present coverage, are those by Storms (1981) on the development of erotic orientation and by Rasmussen (1981) on pair bonding.]

Although these early attempts have whetted the theoretical appetite, one hungers for more nourishing conceptual work (also cf Wittig 1984). Questions of context and process have not yet been thoroughly addressed, and the potential contributions of other disciplines have not been given their due. It is not the function of this chapter to create theory. However I will, in reviewing the research, attempt to identify those pieces that might contribute most to such efforts, as well as to the missing pieces that need to be found.

METHODOLOGY   Following on the heels of demonstrations that the annals of psychological research show numerous signs of bias, ranging from selection of subjects to interpretation of findings, many questions have been raised about the appropriate ways to do research relating to sex and gender (e.g. Roberts 1981, Unger 1983, Wallston & Grady 1984). Some critics have posed broad challenges, suggesting the operation of a double standard in even the newer research formulations (Eichler 1980). Others have more specifically analyzed problems in design and interpretation (e.g. Lloyd 1976, Sherman 1978, Grady 1981, Parlee 1981). Still others have argued that the study of gender requires the use of more descriptive methods such as ethnomethodology (Kessler & McKenna 1978, Atkinson 1982).

In many respects, these arguments parallel those raised in the fields of personality and social psychology in general, reflecting suspicions that a dedicated commitment to laboratory experiments may not be sufficient (and some would argue not even necessary) to develop a full understanding of human behavior (Mishler 1979, Sherif 1979, Rorer & Widiger 1983, Wallston 1983). For sex and gender, these critiques become particularly salient. The social reality of gender cannot be removed from or fully controlled by the laboratory experiment, and recognition of this reality mandates both concern and caution (also cf Unger 1981).

SOCIAL PROBLEMS   Problem-focused research related to issues of sex and gender has emanated primarily from investigators specifically identified as feminist. Not only has this work introduced a variety of new topics into the psychological literature, but it has typically broadened the populations studied as well. Among those issues moved into focus are rape (Albin 1977, Cann et al 1981, Malamuth 1981); the link between pornography and aggression (Donnerstein 1980); sexual harassment (Brewer & Berk 1982); and psychological concomitants of specific biological events such as menstruation (Dan et al 1980, Komnenich 1981). Although these thrusts, generally informed by a feminist perspective, have not always influenced "mainstream" empirical work, they provide a continuing reminder of the scope of human behavior that social scientists must acknowledge. Further, this research has on more than one occasion had significant influence on programs and policy, through demonstrating unfortunate and unwarranted consequences of prevailing gender belief systems.

Scope and Boundaries of Coverage

Recognizing that the topics of sex and gender are inherently multidisciplinary, I will nonetheless restrict my coverage primarily to the psychological literature (although with disciplinary boundary lines broadly defined). Biological and physiological data will not be discussed except as they relate to explanations offered in a particular behavioral area. I will not discuss research falling in the broad areas of clinical and therapy (covered in the earlier Mednick and Weissman review), nor will I deal directly with questions of sexual behavior, an active area of research whose links to more general issues of sex and gender have yet to be forged. As a further restriction, I will focus on adult behavior, leaving questions of the development of gender identity and children's behavior to others (cf Maccoby 1966, Huston 1983). From the plethora of available literature, I will attempt to identify and describe those areas of empirical and theoretical work that are most active and those that in my opinion hold the most promise for understanding the basic processes by which sex and gender influence human behavior. Broadly defined, the major areas of concentration are: 1. sex comparisons; 2. stereotypes and gender belief systems; 3. issues of context, social structure, and process.

SEX COMPARISONS

The longest history and the most extensive list of references within the area of sex and gender in all probability belong to the investigation of sex differences (cf Rosenberg 1982). The accepted terminology itself suggests a belief in the existence of such differences, and failures to find differences are less often regarded as evidence of sex similarities than as a state of confusion or uncertainty. As suggested by the number of references accumulated within the past 15 years, the areas in which such potential differences have been sought are numerous, and only a highly selective sampling will be attempted here.

Maccoby & Jacklin's (1974) compendium has served as the lightning rod for most investigations during the past 10 years, as investigators have tried to verify, modify, and extend the findings of this pair. Relying primarily on child data collected prior to 1970, Maccoby and Jacklin concluded that convincing evidence for sex differences could be found in only four areas: verbal ability, mathematical ability, visual-spatial ability, and aggression. (For a critical analysis of their conclusions, as well as some of the assumptions and procedures that engendered them; cf Block 1976.) Successive waves of investigators, typically focusing on single behavioral domains, frequently compiling larger sets of studies, and often using the increasingly popular meta-analytic techniques, have given increased momentum to this line of study. For the purposes of organization, let me divide this work into three general categories: cognitive skills, personality traits and dispositions, and social behaviors. Within each domain, I will select a few examples, with the choice influenced primarily by the activity level within the field.

Cognitive Skills

A fascination with the distribution of intellectual ability has been a hallmark of American psychological inquiry, perhaps reflecting a belief that a meritocracy depends on the ability to answer the question, "Who is very smart?". Questions of possible differences between the sexes in intellectual capacity have a history nearly as long, with a philosophical underpinning that extends further decades back.[1] Numerous accounts of these early debates are available (Shields 1975, 1982; Sherman 1978; Rosenberg 1982).

The more recent comparisons of the sexes have, in accord with the *zeitgeist* of intelligence research, focused on specific aspects of cognitive ability rather than a global concept of general intelligence. Most typically, following on the heels of Maccoby & Jacklin (1974), investigators have looked for sex differences in verbal, spatial, and mathematical ability. The data are numerous at this point, and the debates as to their meaning have often been acrimonious—an acrimony reflecting the emotional values that come to the fore so readily when issues of nature vs nurture emerge as they do in analyzing intellectual capability. (See Sherman 1978, Wittig & Petersen 1979 for reviews of these positions.)

MATHEMATICAL ABILITY   The question of differences in mathematical ability has been perhaps the most lively area of debate. Maccoby & Jacklin's (1974) conclusion that boys are superior to girls in mathematical performance, but that the differences primarily occur from the period of adolescence onward, was followed by meta-analyses suggesting that only 1% of the variance is explained by this difference (Hyde 1981). More recently, the work of Benbow & Stanley (1980, 1983) has provided new data documenting sex differences in mathematical aptitude, differences that they suggest are evident prior to

[1]It is worth noting in this context that Gustave Le Bon, often considered a founder of social psychology as a discipline, was one of the most virulent in his pronouncements of sex differences. As one example from a lengthier diatribe, published in 1879: "All psychologists who have studied the intelligence of women, as well as poets and novelists, recognize today that they represent the most inferior forms of human evolution and that they are closer to children and savages than to an adult, civilized man" (quoted in S. J. Gould 1980).

adolescence. Using the SAT test as a criterion with a large sample of seventh-grade students, these authors find a mean difference of approximately 30 points between boys and girls. Emphasized in their report is the difference between males and females when one considers the sex ratio at higher levels of performance. Thus at scores of 700 and above (a performance level achieved by 1 of 10,000 students), the ratio of males to females is approximately 13 to 1. Subsequent analyses of these data suggest the male-female difference occurs primarily on algebraic items and is not evident on arithmetical or geometric problems (Becker 1983).

SPATIAL ABILITY   Spatial abilities have also been subject to scrutiny, following Maccoby and Jacklin's report of sex differences and Hyde's (1981) assessment of 4.5% of the variance explained by this factor. In part, this area has been of interest because of the presumed association between spatial skills and achievement in mathematics and science, an association that has not been supported by recent analyses (Meece et al 1982, Linn & Petersen 1983). The sex difference in spatial skill appears to emerge prior to adolescence but is limited to specific types of skills. Specifically, males are found to be superior to females in measures of mental rotation and in tests of horizontality-verticality (such as the rod and frame test), but there are no apparent differences in spatial visualization tasks that require a more analytic, sequential strategy and that are in fact closer to the demands of mathematical and scientific reasoning (Linn & Petersen 1983). Further, as in the case of mathematical ability, there is substantial evidence that training can significantly alter the performance of both women and men (Connor et al 1978, Newcombe et al 1983).

VERBAL ABILITY   Attracting much less attention is the area of verbal skills, in which Maccoby & Jacklin (1974) reported female superiority. Subsequent analyses have suggested that this difference is weak at best (Sherman 1978, Hyde 1981, Benbow & Stanley 1983).

Of further interest is evidence that in each of these three areas of cognitive skills—mathematical, spatial, and verbal—the magnitude of the sex difference is related to the year of study (Rosenthal & Rubin 1982). Thus over the approximately 20-year period of these analyses, females have shown significant gains in cognitive skills relative to males, a finding that certainly cautions against assumptions of immutable differences.

Personality Traits and Dispositions

The ease of administering personality questionnaires and the equal convenience of using sex as a variable in analysis have produced a spate of studies investigating sex differences in almost every imaginable personality trait and disposition. In many cases, these reports can be viewed as atheoretical at best and opportunistic at worst, yielding a random assortment of sex differences in characteristics as diverse as fear of spiders (Cornelius & Averill 1983) and daydreaming styles (Golding & Singer 1983). More concentrated work has been done in some areas, however, such as achievement motivation and the disputed dimensions of masculinity and femininity. Gilligan's work on moral development has also aroused considerable interest as an approach that suggests a broad range of dispositional differences between the sexes (Gilligan 1982, Pollak & Gilligan 1982).

ACHIEVEMENT   Research on achievement motivation was a major topic in the previous Mednick & Weissman (1975) review, with an emphasis on research in the areas of fear of success and causal attributions for performance. That same ground will not be replowed here. In the 10 years since that review, however, the motivation for understanding achievement behaviors has clearly not diminished. The use of fear of success as a conceptual tool for analyzing those behaviors has subsided, however, after a brief period of prominence. Both methodological and conceptual problems have prevented real progress (cf Zuckerman & Wheeler 1975, Condry & Dyer 1976, Tresemer 1977, Hoffman 1982). At the same time, recognition that the consequences of successful performance may be less than unmitigated pleasure for some people has had heuristic importance (cf Mednick 1982), and there have been some intriguing longitudinal findings that suggest the relevance of the concept (e.g. Hoffman 1977).

While the flashier notion of fear of success has waned, more systematic work on achievement motivation has waxed. Real progress has been made both in understanding the nature of the motivational complex and in tracing the patterns of achievement-related behavior across time. Spence & Helmreich (1978, 1983) have developed a measure of achievement tendencies that separates concerns with work, mastery, and competition. In unselected college student populations, women score significantly higher than men in work, while men are significantly higher on both mastery and competition. Comparisons of males and females in selected populations (e.g. varsity athletes, businesspersons, and psychologists) show sex differences in work and mastery diminishing, but men continue to score higher on competitiveness. These investigators have also begun to test the predictive ability of their measures in a variety of achievement settings, including salaries of MBA graduates and citations of scientists, with interesting results (Helmreich et al 1978, 1980).

Recognition of the multidimensional nature of achievement motivation is also evidenced in the work of Lipman-Blumen, Handley-Isaksen & Leavitt (1983). These investigators delineate three domains of achievement styles—direct, instrumental, and relational—and a more differentiated set of substyles that may characterize achievement-related behavior. Also included in this model is the assumption that settings, and particularly the roles and positions defined within those settings, may influence a particular stylistic choice.

The sequence by which aptitude and motivation interact to produce achievement in academic settings has been studied extensively by Eccles and her colleagues [Eccles (Parsons) 1983a,b; Eccles (Parsons) et al 1984; Meece et al 1982]. Beginning with the structure of a traditional expectancy-value model of achievement, Eccles specifies a number of cognitive elements including self-schemata, perceptions of task value, and a child's perceptions of the parents' attitudes and expectations. On the basis of both cross-sectional and longitudinal data, Eccles rejects deficit models of female achievement patterns and points to the importance of subjective task value as a critical predictor of both male and female choices in achievement domains.

Much of this recent work on achievement motivation and behavior offers considerable promise for advances in understanding. Analysis of the multiple components of achievement motivation, longitudinal studies, a focus on choice and attainment in academic and career settings, and a concern with process— all of these strategies represent improvements to models that relied on static states and sex-linked deficits. Further, as the work of Eccles and others demonstrates, models that allow for a test of possible sex differences without postulating different mechanisms may lead to a better understanding of sex and gender as well as of the substantive processes of concern.

MASCULINITY AND FEMININITY   Garnering a great deal of attention during the past decade have been the concepts of masculinity and femininity. Constantinople's (1973) critique of traditional approaches to this topic, with their assumption of a unidimensional bipolar scale of femininity-masculinity, proved to be a watershed for research in this area. In quick succession, a number of investigators developed separate scales to assess masculine and feminine characteristics and demonstrated that the two scales are orthogonal to one another (Bem 1974, Spence et al 1974, Heilbrun 1976, Berzins et al 1978). The greatest excitement was generated by Bem's (1974) introduction of the concept of androgyny, used to refer to those men and women who possess both masculine and feminine qualities in relatively equal proportion.

Although most investigators would now agree on the separate and orthogonal nature of the two dimensions, there has been considerable controversy as to what the measures assess and what significance various combinations of scores on the two measures have. Whereas proponents hailed the androgyny concept as a significant move away from traditional emphases on sex differences (and more than occasionally, as a prescription for social change), critics claimed flaws in both methodology and conceptualization. The full scope of this debate is too extensive to cover here, and interested readers can consult some of the following sources: Kelly & Worell 1977, Sampson 1977, Bem 1979, Lenney

1979, Locksley & Colten 1979, Pedhazur & Tetenbaum 1979, Spence & Helmreich 1979, Lott 1981, Myers & Gonda 1982, Lubinski et al 1983.

At this time, the most appropriate assessment of this area of investigation is conservative. Masculinity and femininity, it is increasingly recognized, are broad multidimensional concepts that are not readily captured in either one- or two-dimensional questionnaires (Constantinople 1973, Spence 1983b, 1984, Deaux 1984b, Feather 1984). The scales on the most commonly used instruments, the BSRI (Bem 1974) and the PAQ (Spence et al 1974), are best viewed as measures of dominance and self-assertion on the one hand and nurturance and interpersonal warmth on the other. (Agency and communion, terms proposed by Bakan 1966, are equally appropriate as descriptors.) As such, these measures show good predictability for behaviors that require either assertive or nurturant behavior, respectively. Less convincing evidence has been offered to support the assumption that these trait measures are substantially related to other classes of gender-related attributes and behaviors associated with the broader concepts of masculinity and femininity (Spence & Helmreich 1980). Nor is there evidence that androgyny, as a specific combination of scores on the two measures (most typically, high scores on both scales arbitrarily defined by the group median), has any unique predictive power (Taylor & Hall 1982, Lubinsky et al 1983). In short, although the visibility of androgyny has been great and the concept has undoubtedly been influential in thought, its empirical status is questionable and it shows little hope of becoming the panacea that many anticipated.

MORAL DEVELOPMENT   Whereas the proponents of androgyny attempted to minimize the significance of sex differences, arguing that measured masculinity and femininity obviate the importance of biological sex, the work of Gilligan (1982) on moral development has given increased attention to the position that males and females differ in significant ways. Using Kohlberg's cognitive-developmental approach to moral development but criticizing its masculine bias, Gilligan argues that there are two distinctly different sequences and principles of moral development. One, identified in Kohlberg's earlier research, emphasizes separation and individuation, while the other is concerned with attachment and caring. Although not claiming that these patterns of moral belief are sexually dimorphic, Gilligan for the most part describes the two in terms of a masculine and feminine voice, respectively. Differences in both the antecedents and the consequences of these two styles are believed to be substantial, in an argument that is consistent with the theorizing of Chodorow (1978). Support for this theory is provided primarily by the descriptive protocols of women and men who responded to moral dilemmas (Gilligan 1982). Additional evidence consistent with the thesis is reported by Pollak & Gilligan (1982), who find that men show more violence imagery in response to affiliation themes, while achievement situations are more likely to elicit violence imagery in women. The latter results are being debated (Benton et al 1983, Pollak & Gilligan 1983, Weiner et al 1983).

Other recent work in moral development suggests that sex differences may be more subtle. Lifton (1984), for example, finds no sex differences in level of moral reasoning, using three different theoretical approaches, but notes that the patterns of interrelationships among personality variables differ for men and women within the same morality level. Work on moral development will undoubtedly continue, prompted by Gilligan's broad-ranging thesis. Among the challenges for investigators in this area is a linkage between moral reasoning and moral behavior, an issue that has long concerned personality theorists working on this problem.

Social Behaviors

As in the case of personality dispositions, the range of social behaviors explored for possible evidence of sex differences has been broader than the present coverage allows. Selected for discussion, primarily on the basis of activity level, are aggression, social influence, and nonverbal behavior.

AGGRESSION   Aggressive behavior, the only social behavior identified by Maccoby & Jacklin (1974) as furnishing clear evidence of a sex difference, has continued to be analyzed during the past decade. The issue has not been resolved to everyone's satisfaction. In a reanalysis of the Maccoby-Jacklin data base, Hyde (1982) found that sex differences in aggression accounted for approximately 5% of the variance. Frodi et al (1977), taking a more careful look at situational variations, reported that sex differences are characteristic of only certain types of situations. They are less likely to be found when aggression is in response to provocation, for example, than when it is initiated by the experimental subject. It has also been suggested that different types of situations may elicit anger in women and men, leading to situationally dependent patterns of aggression (Frodi et al 1977, Towson & Zanna 1982).

In counterpoint to these analyses of laboratory studies are a bevy of statistics suggesting much greater aggression by males than by females in the society. Crime rates for both homicide and rape, for example, show a consistent and wide differential between women and men. Studies of family violence testify to the aggressive behavior of both women and men, although the target of the attacks often varies (cf Breines & Gordon 1983). The disparity between findings obtained in the laboratory versus the field is perhaps more marked in this area of research than in many others, and results from the latter could do much to inform the former type of investigation.

Of more dispute than the existence of sex differences is the possible cause of such differences. Tieger (1980) contested the Maccoby-Jacklin suggestion of a biological predisposition, concluding that reliable differences are observed in humans only after five years of age and that the hormonal, ethological, and anthropological data are unconvincing. In response, Maccoby & Jacklin (1980) provide additional analysis arguing for the existence of differences prior to the age of six and, without minimizing the influential role of socialization, continue to propose some biological contribution.

CONFORMITY AND SOCIAL INFLUENCE   Analysis of possible sex differences in conformity and susceptibility to social influence has been less contentious, perhaps because the possibility of biological determinants has not been salient. Initial reviews by Eagly (1978) and Cooper (1979) were followed by a more complete analysis by Eagly & Carli (1981). The evidence suggests that women are more easily influenced than men and are more likely to conform in group pressure situations that involve surveillance. Approximately 1% of the variance in these behaviors is accounted for by sex (Eagly & Carli 1981). Eagly (1983) has suggested that differing distributions of women and men in status, a difference that exists in society and that may be inferred in the laboratory, may underlie sex differences in social influence.

NONVERBAL BEHAVIOR   Sex differences in nonverbal behavior have been observed in nearly every area studied—personal space, touching, gaze, and posture, to mention only a few. The superiority of women in both encoding and decoding nonverbal cues has also been documented (Hall 1977, 1978, 1979), although explained variance is again relatively small. Female superiority in encoding is particularly marked in the case of visual cues and less marked for vocal expressions (Hall 1979). As decoders, women show less advantage when cues are presented very briefly or when the cues are transmitted through the "leakier" channels of tone or body position as opposed to facial expression. Rosenthal & DePaulo (1979) explain the latter finding in terms of an interpersonal accommodation hypothesis, suggesting that women are more polite in their nonverbal interactions, willing to ignore more revealing cues for the sake of interpersonal harmony.

Other explanations for sex differences in nonverbal communicative skills have included both differential attention (motivated by a need for the less powerful group to be able to predict the behavior of the more powerful group) as well as biological predispositions that may have evolutionary significance (Hall 1978, 1979; Hall & Halberstadt 1981). Within many areas of nonverbal behavior, the parallels between gender and status have been considered (Henley 1977).

Areas of social behavior in which sex differences could be explored are limited only by the ingenuity of investigators and the range of human behavior. Many topics are being ignored in this review, several of which show promise for future developments in theory. Among areas that have been reviewed recently by others are leadership (Hollander 1985), reward allocation (Major & Deaux 1982), causal attribution (Deaux 1976, Frieze et al 1982), helping behavior (Piliavin & Unger 1984), and group interaction (Dion 1984). In each case, careful analysis has suggested the substantial influence of situational factors and the need to interpret the effects of sex and gender within a broader theoretical network.

Central Issues

As a general statement, one might say that evidence of clear and consistent differences is less prominent in the case of social behaviors than it is when differences in cognitive skills are considered. In the former, one immediately confronts the potent influence of situational variables, an influence that readily alters behaviors and makes simple main effect conclusions much less likely than when the focus is on the single individual acting alone, reacting to cognitive tasks. This greater variability may act as a source of frustration or as an important cue to the investigator. Eschewing frustration and beliefs that sex and gender can never be cleanly depicted, the investigator might do well to acknowledge the variability and ponder just what this malleability of behavior signifies.

There are at least three issues that should be considered when evaluating the research on sex comparisons. Briefly stated, these three issues are: (*a*) the meaningfulness of observed differences, (*b*) the distinction between findings obtained in laboratory and field studies, and (*c*) the possible causes of observed sex differences (cf also Deaux 1984a, Jacklin 1981).

MEANINGFULNESS OF DIFFERENCES   Meta-analytic techniques provide a way of calculating the magnitude of difference when a number of diverse studies are combined, obtaining, in effect, an average of the observed differences. Application of such techniques to studies of sex differences has typically yielded relatively low estimates of effect size, generally accounting for less than 5% of the variance. Such analyses are a useful corrective to the somewhat insidious tendency to assume that a reported sex difference implies a bimodal distribution. Further caution is suggested by evidence that these sex differences are not necessarily constant over time, as the Rosenthal & Rubin (1982) analysis of cognitive skills has indicated. At the same time, it should be recognized that even when mean differences between the sexes are small, differences in the proportions of males and females occurring at the extremes of the distribution or even the percentages above the median may be quite substantial and thus have some practical significance (Rosenthal & Rubin 1982, Huston 1983).

There are, of course, some difficulties in combining studies that vary widely in quality, procedures, settings, and a number of other characteristics. Many of the meta-analytic studies have attempted to account for some of these potentially confounding variables, and often investigators have been able to point to significant variables other than sex of subject. Eagly et al (1983), for example, suggest that the particular task is critical in predicting sex effects in prosocial behavior. Among other task attributes, they find that situations which are perceived to involve greater danger for females than males are most likely to elicit sex differences favoring men, while less threatening situations are more apt to show sex similarities. Investigators who have used less quantitative methods of summarizing studies have also pointed to the importance of task characteristics in areas as diverse as aggression (Frodi et al 1977), reward allocation (Major & Deaux 1982), and self-confidence and expectations for performance (Deaux 1976, Lenney 1977).

Interpretation of the importance of sex differences in behavior is also tempered by some reports of a relationship between the sex of the investigator and the direction of findings. Thus Eagly & Carli (1981) report that in their analysis of the social influence literature, as well as in a reanalysis of Hall's (1978) review of nonverbal decoding, sex of author accounts for some variance in the findings. Specifically, both sexes are apparently more likely to report sex differences that are favorable to their own sex, males more likely to report male independence and females more likely to report female superiority in nonverbal decoding. Carli (1983) has observed a similar effect in studies of group behavior and reward allocation. The generality of this pattern is as yet unknown, but it clearly poses a problem for interpretation of specific sex differences and a question for more general issues of scientific procedure.

COMPARISON OF LABORATORY AND FIELD STUDIES   Evidence from many laboratory studies suggests that sex differences, although not insignificant, are relatively small. Such evidence has led many to conclude that recognition of sex similarities should outweigh an emphasis on sex differences. Such conclusions are often met with disbelief among those whose reference point is outside of the psychological laboratory, where differences between women and men are immediately apparent in such areas as occupation, household division of labor, child-caring responsibilities, and the widely heralded "gender gap" in political opinion.

The differences between these two settings in the kinds of information that they can provide need to be more clearly recognized. Within the laboratory, it is possible to vary the degree to which gender is salient. Under some conditions, the role of subject may be most salient and one can conduct a relatively "gender-free" test of sex differences in capability—the ability to perform specific tasks selected by the experimenter (cf also Eagly 1978, Unger 1981). For the most part, this assessment indicates limited sex differences in capability for a wide range of tasks. Alternatively, it is possible to invoke gender considerations quite strongly in the lab through, for example, choice of task, instructions, and sex of interactants, and to obtain dramatic sex differences (e.g. Megargee 1969, Carbonell 1984).

Outside of the laboratory setting, it is more likely that gender-related considerations will always be salient to some degree. Observed differences between women and men thus cannot be considered as simply indices of capability, but rather must be interpreted in terms of individual choice, situational pressures, and structural factors. The multiply determined character of most social behaviors is nowhere more evident than in the case of gender-related behaviors.

Information from both the laboratory and the field is valuable in exploring the range and realm of male-female differences. It is equally important, however, to recognize that somewhat different questions are being asked in the various settings, and that an answer obtained in one setting may not be wholly satisfactory in another. Recognition of the difference between what men and women *can* do and what they *do* do sets the stage for a more probing analysis of the gap between capability and actuality and an appreciation of context as a key element in that analysis.

CAUSES OF SEX DIFFERENCES   The perennial debate among social and behavioral scientists as to the relative influence of nature versus nurture in human behavior finds no more lively forum than that of sex differences. The prevailing tendency among many social scientists to stress nurture, pointing to the inarguable influence of early experience and specific training, has been challenged by many. Most notable in recent years is the impact of modern evolutionary theorists. The simplistic nature of some of the sociobiological accounts have been forcefully and effectively disputed (e.g. Lowe & Hubbard 1983). Yet it would be a mistake, I believe, for psychologists interested in questions of sex and gender to deny any biological influence while quite rightfully attempting to demonstrate the malleability of human behavior.

Biological influences have been invoked in the explanation of a number of observed sex differences, perhaps most prominently for cognitive abilities. Contenders have included pubertal hormones, fetal hormones, brain lateralization, and genetically linked traits. Not unexpectedly, each of these conclusions has been disputed as well. (For discussion of some of these positions, see Sherman 1978, Wittig & Petersen 1979, Henley 1984.) Yet few of those who argue for biological influence would insist upon biological determinism; the malleability and even reversability of human behavior is recognized by most (cf Daly & Wilson 1983).

One senses, within the past few years, some shift in the pendulum of explanation. Emotional debates as to nature and nurture, "mischievous" (Daly & Wilson 1983, p. 266) at best, may be yielding to more thoughtful analyses that acknowledge the multiply determined nature of gender-related behavior.

GENDER BELIEF SYSTEMS

Beliefs about the sexes have a history at least as long as the actual study of those differences, and perhaps longer if one includes statements by those philosophers and social commentators who predated the development of modern psychology. The ways in which people think about women and men can be, and have been, considered from a variety of perspectives, from broad-based attitudinal surveys about the roles of women and men to specific evaluations of individual male and female performance.

Attitudes toward Roles of Women and Men

Following a long psychological tradition of attitudinal research, investigators during the past decade have developed numerous scales to assess attitudes toward the roles, rights, and responsibilities of women and men in this society. Among the more popular offerings are the Attitudes toward Women scale (Spence & Helmreich 1972), the FEM scale (Smith et al 1975), and the more specifically focused Attitudes toward Women as Managers scale (Peters et al 1974). A number of studies in recent years have documented changes in attitudes toward the roles of women and, to a lesser extent, men. In general, these studies indicate a shift toward more egalitarian attitudes and a corresponding movement away from beliefs in traditional roles for women and men (Mason et al 1976, Thornton & Freedman 1979, Cherlin & Walters 1981, Helmreich et al 1982, Thornton et al 1983). Not particularly surprising are data showing that traditional attitudes are more likely to be held by those who are older, less educated, lower in income, and higher in church attendance; for women, egalitarian attitudes are positively associated with labor force experience subsequent to marriage (Beckman & Houser, 1979; Houser & Beckman, 1980; Mason et al, 1976; Morgan & Walker, 1983). However, it is not the case that only the more educated woman, for example, views egalitarianism positively. Rather, movement away from traditional beliefs has been shown in most populations that have been studied.

More specific areas of concern have also been pinpointed with scales developed to tap these areas. Considerable work, for example, has dealt with attitudes toward rape and beliefs about the responsibility of women for their victimization (Feild 1978, Burt 1980, Burt & Albin 1981, Weidner & Griffitt 1983). Beliefs in the responsibility of women for being raped and the sexual, as opposed to aggressive, motivation for rape are more likely to be expressed by men than women and by those with lower education. Patterns of relationship have also been shown among rape mythology, endorsement of traditional stereotypes, and acceptance of interpersonal violence.

Representations of Women and Men

Beliefs about women and men have also been studied extensively through their depiction in various forms of media. Nearly every medium has been analyzed—television shows, children's books, magazine advertisements, and others—showing differences both in the frequency with which men and women are present and in the ways in which they are depicted (cf Busby 1975, Miles 1975, Goffman 1976). Male figures are more common than female figures, in both human and animal forms, and the activities in which males and females are engaged tend to parallel the common stereotypes of the active, work-oriented male and the passive, home-residing female. Differences have even been reported in the relative facial prominence of women and men in periodicals, artwork, and amateur drawings, with the proportionately greater prominence of the male face associated with more favorable evaluations (Archer et al 1983).

Gender Stereotypes

An active area of research in the early 1970s was the evaluation of male and female performance. Numerous studies documented the fact that men and women will be rated differently, even when actual performance is held constant (for a review of these studies, see Wallston & O'Leary 1981). Other investigators used attribution theory to show how explanations for male and female performance differ as well (e.g. Deaux 1976, Frieze et al 1978, Hansen & O'Leary 1983). As an explanation of the different evaluation patterns that were observed, investigators frequently invoked the concept of gender stereotypes, most often making reference to the work of Rosenkrantz and his colleagues (Rosenkrantz et al 1968, Broverman et al 1972).

Satisfaction with simple (yet dramatic) demonstrations of differential evaluation and reliance on perfunctory reference to gender stereotypes have given way in recent years to more systematic efforts to understand the structure and process of gender stereotyping. A number of paths have begun to converge in this recent analysis. The salience of sex as a category, noted by Grady (1977) and others, has been analyzed more thoroughly by Kessler & McKenna (1978), who argue that the process of gender attribution is universal. Recognition of the centrality of the stereotype concept has led many investigators to critically assess past work, pointing to a variety of conceptual and methodological flaws that have impeded understanding (McCauley et al 1980, Ruble & Ruble 1982, Ashmore & Del Boca 1984b). Finally, the recent surge of research in social cognition has provided a new theoretical perspective from which to view questions of gender stereotypy (cf Hamilton 1981, Hastorf & Isen 1982, Miller 1982, Fiske & Taylor 1984).

The "new look" in stereotypy has shifted from a conceptualization of stereotypes as inherently negative and prejudicial to a view of stereotypes as potentially neutral categories that operate in the same way as do other cognitive categories. From this vantage point, questions have been raised not only about the content of gender stereotypes (what might be termed the "old look"), but also about the structure of these categories and the processes by which they operate.

The reliance on trait characteristics to define gender stereotypes, reflected in the original Rosenkrantz et al (1968) methodology and updated by Spence et al (1974), has been questioned in recent years (Ashmore & Del Boca 1979, 1984b; Deaux & Lewis 1983). Deaux & Lewis (1983, 1984) have identified a set of components, including role behaviors, physical characteristics, and occupation in addition to the more typically used traits that are associated with gender stereotypes. These components, although bearing some relationship to one another, nonetheless function with some independence, suggesting a more complex composition than was previously considered. Such findings are consistent with the suggestion of Ashmore & Del Boca (1979) that there are various kinds of attributes associated with gender, including genital and biological features (defining attributes), physical appearance cues (identifying attributes), and the more commonly used trait descriptors (ascribed attributes).

Cross-cultural studies of gender stereotypes, although less concerned with the more detailed analysis of various components, have nonetheless provided valuable information as to both the diversity and the generality of gender stereotypes. In a study of 30 nations, Williams & Best (1982) found a considerable degree of "pancultural generality," evidenced most clearly in the association of instrumental traits with males and expressive traits with females. At the same time, some variations were evident when comparisons were made between groups that differed in religious tradition or in national work-related values. In more descriptive but less systematic explorations of other cultures, anthropologists have also found evidence for both the commonality of instrumentality and expressiveness, as well as for unique attributes that reflect specific cultural contexts (e.g. Strathern 1976, Dwyer 1978).

More analytic work on the structure of gender stereotypes has addressed two questions: (*a*) the interrelationship among various components and their influence relative to simple sex label, and (*b*) the level of categorization at which gender stereotypy occurs. With regard to the first question, it is evident that there are a variety of complex inference processes that operate across various components, although the picture is not yet crystalline. Information about role occupancy can influence the ascription of stereotypic traits, with people identified as in positions of higher influence being accorded more instrumentality, regardless of their sex (Eagly & Wood 1982, Eagly 1983, Eagly & Steffen 1984). The Deaux & Lewis (1984) results suggest that physical characteristics may have some priority as an influence on other inference processes, a suggestion that is consistent with work by social psychologists indicating the general importance of physical appearance cues (McArthur 1982).

It is also becoming apparent that people tend to view men and women in terms of opposites, despite the empirical overlap that they accord to various components of the stereotypes. Thus just as early investigators of self-assessed masculinity and femininity assumed a bipolar model, so do observers tend to assume that what is male is "not female" and vice versa (Foushee et al 1979, Major et al 1981, Deaux & Lewis 1984).

A debate has also surfaced as to the relative influence of gender label in the face of other more diagnostic information (Locksley et al 1980; Grant & Holmes 1981, 1982; Locksley et al 1982; Deaux & Lewis 1984). Experimentally, one can negate the influence of gender label by providing information that is closely linked to the judgment being requested, thus suggesting that the influence of stereotypic beliefs is quite weak. However, the network of associations linked together under the umbrella of gender stereotypes has been shown to influence judgments even when the categorical label loses its potency. [For example, information about gender-related physical characteristics will influence judgments about traits and role behaviors not necessarily related to those characteristics (cf Deaux & Lewis 1984).]

Recent work in cognition, most notably that of Rosch and her colleagues (Rosch 1978, Mervis & Rosch 1981), has also prodded investigators to look beyond the general labels of male and female to search for more specific gender subtypes that may be part of stereotypic thought. In a pre-Roschian investigation, Clifton, McGrath & Wick (1976) noted the existence of "housewife" and "bunny" as distinct female stereotypes. Other investigators have also sought to identify these more specific categories (Ashmore 1981, Deaux et al 1984). Although it is far from clear that gender stereotypes can be ordered in a neat hierarchy in the way that some natural objects line up (cf Lingle et al 1984), consideration of the diversity of stereotypes may yet prove useful. One possibility suggested by Deaux et al (1984) is that the range of female stereotypes is much broader than that of males, showing greater distinctiveness and covering a broader range of attributes.

Yet another line of investigation being pursued in the recent assault on gender stereotypes is the question of individual differences. Whereas earlier concerns with questions of content and assumptions of shared conceptions precluded an analysis of individual variation, the recent social cognition approach is far more amenable to consideration of this variety. Bem's (1981) proposal of gender schema theory assumes that individuals differ in their tendency to use gender as an organizing principle. According to this view, people who are highly sex-typed (masculine males and feminine females, as categorized by scores on the Bem Sex Role Inventory) are more likely to process information and to make distinctions on the basis of gender than are other people. [The relationship between androgeny and gender schema is treated more explicitly by Bem (1984).] The conceptual basis of this formulation has been challenged and its status is somewhat shaky (Spence & Helmreich 1981, Bem 1981, 1982, Markus et al 1982, Crane & Markus 1982, Mills & Tyrrell 1983). Nontheless, the view that individuals differ in their tendency to stereotype is probably acceptable to most and is being studied by a number of investigators (Spence et al 1975, Deaux et al 1984). These latter investigations suggest little relationship between endorsement of gender stereotypes and self-described masculinity (agency) and femininity (communion).

Research on gender stereotyping has moved from the simple demonstrations of discrimination and unequal judgment to a more sophisticated analysis of the components of gender belief systems and the processes by which information is encoded, stored, and retrieved. It can be predicted that this area will generate continued activity within the next decade, pursuing more sophisticated questions about the structure of gender stereotypes (and, by extension, other stereotypic structures) as well as posing new questions about the role of affect, the sources of stereotypes, and the influence of stereotypes on subsequent behavior.

CONTEXT, STRUCTURE, AND PROCESS

Sex comparisons and gender belief systems, although accounting for a large share of the work in sex and gender, are insufficient in themselves to explain the phenomena of interest. Both are often viewed in static terms, stripped of the context from which they arose (cf Mishler 1979). Thus investigators of differences between males and females often assume a stability to these differences; similarly, explorations of gender stereotypes sometimes suggest a search for eternal truths. Yet the research suggests otherwise. Sex differences ebb and flow with changes in situational forces, and stereotypes, it has been shown, vary to some degree across both time and culture. The broader context in which these changes occur, however, has been less salient for the typical psychological investigator, despite evidence from many other social science domains that contextual factors are important.

Sociologists and anthropologists, for example, have explored the influence of economic structure, the distinction between domestic and public spheres of influence, the role of childbearing, and marriage practices as critical factors in the analysis of sex and gender (cf Rosaldo & Lamphere 1974, Quinn 1977, Atkinson 1982). Although extensive review of these areas is beyond the confines of this chapter and is available elsewhere, it is nonetheless important to give some consideration to those factors that frame and define sex and gender. Without recognition of these factors, even a strictly psychological analysis will be impoverished. Particular attention will be given to those "border areas" that have been most closely approached by psychologists: marital roles, occupational distributions, and sex ratios. Attention will also be given to a more "micro" level of psychological analysis that explicitly considers process in the transaction of gender.

Marital Roles

A functionalist view of division of labor within the household is most widely associated with the work of Parsons & Bales (1955). Analyses of research related to this thesis are available elsewhere (Miller & Garrison 1982, Spence et al 1985). Within recent psychological research, perhaps the greatest emphasis has been placed on the dual-career couple, exploring the ways in which this state alters traditional division of labor within the household and the conflicts that may arise between career and family roles (e.g. Bryson & Bryson 1978, Hall & Hall 1979). Most often these analyses have focused on the middle-class career couple, leaving many questions remaining with regard to the more numerous dual-worker couples in the society. Nonetheless, this research makes some contribution to an understanding of some of the broader factors that relate to sex and gender, although its contribution to date has been somewhat limited with respect to the more fundamental issues of sex and gender.

More general work has concerned the relationship between the husband-wife balance of power and marital satisfaction. A recent review of this literature suggests that marital satisfaction is lowest when the wife is dominant and highest in egalitarian couples (Gray-Little & Burks 1983). Although the use of coercive control appears to be most closely associated with marital dissatisfaction, more research on the dynamics of the exchange process within the marital relationship is still needed.

Theoretical advances in understanding marital roles have been relatively few, and the research has typically not been linked to other areas of gender-related research. A promising corrective to this state, however, can be seen in the recent work of Kelley and his colleagues (Kelley 1979, Kelley et al 1983). These investigators offer an ambitious and generative conceptual framework for analyzing close relationships, incorporating both personal and social environmental factors in a process-oriented analysis of dyadic interaction. Although not limited to issues of gender, this theory may prove to be an important framework for exploring such issues.

Occupational Structure

The increasing trends in female employment have prompted a surge of research related to women's place in the occupational hierarchy. Apart from the economic statistics documenting the changing composition of the work force, there are many accounts of the performance of women in various occupations and a comparison of men and women on several dimensions believed to be related to work performance and occupational choice. (For a summary of much of the psychological literature, see Nieva & Gutek 1981). The lack of comparability of the typical male and female job has hampered many of these comparisons. In fact, recent research suggests that occupational segregation is even more severe than had previously been believed. In a comprehensive study of over 400 California work organizations, Bielby & Baron (1984) report that 59% of the companies were perfectly segregated by sex, i.e. there was no overlap between the job titles filled by one sex and those filled by the other. Fewer than 10% of the workforce was in specific jobs that included both sexes. This uneven distribution within the employment realm has important consequences, not only for issues of wage and equity, typified in recent debates about comparable worth, but also for the psychological processes that are activated by disproportionate sex ratios.

Sex Ratios

Kanter (1977), in dissecting the structure of corporate organizations, illuminated the relevance of proportions to the study of sex and gender. In groups in which one of two groups is in a decided majority, members of the minority group can be considered "tokens." Both the behavior of the token members and the behavior of the majority members toward the tokens can be shown to be channeled in systematic ways, independent of the particular identifying characteristics (e.g. sex, race) of the two groups. The consequences of this token status have been explored by Kanter and others (Taylor & Fiske 1978, McArthur 1981) and support the contention that both the behaviors of and the beliefs about males and females may in some cases be a specific example of a more general process that operates when group members are in unequal proportions. Gutek & Morasch (1982) have also used a sex-ratio approach in their analysis of sexual harassment in the workplace.

The potential influence of sex ratios on behavior has been considered further in the work of Guttentag and Secord (Guttentag & Secord 1983; Secord 1982, 1983). Applying a social exchange perspective to the analysis of dyadic relationships between men and women, these authors contend that the ratio of males to females in a society affects the power balance between the sexes. When the ratio of males to females is high, they predict that women are more likely to assume traditional roles of wife and mother and the division of labor would be strong. In contrast, when women are in "oversupply," Guttentag and Secord see the likelihood of greater sexual libertarianism, lower values on marriage and family, and an increased expression of feminist ideology. Focusing their analysis on age cohorts and implied marital opportunities, these investigators note striking changes in the United States sex ratio from the 1960s to the 1970s. Such changes, they argue, have important implications for structural power and social exchange. Although the sex ratio must be considered only one factor influencing male and female behavior, and perhaps is most applicable within the marital system, the work of Guttentag and Secord is intriguing in its consideration of broad structural factors. In addition, it has the salutory effect of highlighting the importance of power in the analysis of sex and gender.

Power and Gender

Issues of power have maintained a remarkably low profile in most psychological accounts of sex and gender, although the need to include this concept is being noted with increasing frequency (Henley 1977, Sherif 1982, Unger 1976, 1982). The most coherent model of status with implications for sex and gender comes from sociology, where the theory of expectation states presents an account of status differentiation in groups (Berger et al 1977, Webster & Driskell 1978, Berger et al 1980). According to this theory, hierarchies of power and prestige develop within the context of group interaction. Beliefs about the competence and ranking of members within a group may develop on the basis of diffuse status characteristics—cues that emanate from differential evaluation of various attributes. Applying this theory to the case of sex, investigators have shown that sex operates as a diffuse status characteristic, implying lesser competence and thus resulting in lower status for females than males within the group (Lockheed & Hall 1976, Meeker & Weitzel-O'Neill 1977). The utility of this model in predicting differential effects has been shown on a number of occasions; it is also the case, however, that specific instructions can counteract this sex-related status hierarchy within an experimental setting (Lockheed et al 1983, Riordan 1983).

Analyses based on power differentials have also appeared within the social psychology literature, including such behavioral domains as social influence and nonverbal behavior (Henley 1977, Eagly 1983). More scattered are studies dealing specifically with sex differences in the use of power strategies and reactions to various power ploys (Johnson 1976, Falbo & Peplau 1980, Falbo et al 1982, Instone et al 1983). It is clear, however, that the full potential of this area has not yet been realized. Concepts of power may in fact provide an important bridge between the more macro-level concerns of sociologists and the more micro-analysis of psychologists.

Gender and Social Interaction

Whereas sociological and structural factors define a broad framework in which gender-related behaviors may be shaped, consideration of the actual process by which gender is enacted provides additional insight. As noted earlier, there is considerable evidence within the sex difference literature as to (*a*) the variability within both males and females with regard to most behaviors, and (*b*) the substantial impact that situational factors can have, sometimes resembling a magician's invocation of "now you see it, now you don't." Such evidence suggests that there is much to be learned from a more careful analysis of the process of gender presentation.

Goffman's (1976) suggestive notions of gender enactment, emphasizing the element of choice in people's portrayal of gender, have found some confirmation in the literature, but the work has generally been scattered and unsystematic. Yet although this particular approach has been mined more shallowly than some of the traditional perspectives, it demonstrates a distinctly psychological contribution to an understanding of sex and gender while also giving more attention to process rather than static elements.

Some investigators have chosen to pit internal dispositions against situational factors in exploring the fluidity of sex differences. For example, it has been shown that fear of success is less predictive of performance than the attitudes of a partner toward accomplishment (Jellison et al 1975). Assessed measures of dominance predict leadership assumption for women paired with other women but not paired with men, at least when the task is masculine in its orientation (Megargee 1969, Carbonell 1984). The influence of normative expectations on the display of dominance behavior has also been shown by Klein & Willerman (1979), although in this case the dispositional tendency continued to exert an effect. Women instructed to be as dominant as possible showed no differences in their behavior toward a male or female partner, whereas the absence of instructions resulted in lower displays of dominance toward a male partner. Each of these studies attests to the flexibility that individuals have in displaying behaviors that are either consistent with an internal disposition or are consistent with the expectations (either implicit or explicit) of others (cf also Deaux 1977, 1984a). It is also interesting to note that women have more often been the subject of these investigations, perhaps reflecting an assumption that women are more likely to be responsive to situational variations. The validity of this assumption remains to be demonstrated. In fact, individuals of both sexes have been shown to be highly responsive to the instrumental or expressive demands of a situation, shaping their behavior in corresponding ways (La France & Carmen 1980, Putnam & McCallister 1980).

Other investigations, while less concerned with specific personality dispositions, have also implicated situational factors as a determinant of gender-related behavior. Zanna and his colleagues have demonstrated that a woman's beliefs about her male partner's attitudes toward women will lead to alterations in self-presentation, both verbal and physical (Zanna & Pack 1975, von Baeyer et al 1981). Still other evidence testifies to the chain of events that may shape gender behavior, wherein expectations of one person can alter the behavior of another in the direction of stereotypically gender-related choices (Skrypnek & Snyder 1982). General models of expectancy confirmation sequences, such as the one presented by Darley & Fazio (1980), may prove valuable in further elucidating the parameters of this process as it relates to gender.

CONCLUDING THOUGHTS

Sex and gender is an area of research whose time has come. The questions, of course, have always existed, but until relatively recently the answers were more likely to be offered by social commentators than by scientists. The very obviousness and assumed natural order of males and females, while producing a surplus of pronouncements on the way things were, may have dulled the sensitivities of scientists to many basic issues. Activity within the past decade or two has surely provided ample evidence that unanswered questions remain.

As an area of research, sex and gender is fraught with dilemmas and decision points. The interface of ideology with the scientific enterprise, long a topic of debate for social science research in general, supplies a tension that pervades the area. What one may wish as a feminist is not necessarily what one sees as a scientist. Yet a clear view of what is, and an understanding of why, become underpinnings for the work of those who seek change. There is, in fact, a perceptible shift in the ideological pendulum in recent years. Attempts to "disprove" the existence of sex differences have given way to arguments, both at the scientific and popular level, that differences do exist (cf Chodorow, Gilligan). Acknowledgment of the existence of differences should not, however, serve as a cap on efforts to understand the processes by which sex and gender become influential in human behavior.

Psychology is not alone in its concern with questions of gender. Historians, anthropologists, sociologists, biologists, and evolutionary theorists all have knowledge and insights to offer to analyses of the questions. Informed by the perspectives of these other disciplines, psychologists too have much to offer. They also have much to gain. The issue of sex and gender is fundamental to an understanding of human behavior, and increased consideration of its parameters and implications can only benefit psychology as a whole. From my own perspective, the best is yet to come and I look forward to the next *Annual Review* chapter that will document that progress.

ACKNOWLEDGMENTS

This chapter was prepared while I was a Fellow at the Center for Advanced Study in the Behavioral Sciences. I am grateful for financial support provided by the John D. and Catherine T. McArthur Foundation and by a grant from the National Science Foundation (BNS-8217313). The insights and suggestions of the following people, commenting on an earlier draft, are recognized with appreciation: Denise Bielby, William Bielby, Alice Eagly, Sheila Kamerman, Marcia Linn, Eleanor Maccoby, Brenda Major, Charles McClintock, Ellen Messer, Paul Rosenkrantz, Janet Spence, Rhoda Unger, and Michelle Wittig.

Literature Cited

Albin, R. S. 1977. Psychological studies of rape. *Signs* 3:423–35

Archer, D., Iritani, B., Kimes, D. D., Barrios, M. 1983. Face-ism: Five studies of sex differences in facial prominence. *J. Pers. Soc. Psychol.* 45:725–35

Ashmore, R. D. 1981. Sex stereotypes and implicit personality theory. See Hamilton 1981, pp. 37–81

Ashmore, R. D., Del Boca, F. K. 1979. Sex stereotypes and implicit personality theory: Toward a cognitive-social psychological conception. *Sex Roles* 5:219–48

Ashmore, R. D., Del Boca, F. K., eds. 1984a. *The Social Psychology of Female-Male Relations: A Critical Analysis of Central Concepts.* New York: Academic. In press

Ashmore, R. D., Del Boca, F. K. 1984b. Gender stereotypes. See Ashmore & Del Boca 1984a

Atkinson, J. M. 1982. Anthropology. *Signs* 8:236–58

Bakan, D. 1966. *The Duality of Human Existence.* Chicago: Rand McNally

Becker, B. J. 1983. *Item characteristics and sex differences on the SAT-M for mathematically able youths.* Presented at Ann. Meet. Am. Educ. Res. Assoc., Montreal

Beckman, L. J., Houser, B. B. 1979. The more you have, the more you do: The relationship between wife's employment, sex-role attitudes, and household behavior. *Psychol. Women Q.* 4:160–74

Bem, S. L. 1974. The measurement of psychological androgyny. *J. Consult. Clin. Psychol.* 42:155–62

Bem, S. L. 1979. Theory and measurement of androgyny: A reply to the Pedhazur-Tetenbaum and Locksley-Colten critiques. *J. Pers. Soc. Psychol.* 37:1047–54

Bem, S. L. 1981. Gender schema theory: A cognitive account of sex typing. *Psychol. Rev.* 88:354–64

Bem, S. L. 1981. The BSRI and gender schema theory: A reply to Spence and Helmreich. *Psychol. Rev.* 88:369–71

Bem, S. L. 1982. Gender schema theory and self-schema theory compared: A comment on Markus, Crane, Bernstein, and Siladi's "Self-schema and gender." *J. Pers. Soc. Psychol.* 43:1192–94

Bem, S. L. 1984. Androgyny and gender schema theory: A conceptual and empirical integration. In *Nebraska Symp. Motiv.: Psychol. Gender,* ed. T. B. Sondregger. Lincoln: Univ. Nebr. Press. In press

Benbow, C. P., Stanley, J. C. 1980. Sex differences in mathematical ability: Fact or artifact? *Science* 210:1262–64

Benbow, C. P., Stanley, J. C. 1983. Sex differences in mathematical reasoning: More facts. *Science* 222:1029–31

Benjamin, J. 1983. Review of *In a Different Voice.* *Signs* 9:297–98

Benton, C. J., Hernandez, A. C. R., Schmidt, A., Schmitz, M. D., Stone, A. J., Weiner, B. 1983. Is hostility linked with affiliation among males and with achievement among females? A critique of Pollak and Gilligan. *J. Pers. Soc. Psychol.* 45:1167–71

Berger, J., Fisek, M. H., Norman, R. Z., Zelditch, M. Jr. 1977. *Status Characteristics and Social Interaction: An Expectation States Approach.* New York: American Elsevier. 196 pp.

Berger, J., Rosenholtz, S. J., Zelditch, M. Jr. 1980. Status organizing processes. *Ann. Rev. Sociol.* 6:479–508

Bernard, J. 1981. *The Female World.* New York: Free Press. 614 pp.

Berzins, J. I., Welling, M. A., Wetter, R. E. 1978. A new measure of psychological androgyny based on the Personality Research Form. *J. Consult. Clin. Psychol.* 46:126–38

Bielby, W. T., Baron, J. N. 1984. A woman's place is with other women: Sex segregation in organizations. In *Sex Segregation in the Workplace: Trends, Explanations, Remedies,* ed. B. Reskin. Washington DC: Natl. Acad. Press. In press

Block, J. H. 1976. Issues, problems, and pitfalls in assessing sex differences: A critical review of "The Psychology of Sex Differences." *Merrill-Palmer Q.* 22:283–308

Breines, W., Gordon, L. 1983. The new scholarship on family violence. *Signs* 8:490–531

Brewer, M. B., Berk, R. A., eds. 1982. Beyond nine to five: Sexual harassment on the job. *J. Soc. Issues* 38(4):1–201

Broverman, I. K., Vogel, S. R., Broverman, D. M., Clarkson, F. E., Rosenkrantz, P. S. 1972. Sex-role stereotypes: A current appraisal. *J. Soc. Issues* 28(2):59–78

Bryson, J. B., Bryson, R. B., eds. 1978. Dual-career couples. *Psychol. Women Q.* 3:1–120

Burt, M. R. 1980. Cultural myths and supports for rape. *J. Pers. Soc. Psychol.* 38:217–30

Burt, M. R., Albin, R. S. 1981. Rape myths, rape definitions, and probability of conviction. *J. Appl. Soc. Psychol.* 11:212–30

Busby, L. J. 1975. Sex-role research on the mass media. *J. Commun.* Autumn:107–31

Cann, A., Calhoun, L. G., Selby, J. W., King, H. E., eds. 1981. Rape. *J. Soc. Issues* 37(4):1–161

Carbonell, J. L. 1984. Sex roles and leadership revisited. *J. Appl. Psychol.* 69:44–49

Carli, L. L. 1983. *Are women more social and men more task oriented? A meta-analytic* review of sex differences in group interaction, reward allocation, coalition formation, and cooperation in the Prisoner's Dilemma game. Univ. Mass. Unpublished manuscript

Cherlin, A., Walters, P. B. 1981. Trends in United States men's and women's sex-role attitudes 1972 to 1978. Am. Sociol. Rev. 46:453–60

Chodorow, N. 1978. The Reproduction of Mothering: Psychoanalysis and the Sociology of Gender. Berkeley: Univ. Calif. Press. 263 pp.

Clifton, A. K., McGrath, D., Wick, B. 1976. Stereotypes of woman: A single category? Sex Roles 2:135–48

Condry, J., Dyer, S. 1976. Fear of success: Attribution of cause to the victim. J. Soc. Issues 32(3):63–83

Connor, J. M., Schackman, M., Serbin, L. A. 1978. Sex-related differences in response to practice on a visual-spatial test and generalization to a related test. Child Dev. 49:24–29

Constantinople, A. 1973. Masculinity-femininity: An exception to a famous dictum? Psychol. Bull. 80:389–407

Cooper, H. M. 1979. Statistically combining independent studies: A meta-analysis of sex differences in conformity research. J. Pers. Soc. Psychol. 37:131–46

Cornelius, R. R., Averill, J. R. 1983. Sex differences in fear of spiders. J. Pers. Soc. Psychol. 45:377–83

Crane, M., Markus, H. 1982. Gender identity: The benefits of a self-schema approach. J. Pers. Soc. Psychol. 43:1195–97

Daly, M., Wilson, M. 1983. Sex, Evolution, and Behavior. Boston: Grant Press. 402 pp. 2nd ed.

Dan, A., Graham, E., Beecher, C., eds. 1980. The Menstrual Cycle: A Synthesis of Interdisciplinary Research, Vol. 1. New York: Springer

Darley, J. M., Fazio, R. H. 1980. Expectancy confirmation processes arising in the social interaction sequence. Am. Psychol. 35:867–81

Deaux, K. 1976. Sex: A perspective on the attribution process. In New Directions in Attribution Research, ed. J. H. Harvey, W. J. Ickes, R. F. Kidd, 1:335–52. Hillsdale, NJ: Erlbaum. 467 pp.

Deaux, K. 1977. Sex differences. In Personality Variables in Social Behavior, ed. T. Blass, pp. 357–77. Hillsdale, NJ: Erlbaum. 405 pp.

Deaux, K. 1984a. From individual differences to social categories: Analysis of a decade's research on gender. Am. Psychol. 39:105–16

Deaux, K. 1984b. Psychological constructions of masculinity and femininity. Presented at Kinsey Conf., Bloomington, Ind.

Deaux, K., Lewis, L. L. 1983. Components of gender stereotypes. Psychol. Doc. 13:25

Deaux, K., Lewis, L. L. 1984. The structure of gender stereotypes: Interrelationships among components and gender label. J. Pers. Soc. Psychol. 46:991–1004

Deaux, K., Lewis, L. L., Kite, M. 1984. Individual differences in gender stereotyping. Presented at Ann. Meet. Am. Psychol. Assoc., Toronto

Deaux, K., Winton, W., Crowley, M., Lewis, L. L. 1984. Level of categorization and content of gender stereotypes. Soc. Cogn. In press

Dion, K. L. 1984. Sex, gender, and groups: Selected issues. See O'Leary et al 1984

Donnerstein, E. 1980. Aggressive erotica and violence against women. J. Pers. Soc. Psychol. 39:269–77

Douvan, E. 1983. Learning to listen to a different drummer. Contemp. Psychol. 28:261–62

Dwyer, D. H. 1978. Images and Self-Images: Male and Female in Morocco. New York: Columbia Univ. Press. 194 pp.

Eagly, A. H. 1978. Sex differences in influenceability. Psychol. Bull. 85:86–116

Eagly, A. H. 1983. Gender and social influence: A social psychological analysis. Am. Psychol. 38:971–81

Eagly, A. H., Carli, L. L. 1981. Sex of researchers and sex-typed communications as determinants of sex differences in influenceability: A meta-analysis of social influence studies. Psychol. Bull. 90:1–20

Eagly, A. H., Renner, P., Carli, L. L. 1983. Using meta-analysis to examine biases in gender-difference research. Presented at Ann. Meet. Am. Psychol. Assoc., Anaheim, CA

Eagly, A. H., Steffen, V. 1984. Gender stereotypes stem from the distribution of women and men into social roles. J. Pers. Soc. Psychol. 46:735–54

Eagly, A. H., Wood, W. 1982. Inferred sex differences in status as a determinant of gender stereotypes about social influence. J. Pers. Soc. Psychol. 43:915–28

Eccles, J. 1983a. Sex differences in achievement patterns. Presented at Nebraska Symp. Motiv., Lincoln, Nebr.

Eccles (Parsons), J. 1983b. Expectancies, values, and academic behaviors. See Spence 1983a, pp. 75–146

Eccles (Parsons), J., Adler, T., Meece, J. L. 1984. Sex differences in achievement: A test of alternate theories. J. Pers. Soc. Psychol. 46:26–43

Eichler, M. 1980. The Double Standard. New York: St. Martin's. 151 pp.

Falbo, T., Hazen, M. D., Linimon, D. 1982. The costs of selecting power bases or messages associated with the opposite sex. *Sex Roles* 8:147–57

Falbo, T., Peplau, L. A. 1980. Power strategies in intimate relationships. *J. Pers. Soc. Psychol.* 38:618–28

Feather, N. T. 1984. Masculinity, femininity, psychological androgyny, and the structure of values. *J. Pers. Soc. Psychol.* In press

Feild, H. S. 1978. Attitudes toward rape: A comparative analysis of police, rapists, crisis counselors, and citizens. *J. Pers. Soc. Psychol.* 36:156–79

Fiske, S. T., Taylor, S. E. 1984. *Social Cognition*. Reading, Mass: Addison-Wesley. 508 pp.

Foushee, H. C., Helmreich, R. L., Spence, J. T. 1979. Implicit theories of masculinity and femininity: Dualistic or bipolar? *Psychol. Women Q.* 3:259–69

Frieze, I. H., Fisher, J. R., Hanusa, B. H., McHugh, M. C., Valle, V. A. 1978. Attributions of the causes of success and failure as internal and external barriers to achievement. In *The Psychology of Women: Future Directions in Research*, ed. J. L. Sherman, F. L. Denmark, pp. 519–52. New York: Psychological Dimensions. 758 pp.

Frieze, I. H., Whitley, B. E. Jr., Hanusa, B. H., McHugh, M. C. 1982. Assessing the theoretical models for sex differences in causal attributions for success and failure. *Sex Roles* 8:333–43

Frodi, A., Macauley, J., Thome, P. R. 1977. Are women always less aggressive than men? A review of the experimental literature. *Psychol. Bull.* 84:634–60

Gilligan, C. 1982. *In a Different Voice*. Cambridge, Mass: Harvard Univ. Press. 184 pp.

Goffman, E. 1976. *Gender Advertisements*. New York: Harper & Row. 84 pp.

Golding, J. M., Singer, J. L. 1983. Patterns of inner experience: Daydreaming styles, depressive moods, and sex roles. *J. Pers. Soc. Psychol.* 45:663–75

Gould, M. 1980. The new sociology. *Signs* 5:459–67

Gould, S. J. 1980. *The Panda's Thumb: More Reflections in Natural History*. New York: Norton

Grady, K. E. 1977. *Sex as a social label: The illusion of sex differences*. PhD thesis. City Univ. New York

Grady, K. E. 1981. Sex bias in research design. *Psychol. Women Q.* 5:628–36

Grant, P. R., Holmes, J. G. 1981. The integration of implicit personality theory schemas and stereotype images. *Soc. Psychol. Q.* 44:107–15

Grant, P. R., Holmes, J. G. 1982. The influence of stereotypes in impression formation: A reply to Locksley, Hepburn, and Ortiz. *Soc. Psychol. Q.* 45:274–76

Gray-Little, B., Burks, N. 1983. Power and satisfaction in marriage: A review and critique. *Psychol. Bull.* 93:513–38

Gutek, B. A., Morasch, B. 1982. Sex-ratios, sex-role spillover, and sexual harassment of women at work. *J. Soc. Issues* 38(4):55–74

Guttentag, M., Secord, P. F. 1983. *Too Many Women? The Sex Ratio Question*. Beverly Hills, Calif: Sage. 277 pp.

Hall, F. S., Hall, D. T. 1979. *The Two-Career Couple*. Reading, Mass: Addison-Wesley. 259 pp.

Hall, J. A. 1977. *Gender effects in encoding nonverbal cues*. Unpublished manuscript. Johns Hopkins Univ.

Hall, J. A. 1978. Gender effects in decoding nonverbal cues. *Psychol. Bull.* 85:845–75

Hall, J. A. 1979. Gender, gender roles, and nonverbal communication skills. See Rosenthal 1979, pp. 32–67

Hall, J. A., Halberstadt, A. G. 1981. Sex roles and nonverbal communication skills. *Sex Roles* 7:273–87

Hamilton, D. L., ed. 1981. *Cognitive Processes in Stereotyping and Intergroup Behavior*. Hillsdale, NJ: Erlbaum. 366 pp.

Hansen, R. D., O'Leary, V. E. 1983. Actresses and actors: The effects of sex on causal attributions. *Basic Appl. Soc. Psychol.* 4:209–30

Hastorf, A. H., Isen, A. M., eds. 1982. *Cognitive Social Psychology*. New York: Elsevier. 362 pp.

Heilbrun, A. B. Jr. 1976. Measurement of masculine and feminine sex role identities as independent dimensions. *J. Consult. Clin. Psychol.* 44:183–90

Helmreich, R. L., Beane, W. E., Lucker, G. W., Spence, J. T. 1978. Achievement motivation and scientific attainment. *Pers. Soc. Psychol. Bull.* 4:222–26

Helmreich, R. L., Spence, J. T., Beane, W. E., Lucker, G. W., Matthews, K. A. 1980. Making it in academic psychology: Demographic and personality correlates of attainment. *J. Pers. Soc. Psychol.* 39:896–908

Helmreich, R. L., Spence, J. T., Gibson, R. J. 1982. Sex-role attitudes: 1972–1980. *Pers. Soc. Psychol. Bull.* 8:656–63

Henley, N. M. 1977. *Body Politics: Power, Sex, and Nonverbal Communication*. Englewood Cliffs, NJ: Prentice-Hall. 214 pp.

Henley, N. M. 1984. Psychology and gender. *Signs*. In press

Hoffman, L. W. 1977. Fear of success in 1965 and 1974: A follow-up study. *J. Consult. Clin. Psychol.* 45:310–21

Hoffman, L. W. 1982. Methodological issues in follow-up and replication studies. *J. Soc. Issues* 38(1):53–64

Hollander, E. P. 1985. Leadership and power. See Lindzey & Aronson 1985. In press

Horner, M. S. 1972. Toward an understanding of achievement-related conflicts in women. *J. Soc. Issues* 28(2):157–75

Houser, B. B., Beckman, L. J. 1980. Background characteristics and women's dual-role attitudes. *Sex Roles* 6:355–66

Huston, A. C. 1983. Sex-typing. In *Handbook of Child Psychology*, ed. P. H. Mussen, E. M. Hetherington, 4:387–467. New York: Wiley. 1043 pp.

Hyde, J. S. 1981. How large are cognitive gender differences? A meta-analysis using ω^2 and d. *Am. Psychol.* 36:892–901

Hyde, J. S. 1982. *Gender differences in aggression: A developmental meta-analysis.* Submitted for publication

Instone, D., Major, B., Bunker, B. B. 1983. Gender, self confidence, and social influence strategies: An organizational simulation. *J. Pers. Soc. Psychol.* 44:322–33

Jacklin, C. N. 1981. Methodological issues in the study of sex-related differences. *Dev. Rev.* 1:266–73

Jellison, J. M., Jackson-White, R., Bruder, R. A., Martyna, W. 1975. Achievement behavior: A situational interpretation. *Sex Roles* 1:369–84

Johnson, P. 1976. Women and power: Toward a theory of effectiveness. *J. Soc. Issues* 32(3):99–110

Kanter, R. M. 1977. *Men and Women of the Corporation.* New York: Basic Books. 348 pp.

Kelley, H. H. 1979. *Personal Relationships: Their Structures and Processes.* Hillsdale, NJ: Erlbaum. 183 pp.

Kelley, H. H., Berscheid, E., Christensen, A., Harvey, J. H., Huston, T. L., et al. 1983. *Close Relationships.* New York: Freeman. 572 pp.

Kelly, J. A., Worell, J. 1977. New formulations of sex roles and androgyny: A critical review. *J. Consult. Clin. Psychol.* 45:1101–15

Kessler, S. J., McKenna, W. 1978. *Gender: An Ethnomethodological Approach.* New York: Wiley. 233 pp.

Klein, H. M., Willerman, L. 1979. Psychological masculinity and femininity and typical and maximal dominance expression in women. *J. Pers. Soc. Psychol.* 37:2059–70

Komnenich, P., ed. 1981. *The Menstrual Cycle: Research and Implications for Women's Health,* Vol. 2. New York: Springer

La France, M., Carmen, B. 1980. The nonverbal display of psychological androgyny. *J. Pers. Soc. Psychol.* 38:36–49

Lenney, E. 1977. Women's self-confidence in achievement settings. *Psychol. Bull.* 84:1–13

Lenney, E. 1979. Androgyny: Some audacious assertions toward its coming of age. *Sex Roles* 5:703–19

Lifton, P. D. 1982. Should Heinz's wife read this book? *J. Pers. Assess.* 46:550–51

Lifton, P. D. 1984. Personality correlates and sex differences in moral reasoning: A comparative approach. *J. Pers. Soc. Psychol.* In press

Lindzey, G., Aronson, E., eds. 1985. *Handbook of Social Psychology.* Reading, Mass: Addison-Wesley. In press. 3rd ed.

Lingle, J. H., Altom, M. W., Medin, D. L. 1984. Of cabbages and kings: Assessing the extendibility of natural object concepts to social things. See Ashmore & Del Boca 1984a

Linn, M. C., Petersen, A. C. 1983. *Emergence and characterization of gender differences in spatial ability: A meta-analysis.* Unpublished manuscript, Univ. Calif., Berkeley

Lipman-Blumen, J., Handley-Isaksen, A., Leavitt, H. J. 1983. Achieving styles in men and women: A model, an instrument, and some findings. See Spence 1983a, pp. 147–204

Lipman-Blumen, J., Tickamyer, A. R. 1975. Sex roles in transition: A ten-year perspective. *Ann. Rev. Sociol.* 1:297–337

Lloyd, B. B. 1976. Social responsibility and research on sex differences. See Lloyd & Archer 1976, pp. 1–23

Lloyd, B. B., Archer, J., eds. 1976. *Exploring Sex Differences.* New York: Academic. 280 pp.

Lockheed, M. E., Hall, K. 1976. Conceptualizing sex as a status characteristic: Applications to leadership training strategies. *J. Soc. Issues* 32(3):111–24

Lockheed, M. E., Harris, A. M., Nemceff, W. P. 1983. Sex and social influence: Does sex function as a status characteristic in mixed-sex groups of children? *J. Educ. Psychol.* 75:877–88

Locksley, A., Borgida, E., Brekke, N., Hepburn, C. 1980. Sex stereotypes and social judgment. *J. Pers. Soc. Psychol.* 39:821–31

Locksley, A., Colten, M. E. 1979. Psychological androgyny: A case of mistaken identity? *J. Pers. Soc. Psychol.* 37:1017–31

Locksley, A., Hepburn, C., Ortiz, V. 1982. On the effect of social stereotypes on judgments of individuals: A comment on Grant and Holmes's "The integration of implicit personality theory schemas and stereotypic images". *Soc. Psychol. Q.* 45:270–73

Lott, B. 1981. A feminist critique of androgyny: Toward the elimination of gender attributions for learned behavior. See Mayo & Henley 1981, pp. 171–80

Lowe, M., Hubbard, R., eds. 1983. *Woman's Nature: Rationalization of Inequality.* New York: Pergamon. 155 pp.

Lubinski, D., Tellegen, A., Butcher, J. N. 1983. Masculinity, femininity, and androgyny viewed and assessed as distinct concepts. *J. Pers. Soc. Psychol.* 44:428–39

Maccoby, E. E., ed. 1966. *The Development of Sex Differences.* Stanford, Calif: Stanford Univ. Press. 351 pp.

Maccoby, E. E., Jacklin, C. N. 1974. *The Psychology of Sex Differences.* Stanford, Calif: Stanford Univ. Press. 634 pp.

Maccoby, E. E., Jacklin, C. N. 1980. Sex differences in aggression: A rejoinder and reprise. *Child Dev.* 51:964–80

Major, B., Carnevale, P. J. D., Deaux, K. 1981. A different perspective on androgyny: Evaluations of masculine and feminine personality characteristics. *J. Pers. Soc. Psychol.* 41:988–1001

Major, B., Deaux, K. 1982. Individual differences in justice behavior. In *Equity and Justice in Social Behavior,* ed. J. Greenberg, R. L. Cohen, pp. 43–76. New York: Academic. 492 pp.

Malamuth, N. M. 1981. Rape proclivity among males. See Cann et al 1981, pp. 138–57

Markus, H., Crane, M., Bernstein, S., Siladi, M. 1982. Self schemas and gender. *J. Pers. Soc. Psychol.* 42:38–50

Mason, K. O., Czajka, J. L., Arber, S. 1976. Change in U. S. women's sex-role attitudes, 1964–1974. *Am. Sociol. Rev.* 41:573–96

Mayo, C. N., Henley, N., eds. 1981. *Gender, Androgyny, and Nonverbal Behavior.* New York: Springer-Verlag

McArthur, L. Z. 1981. What grabs you? The role of attention in impression formation and causal attribution. In *Social Cognition: The Ontario Symposium* ed. C. P. Herman, M. P. Zanna, Vol. 1. Hillsdale, NJ: Erlbaum. 437 pp.

McArthur, L. Z. 1982. Judging a book by its cover: A cognitive analysis of the relationship between physical appearance and stereotyping. See Hastorf & Isen 1982, pp. 149–211

McCauley, C., Stitt, C. L., Segal, M. 1980. Stereotyping: From prejudice to prediction. *Psychol. Bull.* 87:195–208

Mednick, M. T. 1982. Women and the psychology of achievement: Implications for personal and social change. In *Women in the Workforce,* ed. J. Bernardin, pp. 48–69. New York: Praeger. 242 pp.

Mednick, M. T. S., Weissman, H. J. 1975. The psychology of women—Selected topics. *Ann. Rev. Psychol.* 26:1–18

Meece, J. L., Parsons, J. E., Kaczala, C. M., Goff, S. B., Futterman, R. 1982. Sex differences in math achievement: Toward a model of academic choice. *Psychol. Bull.* 91:324–48

Meeker, B. F., Weitzel-O'Neill, P. A. 1977. Sex roles and interpersonal behavior in task-oriented groups. *Am. Sociol. Rev.* 43:91–105

Megargee, E. E. 1969. Influence of sex roles on the manifestation of leadership. *J. Appl. Psychol.* 53:377–82

Mervis, C., Rosch, E. 1981. Categorization of natural objects. *Ann. Rev. Psychol.* 32:89–115

Miles, B. 1975. *Channeling Children: Sex Stereotyping in Prime Time TV.* Princeton, NJ: Women on Words and Images

Miles, C. C. 1935. Sex in social psychology. In *Handbook of Social Psychology,* ed. C. Murchison, pp. 683–797. Worcester, Mass: Clark Univ. Press

Miller, A. G., ed. 1982. *In the Eye of the Beholder: Contemporary Issues in Stereotyping.* New York: Praeger. 531 pp.

Miller, J., Garrison, H. H. 1982. Sex roles: The division of labor at home and in the workplace. *Ann. Rev. Sociol.* 8:237–62

Mills, C. J., Tyrrell, D. J. 1983. Sex stereotypic encoding and release from proactive interference. *J. Pers. Soc. Psychol.* 45:772–81

Mishler, E. G. 1979. Meaning in context: Is there any other kind? *Harvard Educ. Rev.* 49:1–19

Morgan, C. S., Walker, A. J. 1983. Predicting sex role attitudes. *Soc. Psychol. Q.* 46:148–51

Myers, A. M., Gonda, G. 1982. Utility of the masculinity-femininity construct: Comparison of traditional and androgyny approaches. *J. Pers. Soc. Psychol.* 43:514–22

Newcombe, N., Bandura, M. M., Taylor, D. C. 1983. Sex differences in spatial ability and spatial activities. *Sex Roles* 9:377–86

Nieva, V. F., Gutek, B. A. 1981. *Women and Work: A Psychological Perspective.* New York: Praeger. 177 pp.

O'Leary, V. E., Unger, R., Wallston, B. S., eds. 1984. *Women, Gender, and Social Psychology.* Hillsdale, NJ: Erlbaum. In press

Parlee, M. B. 1975. Psychology. *Signs* 1:119–38

Parlee, M. B. 1979. Psychology and women. *Signs* 5:121–33

Parlee, M. B. 1981. Appropriate control groups in feminist research. *Psychol. Women Q.* 5:637–44

Parsons, T., Bales, R. F., eds. 1955. *Family, Socialization, and Interaction.* Glencoe: Free Press

Pedhazur, E. J., Tetenbaum, T. J. 1979. Bem Sex Role Inventory: A theoretical and methodological critique. *J. Pers. Soc. Psychol.* 37:996–1016

Peters, L. H., Terborg, J. R., Taynor, J. 1974. Women as managers scale: A measure of attitudes toward women in management positions. *JSAS Cat. Sel. Doc. Psychol.* 4:27

Philips, S. U. 1980. Sex differences and language. *Ann. Rev. Anthropol.* 9:523–44

Piliavin, J. A., Unger, R. K. 1984. The helpful but helpless female: Myth or reality? See O'Leary et al 1984

Pollak, S., Gilligan, C. 1982. Images of violence in Thematic Apperception Test stories. *J. Pers. Soc. Psychol.* 42:159–67

Pollak, S., Gilligan, C. 1983. Differing about differences: The incidence and interpretation of violent fantasies in women and men. *J. Pers. Soc. Psychol.* 45:1172–75

Putnam, L. L., McCallister, L. 1980. Situational effects of task and gender on nonverbal display. In *Communication Yearbook,* ed. D. Nimno, 4:679–97. New Brunswick, NJ: Transaction

Quinn, N. 1977. Anthropological studies on women's status. *Ann. Rev. Anthropol.* 6:181–225

Rasmussen, D. R. 1981. Pair-bond strength and stability and reproductive success. *Psychol. Rev.* 88:274–90

Riordan, C. 1983. Sex as a general status characteristic. *Soc. Psychol. Q.* 46:261–67

Roberts, H., ed. 1981. *Doing Feminist Research.* London: Routledge & Kegan Paul. 207 pp.

Rorer, L. G., Widiger, T. A. 1983. Personality structure and assessment. *Ann. Rev. Psychol.* 34:431–63

Rosaldo, M. Z., Lamphere, L., eds. 1974. *Woman, Culture, and Society.* Stanford, Calif: Stanford Univ. Press. 352 pp.

Rosch, E. 1978. Principles of categorization. In *Cognition and Categorization,* ed. E. Rosch, B. B. Lloyd, pp. 27–48. Hillsdale, NJ: Erlbaum

Rosenberg, R. 1982. *Beyond Separate Spheres: Intellectual Roots of Modern Feminism.* New Haven: Yale Univ. Press. 288 pp.

Rosenkrantz, P., Vogel, S., Bee, H., Broverman, I., Broverman, D. M. 1968. Sex-role stereotypes and self-concepts in college students. *J. Consult. Clin. Psychol.* 32:287–95

Rosenthal, R., ed. 1979. *Skill in Nonverbal Communication: Individual Differences.* Cambridge, Mass: Oelgeschlager, Gunn & Hain 270 pp.

Rosenthal, R., DePaulo, B. M. 1979. Sex differences in accommodation in nonverbal communication. See Rosenthal 1979, pp. 68–103

Rosenthal, R., Rubin, D. B. 1982. Further meta-analytic procedures for assessing cognitive gender differences. *J. Educ. Psychol.* 74:708–12

Ruble, D. N., Ruble, T. L. 1982. Sex stereotypes. See Miller 1982, pp. 188–251

Sampson, E. E. 1977. Psychology and the American ideal. *J. Pers. Soc. Psychol.* 35:767–82

Sanday, P. R. 1981. *Female Power and Male Dominance: On the Origins of Sexual Inequality.* Cambridge, England: Cambridge Univ. Press. 295 pp.

Secord, P. F. 1982. The origin and maintenance of social roles: The case of sex roles. In *Personality, Roles, and Social Behavior,* ed. W. Ickes, E. S. Knowles, pp. 33–53. New York: Springer-Verlag. 362 pp.

Secord, P. F. 1983. Imbalanced sex ratios: The social consequences. *Pers. Soc. Psychol. Bull.* 9:525–43

Sherif, C. W. 1979. Bias in psychology. In *The Prism of Sex: Essays in the Sociology of Knowledge,* ed. J. A. Sherman, E. T. Beck, pp. 93–133. Madison: Univ. Wisconsin Press. 286 pp.

Sherif, C. W. 1982. Needed concepts in the study of gender identity. *Psychol. Women Q.* 6:375–98

Sherman, J. 1978. *Sex-Related Cognitive Differences.* Springfield, Ill: Thomas. 269 pp.

Shields, S. A. 1975. Functionalism, Darwinism, and the psychology of women: A study in social myth. *Am. Psychol.* 30:739–54

Shields, S. A. 1982. The variability hypothesis: The history of a biological model of sex differences in intelligence. *Signs* 7:769–97

Skrypnek, B. J., Snyder, M. 1982. On the self-perpetuating nature of stereotypes about women and men. *J. Exp. Soc. Psychol.* 18:277–91

Smith, E. R., Ferree, M. M., Miller, F. D. 1975. A short scale of attitudes toward feminism. *Represent. Res. Soc. Psychol.* 6:51–56

Spence, J. T., ed. 1983a. *Achievement and Achievement Motives: Psychological and Sociological Approaches.* San Francisco: Freeman. 381 pp.

Spence, J. T. 1983b. *Gender identity and its implications for concepts of masculinity and femininity.* Presented at Nebraska Symp. Motiv., Lincoln, Nebr.

Spence, J. T. 1984. Masculinity, femininity, and gender-related traits: A conceptual analysis and critique of current research. *Prog. Exp. Pers. Res.* 13:In press

Spence, J. T., Deaux, K., Helmreich, R. L. 1985. Sex roles in contemporary American society. See Lindzey & Aronson 1985

Spence, J. T., Helmreich, R. L. 1972. The Attitudes toward Women Scale: An objective instrument to measure attitudes toward the rights and roles of women in contemporary society. *JSAS Cat. Sel. Doc. Psychol.* 2:667–68

Spence, J. T., Helmreich, R. L. 1978. *Masculinity & Femininity: Their Psychological Dimensions, Correlates, & Antecedents.* Austin: Univ. Texas Press. 297 pp.

Spence, J. T., Helmreich, R. L. 1979. The many faces of androgyny: A reply to Locksley and Colten. *J. Pers. Soc. Psychol.* 37:1032–46

Spence, J. T., Helmreich, R. L. 1980. Masculine instrumentality and feminine expressiveness: Their relationships with sex role attitudes and behaviors. *Psychol. Women Q.* 5:147–63

Spence, J. T., Helmreich, R. L. 1981. Androgyny versus gender schema: A comment on Bem's gender schema theory. *Psychol. Rev.* 88:365–68

Spence, J. T., Helmreich, R. L. 1983. Achievement-related motives and behaviors. See Spence 1983a, pp. 7–74

Spence, J. T., Helmreich, R., Stapp, J. 1974. The personal attributes questionnaire: A measure of sex-role stereotypes and masculinity-femininity. *JSAS Cat. Sel. Doc. Psychol.* 4:43

Spence, J. T., Helmreich, R., Stapp, J. 1975. Ratings of self and peers on sex-role attributes and their relations to self-esteem and conceptions of masculinity and femininity. *J. Pers. Soc. Psychol.* 32:29–39

Storms, M. D. 1981. A theory of erotic orientation development. *Psychol. Rev.* 88:340–53

Strathern, M. 1976. An anthropological perspective. See Lloyd & Archer 1976, pp. 49–70

Taylor, M. C., Hall, J. A. 1982. Psychological androgyny: Theories, methods, and conclusions. *Psychol. Bull.* 92:347–66

Taylor, S. E., Fiske, S. T. 1978. Salience, attention and attribution: Top of the head phenomena. *Adv. Exp. Soc. Psychol.* 11:249–88

Thornton, A., Alwin, D. F., Camburn, D. 1983. Causes and consequences of sex-role attitudes and attitude change. *Am. Sociol. Rev.* 48:211–27

Thornton, A., Freedman, D. 1979. Changes in the sex-role attitudes of women, 1962–1977: Evidence from a panel study. *Am. Sociol. Rev.* 44:832–42

Tieger, T. 1980. On the biological basis of sex differences in aggression. *Child Dev.* 51:943–63

Towson, S. M. J., Zanna, M. P. 1982. Toward a situational analysis of gender differences in aggression. *Sex Roles* 8:903–14

Tresemer, D. W. 1977. *Fear of Success.* New York: Plenum

Unger, R. K. 1976. Male is greater than female: The socialization of status inequality. *Counsel. Psychol.* 6:2–9

Unger, R. K. 1979. Toward a redefinition of sex and gender. *Am. Psychol.* 34:1085–94

Unger, R. K. 1981. Sex as a social reality: Field and laboratory research. *Psychol. Women Q.* 5:645–53

Unger, R. K. 1982. *Controlling out the obvious: Power, status, and social psychology.* Presented at Ann. Meet. Am. Psychol. Assoc., Washington DC

Unger, R. K. 1983. Through the looking glass: No wonderland yet! (The reciprocal relationship between methodology and models of reality.) *Psychol. Women Q.* 8:9–32

Vaughter, R. 1976. Psychology. *Signs* 2:120–46

von Baeyer, C. L., Sherk, D. L., Zanna, M. P. 1981. Impression management in the job interview: When the female applicant meets the male "chauvinist" interviewer. *Pers. Soc. Psychol. Bull.* 7:45–51

Wallston, B. S. 1983. Overview of research methods. In *Sex Role Research: Measuring Social Change,* ed. B. L. Richardson, J. Wirtenberg, pp. 51–76. New York: Praeger. 274 pp.

Wallston, B. S., Grady, K. E. 1984. Integrating the feminist critique and the crisis in social psychology: Another look at research methods. See O'Leary et al 1984

Wallston, B. S., O'Leary, V. E. 1981. Sex and gender make a difference: The differential perceptions of women and men. *Rev. Pers. Soc. Psychol.* 2:9–41

Webster, M. Jr., Driskell, J. E. Jr. 1978. Status generalization: A review and some new data. *Am. Sociol. Rev.* 43:220–36

Weidner, G., Griffitt, W. 1983. Rape: A sexual stigma. *J. Pers.* 51:152–66

Weiner, B., Stone, A. J., Schmitz, M. D., Schmidt, A. C. R., Benton, C. J. 1983. Compounding the errors: A reply to Pollak and Gilligan. *J. Pers. Soc. Psychol.* 45:1176–78

Williams, J. E., Best, D. L. 1982. *Measuring Sex Stereotypes: A Thirty-Nation Study.* Beverly Hills, Calif: Sage. 368 pp.

Wittig, M. A. 1984. *Metatheoretical Dilemmas in the Psychology of Gender.* Manuscript submitted for publication.

Wittig, M. A., Petersen, A. C., eds. 1979. *Sex-Related Differences in Cognitive Functioning.* New York: Academic. 378 pp.

Yanagisako, S. J. 1979. Family and household: The analysis of domestic groups. *Ann. Rev. Anthropol.* 8:161–205

Zanna, M. P., Pack, S. J. 1975. On the self-fulfilling nature of apparent sex differences in behavior. *J. Exp. Soc. Psychol.* 11:583–91

Zuckerman, M., Wheeler, L. 1975. To dispel fantasies about the fantasy-based measure of fear of success. *Psychol. Bull.* 82:932–46

Ann. Rev. Psychol. 1985. 36:83–114

PERSONALITY: CURRENT CONTROVERSIES, ISSUES, AND DIRECTIONS

Lawrence A. Pervin

Department of Psychology, Rutgers University, New Brunswick, New Jersey 08903

CONTENTS

INTRODUCTION

This review of personality theory and research focuses on current controversies and issues. Perhaps the best way to set the tone for such discussion is consideration of past relevant chapters. Reviewing chapters over the past decade leads one to the conclusion that generally all is not well in personality psychology, though some think things may be getting better. With the exception of Carlson's (1975) suggestion of the beginning of a major turnaround in appreciating the complexity of personality, and Helson & Mitchell's (1978) suggestion that we are extending our research and enriching our paradigms, most reviewers have been rather pessimistic about the field. Thus, for example, Sechrest (1976) suggests that personality theory is in sad shape and Phares & Lamiell (1977) suggest that the field is in a period of crisis. In the last review, Loevinger & Knoll (1983) appear to take a dim view of how much the field has advanced

83

0066-4308/85/0201-0083$02.00

and, following Meehl (1978), question whether a really impressive theory of personality is possible. Rorer & Widiger (1983), in their review of personality structure and assessment, appear to be both more critical and optimistic. They suggest that most of the literature deserves to be avoided since it represents a negligible increment to understanding. However, they present a picture of what the field should look like and believe that ultimately their representation will be accepted by most personality psychologists—though only after a period of kicking and screaming. In sum, most recent reviewers have been relatively critical and pessimistic. Where optimism has appeared, it generally has been based on hope for the future rather than on demonstrated gains of the past.

Along with general views of the state of the field, a number of themes stand out. Many of these have particular relevance for the issues to be considered in this chapter. Perhaps the overriding message of past reviewers has been the need for research that appreciates the complexity of individual personality functioning. In various cases the focus of the message is upon the organization of personality variables, in particular relations among cognition and affect (Singer & Singer 1972), and the functioning of people in the natural environment and over extended periods of time. The emphasis is on that which is integrative and dynamic as opposed to that which is fragmented and static. Yet, at the same time, there is recognition of fragmentation in the field and a paucity of studies possessing the desired qualities. Are things getting better now? Are there more studies demonstrating appreciation of the complex, integrated, organized, dynamic, and patterned quality of human personality functioning? If not, why not?

CURRENT CONTROVERSIES AND ISSUES

Much of the current personality literature can be considered in terms of controversies and issues (Pervin 1984b). Though some theories, such as social learning theory, exert considerable influence on the field, we are still without a paradigm as such. Interestingly enough, currently influential theories, such as social learning theory, cognitive-attribution theory, and trait theory, capture little of the integrative, dynamic emphasis suggested by past reviewers. In terms of research, one can point to topics that receive considerable attention in the literature, such as learned helplessness. However, it would be hard to demonstrate that research in the field has coalesced around a few central problems. One is reminded here of Sechrest's (1976) suggestion that the themes of personality research change not so much because issues are resolved and phenomena understood, but rather because investigators run out of steam and interest turns to "newer, more exciting" phenomena. Thus, current work in the field centers around a few hot topics in the field, a few theoretical points of view, a wide variety of rather unrelated topics and concerns, and major concern with a few controversies and issues. Attention here is focused on three such areas of current concern—the person-situation controversy; the issue of relations among cognition, affect, and overt behavior; and concern with the merits of idiographic approaches to research and attention to a wider array of personality phenomena.

The Person-Situation Controversy

The person-situation controversy continues to dominate the attention of personality psychologists, as witnessed in articles in *Psychological Review,* the 1982 edition of the Nebraska Symposium (Page 1983), the second volume of the Michigan State series in honor of Henry Murray (Rabin et al 1982), and the initial issue of *Annals of Theoretical Psychology*. The issue, which in its most recent phase has been with us since publication of Mischel's 1968 book, has now tended to focus on *whether* people are cross-situationally consistent. Before considering the relevant recent literature, two points are noteworthy.

First, trait psychologists do *not* suggest that people will behave the same way in all situations. G. W. Allport (1961) gave specific attention to the relations of situations to traits and concluded that both were important. Traits, defined in terms of frequency, intensity, and range of situations, were regarded as ranges of possible behavior to be activated according to the demands of the situation. In addition, most behavior in a situation was viewed as multi-trait determined. Cattell (1983) emphasized the importance of situational factors and behavioral variability in his specification equation as well as in his emphasis on moods, states, and roles. Finally, Eysenck (1982) suggests that the debate is an unreal one since one always has persons-in-situations and the relative importance of personality and situational factors depends on the nature of the situation, the selection of people, and the particular traits measured. Sometimes it appears as if both attackers and defenders of trait theory are responding to a view that does not exist among major trait theorists.

The second noteworthy point is that the issue is not new, nor is the nature of some of the specific arguments. For example, in 1937 F. H. Allport noted the controversy between generalists (traits) and specifists (situations) and emphasized the need to look at underlying individual consistencies in terms of teleonomic trends. At the same time, Woodworth (1937) asked about the consistency of personality and concluded that people behave similarly in situations they perceive to be similar relevant to what they are trying to do or get out of the situation. Beyond this, one can consider Murray's (1938) discussion of the centralists-peripheralists split and G. W. Allport's (1955) discussion of the division among psychologists concerning whether behavior is governed from within or from without (Pervin, Chap. 1, 1978, 1984a).

Given the long-standing history of the issues concerning person-situation relationships one might have expected research to focus on issues beyond *whether* people are consistent and *whether* situations or persons are more important. Most personality psychologists would have agreed and would still agree that behavior is influenced both by person variables and by situation variables. This would suggest the utility of defining the relevant variables and the processes governing relations between the two. While some attention has been given to such efforts, even greater attention appears to have been given to questions of competing points of view. Trait theory, which many incorrectly view as the only representative of a person emphasis in personality theory, has been attacked by Mischel & Peake (1982, 1983a), who present evidence that behavior is not cross-situationally consistent, and by Shweder (1982), who suggests that traits represent systematic distortions based on conceptual and semantic notions of "what goes with what" rather than actual behavioral co-occurrences—the systematic distortion hypothesis. The response of trait psychologists has taken varied forms, including the following:

1. POOR RESEARCH   The suggestion has been made that most studies that fail to find evidence of consistency and stability are poorly conducted. When such research is properly conducted more supportive evidence can be found (Block 1977, Olweus 1977, 1981). Evidence of stability of aggressive behavior was presented by Olweus (1979, 1980) and of altruistic behavior by Rushton (1981). Mischel (1969, 1983, Mischel & Peake 1982) suggests that temporal stability is less of an issue than cross-situational consistency and that evidence of the latter remains to be provided.

2. REPEATED MEASURES—MULTIPLE OCCASIONS   The trait argument here is that one cannot consider single acts or single-occasion measures as adequate reflections of the presence of a trait. Rather, one must consider aggregate data. The prime proponent of this point of view has been Epstein (1979, 1980, 1982, 1983a,b,c) though the same position has been taken by others as well (Gifford 1982, Jaccard 1974, Moskowitz 1982). The suggestion is that there is too much error involved in the measurement of single acts on single occasions and that reliability and consistency increase as multiple measures are obtained. A study of naturally occurring prosocial and dominance behavior by Small et al (1983) supports the utility of such an approach. Using aggregate data, Diener & Larsen (1984) present evidence of temporal stability and cross-situational consistency of affective, behavioral, and cognitive responses (self-report), though the complexity of person, situation, and response effects involved is also emphasized.

The principle of repeated measures or aggregation has been criticized as failing to distinguish between reliability and consistency (Day et al 1983, Mischel & Peake 1982, 1983a) and as failing to consider situational factors influencing the presence or absence of a trait (Monson et al 1982). In the latter case it is suggested that the relative efficacy of multiple measures may be due to the higher probability of including at least one situation relevant to the trait. Mischel & Peake (1982) suggest that the evidence of consistency offered by Epstein is not very convincing since in the main it consists of functionally related behaviors (e.g. calls made and calls received), a point disputed by Epstein. In addition, the former suggest that aggregating over occasions may serve to bypass rather than resolve critical issues concerning cross-situational consistency: "Although such aggregation is useful for making statements about mean levels of behavior across a range of contexts, cross-situational aggregation also often has the undesirable effect of canceling out some of the most valuable data about a person. It misses the point completely for the psychologist interested in the unique patterning of the individual by treating within-person variance, and indeed the context itself, as if it were error" (p. 738). This is a telling point for personality psychologists interested in processes of person-situation interaction rather than in summary descriptions alone. The issue of aggregation is considered again later in the chapter.

3. PHENOTYPE-GENOTYPE   The above defense on the part of trait theorists suggests a multiple-act criterion for consistency rather than a single-act criterion. A related defense suggests that the multiple acts expressive of a trait may be different topographically or phenotypically while genotypically expressive of the same trait. This argument is made by a number of theorists (Buss & Craik 1980, 1981, 1983a, Fishbein & Ajzen 1974, Moskowitz 1982) and is typified by Loevinger & Knoll's suggestion that "trait theory is more impressive—and more interesting—when it displays not literal consistency from one situation to another but predictability or coherence in what appear to be different behaviors" (1983, p. 209). Particularly noteworthy here is the effort of Buss & Craik (1980, 1981, 1983a) to define traits in terms of acts or behaviors that are more or less defining (prototypicality) of category membership. Distinguishing between *behavioral consistency* (i.e. single-act analyses) and *dispositional consistency* (i.e. multiple-act analysis based on dispositional categories), they demonstrate a relationship between personality scales and multiple-act criteria, particularly where such acts are central rather than peripheral to category membership. However, most correlations (between responses to personality questionnaires and self-reports of act frequencies) reported ranged between .3 and .5. Such relationships may be viewed as more or less problematic depending on whether the two forms of data are seen as different as opposed to corresponding sources of information about the person. In addition, as the authors recognize, the trait concepts emphasized are descriptive rather than representing causal explanations of observed regularities. In a sense, Buss & Craik seem to be suggesting that people will be consistent on "some acts more than others," making use of concepts of category membership and prototypical-

ity from cognitive psychology. It is interesting to speculate on whether the distinction between central and peripheral acts relates at all to the distinction between source traits and surface traits emphasized by factor analysts. Also, the research emphasized going from traits to acts, but it is not clear whether one can go with equal ease from acts to traits; that is, are traits and acts reciprocals or equally defining of one another? Issues such as these have important implications for the validation of personality scales, an issue explored in depth by Buss & Craik (1983 b,c).

The phenotype-genotype distinction is particularly important in psychoanalytic theory, where even opposites can be dynamically related. This broadened definition of consistency has implications for studies of longitudinal stability as well as for cross-situational consistency. Kagan (1980) considers the many different possible meanings of longitudinal stability or consistency and concludes that the evidence is unimpressive in supporting any of the views. On the other hand, Sroufe (1979) comes to a somewhat different conclusion and McClelland (1981) illustrates how the life of a person can take varied turns while expressing the same conflicts and issues.

Mischel (1969), while accepting of longitudinal stability, is not impressed with the above defense of cross-situational consistency. He expresses concern that the phenotype-genotype distinction oversimplifies the complexity of organized behavior. Rather than expressing genotypic consistency, Mischel suggests that behavioral diversity is expressive of the organism's ability to make discriminations among evoking and maintaining conditions in situations—an emphasis on cognitive discriminativeness and situational diversity rather than motivational or trait consistency.

4. SOME PEOPLE MORE THAN OTHERS   Bem & Allen (1974) suggest that some people are more consistent than others. Kenrick & Stringfield (1980) also emphasize this argument and additionally suggest that consistency among judged behaviors will be greatest for publicly observable behaviors. Tellegen et al (1982) favor a linear model over the moderator variable approach suggested above. Mischel & Peake (1982) replicated the findings of Bem & Allen (i.e. subjects describing themselves as consistent show high levels of interrater agreement when rated on relevant traits by others relative to subjects describing themselves as inconsistent), but found that subjects rated as low in variability on a trait did *not* show greater cross-situational consistency in behavior than subjects rated high in variability. Rater reliability was not associated with cross-situational consistency. In addition to these criticisms one may note that using consistency as a moderator variable appears to violate part of the definition of the trait itself—similarity of behavior over a range of situations. In addition, there is no explanation of why some individuals are more consistent than others on particular traits or in relation to particular situations. A some-

what different approach to the issue is taken by Snyder (1979, 1981, 1983, Snyder & Campbell 1982), who suggests that high self-monitoring individuals are more responsive to situational cues for behavior and therefore more variable in their behavior than individuals low in self-monitoring.

5. SOME SITUATIONS MORE THAN OTHERS   The defense of trait theory here suggests that people will be more consistent in some situations than others. Expressive of this argument is the template-matching approach of Bem & Funder (1978, Bem 1983a,b, Funder 1983a). They suggest that people will be consistent to the extent that situations are similar for them. Matching personalities of individuals to personalities of situations leads to consistency of behavior; that is, people behave similarly in situations perceived to be similar in the traits that are relevant to them (Lord 1982). Magnusson (1981, 1984) also emphasizes the perceived situation within an interactional framework and suggests that clusters of situations may be determined within which individuals with certain traits behave similarly. Interestingly enough, social learning theory itself suggests that people behave similarly in situations perceived by them to be similar—in their reinforcement contingencies (Bandura 1977). Reinforcement contingencies include internal (pride, shame) as well as external (praise, criticism) sources of reinforcement. Evidence in support of this hypothesis has been found in terms of self-reported perceptions of behavior similarity and reinforcement contingency similarity (Champagne & Pervin, submitted for publication), though the hypothesis remains in need of further investigation. In particular, it does not account for either purely habitual modes of response or impulsive behavior, that is behavior that may be more or less independent of situation reinforcement contingencies. In addition, behavior may be regulated by long-term goals and reinforcers that extend beyond the immediate situation (Atkinson 1983, Feather 1982, Pervin 1983, Raynor 1974).

Mischel & Peake (1982) report difficulty in replicating the Bem & Funder (1978) results, in fact reporting data that reverse their findings. In addition, they are critical of the atheoretical characteristics of the approach and compare it to Meehl's (1956) cookbook approach to prediction; little is said that is helpful in understanding processes underlying person-situation interaction.

Another approach to the importance of situations for behavioral consistency suggests that people will be more consistent in situations low in constraint (Price & Bouffard 1974) or weak in pressures to conform (Monson et al 1982). Highly structured, norm-regulated situations serve to limit individual differences whereas ambiguous situations and situations weak in normative pressures maximize individual differences. This is interesting in that it is exactly data from the latter kinds of situations that are emphasized by dynamically oriented clinicians.

6. NATURAL SETTINGS, LABORATORY SETTINGS, AND SITUATION SELF-SELECTION   The suggestion by trait supporters that the level of consistency observed is influenced by the nature of the situations involved brings us to suggested differences between data from natural settings and data from laboratory studies. Block (1977) suggests that whether one finds evidence of consistency depends on the data collected and that there is good evidence for consistency when self-report and observer data are used. The consistency problem arises with laboratory data that exaggerate situational forces and limit freedom of individual response (Epstein 1982, Funder & Ozer 1983, Small et al 1983). Even in natural settings it is necessary that the behaviors of the relevant traits be publicly observable for there to be agreement among observers (Kenrick & Stringfield 1980, McCrae 1982).

Another distinction between the laboratory and ordinary social behavior involves the freedom of the person to engage in and otherwise manipulate the situation. G. W. Allport (1961) initially made the suggestion that personality traits were in part defined by the person's selection of situations. The point was again made by Wachtel (1973) in his critique of the situationist position and has recently become a major point of emphasis and research (Cantor et al 1984, Diener et al 1984, Furnham 1981, 1982, Gormly 1982, 1983, 1984, Snyder 1981, 1983, Snyder & Gangestad 1982). The evidence suggests a stronger relationship between trait scores and involvement in chosen or self-selected situations than between such scores and involvement in required situations (Emmons et al, submitted for publication). In other fields it has been suggested that children elicit reactions from mothers as well as respond to them (Lewis & Rosenblum 1974) and that individuals with genetic personality differences self-select and create different environments (Scarr & McCartney 1983). This view of the person as an active participant in life rather than as a passive respondent to evoking and maintaining conditions in the environment has been accepted, indeed championed by social learning theorists such as Bandura and Mischel.

7. IMPLICIT TRAIT THEORIES REFLECT REALITY   The final defense of trait theory concerns the response to suggestions that traits lie "in the eyes of the beholder" and represent systematic distortions or attribution errors. The trait defense here suggests that empirical demonstrations of traits go beyond implicit trait theories of personality, that situation attributions may represent error as much as person attributions (Funder 1982, Funder & van Ness 1983), and that implicit or lay trait theories must represent some high correspondence for them to be maintained. Interestingly enough, Cantor & Mischel (1979) take a quite different theoretical view but generally support this line of reasoning concerning cognitive categories: "Structure exists neither 'all in the head' of the organism nor 'all in the person' perceived; it is instead a function of an

interaction between the beliefs of observers and the characteristics of the observed" (1979, pp. 45–46).

COMMENT   An impressive amount of research has gone into attacking and defending the trait point of view. Despite years of debate and numerous investigations, the person-situation issue has not yet been resolved. Nor, one might venture to guess, will it be in terms of the current framing of the issue. Interestingly enough, the major protagonists in the recent debate agree that there is evidence both for consistency and variability. Epstein (1983b) suggests that situationists and trait theorists can both prove they are right since behavior is both situationally specific and cross-situationally general. He concludes that it is meaningless to argue in favor of one as opposed to the other. Similarly, Mischel (Mischel & Peake 1983a,b) suggests that the data show both behavioral discriminativeness according to the situation and a coherence or pattern of behaviors characteristic of individuals: "At the risk of being repetitious, as well as obvious, surely there is some consistency in behavior, just as surely as there is discriminativeness. . . . Phrasing the discussion in either-or terms, debating whether or not consistency and stability exist, perpetuates an unproductive debate and distracts from the serious tasks of analyzing both the objective structure of human behavior and its psychological construction" (1983a, pp. 241–42). What Epstein and Mischel disagree about is the amount of consistency and variability, and, more significantly, the utility of a trait concept in accounting for regularities that do exist. To a certain extent we are left with differing views as to how much variability in behavior one considers damaging to a trait concept (or, conversely, how much stability is supportive) and how much faith one has that further gains can be made through exploration of trait concepts. At this time, neither trait nor situationist theories do a terribly good job of predicting wide ranges of individual behaviors over varied situations, or of helping us to understand both stability and change in personality functioning.

As previously noted, it is unfortunate that to a great extent current personality theory is equated with trait theory. Whatever the merits of the trait concept, other concepts can be used to emphasize individual differences as well as the patterned, organized aspects of individual psychological functioning. While the trait concept may have value for some purposes, it is unsatisfactory on a number of counts.

First, in many cases the concept is descriptive rather than explanatory. With the exception of trait theories such as that of Eysenck, where the traits emphasized are embedded in a more general theory of personality development and functioning, there is a tendency for trait concepts to represent descriptions of occurrences or co-occurrences of behavior rather than explanatory principles.

Second, the trait concept, in being descriptive, relates to behavior at the overt or manifest level. It may be that this is a poor level at which to consider organizing principles. The issue here is similar to that which concerned Henry Murray: "According to my prejudice, trait psychology is over-concerned with recurrences, with consistency, with what is clearly manifested (the surface of personality), with what is conscious, ordered, and rational" (1938, p. 715). Murray's preference was for the concept of need, which might be a momentary process and which might be present in the organism without becoming manifest directly or overtly. The word "directly" is perhaps of particular significance since it suggests the potential for multiple expressions depending on factors such as the perception of environmental contingencies or internal conditions. Thus, there may be structural organization underlying overt behavior diversity. Similarly, work in the area of artificial intelligence suggests that text material may be organized at the goal level (higher in the system hierarchy) rather than at the plan or behavior level (Carbonell 1981, Schank & Abelson 1977, Wilensky 1978).

Finally, a problem with the trait concept is that it is a static concept and does not provide for an understanding of dynamic processes. This is part of the reason why many trait theorists get caught up in arguing for the sameness of behavior or the structural identity of behavior across situations rather than coming to grips with the issues of diversity and pattern. Perhaps our concepts of personality should reflect patterns of change and variation as well as behavioral consistency and stability (Magnusson 1974, Pervin 1976, 1983).

If traits are not adequate to the task of explaining processes of person-situation interaction, are there other concepts to which we can turn? It is here that future attention will need to be directed. Perhaps the alternative is an emphasis on cognitive variables (Cantor & Kihlstrom 1982). Another possibility is the related concept of scripts (Abelson 1981, Carlson 1981, 1982, Tomkins 1979). A third possibility is an emphasis on goals and plans, concepts that appear in as diverse areas as information-processing theory, psychoanalytic theory, and social learning theory (Bandura & Cervone 1983, Carver & Scheier 1981a,b, 1982, Gedo 1979, King & Sorrentino 1983, Klinger 1977, Mischel 1973, Pervin 1983, Rosenblatt & Thickstun 1977, Schafer 1976, Schank & Abelson 1977, Staats & Burns 1982). Such concepts also show potential for relating cognitive and affective-motivation variables, an issue addressed in the next section. Interestingly enough, Buss & Craik (1983a, 1984) address the question of motivation in relation to their act frequency, disposition approach to personality and specifically compare their approach with purposive-cognitive concepts (desires, beliefs, abilities). Whatever the exact value of the concepts employed, it is clear that we must go beyond debates concerning persons *or* situations and consistency *or* variability to consideration of processes involving persons *and* situations as well as patterns of stability *and* change within the organism.

Information-Processing Models and Personality

Psychology has gone cognitive generally, and personality is no exception. Pulled, on the one hand, by developments in social cognition that are part of social psychology (Hastorf & Isen 1982, Higgins et al 1981, Wyer et al 1984, Zanna et al 1982) and, on the other hand, by developments in cognitive behavior modification that are part of clinical psychology (Wilson & Franks 1982), we have begun to see the development of cognitive social learning theory and cognitive personality theory (Bandura 1982, Cantor 1981, Cantor & Kihlstrom 1981, 1982, Mischel 1973) (See Chap. 14, Pervin 1984a). While there are fuzzy boundaries between these fields, and perhaps at this time it is difficult to point to a specific prototype or examplar, a point of view or emphasis is emerging. The distinguishing characteristics are a link with cognitive experimental psychology (Bower 1978) and an associated emphasis on how people encode, store, and retrieve information. What appears to distinguish it as personality psychology is the content of the information processed and the interest in individual differences, though the latter, including interest in the organization of processes within the individual, has yet to receive the attention it deserves. Consideration here is given to three aspects of the mushrooming literature relevant to cognitive personality theory: conceptual and methodological orientation, content considered, and the question of cognitive style. Attention is then directed toward consideration of relationships with affect and overt behavior.

CONCEPTS AND METHODS   Cognitive, information-processing, personality theory emphasizes concepts such as schema (Neisser 1967, Norman & Rumelhart 1975), plans (Schank & Abelson 1977), prototypes (Rosch 1978), and scripts (Abelson 1981, Schank & Abelson 1977, Tomkins 1979). Simon (1979) reviewed the various information-processing models of cognition available today. Person variables emphasized by cognitive personality psychologists include categories of persons and situations, scripts, attributions, implicit theories of personality (Cantor & Kihlstrom 1982) as well as encoding strategies, expectancies, values, plans, competencies, and self-regulatory systems (Mischel 1981). Also noteworthy in influence has been Heider's thinking and developments in attribution theory, reviewed by Harris & Harvey (1981), as well as Kahneman, Slovic & Tversky's (1982) work on judgmental heuristics and inferential strategies. Rosch's (1978) approach to category formation is of particular interest since it has been utilized both by critics (Cantor & Mischel 1979) and by proponents (Buss & Craik 1983a, 1984) of trait theory. The cognitive, information-processing model is specifically contrasted with trait theory in terms of a greater emphasis on situational specificity of behavior, the discriminativeness and flexibility of human behavior, and the active organization of stimuli into a world that has specific meanings for the individual (Cantor

& Kihlstrom 1981, 1982). Mischel (1981) suggests that George Kelly and Carl Rogers anticipated many current developments and that the wisdom of the former in particular has not yet been fully recognized. On the whole, however, little of the work in this area builds upon or is influenced by works of earlier personality psychologists.

CONTENT CONSIDERED   The content emphasized within the context of a cognitive, information-processing model of personality includes the ways in which people attend to, encode, store, and retrieve information relevant to people (including the self), situations, and events. Rosch's (1978) model has been used in the prototype analysis of trait and situation categories (Cantor & Mischel 1979, Cantor et al 1982), in the analysis of partner preferences in various situations (Cantor et al 1984), and in the analysis of diagnostic categories (Cantor et al 1980, Clarkin et al 1983). Work on impression formation and hypothesis testing in social interaction also appears to have implications for personality psychologists (Bargh 1982, Bargh & Pietromonaco 1982, Ebbesen 1981, Snyder 1981, Snyder & White 1982). Nisbett & Ross' (1980) book on the person as an intuitive scientist is described by Miller & Cantor (1982) as an important work whose implications cannot be ignored. What is important here is the emphasis on how people go about interpreting their world and making relevant decisions based on an implicit causal theory (Nisbett & Wilson 1977), as opposed to an emphasis on trait categories. In addition, there is an emphasis on the nonmotivational sources of error in perception and judgement—a contrast with, and a departure from, the psychoanalytic emphasis (Gur & Sackheim 1979, Sackheim & Gur 1979). Research on the development of children's theory of mind would appear to have important potential implications for this aspect of implicit personality theory (Bretherton & Beeghly 1982, Darby & Schlenker 1982). Among the most important aspects of people's implicit theories of mind and causation are the attributions people make for events and their associated implications for cognition, affect, and motivation (Abelson 1983, Abramson et al 1980, Weiner 1982).

Of particular interest to personality psychologists may be research on the self as a cognitive structure that influences attention, organization or categorization of information, recall, and judgments about others (Bandura 1982, Bargh 1982, Fong & Markus 1982, Ingram et al 1983, Kuiper & Derry 1981, Locksley & Lenauer 1981, Markus 1983, Markus & Sentis 1982, Markus & Smith 1981, Rogers 1981). Early research in this area emphasized the purely cognitive aspects of the self but more recently there has been an interest in the role of affect in the organization of self-relevant information (Fiske 1982). The concept of schema has also been used to investigate gender aspects of the self (S. Bem 1981, 1982, Crane & Markus 1982, Markus et al 1982). While Bem & Markus both employ the concept of schema in relation to self and gender they come to different, in some ways opposite, conclusions concerning relevance for the concept of androgyny. This should serve to alert us to subtle differences in the way that the same concept may be defined and measured, long a problem in personality research.

COGNITION, AFFECT, OVERT BEHAVIOR   Considerable controversy exists concerning relations among cognition, affect, and overt behavior. The issue has relevance for how we conceptualize and investigate personality. Much of the early emphasis was on cognition alone or on cognition as a determinant of affect. Many continue to suggest that cognition has primacy over affect and/or determines how we experience events and ourselves (Abramson et al 1980, Mandler 1982, McFarland & Ross 1982, Smith & Kluegel 1982, Weiner 1982, Weiner et al 1982). The emphasis is on how cognitions, particularly attributions, typically precede and determine emotions. Two developments here are noteworthy. First is articulation of the view that affect has primacy over, and may be a determinant of, cognition (Zajonc 1980, Zajonc et al 1982). Equally important is increased awareness of the importance of considering and investigating relationships between cognition and affect (Clark & Fiske 1982, Higgins et al 1981, Hilgard 1980, Izard et al 1984). Indeed, Kiesler (1982) suggests that an understanding of the relationship of cognition and affect will be a core theoretical problem for the 1980s. A variety of research studies are demonstrating the effects of affect on cognition. Bower's (1981, Bower & Cohen 1982) work has been important in demonstrating the influence of emotion on memory retrieval, selective learning, the organization of perception, and biases in thinking. The effects of affect can be seen on such varied aspects of cognition as expectancy and decision making (Isen et al 1982, Rosenhan & Messick 1966), perception of risk (Tversky & Johnson 1981), attributions (Stephan & Gollwitzer 1981), understanding thematic structures in stories (Dyer 1983), selection of material for entry into consciousness (Clark & Teasdale 1982, Snyder & White 1982), and the processing of self-relevant information (Natale & Hantas 1982, Wright & Mischel 1982). And, while the relation of cognitions, such as self prototypes, to behavior is unclear (Rogers 1981), there is considerable evidence of the influence of affect and mood on behaviors such as helpfulness and aggression (Berkowitz 1983, Isen & Levin 1972, Isen et al 1978, Rosenhan et al 1981).

The relationships among cognition, affect, and behavior undoubtedly are complex. Much of the attribution-emotion literature demonstrates a relation, but considerable question remains about whether a causal connection has been established (Covington & Omelich 1979, Coyne & Gotlib 1983, Stephan & Gollwitzer 1981). The issue continues to be debated, as witnessed in a special issue of the *Journal of Personality* (December 1981) on cognitive and attributional aspects of learned helplessness and depression. While some debate the significance and sequence issue, others emphasize a reciprocal relationship in which one or another element may precede and be more influential at one or another time (Teasdale 1983). Such an emphasis is consistent with a transactional, general systems perspective (Carver & Scheier 1982, Pervin 1983). Sometimes the issue appears to be more semantic (i.e. what constitutes cognition), though at other times the issue appears to be more conceptual and fundamental. In all, we appear to be in for an exciting period ahead as cognitive, social, experimental, and personality psychologists, separately as well as jointly, tackle this fundamental issue.

COMMENT   Cognitive approaches to personality are not new. Kelly's (1955) personal construct theory was published thirty years ago, a cognitive emphasis was present in Blake & Ramsey's (1951) *Perception: An Approach to Personality* and in Messick & Ross' (1962) *Measurement in Personality and Cognition,* and the concept of cognitive style was quite popular during the 1960s (Goldstein & Blackman 1978, Sigel et al 1967). Yet, current cognitive approaches to personality have a fresh spirit to them and in many ways represent an important departure from traditional personality theory (Pervin 1984a, p. 474). Whereas traditional personality theory tends to emphasize stability and consistency, current cognitive, information-processing theory emphasizes discriminativeness and flexibility; whereas the former emphasizes generalized predictions about a person, the latter emphasizes predictions specific to situations; whereas the former emphasizes concepts such as dispositions and needs, the latter emphasizes concepts such as category structures and inferential strategies; whereas the former emphasizes motivation and dynamics, the latter emphasizes cognitive economics and the limitations of everyday cognitive processes; whereas the former emphasizes the self as causal agent and a unitary concept, the latter emphasizes the self as a compound of multiple schema. Taking liberally from the concepts and methods of cognitive psychology, this new approach to personality has begun to dominate the literature in the field.

While making important contributions, current information-processing approaches to personality are not without limitations and potential hazards. First, there is some question whether approaches to natural object category formation are equally suitable for social category formation (Holyoak & Gordon 1984, Lingle, Altom & Medin 1984). Much greater inter-individual variability appears to exist with social object than natural object categorization. In addition, particularly in the former, people appear to be able to form multiple categorical structures for the same objects; that is, the same person may have multiple ways of organizing people and events in the world (Hamilton 1979, Pervin 1981). Furthermore, a number of psychologists have suggested that social cognition is different from natural object cognition in the role of affect

(Cohen 1981, Hoffman 1981). Whether social categories merely have unique features or are fundamentally different from natural object categories remains to be determined.

An emphasis on the importance on affect in social cognition suggests a second concern. With the advent of the cognitive revolution there was for some time a diminished concern with affect and motivation. For example, abstracts listed in *Psychological Abstracts* under cognition surpass those listed under drive, emotion, and motivation by the year 1970. By 1978 there were close to 2000 abstracts listed in association with cognition—about four times the number listed under emotion and approximately ten times the number listed under motivation! A similar picture emerges from analysis of subcategories listed under the concepts of cognition, drive, emotion, and motivation in the *Annual Review of Psychology* for the years 1950–1979. The first chapter focusing on cognition appears in 1966 (Van de Geer & Jaspars 1966). Following that point, references to cognition increase not only in absolute terms, but relative to references to emotion, drive, and motivation as well. In sum, the evidence suggests that psychologists not only have turned toward the study of cognition in addition to other areas, but they have done so to the neglect of others. This would appear to be particularly the case in relation to the concept of motivation. Further evidence of the decline in interest in the concept of motivation comes from a review of 25 years of the Nebraska Symposium on Motivation (Benjamin & Jones 1978). During the 1960s there was a shift in interest from motivational theory to cognition and a serious questioning of the utility of the former concept altogether (Jones 1962, Postman 1956).

A short time ago a number of outstanding social and personality psychologists presented papers on social knowing. Commenting on these papers, Neisser (1980) expressed concern about the narrow perspective taken, the overuse of information-processing concepts, and the neglect of motivation. Norman (1980), in reviewing the results of research following the information-processing model, concludes that there is sterility overall and that a science of cognition cannot afford to continue to ignore areas such as emotion and motivation. Finally, Posner (1981) in reviewing a number of papers on cognition and personality suggests that "just as cognitive psychology presents the danger of leaving the human subject lost in thought without being able to act, so does the current approach leave unsolved the problem of how action occurs" (p. 340). While there are signs of increased concern with the relevant issues, the past history of neglect gives cause for concern.

Third, while current cognitive approaches to personality give lip service to individual differences, the organization of cognitive structures, and idiographics, the fact of the matter is that relevant studies are hard to come by. Is this because it is still early in the game or is there something inherent in the approach, in contrast with much of traditional personality theory, that operates against such research? The concept of cognitive style is interesting in this regard. Much of the thrust of cognitive, information-processing approaches to personality operates against conceptions of personality as stable and consistent. Past conceptualizations of cognitive style in the field generally have faded with the development of a more situation-specific emphasis. Yet, we are presented with the concepts of cognitive style in relation to self-monitoring (Snyder & Campbell 1982) and attribution (Anderson 1983, Peterson et al 1982). Just how these conceptions of cognitive style differ from earlier conceptions remains to be determined.

Finally, a note of caution is in order in relation to the pull from developments in cognitive behavior therapy. Once more we can be impressed with the amount of research activity and signs of promise. However, let us also note that it has been described as involving "a science that does not yet exist" (Mahoney & Arnkoff 1978), that it has been criticized by Eysenck (1982) as lacking in theoretical foundation, and that evidence of its greater effectiveness with difficult cases, relative to other modes of treatment, remains to be developed (Turkat & Forehand 1980). Mahoney (1980), a past and continuing advocate of cognitive behavioral therapies, expresses concern that currently they tend to overlook the importance of unconscious processes, tend to view feelings narrowly, and are poorly integrated with theories of cognition.

Research Strategies

Over the past few years there has been debate concerning content and tactics of research, as well as a general examination of alternatives in data collection and analysis. Hogan (1982) contrasts two distinct traditions in personality, each with its own subject matter, methodology, and theoretical orientation. In the one, rooted in traditional analytic or depth psychology, there is an emphasis on broad aspects of personality functioning as well as on individual differences and integrative aspects of the total personality. In the other, typified by current efforts in cognitive personality, there is an emphasis on part processes, general laws concerning particular processes, and experimental methodology. Is it possible that we have not gone beyond traditional dichotomies in the field noted by Murray (1938), G. W. Allport (1955), and Cronbach (1957)? Probably there is something to the point. However, one also finds evidence of cross-overs on particular issues and generally a greater sense of open-mindedness and flexibility than has often been the case in the past.

IDIOGRAPHIC RESEARCH   What do Allport, Freud, Pavlov, Piaget, and Skinner have in common? And Mischel and Epstein as well? Perhaps the only common factor of scientific significance is the suggested utility of study of the single organism. Does this mean support for an idiographic approach? This depends on what one means by idiographic (Pervin 1984c, Runyan 1983). The term, as used by G. W. Allport (1937) and as associated with later idiographic-nomothetic debate, had at least four different meanings: an approach to research (i.e. intensive study of individuals), an approach to prediction (i.e. clinical vs statistical prediction), a conceptualization of personality (i.e. holistic, dynamic view vs fragmented, static view), and a view of science (i.e. history and biography vs physics and chemistry). While some psychologists have taken a steady path in supporting an idiographic approach (Tyler 1978), at least in the sense of intensive studies of individuals with an eye toward understanding the complexities of individual structures and processes, for perhaps twenty years the term almost disappeared completely from the literature. Not only has it reappeared, but it is becoming a valued term and approach to research for investigators who otherwise differ enormously in theoretical emphasis and methodological approach. Indeed, support for idiographic research may be the one point held in common by trait and social learning psychologists. The renascent interest in idiographic research is clearly seen in the Michigan State series honoring the work of Henry Murray, a chapter on idiographic approaches to personality to be included in the second edition of *Personality and the Behavioral Disorders* (Endler & Hunt 1984), in the special issue of the *Journal of Personality* (September 1983), and a more general utilization of the term throughout the literature.

Lamiell (1981, 1982, Lamiell et al 1983) has formulated what he calls an idiothetic approach to personality, emphasizing individual patterns and what individuals actually do relative to what they can do. His attack upon an individual differences, differential psychology model for personality is considered by Rorer & Widiger (1983) as one of the most important recent papers in the area of personality. Harris (1980) argues for idiovalidation or the validation of individual profiles, but accepts the utilization of nomothetic techniques and dimensions in studying the organization of personality variables within the person. The relative utility of idiographic and nomothetic approaches to assessment and predictions is again a focus of controversy (D. J. Bem 1983c, Kenrick & Braver 1982, Kenrick & Dantchik 1983, Kenrick & Stringfield 1980, Rushton et al 1981). In the meantime, idiographic research is suggested for the study of mood (Zevon & Tellegen 1982), everyday thinking (Neimark & Stead 1981), behavioral patterns (Buss & Craik 1983a,b, Diener & Larsen 1984), motivation (De Boeck, submitted for publication, Pervin 1983), personality types (Carlson 1980), and in behavioral assessment (Cone 1981).

AGGREGATION   Aggregation as an approach to data gathering and analysis is becoming a focal point in personality, touching upon the person-situation controversy as well as the idiographic-nomothetic controversy (Epstein 1983c, Mischel & Peake 1983b). Rushton et al (1983) present an extended argument in favor of aggregation, illustrating its utility in a number of areas. At the same time, it is suggested that there are occasions when aggregation is unnecessary and even harmful—the question of what to aggregate is always an issue! This latter point is emphasized by Diener & Larsen (submitted for publication) in a paper on the limitations of aggregation. Essentially the question is raised as to what is being averaged in and what is being averaged out in aggregation—error, meaningful variation, or what? It is possible to aggregate over subjects, responses, and occasions or situations. It is even becoming increasingly popular to aggregate over studies, as in the meta-analyses of sex differences (Maccoby & Jacklin 1980, Tieger 1980) and the effects of psychotherapy (*Journal of Consulting and Clinical Psychology,* February 1983). Those who favor one kind of aggregation need not be in favor of another kind of aggregation, as in some psychologists favoring aggregating across situations but not across subjects whereas the reverse is true for other psychologists.

TYPE OF DATA   As noted, generally there appears to be an exciting explosion of interest in different kinds of phenomena and data. A theme running throughout this explosion is a recognition of the restrictions to investigation resulting from behaviorism and operationism (Rorer & Widiger 1983, Rychlak 1981). A parallel theme involves an effort to investigate meaningful aspects of people's lives. Thus, there is concern with experience as well as with behavior (Apter 1982, Csikszentmihalyi 1982, Csikszentmihalyi & Figurski 1982, Little 1983, Palys & Little 1983, Rychlak 1982). Lieberman (1979) argues in favor of at least a limited return to introspectionism, a view rejected by Rachlin (1980). Kenrick & Dantchik (1983) express concern about an "overemphasis" on phenomenology. In addition, there is an increasing interest in imagery and the stream of consciousness (Klinger 1978, 1981, Klinger et al 1981, Natsoulas 1981, Vallacher 1983), evidently sufficient to warrant a new journal entitled *Imagination, Cognition, and Personality* edited by Pope & Singer. One finds increasing use of beeper technology (Csikszentmihalyi 1975, Klinger 1978, Palys & Little 1983, Sjoberg 1982) and logs (Brandstätter 1983, Epstein 1983a, Diener & Larsen 1984, Wheeler et al 1983). Within the recent literature one finds support for case studies, psychobiography, and the general utilization of archival data (Anderson 1981, Howe 1982, Runyan 1981, 1982, Simonton 1981, Stolorow & Atwood 1979). Goldberg (1981) argues for the analysis of language to find basic personality terms. Buss & Craik (1984) review the advantages and disadvantages of various categories of data while suggesting act trends as a hybrid category. Lehrer (1982) and Lang et al (1983) express caution concerning the unique information associated with behavioral, self-report, and physiological data.

One of the most critical issues debated today concerns the use of self-report. Gone are the days when most psychologists would eschew the use of self-report. Today, for example, Bandura (1978) and Mischel (1982) support at least some forms of self-report data, and Averill (1983) suggests that many criticisms of self-report data apply to other forms of data as well—including overt behavior and physiological responses. Averill goes so far as to ask "Why are self-reports treated with such skepticism and searching criticism, however valid, while the limitations of other forms of data are often treated with sufferance?" (1983, p. 1155). Funder (1983b) similarly argues for the admissibility of subjective judgments as data and suggests that different sorts of data have distinct uses and limitations associated with them. Rorer & Widiger (1983) suggest that the best way to get information from someone is to ask them—as long as they understand the question, have the information, and are not motivated to deceive you. Sackheim & Gur (1979) suggest that the problem of self-deception may be particularly acute in the use of self-report questionnaires. Qualifications to the utility of introspection and self-report are highlighted in the important paper by Nisbett & Wilson (1977) and in further research by Wilson et al (1981) on the limited awareness in subjects of changes in internal states. These papers emphasize the role of attribution and inference in self-report data, which suggests that subjects are prepared to tell more than they know. Criticism of the approach taken by Nisbett & Wilson and support for at least some kinds of self-report data come from Ericsson & Simon (1980), Sabini & Silver (1981), Smith & Miller (1978), and White (1980).

COMMENT   Are there conclusions to be drawn from these emerging trends? In general one might argue for both enthusiasm and caution. Idiographic research appears to be an important development and so far the idiographic-nomothetic debate appears to have avoided false issues of the past (e.g. one is science while the other is not, one is reductionistic while the other is not, one is humane while the other is not, one is subjective while the other is not, one believes in laws while the other does not, one believes in individuality while the other does not). At the same time, two notes of caution may be suggested. First, it remains unclear as to just what idiographic research is. Some would include all studies utilizing individual data analyses; others would only include intensive studies of individuals with a focus on the organization or integration of variables. Second, in-depth idiographic research is not easy to conduct and such research cannot act as a substitute for theory. In deciding upon the systematic investigation of a few individuals, and there remain remarkably few such efforts being made, one still is faced with the challenging task of what to look at and how to analyze the data obtained. Anyone who has conducted such investigation is familiar with the dilemma between gathering minimal data while feeling that more was needed to understand the person, as opposed to gathering enormous amounts of data without quite knowing how to put it all together. Murray's (1938) efforts included a team approach but for a variety of reasons such programs of research are difficult to establish.

Similarly, aggregation holds both promise and potential for becoming another fad. The greatest potential for the utilization of aggregation would appear to be where it helps to decrease unreliability and clarify general trends. On the other hand, aggregation cannot substitute for competent research or asking penetrating questions. As has been noted by various authors, aggregation provides the potential for lumping together research that has been done well with that which has not, and of canceling out variance that is of interest and significance along with that which is in error.

Finally, the expansion of interest in what can be investigated and the methods of investigation is refreshing. Rather than rejecting entire realms of phenomena and research methods, we appear to be prepared to examine virtually all aspects of human psychological functioning and to consider the circumstances under which varied data collection methods may be particularly appropriate. A strategy of utilizing multiple measures would appear to have particular merit since it is clear that the observations obtained may vary considerably, with important theoretical implications potentially at hand.

BRUSH STROKES OF THE LITERATURE

The literature associated with personality psychology during the past two years is enormous. In a review such as this it is impossible to cover all areas or to do justice to areas that have received considerable attention in the literature. In this section an effort is made to at least touch lightly upon some of these areas.

One of the current focal points of research is the area broadly defined as stress, learned helplessness, and depression. The attribution model of learned helplessness and depression (Abramson et al 1980) clearly has stimulated considerable research, and the recently published *Attributional Style Questionnaire* (Peterson et al 1982) promises to result in even more related research. At this point a central question involves whether attributions are necessary, sufficient, and causal in the way suggested by the model (Alloy 1982, Coyne & Gotlib 1983, Danker-Brown & Baucom 1982, Hammen & de Mayo 1982, Lewinsohn et al 1981, Oakes & Curtis 1982, Raps et al 1982, Teasdale 1983, Tennen et al 1982a,b). Helplessness also is suggested as relevant to the coronary-prone personality (Glass & Carver 1980) and there is a burgeoning literature on the Type A behavior pattern (Matthews 1982). A particularly interesting aspect of some of this research is the effort to relate differences here to characteristic ways of processing information and coping (Humphries et al 1983, Miller & Mangan 1983, Pittner et al 1983).

Interest in the self waxes and wanes; it is currently waxing. Relevant papers can be found in the edited volumes by Cantor & Kihlstrom (1981), Lynch et al (1981), and Suls (1982). Much of the literature involves a schema, information-processing view (Carver & Scheier 1981a,b, 1982, Kihlstrom & Cantor

1983, Scheier & Carver 1981, 1982), though there are signs of an increasing interest in the relevant affective and motivational aspects as well (Markus 1983). The question of one or many selves remains with us (Gergen 1981, Savin-Williams & Demo 1983), as does that of the existence of self-serving biases (Bradley 1978, Gibbons & Wright 1981, McCarrey et al 1982). The concept of self-efficacy has become central to social learning theory and been associated with considerable research (Bandura 1982, 1983). At the same time, the concept has been attacked and some data question its independence from outcome expectancies (Maddux et al 1982, Manning & Wright 1983, Sjoberg 1982, Smedslund 1978). An interesting and important development in self-efficacy theory has been the examination of the relation of self-efficacy to motivation (Bandura & Cervone 1983, Bandura & Schunk 1981). Bandura, it should be noted, is careful to distinguish his views concerning self-efficacy from the seemingly related concepts of learned helplessness and locus of control (Lefcourt 1982).

Interest in situations continues to be present, in part stimulated by environmental psychology and in part by the interactionist model (Magnusson 1974, 1981, 1984, Magnusson & Allen 1984, Magnusson & Endler 1977). A critical question here is whether it will be useful to try to develop a taxonomy of situations relevant to persons (Kenrick & Dantchik 1983). As noted earlier, interest is also increasing in how individuals select and structure situations in terms of their own personalities.

Finally, it should be noted that theory is not dead. Along with active efforts in social learning theory and information-processing theory, there is work going on in relation to psychoanalytic theory (Masling 1983, Silverman 1982, Silverman & Fishel 1981) as well as personal construct theory (Bonarius et al 1981, Epting 1984, Epting & Neimeyer 1983, Landfield & Leitner 1980, Mancuso & Adams-Webber 1982), and there is a presentation of multifactor-systems theory (Powell & Royce 1981, Royce & Powell 1983) as well as logical learning theory (Rychlak 1981, 1982), and we are brought up to date on the thinking of such outstanding theorists as Atkinson (1983, Feather 1982), Cattell (1983), Eysenck (1982, 1983), and Rotter (1982).

CONCLUSION

A review of the recent literature in personality suggests that the field is alive. There is a sense of excitement and vitality, not only in this country but in Europe as well. In relation to the latter, witness the initiation of the European Conference on Personality (Bonarius et al 1984). If the field is alive, more alive than at times in the past, does this mean that it is well? Here one can be less certain. Personality psychologists appear to be debating important issues, but is the field advancing in the course of such debate or, in the words of Jackson &

Paunonen (1980), have the central issues in personality theory been more cogently expressed by earlier pioneers in the field? My own sense is that progress is being made, but not as much as some might suspect. A review of some recent research by Carlson (1984) gives reason for further concern.

Why is there the belief that progress is being made and why the caution concerning enthusiasm? First, why the sense of progress? Personality psychologists appear to be interested in more phenomena, and in exploring these phenomena in a greater variety of ways, than was true in the past. This would appear to be a healthy development despite the potential for confusion and search along blind alleys. The latter have been part of the history of the field in spite of narrow definitions of legitimate research methods and phenomena of interest. A second healthy development would appear to be efforts to relate investigations in the field to developments in other areas, in particular social and cognitive psychology. At times in the past, personality psychology was threatened with the loss of its own identity. Where research from other areas was emphasized, the adaptation appeared to be mechanical and lag behind developments in these other fields. While at times this still is the case, my sense is that there now is a greater effort to adapt concepts and methods to the special concerns of personality psychologists and to stay current with advances in other areas. Finally, there is the sense of an infusion of new blood into the field, a group of young personality psychologists prepared to tackle old problems in both traditional and new ways.

Why, then, the remaining concern and caution? First, there remains concern about the way questions and debate are being framed. To take the person-situation controversy as illustrative, debate has centered on person versus situation and consistency versus variability. As I have noted previously (Pervin 1978), the problem with such debate is that it does not begin to provide us with answers concerning what and how—what in the person, interacts how, with what in the environment? Similarly, debate concerning whether cognition or affect has primacy tells us little about either and less about interrelations between the two. A second, related basis for caution is the remaining paucity of research demonstrating what reviewers over the years have emphasized—concern with the complex, integrated, organized, and patterned behavior of individuals over time. In the introduction to this chapter questions were raised as to whether more such studies were being conducted and, if not, why not? My own sense is that such studies for the most part are not being conducted and the reason for this is that they are conceptually, methodologically, and psychologically difficult. For all its merit, an emphasis on idiographics and the intensive study of the individual tells one neither what to study nor how to study it. If one studies too little, are the gains beyond traditional nomothetic, experimental research substantial? If one studies too much, how is one to organize the data into meaningful statements of relationships? Thus, idiographic research still requires some focusing of concern and selection of research methods. A commitment to idiographics is not a substitute for concern with theory and research strategy. A reading of Murray's pioneering efforts makes clear these points, as well as the value of collaborative efforts among psychologists studying the same individuals. The latter would appear to be not the least of the difficulties encountered in attempting serious, in-depth studies of individuals.

Finally, a concern related to what has been said above. Over the course of the past twenty years I have practiced as a psychotherapist, primarily with a psychodynamic orientation but with some utilization of behavioral techniques in specific problem areas. I continue to be impressed with and distressed by the gap between what I read in the literature and what I see in my office. In particular, I am struck with the power of conflicting motivations in my patients and the absence of concern with such phenomena in the literature, with the diversity of personally significant emotions reported by patients and the more restricted concerns of psychologists with anxiety and depression, with the importance of implicit causal (if-then) beliefs held by people and the narrow perspective of much of attribution theory. On the whole, I continue to feel that I am more in touch with and learn more about people in my office than I do in reading the personality literature. Undoubtedly, some of this is inevitable. However, until the gap is narrowed somewhat I will continue to be concerned about the state of the field.

ACKNOWLEDGMENTS

I would like to express my appreciation to David Buss, Nancy Cantor, Rae Carlson, John Gormly, James Lamiell, Charles Lord, and David Magnusson for their helpful comments on an earlier draft of this chapter.

Literature Cited

Abelson, R. P. 1981. Psychological status of the script concept. *Am. Psychol.* 36:715–29

Abelson, R. P. 1983. Whatever became of consistency theory? *Pers. Soc. Psychol. Bull.* 9:37–54

Abramson, L. Y., Garber, J., Seligman, M. E. P. 1980. Learned helplessness in humans. In *Human Helplessness,* ed. J. Garber, M. E. P. Seligman, pp. 3–34. New York: Academic. 419 pp.

Alloy, L. B. 1982. The role of perceptions and attributions for response-outcome noncontingency in learned helplessness: A commentary and discussion. *J. Pers.* 50:443–79

Allport, F. H. 1937. Teleonomic description in the study of personality. *Charact. Pers.* 6:202–14

Allport, G. W. 1937. *Personality: A Psychological Interpretation.* New York: Holt, Rinehart & Winston. 588 pp.

Allport, G. W. 1955. *Becoming: Basic Considerations for a Psychology of Personality.* New Haven: Yale Univ. Press. 106 pp.

Allport, G. W. 1961. *Pattern and Growth in Personality.* New York: Holt, Rinehart & Winston. 593 pp.

Anderson, C. A. 1983. Motivational and performance deficits in interpersonal settings: The effect of attributional style. *J. Pers. Soc. Psychol.* 45:1136–47

Anderson, J. R. 1981. Psychobiographical methodology: The case of William James. *Rev. Pers. Soc. Psychol.* 2:245–72

Apter, M. J. 1982. *The Experience of Motivation: The Theory of Psychological Reversals.* London: Academic. 378 pp.

Atkinson, J. W. 1983. *Personality, Motivation, and Action.* New York: Praeger. 432 pp.

Averill, J. R. 1983. Studies on anger and

aggression: Implications for theories of emotion. *Am. Psychol.* 38:1145–60

Bandura, A. 1977. *Social Learning Theory.* Englewood Cliffs, NJ: Prentice-Hall. 247 pp.

Bandura, A. 1978. Reflections on self-efficacy. *Adv. Behav. Res. Ther.* 1:237–69

Bandura, A. 1982. Self-efficacy mechanism in human agency. *Am. Psychol.* 37:122–47

Bandura, A. 1983. Self-efficacy determinants of anticipated fears and calamities. *J. Pers. Soc. Psychol.* 45:464–69

Bandura, A., Cervone, D. 1983. Self-evaluative and self-efficacy mechanisms governing the motivational effect of goal systems. *J. Pers. Soc. Psychol.* 45:1017–28

Bandura, A., Schunk, D. H. 1981. Cultivating competence, self-efficacy, and intrinsic interest. *J. Pers. Soc. Psychol.* 41:586–98

Bargh, J. A. 1982. Attention and automaticity in the processing of self-relevant information. *J. Pers. Soc. Psychol.* 43:425–36

Bargh, J. A., Pietromonaco, P. 1982. Automatic information processing and social perception: The influence of trait information presented outside of conscious awareness on impression formation. *J. Pers. Soc. Psychol.* 43:437–49

Bem, D. J. 1983a. Toward a response style theory of persons in situations. See Page 1983, pp. 201–31

Bem, D. J. 1983b. Further déjà vu in the search for cross-situational consistency: A response to Mischel & Peake. *Psychol. Rev.* 90:390–93

Bem, D. J. 1983c. Constructing a theory of the triple typology: Some (second) thoughts on nomothetic and idiographic approaches to personality. *J. Pers.* 51:566–77

Bem, D. J., Allen, A. 1974. On predicting some of the people some of the time: The search for cross-situational consistencies in behavior. *Psychol. Rev.* 81:506–20

Bem, D. J., Funder, D. C. 1978. Predicting more of the people more of the time: Assessing the personality of situations. *Psychol. Rev.* 85:485–501

Bem, S. L. 1981. Gender schema theory: A cognitive account of sex typing. *Psychol. Rev.* 88:354–64

Bem, S. L. 1982. Gender schema theory and self-schema theory compared. *J. Pers. Soc. Psychol.* 43:1192–94

Benjamin, L. T. Jr., Jones, M. R. 1978. From motivational theory to social cognitive development: Twenty-five years of the Nebraska Symposium. In *Nebraska Symp. Motiv.* 26:ix–xix

Berkowitz, L. 1983. Aversively stimulated aggression. *Am. Psychol.* 38:1135–44

Blake, R. R., Ramsey, G. V., eds. 1951. *Perception: An Approach to Personality.* New York: Ronald. 422 pp.

Block, J. 1977. Advancing the psychology of

personality: Paradigmatic shift or improving the quality of research. See Magnusson & Endler 1977, pp. 37–63

Bonarius, H., Holland, R., Rosenberg, S., eds. 1981. *Personal Construct Psychology: Recent Advances in Theory and Practice.* London: Macmillan. 286 pp.

Bonarius, H., Van Heck, G., Smid, N., eds. 1984. *Personality Psychology in Europe: Theoretical and Empirical Developments.* London: Erlbaum. In press

Bower, G. H. 1978. Contacts of cognitive psychology with social learning theory. *Cogn. Ther. Res.* 2:123–46

Bower, G. H. 1981. Mood and memory. *Am. Psychol.* 36:129–48

Bower, G. H., Cohen, P. R. 1982. Emotional influences in memory and thinking: Data and theory. See Clark & Fiske 1982, pp. 291–332

Bradley, G. W. 1978. Self-serving biases in the attribution process: A reexamination of the fact or fiction question. *J. Pers. Soc. Psychol.* 36:56–71

Brandstätter, H. 1983. Emotional responses to other persons in everyday life situations. *J. Pers. Soc. Psychol.* 45:871–83

Bretherton, I., Beeghly, M. 1982. Talking about internal states: The acquisition of an explicit theory of mind. *Dev. Psychol.* 18:906–21

Buss, D. M., Craik, K. H. 1980. The frequency concept of disposition: Dominance and prototypically dominant acts. *J. Pers.* 48:379–92

Buss, D. M., Craik, K. H. 1981. The act frequency analysis of interpersonal dispositions. Aloofness, gregariousness, dominance, and submissiveness. *J. Pers.* 49:175–92

Buss, D. M., Craik, K. H. 1983a. The act frequency approach to personality. *Psychol. Rev.* 90:105–26

Buss, D. M., Craik, K. H. 1983b. The dispositional analysis of everyday conduct. *J. Pers.* 51:393–412

Buss, D. M., Craik, K. H. 1983c. Act prediction and the conceptual analysis of personality scales: Indices of act density, bipolarity, and extensity. *J. Pers. Soc. Psychol.* 45:1081–95

Buss, D. M., Craik, K. H. 1984. Acts, dispositions, & personality. *Prog. Exp. Pers. Res.* 13:241–301

Cantor, N. 1981. A cognitive-social approach to personality. See Cantor & Kihlstrom 1981, pp. 23–44

Cantor, N., Kihlstrom, J. F., eds. 1981. *Personality, Cognition, and Social Interaction.* Hillsdale, NJ: Erlbaum. 362 pp.

Cantor, N., Kihlstrom, J. F. 1982. Cognitive and social processes in personality. See Wilson & Franks 1982, pp. 142–201

Cantor, N., Mackie, D., Lord, C. 1984.

Choosing partners and activities: The social perceiver decides to mix it up. *Soc. Cogn.* 2:256–72

Cantor, N., Mischel, W. 1979. Prototypes in person perception. *Adv. Exp. Soc. Psychol.* 12:3–52

Cantor, N., Mischel, W., Schwartz, J. C. 1982. A prototype analysis of psychological situations. *Cogn. Psychol.* 14:45–77

Cantor, N., Smith, E., French, R., Mezzich, J. 1980. Psychiatric diagnosis as prototype categorization. *J. Abnorm. Psychol.* 89:181–93

Carbonell, J. G. 1981. Politics: An experiment in subjective understanding and integrated meaning. In *Inside Computer Understanding: Five Programs Plus Miniatures,* ed. R. C. Schank, C. K. Riesbeck. Hillsdale, NJ: Erlbaum.

Carlson, R. 1975. Personality. *Ann. Rev. Psychol.* 26:393–414

Carlson, R. 1980. Studies of Jungian typology: Representations of the personal world. *J. Pers. Soc. Psychol.* 38:801–10

Carlson, R. 1981. Studies in script theory: I. Adult analogs of a childhood nuclear scene. *J. Pers. Soc. Psychol.* 40:501–10

Carlson, R. 1982. Studies in script theory: II. Altruistic nuclear scripts. *Percept. Mot. Skills* 55:595–610

Carlson, R. 1984. What's social about social psychology? Where's the person in personality research? *J. Pers. Soc. Psychol.* In press

Carver, C. S., Scheier, M. F. 1981a. *Attention and Self-regulation: A Control-Theory Approach to Human Behavior.* New York: Springer-Verlag. 419 pp.

Carver, C. S., Scheier, M. F. 1981b. A control systems approach to behavioral self-regulation. *Rev. Pers. Soc. Psychol.* 2:107–40

Carver, C. S., Scheier, M. F. 1982. Control theory: A useful conceptual framework for personality-social, clinical and health psychology. *Psychol. Bull.* 92:111–35

Cattell, R. B. 1983. *Structured Personality Learning Theory.* New York: Praeger

Clark, D. M., Teasdale, J. D. 1982. Diurnal variation in clinical depression and accessibility of memories of positive and negative experiences. *J. Abnorm. Psychol.* 91:87–95

Clark, M. S., Fiske, S. T., eds. 1982. *Affect and Cognition.* Hillsdale, NJ: Erlbaum. 357 pp.

Clarkin, J. F., Widiger, T. A., Frances, A., Hurt, S. W., Gilmore, M. 1983. Prototypic typology and the borderline personality disorder. *J. Abnorm. Psychol.* 92:263–75

Cohen, C. 1981. Goals and schemata in person perception: Making sense from the stream of behavior. See Cantor & Kihlstrom 1981, pp. 45–68

Cone, J. D. 1981. Psychometric considerations. In *Behavioral Assessment,* ed. M.

Hersen, A. S. Bellack, pp. 38–68. New York: Pergamon

Covington, M. V., Omelich, C. L. 1979. Are causal attributions causal? A path analysis of the cognitive model of achievement motivation. *J. Pers. Soc. Psychol.* 37:1487–1504

Coyne, J. C., Gotlib, I. H. 1983. The role of cognition in depression: A critical appraisal. *Psychol. Bull.* 94:472–505

Crane, M., Markus, H. 1982. Gender identity: The benefits of a self-schema approach. *J. Pers. Soc. Psychol.* 43:1195–97

Cronbach, L. J. 1957. The two disciplines of scientific psychology. *Am. Psychol.* 12:671–84

Csikszentmihalyi, M. 1975. *Beyond Boredom and Anxiety.* San Francisco: Jossey-Bass. 231 pp.

Csikszentmihalyi, M. 1982. Toward a psychology of optimal experience. *Rev. Pers. Soc. Psychol.* 3:13–36

Csikszentmihalyi, M., Figurski, T. J. 1982. Self-awareness and aversive experience in everyday life. *J. Pers.* 50:1–28

Danker-Brown, P., Baucom, D. H. 1982. Cognitive influences on the development of learned helplessness. *J. Pers. Soc. Psychol.* 43:793–801

Darby, B. W., Schlenker, B. R. 1982. Children's reactions to apologies. *J. Pers. Soc. Psychol.* 43:742–53

Day, H. D., Marshall, D., Hamilton, B., Christy, J. 1983. Some cautionary notes regarding the use of aggregated scores as a measure of behavioral stability. *J. Res. Pers.* 17:907–1109

Diener, E., Larsen, R. J. 1984. Temporal stability and cross-situational consistency of affective, behavioral, and cognitive responses. *J. Pers. Soc. Psychol.* In press

Diener, E., Larsen, R. J., Emmons, R. A. 1984. Person × situation and congruence response models. *J. Pers. Soc. Psychol.* In press

Dyer, M. G. 1983. The role of affect in narratives. *Cogn. Sci.* 7:211–42

Ebbesen, E. B. 1981. Cognitive processes in inferences about a person's personality. See Higgins, Herman & Zanna 1981, pp. 247–76

Endler, N., Hunt, J. McV., eds. 1984. *Personality and the Behavioral Disorders.* New York: Wiley. In press

Epstein, S. 1979. The stability of behavior: I. On predicting most of the people much of the time. *J. Pers. Soc. Psychol.* 37:1097–1126

Epstein, S. 1980. The stability of behavior: II. Implications for psychological research. *Am. Psychol.* 35:790–806

Epstein, S. 1982. The stability of behavior across time and situations. See Rabin et al 1982

Epstein, S. 1983a. A research paradigm for the study of personality and emotions. See Page 1983, pp. 91–154

Epstein, S. 1983b. The stability of confusion: A reply to Mischel & Peake. *Psychol. Rev.* 90:179–84

Epstein, S. 1983c. Aggregation and beyond: Some basic issues on the prediction of behavior. *J. Pers.* 51:360–92

Epting, F. R., ed. 1984. *Personal Construct Counseling and Psychotherapy.* New York: Wiley. 224 pp.

Epting, F. R., Neimeyer, R. A., eds. 1983. Personal meanings of death: Applications of personal construct theory to clinical practice. *Death Educ.* (Spec. Issue) 7:87–327

Ericsson, K. A., Simon, H. A. 1980. Verbal reports as data. *Psychol. Rev.* 87:215–51

Eysenck, H. J. 1982. *Personality Genetics and Behavior.* New York: Praeger. 340 pp.

Eysenck, H. J. 1983. Is there a paradigm in personality research? *J. Pers. Res.* 17:369–97

Feather, N. T., ed. 1982. *Expectations and Actions: Expectancy-Value Models in Psychology.* Hillsdale, NJ: Erlbaum. 436 pp.

Fishbein, M., Ajzen, I. 1974. Attitudes toward objects as predictors of single and multiple behavioral criteria. *Psychol. Rev.* 8:59–74

Fiske, S. T. 1982. Schema-triggered affect: Applications to social perception. See Clark & Fiske 1982, pp. 55–78

Fong, G. T., Markus, H. 1982. Self-schemas and judgments about others. *Soc. Cogn.* 1:191–204

Funder, D. C. 1982. On the accuracy of dispositional versus situational attributions. *Soc. Cogn.* 1:205–22

Funder, D. C. 1983a. Three issues in predicting more of the people: A reply to Mischel & Peake. *Psychol. Rev.* 90:283–89

Funder, D. C. 1983b. The "consistency" controversy and the accuracy of personality judgments. *J. Pers.* 51:346–59

Funder, D. C., Ozer, D. J. 1983. Behavior as a function of the situation. *J. Pers. Soc. Psychol.* 44:107–12

Funder, D. C., van Ness, M. J. 1983. On the nature and accuracy of attributions that change over time. *J. Pers.* 51:17–33

Furnham, A. 1981. Personality and activity preference. *Br. J. Soc. Psychol.* 20:57–68

Furnham, A. 1982. Psychoticism, social desirability, and situation selection. *Pers. Individ. Diff.* 3:43–51

Gedo, J. E. 1979. *Beyond Interpretation: Toward a Revised Theory for Psychoanalysis.* New York: International Universities Press. 280 pp.

Gergen, K. J. 1981. The functions and foibles of negotiating self-conception. See Lynch et al 1981, pp. 59–73

Gibbons, F. X., Wright, R. A. 1981. Motivational biases in causal attributions of arousal. *J. Pers. Soc. Psychol.* 40:588–600

Gifford, R. 1982. Affiliativeness: A trait measure in relation to single-act and multiple-act behavioral criteria. *J. Res. Pers.* 16:128–34

Glass, D. C., Carver, C. S. 1980. Helplessness and the coronary-prone personality. See Abramson et al 1980, pp. 223–43

Goldberg, L. R. 1981. Language and individual differences: The search for universals in personality lexicons. *Rev. Pers. Soc. Psychol.* 2:141–65

Goldstein, K. M., Blackman, S. 1978. *Cognitive Style: Five Approaches to Relevant Research.* New York: Wiley. 279 pp.

Gormly, J. 1982. Behaviorism and the biological viewpoint of personality. *Bull. Psychonom. Soc.* 20:255–56

Gormly, J. 1983. Predicting behavior from personality trait scores. *Pers. Soc. Psychol. Bull.* 9:267–70

Gormly, J. 1984. Correspondence between personality trait ratings and behavioral events. *J. Pers.* In press

Gur, R. C., Sackheim, H. A. 1979. Self-deception: A concept in search of a phenomenon. *J. Pers. Soc. Psychol.* 37:147–69

Hamilton, D. L. 1979. A cognitive-attributional analysis of stereotyping. *Adv. Exp. Soc. Psychol.* 12:53–84

Hammen, C., de Mayo, R. 1982. Cognitive correlates of teacher stress and depressive symptoms: Implications for attributional models of depression. *J. Abnorm. Psychol.* 91:96–101

Harris, B., Harvey, J. H. 1981. Attribution theory: From phenomenal causality to the intuitive social scientist and beyond. In *The Psychology of Ordinary Explanations of Social Behavior,* ed. C. Antaki, pp. 57–95. London: Academic. 350 pp.

Harris, J. G. 1980. Nomovalidation and idiovalidation: A quest for the true personality profile. *Am. Psychol.* 35:729–744

Hastorf, A. H., Isen, A. M., eds. 1982. *Cognitive Social Psychology.* Amsterdam: Elsevier. 362 pp.

Helson, R., Mitchell, V. 1978. Personality. *Ann. Rev. Psychol.* 29:555–85

Higgins, E. T., Herman, C. P., Zanna, M. P., eds. 1981. *Social Cognition.* Hillsdale, NJ: Erlbaum. 437 pp.

Hilgard, E. R. 1980. The trilogy of mind: Cognition, affection, and conation. *J. Hist. Behav. Sci.* 16:107–17

Hoffman, M. L. 1981. Perspectives on the difference between understanding people and understanding things: The role of affect. In *Social Cognitive Development,* ed. J. H. Flavell, L. Ross, pp. 67–81. Cambridge: Cambridge Univ. Press. 322 pp.

Hogan, R. 1982. On adding apples and oranges in personality psychology. *Contemp. Psychol.* 27:851–52

Holyoak, K. J., Gordon, P. C. 1984. Information processing and social cognition. See Wyer et al 1984. In press

Howe, M. J. A. 1982. Biographical evidence and the development of outstanding individuals. *Am. Psychol.* 37:1071–81

Humphries, C., Carver, C. S., Neumann, P. G. 1983. Cognitive characteristics of the Type A coronary-prone behavior pattern. *J. Pers. Soc. Psychol.* 44:177–87

Ingram, R. E., Smith, T. W., Brehm, S. S. 1983. Depression and information processing: self-schemata and the encoding of self-referent information. *J. Pers. Soc. Psychol.* 45:412–20

Isen, A. M., Levin, P. F. 1972. Effect of feeling good on helping: Cookies and kindness. *J. Pers. Soc. Psychol.* 21:384–88

Isen, A. M., Means, B., Patrick, R., Nowicki, G. 1982. Some factors influencing decision-making strategy and risk taking. See Clark & Fiske 1982, pp. 243–62

Isen, A. M., Shalker, T. E., Clark, M., Karp, L. 1978. Affect, accessibility of material in memory and behavior: A cognitive loop? *J. Pers. Soc. Psychol.* 36:1–12

Izard, C., Kagan, J., Zajonc, R., eds. 1984. *Emotions, Cognition, and Behavior.* New York: Cambridge Univ. Press. In press

Jaccard, J. J. 1974. Predicting social behavior from personality traits. *J. Res. Pers.* 7:358–67

Jackson, D. N., Paunonen, S. V. 1980. Personality structure and assessment. *Ann. Rev. Psychol.* 31:503–51

Jones, M. 1962. Introduction. *Nebraska Symp. Motiv.* 10

Kagan, J. 1980. Perspectives on continuity. *In Constancy and Change in Human Development,* ed. O. G. Brim Jr., J. Kagan, pp. 26–74. Cambridge: Harvard Univ. Press. 754 pp.

Kahneman, D., Slovic, P., Tversky, A. 1982. *Judgment Under Uncertainty: Heuristics and Biases.* Cambridge: Cambridge Univ. Press. 555 pp.

Kelly, G. A. 1955. *The Psychology of Personal Constructs.* New York: Norton

Kenrick, D. T., Braver, S. L. 1982. Personality, idiographic and nomothetic! A rejoinder. *Psychol. Rev.* 89:182–86

Kenrick, D. T., Dantchik, A. 1983. Interactionism, idiographics, and the social psychological invasion of personality. *J. Pers.* 51:286–307

Kenrick, D. T., Stringfield, D. O. 1980. Personality traits and the eye of the beholder: Crossing some traditional philosophical boundaries in the search for consistency in all of the people. *Psychol. Rev.* 87:88–104

Kiesler, C. 1982. Comments. See Clark & Fiske 1982, pp. 111–18

Kihlstrom, J., Cantor, N. 1983. Mental representations of the self. *Adv. Exp. Soc. Psychol.* In press

King, G. A., Sorrentino, R. M. 1983. Psychological dimensions of goal-oriented situations. *J. Pers. Soc. Psychol.* 44:140–62

Klinger, E. 1977. *Meaning and Void: Inner Experience and the Incentives in People's Lives.* Minneapolis: Univ. Minn. Press. 412 pp.

Klinger, E. 1978. Modes of normal conscious flow. In *The Stream of Consciousness,* ed. K. S. Pope, J. L. Singer, pp. 225–58. New York: Plenum. 375 pp.

Klinger, E., ed. 1981. *Imagery: Concepts, Results, and Applications.* New York: Plenum. 408 pp.

Klinger, E., Barta, S. G., Maxeiner, M. E. 1981. Current concerns: Assessing therapeutically relevant motivation. In *Assessment Strategies for Cognitive-Behavioral Interventions,* ed. P. C. Kendall, S. D. Hollow, pp. 161–96. New York: Academic

Kuiper, N. A., Derry, P. A. 1981. The self as a cognitive prototype: An application to person perception and depression. See Cantor & Kihlstrom 1981, pp. 215–32

Lamiell, J. T. 1981. Toward an idiothetic psychology of personality. *Am. Psychol.* 36:276–89

Lamiell, J. T. 1982. The case for an idiothetic psychology of personality: A conceptual and empirical foundation. *Prog. Exp. Pers. Res.* 11:1–63

Lamiell, J. T., Foss, N. A., Larsen, R. J., Hempel, A. M. 1983. Studies in intuitive personology from an idiothetic point of view: Implications for personality theory. *J. Pers.* 51:438–67

Landfield, A. W., Leitner, L. M., eds. 1980. *Personal Construct Psychology: Psychotherapy and Personality.* New York: Wiley. 330 pp.

Lang, P. J., Levin, D. N., Miller, G. A., Kozak, M. 1983. Fear behavior, fear imagery, and the psychophysiology of emotion: The problem of affective response integration. *J. Abnorm. Psychol.* 92:276–306

Lefcourt, H. M. 1982. *Locus of Control: Current trends in Theory and Research.* Hillsdale, NJ: Erlbaum. 265 pp.

Lehrer, P. 1982. Problems and promises in behavior therapy. *Contemp. Psychol.* 27:59–60

Lewinsohn, P. M., Steinmetz, J. L., Larson, D. W., Franklin, J. 1981. Depression-related cognitions: Antecedent or consequence. *J. Abnorm. Psychol.* 90:213–29

Lewis, M., Rosenblum, L., eds. 1974. *The Effect of the Infant on Its Caregiver.* New York: Wiley. 264 pp.

Lieberman, D. A. 1979. Behaviorism and the mind. *Am. Psychol.* 34:319–33

Lingle, J. H., Altom, M., Medin, D. L. 1984.

Of cabbages and kings: Assessing the extendibility of natural object concept models to social things. See Wyer et al 1984. In press

Little, B. R. 1983. Personal projects: A rationale and method for investigation. *Environ. Behav.* 15:273–309

Locksley, A., Lenauer, M. 1981. Considerations for a theory of self-inference processes. See Cantor & Kihlstrom 1981, pp. 263–77

Loevinger, J., Knoll, E. 1983. Personality: Stages, traits, and the self. *Ann. Rev. Psychol.* 34:195–222

Lord, C. G. 1982. Predicting behavioral consistency from an individual's perception of situational similarities. *J. Abnorm. Soc. Psychol.* 42:1076–88

Lynch, M. D., Norem-Hebeisen, A., Gergen, K. J., eds. 1981. *Self-concept: Advances in Theory and Research.* Cambridge, Mass: Ballinger. 367 pp.

Maccoby, E. E., Jacklin, C. N. 1980. Sex differences in aggression: A rejoinder and reprise. *Child Dev.* 51:964–80

Maddux, J. E., Sherer, M., Rogers, R. W. 1982. Self-efficacy expectancy and outcome expectancy: Their relationship and their efforts on behavioral intentions. *Cogn. Ther. Res.* 6:207–11

Magnusson, D. 1974. The individual in the situation: Some studies on individual's perception of situations. *Studia Psychologica* 16:124–31

Magnusson, D., ed. 1981. *Toward a Psychology of Situations: An Interactional Perspective.* Hillsdale, NJ: Erlbaum. 464 pp.

Magnusson, D. 1984. Persons in situations: Some comments on a current issue. See Bonarius et al 1984. In press

Magnusson, D., Allen, V. L., eds. 1984. *Human Development: An Interactional Perspective.* New York: Academic. In press

Magnusson, D., Endler, N. S., eds. 1977. *Personality at the Crossroads: Current Issues in Interactional Psychology.* Hillsdale, NJ: Erlbaum, 454 pp.

Mahoney, M. J. 1980. Psychotherapy and the structure of personal revolutions. *In Psychotherapy Process,* ed. M. J. Mahoney. New York: Plenum. 403 pp.

Mahoney, M. J., Arnkoff, D. 1978. Cognitive and self-control therapies. In *Handbook of Psychotherapy and Behavior Change,* ed. S. Garfield, A. E. Bergin, pp. 689–722. New York: Wiley. 1024 pp.

Mancuso, J. C., Adams-Webber, J. R., eds. 1982. *The Construing Person.* New York: Praeger. 317 pp.

Mandler, G. 1982. Cognitive underpinnings of affect. See Clark & Fiske 1982, pp. 3–36

Manning, M. M., Wright, T. L. 1983. Self-efficacy expectancies, outcome expectan-

cies, and the persistence of pain control in childbirth. *J. Pers. Soc. Psychol.* 45:421–31

Markus, H. 1983. Self-knowledge: An expanded view. *J. Pers.* 51:543–65

Markus, H., Crane, M., Bernstein, S., Siladi, M. 1982. Self-schemas and gender. *J. Pers. Soc. Psychol.* 42:38–50

Markus, H., Sentis, K. 1982. The self in social information processing. See Suls 1982, pp. 41–90

Markus, H., Smith, J. 1981. The influence of self-schemata on the perception of others. See Cantor & Kihlstrom 1981, pp. 233–62

Masling, J. M., ed. 1983. *Empirical Studies of Psychoanalytical Theories.* Hillsdale, NJ: Erlbaum. 320 pp.

Matthews, K. A. 1982. Psychological perspectives on the Type A behavior pattern. *Psychol. Bull.* 91:293–323

McCarrey, M., Edwards, H. P., Rozario, W. 1982. Ego relevant feedback, affect, and self-serving attributional bias. *Pers. Soc. Psychol. Bull.* 8:189–94

McClelland, D. C. 1981. Is personality consistent? See Rabin et al 1981, pp. 87–113

McCrae, R. R. 1982. Consensual validation of personality traits: Evidence from self-reports and ratings. *J. Pers. Soc. Psychol.* 43:293–303

McFarland, C., Ross, M. 1982. Impact of causal attributions on affective reactions to success and failure. *J. Pers. Soc. Psychol.* 43:937–46

Meehl, P. E. 1956. Wanted—A good cookbook. *Am. Psychol.* 11:263–72

Meehl, P. E. 1978. Theoretical risks and tabular asterisks: Sir Karl, Sir Ronald, and the slow progress of soft psychology. *J. Consult. Clin. Psychol.* 46:806–34

Messick, S., Ross, J., eds. 1962. *Measurement in Personality and Cognition.* New York: Wiley. 334 pp.

Miller, G. A., Cantor, N. 1982. Review of Nisbett & Ross, Human inference: Strategies and shortcomings of social judgment. *Soc. Cogn.* 1:83–93

Miller, S. M., Mangan, C. E. 1983. Interacting effects of information and coping style in adapting to gynecologic stress: Should the doctor tell all? *J. Pers. Soc. Psychol.* 45:223–36

Mischel, W. 1968. *Personality and Assessment.* New York: Wiley. 365 pp.

Mischel, W. 1969. Continuity and change in personality. *Am. Psychol.* 24:1012–18

Mischel, W. 1973. Toward a cognitive social learning reconceptualization of personality. *Psychol. Rev.* 80:252–83

Mischel, W. 1981. Personality and cognition: Something borrowed, something new? See Cantor & Kihlstrom 1981, pp. 3–19

Mischel, W. 1982. A cognitive-social earning approach to assessment. In *Cognitive Assessment*, ed. T. V. Merluzzi, C. R. Glass, M. Genest, pp. 479–502. New York: Guilford. 532 pp.

Mischel, W. 1983. Alternatives in the pursuit of the predictability and consistency of persons: Stable data that yield unstable interpretations. *J. Pers.* 51:578–604

Mischel, W., Peake, P. K. 1982. Beyond déjà vu in the search for cross-situational consistency. *Psychol. Rev.* 89:730–55

Mischel, W., Peake, P. K. 1983a. Analyzing the construction of consistency in personality. See Page 1983, pp. 233–62

Mischel, W., Peake, P. K. 1983b. Some facets of consistency: Replies to Epstein, Funder, and Bem. *Psychol. Rev.* 90:394–402

Monson, T. C., Hesley, J. W., Chernick, L. 1982. Specifying when personality traits can and cannot predict behavior: An alternative to abandoning the attempt to predict single-act criteria. *J. Pers. Soc. Psychol.* 43:385–99

Moskowitz, D. S. 1982. Coherence and cross-situational generality in personality: A new analysis of old problems. *J. Pers. Soc. Psychol.* 43:754–68

Murray, H. A. 1938. *Explorations in Personality*. New York: Oxford Univ. Press. 761 pp.

Natale, M., Hantas, M. 1982. Effect of temporal mood states on selective memory about the self. *J. Pers. Soc. Psychol.* 42:927–34

Natsoulas, T. 1981. Basic problems of consciousness. *J. Pers. Soc. Psychol.* 41:132–78

Neimark, E. D., Stead, C. 1981. Everyday thinking by college women: Analysis of journal entries. *Merrill-Palmer Q.* 27:471–88

Neisser, U. 1967. *Cognitive Psychology*. New York: Appleton-Century-Crofts. 351 pp.

Neisser, U. 1980. On "social knowing." *Pers. Soc. Psychol. Bull.* 6:601–5

Nisbett, R., Ross, L. 1980. *Human Inference: Strategies and Shortcomings of Social Judgment*. Englewood Cliffs, NJ: Prentice-Hall. 334 pp.

Nisbett, R. E., Wilson, T. D. 1977. Telling more than we know: Verbal reports on mental processes. *Psychol. Rev.* 84:231–79

Norman, D. A. 1980. Twelve issues for cognitive science. *Cogn. Sci.* 4:1–32

Norman, D. A., Rumelhart, D. E. 1975. *Explorations in Cognition*. San Francisco: Freeman. 430 pp.

Oakes, W. F., Curtis, N. 1982. Learned helplessness: Not dependent upon cognitions, attributions, or other such phenomenal experiences. *J. Pers.* 50:387–408

Olweus, D. 1977. A critical analysis of the "modern" interactionist position. See Block 1977, pp. 221–33

Olweus, D. 1979. Stability of aggressive reaction patterns in males: A review. *Psychol. Bull.* 86:852–75

Olweus, D. 1980. The consistency issue in personality psychology revisited—with special reference to aggression. *Br. J. Soc. Clin. Psychol.* 19:377–90

Olweus, D. 1981. Continuity in aggressive and withdrawn, inhibited behavior patterns. *Psychiatr. Soc. Sci.* 1:141–59

Page, M. M., ed. 1983. *Personality: Current Theory and Research*. Lincoln: Univ. Nebraska Press. 276 pp.

Palys, T. S., Little, B. R. 1983. Perceived life satisfaction and the organization of personal project systems. *J. Pers. Soc. Psychol.* 44:1221–30

Pervin, L. A. 1976. A free-response description approach to the analysis of person-situation interaction. *J. Pers. Soc. Psychol.* 34:465–74

Pervin, L. A. 1978. *Current Controversies and Issues in Personality*. New York: Wiley. 313 pp.

Pervin, L. A. 1981. The relation of situations to behavior. See Magnusson 1981, pp. 343–60

Pervin, L. A. 1983. The stasis and flow of behavior: Toward a theory of goals. See Page 1983, pp. 1–53

Pervin, L. A. 1984a. *Personality: Theory and Research*. New York: Wiley. 569 pp. 4th ed.

Pervin, L. A. 1984b. *Current Controversies and Issues in Personality*. New York: Wiley. 2nd ed.

Pervin, L. A. 1984c. Idiographic approaches to personality. See Endler & Hunt 1984. pp. 261–82

Peterson, C., Semmel, A., von Baeyer, C., Abramson, L. Y., Metalsky, G. I., Seligman, M. E. P. 1982. The Attributional Style Questionnaire. *Cogn. Ther. Res.* 6:287–300

Phares, E. J., Lamiell, J. T. 1977. Personality. *Ann. Rev. Psychol.* 28:113–40

Pittner, M. S., Houston, B. K., Spiridigliozzi, G. 1983. Control over stress, Type A behavior pattern, and response to stress. *J. Pers. Soc. Psychol.* 44:627–37

Posner, M. 1981. Cognitions and personality. See Cantor & Kihlstrom 1981, pp. 339–40

Postman, L. 1956. Review of Nebraska Symposium on Motivation. *Contemp. Psychol.* 1:229–30

Powell, A., Royce, J. R. 1981. An overview of a multifactor-system theory of personality and individual differences: I. The factor and system models and the hierarchical factor structure of individuality. *J. Pers. Soc. Psychol.* 41:818–29

Price, R. H., Bouffard, B. L. 1974. Behavioral appropriateness and situational constraint. *J. Pers. Soc. Psychol.* 30:579–86

Rabin, A. I., Aronoff, J., Barclay, A. M., Zucker, R. A., eds. 1981. *Further Explorations in Personality*. New York: Wiley. 277 pp.

Rabin, A. I., Aronoff, A. M., Barclay, A. M., Zucker, R., eds. 1982. *Further explorations in Personality*, Vol. 2. New York: Wiley.

Rachlin, H. 1980. A (stubborn) refusal to return to introspectionism. *Am. Psychol.* 35:473

Raps, C. S., Peterson, C., Reinhard, K. E., Abramson, L. Y., Seligman, M. E. P. 1982. Attributional style among depressed patients. *J. Abnorm. Psychol.* 91:102–8

Raynor, J. O. 1974. Future orientation in the study of achievement motivation. In *Motivation and Achievement*, ed. J. W. Atkinson, J. O. Raynor, pp. 121–54. Washington, DC: Winston. 479 pp.

Rogers, T. B. 1981. A model of the self as an aspect of the human information processing system. See Cantor & Kihlstrom 1981, pp. 193–214

Rorer, L. G., Widiger, T. A. 1983. Personality structure and assessment. *Ann. Rev. Psychol.* 34:431–63

Rosch, E. 1978. Principles of categorization. In *Cognition and Categorization*, ed. E. Rosch, B. B. Lloyd, pp. 27–48. Hillsdale, NJ: Erlbaum. 328 pp.

Rosenblatt, A. D., Thickstun, J. T. 1977. Modern psychoanalytic concepts in a general psychology. *Psychol. Iss. Monogr.* 42–43

Rosenhan, D., Messick, S. 1966. Affect expectation. *J. Pers. Soc. Psychol.* 3:38–44

Rosenhan, D. L., Salovey, P., Karylowski, J., Hargis, K. 1981. Emotion and altruism. In *Altruism and Helping Behavior*, ed. J. P. Rushton, M. P. Sorrentino, pp. 233–48. Hillsdale, NJ: Erlbaum. 471 pp.

Rotter, J. B. 1982. *The Development and Application of Social Learning Theory*. New York: Praeger

Royce, J. R., Powell, A. 1983. *Theory of Personality and Individual Differences: Factors, Systems, and Processes*. Englewood Cliffs, NJ: Prentice Hall. 290 pp.

Runyan, W. M. 1981. Why did Van Gogh cut off his ear? The problem of alternative explanations in psychobiography. *J. Pers. Soc. Psychol.* 40:1070–77

Runyan, W. M. 1982. In defense of the case study method. *Am. J. Orthopsychiatry* 52:440–46

Runyan, W. M. 1983. Idiographic goals and methods in the study of lives. *J. Pers.* 51:413–37

Rushton, J. P. 1981. The altruistic personality. See Rosenhan et al 1981, pp. 251–266

Rushton, J. P., Brainerd, C. J., Pressley, M. 1983. Behavioral development and construct validity: The principle of aggregation. *Psychol. Bull.* 94:18–38

Rushton, J. P., Jackson, D. N., Paunonen, S. V. 1981. Personality: Nomothetic or idiographic? A response to Kenrick & Stringfield. *Psychol. Rev.* 88:582–89

Rychlak, J. F. 1981. *A Philosophy of Science for Personality Theory*. Malibar, Fla: Krieger. 2nd ed.

Rychlak, J. F. 1982. *Personality and Life-style of Young Male Managers: A Logical Learning Analysis*. New York: Academic. 294 pp.

Sabini, J., Silver, M. 1981. Introspection and causal accounts. *J. Pers. Soc. Psychol.* 40:171–79

Sackheim, H. A., Gur, R. C. 1979. Self-deception, other-deception, and self-reported psychopathology. *J. Consult. Clin. Psychol.* 47:213–15

Savin-Williams, R. C., Demo, D. H. 1983. Situational and transituational determinants of adolescent self-feelings. *J. Pers. Soc. Psychol.* 44:824–33

Scarr, S., McCartney, K. 1983. How people make their own environments: A theory of genotype-environment effects. *Child Dev.* 54:424–35

Schafer, R. 1976. *A New Language for Psychoanalysis*. New York: Aronson. 394 pp.

Schank, R. C., Abelson, R. P. 1977. *Scripts, Plans, Goals, and Understanding*. Hillsdale, NJ: Erlbaum. 248 pp.

Scheier, M. F., Carver, C. S. 1981. Private and public aspects of self. *Rev. Pers. Soc. Psychol.* 2:189–216

Scheier, M. F., Carver, C. S. 1982. Cognition, affect and self-regulation. See Clark & Fiske 1982, pp. 157–84

Sechrest, L. 1976. Personality. *Ann. Rev. Psychol.* 27:1–28

Shweder, R. A. 1982. Fact and artifact in trait perception: The systematic distortion hypothesis. *Prog. Exp. Pers. Res.* 11:65–100

Sigel, I. E., Jarman, P., Hanesian, H. 1967. Styles of categorization and their intellectual and personality correlates in young children. *Hum. Dev.* 10:1–17

Silverman, L. H. 1982. A comment on two subliminal psychodynamic activation studies. *J. Abnorm. Psychol.* 91:126–30

Silverman, L. H., Fishel, A. K. 1981. The Oedipus complex: Studies in adult male behavior. *Rev. Pers. Soc. Psychol.* 2:43–68

Simon, H. A. 1979. Information processing models of cognition. *Ann. Rev. Psychol.* 30:363–96

Simonton, D. K. 1981. The library laboratory: archival data in personality and social psychology. *Rev. Pers. Soc. Psychol.* 2:217–43

Singer, J. L., Singer, D. 1972. Personality. *Ann. Rev. Psychol.* 23:375–412

Sjoberg, L. 1982. Logical versus psychological necessity: A discussion of the role of common sense in psychological theory. *Scand. J. Psychol.* 23:65–78

Small, S. A., Zeldin, S., Savin-Williams, R. C. 1983. In search of personality traits: A multimethod analysis of naturally occurring prosocial and dominance behavior. *J. Pers.* 51:1–16

Smedslund, J. 1978. Bandura's theory of self-efficacy: A set of common sense theorems. *Scand. J. Psychol.* 19:1–14

Smith, E. R., Kluegel, J. R. 1982. Cognitive and social bases of emotional experience: Outcome, attributions, and affect. *J. Pers. Soc. Psychol.* 43:1129–41

Smith, E., Miller, P. 1978. Limits on the perception of cognitive processes: A reply to Nisbett and Wilson. *Psychol. Rev.* 85:355–62

Snyder, M. 1979. Self-monitoring processes. *Adv. Exp. Soc. Psychol.* 12:85–128

Snyder, M. 1981. On the influence of individuals on situations. See Cantor & Kihlstrom 1981, pp. 309–29

Snyder, M. 1983. The influence of individuals on situations: Implications for understanding the links between personality and social behavior. *J. Pers.* 51:497–516

Snyder, M., Campbell, M. H. 1982. Self-monitoring: The self in action. See Suls 1982, pp. 185–207

Snyder, M., Gangestad, S. 1982. Choosing social situations: Two investigations of self-monitoring processes. *J. Pers. Soc. Psychol.* 43:123–35

Snyder, M., White, P. 1982. Moods and memories: Elation, depression, and the remembering of the events of one's life. *J. Pers.* 50:149–67

Sroufe, L. A. 1979. The coherence of individual development: Early care, attachment, and subsequent developmental issues. *Am. Psychol.* 34:834–41

Staats, A. W., Burns, G. L. 1982. Emotional personality repertoire as cause of behavior: Specification of personality and interaction principles. *J. Pers.* 43:873–81

Stephan, W. G., Gollwitzer, P. M. 1981. Affect as a mediator of attributional egotism. *J. Exp. Soc. Psychol.* 17:443–58

Stolorow, R. D., Atwood, G. E. 1979. *Faces In A Cloud.* New York: Jason Aronson. 217 pp.

Suls, J., ed. 1982. *Psychological Perspectives on the Self.* Hillsdale, NJ: Erlbaum. 273 pp.

Teasdale, J. D. 1983. Negative thinking in depression: Cause, effect, or reciprocal relationship? *Adv. Behav. Res. Ther.* 5: 3–25

Tellegen, A., Kamp, J., Watson, D. 1982. Recognizing individual differences in predictive structure. *Psychol. Rev.* 89:95–105

Tennen, H., Drum, P. E., Gillen, R., Stanton, A. 1982a. Learned helplessness and the detection of contingency: A direct test. *J. Pers.* 50:421–42

Tennen, H., Gillen, R., Drum, P. E. 1982b. The debilitating effect of exposure noncontingent escape: A test of the learned helplessness model. *J. Pers.* 50:409–25

Tieger, T. 1980. On the biological basis of sex differences in aggression. *Child Dev.* 51:943–63

Tomkins, S. S. 1979. Script theory: Differential magnification of affects. *Nebraska Symp. Motiv.* 26:201–36

Turkat, I. D., Forehand, R. 1980. The future of behavior therapy. *Prog. Behav. Mod.* 9:1–47

Tversky, A., Johnson, E. J. 1981. Affect and the perception of risk. *Proc. 3rd Ann. Conf. Cogn. Sci. Soc.*

Tyler, L. E. 1978. *Individuality.* San Francisco: Jossey-Bass. 274 pp.

Vallacher, R. R. 1983. Thinking is believing. *Contemp. Psychol.* 28:104–6

Van de Geer, J. P., Jaspars, J. M. F. 1966. Cognitive functions. *Ann. Rev. Psychol.* 17:145–76

Wachtel, P. 1973. Psychodynamics, behavior therapy, and the implacable experimenter: An inquiry into the consistency of personality. *J. Abnorm. Psychol.* 82:323–34

Weiner, B. 1982. The emotional consequences of causal attributions. See Clark & Fiske 1982, pp. 185–210

Weiner, B., Graham, S., Chandler, C. 1982. Pity, anger, and guilt: An attribution analysis. *Pers. Soc. Psychol. Bull.* 8:226–32

Wheeler, L., Reis, H., Nezlek, J. 1983. Loneliness, social interaction, and sex roles. *J. Pers. Soc. Psychol.* 45:943–53

White, P. 1980. Limitations of verbal reports of internal events: A refutation of Nisbett and Wilson and of Bem. *Psychol. Rev.* 87:105–12

Wilensky, R. 1978. Why John married Mary: Understanding stories involving recurring goals. *Cogn. Sci.* 2:235–66

Wilson, G. T., Franks, C. M., eds. 1982. *Contemporary Behavior Therapy: Conceptual and Empirical Foundations.* New York: Guilford.

Wilson, T. D., Hull, J. G., Johnson, J. 1981. Awareness and self-perception: Verbal reports on internal states. *J. Pers. Soc. Psychol.* 40:53–71

Woodworth, R. S. 1937. *Psychology.* New York: Holt

Wright, J., Mischel, W. 1982. Influence of affect on cognitive social learning person variables. *J. Pers. Soc. Psychol.* 43:901–14

Wyer, R. S., Srull, T. K., Hartwick, J., eds. 1984. *Handbook of Social Cognition.* Hillsdale, NJ: Erlbaum. In press

Zajonc, R. B. 1980. Feeling and thinking: Preferences need no inferences. *Am. Psychol.* 35:151–75

Zajonc, R. B., Pietromonaco, P., Bargh, J. 1982. Independence and interaction of affect and cognition. See Clark & Fiske 1982, pp. 211–18

Zanna, M. P., Higgins, E. T., Herman, C. P., eds. 1982. *Consistency in Social Behavior.* Hillsdale, NJ: Erlbaum. 314 pp.

Zevon, M. A., Tellegen, A. 1982. The structure of mood change: An idiographic/nomothetic analysis. *J. Pers. Soc. Psychol.* 43:111–22

Ann. Rev. Psychol. 1985. 36:115-40

THE SCHOOL AS A SOCIAL SITUATION

Seymour B. Sarason

Institution for Social and Policy Studies, Yale University, New Haven, Connecticut 06520

Michael Klaber

Department of Psychology, University of Hartford, Hartford, Connecticut 06117

CONTENTS

It would be difficult in 1985, if not irresponsible, to discuss the school as a social situation without giving primary attention to the significance of the fact that schooling has returned near to the top of the national agenda. However one defines the term social, one cannot deny that schooling has again become a social issue: a source of concern and controversy. What schools are, what they should be, who should share responsibility for them, what social-intellectual-vocational functions they should serve for young people—these and related questions are being discussed in books, reports, and the national media. The current discussion is not easy to characterize or to sort out because of the interaction among political, moral, social class, and research data (present or absent). For example, in 1976 the Democratic candidate for the presidency

115

0066-4308/85/0201-0115$02.00

promised, if elected, to create a separate department of education. In the campaign of 1980 Ronald Reagan promised to eliminate the department that President Carter had established. The differences in those positions reflect fundamental differences about who should determine what goes on inside of schools, i.e. how pupils, educators, families, and others in the local community should be interrelated in matters of educational substance and policy.

How can one begin to understand the origins of the one indisputable agreement between people holding these polar positions: that there have been changes in the social ambience of schools that are correlated with poor academic performance, indeed, decreasing levels of educational performance? To some the social changes are causes, to others they are the effects of poor performance, and to still others they are but one set of factors in a horribly complex gestalt rooted in our national history and powered by forces unleashed by World War II (Sarason 1982). Chronologically speaking, there were a number of factors and events in the post World War II era that magnetized public attention to social factors within schools that were considered inimical to quality of education:

1. The population explosion that followed World War II brought overcrowding to the fore. How, it was said, could one expect students to have a productive educational experience in physical quarters unable to accommodate what appeared to be a flood of youngsters? This was also at a time in our urban centers when juvenile delinquency was on the rise, a fact that was seen as correlated with inadequate educational facilities. Indeed, before there was federal legislation, the Ford Foundation's "gray area" projects, centering on youth, education, and employment, were initiated (Maris & Rein 1967).

2. The 1954 Supreme Court desegregation decision highlighted the social-interpersonal-moral consequences of the "separate but equal" doctrine but, no less significant, it set into motion forces that insured that the school as a social situation was in for troubled times.

3. No societal institution was exempt from the influence of the turbulent 1960s and none more than schools was affected by the civil rights, womens', anti-poverty, and anti-Vietnam movements. In the case of schools there was an additional factor: the rise and growth of militant teacher unions, which alone had diverse effects on the social ambience of schools.

4. Beginning in the 1950s, the unprecedented entry of the federal government into the educational arena inevitably had, as it was intended to have, a marked influence on the social climate of schools. Albeit a truism, the influx of new and large sums of money altered relationships within and between different levels in the educational hierarchy as well as those between teachers and specialized personnel, on the one hand, and students, on the other hand.

5. The later falling birth rate had obvious social consequences for schools: reduction in educational personnel, ever-worsening morale, school closings,

conflicts between parents and school boards about how to cope with shrinking resources, increased class size, a rising average age of school personnel, sharpening of conflicts between teacher unions and school boards, the elimination of various school programs (e.g. athletics), and a change in the characteristics of those who sought to make teaching their life career.

6. In 1975 the passage of the Education for All Handicapped Childrens Act (Public Law 94-142) signalled the third revolution in public education (the first was the legitimation of compulsory education by the end of the 19th century and the second was the 1954 desegregation decision). Public Law 94-142, popularly known as the "mainstreaming law," stated that all handicapped children should be integrated into a regular classroom and routine school activities according to the criterion of the least restrictive environment. That is to say, it would no longer be desirable and/or possible to segregate handicapped children simply because they were handicapped, and it became the schools' obligation to study and plan for each handicapped child so that his or her program would meet the criterion of the least restrictive alternative.

In one way or another, directly or indirectly, each of the above factors was seen as contributing to and altering the school as a social situation and, therefore, academic performance. Although some groups argued that over the long run the altered social climate would have beneficial effects on academic performance, the most frequent judgment was that in the short run performance levels would probably be adversely affected. The important point, historically speaking, is that the interaction of these factors set the stage for the return of education to the national agenda.

RESTRICTION OF FOCUS

What has psychology contributed to our understanding of the altered *and* altering social dynamics of schools? What are the major features of those changes and what has psychological research illuminated about them? It should be clear from these questions that in this chapter we restrict ourselves to three major issues: the research basis for characterizing the ways in which the social dynamics and relationships in schools have changed; the relationships of psychological theory and research to the policies that were intended to change the school as a social situation; and the illumination that psychological theory and research have provided about the consequences of those policies. Any one of those issues deserves book-length treatment, not because the research literature is that voluminous but rather because there is a staggeringly large nonresearch literature that seems to assume the existence of a solid psychological basis for what different writers describe, claim, or propose.

The reader should note that in restricting our focus to *changes* in the school as a social situation we therefore, do not refer to research literature that, although sizeable and important, is not directly relevant to social changes that have occurred within schools. Even so, as we endeavor to demonstrate, the restriction in focus we have adopted does not allow us to do justice to the three major issues above, if only because restricting our focus to changes inevitably requires that those changes be described and understood in historical contexts. So, for example, it is impossible to understand how the growth of militant teacher unions altered social relationships among school personnel, between school administrators and boards of education, between parents and school personnel—and the direct and indirect effects of those changes on students—without seeing those changes in terms of larger societal changes. Although the restriction we adopted was a way of achieving manageability—as well as a way of recognizing the importance of educational policy in our society today—we still had to be selective in coverage.

THE SOCIAL SITUATION IN WHICH SCHOOLS?

It is an obvious but neglected focus in the research literature that any generalization must be hedged with many qualifications deriving from the fact that, reflective of the nature of our society, schools vary considerably in many dimensions. Take, for example, public and private schools; the former have been subject of some research, while the latter are more likely to be subjects of fiction, film, and plays. Nonpublic schools are both residential and dayschools. Some are religious schools, some related to a parish, and others to a religious hierarchy (typically Roman Catholic). Other religious schools are essentially independent but follow a certain ideology or denomination (typically Protestant and Jewish). Yet another group of schools is oriented toward a particular life-style, e.g. military academies. The private college preparatory, and often selective, schools are among the oldest schools in America and were until recently sexually segregated.

Another group of schools can be identified as serving the needs of special populations. There are special schools for physically and emotionally handicapped children as well as those with sensory handicaps and perceptual impairments. Few of these schools receive the attention of the researcher. Schools for offenders, on the other hand, have been investigated.

Another group of schools that are a part of our blind spot are vocational and technical schools, and schools with special emphasis on certain cultural or linguistic issues. Further, it is preposterous to lump schools in low-income urban settings with schools in more affluent suburbs and/or rural areas. Moreover, new types of schools (e.g. magnet schools) are devised, staffed and more often than not reorganized (e.g. the open-class school). The purpose of this enumeration is to demonstrate the difficulty of summarizing any research on "the schools."

Schools vary immensely and so do the people who can be found in school buildings at any given moment. In a public school, for example, we are likely to see a very large cast of characters: classroom teachers (male and female, black and white), special teachers for special students (handicapped, gifted) or special subjects (physical education, home economics, computers) or special interests (music, art, drama), and their supervisors and administrators. There are a number of nonteaching professionals in many schools, e.g. the school psychologist, social worker, nurse, and guidance counselor. All of these personnel are supplemented by a variety of professionals who characteristically visit the school, including psychiatrists and other physicians. With the rise of child advocacy, attorneys and officials of child service agencies are in the schools, as are members of state and city agencies, and often federal employees who visit, consult with, and evaluate the school. The students in the school will also interact with large numbers of people who are not designated as professionals. Often these interactions appear to be more significant than teacher-pupil encounters. Thus, teacher aides, cafeteria workers, secretaries, and custodians are significant persons within the school wall. And then there are those who make it possible to go to the school: the crossing guards, police personnel, and the school bus drivers. Many younger children have some intensive interaction with "latch key" personnel.

There are few schools where some parents are not about much of the school day. Yet, parents too are not a homogeneous group. The "traditional" parent shares the school with the single parent (unmarried, divorced, widowed), the foster parent, the step-parent, the surrogate parent, and the legal parent (guardian). In this, admittedly incomplete, panorama we have omitted the group for whom the school has been invented: the student. There are many labels for students, some more useful than others, all presumably devised to extend a service to the labelled person. With PL 94-142 the "mandated student" has come into being: the child who must be served in special ways. There are other designations, such as the bilingual student who may attend bilingual classes taught in his native language or perhaps an ESL (English as a Second Language) class to learn English. Perhaps the most important labels are the unofficial ones, the ones the students use themselves (e.g. hoods, burnouts, jocks).

We must not forget some extrascholastic settings in which academic learning takes place, for example, Sunday schools and religious schools intended to supplement rather than supplant "full-time" schools. Outside the scope of this chapter are educational programs for adults, although it is estimated that so-called adult education is the fastest growing segment of the area termed education. It ranges from adult education and General Education Diploma (GED) classes conducted by the public schools to the Elder Hostels conducted by colleges and universities for senior citizens. The armed forces conduct a vast array of educational programs, as do corporations such as General Electric or Electronic Data Systems. There is no question that education is, to an unusual extent (in terms of hours taught, pupil enrollment, etc), conducted in settings other than public schools.

It is worthy of special note that on January 5, 1983, on national public television a large segment of the MacNeill-Lehrer news hour was devoted to the social, legal, and political significances of independent religious schools, which are estimated to number in the thousands. The sources of this exponential increase are predictably diverse, but there can be no doubt that one such source is beliefs about what should characterize the school as a social situation and how these characteristics should relate to family, community, and church. But, as we have emphasized, these schools are only one type in a crazy-quilt of educational settings. The literature has focused almost exclusively on public schools, and then only on a restricted sample of existing types, so its generalizations may be far from applicable to a truly random selection of school settings. More important, perhaps, this restricted focus may have the unintended effect of diverting attention away from a variety of transformations occurring in our society and, therefore, in our schools.

The restricted focus on the type of school studied is parallelled by another restriction in focus: the emphasis on the individual student. One would expect that the field most directly concerned with schools, namely school psychology, would concern itself with the social situation. This is only marginally the case. In the mammoth *Handbook of School Psychology* (Reynolds & Gutkin 1982) very few chapters have any direct bearing on the school as a social situation. Mearig (1982) pleads for the integration of school and community services, and Schmuck (1981) deals with organizational development of the school as a human system. Emphasis is primarily on the process of consultation. Snapp & Davidson (1982) apply the case study approach to system-level changes in the schools. Gutkin & Curtis (1981) deal with the theories and techniques of school-based consultations by school psychologists. Inevitably, these chapters do illuminate aspects of the school as a social situation, particularly in regard to how reactions to the change process alter relationships within and among different levels of administration. The bulk of the handbook, however, is devoted to diagnosis of and interventions in the lives of individuals. This emphasis on the individual, the neglect of the social surroundings, and the way those surroundings are embedded in larger structured surroundings has long been a characteristic of American psychology (Sarason 1982).

INTEGRATION

One particularly visible aspect of the social climate of the school is the issue of integration. While psychologists have usually taken the position that integration is in general a good thing, they have rarely buttressed their assertions with research. Stephan (1978, 1980) reviewed the research designed to test those assertions of the social scientists that led to the 1954 *Brown vs the Board of Education* decision. He concluded that their predictions had usually not been realized. A number of reviewers took on the task of re-reviewing the evidence and came to the same conclusion, albeit with great reluctance (e.g. Cook 1979). In an article addressing the role of social science in the formation of public policy, Gerard (1983) reviews the most important works published recently. He delineates eleven assumptions that were implicit in the Supreme Court decision to desegregate schools. These include the assumptions that achievement orientations are reversible and that minority children will learn to compete and to strive for higher achievement in desegregated settings. The evidence collected after desegregation does not bear out *any* of the assumptions made by the social scientists. Gerard, however, goes further. He notes that the unresearched assumptions of the social scientists have seriously impaired the credibility of social science. Gerard goes on to recommend that social scientists learn to "engineer effective integration" rather than merely to describe it. In particular, he asserts, we are in need of careful investigations that are first tried out in the laboratory, then applied to selected real-life settings, and finally submitted to longitudinal research on a larger scale. Unfortunately, asserts Gerard, the culture of the school and the culture of psychology departments do not intersect.

The conclusions by Gerard and others are sobering in several respects. First, those who advocated or were responsible for integration vastly underestimated how the culture of the school would present obstacles to and be changed by integration. Second, there was an equal underestimation of the difficulties that would be encountered by virtue of changes in the school as a social situation, difficulties experienced by children, parents, and school personnel. Third, there was and is a chasm between research findings and "real life" in schools. Fourth, the social changes initiated by the 1954 decisions are continuing, and we are far from understanding either what they portend or how we should deal with them. It is our impression that the failure of integration to achieve its major goals has had the effects of lessening research interest in the schools as *changing* social situations.

The problems surrounding school integration are not peculiar to the United States. It is no less a major problem in Israel where, until recently, eastern and central European Jews (Ashkenazi) were socially and politically dominant over Sephardic (so-called mid-Eastern "oriental") Jews. The conflicts, political and religious, between these two groups have intensified in recent years reflected in changes in political power and in criticisms of the educational system. Several Israeli investigators have studied aspects of the integration process. Those studies have been critically reviewed by Sharan (Sharan & Rich 1983), who together with colleagues (Sharan et al 1982) carried out a rather heroic study on the effects of cooperative learning in small groups in the classroom on, among other things, ethnic relations and attitudes. Suffice it to say, neither Sharan's study nor those of others in Israel lend encouragement to the belief that available theory and techniques of intervention have clear effects in diluting negative, inter-ethnic attitudes. It may be, as Sharan suggests, that the general tendency for all students over time to become, as Sharan's data clearly indicate, increasingly disenchanted with school, overwhelms efforts to change inter-ethnic attitudes. Those readers with an interest in the research approach to the problem of altering the school as a social situation are urged to consult Sharan's unusually detailed description of the study: its rationale, modes of analysis, and findings. It is, in our opinion, an important study because of its methodology and the heroic efforts it required to be carried out. For the readers with an interest in desegregration we strongly recommend *School Desegregation: Cross-Cultural Perspectives,* edited by Amir & Sharan (1983).

THE EDUCATIONAL CONSEQUENCES OF EARLY INTERVENTION

The Head Start Programs conceived in 1964, is a particularly clear example of the influential role of psychological theory and research in policy formulation, legislation, implementation, and administration. It was (and is) a project designed, among other purposes, to influence the educational experience and performance of disadvantaged children. Influential in initiating that project was a developmental psychologist, Edward Zigler, who later became the first director of the Office of Child Development (Zigler & Valentine 1979; Zigler, Kagan & Klugman 1983). Among the research, scholarly, and theoretical contributions that Zigler and Anderson (1979) mention as influential in the societal climate that led to the development of Head Start were those by J. McVicker Hunt (1961), Bloom (1964), and Gray (1967). But, as Zigler & Anderson (1979) point out, the conclusions often drawn from these contributions, both by the general public and social-science professionals, were of the nature of a mixed blessing: stimulating efforts for compensating programs and at the same time raising expectations:

> Parents and educators of the mid-sixties were inundated with articles claiming that children could be taught to read by age two and that a child's IQ could be raised by 20 points in a year. Lewis' concept of a culture of poverty was similarly misused. Lewis had introduced the idea of culture into the issue of poverty by describing the behavior and values of economically deprived groups. But the popular interpretation of the relationship between culture and poverty evolved into the term "culturally deprived," as if a group could be deprived of its own culture. At the root of this misunderstanding was the middle-class belief that those who were culturally different were somehow culturally bereft.
>
> Social-science professionals reinforced these popular misconceptions by creating a stereotype of the American poor family on the basis of very meager research. According to

this stereotype, the poor child was deprived not only of the health and nutritional care that the family could not afford, but of proper maternal care and environmental stimulation as well. Poor mothers (fathers were assumed to be absent) were characterized as immature, harsh disciplinarians, unable to love because of their own dependency needs. The environment was either understimulating (insufficient toys, insufficient interaction and attention) or overstimulating (noise, fighting), or both. Verbal activity in the poor household was supposed to consist of body language, monosyllables, shouts, and grunts. . . .

At the time that the War on Poverty and the Head Start Program were created, the stereotypic view of poverty and the environmental view of its cure prevailed. The stereotype of the economically disadvantaged family was so bleak that it made intervention seem the obvious solution. The environmentalists' case for the power of enrichment was so strong that intervention seemed a simple solution as well. Bloom's discovery of the brief, critical period in which intervention could be accomplished filled program planners with a sense of urgency. The ensuing rush to produce programs to enrich the environments of the poor through education overrode the need for research data on which to base these intervention strategies.

The heyday of naive environmentalism left its mark on the nation's social programs for children. Great expectations and promises were based on the view that the young child was a plastic material to be molded quickly and permanently by the proper school environment. Over a decade later, Head Start is still recovering from the days of "environmentalism run amok." (pg. 8–9)

That statement, as we discuss below, underlines the dilemmas that psychologists face when they seek to relate theory and research to societal issues around which passionate differences in view and interest are many and longstanding. And nowhere is this more clear than in the origins of both Head Start and the Office of Child Development (Steiner 1976).

It is not fortuitous that the comprehensive volume *Project Head Start* has the subtitle *A Legacy of the War on Poverty* (1979); nor is it fortuitous that much of that volume deals with the ways that project was intended to alter the experience and performance of young children once they were "graduated" from Head Start and entered schools. Implicitly, Head Start reflected the view that the school as a social situation was inimical to youngsters disadvantaged by race, ethnic background, and economic status. It was also based on the view that unless parents of these preschoolers were encouraged to change their relationships to educational personnel in the schools, educational performance would suffer. In short, Head Start reflected imagery of how social relationships in schools should be altered (Valentine & Stark 1979). Insofar as the consequences of parental involvement in Head Start are concerned, research suggests (*a*) that children do better when their parents are involved, and (*b*) that preschool intervention may only succeed when parents are involved in the educational process. There are no research data on whether the altered role of parents in Head Start has carried over during the ensuing school years, i.e. whether social relationships between parents and school personnel changed. Valentine & Stark (1979, p. 310) conclude: "Basic institutional change would seem to be a minimal prerequisite if individual changes made in childhood are to be sustained through the life cycle. It is noteworthy that in ten years of evaluation research, only two studies have considered institutional change as a potentially significant outcome of a good parent-involvement component."

In 1970 the Westinghouse Learning Corporation issued the first evaluative report on Head Start, concluding that there was no evidence of lasting cognitive gains. As Harman & Hanley (1979) note: "Head Start's administrators could produce virtually no evaluation or even simple quantitative data to counter the Westinghouse Report." The Westinghouse report forced the Head Start administration to review its programs and to initiate a variety of administrative and substantive changes in addition to mandating self-assessment by local programs. It was a bad time for Head Start. But, as Palmer & Andersen (1979) note:

> Fortunately, in the 1960's immediately before and after the beginning of Head Start, a group of intervention studies had been begun by investigators mainly concerned with determining the effects of their particular early-intervention programs on children's performance. Few of these studies were originally conceived of as longitudinal in the sense that they would follow the children through elementary school. But in 1975, alarmed at the prevailing attitudes, the investigators who had made the original studies decided to pool their efforts, relocate the children in the studies they had done earlier, and compare them with their controls with respect to IQ and to performance in the elementary grades. In a 1975 review of the evidence for early intervention for the Education Commission of the States the case was made to withhold judgment until the children in those studies were of sufficient age for reliable and valid measures to be made. ECS and the Office of Child Development subsequently supported the group's efforts to relocate the children and obtain measures of scholastic performance. (p. 436)

In the corridors of administrative-legislative power, as in the halls of science, research findings are both cause and effect, goads to passions and action.

In Table 1, taken from Palmer & Anderson, is summary information on ten longitudinal early childhood studies. These comprise the research consortium galvanized by the jeopardy into which the Westinghouse report and other critics put Head Start. The common characteristics of these studies were:

1. The intervention had been completed before 1969.
2. The original sample size was large enough to allow a recovery rate adequate for statistical purposes.
3. The studies met at least minimal criteria for experimental design (selection of subjects, controls, attrition analysis, etc).
4. The description of the intervention was well documented.
5. Subjects were predominantly poor and black.
6. Each study was able to follow up the sample ten or more years after the initial intervention.

In terms of placement in special education classes, reading levels, and arithmetic achievement, the weight of the evidence favored experimental

Table 1 Summary information on ten longitudinal early child intervention studies[a]

Principal investigator	Location	Latest data	Sample size for latest data	
			Program	Control
E. K. Beller	Philadelphia, Pa.	Grade 4	50	99
M. Deutsch	Harlem, N.Y.	Grade 3	82	166
		Grades 10–13	46	11
I. J. Gordon	Gainesville, Fla.	Grade 3	70	21
S. W. Gray	Nashville, Tenn.	Grade 4	38	41
M. B. Karnes	Champaign, Ill.	Grade 4	48	N.A.
		Grade 3	49	N.A.
P. Levenstein	Freeport, N.Y.	Grade 3	57	51
L. B. Miller	Louisville, Ky.	Grade 2	175	40
		Grades 6, 7	141	
F. H. Palmer	Harlem, N.Y.	Grade 7	185	55
V. Seitz	New Haven, Conn.	Grades 7, 8	63	58
		Grade 7	38	43
D. P. Weikart	Ypsilanti, Mich.	Grade 8	49	46
			110	Total

[a] Adapted from Palmer & Andersen (1979).

controls. "A study-by-study analysis of the effects of early intervention on subsequent IQ must lead to the conclusion that some treatments influenced that variable significantly while others did not. We can only conclude that early intervention frequently affects IQs but does not always do so" (Palmer & Andersen 1979, p. 445).

It should be noted, as Palmer & Andersen emphasize, that impressive evidence favoring early intervention does not mean that Head Start "worked." In regard to the Westinghouse study, they note its conclusion that summer Head Start programs were ineffective, perhaps even counterproductive, but that full-time Head Start programs were beneficial. There have been several critiques of the Westinghouse study (Campbell & Erlebacher 1970) disputing its conclusions.

The studies we have discussed or cited raise a question reminiscent of one that stirred controversy decades ago about the effects of different child-rearing practices on adult personality. That differences in such practices had effects on children was not at issue. What was at issue was whether it made theoretical sense to try to explain adult personality by early parent-child experiences as if the intervening years were a mere playing out of a predetermined script. The conclusion from the early intervention studies and Head Start that the interventions had intended effects later in school raises the same question and for the same reasons: the major conclusions are not confirmed in all of the studies, within each study there is a range of individual differences in later status in school, and there is no theoretical basis for assuming that what happened in the years between the intervention and the follow-up did not contain important events and experiences. Did the schools to which these preschoolers went know about the early interventions? Did those parents who were actively involved in the preschool intervention continue to be involved in the schools to which their children went? What was the nature and substance of the contacts, if any, between the interveners and school personnel? How did the schools vary in terms of social climate, size of class, and student mix? One could ask other questions but the fact is that when these preschoolers entered school they were in a complex social situation that could not be neutral in its effects, i.e. in theory the school as a social situation would be either positive or negative in its relationship to the child's experiences in the intervention program.

The problems facing Head Start children when they entered the public schools requires that we call attention to a research literature on the relationships between school performance and moving of residence. It is a literature that goes back several decades and has relevance to Head Start precisely because moving is amazingly frequent in areas in which these children live. One type of study concerns the relationship between moving and school performance (Corbally 1930, Downie 1953, Evans 1966, Gilliland 1958, Justman 1964, Kasindorf 1963, Levine et al 1966, Sackett 1935). Another type is clinical report (Gabower 1959, Gordon & Gordon 1958, Pedersen & Sullivan 1964, Rakietan 1961, Stubblefield 1955). A third type is experimental analysis of reaction to the unknown or unfamiliar (Arsenian 1943, Berlyne 1960, Ellesor 1933, Gruber 1954, Hudson 1954, Hutt, Hutt, & Ounsted 1965, McReynolds, Acker & Pietila 1961, Mendel 1965, Pielstrick & Woodruff 1964, Smock & Holt 1962). These studies provide important clues about how a lower-class child may respond to an unfamiliar school setting. This literature and Fox's *Entering a new school* (1968) leave no doubt that entering a new school situation is far from a matter of indifference to the lower-class child. There is abundant evidence that inner-city schools have a very high turnover of children that very much affects the school as a social situation for children and teachers. Fox noted in 1968 that some schools in New York City reported a turnover of 100% in a single year, and figures of 50% were not uncommon in other urban school systems. (There is no reason to believe that the situation has dramatically improved.)

It is safe to assume that, because the early intervention studies and Head Start began in the 1960s, for which the depressing data on turnover are available, an undetermined number of the children were entering an unfamiliar, ever-changing social situation. One is tempted to argue, in light of what the school as a social situation may have been for many children, that the findings from the different intervention studies reported by Palmer & Anderson are far stronger than they appear. However understandable it may be that so much attention is given to points separated by years, it distracts attention away from studying not only the school experience but the differences among schools as social situations.

SOCIAL ASPECTS OF EDUCATIONAL DECISION MAKING

One mandated feature of Public Law 94-142 is especially relevant to the school as a social situation: school personnel must meet in multidisciplinary *teams* to make placement and instructional planning decisions about handicapped or potentially handicapped students. It has been noted (e.g. Sarason et al 1966, Sarason 1982) that the tradition of the case conference has never taken hold in the culture of the school. By case conference we mean a regularly scheduled meeting (*a*) at which available data on problem children are presented and discussed, and recommendations are made, and (*b*) to which come those school personnel who have significant contact with or knowledge of these children and families. In the culture of the school, the decision-making process largely reflected the style of the school principal, who might talk with the child's teacher, with a designated member of the pupil personnel department "downtown," or essentially with no one. Almost always the decisions were made without parent involvement and the main task of the principal or his-her surrogate was to convince the parent of the wisdom of the decision. Another way of putting it is that decision making was from the top down, reflecting the more general tendency: superintendent → district superintendent → principal → teacher → parent. Indeed, in regard to this general tendency, the larger the school system the more likely that each level of the hierarchy felt unrelated to decisions made by those above them.

One cannot understand the rise in size and strength of teacher unions and militant parent groups in the 1960s without paying attention to the long-smoldering resentment on the part of teachers and parents to the modal decision-making process in the schools. In the case of teacher unions, far more than money was at stake. There was also the absence of the sense of professional worth, of a social and professional cohesiveness within the school, and other correlates of a kind of learned helplessness.

For teachers (if not for all other credentialled personnel) there is no fine line between the school as a social and professional situation. However, although there is a forbiddingly massive literature on the school as a social situation for students, there has been little or no systematic research on that topic for the professionals who work in schools, among whom, of course, teachers are by far the most numerous. There are anecdotes, narratives, and case studies but nothing resembling the systematic research done on children. For example, in 1966 Sarason et al described in detail their experiences (via the Yale Psychoeducational Clinic) in and conclusions drawn from their intensive work in schools, largely elementary schools. One of the chapters (written by Murray Levine) was titled: "Teaching is a Lonely Profession," a title that referred to several factors: what teachers had said to clinic staff, the fleeting and superficial social and professional relationships among teachers, and what it meant to spend the bulk of the day only with young children. That chapter, more than any other, drew spontaneous approving letters from teachers. The degree to which one can generalize from the conclusions in that chapter is, of course, limited by the anecdotal and narrative kinds of "data" it contains. Over the years several books (Waller, 1961, Sarason 1982, second edition, Lortie 1975) have, from different but overlapping points of view, been influential in directing attention to the school as a social situation and to the ways that different classes of personnel confront and are affected by the decision-making process. There have been case studies of innovative schools (e.g. Smith & Keith 1971, Gold & Miles 1981) that describe in comprehensive detail the complexity, ambiguity, and problematic nature of the decision-making process. More to the point, these studies, despite their focus on new schools, leave no doubt that the decision-making process is a most productive focus for those seeking to understand the school as a social situation.

The fact is that systematic research on the decision-making process in the modal school received little attention until Public Law 94-142 in 1975 mandated a formal vehicle for making decisions about handicapped children. As we indicated earlier, that legislation was an explicit attempt to remedy what was seen as an informal, discriminatory decision-making process affecting parents, children, teachers, and administrative personnel. The research on team decision making stimulated by Public Law 94-142 employed self-report methodologies, sometimes accompanied by observation (Fenton et al 1979, Goldstein et al 1980, Hoff et al 1978, Holland 1980, Yoshida et al 1978a,b). Other investigators employed teams of researchers who used specific observational systems to answer questions about the effectiveness of the team process (Mitchell 1980), the domains of data discussed (Rostollan 1980), the assessment data discussed (Shinn 1980), the extent to which team decisions were based on data (Richey & Graden 1980), the participation of other than special-educators or personnel (Allen 1980), and the generation of intervention statements (Poland & Mitchell 1980). There are four conclusions these studies support: individuals rather than the team are influential in determining the outcome of meetings; parents tend to be involved minimally despite the explicit wording of PL 94-142; there do not seem to be criteria to guide decision making; not infrequently, decisions seem to be made before the team meeting, with the meeting serving only to approve them.

In 1979 Poland et al asked directors of special-education from across the nation to list the major steps followed in the assessment and decision-making process (Poland et al 1979). They studied special-education directors because previous research (Fenton et al 1979) indicated they were the most aware of the responsibilities of the team. Poland et al (1979) found that the descriptions of the directors varied considerably; few directors described pre-referral intervention efforts; few noted strategies to implement the education program for individuals; less than 25% reported that parents were contacted after the assessment of the students; about the same percentage said that parent permission for a placement was obtained. Poland et al state that their data do not allow one to separate what actually occurs from the directors' perception of current practice.

In a subsequent study Ysseldyke et al (1980) received permission from five elementary schools to observe their decision-making process for one year. The observers obtained data by "(a) observing meetings at which a (previously selected) target student was discussed, (b) reviewing reports or other written documents about the student, and (c) interviewing key school personnel and the student's parent(s). Written notes on their observations and interviews were maintained by the observers; these were then used to develop the reports on the seven students who were followed." The major findings included the following: there was considerable variation in the extent to which the requirements of PL 94-142 were used as an opportunity for substantive decision making; in terms of eligibility criteria, there were as many different criteria as there were school districts; the cost of the process in terms of time and money varied but was never small; there was enormous variation in the number and type of assessment devices utilized; some teams appeared to be actively involved in the direction of the assessment, others appeared indecisive, "expressing lack of clarity as to the purpose of the meeting"; in a majority of cases the process did not result in a substantive change in program or services for the student; some students did seem to benefit from the process and some seemed to have been affected negatively; the primary decision-making role of the teams appeared to be one of determining eligibility for service rather than one of cooperative problem solving for the purpose of developing strategies to serve children and teachers more effectively.

One must be cautious about generalizing from this study because the data were obtained from schools willing to be studied over a period of a year. It would not be unreasonable to assume that these schools may be atypical in the degree of security they had about the quality of their decision making in relation to PL 94-142. Even though the results do not provide a basis for general satisfaction about the quality of team decision making, they may be conveying a more optimistic picture than studies of randomly chosen schools would show. In this connection mention must be made of the study spearheaded by Ysseldyke et al (1980) in which 38 team meetings in 16 school districts were videotaped. The analyses of the tapes indicate that these team meetings left much to be desired, e.g. in only 27% of the meetings was language at a level that parents could be expected to understand, the purpose of the meeting was seldom stated, and there was almost never a statement of the decisions to be reached. In their recent publication Ysseldyke & Algozzine (1982, pp. 147–48) conclude the following from their studies using videotapes:

> The videotape studies of each placement team's decision-making process provided especially enlightening information. It was very difficult to find meetings that could be called placement decision-making sessions. Many team meetings were held, but most can be described as meetings to get ready for the meeting. Often, placement decisions were made at the same meetings at which many other kinds of decisions were made. We repeatedly had difficulty attempting to specify decisions that were actually made at meetings because in most instances it was apparent that the decisions were made before the actual meetings took place. We also had difficulty getting individuals to assume responsibility for the decisions that were made. When we asked people after the meetings, "Who actually made the decision," nearly all claimed that someone else had been responsible for it, and that they, personally, had little power in the process. We learned to refer to this finding as the "Little Red Hen" phenomenon. (When we asked who made decisions, we consistently were told, "Not I!")

There can be no doubt that the mandating in Public Law 94-142 of placement teams has altered social-professional relationships within schools. That the studies cited and described above are not heartening in regard to the quality of performance has to be seen in the light of long-standing tradition in which decision making was the province of individuals. On the one hand, one could argue that, given long-standing tradition, the results to date are as good or better than one might have expected; on the other hand, one could argue that the "new tradition" is developing in ways unlikely to meet the purposes for which this new vehicle was established. There is a sizeable literature comparing the behavior and performance of children in two types of classrooms: the traditional ones and those in which children are members of small, cooperative, problem-solving groups. Sharan et al (1982) in particular has described in eloquent detail the obstacle course the researcher has to run, first to reach the point where it is possible to begin to alter the classroom in terms of its social organization and, second, to find the time and energy it takes to help teachers act consistently with the rationale for small-group, cooperative learning, which is so different from customary practice. What Sharan has described is precisely what could have been predicted when school personnel who, daily performing their duties as *individuals,* are catapulted into *teams.* The difference, of course, is that in the formation of these teams there was no external agent to guide or help the participants. As with so many efforts to change schools as a social situation, the introduction of placement teams did not take the culture of schools into account (Sarason 1982).

THE EFFECTS OF UNIONIZATION

The previous section is an example of a social-cultural change in schools due primarily to organized, external forces. Public Law 94-142 in no way represented a ground swell of opinion in schools supportive of that legislation. In contrast, the rise of powerful and militant teacher unions stems exclusively, as we indicated above, from teacher dissatisfaction with their sense of powerlessness and their absence from decision making that affected them socially, professionally, and financially. If boards of education and administrative personnel were largely opposed to unionization, their reasons held no mystery. It was obvious that if unions were successful in their organizing efforts, many changes would take place, i.e. there would be changes in the balance and uses of power; budgets (and, therefore, taxes) would likely increase; constraints would be placed, directly or indirectly, on existing and new programs; and procedures (e.g. grievance and face-to-face bargaining) costly in time and money would have to be institutionalized. What heretofore had been a muted, informal, conflictful relationships between teachers and policy-makers would, it was clear, become an openly formal and adversarial one.

That unionization has dramatically changed the school as a social situation no one doubts. That unions have played the major role in increasing salaries, no one questions. That teachers have an altered perception of their power and rights, which has in turn altered their perception of and the quality of their relationships with those administratively above them, can be safely assumed. That policy-makers and school administrators rarely make a school or system-wide decision without serious thought to "how will the unions react?" is probably also a valid assumption. Nor has anyone questioned the assumption that the cost of collective bargaining *and* of the implementation of the contract is not miniscule either for the union or the school system. (Most people think of collective bargaining as a process taking place when the two sides face each other and put their demands on the table. The process begins long before the face-to-face meetings begin).

Unionization has indeed altered the school as a social situation, but this has not been demonstrated in research. The opponents of unionization predicted adverse consequences both for the educator and the student; the advocates for unionization predicted improvements in the quality of education. It is fair to state that neither opponents nor advocates have an empirical basis for their claims or predictions. It goes without saying that the issues involved are very important, theoretically and practically, if only because they bear directly on the more general question of how a major societal institution, or for that matter any complicated organization, responds to change efforts from within or without.

Lieberman (1980), once a vigorous advocate for teacher unions and someone with much experience as an arbitrator involving boards of education and teacher unions, has become a critic of teacher unions, asserting that it was inherent in collctive bargaining to demand "less work for more pay" and to resist administrative control over assignments and transfers, even when such changes might improve the overall functioning of schools. Johnson's (1982) observations led her to conclude that the effects of collective bargaining were less extensive than was generally believed. She notes that "principals' formal authority had been restricted and teachers' formal authority had been increased." However, the effects varied considerably from school to school. The observations of Lieberman and Johnson, together with those of Rosenthal (1969) and McDonnell & Pascal (1979), may not agree on the degree and consistency of effects of unionization, but they in no way invalidate the assumption that unionization has had diverse and pervasive effects on social and professional relationships within schools.

What evidence other than informal observation, would be relevant to the assessment of how unionization has changed the school as a social situation? Questionnaires and interviews can be productive, assuming that the researcher can overcome the difficult obstacle of securing the cooperation of the unions, administrators, boards of education, and other partisans. There remains, of course, the problem of determining the relationship of these kinds of data to observable practices and social interactions. Ethnographic and participant observation methodologies along the lines illustrated by Wolcott (1973, 1977) and Porter-Gehrie (1979) would be relevant, again assuming that the unions and school boards were willing to become objects of sustained study. Sarason (1982, pp. 150–52) suggested that a wealth of unanalyzed data exists in the form of (a) formal contracts between unions and schools and school systems and (b) *Arbitration in the Schools,* published monthly by the American Arbitration Association and containing summaries of decisions rendered by arbitrators of education under existing contracts. Since the readers of this chapter may be unfamiliar with the type of "data" these summaries contain, we give here three summaries used by Sarason (1982, pp. 150–52).

Administrative Transfer of Teacher-Parent Conflict

The District did not violate the agreement, which states that an administrative transfer must be made for just cause, when it transferred a teacher who had personality conflicts with her principal and with other teachers. The District's action was not punitive where the grievant's conduct was deemed to be uncooperative, challenging and disruptive. 'A severe personality conflict may well be the most legitimate basis for administrative behavior.'

The evidence supported the contentions that the grievant: (1) was unable to accept and to adjust to her assignment; (2) was uncooperative with her department head; and (3) had irreconcilable differences with her principal.

The grievant objected to being assigned to first period preparation time. This assignment led to the grievant's resigning her stewardship of the reading department and to the alienation of her teaching associates.

In addition, the teacher did not cooperate with her department head. She failed to attend essential department meetings and her relationship with other teachers in her department deteriorated to the point where the reading program was affected.

Finally, she refused to cooperate with the principal, claiming that the first period assignment was the result of her failure to comply with several prior requests of the principal. As to whether the transfer was punitive, the reasons urged by the grievant are 'remote and unpersuasive. Feeling wronged the grievant did everything she could think of to antagonize the principal. That her antagonism was ultimately successful cannot be doubted, but her transfer could scarcely be described as punitive.'

Evaluation-Change in Rating

Although the Department did not act arbitrarily or capriciously in its evaluation of a teacher, it did violate three sections of the contract's evaluation provision by its failure to give the grievant written notification of the criteria used, by not actually observing the grievant on the job, and by not listing the names of the teachers who made criticisms or the incidents for which the grievant was criticized. The Department was directed to void the evaluation in its entirety and to give the grievant a satisfactory rating for the year.

The grievant was given the overall 'improvement necessary' rating based on (1) critical comments received from other teachers; (2) the grievant's failure to post his schedule and to mark the equipment in the audio-visual department; and (3) his being observed playing backgammon during school hours. The principal, however, never mentioned any specific names or dates in his written evaluation. This violated language which states that 'teacher evaluations . . .(must) . . .be based on documented facts from actual observation.'

Termination of Probationary Music Teacher

The termination of a third-year probationary music teacher was not for good cause where the grievant's unsatisfactory rating was the result of her teaching a combined class in piano, guitar and drums. This class was oustide her normal teaching routine. For the two other years of her probation, she had been rated satisfactory. The grievant was to be reinstated to another year of probation so that she may be properly evaluated for consideration of tenure.

The grievant was assigned to teach an instrumental music class during her third year, a class she had not taught in the two previous years. 'This was a class of beginning students and grievant was expected to teach piano/drums/guitar to these students in a single classroom environment.' It was with this class that she had problems.

Not being an authority on music, the arbitrator relied on the opinion of a college music professor who stated that 'under no circumstances could a probationer teach such a class in her third year as it placed upon her a burden beyond the usual abilities of a teacher.'

Thousands of these summaries exist—summarized by the arbitrator from much more lengthy and available decisions—and numerous communities also make available consecutive contracts over a period of years. It is unfortunate that these documents have not been systemically studied because they could illuminate how the school as a social situation has changed.

THE ETHOS OF SCHOOLS

There have been very few attempts to study schools as total social entities. As Goodlad (1983, p. 17) notes: "There have been rather, thousands of studies of various pieces, most of them seeking to determine the effects of some classroom practice on student achievement. Researchers criticize *schools* but tend to study students, teachers, or methods of teaching." In the past decade one can discern a shift in research toward studying schools in comprehensive ways. In part, this shift was a reaction on the part of the federal educational policy makers to what they perceived to be the failure of past efforts to change and improve schools. This reaction took the form of the Experimental Schools Program (ESP) initiated in the early 1970s with much fanfare (Cowden & Cohen 1981). Unlike the programs assessed by Berman & McLaughlin (1978), which did not genuinelly stem from a clearly articulated conception of change, the ESP was based explicitly on a recognition of the inadequacies of past efforts. Briefly, the ESP was based on several considerations:

1. Past federal efforts to improve and change schools were largely failures.

2. Federal programs had a buckshot quality: there was a program for this part of the school system and for that one; there was a program for this educational problem and for that one. It was as if the federal government kept reacting to whatever problem was brought to its attention. Sequence and interconnectedness were not important.

3. The federal government should provide the resources for *comprehensive* change in a school system, i.e. sufficient resources to permit a school district more meaningfully and efficiently "to put it all together" in a single direction.

4. There was merit in the complaints of local districts that federal imposition of programs, or too many intrusions by federal personnel into planning at the local level, robbed local people of initiative, creativity, and control. In the ESP local people would have more control over ESP projects. If local districts were sincerely given the opportunity to change their schools in ways they considered most appropriate, one could then count on their commitment to initiate and sustain the change process.

5. Federal efforts to evaluate past reform efforts had been inadequate and they bore no relationship either to changes in federal policy or local program management. The ESP would use innovative and rigorous social science methodology to understand and assess the change process better. Indeed, somewhat less than one third of the 60 to 70 million dollars that the ESP would cost would go to an evaluation scheme no less comprehensive than the changes that local districts would bring about in their schools.

Cowden & Cohen (1981) described the disaster the ESP became, concentrating on several facts: the sources of friction between Washington and the schools; the federal officials' lack of understanding of the schools; and how characteristics of the school culture (varying little among schools different in size, urban-rural placement, and student composition) subverted the aims of the program. At the very least, the ESP experience confirmed Sarason's (1982) contention that both those from without who seek to change schools and those from within with similar aims have far from an adequate understanding of the social complexity of schools. That conclusion was identical to Goodlad's (1983) which was the basis for undertaking the most systematic and comprehensive study of schools to date.

Rutter's (1979) study of twelve London schools is very similar to that of Goodlad's, both in rationale and major findings, but because Goodlad studied more schools in more different ways we shall concentrate on his study. Goodlad selected thirteen communities from different parts of the country. In each of these communities he selected a "triplet": an elementary, a middle, and a high school, resulting in a sample of 38 schools. Data came from 8,624 parents, 1,350 teachers, and 17,163 students. Detailed observations of 1,000 classrooms were made. Research teams spent at least one month in each school: observing, interviewing, and collecting data. It is impossible to do justice here to what Goodlad and his colleagues did. Although they started with conceptions about what would be data relevant to understanding the ethos of a school, and they intended and did collect comparable data in all schools, their major focus was always on capturing not only differences among schools but ways in which the data permitted one to understand what was distinctive about each school as a complex social organization. The methodological problem did not inhere in the techniques for data gathering but in how data from different sources suggested hypotheses that could be tested by new ways of looking at and recombining data. For the purposes of this chapter the following of Goodlad's findings are relevant.

The first has to do with what has not changed in schools: whichever single variable, or combination of variables, were used to categorize school differences, there was no relationship to the tradidional regularities in the classroom, i.e. there was an extraordinary sameness of instructional practices: teachers lectured and questioned, students listened, and textbooks were the most common medium for teaching and learning. What Goodlad describes is very similar to the picture evoked by reading Susskind's (1969) study of question asking in the classroom.

The second conclusion is that the satisfaction level of students about the school and classroom is highly correlated to the satisfaction level of other persons in and close to the schools. The three senior high schools rated highest by teachers, students, and parents on indicators of satisfaction also were the three senior highs in which students had the most positive views of their classroom climate. All four elementary schools ranking lowest on satisfaction indicators were also the four elementary schools in which students had the most negative views of their institution.

The third conclusion is that, although the data support the stereotype of the most satisfying schools (small, rural or suburban, predominantly white, supported by parents who are above average in education and income), the parallel stereotype—that the least satisying schools are large, urban, with a predominantly minority population, and serve families of a low educational level—stands up less well. Finally, various analyses indicated that those schools in which teachers perceived that significant and positive changes had occurred during the last three years, in contrast to those in which teachers did not perceive change, fitted the picture of "the renewing school." On the surface, Goodlad asserts, although schools are monotonously similar in terms of behavioral and programmatic regularities "schools do differ . . . in the ways humans in them, individually and collectively, cope with these regularities and relate to each other" (p. 267).

Boyer's (1983) *High School* and Lightfoot's (1983) *The Good High School* were published within a few months of Goodlad's *A Place Called School*. Neither of those publications presents and analyzes data comparable to those of Goodlad's. In Boyer's study a team of twenty-five educators was chosen to visit preselected schools. Visits were scheduled for twenty school days at each school. Team members talked with principals, teachers, students, and parents. They went to classes, attended pep rallies and sports events, sat in on faculty and PTA meetings, observed counselors and principals at work. The major themes and issues contained in these reports were derived from an analysis of the reports by one person. Lightfoot's book, as its title suggests, is explicitly a reaction to the tendency of the social scientist to focus on "pathology rather than health" (p. 11). Unlike Boyer and Goodlad, Lightfoot had no staff. She visited each of six high schools and wrote up her observations and impressions, which she describes as a mixture of the artist's intuition and the ethnographer's attention to structure and culture. Although they come to their conclusions in very different ways, using very different types of methodology and data, Goodlad and Lightfoot appear to agree that the good school (not only the good high school in Goodlad's study) has the features of the ever "renewing" school, i.e. they have the vehicles and ambience that make for sensitivity to existing or developing problems and that dilute anxiety and resistance so often associated with change.

The almost simultaneous appearance of three major publications relevant to improving and changing high schools is unprecedented. Indeed, the research and theoretical literature bearing on schools have overwhelmingly concerned elementary and, to a lesser degree, middle schools. If there has been a renewed concern for the status and adequacy of high schools, it is in large part because of the widespread impression that in terms of curriculum, social attitudes, and relationships high schools have undergone significant changes in the post World War II period. Curriculum changes were catalyzed by Conant's studies and recommendations in 1959 (Conant 1959). In his 1961 book comparing conditions in urban slums and suburbs, Conant referred to the inequities, including those in schools, as "social dynamite" (Conant 1961). The dynamite exploded in the turbulent 1960s when high schools became sites for conflicts around issues of community control, student rights, the "relevance" of the curriculum to the "real world," social discrimination and the Vietnam era.

If it is difficult to come to any secure conclusions about the major ways schools as social situations have changed, it is less difficult to indicate why this is so. For one thing, any school, large or small, is a very complicated social organization that cannot be comprehended by one individual or from one perspective. Second, the social organization of a school has transactions with a social-community surround that is never static. Third, it follows from the first two points that a serious effort to comprehend the school as a *changing* social situation has to have a historical basis or starting point, i.e. from what and to what has it changed? Fourth, it is obvious that any such serious effort would require a rather large research team sustained over a period of years. Fifth, to be able to make generalizations—to be able to go somewhat beyond the limitations of what would be a case study—it would be necessary to study more than one school. In light of these and other factors, it should not be surprising that our knowledge is as sparse and as fragmented as it is.

In this review we have endeavored to point to aspects of the school that signify important changes in and around the school. The reader will be aware that we were unable to indicate how these aspects interrelate to give a more integrated picture. Although each of these aspects has been studied and has illuminated and suggested important social changes in the school, we are left with pieces of the conceptual puzzle. This situation would not in itself be troubling were it not for the fact that we are again in a time when policies are being recommended to change and improve schools precisely because they are perceived as having social characteristics inimical to student achievement. These policies have the most flimsy basis in research and it is worthy of emphasis that those who are pressuring for change are not saying that there is much we need to learn either about schools as social organizations or about effective ways of bringing about desired change. Nor has there been a call for discussion about why over the decades schools have seemed to be intractable to proposed changes. Sarason (1982) has suggested that our efforts at change are doomed to failure because of the inability to expose and examine certain axioms undergirding our world view of schools. He examines the axiom that education should and best takes place inside of encapsulated classrooms in encapsulated schools, and he concludes that the axiom is largely invalid.

As social situations, schools have changed and will continue to change. The potential for psychological research to enlarge our understanding of these changes is vast but has hardly been developed. Indeed, as Gerard (1983) suggests, the research bearing on the nature and consequences of some of these changes has been inadequate in conception and baleful in its policy consequences. Why that is probably the case is beyond the scope of this chapter. We offer the opinion that this situation will not be clarified until we recognize that education, wherever it takes place, is inherently and complicatedly social in its structure, dynamics, and purposes. And in using the word "complicatedly" we mean to counter the dominant tendency in American psychology to rivet on the ahistorical, individual organism (Sarason 1981). Why did it take so long for the clinical community to accept family therapy, to act on the fact that the problems of the individual were embedded in a social system we call a family? How long will it take for us to take seriously that we can understand little about anyone in a school as long as we see the individual (or a group or a problem) apart from the family we call a school? The traditional family is no easy unit to conceptualize or to change. Neither is the school as a social unit. At this point one is tempted to say that what we need is not research or the amassing of facts but serious and bold conceptualizations that give us a less astigmatic picture of a very complex social institution. We have glimpses of pieces of the picture. How do we start to integrate these pieces?

Literature Cited

Allen, D. 1980. Participation of regular education teachers in special education team decision making. See Ysseldyke, Algozzine & Thurlow 1980

Amir, Y., Sharan, S., eds. 1983. *School Desegregation: Cross-Cultural Perspectives.* Hillsdale, NJ: Erlbaum

Arsenian, J. M. 1943. Young children in an insecure situation. *J. Abnorm. Soc. Psychol.* 38:225–49

Berlyne, D. E. 1960. *Conflict, Arousal, and Curiosity.* New York: McGraw-Hill

Berman, P., McLaughlin, M. W. 1978. *Federal Programs Supporting Educational Change*, Vol. 8: *Implementing and Sustaining Innovations.* Santa Monica, Calif: Rand Corp.

Bloom, B. S. 1964. *Stability and Change in Human Characteristics.* New York: Wiley

Boyer, E. L. 1983. *High School.* New York: Harper & Row

Campbell, D. T., Erlebacher, A. 1970. How regression artifacts can mistakenly make compensatory education look harmful. In *Disadvantaged Child*, Vol. 3, *Compensatory Education*, ed. J. Hellmuth. New York: Brunner/Mazel

Conant, J. B. 1959. *The American High School Today.* New York: McGraw-Hill

Conant, J. B. 1961. *Slums and Suburbs. A Commentary on Schools in the Metropolitan Area.* New York: McGraw Hill

Cook, S. W. 1979. Social science and school desegregation: Did we mislead the Supreme Court? *Pers. Soc. Psychol. Bull* 5:420–37

Corbally, J. E. 1930. Pupil mobility in the public schools of Washington. *Univ. Wash. Publ. Soc. Sci.* 5:95–180

Cowden, P., Cohen, D. 1981. *Divergent Worlds of Practice. The Federal Reform of Schools in the Experimental Schools Program.* Cambridge, Mass: Huron Inst.

Downie, N. M. 1953. A comparison between children who have moved from school to school with those who have been in continuous residence on various factors of adjustment. *J. Educ. Psychol.* 44:50–53

Ellesor, M. V. 1933. Children's reactions to novel visual stimuli. *Child Dev.* 4:95–105

Evans, J. W. 1966. The effect of pupil mobility upon academic achievement. *Natl. Elem. Princ.* 45:18–22

Fenton, K. S., Yoshida, R. K., Maxwell, J. P., Kaufman, M. J. 1979. Recognition of team goals: An essential step toward rational decision making. *Except. Child.* 45:538–44

Fox, E. M. 1968. *Entering a new school.* PhD thesis. Yale Univ., New Haven, Conn.

Gabower, G. 1959. *Behavior Problems of Children in Navy Officers' Families.* Washington DC: Catholic Univ. Am. Press

Gerard, H. B. 1983. School desegregation: the social science role. *Am. Psychol.* 38:869–77

Gilliland, C. H. 1958. *The relationships of pupil mobility to achievement in the elementary school.* PhD thesis. Colorado State Univ., Fort Collins

Gold, B. A., Miles, M. B. 1981. *Whose School Is It Anyway? Parent-Teacher Conflict over an Innovative School.* New York: Praeger

Goldstein, S., Strickland, B., Turnbull, A. P., Curry, L. 1980. An observational analysis of the IEP conference. *Except. Child.* 46:278–86

Goodlad, J. L. 1983. *A Place Called School.* New York: McGraw-Hill

Gordon, R. E., Gordon, K. K. 1958. Emotional disorders of children in a rapidly growing suburb. *Int. J. Soc. Psychol.* 4:85–97

Gray, S. W. 1967. *The early training project.* Washington, DC: Research and Evaluation Office, Project Head Start, OEO

Gruber, S. 1954. The concept of task orientation in the analysis of play behavior of children entering kindergarten. *Am. J. Orthopsychiatry* 24:326–35

Gutkin, T. B., Curtis, J. J. 1981. School-based consultation: Theory and techniques. In *The Handbook of School Psychology*, ed. C. R. Reynolds, T. B. Gutkin. New York: Wiley

Harman, C., Hanley, E. J. 1979. Administrative aspects of the Head Start program. See Zigler & Valentine 1979

Hoff, M. K., Fenton, K. S., Yoshida, R. K., Kaufman, M. J. 1978. Notice and consent: The school's responsibility to inform parents. *J. Sch. Psychol.* 16:265–78

Holland, R. P. 1980. An analysis of the decision-making processes in special education. *Except. Child.* 46:551–54

Hudson, B. B. 1954. Anxiety in response to the unfamiliar. *J. Soc. Issues* 10(3):53–60

Hunt, J. McV. 1961. *Intelligence and Experience.* New York: Ronald Press

Hutt, C., Hutt, S. J., Ounsted, C. 1965. The behaviour of children with and without upper CNS lesions. *Behaviour* 24(3–4):246–68

Johnson, S. M. 1982. *Teacher unions and the schools.* Cambridge, Mass: Inst. for Educ. Policy Stud. Harvard Univ.

Justman, J. 1964. *Stability of academic aptitude and reading test scores of movile and non-mobile disadvantaged children.* Rep. from Bureau of Educ. Program Res. Statistics, New York City Board of Education

Kasindorf, B. R. 1963. *The effects of pupil transiency on pupil functioning.* Bureau of Educ. Program Res. Statistics, Publ. No. 202. New York City Board of Education

Levine, M., Wesolowski, J., Corbett, F. J. 1966. Pupil turnover and academic performance in an inner city elementary school. *Psychol. Sch.* 3:153–58

Lieberman, M. 1980. *Public Sector Bargaining. A Policy Reappraisal.* Lexington, Mass: Heath

Lightfoot, S. L. 1983. *The Good High School.* New York: Basic Books

Lortie, D. C. 1975. *School Teacher.* Chicago: Univ. Chicago Press

Maris, P., Rein, M. 1967. *Dilemmas of Social Reform.* New York: Atherton

McDonnell, L., Pascal, A. 1979. *Organized Teachers in American Schools.* Santa Monica, Calif: Rand Corp.

McReynolds, P. J., Acker, M., Pietila, C. 1961. Relation of object curiosity to psychological adjustment. *Child Dev.* 32:393–400

Mearig, J. S. 1982. Integration of school and community services. See Reynolds & Gutkin 1982

Mendel, G. 1965. Children's preferences for differing degrees of novelty. *Child Dev.* 36(2):453–65

Mitchell, J. 1980. The special education team process: To what extent is it effective? See Ysseldyke, Algozzine & Thurlow 1980

Palmer, F., Andersen, L. W. 1979. Long-term gains from early intervention: findings from longitudinal studies. See Zigler & Valentine 1979, pp. 433–66

Pedersen, F. A., Sullivan, E. J. 1964. Relationships among geographic mobility, parental attitudes and emotional disturbances in children. *Am. J. Orthopsychiatry* 34:575–80

Pielstrick, N. L., Woodruff, A. B. 1964. Exploratory behavior and curiosity in two age and ability groups of children. *Psychol. Rep.* 14(3):831–38

Poland, S., Mitchell, J. 1980. Generation of intervention statements by decision-making teams in school settings. See Ysseldyke, Algozzine & Thurlow

Poland, S., Ysseldyke, J., Thurlow, M., Mirkin, P. 1979. *Current assessment and decision-making practices in school settings as reported by directors of special education.* (Res. Rep. No. 14). Minneapolis: Univ. Minnesota, Inst. for Res. on Learning Disabil. (ERIC Document Reproduction Service No. ED 185 758)

Porter-Gehrie, C. 1979. (Book review article) "Ethnographic data and educational policy analysis: recent qualitative research." *Educ. Theory* 29(3):255–62

Rakietan, H. 1961. The reactions of mobile elementary school children to various elementary school induction and orientation procedures. Unpublished doctoral dissertation, Columbia Teachers College

Reynolds, C. R., Gutkin, T. B., eds. 1982. *The Handbook of School Psychology*. New York: Wiley

Richey, L., Graden, J. 1980. The special education team process: To what extent is it data based? See Ysseldyke, Algozzine & Thurlow 1980

Rosenthal, A. 1969. *Pedagogues and Power: Teachers Groups in School Politics*. Syracuse, NY: Syracuse Univ. Press

Rostollan, D. 1980. Domains of data discussed at special education team meetings. See Yzzeldyke, Algozzine & Thurlow 1980

Rutter, M. 1979. *Fifteen Thousand Hours*. Cambridge, Mass: Harvard Univ. Press

Sackett, E. G. 1935. The effect of moving one educational status of children. *Elementary Sch. J.* 35:517–26

Sarason, S. B. 1981. *Psychology Misdirected*. New York: Free Press

Sarason, S. B. 1982. *The Culture of the School and the Problem of Change*. Boston: Allyn & Bason. 2nd ed.

Sarason, S. B., Levine, M., Goldenberg, I., Cherlin, D., Bennett, E. 1966. *Psychology in Community Settings*. New York: Wiley

Schmuck, R. A. 1981. Organizational development in the schools. See Reynolds & Gutkin 1981

Sharan, S., Kussell, P., Berjerano, Y., Hertz-Lazarowitz, R., Brosh, T. 1982. *Cooperative learning, whole-class instruction, and the academic achievement and social relations of pupils in ethnically-mixed junior high schools in Israel*. Final rep. to Ford Found. and Israel Ministry of Educ. Culture

Sharan, S., Rich, Y. 1983. Field experiments on ethnic integration in Israeli schools. See Amir & Sharan 1983

Shinn, M. 1980. Domains of assessment data discussed during placement team decision making. See Ysseldyke, Algozzine & Thurlow 1980

Smith, L. M., Keith, P. M. 1971. *The Anatomy of an Educational Innovation*. New York: Wiley

Smock, C. D., Holt, B. G. 1962. Children's reactions to novelty: an experimental study of "curiosity motivation." *Child Dev.* 33(3):631–42

Snapp, M., Davidson, J. L. 1982. System interventions for school psychologists: A case study approach. See Reynolds & Gutkin 1982

Steiner, G. Y. 1976. *The Children's Cause*. Washington DC: Brookings Inst.

Stephan, W. G. 1978. School desegregation: An evaluation of predictions made in *Brown vs. Board of Education*. *Psychol. Bull.* 85:217–38

Stephan, W. G., Feagin, J. R., eds. 1980. *School Desegregation: Past, Present, and Future*. New York: Plenum

Stubblefield, R. L. 1955. Children's emotional problems aggravated by family moves. *Am. J. Orthopsychiatry* 25:120–26

Susskind, E. 1969. *Questionning and curiosity in the elementary school classroom*. Doctoral dissertation. Yale Univ.

Valentine, J., Stark, E. 1979. The social context of parent involvement in headstart. See Zigler & Valentine 1979

Waller, W. 1961. *The Sociology of Teaching*. New York: Russell & Russell

Wolcott, H. F. 1973. *The Man in the Principal's Office*. New York: Holt, Rinehart, and Winston

Wolcott, H. F. 1977. *Teachers vs. technocrats*. Eugene, Ore: Cent. for Educ. Policy and Management, Univ. Ore.

Yoshida, R. K., Fenton, K. S., Maxwell, J. P., Kaufman, M. J. 1978a. Group decision making in the planning team process: Myth or reality? *J. Sch. Psychol.* 16:237–44

Yoshida, R. K., Fenton, K. S., Maxwell, J. P., Kaufman, M. J. 1978b. Ripple effect: Communication of planning team decisions to program implementers. *J. Sch. Psychol.* 16:177–83

Ysseldyke, J. E., Algozzine, B. 1982. *Critical Issues in Special and Remedial Education*. Boston: Houghton-Mifflin

Ysseldyke, J. E., Algozzine, B., Thurlow, M., eds. 1980. *A naturalistic investigation of special education team meetings* (Res. Rep. No. 40). Minneapolis: Univ. Minn. Inst. for Res. on Learn. Disabil.

Zigler, E., Anderson, K. 1979. An Idean whose time had come. The intellectual and political climate for Head Start. See Zigler & Valentine 1979.

Zigler, E., Valentine, J., eds. 1979. *Project Head Start*. New York: Free Press

Zigler, E., Kagan, S. L., Klugman, E., eds. 1983. *Children, Families, and Government*. New York: Cambridge Univ. Press

Ann. Rev. Psychol. 36:141–69

THE ECOLOGY OF FORAGING BEHAVIOR: IMPLICATIONS FOR ANIMAL LEARNING AND MEMORY

Alan C. Kamil

Departments of Psychology and Zoology, University of Massachusetts, Amherst, Massachusetts 01003

Herbert L. Roitblat

Department of Psychology, Columbia University, New York, New York 10027

CONTENTS

0066-4308/85/0201-0141$02.00

INTRODUCTION

In his recent *Annual Review of Psychology* article, Snowdon (1983) discussed the synthesis of ethology and comparative psychology. A similar synthesis of behavioral ecology and animal learning is beginning to take place. This article reviews developments in the behavioral ecology and ethology of foraging behavior relevant to psychological research on animal learning.

The psychological literature shows that animals possess a wide range of learning abilities, including "simple" classical and operant conditioning; they acquire spatial, nonspatial, and temporal discriminations; they exhibit various forms of rule learning (e.g. matching-to-sample and learning set), and may even in certain senses learn language. Why does this widespread animal ability to modify behavior on the basis of previous experience exist? The answer to this question must include both a mechanistic (proximate) and a functional (ultimate) aspect (Tinbergen 1951; Alcock 1979). The mechanistic answer seeks to explain learning in terms of the mechanisms and processes that enable the animal to learn. The functional answer seeks to explain learning in terms of the role learning plays in conferring a selective advantage on organisms possessing those mechanisms.

Psychological investigations of animal learning have emphasized mechanistic explanations whereas ecological and ethological investigations have tended to emphasize functional explanations. Complete understanding requires both kinds of answers, however, and the synthesis of behavioral ecology and psychology suggested here provides a basis for both kinds of analysis.

Several recent articles have discussed the relationship between behavioral ecology and animal learning in general terms (Johnston 1981, Kamil & Yoerg 1982, Shettleworth 1983, 1984). Here we review those portions of the ecological and ethological literature on foraging behavior most relevant to animal learning and memory.

ON OPTIMAL DECISION THEORY

MacArthur & Pianka (1966) introduced the notion that animals seeking food are attempting to solve a maximization problem, obtaining the maximum amount of food per unit time. They suggested that foraging animals could be conceptualized as optimal decision makers. Because optimal decision theory is central to understanding recent developments in the study of foraging, it deserves discussion in the present context (see also Maynard Smith 1978).

Life is a compromise. It is a compromise among competing demands (e.g. whether to spend time seeking food or seeking a mate) and among potential and realizable goals. Every behavior has both costs and benefits, and the animal must always compromise between minimizing costs and maximizing benefits.

According to modern views of evolution, the successful organism is the one that maximizes its contribution to the gene pool (e.g. Wilson 1975, Dawkins 1976). Life, in this view, is also a maximization problem, as expressed in the tautology that animals have been selected so as to maximize their fitness. From these two premises, compromise and maximization, comes the essence of optimality theory. The optimal decision maker adopts the compromise that maximizes fitness given the organism's limitations.

If there were no competing demands on an organism—if it had only one life problem to solve—then its life (and ours) would be simple. For example, if an organism's single problem were to get as much food as it could, then the most successful organism would be the one that got the most food. Even if life were so simple, however, no animal could possibly obtain food at an infinite rate and thereby achieve infinite fitness. Its life would still be a compromise between its goal of an infinite food intake rate and the practical limits on food intake. We usually think of these limits as constraints. Among the constraints that prevent an animal from achieving a "perfect" solution to its optimization problem are (a) "accidents" of its ancestry, (b) limits on the speed with which it can change the form of its compromises, (c) limits on the ability to obtain information from the environment, and many others (Roitblat 1982a). Optimality theory seeks to determine not whether organisms are "nicely adapted to their environmental niche" but what competing demands and constraints they face and what means they employ to meet them.

As psychologists we tend to concentrate on one kind of constraint: that produced by limits on the organism's ability to process relevant information. Some organisms, for example deal with a range of situations by using such relatively rigid mechanisms as reflexes and fixed action patterns. Many approaches to foraging behavior, however, imply that organisms have more dynamic mechanisms for assessing and responding to changes in the environment. For example, many of the models considered below assume that organisms can measure both time and the density of prey items in a patch. Although animals in the laboratory have been found to discriminate time and number, their performance on these two dimensions is seldom perfect (e.g. Gibbon & Church 1981, 1984; Church & Meck 1984). Imperfections in either of these estimation tasks would yield less than perfectly efficient behavior.

Optimal decision models of an activity like searching for food in a patchy environment represent assumptions about the compromises being effected by the organism, about its limitations and constraints, and about the maximization problem(s) it faces. Given these important assumptions we can specify, in a formal and often mathematical way, what that organism should do in various situations. The observations we then make in those situations are tests of the assumptions in the model; they do not test the optimization principle itself (e.g. Maynard Smith 1978, Roitblat 1982a).

Behavioral ecologists have varied in the extent to which they are explicit in specifying the type and content of information they suppose a predator to possess. Some models assume the predator to be less than omniscient. These are sometimes called "rule of thumb" models. This application of the phrase seems inappropriate (Krebs et al 1983), however, if it suggests that the animal is "satisficing" (Simon 1956)—i.e. merely choosing a course of action that is "good enough." Such models are not rules of thumb in this sense. A rule of thumb, as the term is used here, is not a rule that does well enough but rather a hypothesis about the best choices the organism can make, assuming various constraints.

By a rule of thumb model, then, we mean a hypothesis that specifies precisely the variables controlling the animal's behavior, the information it has, and how that information is represented (Roitblat 1982b). For example, Hubbard & Cook (1978) found that the parasitoid *Nemeritis canescens* allocates its search time for hosts approximately as specified by an optimal decision model based on an ability to measure the rate at which it encountered hosts. Waage (1979) subsequently found that this parasitoid's "rule" for "deciding" when to stop searching in a particular patch is based on its habituation to the host's scent. Laying eggs results in dishabituation, after which searching resumes until a certain level of habituation is again reached. Thus a potentially complex ability—i.e. to keep track of one or more intercapture intervals, is instantiated by a relatively simple mechanism.

Rules of thumb differ in the extent to which they approximate "ideal" performance (Houston et al 1982; Krebs et al 1983). For example, all other things being equal, a predator with more information about the distribution of prey will do better than one without that information (Iwasa et al 1981). The ability to process additional information, however, is not itself without costs. At some point, the marginal benefits (ultimately in terms of increased fitness) of additional information processing capacity may not justify its costs (e.g. Janetos & Cole 1981; Orians 1981). This argument is also an optimality argument, not an argument against optimality.

Psychologists are particularly well suited to discovering the kinds of information used by a predator and the mechanisms it has for dealing with that information. For example, laboratory studies of sequential patterns of reinforcement indicate that animals do not simply average the outcome of a set of trials. Rather, different patterns of reinforcement and nonreinforcement, each leading to the same average rate, can result in widely different patterns of behavior, such as resistence to extinction (Capaldi 1966, 1971). Application of such laboratory findings to foraging situations will elucidate both foraging and the mechanisms of animal learning (Kamil & Yoerg 1982).

Although all organisms must ultimately maximize their fitness, measuring fitness and the effects of various individual actions on it is problematical. For this reason, students of animal behavior typically make simplifying assumptions. For example, many of the models described below assume that animals attempt to maximize their net rate of energy intake, usually measured in calories per unit time. This is a simplifying assumption dictated by the difficulties of estimating the effect of a behavior on the organism's ultimate fitness, the complexity of solving multidimensional maximization problems (McCleery 1978), and so forth. We must recognize, however, that the animal faces a situation far more complex than our simplifications. For any real predator, energy intake always competes with many other demands. These competing demands include balancing the danger of becoming prey against the success of obtaining prey (e.g. Milinski & Heller 1978, Sih 1980, Grubb & Greenwald 1982). That the world is less simple than our models does not falsify the optimization hypothesis, but it does make the process of developing optimal decision rules more difficult. Fortunately, many systems can be studied in which our simplifying assumptions do not invalidate analysis.

PATCH SELECTION

In nature, food is often distributed in discrete patches (e.g. different trees, branches, pieces of lawn, etc). When food is not uniformly distributed in the environment, the predator must decide in which of these concurrently available patches to forage and how long to spend in each.

The nature of the predator's problem depends on the reliability of the distribution of prey within patches. In order to maximize food intake, the predator must identify and then choose the patch that will yield the highest rate of return. In some cases, the predator can determine the richness of a patch before it begins to forage, by means of perceptual cues or memory. Quite another problem arises when the quality of a patch can vary significantly in a stochastic manner. In that case, the predator must "invest" effort to discover the value of the available patches before it can concentrate on the richer patches.

Foraging in Reliable Patches

Predators have been found to take advantage of uneven prey distribution. For example, redshank (*Tringa totanus*) tend to concentrate their search for worms in areas containing relatively high prey densities, selecting areas that appear to maximize their rate of food intake (Goss-Custard 1981). Wagtails (*Motacilla flava* and *M. alba*) select foraging sites as a function of prey density (Davies 1977a). Blackbirds (*Turdus merula*) and song thrushes (*Turdus philomelos*) choose foraging sites on the basis of location and time of day (Greenwood & Harvey 1978). As the shadows cast by trees moved during the day, the prey density and the preferred foraging sites of the thrushes also moved. The reliability of these diurnal variations presumably allowed the birds to take advantage of their past experience and to allocate their foraging effort in response to variations in patch quality. Similar behaviors have been observed in ovenbirds (*Seirus aurocapillus;* Zach & Falls 1976), great tits (*Parus major;* Smith & Sweatman 1974), kangaroos *(Macropus giganteus)* and wallaroos (*Macropus robustus;* Taylor 1984), and in bees *(Apis mellifer)* selecting among flower types (Waddington & Holden 1979).

Foraging in Variable Patches

When the quality of a patch is not predictable, a predator must invest effort to discover value of the patch. There should be an optimal tradeoff between time spent assessing and time spent exploiting patches. This expectation has begun to be studied in the laboratory (Krebs et al 1978; Kacelnik 1979).

Foraging in concurrently available patches resembles the probem faced by a laboratory animal on a concurrent reinforcement schedule. These schedules have been studied extensively in the operant laboratory (de Villiers 1977, Staddon & Motheral 1978, Herrnstein & Heyman 1979, Heyman & Luce 1979, Staddon 1980). Kamil & Yoerg (1982) have questioned the generality of these studies because of peculiarities of the schedules employed. They argue for cautious interpretation of the operant studies because of peculiarities of the variable interval schedules typically selected for study.

The patch-selection problem faced by a foraging predator is also similar to that studied in probability learning (for reviews see Bitterman 1965, 1969, Mackintosh 1969).

Laboratory studies of patch selection typically use concurrent variable ratio (VR) schedules. Despite controversy over many other combinations of concurrent schedules, there is widespread agreement (Rachlin et al 1976) that the optimal response pattern on concurrent VR schedules is to respond exclusively to the alternative with the richer schedule (i.e. the lower average response requirement). Laboratory studies of patch selection differ from typical operant studies, however, in that the schedule associated with a given response varies stochastically from one session to the next. At the start of a patch-selection session, the predator typically does not know which alternative is associated with the richer VR schedule. Such studies concern the process by which information about the schedules is acquired, rather than the steady-state behavior of the organism following acquisition.

Strategies that maximize reward on these schedules have been explored by mathematicians in the form of the "two-armed bandit" problem (Bellman 1956, Lindley & Barnett 1965, De Groot 1970, Jones 1976, Wahrenberger et al 1977). Each alternative is conceived as a slot machine (or one-armed bandit) with a fixed but unknown probability of payout. By extension, a "machine" with two alternatives is called a two-armed bandit. The problem is to find a rule specifying which arm to choose in order to maximize the overall rate of return in a fixed number of trials. The fixed number of trials is called the time horizon.

Optimal terminal performance on a two-armed bandit problem allocates all responses to the alternative with the higher probability of reinforcement. To achieve this, the predator must first discover which alternative is better, sampling the two until a decision can be made. Hence, the task can be divided into a sampling phase and an exploitation phase; the problem is to determine how much time to spend sampling.

The optimal sampling time depends on the difference between the reward distributions on the two alternatives and on the total time available for foraging. The more of its limited time the animal spends sampling, the less time it will have to exploit the better patch; the less time it spends sampling, the higher the probability of exploiting the wrong patch. Even small differences in the reward probabilities can have a substantial effect as they cumulate over the exploitation period. The cumulative difference between the richer and the poorer alternative is the cost of concentrating on the poorer alternative. The optimal duration of the sampling period is a trade-off of the probability of a correct decision against the cumulative effects of that decision, and depends on the number of responses or time that can be spent—the time window. With longer available durations, the sampling period is expected to be longer (Krebs et al 1978, Kacelnik 1979).

Kacelnik (1979) tested great tits *(Parus major)* who foraged by hopping on one of two perches. Each perch was associated with a characteristic, but unknown, variable ratio reinforcement schedule. The probabilities of reinforcement assigned to the two alternatives varied randomly from session to session. Sessions were terminated when 90% of a sequence of 100 hops were to one of the alternatives or when all 72 of the available reinforcers were obtained without reaching this criterion. The last hop before the beginning of a block of 100 responses with a bias of more than 90% was taken to be the switch point separating the sampling from the exploitation period.

Kacelnik found that the birds' sampling performance fit very closely an optimizing model based on a time window of 150 responses, which was the modal number of responses emitted in a session before reaching one of the stopping criteria. The greater the difference between the probabilities of reward on the two responses, the sooner the birds switched from sampling to exploitation. Furthermore, explicit manipulation of the session duration, in a second experiment, resulted in changes in the estimated tine window, and in the duration of the sampling period. Finally, Kacelnik also found that the birds' performance was poorly fit by a momentary maximizing model (Shimp 1969), which predicted choice of the alternative with the currently higher expected reward probability.

Such studies raise a number of interesting possibilities for future research. First, unlike typical operant experiments, these are concerned with the dynamic rather than steady-state properties of animals' behavior. There has been little operant research, for example, on concurrent variable ratio schedules because terminal performance on them presents a trivial problem. Studies on foraging, in contrast, show that the means by which animals arrive at this trivial solution can itself be interesting.

Two further opportunities for research derive from an elaboration of the simplifying assumptions used in designing the experiments on patch selection. For example, all the patch-selection experiments known to us have used only two alternatives. Leaving one "patch," therefore, is equivalent to entering another. Although this simplification makes the mathematics of prediction tractable, it risks simplifying the problem out of existence. At least three alternatives are probably necessary to mimic, in any significant sense, the kind of situation faced by a predator in the field.

A second limitation in the methods used so far is the lack of a variable representing significant travel costs between patches. Although these studies generally assume that multiple patches are simultaneously available, outside the laboratory it takes time and energy to move from one patch to another. If the effort required is significant, it will have an important impact on the pattern of behavior observed.

The importance of travel time and its impact on the validity of using concurrent reinforcement schedules to mimic patch choice is most apparent when "central place" foragers are considered. These animals must travel frequently between a foraging site and a central place, such as a nest or den. A pair of brooding birds, for example, must frequently bring food gathered in a distant patch back to their nestlings. The significant time spent traveling between the central place and the foraging sites presents special problems (Orians & Pearson 1979, Andersson 1981, Bryant & Turner 1982, Evans 1982, Giraldeau & Kramer 1982, Kasuya 1982, Aronson & Givnish 1983, Kacelnik 1984).

PATCH PERSISTENCE

In the previous section we assumed that multiple patches were concurrently available; the value of each patch was predictable and stable. Effort may have been required to discover the value of a patch, but during exploitation that value remained stable. None of these assumptions is universally appropriate. For many predators it is more reasonable to assume that the predator encounters patches one at a time (e.g. because of substantial costs of traveling between patches), that the value of patches is a random variable, and that the marginal or conditional within-patch capture rate declines with foraging time (e.g. because the predator consumes or frightens off the available prey). Under these conditions, the predator cannot rationally control the selection of patches, but it can control time spent in each.

In general, an efficient predator should search a patch only so long as the expected rate of return (e.g. measured in prey captured per minute) for remaining in a patch is higher than the rate of return that can be expected after leaving the patch. The predator (and anyone trying to understand it) must devise rules for inferring future events (i.e. expected rates of prey capture) from past experience. One of the first hypotheses attempting to describe the rules used by predators in determining how much time to spend searching a patch was the marginal value theorem proposed by Charnov (1976; see also Krebs et al 1974, Charnov et al 1976 for simplified versions of the theorem).

The marginal value theorem assumes: (a) The predator spends all its time either searching for prey within a patch or traveling between patches. (b) The patches vary in their profitability. (c) The rate of food intake for the patch declines gradually as the predator depletes it of prey. (d) The number of prey present in a patch cannot be observed directly but must be "discovered" by sampling. Therefore, the expected value (number of prey) of a patch before it has been visited is simply the average value of all patches. (e) The predator has information about the overall average capture rate and the instantaneous marginal capture rate (i.e. conditional on the time already spent in the patch). The theorem predicts that the predator should leave a patch when the marginal value has declined to the average rate of intake for the habitat. Time spent within patches and time spent traveling between patches are both included in calculating the average rate of intake for the habitat.

The marginal value theorem assumes prey are captured continuously and an instantaneous rate of capture can be calculated. For most predators, however, a more reasonable assumption is that prey are captured at discrete instances and the predator can only approximate the continuous distribution. Krebs et al (1974) and others have suggested that predators can use the interval between successive captures as as a measure of the capture rate. According to this "rule of thumb" (see above), the predator should leave a patch when the interval since the last prey capture exceeds a criterion period; this period should be constant and independent of the actual value of the patch (see McNair 1982).

Krebs et al (1974) investigated this optimal "giving-up-time" hypothesis with chickadees (Parus atricapillus) foraging in an indoor aviary. Patches were artificial "pine cones," made from small blocks of wood with holes drilled in them and pieces of mealworm concealed in these holes. The birds were initially trained with one prey per patch and then tested in a mixed environment with two kinds of patches containing either one or three prey per patch. Krebs et al (1974) compared the predictions of their giving-up-time version of the marginal value theorem with a hypothesis that predators hunt by expectation (Gibb 1958, 1960, 1962; see also Hodges 1981, Lima 1983). According to the expectation hypothesis, predators learn how many prey they can expect in a patch and stop searching when the expected number of prey have been found. Contrary to the expectation hypothesis, however, during the mixed condition the birds studied by Krebs et al (1974) did not give up immediately after finding the single prey they had learned to expect. Rather, they searched longer when a patch contained three, as opposed to one prey. Their giving-up time depended on the average number of prey per patch (i.e. it was longer in the mixed than in the single-prey condition) but not on the number of prey in any particular patch. The same giving-up time was observed in both one-prey and three-prey patches. These results are all consistent with the predictions of the marginal value theorem and with the optimal giving-up-time rule of thumb.

Cowie (1977) investigated these hypotheses further in a test designed to simulate the effects of travel time (the amount of time necessary to leave one patch and begin foraging in another). Longer travel time between patches reduces the average profitability of an environment without affecting the rate of capture within a patch. The greater the travel time, therefore, the longer the predator should spend in a patch. Cowie tested great tits in an indoor aviary. Patches consisted of cups filled with sawdust in which pieces of mealworm were hidden. Long travel times were simulated by covering all cups in the environment with tight-fitting lids. Short travel times were simulated by covering all cups in the environment with loose-fitting lids. The birds spent more time searching in a patch when all patches were covered by tight lids than when they were covered by loose lids. Thus when the energetic costs of searching and traveling between patches were considered, the data fit closely the quantitative predictions of the marginal value theorem.

Other experiments, using methods similar to that used by Krebs et al (1974), have yielded results inconsistent with the optimal giving-up-time version of the marginal value theorem. Zach & Falls (1976) tested ovenbirds *(Seiurus aurocapillus)* in an artificial environment consisting of six "golf-course" patches made of plywood, each containing 99 holes in which freeze-killed flies were hidden as prey. Zach & Falls found no evidence that the birds used either a number-of-prey or a searching-time expectation to control the time they spent in searching a patch. The birds spent more time searching patches when the environment as a whole contained more prey, but, contrary to the optimal giving-up-time hypothesis, their giving-up time did not depend on the overall prey density.

Hypotheses that do not rely on the assumptions of the marginal value theorem have also been used to predict how long an efficient predator should continue searching a patch. In a field experiment analogous to that of Krebs et al (1974), Lima (1984) studied free-ranging downy woodpeckers *(Picoides pubescens)* foraging for sunflower seeds in artificial patches. Each patch was made by drilling 24 holes in a piece of log. During pretraining, a single seed was placed in each hole, then covered with masking tape, and the birds learned to retrieve the seeds. The birds were then tested with patches containing either 0 prey or a fixed number of prey. The bird could not predict which of the patches contained prey without pecking through the masking tape covering some of the holes. Hence, this experiment provided the birds with a stochastic environment in which the number of prey in a patch was a random variable (with a value of 0 or n).

By simulation, Lima predicted the number of holes a bird should peck open to optimize its discrimination between empty and nonempty patches. This number varied with the number of prey hidden in the nonempty patches. He found that the birds quit an empty patch after searching approximately the predicted number of holes but continued to search a nonempty patch until all of the holes had been opened. Thus their performance on empty patches was approximately as predicted, but their performance on nonempty patches was not. This result may indicate that the birds could not change their searching strategy from the one appropriate during pretraining, when all patches were full. Alternatively, these data could mean that the birds "knew" the average prey density in the environment as a whole but could not keep track of the individual counts within a certain patch. A number of mechanisms that do not rely on counting prey might provide an estimate of the overall value of an environment (e.g. stomach load, energetic gain, etc).

Knowing the average density, but not the number of prey already found within the patch, would allow an optimal giving-up strategy on empty patches but would not be sufficient to yield an optimal giving-up strategy on nonempty patches. The difference between the predicted optimal strategy and the observed strategy could be attributable to an information constraint (see also Lima 1983). When information about the exact number of prey already found in a patch is not available, then the optimal strategy (in Lima's experiment as in that of Krebs et al 1974 and that of Zach & Falls 1976) is to search every available site exactly once. Without information that the last prey has been discovered, the predator's best guess is that the probability of a prey in the next hole remains constant.

Iwasa et al (1981) showed that the stopping rule to maximize the number of prey captured per unit foraging time depends on the distribution of prey in the patches. An optimal giving-up-time rule of the sort investigated by Krebs et al (1974) is best when the variance of the prey distribution is high, but worst when the variance is low. Iwasa et al showed that if the prey are binomially distributed, then the optimal stopping rule says to quit after discovering a fixed number of prey. If the prey are Poisson distributed, then the optimal stopping rule is to quit a patch after a fixed time spent. Because different rules are appropriate with different prey distributions, we should expect predators to show stopping rules characteristic of the distribution patterns of their typical prey.

The general model underlying the predictions by Iwasa et al (1981) is related to the stochastic giving-up-time model proposed by Oaten (1977) and McNamara (1982). The stochastic giving-up-time model assumes that the predator knows (*a*) the distribution of the number of prey per patch (i.e. what proportion of patches have 0 prey, 1 prey, 2 prey, etc) and (b) the distribution of the intercapture interval, conditional on the number of prey already captured in the patch and on the distribution of the number of prey in the patch. The predator uses this information and the remembered intercapture intervals for the current patch to estimate the expected period until capture of the next prey. Analogous to the marginal value theorem, the stochastic giving-up-time model assumes that the predator will leave the patch when it fails to capture a prey within the expected period. Unlike the marginal value theorem, the stochastic model does not assume any particular relationship between successive intercapture intervals and does not necessarily set the criterial intercapture interval to a constant value such as the environmental average intercapture interval.

Although these stochastic models have not been investigated rigorously, they appear to be more general and potentially more powerful than the marginal value theorem proposed by Charnov (1976). In order to obtain this increased power, however, we must assume that the predator possesses vast amounts of data about both the distribution of patches and its own history on the current patch (e.g. the distribution of numbers of prey per patch, the pattern of intercapture intervals, etc). Animals can sometimes possess surprising amounts and types of information (e.g. Kamil 1978, Olton 1978, Roitblat 1982b, Shettleworth & Krebs 1982, Balda & Turek 1984, Kamil & Balda 1985, Roberts 1984), so it is not reasonable to dismiss, out of hand, models that assume large stores of data. On the other hand, models that assume less sophisticated cognitive capacities may be more appropriate.

DIET SELECTION

Theoretical Models

One of the earliest optimal foraging models (MacArthur & Pianka 1966; see also Emlen 1966) analyzed the problem faced by a forager encountering different food types (e.g. different species of insects or seeds), each of which is characterized by a particular handling time (time to approach, capture, and consume) and energetic value. MacArthur & Pianka (1966) found a relatively simple way to calculate which prey types should and should not be included in the diet, provided the forager knows a lot about the prey types and is attempting to maximize its net rate of energy gain.

The MacArthur & Pianka (1966) model is most appropriate for a forager that encounters prey sequentially and must decide, in each case, whether or not to capture and consume it. The model partitions foraging time into search time and handling time. Search time is spent looking for prey, while handling time is spent pursuing, capturing, and consuming it. If the prey types available are ranked from best to worst in terms of energetic value per unit of handling time (E/H), the solution that maximizes net energy intake is easily seen. For a forager that presently includes only the highest ranking item in its diet, adding the item ranked second highest will have two effects. Search time between items will decrease, since more items are now included in the diet; but handling time per unit of intake will increase, because the second item provides less energetic value per unit handling time than the first. The diet that maximizes rate of intake will add lower-ranked items only when the decrease in search time compensates for the increase in average handling time. This point is reached when the next prey in the ranking has an E/H value less than the rate of intake being achieved without that prey in the diet (this overall rate includes search time in the denominator).

Three of the major predictions of this model are: (*a*) Under a given set of conditions, a prey type should either always be included in the diet or always excluded. There should be "no partial preferences" in which a prey type is sometimes included and sometimes excluded. (*b*) The inclusion of any prey type should depend only upon the density of higher-ranked prey types, not on the density of either the prey type in question or any lower-ranking types. (*c*) By implication, the predator must be able to rank the prey items it encounters in E/H order.

Hughes (1979) developed a model that incorporates recognition time and learning effects. Hughes added a recognition time component to the denominator of E/H and considered how experience might affect the time required to recognize and/or capture a prey type. Ollason (1980) and McNair (1981) have also considered possible learning effects. The McNair paper is particularly interesting because it considers the effects of learning on diet selection in a stochastic environment. Another approach to the diet selection problem has been advanced and tested by Belovsky (1978, 1981, 1984a,b), based on linear programming techniques (see below).

These models have been tested often in both laboratory and field, and the resulting literature is much larger than we can review here, given space limitations (see Pyke et al 1977, Krebs et al 1983 for reviews). Therefore we emphasize some of the papers of most interest to psychologists.

Field Studies

Many studies have tested the predictions of diet selection models in the field (e.g. Davies 1977b, Goss-Custard 1977a,b, Waddington & Holden 1979, Pulliam 1980, Pleasants 1981, Tinbergen 1981; see Krebs et al 1983 for review, especially Table 6.1). In general, these studies have found either qualitative or quantitative support for predictions of the MacArthur & Pianka (1966) approach (but see Goss-Custard 1977b, Schluter 1981, 1982, Zach & Smith 1981). For those first reading this literature, Goss-Custard (1981) and Werner & Mittelbach (1981) provide well-written overviews of extensive research projects on diet selection.

Goss-Custard (1981) studied the behavior of redshanks *(Tringa totanus)* foraging on mud flats for polychaete worms and amphipod crustaceans buried in the mud. Goss-Custard first studied the selection of different size classes of polychaetes by the redshanks. Several of the basic predictions of the MacArthur & Pianka model received support. The proportion of larger worms taken was affected only by their own density, and not by the density of smaller (lower E/H value) worms; but, as predicted, smaller worms were preyed upon by the redshanks only when larger worms were relatively rare. Prey selections were affected by neither day length nor the amount of foraging already accomplished. This is consistent with the model since the birds should always be taking the diet that maximizes rate of intake.

Goss-Custard (1981) also found two major deviations from predictions of the model. The redshanks sometimes showed partial preferences for small or medium-sized worms. In addition, when amphipods were present in the same area as polychaete worms, the redshanks often took the amphipods at a high rate, although the amphipods had relatively low E/H values. This may be because the amphipods provide a needed nutritional component (see Goss-Custard 1977b, Rapport 1981).

Werner and his associates (Werner & Hall 1974, 1976, 1979; Mittelbach 1981, 1983; Werner et al 1981, 1983a,b) have studied the foraging behavior of bluegill sunfish *(Lepomis macrochirus)* feeding on various food, especially *Daphnia,* in natural lakes and artificial ponds. These investigators have sought to understand natural patterns of foraging behavior in bluegills and their implications for species interactions and community structure. In general terms, they have found that a modified form of the MacArthur & Pianka (1966) model accurately predicts the different diet compositions and habitat usages of different size classes of bluegills. The diets of these different classes are different because each size class differs in the size prey it can efficiently handle. These differences, in turn, predict which part of the pond or lake the fish will be found in.

Field tests of optimal diet models suggest that learning plays a central role in efficient diet selection. The factors that affect diet selection, particularly relative prey density, can change rapidly under natural conditions, and predators often deal flexibly with these changes, tracking environmental change closely. "Sampling" behavior, spending time in relatively unprofitable areas (see above, Goss-Custard 1981, Werner & Mittelbach 1981), or occasionally taking a relatively unprofitable prey type, is probably essential to this learning. As Werner & Mittelbach state, "Our studies with fish also call attention to several areas critical to the further development of foraging theory. Specifically the role learning and sampling play in the foraging behavior of animals is crucial" (p. 826; see also Dill 1983 for broader discussion of learning and foraging in fishes).

Belovsky (1978, 1984a,b) has provided substantial data testing a linear programming approach to diet selection that appears to better account for characteristics of the foraging behavior of herbivores than several alternative models (Belovsky 1984a). The linear programming approach allows the inclusion into the model of several factors of particular importance for herbivores, such as constraints upon daily digestive capacity and nutrient requirements. While some have treated such factors as inherently incompatible with optimal foraging approaches (Rapport 1981), Belovsky's work shows that they can be incorporated into a single maximization model. The model appears to account for the diet selection of moose (Belovsky 1978, 1981), beaver (Belovsky 1984b), kudu, and microtine rodents (Belovsky 1984a). The evidence for the importance of nutritional constraints suggests that important connections to the psychological literature on "nutritional wisdom" could be made (e.g. Rozin & Kalat 1971).

Laboratory Studies

Tests of the predictions of diet selection models under laboratory conditions (e.g. Krebs et al 1977, Elner & Hughes 1978, Erichsen et al 1980, Houston et al 1980, Jaeger & Barnard 1981, Kaufman & Collier 1981, Moermond & Denslow 1983) generally support such models, at least qualitatively (but see Hughes & Elner 1979, Rapport 1980, Barnard & Brown 1981).

Only Moermond & Denslow (1983) have rigorously tested the assumption that foragers rank their food types in a monotonic fashion. These researchers offered individual fruit-eating, wild-caught birds choices between pairs of different fruits in an aviary. The birds were sensitive to fruit differences, showing preferences on 67–100% of the trials. In addition, the choices of the birds were transitive; if the birds preferred fruit A to fruit B, and preferred fruit B to fruit C, then they always preferred fruit A to fruit C. These data strongly support the hypothesis of an underlying monotonic ranking. Moermond & Denslow (1983) also obtained data suggesting that the concept of handling time is too simple. Relatively small changes in the accessibility of fruit above or below the branches on which the birds stood sometimes had large effects on choice, even though the effects on handling *time* were small. Thus time may sometimes be an inappropriate measure of the costs of handling food items. In this case, the risk of falling or the physical difficulty of movement may play a large role in determining the denominator of the E/H ratio.

Krebs et al (1977) tested the diet selection model with great tits *(Parus major)* in an interesting and clever experimental apparatus. The bird sat on a perch while prey went by on a conveyer belt. The prey were large and small pieces of mealworm. As predicted, when the encounter rate with prey was low the birds were nonselective, taking both sizes, but they specialized on the large prey when the encounter rate was high. However, the birds did not switch from a mixed to a pure diet in a single step. Krebs et al suggest that this may represent sampling by the birds.

In another experiment utilizing the same apparatus, Erichsen et al (1980) tested the model of Hughes (1979). They placed large and small pieces of mealworm inside opaque and clear pieces of plastic straw, respectively, which were then placed on the conveyor belt along with opaque straws containing only string. The larger prey thus resembled "twigs." In this same twig-like guise the birds might also find pieces of straw containing only string. The birds could only discriminate between the string-filled "twigs" and the large prey by picking up the straw and inspecting it. As predicted by the model, the birds switched their preference from the larger to the smaller prey as the proportion of mealworm pieces present in the opaque straws on the conveyor belt decreased.

Lea (1979) used more traditional operant procedures to test the diet selection model with pigeons. Each trial consisted of a series of events designed to mimic search time and handling time. After completing a preliminary fixed interval (FI) search requirement, the birds were presented with one of two stimuli (the prey types), each associated with a particular FI requirement (short or long) that produced access to food at the end. The pigeon could choose either to include the prey by pecking at the colored key or to exclude it by pecking at another key. This procedure gave Lea control over several parameters relevant to diet selection models: E/H values could be manipulated by varying either the FI requirements or the food access; relative density could be manipulated by controlling the probability of the long and short FI schedules. The results were qualitatively in agreement with diet selection model predictions, but there were significant departures from the MacArthur & Pianka (1966) predictions. As usual, partial preferences were observed, and the birds showed a marked bias against accepting the long FI (low E/H) alternative. The density of the worse prey type affected the choices of the birds.

Abarca & Fantino (1982) used similar techniques but employed a variable interval (VI) schedule for search rather than an FI. Their results were qualitatively similar to those predicted both by diet selection theory and by the delay-reduction hypothesis (Fantino 1981). Using operant procedures to investigate the diet selection model in pigeons, Snyderman (1983a) found that extended exposure to a stable set of conditions produced all-or-none prey selection, and that increasing deprivation decreased the selectivity of the pigeons (1983b).

As these studies make clear, the predictions of diet selection theory can be translated into psychological experiments. The critical parameters of the models, such as prey value, handling time, and search time, can easily be mimicked and manipulated with suitable adaptations of operant techniques. It is interesting to note that diet selection models make predictions about successive choice situations in which the predator must decide either to attack or pass up a prey.

This contrasts with patch selection and patch persistence models, which apply to simultaneous choice situations in which the predator must choose between or among patches available at the same time.

RISK-PRONE AND RISK-AVERSE BEHAVIOR

As discussed earlier, the problem of stochasticity has become a focus for recent theory and research in behavioral ecology. The study of risk-averse and risk-prone behavior has shown that the choices of a forager can be affected by the variability of reward.

Caraco (1980) explored this problem theoretically, using the concepts of utility theory (e.g. Keeney & Raiffa 1976). Caraco analyzed the problem of a forager with a fixed amount of foraging time—e.g. a small bird during winter, with foraging limited to daylight hours. How should the forager allocate its time among the available patch or prey types? Caraco's model predicts that preference for the more variable patch (risk-prone) or for the less variable patch (risk-averse) should depend upon resource availability. If resources are readily available, so that the forager can reasonably expect to obtain enough food to meet its needs, Caraco predicts risk-aversion. But if resource availability is low, so that the forager cannot expect to meet its needs, Caraco predicts risk-prone behavior.

One useful if simplified way to conceptualize this model is by thinking in terms not of maximizing energy intake but of minimizing risk of starvation. When things are good, and the average benefit realized from the available patches is sufficient to meet energetic/dietary needs, choosing the more variable patch will increase the risk of starving, through a run of bad luck. If things are bad, and the patch average is insufficient, the gamble of choosing the more variable patch type becomes worthwhile. With a run of good luck, starvation may be avoided.

Other papers have addressed this problem theoretically. Real (1980a,b) has dealt with uncertainty in more general terms. For example, he has explored the idea of variance discounting, in which the mean value of a behavioral option is discounted in proportion to its variance. He finds that under uncertain conditions, organisms should engage in more diverse behaviors, whereas under conditions of certainty, a single behavior should dominate. Stephens's (1981) analytical model, which minimizes starvation risk, agrees with Caraco's (1980) in many respects, including the prediction that the occurrence of risk-prone and risk-averse behavior should depend on mean food availability. One interesting additional implication of this model is that the risk-taking decision may be affected by the number of decisions left to make—by, for example, the time of day with a diurnal feeder. Stephens (1981) suggests that risk-prone behavior may be less likely when few decisions remain. Houston &

McNamara's (1982) sequential version of Stephens's (1981) model suggests that a forager may switch back and forth frequently between risk-prone and risk-averse behavior during foraging, depending upon current energy reserves.

Three papers have reported experiments testing the effects of variability in nectar supply on the foraging behavior of insect pollinators. Waddington et al (1981) gave bumblebees *(Bombus edwardsii)* a choice between two flower types, one offering constant reward, the other variable reward. The mean nectar contents of the two flower types were equal. In each of three experiments the bumblebees preferred the more constant flower. Because this risk-aversion developed as the bees gained experience with the flower types, learning appeared to be involved.

In a similar experiment, Real (1981) found that bumblebees *(Bombus sandesdoni)* and paper wasps *(Vespula vulgaris)* also preferred constant flowers. In this experiment, flower type was signaled by color. In the initial phase of the experiment, blue flowers were variable while yellow flowers were constant, and the foragers preferred yellow. When these values were reversed, the preference reversed. This again implies learning.

The effects on choice of variance in amount of reward have been studied extensively in small, granivorous birds (see Caraco & Lima 1985 for the most recent review). In most of these experiments, the same basic discrete-choice procedures have been used. Each bird receives a series of tests under different experimental conditions. Each test consists of a preliminary set of forced-choice trials, during which each alternative is presented equally often. These are followed by a preference test, consisting of free-choice trials. On each free-choice trial the bird can choose one feeder.

Caraco et al (1980) tested yellow-eyed juncos *(Junco phaeonotus)* in two experiments. In each experiment, the birds were given a series of tests with constant rewards vs variable rewards with the same mean value. For example, in one test, the juncos received a constant 2 seeds per trial at one feeder, a variable 0 or 4 seeds at the other feeder (with a mean of two seeds). During the first experiment, the birds were food deprived for 1 hr before each session, and there was a delay of 30 sec per seed eaten between trials. These conditions were chosen because they should have maintained the birds in a positive energy budget (intake exceeding expenditures). The juncos showed consistent, significant preferences for the constant feeder—risk-aversion. In the second experiment, the birds were deprived for 4 hr before each session. The intertrial interval was 1 min per seed eaten. These conditions maintained the birds in a negative energy budget (rate of intake below energy expenditures). The birds now showed consistent, significant risk-prone behavior, reliably choosing the more variable feeder. The results support models predicting switches between risk-prone and risk-averse behavior as a function of energy budget (e.g. Caraco 1980, Stephens 1981).

Caraco (1981) obtained similar results with dark-eyed juncos *(J. hyemalis)*. These birds also were risk-averse when maintained under a positive energy budget, and risk-prone under a negative energy budget. When tested under a balanced energy budget, the birds showed mixed results, with more indifference than observed in other experiments. The details of the choices of individual birds in this condition suggested that certain mean-variance combinations might be particularly attractive to the birds.

Caraco (1982, 1983) has also worked with white-crowned sparrows *(Zonotrichia leucophrys),* a bird half again as large as a junco. In the first of these papers, Caraco (1982) reported the results of two experiments. In the first experiment, the sparrows, like the juncos, showed risk-aversion under a positive energy budget. In the second experiment, a new procedure was used. All feeders were present simultaneously, and the bird could visit them in any order. The different feeder types were signalled by colored pieces of paper. Under these conditions, one might expect risk aversion to be reduced, since a visit to a low-quality feeder would be less costly—i.e another feeder can be visited immediately. However, the results again showed risk aversion under positive energy budgets. Caraco (1983) found risk aversion under positive energy budgets, and risk proneness under negative budgets, even when both feeders were variable, but with different variances.

Recently, Caraco & Chasin (1984) extended the general finding that birds are sensitive to the distribution of rewards about the mean. Using the choice procedures developed in Caraco's studies of risk, Caraco & Chasin showed that white-crowned sparrows were sensitive to the skew of the distribution of rewards, with the mean and variance held constant. For example, the sparrows were given a choice between two feeders: Feeder 1 delivered either no seeds with probability 0.25 or delivered 2 seeds with probability 0.75. Feeder 2 delivered either 1 seed with probability 0.75 or 3 seeds with probability 0.25. Each feeder thus had a mean number of seeds per choice of 1.5 and a variance of 0.87, but feeder 2 was positively skewed. The birds showed significant preference for the positively skewed feeders when maintained under a positive energy budget.

What general conclusions of interest to psychologists can be drawn from this work? First of all, many questions about risk-prone and risk-averse behavior in the ecological context remain unanswered. The only experimental demonstrations of risk-prone behavior have been with relatively small seed-eating birds. Several studies with insect and nectar feeders have found only risk aversion (although energy budget was not manipulated directly). It remains to be established whether the phenomenon of switching between risk preference and risk avoidance as a function of energy balance is general among animals. However, the existence of sensitivity to reward variance and skew raises interesting psychological questions. Clearly animals can be quite sensitive to the characteristics of the distribution of reward about the mean. Psychological experiments with rats have reported risk-prone behavior when number of food pellets was varied (Leventhal et al 1959), but these studies used relatively severe deprivation conditions, and one wonders whether risk aversion would otherwise have been shown. The strength of the risk preference decreased as mean number of food pellets per choice increased (Leventhal et al 1959).

A number of authors (e.g. Krebs et al 1983; Caraco & Lima 1985) have pointed out a potential relationship between the results of (a) experiments on risk and (b) operant experiments investigating preference for variable vs constant ratio or interval schedules (e.g. Herrnstein 1964; Fantino 1967; Davison 1969). This relationship is tenuous because there are so many procedural differences between the two sets of experiments. The biggest difference is that the risk experiments have manipulated the distribution of amount of reward. (It should be noted that in most of Caraco's experiments variable reward was associated with variable intertrial intervals whose duration was defined in time per seed obtained.) Different relationships might hold for other aspects of food delivery. However, because prey types are apparently often ranked on the basis of the ratio of food value to handling time, and interval or ratio schedules may be reasonable simulations of handling time, the effects on preference of the distribution of intervals or ratios within schedules of reinforcement certainly deserve more intensive investigation.

CACHE RECOVERY AND MEMORY IN BIRDS

Field workers have long known that members of two families of birds, the Paridae and the Corvidae, frequently cache food which is later recovered and eaten (e.g. Lohrl 1950, Swanberg 1951, Turcek & Kelso 1968). Most of the experimental research on cache recovery and memory in birds has concentrated upon the *Parus* and *Nucifraga* genera (but see Bossema 1979 for work with the European jay, *Garrulus glandarius*). Since the two genera show somewhat different natural patterns of cache recovery, we review the work with each separately, then conclude with a section on comparative implications.

Parids

The basic pattern of food caching shown by parids is probably best described as scatter-hoarding, dispersing food items over a wide area and making no attempt to defend them (Sherry et al 1982). Most of the cached food is usually recovered and eaten within 24 hr (Cowie et al 1981). Some field data have suggested that parids may find their caches using memory (Lohrl 1950; but because many cache sites are usually involved, others have doubted that memory guides these birds back to the scattered food (Gibb 1960, Haftorn 1974).

This disagreement cannot be resolved through field data alone. One cannot assign a central role to memory until reliance on other possible mechanisms has been eliminated. For example, direct cues emanating from the seeds, site preferences, or systematic patterns of movement could all account for most field observations. The best field data indicating the potential role of memory in cache recovery by parids comes from a clever experiment by Cowie et al (1981). Radioactively labelled sunflower seeds were dispensed to marsh tits *(Parus palustris)* from feeders placed in Wytham wood outside Oxford. Many of these seeds were cached by the marsh tits, and subsequently located by the experimenters using oscillation counters. Control seeds were then placed near (within 10 cm) or far (100 cm) from each located cached seed. Both types of control seeds remained undiscovered longer than the seeds cached by the birds, but this difference was significant only for the far control seeds. Although not conclusive, this evidence is consistent with the hypothesis that memory plays an important role in the cache recovery of marsh tits. Since birds discovered the seeds placed close to the original cached seeds less frequently than they did the original seeds, this argues against use of direct cues. Furthermore, several aspects of the data argue against specific site preferences. For example, although the marsh tits showed preferences for particular types of locations (e.g. moss or tree bark), these preferences often changed from day to day. Nonetheless, only by means of the control offered by laboratory studies can we determine whether or not parids remember cache site locations.

LABORATORY STUDIES   The role of memory in the cache recovery of parids has been clearly established by several laboratory experiments with marsh tits (*P. palustris*) and chickadees (*P. atricapillus*) (Sherry et al 1981, Sherry 1982, 1984a, Shettleworth & Krebs 1982). Individually and collectively, these experiments leave little doubt that memory is a primary mechanism of cache recovery in this genus.

In an aviary experiment, Sherry et al (1981) presented marsh tits with moss trays in which sunflower seeds could be cached. Following the caching session, all seeds were removed by the experimenters, and recovery sessions were conducted 3 and 24 hr after the caches had been created. The marsh tits made more visits to, and spent more time at, the quadrants of the moss trays in which they had cached seeds.

In a second experiment, Sherry et al (1981) tested the effect of interocular transfer on cache recovery. Because in the visual system of birds the two optic nerves show complete decussation at the optic chiasma, memory cues stored using one eye would only be useful if the stimuli to be remembered were again seen by that eye. In this experiment with marsh tits one eye was covered during caching and one eye covered during recovery. In the control condition the same eye was covered during both caching and recovery; in the transfer condition, different eyes were covered. The marsh tits performed accurately (found their caches) during control tests but randomly when interocular transfer was required. They therefore seemed to be relying on information stored in the brain.

Sherry (1982) extended these results, employing a similar technique using moss trays. In this experiment, he tested marsh tits with two recovery sessions after a single caching session. While cached seeds were present during the first recovery session, all seeds were removed for the second. He found that during the second recovery session, the birds avoided the sites they had emptied during the first.

Memory is clearly important in the cache recovery of marsh tits. Several experiments found accurate performance in the absence of any possible direct cues from the seeds. The lack of interocular transfer suggests that information is stored in the brain. The avoidance of already emptied cache sites during a second recovery session eliminates simple rules of movement, and implies a dynamic memory system.

Shettleworth & Krebs (1982) have further documented the role of memory in cache recovery in marsh tits using a more sophisticated experimental technique. They presented marsh tits with a large set of cloth-covered holes in artificial trees. They replicated many of the findings reviewed above. In addition, they found that the number of errors per seed increased with successive seeds found, that the birds avoid holes in which they have already cached seeds when caching more seeds, and that there was a slight recency effect when recovering seeds cached at two separate times. All of these results are consistent with the use of memory.

Sherry (1984a) has extended research on cache recovery to another parid species, the black-capped chickadee *(P. atricapillus),* employing a technique similar to that used by Shettleworth & Krebs (1982). In addition to replicating many of the results previously obtained with marsh tits, Sherry (1984a) reported two new findings. When given a second recovery session, not only did the chickadees avoid sites they had emptied during the first recovery session, but they also avoided sites they had found to be empty (seeds removed by the experimenter) during the first recovery session. In an experiment in which the chickadees stored two different types of seeds, they tended to visit those containing the preferred seeds during recovery, suggesting memory for the contents of food caches.

Nutcrackers

In contrast to the parids, which appear to recover most of their cached food within 24 hr (Cowie et al 1981), the nutcrackers (the Eurasian nutcracker, *Nucifraga caryocatactes,* and Clark's nutcracker, *N. columbiana*) usually leave food caches in place for months before recovering them. These birds harvest pine seeds and store them in caches in the ground during the late summer and fall (Tomback 1977, Vander Wall & Balda 1977). These cached seeds then provide most or all of the diet during the following winter and breeding season (Giuntoli & Mewaldt 1978) and are fed to nestlings and fledglings during the following spring and summer (Mewaldt 1956). An individual Clark's nutcracker stores from 22,000 to 33,000 pine seeds a year (Vander Wall & Balda 1977, Tomback 1983), while estimates for Eurasian nutcrackers are as high as 86,000 to 100,000 (Mezhenny 1964, Mattes 1978). The nutcrackers possess a number of morphological and behavioral specializations for the harvesting and storage of pine seeds, including a stout, strong bill and a sublingual pouch used in seed transport (Bock et al 1973, Vander Wall & Balda 1977, 1981, Conrads & Balda 1979).

As in the case of the parids, field observations suggest that memory may be involved in the cache recovery of nutcrackers. For example, since nutcrackers usually husk recovered pine seeds by the cache site, Tomback (1980) was able to estimate what percentage of probes in the ground result in recovery of seeds. Her estimate, 72%, must be regarded as a lower bound since rodents may steal some caches and nutcrackers may sometimes carry unhusked seeds away from cache sites (see also Swanberg 1951, Mezhenny 1964, Mattes 1978).

LABORATORY STUDIES   Four experiments have examined the cache recovery performance of nutcrackers in laboratory settings (Balda 1980, Vander Wall 1982, Balda & Turek 1984, Kamil & Balda 1985). Balda (1980) worked with a single Eurasian nutcracker in an aviary with a dirt floor. Using retention intervals of 7–31 days, he found that cache recovery was highly accurate, even when cached seeds had been removed by the experimenter to eliminate any cues emanating from the seeds themselves.

Vander Wall (1982) allowed two Clark's nutcrackers to cache in a single dirt-floored aviary. During recovery, each bird accurately recovered its own caches but virtually never found caches created by the other. Two additional nutcrackers, which did not cache themselves but were allowed to watch the other birds cache seeds, found caches at levels above chance but well below the levels of the cachers themselves. Vander Wall (1982) also found that when he moved landmarks within the room (logs and rocks), the cache recovery of the nutcrackers was disrupted. In a similar vein, Balda & Turek (1984) found that cache recovery accuracy declined when local landmarks were removed. These results strongly support the memory hypothesis and implicate visual cues as the stimuli controlling recovery performance.

Kamil & Balda (1985) studied four Clark's nutcrackers in a room with 180 sand-filled holes, each of which could be made inaccessible with a wooden plug. Using retention intervals of 10–15 days, they found that the nutcrackers recovered their caches accurately even when the experimenters forced the birds to cache in randomly selected holes. These results show accurate recovery even when site preferences have been eliminated.

Comparative Implications

The data reported to date suggest two important differences between parids and nutcrackers in their use of memory to recover caches. The first is the duration of the memory. The nutcracker experiments have used retention intervals of up to 31 days with good results, and Balda & Kamil have a study in progress using much longer retention intervals and have observed accurate cache recovery after 91 days. The parid experiments have used retention intervals of 3–24 hr. While the parids have not been tested with longer delays, the field data (Cowie et al 1981) stongly suggest that they would not perform well if the interval between caching and recovery were several days or weeks. The second difference concerns revisits to cache sites previously emptied by the birds. Parids avoid such revisits (Sherry 1982, 1984a) while nutcrackers do not (Balda 1980, Kamil & Balda 1985). While both of these differences require further study, they raise substantial comparative questions, especially since the differences appear to correlate with differences in caching behavior shown in the field (Kamil & Balda 1985). These comparative implications, and the relationship between cache recovery and more traditional psychological tests of animal memory, are discussed in more detail by Sherry (1984b). Further research with other caching species, as well as research with caching species in more traditional tests of animal memory, is needed.

CONCLUDING REMARKS

The ecological and ethological literatures on foraging behavior contain ideas and data that raise significant issues for the study of animal learning and memory. This functionally oriented literature will not be integrated easily with the mechanistically oriented psychological literature on animal learning and memory. It is always difficult to combine different levels of explanation (Lehrman 1974, Shettleworth 1983, 1984).

Perhaps recent recearch on kin recognition provides an example of how such integration could occur. Functional considerations led Hamilton (1964) to argue that animals could gain significant adaptive advantage if they could recognize their relatives. That mechanisms for kin recognition exist was later confirmed (Lewin 1984). The foraging literature suggests many learning and memory mechanisms, such as risk sensitivity when rewards vary, and sampling of the environment in the face of uncertainty. Psychologists possess experimental skills and specific techniques well-suited to the investigation of the phenomena implicit in the foraging literature. But in doing such research, psychologists must be aware of the biological, adaptive implications of the research. Such ecologically oriented research will likely alter significantly our ideas about the capabilities of animals.

ACKNOWLEDGMENTS

Preparation of this manuscript was supported by NSF grants BNS 82-03017 and BNS 81-02335, and by NIMH grant R01-MH37070.

Literature Cited

Abarca, N., Fantino, E. 1982. Choice and foraging. *J. Exp. Anal. Behav.* 38:117–23

Alcock, J. 1979. *Animal Behavior: An Evolutionary Approach.* Sunderland, Mass: Sinauer. 2nd ed.

Andersson, M. 1981. Central place foraging in the whinchat, *(Saxicola rubetra). Ecology* 62:538–44

Aronson, R. B., Givnish, T. J. 1983. Optimal central place foragers: A comparison with null hypotheses. *Ecology* 64:395–99

Balda, R. P. 1980. Recovery of cached seeds by a captive *Nucifraga caryotactes. Z. Tierpsychol.* 52:331–46

Balda, R. P., Turek, R. J. 1984. The cache-recovery system as an example of memory capabilities in Clark's nutcracker. See Roitblat et al 1984, pp. 513–32

Barnard, C. J., Brown, C. A. J. 1981. Prey size selection and competition in the common shrew *(Sorex araneus* L.). *Behav. Ecol. Sociobiol.* 8:239–43

Bellman, R. 1956. A problem in the sequential design of experiments. *Sankhya* 16:221–29

Belovsky, G. E. 1978. Diet optimization in a generalist herbivore, the moose. *Theor. Popul. Biol.* 14:105–34

Belovsky, G. E. 1981. Optimal activity times and habitat choice of moose. *Oecologia* 48:22–30

Belovsky, G. E. 1984a. Herbivore optimal foraging: A comparative test of three models. *Am. Nat.* In press

Belovsky, G. E. 1984b. Summer diet optimization by beaver. *Am. Midl. Nat.* In press

Bitterman, M. E. 1965. Phyletic differences in learning. *Am. Psychol.* 20:396–410

Bitterman, M. E. 1969. Habit-reversal and probability-learning: Rats, birds and fish. In *Animal Discrimination Learning,* ed. R. M. Gilbert, N. S. Sutherland. New York: Academic

Bock, W. J., Balda, R. P., Vander Wall, S. B. 1973. Morphology of the sublingual pouch and tongue musculature in Clark's nutcracker. *Auk* 90:491–519

Bossema, I. 1979. Jays and oaks: An eco-ethological study of a symbiosis. *Behaviour* 70:1–17

Bryant, D. M., Turner, A. K. 1982. Central place foraging by swallows *(Hirundinidae):* The question of load size. *Anim. Behav.* 30:845–56

Capaldi, E. J. 1966. Partial reinforcement: A hypothesis of sequential effects. *Psychol. Rev.* 73:459–79

Capaldi, E. J. 1971. Memory and learning: A sequential viewpoint. In *Animal Memory,* ed. W. K. Honig, P. H. R. James. New York: Academic

Caraco, T. 1980. On foraging time allocation in a stochastic environment. *Ecology* 61:119–28

Caraco, T. 1981. Energy budgets, risk, and foraging preferences in dark-eyed juncos *(Junco hyemalis). Behav. Ecol. Sociobiol.* 8:213–17

Caraco, T. 1982. Aspects of risk-aversion in foraging white-crowned sparrows. *Anim. Behav.* 30:719–27

Caraco, T. 1983. White-crowned sparrows *(Zonatrichia leucophrys):* Foraging preferences in a risky environment. *Behav. Ecol. Sociobiol.* 12:63–69

Caraco, T., Chasin, M. 1984. Foraging preferences: response to reward skew. *Anim. Behav.* 32:76–85

Caraco, T., Lima, S. L. 1985. Survivorship, energy budgets and foraging risk. In *Quantitative Analysis of Behavior,* Vol. 6, ed. M. Commons, S. J. Shettleworth, T. Nevin. In press

Caraco, T., Martindale, S., Whittam, T. S. 1980. An empirical demonstration of risk-sensitive foraging preferences. *Anim. Behav.* 28:820–30

Charnov, E. L. 1976. Optimal foraging: The marginal value theorem. *Theor. Popul. Biol.* 9:129–36

Charnov, E. L., Orians, G. H., Hyatt, K. 1976. Ecological implications of resource depression. *Am. Nat.* 110:141–51

Church, R. M., Meck, W. 1984. The numerical attribute of stimuli. See Roitblat et al 1984, pp. 445–64

Conrads, K., Balda, R. P. 1979. Überwinterungschancen Siberischer Tannenhaher *(Nucifraga caryocatactes macrorhynchos)* im Invasionsgebiet. *Ber. Naturwissensch. Ver. Bielefeld* 24:115–37

Cowie, R. J. 1977. Optimal foraging in great tits *(Parus major). Nature* 268:137–39

Cowie, R. J., Krebs, J. R., Sherry, D. F. 1981. Food storing by marsh tits. *Anim. Behav.* 29:1252–59

Davies, N. B. 1977a. Prey selection and social

behavior in wagtails (Aves:Motacillidae). *J. Anim. Ecol.* 46:37–57

Davies, N. B. 1977b. Prey selection and the search strategy of the spotted flycatcher *(Muscicapa striata):* A field study of optimal foraging. *Anim. Behav.* 25:1016–33

Davison, M. 1969. Preference for mixed-interval versus fixed-interval schedules. *J. Exp. Anal. Behav.* 12:247–52

Dawkins, R. 1976. *The Selfish Gene.* Oxford: Oxford Univ. Press

De Groot, M. H. 1970. *Optimal Statistical Decisions.* New York: McGraw-Hill

de Villiers, P. 1977. Choice in concurrent schedules and a quantitative formulation of the law of effect. In *Handbook of Operant Behavior,* ed. W. K. Honig, J. E. R. Staddon. Englewood Cliffs, NJ: Prentice Hall

Dill, L. M. 1983. Adaptive flexibility in the foraging behavior of fishes. *Can. J. Fish. Aquat. Sci.* 40:398–408

Elner, R. W., Hughes, R. N., 1978. Energy maximization in the diet of the shore crab *Carcinus maenas. J. Anim. Ecol.* 47:103–16

Emlen, J. M. 1966. The role of time and energy in food preference. *Am. Nat.* 100:611–17

Erichsen, J. T., Krebs, J. R., Houston, A. I. 1980. Optimal foraging and cryptic prey. *J. Anim. Ecol.* 49:271–76

Evans, R. M. 1982. Efficient use of food patches at different distances from a breeding colony in black-billed gulls. *Behaviour* 79:28–38

Fantino, E. 1967. Preference for mixed- versus fixed-ratio schedules. *J. Exp. Anal. Behav.* 10:35–43

Fantino, E. 1981. Contiguity, response strength, and the delay reduction hypothesis. In *Advances in the Analysis of Behavior, Vol. 2: Predictability, Correlation and Contiguity,* ed. P. Harzem, M. D. Zeiler. Chichester: Wiley

Gibb, J. A. 1958. Predation by tits and squirrels on the eucosmimid *Ernarmonia conicolana* (Heyl.). *J. Anim. Ecol.* 27:275–96

Gibb, J. A. 1960. Populations of tits and goldcrests and their food supply in pine plantations. *Ibis* 102:163–208

Gibb, J. A. 1962. L. Tinbergen's hypothesis of the role of specific search images. *Ibis* 104:106–11

Gibbon, J., Church, R. M. 1981. Time left: Linear vs logarithmic subjective time. *J. Exp. Psychol.: Anim. Behav. Proc.* 7:87–107

Gibbon, J., Church, R. M. 1984. Sources of variance in an information processing theory of timing. See Roitblat et al 1984, pp. 465–88

Giraldeau, L., Kramer, D. L. 1982. The marginal value theorem: A quantitative test using load size variation in a central place forager, the eastern chipmunk, *(Tamias striatus). Anim. Behav.* 30:1036–42

Giuntoli, M., Mewaldt, L. R. 1978. Stomach contents of Clark's nutcrackers collected in Western Montana. *Auk* 95:595–98

Goss-Custard, J. D. 1977a. Optimal foraging and the size selection of worms by redshank, *Tringa totanus,* in the field. *Anim. Behav.* 25:10–29

Goss-Custard, J. D. 1977b. The energetics of prey selection by redshank, *Tringa totanus* (L.), in relation to prey density. *J. Anim. Ecol.* 46:1–19

Goss-Custard, J. D. 1981. Feeding behavior of redshank, *Tringa totanus,* and optimal foraging theory. See Kamil & Sargent, 1981, pp. 115–34

Greenwood, P. J., Harvey, P. H. 1978. Foraging and territory utilization of blackbirds *(Turdus merula)* and song thrushes *(Turdus philomelos). Anim. Behav.* 26:1222–36

Grubb, T. C., Greenwald, L. 1982. Sparrows and a brushpile: Foraging responses to different combinations of predation risk and energy cost. *Anim. Behav.* 30:637–40

Haftorn, S. 1974. Storage of surplus food by the boreal chickadee *Parus hudsonicus* in Alaska, with some records on the mountain chickadee *Parus gambeli* in Colorado. *Ornis. Scand.* 5:145–61

Hamilton, W. D. 1964. The genetical theory of social behavior, I, II. *J. Theor. Biol.* 7:1–52

Herrnstein, R. 1964. Aperiodicity as a factor in choice. *J. Exp. Anal. Behav.* 7:179–89

Herrnstein, R. J., Heyman, G. M. 1979. Is matching compatible with reinforcement maximization on concurrent variable interval variable ratio? *J. Exp. Anal. Behav.* 31:209–23

Heyman, G. M., Luce, R. D. 1979. Operant matching is not a logical consequence of maximizing reinforcement rate. *Anim. Learn. Behav.* 7:133–40

Hodges, C. M. 1981. Optimal foraging in bumblebees: Hunting by expectation. *Anim. Behav.* 29:1166–71

Houston, A., Kacelnik, A., McNamara, J. 1982. Some learning rules for acquiring information. In *Functional Ontogeny,* ed. D. J. McFarland, pp. 140–91. London: Plenum

Houston, A. I., Krebs, J. R., Erichsen, J. T. 1980. Optimal prey choice and discrimination time in the great tit *(Parus major* L.). *Behav. Ecol. Sociobiol.* 6:169–75

Houston, A. I., McNamara, J. 1982. A sequential approach to risk-taking. *Anim. Behav.* 30:1260–61

Hubbard, S. F., Cook, R. M. 1978. Optimal foraging by parasitoid wasps. *J. Anim. Ecol.* 47:593–604

Hughes, R. N. 1979. Optimal diets under the energy maximization premise: The effects of recognition time and learning. *Am. Nat.* 113:209–21

Hughes, R. N., Elner, R. W. 1979. Tactics of a

predator, *Carcinus maenas,* and morphological responses of the prey, *Nucella lapillus.* *J. Anim. Ecol.* 48:65–78

Iwasa, Y., Higashi, M., Yamamura, N. 1981. Prey distribution as a factor determining the choice of optimal foraging strategy. *Am. Nat.* 117:710–23

Jaeger, R. G., Barnard, D. E. 1981. Foraging tactics of a terrestrial salamander: Choice of diet in structurally simple environments. *Am. Nat.* 117:639–64

Janetos, A. C., Cole, B. J. 1981. Imperfectly optimal animals. *Behav. Ecol. Sociobiol.* 9:203–10

Johnston, T. D. 1981. Contrasting approaches to a theory of learning. *Behav. Brain Sci.* 4:125–39

Jones, P. W. 1976. Some results for the two-armed bandit problem. *Math. Operat. Forsch. Stat.* 7:471–75

Kacelnik, A. 1984. Central place foraging in starlings *(Sturnus vulgaris).* I. Patch residence time. *J. Anim. Ecol.* 53:283–99

Kacelnik, A. 1979. *Studies of foraging behavior and time budgeting in great tits (Parus major).* DPhil thesis. Oxford Univ., Oxford, Great Britain

Kamil, A. C. 1978. Systematic foraging by a nectar-feeding bird, the amakihi *(Loxops virens). J. Comp. Physiol. Psychol.* 92:388–96

Kamil, A. C., Balda, R. P. 1985. Cache recovery and spatial memory in Clark's nutcrackers *(Nucifraga columbiana). J. Exp. Psychol.: Anim. Behav. Proc.* In press

Kamil, A. C., Sargent, T. D. 1981. *Foraging Behavior: Ecological, Ethological and Psychological Approaches.* New York: Garland STPM Press

Kamil, A. C., Yoerg, S. J. 1982. Learning and foraging behavior. In *Perspectives in Ethology,* ed. P. P. G. Bateson, P. H. Klopfer, 5:325–64. London/New York: Plenum

Kasuya, E. 1982. Central place water collection in a Japanese paper wasp, *Polistes chinensis antennalis. Anim. Behav.* 30:1010–14

Kaufman, L. W., Collier, G. 1981. The economics of seed handling. *Am. Nat.* 118:46–60

Keeney, R. L., Raiffa, H. 1976. *Decisions with Multiple Objectives: Preference and Value Tradeoffs.* New York: Wiley

Krebs, J. R., Erichsen, J. T., Webber, J. I., Charnov, E. L. 1977. Optimal prey selection in the great tit *(Parus major). Anim. Behav.* 25:30–38

Krebs, J. R., Kacelnik, A., Taylor, P. 1978. Test of optimal sampling by foraging great tits. *Nature* 275:27–31

Krebs, J. R., Ryan, J. C., Charnov, E. L. 1974. Hunting by expectation or optimal foraging? A study of patch use by chickadees. *Anim. Behav.* 22:953–64

Krebs, J. R., Stephens, D. W., Sutherland, W. J. 1983. Perspectives in optimal foraging. In *Perspectives in Ornithology,* ed. A. H. Brush, G. A. Clark, Jr., pp. 165–215. Cambridge: Cambridge Univ. Press

Lea, S. E. G. 1979. Foraging and reinforcement schedules in the pigeon: Optimal and non-optimal aspects of choice. *Anim. Behav.* 27:875–86

Lehrman, D. S. 1974. Can psychiatrists use ethology? In *Ethology and Psychiatry,* ed. N. F. White, pp. 187–96. Toronto: Univ. Toronto Press

Leventhal, A. M., Morrell, R. F., Morgan, E. F. J., Perkins, C. C. J. 1959. The relation between mean reward and mean reinforcement. *J. Exp. Psychol.* 57:284–87

Lewin, R. 1984. Practice catches theory in kin recognition. *Science* 223:1049–51

Lima, S. L. 1983. Downy woodpecker foraging behavior: Foraging by expectation and energy intake rate. *Oecologia* 58:232–37

Lima, S. L. 1984. Downy woodpecker foraging behavior: Efficient sampling in simple stochastic environments. *Ecology* 65:166–74

Lindley, D. V., Barnett, V. 1965. Sequential sampling: Two decision problems with linear losses in binomial and normal random variables. *Biometrika* 52:507–32

Lohrl, H. 1950. Beobachtungen zur Soziologie und Verhaltensweige von Sumpfmeisen *(Parus palustris communis)* im Winter. *Z. Tierpsychol.* 7:417–24

MacArthur, R. H., Pianka, E. R. 1966. On optimal use of a patchy environment. *Am. Nat.* 100:603–9

Mackintosh, N. J. 1969. Comparative studies of reversal and probability-learning: Rats, birds and fish. In *Animal Discrimination Learning,* ed. R. M. Gilbert, N. S. Sutherland, pp. 137–62. New York: Academic

Mattes, H. 1978. Der Tannenhaher im Engadin. *Münster. Geogr. Arbeit.* 3:87

Maynard Smith, J. 1978. Optimization theory in evolution. *Ann. Rev. Ecol. Syst.* 9:31–56

McCleery, R. H. 1978. Optimal behaviour sequences and decision making. In *Behavioural Ecology: An Evolutionary Approach,* ed. J. R. Krebs, N. B. Davies, pp. 377–410. Sunderland, Mass: Sinauer

McNair, J. N. 1981. A stochastic foraging model with predator training effects. 2. Optimal diets. *Theor. Popul. Biol.* 19:147–62

McNair, J. N. 1982. Optimal giving-up-times and the marginal value theorem. *Am. Nat.* 119:511–29

McNamara, J. 1982. Optimal patch use in a stochastic environment. *Theor. Popul. Biol.* 21:269–88

Mewaldt, R. L. 1956. Nesting behavior of the Clark's nutcracker. *Condor* 58:3–23

Mezhenny, A. A. 1964. Biology of the nutcracker *Nucifraga caryocatactes macrorhynchos* in South Yakutia. *Zool. Zh.* 43:167–68

Milinski, M., Heller, R. 1978. Influence of a predator on the optimal foraging behavior of sticklebacks (*Gasterosteus aculeatus* L.). *Nature* 275:642–44

Mittelbach, G. G. 1981. Foraging efficiency and body size: A study of optimal diet and habitat use by bluegills. *Ecology* 62:1370–86

Mittelbach, G. G. 1983. Optimal foraging and growth in bluegills. *Oecologia* 59:157–62

Moermond, T., Denslow, J. S. 1983. Fruit choice in neotropical birds: Effects of fruit type and accessibility on selectivity. *J. Anim. Ecol.* 52:407–20

Oaten, A. 1977. Optimal foraging in patches: A case for stochasticity. *Theor. Popul. Biol.* 12:263–85

Ollason, J. G. 1980. Learning to forage optimally? *Theor. Popul. Biol.* 18:44–56

Olton, D. S. 1978. Characteristics of spatial memory. In *Cognitive Processes in Animal Behavior*, ed. S. H. Hulse, H. F. Fowler, W. K. Honig, pp. 341–73. Hillsdale, NJ: Erlbaum

Orians, G. H. 1981. Foraging behavior and the evolution of discriminatory abilities. See Kamil & Sargent 1984, pp. 389–406

Orians, G. H., Pearson, N. E. 1979. On the theory of central place foraging. In *Analysis of Ecological Systems,* ed. D. J. Horn, G. R. Stairs, R. D. Mitchell, pp. 155–77. Columbus: Ohio State Univ. Press

Pleasants, J. M. 1981. Bumblebee response to variation in nectar availability. *Ecology* 62:1648–61

Pubols, B. H. J. 1962. Constant versus variable delay of reinforcement. *J. Comp. Physiol. Psychol.* 55:52–56

Pulliam, H. R. 1980. Do chipping sparrows forage optimally? *Ardea* 68:75–82

Pyke, G. H., Pulliam, H. R., Charnov, E. L. 1977. Optimal foraging: A selective review of theory and tests. *Q. Rev. Biol.* 52:137–54

Rachlin, H., Green, L., Kagel, J. H., Battalio, R. C. 1976. Economic demand theory and psycophysical studies of choice. In *The Psychology of Learning and Motivation,* ed. G. Bower, 10:129–54. New York: Academic

Rapport, D. J. 1980. Optimal foraging for complementary resources. *Am. Nat.* 116:324–46

Rapport, D. J. 1981. Foraging behavior of *Stentor coeruleus:* A microeconomic interpretation. See Kamil & Sargent 1981, pp. 77–94

Real, L. A. 1980a. Fitness, uncertainty, and the role of diversification in evolution and behavior. *Am. Nat.* 115:623–38

Real, L. A. 1980b. On uncertainty and the law of diminishing returns in evolution and behavior. In *Limits to Action: The Allocation of Individual Behavior,* ed. J. E. R. Staddon, pp. 37–64. New York: Academic

Real, L. A. 1981. Uncertainty and pollinator-plant interactions: The foraging behavior of bees and wasps on artificial flowers. *Ecology* 62:20–26

Roberts, W. A. 1984. Some issues in animal spatial memory. See Roitblat et al 1984, pp. 425–43

Roitblat, H. L. 1982a. The meaning of representation in animal memory. *Behav. Brain Sci.* 5:353–72

Roitblat, H. L. 1982b. Decision making, evolution and cognition. In *Evolution and Determination of Animal and Human Behavior,* ed. H. D. Schmidt, G. Tembrock, pp. 108–16. Berlin:VEB Deutscher Verlag der Wissenschaften

Roitblat, H. L., Bever, T. G., Terrace, H. S. 1984. *Animal Cognition.* Hillsdale, NJ: Erlbaum

Rozin, P., Kalat, J. W. 1971. Specific hungers and poison avoidance as adaptive specializations of learning. *Psychol. Rev.* 78:459–86

Schluter, D. 1981. Does the theory of optimal diets apply in complex environments? *Am. Nat.* 118:139–47

Schluter, D. 1982. Seed and patch selection by Galapagos ground finches: Relation to foraging efficiency and food supply. *Ecology* 63:1106–20

Sherry, D. F. 1982. Food storage, memory and marsh tits. *Anim. Behav.* 30:631–33

Sherry, D. F. 1984a. Food storage by black-capped chickadees: Memory for the location and contents of caches. *Anim. Behav.* 32:451–64

Sherry, D. F. 1984b. What food-storing birds remember. *Can. J. Psychol.* In press

Sherry, D. F., Avery, M., Stevens, A. 1982. The spacing of stored food by marsh tits. *Z. Tierpsychol.* 58:153–62

Sherry, D. F., Krebs, J. R., Cowie, R. J. 1981. Memory for the location of stored food in marsh tits. *Anim. Behav.* 29:1260–66

Shettleworth, S. J. 1983. Function and mechanism in learning. In *Advances in Analysis of Behavior, Vol. 3. Biological Factors in Learning,* ed. M. D. Zeiler, P. Harzem, pp. 1–39. New York: Wiley

Shettleworth, S. J. 1984. Learning and behavioral ecology. In *Behavioral Ecology,* ed. J. R. Krebs, N. B. Davies, pp. 170–94. Sunderland, Mass: Sinauer. 2nd ed.

Shettleworth, S. J., Krebs, J. R. 1982. How marsh tits find their hoards: The roles of site preference and spatial memory. *J. Exp. Psychol.: Anim. Behav. Proc.* 8:354–75

Shimp, L. P. 1969. Optimal behavior in free-operant experiments. *Psychol. Rev.* 76:97–112

Sih, A. 1980. Optimal behavior: Can foragers

balance two conflicting demands? *Science* 210:1041–43

Simon, H. A. 1956. Rational choice and the structure of the environment. *Psychol. Rev.* 63:129–38

Smith, J. N. M., Sweatman, H. P. A. 1974. Food searching behavior of titmice in patchy environments. *Ecology* 55:1216–32

Snowdon, C. 1983. Ethology, comparative psychology, and animal behavior. *Ann. Rev. Psychol.* 34:63–94

Snyderman, M. 1983a. Optimal prey selection: Partial selection, delay of reinforcement and self control. *Behav. Anal. Lett.* 3:131–48

Snyderman, M. 1983b. Optimal prey selection: The effects of deprivation. *Behav. Anal. Lett.* 3:359–70

Staddon, J. E. R. 1980. Optimality analyses of operant behavior and their relation to optimal foraging. In *Limits to Action: The Allocation of Individual Behavior*, ed. J. E. R. Staddon, pp. 101–42. New York: Academic

Staddon, J. E. R., Motheral, S. 1978. On matching and maximizing in operant choice experiments. *Psychol. Rev.* 85:436–44

Stephens, D. W. 1981. The logic of risk-sensitive foraging preferences. *Anim. Behav.* 29:628–29

Swanberg, P. 1951. Food storage, territory and song in the thick-billed nutcracker. *Proc. 10th Int. Ornithol. Congr.* 10:545–54

Taylor, R. J. 1984. Foraging in the eastern gray kangaroo and the wallaboo. *J. Anim. Ecol.* 53:65–74

Tinbergen, J. M. 1981. Foraging decisions in starlings, *Sturnus vulgaris* L. *Ardea* 69:1–67

Tinbergen, N. 1951. *The Study of Instinct.* Oxford: Oxford Univ. Press

Tomback, D. F. 1977. Foraging strategies of Clark's nutcrackers. *Living Bird* 16:123–61

Tomback, D. F. 1980. How nutcrackers find their seed stores. *Condor* 82:10–19

Tomback, D. F. 1983. Nutcrackers and pines: Coevolution or coadaptation? In *Coevolution*, ed. M. H. Nitecki, pp. 179–223. Chicago: Univ. Chicago Press

Turcek, F., Kelso, L. 1968. Ecological aspects of food transportation and storage in the Corvidae. *Comm. Behav. Biol., Part A* 1:277–97

Vander Wall, S. B. 1982. An experimental analysis of cache recovery in Clark's Nutcracker. *Anim. Behav.* 30:84–94

Vander Wall, S. B., Balda, R. P. 1977. Codaptations of the Clark's nutcracker

and the pinon pine for efficient seed harvest and dispersal. *Ecol. Monogr.* 47:89–111

Vander Wall, S. B., Balda, R. P. 1981. Ecology and evolution of food-storage behavior in conifer-seed-caching corvids. *Z. Tierpsychol.* 56:217–42

Waage, J. K. 1979. Foraging for patchily-distributed hosts by the parasitoid, *Nemeritis canescens. J. Anim. Ecol.* 48:353–71

Waddington, K. D., Allen, T., Heinrich, B. 1981. Floral preferences of bumblebees (*Bombus edwardsii*) in relation to intermittent versus continuous rewards. *Anim. Behav.* 29:779–84

Waddington, K. D., Holden, L. R. 1979. Optimal foraging: On flower selection by bees. *Am. Nat.* 114:179–96

Wahrenberger, D. L., Antle, C. E., Klimko, L. A. 1977. Bayesian rules for the two-armed bandit. *Biometrika* 64:172–74

Werner, E. E., Gilliam, J. F., Hall, D. J., Mittelbach, G. G. 1983b. An experimental test of the effects of predation risk on habitat use in fish. *Ecology* 64:1540–48

Werner, E. E., Hall, D. J. 1974. Optimal foraging and size selection of prey by the bluegill sunfish (*Lepomis macrochirus*). *Ecology* 55:1042–52

Werner, E. E., Hall, D. J. 1976. Niche shifts in sunfishes: Experimental evidence and significance. *Science* 191:404–6

Werner, E. E., Hall, D. J. 1979. Foraging efficiency and habitat switching in competing sunfishes. *Ecology* 60:256–64

Werner, E. E., Mittelbach, G. G. 1981. Optimal foraging: Field tests of diet choice and habitat switching. *Am. Zool.* 21:813–29

Werner, E. E., Mittelbach, G. G., Hall, D. J. 1981. The role of foraging profitability and experience in habitat use by the bluegill sunfish. *Ecology* 62:116–25

Werner, E. E., Mittelbach, G. G., Hall, D. J., Gilliam, J. F. 1983a. Experimental tests of optimal habitat use in fish: The role of relative habitat profitability. *Ecology* 64:1525–39

Wilson, E. O. 1975. *Sociobiology: The New Synthesis.* Cambridge: Harvard Univ. Press

Zach, R., Falls, J. B. 1976. Ovenbird (Aves: Parulidae) hunting behavior in a patchy environment: An experimental study. *Can. J. Zool.* 54:1863–79

Zach, R., Smith, J. 1981. Optimal foraging in wild birds? See Kamil & Sargent 1981, pp. 95–110

Ann. Rev. Psychol. 1985. 36:171–218

ANIMAL BEHAVIOR GENETICS: A Search for the Biological Foundations of Behavior

R. E. Wimer and C. C. Wimer[1]

Division of Neurosciences, Beckman Research Institute, City of Hope, Duarte, California 91010

CONTENTS

[1] Preparation of this review was supported in part by Grant NS-18860 from the National Institutes of Neurological and Communicative Disorders and Stroke.

171

0066-4308/85/0201-0171$02.00

INTRODUCTION

Behavior genetics is the study of the hereditary bases of behavior. A comprehensive description of a genetically associated behavior would obviously include genes; primary gene products and their developmental interactions; chemical, physiological, and morphological effects; and—ultimately—evolutionary implications. People who consider themselves behavior geneticists may be found working at each of the levels of description mentioned above, and with species ranging from bacteria to man. Such a comprehensive description as that indicated above extends far beyond psychology as it is currently conceived, but we limit this review to topics within the province of psychology.

Because of the great diversity of interests represented by just those animal behavior geneticists working on topics of historical or potential interest to psychologists, there is a corresponding marked diversity of opinion as to which levels of description should be assigned the highest immediate priority, and which genetic strategies should be employed. Predictably, geneticists have tended to be enchanted by the genetic level, and chemists to be engrossed by the chemical. A good case can be made that many of the greatest discoveries of twentieth century biology have resulted from the use of mutant stocks of simple organisms (Davis 1980), and that—on the basis of prior success—this is a tradition that should be continued most vigorously (Quinn & Gould 1979, Burnet & Connolly 1981, Hall et al 1982). Others may point with justifiable enthusiasm to the great attainments of biometrical genetics and population-biological thinking in this century (Davis 1980), and advocate the pursuit of those levels of analysis and description (Fulker 1981). We will do our best to present an integrated perspective.

THE BEHAVIOR GENETICIST'S TOOLBOX

The purpose of this section is to introduce some major terms, concepts, and experimental techniques currently in use in animal behavior genetics.

Basic Definitions and Concepts

A *gene* is a functionally defined sequence of DNA which, through processes including transcription and translation, results in a chain of amino acids called a polypeptide. Genes are arranged in linear sequences in larger aggregates called *chromosomes*. The X and Y chromosomes are involved in primary sex determination. The other chromosomes are referred to collectively as *autosomes*. *Recombination* is the consequence of exchange of segments between two chromosome members of the homologous set. The result can be new combinations of genes upon each chromosome. Genes on the same chromosome tend to show *linkage*, nonrandom assortment. Genes close to each other are less likely to undergo recombination. Knowledge of recombination frequencies between linked genes may be used to deduce their linear sequence, and thus construct a *linkage map*.

Alternate gene forms capable of occupying the equivalent chromosomal location *(locus)* are called *alleles*. A *point mutation,* an alteration in genetic code within a gene, involves base-pair substitutions, additions, or deletions. *Mutation* may be used more broadly to refer to any genetic change, including changes in chromosome number *(ploidy)* and structural alterations of large chromosome segments. In *diploid* organisms, those possessing two of each chromosome, the pair of genes present at any locus may be the same *(homozygous),* or different *(heterozygous)*. In the formation of *Drosophila* and human sperm cells and eggs, a process called *meiosis* eventually involves the sorting of one, and ordinarily only one, member of each chromosome pair to each germ cell. This is the physical basis for the *segregation* of two alleles. Separation between each chromosomal pair occurs independently of other chromosome pairs, and this is the physical basis for the genetic phenomenon of *independent assortment* of nonalleles.

Phenotype and *character* refer to some observable feature of an organism, while *genotype* refers to the complete set of genes it possesses. *Dominance* occurs when heterozygotes resemble one of the two possible homozygotes. A character may be a quantifiable and continuous phenotype or it may occur in two or more relatively common and qualitatively different states, i.e. *polymorphisms*. A *major gene* has detectable phenotypic consequences by itself, though a phenotype may be associated with the actions of several such genes, i.e. be *multifactorial*. In many instances of multifactorial inheritance, the effects of the individual genes *(polygenes)* may not be detectable at the level of the character, the effects of gene substitutions may be equivalent, and the phenotype may be determined by the cumulative effects of large numbers of these genes, i.e. be *polygenic* (Mather & Jinks 1971, Thoday 1979). Mather & Jinks (1971) have likened major genes to the genetic skeleton of an organism, and polygenes to the clothing that covers it. Polygenic systems are thought of as providing adaptive changes for fine adjustment.

Selection is the differential production of genotypes on the basis of phenotype. Practically, it is the process of rendering characters more or less common through differential breeding to alter their frequency. A *line* or *stock* is a group of animals maintained for some purpose. *Inbreeding* is the mating of genetically similar individuals. A line becomes an *inbred strain* when it has been consistently brother-sister mated for (in mice) no less than 20 generations so that the animals become homogeneous. Different inbred strains may vary from one another greatly. Because of knowledge of definite or highly probable genetic differences between them, inbred strains are sometimes divided into subdivision called *substrains*. The term *subline* is used to identify separately animals within a strain or substrain that have been treated differently. Maintenance in laboratories of different investigators is sufficient to produce different sublines (Green 1981).

A mutation may occur in a mouse that is a member of an inbred strain, creating two substrains differing at a single locus. The two substrains are said to be *coisogenic*. It is also possible to transfer a gene residing in one stock to a specific inbred strain by a mating system involving repeated *backcrossing*, which (in the simplest case) involves repeated mating of the heterozygote to the inbred strain. After a number of backcross generations (at least 10) two specific substrains will have resulted: the original inbred strain, and another possessing the transferred gene and genes closely linked to it. The genetic difference between these two *congenic* substrains is greater than is the difference between coisogenic substrains. Inbred strains are extremely useful for establishing the fact that variation in some phenotype is genotype dependent. Further, inbred strains represent gene banks, stable repositories of genes for extreme phenotypes, which can be unlocked through crossing to provide progeny for precise genetic analyses. If two different inbred strains are mated, the resulting progeny (F_1 hybrids) will be of uniform composition genetically. They will be consistently homozygous for alleles for which the parental strains do not differ and uniformly heterozygous for alleles for which they do. Intercrossing F_1 animals produces a second filial generation (F_2), in which alleles have an opportunity to display segregation and independent assortment.

Special Genetic Techniques

RECOMBINANT INBRED STRAINS   This technique is extremely powerful (Bailey 1971, 1981). Two progenitor inbred strains are crossed and the resulting F_1 progeny are intercrossed. The resulting F_2 progeny are organized into sets of one brother-sister pair each. Inbreeding is pursued separately within each newly established line for 20 generations. The genes initially frozen together by inbreeding into separate combinations in the progenitor strains are provided with a large number of opportunities to recombine and thus come together in the newly forming recombinant inbred (RI) strains. The result is a series of new inbred strains, each limited to a sampling of genes originally present in the two progenitor inbred strains, but now in new combinations that may vary for each RI strain. Consider any two characteristics for which the two progenitor strains differ. Examination of the distribution of those characters among the RI strains can reveal whether they are likely to be under common or separable genetic control, and whether the genetic association is likely to involve a major gene or a polygenic system. Biochemical polymorphisms whose gene locations are known may be used to establish the chromosomal locations of genes associated with characters of interest. This basic process may be repeated indefinitely for any two characters for which the progenitor strains are found to differ.

CHIMERAS AND MOSAICS   *Chimeras* are animals whose cells originate from more than one fertilized egg. They are formed by putting together cells from different embryos at a very early stage of development. The composite embryos that result are transferred to the uterus of a pseudopregnant female to complete their development. If a pair of mouse embryos, one mutant and the other normal, are fused to produce a chimeric fetus, the resulting adult represents a composite of normal and mutant cells. Chimeras offer the possibility of establishing the critical tissue for gene action because, if the primary site of mutant action involves that tissue, all behaviorally affected individuals should possess cells of mutant embryonic origin within it (McLaren 1976). The use of chimeras to study neurological mutant rats and mice is summarized by Mullen & Herrup (1979). Nesbitt et al (1979, 1981) performed behavioral studies using mouse chimeras composed of cells from two inbred strains. The chimeric mice were tested behaviorally for open-field activity, alcohol preference, attacking crickets, and rope climbing—all behaviors in which the two progenitor strains differed substantially. Evidence for three separate groupings of behavioral measures were obtained, suggesting that the neurobiological foundations for the behaviors involve three different biological systems. Cellular compositions of chimeric tissues were studied to identify strain of origin, and this information was used to tentatively identify associations between specific sets of tissues and groups of behaviors.

A *mosaic* is an animal derived from a single embryo, but composed of cells of at least two genotypes. Genetic variegation occurs during development as a result of genetic changes occurring in individual cells. Female mammals are mosaics for any X-linked gene for which they are heterozygotes because a process largely inactivates one X in each cell of the female body. The mosaicism that results is relatively fine. Mosaicism in *Drosophila* can be generated by several techniques, including use of an unstable ring-X chromosome, or use of chromosome-destabilizing mutants (Benzer 1973, Hall et al 1976). For example, the ring-X chromosome may be used to carry normal alleles not of interest. A mutant gene that is of interest is located upon a stable X. The ring-X (X_R) tends to be lost during the first division of the nucleus of the female *Drosophila* embryo, and can result in two clones of nuclei, those that are XX_R and those that are X0. XX_R cells have gene products of normal alleles contained on the X_R chromosome, while X0 cells have only abnormal products of the mutant gene on the stable X. The number and identities of progenitor cells affected varies between embryos, and the location and extensiveness of mosaicism varies between individual adult *Drosophila* in a corresponding manner. A great variety of mosaics are formed. Examination of the adult *Drosophila*, and knowledge of the embryonic origins of various portions are used in a mathematical process called *fate mapping*. Fate mapping permits estimates of the locations of mutant embryonic cells (the *focus*). This in turn permits deductions concerning the locations of adult tissues likely to have been affected. Hotta and Benzer (1972) employed these techniques to identify essential tissues for such *Drosophila* mutants as drop-dead and wings-up. The number of progenitor cells giving rise to a structure may be estimated through observing the fineness of the mosaicism exhibited by the structure (Hall et al 1982).

BIOMETRICAL GENETICS   There are two great traditions in genetics: Mendelian genetics and biometrical genetics (Jinks & Broadhurst 1974, Jinks 1979). Mendelian genetics is concerned with major genes. Classic Mendelian analyses are initiated by a *cross,* a mating of unlike homozygotes, to establish dominance and recessivity in the F_1 hybrid. Intercrosses between F_1 hybrids result in segregating F_2 progeny in the ratios 1:2:1 of genotypes and—with dominance—3:1 for phenotypes. The classic confirming *testcross,* and backcross of the F_1 hybrid to the homozygous recessive parent, has an expected ratio of 1:1 both for genotype and for phenotype.

Biometrical genetics deals primarily with continuous variation and is concerned with making quantitative statements about polygenic inheritance. Phenotypic variation results from a combination of genotypic and environmental variation. Genetic and environmental terms are each partitioned into a number of quantifiable components. Thus, the genetic term is divided into fixable (additive), nonfixable (dominance), and nonallelic (interlocus or *epistatic*) interaction components. The environmental term has its components as well, and a genotype-environment ($G \times E$) interaction term is included. Genetic materials and environments are selected to suit this components-of-variance model. Answers that directly result from biometrical analyses are a series of numbers representing the relative contributions of the various genetic and environmental components to total phenotypic variation. *Heritability* of a phenotype is defined as the ratio of an additive (fixable) component to the total phenotypic variance. The *coefficient of genetic determination* (heritability in the broad sense) is the ratio of the sum of *all* the various genetic components to total phenotypic variance.

GENETIC ARCHITECTURE   The *genetic architecture* of a character is the patterning of its genetic determinants. The relative sizes of the quantitative additive, dominance, and (duplicate) nonallelic interaction terms provided by biometrical genetics have been used in an attempt to learn more about the evolutionary histories of behavioral characters (Mather 1973, Broadhurst & Jinks 1974, Broadhurst 1979)

Animals are subject to three types of selection pressures. *Stabilizing* selection favors the intermediate phenotype. *Directional* selection, occurring during occasions of large-scale environmental change, favors one phenotypic extreme over the other and moves the entire population in that direction. *Disruptive* selection favors sharply differing optimal phenotypes and can occur on the basis of, say, environmental variation over the range of a diverse territory. Each type of selection may be anticipated to result in distinctive genetic architectures. For example, stabilizing selection for a character should result in a large additive term, relative to the dominance term. Directional selection should result in dominance of genes toward one phenotypic extreme. Disruptive selection should result in sex dimorphisms and polymorphisms, phenotypic states not particularly appropriate for biometrical genetic analysis, but with distinctive genetic architectures nevertheless.

When defined with regard to genetic architecture, characters are of three types. First, there is *fitness*, i.e. reproductive success. Fitness is a composite character, and one can never have too much. Thus, there should always be directional dominance toward high fitness. The fitness composite consists of a number of subcharacters—*fitness-related* characters—which jointly determine it, and these should also exhibit some directional dominance. Finally, there are *peripheral* characters not directly comprising fitness, but only affecting it when they deviate from some intermediate optimum. These characters should show a large additive component of genetic variation.

The topic of genetic architecture has been the subject of two thoughtful critiques. Maxson (1973) examined assumptions underlying the expected relations between types of selection pressure and kinds of genetic architecture. These are (*a*) that the entire experimental population is derived from a single potentially interbreeding natural population, and (*b*) that the laboratory population is a representative sample of the natural population. Maxson shows that neither assumption can be met even approximately by existing studies. Henderson (1979) basically agrees, but argues that violation of this assumption may not be as critical as Maxson suggests. Henderson's robustness argument is based upon the intuitive rightness of fitness values that have actually been obtained for various characters.

SOME GENERAL TOPICS

Recent Books and General Reviews

Since the last *Annual Review of Psychology* chapter covering animal behavior genetics (DeFries & Plomin 1978), there have been several comprehensive reviews of the field, both experimental and theoretical. Fuller & Thompson's *Foundations of Behavior Genetics* (1978) brought up to date their classic 1960 text and provided broad coverage of advances in the field. General surveys can also be found in Plomin et al (1980) and Ehrman & Parsons (1981). In 1979, Royce & Mos published the proceedings of a symposium on the latest theoretical advances, a landmark compilation of some of the major approaches to the field. Reviews by Hall (1984) and Quinn & Greenspan (1984) covered *Drosophila,* especially learning and courtship behavior, with emphasis on biological foundations. Partridge's excellent review (1984) emphasized recent developments and new techniques. Fuller & Simmel (1983) provided multiauthor coverage of subfields of behavior genetics. Because several of these subfields have been reviewed so recently, we cover them only briefly below.

Ethology and Ecology

The study of species-typical behaviors and their interactions with environment can be of great value to behavior geneticists, while behavior-genetic analysis, in turn, has considerable potential in the study of ethology and ecology (van Abeelen 1979, Fuller 1983a). One of the advantages of an ethological approach is that it encourages the exploration of qualitative variation. Most laboratory tasks, and the measures and analyses employed in the assessment of performance on laboratory tasks, are structured to emphasize quantitative variation. Observations of behavior in a natural environment are not necessarily so restricted. Immelmann's (1979) studies of the development of imprinting in zebra finches do not involve genetic "experiments" per se, but the careful analysis of individual differences permits inferences about the evolution of the trait and hypotheses about the genetic bases of variation. They also provide a solid ground for subsequent genetic analysis.

Feeding and foraging strategies and patterns have been of considerable interest to animal behaviorists (e.g. Kamil & Roitblat 1985), but they have not often been studied by behavior-genetic methods. An exception is the work of Gray and his associates. In an ingeniously designed study, Gray (1979) investigated feeding behavior in two related subspecies of deermice from differing natural environments. Although there was considerable between-individual variation in both subspecies, one of them showed significantly more *within*-individual diversity in both obtaining and consuming food. Gray suggested that the more diverse subspecies may have evolved in a more unpredictable environment, in which a variety of feeding responses in an individual's repertoire would be more adaptive. A study of the development of feeding diversity in four species of deermice (Gray & Tardif 1979) revealed that all species became more specialized with age, but that they varied with respect to the susceptibility to developmental change of each behavior. Results of these studies point to the necessity of examining the interplay among genes, environment, and development in the study of feeding behavior (Gray 1981).

Sokolowski and her associates have studied larval foraging behavior in *Drosophila.* They identified a genetic difference in locomotor behavior that resulted in differences in foraging strategy (Sokolowski 1980). Subsequent species comparisons (Sokolowski & Hansell 1983) and selection studies (Soko-lowski et al 1983) led to inferences about the evolution of a "roving" vs a "sitting" strategy. Recent studies (Sokolowski et al 1984) have examined environmental effects on foraging behavior and traced developmental changes.

Social Behavior

Because of the complex nature of social systems, it has not been feasible to subject them to genetic analysis; instead, the approach has been to manipulate genotype and study the effects on social systems (Scott 1983). Sociobiology (Wilson 1975) may be an exception, but we leave exploration of that possibility to other reviewers (see Thiessen 1979, Fuller 1983b). Gurski (1983, Gurski & Scott 1980) reviewed social aspects of parent-offspring relationships in a range of species from invertebrates to primates. A long-term program on social behavior in various breeds of dogs was reviewed by Scott (1977), who pre-sented a strong case for their use in the study of social behavior genetics. A philosophical and theoretical introduction to the field was provided by Gins-burg (1978).

Psychopharmacology

The existence of genetically associated differences in drug effects has provided the basis for extensive research, involving a variety of approaches (Petersen 1982). With the exception of the work on alcohol (see below) few conclusive results have emerged. Genes that determine behavioral drug response have not been identified (Lush 1981). Critical reviews of research are provided by Broadhurst (1978), Shuster (1982), and Horowitz & Dudek (1983). Crabbe & Belknap (1980) reviewed the literature on genetic determinants of drug depen-dence for a variety of substances. They found few studies of stimulants, but a number involving opiates and barbiturates. A problem with opiates has been that the established genetic differences in sensitivity do not seen to be corre-lated with variations in the substrate of opiate receptor binding. With respect to barbiturates, sensitivity is independent of sensitivity to ethanol and is apparent-ly controlled in a different way from the development of tolerance. One major difficulty is that genetic variation in behavioral response has often proved to be based on "dispositional" differences, such as metabolic rate, rather than on functional differences in neurosensitivity.

ANIMAL MODELS FOR HUMAN DISEASE AND BEHAVIOR DISORDERS

Animals models are clearly of value in the study of etiology of human diseases and in the search for effective treatments. The study of animal models has taken several forms. There are studies of alterations in brain and behavior in diseases with a known (or suspected) genetic basis, e.g. autoimmune disorders, Down's

Syndrome (Cox et al 1984), hypertension (Nelson & Boulant 1981), and obesity (Ramirez & Sprott 1978, 1979, Burkhart et al 1983). Major gene effects on behavior are sometimes discovered by accident, then subsequently exploited in the search for mechanisms. Neurological mutants fall into this category, as do a number of animal models for epilepsy. There are also models in which animals have been selectively bred for extreme behavioral traits, such as the Maudsley strains of rats bred for high and low reactivity or emotionality, and the "nervous pointer dogs." Finally, there are research programs that combine a number of these techniques to achieve a clearer comprehension of a clinical syndrome. This approach is best exemplified in the long series of studies on alcohol dependence. Recent research in each of these categories is discussed below.

Convulsive Disorders

Behavioral disorders characterized by recurrent seizure activity—the epilepsies—occur in many species of animals. Thus there are a number of animal models for inherited epilepsy, and much research has been devoted to establishing parallels between animal and human disorders. Seyfried (1982a) published an extensive review of this work. A 1979 symposium on genetic models, sponsored by the American Society for Pharmacology and Experimental Therapeutics, was reported in the 1979 *Federation Proceedings*; among other speakers, Noebels (1979) presented arguments for the use of single-gene mutations in mice, and Consroe et al (1979) described the derivation and use of seizure-susceptible rats. Jobe & Laird (1981) reviewed the evidence for neurotransmitter abnormalities in a variety of genetic seizure models. Löscher & Meldrum (1983) summarized an international symposium concerned with the use of various models in the evaluation of anticonvulsant drugs. Because of the availability of extensive recent reviews, only the most recent research reports are mentioned here.

The most widely used model is the audiogenic-seizure-prone mouse (see reviews by Seyfried 1979, 1982b). Research began with Hall's discovery in 1947 of a difference in susceptibility to seizures triggered by sound between two inbred strains, DBA/2 (susceptible) and C57BL/6 (nonsusceptible). Extensive comparison of these strains has led to a variety of hypotheses about the genetic basis of the variation, its developmental course, and environmental influences on its expression. While most investigators accept a polygenic inheritance for the susceptibility trait, some experiments suggest the involvement of major genes. Seyfried & Glaser (1981) proposed a major gene that inhibits seizure susceptibility on the basis of studies of recombinant inbred strains, congenic lines, and backcrosses involving DBA/2 and C57BL/6. It has subsequently been found (Seyfried 1983) that this gene is associated only with juvenile-onset susceptibility; adult-onset susceptibility is controlled by a different genetic mechanism. There have been a number of neurochemical and endocrine studies on these two strains of mice, implicating the involvement of, for example, variations in neurotransmitter metabolism, abnormalities in ion transport, and levels of thyroid hormone (Seyfried 1982a). Most recently, Dailey & Jobe (1984) found that the anticonvulsant effects of L-dopa in seizure-prone DBA/2 were mediated by its conversion to dopamine. They concluded that the mechanism of seizure regulation is different in these mice than in audiogenic-seizure-prone rats, in which dopamine must be converted to norepinephrine to reduce seizure susceptibility (Jobe et al 1982, Ko et al 1982).

The various lines of audiogenic-seizure-susceptible rats, developed by unidirectional selective breeding of Sprague-Dawley stocks, are not as genetically defined as are the mouse strains, and studies have primarily concentrated on development, biological bases, and effects of anticonvulsant agents (Consroe et al 1979, 1980). The Shreveport lines have low thresholds for convulsions induced by hypothermia, electrical stimulation, and convulsive drugs in addition to sound; these lines are now called "genetically epilepsy-prone" (Penny et al 1983). They have abnormalities in noradrenergic (Jobe et al 1984a) and monoaminergic (Dailey et al 1982, Ko et al 1984) function in the central nervous system. Some noradrenergic abnormalities are present in seizure-prone mice before they have had a seizure, and thus may provide a basis for increased seizure susceptibility; others are apparent only after a seizure, which suggests that they have been induced by the seizure or the treatment that produced it (Dailey & Jobe 1983). Morphological abnormalities were found in the cochlea (Penny et al 1983), and it has been suggested that hyperreactivity to acoustic stimulation is related to mechanisms compensating for the hearing loss associated with cochlear damage (Faingold et al 1983). The utility of this stock for the testing of anticonvulsant drugs was demonstrated by Jobe et al (1984b).

There are other less well-established genetic models. Rabbits susceptible to seizures induced by tetrahydrocannabinol, the major psychoactive ingredient in marijuana, have been bred at the University of Arizona (Consroe & Fish 1980). EEG patterns are comparable to those produced by marijuana in humans (Consroe & Martin 1981). Seizure susceptibility is attributed to a single gene (Fish et al 1981).

Most of the models for inherited epilepsy heretofore described were triggered by a defined stimulus or treatment. But many human epilepsies are "spontaneous" (that is, the precipitating event is either nonexistent or unknown). Some mouse mutants, not extensively studied, also exhibit spontaneous (or perhaps normal handling-induced) seizures. These include some described by Noebels (1979), "tottering" (Kaplan et al 1979), a new single-gene mutation described by Maxson et al (1983a), and one of a set of recombinant inbred strains currently being developed in our laboratory (unpublished).

Alcoholism

Behavioral response to alcohol has been extensively studied in animal models (for recent reviews see Horowitz & Dudek 1983, Crabbe et al 1984). We compare here four mouse models—developed by genetic selection—designed for the investigation of three aspects of the alcohol response: preference, sensitivity, and dependence. Some of the earliest behavior-genetic studies on alcoholism resulted from the discovery of a difference between inbred mouse strains in preference for alcohol (McClearn & Rodgers 1961). When given a choice, some strains consume substantial amounts of alcohol, while others drink only water. A major metabolic substrate for this difference appears to be alcohol dehydrogenase activity in the liver, with alcohol-preferring strains having higher activity (Anderson et al 1979). Genetic analyses have generally found voluntary alcohol consumption to be a polygenic trait, with low heritability and dominance for low consumption (e.g. Drewek & Broadhurst 1983). Two lines of mice have been selected for high and low ethanol preference (Anderson & McClearn 1981; see also rats selected by Lumeng et al 1977). In spite of some difficulties in defining the nature of the difference between the two lines, they may prove to represent a useful model for the first stage of alcoholism, preference.

Behavioral sensitivity to alcohol can be measured in a number of different ways. Crabbe (1983) found evidence for separate genetic control of at least two distinct classes of behavioral effects: "Hypothermic sensitivity" includes loss of body temperature, ataxia, and long-lasting loss of righting reflex; "activity change" includes either increases or decreases in several activity measures. A representative behavior from the hypothermic class is the duration of "sleep time" (sleep being defined as failure of the righting reflex) following a hypnotic dose of ethanol. The Colorado Long and Short Sleep lines of mice have been genetically selected for this phenotype (McClearn & Kakihana 1981; for a review of research on these lines, see Collins 1981). There was considerable additive genetic variance available for selection, and thus the selected lines diverged considerably (Dudek & Abbott 1981). Several possible neurochemical associations have been pursued, including dopaminergic involvement (e.g. Dudek & Fanelli 1980, Dudek et al 1984). Neurophysiological studies suggest that the sedative effect may result from depression of activity in cerebellar Purkinje neurons (Spuhler et al 1982).

There have been two major selection studies for alcohol dependence. The Colorado lines, called Mild and Severe Ethanol Withdrawal, were developed according to a complex selection criterion based on a multivariate analysis (McClearn et al 1982, Allen et al 1983). The selection index includes pharmacological measures, hypothermia, seizure severity during withdrawal, and several behavioral measures from a battery described by Hutchins et al (1981). Alcohol is administered via a forced liquid diet, then withheld during withdrawal testing. These lines are still undergoing selection. Preliminary results indicate that alcohol consumption has increased in all lines. The Mild Withdrawal lines appear to have reduced sensitivity to acute doses of ethanol as indicated by sleep time, but no relation has been found between severity of withdrawal and hypothermia (Wilson et al 1984). The Oregon lines, called Withdrawal Seizure Prone and Resistant, are a recent development (Crabbe et al 1983a). Dependence is induced via ethanol vapor inhalation, and the selection criterion is seizure severity during withdrawal. In contrast to the Colorado lines, withdrawal severity appears to be *negatively* correlated with initial sensitivity, as measured by hypothermia. Lack of hypothermic sensitivity has been suggested as a marker for potential alcoholism (Crabbe et al 1983c,d). Harris et al (1984) reported that the lines do not differ in ethanol metabolism or levels of ethanol in blood or brain during either dietary or inhalation treatment.

In selecting a model for alcoholism, it would seem that the central phenotype should be dependence. The most direct approach should be to select for that phenotype, as the last two studies described did. Supporting this is evidence that the phenotypes of preference and sensitivity (at least according to some indices) are only moderatly related to dependence. For example, Allen et al (1982) found that preference for alcohol in a hererogeneous stock of mice was not related to seizure severity during withdrawal after forced ingestion, although there was a drop in preference after withdrawal. Crabbe et al (1983b) compared recombinant inbred strains of mice constructed from the two strains originally found to represent opposite ends of the preference scale. Strain distribution patterns for alcohol acceptance or intake and for withdrawal severity were uncorrelated. Similarly, two measures of sensitivity, activity change and ataxia, were also unrelated to each other. These and other results suggest that sensitivity to the effects of alcohol is a very complex phenotype, and one that is poorly understood as yet. Of the two selection studies for dependence, it would seem that the Colorado lines, with a broadly based selection criterion, might provide a particularly useful model. On the other hand, the complexities of interpretation apparent in studies with these lines suggest that generalizations about human alcoholism may be difficult to make from this model.

Emotionality: The Maudsley Model

The Maudsley reactive (MR) and nonreactive (MNR) strains of rats were selected not so much to model a behavior disorder, but to provide a tool for the study of Eysenck's (1967) emotionality dimension of human personality. The phenotype selected for was defecation in the open field, based on the rationale that a bright, open test arena would be an aversive stimulus for the rat, and the response of defecation would be an index of emotionality (Blizard 1981). There is some disagreement about the validity of the rationale (and thus, the validity of the model for human emotionality), but in any case, the lines have been used extensively for the investigation of reactivity to stress. Selection was bidirectional, but the response was asymmetrical: there was little increase in defecation in the MRs, while number of boli in the MNRs rapidly decreased to near zero. Three North American sets of lines were derived from the original British set, and have been used extensively. The Iowa lines (Harrington 1981) are particularly useful, since two replications of the MNRs differ from each other on several measures, thus providing a test of hypotheses derived from the original unreplicated lines. In addition, Blizard (1981) developed a set of recombinant inbred strains from a cross between MRs and MNRs. These lines, when fully inbred, should be particularly useful in the study of biological substrates of stress reactivity.

Surveys, discussions of results, and comparisons of sublines have been published by Broadhurst (1975) and Blizard (1981). In general, the differences in behavior between the MRs and the MNRs are apparent under stressful but not under normal conditions. The variation in stress response is thought to reflect variation in autonomic arousal. High open-field defecation is associated with low levels of norepinephrine in tissues innervated by the peripheral sympathetic nervous system (Blizard et al 1982a,b). This is something of a paradox, since stress response is usually associated with heightened sympathetic activity. The paradox was partially resolved by Liang et al (1982), who showed that release of norepinephrine could have potentially greater physiological and behavioral consequences in the reactive lines. Blizard et al (1983) proposed that selection has altered the adaptability of the central and peripheral noradrenergic systems to chronic stress. Whether these findings are relevant to Eysenck's emotionality dimension remains to be determined, but selection for defecation in the open field has produced biologically significant variation in response to stress.

A Model in Search of a Disease: The Nervous Pointer Dogs

A selection experiment at the University of Arkansas has resulted in a line of dogs that is, in comparison to a control line, extremely "nervous." The strain has been proposed as a model for human psychopathology, but the parallel between the animal phenotype and the human behavior disorder is not clear. A marvelous description of the behavior of these dogs is provided by Reese et al (1983). Although they are normally active in the company of other dogs, nervous dogs respond to man as to a predator: they are timid and fearful, exhibiting freezing and immobility bordering on catatonia. The case for these dogs as a model for a phobia (specifically, anthropophobia) has been promoted by Dykman et al (1979). Nervous dogs are poor at operant-conditioning, have a very low heart rate with some cardiac dysrhythmias, and respond to some psychoactive drugs by a decrease in their "antisocial behavior" (Reese 1979). Reese proposed that the dogs respond more to negative than to positive reinforcement, and thus condition aversively to man. Frequent exposure to man eventually leads to a state resembling anxiety neurosis. Lucas et al (1981) reviewed physiological and biochemical characteristics of the dogs. Reduced sensitivity to morphine may reflect a lower density of opioid receptors in brain (Angel et al 1983). It appears that alterations in catecholaminergic, cholinergic, and serotonergic neurotransmitter systems are all involved. The reduced heart-rate response to humans, described by Newton & Lucas (1982), is thought to reflect abnormal dopaminergic function (Shideler et al 1983), perhaps specifically involving a dopaminergic nervous pathway to the heart (Seifen & Newton 1982).

There is also a canine model for a behavior disorder at the other end of the spectrum: hyperkinesis. Corson et al (1973) discovered that some dogs that were extremely agitated and could not be trained in a conditioning task responded to administration of amphetamine, as do hyperkinetic children. Ginsburg et al (1976) developed the model in Telomian-beagle hybrids. Results of several years of research were summarized and implications for dopaminergic involvment reviewed by Corson et al (1980) and by Ginsburg et al (1984).

Autoimmune Disorders

Among the potential disorders of the immune system is the failure to recognize one's own cells. The result is formation of antibodies that attack specific tissues, and lead to a group of diseases known as autoimmune disorders— among them systemic lupus erythematosus (SLE), myasthenia gravis, and rheumatoid arthritis. Autoimmune disease is more common in females than in males. Immune regulation has been shown to be associated with sex hormones, with androgen providing protection against SLE (Roubinian et al 1977). SLE in humans is known to affect the central nervous system and to have behavioral manifestations (e.g. Carr et al 1978). Geschwind & Behan reported an association between autoimmune disease, left-handedness, and a learning disorder— developmental dyslexia (Geschwind & Behan 1982). Galaburda & Kemper (1979) had already shown morphological abnormalities in the brain of a left-handed dyslexic patient, especially in regions associated with speech and language in the left hemisphere. Here, then, was a potential model for research: a genetically associated autoimmune disorder, subject to hormonal modulation, possibly resulting in neuroanatomical abnormalities, and leading to intellectual deficits.

An animal model for autoimmune disease had been known for some time— the New Zealand mouse strains NZB and NZW and their F_1 hybrid. (For summaries of research on these mice, see Milich & Gershwin 1981, Talal 1983.) It remained to demonstrate morphological abnormalities and behavioral deficits. Sherman et al (1983a) examined brains of mice from several strains and found clusters of out-of-place (ectopic) neurons in layer one of soma-tosensory cortex of young NZB mice. Nandy et al (1983) compared NZB mice (the autoimmune prototype) with C57BL/6 (a strain that is free of immune deficiencies until senescence) on an avoidance conditioning task. While they found a steady decline in learning ability with age in C57BL/6, NZB mice were unable to learn the task at *any* age. Deficits in performance were associated with increased levels of brain-reactive antibodies in serum—a normal accompaniment of aging, but one occurring precociously in NZB. On the basis of these results, the authors suggested NZB as a model for the study of Alzheimer's disease. Whether or not the strain proves to be useful in this respect, it is clear that it can shed light on the behavioral consequences of autoimmune disorders.

Aging

Aging may prove to be a productive research area for behavior genetics. Current aging research involves two major directions that have possibilities. The first concerns genetic effects on behavioral changes in normal aging. The second involves the search for genetic defects that may be associated with behavioral pathologies accompanying aging, especially senile dementia of the Alzheimer type. Major efforts have been devoted to the development of mammalian models for research (Committee on Animal Models for Research on Aging 1981; Brizzee et al 1978, Wisniewski 1979). The house mouse is the model most often used in studies of genetic aspects of aging (cf Zurcher et al 1982). Bellamy's (1981) discussion of the house mouse as a model for normal aging describes differing biological concepts of normal aging and explores various experimental approaches. The original hope was that long-lived and short-lived inbred mouse strains would help identify genes controlling the normal aging process, but research based on this hope has not been particularly productive. The search for primary genetic effects on age-dependent changes in learning and memory has been disappointing, although a number of secondary effects, e.g. genotype-dependent changes in motor ability, have been found (Sprott 1983). It may become possible to identify appropriate animal models once the neurobiological correlates of behavioral decline are better understood.

THE DISSECTION OF NORMAL BEHAVIOR

This section is devoted to the application of experimental genetics to the analysis of normal behavior. Topics include organization and development, individual variation, interactions with the environment, and adaptive value. Two major (and very general) phenotypes that have been extensively studied are activity and learning. Studies described below rely on comparisons of inbred strains, selection experiments, recombinant inbred strains, and biometrical genetic analyses.

Locomotor Activity and Exploratory Behavior

In behavior genetics, activity has been studied both as a trait with interrelated components and as a component (sometimes a confounding component) of other traits. Activity encompasses a variety of distinct behaviors. Simmel & Bagwell (1983) distinguish between locomotor activity and exploratory behavior. Rather than maintaining that distinction here, we mix the two categories together, where possible specifying behaviors operationally and leaving it to the reader to classify them.

STRAIN COMPARISONS   Comparisons of activity measures for sets of inbred strains tend to be early experiments. Several classic studies (Thompson 1956, McClearn 1959, 1961, Southwick & Clark 1968) established that there is a strong genetic component in several types of activity in inbred mice. Harrington (1972, 1979, 1981) established a stable genetic component among strains of rats for both locomotor and exploratory behavior. Although specific orderings of strains are not always consistent from experiment to experiment, most studies show strong positive correlation between most measures. In an unpublished study in our laboratory (reported in Tunnicliff et al 1973), however, we compared seven strains of mice on a number of measures. While there was consistency among tasks, we found two independent factors that cut across tasks: initiation and maintenance of activity. That is, a strain that has low latency of activity may or may not show a rapid decline in activity over time. Lassalle & LePape (1978) pointed out the necessity of taking housing conditions into account: They found that two mouse strains reversed order with respect to amount of diurnal activity, depending on whether they were tested in a breeding cage or a "seminatural" environment.

SELECTION STUDIES   Several major selection experiments have bred animals on the basis of some aspect of activity. The largest is a study of bidirectional selection for open-field activity, performed at the Institute for Behavioral Genetics, University of Colorado (DeFries et al 1978). Strong response to selection was obtained. There was no overlap between the means of the two high lines, two controls, and two lows after eight generations, and after 30 generations the lines continued to separate. At that point a mouse from the high-activity line could run the length of a football field in six minutes (Plomin et al 1980), while the lows were very nearly motionless in the open field. Van Abeelen (1975) selected for rearing frequency, also beginning with a cross between two strains of mice. After 40 generations there was about a three-fold difference in rearing frequency in the two lines (van Abeelen & van Nies 1983). These lines are now inbred, and have been used in genetic analyses and in studies of biological substrates of exploratory behavior. The Bethlem lines of rats (Sanders 1981) were also selected for rearing frequency. The foundation stock was a random-bred stock derived from nine different strains. By the tenth generation there was about a four-fold difference between highs and lows, and controls were intermediate. These relatively new lines have not yet been used extensively in behavioral research.

Van Dijken & colleagues bred *Drosophila* for high and low locomotor activity (van Dijken & Scharloo 1979a,b, van Dijken et al 1979). They concluded that a large part of the activity difference between lines was associated with genes on the X chromosome. Although genetic analyses indicated dominance for low activity, females apparently preferred to mate with high-activity males.

One of the interesting observations that can be made on selected lines is that of other traits also responding to selection, thereby indicating a genetic correlation. In both the open-field study and selection for rearing in rats, the low-activity lines are completely albino, while there are few albinos in the high-activity lines. This result is in accord with a theme that is recapitulated in many experiments: the albino locus has a number of behavioral effects, perhaps associated with visual system in this instance. In selection studies, of course, all genes associated with the selected trait tend to be selected for—and they tend to take on an apparent importance that is perhaps out of proportion to their association with the trait in unselected populations. Van Abeelen (1977) found that selection for rearing frequency was accompanied by a change in locomotor activity and suggested a common genetic basis for these two behaviors. There was also a strong negative relationship between defecation and activity in the open-field lines, in agreement with many other studies (including a definitive analysis using recombinant inbred strains; Blizard & Bailey 1979) that show a negative genetic correlation between these two phenotypes.

GENETIC ANALYSES   Different forms or levels of a behavior may be more or less adaptive at different stages of development. One might therefore expect the genetic architecture of those behaviors to exhibit concordant changes. Henderson (1978, 1981) demonstrated this phenomenon in studies of locomotor activity in the home-nest environment in 4- and 11-day-old infant mice. He found dominance for *low* activity in 4–5-day-old mice, at a stage when a pup that strays from the nest might be expected to have difficulty returning. From 8–9 days until eye opening, when motor ability is better developed, pups frequently stray from the nest but return rapidly. In this period, Henderson found dominance for *high* activity.

RECOMBINANT INBRED STRAINS   Two strains of mice are used extensively in studies of activity: BALB/c, a relatively inactive albino strain, and C57BL/6, the "standard" black strain, which is more active under most conditions. A set of recombinant inbred (RI) strains developed from a cross between these two lines (Bailey 1971) has proved useful in examining the genetic basis for the activity difference.

The initial study (Oliverio et al 1973) concluded from the strain distribution pattern that there is a single gene controlling "short-term exploratory activity." Probably because of the precision of the genetic technique, this gene is widely accepted, but it is not clear how the specific behavioral measure used—basically locomotor activity in a shuttle box—relates to any broader definition of exploratory activity or to other more traditional measures. Furthermore, behavioral testing was preceded by an IP injection of saline (as a control for drug administration in another group of mice). A subsequent experiment using the same strains and apparatus, but without the injection (Simmel & Bagwell 1983), failed to replicate the strain-distribution pattern found in the original study, and results did not lead to the conclusion of single-gene control. Simmel & Eleftheriou (1977) conducted a factor-analytic study of activity in the RI lines and found two orthogonal factors: (a) "Reactivity to novel stimuli" was confirmed (via congenic histocompatibility stocks) to be controlled by a gene or genes in a specific chromosomal segment; (b) "General activity" (which included the behavioral measure used by Oliverio et al) was found to fit a polygenic model.

These studies reflect a progression common in many areas of behavior genetics: from the establishment of a genetic component in a behavior, through exploration of its mode of inheritance, to the attempt to identify specific genes that are involved. They also illustrate the fact that increased precision in defining behavioral phenotypes must go hand-in-hand with increased genetic precision.

Learning

Probably the single most-researched topic in animal behavior genetics is learning, and there have been a number of very thorough reviews of the field (e.g. Wahlsten 1972, 1978, Bovet 1977; see also Broadhurst's 1979 survey of genetic architecture). We concentrate here on the association between learning and "central excitatory state" in insects and the analysis of avoidance performance in rats.

CONDITIONING IN THE BLOWFLY   The blowfly, *Phormia regina,* has taste receptors on hairs located on its lips (labellae) and feet (tarsi). For a food-deprived fly, application of sugar to these hairs typically produces an immediate extension of its proboscis. Food-deprived water-satiated blowflies do not ordinarily respond with proboscis extension when water is applied to these hairs, but they temporarily become likely to do so if their hairs have recently been stimulated by sugar (Dethier et al 1965). There is evidence that this phenomenon reflects a continuing central neural activity that declines over the course of a couple of minutes, a central excitatory state (CES). Nelson (1971) described a conditioning paradigm for the blowfly utilizing this phenomenon.

Conditioning consisted of the sequential application of two different conditioning stimuli (CS), distilled water or salt solution, to the tarsi. A drop of sucrose was applied to the labellum prior to termination of the second CS, and this resulted in extension of the proboscis and ingestion of the sugar. By the end of training, approximately half the blowflies were responding to the second CS while about a quarter were responding to the first CS. Since the first CS had been closer in time to the *last* application of sugar, but the second CS was much more effective in eliciting the proboscis extension, some associative learning appears to have occurred.

Hirsch and his associates conducted two selection experiments based upon magnitude of response to the second CS (Hirsch & McCauley 1977, McGuire & Hirsch 1977). Bidirectional selection for conditioning "brightness" and "dullness" resulted in gradual progressive divergence of the "brights" and "dulls." To examine the association between conditioning and CES, two selection experiments (McGuire 1981, Tully & Hirsch 1982a) used water-induced proboscis extension by "priming" with sucrose as the selection criterion. Extremely rapid response to selection for CES favored major gene involvement. Tully & Hirsch (1982b) crossed blowflies of their high and low CES lines. The resulting F_1 hybrids were backcrossed to the high and low lines, and intercrossed to produce segregating F_2 populations. CES testing was performed on these specimens. Analysis revealed a strong additive genetic component and a moderate environmental component. Supporting previous indications, these results once again favored involvement of segregation at a single locus.

Tully et al (1982) examined individual F_2 specimens initiated by the cross of selected high and low CES lines, and unselected free-mating blowflies. Specimens were tested for both CES and for conditioning. Correlations between the two measures for the two segregating populations were very similar ($+.51$ and $+.55$). McGuire (1983) also examined the association between CES and conditioning in individual specimens. Once again, CES and conditioning were found to be associated. The magnitudes of the correlations obtained, however, suggest that conditioning may involve other substantial determinants besides CES. Tully & Hirsch (1983) provided evidence for three nonassociative components of proboscis extension: base-level responsiveness, water-induced CES, and sucrose-induced CES. A line selected for high sucrose-induced CES exceeded selected lows not only for the selected trait, but also for water-induced CES level of reponsiveness. All three components may contribute to differences in conditionability among blowflies.

In an attempt to avoid the confounding effects of nonassociative factors, Zawistowski & Hirsch (1984) developed a conditioned discrimination procedure in which the positive and negative CS were switched during training, requiring the flies to make a discrimination reversal. A bidirectional selection experiment succeeded in producing lines of flies differing significantly in conditioned discrimination performances. Analysis of these lines is now underway.

Vargo & Hirsch (1982) presented evidence that sucrose-induced CES can be obtained in *Drosophila,* though there appear to be some interesting species differences. For example, water posttest for sucrose-CES appears to make this excitatory state disappear.

SELECTION FOR AVOIDANCE PERFORMANCE   Probably the most widely used lines of rats selected for avoidance performance are the Roman highs (RHA) and lows (RLA). These lines originated from an experiment initiated by Bignami (1965) in Rome and were later transferred to Birmingham, England, where a control line was added (Hewitt et al 1981). A number of different stocks of these lines have now been inbred or further selected in other laboratories.

Avoidance conditioning is a phenotype that badly needs to be dissected. There are many components, e.g. escape learning, basic activity level, response to shock, that need to be explored. Thus, there have been a number of studies on the Roman lines looking for correlated responses to selection for avoidance behavior. For example, Driscoll et al (1980) showed that the typical response to shock in the low-avoidance line is freezing. There is apparently no difference between the two lines in sensitivity to shock, but the RHAs respond actively to the stimulus, while the RLAs suppress active responding—obviously not an adaptive response in the avoidance conditioning paradigm. Satinder (1976) conducted a series of studies on another set of substocks. He also found that RLAs freeze in response to shock. A subsequent experiment (Satinder 1977) showed that the difference between lines decreased as the complexity of the task decreased; as the task was made simpler, freezing was less likely to occur in the lows. Satinder attributed this finding to differences in arousal level between lines. Later studies (Satinder 1980, 1981) showed that there is also a difference between lines in responsiveness to visual stimuli. These several experiments led to the conclusion that selection has been for *task-specific* avoidance learning, rather than avoidance learning in general. For further discussion of this issue and a summary of pharmacological studies on the Roman lines, see Driscoll & Battig (1982).

There have been two other major selection experiments for avoidance performance in rats. The Syracuse high- and low-avoidance lines were selectively bred from a foundation stock of Long-Evans rats (Brush et al 1979). These lines are also differentiated for pain sensitivity under varying stress conditions (Nagase et al 1984). The primary correlated response appears to be greater reactivity or emotionality in the lows, as reflected in conditioned suppression of instrumental responding (Brush et al 1984a,b). Like the RLAs, the Syracuse lows suppress activity in response to shock. Differences between the lines are thought to be hormonally mediated (Brush et al 1980). Bammer (1983) reported that two new lines of rats selected for high and low active avoidance do not differ in activity, "emotionality," escape latency, or passive avoidance responding. The Brush and Bammer lines may provide informative contrasts to the Roman highs and lows.

GENETIC ANALYSES   A recent series of studies compared several inbred strains of mice and hybrids between them on a number of different learning tasks. For shuttle-avoidance conditioning (Buselmaier et al 1978), a single gene was implicated, but it was not considered a "general avoidance" gene—rather, more conservatively, a gene associated with speed of learning under the particular experimental conditions. A subsequent study, in which a number of environmental parameters were manipulated (Buselmaier et al 1981), however, led to the more general conclusion that strain differences in avoidance learning in both shuttle box and Skinner box are associated with allelic differences at this single locus. In view of the qualifications discussed above, this conclusion would appear to be somewhat too general for the present stage of our understanding of the avoidance phenotype. This group of investigators also studied discrimination learning in a water-filled T-maze (Schwegler & Buselmaier 1981), and concluded that its genetic determinants are multifactorial, one of the genes being the single gene for avoidance conditioning. Van Abeelen & Schetgens (1981) also investigated discrimination learning, but obtained inconclusive results. They proposed single-gene control for retention of the discrimination task.

The genetic architecture of avoidance learning in the rat was investigated in the Roman highs and lows and other strains in a progressive series of studies summarized by Hewitt et al (1981). These studies, which stand as a model for the application of biometrical genetic techniques to a behavioral phenotype, provided a complex picture that is not yet fully understood. As defined by genetic architecture, the fittest rat initially freezes in response to stressful stimulation and is thus an unsuccessful early avoider. Later in conditioning, high avoidance has the adaptive advantage. Throughout conditioning, the most fit rat escapes shock quickly and makes few intertrial crossings. The results provide a genetic basis for Mowrer's (1960) two-factor theory of escape-avoidance conditioning, a theory involving a classically conditioned emotional response to stimuli preceding shock with subsequent instrumental conditioning leading to successful stimulus termination and shock avoidance. Many of the conclusions from these studies can be applied to wild as well as domesticated populations of rats (Wilcock et al 1981, Hewitt & Fulker 1983).

SEXUAL AND SEX-RELATED BEHAVIORS
Mice and Rats

MATE SELECTION   Mate selection is not a random process among house mice. Mice have preferences, which can be based on difference in genotype. One small chromosome segment, *H-2,* which includes the major histocompatibility complex (MHC) of the house mouse, is definitely involved. The discovery of the phenomenon and the elegant behavioral and genetic experiments performed to explore it represent a lovely continuing scientific detective story of great potential significance. Studies may eventually lead to insights into many other phenomena such as imprinting, kin recognition, and pregnancy blocking (Boyse et al 1982, 1983).

The story began with two threads (Yamazaki et al 1976). First was the proposal by Thomas—theorizing on processes of molecular identity—that histocompatibility genes (which are involved in rejection of tissue transplants) might cause each individual to have a characteristic scent. Second was the informal observation by animal care staff working with congenics that male and female mice of dissimilar *H-2* types tended to associate and nest with each other. Early experimental work employing congenics was directed toward empirical verification of the mate selection phenomenon. A male mouse of one *H-2* haplotype (a term analogous to allele, but used to designate the genotype of a complex of genes in a chromosomal region) was caged with two congenic female mice offering the same and a different haplotype. Three pairs of MHC-dissimilar congenic substrains were examined in this manner. Systematic preference for mating with a female of unlike haplotype was shown for two of the three pairs of substrains; some males in the third pair showed a preference for females of the same haplotype whereas others preferred the different haplotype. Thus, while preference was variable, it was consistent nevertheless for each male. Differences between male congenics suggested that there are genetically associated differences in responding, as well as in signalling.

Three subsequent mating-preference studies were performed. Yamazaki et al (1978) studied mate selection in segregating F_2 or F_3 stocks initiated by the crosses of two sets of MHC-dissimilar congenic substrains, and obtained some additional evidence for MHC-related mate preference. Taking advantage of a crossover between *H-2* and an adjacent region *(Qa:Tla)* of chromosome 17, Andrews & Boyse (1978) obtained evidence that this adjacent region could also be involved. Mice of strains congenic for it preferred to mate with females with one haplotype, which indicated that this chromosome region is somehow involved in the *signalling* of mouse identity *(Ris)*. Andrews & Boyse proposed that *recognition* of identity may be associated with genes *(Rir)* outside the signalling region. The experiments of Yamaguchi et al (1978) supported the findings of Andrews & Boyse with respect to the location of gene(s) affecting recognition of female identity in one region and gene(s) affecting male preference in another.

Pregnant female mice tend to abort if they are exposed to a strange male or its urine before implantation. Yamazaki et al (1983c) demonstrated that pregnancy blocking is strongly responsive to differences in MHC haplotype. Females were mated with a stud male of one haplotype and later exposed to a stimulus male of the same or a different one. A spectacular increase in blocking occurred when stud and stimulus males were of unlike MHC haplotypes.

The mate-selection technique was complemented by the easier-to-use Y-maze procedure. Mice were trained to select one of the two arms for a water reward on the basis of odor cues provided by air flowing through chambers occupied by MHC-dissimilar congenic mice (Yamazaki et al 1979). Stimulus mice were congenic substrains and F_2 segregants initiated by crosses between them. Discrimination performance was excellent. Equally good results were obtained when urine was used to provide odor cues (Yamaguchi et al 1981). Thus, study of recombinants showed that genetic differences in either chromosomal region can result in discriminable olfactory cues (Yamazaki et al 1982).

Ability to discriminate need not be limited to unlike homozygotes. Yamazaki et al (1983a,b) showed that mice discriminate between the mixed urine of two MHC-dissimilar homozygotes and that of their heterozygote. They can detect an odor difference associated with a mutation known to result in three amino acid substitutions in a cell surface glycoprotein. This finding can only be regarded as suggestive, however. Because the stocks used were congenic, effects of other closely linked genes cannot be excluded.

Taken together, these studies clearly implicate genes located in this entire region of mouse chromosome 17 *(H-2:Qa:Tla)* in mating preference and pregnancy block, and thus in processes of preference and recognition of individual identity. The associated chemosensory differences are not understood. The odorants involved need not be single (or multiple) chemical derivatives of gene products. The ability of the mouse to discriminate the urine of a heterozygote from a mixed-urine sample of the two homozygotes suggests a variation in steroid metabolism. Changes in concentrations of odorants, or in their relative proportions, may be sufficient.

The adjacent T-locus region of chromosome 17 may be the evolutionary precursor of *H-2* (e.g. Bennett 1975). T-locus gene products have only been detected in young embryos, whereas *H-2* gene products have only been detected in later embryos and, of course, in adults. T-locus variants affect sperm production and function, genetic recombination, and embryonic development. A large number of recessive *t*-alleles have been identified, most being homozygous lethals, causing death in early fetal development. Recent evidence shows that female mice can discriminate between $+/+$ (wild type) and $t/+$ (heterozygous at the T-locus) male mice, and that they prefer to associate with $+/+$ males. Both $+/+$ and $t/+$ male mice have a preference for mounting $+/+$ females (Levine et al 1980, Lenington 1983). Female preference testing for air flowing over soiled bedding of $+/+$ versus $t/+$ males clearly shows that at least a portion of this preference could be based upon odor (Lenington 1983).

COPULATION   Copulation in male mice consists of a series of female mounts, followed by mounts with intromission and ejaculation. Male mouse sexual behavior is genotype dependent (Batty 1978, McGill 1978, Shrenker & Maxson 1983), and castration of the adult male mouse tends to eliminate sexual behavior in a genotype-dependent manner (McGill & Manning 1976). Two mechanisms may be involved in the total act of copulation: one concerned with the arousal of sexual behavior, and the other with copulation itself (Shrenker & Maxson 1983). Measures of sexual behavior and plasma testosterone levels were obtained for males of strains varying in mounting (presumably activational) and ejaculatory (copulatory) behavior, and in two different segregating populations of F_2 mice initiated by crosses between them. Study of the inbred strains showed a very strong negative association, i.e. high testosterone levels associated with lower sexual activity. Results of the F_2 analyses supported a higher negative association of testosterone levels with activational than with copulatory mechanisms.

Placement of the DBA/1Bg Y chromosome on a DBA/2Bg genetic background also supports the existence of two mechanisms because it results in reduced mounting, but not reduced intromission or ejaculation (Shrenker & Maxson 1983). The DBA/1 Y chromosome can result in an increase in plasma testosterone levels (Shrenker & Maxson 1983). Since males of DBA/1Bg and DBA/2Bg do not differ in sexual vigor, other genetic factors in the genome must be involved as well.

NEST BUILDING   Female house mice tend to build small individual (thermoregulatory) nests to keep themselves warm, and much larger (maternal) nests when they become pregnant. Males tend to build a somewhat larger thermoregulatory nest all the time. Some inbred strains show a greater amount of thermoregulatory nest building than do others, and heterozygotes created by crossing strains tend to show even more (Lynch & Hegmann 1972, Wainwright 1981, Broida & Svare 1982). The last is a genetic architecture to be expected for a fitness-related trait. In a replicated bidirectional selection experiment for thermoregulatory nest building, Lynch (1980) achieved substantial progressive response to selection. Maternal nest building for pregnant females of later generations of selection was a correlated alteration, thus indicating substantial common genetic determination (Lynch 1981).

Progesterone is a primary hormone of pregnancy, and progesterone treatment of female house mice increases nest building. Schneider et al (1983) found that progesterone treatment discernably increased thermoregulatory nest building levels of lows and controls, but not of highs. Maternal nest-building levels were slightly less than progesterone-induced levels for highs and controls, slightly higher for lows. A study of inbred strains (Schneider et al 1982) supports the presence of mechanisms common to all three types of nest building, as well as showing striking similarities in levels of each type between substrains. It is clear that there are common nest-building mechanisms with substantial effect, but that other factors—for example, different endogenous levels of circulating progesterone, or different degrees of progesterone tissue sensitivity—must be involved as well. Inbred strains are known to vary in other parental-care characteristics, such as pup retrieval, as well (Carlier et al 1982).

MECHANISMS OF PRIMARY AND SECONDARY SEX DETERMINATION   Sex chromosomes of female mice are XX, while those of males are XY. Genes located upon these sex chromosomes are usually responsible for establishing the (primary) sex of the gonads (Gordon & Ruddle 1981). Gonadal sex is female in the absence of the Y. Gonadal products are subsequently responsible for determining secondary sex characteristics (Wilson et al 1981). The H-Y antigen has been proposed as the testis-producing substance; and one of the genes associated, perhaps through regulation, with production of this antigenic substance is located upon the Y chromosome (Haseltine & Ohno 1981). Two hormones present in fetal testes—Müllerian regression hormone and testosterone—are responsible for male secondary sex phenotype. It is common to view the developing mammalian brain as intrinsically female, with divergence in organization toward the male (masculinization and defeminization) originating in perinatal exposure to testosterone (Harlan et al 1979, MacLusky & Naftolin 1981, Olsen 1983, vom Saal 1983).

NEUROBIOLOGICAL DIFFERENCES   What neurobiological differences may result from perinatal exposure to testosterone? A number have been identified in recent years. Differences involving neuron number or regional size have been reported for the following areas: preoptic area (Gorski et al 1978), suprachiasmatic nucleus (Gorski et al 1978), spinal cord (Henry & Calaresu 1972, Breedlove & Arnold 1980), cerebellum (Yanai 1979), and granule cell layer of the hippocampus (Wimer & Wimer 1984). Adult variations directly implicating connectivity have been reported as well: preoptic area (Raisman & Field 1971, Greenough et al 1977), arcuate nucleus of hypothalamus (Matsumoto & Arai 1980), lateral divisions of septal and habenular nuclei (De Vries et al 1981), and amygdala (Nishizuka & Arai 1981).

DIFFERENCES IN LATERALITY   Sex differences in brain development and lateralization of characteristics have been observed. Thicknesses of neocortex and hippocampus are greater on the right side for Long-Evans male rats, but show a tendency to be thicker on the left for females. Degree of lateralization is age dependent (Diamond et al 1982, 1983). Gregory (1975) observed a different postnatal developmental time course in the sizes of pyramidal neurons of somatosensory cortex. Juraska (1984) found that sex-characteristic dendritic patterns of neurons can change by brain region, and that presence of sex differences depends upon the richness of the postnatal rearing environment. Ross et al (1982) found a marked sex difference in cerebral glucose incorporation (a measure of brain activity) to develop at about the sixth postnatal week in Sprague-Dawley rats. Ross et al (1981) found left-right asymmetries among neonatal females, but not among males. They also observed neonatal asymmetries in tail position. Sprague-Dawley females were right-biased, while males were biased to the left.

The study of neonatal tail position, and/or adult turning direction in an open field, has proved to be fruitful. Biases in tail position of neonates are highly predictive of adult turning preferences (Ross et al 1981, Denenberg et al 1982). Denenberg et al (1982) studied tail-position bias of neonatal Purdue-Wistar rats and found both sexes to be left-biased, though females showed the stronger bias. Prenatal treatment with testosterone shifted female Purdue-Wistar tail position bias to the right (Rosen et al 1983). Handling of male Purdue-Wistar rats before weaning produced a later left-turning bias in the open field in comparison to nonhandled controls, which show no bias (Sherman et al 1980). But female Purdue-Wistar rats appear to respond quite differently, for preweaning handling and rearing in an enriched environment eliminates their left-turning bias (Sherman et al 1983b). Not only does there appear to be sex-related bias, but the direction of adult turning bias depends upon line. Thus, Glick & Ross (1981) report that their Sprague-Dawley female rats show a rotation bias to the right, in contrast to the left bias observed for Purdue-Wistars. Mice also exhibit behavioral asymmetries. Female C57BL/6J mice display stronger paw preferences than do the males (Collins 1977), and adult male ICR mice have a turning bias to the left as determined by a rotometer (Korczyn & Eshel 1979).

AGGRESSION   It has long been known that male mice of different inbred strains vary in their aggressiveness toward other males (Lagerspetz & Lagerspetz 1974, Hahn & Haber 1982, Hyde 1983). The determinants of intermale aggression are complex (Fuller & Thompson 1978, Selmanoff & Ginsburg 1981), however, and a great deal remains to be understood about the environmental, genetic, and hormonal determinants that are all involved. Castration reduces aggression (e.g. Selmanoff & Ginsburg 1981), and testosterone replacement may cause it to reappear (Maxson et al 1983b). Tissue sensitivity to testosterone itself may be variable and dependent upon genotype (Maxson et al 1983b, Shrenker & Maxson 1983), and attempts to relate circulating levels of testosterone to differences in aggression have been equivocal (Selmanoff et al 1977, Stewart et al 1980, Selmanoff & Ginsburg 1981). There is accumulating evidence that genes located on the Y chromosome and elsewhere in the genome (on the X, or on the autosomes) are both involved (e.g. Maxson et al 1982). Reciprocal F_1 hybrids (which would be identical with respect to their autosomes) of peaceful strain C57BL/10 are more aggressive when the male progenitor strain is DBA/1 (Maxson 1981). Reciprocal F_1 hybrids of strains C57BL/10 and DBA/2 do not differ.

These outcomes could be interpreted as supporting direct association of the DBA/1 Y chromosome with aggression, and of the DBA/2 Y chromosome with relative pacifism. But, transferring the DBA/1 Y to a C57BL/10 background (by mating a C5BL/10 female to a male DBA/1 and continuing to backcross F_1, F_2, etc males exclusively to C57BL/10 females) does *not* change intermale aggression levels. However, when a male produced by this method is mated with a DBA/1 female, the resulting F_1 hybrid males are more aggressive than hybrids of DBA/1 females and standard C57BL/10 males (Maxson et al 1979). The Y-dependent behavioral difference between the hybrid groups is clearcut. Clearly, both Y chromosomes and genes located elsewhere are involved. It has been suggested that DBA/1 and DBA/2 Y chromosomes may be similar in their potential effects on aggression, but that autosomal differences between the strains may lead to different consequences (Shrenker & Maxson 1982). Stewart et al (1980) provide independent evidence for interactions between genes on the Y chromosome and genes located elsewhere. Testis weight exhibits a direct association with genetic differences involving the Y, while plasma testosterone levels involve other chromosomes.

Recently, there has been a good deal of interest in other types of aggression (Ebert 1983) exhibited by house mice: predatory aggression (Ebert & Green 1984), pre- and postnatal maternal aggression (Green 1978, Hyde & Sawyer 1979, Hedricks & Daniels 1981, Mann & Svare 1982, Ogawa & Makino 1981, 1984), and interfemale aggression (Hyde & Sawyer 1977, 1980). Results of 11 generations of bidirectional selection for isolation-induced interfemale aggression have been reported (Hyde & Sawyer 1980, Ebert 1983). Response to selection was asymmetrical, consisting in large part of a gradual progressive decline in interfemale aggression scores of low-line females. With respect to maternal aggression, displayed by a lactating female toward an unfamiliar female, separation between lines was extremely clear, and correlated with interfemale aggression (Hyde & Sawyer 1979).

Intermale aggression may be associated with interfemale aggression, but the high variability of results obtained in different generations renders the status of the association uncertain. The failure to find a genetic correlation between male and female aggression is supported by a recent selection study for intermale aggressive behavior, which, though it appears to have been very successful, failed to result in a correlated response in interfemale aggression (van Oort-merssen & Bakker 1981). Yet an earlier study (St. John & Corning 1973) found a genetic correlation between maternal aggression and male aggression in inbred and heterogeneous lines of mice. Results obtained for predatory aggression (killing and eating a live cricket) appear to be less ambiguous. Male and female descendants of the interfemale aggression lines fail to show predatory aggression patterns consistent with their selection histories. In sum, the recent research favors mouse maternal aggression as a central character, with the very real possibility that all other recognized forms of aggression may be correlated with it genetically.

OTHER SEX-RELATED BEHAVIORS   Sex differences in a variety of nonreproductive behaviors of rodents (mainly rats) were subjects of major reviews by Archer (1975) and by Beatty (1979). Results for mouse appear to be much less definite, and there may be substantial species differences. Female rats spend less time in rough and tumble play than do males, and they do less scent marking. Females exhibit higher levels of activity in open fields. They also tend to run in threatening situations, while males are more likely to freeze. Female rats are better at learning one-way, two-way, and free-operant shock avoidance, and do better on DRL. They are, however, poorer than males on passive avoidance tasks and on spatial maze learning.

Fruit Flies

COURTSHIP AND COPULATION   *Drosophila* courtship has long been a topic of interest to evolutionary biologists and ethologists (Ewing 1983). It has come to represent an intense research area for behavior geneticists as well (Hall 1984, Quinn & Greenspan 1984). Some elements of male courtship are orienting to the female's abdomen, tapping her with his forelegs, extending and vibrating one of his wings, licking her genitalia and mounting and copulating. Female acceptance behavior includes becoming inactive during the later courtship stages, wing spreading, and opening of vaginal plates to permit intromission. Females also exhibit behaviors such as wing flicking or kicking that can decrease mating probability.

Chemosensory cues are very important. Virgin females produce a pheromone that excites males to courtship (Nissani 1977, Tompkins et al 1980, Venard & Jallon 1980). Jallon & Hotta (1979) used mosaics to obtain evidence that fat bodies may be involved in pheromone production. Males produce a pheromone that inhibits the courtship of other males (Ewing 1983). Inseminated females emit a male-derived antiaphrodisiac (Mane et al 1983). Exposure to antiaphrodisiac extracts, in the presence of either male or virgin female flies, markedly reduces subsequent male courtship. Mutant males with olfactory defects are much less affected (Tompkins et al 1983).

Visual stimuli are also important for both sexes. Tompkins et al (1982) used several mutants to study the role of vision in male courtship. Females of a temperature-sensitive paralytic mutant were used with mutant males that were either totally blind or had substantial visual defects. Less courtship behavior was displayed toward temperature-paralyzed females, and male visual mutants exhibited courtship abnormalities. Willmund & Ewing (1982) showed that interference with visual input causes female *Drosophila* to be less receptive to copulation.

The courtship songs produced by the male's wing vibration consist of a series of pulses and a sinusoidal hum (Kyriacou & Hall 1982). In wild-type *Drosophila*, both the number of bouts of wing vibration and their average durations are heavily influenced by the female. Number of bouts of genital licking is influenced by characteristics of both sexes. PWV, the proportion of time spent in wing vibration—in contrast to orientation to the female abdomen, genital licking, and attempting copulation—is more male-determined (Crossley & McDonald 1979). McDonald & Crossley (1982) analyzed flies selected for PWV (McDonald 1979) for correlated alteration in other activities, and found that the frequency of genital licking and copulation (they very rarely occurred apart) varied with PWV. The basis for the association, response chaining or common central process, is unknown.

MECHANISMS OF SEX-DETERMINATION   Sex determination in *Drosophila* is based upon the X chromosome:autosome ratio. The Y has no role. A number of regulatory genes are involved in sensing this ratio (Belote & Baker 1982). Genes on both X chromosomes of females are active, so that the female is not intrinsically a mosaic as in, say, a female mouse. The single X chromosome in males produces the same amount of messenger RNA as do the combined Xs of the female (Baker & Belote 1983).

USE OF MOSAICS TO IDENTIFY NEUROBIOLOGICAL DETERMINANTS   The search for sex dimorphisms in tissues underlying *Drosophila* behavior has been based almost solely on the use of mosaics: XX cells are females, while X0 cells are male. Employing this phenomenon and an unstable ring-X chromosone in combination with three externally observable markers, Hotta & Benzer (1976) set out to determine the foci (locations of progenitor cells in the embryo) for male and female courtship patterns. Two behavioral courtship elements that occur early are orientation and wing vibration. Attempted copulation (curling the abdomen and following closely behind a female) is a later behavioral sequence that tends not to occur in the absence of earlier ones. Thus, a search for the focus for attempted copulation had to take place among mosaic flies that had previously displayed orientation and wing vibration. Mosaic female flies were scored for their ability to evoke courtship behavior in normal males. Fate mapping of males indicated the involvement of an anterior region in orientation and wing vibration which may be common to both behaviors, while attempted copulation involved a midregion. Receptivity to copulation appears to involve an anterior focus in the female. Reasonably normal genitalia of both sexes are, of course, a requirement for successful copulation.

Fate mapping reveals association between parts of embryonic blastoderm and does not specify the precise adult locations of neurobiological differences, but it does indicate where one should look. Study of neural determinants of male courtship has proceeded rapidly to more detailed examination of tissues of brain and thoracic ganglia through the use of internal enzyme markers, e.g. acid phosphate histochemistry (Kankel & Hall 1976). Hall (1977) verified the very close association between foci for wing vibration and following, and found a clear separation between wing extension and attempted copulation. Examination of neural tissues suggested that dorsal male brain, and not ventral brain or optic lobes, is essential for following and wing extension. Small patches of male tissues in thoracic ganglia appear adequate for the occurrence of attempted copulation, though the dependence of this behavior on the prior occurrence of orientation and wing vibration could implicate dorsal brain as well. A subsequent study (Hall 1979) supports these findings, as well as providing evidence that genital licking is also associated with dorsal brain. Von Schilcher & Hall (1979) examined wing extension and characteristics of courtship song for sex mosaics with male tissue on external head. Wing extension involved dorsal posterior brain, and the prothoracic region. Song characteristics involved one brain site (the subesophageal region) and the thoracic ganglia.

What of the female *Drosophila?* Female brain tissue is a requirement for the occurrence of female sexual receptivity. Bilateral femaleness for a site in the supraesophageal ganglion appears to be essential (Tompkins & Hall 1983).

A sex dimorphism was recently reported (Technau 1984) for two structures in the *Drosophila* brain, the mushroom bodies (Howse 1975). Functions of these brain structures are presently unknown (Siegel et al 1984).

THE SEARCH FOR NEUROBIOLOGICAL FOUNDATIONS OF LEARNING

The search for neurobiological foundations of animal learning can begin with variations in brain and then proceed to search for associated variations in behavior, or it can follow the reverse order. This section begins with studies of morphological variations in brain and ends with *Drosophila* learning mutants. It should be noted that one *Drosophila* mutant *(Ddc)* really belongs to the first category, but has been reviewed with mutants identified by their behaviors for convenience.

From Brain to Behavior

This portion will deal with morphological variations observed in hippocampi of house mice, and with the determination of behavioral consequences.

VARIATION IN DISTRIBUTION OF MOSSY FIBERS   Mossy fibers are axons of granule cells of the dentate gyrus, and they form synaptic connections with target neurons in the hilar region of the dentate gyrus and with pyramidal neurons of the hippocampus. These target hippocampal neurons have both apical and basal dendritic fields. Typically, the majority of mossy fiber synaptic connections within the hippocampus are made with apical dendrites (the *supra*pyramidal system) along the entire extent of the target pyramids, while a lesser number of synaptic connections are made with basal dendrites (the *infra*pyramidal system). Barber et al (1974) found evidence for a very substantial genetically associated variability in the patterning of mossy fiber synapses between inbred mouse strains. One strain did not have any appreciable infrapyramidal mossy fiber field, but possessed a substantial *intra*pyramidal field instead. Mice of another strain represented an opposing extreme, exhibiting an extensive infrapyramidal field and a very limited intrapyramidal field. More modest quantitative variations occurred between specimens of the other strains.

Schwegler et al (1981) and Schwegler & Lipp (1983) compared the mossy fiber patterning of Roman High-Avoidance and Roman Low-Avoidance rats. Lows were found to have a modestly higher, but statistically significant, proportion of mossy fiber terminals in the within (intrapyramidal) and below (infrapyramidal) pyramidal regions than did highs. A morphological phenotype consisting of the ratio of the areas of mossy fiber synapses in those two fields, divided by the total area of the mossy-fiber territory (including the hilus of dentate gyrus), was devised. This is their IIP score. Mice of seven inbred strains known to vary either in mossy fiber patterning or in shuttle-box performance were also tested in shuttle boxes and then processed for morphological phenotyping. Strain means for IIP and shuttle-box learning exhibited an amazing correlation of $r=-.97$. Independent verification of the association was sought in two different ways. First, individual mice belonging to a genetically heterogeneous stock were tested behaviorally, then examined histologically. They yielded a value of only $r=-.80$. Second, Roman High-Avoidance rats were treated with thyroxine, a hormone that increases the value of IIP if administered during the first 15 postnatal days, then tested behaviorally and examined histologically (Lipp & Schwegler 1982). Thyroxine treatment increased both IIP and number of trials to criterion. Correlations between IIP and learning performance were $r=-.91$ for saline controls and $r=-.87$ for thyroxine-treated experimentals.

Lipp & Schwegler (1982) believe that the target pyramids represent a highly significant portion of the hippocampus with respect to shuttle-box performance, and that the mossy fiber variations represent shifting balances of dentate input to this critical neuronal region. Gozzo & Ammassari-Teule (1983) recently began to examine mossy-fiber variations, but the range of genotypes with which they have worked is limited. Their work would seem to confirm, perhaps advance, that of Schwegler & Lipp.

VARIATIONS IN GRANULE CELL NUMBER AND DENSITY   Granule cells vary in number (Wimer et al 1978, Wimer & Wimer 1982) and in density (Wimer et al 1983); these variations allow researchers to shift the quantity and informational content of dentate inputs to hippocampal pyramids. Inbred mouse strains C57BL/6J and C58/J are stikingly different for both. C57BL/6 has an unusually large and densely populated granule cell layer, while that of C58 is both smaller in volume and less dense. The two inbred strains were used in a breeding design that produced F_3 and second backcross progeny. Both types of progeny provide two opportunities for recombination to break looser linkages between genes associated in the progenitor strains. Mice were first tested behaviorally for open-field activity, spatial maze learning, and shuttle-box learning, and then examined histologically. Examination of these two types of genetically heterogeneous stocks revealed that granule cell number and density are essentially unrelated characters, and that granule cell number was not related to any behavior measured. Granule cell density, however, was negatively related to shuttle-box performance: the higher the density, the poorer was performance in the shuttle box. This moderate association between granule cell density and behavior (typically correlations of about .6) appears to be weaker than that for mossy fiber terminals described above. Division of the granule cell layer along its longitudinal ("septo-occipital") axis produced results suggesting that septal granule cell density might be associated with shuttle-box performance later in learning, and that occipital density might be associated with early learning. It was suggested that variations in granule cell density may be due to variations in the quantity of afferent inputs surrounding granule cell bodies.

EVALUATION   Taken together, the results of studies of mossy fiber patterning and granule cell density lead to two major conclusions. First, the mouse brain represents a genetically differentiated system, with various morphological characters under separable genetic control. Second, morphological variations can have very substantial behavioral associations. A variety of identified morphological variations in mouse hippocampus remain to be explored (Fredens 1981).

From Behavior to Brain

Over a decade ago, Benzer launched an intellectually and technically formidable program to identify the biological bases of learning and memory in

Drosophila. A chemical mutagen was used to treat males, which were then mated to untreated attached-X females. This program was used to produce and isolate X-linked mutants affecting learning.

MASS TESTING STUDIES   In 1974, Quinn et al reported the development of a learning task for *Drosophila*. Flies driven by phototaxis were allowed to enter test tubes that separately exposed them to two odors, one of which was accompanied by electric shock. Testing for learning consisted of allowing flies a subsequent opportunity to enter two tubes, each containing one of the original odors. Training and testing were performed in groups.

A review of many findings may be found in Aceves-Piña et al (1983). The first learning mutant was "dunce." Additional learning mutants "rutabaga," "cabbage," and "turnip" and a memory mutant, "amnesiac," were subsequently produced and isolated (Aceves-Piña & Quinn 1979, Quinn et al 1979). Mutants resulting in acquisition deficits in adult *Drosophila* also resulted in acquisition defects in larvae. Livingstone & Tempel (1983) subsequently found that flies with dopa decarboxylase mutations on the second chromosome also fail to learn.

Much has been done subsequently to clarify both the behavioral and neurobiological phenotypes involved. Dudai (1983) attempted to discriminate between acquisition and retention defects. Cabbage mutants exhibited the most severe acquisition deficit. Dunce, rutabaga, and cabbage mutants all exhibited severe retention defects. A second experiment attempted to increase precision of measurement of retention deficits and to discriminate between storage and retrieval. A retroactive interference paradigm led Dudai to suggest that rutabaga and cabbage are retrieval mutants, while dunce is a storage mutant.

A question of considerable interest is whether learning mutants are "shallow," highly task-specific, or whether they are "deep," affecting learning tasks that involve a variety of discriminative stimuli, reinforcers, and responses (Aceves-Piña et al 1983). Tempel et al (1983) paired one of two odors with an opportunity to feed on sucrose. Turnip, *Ddc* (dopa decarboxylase), and amnesiac are relatively deep mutants, showing acquisition or retention deficits with both reward and punishment. The mutants dunce and rutabaga are shallow with respect to acquisition, showing substantial deficits when punished, but not when rewarded. They are, however, deeper with respect to retention. Retention was measureable for about four times as long in normal flies when reward was used instead of punishment. When reward and punishment are both used (one odor punished, the other rewarded), their behavioral effects appear to be independent and additive for both acquisition and retention. It is as though two separate memory mechanisms were involved. Viewed in this light, the shallowness (with respect to acquisition) and deepness (with respect to retention) of dunce and rutabaga suggest a still greater functional dissociation within reward and punishment systems. Shallow need not mean less significant.

Folkers (1982) studied acquisition and retention of a visual association in dunce, amnesiac, rutabaga, and turnip mutants. Conditioning trials consisted of shaking flies vigorously in the presence of either violet or green light. Group acquisition and retention testing consisted of choice between halves of a chamber, each separately illuminated by one of the two lights. Durcan & Fulker (1983) found that performances of wild-type *Drosophila* strains on this type of learning task can be genetically independent of their performances on the Quinn et al (1974) task originally used to identify the learning mutants. However, while Folkers found all mutants to exhibit some learning on her task, no mutant group learned as well as her wild-types. Once again, the mutants were found to be at least moderately deep. The mutant turnip appeared to be the worst at acquisition. Degree of acquisition was not standardized for retention comparisons, but both turnip and dunce appeared to possess atypical retention curves.

STUDIES OF LEARNING IN INDIVIDUAL FLIES   Duerr & Quinn (1982) studied two forms of nonassociative memory. Mutants dunce and rutabaga showed both decreased habituation and brief sensitization, while turnip exhibited only decreased habituation. Results for amnesiac were complicated by an increased threshold for sucrose, but this mutant appears to have decreased habituation and, possibly, decreased sensitization as well.

Booker & Quinn (1981) adopted a procedure originally devised for the cockroach (Horridge 1962). Mutant dunce, cabbage, and turnip flies were shocked every time they extended a leg. The objective was to train them to maintain their legs in a flexed position. Viewed as groups, no mutant stocks exhibited appreciable learning, though normal flies did. When viewed as individuals, mutants were much more variable than normals, which suggests that the neurobiological expression of the mutant gene is not uniform in all flies possessing the genotype.

Learning tasks have also been based on *Drosophila* reproductive behaviors. Thus, *Drosophila* males produce a courtship song with their wings, which consists of a low frequency hum and a train of pulses. Artificial stimulation ("priming") of females with a pulse song or a hum song prior to male courtship enhances mating success. Kyriacou & Hall (1984) used this technique to study acquisition and retention differences. They found that amnesiac females exhibited priming effects for a much shorter interval than normals. Neither dunce nor rutabaga females showed priming at all.

Drosophila males normally attempt to mate with virgin *Drosophila* females vigorously, but they show very little courtship for about three hours following exposure to an unreceptive fertilized female. This courtship depression phenomenon is thought to be based upon an aversive chemical produced by the fertilized female and to involve association of that aversive cue with courtship-stimulating ones produced by virgin females. Siegel & Hall (1979) used this learning situation to compare normal and amnesiac stocks. They found courtship depression in amnesiac stocks to last only briefly compared to normals.

EVALUATION OF FLY STUDIES   The behavioral findings we have reviewed are impressive. Every behavioral paradigm has detected a behavioral effect for almost every mutant. Characterization of defects (acquisition vs retention, storage vs retrieval) hardly seem definitive yet; though—with the exception of visual associative learning (Folkers 1982)—every study of mutant amnesiac shows it to possess a retention deficit. A part of the complexity originates in the taxonomy of behaviors. It appears, for example, that acquisition defects may appear or not depending on whether reward or punishment systems are involved (dunce and rutabaga in Tempel et al 1983). In other instances, differences in outcomes may reflect the relative involvement of excitatory or inhibitory processes (turnip, in Duerr & Quinn 1982). The recognition and definition of behavioral phenotypes must always place limits on the precise definitions of the mutants, and so it is a topic with which behavior geneticists studying *Drosophila* are likely to wrestle continually. It is also a topic to which they are very likely to make a substantial contribution. A thoughful review of problems in the design of insect learning experiments, along with criteria for establishing the occurrence of learning, was provided by Tully (1984).

What of the neurobiological basis for these mutants? Involvement of the adenylate cyclase pathway has been indicated for rutabaga and of a cAMP-phosphodiesterase for dunce (Dudai et al 1983, Livingstone et al 1984). Useful recent summaries are provided by Hall (1982) and by Quinn & Greenspan (1984).

CONCLUDING REMARKS

Genetic influences on behavior are pervasive. We have reviewed genetically associated differences in brain chemistry and morphology, in sex and courtship, in preferences for alcohol and for mate, in emotionality and aggression, in learning and laterality, and much more. Every aspect of contemporary animal behavior genetics exhibits increased precision in genetic resolution and in experimental control. The subtleties and complexities of hereditary contributions to behavioral processes are becoming increasingly well defined.

The potential for establishing brain-behavior associations is great: Correlations between hippocampal mossy fiber distributions and learning performance are remarkably near unity. The involvement of errors in cyclic AMP metabolism with defects in *Drosophila* learning may also prove to be substantial.

There have been many and varied satisfactions in writing this review. Describing the relation between neonatal tail position, a small sign of a nervous system already lateralized, and adult turning preference was one. Calling attention to what may prove to be a major discovery—the involvement of autoimmune disorders with marked aberrations in nervous system morphology and behavior—was another. Delineating the elegant behavioral and genetic demonstrations that genes identified through studies of tissue transplantation may have profound consequences for such phenomena as mate selection and pregnancy blocking was particularly rewarding. It has been gratifying to have the privilege of presenting these and so many other instances of progress being made toward understanding the role genes can play in intact animals living in a real world.

Literature Cited

Aceves-Piña, E. O., Booker, R., Duerr, J. S., Livingstone, M. S., Quinn, W. G., et al. 1983. Learning and Memory in *Drosophila*, studied with mutants. *Cold Spring Harbor Symp. Quant. Biol.* 48:831–40

Aceves-Piña, E. O., Quinn, W. G. 1979. Learning in normal and mutant *Drosophila* larvae. *Science* 206:93–96

Allen, D. L., Fantom, H. J., Wilson, J. R. 1982. Lack of association between preference for and dependence on ethanol. *Drug Alcohol Depend.* 9:119–24

Allen, D. L., Petersen, D. R., Wilson, J. R., McClearn, G. E., Nishimoto, T. K. 1983. Selective breeding for a multivariate index of ethanol dependence in mice: Results from the first five generations. *Alcoholism: Clin. Exp. Res.* 7:443–47

Anderson, S. M., McClearn, G. E. 1981. Ethanol consumption: Selective breeding in mice. *Behav. Genet.* 11:291–301

Anderson, S. M., McClearn, G. E., Erwin, V. G. 1979. Ethanol consumption and hepatic enzyme activity. *Pharmacol. Biochem. Behav.* 11:83–88

Andrews, P. W., Boyse, E. A. 1978. Mapping of an *H-2*-linked gene that influences mating preference in mice. *Immunogenetics* 6:265–68

Angel, C., McMillan, D. E., Newton, J. E. O., Reese, W. G. 1983. Differential sensitivity to morphine in nervous and normal pointer dogs. *Eur. J. Pharmacol.* 91:485–91

Archer, J. 1975. Rodent sex differences in emotional and related behavior. *Behav. Biol.* 14:451–79

Bailey, D. W. 1971. Recombinant inbred strains. *Transplantation* 11:325–27

Bailey, D. W. 1981. Strategic uses of recombinant inbred and congenic strains in behavior genetics research. See Gershon et al 1981, pp. 189–98

Baker, B. S., Belote, J. M. 1983. Sex determination and dosage compensation in *Dro-*

sophila melanogaster. Ann. Rev. Genet. 17:345–93

Balthazart, J., Pröve, E., Gilles, R., eds. 1983. *Hormones and Behavior in Higher Vertebrates.* Berlin/Heidelberg: Springer-Verlag

Bammer, G. 1983. The Australian high and low avoidance rat strains: Differential effects of ethanol and α-methyl-*p*-tyrosine. *Behav. Brain Res.* 8:317–33

Barber, R. P., Vaughn, J. E., Wimer, R. E., Wimer, C. C. 1974. Genetically associated variations in the distribution of dentate granule cell synapses upon the pyramidal cell dendrites in mouse hippocampus. *J. Comp. Neurol.* 156:417–34

Batty, J. 1978. Plasma levels of testosterone and male sexual behaviour in strains of the house mouse *(Mus musculus). Anim. Behav.* 26:339–48

Beatty, W. W. 1979. Gonadal hormones and sex differences in nonreproductive behaviors in rodents: Organizational and activational influences. *Horm. Behav.* 12:112–63

Bellamy, D. 1981. Aging: With particular reference to the use of the house mouse as a mammalian model. See Berry 1981, pp. 267–300

Belote, J. M., Baker, B. S. 1982. Sex determinations in *Drosophila melanogaster*. Analysis of transformer-2, a sex-transforming locus. *Proc. Natl. Acad. Sci. USA* 79:1568–72

Bennett, D. 1975. The T-locus of the mouse. *Cell* 6:441–54

Benzer, S. 1973. Genetic dissection of behavior. *Sci. Am.* 229:24–37

Berry, R. J., ed. 1981. *Biology of the House Mouse.* London: Academic. 715 pp.

Bignami, G. 1965. Selection for high and low rates of conditioning in the rat. *Anim. Behav.* 13:221–27

Blizard, D. A. 1981. The Maudsley Reactive and Nonreactive strains: A North American perspective. *Behav. Genet.* 11:469–89

Blizard, D. A., Altman, H. J., Freedman, L. S. 1982a. The peripheral sympathetic nervous system in rat strains selectively bred for differences in response to stress. *Behav. Neural Biol.* 34:319–25

Blizard, D. A., Bailey, D. W. 1979. Genetic correlation between open-field activity and defecation: Analysis with the C×B recombinant-inbred strains. *Behav. Genet.* 9:349–57

Blizard, D. A., Freedman, L. S., Liang, B. 1983. Genetic variation, chronic stress, and the central and peripheral noradrenergic systems. *Am. J. Physiol.* 245:R600–5

Blizard, D. A., Hansen, C. T., Freedman, L. S. 1982b. Open-field behavior and the peripheral sympathetic nervous system in the MR/N and MNR/N rat strains. *Behav. Genet.* 12:459–66

Booker, R., Quinn, W. G. 1981. Conditioning of leg position in normal and mutant *Drosophila. Proc. Natl. Acad. Sci. USA* 78: 3940–44

Bovet, D. 1977. Strain differences in learning in the mouse. In *Genetics, Environment and Intelligence,* ed. A. Oliverio, pp. 79–92. Amsterdam: North Holland

Boyse, E. A., Beauchamp, G. K., Yamazaki, K. 1983. The sensory perception of genotypic polymorphism of the major histocompatibility complex and other genes: Some physiological and phylogenetic implications. *Hum. Immunol.* 6:177–83

Boyse, E. A., Beauchamp, G. K., Yamazaki, K., Bard, J., Thomas, L. 1982. Chemosensory communication. A new aspect of the major histocompatibility complex and other genes in the mouse. *Oncodev. Biol. Med.* 4:101–16

Breedlove, S. M., Arnold, A. P. 1980. Hormone accumulation in a sexually dimorphic motor nucleus of the rat spinal cord. *Science* 210:564–66

Brizzee, K. R., Ordy, J. M., Hofer, H., Kaack, B. 1978. Animal models for the study of senile brain disease and aging changes in the brain: In *Alzheimer's Disease: Senile dementia and Related Disorders,* ed. R. Katzman, R. D. Terry, K. L. Bick, 7:515–53. New York: Raven

Broadhurst, P. L. 1975. The Maudsley Reactive and non-reactive strains of rats: A survey. *Behav. Genet.* 5:299–319

Broadhurst, P. L. 1978. *Drugs and Inheritance of Behavior.* New York: Plenum

Broadhurst, P. L. 1979. The experimental approach to behavioral evolution. See Royce & Mos 1979, pp. 43–95

Broadhurst, P. L., Jinks, J. L. 1974. What genetical architecture can tell us about the natural selection of behavioral traits. See van Abeelen 1974, pp. 43–63

Broida, J., Svare, B. 1982. Strain-typical patterns of pregnancy-induced nestbuilding in mice: Maternal and experiential influences. *Physiol. Behav.* 25:153–57

Brush, F. R., Baron, S., Froehlich, J. C., Ison, J. R., Pellegrino, L. J., et al. 1984a. Genetic differences in avoidance behavior: Escape/avoidance responding, sensitivity to electric shock, discrimination learning and open-field behavior. Submitted to *J. Comp. Psychol.*

Brush, F. R., Froehlich, J. C., Baron, S. 1980. Hormonal mediation of genetic differences in avoidance behavior. In *Adv. Physiol. Sci.,* Vol. 13: *Endocrinology, Neuroendocrinology, Neuropeptides,* ed. E. Stark, G. B. Makara, Zs. Acs, E. Endröczi, I:269–72. Budapest: Akadémiai Kiadó (Pergamon)

Brush, F. R., Froehlich, J. C., Sakellaris, P. C. 1979. Genetic selection for avoidance behavior in the rat. *Behav. Genet.* 9:309–16

Brush, F. R., Pellegrino, L. J., Rykazewski, I. M. 1984b. Genetic differences in avoidance behavior. Submitted to *J. Exp. Anal. Behav.*

Burkhart, C. A., Cherry, J. A., Van Krey, H. P., Siegel, P. B. 1983. Genetic selection for growth rate alters hypothalamic satiety mechanisms in chickens. *Behav. Genet.* 13: 295–300

Burnet, B., Connolly, K. J. 1981. Gene action and the analysis of behaviour. *Br. Med. Bull.* 37:107–13

Buselmaier, W., Geiger, S., Reichert, W. 1978. Monogene inheritance of learning speed in DBA and C3H mice. *Hum. Genet.* 40:209–14

Buselmaier, W., Vierling, T., Balzereit, W., Schwegler, H. 1981. Genetic analysis of avoidance learning by means of different psychological testing systems with inbred mice as model organisms. *Psychol. Res.* 43:317–33

Carlier, M., Roubertoux, P., Cohen-Salmon, C. 1982. Differences in patterns of pup care in *Mus musculus domesticus* I—Comparisons between eleven inbred strains. *Behav. Neural. Biol.* 35:205–10

Carr, R. I., Shucard, D. W., Hoffman, S. A., Bardana, E. J., Harbeck, R. J. 1978. Neuropsychiatric involvement in systemic lupus erythematosus. In *Neurochemical and Immunologic Components in Schizophrenia,* ed. D. Bergsma, A. L. Goldstein, pp. 209–35. New York: Liss

Collins, A. C. 1981. A review of research using the short-sleep and long-sleep mice. See McClearn et al 1981

Collins, R. L. 1977. Toward an admissible genetic model for the inheritance of the degree and direction of asymmetry. In *Lateralization in the Nervous System,* ed. S. Harnad, R. W. Doty, L. Goldstein, J. Jaynes, G. Krauthamer, pp. 137–50. New York: Academic

Committee on Animal Models for Research on Aging. 1981. *Mammalian Models for Research on Aging.* Washington: National Academy. 587 pp.

Consroe, P., Fish, B. S. 1980. Behavioral pharmacology of tetrahydrocannabinol convulsions in rabbits. *Commun. Psychopharmacol.* 4:287–91

Consroe, P., Kudray, K., Schmitz, R. 1980. Acute and chronic antiepileptic drug effects in audiogenic seizure-susceptible rats. *Exp. Neurol.* 70:626–37

Consroe, P., Martin, P. 1981. EEG profile of tetrahydrocannabinol seizure-susceptible rabbits. *Proc. West. Pharmacol. Soc.* 24:11–13

Consroe, P., Picchioni, A., Chin, L. 1979. Audiogenic seizure susceptible rats. *Fed. Proc.* 38:2411–16

Corson, S. A., Corson, E. O'L., Becker, R. E., Ginsburg, B. E., Trattner, A., et al. 1980. Interaction of genetics and separation in canine hyperkinesis and in differential responses to amphetamine. *Pavlovian J. Biol. Sci.* 15:5–11

Corson, S. A., Corson, E. O'L., Kirilcuk, V., Kirilcuk, J., Knopp, W., Arnold, L. E. 1973. Differential effects of amphetamines on clinically relevant dog models of hyperkinesis and stereotypy: Relevance to Huntington's chorea. In *Advances in Neurology,* ed. A. Barbeau, T. N. Chase, G. W. Paulson, 1:681–97. New York: Raven

Cox, D. R., Smith, S. A., Epstein, L. B., Epstein, C. J. 1984. Mouse Trisomy 16 as an animal model of human Trisomy 21 (Down syndrome): Production of viable Trisomy 16↔diploid mouse chimeras. *Dev. Biol.* 101:416–24

Crabbe, J. C. 1983. Sensitivity to ethanol in inbred mice: genotypic correlations among several behavioral responses. *Behav. Neurosci.* 97:280–89

Crabbe, J. C., Belknap, J. K. 1980. Pharmacogenetic tools in the study of drug tolerance and dependence. *Subst. Alcohol Actions/Misuse* 1:385–413

Crabbe, J. C., Kosobud, A., Young, E. R. 1983a. Genetic selection for ethanol withdrawal severity: Differences in replicate mouse lines. *Life Sci.* 33:955–62

Crabbe, J. C., Kosobud, A., Young, E. R., Janowsky, J. S. 1983b. Polygenic and single-gene determination of responses to ethanol in B×D/Ty recombinant inbred mouse strains. *Neurobehav. Toxicol. Teratol.* 5:181–87

Crabbe, J. C., McSwigan, J. D., Belknap, J. K. 1984. The role of genetics in substance abuse. In *Determinants of Substance Abuse: Biological, Psychological and Environmental Factors,* ed. M. Galizio, S. Maisto. New York: Plenum. In press

Crabbe, J. C., Young, E. R., Kosobud, A. 1983c. Genetic correlations with ethanol withdrawal severity. *Pharmacol. Biochem. Behav.* 18(Suppl. 1):541–47

Crabbe, J. C., Young, E. R., Kosobud, A. 1983d. Genetic studies of the role of temperature in physical dependence on ethanol in mice. In *Environment, Drugs and Thermoregulation. 5th Int. Symp. Pharmacol. Thermoregulation, Saint-Paul-de-Vence, 1982,* pp. 171–75. Basel: Karger

Crossley, S., McDonald, J. 1979. The stability of *Drosophila melanogaster* courtship across matings. *Anim. Behav.* 27:1041–47

Dailey, J. W., Battarbee, H. D., Jobe, P. C. 1982. Enzyme activities in the central nervous system of the epilepsy-prone rat. *Brain Res.* 231:225–30

Dailey, J. W., Jobe, P. C. 1983. Noradrenergic abnormalities in the genetically epilepsy-prone rat: Do they cause or result from seizures? *Neurosci. Abstr.* 9:400

Dailey, J. W., Jobe, P. C. 1984. Effect of increments in central nervous system dopamine concentration on audiogenic seizures in DBA/2J mice. *Neuropharmacology.* In press

Davis, B. D. 1980. Frontiers of the biological sciences. *Science* 209:78–89

DeFries, J. C., Gervais, M. C., Thomas, E. A. 1978. Response to 30 generations of selection for open-field activity in laboratory mice. *Behav. Genet.* 8:3–13

DeFries, J. C., Plomin, R. 1978. Behavioral genetics. *Ann. Rev. Psychol.* 29:473–515

Denenberg, V. H., Rosen, G. D., Hofmann, M., Gall, J., Stockler, J., Yutzey, D. A. 1982. Neonatal postural asymmetry and sex differences in the rat. *Dev. Brain Res.* 2:417–19

Dethier, V. G., Solomon, R. L., Turner, L. H. 1965. Sensory input and central excitation and inhibition in the blowfly. *J. Comp. Physiol. Psychol.* 60:303–13

De Vries, G. J., Buijs, R. M., Swaab, D. F. 1981. Ontogeny of the vasopressinergic neurons of the suprachiasmatic nucleus and their extrahypothalamic projections in the rat brain—presence of a sex difference in the lateral septum. *Brain Res.* 218:67–78

Diamond, M. C., Johnson, R. E., Young, D., Singh, S. S. 1983. Age-related morphologic differences in the rat cerebral cortex and hippocampus: Male-female; right-left. *Exp. Neurol.* 81:1–13

Diamond, M. C., Murphy, G. M., Akiyama, K., Johnson, R. E. 1982. Morphologic hippocampal asymmetry in male and female rats. *Exp. Neurol.* 76:553–65

Drewek, K. J., Broadhurst, P. L. 1983. The genetics of alcohol preference in the female rat confirmed by a full triple test cross. *Behav. Genet.* 13:107–16

Driscoll, P., Battig, K. 1982. Behavioral, emotional and neurochemical profiles of rats selected for extreme differences in active, two-way avoidance performance. See Lieblich 1982, pp. 95–123

Driscoll, P., Woodson, P., Fuemm, H., Battig, K. 1980. Selection for two-way avoidance deficit inhibits shock-induced fighting in the rat. *Physiol. Behav.* 24:793–95

Dudai, Y. 1983. Mutations affect storage and use of memory differentially in *Drosophila*. *Proc. Natl. Acad. Sci. USA* 80:5445–48

Dudai, Y., Uzzan, A., Zvi, S. 1983. Abnormal activity of adenylate cyclase in the *Drosophila* memory mutant rutabaga. *Neurosci. Lett.* 42:207–12

Dudek, B. C., Abbott, M. E. 1981. A biometrical genetic analysis of ethanol response in selectively bred long-sleep and short-sleep mice. *Behav. Genet.* 14:1–20

Dudek, B. C., Abbott, M. E., Phillips. T. J. 1984. Stimulant and depressant properties of sedative-hypnotics in mice selectively bred for differential sensitivity to ethanol. *Psychopharmacology*. In press

Dudek, B. C., Fanelli, R. J. 1980. Effects of gamma-butyrolactone, amphetamine and haloperidol in mice differing in sensitivity to alcohol. *Psychopharmacology* 68:89–97

Duerr, J. S., Quinn, W. G. 1982. Three *Drosophila* mutations that block associative learning also affect habituation and sensitization. *Proc. Natl. Acad. Sci. USA* 79:3646–50

Durcan, M. J., Fulker, D. W. 1983. A comparative study of two *Drosophila* learning tasks. *Behav. Genet.* 13:179–90

Dykman, R. A., Murphree, O. D., Reese, W. G. 1979. Familial anthropophobia in pointer dogs? *Arch. Gen. Psychiatry* 36:988–93

Ebert, P. D. 1983. Selection for aggression in a natural population. In *Aggressive Behavior: Genetic and Neural Approaches,* ed. E. C. Simmel, M. E. Hahn, J. K. Walters, pp. 103–27. New Jersey: Erlbaum

Ebert, P. D., Green, Y. V. 1984. Predatory aggression in lines of wild mice selected for interfemale aggression. *Aggressive Behav.* 10:21–26

Ehrman, L., Parsons, P. A. 1981. *Behavior Genetics and Evolution.* New York: McGraw-Hill

Ewing, A. W. 1983. Functional aspects of *Drosophila* courtship. *Biol. Rev.* 58:275–92

Eysenck, H. J. 1967. *The Biological Basis of Personality.* Springfield, Ill: Thomas

Faingold, C. L., Travis, M. A., Jobe, P. C., Laird, H. E. 1983. Abnormalities of the auditory responses of neurons in the inferior colliculus of genetically epilepsy prone rats. *Neurosci. Abstr.* 9:400

Fish, B. S., Consroe, P., Fox, R. R. 1981. Inheritance of Δ^9-tetrahydrocannabinol sei-

zure susceptibility in rabbits. *J. Hered.* 72:215–16

Folkers, E. 1982. Visual learning and memory of *Drosophila melanogaster* wild type C-S and the mutants *dunce, amnesiac, turnip, and rutabaga*. *J. Insect Physiol.* 28:535–39

Foster, H. L., Small, J. D., Fox, J. G., eds. 1982. *The Mouse in Biomedical Research,* Vol. IV, *Experimental Biology and Oncology.* New York: Academic. 561 pp.

Fredens, K. 1981. Genetic variation in the histoarchitecture of the hippocampal region of mice. *Anat. Embryol.* 161:265–81

Fulker, D. W. 1981. Biometrical genetics and individual differences. *Br. Med. Bull.* 37:115–20

Fuller, J. L. 1983a. Ethology and behavior genetics. See Fuller & Simmel 1983, pp. 337–62

Fuller, J. L. 1983b. Sociobiology and behavior genetics. See Fuller & Simmel 1983, pp. 435–77

Fuller, J. L., Simmel, E. C., eds. 1983. *Behavior Genetics: Principles and Applications.* Hillsdale, NJ: Erlbaum. 498 pp.

Fuller, J. L., Thompson, W. R. 1978. *Foundations of Behavior Genetics.* St. Louis: Mosby. 533 pp.

Galaburda, A. M., Kemper, T. L. 1979. Cytoarchitecture abnormalities in developmental dyslexia: A case study. *Ann. Neurol.* 6:94–100

Gershon, E. S., Matthysee, S., Breakefield, X. O., Ciaranello, R. D., eds. 1981. *Genetic Research Strategies in Psychobiology and Psychiatry.* Pacific Grove, Calif: Boxwood. 469 pp.

Geschwind, N., Behan, P. 1982. Left-handedness: Association with immune disease, migraine, and developmental learning disorder. *Proc. Natl. Acad. Sci.* 79:5097–5100

Ginsburg, B. E. 1978. The genetics of social behavior. In *Perspectives in Ethology,* ed. P. P. G. Bateson, P. H. Klopfer, 3:1–15. New York: Plenum

Ginsburg, B. E., Becker, R. E., Trattner, A., Bareggi, S. R. 1984. A genetic taxonomy of hyperkinesis in the dog. *Dev. Neurosci.* In press

Ginsburg, B. E., Becker, R. E., Trattner, A., Dutson, J., Bareggi, S. R. 1976. Genetic variation in drug responses in hyrid dogs: A possible model for the hyperkinetic syndrome. *Behav. Genet.* 6:107 (Abstr.)

Glick, S. D., Ross, D. A. 1981. Right-sided population bias and lateralization of activity in normal rats. *Brain Res.* 205:222–25

Gordon, J. W., Ruddle, F. H. 1981. Mammalian gonadal determination and gametogenesis. *Science* 211:1265–71

Gorski, R. A., Gordon, J. H., Shryne, J. E., Southam, A. M. 1978. Evidence for a morphological sex difference within the medial preoptic area of the rat brain. *Brain Res.* 148:333–46

Gozzo, S., Ammassari-Teule, M. 1983. Different mossy fiber patterns in two inbred strains of mice: A functional hypothesis. *Neurosci. Lett.* 36:111–16

Gray, L. 1979. The feeding diversity of deermice. *J. Comp. Physiol. Psychol.* 93:1118–26

Gray, L. 1981. Genetic and experiential differences affecting foraging behavior. See Kamil & Sargent 1981, pp. 409–54

Gray, L., Tardif, R. R. 1979. The development of feeding diversity of deermice. *J. Comp. Physiol. Psychol.* 93:1127–35

Green, E. L. 1981. *Genetics and Probability in Animal Breeding Experiments.* New York: Oxford. 271 pp.

Green, J. A. 1978. Experiential determinants of postpartum aggression in mice. *J. Comp. Physiol. Psychol.* 92:1179–87

Greenough, W. T., Carter, C. S., Steerman, C., De Voogd, T. J. 1977. Sex differences in dendritic patterns in hamster preoptic area. *Brain Res.* 126:63–72

Gregory, E. 1975. Comparison of postnatal CNS development between male and female rats. *Brain Res.* 99:152–56

Gurski, J. C. 1983. Epimeletic and et-epimeletic behavior in animals. See Fuller & Simmel 1983, pp. 373–408

Gurski, J. C., Scott, J. P. 1980. Individual vs. multiple mothering in mammals. In *Maternal Influences and Early Behavior*, ed. W. P. Smotherman, R. W. Bell, pp. 403–38. Jamaica, NY: Spectrum

Hahn, M. E., Haber, S. B. 1982. The inheritance of agonistic behavior in male mice: A diallel analysis. *Aggressive Behav.* 8:19–38

Hall, C. S. 1947. Genetic differences in fatal audiogenic seizures. *J. Hered.* 38:2–6

Hall, J. C. 1977. Portions of the central nervous system controlling reproductive behavior in *Drosophila melanogaster*. *Behav. Genet.* 7:291–312

Hall, J. C. 1979. Control of male reproductive behavior by the central nervous system of *Drosophila:* Dissection of a courtship pathway by genetic mosaics. *Genetics* 92:437–57

Hall, J. C. 1982. Genetics of the nervous system in *Drosophila*. *Q. Rev. Biophys.* 2:223–479

Hall, J. C. 1984. Genetic analysis of behavior in insects. In *Comp. Insect Physiol. Biochem. Pharmacol.*, ed. G. A. Kerkut, L. I. Gilbert, 9:1–87. Oxford: Pergamon

Hall, J. C., Gelbart, N. M., Kankel, D. R. 1976. Mosaic systems. In *Genetics and Biology of Drosophila*, ed. M. Ashburner, E. Novitski, 1A:265–314. London: Academic

Hall, J. C., Greenspan, R. J., Harris, W. A.,

eds 1982. *Genetic Neurobiology.* Cambridge, Mass: MIT. 284 pp.

Harlan, R. E., Gordon, J. H., Gorski, R. A. 1979. Sexual differentiation of the brain: Implications for neuroscience. *Rev. Neurosci.* 4:31–71

Harrington, G. M. 1972. Strain differences in open-field behavior of the rat. *Psychon. Sci.* 27:51–53

Harrington, G. M. 1979. Strain differences in open-field behavior of the rat. II. *Bull. Psychon. Soc.* 13:85–86

Harrington, G. M. 1981. The Har strains of rats: Origins and characteristics. *Behav. Genet.* 11:445–68

Harris, R. A., Crabbe, J. C., McSwigan, J. 1984. Relationship of membrane physical properties to alcohol dependence in mice selected for genetic differences in alcohol withdrawal. Submitted to *Life Sci.*

Haseltine, F. L., Ohno, S. 1981. Mechanisms of gonadal differentiation. *Science* 211:1272–78

Hedricks, C., Daniels, C. E. 1981. Agonistic behavior between pregnant mice and male intruders. *Behav. Neural Biol.* 31:236–41

Henderson, N. D. 1978. Genetic dominance for low activity in infant mice. *J. Comp. Physiol. Psychol.* 92:118–25

Henderson, N. D. 1979. Adaptive significance of animal behavior: The role of gene-environment interaction. See Royce & Mos 1979, pp. 243–87

Henderson, N. D. 1981. Genetic influences on locomotor activity in 11-day-old housemice. *Behav. Genet.* 11:209–26

Henry, J. L., Calaresu, F. R. 1972. Topography and numerical distribution of neurons of the thoraco-lumbar intermediolateral nucleus in the cat. *J. Comp. Neurol.* 144:205–14

Hewitt, J. K., Fulker, D. W. 1983. Using the triple test cross to investigate the genetics of behavior in wild populations. II. Escape-avoidance conditioning in *Rattus norvegicus*. *Behav. Genet.* 13:1–15

Hewitt, J. K., Fulker, D. W., Broadhurst, P. L. 1981. Genetics of escape-avoidance conditioning in laboratory and wild populations of rats: A biometrical approach. *Behav. Genet.* 11:533–44

Hirsch, J., McCauley, L. A. 1977. Successful replication of, and selective breeding for, classical conditioning in the blowfly *Phormia regina*. *Anim. Behav.* 25:784–85

Horowitz, G. P., Dudek, B. C. 1983. Behavioral pharmacogenetics. See Fuller & Simmel 1983, pp. 117–54

Horridge, G. A. 1962. Learning of leg position by headless insects. *Nature* 193:697–98

Hotta, Y., Benzer, S. 1972. Mapping of behavior in *Drosophila* mosaics. *Nature* 240:527–35

Hotta, Y., Benzer, S. 1976. Courtship in *Drosophila* mosaics: Sex-specific foci for sequential action patterns. *Proc. Natl. Acad. Sci. USA* 73:4154–58

Howse, P. E. 1975. Brain structure and behavior in insects. *Ann. Rev. Entomol.* 20: 359–79

Hutchins, J. B., Allen, D. L., Cole-Harding, L. S., Wilson, J. R. 1981. Behavioral and physiological measures for studying ethanol dependence in mice. *Pharmacol. Biochem. Behav.* 15:55–59

Hyde, J. S. 1983. The genetics of agonistic and sexual behavior. See Fuller & Simmel 1983, pp. 409–34

Hyde, J. S., Sawyer, T. F. 1977. Estrous cycle fluctuations in aggressiveness of house mice. *Horm. Behav.* 9:290–95

Hyde, J. S., Sawyer, T. F. 1979. Correlated characters in selection for aggressiveness in female mice. II. Maternal agressiveness. *Behav. Genet.* 9:571–77

Hyde, J. S., Sawyer, T. F. 1980. Selection for agonistic behavior in wild female mice. *Behav. Genet.* 10:349–59

Immelmann, K. 1979. Genetical constraints on early learning: A perspective from sexual imprinting in birds. See Royce & Mos 1979, pp. 121–33

Jallon, J.-M., Hotta, Y. 1979. Genetic and behavioral studies of female sex appeal in *Drosophila. Behav. Gen.* 9:257–75

Jinks, J. L. 1979. The biometrical approach to quantitative variation. See Thompson & Thoday 1979, pp. 81–109

Jinks, J. L., Broadhurst, P. L. 1974. How to analyse the inheritance of behavior in animals—the biometrical approach. See van Abeelen 1974, pp. 1–41

Jobe, P. C., Ko, K. H., Dailey, J. W. 1984a. Abnormalities in norepinephrine turnover rate in the central nervous system of the genetically epilepsy-prone rat. *Brain Res.* 290:357–60

Jobe, P. C., Laird, H. E. 1981. Neurotransmitter abnormalities as determinants of seizure susceptibility and intensity in the genetic models of epilepsy. *Biochem. Pharmacol.* 30:3137–44

Jobe, P. C., Laird, H. E. II, Ko, K. H., Ray, T., Dailey, J. W. 1982. Abnormalities in monoamine levels in the central nervous system of the genetically epilepsy-prone rat. *Epilepsia* 23:359–66

Jobe, P. C., Woods, T. W., Dailey, J. W. 1984b. Proconvulsant and anticonvulsant effects of tricylcic antidepressants in genetically epilepsy-prone rats. *Adv. Epileptol.* 15: In press

Juraska, J. M. 1984. Sex differences in developmental plasticity in the visual cortex and hippocampal dentate gyrus. *Prog. Brain Res.* 61: In press

Kamil, A. C., Roitblat, H. L. 1985. The ecology of foraging behavior: Implications for animal learning and behavior. *Ann. Rev. Psychol.* 36:141–69

Kankel, D. R., Hall, J. C. 1976. Fate mapping of nervous system and other internal tissues in genetic mosaics of *Drosophila melanogaster. Dev. Biol.* 48:1–24

Kaplan, B. J., Seyfried, T. N., Glaser, G. H. 1979. Spontaneous polyspike discharges in an epileptic mutant mouse (tottering). *Exp. Neurol.* 65:577–86

Ko, K. H., Dailey, J. W., Jobe, P. C. 1982. Effect of increments in norepinephrine concentrations on seizure intensity in the genetically epilepsy-prone rat. *J. Pharmacol. Exp. Ther.* 222:662–69

Ko, K. H., Dailey, J. W., Jobe, P. C. 1983. Evaluation of monoaminergic receptors in the genetically epilepsy prone rat. *Experientia* 40:70–73

Korczyn, A. D., Eshel, Y. 1979. Dopaminergic and non-dopaminergic circling activity of mice. *Neuroscience* 4:1085–88

Kyriacou, C. P., Hall, J. C. 1982. The function of courtship song rhythms in *Drosophila. Anim. Behav.* 30:794–801

Kyriacou, C. P., Hall, J. C. 1984. Learning and memory mutations impair acoustic priming of mating behaviour in *Drosophila. Nature* 308:62–65

Lagerspetz, K. M. J., Lagerspetz, K. Y. H. 1974. Genetic determination of aggressive behavior. See van Abeelen 1974, pp. 321–46

Lassalle, J. M., LePape, G. 1978. Locomotor activity of two inbred strains of mice in a seminatural and a breeding cage environment. *Behav. Genet.* 8:371–76

Lenington, S. 1983. Social preferences for partners carrying "good genes" in wild house mice. *Anim. Behav.* 31:325–33

Levine, L., Rockwell, R. F., Grossfield, J. 1980. Sexual selection in mice. V. Reproductive competition between $+/+$ and $+/t^{w5}$ males. *Am. Nat.* 116:150–56

Liang, B., Dunlap, C. E. III, Freedman, L. S., Blizard, D. A. 1982. Cardiac β-receptor variation in rat strains selectively bred for differences in susceptibility to stress. *Life Sci.* 31:533–39

Lieblich, I., ed. 1982. *Genetics of the Brain.* Amsterdam: Elsevier. 491 pp.

Lipp, H. P., Schwegler, H. 1982. Hippocampal mossy fibers and avoidance learning. See Lieblich 1982, pp. 325–64

Livingstone, M. S., Sziber, P. P., Quinn, W. G. 1984. Loss of calcium/calmodulin responsiveness in the adenylate cyclase of *rutabaga,* a *Drosophila* learning mutant. *Cell* 37:205–15

Livingstone, M. S., Tempel, B. L. 1983. Genetic dissection of monoamine neurotransmitter synthesis in *Drosophila*. *Nature* 303:67–70

Löscher, W., Meldrum, B. S. 1983. Evaluation of anticonvulsant drugs in genetic animal models of epilepsy. *Fed. Proc.* 43:276–84

Lucas, L. A., DeLuca, D. C., Newton, J. E. O., Angel, C. A. 1981. Animal models for human psychopathology: The nervous pointer dog. See Gershon et al 1981, pp. 241–52

Lumeng, L., Hawkins, T. D., Li, T. K. 1977. New strains of rats with alcohol preference and non-preference. In *Alcohol and Aldehyde Metabolizing Systems*, ed. R. G. Thurman, J. R. Williamson, H. R. Drott, B. Chance. New York: Academic

Lush, I. E. 1981. Mouse pharmacogenetics. See Berry 1981, pp. 517–46

Lynch, C. B. 1980. Response to divergent selection for nesting behavior in *Mus musculus*. *Genetics* 96:757–65

Lynch, C. B. 1981. Genetic correlation between two types of nesting in *Mus musculus*: Direct and indirect selection. *Behav. Genet.* 11:267–72

Lynch, C. B., Hegmann, J. P. 1972. Genetic differences influencing behavioral temperature regulation in small mammals. I. Nesting by *Mus musculus*. *Behav. Genet.* 2:43–53

MacLusky, N. J., Naftolin, F. 1981. Sexual differentiation of the central nervous system. *Science* 211:1294–1303

Mane, S. D., Tompkins, L., Richmond, R. C. 1983. Male esterase 6 catalyzes the synthesis of a sex pheromone in *Drosophila melanogaster* females. *Science* 222:419–21

Mann, M. A., Svare, B. 1982. Factors influencing pregnancy-induced aggression in mice. *Behav. Neural Biol.* 36:242–58

Mather, K. 1973. *Genetic Structure of Populations*. London: Chapman & Hall. 189 pp.

Mather, K., Jinks, J. L. 1971. *Biometrical Genetics: The Study of Continuous Variation*. New York: Cornell Univ. Press. 376 pp.

Matsumoto, A., Arai, Y. 1980. Sexual dimorphism in "wiring pattern" in the hypothalamic arcuate nucleus and its modification by neonatal hormonal environment. *Brain Res.* 190:238–42

Maxson, S. C. 1973. Behavioral adaptations and biometrical genetics. *Am. Psychol.* 28:268–69

Maxson, S. C. 1981. The genetics of aggression in vertebrates. In *The Biology of Aggression*, ed. P. F. Brain, D. Benton, pp. 69–104. Alphen aan den Rijn, The Netherlands: Sythoff & Noordhoff

Maxson, S. C., Fine, M. D., Ginsburg, B. E., Koniecki, D. L. 1983a. A mutant for spontaneous seizures in C57BL/10Bg mice. *Epilepsia* 24:15–24

Maxson, S. C., Ginsburg, B. E., Trattner, A. 1979. Interaction of Y-chromosomal and autosomal gene(s) in the development of intermale aggression in mice. *Behav. Genet.* 9:219–26

Maxson, S. C., Platt, T., Shrenker, P., Trattner, A. 1982. The influence of the Y-chromosome of Rb/1Bg mice on agonistic behaviors. *Aggressive Behav.* 8:285–91

Maxson, S. C., Shrenker, P., Vigue, L. C. 1983b. Genetics, hormones, and aggression. In *Hormones and Aggressive Behavior*, ed. B. B. Svare, pp. 179–96. New York: Plenum

McClearn, G. E. 1959. The genetics of mouse behavior in novel situations. *J. Comp. Physiol. Psychol.* 49:90–92

McClearn, G. E. 1961. Genotype and mouse activity. *J. Comp. Physiol. Psychol.* 54:674–76

McClearn, G. E., Deitrich, R. A., Erwin, V. G., eds. 1981. *The Development of Animal Models as Pharmacogenetic Tools*. Washington: NIAAA Monograph

McClearn, G. E., Kakihana, R. 1981. Selective breeding for ethanol sensitivity: SS and LS mice. See McClearn et al 1981, pp. 147–59

McClearn, G. E., Rodgers, D. A. 1961. Genetic factors in alcohol preference of laboratory mice. *J. Comp. Physiol. Psychol.* 54:116–19

McClearn, G. E., Wilson, J. R., Petersen, D. R., Allen, D. L. 1982. Selective breeding in mice for severity of the ethanol withdrawal syndrome. *Subst. Alcohol Actions/Misuse* 3:135–43

McDonald, J. 1979. Genetic analysis of lines selected for wing vibration in *Drosophila melanogaster*. *Behav. Genet.* 9:579–84

McDonald, J., Crossley, S. 1982. Behavioural analysis of lines selected for wing vibration in *Drosophila melanogaster*. *Anim. Behav.* 30:802–10

McGill, T. E. 1978. Genetic factors influencing the action of hormones on sexual behavior. In *Biological Determinants of Sexual Behavior*, ed. J. B. Hutchison, pp. 7–28. New York: Wiley

McGill, T. E., Manning, A. 1976. Genotype and retention of the ejaculatory reflex in castrated male mice. *Anim. Behav.* 24:507–18

McGuire, T. R. 1981. Selection for central excitatory state (CES) in the blow fly *Phormia regina*. *Behav. Genet.* 11:331–38

McGuire, T. R. 1983. Further evidence for a relationship between central excitatory state and classical conditioning in the blow fly *Phormia regina*. *Behav. Genet.* 13:509–15

McGuire, T. R., Hirsch, J. 1977. Behavior-genetic analysis of *Phormia regina*: Conditioning, reliable individual differences, and selection. *Proc. Natl. Acad. Sci. USA* 74:5193–97

McLaren, A. 1976. *Mammalian Chimaeras.* New York: Cambridge Univ. Press. 148 pp.

Milich, D. R., Gershwin, M. E. 1981. The pathogenesis of autoimmunity in New Zealand mice. In *Immunologic Defects in Laboratory Animals,* ed. M. E. Gershwin, B. Merchant, 2:77–123. New York: Plenum

Mowrer, O. H. 1960. *Learning Theory and Behavior.* New York: Wiley. 555 pp.

Mullen, R. J., Herrup, K. 1979. Chimeric analysis of mouse cerebellar mutants. In *Neurogenetics: Genetic Approaches to the Nervous System,* ed. X. O. Breakefield, pp. 173–96. New York: Elsevier

Nagase, C. S., Randick, A., Brush, F. R. 1984. Genetic differences in avoidance behavior: Cardiovascular activity, pain sensitivity and stress-induced analgesia. Submitted to *Peptides*

Nandy, K., Lal, H., Bennett, M., Bennett, D. 1983. Correlation between a learning disorder and elevated brain-reactive antibodies in aged C57BL/6 and young NZB mice. *Life Sci.* 33:1499–1503

Nelson, D. O., Boulant, J. A. 1981. Altered CNS neuroanatomical organization of spontaneously hypertensive (SHR) rats. *Brain Res.* 226:119–30

Nelson, M. C. 1971. Classical conditioning in the blowfly *(Phormia regina):* Associative and excitatory factors. *J. Comp. Physiol. Psychol.* 77:353–68

Nesbitt, M. N., Guthrie, D., Spence, M. A., Butler, K. 1981. Use of chimeric mice to study behavior. See Gershon et al 1981, pp. 105–12

Nesbitt, M. N., Spence, M. A., Butler, K. 1979. Behavior in chimeric mice combining differently behaving strains. *Behav. Genet.* 9:277–88

Newton, J. E. O., Lucas, L. A. 1982. Differential heart-rate responses to person in nervous and normal pointer dogs. *Behav. Genet.* 12:379–93

Nishizuka, M., Arai, Y. 1981. Sexual dimorphism in synaptic organization in the amygdala and its dependence on neonatal hormone environment. *Brain Res.* 212:31–38

Nissani, M. 1977. Gynandromorph analysis of some aspects of sexual behavior of *Drosophila melanogaster. Anim. Behav.* 25:555–66

Noebels, J. 1979. Analysis of inherited epilepsy using single locus mutations in mice. *Fed. Proc.* 38:2405–10

Ogawa, S., Makino, J. 1981. Maternal aggression in inbred strains of mice: Effects of reproductive states. *Japanese J. Psychol.* 52:78–84

Ogawa, S., Makino, J. 1984. Aggressive behavior in inbred strains of mice during pregnancy. *Behav. Neural Biol.* 40:195–204

Oliverio, A., Eleftheriou, B. E., Bailey, D. W. 1973. Exploratory activity: Genetic analysis of its modification by scopolamine and amphetamine. *Physiol. Behav.* 10:893–99

Olsen, K. L. 1983. Genetic determinants of sexual differentiation. See Balthazart et al 1983, pp. 138–58

Partridge, L. 1984. Genetics and behaviour. In *Animal Behaviour: Genes, Development and Learning,* ed. T. R. Halliday, P. J. B. Slater, 3:11–51. Oxford: Blackwell

Penny, J. E., Brown, R. D., Hodges, K. B., Kupetz, S. A., Glenn, D. W., Jobe, P. C. 1983. Cochlear morphology of the audiogenic-seizure susceptible (AGS) or genetically epilepsy prone rat (GEPR). *Acta Otolaryngol.* 95:1–12

Petersen, D. R., ed. 1982. Boulder Symposium on Behavioral Pharmacogenetics. *Behav. Genet.* Vol. 12, No. 1

Plomin, R., DeFries, J. C., McClearn, G. E. 1980. *Behavior Genetics: A Primer.* San Francisco: Freeman. 415 pp.

Quinn, W. G., Gould, J. L. 1979. Nerves and genes. *Nature* 278:19–23

Quinn, W. G., Greenspan, R. J. 1984. Learning and courtship in *Drosophila:* Two stories with mutants. *Ann. Rev. Neurosci.* 7:67–93

Quinn, W. G., Harris, W. A., Benzer, S. 1974. Conditioned behavior in *Drosophila melanogaster. Proc. Natl. Acad. Sci. USA* 71:708–12

Quinn, W. G., Sziber, P. P., Booker, R. 1979. The *Drosophila* memory mutant *amnesiac. Nature* 277:212–14

Raisman, G., Field, P. M. 1971. Sexual dimorphism in the preoptic area of the rat. *Science* 173:731–33

Ramirez, I., Sprott, R. L. 1978. Food intake and body weight regulation in diabetes *(db/db)* and obese *(ob/ob)* mice. *Physiol. Psychol.* 6:187–90

Ramirez, I., Sprott, R. L. 1979. Regulation of caloric intake in yellow mice (C57BL/6J-Ay/a). *Physiol. Behav.* 22:507–11

Reese, W. G. 1979. A dog model for human psychopathology. *Am. J. Psychiatry* 136:1168–72

Reese, W. G., Newton, J. E. O., Angel, C. 1983. A canine model of psychopathology. In *Psychomatic Medicine,* ed. A. J. Krakowski, C. P. Kimball, pp. 25–31. New York: Plenum

Rosen, G. D., Berrebi, A. S., Yutzey, D. A., Denenberg, V. H. 1983. Prenatal testosterone causes shift of asymmetry in neonatal tail posture of the rat. *Dev. Brain Res.* 9:99–101

Ross, D. A., Glick, S. D., Meibach, R. C. 1981. Sexually dimorphic brain and behavioral asymmetries in the neonatal rat. *Proc. Natl. Acad. Sci. USA* 78:1958–61

Ross, D. A., Glick, S. D., Meibach, R. C. 1982. Sexually dimorphic cerebral asymmetries in 2-deoxy-D-glucose uptake during postnatal development of the rat: Correlations with age and relative brain activity. *Dev. Brain Res.* 3:341–47

Roubinian, J. R., Papoian, R., Talal, N. 1977. Angrogenic hormones modulate autoantibody response and improve survival in murine lupus. *J. Clin. Invest.* 59:1066–70

Royce, J. R., Mos, L. P., eds. 1979. *Theoretical Advances in Behavior Genetics.* Alphen aan den Rijn, The Netherlands: Sijthoff & Noordhoff. 707 pp.

Sanders, D. C. 1981. The Bethlem lines: Genetic selection for high and low rearing activity in rats. *Behav. Genet.* 11:491–504

Satinder, K. P. 1976. Sensory responsiveness and avoidance learning. *J. Comp. Physiol. Psychol.* 90:946–57

Satinder, K. P. 1977. Arousal explains difference in avoidance learning of genetically selected rat strains. *J. Comp. Physiol. Psychol.* 91:1326–36

Satinder, K. P. 1980. Interaction among scopolamine, conditioned stimulus modality, genotype, and either-way avoidance behavior of rats. *Psychopharmacology* 67:97–99

Satinder, K. P. 1981. Interaction among *d*-amphetamine, scopolamine and genotype in avoidance behavior of rats. *Pharmacol. Biochem. Behav.* 14:121–24

Schneider, J. E., Lynch, C. B., Gundaker, C. L. 1983. The influence of exogenous progesterone on selected lines of mice divergent for maternal nesting. *Behav. Genet.* 13:247–56

Schneider, J. E., Lynch, C. B., Possidente, B., Hegmann, J. P. 1982. Genetic association between progesterone-induced and maternal nesting in mice. *Physiol. Behav.* 29:97–105

Schwegler, H., Buselmaier, W. 1981. Behavior genetic analysis of water-T-maze learning in inbred strains of mice, their hybrids, and selected second generation crosses. *Psychol. Res.* 43:335–45

Schwegler, H., Lipp, H. P. 1983. Hereditary covariations of neuronal circuitry and behavior: Correlations between the proportions of hippocampal synaptic fields in the regio inferior and two-way avoidance in mice and rats. *Behav. Brain Res.* 7:1–38

Schwegler, H., Lipp, H. P., van der Loos, H., Buselmaier, W. 1981. Individual hippocampal mossy fiber distribution in mice correlates with two-way avoidance performance. *Science* 214:817–18

Scott, J. P. 1977. Social genetics. *Behav. Genet.* 7:327–46

Scott, J. P. 1983. Genetics of social behavior in nonhuman animals. See Fuller & Simmel 1983, pp. 363–72

Seifen, E., Newton, J. E. O. 1982. Abnormal

autonomic nervous system functions in inbred dogs. *Pharmacologist* 24:233

Selmanoff, M., Ginsburg, B. E. 1981. Genetic variability in aggression and endocrine function in inbred strains of mice. In *Multidisciplinary Approaches to Aggression,* ed. P. F. Brain, D. Benton, pp. 247–68. New York: Elsevier

Selmanoff, M. K., Golman, B. D., Maxson, S. G., Ginsburg, B. E. 1977. Correlated effects of the Y-chromosome of mice on developmental changes in testosterone levels and intermale aggression. *Life Sci.* 20:359–66

Seyfried, T. 1979. Audiogenic seizures in mice. *Fed. Proc.* 38:2399–2404

Seyfried, T. N. 1982a. Convulsive disorders. See Foster et al 1982, pp. 97–124

Seyfried, T. N. 1982b. Developmental genetics of audiogenic seizure susceptibility in mice. In *Genetic Basis of the Epilepsies,* ed. V. E. Anderson, W. A. Hauser, J. K. Penry, C. F. Sing, pp. 199–210. New York: Raven

Seyfried, T. N. 1983. Genetic heterogeneity for the development of audiogenic seizures in mice. *Brain Res.* 271:325–29

Seyfried, T. N., Glaser, G. H. 1981. Genetic linkage between the AH locus and a major gene that inhibits susceptibility to audiogenic seizures in mice. *Genetics* 99:117–26

Sherman, G. F., Galaburda, A. M., Geschwind, N. 1983a. Ectopic neurons in the brain of the autoimmune mouse: A neuropathological model of dyslexia? *Neurosci. Abstr.* 9:939

Sherman, G. F., Garbanati, J. A., Rosen, G. D., Hofmann, M., Yutzey, D. A., Denenberg, V. H. 1983b. Lateralization of spatial preference in the female rat. *Life Sci.* 33:189–93

Sherman, G. F., Garbanati, J. A., Rosen, G. D., Yutzey, D. A., Denenberg, V. H. 1980. Brain and behavioral asymmetries for spatial preference in rats. *Brain Res.* 192:61–67

Shideler, C. E., DeLuca, D. C., Newton, J. E. O., Angel, C. 1983. Effects of naloxone and neuroleptic drugs on muscle rigidity and heart rate of the nervous pointer dog. *Pavlovian J. Biol. Sci.* 18:211–15

Shrenker, P., Maxson, S. C. 1982. The Y chromosomes of DBA/1Bg and DBA/2Bg compared for effects on intermale aggression. *Behav. Genet.* 12:429–34

Shrenker, P., Maxson, S. C. 1983. The genetics of hormonal influences on male sexual behavior of mice and rats. *Neurosci. BioBehav. Rev.* 7:349–59

Shuster, L. 1982. A pharmacogenetic approach to the brain. See Lieblich 1982, pp. 159–73

Siegel, R. W., Hall, J. C. 1979. Conditioned responses in courtship behavior of normal and mutant *Drosophila. Proc. Natl. Acad. Sci. USA* 76:3430–34

Siegel, R. W., Hall, J. C., Gailey, D. A., Kyriacou, C. P. 1984. Genetic elements of courtship in *Drosophila* mosaics and learning mutants. *Behav. Genet.* In press

Simmel, E. C., Bagwell, M. 1983. Genetics of exploratory behavior and activity. See Fuller & Simmel 1983, pp. 89–116

Simmel, E. C., Eleftheriou, B. E. 1977. Multivariate and behavior genetic analysis of avoidance of complex visual stimuli and activity in recombinant inbred strains of mice. *Behav. Genet.* 7:239–50

Sokolowski, M. B. 1980. Foraging strategies of *Drosophila melanogaster:* A chromosomal analysis. *Behav. Genet.* 10:291–302

Sokolowski, M. B., Hansell, R. I. C. 1983. *Drosophila* larval foraging behavior. I. The sibling species, *D. melanogaster* and *D. simulans. Behav. Genet.* 13:159–68

Sokolowski, M. B., Hansell, R. I. C., Rotin, D. 1983. *Drosophila* larval foraging behavior. II. Selection in the sibling species, *D. melanogaster* and *D. simulans. Behav. Genet.* 13:169–77

Sokolowski, M. B., Kent, C., Wong, J. 1984. *Drosophila* larval foraging behaviour: Developmental stages. *Anim. Behav.* In press

Southwick, C. H., Clark, L. H. 1968. Interstrain differences in aggressive behavior and exploratory activity of inbred mice. *Commun. Behav. Biol.* A 1:49–59

Sprott, R. L. 1983. Genetic aspects of aging in *Mus musculus:* January 1981-February 1982. *Rev. Biol. Res. Aging* 1:73–80

Spuhler, K., Hoffer, B., Weiner, N., Palmer, M. 1982. Evidence for genetic correlation of hypnotic effects and cerebellar Purkinje neuron depression in response to ethanol in mice. *Pharmacol. Biochem. Behav.* 17:569–78

St. John, R. D., Corning, P. A. 1973. Maternal aggression in mice. *Behav. Biol.* 9:635–39

Stewart, A. D., Manning, A., Batty, J. 1980. Effects of Y-chromosome variants on the male behaviour of the mouse *Mus musculus. Genet. Res.* 35:261–68

Talal, N. 1983. Immune response disorders. In *The Mouse in Biomedical Research: Normative Biology, Immunology, and Husbandry,* ed. H. L. Foster, J. D. Small, J. G. Fox, 3:391–401. New York: Academic

Technau, G. M. 1984. Fiber number in the mushroom bodies of adult *Drosophila melanogaster* depends on age, sex, and experience. *J. Neurogenet.* 1:113–26

Tempel, B. L., Bonini, N., Dawson, D. R., Quinn, W. G. 1983. Reward learning in normal and mutant *Drosophila. Proc. Natl. Acad. Sci. USA* 80:1482–86

Thiessen, D. 1979. Biological trends in behavior genetics. See Royce & Mos 1979, pp. 169–212

Thoday, J. M. 1979. Polygenic mapping: Uses and limitations. See Thompson & Thoday 1979, pp. 219–33

Thompson, J. N. Jr., Thoday, J. M., eds. 1979. *Quantitative Genetic Variation.* San Francisco: Academic. 305 pp.

Thompson, W. R. 1956. The inheritance of behavior (activity differences in five inbred mouse strains). *J. Hered.* 47:147–48

Tompkins, L., Gross, A. C., Hall, J. C., Gailey, D. A., Siegel, R. W. 1982. The role of female movement in the sexual behavior of *Drosophila melanogaster. Behav. Genet.* 12:295–307

Tompkins, L., Hall, J. C. 1983. Identification of brain sites controlling female receptivity in mosaics of *Drosophila melanogaster. Genetics* 103:179–95

Tompkins, L., Hall, J. C., Hall, L. M. 1980. Courtship-stimulating volatile compounds from normal and mutant *Drosophila. J. Insect Physiol.* 26:689–97

Tompkins, L., Siegel, R. W., Gailey, D. A., Hall, J. C. 1983. Conditioned courtship in *Drosophila* and its mediation by association of chemical cues. *Behav. Genet.* 13:565–78

Tully, T. 1984. Conceptual and experimental evaluation of issues in *Drosophila* learning. *Behav. Genet.* In press

Tully, T., Hirsch, J. 1982a. Behavior-genetic analysis of *Phormia regina.* I. Isolation of pure-breeding lines for high and low levels of the central excitatory state (CES) from an unselected population. *Behav. Genet.* 12:395–415

Tully, T., Hirsch, J. 1982b. Behaviour-genetic analysis of *Phormia regina* II. Detection of a single, major-gene effect from behavioural variation for central excitatory state (CES) using hybrid crosses. *Anim. Behav.* 30: 1193–1202

Tully, T., Hirsch, J. 1983. Two nonassociative components of the proboscis extension reflex in the blow fly, *Phormia regina,* which may affect measures of conditioning and of the central excitatory state. *Behav. Neurosci.* 97:146–53

Tully, T., Zawistowski, S., Hirsch, J. 1982. Behavior-genetic analysis of *Phormia regina.* III. A phenotypic correlation between the central excitatory state (CES) and conditioning remains in replicated F_2 generations of hybrid crosses. *Behav. Genet.* 12: 181–91

Tunnicliff, G., Wimer, C. C., Wimer, R. E. 1973. Relationships between neuro-transmitter metabolism and behaviour in seven inbred strains of mice. *Brain Res.* 61:428–34

van Abeelen, J. H. F., ed. 1974. *The Genetics of Behavior.* New York: Elsevier. 450 pp.

van Abeelen, J. H. F. 1975. Genetic analysis of

behavioural responses to novelty in mice. *Nature* 254:239–41

van Abeelen, J. H. F. 1977. Rearing responses and locomotor activity in mice: Single-locus control. *Behav. Biol.* 19:401–4

van Abeelen, J. H. F. 1979. Ethology and the genetic foundations of animal behavior. See Royce & Mos 1979, pp. 101–12

van Abeelen, J. H. F., van Nies, J. H. M. 1983. Effects of intrahippocampally-injected naloxone and morphine upon behavioural responses to novelty in mice from two selectively-bred lines. *Psychopharmacology* 81:232–35

van Abeelen, J. H. F., Schetgens, T. M. P. 1981. Inheritance of discrimination learning ability and retention in BA and DBA mice. *Behav. Genet.* 11:173–77

van Dijken, F. R., Scharloo, W. 1979a. Divergent selection on locomotor activity in *Drosophila melanogaster*. I. Selection response. *Behav. Genet.* 9:543–54

van Dijken, F. R., Scharloo, W. 1979b. Divergent selection on locomotor activity in *Drosophila melanogaster*. II. Test for reproductive isolation between selected lines. *Behav. Genet.* 9:555–62

van Dijken, F. R., van Sambeek, M. P. J. W., Scharloo, W. 1979. Divergent selection on locomotor activity in *Drosophila melanogaster*. III. Genetic analysis. *Behav. Genet.* 9:563–70

van Oortmerssen, G. A., Bakker, T. C. M. 1981. Artificial selection for short and long attack latencies in wild *Mus musculus domesticus. Behav. Genet.* 11:115–26

Vargo, M., Hirsch, J. 1982. Central excitation in the fruit fly *(Drosophila melanogaster). J. Comp. Physiol. Psychol.* 96:452–59

Venard, R., Jallon, J.-M. 1980. Evidence for an aphrodisiac pheromone of female *Drosophila. Experientia* 36:211–13

vom Saal, F. S. 1983. The interaction of circulating oestrogens and androgens in regulating mammalian sexual differentiation. See Balthazart et al 1983, pp. 159–77

von Schilcher, F., Hall, J. C. 1979. Neural topography of courtship song in sex mosaics of *Drosophila melanogaster. J. Comp. Physiol.* 129:85–95

Wahlsten, D. 1972. Genetic experiments with animal learning: A critical review. *Behav. Biol.* 7:143–82

Wahlsten, D. 1978. Behavioral genetics and animal learning. In *Psychopharmacology of Aversively Motivated Behavior,* ed. H. Anisman, G. Bignami, pp. 63–118. New York: Plenum

Wainwright, P. E. 1981. Maternal performance of inbred and hybrid laboratory mice *(Mus musculus). J. Comp. Physiol. Psychol.* 95:694–707

Wilcock, J., Fulker, D. W., Broadhurst, P. L.

1981. Analysis of two-way escape-avoidance conditioning measures from a diallel cross of eight strains of rats. *Behav. Genet.* 11:339–58

Willmund, R., Ewing, A. 1982. Visual signals in the courtship of *Drosophila melanogaster. Anim. Behav.* 30:209–15

Wilson, E. O. 1975. *Sociobiology: The New Synthesis.* Cambridge: Harvard. 697 pp.

Wilson, J. D., George, F. W., Griffin, J. E. 1981. The hormonal control of sexual development. *Science* 211:1278–94

Wilson, J. R., Erwin, V. G., DeFries, J. C., Petersen, D. R., Cole-Harding, S. 1984. Ethanol dependence in mice: Direct and correlated responses to 10 generations of selective breeding. *Behav. Genet.* In press

Wimer, C., Wimer, R. E., Wimer, J. S. 1983. An association between granule cell density in the dentate gyrus and two-way avoidance conditioning in the house mouse. *Behav. Neurosci.* 97:844–56

Wimer, R. E., Wimer, C. C. 1982. A geneticist's map of the mouse brain. See Lieblich 1982, pp. 395–420

Wimer, R. E., Wimer, C. 1984. Three sex dimorphisms in the granule cell layer of the hippocampus in house mice. *Brain. Res.* In press

Wimer, R. E., Wimer, C. C., Vaughn, J. E., Barber, R. P., Balvanz, B. A., Chernow, C. R. 1978. The genetic organization of neuron number in the granule cell layer of the area dentata in house mice. *Brain Res.* 157:105–22

Wisniewski, H. M. 1979. The aging brain. In *Spontaneous Animal Models of Human Disease,* ed. E. J. Andrews, B. C. Ward, N. H. Altman, 2:148–52. New York: Academic

Yamaguchi, M., Yamazaki, K., Beauchamp, G. K., Bard, J., Thomas, L., Boyse, E. A. 1981. Distinctive urinary odors governed by the major histocompatibility locus of the mouse. *Proc. Natl. Acad. Sci. USA* 78:5817–20

Yamaguchi, M., Yamazaki, K., Boyse, E. A. 1978. Mating preference tests with the recombinant congenic strain BALB.HTG. *Immunogenetics* 6:261–64

Yamazaki, K., Beauchamp, G. K., Bard, J., Thomas, L., Boyse, E. A. 1982. Chemosensory recognition of phenotypes determined by the *Tla* and *H-2K* regions of chromosome 17 of the mouse. *Proc. Natl. Acad. Sci. USA* 79:7828–31

Yamazaki, K., Beauchamp, G. K., Egorov, I. K., Bard, J., Thomas, L., Boyse, E. A. 1983a. Sensory distinction between $H-2^b$ and $H-2^{bml}$ mutant mice. *Proc. Natl. Acad. Sci. USA* 80:5685–88

Yamazaki, K., Beauchamp, G. K., Thomas, L., Boyse, E. A. 1983b. Chemosensory identity of *H-2* heterozygotes. *Mol. Cell Immunol.* In press

Yamazaki, K., Beauchamp, G. K., Wysocki, C. J., Bard, J., Thomas, L., Boyse, E. A. 1983c. Recognition of *H-2* types in relation to the blocking of pregnancy in mice. *Science* 221:186–88

Yamazaki, K., Boyse, E. A., Mike, V., Thaler, H. T., Mathieson, B. J., et al. 1976. Control of mating preferences in mice by genes in the major histocompatibility complex. *J. Exp. Med.* 144:1324–35

Yamazaki, K., Yamaguchi, M., Andrews, P. W., Peake, B., Boyse, E. A. 1978. Mating preferences of F_2 segregants of crosses between MHC-congenic mouse strains. *Immunogenetics* 6:253–59

Yamazaki, K., Yamaguchi, M., Baranoski, L., Bard, J., Boyse, E. A., Thomas, L. 1979. Recognition among mice: Evidence from the use of a Y-maze, differentially scented by congenic mice of different major histocompatibility types. *J. Exp. Med.* 150:755–60

Yanai, J. 1979. Strain and sex differences in the rat brain. *Acta Anat.* 103:150–58

Zawistowski, S., Hirsch, J. 1984. Conditioned discrimination in the blowfly, *Phormia regina:* Controls and bidirectional selection. *Anim. Learn. Behav.* In press

Zurcher, C., van Zweiten, M. J., Solleveld, H. A., Hollander, C. F. 1982. Aging research. See Foster et al 1982, pp. 11–36

Ann. Rev. Psychol. 1985. 36:219–43

THE PSYCHOLOGY OF INTERGROUP ATTITUDES AND BEHAVIOR

Marilynn B. Brewer and Roderick M. Kramer

Department of Psychology, University of California, Los Angeles, CA 90024

CONTENTS

INTRODUCTION

The study of social relationships between members of different social groups or categories is a disciplinary hybrid that needs to be distinguished from other related research orientations. In the absence of appropriate qualifiers, the phrase "intergroup relations" is generally taken to refer to the collective behavior of groups *qua* groups—international conflict, status stratification, and institutional discrimination—the study of which is traditionally regarded as the domain of sociology and political science. At the other extreme, the traditional psychological orientation toward the study of intergroup relations has been to regard such phenomena as extensions of intraindividual processes (such as attraction formation, hostility, and aggression) to the level of groups. In this conceptualization the study of group relations is simply a particular application of the psychology of personality or interpersonal processes.

0066-4308/85/0201-0219$02.00

A third representation of the nature of intergroup relations is that proposed by Sherif (1966): "Whenever individuals belonging to one group interact, collectively or individually with another group or its members *in terms of their group identification,* we have an instance of intergroup behavior" (p. 12). Seen from this perspective, the study of intergroup relations occupies a special niche at the intersection of individual and group level processes—how interpersonal perceptions, attitudes, or behaviors are shaped or transformed by the presence of group boundaries. It was this conceptualization of the domain of study that provided the focus for Tajfel's (1982a) review, which is the point of departure for the present article. Because of the similarity of focus, much of the research reviewed here represents extensions of prior work covered in the earlier review. To avoid overlap, we will report only studies published since that review or in areas not covered extensively by Tajfel.

Although the view represented here is only one of the multilevel approaches that can be taken to the study of intergroup relations, it is characterized by a number of distinctive, largely independent research traditions or thematic perspectives. In general, these traditions can be grouped into those that are primarily concerned with the intraindividual *processes* underlying the formation and maintenance of intergroup orientations and those that are concerned with the perceptual and behavioral consequences or *outcomes* of such processes. The purpose of this chapter is to characterize these different traditions, reviewing recent theory and research undertaken within each, and then to attempt to identify some integrative or common themes that emerge from the different perspectives.

PROCESS-ORIENTED INTERGROUP RESEARCH

Historically, process orientations to the study of intergroup relations were dominated by motivational theories that stressed the role of attitudes toward own and other social groups in maintaining individual self-esteem or ego defenses (e.g. Adorno et al 1950, Smith et al 1956). More recently, motivation-based explanations have given way to an emphasis on cognitive underpinnings, including extensions of theories of categorization and social cognition to the study of group stereotypes and intergroup biases (e.g. Tajfel 1969, Hamilton 1976, 1979).

Cognitive Underpinnings

SOCIAL COGNITION   As a general field of study, social cognition is concerned with the role of mental representations—or cognitive schemata—in guiding the processing of information about persons or social events. It is characterized by the application of cognitive research methods—particularly measures of reaction time, recall, and recognition—to social contexts. Social cognition research is relevant to the study of intergroup behavior when the cognitive representations under examination are group stereotypes and how they affect the encoding, storage, and retrieval of information about individual group members. The application of social cognition theory and procedures to our understanding of the nature of intergroup stereotyping is represented in recent reviews by Cantor et al (1982), R. Jones (1982), and an edited volume devoted to stereotyping and intergroup behavior (Hamilton 1981). An excellent critical review of the use of cognitive research methods in this line of research is provided by Taylor & Fiske (1981).

A number of different cognitive paradigms have been employed in the search for evidence of social category-based information processing. On the input side, speed of processing visual (facial) information has been found to be influenced by occupational stereotypes (Klatzky et al 1982). On the output side, both recall and recognition of information provided about individual category members are affected by prevailing category stereotypes, such that traits or behaviors relevant to stereotypes are more likely to be correctly remembered than are stereotype-irrelevant characteristics (Brewer et al 1981, C. Cohen 1981, Lui & Brewer 1983). Recent experiments indicate that the facilitating effect of category consistency on memory occurs only when category information is available at the time of encoding (or immediately after) and not when it is presented only at the time of later retrieval from memory (Bellezza & Bower 1981, Clark & Woll 1981).

Social category identification has also been found to affect inferences that are made about individuals in the absence of relevant information. Gender, for instance, is highly associated with position status in our society, leading to expectations that women will be more compliant and easily influenced than men, particularly when an individual's actual job status is unknown (Eagly & Wood 1982). Such expectations can, in turn, foster interactive orientations that elicit stereotype-confirming behaviors, thus contributing to a self-perpetuating cycle (Eagly 1983, Skrypnek & Snyder 1982).

When relevant but ambiguous information is presented in association with category identification, category stereotypes affect the judgments or interpretations that are made about that information. Sagar & Schofield (1980) demonstrated, for example, that pictures of ambiguously aggressive behaviors were interpreted as more hostile and threatening when performed by a black stimulus figure than when the perpetrator was portrayed as white. Interestingly, Darley & Gross (1983) found that information regarding social class membership alone was not sufficient to elicit category-based attributions about the academic ability of an individual child. When combined with ambiguous information in the form of a video-tape of the child's test-taking performance, however, category membership influenced judgments of the performance in a direction that confirmed category-based expectations.

Whereas information that is ambiguous or unrelated to category stereotypes tends to be interpreted or recalled (if at all) in a manner consistent with prior expectancies, information about an individual that is unambiguously inconsistent or incongruent with social category stereotypes is not so easily absorbed or ignored. Such information apparently overrides social stereotypes in judgments about specific individuals (Locksley et al 1980a, 1982) and is remembered as well or better than stereotype-consistent information about the same individual (Brewer et al 1981, C. Cohen 1981). Given that highly discrepant information is attended to, it is logical to ask how exposure to such disconfirming instances feeds back to or alters the perceiver's category stereotypes. A series of experiments by Weber & Crocker (1983) indicates that the effect of stereotype-inconsistent evidence depends on the frequency and distribution of its occurrence. When disconfirming information is concentrated in a single individual or small subgroup, such individuals may be "subtyped" and hence disassociated from the category as a whole. When the inconsistent traits are dispersed across many members of a category, on the other hand, they may be easily ignored unless they are highly salient or represent a high proportion of the total information available. By either mechanism, base-rate stereotypes prove to be relatively resistant to disconfirming case information.

Further indication of the resistance of category stereotypes to disconfirmation comes from research on the phenomenon of "illusory correlation." Illusory correlations derive from memory biases whereby the relative frequency of particular pairings of stimuli is overestimated, resulting in a perceived correlation between the two that exceeds their actual correlation. Illusory correlation processes perpetuate stereotype beliefs when the pairing involved is that between a group label and the presence of traits or characteristics congruent with category expectancies. In the illusory correlation research paradigm, stimulus sets are constructed so that the number of pairings of a particular group label with stereotype-consistent and nonconsistent traits is proportionally the same as the pairings of the same traits with other group labels. Thus the data presented to subjects contain no correlation between group identity and traits. Subjects' memory of the frequency with which they have seen group-trait pairings, however, tends to be biased in the direction of overestimating the occurrence of congruent pairings, thus perpetuating the perceived association (Hamilton & Rose 1980, McArthur & Friedman 1980, Wampold et al 1981).

CATEGORIZATION THEORY   Apart from the effects of prior knowledge structures on our interpretation and recall of information about individual persons, cognitive processes are also represented in research on the perceptual and affective consequences of category differentiation per se (e.g. Wilder & Cooper 1981). It has been demonstrated, in both the physical and social domains, that the imposition of a category boundary on a variable stimulus array alters the perceived values of the stimuli and the differences among them (Tajfel 1957, 1959). Specifically, the assignment of stimuli to distinct categories tends to attenuate perceived differences among stimuli within categories while accentuating intercategory differences. Analogous perceptual processes are presumed to apply to the perception of social categories and category members.

Research on social categorization effects consistently reveals interesting reciprocal relationships between formation of categories and consequences of categorization. Inclusion of individuals in a category boundary, for instance, tends to create a perception of common fate among category members (Larsen 1980), while, conversely, exposure to common fate (such as the outcome of a single lottery) generates feelings of shared category membership (Locksley et al 1980b, Kramer & Brewer 1984). The relationship between intergroup differentiation and distinctiveness seems to be similarly reciprocal. On the one hand, differentiation of a group into separate social categories reduces discriminability among individuals within categories and enhances perceived distinctiveness between members of different categories (Arcuri 1982, Taylor & Falcone 1982). On the other hand, distinctiveness within a social collective tends to induce categorization (Taylor et al 1978). This latter phenomenon is the basis of the so-called "solo effect" whereby salience and recall for information about a single representative of a distinctive category within an interacting group is enhanced relative to that for other members of the group (e.g. Crocker & McGraw 1984). Although there appears to be no simple relationship between these categorization effects and negative prejudice toward distinctive group members (South et al 1982, Taylor & Falcone 1982), categorized minorities have been found to exert less influence in group discussion than minority group members who do not belong to a distinctive category (Maass et al 1982, Mugny & Papastamou 1982).

The tendency to accentuate the degree of homogeneity among members of a common social category exhibits an interesting asymmetry when category membership of the perceiver is taken into account. In general, individuals demonstrate greater differentiation among members of groups to which they themselves belong (ingroups) than they do among members of outgroups. Numerous studies have shown, for instance, that ability to discriminate among and accurately recognize faces is superior for own-race faces than for other races, and recent research indicates that this differential performance increases with age (Chance et al 1982). Individuals also perceive more variability in personality and behavioral characteristics among members of their own groups than within outgroups (Jones et al 1981, Park & Rothbart 1982) and are more likely to recall differentiating information about ingroup than about outgroup stimulus persons (Park & Rothbart 1982, Experiment 4). As further indication of differences in perceived variability among group members, Higgins & Bryant (1982) found that older children and adults are more likely to use group baserate information to account for the choice behavior of an outgroup member than they are for an ingroup member.

Some theorists attribute the differential discriminability among ingroup and outgroup category members to the possibility that cognitive representations of ingroup categories are more complex or differentiated than those of outgroup categories. Linville & Jones (1980) have speculated that such differences in category complexity lead to differences in extremity of evaluation of individual group members. Linville (1982) found, for example, that young (college-aged) subjects exhibited greater dimensional complexity in sorting traits associated with "college-aged males" than in sorting the same traits in association with "males in their 60s or 70s," and, further, that less complexity was correlated with greater polarization of evaluations (positive or negative) of individual elderly persons. Thus, on a number of different measures individuals exhibit greater differentiation in responding to ingroup than to outgroup members. Such findings, however, do not indicate clearly whether these differences stem from the degree of differentiation available in subjects' knowledge structures or from differences in motivation to utilize the distinctions that might be available.

Social Identity Theory

The social cognition approach is based on the premise that knowledge of the relevant cognitive processes alone is sufficient to account for intergroup stereotyping. The appearance of significant asymmetries associated with ingroup and outgroup perceptions, however, suggests the limitations of an approach that does not take account of the affective significance of category membership as a potential moderating factor. Such asymmetries appear in connection with many of the cognitive phenomena that have been studied. In addition to the differential perceived homogeneity effect described above, illusory correlation effects are influenced by the evaluative connotations of the stimuli presented. Overestimation of frequency is most likely to be obtained for distinctive pairings of outgroup categories with *undesirable* behaviors and for ingroup categories with *desirable* behaviors (McArthur & Friedman 1980).

Social identity theory (Tajfel 1974, Tajfel & Turner 1979, Tajfel 1982b) explicitly recognizes the need to consider both basic motivational and cognitive processes in order to explain intergroup perceptions and behavior. As Tajfel & Forgas (1981) put it, "social categorization entails much more than the cognitive classification of events, objects, or people. It is a process impregnated by values, culture and social representations . . ." (p. 114). Most important is the role of social category membership, and of social comparison between categories, in the maintenance of a person's positive social identity, a role which leads individuals to *seek* distinctiveness between their own group and others, particularly on dimensions that are positively valued.

The tenets of social identity theory presume a basic feedback loop in the social categorization process. The presence of a salient basis for categorization in a given social setting induces individuals to incorporate their respective category memberships as part of their social identity in that setting (Meindl & Lerner 1984, Turner 1984). This identification in turn leads them to adopt interpersonal strategies that enhance the distinctiveness between the social categories in ways that favor their own group, a process which produces social competition between groups and further accentuation of category salience. Evidence for this postulated reciprocal relationship between category identification and category differentiation has been established in both laboratory and naturalistic research settings. Discrimination in favor of members of one's own category relative to members of another category has been demonstrated consistently even when the basis for categorization is minimal or arbitrary, and this effect does not seem to be accounted for by experimental "demand characteristics" (St. Claire & Turner 1982).

Discrimination in favor of the ingroup is particularly pronounced when ingroup and outgroup are to be evaluated on the same dimension, with the basis for evaluation provided by the researcher. When Mummendey & Schreiber (1983) gave subjects a choice of rating scales, they showed differentiation in favor of their own category only on selected dimensions, but differentiated in favor of the outgroup category on other, noncorresponding dimensions. Dion (1979) obtained a sex difference in preferred bases for intergroup differentiation. Groups composed entirely of males, who tend to be task-oriented, showed most ingroup favoritism on measures of group product evaluation, whereas groups composed of females showed more bias in interpersonal evaluations of ingroup and outgroup members. Thus, distinguishing ingroup from outgroup is not uniformly biased in favor of the ingroup, as long as *some* basis for positive ingroup distinction is available.

The availability of multiple alternative bases for intergroup differentiation is obvious when research focuses on natural rather than experimentally induced social categories. Perceived differences between ethnic groups, for example, tend to be multidimensional and do not always correspond closely to objective dissimilarities (Foster & White 1982). As a consequence, the relationship between category distinctiveness and intergroup similarity (in attitudes, values, etc) is quite complex. In some laboratory studies, category differentiation has been found to override interpersonal similarity as a determinant of allocation of rewards and penalties (e.g. Hewstone et al 1981), but in other settings attitudinal similarity between groups has been found sometimes to decrease intergroup competition and sometimes to increase it (Brown 1984a,b). Contradictory findings of this kind led Brown (1984a) to conclude that intergroup similarity functions differently depending on social context. When the situation is non-competitive, similarity serves as a source of social validation and reduces intercategory differentiation, as do other forms of reward from the outgroup (Locksley et al 1980b). When competitive orientations are salient, however, the presence of similarity enhances the concern for ingroup distinctiveness and increases intergroup rivalry.

The experience of joint effort to reach a superordinate goal may also be predicted to have potentially opposing effects on intergroup attitudes. Deschamps & Brown (1983) found that when members of two different social categories were given a cooperative task to work on and were assigned differentiated, noncomparable roles to perform, intergroup biases in evaluative ratings decreased following the cooperative effort. However, when the task was undertaken with both groups having comparable roles, differentiation in favor of the ingroup *increased* after cooperation. Thus, under some circumstances the presence of shared superordinate goals appears to enhance rather than decrease the need for intercategory distinctiveness.

ALLOCATION BIASES   While ingroup favoritism is most frequently assessed in terms of biases on evaluative ratings, much of the research in social identity theory has demonstrated ingroup favoritism on behavioral measures as well, particularly on decisions regarding allocation of resources (such as points or money) to individuals as a function of their category membership. Of most interest is the nature of the choice strategy employed by subjects when given an opportunity to allocate resources to an ingroup member (other than self) and an outgroup member. According to social identity theory, the drive toward intergroup social competition should lead allocators to seek to maximize the difference in resources allotted to ingroupers relative to outgroupers in order to achieve positive distinctiveness between groups. When social category identity is salient, individual decision makers should eschew alternative allocation strategies, such as equality or total joint allocation, in favor of those options that provide relatively greater allocation to members of their own category.

Although methodological controversies still persist regarding the appropriate measurement of allocation strategies (Bornstein et al 1983a,b, Turner 1983a,b), over a decade of research employing the "minimal intergroup paradigm" (as initially defined by Tajfel et al 1971) has demonstrated the pervasive influence of relative advantage to the ingroup as a factor in resource allocation decisions, even when no direct self-interest is involved in the outcome, and even when category membership is associated with negative interpersonal attraction (Turner et al 1983). The tendency to favor one party over another has been found to be equally strong when the parties are members of arbitrary social categories as when one party is a close personal friend (Vaughan et al 1981). When members of distinct social categories or subgroups are placed in situations involving interdependence—such as shared access to a common resource pool—this tendency to seek relative advantage for the ingroup persistently interferes with achievement of maximum collective outcomes for the group as a whole, even when cooperative goals have been made salient (Komorita & Lapworth 1982, Kramer & Brewer 1984).

Implicit intergroup comparison also influences judgments of equity and decisions to redistribute rewards in order to preserve or establish equity (Ng 1981). If intergroup competition is present, ingroup loyalties tend to override equity considerations when individuals are given the power to allocate rewards to other performers who have been differentially productive with respect to task contribution (Towson et al 1981, Ancok & Chertkoff 1983). Furthermore, the category membership of the person benefited or deprived by inequitable distributions influences the degree of distress expressed by noninvolved observers over the fact of the inequity (Gray-Little 1980). In the political arena, concerns over relative deprivation of one's own group in intergroup comparisons prove to be more important in predicting intergroup hostility and support for protest movements than do feelings of personal deprivation (Tripathi & Srivastava 1981, Guimond & Dubé-Simard 1983). These findings support one of the major tenets of social identity theory, namely that *intergroup* comparisons must be considered above and beyond *interpersonal* factors in predicting social behavior in group contexts.

OUTCOME-ORIENTED INTERGROUP RESEARCH

Methodologically, process-oriented research is characterized by a predominance of laboratory experiments designed to test hypothesized causal mechanisms. A move from laboratory to field settings tends to be accompanied by a shift of research emphasis, away from a focus on causes as the starting point for hypothesis-testing to a focus on effects, from which causes are to be inferred. In the case of field research on the social psychology of intergroup relations, the effects or outcomes of most interest have been of two types. One is the study of the structure and content of *social representations*—the shared beliefs, images, and affect that persons in a particular society hold about the various social categories or subgroupings recognized in the society. The other is the study of the attitudinal and behavioral consequences of *intergroup contact,* particularly among persons in the contact setting.

Social Representations

GROUP STEREOTYPES   Although much of recent research on social stereotypes has been undertaken within the framework of social cognition studies, there is still considerable interest in more traditional approaches to the study of stereotypes where the focus is on assessment of the structure and content of stereotypes of specific social groups. In this tradition, the mutual perceptions that members of different groups hold of each other are viewed as one aspect of intergroup relations existing within a particular social system. Recent applications of this research approach include the study of interethnic attitudes and perceptions within the context of cultural pluralism in Canada (Gardner & Kalin 1981, Samuda et al 1983) and studies of the mutual perceptions of specific subgroups such as Jews and Arabs in Israel (Bizman & Amir 1982), Hispanics and Anglos in the United States (Triandis et al 1982), and the Chipewyan and Cree Indians in Northern Canada (Jarvenpa 1982).

In addition to stereotypes of groups defined by racial or ethnic identity, similar research has been addressed to stereotyping of demographically defined social categories, particularly gender (Del Boca & Ashmore 1980, Wallston & O'Leary 1981, Ruble & Ruble 1982, Deaux & Lewis 1984), age (Branco & Williamson 1982, Rothbaum 1983), and social class (Morris & Williamson 1982). The methodology associated with most of this research is similar to that employed in the classic study by Katz & Braly (1933)—the assessment (by checklist or rating scale) of associations between group labels and trait characteristics. While the methodology has stayed fairly constant, however, there has been a discernible shift over time in the ways in which stereotypes have been defined or conceptualized (see A. Miller 1982 for overview). Whereas earlier views tended to emphasize negative evaluative connotations and inaccuracy as defining features of stereotypes, more recent conceptualizations tend to be nonevaluative, emphasizing the cognitive functions served by stereotypes (Stephan & Rosenfield 1982). One important consequence of this change of emphasis has been the recognition that "stereotyping" and "prejudice" are both conceptually and empirically distinguishable processes.

The shift in definition at the conceptual level has also brought some criticisms of traditional methods for defining stereotypes operationally. Specifically, the assumption that stereotypes are best assessed through group-based measures (such as mean ratings on evaluative trait scales) is being challenged by those who advocate individualized quantitative measures based on defining stereotypes as probabilistic predictions that distinguish the target group from other groups (McCauley & Stitt 1978, McCauley et al 1980). Other new approaches to assessment of stereotypes replace the traditional emphasis on abstract personality traits as the basic content of group stereotypes with visual or behavioral associations as the basic content (see Brewer et al 1981, Klatzky et al 1982, Deaux & Lewis 1984).

Changes in the way in which stereotypes are conceptualized are also reflected in theory and research on the formation of stereotypic beliefs. Instead of seeking the origin of stereotypes in normatively based prejudice (e.g. Morland & Suthers 1980), current research emphasizes cognitive "overload" and the use of mental heuristics as fundamental to the formation of stereotypes (e.g. Rothbart et al 1984). In this vein, Kruglanski & Freund (1983) predicted and found that ethnic stereotyping—along with other cognitive biases such as primacy effects—increase in magnitude with an increase in time pressure on the individual to make a judgment or prediction. Read (1983) found that assumptions about the behavior of members of a foreign culture could be derived from experience with a single, concrete instance and that the tendency to generalize from a single instance was greater the more complex the rule governing the behavior. Along the same lines, individual differences in stereo-typing and negative evaluations of ethnic outgroups have been found to be related to differences in cognitive complexity (Schönbach et al 1981, Berry 1984, Wagner & Schönbach 1984).

ETHNOCENTRIC ATTRIBUTIONS   Despite the current emphasis on cognitive functions of stereotypes and intergroup perceptions, evidence persists for the influence of ingroup-outgroup biases on the content of such beliefs. In addition to the evaluative biases associated with research on social identity theory, ethnocentric perspectives are also evident in the causal attributions individuals make about the behavior of other individuals as a function of their social category membership. Probably the strongest form of bias is represented by what Pettigrew (1979) referred to as "the ultimate attribution error" in causal attributions for socially desirable versus undesirable behaviors. Desirable be-haviors on the part of ingroup members tend to be attributed to internal, dispositional causes, whereas similar behaviors by outgroup members are more likely to be attributed to transitory causes such as situational influences or exceptional effort. Conversely, undesirable behaviors are more likely to be seen as dispositionally caused when exhibited by outgroup members than by ingroup members.

Attributional biases also appear in explanations for the positive or negative consequences of behavior. Wang & McKillip (1978) found that responsibility for an automobile accident was more likely to be attributed to personality characteristics of the driver when the driver was of a different ethnic identity than the subject than when the driver was of the same ethnic identity. Category membership of the actor also influences whether success or failure are attri-buted to factors such as ability, effort, or luck (Hewstone et al 1982). Green-berg & Rosenfield (1979) found that people who differ in ethnocentrism also differ in their attributions for performance on an ESP task by black and white stimulus persons. The more ethnocentric the perceiver, the more they tended to give whites greater credit (internal attributions) for success than blacks and the more they tended to give whites less blame for failure.

The tendency to assume that success in achievement situations on the part of outgroup members is attributable to situational or other exceptional causes has implications for the effects of affirmative action programs. Garcia et al (1981) demonstrated that when subjects were given information that a minority appli-cant had been admitted to a particular graduate program, they assumed that the applicant was less qualified when the university had an affirmative action program than when it did not have such a program. No such effects were found for evaluations of nonminority candidates.

Apart from the attributions we make about individual behaviors and their consequences, another important aspect of social representations is the explanations members of different groups hold regarding the differences that exist among them (Moscovici 1981), particularly regarding differences in status or power. Hewstone et al (1983) found that group members' explanations for characteristics that distinguished between two different university groups in Hong Kong showed group-serving attributional biases, particularly on the part of the lower status group. More specifically, Hewstone & Jaspars (1982) found that black adolescents tended to blame the white authority system for instances of racial discrimination more than did white adolescents and, further, that such differential explanations tended to become more polarized following intragroup discussion.

One way to account for intergroup differences in outcomes and life styles is to attribute such differences to the beliefs and values held by group members. Such attributions may be particularly important to intergroup relations because of the close relationship between assumed similarity of beliefs and the perceived ease and desirability of social interaction. The belief-congruence model of racial attitudes (Rokeach et al 1960) specifically contends that prejudice and social distance between racial-ethnic groups are mediated by perceived dissimilarity in beliefs and values (see Insko et al 1983 for review). When information about a stimulus person's racial identity is provided simultaneously with information indicative of cultural similarity or dissimilarity to the perceiver, similarity tends to override racial label as a determinant of interpersonal attraction and social distance, at least in situations involving low social pressure and no intergroup competition (Moe et al 1981, McKirnan et al 1983). However, when specific information about personal beliefs is not provided, beliefs attributed to members of distinct social categories tend to exhibit contrast effects (Granberg et al 1981). Thus, in natural contexts the direction of the causal relationship between perceived dissimilarity and intergroup attitudes is ambiguous.

PREJUDICE   The mutual interrelationship between affective and cognitive components of intergroup perceptions is extensively demonstrated in the study of social representations, but the two are conceptually separable. The affective component is best represented in the shared feelings of acceptance-rejection, trust-distrust, and liking-disliking that characterize attitudes toward specific groups in a social system. While technically the term "prejudice" could be applied to the cognitive content of intergroup perceptions as well, typically it is used with reference to this affective or emotional component of intergroup relations. And although affect in this sense is closely associated with the evaluative content of beliefs about different groups, affect and evaluation are not necessarily fully congruent (Abelson et al 1982).

While any social category may be the object of negative prejudice, the preponderance of research in this area has continued to be directed to the study of racial and ethnic prejudice in ethnically mixed societies such as the United States. Most of the research has focused on intergroup relations within a particular society, although proposals for comparative, cross-cultural studies of race and ethnic relations have been developed (Kinloch 1981).

The contribution of psychological research to the study of prejudice has been most evident in the development of methods for assessing prejudicial attitudes and in research on the intercorrelations among measures of ethnic identification, general ethnocentrism, and attitudes toward particular outgroups (e.g. Gallois et al 1982, Hofman 1982). Considerable interest has been focused recently on documenting or tracing historical changes in the extent of prejudice and the form of expression, particularly of racist attitudes in the United States (see Bowser & Hunt 1981 for overview). Many of the more direct expressions of racial hostility and acceptance of racial discrimination and segregation have declined over the past two decades. A number of researchers have suggested, however, that the underlying racist values have not really changed but have merely been rechanneled into less direct forms of expression, variously called "symbolic racism" (Kinder & Sears 1981) or "modern racism" (McConahay et al 1981). The argument here is that "old-fashioned" racial beliefs, now widely recognized as blatantly racist and hence socially undesirable, have been supplanted by new sets of beliefs for which the underlying racial content is not recognized. Such symbolic beliefs include attitudes toward indirectly relevant social issues and policies, such as law and order, busing, and affirmative action.

The basic assumption of symbolic racism theory is that attitudes toward issues such as these, that appear on the surface to be motivated by concerns over self-interest, are actually reflections of residual racial resentments and resistance to racial integration. In support of this view, Kinder & Sears (1981) found that direct threats to whites' personal lives bore little relation to voting patterns in mixed-race elections. Furthermore, both McConahay (1982) and Sears et al (1979, 1980) report that white opposition to busing for school desegregation is only weakly related to direct self-interest factors (living in affected neighborhoods, having school-aged children, etc) but is strongly and consistently related to more general measures of modern racial attitudes. A reanalysis by Bobo (1983), however, challenges the symbolic racism position, arguing that realistic group conflict issues do explain opposition to busing, particularly if threats to ingroup status and distinctiveness are taken into account.

One implication of the symbolic racism concept is that traditional self-report measures of racial bias and prejudice should be replaced by indirect or unobtrusive behavioral measures that are less subject to conscious control and social desirability response biases. Evidence for discrimination against blacks by white subjects has been obtained from experimental studies of nonverbal communication, helping behavior, and aggression (see Crosby et al 1980 for review). Such discrimination is particularly evident when conflicting norms are present in the situation. In an experiment on the effects of the presence of other, nonresponsive bystanders on intervention in an apparent emergency, Gaertner et al (1982) found that white subjects conformed to nonintervention pressures more readily when the victim was black than when she was white. Rogers & Prentice-Dunn (1981) found that nonangered whites were less likely to express aggression against black than white targets, but angered whites were more aggressive against blacks than whites—a pattern of behavior indicative of what they called "regressive racism." Race has also been found to be a factor in competitive responding in mixed-motive games (e.g. Longshore & Beilin 1980).

Underlying racial attitudes can also be revealed in "ambivalence-induced behavioral amplification" (Gaertner & Dovidio 1981, Katz 1981)—the tendency to overreact to blacks (or other stigmatized individuals) such that ambivalent individuals behave more negatively than unambivalent individuals under conditions fostering negative reactions but behave more positively under conditions fostering positive response. McConahay (1983) found such amplification to be predicted from scores on his "modern racism" scale. In a study involving simulated hiring decisions by white subjects, when the job candidate was black, racism scale scores were negatively correlated with hiring evaluations in negative contexts but positively correlated with hiring evaluations in positive contexts. When the job candidate was white, neither context nor modern racism scores were related to hiring evaluations.

Contact Effects

Research on behavioral measures of racial attitudes provides a bridge between studies of social representations and studies of intergroup contact. Whereas social representations of groups can be developed and transmitted in the absence of direct experience with group members, the presence of extended contact between members of different social groups or categories necessitates a shift from representations at the level of the group as a whole to the level of interpersonal perceptions and behavior. The so-called "contact hypothesis" rests on the general assumption that this very shift from the abstract and unfamiliar to the interpersonal and familiar will engender more positive intergroup attitudes and social acceptance. With appropriate qualifications regarding the necessary conditions for positive contact, this hypothesis provided the foundation for the Social Science Statement submitted to the U. S. Supreme

Court in connection with the *Brown vs. Board of Education* decision of 1954 and has guided much of the research since then on the effects of school desegregation in the United States and elsewhere. (For reviews see Schofield 1978, Stephan 1978, Cook 1979, Stephan & Feagin 1980, Hawley 1981, Patchen 1982, Thomas & Brown 1982, Lacy et al 1983, Walberg & Genova 1983, Amir & Sharan 1984, Miller & Brewer 1984).

Although empirical research on the contact hypothesis is dominated by studies in naturalistic desegregation settings, laboratory analogs have been developed for experimental tests of aspects of the hypothesis (e.g. Wilder & Thompson 1980, Brewer & Miller 1984). Field research has involved a variety of research strategies, ranging from descriptive case studies employing ethnographic perspectives (e.g. Clement 1978, Schofield 1982) to correlational case surveys involving natural variations in policy implementation across schools or school districts (e.g. Crain & Mahard 1982, Longshore 1982, Morgan & England 1982), to field experiments testing specific interventions within a given school or classroom (e.g. Slavin 1979, Cohen & Sharan 1980, Riordan & Ruggiero 1980, Rogers et al 1981). Because of its direct policy relevance, results from much of this research have been reviewed and packaged in the form of policy recommendations for designing more effective desegregation programs (e.g. Slavin & Madden 1979, Mercer et al 1980, N. Miller 1980).

Research on the overall correlation between contact and general intergroup attitudes has produced mixed results. Findings from a national probability sample of high school-aged respondents in the U.S. indicated that racial tolerance is positively related to desegregation for both blacks and whites (Scott & McPartland 1982), and Stephan & Rosenfield (1978) found that increases in interethnic contact related positively to changes in racial attitudes of children when combined with low parental authoritarianism. Other studies, however, have found less effect of contact per se on general attitudes (e.g. Amir et al 1980, Barnea & Amir 1981), and results of laboratory experiments on contact experiences suggest that attitude changes do not generalize beyond the contact setting to the outgroup as a whole (Wilder & Thompson 1980), particularly if the contact involves an outgroup member who is regarded as "atypical" (Wilder 1984).

Greater insight into the mixed effects of contact on intergroup attitudes is achieved when outcomes are assessed within the contact setting itself. Particularly relevant are studies of friendship choices and patterns of interaction within racially desegregated schools. In their longitudinal study of one school district, Gerard & Miller (1975) observed that racial encapsulation in friendship choices actually increased rather than decreased in successive years following desegregation, and a number of observational and sociometric studies since then have documented similar patterns of "resegregation" (Tuma & Hallinan 1979, Davey & Mullin 1982, Miller et al 1983). This effect is qualified somewhat by both methodological and situational considerations. With sociometric studies, the extent of racial cleavage in friendships is found to be less when roster-and-rating scale measures are used instead of peer nomination measures (Thomas 1982, Schofield & Whitley 1983), and when relationships are assessed dyadically rather than aggregated by group (Whitley et al 1984). Observational studies of same- versus cross-race interactions indicate that the extent of cross-racial associations is related to gender and to setting. Overall, own-race preference is greater among girls than among boys (Schofield & Francis 1982, Miller et al 1983) and greater in nonacademic social settings than in task-oriented classroom settings (Schofield & Francis 1982, Howe et al 1983).

The evidence for natural resegregation in contact settings has led investigators to address the questions of what structural features of the situation affect category differentiation and how they may be altered to promote greater intergroup acceptance. Most attention has been given to the potential effects of (a) group composition or representation within the desegregated setting, (b) classroom climate and structure, and (c) status differences between groups both within and outside the contact situation.

COMPOSITION   There is surprisingly little systematic information on the effects of proportional representation of different social categories in desegregated settings, particularly considering the theoretical importance of this variable as a factor in category salience and social competition. Experimental studies indicate that, in comparison to equal representation of two categories, the presence of a distinct minority makes minority category identity more salient to nonminority perceivers and increases the self-focus of minority group members (Mullen 1983) and is associated with enhanced ingroup favoritism (Sachdev & Bourhis 1984). In racially desegregated settings, however, the form of the functional relationship between intergroup hostility and racial composition of enrollment is not entirely clear, in part because proportional representation is evaluated relative to past experience and related expectations. Some studies indicate that intergroup hostility is greatest on the part of minority group members in the presence of a clear outgroup majority (e.g. Rogers et al 1984), while other studies find that attitudes are least favorable when racial composition is approximately equal so that neither group clearly controls the "turf" in the desegregated school (Longshore 1982). The situation is further complicated when the setting is multiethnic rather than biracial. Brewer & Miller (1984) have suggested some hypotheses about the interactions among number of categories, their proportional representation, and total group size as determinants of resulting intergroup attitudes, but these have yet to be tested systematically in field settings.

ORGANIZATIONAL STRUCTURE   Results of a number of correlational and observational studies of desegregated schools have suggested that variations in classroom structure and climate have important bearing on the expression of intergroup hostilities and the frequency of cross-ethnic friendship choices (Serow & Solomon 1979, Damico et al 1981, Gumbiner et al 1981, Rosenfield et al 1981). As a consequence, interventions aimed at altering critical aspects of the classroom environment have been among the most frequently assessed in desegregation research. Such interventions range from the introduction of human relations services in the school (see Longshore & Wellisch 1982 for review) to more direct interventions affecting intergroup interactions within the classroom. Among the latter, the most commonly studied are various forms of cooperative learning programs where students are placed in ethnically mixed work groups in which their outcomes are positively interdependent (see Sharan 1980 for review). Meta-analyses of studies comparing such cooperative learning techniques with more traditional competitive or individualistic learning environments document a generally positive effect on intergroup acceptance (Johnson et al 1984). Of particular importance are studies indicating that the impact of cooperative learning experiences on cross-ethnic interactions and sociometric friendship choices extends beyond the immediate workteam setting (Slavin 1979, Hansell & Slavin 1981, Johnson & Johnson 1981). Similar effects have been observed for the introduction of cooperative games in playground settings (Rogers et al 1981).

The generally positive effects of structures that promote intergroup cooperation are not without qualification. First of all, we do not know whether the effects are limited to the interpersonal relations that develop within the cooperative work group, or class, or whether these experiences influence intergroup relations and attitudes in general. Earlier work on positive contact experiences indicates that increasing interpersonal attraction toward specific members of outgroups does not necessarily result in reductions in prejudicial attitudes toward the group as a whole (Cook 1984). Further, there is experimental evidence that if the environment is clearly designed to facilitate successful cooperation, positive effects on intergroup attraction are reduced, since participants can attribute their outcomes to the environment rather than to the cooperation of outgroup team members (Worchel & Norvell 1980). And, as discussed in the preceding section on social identity theory, there are conditions under which cooperative interdependence may enhance motivations for intergroup differentiation rather than reduce them.

GROUP STATUS   In sharp contrast to the manipulation of classroom environment by the introduction of cooperative learning groups is the effect of academic tracking on intergroup behavior in desegregated schools. Schofield (1979) found that the effects of positively structured contact on intergroup interactions eroded when accelerated tracking was introduced. Studies of the effects of desegregation on interethnic acceptance in Israel have also found academic tracking to be a strong moderating factor (Schwarzwald & Cohen

1982). The dampening effect of tracking on intergroup contact and acceptance is generally attributed to the correlation between academic status (as represented in track placement) and group membership. Unequal status within the contact situation has long been recognized as a barrier to promotion of positive intergroup acceptance.

Until recently, most research related to intergroup status effects has concentrated on producing equal-status conditions within the contact setting. It is now recognized, however, that equal status at the structural level does not necessarily correspond to equal status at the psychological level and that it is necessary to take into account both historical status differences and immediate status differences as determinants of intergroup acceptance (Norvell & Worchel 1981). Expectation states theory (Berger et al 1980) holds that the differential status associated with general characteristics such as race (E. Cohen 1982) or sex (Lockheed et al 1983) carry over into new situations even when those characteristics are irrelevant to competence in that setting. As a consequence, it is difficult to achieve equal-status conditions within contact settings without taking into account preexisting status differences between the groups involved (Riordan & Ruggiero 1980).

Direct attempts to compensate for preexisting status differences meet with a number of problems. Norvell & Worchel (1981) found that compensatory advantages to members of any group were universally regarded as unfair, even when they redressed historical imbalances. When status differences between groups are securely established, it is generally the case that high status groups exhibit less ingroup favoritism than low status groups (e.g. Vleming 1983). When status differences are threatened, however, motivations to establish positive intergroup differentiation are heightened on both sides. Thus, the structuring of status relationships within contact settings must be particularly sensitive to the need to provide opportunities for reversing prior status differences without reinforcing category distinctions at the same time (e.g. Amir et al 1979, E. Cohen 1984).

INTEGRATIVE THEMES

Thus far in this review we have focused attention on the distinctive features of the various research traditions that have developed in the study of intergroup attitudes and behavior. There are some common themes, however, that supercede differences in methodological orientation and problem focus. In that vein, we will conclude this review with some thoughts on how research from the process domain might be brought to bear more directly on the problems associated with intergroup contact and desegregation.

One observation that emerges from a number of lines of research is the extent to which group membership influences the attributions we make about our own and others' behavior, intentions, and values. This suggests that the knowledge structures or "subjective culture" (Triandis 1972) that individuals bring *to* an intergroup contact situation may be as important as the structure of the situation itself in shaping the behavioral and attitudinal outcomes. Information gained from direct experience with outgroup members may be rejected or assimilated to prior expectations unless alternative knowledge structures or schemata have been provided in advance of the contact experience. Intercultural training methods such as the "cultural assimilator" (see Landis & Brislin 1983) may provide a model for interventions along these lines.

Other implications for the design of interventions in intergroup contact situations may be drawn from research on social identity and categorization effects. One important factor in the reduction of ingroup biases is the presence of *cross-cutting* category distinctions. When multiple category boundaries are available in a situation, competing bases for ingroup-outgroup classification reduce the importance of any one category membership as a source of social identity and intergroup comparison. Yet interventions in desegregated settings are rarely sensitive to the need for salient cross-cutting categorization schemes that realign individuals along different dimensions at different times. Even cooperative learning programs are usually designed with the intent of subsuming existing social groupings within a common superordinate category rather than creating alternative category alignments. This leaves open the potential for role differentiation and task assignment within cooperative work groups that may reinforce rather than replace prior category distinctions.

Literature Cited

Abelson, R. P., Kinder, D. R., Peters, M. D., Fiske, S. T. 1982. Affective and semantic components in political person perception. *J. Pers. Soc. Psychol.* 42:619–30

Adorno, T., Frenkel-Brunswick, E., Levinson, D., Sanford, R. 1950. *The Authoritarian Personality*. New York: Harper

Amir, Y., Bizman, A., Ben-Ari, R., Rivner, M. 1980. Contact between Israelis and Arabs: A theoretical evaluation of effects. *J. Cross-Cult. Psychol.* 11:426–43

Amir, Y., Sharan, S., eds. 1984. *School Desegregation: Cross-Cultural Perspectives*. Hillsdale, NJ: Erlbaum

Amir, Y., Sharan, S., Rivner, M., Ben-Ari, R., Bizman, A. 1979. Group status and attitude change in desegregated classrooms. *Int. J. Intercult. Relat.* 3:137–52

Ancok, D., Chertkoff, J. M. 1983. Effects of group membership, relative performance, and self-interest on the division of outcomes. *J. Pers. Soc. Psychol.* 45:1256–62

Arcuri, L. 1982. Three patterns of social categorization in attribution memory. *Eur. J. Soc. Psychol.* 12:271–82

Barnea, M., Amir, Y. 1981. Attitudes and attitude change following intergroup contact of religious and nonreligious students in Israel. *J. Soc. Psychol.* 115:65–71

Bellezza, F. S., Bower, G. H. 1981. Person stereotypes and memory for people. *J. Pers. Soc. Psychol.* 41:856–65

Berger, J., Rosenholtz, S. J., Zelditch, M. Jr. 1980. Status organizing processes. *Ann. Rev. Sociol.* 6:479–508

Berry, J. W. 1984. Cultural relations in plural societies: Alternatives to segregation and their sociopsychological implications. See Miller & Brewer 1984, pp. 11–27

Bizman, A., Amir, Y. 1982. Mutual perceptions of Arabs and Jews in Israel. *J. Cross-Cult. Psychol.* 13:461–69

Bobo, L. 1983. Whites' opposition to busing: Symbolic racism or realistic group conflict? *J. Pers. Soc. Psychol.* 45:1196–1210

Bornstein, G., Crum, L., Wittenbraker, J., Harring, K., Insko, C., Thibaut, J. 1983a. On the measurement of social orientations in the minimal group paradigm. *Eur. J. Soc. Psychol.* 13:321–50

Bornstein, G., Crum, L., Wittenbraker, J., Harring, K., Insko, C., Thibaut, J. 1983b. Reply to Turner's comments. *Eur. J. Soc. Psychol.* 13:369–81

Bowser, B. P., Hunt, R. G., eds. 1981. *Impacts of Racism on White Americans.* Beverly Hills: Sage

Branco, K. J., Williamson, J. B. 1982. Stereotyping and the life cycle: Views of aging and the aged. See Miller 1982, pp. 364–410

Brewer, M. B., Dull, V., Lui, L. 1981. Perceptions of the elderly: Stereotypes as prototypes. *J. Pers. Soc. Psychol.* 41:656–70

Brewer, M. B., Miller, N. 1984. Beyond the contact hypothesis: Theoretical perspectives on desegregation. See Miller & Brewer 1984, pp. 281–302

Brown, R. J. 1984a. The effects of intergroup similarity and cooperative versus competitive orientation on intergroup discrimination. *Br. J. Soc. Psychol.* 23:21–33

Brown, R. J. 1984b. The role of similarity in intergroup relations. In *The Social Dimension: European Developments in Social Psychology,* ed. H. Tajfel, pp. 603–23. London: Cambridge Univ. Press

Cantor, N., Mischel, W., Schwartz, J. 1982. Social knowledge: Structure, content, use, and abuse. In *Cognitive Social Psychology,* ed. A. H. Hastorf, A. M. Isen. pp. 33–72. New York: Elsevier/North Holland

Chance, J. E., Turner, A. L., Goldstein, A. G. 1982. Development of differential recognition for own- and other-race faces. *J. Psychol.* 112:29–37

Clark, L. F., Woll, S. B. 1981. Stereotype biases: A reconstructive analysis of their role in reconstructive memory. *J. Pers. Soc. Psychol.* 41:1064–72

Clement, D. C. 1978. Ethnographic perspective on desegregated schools. *Anthropol. Educ. Q.* 9:245–47

Cohen, C. E. 1981. Person categories and social perception: Testing some boundaries of the processing effects of prior knowledge. *J. Pers. Soc. Psychol.* 40:441–52

Cohen, E. G. 1982. Expectation states and interracial interaction in school settings. *Ann. Rev. Sociol.* 8:209–35

Cohen, E. G. 1984. The desegregated school: Problems in status power and interethnic climate. See Miller & Brewer 1984, pp. 77–96

Cohen, E. G., Sharan, S. 1980. Modifying status relations in Israeli youth. *J. Cross-Cult. Psychol.* 11:364–84

Cook, S. W. 1979. Social science and school desegregation: Did we mislead the Supreme Court? *Pers. Soc. Psychol. Bull.* 5:420–37

Cook, S. W. 1984. Cooperative interaction in multi-ethnic contexts. See Miller & Brewer 1984, pp. 155–85

Crain, R. L., Mahard, R. E. 1982. The consequences of controversy accompanying institutional change: The case of school desegregation. *Am. Sociol. Rev.* 47:697–708

Crocker, J., McGraw, K. M. 1984. What's good for the goose is not good for the gander: Solo status as an obstacle to occupational achievement for males and females. *Am. Behav. Sci.* 27:357–69

Crosby, F., Bromley, S., Saxe, L. 1980. Recent unobtrusive studies of black and white discrimination and prejudice: A literature review. *Psychol. Bull.* 87:546–63

Damico, S. B., Bell-Nathaniel, A., Green, C. 1981. Effects of school organizational structure on interracial friendships in middle schools. *J. Educ. Res.* 74:388–93

Darley, J. M., Gross, P. H. 1983. A hypothesis-confirming bias in labeling effects. *J. Pers. Soc. Psychol.* 44:20–33

Davey, A. G., Mullin, P. N. 1982. Inter-ethnic friendship in British primary schools. *Educ. Res.* 24:83–92

Deaux, K., Lewis, L. L. 1984. The structure of gender stereotypes: Interrelationships among components and gender label. *J. Pers. Soc. Psychol.* 46:991–1004

Del Boca, F. K., Ashmore, R. D. 1980. Sex stereotypes through the life cycle. In *Review of Personality and Social Psychology,* ed. L. Wheeler, 1:163–92. Beverly Hills: Sage

Deschamps, J-C., Brown, R. J. 1983. Superordinate goals and intergroup conflict. *Br. J. Soc. Psychol.* 22:189–95

Dion, K. L. 1979. Status equity, sex composition of group, and intergroup bias. *Pers. Soc. Psychol. Bull.* 5:240–44

Eagly, A. H. 1983. Gender and social influence: A social psychological analysis. *Am. Psychol.* 38:971–81

Eagly, A. H., Wood, W. 1982. Inferred sex differences in status as a determinant of gender stereotypes about social influence. *J. Pers. Soc. Psychol.* 43:915–28

Foster, B. L., White, G. M. 1982. Ethnic identity and perceived distance between ethnic categories. *Hum. Organ.* 41:121–30

Gaertner, S. L., Dovidio, J. F. 1981. Racism among the well-intentioned. In *Pluralism, Racism, and Public Policy: The Search for Equality,* ed. E. Clausen, J. Bermingham, pp. 208–22. Boston: Hall

Gaertner, S. L., Dovidio, J. F., Johnson, G. 1982. Race of victim, nonresponsive bystanders, and helping behavior. *J. Soc. Psychol.* 117:69–77

Gallois, C., Callan, V. J., Parslow, L. A. 1982. Evaluations of four ethnic groups: Level of ethnocentrism, favourability, and social distance. *Aust. J. Psychol.* 34:369–74

Garcia, L. T., Erskine, N., Hawn, K., Casmay, S. 1981. The effect of affirmative action on attributions about minority group members. *J. Pers.* 49:427–37

Gardner, R. C., Kalin, R., eds. 1981. *A Cana-*

dian Social Psychology of Ethnic Relations. New York: Methuen

Gerard, H. B., Miller, N. 1975. *School Desegregation.* New York: Plenum

Granberg, D., Jefferson, N. L., Brent, E. E., King, M. 1981. Membership group, reference group, and the attribution of attitudes to groups. *J. Pers. Soc. Psychol.* 40:833–42

Gray-Little, B. 1980. Race and inequity. *J. Appl. Soc. Psychol.* 10:468–81

Greenberg, J., Rosenfield, D. 1979. Whites' ethnocentrism and their attributions for the behavior of blacks: A motivational bias. *J. Pers.* 47:643–57

Guimond, S., Dubé-Simard, L. 1983. Relative deprivation theory and the Quebec Nationalist Movement: The cognition-emotion distinction and the personal-group deprivation issue. *J. Pers. Soc. Psychol.* 44:526–35

Gumbiner, J., Knight, G. P., Kagan, S. 1981. Relations of classroom structures and teacher behaviors to social orientation, self-esteem, and classroom climate among Anglo-American and Mexican-American children. *Hisp. J. Behav. Sci.* 3:19–40

Hamilton, D. L. 1976. Cognitive biases in the perception of social groups. In *Cognition and Social Behavior,* ed. J. S. Carroll, J. W. Payne, pp. 81–93. Hillsdale, NJ: Erlbaum

Hamilton, D. L. 1979. A cognitive-attributional analysis of stereotyping. *Adv. Exp. Soc. Psychol.* 12:53–84

Hamilton, D. L., ed. 1981. *Cognitive Processes in Stereotyping and Intergroup Behavior.* Hillsdale, NJ: Erlbaum

Hamilton, D. L., Rose, T. L. 1980. Illusory correlation and the maintenance of stereotypic beliefs. *J. Pers. Soc. Psychol.* 39:832–45

Hansell, S., Slavin, R. E. 1981. Cooperative learning and the structure of interracial friendships. *Sociol. Educ.* 54:98–106

Hawley, W. D., ed. 1981. *Effective School Desegregation: Equity, Quality, and Feasibility.* Beverly Hills: Sage

Hewstone, M., Bond, M. H., Wan, K. 1983. Social facts and social attributions: The explanation of intergroup differences in Hong Kong. *Soc. Cognit.* 2:142–57

Hewstone, M., Fincham, F., Jaspars, J. 1981. Social categorization and similarity in intergroup behaviour: A replication with 'penalties'. *Eur. J. Soc. Psychol.* 11:101–7

Hewstone, M., Jaspars, J. 1982. Explanations for racial discrimination: The effect of discussion on intergroup attributions. *Eur. J. Soc. Psychol.* 12:1–16

Hewstone, M., Jaspars, J., Lalljee, M. 1982. Social representations, social attribution, and social identity: The intergroup images of 'public' and 'comprehensive' schoolboys. *Eur. J. Soc. Psychol.* 12:241–69

Higgins, E. T., Bryant, S. L. 1982. Consensus information and the fundamental attribution error: The role of development and in-group versus out-group knowledge. *J. Pers. Soc. Psychol.* 43:889–900

Hofman, J. E. 1982. Social identity and the readiness for social relations between Jews and Arabs in Israel. *Hum. Relat.* 35:727–41

Howe, A. C., Hall, V., Stanback, B., Seidman, S. 1983. Pupil behaviors and interactions in desegregated urban junior high activity-centered science classrooms. *J. Educ. Psychol.* 75:97–103

Insko, C. A., Nacoste, R. W., Moe, J. L. 1983. Belief congruence and racial discrimination: Review of the evidence and critical evaluation. *Eur. J. Soc. Psychol.* 13:153–74

Jarvenpa, R. 1982. Intergroup behavior and imagery: The case of Chipewyan and Cree. *Ethnology* 21:283–99

Johnson, D. W., Johnson, R. T. 1981. Effects of cooperative and individualistic experiences on interethnic interaction. *J. Educ. Psychol.* 73:444–49

Johnson, D. W., Johnson, R. T., Maruyama, G. 1984. Goal interdependence and interpersonal attraction in heterogeneous classrooms: A meta-analysis. See Miller & Brewer 1984, pp. 187–212

Jones, E. E., Wood, G. C., Quattrone, G. A. 1981. Perceived variability of personal characteristics in in-groups and out-groups: The role of knowledge and evaluation. *Pers. Soc. Psychol. Bull.* 7:523–28

Jones, R. A. 1982. Perceiving other people: Stereotyping as a process of social cognition. See Miller 1982, pp. 41–91

Katz, D., Braly, K. W. 1933. Racial stereotypes of 100 college students. *J. Abnorm. Soc. Psychol.* 28:280–90

Katz, I. 1981. *Stigma: A Social Psychological Analysis.* Hillsdale, NJ: Erlbaum

Kinder, D. R., Sears, D. O. 1981. Prejudice and politics: Symbolic racism versus racial threats to the good life. *J. Pers. Soc. Psychol.* 40:414–31

Kinloch, G. C. 1981. Comparative race and ethnic relations. *Int. J. Comp. Sociol.* 22:3–4

Klatzky, R. A., Martin, G. L., Kane, R. A. 1982. Influence of social-category activation on processing of visual information. *Soc. Cognit.* 1:95–109

Komorita, S. S., Lapworth, C. W. 1982. Cooperative choice among individuals versus groups in an n-person dilemma situation. *J. Pers. Soc. Psychol.* 42:487–96

Kramer, R. M., Brewer, M. B. 1984. Effects of group identity on resource use decisions in a simulated commons dilemma. *J. Pers. Soc. Psychol.* 46:1044–57

Kruglanski, A. W., Freund, T. 1983. The freezing and unfreezing of lay-inferences: Effects on impressional primacy, ethnic stereotyping, and numerical anchoring. *J. Exp. Soc. Psychol.* 19:448–68

Lacy, W. B., Mason, E. J., Middleton, E. 1983. Fostering constructive intergroup contact in desegregated schools: Suggestions for future research. *J. Negro Educ.* 52:113–41

Landis, D., Brislin, R. W., ed. 1983. *Handbook of Intercultural Training*, Vols. 1–3. Elmsford, NY: Pergamon

Larsen, K. S. 1980. Social categorization and attitude change. *J. Soc. Psychol.* 111:113–18

Linville, P. W. 1982. The complexity-extremity effect and age-based stereotyping. *J. Pers. Soc. Psychol.* 42:193–211

Linville, P. W., Jones, E. E. 1980. Polarized appraisals of out-group members. *J. Pers. Soc. Psychol.* 38:689–703

Lockheed, M. E., Harris, A. M., Nemceff, W. P. 1983. Sex and social influence: Does sex function as a status characteristic in mixed-sex groups of children? *J. Educ. Psychol.* 75:877–88

Locksley, A., Borgida, E., Brekke, N., Hepburn, C. 1980a. Sex stereotypes and social judgment. *J. Pers. Soc. Psychol.* 39:821–31

Locksley, A., Ortiz, V., Hepburn, C. 1980b. Social categorization and discriminatory behavior: Extinguishing the minimal intergroup discrimination effect. *J. Pers. Soc. Psychol.* 39:773–83

Locksley, A., Hepburn, C., Ortiz, V. 1982. Social stereotypes and judgments of individuals: An instance of the base-rate fallacy. *J. Exp. Soc. Psychol.* 18:23–42

Longshore, D. 1982. School racial composition and blacks' attitudes towards desegregation: The problem of control in desegregated schools. *Soc. Sci. Q.* 63:674–87

Longshore, D., Beilin, R. 1980. Interracial behavior in the prisoner's dilemma. The effect of color connotations. *J. Black Stud.* 11:105–20

Longshore, D., Wellisch, J. B. 1982. Human relations programs in desegregated elementary schools. *Eval. Rev.* 6:789–99

Lui, L., Brewer, M. B. 1983. Recognition accuracy as evidence of category-consistency effects in person memory. *Soc. Cognit.* 2:89–107

Maass, A., Clark, R. D., Haberkorn, G. 1982. The effects of differential ascribed category membership and norms on minority influence. *Eur. J. Soc. Psychol.* 12:89–104

McArthur, L., Friedman, S. A. 1980. Illusory correlation in impression formation: Variations in the shared distinctiveness effect as a function of the distinctive person's age, race, and sex. *J. Pers. Soc. Psychol.* 39:615–24

McCauley, C., Stitt, C. L. 1978. An individual and quantitative measure of stereotypes. *J. Pers. Soc. Psychol.* 36:929–40

McCauley, C., Stitt, C. L., Segal, M. 1980. Stereotyping: From prejudice to prediction. *Psychol. Bull.* 87:195–208

McConahay, J. B. 1982. Self-interest versus racial attitudes as correlates of anti-busing attitudes in Louisville: Is it the buses or the blacks? *J. Polit.* 44:692–720

McConahay, J. B. 1983. Modern racism and modern discrimination: The effects of race, racial attitudes, and context on simulated hiring decisions. *Pers. Soc. Psychol. Bull.* 9:551–58

McConahay, J. B., Hardee, B. B., Batts, V. 1981. Has racism declined in America? It depends on who is asking and what is asked. *J. Conflict Resolut.* 25:563–79

McKirnan, D. J., Smith, C. E., Hamayan, E. V. 1983. A sociolinguistic approach to the belief-similarity model of racial attitudes. *J. Exp. Soc. Psychol.* 19:434–47

Meindl, J. R., Lerner, M. J. 1984. Exacerbation of extreme responses to an outgroup. *J. Pers. Soc. Psychol.* 47:71–84

Mercer, J. R., Iadicola, P., Moore, H. 1980. Building effective multiethnic schools. See Stephan & Feagin 1980, pp. 281–307

Miller, A. G. 1982. Historical and contemporary perspectives on stereotyping. In *In the Eye of the Beholder: Contemporary Issues in Stereotyping*, ed. A. G. Miller, pp. 1–39. New York: Praeger

Miller, N. 1980. Making school desegregation work. See Stephan & Feagin 1980, pp. 309–57

Miller, N., Brewer, M. B., eds. 1984. *Groups in Contact: The Psychology of Desegregation*. San Diego: Academic

Miller, N., Rogers, M., Hennigan, K. 1983. Increasing interracial acceptance: Using cooperative games in desegregated elementary schools. *Applied Social Psychology Annual*, ed. L. Bickman, 4:199–216. Beverly Hills: Sage

Moe, J. L., Nacoste, R. W., Insko, C. A. 1981. Belief versus race as determinants of discrimination: A study of Southern adolescents in 1966 and 1979. *J. Pers. Soc. Psychol.* 41:1031–50

Morgan, D. R., England, R. E. 1982. Large district school desegregation: A preliminary assessment of techniques. *Soc. Sci. Q.* 63:688–700

Morland, J. K., Suthers, E. 1980. Racial attitudes of children: Perspectives on the structural-normative theory of prejudice. *Phylon* 41:267–75

Morris, M., Williamson, J. B. 1982. Stereotypes and social class: A focus on poverty. See Miller 1982, pp. 411–504

Moscovici, S. 1981. On social representations. In *Social Cognition: Perspectives on Everyday Understanding*, ed. J. P. Forgas, pp. 181–209. New York: Academic

Mugny, G., Papastamou, S. 1982. Minority

influence and psycho-social identity. *Eur. J. Soc. Psychol.* 12:379–94

Mullen, B. 1983. Operationalizing the effect of the group on the individual: A self-attention perspective. *J. Exp. Soc. Psychol.* 19:295–322

Mummendey, A., Schreiber, H. 1983. Better or just different? Positive social identity by discrimination against, or by differentiation from outgroups. *Eur. J. Soc. Psychol.* 13:389–97

Ng, S. H. 1981. Equity theory and the allocation of rewards between groups. *Eur. J. Soc. Psychol.* 11:439–43

Norvell, N., Worchel, S. 1981. A reexamination of the relation between equal status contact and intergroup attraction. *J. Pers. Soc. Psychol.* 41:902–8

Park, B., Rothbart, M. 1982. Perception of out-group homogeneity and levels of social categorization: Memory for the subordinate attributes of in-group and out-group members. *J. Pers. Soc. Psychol.* 42:1051–68

Patchen, M. 1982. *Black-White Contact in Schools: Its Social and Academic Effects.* West Lafayette, Ind: Purdue Univ. Press

Pettigrew, T. F. 1979. The ultimate attribution error: Extending Allport's cognitive analysis of prejudice. *Pers. Soc. Psychol. Bull.* 5:461–76

Read, S. J. 1983. Once is enough: Causal reasoning from a single instance. *J. Pers. Soc. Psychol* 45:323–34

Riordan, C., Ruggiero, J. 1980. Producing equal-status interracial interaction: A replication. *Soc. Psychol. Q.* 43:131–36

Rogers, M., Hennigan, K., Bowman, C., Miller, N. 1984. Intergroup acceptance in classroom and playground settings. See Miller & Brewer 1984, pp. 213–27

Rogers, M., Miller, N., Hennigan, K. 1981. Cooperative games as an intervention to promote cross-racial acceptance. *Am. Educ. Res. J.* 18:513–16

Rogers, R. W., Prentice-Dunn, S. 1981. Deindividuation and anger-mediated interracial aggression: Unmasking regressive racism. *J. Pers. Soc. Psychol.* 41:63–73

Rokeach, M., Smith, P. W., Evans, R. I. 1960. 'Two kinds of prejudice or one?' In *The Open and Closed Mind,* ed. M. Rokeach, pp. 132–68. New York: Basic Books

Rosenfield, D., Sheehan, D. S., Marcus, M. M., Stephan, W. G. 1981. Classroom structure and prejudice in desegregated schools. *J. Educ. Psychol.* 73:17–26

Rothbart, M., Dawes, R., Park, B. 1984. Stereotyping and sampling biases in intergroup perception. In *Attitudinal Judgment,* ed. J. R. Eiser, pp. 109–34. New York: Springer-Verlag

Rothbaum, F. 1983. Aging and age stereotypes. *Soc. Cognit.* 2:171–84

Ruble, D. N., Ruble, T. L. 1982. Sex stereotypes. See Miller 1982, pp. 188–252

Sachdev, I., Bourhis, R. Y. 1984. Minimal majorities and minorities. *Eur. J. Soc. Psychol.* 14:35–52

Sagar, H. A., Schofield, J. W. 1980. Racial and behavioral cues in white children's perceptions of ambiguously aggressive acts. *J. Pers. Soc. Psychol.* 39:590–98

St. Claire, L., Turner, J. C. 1982. The role of demand characteristics in the social categorization paradigm. *Eur. J. Soc. Psychol.* 12:307–14

Samuda, R., Berry, J., Laferriere, M., eds. 1983. *Multiculturalism in Canada: Social and Educational Perspectives.* Toronto: Allyn & Bacon

Schofield, J. W. 1978. School desegregation and intergroup relations. In *The Social Psychology of Education: Theory and Practice,* ed. D. Bar-Tal, L. Saxe. pp. 329–63. New York: Halstead

Schofield, J. W. 1979. The impact of positively structured contact on intergroup behavior: Does it last under adverse conditions? *Soc. Psychol. Q.* 42:280–84

Schofield, J. W. 1982. *Black and White in School: Trust, Tension, or Tolerance.* New York: Praeger

Schofield, J. W., Francis, W. D. 1982. An observational study of peer interaction in racially mixed "accelerated" classrooms. *J. Educ. Psychol.* 74:722–32

Schofield, J. W., Whitley, B. E. 1983. Peer nomination versus rating scale measurement of children's peer preferences. *Soc. Psychol. Q.* 46:242–51

Schönbach, P., Gollwitzer, P., Stiepel, G., Wagner, U. 1981. *Education and Intergroup Attitudes.* New York: Academic

Schwarzwald, J., Cohen, S. 1982. Relationship between academic tracking and the degree of interethnic acceptance. *J. Educ. Psychol.* 74:588–97

Scott, R. R., McPartland, J. M. 1982. Desegregation as national policy: Correlates of racial attitudes. *Am. Educ. Res. J.:* 19:397–414

Sears, D. O., Hensler, C. P., Speer, L. 1979. Whites' opposition to busing: Self-interest or symbolic politics? *Am. Polit. Sci. Rev.* 73:369–84

Sears, D. O., Lau, R. R., Tyler, T. R., Allen, H. M. 1980. Self-interest or symbolic politics in policy attitudes and presidential voting. *Am. Polit. Sci. Rev.* 74:670–84

Serow, R. C., Solomon, D. 1979. Classroom climates and students' intergroup behavior. *J. Educ. Psychol.* 71:669–76

Sharan, S. 1980. Cooperative learning in small groups: Recent methods and effects on achievement, attitudes, and ethnic relations. *Rev. Educ. Res.* 50:241–71

Sherif, M. 1966. In Common Predicament: Social Psychology of Intergroup Conflict and Cooperation. New York: Houghton Mifflin

Skrypnek, B. J., Snyder, M. 1982. On the self-perpetuating nature of stereotypes about women and men. J. Exp. Soc. Psychol. 18:277–91

Slavin, R. E. 1979. Effects of biracial learning teams on cross-racial friendships. J. Educ. Psychol. 71:381–87

Slavin, R. E., Madden, N. A. 1979. School practices that improve race relations. Am. Educ. Res. J. 16:169–80

Smith, M. B., Bruner, J. S., White, R. W. 1956. Opinions and Personality. New York: Wiley

South, S. J., Bonjean, C. M., Markham, W. T., Corder, J. 1982. Social structure and intergroup interaction: Men and women of the federal bureaucracy. Am. Sociol. Rev. 47:587–99

Stephan, W. G. 1978. School desegregation: An evaluation of predictions made in Brown v. Board of Education. Psychol. Bull. 85: 217–38

Stephan, W. G., Feagin, J. R., eds. 1980. School Desegregation: Past, Present, and Future. New York: Plenum

Stephan, W. G., Rosenfield, D. 1978. Effects of desegregation on racial attitudes. J. Pers. Soc. Psychol. 36:795–804

Stephan, W. G., Rosenfield, D. 1982. Racial and ethnic stereotypes. See Miller 1982, pp. 92–135

Tajfel, H. 1957. Value and the perceptual judgment of magnitude. Psychol. Rev. 64:192–204

Tajfel, H. 1959. Quantitative judgment in social perception. Br. J. Psychol. 50:16–29

Tajfel, H. 1969. Cognitive aspects of prejudice. J. Soc. Issues 25:79–97

Tajfel, H. 1974. Social identity and intergroup behavior. Soc. Sci. Inf. 13:65–93

Tajfel, H. 1982a. Social psychology of intergroup relations. Ann. Rev. Psychol. 33:1–39

Tajfel, H., ed. 1982b. Social Identity and Intergroup Relations. Cambridge: Cambridge Univ. Press

Tajfel, H., Billig, R., Bundy, C., Flament, C. 1971. Social categorization and intergroup behavior. Eur. J. Soc. Psychol. 1:149–78

Tajfel, H., Forgas, J. P., eds. 1981. Social categorization: Cognitions, values and groups. In Social Cognition: Perspectives on Everyday Understanding, ed. J. P. Forgas, pp. 113–40. New York: Academic

Tajfel, H., Turner, J. C. 1979. An integrative theory of intergroup conflict. In The Social Psychology of Intergroup Relations, ed. W. Austin, S. Worchel, pp. 33–47. Monterey, Calif: Brooks/Cole

Taylor, S. E., Falcone, H. 1982. Cognitive bases of stereotyping: The relationship between categorization and prejudice. Pers. Soc. Psychol. Bull. 8:426–32

Taylor, S. E., Fiske, S. T. 1981. Getting inside the head: Methodologies for process analysis in attribution and social cognition. In New Directions in Attribution Research, ed. J. H. Harvey, W. Ickes, R. F. Kidd, 3:459–524. Hillsdale, NJ: Erlbaum

Taylor, S. E., Fiske, S. T., Etcoff, N. L., Ruderman, A. J. 1978. Categorical and contextual bases of person memory and stereotyping. J. Pers. Soc. Psychol. 36:778–93

Thomas, G. E., Brown, F. 1982. What does educational research tell us about school desegregation effects? J. Black Stud. 13:155–74

Thomas, K. C. 1982. The influence of race on adolescent friendship patterns. Educ. Stud. 8:175–83

Towson, S. M., Lerner, M. J., de Carufel, A. 1981. Justice rules or ingroup loyalties: The effects of competition on children's allocation behavior. Pers. Soc. Psychol. Bull. 7:696–700

Triandis, H. 1972. The Analysis of Subjective Culture. New York: Wiley

Triandis, H., Lisansky, J., Setiadi, B., Chang, B., Marin, G., et al. 1982. Stereotyping among hispanics and anglos: The uniformity, intensity, direction, and quality of auto- and hetereostereotypes. J. Cross-Cult. Psychol. 13:409–26

Tripathi, R. C., Srivastava, R. 1981. Relative deprivation and intergroup attitudes. Eur. J. Soc. Psychol. 11:313–18

Tuma, N. B., Hallinan, M. T. 1979. The effects of sex, race, and achievement on schoolchildren's friendships. Soc. Forces 57:1265–85

Turner, J. C. 1983a. Some comments on . . . "the measurement of social orientations in the minimal group paradigm." Eur. J. Soc. Psychol. 13:351–67

Turner, J. C. 1983b. A second reply to Bornstein, Crum, Wittenbraker, Harring, Insko and Thibaut on the measurement of social orientations. Eur. J. Soc. Psychol. 13:383–87

Turner, J. C. 1984. Social identification and psychological group formation. See Brown 1984b, pp. 518–38

Turner, J. C., Shaver, I., Hogg, M. A. 1983. Social categorization, interpersonal attraction and group formation. Br. J. Soc. Psychol. 22:227–39

Vaughan, G. M., Tajfel, H., Williams, J. 1981. Bias in reward allocation in an intergroup and an interpersonal context. Soc. Psychol. Q. 44:37–42

Vleeming, R. G. 1983. Intergroup relations in a simulated society. J. Psychol. 113:81–87

Wagner, U., Schönbach, P. 1984. Links between educational status and prejudice:

Ethnic attitudes in West Germany. See Miller & Brewer 1984, pp. 29–52

Walberg, H. J., Genova, W. J. 1983. School practices and climates that promote integration. *Contemp. Educ. Psychol.* 8:87–100

Wallston, B. S., O'Leary, V. E. 1981. Sex makes a difference: Differential perceptions of women and men. *Rev. Pers. Soc. Psychol.* 2:9–41

Wampold, B. E., Casas, J. M., Atkinson, D. R. 1981. Ethnic bias in counseling: An information processing approach. *J. Couns. Psychol.* 28:498–503

Wang, G., McKillip, J. 1978. Ethnic identification and judgements of an accident. *Pers. Soc. Psychol. Bull.* 4:296–99

Weber, R., Crocker, J. 1983. Cognitive processes in the revision of stereotypic beliefs. *J. Pers. Soc. Psychol.* 45:961–77

Whitley, B. E., Schofield, J. W., Snyder, H. N. 1984. Peer preferences in a desegregated school: A round robin analysis. *J. Pers. Soc. Psychol.* 46:799–810

Wilder, D. A. 1984. Intergroup contact: The typical member and the exception to the rule. *J. Exp. Soc. Psychol.* 20:177–94

Wilder, D. A., Cooper, W. E. 1981. Categorization into groups: Consequences for social perception and attribution. In *New Directions for Attribution Research*, ed. J. H. Harvey, W. Ickes, R. F. Kidd, 3:247–77. Hillsdale, NJ: Erlbaum

Wilder, D. A., Thompson, J. E. 1980. Intergroup contact with independent manipulations of in-group and out-group interaction. *J. Pers. Soc. Psychol.* 38:589–603

Worchel, S., Norvell, N. 1980. Effect of perceived environmental conditions during cooperation on intergroup attraction. *J. Pers. Soc. Psychol.* 38:764–72

Ann. Rev. Psychol. 1985. 36:245–74

PROGRESS IN NEUROPHYSIOLOGY OF SOUND LOCALIZATION

Dennis P. Phillips

Department of Psychology, Dalhousie University, Halifax, Nova Scotia,
Canada B3H 4J1

John F. Brugge

Department of Neurophysiology and Waisman Center on Mental Retardation
and Human Development, University of Wisconsin, Madison, Wisconsin 53705

CONTENTS

INTRODUCTION

In 1972, Erulkar provided a detailed review of sound localization mechanisms in a wide variety of species. Classical psychoacoustics pointed to the importance of interaural time and intensity disparities in the perception of sound source location, and, in the decades immediately preceding Erulkar's review, considerable attention was devoted to the question of whether central auditory

0066-4308/85/0201-0245$02.00

neurons were sensitive to these dichotic sound localization cues. The 1960s brought forward a number of single-neuron recording studies (e.g. Rose et al 1966, Boudreau & Tsuchitani 1968, Brugge et al 1969, Goldberg & Brown 1969), which demonstrated that some binaural neurons in the mammalian central nervous system were indeed sensitive to interaural time and intensive disparities, and, moreover, that the tonal frequencies for which those disparities significantly influenced neural responses were also those predicted by physical and psychological acoustics. In addition, behavioral-lesion experiments (e.g. Masterton et al 1967) had revealed that ablation of the central nervous system loci responsible for the initial encoding of those binaural disparities severely impaired, or abolished, localization ability. In this regard, therefore, a firm correspondence was established between the types of sound localization cues available, the sensitivity of central neural elements to those cues, and the locations in the central auditory pathway of the relevant neural elements.

Since that time, there have been substantial advances in our understanding of the neurophysiology of sound localization. New data are available on the range of interaural time and intensive disparities generated by the cat's head and pinnae, on the mechanisms responsible for the sensitivity of central nervous system cells to those disparities, and on the range of those disparities to which central auditory cells are most sensitive. A second line of recent investigation has been based predominantly on the use of free-field stimuli in animals possessing peripheral acoustic specializations that might subserve sound localization. One series of such studies, on the barn owl, demonstrated the significance of asymmetrically located external ear canals in providing that species with cues for sound source elevation as well as sound source azimuth. This line of research is particularly interesting because it led to the discovery of a neural "map" of auditory space in that species' central nervous system. Another series of studies, in the cat, has provided insight into the directional properties of the pinna, and into the manner in which pinna directionality may influence the spatial selectivity of central auditory neurons. Taken together, these and related lines of research have drawn closer the correspondence between the specific behavioral capacities of animals and human beings in sound localization, and our knowledge of the neurophysiological mechanisms that might be subserving those functions.

In the following review, we have tried to evaluate critically some of this material. Limitations on space preclude an exhaustive review of all of the recent work in this area, and we refer the reader to other authors for more detailed accounts of specific issues not covered here (Erulkar, 1972, Møller 1972, Goldberg 1975, Webster & Aitkin 1975, Brugge & Geisler 1978, Suga 1978, 1982, Tsuchitani 1978, Phillips & Gates 1982, Masterton & Imig 1984). We begin by sketching summarily the nature and magnitudes of the dichotic cues used in sound localization; thereafter we examine in detail the physiological mechanisms that give rise to neural sensitivity to those cues. We turn then to the free-field studies of the cat and the barn owl that have provided new information on the nature and coding of cues provided by peripheral specializations. We then examine some recent evidence from behavioral-lesion studies. Finally, we draw together these lines of evidence in an attempt to indicate that they represent the neurophysiological and behavioral instantiations of two fundamental principles of central auditory stimulus processing.

NATURE AND MAGNITUDES OF THE DICHOTIC SOUND LOCALIZATION CUES

The dichotic cues for sound localization derive principally from the fact that the tympanic membranes are separated by an interaural distance, and that the interaural space is occupied by the head, which, for a wide range of stimulus frequencies, is acoustically opaque. The physical separation of the ears imposes an interaural time delay (ITD) on the stimuli arriving at the tympanic membranes from a sound source located at any point not equidistant from the two ears. The ITDs may usefully be divided into interaural arrival-time disparities and ongoing phase disparities. Arrival-time disparities are present for all tonal frequencies. Interaural phase disparities, while physically present for all stimulus frequencies, are ambiguous for frequencies whose wavelengths are shorter than the head diameter. This is because the interaural time delay may rapidly exceed the period of one stimulus cycle with only small changes in stimulus azimuth. Moreover, as is discussed below, the central auditory nervous system does not have the temporal resolving power necessary to discriminate interaural phase-angle disparities generated by high stimulus frequencies. The nervous system may, however, detect ongoing temporal disparities in high-frequency signals if those signals also contain low-frequency elements, as might be found in the shape of the stimulus envelope or in the low-frequency content of a spectrally complex signal otherwise containing predominantly high-frequency information (Mills 1972, McFadden & Pasanen 1976). Interaural intensity differences (IIDs) are generated largely by the acoustic shadow of the head and the pinnae, and are significant only for frequencies whose wavelength is smaller than the head diameter or pinna height.

Two recent studies have provided parametric data on the frequency and azimuthal dependence of interaural time (Roth et al 1980) and intensity (Moore & Irvine 1979) differences in cats. In each case, measurements were taken at the tragus and were made for a range of tonal frequencies. Interaural time differences were measured in adult cats for tonal frequencies from 400 Hz to 7.0 kHz, and for stimulus azimuths from 0 to 90° (plane of interaural axis). The magnitude of these disparities is frequency dependent, being slightly higher for frequencies below about 2.0 kHz. The largest measured ITD in the cat was 435 μsec. This obviously depends on interaural separation, and therefore on the size of the cat. The measured ITDs were generally greater than those predicted by the spherical-head model of Woodworth (1938). The frequency parameter was responsible for as much as 100 μsec of this delay, confirming the similar effect of tonal frequency on interaural delay reported for human manikins (Kuhn 1977). Interaural delays increase steeply with changes in stimulus azimuth from the midline to about 45°, and then remain relatively constant for azimuthal ranges between 45 and 90°. This finding agrees with the psychophysical data, which indicates that the ability to localize sounds is greatest for sounds located near the midline. The effect of azimuth alone may be as great as 350 μsec at low frequencies, and 300 μsec at high frequencies. Apparently, the pinna has little effect on ITDs although it can, as is discussed below, have a significant influence in the generation of interaural intensity differences. The acoustic considerations alone indicate that two distinct ITDs, onset delays and ongoing phase differences, are available for encoding the location of a sound source in space. Neurophysiological data, examined in detail below, indicate that the nervous system is able to detect both cues.

Interaural intensity differences measured at the cat's tragi were reported by Moore & Irvine (1979) for tone frequencies from 200 Hz to 20.0 kHz, and for azimuths from 0° (midline, in front of the animal) to 180° (midline, behind the head). Like interaural onset-time disparities, interaural intensity differences show marked influences attributable to both the frequency of the stimulus and the azimuth of the sound source. For frequencies below about 4.0 kHz, IIDs generated by stimuli at any azimuth rarely exceed about 10 dB, but for higher frequencies, intensity disparities may approach 30 dB. In general, intensity disparity-versus-azimuth functions are steep for azimuths within about 45° of the midline, and, particularly for frequencies above 7.0 kHz, may plateau for wide ranges of azimuths in the lateral hemifields. Qualitatively similar data have been presented for human beings (Feddersen et al 1957, Shaw 1974).

The extant data on the magnitude and "directionality" of interaural disparities should be qualified to the extent that, with few exceptions (Wiener et al 1966, Djupesland & Zwislocki 1973), parametric studies of the azimuthal dependence of interaural disparities have been based on measurements at the tragus or ear canal entrance (Shaw 1974, Moore & Irvine 1979, Roth et al 1980). The extent to which these data are representative of those that might be obtained at the tympanum using a nonintrusive recording system is unclear. This would appear to be a problem more for the measurement of intensive disparities than for temporal ones (Shaw 1974, Kuhn 1977). Second, few data have been presented on the dependence of interaural disparities on stimulus elevation (i.e. loci above or below the horizontal plane). It is noteworthy, however, that while human beings are capable of localizing elevated sound sources (e.g. Blauert 1969, Butler 1973), it is by no means obvious that the cues used are restricted to those of a dichotic kind.

NEURAL CODING OF INTERAURAL TIME AND INTENSITY DIFFERENCES

Most evidence on the physiological mechanisms generating neural sensitivity to interaural time and intensity disparities has come from studies in the cat. This is perhaps fortunate because this species' acuity in both lateralization (Wakeford & Robinson 1974, Cranford 1979) and free-field localization (Jenkins & Masterton 1982) shows some qualitative and quantitative similarities to that of human beings.

The principal sites of binaural convergence in the central nervous system are in the superior olivary complex (SOC), which contains several major auditory cell groups. Two of them, the medial (MSO) and lateral (LSO) superior olivary nuclei, are known to receive substantial input from the two ears by way of the cochlear nuclear complexes (Stotler 1953, Goldberg & Brown 1968). Physiological (Boudreau & Tsuchitani 1968, Goldberg & Brown 1968, Guinan et al 1972a,b) and comparative anatomical (Masterton 1974) evidence suggests that the MSO and LSO are relatively specialized for processing low- and high-frequency information, respectively. Correlated with these data is the finding that many MSO cells are sensitive to interaural time disparities (Goldberg & Brown 1969) whereas LSO cells are commonly sensitive to interaural intensity differences (Boudreau & Tsuchitani 1968, Guinan et al 1972a). Partly because of the difficulty in recording single MSO cells, most quantitative data on the coding of interaural time disparities have come from studies of higher auditory nuclei, with the understanding that the binaural properties visualized at these more rostral levels is presumed to reflect the sensitivity of cells in the superior olivary nuclei from which they receive a major part of their afferent supply.

Sensitivity to Interaural Time Differences

Sensitivity to interaural time disparities of low-frequency tonal stimuli has been described for single neurons in a variety of auditory nuclei in several species including the cat (Rose et al 1966, Brugge et al 1969, 1970, Geisler et al 1969, Aitkin & Webster 1972, Aitkin 1973, Aitkin & Boyd 1975), dog (Goldberg & Brown 1969), rabbit (Aitkin et al 1972), kangaroo rat (Stillman 1971), chinchilla (Benson & Teas 1976), and marsupial possum (Aitkin et al 1978). Inspection of these data suggests that the shape of the functions relating neural spike count (i.e. response strength) to variations in interaural phase delay is similar at the various levels of the auditory pathway in a broad range of mammalian species. We shall, therefore, tentatively assume that the mechanisms generating this sensitivity are similarly general.

Recall that an acoustic signal that generates an interaural time disparity actually produces two differences in the timing of the signals at the two ears. One is the difference in the onset time, the other is the difference in ongoing interaural phase. These two time delays are linked: the onset-time delay determines the steady-state ongoing phase difference. As Roth and his colleagues (1980) point out, under natural conditions these two components may behave differently and thereby function as competing cues for sound localization, if, of course, neurons in the auditory pathway are equally sensitive to both. Kuwada & Yin (1983), in an extensive study of this problem, found that the great majority (93%) of cells sensitive to low tonal frequencies that they studied in the cat's inferior colliculus (IC), and that *were* sensitive to interaural phase disparities, were *not* also sensitive to arrival-time differences at the two ears. This is not to say, however, that central auditory cells are generally insensitive to interaural arrival-time disparities. As is discussed below, many brainstem and cortical neurons *do* show marked sensitivity to onset-time disparities (Benevento et al 1970, Benson & Teas 1976, Kitzes et al 1980), although most of these cells that have been described tend to be more sensitive to higher tonal frequencies than those neurons sensitive to interaural phase-angle disparities.

Neural sensitivity to interaural phase disparities of tonal stimuli necessarily requires that each of the monaural inputs to the binaural neuron preserve temporal information about the stimulus at the tympanum. For tonal frequencies up to at least 2500 Hz, the periodicity of the stimulus waveform is encoded by "locking" of neural responses to a particular point in the period of each cycle of the stimulus (Rose et al 1967, Johnson 1980). If this temporal information is preserved in the inputs to a binaural neuron, then a comparison of the two inputs for the timing of discharges provides the binaural neuron with information regarding the interaural phase delay.

That such is in fact the case has been revealed in studies of the dog MSO (Goldberg & Brown 1969) and cat dorsal nucleus of the lateral lemniscus (Brugge et al 1970). Neurons in these nuclei commonly are excited by independent stimulation of each ear, and the discharges to the monaural stimuli may be locked to a preferred half-cycle of the stimulating waveforms, though not necessarily to the same preferred phase. If the frequency and the intensity of the tones delivered to the two ears are held constant, while only the interaural phase delay is varied, the response rate of the binaural neuron is a periodic function of interaural delay. Response rate reaches a maximum when the preferred phases of the monaural inputs are in synchrony at the cell of convergence ("favorable delays") and falls to a minimum when the monaural inputs arrive 180° out of phase ("unfavorable delays"). The shape of the function relating spike count to delay assumes a cyclical form, with the period of the cycle being equal to that of the stimulating waveform (e.g. Rose et al 1966, Brugge et al 1969, 1970, Goldberg & Brown 1969, Orman & Phillips 1984).

Careful examination of the number of discharges and their temporal organization over a range of interaural delays provides further information about the genesis of this sensitivity in binaural neurons (Brugge et al 1970). At favorable delays, the responses of a binaural neuron are at least as strong, and sometimes stronger, than the sum of the monaural responses. At unfavorable delays, response rate may be weaker than the response to either ear alone, which suggests that active neural suppression may be a mechanism contributing to interaural delay sensitivity (Rose et al 1966). The use of period histograms (i.e. histograms showing the temporal disposition of neural discharges in relation to the period of the cycle) provides further information on these mechanisms. Such analyses reveal that the monaural inputs each have an excitatory preferred half-cycle, and that the remainder of the stimulus cycle may be associated with an absence of discharges or with a suppression of spontaneous discharges, i.e. with an inhibitory response. Accordingly, when the interaural delay is varied from the optimal delay for the neuron, the excitatory and inhibitory half-cycles of one monaural input are shifted in time relative to those of the other, so that the inhibitory response period of one input coincides temporally with the excitatory response period of the other. The result is an active cancellation of one or both monaural responses. These mechanisms serve to enhance the peak-to-peak amplitude of the periodicity in the relation of spike count to interaural delay. It is apparent, therefore, that sensitivity to interaural phase delays reflects a temporal interlacing of excitatory and inhibitory events that is locked to the phase of the signals at the two ears, and that the analysis of the disparity is performed cycle by cycle of the stimulus.

In a now-classic study of the binaural interactions of low-frequency neurons, Rose et al (1966) provided evidence for a class of neurons within the inferior colliculus that detects a specific interaural time delay. The "characteristic delay" that each of these neurons was postulated to possess describes the distribution of sound sources that would lie on the surface of a hyperboloid extending laterally from the midpoint of the interaural axis (the "cone of confusion"). Although the concept of the "characteristic delay" has been widely accepted, until recently, there has been little strong experimental evidence to support it. Yin & Kuwada (1983b) reexamined this issue in a detailed study of low-frequency delay-sensitive neurons in the cat's inferior colliculus. Their work replicated and extended the results of others and supported, in general, the concept of a "characteristic delay" [see Kuwada & Yin (1984) and Yin & Kuwada (1984) for recent reviews of this work]. Sensitivity to interaural delay is preserved at tonal frequencies away from a neuron's best frequency, though generally not for frequencies above about 2500 Hz. For some of these neurons, there is, regardless of stimulus frequency a particular interaural delay to which the neuron responds maximally (characteristic "peak" delay); for some others, the common response is a minimum (characteristic "trough" delay). For still other neurons, the point of the characteristic delay may be elsewhere on the delay curve.

Because the characteristic delay may occur at any point on a given neuron's delay function, it is not an unqualified indicator of which delays might be expected to elicit the strongest, or weakest, responses from a neuron. For this reason, Yin & Kuwada (1983b) performed an alternative analysis of their data to provide evidence on the range of delays to which inferior colliculus cells were most sensitive, while circumventing the otherwise confounding factor of the precise locus of the characteristic delay on the delay function. For each cell studied with a wide range of tonal frequencies, these authors produced a "composite delay curve" that represented an equally weighted average of those obtained for each tonal frequency tested separately. In general, these composite delay curves had well-defined peaks and troughs. The peaks of these functions, and therefore the interaural delays most likely to elicit vigorous neural responses, were generally associated with delays of the ipsilateral stimulus relative to the contralateral one, i.e. delays favoring the contralateral ear. Their absolute values were usually less than 250 μsec and rarely exceeded 500 μsec, which is perhaps the upper limit of interaural time delays expected to be generated by the interaural separation of a large cat (Roth et al 1980). In contrast, the troughs in the composite delay functions, and therefore the interaural delays likely to elicit the weakest neural responses, were typically associated with delays favoring the ipsilateral ear, i.e. stimuli in which the phase of the ipsilateral stimulus led that of the contralateral stimulus. These delays also only infrequently exceeded about 500 μsec.

Similar data from studies of low-frequency, delay-sensitive neurons in the inferior colliculus and superior olivary complex of the kangaroo rat (Moushegian et al 1971, Stillman 1971) and auditiory cortex of the chinchilla (Benson & Teas 1976) have, because of the small interaural distance in these animals, raised questions about the efficacy of the characteristic delay in transmitting localization information. In the kangaroo rat, the 3.5 cm interaural distance would be expected to create about 105 μsec of interaural arrival-time difference. The direct measurements made by von Bismarck (1967) indicate a maximal delay of 260 μsec in the chinchilla. The characteristic peak and trough delays displayed by neurons in the auditory cortex and brainstem of these animals are often at delays whose magnitudes exceed those that the animals can encounter in the free field. In addition, the characteristic delay is rarely a well-defined peak in the function, but is a broad plateau in which the maximal or minimal firing level is relatively constant over a range of several hundred microseconds. It is of interest to note, however, that the delay function frequently is steepest around zero delay, so that only small changes in interaural delay over a relatively narrow range (centered around zero delay) might be expected to have a great influence on the cell's discharge rate. We shall return to this general issue after further consideration of the neural encoding of other interaural disparities.

Some delay-sensitive neurons are excited by interaural phase shifts that simulate movement of a sound source in the horizontal plane. This stimulus can be simulated using dichotic stimulus systems if a low-frequency tone (e.g. of 500 Hz) is presented to one ear while a slightly disparate frequency (e.g. 501 Hz) is presented to the other. This creates a "rotating tone" or "binaural beat" in which continuous and graded changes in interaural phase are generated. Pure tones moving along the azimuth will generate phase delays similar to those set up by the binaural beat. The rate of motion is determined by the frequency disparity between the two ears (1 Hz, in the example), and the sensation experienced by a listener is that of a tone moving from one ear to the other, with the tone then "jumping" back to the ear of origin (Licklider et al 1950, Perrott & Musicant 1977). Both aspects of this apparent movement are explicable in terms of the continuously varying interaural phase delay produced by the stimulus.

Kuwada & Yin (1983) and Yin & Kuwada (1983a) described in detail the responses of cat inferior colliculus neurons both to static tonal stimuli varying in interaural phase delay and to binaural beat stimuli. The characteristic peak and trough delays seen in studies using static tones are similar or identical to those revealed in the same neurons studied with binaural beats. This stimulus, therefore, provides a particularly time-efficient means of collecting data on neural sensitivity to interaural delays (Kuwada et al 1979).

The fact that the binaural beat stimulus reasonably simulates the temporal features of a moving tonal stimulus has provided a means of examining the coding of various parameters of dynamic acoustic stimuli. Not the least of these is the direction of stimulus movement, for which Yin & Kuwada have presented evidence on neural selectivity. Some neurons in the inferior colliculus are sensitive to the direction of interaural phase change, responding more strongly, or only, when the direction of the beat is toward the ipsilateral ear, i.e. when the frequency of the tone to the contralateral ear is lower than that delivered to the ipsilateral ear. This finding takes on special significance because neural selectivity to the direction of a binaural beat is not a property predictable from knowledge of a neuron's responses to static tonal stimuli of differing interaural delays. This is because binaural beat stimuli that differ only in the direction of the interaural phase change also differ only in the temporal ordering of interaural delays with which they present the central nervous system, and not in the actual interaural delays that are provided. Neurons that are selective to the direction of a binaural beat are responding preferentially to the particular *temporal ordering* of interaural delays impinging on the two ears. Selectivity to direction of a binaural beat, therefore, represents a more sophisticated level of stimulus processing than selectivity to a particular interaural delay alone.

The classical view that high-frequency sounds are localized using interaural intensity cues alone holds only for pure tones. There is ample psychophysical evidence that human listeners can lateralize complex high-frequency signals on the basis of interaural time cues, and recently Yin et al (1984) provided data from single-neuron studies in the cat inferior colliculus that bear directly on this issue. Using amplitude-modulated signals with high-frequency carriers (>3.5 kHz), Yin and his colleagues found that in 41% of the IC neurons studied the discharge varied cyclically as a function of interaural time delay. The period of the cycle corresponded to that of the modulation frequency and, hence, they concluded that such cells respond to the interaural phase difference of the envelope waveform and that the information provided by the high-frequency carrier wave form is not relevant to the neuron's cyclic response. This interaural phase sensitivity to the modulation waveform at the cell of convergence apparently requires inputs that are phase locked to the modulation envelope, a mechanism that is analogous to that which mediates discrimination of interaural phase disparities of a low-frequency tone.

Rather less evidence has been presented on neural sensitivity to interaural onset-time disparities (Brugge et al 1969, Benevento et al 1970, Benson & Teas 1976, Kitzes et al 1980). The available data, however, point to a relation of neural spike count to arrival-time disparity which is qualitatively different from that relating spike count to phase disparity and which, like that for intensity disparities (see below), does not suggest a cycle-by-cycle comparison of the stimuli at the two eardrums. The function relating interaural onset-time disparities and spike discharge rate is usually sigmoidal, with responses strongest when the arrival time of the contralateral stimulus precedes that of the ipsilateral stimulus. There may be an active suppression of spontaneous discharges when the ipsilateral stimulus precedes the contralateral one. These data suggest that the contralateral ear provides a net excitatory input while the ipsilateral ear provides a net inhibitory influence. The relative times of arrival of the excitatory and inhibitory inputs at the binaural neuron reflect, at least in part, the relative times of arrival of the stimuli at the two tympanic membranes, and the latter thereby dictates the discharges of the neuron.

It is of interest to examine the range of interaural onset-time delays over which spike counts are most sensitive to changes in that parameter. The most detailed evidence on this issue is that of Kitzes et al (1980) in the awake cat's auditory cortex. As in cells described by other authors, the delay functions for cortical neurons often were roughly sigmoidal in shape, with the strongest responses being associated with ipsilateral delays. In general, the cells were most sensitive to changes in delay over ranges very close to zero milliseconds, or over ranges of ipsilateral delays (i.e. delays that would be generated by a sound source in the contralateral acoustic hemifield).

Kitzes and his colleagues (1980) described a further group of cortical neurons, which they termed "predominantly binaural." These cells tended not to be excitable by monaural stimuli, but responded preferentially to binaural stimuli with zero, or near-zero, interaural delay. That is, the delay functions for these neurons were markedly nonmonotonic in shape, peaking at or near zero disparity. These neurons were presumably excited by brief-duration subthreshold inputs from each ear; when interaural delays were sufficiently small, the inputs may have been coincident at the neuron and summed to generate spike discharges.

Sensitivity to Interaural Intensity Differences

Coding of interaural intensity disparities has been studied in detail in a number of central auditory system nuclei in a range of species (Rose et al 1966, Brugge et al 1969, 1970, Goldberg & Brown 1969, Benevento et al 1970, Aitkin & Webster 1972, Stillman 1972, Brugge & Merzenich 1973, Benson & Teas 1976, Phillips & Irvine 1981, 1982, Orman & Phillips 1984). The sensitivity of a neuron to IIDs is most commonly manifested as a sigmoidal relation of spike count to intensive disparity. At levels rostral to the decussating outputs of the SOC, spike counts are generally greater when the contralateral stimulus intensity exceeds the ipsilateral stimulus intensity.

For many, but not all, such neurons (Stillman 1972, Phillips & Irvine 1981), this sensitivity may be explained by a net excitatory input being derived from the contralateral ear and a net inhibitory input being derived from the ipsilateral ear. For these cells, if the contralateral, excitatory, stimulus intensity is held constant while the ipsilateral stimulus intensity is raised from zero, then, as the latter approaches the contralateral stimulus level, the response rate of the binaural neuron falls below that expected of the contralateral input alone. With intensity disparities significantly favoring the ipsilateral, inhibitory, ear, the response rate of the binaural neuron may fall to zero.

It seems likely that at least two factors contribute to sensitivity of this kind. First, it is probable that the strength of the inhibitory "volley" increases with the intensity of the stimulus delivered to the ipsilateral ear. Second, increments in stimulus intensity shorten the latency of the afferent "volley" at the binaural neuron. This latter effect is perhaps best illustrated by the observation that the effect on spike count of an intensity disparity favoring one ear can be offset by the introduction of an arrival-time disparity favoring the other (e.g. Brugge et al 1969). Thus, for a neuron securely driven by monaural contralateral stimuli, but whose responses have been suppressed by an intensity disparity favoring the ipsilateral ear, responsiveness may be restored by an arrival-time delay imposed on the (inhibitory) ipsilateral stimulus. It seems likely that this neural mechanism may be the substrate of the well-known psychoacoustic phenomenon of "time-intensity trading" in auditory lateralization (Durlach & Colburn 1978).

There appears to be a second group of neurons sensitive to interaural intensity differences whose sensitivity reflects facilitative rather than suppressive binaural interactions (Phillips & Irvine 1981, Orman & Phillips 1984). These neurons probably correspond to the "predominantly binaural" class of Kitzes et al (1980), since they are virtually unresponsive to monaural tones, but respond well to binaural stimuli with zero, or near zero, intensive disparity (Phillips & Irvine 1981, 1983). Cells with an apparent preference for sounds located at the midline in the direction of frontal gaze have also been described for the cat's cerebellar vermis (Aitkin & Rawson 1983).

Two additional features of neural sensitivity to interaural intensity disparities are of interest. First, for some neurons showing sigmoidal relations of spike count to intensity disparity (Brugge et al 1969, 1970), the range of intensive disparities over which spike count is a sensitive function of disparity (i.e. the steeply declining portion of the sigmoidal function) may be independent of overall stimulus level. Thus, for example, regardless of the absolute level at which the (excitatory) contralateral stimulus is held, the same intensive disparity range is required to elicit the declining part of the spike count function. The second feature of interest is the absolute range of intensive disparities over which neurons are indeed most sensitive to changes in that parameter. For the cat's primary auditory cortex (Phillips & Irvine 1981), the majority of neurons show greatest sensitivity to changes in intensity disparity over ranges that correspond to those generated by free-field stimuli located at contralateral azimuths extending from the midline to about 45°.

Head Size, Interaural Disparities, and the Problem of Long Characteristic Delays

The preceding discussion revealed that animals drawn from diverse mammalian families have auditory nervous systems containing binaural neurons sensitive to changes in the major dichotic cues for sound localization. One problematic issue that has evolved from analysis of the range of interaural disparities encoded by the nervous systems in these species relates to the fact that this range seems to be relatively constant across species. This finding is problematic because the species studied vary widely in their head sizes and, therefore, in the range of interaural disparities that they can be expected to encounter in the free field. Accordingly, some animals, perhaps particularly those with small heads, appear to have nervous systems that encode interaural disparities over a range at least part of which should be inappropriate for the size of the animal's head. The question that arises, therefore, concerns the utility of the neural codes that have been described for the localization of sounds by these species. Perhaps because cells that are sensitive to interaural intensity disparities are generally most sensitive to changes in that parameter over ranges near zero, this critique has most commonly been addressed to the cells that are sensitive to interaural phase disparities and that have very long characteristic delays (Stillman 1971, McFadden 1973).

This critique of the efficacy of long—and presumably, therefore, all—characteristic delays in providing the animal with information regarding the azimuthal location of an acoustic stimulus appears to be predicated on two assumptions. The first is that the code for interaural phase disparity is the characteristic delay itself. As mentioned previously, the sensitivity of a neuron to interaural phase delays is almost always manifested as a cyclical relation of spike count to interaural delay, so that a neuron has a continuous sensitivity to variations in interaural delay. Moreover, for many such cells, the slopes of the delay functions are steepest near zero disparity so that although the *peak* response might be obtained at an interaural delay never encountered by the animal in nature, the cell nevertheless may be sensitive to changes in interaural delays over the range that it *is* likely to encounter in the free field. The second assumption is the view that the spike output of a neuron uniquely specifies interaural delay and, therefore, sound source azimuth. Since the discharges of an auditory neuron are also controlled by a variety of stimulus parameters other than interaural disparities (e.g. the frequency and intensity of the stimulus), and since these may vary independently, it is perhaps unlikely that the spike output of a single neuron uniquely specifies anything in the "real world." An alternative view is that the animal's detection of sound source location (or any other parameter of acoustic or other sensory stimulation) is based on the activity of the ensemble of neural elements activated by a specified stimulus (see also Suga 1982, Yin & Kuwada 1983b, Phillips & Orman 1984). Concerning the present discussion, the population of neurons excited by an acoustic stimulus will vary with the location of that stimulus. This is a necessary consequence of the fact that many auditory neurons have characteristic delays.

This hypothesis does not alter the fact, however, that the total range of disparities encoded by an animal's auditory nervous system may, at least in part, exceed that expected on the basis of the animal's head size alone. Consequently, animals with small heads might be expected to have poorer sound localization acuity than animals with larger heads. This is because the range of disparities that small-headed animals can expect to encounter in the free field is relatively narrow and centered close to zero. Accordingly, one might expect that since the only disparities that small animals may encounter are themselves small, those disparities may be too small to alter significantly the ensemble of neural elements activated by the stimulus unless the stimulus undergoes relatively wide changes in azimuth or location. This view was supported by the behavioral finding that there may be a graded, inverse relation between head size and localization acuity (Heffner & Heffner 1982). Thus, minimum audible angles for dolphins, humans, and elephants are on the order of one degree of azimuth, whereas those for a variety of species of rodents are closer to 20 degrees. Animals with intermediate head sizes occupy intermediate positions on the scale of localization acuity. The exception to this general rule is the horse, which has a sound-localizing ability that is no better than that of a rat, indicating that localization acuity is not determined simply by interaural distance or the availability of large binaural cues (Heffner & Heffner 1984). From the phylogenetic standpoint, these data engender the speculation that evolutionary pressures might have resulted in mammals, as a class, acquiring a single set of neural mechanisms for localizing sound sources on the basis of interaural disparities, and that these mechanisms represent a compromise meeting the localization needs of many, if not all, mammalian species.

NEURAL CODING OF THE SPATIAL LOCATION OF ACOUSTIC STIMULI

It has been recognized for many years that the dichotic cues alone are ambiguous with regard to both the elevation of a sound source and its location in the frontal or caudal hemifields. The loci expected to generate any specified interaural disparity are disposed on a conical surface in the lateral hemifield, and the phrase "cone of confusion" has been used to describe these loci and their geometric projection to the midpoint of the head. Psychoacoustic studies have emphasized the contributions of the pinnae to the resolution of this confusion and have indicated the deleterious effects of pinna manipulation on sound localization accuracy (e.g. Batteau 1967, Musicant & Butler 1984). Moreover, the well-established finding that human beings can show considerable acuity in monaural sound localization (Angell & Fite 1901, Butler 1969, 1971, Musicant 1982) points directly to monaural cues, which, at least in part, must reflect the acoustic properties of the pinna.

A number of single-neuron recording studies in awake cats (Evans 1968, Bock & Webster 1974, Eisenman 1974) and monkeys (Benson et al 1981) examined the spatial "tuning" of central auditory neurons, generally using an array of speakers disposed at various azimuthal locations in the frontal sound field. Typically, these studies revealed that neurons respond more strongly to stimuli located in the contralateral acoustic hemifield than to identical stimuli located in the ipsilateral hemifield. For the majority of such neurons, response strength is a graded function of azimuth, peaking at far contralateral azimuths, and this is perhaps the kind of spatial sensitivity that might have been predicted on the basis of the known sensitivity to dichotic cues alone. However, at least some neurons in the cat (Evans 1968) and monkey (Benson et al 1981) auditory cortex show spatial selectivity to relatively specific locations in the frontal contralateral quadrant of auditory space, which suggests that factors other than the interaural disparities alone may have been contributing to the neurons' responses.

Grinnell & Grinnell (1965) presented neurophysiological evidence for pinna directionality in the echo-locating bat almost two decades ago. Only recently, however, has there been a concerted effort to examine the contribution of pinna directionality to the spatial selectivity of central auditory neurons in an acoustically less specialized mammal. The first major insight into this question was provided by Middlebrooks & Pettigrew (1981). These authors examined the sensitivity of cat cortical neurons to the location of a free-field stimulus in a spatially calibrated anechoic environment using a stimulating system designed for remote control of stimulus movements in both azimuth and elevation referred to the cat's median plane and interaural axis. They found three groups of neurons distinguishable by the nature of their selectivity to sound source location. The first group was termed "omnidirectional." Cells in this class showed little or no spatial selectivity, and appeared to respond to a stimulus regardless of its spatial location. These neurons had best frequencies that varied over a very wide range. Neurons of the second group were termed "hemifield" units. These neurons responded to an acoustic stimulus only if it was located in the contralateral auditory hemifield. The medial borders of these cells' spatial receptive fields were well defined and usually located very close to the midsagittal plane. Hemifield cells almost always had best frequencies below 12.0 kHz. Neurons in the third category had rather small spatial receptive fields that were invariably located in the direction in which the contralateral pinna was oriented. If the contralateral pinna was mechanically displaced, then the location of the receptive fields moved correspondingly. Because their receptive fields were located on an apparent acoustical "axis" of the contralateral pinna, this class of neurons was termed "axial." Almost all of these cells had best frequencies above 12.0 kHz.

Hemifield spatial selectivity would appear to be the form expected from binaural interactions of the classical kind (Middlebrooks & Pettigrew 1981). The common sensitivity of cortical neurons to variations in interaural time (Kitzes et al 1980) and intensive (Phillips & Irvine 1981) disparities associated with midline or near-midline azimuths seems a plausible mechanism to account for the location of the medial borders of these receptive fields. The genesis of spatial selectivity of the axial kind was less clear but might have been more readily explained by directionality inherent in the pinnae.

This latter issue was addressed in a recent study in which the directionality of sound pressure transformation at the cat's pinna was reexamined using the amplitude of cochlear potentials as a nonintrusive measure of tympanic sound pressure level (Phillips et al 1982). These authors used a stimulating system identical to that used by Middlebrooks & Pettigrew, and examined the dependence of tympanic sound pressure level on the azimuth and elevation of a tonal sound source. The directionality of sound pressure transformations was inversely related to tone frequency. At low frequencies, the pinna produced little in the way of interference effects on tympanic sound pressure level. With increasing tone frequency, the pinna became more strongly directional such that at frequencies above about 10 to 12 kHz only small displacements of a sound source were needed to attenuate the stimulus at the tympanum by more than 10 to 15 dB. By connecting loci associated with any specific tympanic sound pressure level for any single-tone frequency, it was shown that the "optimal area" for tympanic sound pressure level was completely circumscribed. Its location varied correspondingly with pinna displacements, and was abolished by pinna excision. These data confirmed that the pinna has an accoustical axis. The frequency at which the pinna began to show directionality (about 3.5 kHz) has a wavelength corresponding roughly with the long dimension of the pinna, and the acoustical axis studied with the pinnae in a forward, resting orientation generally corresponded with the visual plane in the same species (Bishop et al 1962).

Experiments examining the mechanisms generating pinna directionality (Phillips et al 1982) revealed that the pinna's acoustical axis is the product of at least two passive acoustic processes. For stimuli delivered "on axis," i.e. for stimuli originating from a source in the direction of the acoustical axis, the pinna and external auditory meatus amplify the acoustic signal. The amount of amplification depends on the frequency content of the signal, but may be as high as 30 dB. Second, for stimuli delivered "off axis," the pinna's own acoustic shadow may result in an attenuation of the acoustic signal at the tympanum.

The studies of Phillips et al (1982) and Calford & Pettigrew (1984) revealed that with the pinna in a drooped position the precise direction in which the pinna's acoustical axis lay varied with tone frequency; it tended to be more lateral for higher-frequency stimuli. With the pinna in an upright posture, the axes for all frequencies tested tended to be tightly clustered. Because the cat has mobile pinnae, it may bring these various axes into alignment by active pinna movements. Nevertheless, these data engender the speculation that the human pinna may also have an acoustical axis whose precise orientation may vary with the spectral content of the acoustic signal. In this regard, therefore, it is of interest that research from Butler's laboratory has for some years indicated not only that humans are capable of relatively accurate monaural sound localization, but that the monaurally perceived azimuthal location of a stationary sound source varies with tone frequency, being more lateral for higher-frequency stimuli (Butler & Flannery 1980, Flannery & Butler 1981). In humans, the contribution of such spectral cues to monaural localization seems to be strongest for stimulus locations outside the range to which the dichotic cues would otherwise normally contribute, i.e. azimuthal ranges beyond 45° from the midline, and perhaps also for elevation (Butler 1973, 1974, Butler & Flannery 1980, Flannery & Butler 1981). In animals with mobile pinnae, such as cats, the azimuthal range within which the pinnae contribute to localization presumably depends on the orientation of the pinnae.

The strong directionality of the cat's pinna, particularly at high frequencies, no doubt contributes to the genesis of axial receptive fields of the type described for the auditory cortex (Middlebrooks & Pettigrew 1981) and inferior colliculus (Semple et al 1983). In particular, the central auditory cells with the smallest spatial receptive fields are those with best frequencies in the range where the pinna is most strongly directional. One recent study of the cat's IC (Moore et al 1984) provides quantitative evidence indicating that pinna directionality is manifested not only in the shape of "axial" receptive fields, but also in the dependence of spike counts on stimulus location within the receptive field. Moore et al (1984) reported that for a large number of inferior colliculus neurons, spike counts were maximal in the direction of the acoustical axis of the contralateral ear, regardless of the absolute size of receptive fields, and for some neurons, regardless of the shape of the receptive field. These data suggest that the directionality of the cat's pinna is imposed on the spatial selectivity that might otherwise result from binaural interactions alone, and that the presence of a conical pinna might substantially enhance the spatial selectivity of central auditory neurons.

The fact that the pinna does indeed have an acoustical axis has an interesting implication for those animals with mobile pinnae. As pointed out first by Middlebrooks & Pettigrew (1981), and later by Phillips and his colleagues (1982), mobile pinnae provide the animal not only with cues for sound localization, but also with a mechanism for significantly enhancing the signal-to-noise ratio deriving from a source at which the pinnae are directed. These animals could, therefore, use active pinna movements for the selective scrutiny of sound sources of interest. In humans, capitalizing on pinna directionality for the detection or analysis of acoustic signals might necessarily have to be achieved by head movements.

Konishi, Knudsen, and their colleagues (Konishi 1973, Knudsen et al 1977, Knudsen & Konishi 1978, 1979, 1980, Knudsen 1980, Moiseff & Konishi 1981, 1983a,b) presented a detailed series of reports on the neurophysiology of sound localization by the barn owl *(Tyto alba)*. This bird perches above the ground and is quite capable of localizing and striking prey on the gound (e.g. mice) using only acoustic cues for the prey's whereabouts (Konishi 1973).

Tyto alba, like many owls, shows a number of peripheral auditory specializations. Among these is the asymmetry of its external ear canals. These asymmetries may take a number of forms (Knudsen 1980). In the barn owl, one of the most obvious is that the left external auditory meatus opens on the face rather higher than does the right canal. It has subsequently become clear that the left ear is more sensitive to sounds originating from the lower sound field, whereas the right ear is more sensitive to acoustic stimuli in the upper sound field (Knudsen 1980). Thus, when the right ear canal is partially occluded, the owl's head orienting response and therefore its sound localization accuracy are caused to err in the direction of the left ear and below the actual sound source, while the converse behavior results from occlusion of the left meatus. In each case, the vertical errors are the more severe (Knudsen & Konishi 1979).

In the barn owl's telencephalon (Knudsen et al 1977) and midbrain (Knudsen & Konishi 1978), some single auditory neurons have relatively small spatial receptive fields. These receptive fields are not, like those of the cat, located uniformly in the acoustical axis of any contralateral pinna (since the owl has none), but vary with regard to their location in both azimuth and elevation. Collectively, they occupy much of the frontal sound hemifield. There is, however, in each side of the owl's auditory system, an almost exclusive representation of the contralateral acoustic hemifield, with a disproportionate number of neurons with receptive fields in the inferior and midline region of the frontal contralateral quadrant (Knudsen & Konishi 1978). The vast majority of these neurons have best frequencies in the range of 6 to 8 kHz, the frequency range over which the owl has the greatest absolute sensitivity and over which it shows its greatest acuity in sound localization (Konishi 1973). Occlusion of one or the other external auditory meatus shifts the locations of these receptive fields in directions favoring the directionality of the unoccluded ear (Knudsen & Konishi 1980).

Of particular interest has been the finding that the anterior and lateral division of the owl's auditory midbrain (nucleus mesencephalicus lateralis dorsalis, MLD) contains, almost exclusively, neurons with small receptive fields, and that these neurons are topographically arranged such that the nucleus contains an orderly neural "map" of contralateral auditory space (Knudsen & Konishi 1978). This map contains a disproportionate representation of midline azimuths and inferior elevations. In this regard, it is noteworthy that the owl's localization accuracy is greatest for sound source locations in and near the median plane, although any superiority of performance for stimuli in the inferior elevations is less clear (Knudsen et al 1979).

Since the owl does not possess pinnae, the neural mechanisms generating these spatial receptive fields are of particular interest. Evidence on this issue has been presented by Moiseff & Konishi (1981, 1983a,b). These authors reported that the interaural time disparity generated by a 7-kHz tone—the frequency around which most space-mapped neurons were most sensitive—was an almost linear function of azimuth over a range of at least 60° from the midline. Single neurons shown in free-field examination to be space-mapped were also shown under dichotic conditions (using ring inserts in each meatus) to be sensitive to ongoing interaural phase disparities in this frequency range. Over the range of interaural delays with which these cells were tested, these cells displayed relatively distinct peaks in their responses at some optimal interaural delay; the optimal delays varied among neurons but were generally in the behaviorally relevant range, i.e. less than about 100 μsec. In the same cells, the centers of receptive fields—and hence encoded auditory azimuth—were linearly related to the optimal ongoing time disparity to which the neurons were most sensitive. These data suggest that, in the owl, ITDs are critical determinants of the azimuthal centers of spatial receptive fields.

As mentioned earlier, interaural phase sensitivity in the mammalian auditory system is the result of the relative time of arrival of phase-locked spikes at the cell of convergence and is, therefore, limited to frequencies below about 4 kHz. In the owl, this limit is extended to near 9 kHz by virtue of the fact that the outputs of neurons in the nucleus magnocellularis (homolog of the mammalian anteroventral cochlear nucleus) are phase-locked at these relatively high frequencies (Sullivan & Konishi 1983). While the mechanisms that permit encoding of waveform timing at high frequencies are not well understood, the mechanisms involved in the binaural interactions appear to be the same as those operating in the mammalian auditory brainstem.

Moiseff & Konishi (1981) also reported that MLD neurons do not exhibit time intensity trading (see above) of the kind seen in the mammalian central auditory nervous system. This observation suggested to them that time and intensity cues for localization are processed separately by the owl's nervous system. Corroborative evidence for this view derives from the behavioral experiments of Knudsen & Konishi (1979) in which partial occlusion of one meatus—creating attenuation but not necessarily delay of the stimulus to the occluded tympanum—resulted in more severe vertical than lateral errors in localization. In a more recent electrophysiological study of the owl brainstem, Moiseff & Konishi (1983a,b) arrived at the same conclusion and further suggested that space selectivity emerges where these two pathways converge in the MLD. Taking these data together, there are grounds for believing that while interaural time disparities to which neurons are most sensitive specify the azimuthal center of receptive fields, interaural intensity differences might play an important role in determining the elevation of receptive field centers (Moiseff & Konishi 1981).

BEHAVIORAL-LESION STUDIES OF SOUND LOCALIZATION MECHANISMS

The observation that animals with bilateral lesions of the auditory cortex "hear less distinctly" is an old one (Ferrier 1876, 1890). The intensive study of the effects on auditory lateralization and localization of brain lesions began in the 1950s (e.g. Neff et al 1956, Riss 1959). The studies in the three decades since then may usefully be divided into those before and after about 1972. This is for two reasons. First, the studies before the early 1970s have been reviewed in detail by Neff, Diamond & Casseday (1975) and, accordingly, are treated only summarily here. Second, the 1970s saw the introduction, in a wide range of species, of behavioral paradigms designed to enable a more definitive specification of the nature of the deficits consequent to brain lesions.

Many of the earlier behavioral-lesion studies required animals (usually cats) with lesions (usually bilateral) of the central auditory nervous system to indicate their ability to localize or to lateralize a sound source in one of two behavioral paradigms. In the case of localization tasks, the animal was restrained in a start box facing an environment in which a free-field speaker was located in the left and right auditory hemifields. One of these would be activated briefly, after which the animal would be released from the start box and would approach the appropriate sound source for food or other reward. Varying the separation of the speakers in different trials enabled estimations of minimum audible angles for pre- and post-operated animals (Neff et al 1956, Strominger 1969a,b, Strominger & Oesterreich 1970, Moore et al 1974, Casseday & Neff 1975). In the case of lateralization tasks, cats fitted with earphones were usually trained in a double grill-box avoidance task in which dichotic stimuli favoring one laterality (left or right) constituted a neutral signal; a reversal of the interaural disparity comprised a warning signal to which the animal was required to respond by leaving its starting chamber of the box for the other in order to avoid electric shock (e.g. Masterton & Diamond 1964, Masterton et al 1967).

These studies were consistent in revealing that cats with bilateral lesions of the auditory cortex (Neff et al 1956, Strominger 1969a,b) or inferior colliculus (Strominger & Oesterreich 1970) displayed impaired performance in localization tasks, and in the lateralization of transients (Masterton & Diamond 1964, Masterton et al 1968). It is of particular interest that section of the trapezoid body (the fiber pathway providing the major source of contralateral input to the MSO) in cats elevated the threshold interaural time difference to levels beyond those normally encountered in nature, i.e. beyond about 500 μsec (Masterton et al 1967) and led to poor free-field localization performance (Casseday & Neff 1975, Jenkins & Masterton 1982). In contrast, animals with lesions of the lateral lemnisci (the major output of the SOC) are able to relearn lateralization using interaural time differences (Masterton et al 1967). Lesions of the other major commissural connections in the auditory system of cats (the corpus callosum and the commissure of the inferior colliculi) were without marked effect on auditory localization in the two-speaker paradigm (Moore et al 1974). These data are significant not only because they point to the importance of the SOC in the initial encoding of interaural time differences, but because in conjunction with related evidence on the effects of deep midbrain lesions in the same species (Masterton et al 1968) they suggest that separate anatomical pathways may be involved in the encoding of interaural time and intensity disparities.

Deficits that result from unilateral brain lesions have also been studied. Unilateral lesions of the SOC or nuclei caudal to it (Masterton et al 1967, 1981, Casseday & Neff 1975, Casseday & Smoak 1981, Jenkins & Masterton 1982) result in impairments in the performance of tasks requiring sound localization in either the acoustic hemifield ipsilateral to the lesion, or in both the ipsilateral and the contralateral hemifields. Unilateral lesions rostral to the SOC (Strominger 1969a, Strominger & Oesterreich 1970, Jenkins & Masterton 1982) result in deficits predominantly when the stimulus to which the animal must respond is located in the sound field contralateral to the lesion.

The nature of the deficits exhibited by such animals in these kinds of tasks seems relatively clear for lesions of, and caudal to, the SOC. In each of these cases, binaural comparisons have been prevented, either by elimination of one input (as in lesions of the cochlear nucleus or trapezoid body), or by direct ablation of the binaural comparator (the SOC). The deficit, therefore, appears to be a sensory one (i.e. in the *detection* of sound source location) if for no other reason than that the independent anatomical and physiological evidence on the lesioned structures points directly to their critical importance in the initial encoding of interaural disparities.

The case with lesions of more rostral regions of the auditory nervous system is less clear because the independent evidence on the anatomy and physiology of the structures concerned (particularly the cortex and thalamus) does not point to any major binaural convergence taking place in those structures. Perhaps especially in the instances of cortical lesions, independent evidence is required to eliminate the possibility that the poor "localization" performance of lesioned animals is not secondary to attentive, memory or sensory-motor integrative dysfunctions that have been caused by the ablations without necessarily interfering in the detection of sound source location per se.

This question is addressed in a number of recent studies that paid careful attention to procedural variables in behavioral experiments. An important development in this regard came with the report of Ravizza & Masterton (1972) on the opossum *(Didelphis virginiana)*. This species, when provided with a novel, threatening, or noxious stimulus, ceases its ongoing behavior and "freezes"—a behavior doubtless responsible for the expression "playing 'possum." Ravizza & Masterton (1972) capitalized on this phenomenon by designing a behavioral paradigm that used this response of behavior suppression as an indicator of the animal's ability to localize sound sources. A water-deprived opossum licked at a water spout (which also ensured the orientation of the head) in the presence of a neutral acoustic stimulus from one hemifield (left or right). A warning stimulus, associated with unavoidable shock to the feet, was an identical signal from a speaker located symmetrically in the opposite hemifield. Decorticate opossums were capable of discriminating between the two sound source locations, although there was some loss of azimuth acuity, an important finding to which we shall return below. Similar data, obtained using a similar suppression-of-drinking paradigm, were presented for the rat (Kelly & Glazier 1978). In this species, the minimum audible angles for lesioned animals and unoperated controls were comparable. These data raise the possibility that the deficits seen in other studies using behavioral paradigms requiring the animal to move toward a sound source may not have been purely sensory ones.

Recent studies by Heffner & Masterton (1975) in the macaque monkey and by Heffner (1978) in dogs provide corroborative evidence for this line of argument. Using the two-speaker paradigm, a monkey with bilateral auditory cortical lesions was unable to "localize" a sound source when "localization" required the animal to move toward the speaker that had provided a transient stimulus. The same monkey, however, was able to indicate correctly which of the speakers had been activated if it did so by pressing one of two proximally located response keys. These results, and those from a conceptually similar series of experiments on bilaterally lesioned dogs (Heffner 1978), suggested that the deficits exhibited by animals with bilateral cortical lesions in this kind of sound localization task were not purely sensory, but were probably the result of disrupted sensory-motor integrative functions otherwise required for the performance of some, but not all, motor responses. These findings have been complemented by the finding that under appropriate training conditions, cats with bilateral cortical lesions are able to regain normal thresholds for interaural intensity and phase-angle discriminations in a double grill-box avoidance task (Cranford 1979).

There seem to be two difficulties in the interpretation of the data adduced from this line of investigation. The first, indicated initially by Heffner (1978) and subsequently by Cranford (1979), is that there is currently no viable hypothesis capable of predicting precisely which motor responses, or even classes thereof, should be affected by cortical lesions in these kinds of experiments. A second problem with many of these experiments concerns the fact that, in the two-speaker paradigm, the animals were essentially required only to *lateralize* the stimulus: since there was only one appropriate goal in each hemifield, detection of the laterality of the sound source may have been sufficient to obtain an apparently normal "localization" performance. Accordingly, the implications of those studies for the role of the auditory cortex in the *localization* of free-field sound sources are less than clear. In this context, Ravizza & Masterton (1972) in their study of opossums reported that decorticate animals showed poorer azimuth acuity than did unoperated animals.

Jenkins & Masterton (1982) recently re-addressed the question of the effects of unilateral brain lesions on auditory localization. They used a behavioral paradigm in which cats were required to move toward the source of a brief sound, but with the difference that the cats had to select between seven possible speakers disposed in 30° intervals in auditory azimuth. They confirmed that animals with lesions rostral to the SOC showed deficits only in responses to stimuli originating in the sound field contralateral to the lesion, but revealed that the animals showing these azimuth acuity deficits were still able to perform the two-speaker task at normal levels. Jenkins & Merzenich (1984) extended and refined these studies. Normal sound localization behavior was studied in cats using a seven-speaker apparatus similar to that used in the Jenkins & Masterton (1982) study. Lesions were produced in a part of cortical region AI representing a restricted band of frequencies, the site and extent of the lesion being guided by prior electrophysiological mapping. The animal was again evaluated to determine the consequences of such a lesion on localization acuity. The results showed not only that the integrity of AI is necessary and sufficient for normal azimuthal sound localization behavior but suggested that sound localization is accomplished over frequency-specific pathways.

CONCLUSIONS AND DIRECTIONS FOR FUTURE RESEARCH

The preceding brief overview of some recent literature on the neurophysiology of sound localization enables us to draw two important general principles.

The first concerns the correspondence between the azimuthal dependence of the dichotic sound localization cues, the ranges of those cues that central auditory neurons most commonly encode, and the azimuthal dependence of sound localization and lateralization acuity. Recall that physical measurements of interaural time and intensity disparities are, in cats at least, a relatively steep function of azimuth over azimuthal ranges within about 45° of the midsagittal plane. The recent neurophysiological studies on the coding of onset-time and intensity disparities revealed that the ranges of those cues that neurons encoded (i.e. the ranges of the disparities over which response strength was a most sensitive function of disparity) were those associated with the same ranges of azimuths, namely those near the midline. That is to say, *the auditory nervous system seems to be most sensitive to the dichotic cues for azimuth over ranges where the cues themselves most precisely specify sound source azimuth*. This proposition raises the intriguing question of whether the neural circuitry for the coding of these dichotic cues is "hard-wired," is sensitive to experimental manipulation, or, indeed, whether it undergoes developmental changes concordant with the postnatal growth of the head (e.g. Moore & Irvine 1981).

These mechanisms appear likely to be the neurophysiological substrates of two related psychophysical findings. First, recent psychoacoustic studies in human beings (Yost 1974, 1981) indicate that interaural intensive and temporal cues are most effective in determining the apparent azimuth of "intracranial" acoustic perceptions near the midsagittal plane. The relationship between apparent intracranial azimuth and interaural disparity is linear for small and medium disparities, and becomes markedly nonlinear with larger intensive or temporal differences. Second, behavioral studies in both humans (Mills 1958) and cats (Jenkins & Masterton 1982) indicate that the greatest acuity in free-field sound localization is for azimuths at or near the median plane.

The recent evidence on the barn owl provides a particularly striking example of covariation of neural stimulus selectivity, peripheral acoustic specializations, and the acoustic "ethology" of a species. There is a strong correspondence between the fact that this bird perches at some distance above the ground on which its prey are usually located, and the fact that its central auditory nervous system is particularly sensitive to the spatial location of acoustic stimuli in the lower frontal quadrant. At least in part, this correspondence reflects, first, the asymmetry of the owl's external ear canals, which provides cues for sound source elevation as well as sound source azimuth, and second, neural sensitivity to dichotic cues that the avian auditory periphery is capable of both producing and encoding (e.g. interaural phase-angle disparities in high-frequency signals).

It is, however, precisely the presence of these specializations that raises the question of how general the neural map of auditory space is across species. Moreover, so far as the neural circuitry required for such a map is concerned, the owl does not have the added complication of the orientation of mobile pinnae to include in the analysis of interaural disparities. In animals with mobile pinnae, this information could be provided by efference copy or by proprioception (Phillips et al 1982), although attempts to find an auditory space map in the cat's auditory cortex (Middlebrooks & Pettigrew 1981), inferior colliculus (Semple et al 1983), and superior colliculus (Irvine & Wise 1983) have thus far been unsuccessful. There may be a topographic organization according to azimuth of acoustic spatial receptive fields in the guinea pig's deep superior colliculus (Palmer & King 1982), and this may overlay the topographic visual map in the same structure. It is noteworthy, however, that the guinea pig's pinnae are considerably less mobile, less conical, and less substantial than those of cats or bats. Pinnae of this physical structure might not be expected to generate the strong directionality of sound pressure transformations seen in larger, more conical, pinnae. If this is in fact the case, then the effects of pinna directionality on the spatial selectivity of central neurons might be less profound.

In contrast to those presented for the owl, the bulk of data on the neural mechanisms for sound localization in mammals suggests that the neural encoding of interaural time and intensive disparities provides the animal with information on the azimuth of a sound source. Because of the "cone of confusion" phenomenon, this information is ambiguous. It seems likely, however, that the ambiguity is resolved by directionality inherent in the pinnae, since pinna directionality is imposed on the spatial selectivity of central neurons that otherwise results from their sensitivity to the dichotic cues alone.

The second general principle concerns a model of sound localization mechanisms that has been derived independently from both the neurophysiological (Phillips & Irvine 1982, Phillips & Gates 1982) and behavioral-lesion (Strominger & Oesterreich 1970, Masterton et al 1981, Jenkins & Masterton 1982) evidence. A number of authors have remarked that central auditory neurons rostral to the SOC respond most strongly, or solely, when interaural disparities favor the contralateral ear, and have suggested, therefore, that such neurons may form a mechanism for the discrimination of sound source laterality (Benevento et al 1970, Stillman 1972, Starr 1974, Benson & Teas 1976). The present review, however, reveals that not only do these neurons respond more strongly when interaural disparities favor the contralateral ear, but that the ranges of those disparities over which response strength was a most sensitive function of that parameter were also associated with contralateral azimuths. This phenomenon is perhaps most readily visualized in the relationship of spike count to interaural intensity disparity. It is also manifested in neural sensitivity to interaural phase delays, since the peak of averaged delay curves for any given neuron is typically at a delay favoring the contralateral ear, so that the steeply declining part of the function is also associated with delays favoring the contralateral ear. These data suggest that these neurons may not simply encode sound source laterality, but that they may encode the dichotic cues for *azimuth* within the contralateral acoustic hemifield. The strong bias toward the coding of the cues for contralateral azimuths is consistent with the finding that those cells in the auditory cortex (Middlebrooks & Pettigrew 1981) and inferior colliculus (Semple et al 1983, Moore et al 1984) with circumscribed spatial receptive fields have those fields located exclusively in contralateral auditory space. Taken together, these data have engendered the hypothesis that *cells in levels of the auditory nervous system rostral to the decussating outputs of the SOC encode spatial information only for the contralateral auditory hemifield* (Phillips & Irvine 1981, Phillips & Gates 1982). The same conclusion has been reached independently on the basis of the behavioral deficits consequent to unilateral lesions at levels rostral to the SOC, since those animals show deficits almost exclusively in the responses to stimuli originating in the sound field contralateral to the lesion (Strominger 1969a,b, Strominger & Oesterreich 1970, Thompson & Masterton 1978, Masterton et al 1981, Jenkins & Masterton 1982).

This hypothesis of central auditory system function parallels the well-known representation of the contralateral visual field and body surface in the levels of those sensory systems rostral to their decussations. A primary difference between the acoustic modality on the one hand, and the visual and somatic modalities on the other, derives from the fact that, whereas contralateral spatial representation in the latter modalities has been achieved simply by crossed central projections of afferent nerve fibers (and the retention of their topographic relationships), spatial representation in the auditory system may be necessarily computational in requiring inputs from both ears.

ACKNOWLEGMENTS

We thank Drs. T. C. T. Yin, D. Oertel, and A. D. Musicant for their helpful critiques of the manuscript. This review was prepared while Dr. Phillips was supported by NIH International Research Fellowship FO5 TW03102. The work was also partly supported by NSF Grant BNS19893 and NIH Grants NS12732 and HD03352.

Literature Cited

Aitkin, L. M. 1973. Medial geniculate body of the cat: responses to tonal stimuli of neurons in medial division. *J. Neurophysiol.* 36:275–83

Aitkin, L. M., Blake, D. W., Fryman, S., Bock, G. R. 1972. Responses of neurones in the rabbit inferior colliculus. II. Influence of binaural tonal stimulation. *Brain Res.* 47:91–101

Aitkin, L. M., Boyd, J. 1975. Responses of single units in cerebellar vermis of the cat to monaural and binaural stimuli. *J. Neurophysiol.* 38:418–29

Aitkin, L. M., Bush, B. M., Gates, G. R. 1978. The auditory midbrain of a marsupial: the brush-tailed possum *(Trichosurus vulpecula)*. *Brain Res.* 150:29–44

Aitkin, L. M., Rawson, J. A. 1983. Frontal sound source location is represented in the cat cerebellum. *Brain Res.* 265:317–21

Aitkin, L. M., Webster, W. R. 1972. Medial geniculate body of the cat: organization and responses to tonal stimuli of neurons in ventral division. *J. Neurophysiol.* 35:365–80

Angell, J. R., Fite, W. 1901. The monaural localization of sound. *Psychol. Rev.* 8:225–46

Batteau, D. W. 1967. The role of the pinna in human localization. *Proc. R. Soc. London Ser. B* 168:158–80

Benevento, L. A., Coleman, P. D., Loe, P. R. 1970. Responses of single cells in cat inferior colliculus to binaural click stimuli: combinations of intensity levels, time differences and intensity differences. *Brain Res.* 17:387–405

Benson, D. A., Heinz, R. D., Goldstein, M. H. Jr. 1981. Single-unit activity in the auditory cortex of monkeys actively localizing sound sources: spatial tuning and behavioral dependency. *Brain Res.* 219:249–67

Benson, D. A., Teas, D. C. 1976. Single unit study of binaural interaction in the auditory cortex of the chinchilla. *Brain Res.* 103:313–38

Bishop, P. O., Kozak, W., Vakkur, G. 1962. Some quantitative aspects of the cat's eye: axis and place of reference, visual field coordinates, and optics. *J. Physiol.* 163:466–502

Bismarck, G. von. 1967. *The sound pressure transformation function from free-field to the eardrum of the chinchilla.* MS Thesis. MIT, Cambridge, Mass.

Blauert, J. 1969/1970. Sound localization in the median plane. *Acustica* 22:205–13

Bock, G. R., Webster, W. R. 1974. Coding of spatial location by single units in the inferior colliculus of the alert cat. *Exp. Brain Res.* 21:387–98

Boudreau, J. C., Tsuchitani, C. 1968. Binaural interaction in the cat superior olive S segment. *J. Neurophysiol.* 31:442–54

Brugge, J. F., Anderson, D. J., Aitkin, L. M. 1970. Responses of neurons in the dorsal nucleus of the lateral lemniscus of cat to binaural tonal stimulation. *J. Neurophysiol.* 33:441–58

Brugge, J. F., Dubrovsky, N. A., Aitkin, L. M., Anderson, D. J. 1969. Sensitivity of single neurons in auditory cortex of cat to binaural tonal stimulation; effects of varying interaural time and intensity. *J. Neurophysiol.* 32:1005–24

Brugge, J. F., Geisler, C. D. 1978. Auditory mechanisms of the lower brainstem. *Ann. Rev. Neurosci.* 1:363–94

Brugge, J. F., Merzenich, M. M. 1973. Responses of neurons in auditory cortex of the macaque monkey to monaural and binaural stimulation. *J. Neurophysiol.* 36:1138–58

Butler, R. A. 1969. On the relative usefulness

of monaural and binaural cues in locating sound in space. *Psychon. Sci.* 17:245–46

Butler, R. A. 1971. The monaural localization of tonal stimuli. *Percept. Psychophys.* 9:99–101

Butler, R. A. 1973. The relative influence of pitch and timbre on the apparent location of sound in the median sagittal plane. *Percept. Psychophys.* 14:255–58

Butler, R. A. 1974. Does tonotopicity subserve the perceived elevation of a sound? *Fed. Proc.* 33:1920–23

Butler, R. A., Flannery, R. 1980. The spatial attributes of stimulus frequency and their role in monaural localization of sound in the horizontal plane. *Percept. Psychophys.* 28:449–57

Calford, M. B., Pettigrew, J. D. 1984. Frequency dependence of directional amplification of the cat's pinna. *Hearing Res* 14:13–19

Casseday, J. H., Neff, W. D. 1975. Auditory localization: role of auditory pathways in brain stem of the cat. *J. Neurophysiol.* 38:842–58

Casseday, J. H., Smoak, H. A. 1981. Effects of unilateral ablation of anteroventral cochlear nucleus on localization of sound in space. In *Symposium on Neuronal Mechanisms of Hearing,* ed. J. Syka, L. Aitkin, pp. 277–82, New York: Plenum

Cranford, J. L. 1979. Auditory cortex lesions and interaural intensity and phase-angle discrimination in cats. *J. Neurophysiol.* 42:1518–26

Djupesland, G., Zwislocki, J. J. 1973. Sound pressure distribution in the outer ear. *Acta Otolaryngol.* 75:350–52

Durlach, N. I., Colburn, H. S. 1978. Binaural phenomena. In *Handbook of Perception, Vol. 4, Hearing,* ed. E. C. Carterette, M. P. Friedman. pp. 365–466. New York: Academic

Eisenman, L. M. 1974. Neural encoding of sound location: an electrophysiological study in auditory cortex (AI) of the cat using free-field stimuli. *Brain Res.* 75:203–14

Erulkar, S. D. 1972. Comparative aspects of spatial localization of sound. *Physiol. Rev.* 52:237–360

Evans, E. F. 1968. Cortical representation. In *Hearing Mechanisms in Vertebrates,* ed. A. V. S. de Reuck, J. Knight, pp. 272–95. Boston: Little, Brown

Feddersen, W. C., Sandel, T. T., Teas, D. C., Jeffress, L. A. 1957. Localization of high-frequency tones. *J. Acoust. Soc. Am.* 29:988–91

Ferrier, D. 1876. *The Functions of the Brain.* London: Smith, Elder

Ferrier, D. 1890. *The Croonian Lectures on Cerebral Localization.* London: Smith, Elder

Flannery, R., Butler, R. A. 1981. Spectral cues provided by the pinna for monaural localization in the horizontal plane. *Percept. Psychophys.* 29:438–44

Geisler, C. D., Rhode, W. S., Hazelton, D. W. 1969. Responses of inferior colliculus neurons in the cat to binaural acoustic stimuli having wide-band spectra. *J. Neurophysiol.* 32:960–74

Goldberg, J. M. 1975. Physiological studies of auditory nuclei of the pons. In *Handbook of Sensory Physiology, Vol. V/2,* ed. W. D. Keidel, W. D. Neff, pp. 109–44. New York: Academic

Goldberg, J. M., Brown, P. B. 1968. Functional organization of the dog superior olivary complex: an anatomical and electrophysiological study. *J. Neurophysiol.* 31:639–56

Goldberg, J. M., Brown, P. B. 1969. Response of binaural neurons of dog superior olivary complex to dichotic tonal stimuli: some physiological mechanisms of sound localization. *J. Neurophysiol.* 32:613–36

Grinnell, A. D., Grinnell, V. S. 1965. Neural correlates of vertical localization by echo-locating bats. *J. Physiol.* 181:830–51

Guinan, J. J. Jr., Guinan, S. S., Norris, B. E. 1972a. Single auditory units in the superior olivary complex I: Responses to sounds and classifications based on physiological properties. *Int. J. Neurosci.* 4:101–20

Guinan, J. J. Jr., Norris, B. E., Guinan, S. S. 1972b. Single auditory units in the superior olivary complex II: Locations of unit categories and tonotopic organization. *Int. J. Neurosci.* 4:147–66

Heffner, H. 1978. Effect of auditory cortex ablation on localization and discrimination of brief sounds. *J. Neurophysiol.* 41:963–76

Heffner, H., Masterton, R. B. 1975. Contribution of auditory cortex to sound localization in the monkey *(Macaca mulatta). J. Neurophysiol.* 38:1340–58

Heffner, H. E., Heffner, R. S. 1984. Sound localization in large mammals, I. Localization of complex sounds by horses. *Behav. Neurosci.* 98:541–55

Heffner, R. S., Heffner, H. E. 1982. Hearing in the elephant *(Elephas maximus):* absolute sensitivity, frequency discrimination, and sound localization. *J. Comp. Physiol. Psychol.* 96:926–44

Irvine, D. R. F., Wise, L. Z. 1983. Topographic organization of interaural-intensity–difference sensitivity and the representation of auditory azimuthal location in the deep layers of the superior colliculus. In *Mechanisms of Hearing,* ed. W. R. Webster, L. M. Aitkin, pp. 101–6. Clayton, Victoria, Australia: Monash Univ. Press

Jenkins, W. M., Masterton, R. B. 1982. Sound localization: effects of unilateral lesions in central auditory system. *J. Neurophysiol.* 47:987–1016

Jenkins, W. M., Merzenich, M. M. 1984. Role of cat primary auditory cortex for sound localization behavior. *J. Neurophysiol.* In press

Johnson, D. H. 1980. The relationship between spike rate and synchrony in responses of auditory-nerve fibers to single tones. *J. Acoust. Soc. Am.* 68:1115–22

Kelly, J. B., Glazier, S. J. 1978. Auditory cortex lesions and discrimination of spatial location by the rat. *Brain Res.* 145:315–21

Kitzes, L. M., Wrege, K. S., Cassady, J. M. 1980. Patterns of responses of cortical cells to binaural stimulation. *J. Comp. Neurol.* 192:455–72

Knudsen, E. I. 1980. Sound localization in birds. In *Comparative Studies of Hearing in Vertebrates,* ed. A. N. Popper, R. R. Fay, pp 289–322. New York: Springer-Verlag

Knudsen, E. I., Blasdel, G. G., Konishi, M. 1979. Sound localization by the barn owl (*Tyto alba*) measured with the search coil technique. *J. Comp. Physiol.* 133:1–11

Knudsen, E. I., Konishi, M. 1978. Space and frequency are represented separately in auditory midbrain of the owl. *J. Neurophysiol.* 41:870–84

Knudsen, E. I., Konishi, M. 1979. Mechanisms of sound localization in the barn owl (*Tyto alba*). *J. Comp. Physiol.* 133:13–21

Knudsen, E. I., Konishi, M. 1980. Monaural occlusion shifts receptive-field locations of auditory midbrain units in the owl. *J. Neurophysiol.* 44:687–95

Knudsen, E. I., Konishi, M., Pettigrew, J. D. 1977. Receptive fields of auditory neurons in the owl. *Science* 198:1278–80

Konishi, M. 1973. How the owl tracks its prey. *Am. Sci.* 61:414–27

Kuhn, G. F. 1977. Model for the interaural time differences in the azimuthal plane. *J. Acoust. Soc. Am.* 62:157–67

Kuwada, S., Yin, T. C. T. 1983. Binaural interaction in low-frequency neurons in inferior colliculus of the cat. I. Effects of long interaural delays, intensity, and repetition rate on the interaural delay function. *J. Neurophysiol.* 50:981–99

Kuwada, S., Yin, T. C. T. 1984. Physiological studies of directional hearing. In *Directional Hearing,* ed. W. A. Yost, G. Gourevitch. Maryland: Univ. Park Press

Kuwada, S., Yin, T. C. T., Wickesberg, R. E. 1979. Response of cat inferior colliculus neurons to binaural beat stimuli: possible mechanisms for sound localization. *Science* 206:586–88

Licklider, J. C. R., Webster, J. C., Hedlun, J. M. 1950. On the frequency limits of binaural beats. *J. Acoust. Soc. Am.* 22:468–73

Masterton, R. B. 1974. Adaptation for sound localization in the ear and brainstem of mammals. *Fed. Proc.* 33:1904–10

Masterton, R. B., Diamond, I. T. 1964. Effects of auditory cortex ablation on discrimination of small binaural time differences. *J. Neurophysiol.* 27:15–36

Masterton, R. B., Glendenning, K. K., Nudo, R. J. 1981. Anatomical-behavioral analyses of hindbrain sound localization mechanisms. In *Symposium on Neuronal Mechamisms of Hearing,* ed. J. Syka, L. Aitkin, pp. 263–75. New York: Plenum

Masterton, R. B., Imig, T. J. 1984. Neural mechanisms for sound localization. *Ann. Rev. Physiol.* 46:275–87

Masterton, R. B., Jane, J. A., Diamond, I. T. 1967. Role of brainstem auditory structures in sound localization. I. Trapezoid body, superior olive, and lateral lemniscus. *J. Neurophysiol.* 30:341–59

Masterton, R. B., Jane, J. A., Diamond, I. T. 1968. Role of brainstem auditory structures in sound localization. II. Inferior colliculus and its brachium. *J. Neurophysiol.* 31:96–108

McFadden, D. 1973. Precedence effects and auditory cells with long characteristic delays. *J. Acoust. Soc. Am.* 54:528–30

McFadden, D., Pasanen, E. G. 1976. Lateralization at high frequencies based on interaural time differences. *J. Acoust. Soc. Am.* 59:634–39

Middlebrooks, J. C., Pettigrew, J. D. 1981. Functional classes of neurons in primary auditory cortex (AI) of the cat distinguished by sensitivity to sound location. *J. Neurosci.* 1:107–20

Mills, A. W. 1958. On the minimum audible angle. *J. Acoust. Soc. Am.* 30:237–46

Mills, A. W. 1972. Auditory localization. In *Foundations of Modern Auditory Theory,* ed. J. V. Tobias, 2:301–48. New York: Academic

Moiseff, A., Konishi, M. 1981. Neuronal and behavioral sensitivity to binaural time differences in the owl. *J. Neurosci.* 1:40–48

Moiseff, A., Konishi, M. 1983a. The neural mechanisms of sound localization in the barn owl. In *Mechanisms of Hearing,* ed. W. R. Webster, L. M. Aitkin, pp. 107–10. Clayton, Victoria, Australia: Monash Univ. Press

Moiseff, A., Konishi, M. 1983b. Binaural characteristics of units in the owl's brainstem auditory pathway: precursors of restricted spatial receptive fields. *J. Neurosci.* 3:2553–62

Møller, A. R. 1972. Coding of sounds in lower levels of the auditory system. *Q. Rev. Biophys.* 5:59–155

Moore, C. N., Casseday, J. H., Neff, W. D. 1974. Sound localization: the role of the commissural pathways of the auditory system of the cat. *Brain Res.* 82:13–26

Moore, D. R., Irvine, D. R. F. 1979. A developmental study of the sound pressure transformation by the head of the cat. *Acta Otolaryngol.* 87:434–40

Moore, D. R., Irvine, D. R. F. 1981. Development of responses to acoustic interaural intensity differences in the cat inferior colliculus. *Exp. Brain Res.* 41:301–9

Moore, D. R., Semple, M. N., Addison, P. D., Aitkin, L. M. 1984. Properties of spatial receptive fields in the central nucleus of the cat inferior colliculus. I. Responses to tones of low intensity. *Hearing Res.* 13:159–74

Moushegian, G., Stillman, R. D., Rupert, A. L. 1971. Characteristic delays in superior olive and inferior colliculus. In *Physiology of the Auditory System*, ed. M. B. Sachs, pp. 245–54. Baltimore, Md: Natl. Educ. Consult.

Musicant, A. D. 1982. *Contribution of spectral cues to directional hearing*. PhD Thesis, Univ. Chicago.

Musicant, A. D., Butler, R. A. 1984. The influence of pinnae-based spectral cues on sound localization. *J. Acoust. Soc. Am.* 75:1195–1200

Neff, W. D., Diamond, I. T., Casseday, J. H. 1975. Behavioral studies of auditory discrimination: central nervous system. In *Handbook of Sensory Physiology, Vol. V/2*, ed. W. D. Keidel, W. D. Neff. Berlin: Springer-Verlag

Neff, W. D., Fisher, J. F., Diamond, I. T., Yela, M. 1956. Role of auditory cortex in discrimination requiring localization of sound in space. *J. Neurophysiol.* 19:500–12

Orman, S. S., Phillips, D. P. 1984. Binaural interactions of single neurons in posterior field of cat auditory cortex. *J. Neurophysiol.* 51:1028–39

Palmer, A. R., King, A. J. 1982. The representation of auditory space in the mammalian superior colliculus. *Nature* 299:248–49

Perrott, D. R., Musicant, A. D. 1977. Rotating tones and binaural beats. *J. Acoust. Soc. Am.* 61:1288–92

Phillips, D. P., Calford, M. B., Pettigrew, J. D., Aitkin, L. M., Semple, M. N. 1982. Directionality of sound pressure transformation at the cat's pinna. *Hearing Res.* 8:13–28

Phillips, D. P., Gates, G. R. 1982. Representation of the two ears in the auditory cortex: a re-examination. *Int. J. Neurosci.* 16:41–46

Phillips, D. P., Irvine, D. R. F. 1981. Responses of single neurons in physiologically defined area AI of cat cerebral cortex: sensitivity to interaural intensity differences. *Hearing Res.* 4:299–307

Phillips, D. P., Irvine, D. R. F. 1982. Properties of single neurons in the anterior auditory field (AAF) of cat cerebral cortex. *Brain Res.* 248:237–44

Phillips, D. P., Irvine, D. R. F. 1983. Some features of binaural input to single neurons in physiologically defined area AI of cat cerebral cortex. *J. Neurophysiol.* 49:383–95

Phillips, D. P., Orman, S. S. 1984. Responses of single neurons in posterior field of cat auditory cortex to tonal stimulation. *J. Neurophysiol.* 51:147–63

Ravizza, R. J., Masterton, R. B. 1972. Contribution of neocortex to sound localization in opossum *(Didelphis virginiana)*. *J. Neurophysiol.* 35:344–56

Riss, W. 1959. Effect of bilateral temporal cortical ablation on discrimination of sound direction. *J. Neurophysiol.* 22:374–84

Rose, J. E., Brugge, J. F., Anderson, D. J., Hind, J. E. 1967. Phase-locked response to low-frequency tones in single auditory nerve fibers of the squirrel monkey. *J. Neurophysiol.* 30:769–93

Rose, J. E., Gross, N. B., Geisler, C. D., Hind, J. E. 1966. Some neural mechanisms in the inferior colliculus of the cat which may be relevant to localization of a sound source. *J. Neurophysiol.* 29:288–314

Roth, G. L., Kochhar, R. K., Hind, J. E. 1980. Interaural time differences: implications regarding the neurophysiology of sound localization. *J. Acoust. Soc. Am.* 68:1643–51

Semple, M. N., Aitkin, L. M., Calford, M. B., Pettigrew, J. D., Phillips, D. P. 1983. Spatial receptive fields in the cat inferior colliculus. *Hearing Res.* 10:203–15

Shaw, E. A. G. 1974. Transformation of sound pressure level from the free field to the eardrum in the horizontal plane. *J. Acoust. Soc. Am.* 56:1848–61

Starr, A. 1974. Neurophysiological mechanisms of sound localization. *Fed. Proc.* 33:1911–14

Stillman, R. D. 1971. Characteristic delay neurons in the inferior colliculus of the kangaroo rat. *Exp. Neurol.* 32:404–12

Stillman, R. D. 1972. Responses of high-frequency inferior colliculus neurons to interaural intensity differences. *Exp. Neurol.* 36:118–26

Stotler, W. A. 1953. An experimental study of the cells and connections of the superior olivary complex of the cat. *J. Comp. Neurol.* 98:401–32

Strominger, N. L. 1969a. Subdivisions of auditory cortex and their role in localization of sound in space. *Exp. Neurol.* 24:348–62

Strominger, N. L. 1969b. Localization of sound in space after unilateral and bilateral ablation of auditory cortex. *Exp. Neurol.* 25:521–33

Strominger, N. L., Oesterreich, R. E. 1970. Localization of sound after section of the brachium of the inferior colliculus. *J. Comp. Neurol.* 138:1–18

Suga, N. 1978. Specialization of the auditory

system for reception and processing species-specific sounds. *Fed. Proc.* 37:2342–54

Suga, N. 1982. Functional organization of the auditory cortex. Representation beyond tonotopy in the bat. In *Cortical Sensory Organization, Vol. 3, Multiple Auditory Areas,* ed. C. N. Woolsey, pp. 157–218. Clifton, NJ: Humana Press

Sullivan, W. E., Konishi, M. 1983. High frequency phase coding in the cochlear nucleus of the barn owl. *Neurosci. Abstr.* 9:496

Thompson, G. C., Masterton, R. B. 1978. Brain stem auditory pathways involved in reflexive head orientation to sound. *J. Neurophysiol.* 41:1183–1202

Tsuchitani, C. 1978. Lower auditory brain stem structures of the cat. In *Evoked Electrical Activity in the Auditory Nervous System,* ed. R. Naunton. New York: Academic

Wakeford, O. S., Robinson, D. E. 1974. Lateralization of tonal stimuli by the cat. *J. Acoust. Soc. Am.* 55:649–52

Webster, W. R., Aitkin, L. M. 1975. Central auditory processing. In *Handbook of Psychobiology,* ed. M. S. Gazzaniga, C. Blakemore. New York: Academic

Wiener, F. M., Pfeiffer, R. R., Backus, A. S. N. 1966. On the sound pressure transformation by the head and auditory meatus of the cat. *Acta Otolaryngol.* 61:255–69

Woodworth, R. S. 1938. *Experimental Psychology.* New York: Holt, Rinehart & Winston

Yin, T. C. T., Kuwada, S. 1983a. Binaural interaction in low-frequency neurons in inferior colliculus of the cat. II. Effects of changing rate and direction of interaural phase. *J. Neurophysiol.* 50:1000–19

Yin, T. C. T., Kuwada, S. 1983b. Binaural interaction in low-frequency neurons in inferior colliculus of the cat. III. Effects of changing frequency. *J. Neurophysiol.* 50:1020–42

Yin, T. C. T., Kuwada, S. 1984. Neuronal mechanisms of binaural interaction. In *Dynamic Aspects of Neocortical Function,* ed. G. M. Edelman, W. M. Cowan, W. E. Gall. New York: Wiley

Yin, T. C. T., Kuwada, S., Sujaku, Y. 1984. Interaural time sensitivity of high-frequency neurons in the inferior colliculus. *J. Acoust. Soc. Am.* 76:1401–10

Yost, W. A. 1974. Discriminations of interaural phase differences. *J. Acoust. Soc. Am.* 55:1299–1303

Yost, W. A. 1981. Lateral position of sinusoids presented with interaural intensive and temporal differences. *J. Acoust. Soc. Am.* 70:397–409

Ann. Rev. Psychol. 1985. 36:275-305
Copyright © 1985 by Annual Reviews Inc. All rights reserved

SOCIAL COGNITION: A LOOK AT MOTIVATED STRATEGIES

Carolin Showers and Nancy Cantor

Institute for Social Research, University of Michigan, Ann Arbor, Michigan 48106

CONTENTS

INTRODUCTION

Motivation and Social Cognition

The present review takes as a starting point the interface between motivation and social cognition (Lewin et al 1944, Bruner & Tagiuri 1954, Kelly 1955,

0066-4308/85/0201-0275$02.00

Zajonc 1980, Lazarus 1982). As we gain an understanding of basic cognitive structures and processes, we move toward analyzing social cognition in more complex, personally involving contexts, with an eye for how motivation is translated into strategic cognitive activity (Clark & Fiske 1982, Isen & Hastorf 1982, Kelley et al 1983, Sorrentino & Higgins 1984). Investigators increasingly attend to the motivational elements—goals, mood, expertise—that carry positive and negative incentives for behavior and guide individuals' interpretations and plans.

Interest is shifting to questions about the cognitive representations of *dynamic self-knowledge*—the self as I want to be, should be, or dread becoming (Markus 1983, Higgins et al 1984); of *personal goals* associated with the self in different life contexts (Little 1983, Kihlstrom & Cantor 1984, Greenwald & Pratkanis 1984); of the *mood states* and affect connected with stereotypes and prototypes and past episodes (Kihlstrom 1981, Clark & Isen 1982, Fiske & Pavelchak 1984); and of personal efficacy or *expertise* or involvement in a task domain (Bandura 1977, Chaiken 1980, Fazio & Zanna 1981). Complementary endeavors are based on the assumption that these motivational-cognitive elements drive *cognitive strategies* for interpreting situations and planning action (Greenwald 1982). Individuals use specific self-presentation and communication strategies to effect particular goals (Higgins 1981, Jones & Pittman 1982, Schlenker 1982); mood states direct decision-making strategies and those strategies may serve to perpetuate moods (Abramson et al 1978, Isen et al 1982); expertise from direct experience and personal involvement mediates the link between attitudes and behaviors (Fazio et al 1982, Petty & Cacioppo 1984). From this perspective, much of social cognition looks motivated. Cognitive strategies translate goals, mood, and expertise into "appropriate" action in particular contexts (Figure 1).

As an added benefit, the "energizing" of social cognition has not gone unnoticed by those primarily interested in individual differences (Pervin 1985). Personality researchers often refer to the individual's repertoire of self-knowledge and social knowledge in building links between dispositions and behavior. (See Bem & Funder 1978 and Lord 1982 on perceptions of situations; Cantor et al 1982 and Buss & Craik 1983 on prototypes; Buss 1980 on the

Motivational Elements ⇒ Flexible Cognitive Strategies ⇒ "Appropriate" Action

Goals	— Responsiveness to situations
Mood	— Multiple interpretations
Expertise	— Active control
	— Change in repertoire

Figure 1 Motivated social cognition: Cognitive strategies for interpreting situations and planning behavior translate goals, mood, and expertise into "appropriate" action in particular contexts.

private and public self; Trzebinski 1984 on "action-oriented" representations.) Analyses of cognitive strategies reveal meaningful patterns of behavioral variation; but those strategies can and will change in line with situational contingencies and individuals' goals. (See Carver & Scheier 1981 and Mischel 1983 on self-control strategies; Kuhl 1984 on achievement strategies; Lewinsohn et al 1980 on self-defeating or depressive strategies.) Some even suggest that the cognitive analysis of strategies provides special access to the *process* by which an individual's goals, motives, or competencies (whether stable or changeable) get translated into unique patterns of behavior (Cantor & Kihlstrom 1982, 1983, Hampson 1982).

Flexibility in Social Cognition

Renewed interest in motivated social cognition has introduced other changes in our analyses as well. Researchers pay increased attention to the flexibility people sometimes demonstrate as they interpret situations (Gilovich 1983), reflect on the past (Kahneman & Tversky 1982), and plan for the future (Markus 1983). We are interested in the mixing of prior knowledge and information culled from the situation, as the individual attempts to understand what is happening and why, who is involved and how, what are the potential outcomes and when, what opportunities are afforded and for whom. Under some circumstances, especially when central goals, mood, or expertise are engaged by events in the situation, people show flexibility in (*a*) adjusting interpretations in response to situational features; (*b*) taking control of their thoughts and their plans; (*c*) seeing multiple alternatives for interpreting the same event or outcome; and (*d*) changing their own knowledge repertoire by adding new experiences and by reworking cherished beliefs, values, and goals.

These four aspects of flexibility in interpretive activity form the focus of our reading of the social cognition literature (Figure 1). The situations and outcomes of interest range, broadly, from negotiating with spouses and roommates (e.g. Kelley 1979, Klos et al 1983) to buying a car or evaluating a housing option (e.g. Isen & Means 1983) and to coping with a major illness (Taylor et al 1984) or helping a person in distress (Schwartz 1977). The common thread in these cases is that individuals in such situations will often actively embrace cognitive strategies that seem to fit their goals, mood, or expertise at the time.

To those familiar with this literature it may seem odd that we focus on flexibility and strategic cognition, since the preponderance of evidence in social cognition paints a very different portrait (e.g. Langer 1978). Numerous counter examples exist for all four forms of flexibility: (*a*) The literature has emphasized people's tendencies to cling to favorite interpretations, rather than show responsiveness to situations (Ross et al 1975, Lord et al 1979, Anderson et al 1980, Swann & Read 1981, Jelalian & Miller 1984). (*b*) Cognitive therapists despair over attempts to teach people to exercise more active control over moods, self-defeating cognitions, and dysfunctional strategies (Raimy 1975, Wachtel 1977, Schachter 1982). (*c*) The prevailing assumption is that people miss the multiple possible interpretations of an event because they are "trapped" by perceptually salient and cognitively available stimuli (Taylor & Fiske 1978, Nisbett & Ross 1980). And (*d*) schemas, stereotypes, and impressions in a person's knowledge repertoire may be remarkably resistant to change (Hastie 1981, Taylor & Crocker 1981, Fiske & Taylor 1984). As a whole, the literature on social cognition is heavily skewed toward representing the more passive, less flexible ways in which prior knowledge contributes to present interpretations and strategies for action.

Indeed, good evidence exists for the stability and entrenchment of well-organized memory structures and for the power of contextual cues to prime those structures (or bring them to mind) in a rather direct manner (e.g. Higgins & King 1981, Wyer & Gordon 1984). The direct priming of self-schemas in response to unobtrusive environmental cues (Bargh & Pietromonaco 1982) or the retrieval, rather passively, of mood-congruent memories (Bower 1981) must be taken to be the foundation upon which they more active and strategic processes operate. However, despite passive priming, it is unsafe to assume one-to-one mappings from situational cues to memory organizations to interpretations of those situations. When pressing goals, affective states, or cherished beliefs intervene, it is likely that the individual can fly in the face of the most obvious interpretations of situations, actively retrieving additional information and selectively combining the available information so as to construct an interpretation in accordance with overriding goals or feelings (Anderson & Hastie 1974, Herstein et al 1980; also cf Kelly 1955, Landman & Manis 1983). In such cases, the passively primed material serves as one source of input to the ultimate interpretive strategies. In actuality, however, the active cognitive processes of selection, combination, and reinterpretation are often neither necessary nor efficient; individuals seem to do just fine using the most available and ready-made interpretations (Taylor & Fiske 1978). However, as we look at more costly and personally involving tasks, in which there are self-evident consequences for the social perceiver, we may begin to see the benefits of a more active and strategic interpretive process. The social perceiver works with a well-structured and easily primed repertoire of knowledge; but, we may only have begun to see the full extent of what he does with that knowledge in the service of personal goals and beliefs and affective states.

Individuals Making Sense of Situations

Individuals' interpret situations by combining information drawn from a vast repertoire of prior knowledge with new information from the situation itself. Here we consider three factors—goals, mood, and expertise—that sometimes motivate individuals to use prior knowledge and new information in a flexible manner. We first look briefly at how each factor has been defined within a cognitive perspective. In some cases, these definitions include assumptions about the representation of goals, mood, or expertise as part of the individual's knowledge repertoire. However, we do not concentrate here on models of cognitive structure (cf Hastie et al 1984). Instead, we emphasize the role that goals, mood, and expertise may play in guiding interpretations and shaping strategies for action.

Each factor illustrates one or more of the four forms of flexibility in strategic interpretation: *responsiveness* of interpretations to situational features; *active control* over the direction an interpretation takes; *multiple interpretations* of the same situation; or *substantive change* in the individual's repertoire of knowledge and beliefs. In all cases the direction of research interest is clear, though the evidence base is often still meager.

In the end, the extent of flexible social cognition—constructive alternativism—is still an open question (Kelly 1955). We close this review by speculating about the relevance of this literature to analyses of individual differences, the relations between automaticity and flexibility in cognition, and the adaptiveness of flexibility in different settings and tasks. But first, we must consider briefly the features of *social situations* that must influence interpretive activity and that enable or encourage certain goals, moods, or expertise to press for action.

SITUATIONS

Research on motivated cognition accompanies a growing interest in complex, personally involving situations (Forgas 1982, Stokols 1982, Mehrabian & Russell 1974). In these situations, the flexibility of cognitive strategies may be especially apparent. On one hand, contextual features prime relevant knowledge automatically. Individuals may base their interpretations on this information simply because it is easily accessible (Ferguson & Wells 1980, Higgins & King 1981, Wyer & Srull 1981, Snyder 1982). On the other hand, motivational analyses suggest that people can adapt their interpretive strategies to fit the situation. Specific tasks and goals are not just cued by the situation; the individual *sets them up* in response to the constraints he perceives in reading the situation (cf Jones & Thibaut 1958, King & Sorrentino 1983). Goals, mood, or expertise may affect what information becomes accessible and how it is used (Fazio et al 1982). Moreover, the individual may select additional information from his knowledge repertoire or reject contextually salient information in constructing interpretations (Higgins et al 1977, Fazio et al 1983). In this view, individuals sometimes intelligently and flexibly adapt their interpretations to the situation, rather than being inevitably swayed by salient features.

Of course, it is often difficult to disentangle straightforward priming effects from instances in which the perceiver selectively and flexibly works with the primed material. Consider the ways in which recent experience affects interpretations of new situations. For example, Baum et al (1982) suggest that the recent experience of a crowded dormitory setting caused some subjects to view a bargaining game as uncontrollable and to adopt strategies of giving up. However, this was only true for subjects who did not have well-developed "screening" strategies for coping with the crowded environment. Now, it could be said that this is a simple priming effect—the game primes the uncontrollable dormitory experience for nonscreeners (who subsequently give up in the game) and a controllable dormitory experience for screeners (who actively compete in the game). However, a motivational view of these results also considers that screeners and nonscreeners may attend to different kinds of information about the game; they may bring to bear different hypotheses about the controllability of situations, based on their dormitory experiences. They may also have different behavioral strategies available to them. It may be that the current situation primes different information for screeners and nonscreeners. Still, their distinct game strategies may be actively constructed on the basis of their selective readings of the current situation, the different goals they see as feasible, and selective use of primed material and prior knowledge. Like most of the literature we review here, alternative views of priming effects are just beginning to get attention. This may be due in part to the fact that people are looking at complex contexts where motivated strategies operate.

Affordances in Situations

Individuals construct interpretations according to the structures embedded in a situation. The theory of social perception states that perception is guided by opportunities for action in the environment (McArthur & Baron 1983). In a similar vein, the development of cognition in children is said to be shaped by the structure of their social lives ("age subcultures") in addition to cognitive growth or acquisition of skills (Higgins & Parsons 1983).

The literature offers a variety of examples of how individuals respond to specific situational constraints. The most obvious examples are manipulations in psychological laboratories [e.g. public vs private contexts of evaluation (Baumeister & Jones 1978)]. Wording of questions affects the way individuals construe the task at hand, thereby framing interpretations of risk (Tversky & Kahneman 1981) or perceptions of a target's extraversion (Snyder & Swann 1978, Snyder & Cantor 1979). Norms and standards for judgment in different settings affect the way people evaluate themselves and others (Carlston 1980, Higgins & King 1981, Higgins & Lurie 1983). The degree of contrast between a social stimulus and the current context may affect judgments and subsequent behavior (Sherman et al 1978). The availability of situational attributions for incongruent information about a target affects impressions formed (Crocker et al 1983). Individuals differ in their responsiveness to situational constraints; for instance, individuals who are high self-monitors are especially likely to adjust their behavior to fit the current context (Snyder 1982).

The actual cast of characters in a situation is an especially important feature since many tasks depend on others' behaviors. The presence of others may motivate an individual to use knowledge about his public self and focus on impression-management tasks (Baumeister 1982, Schlenker & Leary 1982, McFarland et al 1984). Audience composition guides the selection and construction of particular self-presentational strategies (Jackson & Latane 1981, Tedeschi 1981). For example, the presence of informed observers moderates the use of self-serving attributions (Weary 1980). [Jones & Pittman (1982) also cite examples of settings in which strategic self-presentation is minimal.] Individuals alter the messages used to convey information to others according to their relationship to the listener (Higgins & McCann 1984), the listener's prior knowledge (Higgins et al 1982), and the audience's attitude (Manis et al 1974, Newtson & Czerlinsky 1974, Higgins & Rholes 1978). These messages constructed in specific contexts may subsequently have long-term effects on individuals' interpretations of information (Higgins & Rholes 1978, Higgins & McCann 1984). Individuals are also responsive to the perceived roles of others in the situation. For example, the perceived role of teacher to control, inform, or reward may affect how a student interprets his motives in an achievement situation (Deci et al 1981).

Constructing Situations

Individuals not only adjust their interpretations to fit situational constraints, but also actively take control in constructing the situation (Snyder 1981). Some situations are more responsive to the individual's behavior than others. Social interactions are usually highly influenced by the individual (Snyder et al 1977, Snyder 1983). For example, belief in one's control or mastery in a stressful situation may lead to successful adjustment only so long as the situation is actually controllable or the illusory belief can be maintained (Wortman 1976, Wortman & Dintzer 1978, Collins et al 1983, Taylor et al 1984). Similarly, individuals may be able to control the way tasks are set up in a situation, e.g. by rethinking extrinsic motivation to fit and fulfill personal goals (Deci & Ryan 1984). At the extreme of this kind of flexibility, individuals may choose the kinds of situations they enter (Snyder & Kendzierski 1982, Snyder et al 1983, Cantor et al 1984, Diener et al 1984), thereby actively controlling the likelihood that some kinds of goals, tasks, and self-knowledge are chronically activated, while others languish from disuse (Wyer & Srull 1981, Higgins et al 1982).

GOALS AND MOTIVATED STRATEGIES
Implicit Definition

The importance of goal setting for motivating behavior was recognized in early work on "levels of aspiration" in achievement situations (Lewin et al 1944). Zajonc (1960) demonstrated that the communication goals of subjects who expect to "transmit" or "receive" activate distinct cognitive structures. Current literature identifies a variety of goals that affect how people interpret information and plan behavior (Kruglanski et al 1978, Locke et al 1981, Carver & Scheier 1983). Most of the goals that have been linked to specific cognitive processes are "imposed" by situations (Wyer et al 1982). For example, when subjects adopt goals of impression formation as opposed to direct memory, they encode, retrieve, and hence interpret information differently (Hamilton et al 1980, Hoffman et al 1981, Srull 1983). The schemas activated in person perception and social judgment serve observational goals (Cohen & Ebbesen 1979). Communication goals (e.g. interpreting vs describing stimulus information) alter a person's own interpretations of information (Higgins et al 1982).

Goals are not only imposed by the environment; they may also be actively constructed by the individual in the situation. [Consider extrinsic vs intrinsic motives (Lepper & Greene 1978, Deci & Ryan 1984).] Personally constructed goals are usually self-relevant, and may represent important features of the self-concept. Goals may be embedded in a set of *possible selves* (Markus 1983)—those images of self that may not be actually or presently true but that may be descriptive in the future (Schutz 1964, Gordon 1968). A person's goals in any given situation may be represented in her "working self-concept," constructed from the set of all current and possible selves (Markus & Nurius 1983). For example, when visiting a child, one may construct a working self-concept based on one's desired, but not yet actualized "maternal self" and one's current, but infrequently realized "playful self." Possible selves represent both attractive and threatening end-states and may guide behavior accordingly.

Self-relevant goals vary from those that are global, abstract, and used in a variety of situations to those that are concrete and context-specific. The literature defines several global goals pertaining to the maintenance of self-esteem or the self-concept: self-evaluation maintenance (Tesser & Campbell 1984), self-verification (Swann & Read 1981), and self-esteem enhancement (Weary 1979). These global goals may lead to the formation of more specific goals. Causal attributions in specific situations are often motivated by underlying goals associated with self-esteem, self-presentation, or mastery and control (Harvey & Weary 1984). Children seem to be guided by an abstract goal of self-socialization, which motivates the use of social comparison in concrete contexts to determine areas of competence (Ruble 1983). At a more instrumental level, individuals construct self-relevant goals such as *life tasks*

(Cantor & Kihlstrom 1983), or Levinson's (1978) concept of the *Dream* (an imagined self). These include concrete achievement and interpersonal goals (e.g. becoming a professor, raising children) or abstract concerns (e.g. becoming a more likable person or forging an identity). Like possible selves, life tasks concretely specify a number of desired and feared behaviors relevant to a particular life context or event. Similarly, *personal projects* focus on a single task or accomplishment (Little 1983), as when the college student sets himself the task of getting over computer anxieties or the overweight dieter establishes a project of shedding pounds.

In a few cases, individual differences in interpretation or behavior have been linked specifically to individuals' goals. For some parole board members and judges, the primary goal of imprisonment is incapacitation of criminals; for others, the objective is rehabilitation, prison stability, or punishment. These goals lead to differences in sentencing strategies and attributions for crime (Carroll & Wiener 1982). Similarly, for some college students, choice of housing is an interpersonal task; for others, the choice depends upon more practical concerns. These individual differences in goals predict the use of a self-to-protoype matching strategy that maximizes interpersonal comfort (Niedenthal & Cantor 1984). In other cases, research has described dynamic strategies for behavior, without focusing on individual differences in underlying goals (e.g. Mischel 1983). In those instances, the strategies are viewed as cognitive processes that link a person's initial goals to his observable behavior. To understand individual differences, we need to know more about corresponding variations in goals and how they are established. Additional research on underlying goals would contribute to our understanding of strategies like information-seeking or avoidance (Miller & Mangan 1983) and assertiveness (Rudy et al 1982). Thus, individuals use goals to develop "appropriate" *strategies* for processing information and planning behavior in that context.

Flexible Strategies

Examples of goal-motivated strategies in the literature illustrate two kinds of flexibility in the way individuals may interpret situations and plan behavior: (*a*) Individuals are responsive to situational features and adjust their strategies to fit the situation. In other words, they are able to construct alternative strategies. (*b*) Individuals construct different strategies for behavior as their personal goals or the contents of their knowledge repertoires change.

RESPONSIVENESS TO SITUATIONS   Goals are usually embedded in situational contexts. For example, the life task of achieving professional recognition may apply to behavior at an annual convention but not at a family reunion. Similarly, individuals' strategies for behavior are responsive to context-specific goals. For example, when success at a joint task depends on a partner's performance, the subject's goal is to predict and control the partner's behavior; she therefore pays increased attention to discrepant information about the partner's skill. When success does not depend on the partner, the subject's goal is simply to maintain her impressions of the partner, and so she is less attentive to discrepant information (Erber & Fiske 1984).

People are also flexible in adjusting their strategies to different situations in the service of the same abstract goal. This is done by setting concrete goals that represent ways of achieving a higher goal *in that specific situation*. Ego tasks (impression management, self-image management, and value management) encompass those situation-specific strategies that serve global ego-involvement goals (Greenwald 1982). Some more specific strategies are the modes of self-presentation, including ingratiation, intimidation, and supplication (Jones & Pittman 1982); self-handicapping (Jones & Berglas 1978); and strategies associated with self-awareness, such as opinion moderation (Scheier 1980) or responses to negative evaluation (Fenigstein 1979). The self-serving biases are a set of optimistic strategies motivated by a global goal of preserving and enhancing self-esteem (Kelley & Michela 1980, Harvey & Weary 1984). They include the illusion of control (Alloy & Abramson 1982, Martin et al 1984), attributional egotism (Snyder et al 1978), illusory glow (Lewinsohn et al 1980), downward social comparison (Wills 1981), and the egocentric "contribution" bias (Ross & Sicoly 1979). Each strategy may be viewed as an appropriate way of achieving the global goal in a certain kind of situation.

Of course, it is difficult to prove definitively that global goals—such as self-esteem maintenance—underlie these diverse behavioral reactions (Tetlock & Levi 1982). However, when individuals selectively rely on "just the right" self-serving cognitive bias in each of a variety of contexts, it seems parsimonious to infer that the behavior as a whole fulfills an underlying global goal. Future research must demonstrate more precisely this pattern of situational adjustment in the use of particular self-serving strategies (Sherman et al 1984). For instance, since self-esteem goals may not be predominant for an individual in all his life contexts, he should demonstrate selectivity in the use of self-serving strategies, even across situations that are equally likely to elicit those behaviors (Greenwald 1982).

In making interpretations and planning behavior, we often imagine or play through situations and fit our strategies to the imagined outcomes (Nuttin 1984). We may run through our repertoire of scripts, mentally testing their rules for action (Abelson 1981, Abelson & Levi 1984). The simulation heuristic is a strategy of constructing scenarios of events, often in order to "undo" the past (Kahneman & Tversky 1982). Defensive pessimism is a strategy that may be used by someone who selectively plays through bad outcomes. Defensive pessimists set low expectations for themselves and at the same time increase effort in order to cushion themselves against negative outcomes (Showers &

Cantor 1984, Norem & Cantor 1984). Cacioppo et al (1979) also showed how people cognitively prepare themselves for upcoming interactions by playing through the situation; they found that protocols of persons high in social anxiety contained more negative self-relevant thoughts than those of low-anxiety subjects. Playing through possible personal futures contributes to major life decisions (Sloan 1983). Imagining specific future actions is likely to lead to that behavior (Bandura & Jeffery 1973, Wright 1979, Sherman et al 1981, Gregory et al 1982, Anderson 1983).

People are particularly responsive to the current situation when they are looking back at past experience (Fischoff & Beyth 1975, Kihlstrom 1981). Research on biases in interpreting the past indicates that a person's current goals organize his use of prior knowledge and guide his interpretations. Hindsight bias has been linked to motives of predictability and self-presentation (Campbell & Tesser 1983). Recall of past behavior is often biased to be consistent with present salient attitudes (Ross et al 1983).

CHANGE IN THE REPERTOIRE   Individuals show flexibility in being able to develop new strategies for interpretation and behavior when their repertoires of prior knowledge change. The goals represented in a person's repertoire capture dynamic elements of his personality and behavior. They are likely to change and precipitate changes in strategies (Miller & Porter 1980, cf Weber & Crocker 1984). Transient goals—e.g. impressing a visting colleague—tend to be set up in specific situations and are quickly satisfied or abandoned. Life tasks are fairly enduring goals that are likely to change (albeit infrequently) over the life cycle (Cantor & Kihlstrom 1983). Completion or change of life tasks may occasion dramatic shifts in how individuals interpret new life situations (Neugarten 1976, Brim 1976, Veroff & Veroff 1980). Consider how a stern, strict parent may become a doting grandparent. Even the most enduring goals—e.g. self-esteem maintenance—may be instantiated in diverse behaviors as people's historical, cultural, organizational, and interpersonal contexts change. For example, achievement motives were expressed in terms of task accomplishments in 1957, but in terms of personal actualization in 1976 (Veroff 1983).

Certain features in the repertoire (other than goals) may change, precipitating changes in goal-directed strategies. Interpersonal negotiation or confrontation may involve continually updating one's knowledge and expectations about the other(s) (Moreland & Levine 1982). Niemeyer & Merluzzi (1982) propose that group development depends on individuals' adjusting their schemas for the group through successive interchanges until a shared perception is negotiated. On a more dramatic scale, tragic and stressful life events (such as loss of a spouse or a paralyzing accident) radically alter a person's self-concept and his view of the environment. In coping with these changes in their repertoires, people show flexibility by developing new goals and strategies for interpreting their experience and controlling their behavior (Silver et al 1983, Wortman 1983). For example, victims search for meaning in threatening events, they develop strategies to gain mastery and control, or they engage in self-enhancing evaluations to restore self-esteem (Taylor 1982).

MOOD

Implicit Definition

Moods in the form of low-level feeling states may have both subtle and pervasive effects on social cognition (Clark & Isen 1982). Research has also looked at the cognitive consequences of chronic, intense moods like depression (e.g. Kuiper et al 1984) and specific emotions like anxiety (e.g. Goldfried et al 1984) and anger (Klos et al 1983).

Moods may be represented in the knowledge repertoire as affective "tags" to other cognitive elements (Bower 1981). These tags may be linked among themselves in an especially strong associative network, possibly activated by the physiological states of arousal that accompany affect (Clark et al 1983, 1984). Mood effects may result from direct priming of other mood-related material, such as prior experience during a similar mood state (Teasdale & Fogarty 1979, Bower 1981). Positive affect may increase helpful and generous behavior, possibly because the positive consequences of helping are primed (Isen et al 1978, Cialdini et al 1982).

The motivated-cognitive approach emphasizes how mood can be used to guide other cognitive constructions (e.g. Weiner 1980). For instance, a sense of self-esteem or self-efficacy at a task may be constructed selectively from the array of affective tags on relevant knowledge in the repertoire (cf Bandura 1977). Moods linked to autobiographical memories should be especially influential (Kihlstrom & Cantor 1984). In this view, self-esteem need not imply a stable positive or negative evaluation of oneself across domains. Instead, it may vary across task domains and even change with the valence of recent experience in a particular domain (McFarland & Ross 1982, Harter 1984).

Mood-Directed Strategies

The kinds of intelligent, interpretive strategies that have been linked to mood illustrate two kinds of flexibility: (a) the ability to see multiple ways of interpreting a situation (and choose among them intelligently); and, similarly, (b) the ability to take control of the strategies one uses in particular situations and, in doing so, to choose to maintain or alter moods and their effects.

MULTIPLE ALTERNATIVES   Evidence for the first kind of flexibility is provided by work on the characteristic cognitive processes of positive mood.

These include use of broad categories, recognition of more (and weaker) relationships among objects, and development of more creative solutions to problems (Isen et al 1984). Positive moods may also facilitate learning of simple tasks (Masters et al 1979). Thus, positive mood may have direct effects on the number of alternative interpretations perceived in a situation. Although these effects may be due in part to priming or arousal, the processes themselves afford the individual greater flexibility.

In contrast, chronic depression is associated with narrow, inflexible cognitive processes (cf Patsiokas et al 1979). The negative content of a depressed person's repertoire may result from failure to see the multiple possibilities in situations, especially potential positive outcomes for herself (Markus & Nurius 1983). Depressed persons have negative perceptions of themselves, schematically organized (Beck 1974, Lewinsohn et al 1980, Kuiper & Derry 1981, Tabachnik et al 1983, Kuiper et al 1984). The depressive uses this "negative self" rigidly and may be unable to draw on or construct alternative self-perceptions. The characteristic cognitive processes of depressives are rigid and narrowly focused: pervasive organization of information by negative affect (Pietromonaco, unpublished manuscript); singular focus of attention on the self (Smith & Greenberg 1981); selective memory for negative information about the self (Derry & Kuiper 1981); and reliance on internal attributions for failure (Kuiper 1978, Raps et al 1982).

Cognitive modes of psychotherapy treat mood disorders by helping patients construct alternative interpretations for their own feelings and behavior, as well as for distressing situations (Goldfried & Goldfried 1975, Ellis & Harper 1975, Meichenbaum 1977, Rush 1982). For instance, depressed patients may be taught to interpret information in self-enhancing ways (Beck 1976). Test-anxious persons may experience a flooding of negative affect that interferes with their ability to interpret the situation in less threatening ways or to use their aroused feelings constructively (Meichenbaum 1977, Lazarus & Launier 1978). Treatment involves substitution of less extreme thoughts and behaviors for old "irrational" ones, thereby providing the flexibility necessary to cope. Social anxiety has been linked to the specific categories used in interpreting situations; it, too, may be dealt with by restructuring those interpretations (Goldfried et al 1984).

Some theoretical support for the adaptiveness of multiple interpretations is offered by Linville's (1982a) work on cognitive complexity. Individuals who organize self-relevant information into numerous categories report less variability in mood than individuals with "simpler" organization. Multiple categories may buffer emotional responses to events in a single domain. For example, the "empty nest" may be less threatening to parents' self-concepts if they see other nurturing roles for themselves in the family or at work. In a related vein, Landau (1980) found that phobics' knowledge about a feared object is less extensive than the knowledge of control subjects and is organized by fewer dimensions. The simple structure of phobics' knowledge in that domain may exacerbate their negative arousal reactions.

TAKING CONTROL   When an individual perceives multiple alternatives in a situation, he has the flexibility to take control in generating an appropriate strategy for the situation. This kind of flexibility is different from adjustment of one's interpretation to context-specific goals. In that case, an appropriate strategy is formed in response to situational features. In the present case, the individual is not just responding to situational cues, but is actively choosing among alternative interpretations and strategies. The process is analogous to piecemeal processing at a strategic level. When categorization fails, individuals have the ability to abandon category-based processing, take control, and construct their affective responses using piecemeal attribute-by-attribute judgments (Fiske & Pavelchak 1984).

This kind of flexibility is evident in the use of strategies for decision making. Positive mood has been linked to simple, fast, and efficient choice strategies, and may affect perception of risk (Isen et al 1982, Isen & Means 1983, Johnson & Tversky 1983). Good mood may increase risk taking, but only when the stakes are low (Isen & Patrick 1983). People may have both risk-taking and risk-avoiding strategies available to them; they may be able to control mood effects by selecting the strategy that serves their goals in the situation. Flexible use of risk-taking strategies is represented in cost/benefit models of choice (Payne 1982).

Moods themselves may incite the individual to take control of his behavioral strategies. In particular, anxiety about the outcomes of one's behavior or frustration of one's goals can motivate individuals to increase efforts to control behavior. Control theory of self-regulation predicts that these moods interrupt current behavior and lead to either increased effort or withdrawal, depending on expectations for a favorable outcome (Carver et al 1979, Scheier et al 1981, Carver & Scheier 1983). In a study of role-played confrontations with roommates, anger in response to frustration of participants' goals for the interaction may have cued use of alternative problem-solving strategies (Klos et al 1983). For recent crime victims, affect has a major, distinct influence on beliefs about future danger as well as crime prevention behaviors (Tyler & Rasinski (1984).

People may also choose strategies designed to maintain or alter a mood, thereby exercising flexible control over mood effects. In fact, many self-serving biases and strategies for self-esteem enhancement may be geared toward maintaining a positive mood (Abramson et al 1978, Weary 1980). People in good moods are less willing than controls to jeopardize their positive state by doing certain helping tasks (Isen & Simmons 1978). On the other hand, altruism may be part of a strategy for improving negative mood (Cialdini et al 1982, Manucia et al 1984). Moods, of course, do tend to be perpetuated by priming of congruent memories (Snyder & White 1982). This makes it all the more surprising when moods are intentionally changed (Hochschild 1979).

At times, even depressed moods may be maintained by motivated strategies, as well as by priming of negative material, rigid cognitive processes, and negative self-schemas. For instance, the same cognitive process that contribute to chronic depression may serve other goals, such as maintaining high standards for oneself (cf Beck & Burns 1979, Wright & Mischel 1982, Higgins et al 1984). In this sense, the individual may actively contribute to his depressed state until he adopts new goals. Moreover, if depression is maintained by context-specific goals, that mood may be more bounded by situational contexts than has previously been supposed.

EXPERTISE

Implicit Definition

Expertise is an especially fuzzy concept, and is loosely applied to a variety of cognitive skills. Experts have a great deal of well-organized knowledge in their preferred domains. Typically, the articulation of schemas, stereotypes, scripts, or prototypes has been linked to expertise (Cantor et al 1980, Fiske & Kinder 1981, Markus et al 1984). The processing efficiency of self-schemas illustrates people's skill at handling information relevant to the self (Markus 1977). Efficient schematic organization characterizes expertise in other domains, from politics (Fiske et al 1983) to shoplifting (Weaver & Carroll 1984). Of course, the mere use of knowledge structures like stereotypes implies only a minimal ability to generalize and structure information; expertise also usually implies considerable knowledge and extensive experience in a given domain (Fiske & Kinder 1981, Linville 1982b). In attitude research, expertise has been addressed in terms of level of involvement (Lastovicka & Gardner 1978, Chaiken 1980), direct experience (Bettman & Park 1980, Beattie 1981, Fazio & Zanna 1981), and attitude centrality (Converse 1970).

Experts are especially likely to make generalizations and inferences on the basis of their extensive concrete knowledge and store these as abstract concepts and rules (Chi et al 1981). They also chunk information into larger organizational units (Chase & Simon 1973, Newtson & Engquist 1976, Markus et al 1984). These skills may enable the expert to construct an overlaying structure that allows easy, frequent, speedy access to a complex underlying body of knowledge (Tesser & Leone 1977, Ostrom et al 1980, Linville 1982a, Burnstein & Schul 1983). On one hand, experts have sufficient knowledge to make unusually fine discriminations among stimuli in their domains (Lippa 1977). On the other hand, their efficient organization frees cognitive capacity to elaborate knowledge or process schema-inconsistent information that might otherwise be ignored (Hastie 1981, Fiske et al 1983).

This brief overview of the literature points to some cognitive characteristics of expertise—amount of knowledge, well-organized structure, and efficient processing. The motivational aspects of expertise seem to be derived from personal involvement in a domain, or the perceived importance of a situation. In order to see how an expert uses special processing skills, we need to consider the motivational factor of involvement. For example, self-schemas for gender are developed by individuals who masculinity or femininity is centrally important to them (Bem 1981, Markus et al 1982). In the next section, we consider both the expert's cognitive skills and his involvement in specific situations in reviewing the issue of the expert's flexibility. There is evidence that highly involved experts can at times see multiple interpretations in a situation and control their use of strategies by choosing among alternatives. In particular, some research suggests that experts may choose actively controlled strategies when the situation is important, and more passive, automatic processing when they are less involved.

Expert Strategies

It is difficult not only to define the characteristics of expertise but also to predict the consequences of using expert strategies. For instance, is an experienced psychotherapist flexible in the way she perceives and interprets new case material, or is she prone to fit it into a set, optimal structure for the patient's problem? Given her well-organized knowledge and extensive experience, the expert may be able to see multiple alternatives in a situation; or she may automatically use rigid (albeit "optimal") interpretations (cf Langer & Abelson 1974). The literature suggests one resolution to this controversy, namely that the expert has the flexibility to choose a more effortful or more automatic strategy depending on his involvement in the situation.

The issue of experts' flexibility is well illustrated by the typical pattern of development of academic expertise over the course of a lifetime. On entering graduate school, we might be labeled "ignorant generalists." We have a basic, broad background that links the areas of psychology to other fields and is unencumbered by detail. All theories, all possible models are entertained. Throughout graduate school and the early professional years, we become "refined specialists," solving narrowly focused problems using a growing body of increasingly detailed and complex knowledge. Here, we may tend to focus on single, set ways of interpreting theories, although we also learn to see deeper implications. Gradually, we find ourselves making the transition to "mature generalists," reorganizing our knowledge using fewer, more abstract concepts that span seemingly unrelated domains (Markus et al 1984). Is this the most flexible stage?

MULTIPLE ALTERNATIVES   Considerable research shows that schemas, stereotypes, and prototypes in a person's repertoire guide the interpretation of new information to be consistent with these structures (Hamilton 1981, Fiske 1982, Schneider & Blankmeyer 1983). Schematics elaborate on stimulus information, filling in missing pieces to be congruent with the schema (Cohen 1981, Hastie 1981). Moreover, they recall their own elaborations as presented material and are equally confident in their mistaken and accurate memories (Bower et al 1979, Graesser et al 1980, Raye et al 1980). These errors are carried over into judgments and behaviors (Sherman et al 1978, 1981, Taylor & Crocker 1981, Wyer et al 1984).

While these characteristics of schematic processing should restrict interpretations, they may be balanced by features that enable experts to generate multiple interpretations. Easy access to a large amount of knowledge should facilitate alternative interpretations depending on the subset of information (or specific schema) used. Using schemas to elaborate stimulus information also provides the expert with additional relevant information. The efficiency of schematic processing should free up cognitive capacity to generate other alternatives.

The consequences for experts of using automatic, uncontrolled processing are equally debatable. On one hand, experts have the skills to process information and execute behaviors automatically (Schneider & Shiffrin 1977, Shiffrin & Schneider 1977, Neves & Anderson 1981, Bargh 1982, Bargh & Pietromonaco 1982). Automatic processing has the advantage of being fast and efficient and freeing cognitive capacity for other activities. However, it may be inflexible in contrast to controlled processing, which may engender multiple interpretations. Automatic processing may preclude access to the underlying details and components of the process (cf Langer & Imber 1979). Thus, the individual may not see possible alternatives as he makes his interpretation. In fact, when subjects focus on the details of an action (rather than its meaning), they are more open to suggestion of alternative interpretations of the act (Wegner et al 1984).

TAKING CONTROL   Experts may use automatic processing while retaining the flexibility to generate alternative interpretations when they are motivated to do so (Posner & Snyder 1975, Logan 1980; cf Lingle & Ostrom 1981, Tetlock 1983). For instance, subjects highly involved with the topic of a persuasive message tend to process message content systematically; less involved subjects use more superficial (and automatic) heuristic processes (Chaiken 1980, Chaiken & Baldwin 1981, Petty & Cacioppo 1984). Highly involved subjects expend effort in elaborating the message content and bringing extensive prior knowledge to bear in interpreting it (Petty & Cacioppo 1979, Petty et al 1981, Tybout & Scott 1983). Thus, systematic processing affords the expert considerable control over interpretations made. Experts may choose controlled, systematic processing or heuristic processing, depending on the importance of the situation (Cantor & Showers 1983). Borgida & Howard-Pitney (1983) demonstrated that highly involved subjects process messages systematically and are less influenced by the perceptual salience of information than are less involved subjects.

People can also increase effort and take control of their interpretations in their selective use of schemas, stereotypes, and (expert) self-knowledge. When subjects can pay more attention to an actor, they rely less on schemata in making impression judgments (White & Carlston 1983). Stereotypes are less likely to affect judgments about individuals when other diagnostic information is available (Locksley et al 1980, 1982, Zukier 1982). For example, the effects of sex stereotypes on clinical judgments are mitigated by target case information (Abramowitz & Dokecki 1977, Stricker 1977). Similarly, people can control their tendencies to generalize from expert knowledge about themselves. For instance, one has expertise about one's peer group relative to nonpeers. Higgins & Bryant (1982) find that people are more likely to use (expert) self-knowledge in judging peers than nonpeers. Expertise about one's group may underlie in-group biases (Brewer 1979, Linville & Jones 1980, Quattrone & Jones 1980); in-group "experts" may regulate the use of their expertise according to its appropriateness in a particular context. People can also use either statistical (e.g. base-rate) or nonstatistical (case) information, depending on its perceived relevance in the situation (Borgida & Nisbett 1977, Borgida & Brekke 1981, Nisbett et al 1983, Kruglanski et al 1984; cf Miller & Cantor 1982).

In general, these examples of flexibility imply that individuals can control the trade-off between efficiency and accuracy that comes with schematic processing. It is almost as if the individual is willing to allow some of the errors associated with rigid use of schemas (e.g. mistaken recall of congruent material) in situations where speed, automaticity, and low effort are valued. In some situations, "errors" have adaptive value. For example, the mistaken belief that one can monitor a long-term, asymptomatic illness may be adaptive in coping with the illness because it provides a therapeutic sense of mastery and control (Leventhal et al 1984a). Experts may be especially skillful at identifying situations in which, say, precise memory for detail is important; consequently, they may exert themselves to encode and recall information accurately, aided but not controlled by their schematic expertise (cf Markus et al 1984). Further research might clarify the kind and number of situations where "accuracy" of interpretation, precise recall, and effortful processing are advantageous. Such occasions may be rare compared to those where efficient, elaborated memory and confidence in one's knowledge have the adaptive advantage.

Mindless, automatic forms of processing (like priming or schematic processing) may occur spontaneously for experts in most situations. The expert's advantage may be that he can intervene and check the progress of automatic interpretations. He may be able to recognize and generate other ways of reading a situation when motivated to do so. In this way, the expert has the flexibility to take advantage of automaticity without losing control.

CONCLUSION

Summary: Flexibility in Motivated Cognition

This chapter reviews selected literature on social cognition pertaining to three motivational elements—goals, mood, and expertise—and associated flexible strategies for interpreting situations and planning behavior. In summary, we present specific strategies as examples of the four kinds of flexibility.

RESPONSIVENESS TO SITUATIONS   According to Greenwald's notion of ego tasks, individuals use a variety of specific strategies (depending on the situation) to achieve more abstract goals (Greenwald 1982). For example, an individual may use different strategies to maintain his self-image in different achievement situations. Carver & Scheier (1983) describe two alternative strategies for regulating behavior in light of one's goals: (*a*) In situations where the individual expects positive outcomes (satisfying his goals), he will increase effort; and (*b*) in situations where he expects negative outcomes (failing his goals), he will withdraw.

Perhaps the ultimate example of the responsiveness of an individual to situations is the flexibility with which he attends to, alters, or ignores aspects of his self-concept. To some degree, an individual constructs his current self-concept from the features of his total self-knowledge that are most useful or informative in the present situation (Gergen 1972, McGuire et al 1978, McGuire & McGuire 1981). Clearly, the perception of oneself at a given time in a given situation affects interpretations of situations and behavior.

TAKING CONTROL   Individuals can choose interpretive strategies that are either effortful and actively controlled or more efficient and automatic. This skill is characteristic of expertise or high involvement in a particular domain (Chaiken 1980, Petty et al 1981). People also frequently take control of their needs and emotions. We actively induce or inhibit feelings (not just expressions of them) until our emotions are appropriate for the situation—e.g. we psych ourselves up for a football game or become serious for a seminar. Hochschild (1979) emphasizes that this need not be a passive process; the individual assesses the fit of his feelings to a situation and then works on his emotions by altering his cognitions, his physiological state, and his expressions of feeling.

MULTIPLE ALTERNATIVES   In the section on moods, we suggested that people in positive moods may see more alternatives for interpreting a situation and planning behavior, while depression may be associated with more rigid strategies (cf Spivack et al 1976). Many coping styles as well as therapy techniques involve learning alternative strategies of interpretation (Meichenbaum 1977, Silver et al 1983, Wortman 1983, Taylor et al 1984). For instance, attribution therapy trains individuals to attribute negative events to unstable factors (Dweck 1975, Wilson & Linville 1982, 1984). In fact, some theorists, notably Haan (1977, 1982), go so far as to define *coping* as "open" consideration of options and flexible and inventive creation of response alternatives. People who tend to use active cognitive coping strategies (e.g. redefinition of the problem or restructuring the situation) rather than denial or avoidance typically find it easier to weather stressful life events (Singer 1974, Lazarus & Launier 1978, Billings & Moos 1981).

CHANGE IN THE REPERTOIRE   This kind of flexibility is seen over fairly long periods, as the individual's knowledge, self-perceptions, goals, and experience grow and change (Kihlstrom & Nasby 1981, Landau & Goldfried 1981). Substantive changes in the knowledge repertoire can promote different interpretive strategies or necessitate new action plans. For example, preferred coping styles change over the life cycle. Older persons are more likely than younger persons to use affective appraisal and control of emotional reactions as coping mechanisms. This change may be linked to people's experiences with illness, their health expectations, and their models for illness (Leventhal et al 1984b). Old ways of thinking and feeling may never be lost, as a visit to one's parents will undoubtedly show. However, people do have the flexibility to adapt old strategies and learn new ones that reflect changing knowledge and experience.

Levels of Awareness

Motivated cognitive strategies need not be formed at a conscious level (Isen & Hastorf 1982, Kihlstrom 1983). In some cases, conscious awareness of a goal may actually interfere with a person's ability to achieve it. In the strategy of self-handicapping (Jones & Berglas 1978), a person must be aware that he was incapacitated in order to make an external attribution for failure; yet, it is not clear how successful this strategy would be if the person were aware of his underlying intent to disadvantage himself.

Even the kinds of flexibility that involve multiple interpretations and taking control of the interpretive process need not imply conscious awareness. All the aspects of taking control—e.g. actively selecting information and strategies that serve one's goals, moods, or expertise—can take place outside of awareness (Dennett 1969, Mandler 1975, Wilson 1984). Yet these processes are still controlled, in contrast to automatic processes (like priming) that resist intervention by the individual.

Individual Differences

Goal-directed strategies for interpretation may be viewed as cognitive process-es that link an individual's competencies, motives, or predispositions to be-havior (Nuttin 1984, Kuhl & Beckmann 1984). By tracking individuals' goals, moods, and expertise, we see the dynamics of individiual differences over time and perceive flexibility in the kinds of strategies used.

Individual differences in goal-directed strategies have been studied exten-sively in achievement domains (Heckhausen et al 1984). When an individual's goals are discrepant with present or perceived reality, he may be motivated to adopt the following kinds of strategies: self-handicapping (Berglas & Jones 1978; cf Hull & Young 1983), defensive pessimism (Showers & Cantor 1984), increased effort or withdrawal (Carver & Scheier 1983), reevaluation of intrin-sic interest (e.g. Deci & Ryan 1984), and adjustment of goals (Lewin et al 1944, Spates & Kanfer 1977, Meece et al 1982, Pittman et al 1982, Eccles et al 1984) or attributional strategies (e.g. Diener & Dweck 1980, Alloy et al 1984). Why does an individual adopt the strategy he does? To answer this, we must consider the motivational elements (e.g. goals, mood, and expertise), the situation, and the individual's interpretations of it. The strategies represent the process that leads to behavior; by focusing on them, we may be better able to predict and make sense of an individual's behavior (Cantor & Kihlstrom 1982, Mischel 1984; cf also Andersen & Ross 1984, Andersen 1984).

Adaptiveness

In highlighting flexibility, the motivational-cognitive approach raises some age-old issues about the adaptiveness of flexibility in certain situations: (a) The identity issue. Individuals must be responsive to situations; yet they desire to possess and project a coherent identity. What are the adaptive limits on the flexibility of selfhood? (James 1890, Allport 1961). (b) the laissez-faire issue. Experts often confront the trade-offs between efficient automaticity and con-trolled processing. How adaptive is it to try to take control when skills may be inadequate or expertise is mistaken? (Skinner 1953, Hartmann 1958). (c) The specialist vs generalist issue. What are the relative merits of being a specialist or a generalist? Seeing multiple alternatives is an effortful and time-consuming process. Consideration of some options may lead to brilliant innovation and creativity; others will surely lead down blind alleys (Duncker 1945, Kelly 1955). (d) The life cycle change issue. To what extent should people change their strategies in response to new experience over time? Frequently, it is important to work with well-worn strategies in order to fulfill goals and desires carried from childhood (Freud 1901, Erikson 1950).

A look at motivated strategies not only raises these issues, but also may afford new means of addressing questions of human adaptiveness (Bruner

1983). By considering motivational underpinnings, we can see how cognitive strategies translate goals, mood, and expertise into appropriate action in particular contexts. Increasingly, we are drawn to study dynamic, personally involving situations where adaptiveness and flexibility come into play.

ACKNOWLEDGMENTS

The authors are indebted to Sara Freeland for her painstaking care in preparation of this manuscript. We appreciate discussion of these issues with Aaron Brower, Susan Fiske, Nancy Genero, Alice Isen, John Kihlstrom, Hazel Markus, Paula Niedenthal, and Julie Norem.

Literature Cited

Abelson, R. P. 1981. The psychological status of the script concept. *Am. Psychol.* 36:715–29

Abelson, R. P., Levi, A. 1984. Decision-making and decision theory. In *Handbook of Social Psychology,* ed. G. Lindzey, E. Aronson. Reading, Mass: Addison-Wesley. In press

Abramowitz, C., Dokecki, P. 1977. The politics of clinical judgment: Early empirical returns. *Psychol. Bull.* 84:460–76

Abramson, L. Y., Seligman, M. E. P., Teasdale, J. D. 1978. Learned helplessness in humans: Critique and reformulation. *J. Abnorm. Psychol.* 87:49–74

Alloy, L. B., Abramson, L. Y. 1982. Learned helplessness, depression, and the illusion of control. *J. Pers. Soc. Psychol.* 42:1114–26

Alloy, L. B., Peterson, C., Abramson, L. Y., Seligman, M. E. P. 1984. Attributional style and the generality of learned helplessness. *J. Pers. Soc. Psychol.* 46:681–87

Allport, G. W. 1961. *Pattern and Growth in Personality.* New York: Holt, Rinehart & Winston

Andersen, S. M. 1984. Self-knowledge and social inference: II. The diagnosticity of cognitive/affective and behavioral data. *J. Pers. Soc. Psychol.* 46:294–307

Andersen, S. M., Ross, L. 1984. Self-knowledge and social inference: I. The impact of cognitive/affective and behavioral data. *J. Pers. Soc. Psychol.* 46:280–93

Anderson, C. A. 1983. Imagination and expectation: The effect of imagining behavioral scripts on personal intentions. *J. Pers. Soc. Psychol.* 45:293–305

Anderson, C. A., Lepper, M. R., Ross, L. 1980. The perseverance of social theories: The role of explanation in the persistence of discredited information. *J. Pers. Soc. Psychol.* 39:1037–49

Anderson, J. R., Hastie, R. 1974. Individuation and reference in memory: Proper names and definitive descriptions. *Cognit. Psychol.* 6:495–514

Bandura, A. 1977. Self-efficacy: Toward a unifying theory of behavioral change. *Psychol. Rev.* 84:191–215

Bandura, A., Jeffery, R. W. 1973. Role of symbolic coding and rehearsal processes in observational learning. *J. Pers. Soc. Psychol.* 26:122–30

Bargh, J. A. 1982. Attention and automaticity in the processing of self-relevant information. *J. Pers. Soc. Psychol.* 43:425–36

Bargh, J. A., Pietromonaco, P. 1982. Automatic information processing and social perception: The influence of trait information presented outside of conscious awareness on impression formation. *J. Pers. Soc. Psychol.* 43:437–49

Baum, A., Calesnick, L. E., Davis, G. E., Gatchel, R. J. 1982. Individual differences in coping with crowding: Stimulus screening and social overload. *J. Pers. Soc. Psychol.* 43:821–30

Baumeister, R. F. 1982. A self-presentational view of social phenomena. *Psychol. Bull.* 91:3–26

Baumeister, R. F., Jones, E. E. 1978. When self-presentation is constrained by the target's prior knowledge: Consistency and compensation. *J. Pers. Soc. Psychol.* 14:23–31

Beattie, A. E. 1981. Effects of product knowledge on comparison, memory, evaluation, and choice: A model of expertise in consumer decision-making. In *Advances in Consumer Research,* Vol 10, ed. A. A. Mitchell. St. Louis: Assoc. Consumer Res.

Beck, A. T. 1974. The development of depression: A cognitive model. In *Psychology of Depression: Contemporary Theory and Research,* ed. R. Friedman, M. Katz, pp. 3–20. New York: Winston-Wiley

Beck, A. T. 1976. *Cognitive Therapy and the Emotional Disorders.* New York: Int. Univ. Press

Beck, P., Burns, D. 1979. Anxiety and depression in law students: Cognitive intervention. *J. Legal. Educ.* 30:270–90

Bem, D. J., Funder, D. 1978. Predicting more of the people more of the time: Assessing the personality of a situation. *Psychol. Rev.* 85:484–501

Bem, S. L. 1981. Gender schema theory: A cognitive account of sex typing. *Psychol. Rev.* 88:354–64

Berglas, S., Jones, E. E. 1978. Drug choice as an internalization strategy in response to noncontingent success. *J. Pers. Soc. Psychol.* 36:405–17

Bettman, J. R., Park, C. W. 1980. Effects of prior knowledge and experience and phase of the choice process on consumer decision processes: A protocol analysis. *J. Consum. Res.* 7:234–48

Billings, A., Moos, R. 1981. The role of coping responses in attenuating the impact of stressful life events. *J. Behav. Med.* 4:139–57

Borgida, E., Brekke, N. 1981. The base rate fallacy in attribution and prediction. See Harvey et al 1981, pp. 63–95

Borgida, E., Howard-Pitney, B. 1983. Personal involvement and the robustness of perceptual salience effects. *J. Pers. Soc. Psychol.* 45:560–70

Borgida, E., Nisbett, R. E. 1977. The differential impact of abstract vs. concrete information on decisions. *J. Appl. Soc. Psychol.* 7:258–71

Bower, G. H. 1981. Mood and memory. *Am. Psychol.* 36:129–48

Bower, G. H., Black, J. B., Turner, T. J. 1979. Scripts in memory for text. *Cognit. Psychol.* 11:177–220

Brewer, M. B. 1979. In-group bias in the minimal intergroup situation: A cognitive-motivational analysis. *Psychol. Bull.* 86:307–24

Brim, O. 1976. Theories of the male mid-life crisis. *Couns. Psychol.* 6:2–9

Bruner, J. S. 1983. *The pragmatics of language and the language of pragmatics.* Katz-Newcomb Lecture, Univ. Mich, Ann Arbor

Bruner, J. S., Tagiuri, R. 1954. The perception of people. In *Handbook of Social Psychology,* Vol 2, ed. G. Lindzey, Reading, Mass: Addison-Wesley

Burnstein, E., Schul, Y. 1983. The informational basis of social judgments: Memory for integrated and nonintegrated trait descriptions. *J. Exp. Soc. Psychol.* 19:49–57

Buss, A. H. 1980. *Self-Consciousness and Social Anxiety.* San Francisco: Freeman

Buss, D. M., Craik, K. H. 1983. The act frequency approach to personality. *Psychol. Rev.* 90:105–26

Cacioppo, J. T., Glass, C. R., Merluzzi, T. V. 1979. Self-statements and self-evaluations:

A cognitive-response analysis of heterosocial anxiety. *Cognit. Ther. Res.* 3:249–63

Campbell, J. D., Tesser, A. 1983. Motivational interpretations of hindsight bias: An individual-difference analysis. *J. Pers.* 51:605–20

Cantor, N., Kihlstrom, J. F. 1981. *Personality, Cognition, and Social Interaction.* Hillsdale, NJ: Erlbaum

Cantor, N., Kihlstrom, J. F. 1983. *Social intelligence: The cognitive basis of personality.* Tech. Rep. 60, Cognit. Sci. Cent., Univ. Mich.

Cantor, N., Kihlstrom, J. 1982. Cognitive and social processes in personality: Implications for behavior therapy. In *Handbook of Behavior Therapy,* ed. E. M. Franks, G. T. Wilson. New York: Guilford

Cantor, N., Mackie, D., Lord, C. 1984. Choosing partners and activities: The social perceiver decides to mix it up. *Soc. Cognit.* 2:

Cantor, N., Mischel, W., Schwartz, J. 1982. A prototype analysis of psychological situations. *Cognit. Psychol.* 14:45–77

Cantor, N., Showers, C. 1983. *Consumer communications and driving behavior.* Tech. rep. under private contract, Univ. Mich.

Cantor, N., Smith, E. E., French, R. Mezzich, J. 1980. Psychiatric diagnosis as prototype categorization. *J. Abnorm. Psychol.* 89:181–93

Carlston, D. E. 1980. The recall and use of trait and events in social inference processes. *J. Exp. Soc. Psychol.* 16:303–28

Carroll, J. S., Wiener, R. L. 1982. Cognitive social psychology in court and beyond. See Hastorf & Isen 1982, pp. 213–53

Carver, C. S., Blaney, P. H., Scheier, M. F. 1979. Focus of attention, chronic expectancy, and responses to a feared stimulus. *J. Pers. Soc. Psychol.* 37:1186–95

Carver, C. S., Scheier, M. F. 1981. *Attention and Self-Regulation: A Control-Theory Approach to Human Behavior.* New York: Springer-Verlag

Carver, C. S., Scheier, M. F. 1983. A control-theory approach to human behavior and implications for problems in self-management. *Adv. Cognit. Behav. Res. Ther.* 2:127–93

Chaiken, S. 1980. Heuristic versus systematic information processing and the use of source versus message cues in persuasion. *J. Pers. Soc. Psychol.* 39:752–56

Chaiken, S., Baldwin, M. W. 1981. Affective-cognitive consistency and the effect of salient behavioral information on the self-perception of attitudes. *J. Pers. Soc. Psychol.* 41:1–12

Chase, W. G., Simon, H. A. 1973. The mind's eye in chess. In *Visual Information Processing,* ed. W. G. Chase. New York: Academic

Chi, M. T. H., Feltovich, P. J., Glaser, R. 1981. Categorization and representation of physics problems by experts and novices. *Cognit. Sci.* 5:121–52

Cialdini, R. B., Kenrick, D. T., Baumann, D. J. 1982. Effects of mood on prosocial behavior in children and adults. In *The Development of Prosocial Behavior,* ed. N. Eisenberg, pp. 339–59. New York: Academic

Clark, M. S., Fiske, S. T., eds. 1982. *Affect and Cognition: The 17th Annual Carnegie Symposium.* Hillsdale, NJ: Erlbaum

Clark, M. S., Isen, A. M. 1982. Toward understanding the relationship between feeling states and social behavior. See Hastorf & Isen 1982, pp. 73–108

Clark, M. S., Milberg, S., Erber, R. 1984. Effects of arousal on judgments of others' emotions. *J. Pers. Soc. Psychol.* 46:551–60

Clark, M. S., Milberg, S., Ross, J. 1983. Arousal cues arousal-related material in memory: Implications for understanding effects of mood on memory. *J. Verb. Learn. Verb. Behav.* 22:633–49

Cohen, C. E. 1981. Goals and schemata in person perception: Making sense from the stream of behavior. See Cantor & Kihlstrom 1981, pp. 45–68

Cohen, C. E., Ebbesen, E. B. 1979. Observational goals and schema activation: A theoretical framework for behavior perception. *J. Exp. Soc. Psychol.* 15:305–29

Collins, D. L., Baum, A., Singer, J. E. 1983. Coping with chronic stress at Three Mile Island: Psychological and biochemical evidence. *Health Psychol.* 2:149–66

Converse, P. E. 1970. Attitudes and nonattitudes: Continuation of a dialogue. In *The Quantitative Analysis of Social Problems,* ed. E. R. Tufte. Reading, Mass: Addison-Wesley

Crocker, J., Hannah, D. B., Weber, R. 1983. Person memory and causal attributions. *J. Pers. Soc. Psychol.* 44:55–66

Deci, E. L., Nezlek, J., Sheinman, L. 1981. Characteristics of the rewarder and intrinsic motivation of the rewardee. *J. Pers. Soc. Psychol.* 40:1–10

Deci, E. L., Ryan, R. M. 1984. The dynamics of self-determination in personality and development. In *Self-Related Cognition in Anxiety and Motivation,* ed. R. Schwarzer. Hillsdale, NJ: Erlbaum. In press

Dennett, D. C. 1969. *Content and Consciousness.* London: Routledge & Kegan

Derry, P. A., Kuiper, N. A. 1981. Schematic processing and self-references in clinical depression. *J. Abnorm. Psychol.* 90:286–97

Diener, C. I., Dweck, C. S. 1980. An analysis of learned helplessness: II. The processing of success. *J. Pers. Soc. Psychol.* 39:940–52

Diener, E., Emmons, R. A., Larsen, R. J. 1984. Person x situation interactions: Choice of situations and congruence response models. *J. Pers. Soc. Psychol.* In press

Duncker, K. 1945. On problem-solving. *Psychol. Monogr.* 58:Whole No. 5

Dweck, C. S. 1975. The role of expectations and attributions in the alleviation of learned helplessness. *J. Pers. Soc. Psychol.* 31:674–85

Eccles, J., Adler, T., Meece, J. L. 1984. Sex differences in achievement: A test of alternate theories. *J. Pers. Soc. Psychol.* 46:26–43

Ellis, A., Harper, R. A. 1975. *A New Guide to Rational Living.* N. Hollywood, Calif: Wilshire Book Co.

Erber, R., Fiske, S. T. 1984. Outcome dependency and attention to inconsistent information. *J. Pers. Soc. Psychol.* In press

Erikson, E. H. 1950. *Childhood and Society.* New York: Norton

Fazio, R. H., Chen, J., McDonel, E. C., Sherman, S. J. 1982. Attitude accessibility, Attitude-behavior consistency, and the strength of the object-evaluation association. *J. Exp. Soc. Psychol.* 18:339–57

Fazio, R. H., Powell, M. C., Herr, P. M. 1983. Toward a process model of the attitude-behavior relation: Accessing one's attitude upon mere observation of the attitude object. *J. Pers. Soc. Psychol.* 44:723–35

Fazio, R. H., Zanna, M. P. 1981. Direct experience and attitude-behavior consistency. *Adv. Exp. Soc. Psychol.* 14:161–202

Fenigstein, A. 1979. Self-consciousness, self-attention, and social interaction. *J. Pers. Soc. Psychol.* 37:75–86

Ferguson, T. J., Wells, G. L. 1980. Priming of mediators in causal attribution. *J. Pers. Soc. Psychol.* 38:461–70

Fischoff, B., Beyth, R. 1975. "I knew it would happen"—Remembered probabilities of once-future things. *Organ. Behav. Hum. Perform.* 13:1–16

Fiske, S. T. 1982. Schema-triggered affect: Applications to social perception. See Clarke & Fiske 1982, pp. 55–78

Fiske, S. T., Kinder, D. R. 1981. Involvement, expertise, and schema use: Evidence from political cognition. See Cantor & Kihlstrom 1981, pp. 171–90

Fiske, S. T., Kinder, D. R., Larter, W. M. 1983. The novice and the expert: Knowledge-based strategies in political cognition. *J. Exp. Soc. Psychol.* 19:381–400

Fiske, S. T., Pavelchak, M. A. 1984. Category-based versus piecemeal-based affective responses: developments in schema-triggered affect. See Sorrentino & Higgins 1984

Fiske, S. T., Taylor, S. E. 1984. *Social Cognition.* Reading, Mass: Addison-Wesley

Forgas, J. P. 1982. Episode cognition: Internal

representations of interaction routines. *Adv. Exp. Soc. Psychol.* 15:59–102

Freud, S. (1901) 1960. The psychopathology of everyday life. In *The Standard Edition of the Complete Psychological Works,* Vol. 6, ed. J. Strachey. London: Hogarth

Gergen, K. J. 1972. Multiple identity: The healthy, happy human being wears many masks. *Psychol. Today* 5:31–35, 64–66

Gilovich, T. 1983. Biased evaluation and persistence in gambling. *J. Pers. Soc. Psychol.* 44:1110–27

Goldfried, M. R., Goldfried, A. P. 1975. Cognitive change methods. In *Helping People Change: A Textbook of Methods,* ed. F. H. Kanfer, A. P. Goldstein, pp. 89–116. New York: Pergamon

Goldfried, M. R., Padawer, W., Robins, C. 1984. Social anxiety and the semantic structure of heterosocial interactions. *J. Abnorm. Psychol.* 93:87–97

Gordon, C. 1968. Self-conceptions: Configuration of content. In *The Self in Social Interaction,* ed. C. Gordon, K. J. Gergen, New York: Wiley

Graesser, A. C., Woll, S. B., Kowalski, D. J., Smith, D. A. 1980. Memory for typical and atypical action in scripted activities. *J. Exp. Psychol: Hum. Learn. Mem.* 6:503–15

Greenwald, A. G. 1982. Ego-task analysis: An integration of research on ego-involvement and self-awareness. See Hastorf & Isen 1982, pp. 109–47

Greenwald, A. G., Pratkanis, A. R. 1984. The self. See Wyer & Srull 1984

Gregory, W. L., Cialdini, R. B., Carpenter, K. M. 1982. Self-relevant scenarios as mediators of likelihood estimates and compliance: Does imagining make it so? *J. Pers. Soc. Psychol.* 43:89–99

Haan, N. 1982. The assessment of coping, defense, and stress. In *Handbook of Stress: Theoretical and Clinical Aspects,* ed. L. Goldberger, S. Breznitz. New York: Free Press

Haan, N., ed. 1977. *Coping and Defending: Processes of Self-Environment Organization.* New York: Academic

Hamilton, D. L. 1981. *Cognitive Processes in Stereotyping and Intergroup Behavior.* Hillsdale, NJ: Erlbaum

Hamilton, D. L., Katz, L. B., Leirer, V. O. 1980. Cognitive representation of personality impressions: Organizational processes in first impression formation. *J. Pers. Soc. Psychol.* 39:1050–63

Hampson, S. E. 1982. *The Construction of Personality: An Introduction.* London: Routledge & Kegan Paul

Harter, S. 1984. Developmental perspectives on the self-system. In *Carmichael's Manual of Child Psychology: Social and Personality Development,* ed. M. Hetherington. New York: Wiley

Hartmann, H. 1958. *Ego-Psychology and the Problem of Adaptation.* New York: Int. Univ. Press

Harvey, J. H., Ickes, W., Kidd, R. F., eds. 1978. *New Directions in Attribution Research,* Vol. 2. Hillsdale, NJ: Erlbaum

Harvey, J. H., Ickes, W., Kidd, R. F., eds. 1981. *New Direction in Attribution Research,* Vol. 3. Hillsdale, NJ: Erlbaum

Harvey, J. H., Weary, G. 1984. Current issues in attribution theory and research. *Ann. Rev. Psychol.* 35:427–59

Hastie, R. 1981. Schematic principles in human memory. See Higgins et al 1981, pp. 39–87

Hastie, R., Park, B., Weber, R. 1984. Social memory. See Wyer & Srull 1984

Hastorf, A., Isen, A., eds. 1982. *Cognitive Social Psychology.* New York: Elsevier

Heckhausen, H., Schmalt, H.-D., Schneider, K. 1984. *Advances in Achievement Motivation Research.* New York: Academic. In press

Herstein, J. A., Carroll, J. S., Hayes, J. R. 1980. The organization of knowledge about people and their attributes in long-term memory. *Rep. Res. Soc. Psychol.* 11:17–37

Higgins, E. T. 1981. The "communication game": Implications for social cognition and persuasion. See Higgins et al 1981, pp. 343–91

Higgins, E. T., Bryant, S. L. 1982. Consensus information and the fundamental attribution error: The role of development and in-group versus out-group knowledge. *J. Pers. Soc. Psychol.* 43:889–900

Higgins, E. T., Herman, C. P., Zanna, M. P. 1981. *Social Cognition: The Ontario Symposium,* Vol. 1. Hillsdale, NJ: Erlbaum

Higgins, E. T., King, G. 1981. Accessibility of social constructs: Information-processing consequences of individual and contextual variability. See Cantor & Kihlstrom 1981, pp. 69–121

Higgins, E. T., Klein, R., Strauman, T. 1984. Self-concept discrepancy theory: A psychological model for distinguishing among different aspect of depression and anxiety. *Soc. Cognit.* In press

Higgins, E. T., Lurie, L. 1983. Context, categorization, and recall: The "change-of-standard" effect. *Cognit. Psychol.* 15:525–47

Higgins, E. T., McCann, C. D. 1984. Social encoding and subsequent attitudes, impressions, and memory: "Context-driven" and motivational aspects of processing. *J. Pers. Soc. Psychol.* 47:26–39

Higgins, E. T., McCann, C. D., Fondacaro, R. 1982. The "communication game": Goal-directed encoding and cognitive consequences. *Soc. Cognit.* 1:21–37

Higgins, E. T., Parsons, J. E. 1983. Social cognitions and the social life of the child: Stages as subcultures. See Higgins et al 1983, pp. 15–62

Higgins, E. T., Rholes, W. S., Jones, C. R. 1977. Category accessibility and impression formation. *J. Exp. Soc. Psychol.* 13:141–54

Higgins, E. T., Rholes, W. S. 1978. "Saying is believing": Effects of message modification on memory and liking for the person described. *J. Exp. Soc. Psychol.* 14:363–78

Higgins, E. T., Ruble, D. N., Hartup, W. W., eds. 1983. *Social Cognition and Social Development.* New York: Cambridge Univ. Press

Hochschild, A. R. 1979. Emotion work, feeling rules, and social structure. *Am. J. Sociol.* 85:551–75

Hoffman, C., Mischel, W., Mazze, K. 1981. The role of purpose in the organization of information about behavior: Trait-based versus goal-based categories in person cognition. *J. Pers. Soc. Psychol.* 40:211–25

Hull, J. G., Young, R. D. 1983. Self-consciousness, self-esteem, and success-failure as determinant of alcohol consumption in male social drinkers. *J. Pers. Soc. Psychol.* 44:1097–109

Isen, A. M., Daubman, K. A., Gorgoglione, J. M. 1984. The influence of positive affect on cognitive organization. In *Aptitude, Learning, and Instruction: Cognitive and Affective Factors*, ed. R. Snow, M. Farr. Hillsdale, NJ: Erlbaum. In press

Isen, A. M., Hastorf, A. H. 1982. Some perspectives on cognitive social psychology. See Hastorf & Isen 1982, pp. 1–31

Isen, A. M., Means, B. 1983. The influence of positive affect on decision-making strategy. *Soc. Cognit.* 2:18–31

Isen, A. M., Means, B., Patrick, R., Nowicki, G. 1982. Some factors influencing decision-making strategy and risk taking. See Clark & Fiske 1982, pp. 243–61

Isen, A. M., Patrick, R. 1983. The effect of positive feelings on risk taking: When the chips are down. *Organ. Behav. Hum. Perform.* 31:194–202

Isen, A. M., Shalker, T. E., Clark, M., Karp, L. 1978. Affect, accessibility of material in memory, and behavior: A cognitive loop? *J. Pers. Soc. Psychol.* 36:1–12

Isen, A. M., Simmons, S. 1978. The effect of feeling good on a helping task that is incompatible with good mood. *Soc. Psychol.* 41:346–49

Jackson, J. M., Latane, B. 1981. All alone in front of all those people: Stage fright as a function of number and type of co-performers and audience. *J. Pers. Soc. Psychol.* 40:74–85

James, W. 1890. *Principles of Psychology.* New York: Holt

Jelalian, E., Miller, A. G. 1984. The perseverance of beliefs: Conceptual perspectives and research developments. *J. Soc. Clin. Psychol.* In press

Johnson, E. J., Tversky, A. 1983. Affect, generalization, and the perception of risk. *J. Pers. Soc. Psychol.* 45:20–31

Jones, E. E., Berglas, S. 1978. Control of attributions about the self through self-handicapping strategies: The appeal of alcohol and the role of underachievement. *Pers. Soc. Psychol. Bull.* 4:200–6

Jones, E. E., Pittman, T. S. 1982. Toward a general theory of strategic self-presentation. In *Psychological Perspectives on the Self*, ed. J. Suls, 1:231–62. Hillsdale, NJ: Erlbaum

Jones, E. E., Thibaut, J. W. 1958. Interaction goals as bases of human inference in interpersonal perception. In *Person Perception and Interpersonal Behavior*, ed. R. Tagiuri, L. Petrullo. Stanford, Calif: Stanford Univ. Press

Kahneman, D., Tversky, A. 1982. The simulation heuristic. In *Judgment Under Uncertainty: Heuristics and Biases*, ed. D. Kahneman, P. Slovic, A. Tversky, pp. 201–8. New York: Cambridge Univ. Press

Kelley, H. H. 1979. *Personal Relationships.* Hillsdale, NJ: Erlbaum

Kelley, H. H., Berscheid, E., Christensen, A., Harvey, J., Huston, T., et al 1983. *Close Relationships.* San Francisco: Freeman

Kelley, H. H., Michela, J. L. 1980. Attribution theory and research. *Ann. Rev. Psychol.* 31:457–501

Kelly, G. A. 1955. *The Psychology of Personal Constructs.* New York: Norton

Kendall, P. C., Hollon, S. D., eds. 1981. *Cognitive-Behavorial Interventions: Assessment Methods.* New York: Academic

Kihlstrom, J. F. 1981. On personality and memory. See Cantor & Kihlstrom 1981, pp. 123–49

Kihlstrom, J. F. 1983. Conscious, subconscious, unconscious. In *Unconscious Processes: Several Perspectives*, ed. K. S. Bowers, D. Meichenbaum. New York: Wiley

Kihlstrom, J. F., Cantor, N. 1984. Mental representations of the self. *Adv. Exp. Soc. Psychol.* 17:

Kihlstrom, J. F., Nasby, W. 1981. Cognitive tasks in clinical assessment: An exercise in applied psychology. See Kendall & Hollon 1981

King, G. A., Sorrentino, R. M. 1983. Psychological dimensions of goal-oriented interpersonal situations. *J. Pers. Soc. Psychol.* 44:140–62

Klos, D. S., Loomis, J. W., Ruhrold, R. E. 1983. *Anger and strategic thinking during interpersonal conflict.* Presented at Am. Psychol. Assoc. meet., Anaheim

Kruglanski, A. W., Friedland, N., Farkash, E. 1984. Lay persons' sensitivity to statistical information: The case of high perceived applicability. *J. Pers. Soc. Psychol.* 46: 503–18

Kruglanski, A. W., Hamel, I. Z., Maides, S. A., Schwartz, J. M. 1978. Attribution theory as a special case of lay epistemology. See Harvey et al 1978

Kuhl, J. 1984. Volitional aspects of achievement motivation and learned helplessness: Toward a comprehensive theory of action control. *Prog. Exp. Pers. Res.* 13:99–171

Kuhl, J., Beckmann, J., eds. 1984. *Action Control: From Cognition to Behavior.* New York: Springer. In press

Kuiper, N. A. 1978. Depression and causal attributions for success and failure. *J. Pers. Soc. Psychol.* 36:236–46

Kuiper, N. A., Derry, P. A. 1981. The self a a cognitive prototype: An application to person perception and depression. See Cantor & Kihlstrom 1981, pp. 215–32

Kuiper, N. A., MacDonald, M. P., Derry, P. A. 1984. Parameters of a depressive self-schema. In *Psychological Perspectives on the Self,* ed. J. Suls, A. Greenwald, Vol. 2. Hillsdale, NJ: Erlbaum. In press

Landau, R. J. 1980. The role of semantic schemata on phobic-word interpretations. *Cognit. Ther. Res.* 4:427–34

Landau, R. J., Goldfried, M. R. 1981. The assessment of schemata: A unifying framework for cognitive, behavioral, and traditional assessment. See Kendall & Hollon 1981, pp. 363–99

Landman, J., Manis, M. 1983. Social cognition: Some historical and theoretical perspectives. *Adv. Exp. Soc. Psychol.* 16:49–123

Langer, E. J. 1978. Rethinking the role of thought in social interaction. See Harvey et al 1978, pp. 36–57

Langer, E. J., Imber, L. 1979. When practice makes imperfect: Debilitating effects of over-learning. *J. Pers. Soc. Psychol.* 37: 2014–24

Langer, E. J., Abelson, R. P. 1974. A patient by any other name . . .: Clinician group difference in labeling bias. *J. Consult. Clin. Psychol.* 42:4–9

Lastovicka, J. L., Gardner, D. M. 1978. Low involvement vs. high involvement cognitive structures. In *Advances in Consumer Research,* ed. H. K. Hunt, 5:87–92. Ann Arbor, Mich: Assoc. Consumer Res.

Lazarus, R. S. 1982. Thoughts on the relations between emotions and cognition. *Am. Psychol.* 37:1019–24

Lazarus, R. S., Launier, R. 1978. Stress-related transactions between person and environment. In *Internal and External Determinators of Behavior,* ed. L. A. Pervin, M. Lewis. New York: Plenum

Lepper, M. R., Greene, D., eds. 1978. *The Hidden Costs of Reward.* Morristown, NJ: Erlbaum

Leventhal, H., Nerenz, D. R., Steele, D. J. 1984a. Illness representations and coping with health threats. In *A Handbook of Psychology and Health,* ed. A. Baum, J. Singer, Vol. 4. Hillsdale, NJ: Erlbaum. In press

Leventhal, H., Prohaska, T. R., Hirschman, R. S. 1984b. Preventive health behavior across the life-span. In *Preventing Health Risk Behaviors and Promoting Coping with Illness,* Vol. 8. Vermont Conf. Primary Prevention of Psychopathol. Hanover, NH: Univ. Press New England

Levinson, D. 1978. *The Seasons of a Man's Life.* New York: Knopf

Lewin, K., Dembo, T., Festinger, L., Sears, P. S. 1944. Level of aspiration. In *Personality and the Behavior Disorders,* ed. J. M. Hunt, pp. 333–78. New York: Ronald Press

Lewinsohn, P. M., Mischel, W., Chaplain, W., Barton, R. 1980. Social competence and depression: The role of illusory self-perceptions. *J. Abnorm. Psychol.* 89:203–12

Lingle, J. H., Ostrom, T. M. 1981. Principles of memory and cognition in attitude formation. In *Cognitive Responses in Persuasion,* ed. R. E. Petty, T. M. Ostrom, T. C. Brock, pp. 399–420. Hillsdale, NJ: Erlbaum

Linville, P. W. 1982a. Affective consequences of complexity regarding the self and others. See Clark & Fiske 1982

Linville, P. W. 1982b. The complexity-extremity effect and age-based stereotyping. *J. Pers. Soc. Psychol.* 42:193–211

Linville, P. W., Jones, E. E. 1980. Polarized appraisals of outgroup members. *J. Pers. Soc. Psychol.* 38:689–703

Lippa, R. 1977. Androgyny, sex-typing, and the perception of masculinity-femininity in handwritings. *J. Res. Pers.* 11:21–37

Little, B. R. 1983. Personal projects—A rationale and methods for investigation. *Environ. Behav.* 15:273–309

Locke, E. A., Shaw, K. N., Saari, L. M., Latham, G. P. 1981. Goal setting and task performance: 1969–1980. *Psychol. Bull.* 90:125–52

Locksley, A., Borgida, E., Brekke, N., Hepburn, C. 1980. Sex stereotypes and social judgment. *J. Pers. Soc. Psychol.* 39:821–31

Locksley, A., Hepburn, C., Ortiz, V. 1982. Social stereotypes and judgments of individuals: An instance of the base-rate fallacy. *J. Exp. Soc. Psychol.* 18:23–42

Logan, G. D. 1980. Attention and automaticity in Stroop and priming tasks: Theory and data. *Cognit. Psychol.* 12:523–53

Lord, C. G. 1982. Predicting behavioral consistency from an individual's perception of situational similarities. *J. Pers. Soc. Psychol.* 43:1076–88

Lord, C. G., Lepper, M. R., Ross, L. 1979. Biased assimilation and attitude polarization: The effects of prior theories. *J. Pers. Soc. Psychol.* 37:2098–110

Mandler, G. 1975. *Mind and Emotion.* New York: Wiley

Manis, M., Cornell, S. D., Moore, J. C. 1974. Transmission of attitude-relevant information through a communication chain. *J. Pers. Soc. Psychol.* 30:81–94

Manucia, G. K., Baumann, D. J., Cialdini, R. B. 1984. Mood influences on helping: Direct effects or side effects? *J. Pers. Soc. Psychol.* 46:357–64

Markus, H. 1977. Self-schemata and processing information about the self. *J. Pers. Soc. Psychol.* 35:63–78

Markus, H. 1983. Self-knowledge: An expanded view. *J. Pers.* 51:543–65

Markus, H., Crane, M., Bernstein, S., Siladi, M. 1982. Self-schemas and gender. *J. Pers. Soc. Psychol.* 42:38–50

Markus, H., Nurius, P. 1983. *Possible selves.* Presented at Soc. Exp. Soc. Psychol. Meet., Pittsburgh

Markus, H., Smith, J., Moreland, D. 1984. The role of the self in social perception: A cognitive analysis. In press

Martin, D. J., Abramson, L. Y., Alloy, L. B. 1984. Illusion of control for self and others in depressed and nondepressed college students. *J. Pers. Soc. Psychol.* 46:125–36

Masters, J. C., Barden, R. C., Ford, M. E. 1979. Affective states, expressive behavior and learning in children. *J. Pers. Soc. Psychol.* 37:380–90

McArthur, L. Z., Baron, R. M. 1983. Toward an ecological theory of social perception. *Psychol. Rev.* 90:215–38

McFarland, C., Ross, M. 1982. Impact of causal attributions on affective reactions to success and failure. *J. Pers. Soc. Psychol.* 43:937–46

McFarland, C., Ross, M., Conway, M. 1984. Self-persuasion and self-presentation as mediators of anticipatory attitude change. *J. Pers. Soc. Psychol.* 46:529–40

McGuire, W. J., McGuire, C. V. 1981. The spontaneous self-concept as affected by personal distinctiveness. In *Self-Concept: Advances in Theory and Research,* ed. M. D. Lynch, A. A. Norem-Hebeisen, K. Gergen. New York: Ballinger

McGuire, W. J., McGuire, C. V., Child, P., Fujioka, T. 1978. Salience of ethnicity in the spontaneous self-concept as a function of one's ethnic distinctiveness in the social environment. *J. Pers. Soc. Psychol.* 36:511–20

Meece, J. L., Eccles-Parsons, J., Kaczala, C. M., Goff, S. B., Futterman, R. 1982. Sex differences in math achievement: Toward a model of academic choice. *Psychol. Bull.* 91:324–48

Mehrabian, A., Russell, J. A. 1974. *An Approach to Environmental Psychology.* Cambridge, Mass: MIT Press

Meichenbaum, D. 1977. *Cognitive Behavior Modifications: An Integrated Approach.* New York: Plenum

Miller, D. T., Porter, C. A. 1980. Effect of temporal perspective on the attribution process. *J. Pers. Soc. Psychol.* 39:532–41

Miller, G. A., Cantor, N. 1982. Book review of *Human Inference: Strategies and Shortcomings of Social Judgment,* by R. Nisbett & L. Ross. *Soc. Cognit.* 1:83–93

Miller, S. M., Mangan, C. E. 1983. Interacting effects of information and coping style in adapting to gynecologic stress: Should the doctor tell all? *J. Pers. Soc. Psychol.* 45:223–36

Mischel, W. 1983. Delay of gratification as process and as person variable in development. In *Human Development: An Interactional Perspective,* ed. D. Magnusson, V. P. Allen. New York: Academic

Mischel, W. 1984. Convergences and challenges in the search for consistency. *Am. Psychol.* 39:351–64

Moreland, R. L., Levine, J. M. 1982. Socialization in small groups: Temporal changes in individual-group relations. *Adv. Exp. Soc. Psychol.* 15:137–92

Neugarten, B. L. 1976. Adaptation and the life cycle. *Couns. Psychol.* 6:16–20

Neves, D. M., Anderson, J. R. 1981. Knowledge compilation: Mechanisms for the automization of cognitive skills. In *Cognitive Skills and their Acquisition,* ed. J. R. Anderson. Hillsdale, NJ: Erlbaum

Newtson, D., Czerlinsky, T. 1974. Adjustment of attitude communications for contrasts by extreme audiences. *J. Pers. Soc. Psychol.* 30:829–37

Newtson, D., Engquist, G. 1976. The perceptual organization of ongoing behavior. *J. Pers. Soc. Psychol.* 12:436–50

Niedenthal, P. M., Cantor, N. 1984. Making use of social prototypes: From fuzzy concepts to firm decisions. *Fuzzy Sets & Syst.* 13:1–23

Niemeyer, G. J., Merluzzi, T. V. 1982. Group situation and group process: Personal construct theory and group development. *Small Group. Behav.* 13:150–64

Nisbett, R. E., Krantz, D. H., Jepson, C., Kunda, Z. 1983. The use of statistical heuristics in everyday inductive reasoning. *Psychol. Rev.* 90:339–63

Nisbett, R. E., Ross, L. 1980. *Human Inference: Strategies and Shortcomings in Social*

Judgment. Englewood Cliffs, NJ: Prentice-Hall

Norem, J., Cantor, N. 1984. Anticipatory and post-hoc cushioning strategies. *Cognit. Ther. Res.* In press

Nuttin, J. R. 1984. *Motivation, Planning, and Action: A Relational Theory of Behavioral Dynamics.* Hillsdale, NJ: Erlbaum

Ostrom, T. M., Lingle, J. H., Pryor, J. B., Geva, N. 1980. Cognitive organization of person impressions. In *Person Memory: The Cognitive Basis of Person Perception,* ed. R. Hastie, T. M. Ostrom, E. B. Ebbesen, R. S. Wyer Jr., D. L. Hamilton, D. E. Carlston. Hillsdale, NJ: Erlbaum

Patsiokas, A. T., Clum, G. A., Luscomb, R. L. 1979. Cognitive characteristics of suicide attempters. *J. Consult. Clin. Psychol.* 47:478–84

Payne, J. W. 1982. Contingent decision behavior. *Psychol. Bull.* 92:382–402

Pervin, L. A. 1985. Personality: Current controversies, issues, and directions. *Ann. Rev. Psychol.* 36:83–114

Petty, R. E., Cacioppo, J. T. 1984. The effects of involvement on responses to argument quantity and quality: Central and peripheral routes to persuasion. *J. Pers. Soc. Psychol.* 46:69–81

Petty, R. E., Cacioppo, J. T. 1979. Issue involvement can increase or decrease persuasion by enhancing message-relevant cognitive responses. *J. Pers. Soc. Psychol.* 37:1915–26

Petty, R. E., Cacioppo, J. T., Goldman, R. 1981. Personal involvement as a determinant of argument-based persuasion. *J. Pers. Soc. Psychol.* 41:847–55

Pittman, T. S., Emery, J., Boggiano, A. K. 1982. Intrinsic and extrinsic motivational orientations: Reward-induced changes in preference for complexity. *J. Pers. Soc. Psychol.* 42:789–97

Posner, M. I., Snyder, C. R. R. 1975. Attention and cognitive control. In *Information Processing and Cognition: The Loyola Symposium,* ed. R. L. Solso. Hillsdale, NJ: Erlbaum

Quattrone, G. A., Jones, E. E. 1980. The perception of variability within in-groups and out-groups: Implications for the law of large numbers. *J. Pers. Soc. Psychol.* 38:141–52

Raimy, V. 1975. *Misunderstanding of the Self: Cognitive Psychotherapy and the Misconception Hypothesis.* San Francisco: Jossey-Bass

Raps, C. S., Peterson, C., Reinhard, K. E., Abramson, L. Y., Seligman, M. E. P. 1982. Attributional style among depressed patients. *J. Abnorm. Psychol.* 91:102–8

Raye, C. L., Johnson, M. K., Taylor, T. H. 1980. Is there something special about memory for internally-generated information? *Mem. Cognit.* 8:141–48

Ross, L., Lepper, M. R., Hubbard, M. 1975. Perseverance in self-perception and social perception: Biased attribution processes in the debriefing paradigm. *J. Pers. Soc. Psychol.* 32:880–92

Ross, M., McFarland, C., Conway, M., Zanna, M. P. 1983. Reciprocal relations between attitude and behavior recall: Committing people to newly formed attitudes. *J. Pers. Soc. Psychol.* 45:257–67

Ross, M., Sicoly, F. 1979. Egocentric biases in availability and attribution. *J. Pers. Soc. Psychol.* 37:322–37

Ruble, D. N. 1983. The development of social-comparison processes and their role in achievement-related self-socialization. See Higgins, et al 1983, pp. 134–57

Rudy, T. E., Merluzzi, T. V., Henahan, P. T. 1982. Construal of complex assertion situations: An MDS analysis. *J. Consult. Clin. Psychol.* 50:125–37

Rush, A. J., ed. 1982. *Short-term Psychotherapies for Depression: Behavioral, Interpersonal, Cognitive, and Psychodynamic Approaches.* New York: Guilford

Schachter, S. 1982. Recidivism and self-cure of smoking and obesity. *Am. Psychol.* 37:436–44

Scheier, M. F. 1980. The effects of public and private self-consciousness on the public expression of personal beliefs. *J. Pers. Soc. Psychol.* 39:514–21

Scheier, M. F., Carver, C. S., Gibbons, F. X. 1981. Self-focused attention and reactions to fear. *J. Res. Pers.* 15:1–15

Schlenker, B. R. 1982. Translating actions into attitudes: An identity-analytic approach to the explanation of social conduct. *Adv. Exp. Soc. Psychol.* 15:194–247

Schlenker, B. R., Leary, M. R. 1982. Social anxiety and self-presentation: A conceptualization and model. *Psychol. Bull* 92:641–69

Schneider, D. J., Blankmeyer, B. L. 1983. Prototype salience and implicit personality theories. *J. Pers. Soc. Psychol.* 44:712–22

Schneider, W., Shiffrin, R. M. 1977. Controlled and automatic human information processing: I. Detection, search, and attention. *Psychol. Rev.* 84:1–66

Schutz, A. 1964. On multiple realities. In *Collected Papers of Alfred Schutz,* Vol. 1, ed. M. Natanson. The Hague: Martinus Nijhoff

Schwartz, S. H. 1977. Normative influences on altruism. *Adv. Exp. Soc. Psychol.* 10:221–79

Sherman, S. J., Ahlm, K., Berman, L., Lynn, S. 1978. Contrast effects and their relationship to subsequent behavior. *J. Exp. Soc. Psychol.* 14:340–50

Sherman, S. J., Presson, C. C., Chassin, L.

1984. Mechanisms underlying the false consensus effect: The special role of threats to the self. *Pers. Soc. Psychol. Bull.* 10:127–38

Sherman, S. J., Skov, R. B., Hervitz, E. F., Stock, C. B. 1981. The effects of explaining hypothetical future events: From possibility to probability to actuality and beyond. *J. Exp. Soc. Psychol.* 17:142–58

Shiffrin, R. M., Schneider, W. 1977. Controlled and automatic human information processing. II. Perceptual learning, automatic attending, and a general theory. *Psychol. Rev.* 84:127–90

Showers, C., Cantor, N. 1984. *The effects of best- and worst-case strategies: Making sense of judgment "bias."* Presented at Midwest Psychol. Assoc. meet., Chicago

Silver, R., Wortman, C. B., Klos, D. 1983. Cognitive, affective, and coping responses: New direction for human helplessness research. *J. Pers.* 51:123–26

Singer, J. L. 1974. *Imagery and Daydream Methods in Psychotherapy and Behavior Modification.* New York: Academic

Skinner, B. F. 1953. *Science and Human Behavior.* New York: Macmillan

Sloan, T. S. 1983. The aura of projected futures: A neglected aspect of major life decisions. *Pers. Soc. Psychol. Bull.* 9:551–66

Smith, T. W., Greenberg, J. 1981. Depression and self-focused attention. *Motiv. Emot.* 5:323–31

Snyder, M. L., Stephan, W. G., Rosenfield, D. 1978. Attributional egotism. See Harvey et al 1978, pp. 91–117

Snyder, M. 1981. On the influence of individuals on situations. See Cantor & Kihlstrom 1981, pp. 309–29

Snyder, M. 1982. When believing means doing: Creating links between attitudes and behavior. In *Consistency in Social Behavior: The Ontario Symposium,* vol. 2, ed. M. P. Zanna, E. T. Higgins, C. P. Herman. Hillsdale, NJ: Erlbaum

Snyder, M. 1983. The influence of individuals on situations: Implications for understanding the links between personality and social behavior. *J. Pers.* 51:497–526

Snyder, M., Cantor, N. 1979. Testing hypotheses about other people: The use of historical knowledge. *J. Exp. Soc. Psychol.* 15:330–42

Snyder, M., Gangestad, S., Simpson, J. 1983. Choosing friends as activity partners: The role of self-monitoring. *J. Pers. Soc. Psychol.* 45:1061–72

Snyder, M., Kendzierski, D. 1982. Choosing social situations: Investigating the origins of correspondence between attitudes and behavior. *J. Pers.* 50:280–95

Snyder, M., Swann, W. B. Jr. 1978. Behavioral confirmation in social interaction: From social perception to social reality. *J. Exp. Soc. Psychol.* 14:148–62

Snyder, M., Tanke, E., Berscheid, E. 1977. Social perception and interpersonal behavior: On the self-fulfilling nature of social stereotypes. *J. Pers. Soc. Psychol.* 35:656–66

Snyder, M., White, P. 1982. Moods and memories: Elation, depression, and the remembering of the events of one's life. *J. Pers.* 50:149–67

Sorrentino, R. M., Higgins, E. T., eds. 1984. *The Handbook of Motivation and Cognition: Foundations of Social Behavior.* New York: Guilford. In press

Spates, C., Kanfer, F. 1977. Self-monitoring, self-evaluation and self-reinforcement in children's learning: A test of a multistage self-regulation model. *Behav. Ther.* 8:9–16

Spivack, G., Platt, J. J., Shure, M. B. 1976. *The Problem-Solving Approach to Adjustment.* San Francisco: Jossey-Bass

Srull, T. K. 1983. Organizational and retrieval processes in person memory: An examination of processing objectives, presentation format, and the possible role of self-generated retrieval cues. *J. Pers. Soc. Psychol.* 44:1157–70

Stokols, D. 1982. Environmental psychology: A coming of age. In *The G. Stanley Hall Lecture Series,* ed. A. G. Kraut, 2:155. Washington DC: Am. Psychol. Assoc.

Stricker, G. 1977. Implications of research for psychotherapeutic treatment of women. *Am. Psychol.* 32:14–22

Swann, W. B., Read, S. J. 1981. Self-verification processes: How we sustain our self-conceptions. *J. Exp. Soc. Psychol.* 17:351–72

Tabachnik, N., Crocker, J., Alloy, L. B. 1983. Depression, social comparison, and the false-consensus effect. *J. Pers. Soc. Psychol.* 45:688–99

Taylor, S. E. 1982. Adjustment to threatening events: A theory of cognitive adaptation. *Am. Psychol.* 38:1161–73

Taylor, S. E., Crocker, J. 1981. Schematic bases of social information processing. See Higgins et al 1981, pp. 89–133

Taylor, S. E., Fiske, S. T. 1978. Salience, attribution, and attention: Top of the head phenomena. *Adv. Exp. Soc. Psychol.* 11: 250–88

Taylor, S. E., Lichtman, R. R., Wood, J. V. 1984. Attributions, beliefs about control, and adjustment to breast cancer. *J. Pers. Soc. Psychol.* 46:489–502

Teasdale, J. D., Fogarty, S. J. 1979. Differential effect of induced mood on retrieval of pleasant and unpleasant events from episodic memory. *J. Abnorm. Psychol.* 88:248–57

Tedeschi, J. T., ed. 1981. *Impression Management Theory and Social Psychological Research.* New York: Academic

Tesser, A., Campbell, J. 1984. Self-definition and self-evaluation maintenance. In *Social*

Psychological Perspectives on the Self, Vol. 2, ed. J. Suls, A. Greenwald. Hillsdale, NJ: Erlbaum. In press

Tesser, A., Leone, C. 1977. Cognitive schemas and thought as determinants of attitude change. *J. Exp. Soc. Psychol.* 13:340–56

Tetlock, P. E. 1983. Accountability and complexity of thought. *J. Pers. Soc. Psychol.* 45:74–83

Tetlock, P. E., Levi, A. 1982. Attribution bias: On the inconclusiveness of the cognition-motivation debate. *J. Exp. Soc. Psychol.* 18:68–88

Trzebinski, J. 1984. Action oriented representation of implicit personality theories. *J. Pers. Soc. Psychol.* In press

Tversky, A., Kahneman, D. 1981. The framing of decision and the psychology of choice. *Science* 211:453–58

Tybout, A. M., Scott, C. A. 1983. Availability of well-defined internal knowledge and the attitude formation process: Information aggregation versus self-perception. *J. Pers. Soc. Psychol.* 44:474–91

Tyler, T. R., Rasinski, K. 1984. Comparing psychological images of the social perceiver: Role of perceived informativeness, memorability, and affect in mediating the impact of crime victimization. *J. Pers. Soc. Psychol.* 46:308–28

Veroff, J. 1983. Contextual determinants of personality. *Pers. Soc. Psychol. Bull.* 9:331–44

Veroff, J., Veroff, J. 1980. *Social Incentives.* New York: Academic

Wachtel, P. L. 1977. *Psychoanalysis and Behavior Therapy.* New York: Basic Books

Weary, G. 1979. Self-serving attributional biases: Perceptual or response distortions. *J. Pers. Soc. Psychol.* 37:1418–20

Weary, G. 1980. Examination of affect and egotism as mediators of bias in causal attributions. *J. Pers. Soc. Psychol.* 38:348–57

Weaver, F. M., Carroll, J. S. 1984. *Crime perception in a natural setting by expert and novice shoplifters.* Alfred P. Sloan Sch. Manage. Work. Pap. 1535–84. Cambridge, Mass: MIT

Weber, R., Crocker, J. 1984. Cognitive processes in the revision of stereotypic beliefs. *J. Pers. Soc. Psychol.* In press

Wegner, D. M., Vallacher, R. R., Macomber, G., Wood, R., Arps, K. 1984. The emergence of action. *J. Pers. Soc. Psychol.* 46:269–79

Weiner, B. 1980. A cognitive (attribution)-emotion-action model of motivated behavior: An analysis of judgments of help-giving. *J. Pers. Soc. Psychol.* 39:186–200

White, J. D., Carlston, D. E. 1983. Consequences of schemata for attention, impressions, and recall in complex social interactions. *J. Pers. Soc. Psychol.* 45:538–49

Wills, T. A. 1981. Downward comparison principles in social psychology. *Psychol. Bull.* 18:68–88

Wilson, T. D. 1984. Strangers to ourselves: The origins and accuracy of beliefs about one's own mental states. In *Attribution in Contemporary Psychology*, ed. J. H. Harvey, G. Weary. In press

Wilson, T. D., Linville, P. 1982. Improving the academic performance of college freshmen: Attribution therapy revisited. *J. Pers. Soc. Psychol.* 42:367–76

Wilson, T. D., Linville, P. 1984. Improving the performance of college freshmen with attributional techniques. *J. Pers. Soc. Psychol.* In press

Wortman, C. B. 1976. Causal attributions and personal control. In *New Directions in Attribution Research*, Vol. 1, ed. J. H. Harvey, W. J. Ickes, R. F. Kidd. Hillsdale, NJ: Erlbaum

Wortman, C. B. 1983. Coping with victimization. *J. Soc. Issues* 39:197–223

Wortman, C. B., Dintzer, L. 1978. Is an attributional analysis of the learned helplessness phenomena viable? A critique of the Abramson-Seligman-Teasdale reformulation. *J. Abnorm. Psychol.* 87:75–90

Wright, J., Mischel, W. 1982. Influence of affect on cognitive social learning person variables. *J. Pers. Soc. Psychol.* 43:901–14

Wright, P. 1979. Concrete action plans in television messages to increase reading of drug warnings. *J. Consult. Res.* 6:256–70

Wyer, R. S., Gordon, S. E. 1984. The cognitive representation of social stimulus information. See Wyer & Srull 1984

Wyer, R. S. Jr., Srull, T. K. 1981. Category accessibility: Some theoretical and empirical issues concerning the processing of social stimulus information. See Higgins et al 1981, pp. 161–97

Wyer, R. S., Srull, T. K., Gordon, S. 1984. The effects of predicting a person's behavior on subsequent trait judgments. *J. Exp. Soc. Psychol.* 20:29–46

Wyer, R. S., Srull, T. K., Gordon, S. E., Hartwick, J. 1982. Effects of processing objectives on the recall of prose material. *J. Pers. Soc. Psychol.* 43:674–88

Wyer, R. S., Srull, T. K., eds. 1984. *Handbook of Social Cognition.* Hillsdale, NJ: Erlbaum

Zajonc, R. B. 1960. The process of cognitive tuning and communication. *J. Abnorm. Soc. Psychol.* 61:159–67

Zajonc, R. B. 1980. Feeling and thinking: Preferences need no inferences. *Am. Psychol.* 35:151–75

Zukier, H. 1982. The dilution effect: The role of the correlation and the dispersion of predictor variables in the use of non-diagnostic information. *J. Pers. Soc. Psychol.* 43:1163–74

Ann. Rev. Psychol. 1985. 36:307–48

ENGINEERING PSYCHOLOGY

C. D. Wickens and A. Kramer

Department of Psychology, University of Illinois at Urbana-Champaign, Champaign, Illinois 61820

CONTENTS

INTRODUCTION

Engineering psychology is the study of human behavior with the objective of improving human interaction with systems. The field is partner to at least three related disciplines, overlapping but not synonymous. *Human factors engineering* considers the role of human limits, constraints, and characteristics in system design. These may include, but are not restricted to, characteristics of the brain in processing information. Thus for example, the discipline includes anthropometry—designing to accomodate the form of the human body—or the role of muscle strength and fatigue in system design. The ultimate goal of human factors engineering, however, is to improve system design, not to understand human behavior. The latter of course is the primary objective of engineering psychology. In Europe *ergonomics* is nearly synonymous with human factors and has, as its name suggests, a major component related to work physiology: the response of various physiological subsystems to task and environmental influences. Finally, while the psychology of *human skilled performance* addresses issues of performance in complex tasks, it does not necessarily aim its findings toward the production of better systems.

Our review focuses on the trends in engineering psychology that have emerged since Alluisi & Morgan's (1976) comprehensive review. Four major factors have produced these trends.

First, the last 15 years have seen major advances in cognitive psychology, which are finding their way into engineering-design applications. The term cognitive engineering has been proposed to describe these applications, while DeGreen (1980) has forcefully argued that the major focus of engineering psychology research must shift from sensory-motor concerns to cognitive factors. Recently the field has seen the incorporation of cognitive concepts such as attention allocation and internal models (Pew & Baron 1978, Sheridan 1981, Rasmussen 1983) into fairly rigorous engineering models of manual and process control.

Second, the revolution in computer technology has produced exponential growth in the frequency with which humans interact with computers. This growth has spawned a concomitant increase in the application of engineering psychology to human-computer interaction.

Third, computers are becoming more capable of taking over tasks once assigned to humans. Besides forcing a rethinking of the classical "allocation of function" (Eason 1980, Hart & Sheridan 1984), the resulting automation has gradually changed the roles of human operators. In many systems, humans were once active controllers and responders, bearing a heavy physical workload. Now they are becoming instead monitors and supervisors of such complex semiautomated systems as nuclear power plants and computerized manufacturing systems. Such environments impose their greatest demands on perception and attention, with critical skills of decision making and diagnosis required when automation fails. Such a trend is reflected in two important NATO-sponsored workshops, which resulted in *Monitoring Behavior and Supervisory Control* (Sheridan & Johannsen 1976) and *Detection and Diagnosis of System Failures* (Rasmussen & Rouse 1981).

Finally, the disaster at the Three Mile Island nuclear power plant (Rubenstein & Mason 1979) has directed attention to the human factors issues in the nuclear power industry. It has also made more relevant in this country the engineering psychology research on the process control industry, which was more visible in Europe during the 1970s. This interest in monitoring, supervising, and fault diagnosis in complex, heavily automated, and slowly responding systems involves all three areas mentioned above.

SCOPE AND LIMITS OF THE REVIEW

In this review we emphasize: the cognitive aspects of engineering psychology (perception, decision making, attention), issues in human-computer interaction, process control, and automation. Owing to length limitations we must neglect other research within or close to the purview of engineering psychology. Many of these areas have been addressed in special issues of *Human Factors* or *Ergonomics,* including the effects of stressors, individual differences and selection, safety research, highway transportation (*Human Factors,* Dec. 1976), aging (*Human Factors,* Feb. 1981), the handicapped (*Human Factors,* June 1978; *Ergonomics,* Nov. 1981), research methodology (*Human Factors,* June 1977), and training (*Human Factors,* April 1978).

APPROACH

The interface between humans and machines can be addressed from two different perspectives. From the viewpoint of the human factors engineer, the *systems* perspective focuses on a system (e.g. an aircraft) or a task (e.g. debugging a computer program) as a starting point and brings to bear all the human performance data that may be relevant, no matter how diverse the mental or physical operations involved. From the viewpoint of the experimental/cognitive psychologist, the *human performance* perspective models different mental operations, stages, or processes in human performance (e.g. decision making, recognition, motor control) independently of any specific physical system.

During the last decade research efforts on both sides have sought to fuse the two approaches. Human factors engineers have focused on specific component processes, while human performance researchers have examined these component processes within the framework of real-world tasks. Our review, however, still reflects the dichotomy to some degree. We adopt as a framework Wickens's (1984) model of human information processing, in which information is first perceived (detected and recognized), decisions are made on the basis of that information (relying upon working memory if necessary), and then responses are selected and executed. All of these processes depend to some extent upon the human's limited attentional resources. In the first section of this review we consider the investigation of each of these stages and the application of research to particular systems problems. In the second half of the review we discuss research more directly from the systems framework, as both the research and the tasks involved encompass all phases of human information processing, including human-computer interaction, process control, and automation.

A number of books address problems of engineering psychology from a human information processing framework. Some emphasize the human information processing perspective (i.e. Welford 1976, Anderson 1979, Lachman et al 1979, Holding 1981); some stress the systems and human factors perspective (Bailey 1982, McCormick & Sanders 1982, Kantowitz & Sorkin 1983); and some fall in between (Sheridan & Ferrell 1974, Underwood 1978, Wickens 1984). Sheridan & Ferrell's book has a heavy mathematical flavor, while Wickens' book adopts a framework similar to that presented below for organizing research on human information processing limits and their implications for system design.

HUMAN PERFORMANCE LIMITS

Perception

DETECTION   Engineering psychology research in this area has been heavily vision-oriented, with major research trends in two closely related areas: vigilance and visual search. The topic of human vigilance—why people fail to detect sometimes salient visual events after a long watch period—has been at the forefront of research during the past 20 years. While the intensity of research has declined somewhat, the subject still receives scrutiny. Methodological questions related both to dependent variables (e.g. Craig 1979, Long & Waag 1981) and to experimental artifacts (Craig 1978), as well as experimental questions regarding the detection of multiple targets (Craig 1981), redundancy of signal representation (Colquhoun 1975), and the role of working memory (Parasuraman 1979), have been investigated. Murrell (1977) has considered machine aids in vigilance, while Parasuraman's (1979) paper reflects an important new effort to account for the vigilance decrement in terms of working memory deficits. Books by Mackie (1977) and Davies & Parasuraman (1980) summarize much of the recent research in the field.

Unfortunately, much of this research has still failed to clarify how relevant the phenomena examined in the laboratory are to real-world vigilance problems. Both Ruffle-Smith (1979) and Lees & Sayers (1976) have addressed vigilance more directly from the complex perspectives of the aviation environment and the nuclear process control room, respectively. Sheridan & Johannsen's (1976) book, *Monitoring Behavior and Supervisory Control,* integrating the papers of a NATO conference, extends classic vigilance research to the general environment faced by the supervisor/monitor of the nuclear power reactor. Here an operator monitors a complex system, interacting little with it until the infrequent events occur that must be detected, diagnosed, and acted upon.

Visual search differs from vigilance by involving the important element of stimulus location within the visual field. Two contexts—that of the industrial inspector and of the Air Force pilot—have been thoroughly investigated. Excellent work on the former has been carried out by Drury and his associates [as reviewed in Drury (1982)]. In this research, fruitful models predicting the latency and accuracy of the detection of flaws in industrial products like sheet metal have been proposed, and experimental variables have been examined related to the effect of multiple targets on search performance (Morowski et al 1980), the influence of different training programs (Czaja & Drury 1981) and display aids (Liuzzo & Drury 1980), and the merits of human versus machine inspection (Drury & Sinclair 1983).

Recent research on airborne visual search also attempts to derive predictive models of the search time and accuracy of an airborne observer spotting a terrestrial or flying target. In formulating these models, researchers are recognizing the importance of such cognitive factors as expectancy and target uncertainty, as well as such physical ones as intensity and acuity (Greening 1976). The entire June 1979 issue of *Human Factors* is devoted to visual search and target acquisition. In this issue, Teichner & Mocharnuk (1979) present a valuable overview and summary of existing models.

Finally, signal detection theory remains a strong and healthy tool, applicable to a diverse array of detection problems. The theory's ever-critical distinction between sensitivity and response bias and the variables that influence each has proved useful not only to work on vigilance and search, but also to that on an air traffic controller's detection of impending collisions (Bisseret 1981), a pilot's detection of air targets (Gai & Curry 1978), polygraph lie detection (Ben-Shakhar et al 1982), eyewitness testimony in criminal proceedings (Malpass & Devine 1981), and medical detection and diagnosis (Swennsen et al 1977). Swets & Pickett (1982) offer an excellent overview of these applications of signal detection theory, with strong emphasis on the medical field.

DISPLAY CONCEPTS AND MEMORY   Rapid advances in computers and display technology have made a host of new display concepts available for presenting complex information to the human operator. More research is urgently needed on how this technology can best exploit the strengths and avoid the weaknesses of human perceptual and cognitive processing. Critical reports have examined the roles of color (Christ 1975, Christ & Corso 1983), three-dimensional graphics (Getty 1982), "holistic" object-like displays (Jacob et al 1976, Goodstein 1981, Woods et al 1981, Wickens 1984), "face" displays (Jacob et al 1976), synthetic voice displays (Nakatani & O'Conner 1980, Simpson & Williams 1980, Luce et al 1983, McCauley 1984, Wickens et al 1983b, 1984), and integrated computer graphics (Goodstein 1981, Mitchell & Miller 1983).

Unfortunately, new display technologies may be implemented without theory-based empirical guidelines having been developed to indicate when they are more and less useful. Such guidelines should be based in part upon the working memory demands of the task and the integrative power of the display. For example, Wickens et al (1983b, 1984) have attempted to provide such guidelines on the appropriateness of speech displays to tasks involving a continuum of working memory operations from the spatial to the verbal. These investigators propose that verbal tasks are better served than spatial ones by speech displays. Predictive displays are most successful in decreasing the working memory demanded by the mental processes of prediction (Wickens 1984). The utility of such displays has been demonstrated in the contexts of aviation (Grunwald & Merhav 1978, Jensen 1981), air traffic control (Whitfield et al 1980), industrial scheduling (Smith & Crabtree 1975, Gibson & Liaos 1978, Liaos 1978, Mitchell & Miller 1983), and process control (West & Clark 1974, Sheridan 1981).

Two additional areas of engineering psychology research have integrated perceptual and memory processes:

1. Several investigators have compared the efficacy of verbal instructions with that of pictures and flowcharts in instruction (e.g. Booher 1975, Kamman 1975, Krohn 1983), and in assisting computer programming or fault diagnosis tasks (Ramsey et al 1978, Brooke & Duncan 1980a,b; see the section below on Human–Computer Interaction). A redundant combination of both formats consistently provides more effective performance than either alone. Fitter & Green (1979) offer an excellent discussion of the use of pictures and diagrams in computer systems. They argue for the benefits of redundancy and discuss what makes graphics and flowcharts effective supplements to printed instructions.

2. A recent interest has developed in the role of *spatial cognition* in constructing maps and other navigational aids. Relevant here is fundamental research in the human factors of map layout (e.g. Potash, 1977, Noyes 1980) and the optimal format for conveying geographical information to suit specific tasks. Is it better to use maps or verbal "route lists" (Bartram 1980), or to use map study or navigation through an area (simulated or actual) to learn its geographical features (Goldin & Thorndyke 1982, Thorndyke & Hayes-Roth 1982)? What distortions of spatial cognition are imposed by the limitations of human memory, and how do they affect the performance of geographical/navigational tasks (Howard & Kerst 1981, Tversky 1981)? Thorndyke's research addresses these questions within the framework of a three-phase model describing the acquisition of geographical knowledge (Thorndyke & Hayes-Roth 1982). First, *landmark knowledge* (visual images of major landmarks) is attained. *Route-knowledge* is developed next, enabling navigation from place to place. Finally, at the most abstract level, *survey knowledge* typifies the true "cognitive" map of an area.

Response Process

Two research areas relevant to the selection and execution of responses are currently important: voice control and models of manual control.

VOICE CONTROL   Advances in speech recognition technology have made feasible voice control of, or voice interaction with, inanimate systems. Lea (1980) offers a good overview of issues in this area, and McCauley (1984), along with several papers in the 1982 and 1983 *Proceedings of the Human Factors Society Annual Meeting,* describes guidelines for task interfacing with speech control. The use of speech control in severe environments has also been discussed (National Research Council 1984). Speech control can improve performance in environments when the hands are already busy with other tasks (Wickens 1980, Wickens et al 1983b), but beyond this no strong guidelines are available to indicate which tasks are best and worst suited to voice control. Wickens et al (1983b, 1984) have found that inherently verbal tasks are better suited for voice control. Ballantine (1980) discusses the use of voice channels in human–computer interactions, while Gould & Boies (1978) compare the advantages of voice and writing as means of creating text.

MANUAL CONTROL AND AVIATION   The study of manual control and tracking has always been a cornerstone of engineering psychology, and the last decade has seen a continuation of interest in how people control aircraft, automobiles, and ships. Poulton's (1974) book summarizes much of the prior research in this area, while various volumes of the NASA-sponsored *Annual Conference on Manual Control* provide current compendia of research papers. Basic laboratory research in manual control has evolved from an interest in the human as an error nullifying compensatory tracker, to a consideration of the "four Ps": pursuit, prediction, preview, and precognition. Thus, recent investigations have examined *predictive* displays (Grunwald & Merhav 1978, Jensen 1981); *preview* and *precognitive* tracking, in which the human can either see ahead of time or has stored in memory the course to be tracked (Pew 1974, Kleinman et al 1980, McRuer 1980, Hess 1981b); and *pursuit* tracking, where the target can be pursued directly in an "open-loop" rather than a compensatorily error-correcting fashion (Hess 1981b). The differences between compensatory, pursuit, and predictive tracking in the context of aviation displays are coherently addressed by Roscoe et al (1981).

Manual control research continues to focus on modeling. McRuer (1980) surveys and contrasts two of the most successful approaches: (*a*) the classical "crossover" model, based upon linear feedback control theory (Wickens & Gopher 1977), and (*b*) the more recently developed "optimal control" model, which is both more mathematical than the crossover model and more attuned to human cognitive processes and limitations (see Pew & Baron 1978 for an intuitive overview of this model). A series of articles in the special August and October 1977 issues of *Human Factors* describe the use of these models to predict control performance and guide display design in aviation, automobile driving, target acquisition, and ship control. Intensive modeling efforts have been devoted to the first two areas. A series of studies (e.g. McRuer et al 1975, Donges 1978, Reid et al 1981b) have modeled the automobile driving process. Meanwhile, the optimal control model has been applied by Hess (1981a) to the design of flight director displays, by Baron & Levison (1975) to the design of flight attitude displays, by Stengel & Broussard (1978) to predict aircraft handling qualities and stability problems, and by Bergman (1976) and Merhav & Ben Ya'acov (1976) to design more effective flight controls.

Manual control is not the only component of the processing demands made on the pilot. A number of investigators have called attention to the more decisional/cognitive characteristics of aviation. Johannsen & Rouse (1979) offer a framework for developing more complex models of the control, planning, and decisional processes, while Govinderaj & Rouse (1981) model the time-sharing between discrete and continuous aviation tasks typical of air transport carriers. Johannsen & Rouse (1983) address the critical issue of *planning* in aviation, and Jensen (1982) reviews the literature on pilot judgment and decision making. Finally, we note five interesting and integrative treatments of human performance in aviation: Roscoe's (1981) textbook on aviation psychology, Hurst's (1976) fascinating book on *Pilot Error,* Wiener & Curry's (1980) critical discussion of flight deck automation, the October and December 1980 special issues of *Human Factors,* devoted to research and analysis of air traffic control, and the December 1984 special issue of *Human Factors,* devoted to aviation psychology. All five of these do a good job of integrating analysis of task demands with experimental research on the basic limits of human performance.

Attention

The properties and limits of human attention have been examined and applied to system design questions with increasing frequency in recent years. Designers have begun to realize that many systems impose more monitoring and processing demands on the operator than his attentional resources can meet. The recent volume edited by Parasuraman & Davies (1984) offers an excellent perspective on the current status of attention research and theory, while Wickens's (1984) two chapters on the topic specify four areas where attention research has been applied: selective attention, task configuration, individual differences, and workload.

SELECTIVE ATTENTION   Engineers are currently interested in models of the attention selection process. How does the operator choose which of a vast array of instruments or tasks to observe or perform at a given time? A good portion of Sheridan & Johannsen's (1976) book is devoted to this question, and Moray presents highly readable discussions of the issues both in general (1979) and in the context of the process control environment (1981).

More specific quantitative models of the attention allocation process have been developed by Walden & Rouse (1978) based on cueing theory, by Tulga & Sheridan (1980) based upon dynamic programming, and by Pattipati et al (1982) based upon the optimal control model. These efforts examine performance in terms of how humans depart from optimal attention control. Research on the limits of selective attention has been applied to analysis of the processing of information in television ads (Warshaw 1978), to the perception of important and irrelevant details by eyewitnesses viewing crimes (Wells & Leippe 1981), and to the detection of objects outside the cockpit through "heads-up" aviation displays (Fischer et al 1980).

ATTENTION AND TASK CONFIGURATION   In 1979 Navon & Gopher proposed that humans have several types of attention—they referred to these as multiple resources—and that tasks requiring different resources are more efficiently time-shared than tasks imposing their demands on the same resource. Wickens and his colleagues (Wickens et al 1981, 1983b) have examined the implications of this view for configuring complex multitask environments to distribute demands across, rather than focussing demands within, resources. For example, if audition and vision employ different perceptual resources, and speech and manual control depend on different response resources, then the use of auditory displays and speech control in otherwise heavy visual-manual environments may increase operator efficacy (Hammerton 1975, McLeod 1977, Wickens 1980, Wickens et al 1981, 1983b). The distribution of demands across other dimensions defining separate resources may have a similar effect. For example, since spatial and verbal tasks may require different resources, asking an operator to perform two spatial tracking tasks will produce poorer time-sharing than the concurrent performance of a tracking with a verbal task (Wickens et al 1983b).

INDIVIDUAL DIFFERENCES AND LEARNING   Why do some people perform complex tasks better than others? The difference may derive from a difference in time-sharing capability, either inherent or developed through practice and training. The search for a "general" stable time-sharing ability that differentiates people across diverse multitask situations has generally produced more failures (Jennings & Chiles 1977, Wickens et al 1981) than successes (Sverko et al 1983). On the other hand, people may differ in terms of time-sharing abilities relevant to specific dual-task environments [e.g. time-sharing of two discrete keypress tasks, or dual-axis tracking (Damos, Smist & Bittner 1983)]. Specific attentional skills assessed in "pure" laboratory environments appear to predict performance in more complex multitask environments (Fournier & Stager 1976, North & Gopher 1976, Gopher 1982). Time-sharing performance increases as people practice in a dual-task environment (Gopher & North 1977, Damos & Wickens 1980) or as expert pilots are compared with novices (Damos 1978, Crosby & Parkinson 1979). Many of these differences result from increased automaticity (decreased resourse demand) of the single-task components, in addition to the development of time-sharing skill (Damos & Wickens 1980).

WORKLOAD   The metaphor of attention as a limited commodity or set of resources underlies the concept of *mental workload,* one of the most prolific research areas in the last decade. The study of mental workload has been to the 1970s and early 1980s what research on the topic of vigilance was to the 1960s. Hundreds of empirical and theoretical articles on the subject have appeared in the last ten years, and mental workload has been the main topic or at least a major issue at several recent conferences [e.g. the NATO Conference on Mental Workload (1977), the NASA/Industry Workshop on Flight Deck Automation (1980), the USAF Workshop on Flight Testing to Identify Pilot Workload and Pilot Dynamics (1983), and the First Annual Conference on Mental Workload (1984)].

The definition of mental workload remains somewhat uncertain, though there seems to be agreement on what mental workload is not: It cannot be represented as a scalar but instead is best viewed as a multidimensional construct that includes behavioral, physiological, and subjective aspects (Le-Plat 1978, Johannsen et al 1979, Wickens 1979, Williges & Wierwille 1979, Eggemeier 1980, Kramer et al 1983).

The equivocal nature of the concept of mental workload is perhaps best illustrated by a survey of theoretical and empirical definitions found in the literature. Mental workload has been equated with the arousal level of the operator (Wierwille 1979); defined as a person's subjective experience of cognitive effort (Sheridan 1980); measured as the time taken to perform a task (Welford 1978); and conceptualized as the demands imposed upon the limited information-processing capabilities of the human operator (Wickens 1979). Several literature reviews also illustrate the equivocal nature of the concept of mental workload. Rolfe (1971), Brown (1978) and Ogden et al (1979) review some of the applications of dual-task techniques. Reviews by Roscoe (1978) and Wierwille (1979) are concerned solely with physiological measures. Ellis (1978), Borg (1978), and Moray (1982) concentrate on subjective measures of mental workload. Chiles (1978) and Williges & Wierwille (1979) review the behavioral techniques. That so many measurement techniques are available implies a diversity of definitions.

Such measurement techniques can be classified as: primary task measures, secondary task indexes, subjective techniques, and physiological measurements.

Primary task measures equate mental workload with performance on a single task. It is assumed that increasing the difficulty of a task will decrease the operator's performance (Hurst & Rose 1978, Wierwille & Gutmann 1978, Hicks & Wierwille 1979, Wierwille & Connor 1983). The primary task measure provides high face validity as a workload metric, does not impose additional demands on the operator, and is relatively simple to apply in operational environments. Furthermore, generic categories of task variables can be tabulated and used to predict drops in primary task performance (Johannsen et al 1979). Although primary task measures provide a reliable index of performance it is difficult to say precisely how primary task difficulty influences workload. For example, two subjects may produce the same performance scores with a different investment of resources. A second shortcoming of the primary task method of workload assessment is the difficulty of generalizing or equating the workload effects across different primary tasks.

Secondary tasks   The importance of the secondary task workload methodology is illustrated by the numerous critical reviews and research articles devoted to the topic (Brown 1978, Ogden et al 1979, Pew 1979, Williges & Wierwille 1979). The several variants of the secondary task method all require subjects to perform two tasks concurrently. One task is usually designated as primary, the other as secondary. Subjects are instructed to protect their performance on the primary task by allocating sufficient resources. Increases in the difficulty of the primary task are presumed to decrease performance on the secondary task from its single task level. Hence, workload or inferred resource demands of different primary tasks may be compared. The major disadvantage of the secondary task technique is its intrusion on primary task performance. Commonly used secondary tasks include active and retrospective time estimation (Hart 1975, Wierwille & Conner 1983); tracking (Jex & Clement 1979, Wickens & Kessel 1979, Burke et al 1980); memory and classification tasks (Crosby & Parkinson 1979, Logan 1979, Schiflett 1980); monitoring (Becker 1976), probe reaction time (McLeod 1978); and random digit generation (Zeitlin & Finkelman 1975, Savage et al 1978).

Recent conceptualizations of mental workload have suggested that two tasks can be time-shared successfully to the extent that they require separate types of processing resources (Kinsbourne & Hicks 1978, Freidman & Polson 1981). Wickens (1980) has proposed that resources may be represented by three dimensions: stages of processing (perceptual/cognitive and response stages), modalities of processing (auditory and visual), and codes of processing (spatial and verbal). This theoretical approach in conjunction with empirical validation has increased the predictive power of the secondary-task technique, by allowing the practitioner to choose secondary tasks that have the same resource demands as primary tasks (Wickens & Kessel 1979, Isreal et al 1980a,b).

Subjective measures   Several new or modified scales have been developed for subjective rating of mental workload. Wierwille & Casali (1983) modified the Cooper-Harper scale of Aircraft Handling Quality to assess perceptual, cognitive, and communication load. Ratings based on this scale varied systematically with task difficulty in three separate experiments. Sheridan (1980) has proposed that the subjective experience of mental workload comprises three dimensions (see also Sheridan & Simpson 1979): the time stress of the task, the amount of mental effort invested in the task, and the psychological/emotional stress imposed upon the subject by the task. Reid et al (1981a) employed conjoint analysis to derive a scale based on these three dimensions. Subjects were able to rate tasks along the three dimensions. At present, however, both the independence of the dimensions and the percentage of variance in the subjective experience of mental workload accounted for by the scale appear uncertain (Boyd 1983). A theoretically based approach to the assessment of the subjective aspects of mental workload has also been proposed (Derrick 1983). Subjects performed four tasks, singly and in all four pairwise combinations. The tasks were selected on the basis of their resource requirements, as suggested by multiple resource theory (Wickens 1980, 1984). A multidimensional scaling analysis of the subjective data produced three dimensions. The dimensions presumed to underlie the subjective difficulty ratings related to the competition for resources of the dual-task pairs, the adequacy of feedback, and a measure of heart-rate variability that appears to index the total resource demands. Recent innovations in the methodology of subjective workload assessment have produced potentially useful measurement devices. However, these scales require further validation in terms of their correspondence to other methods of workload assessment (Wickens & Yeh 1983).

Physiological techniques   The major advantage of physiological workload assessment techniques is their relative lack of intrusion on primary-task performance. Since excellent reviews of these techniques are available, only a few are discussed here (Roscoe 1978, Wierwille 1979). Physiological workload assessment techniques are of two types: those sensitive to overall workload, and those reflecting one aspect of mental workload. Pupil diameter correlates highly with many different cognitive tasks (Beatty 1982). Similarly, heart-rate variability is systematically influenced by various task manipulations (Mulder & Mulder 1981, Sharit & Salvendy 1982). The P300 component of the

event-related brain potential appears to index the perceptual/cognitive processing demands of a task while being relatively insensitive to the manipulation of
response load (Isreal et al 1980a,b, Natani & Gomer 1981, Donchin et al 1982,
Kramer et al 1983). Furthermore, the P300 can provide a measure of the
resource trade-offs between two concurrently performed tasks (Wickens et al
1983a). Although physiological measures provide a continuous and relatively
unobtrusive measure of workload, their cost and artifact problems preclude
their use in some operational settings. These technological disadvantages
should be solved in the near future.

Strategies and dissociation   Research in the workload area is beginning to
investigate what happens when workload measures *dissociate* (Wickens & Yeh
1983)—e.g. when two tasks are compared and one produces both better
primary task performance and higher ratings of subjective difficulty. Examples
such as these of lack of agreement between workload measures call for a better
understanding of the information processing mechanisms that "drive" different
indexes (Wickens & Yeh 1983).

The investigation of the strategy changes subjects invoke to cope with high
workloads has produced interesting findings in both operational and laboratory
tasks. In a series of field studies Sperandio (1978) observed the performance of
air traffic controllers under different workload levels. As the workload increased, air traffic controllers gradually shifted their attention to fewer and
presumably more important operational objectives. Under low workload, controllers can monitor several objectives, such as collision avoidance, rate of
progress of aircraft through the system, choice of the shortest flight paths for
economy of time and fuel, and the preferred altitudes of pilots. Under high
workload, however, controllers shift to the primary objective of collision
avoidance. Welford (1978) has suggested that at least three different types of
strategies may prove useful in dealing with high workloads: (*a*) perceptual
coding and motor programming, (*b*) methods of search, and (*c*) balancing
conflicting factors (e.g. speed and accuracy, or errors of ommission and
commission). The selection and implementation of effective and economical
strategies to cope with high workloads may be a useful indicator of a highly
skilled operator (Bainbridge 1978, Rasmussen 1981).

Decision Making

Two major causes account for the increasing concern in the last decade with
decision making in human–systems interactions. First, greater system complexity and automation require operators to integrate massive amounts of
information and make decisions. Second, cognitive psychology has advanced
beyond the classical view of the human as a normative decision maker (a view
that dominated the 1950s and 1960s) to a consideration of how limitations on

human attention and memory affect decision making, forcing humans to employ decision making *heuristics* (Tversky & Kahneman 1974, Slovic et al 1977, Einhorn & Hogarth 1981, Kahneman et al 1982). Slovic et al's (1977) review of the decision-making literature provides an overview of the contrast between these two approaches.

DECISION AIDS   Classical decision theory has had its greatest impact on engineering psychology in the area of *decision aids*, which offer a methodology and framework for breaking the global decision problem down into its basic elements—what Slovic et al (1977) call the "divide and conquer" strategy. Two related applications have proven particularly fruitful in decision aiding: decision tree analysis and multiattribute utility theory. Decision tree analysis—a procedure for choosing courses of action given problabistic estimates of the state-of-the-world and utilities assigned to different outcomes—is clearly outlined in the *Handbook for Decision Analysis* (Barclay et al 1977). Steeb & Johnston (1981) offer a computer-based system to aid group decision making within this framework, while Fischoff et al (1979a) examines the cognitive processing involved in using decision trees.

In multiattribute utility theory (MAU), the choice of a course of action, or object is supposed to be facilitated by an analysis of the attributes and relative importance of all competing alternatives. The special May 1977 issue of *IEEE Transactions on Systems, Man, and Cybernetics* was devoted to decision processes. It contains several examples of the MAU approach, including Edwards's (1977) overview of the technique and the description and validation by Weisbroad et al (1977) of an adaptive decision-aiding system employing MAU that models humans' utilities for different information sources on-line. Steeb (1980) applies the same procedures to the decision-making problem facing a supervisor of remotely controlled vehicles.

Other investigations have shown the advantage of MAU over "holistic" decision making in apartment selection (Pitz et al 1980), credit application evaluation (Stillwell et al 1983), energy policy development (Keeney 1977), and government research program evaluation (Edwards 1977). A related approach focuses more directly on the appropriate methodology for assessing the utilities employed in MAU (Edwards 1977, Keeney 1977, Beach & Barnes 1983). An overview of decision-aiding procedures that may be used in information systems is presented by Sage (1981), while Wohl (1981) has discusses the role of decision aids in Air Force command and control environments.

HEURISTICS AND COGNITIVE LIMITS   Tversky & Kahneman's (1974) influential article on decision-making heuristics has generated a wave of research and theory on the decision-making process from a "non-classical" perspective. Such work examines non-optimal decision making in terms of fundamental limitations on human memory and attention (Wickens 1984). Wallsten's (1980) edited volume contains good overviews of these limitations and biases in the decision-making process.

Specific information-processing limitations affect decision making in such areas as seeking out information sources (Payne 1980), properly combining base-rate frequency information with new data in diagnosis (Carroll & Siegler 1977, Fischoff et al 1979b, Edgell & Hennessey 1980, Christenssen-Szalanski & Bushyhead 1981), changing hypotheses on the basis of new data (Arkes et al 1981, Einhorn & Hogarth 1981, 1982, Schustack & Sternberg 1981), generating diagnostic hypotheses to test (Gettys & Fisher 1978, Rasmussen 1981, Mehle 1982), integrating information concerning data reliability with the data itself (Schum 1975, 1980, Lindsay et al 1981), using negative diagnostic evidence (Balla 1980, Rouse & Hunt 1984), and revising the rules for decision making on the basis of incorrect outcomes (Einhorn & Hogarth 1978, Brehmer 1981). Many of these limitations have been identified in laboratory investigations; but psychologists and decision theorists can also demonstrate their presence outside the lab in such fields as medicine, criminal justice, and equipment troubleshooting.

APPLICATIONS TO CRIMINAL JUSTICE AND FORECASTING   Books by Ellison & Buckhout (1981) and Loftus (1979) comprehensively cover applications of decision theory to the legal field. Ebbeson & Konecki's (1980) chapter surveys applications of this research to judicial decisions concerning parole and sentence setting. One productive approach has examined biases in eyewitness testimony. Some of this research has focused directly on the factors that affect the initial perceptions accuracy—for example, physical conditions, number of people involved, or time of day (e.g. Tickner & Poulton 1975), whether the crime was violent or not (Clifford & Hollin 1981), or whether many irrelevant details were perceived (Wells & Leippe 1981). Other studies have examined the influence of memory distortions on later accuracy of recall (Loftus 1979, 1980, Malpass & Devine 1981), focusing on biases imposed by events occurring between the crime and the testimony (Gorenstein & Ellsworth 1980) and studying how initial accuracy can be restored (Malpass & Devine 1981).

Schum (1975, 1980) has presented a formal model for how reliability information should be integrated. Others have noted that the eyewitness's asserted confidence seems unrelated to the accuracy of recall (Leippe et al 1978, Lindsay et al 1981), a tendency that is more pronounced with violent than with nonviolent incidents (Clifford & Hollin 1981). Some studies have employed mock jurors who interrogate the eyewitness. Such jurors are relatively insensitive to discrepancies between the witness's claims to reliability and his testimony's actual accuracy (Schum 1975, Lindsay et al 1981). Loftus (1980) has found that exposure to expert testimony on the unreliability of eyewitnesses can somewhat improve jurors' sensitivity to witness bias.

The relation between confidence and accuracy has also been examined in studies of forecasting (Murphy & Winkler 1974, Fischoff & MacGregor 1981). *Overconfidence* in forecasting occurs when the probability that a forecast will turn out to be correct is considerably less than the prior expression of confidence in the forecast. Finally, Fischoff & MacGregor (1981) have examined techniques for improving forecasting, including feedback about overconfident forecasts and prescriptions to be cautious.

Causal Inference and Diagnosis in Medicine and Troubleshooting

How well do humans (*a*) predict symptoms from known causes and (*b*) diagnose causes from known symptoms? Much of the human engineering work in these areas is either basic research on human biases, research applied to medical diagnosis, or the application of knowledge to equipment troubleshooting.

Einhorn & Hogarth (1982, 1983) have integrated their research on how humans infer causality into a theory identifying the factors that induce spurious perceptions of causal relations—e.g. the contiguity of two events in time and space. The excellent collection of readings edited by Kahneman et al (1982) devotes four papers to the inference of causality. In one, Tversky & Kahneman describe a human bias toward causal rather than diagnostic inference (but see Burns & Pearl 1981). Perhaps the most integrative treatment of diagnosis in applied contexts appears in Rasmussen & Rouse's (1981) *Human Detection and Diagnosis of System Failures*, summarizing the proceedings of a 1980 conference on that topic.

Specific applications of decision theory to medical decision making have taken several forms. Signal detection theory has been used to model the detection of tumors and other abnormalities (Lusted 1976, Swennsen et al 1977). Investigators have studied the use or disuse of disease prevalence rate information in medical diagnosis (Lusted 1976, Balla 1980, Christenssen-Szalanski & Bushyhead 1981, Christenssen-Szalanski & Beach 1982), and the influence of overconfidence and poor feedback on physician's diagnostic ability (Arkes et al 1981, Brehmer 1981). Eddy (1982) addresses the influence of confusions between causal inference (probability of symptoms given a disease) and diagnostic inference (probability of disease given the symptoms) on the diagnosis and treatment of breast cancer. The book edited by Dombal & Grevy (1976) summarizes research and theory concerning medical decision making, while Fitter & Cruickshank (1983) offer explicit guidelines for the use of computers in the decision making process.

In an integrated program of research, Rouse and his colleagues (Rouse

1979a,b, Rouse & Rouse 1979, Hunt & Rouse 1981, Johnson & Rouse 1982b, Rouse & Hunt 1984) have examined the nature of human troubleshooting abilities. Experimental results have been obtained both in a generic or "context-free" network of nodes and logical operations known as *TASK* (Rouse 1979a,b,) and in simulations of more context-specific environments related to identifiable systems (Hunt & Rouse 1981, Johnson & Rouse 1982b). These investigations have explored the use of non-optimal tests and the effects of system complexity, computer aiding, and forced-pacing on the process of fault location. Findings of these studies reviewed by Rouse (1981a) and Rouse & Hunt (1984), indicate that the human is good at recognizing familiar patterns of symptoms in context-specific environments but often neglects to use evidence about healthy components to limit the possible alternatives. Troubleshooting aids that unburden memory by keeping track of test outcomes seem particularly helpful in diagnostic tasks.

How well can troubleshooting skills acquired in context-free training be transferred to context-specific environments? Rouse notes positive transfer to diagnosis of both aircraft power plant failures (Johnson & Rouse 1982b) and automotive failures (Hunt & Rouse 1981). Johnson & Rouse (1982b) demonstrate the advantage of incorporating generic troubleshooting training with conventional video instruction. Brooke & Duncan (1983) also describe generic trainers for use in troubleshooting.

Efforts have also been made to model both the troubleshooting task and the performance of the human operator. Rouse & Rouse (1979) and Wohl (1983) have attempted to model the complexity of troubleshooting problems in a manner that can predict both the time to identify failures (Wohl 1983) and the qualitative nature of tests and actions taken (Rouse 1979b). According to Wohl's data, the distribution of repair time is accurately predicted by the complexity of component interrelations. Here the upper bound to repair time seems to be predicted by the limits of human working memory (7 ± 2 chunks). Since the computer, unlike the human designer, is not constrained by these limits in conceptualizing a system, Wohl worries that "unsolvable" diagnostic problems may become more prevalent as computers design more complex circuitry.

Wohl's model takes into account Rasmussen's distinction (1981; Rasmussen & Jensen 1974) between "S-rules" and "T-rules" in troubleshooting. S-rules involve familiar patterns of symptoms that automatically trigger the appropriate fault category by a pattern recognition procedure. T-rules, used when S-rules fail, require systematic, attention-demanding applications of sequential tests. S-rules tend to be context-specific; T-rules are context-free.

Other important work in troubleshooting and diagnosis has addressed the role of familiarity and memory in diagnosing circuit wiring problems (Egan & Schwartz 1979), the role of hypothesis generation in the diagnostic process

(Gettys & Fisher 1978, Mehle 1982), the reluctance of diagnosticians to revise or change diagnostic hypotheses on the basis of contradictory data (Rasmussen 1981, Einhorn & Hogarth 1982), the limiting role of working memory in constraining the tests made in electronics troubleshooting (Rasmussen & Jensen 1974), and the incorporation of time and expected cost into a model predicting the selection of different problem-solving or troubleshooting strategies (Smith et al 1982). Bond's (1981) discussion of troubleshooting in the computer industry focuses less on human limitations as the cause of diagnostic failures and more on the avoidance of such failures by a profit-oriented industry attentive to its customers' desire for equipment easy to troubleshoot.

Errors and Internal Models in Human Performance

ERRORS   Before turning to research on specific systems, a word should be said concerning the dependent variables used in human performance research. In much of this research, processing latency has been viewed as the primary dependent variable of interest. Error has been seen as a "nuisance variable" to be kept low and constant across conditions, or as a variable to be converted to percentage scores or transmitted information, as a second indicator of performance. While some recent work treats the systematic relation between error rate and latency—the so-called speed-accuracy trade-off—(see Pachella 1974 and Wickelgren 1977 for overviews), a growing number of studies examine the nature of human error per se. Rouse & Rouse (1983b) have distinguished two approaches to human error:

1. The probabilistic approach is typified by the work on human reliability analysis, applied by Swain (1977, Swain & Guttman 1980) to the nuclear power plant environment. Swain attempts to combine task-specific human error probabilities with machine error probabilities to derive measures of total system reliability. Adams (1982) has pointed out the current constraints and limitations of this potentially useful technique.

2. The second approach views errors as caused by breakdowns in the natural course of human information processing. Much of this work follows from the classic analysis of aircraft errors by Fitts & Jones (1961). An integrative overview by Norman (1981a,b) distinguished errors occurring early from those occurring late in the processing sequence and provides numerous anectdotal examples, as does Reason (1984). Roberts et al (1980) have used multi-dimensional clustering techniques to categorize errors of the P-3 pilot into those of judgment, oversight, and skills. Rouse & Rouse (1983a) have presented a more elaborate error classification and analysis methodology that considers errors in terms of several different stages of information processing, with different contributing causes at each stage. Johnson & Rouse (1982a) applied

this scheme to the analysis of troubleshooting errors made by maintenance trainees. McRuer et al (1981) have offered a similar information processing framework for errors in manual control tasks, while Fegetter (1982) presents a methodology for collecting and analyzing errors in aviation. More specific analysis of error data has been undertaken by Roberts et al (1980) in the task of the P-3 pilot, by Brooke & Duncan (1980a) for fault diagnosis, and by Van Es (1976) and Rabbitt (1978) in keying tasks. Both of the latter investigators point to the prevalence of errors of response selection and execution (the right intention but the wrong response) and to the efficiency with which they may be monitored and corrected, provided they are not indelibly transmitted to the system.

Beyond the obvious catastrophies that sometimes result from human error, Rouse & Rouse (1983b) propose two further reasons for interest in the topic: Understanding the nature and causes of error can lead to effective redesign of systems and can guide the training of human operators. The kinds of mistakes humans make when interacting with systems can also offer insight into the nature of the human's internal model of the system.

INTERNAL MODELS   Engineering interest in the concept of an internal model is a result of the growing concern for the role of strategies and expectancies in human–machine interaction. In simple terms, an internal or mental model describes an operator's concept of how a system operates; expectancies comprise the operator's view of how it responds to control and environmental inputs. The internal-model concept has recently been addressed from a variety of perspectives in Gentner & Stevens' (1983) edited volume and forms the basis of optimal control models of manual control (Pew & Baron 1978), ship control (Veldhuyzen & Stassen 1977), tracking semipredictable environmental signals (Kleinman et al 1980), human–computer interaction (Carey 1982), operation of pocket calculators (Young 1981), and, qualitatively, process control (Rasmussen 1983). The internal-model concept can guide the design of operator training programs and improved display interfaces. Instructional programs and display interfaces should be made compatible with the internal model so that a system is perceived to respond as it is expected to respond (Roscoe 1968). The internal model has also been used to describe and model how operators control dynamic systems (Jagacinski & Miller 1978) and how they detect failures in systems dynamics (Gai & Curry 1976, Wickens & Kessel 1981).

PROCESS CONTROL

Research on the human–machine interface confronting the supervisor/monitor of complex chemical and industrial processes has increased in the last decade. Edwards and Lees's (1974) book summarizes research performed prior to 1975, and some process-control research was carried out in Europe during the early and mid 1970s. The disaster at the Three Mile Island nuclear power plant in 1979 (Rubenstein & Mason 1979) provided a major impetus for process-control research in this country. General overviews of the nature of the process controller's task and of research in the area are offered by Baum & Drury (1976), Morris (1982), Umbers (1979b), and Wickens (1984). Sheridan (1981) focuses explicitly on the nuclear power plant monitor's task; Moray (1981) examines the role of human attention in this environment; and Cuny (1979) offers a framework for task analysis. A comprehensive report by Hopkins et al (1982) summarizes the conclusions drawn by a panel of experts on priorities for human factors research in nuclear power plant supervision. Priority should be placed on the design of annunciator and alarm systems, the development of advanced display technology, and the use of color coding.

Control

The process controller's job has been described as hours of boredom punctuated by a few minutes of pure hell. This dichotomy between routine and failure mode can be used to classify research in the area. Research in the former category has examined operators' strategies in controlling and adjusting process variables in such tasks as steel pitsoaking (Liaos 1978), distillation (Patternote & Verhagen 1979), gas grid controlling (Umbers 1979a), nuclear reactor control (McLeod & McCallum 1975, Sheridan 1981), industrial scheduling (Mitchell & Miller 1983), and more "generic" simulated process plants (Brigham & Liaos 1975, Morris & Rouse 1983). Some of these studies have examined the relative use of different controlling strategies (e.g. West & Clark 1974, McLeod & McCallum 1975), while many have focused on the nature of the display interface. Predictive information is important (Shackel 1976, Liaos 1978), and computer technology should be used to derive and present integrated display information, a point considered below (Goodstein 1981).

Detection and Diagnosis

Failure detection and diagnosis in process control have received more extensive treatment. In fact, many of the chapters in Rasmussen & Rouse's (1981) book concern the process-control environment. The research in this area falls into three overlapping areas: the nature of alarm indicators, the diagnostic process, and diagnosis training.

NATURE OF ALARM INDICATORS   Reducing the confusion caused when scores of auditory and visual annunciators change state following a failure is a high priority item for research in process control (Hopkins et al 1982). Since the overwhelming array of information in conventional electromechanical displays offers little diagnostic assistance, research must determine how a computer with a flexible video display can be programmed to integrate information to best serve the operator's diagnostic need. Research has addressed the use of physical variables like color (Osborne et al 1981) and composition of display elements (Benel et al, 1981), as well as cognitive factors. In what form should the computer present the system's raw physical signals in order best to meet the operator's need for information (Kiguchi & Sheridan 1979)? As one example, some investigators have advocated probabilistic displays portraying the *likelihood* that a system or component will fail (Gonzalez & Howington 1977, Moray 1981, Sheridan 1981). Goodstein (1981) and Lees (1981) have considered the role of computer support in preserving and interpreting the *sequence* in which events occur, thereby reducing the load imposed on human memory. Rasmussen & Lind (1981) recommend displays that can present information according to the *level of abstraction* of the operator's needs—that can, for example, display either physical quantitites like pressure and temperature (low level of abstraction) or more abstract ones like energy flow and cost.

THE NATURE OF THE DIAGNOSTIC PROCESS   Much research in process control is related to troubleshooting, discussed above. Beyond this, however, Rasmussen's (1981, 1983) qualitative model has influenced research on complex systems. Besides stressing the importance of mental models, Rasmussen emphasizes the information needs and decision-making processes associated with three modes of behavior: *skill-based:* highly automatic, involving well-learned actions; *rule-based:* attention-demanding, but grounded in following routine procedures; and *knowledge-based:* complex, creative, and innovative. Rasmussen (1983) has integrated this trichotomy into descriptions of the process-control task, and Pew et al (1981) have used it as a framework for analysis of specific critical incidents in nuclear power plants.

The last ten years have also witnessed an interest in the methodology for obtaining data relevant to process control and diagnostic models. Given that the ratio of observable responses to unobservable cognition is low, verbal protocols provide a logical source of such data, and several studies have argued the merits (Umbers 1979a, Bainbridge 1979, 1981, LePlat & Hoc 1981) and shortcomings (Brigham & Liaos 1975, Broadbent 1977, Umbers 1981) of this technique in deriving valid models of the process-control operator.

TRAINING AND INDIVIDUAL DIFFERENCES   Operator differences due to training and abilities are beyond the scope of this review. Since they are relevant to cognitive models describing operator performance, however, process-control research in this area is worth mentioning. Landeweerd (1979) has found that subjects with high verbal ability perform better at process control tasks, while those with high spatial ability excel at diagnostic tasks. Marshall et al (1981) have examined different strategies for training process controllers, while Lees & Sayers (1976) have considered the importance of embedded diagnostic training in real simulators. Research concerning the level of operator sophistication and knowledge required for effective control and diagnosis indicates that minimal instruction in plant input-output relations is insufficient to produce good diagnosticians (Brigham & Liaos 1975, Shepherd et al 1977, Landeweerd et al 1981). However, instruction on troubleshooting procedures and heuristics related to the specific process appears to be adequate. Additional instruction in the general theory of plant operations appears to do little to enhance control or diagnostic capabilities (Kragt & Landeweerd 1974, Morris & Rouse 1983).

COMPUTERS AND AUTOMATION: THE INTERFACE AND THE LOGIC

The computer explosion has exerted two profound influences on human factors during the last ten years. First, it has made computer services such as scheduling, text editing, record keeping, and entertainment available to a wider range of users. This has brought to the forefront a whole array of research and design issues concerning the interface between humans and computers. Second, because of their increased sophistication and steadily declining cost and weight, computers are replacing humans in certain interactions with complex processes.

Human-Computer Interaction

Numerous guidelines have been compiled for designers of human-computer interfaces (Engel & Granda 1975, Smith & Aucella 1982, Towstopiat 1983). Although most incorporate psychological principles where possible, many of the design principles appear to be based on intuition and experience. Validation of such guidelines in both laboratory and operational environments has been sparse and will require substantial work over the next decade. Several investigators have recommended a more systematic construction of guidelines than is generally found in the literature. We endorse this call for development of a cognitively based performance theory of the human-computer interaction enabling the derivation and empirical validation of design principles (Fitter 1979, Moran 1981a, Card et al 1983). Some existing attempts to develop and validate human performance models are described below.

The magnitude and breadth of interest in the topic of the human-computer interaction are also illustrated by reviews on subtopics such as software design and programming (Ramsey et al 1978, Atwood et al 1979, Shneiderman 1980, Curtis 1981, Sheil 1981). These examine the effects of structural and stylistic changes in programming languages on performance, as well as the use of programming aids and debugging procedures. Others have evaluated query languages for nonprofessional programmers (Ehrenreich 1981, Reisner 1981). In many cases these reviews concern primarily the advantages and disadvantages of natural and structured query languages (Harris 1983, Hill 1983).

The methods by which subjects encode and later retrieve information relevant to the operation of computer systems have generated theoretical and empirical interest (Durding et al 1977, Carroll & Thomas 1982, Jagodzinski 1983). These reviews evaluate cognitive models of information representation for efficiency in helping the user learn new computer systems and languages. Numerous investigations of data input and retrieval devices have also been reviewed (Norman & Fisher 1982, Card et al 1983, Noyes 1983). Entire journal issues have been devoted to human-computer interaction. Special issues of the *International Journal of Man-Machine Studies* have addressed problems in software psychology (April 1981) and presented selected papers from several computer conferences (May 1978). *AMC Computing Surveys* (March 1981) devoted an issue to the human-factors considerations involved in programming and design of text editors and query languages.

PROGRAMMING   Weinberg's classic text, *The Psychology of Computer Programming* (1971), provided one of the first systematic treatments of the human aspects of programming. He focused attention on individual differences in programming style and abilities, procedures for motivation and training, and social influences and personality factors relevant to the programming endeavor. Although Weinberg's book provided a wealth of information on the human side of programming, the discussion was based primarily on anecdote and insight rather than experimental results. Shneiderman's more recent text, *Software Psychology: Human Factors in Computer and Information Systems* (1980), provides an update on psychological research relevant to programming and software design, focusing whenever possible on empirical investigations of programming practices. The text examines topics such as programming language features, software quality evaluation, database query and manipulation languages, and team organization and group processes.

The discovery of large individual differences in programmer productivity has prompted examination of the learning and comprehension of the computer programming process (Brooks 1977, Barfield et al 1981, Salvendy et al 1983). Estimates of the magnitude of these differences range from a factor of 5 to a factor of 90 with programmers of comparable experience. Several investigators have suggested that a programmer's comprehension might be enhanced by the construction of a mental model of the task (Mayer 1975, Carey 1982). One method for cognitively representing the programming task is the use of metaphor. Carroll & Thomas (1982) reviewed research on the development of new cognitive structures by metaphorical extension of previously learned structures and recommended employing metaphors to enhance the learning and comprehension of computer programmers. Examples of the use of conceptual models to help the programmer learn a computer system can be found in the literature (Moran 1981b, Young 1981). DuBoulay et al (1981) instructed children in the language LOGO by using a conceptual model of a computer system which consisted of memory locations, switches, and work space. Unfortunately, the investigators did not evaluate the effectiveness of their instructional technique relative to other methods. Mayer (1981) provided naive programmers with concrete models of a computer as an aid in learning Basic-like and file management languages. These models represented the structure of the computer in terms of familar objects. For example, input was represented as a ticket window, memory was depicted as an eraseable scoreboard, and output was represented as a note pad. The use of the models enhanced the learning of complex programming tasks.

Investigators have also examined the cognitive processes involved in debugging computer programs. In these studies programmers are usually required to detect and in some cases correct syntatic, structural, and semantic bugs that have been introduced into programs. Syntatic bugs are relatively easy to detect (Boies & Gould 1974). Structural and semantic bugs, however, appear difficult to detect, and detection accuracy seems to depend on the search strategy, the kind of bug, and the aids provided to the programmers (Gould & Drongowski 1974, Gould 1975, Green et al 1980). Flowcharts of program structure aid debugging in some situations, especially with complex programs (Shneiderman et al 1977, Brooke & Duncan 1980a,b).

The increase in the cost of software development and the decrease in expenses associated with computer hardware have focused attention on the prediction of programmer ability. Although several standardized tests of programming ability have been constructed, their effectiveness is uncertain (Shneiderman 1980). Other indexes of programming ability such as SAT scores and college grades in math, science, and English account for only a small proportion of variance in performance on programming tasks (Barfield et al 1981). A syntatic/semantic model of programmer behavior, which suggests that experience in programming results in an increased capacity for recognizing and abstracting program structures, has led to the construction of a memorization/reconstruction test of programmer ability (Shneiderman & Mayer 1979). The task requires programmers to memorize and later reconstruct a section of code. As predicted by the syntatic/semantic model, experienced programmers and students with high grades in computer classes are significantly better at reconstructing code than less experienced programmers and students with lower grades (Shneiderman 1977, DiPersio et al 1980). Also consistent with the model, the number of lines perfectly recalled does not vary significantly between groups of programmers (Atwood & Ramsey 1977). The generation of tests on the basis of a theoretical framework appears to offer a promising alternative to the traditionally atheoretical investigation of programming ability.

TEXT EDITORS   Text editors offer an ideal medium for studying human performance characteristics and cognitive processes. The editing of a manuscript includes a variety of information processing activities from the encoding of text on a CRT, through the retrieval of information from memory and its integration with new material, to the selection and execution of data entry and modificaion commands. Embley & Nagy (1981) review recent studies of the behavioral aspects of text editing. The review outlines several theoretical models of the editing process, emphasizing the potential contribution of cognitive psychology to the design of text editors.

Card et al in their recent text, *The Psychology of Human-Computer Interaction* (1983), propose a cognitively based model of text editing. Their GOMS model describes a user's cognitive structure in terms of goals, operators, methods for achieving goals, and the selection rules for choosing among competing methods. The model has been tested with several text editors and provides a reasonable account of user performance. One interesting aspect of the model is its flexibility in analyzing editing tasks at different levels of detail. The model can predict performance from the single keystroke level to the level of a unit task. A set of user-interface design principles has been derived from the model. Robertson & Black (1983) proposed a model to represent the goals and plans of text editor users. Their model, based on goal-fate analysis (Schank & Abelson 1977), represents the relationships among a user's multiple goals and shows how errors can result from poorly conceived plans. Although the model still requires additional empirical validation, it offers a potentially useful method for examining the learning of text editors and provides information on user's text editing strategies.

The learning of text editors has also been explored by examining the analogies users employ while building a representaton of the text editing commands. Douglas & Moran (1983) argue that novices use a typewriter analogy to aid them in learning editing commands. An analysis technique is proposed and data are presented suggesting that errors can be predicted on the basis of the correspondence between typewriting and text editing commands. Other investigators have compared screen editors with line editors (Gomez et al 1983) and examined the effects of differences in screen formatting (Darnell & Neal 1983) on the learning of text editors.

DATA MANIPULATION AND RETRIEVAL   The continuing increase in the number of casual users of computer systems has prompted examination of the human–computer interface (Nickerson 1981). In most cases it is not necessary for casual users to specify (using a procedural query language) the procedures by which the computer accesses the information they require but only to state (using a nonprocedural query language) the result they want the computer to accomplish. Query languages are special-purpose languages constructed to retrieve information from a database. The language is usually intended for nonprofessional programmers and consists of a set of syntatic and lexical rules by means of which the user can question the computer. What is the best structure for nonprocedural query languages? This is one of the most frequently debated issues in computer science. Query languages occupy a continuum from unrestricted natural languages with grammatical rules and vocabulary similar to English to formal computer languages with highly restricted syntaxes and vocabularies. Natural languages have their share of proponents (Harris 1983) and detractors (Hill 1983, Small & Weldon 1983). Excellent reviews of the issue can be found in the literature (Petrick 1976, Shneiderman 1980, Ehrenreich 1981). Some investigators believe that English-based natural languages are too ambiguous for correct interpretation by a computer, while others suggest that natural languages are ideal for casual computer users since the language is already learned. Other reviews describe and evaluate the advantages and disadvantages of various formal query languages (Reisner 1981).

Although the controversy over the relative merits of query languages has been focused on the endpoints of the continuum (unrestricted natural languages and formal query languages), attention appears to be shifting toward a midpoint. How, then, shall natural languages be restricted to remedy such problems as semantic ambiguity? Natural languages have been restricted both in their grammar and vocabulary and in the domains they access. Both the number of grammatical rules and the size of the vocabulary can be substantially reduced without adverse effects on user performance (Kelly & Chapanis 1977, Hendler & Michaelis 1983, Ogden & Brooks 1983). Domain-specific natural languages have been constructed to access aircraft maintenance information (PLANES: Waltz 1978), mimic a Rogerian psychotherapist (DOCTOR: Weizenbaum 1976), and provide information on a supplier-parts-project database (RENDEZVOUS: Codd 1978). Several restricted-domain natural language systems have also become commercially available (e.g. ROBOT: Harris 1977).

An alternative to the use of query languages for data access is menu selection. In menu selection, users choose among several preprogrammed alternatives to access the desired information. It has been suggested that menus are particularly useful for novices because the database structure provided by the menu reduces memory demands (Simpson 1982). Menu hierarchies are arranged on the basis of an interaction between breadth and depth. Breadth refers to the number of items on a single menu level while depth refers to the number of hierarchically arranged menus. What is the optimal combination of breadth and depth? Some investigators have suggested that intermediate levels of breadth and depth lead to optimal performance (Miller 1981), while others argue that performance accuracy is best with high levels of breadth and low levels of depth (Snowberry et al 1983). Two techniques aid novices in accessing deeply embedded menus. The availability of a pictorial representation of the menu structure appears to facilitate development of a useful mental model of the system (Billingsley 1982). Natural-language menus have also been found easy to use with deeply embedded menus, presumably because sentences provide an understandable structure (Tennant et al 1983).

The structure of information in the database has a powerful influence on user performance in data manipulation and retrieval tasks. Most databases use one of the three common data-storage models: the network model, the relational model, or the hierarchical model. Evaluations of the effects of data models on user performance have not found a clear superiority for any of these three. Lochovsky (1978) employed three separate data manipulation languages that reflected the three data models and found that novices' queries were best with the relational language. Brosey & Shneiderman (1978) discovered that novices comprehended database elements best when they used a hierarchical model. Durding et al (1977) found that the structure of the database strongly influenced how people organize data. Data represented in relational, network, or hierarchical formats on the basis of semantic relations was usually organized in those formats by the subjects. Thus, it appears that the selection of a data model should be based on the relations among the database elements.

DATA INPUT AND RETRIEVAL DEVICES   The proliferation of computer-related tasks and the diversity of computer users have made it necesary to evaluate different input and retrieval devices. From the mid-1800s to the 1970s such evaluations involved primarily comparing different keyboard layouts (Noyes 1983). Although keyboards are still the most frequently employed input devices, other devices are rapidly becoming popular. The studies conducted to evaluate data input and retrieval devices are of two kinds: those primarily concerned with the performance characteristics of different devices, (Neal 1977, Butterbaugh & Rockwell 1982, Price & Cordova 1983, Whitfield et al 1983) and those involving predictive models. The former have compared various touch input devices, evaluated the relative advantages of different keyboard layouts, and investigated the response characteristics of multiple-button mice. In one such study, Goodwin (1975) compared subjects' performance with a lightpen, lightgun, and keyboard across several tasks. The lightpen and lightgun were at least twice as fast as the keyboard in the cursor-positioning tasks. Although these studies provide valuable information concerning the relative merits of different input and retrieval devices, they did not attempt to develop models from which performance could be predicted.

In a series of studies, Card and coworkers (Card et al 1978, 1983) examined text selection performance with four different devices: a mouse, a rate-controlled isometric joystick, step keys, and text keys. Performance on these devices was evaluated in terms of its correspondence to predictions derived from a Human Processor Model (Card et al 1983). This model, which incorporates a number of psychological principles, enables system designers to estimate the latencies of perceptual, cognitive, and motor activities. One principle, Fitt's Law, describes the time it takes to make a goal-oriented movement on the basis of the goal's size and distance from the subject. The positioning time for the continuous devices, the mouse and the joystick, was consistent with Fitt's Law. Knowledge of this relationship allowed investigators to estimate the maximum velocity with which a user could move a cursor across a cathode ray tube with a mouse. This information led to the redesign of a piece of hardware prior to the production of a text-editing system.

Other investigators have also successfully used models of human performance for the design and evaluation of data input devices. Gopher (1985) employed models of visual imagery in his design of a two-hand chord keyboard (Gopher & Koenig 1983). Norman & Fisher (1982) evaluated a number of keyboard layouts using computer simulation of the hand and finger movements of a skilled typist. By using predictive models of human performance, experimental and cognitive psychologists can aid the designer of human-computer interfaces.

Automation

Wickens (1984) describes three reasons why automation may be implemented: (*a*) to carry out dangerous functions (e.g. remotely manipulate radioactive material) or do things humans cannot do; (*b*) to do things humans sometimes do poorly because of high workload or boredom (e.g. diagnose failure or pilot certain aircraft); and (*c*) to supplement or augment human perception, memory, attention, or motor skill.

ROBOTICS   The use of robots falls into the first two categories. Robots and remote manipulators are increasingly used in hazardous environments (undersea, around hazardous materials, in outer space) (Johnson et al 1983). They are also replacing factory workers in more mundane assembly jobs. Yet robots obviously need to be taught and supervised, and here human-factors issues become relevant. Birk & Kelley (1981) have summarized a conference workshop on human factors in robotics, emphasizing the importance of research on communications between robot and human, while Parsons & Kearsley (1982) and Salvendy (1983) have offered more general overviews of the state of robotics and human factors. Salvendy reviews both the social issues associated with the introduction of robots and the technical issues related to human performance characteristics. Others have examined specifically the human-factors problem associated with robotics in industrial assembly lines (Noro &

Okada 1983), undersea environments (Sheridan 1982), and outer space (Bejszy 1980). Several recent treatments of human factors in robotics are offered in recent volumes from the NASA Annual Conference on Manual Control. Other articles consider the partitioning of intelligence between humans and robots (Sheridan 1982), and sensory-motor feedback between human and robot (e.g. Book & Hannema 1980, Bejszy 1980).

AUTOMATION THAT ASSISTS   A continuum exists from automation that assists to automation that replaces human beings. Automation assists with *predictive* tasks (see the section above on Display Concepts and Memory). Voice input unburdens the hands (Wickens et al 1983a), helps humans to converse with computers (Ballantine 1980), and enhances the creative composition process (Gould & Boies 1978). Computer graphics assist in proceeding through flight checklists (Rouse et al 1982) and in medical diagnosis (Fitter & Cruickshank 1983). Computer support augments an array of office functions (Chapanis 1979). The July/August (1982) issue of *IEEE Transactions on Systems, Man, and Cybernetics* contains a special section on displays for information management systems, which aid in information integration. Wohl (1981) has considered the use of computer aids for decision support in command and control situations. Felson (1978) has done the same for the investment decision maker. The consensus is that automation in these roles is beneficial.

AUTOMATION THAT REPLACES: PROBLEMS   In some situations, computers replace people in functions that people perform adequately. This controversial aspect of automation forces a rethinking of the classic allocation of function between human and machine. An excellent analysis of such automation in commercial aviation (Wiener & Curry 1980) distinguished between automation of monitoring and of control functions on the flight deck. Hart & Sheridan (1984) considered the impact of automation on workload, while Rouse & Rouse (1983b) addressed the automation of decision making. While there is little doubt that automation is a necessity in such high-demand environments as the combat aircraft (Air Force Studies Board Committee 1982), several investigators have cautioned that analysis of the total system must be carried out before tasks are assigned to computers or humans (DeGreen 1980, Eason 1980, Hart & Sheridan 1984). Others have considered the specific costs and benefits of assigning tasks to one or the other (Air Force Studies Board Committee 1982, Wiener & Curry 1980), while Boehm-Davis et al (1983) have identified salient issues for human-factors research in flight deck automation. Two questions are foremost among these: How can decision-aiding techniques be used and information transfer between human and computer be improved? How can monitoring of automated systems be improved to help the operator deal with unforeseen situations? Finally, the summary review of the study panel on automation in combat aircraft (Air Force Studies Board Committee 1982), along with Wiener & Curry (1980) and Wickens (1984), has tried to specify the costs or dangers associated with automation. Wiener & Curry's review, in addition to several articles in the October and December 1981 special issues of *Human Factors* dealing with Air Traffic Control (see particularly Wiener 1977, Danaher 1980, Fowler 1980) offers salient examples of how automation has led to disasters or near disasters in aviation.

While much has been done to identify automation-related dangers, few systematic empirical investigations have been carried out. Ephrath & Young (1981) and Wickens & Kessel (1981) have examined the losses in failure-detection ability that may occur when the human operator is removed as an active participant from a flight-control loop, while Gai & Curry (1976) have tried to model the failure-detection process. Also, as noted in the section on process control, several investigators have dealt with the problems of automated information integration in alarm and other alerting systems (see Gonzalez & Howington 1977, Kiguchi & Sheridan 1979, and several chapters in Rasmussen & Rouse 1981).

ADAPTIVE SYSTEMS   There seems to be a growing consensus that automation will be more effective and more accepted if (*a*) it functions in a manner qualitatively similar to that of the human operator (Air Force Studies Board Committee 1982; Wiener & Curry 1980, Hart & Sheridan 1984), and (*b*) the automation is flexible and adaptive. In a discussion of adaptive decision systems, Rouse & Rouse (1983b) comment that most decision aids are designed for the average person under the average circumstances, which greatly limits their flexibility. In a series of articles, Rouse describes the characteristics of good adaptive systems in the control of dynamic systems (Rouse 1981b), in decision aiding (Rouse & Rouse 1984), and in multitask situations in which certain tasks can be assigned either to the computer or to the human as a function of the operator's momentary workload (Chu & Rouse 1979; Rouse 1977).

Four critical research questions concerning such systems are beginning to be addressed:

1. *What task characteristics to adapt?* As noted above in the section on decision aids, Weisbroad et al (1977) and Madni et al (1982) have adapted information presentation in decision making, while Adelman et al (1982) have considered an adaptive Bayesian decision aid. Chu & Rouse (1979) have adapted the responsibility for performing the decision-making task by computer or human to the workload of the operator. Geiselman & Samet (1982) have adapted intelligence message format to operator preferences, while Lintern & Gopher (1978) have summarized a host of studies related to adapting difficulty variables to learner progress in adaptive training.

2. *What is the time frame for the adaptation?* Is it done on-line in real time, according to the momentary state of the operator, or off-line between time periods, according to the ability or preference of different operators (Rouse & Rouse 1983b)?

3. *What is the command for adaptation?* Does the operator overtly request automation when needed, or does the computer infer its need through covert channels of communication from humans to computer, interpreted within the framework of a computer's internal model of the human? Various possible channels of this communication that can be monitored on-line have been investigated, including control theory estimates of tracking behavior (Enstrom & Rouse 1977, Merhav & Gabay 1975, Wickens & Gopher 1977), decision choice preference (Madni et al 1982), voice quality (Levin & Lord 1975), tasks left undone (Rouse 1977), or physiological signals (Isreal et al 1980b).

4. *Who is in charge?* All-important is the issue of who is ultimately in charge, computer or human. How can we provide clear communications from computer to human regarding the current partitioning of responsibility? This question is discussed clearly in a review of adaptive systems by Steeb et al (1976).

Adaptive systems are worthy of far more research than they have received. Whether desirable or not, computer automation is inevitable. If they can be successfully implemented, adaptive systems provide the most flexible and graceful means of incorporating automation into complex systems for all concerned.

Literature Cited

Adams, J. A. 1982. Issues in human reliability. *Hum. Factors* 24:1–10

Adelman, L., Donnell, M. L., Phelps, R. H., Paterson, J. F. 1982. An iterative Bayesian decision-aid: Towards improving the user-aid and user organization interface. *IEEE Trans. Syst. Man Cybern.* 12:733–43

Air Force Studies Board Committee. 1982. Automation in combat aircraft. Washington DC: Natl. Acad. Press

Alluisi, E., Morgan, B. 1976. Engineering psychology and human performance. *Ann. Rev. Psychol.* 27:305–30

Anderson, J. R. 1979. *Cognitive Psychology.* New York: Academic

Arkes, H., Wortmann, R. L., Saville, P. D., Harkness, A. R. 1981. Hindsight bias among physicians weighing the likelihood of diagnosis. *J. Appl. Psychol.* 87:252–54

Atwood, M. E., Ramsey, H. R. 1977. Cognitive structures in the comprehension and memory of computer programs. *Tech. Memo. SAI-77-025 DEN,* Science Applications, Inc.

Atwood, M. E., Ramsey, H. R., Hooper, J. N., Kollas, D. A. 1979. Annotated bibiolgraphy on human factors in software. ARI

Tech. Rep. P-79-1. Alexandria, Va: U.S. Army Res. Inst.

Bailey, R. W. 1982. *Human Performance Engineering: A Guide for System Designers.* Englewood Cliffs, NJ: Prentice-Hall

Bainbridge, L. 1978. Forgotten alternatives in skills and workload. *Ergonomics* 21:169–85

Bainbridge, L. 1979. Verbal reports as evidence of the process operator's knowledge. *Int. J. Man-Machine Stud.* 11:411

Bainbridge, L. 1981. Mathematical equations or processing routines? See Rasmussen & Rouse 1981, pp. 259–86

Balla, J. 1980. Logical thinking and the diagnostic process. *Methodol. Inform. Med.* 19:88–92

Ballantine, M. 1980. Conversing with computers—the dream and the controversy. *Ergonomics* 23:935–46

Barclay, S. et al. 1977. *Handbook for Decision Analysis.* McLean, Va: Decisions and Designs

Barfield, W., LeBold, W. K., Salvendy, G., Shodja, S. 1981. Cognitive factors related to computer programming and software productivity. See Pope & Haugh 1983, pp. 647–51

Baron, S., Levison, W. 1975. An optimal control methodology for analyzing the effects of display parameters on performance and workload in manual flight control. *IEEE Trans. Syst. Man Cybern.* 5:423–30

Bartram, J. D. 1980. Comprehending spatial information: The relative efficiency of different methods of presenting information about bus routes. *J. Appl. Psychol.* 65:103–10

Baum, A. S., Drury, C. G. 1976. Modelling the human process operation. *Int. J. Man-Machine Stud.* 8:1–12

Beach, L. R., Barnes, V. 1983. Approximate measurement in multiattribute utility context. *Organ. Behav. Hum. Perform.* 32:417–24

Beatty, J. 1982. Task-evoked pupillary responses, processing load, and the structure of processing resources. *Psychol. Bull.* 91:276–92

Becker, C. A. 1976. Allocation of attention during visual work recognition. *J. Exp. Psychol: Hum. Percept. Perform.* 2:556–66

Bejszy, A. K. 1980. Manipulation of large objects. In *Proc. 3rd Symp. on Theory and Practice of Robots and Manipulators*, ed. A. Morecki, G. Biachi, K. Kedzior. Amsterdam/New York: Elsevier

Benel, D. C. R., McCafferty, D. B., Neal, V., Mallory, K. M. 1981. Issues in the design on annunciator systems. See Sugerman 1981, pp. 122–26

Ben-Shakhar, G., Lieblich, I., Bar-Hillel, M. 1982. An evaluation of polygraph's judgments: A review from a decision theoretic perspective. *J. Appl. Psychol.* 67:701–13

Bergman, C. A. 1976. An airplane performance control system: A flight experiment. *Hum. Factors* 18:173–82

Billingsley, P. 1982. Navigation through hierarchical menu structures: Does it help to have a map? *Proc. 26th Ann. Meet. Hum. Factors Soc., Santa Monica, CA,* pp. 103–7

Birk, H., Kelley, R. 1981. Overview of the basic research needed to advance the state of knowledge in robotics. *IEEE Trans. Syst. Man Cybern.* 11:574–79

Bisseret, A. 1981. Application of signal detection theory to decision making in air traffic control. *Ergonomics* 24:81–94

Boehm-Davis, D., Curry, R. E., Wiener, E. L., Harrison, R. L. 1983. Human factors of flight deck automation: Report on NASA-industry workshop. *Ergonomics* 26:953–62

Boies, S. J., Gould, J. D. 1974. Syntatic errors in computer programming. *Hum. Factors* 16:253–57

Bond, N. A. 1981. Troubleshooting in the commercial computer industry: A success story. See Rasmussen & Rouse 1981, pp. 75–86

Booher, H. R. 1975. Relative comprehensibility of pictorial information and printed words

in proceduralized instructions. *Hum. Factors* 17:266–77

Book, W. J., Hannema, D. P. 1980. Master-slave performance for various dynamic characteristics and positioning task parameters. *IEEE Trans. Syst. Man Cybern.* 8:764–71

Borg, G. 1978. Subjective aspects of physical and mental load. *Ergonomics* 21:215–20

Boyd, S. P. 1983. Assessing the validity of SWAT as a workload assessment instrument. See Pope & Haugh 1983, pp. 124–28

Brehmer, B. 1981. Models of diagnostic judgment. See Rasmussen & Rouse 1981, pp. 231–40

Brigham, F. R., Liaos, L. 1975. Operator performance in the control of the laboratory process plant. *Ergonomics* 29:181–201

Broadbent, D. E. 1977. Levels, hierarchies, and the locus of control. *Q. J. Exp. Psychol.* 29:181–201

Brooke, J. B., Duncan, K. D. 1980a. Experimental studies of flowchart use at different stages of program debugging. *Ergonomics* 23:1057–91

Brooke, J. B., Duncan, K. D. 1980b. Flowcharts versus lists as aids in program debugging. *Ergonomics* 23:387–99

Brooke, J. B., Duncan, K. D. 1983. Effects of prolonged practice on performance in a fault location task. *Ergonomics* 26:379–94

Brooks, R. E. 1977. Towards a theory of cognitive processes in computer programming. *Int. J. Man-Machine Stud.* 9:737–51

Brosey, M., Shneiderman, B. 1978. Two experimental comparisons of relational and hierarchical models. *Int. J. Man-Machine Stud.* 10:625–37

Brown, I. D. 1978. Dual task methods of assessing workload. *Ergonomics* 21:221–24

Burke, M. W., Gilson, R. D., Jagacinski, R. J. 1980. Multiple information processing for visual workload relief. *Ergonomics* 23:961–75

Burns, M., Pearl, J. 1981. Causal and diagnostic inferences: A comparison of validity. *Organ. Behav. Hum. Perform.* 28:379–94

Butterbaugh, L. C., Rockwell, T. H. 1982. Evaluation of alternative alphanumeric keying logics. *Hum. Factors* 24:521–34

Card, S. K., English, W. K., Burr, B. J. 1978. Evaluation of mouse, rate controlled isometric joystick, step keys and text keys for text selection on a CRT. *Ergonomics* 21:601–13

Card, S. K., Moran, T. P., Newell, A. P. 1983. *The Psychology of Human-Computer Interaction*. Hillsdale, NJ: Erlbaum Assoc.

Carey, T. 1982. User differences in interface design. *Computer* 15:14–20

Carroll, J. S., Siegler, R. S. 1977. Strategies for the use of base-rate information. *Organ. Behav. Hum. Perform.* 19:392–402

Carroll, J. M., Thomas, J. C. 1982. Metaphor

and the cognitive representation of computing systems. *IEEE Trans. Syst. Man Cybern.* 12:107–16

Chapanis, A. 1979. Quo Vadis. *Ergonomics* 22:595–606

Chiles, W. D. 1978. Objective methods. See Roscoe 1978

Christ, R. 1975. Review and analysis of color coding for visual displays. *Hum. Factors* 17:542–70

Christ, R. E., Corso, G. 1983. The effects of extended practice on the evaluation of visual display codes. *Hum. Factors* 25:71–84

Christenssen-Szalanski, J. J., Beach, L. R. 1982. Experience and the base-rate fallacy. *Organ. Behav. Hum. Perform.* 29:270–78

Christenssen-Szalanski, J. J., Bushyhead, J. B. 1981. Physician's use of probabilistic information in a real clinical setting. *J. Exp. Psychol: Hum Percept. Perform.* 7:928–36

Chu, Y. Y., Rouse, W. B. 1979. Adaptive allocation of decision making responsibility between human and computer in multitask situations. *IEEE Trans. Syst. Man Cybern.* 9:769–78

Clifford, B. R., Hollin, C. R. 1981. Effects of the type of incident and number of perpetrators on eyewitness testimony. *J. Appl. Psychol.* 67:364–70

Codd, E. F. 1978. How about recently? (English dialogue with relational database using RENDEZVOUS version 1). In *Databases: Improving Usability and Responsiveness*, ed. B. Shneiderman, pp. 3–28. New York: Academic

Colquhoun, W. P. 1975. Evaluation of auditory, visual, and dual-mode displays for prolonged sonar monitoring in repeated sessions. *Hum. Factors* 17:425–37

Craig, A. 1978. Is the vigilance decrement simply a response adjustment toward probability matching? *Hum. Factors* 20:441–46

Craig, A. 1979. Non-parametric sensitivity measures. *Hum. Factors* 21:69–78

Craig, A. 1981. Monitoring for one kind of signal in the presence of another: The effects of signal mix on detectability. *Hum. Factors* 23:191–98

Crosby, J. V., Parkinson, S. R. 1979. A dual task investigation of pilots' skill level. *Ergonomics* 22:1301–13

Cuny, X. 1979. Different levels of analyzing process control tasks. *Ergonomics* 22:425–526

Curtis, B. 1981. *Tutorial: Human Factors in Software Development.* Los Alamitos, Calif: IEEE Computer Soc. Press

Czaja, S. J., Drury, C. 1981. Training programs for inspection. *Hum. Factors* 23:485–94

Damos, D. 1978. Residual attention as a predictor of pilot performance. *Hum. Factors* 20:435–40

Damos, D., Wickens, C. D. 1980. The acquisition and transfer of timesharing skills. *Acta Psychol.* 6:569–77

Damos, D., Smist, T., Bittner, A. C. 1983. Individual differences in multiple task performance as a function of response strategies. *Hum. Factors* 25:215–26

Danaher, J. W. 1980. Human error in ATC systems operations. *Hum. Factors* 22:535–45

Darnell, M. J., Neal, A. S. 1983. Text editing performance with partial and full page displays. See Pope & Haugh 1983, pp. 821–25

Davies, R., Parasuraman, R. 1980. *The Psychology of Vigilance.* London: Academic

DeGreen, K. B. 1980. Major conceptual problems in the systems management of human factors/ergonomics research. *Ergonomics* 23:3–12

Derrick, W. 1983. Examination of workload measures with subjective task clusters. See Pope & Haugh 1983, pp. 134–38

DiPersio, T., Isbister, B., Shneiderman, B. 1980. An experiment using memorization/ reconstruction as a measure of programmer ability. *Int. J. Man-Machine Stud.* 13:339–54

Dombal, D., Grevy, J., eds. 1976. *Decision Making and Medical Care.* Amsterdam: North Holland

Donchin, E., Kramer, A., Wickens, C. D. 1982. Probing the cognitive infrastructure with event-related brain potentials. In *Proceedings of the Workshop on Flight Testing to Identify Pilot Workload and Pilot Dynamics*, pp. 371–87. ed. M. L. Frazier, R. C. Crombie. AFFTC-TR-82-5. Edwards Air Force Base, CA

Donges, E. 1978. A two level model of driver steering behavior. *Hum. Factors* 20:691–708

Douglas, S. A., Moran, T. P. 1983. Learning text editor semantics by analogy. See Janda 1983, pp. 207–11

Drury, C. 1982. Improving inspection performance. In *Handbook of Industrial Engineering*, ed. G. Salvendy. New York: Wiley

Drury, C., Sinclair, M. A. 1983. Human and machine performance in an inspection task. *Hum. Factors* 25:391–400

DuBoulay, B., O'Shera, T., Monk, J. 1981. The black box inside the glass box: Presenting computing concepts to novices. *Int. J. Man-Machine Stud.* 14:237–50

Durding, B. M., Becker, C. A., Gould, J. D. 1977. Data organization. *Hum. Factors* 19:1–14

Eason, K. D. 1980. Dialogue design implications of task allocation between man and computer. *Ergonomics* 23:881–93

Ebbeson, E. B., Konecki, V. 1980. On external validity in decision-making research. See Wallsten 1980, pp. 21–46

Eddy, D. M. 1982. Probabilistic reasoning in clinical medicine: Problems and opportunities. See Kahneman et al 1982, pp. 249–67

Edgell, S. E., Hennessey, J. E. 1980. Irrelevant information and utilization of event base-rates in non-metric multiple cue probability learning. *Organ. Behav. Hum. Perform.* 26:1–6

Edwards, E., Lees, F. P., eds. 1974. *The Human Operator in Process Control.* London: Taylor & Francis

Edwards, W. 1977. How to use multiattribute utility measurement for social decision making. *IEEE Trans. Syst. Man Cybern.* 17:326–40

Egan, D. E., Schwartz, B. S. 1979. Chunking in recall of symbolic drawings. *Mem. Cognit.* 7:149–58

Eggemeier, F. T. 1980. Some current issues in workload assessment. *Proc. 24th Ann. Meet. Hum. Factors Soc., Santa Monica, CA*, pp. 667–73

Ehrenreich, S. L. 1981. Query languages: Design recommendations derived from the human factors literature. *Hum. Factors* 23: 709–26

Einhorn, H. J., Hogarth, R. M. 1978. Confidence in judgment: Persistence of the illusion of validity. *Psychol. Rev.* 85:395–416

Einhorn, H. J., Hogarth, R. M. 1981. Behavioral decision theory. *Ann. Rev. Psychol.* 32:53–88

Einhorn, H. J., Hogarth, R. M. 1982. Prediction, diagnosis, and causal thinking in forecasting. *J. Forecasting* 1:23–36

Einhorn, H. J., Hogarth, R. 1983. *A theory of diagnostic inference: Studying causality.* Tech. Rep. No. 4. Chicago: Univ. of Chicago Bus. Sch. Cent. Decision Res.

Ellis, G. A. 1978. Subjective assessment pilot opinion measures. See Roscoe 1978

Ellison, K. W., Buckhout, R. 1981. *Psychology and Criminal Justice.* New York: Harper & Row

Embley, D. W., Nagy, G. 1981. Behavioral aspects of text editors. *Comput. Surv.* 13:33–70

Engel, S., Granda, R. 1975. Guidelines for man/display interfaces. Tech. Rep. TR 00.2720. Poughkeepsie, NY: IBM

Enstron, K., Rouse, W. 1977. Real time determination of how a human has allocated his attention between control and monitoring tasks. *IEEE Trans. Syst. Man Cybern.* 7: 153–61

Ephrath, A. R., Young, L. R. 1981. Monitoring vs. man-in-the-loop detection of aircraft control failures. See Rasmussen & Rouse 1981

Fegetter, A. J. 1982. A method of investigating human factor aspects of aircraft accidents and incidents. *Ergonomics* 25:1065–76

Felson, J. 1978. A man-machine investment decision system. *Int. J. Man-Machine Stud.* 8:169–93

Fischer, E., Haines, R., Price, T. 1980. Cognitive issues in heads-up displays. NASA Tech. Pap. 1711. Washington DC: NASA

Fischoff, B., Slovic, P., Lichtenstein, S. 1979a. Fault trees: Sensitivity of estimated failure probabilities to problem representation. *J. Exp. Psychol.: Hum. Percept. Perform.* 4:330–44

Fischoff, B., Slovic, P., Lichtenstein, S. 1979b. Subjective sensitivity analysis. *Org. Behav. Hum. Perform.* 23: 339–59

Fischoff, B., MacGregor, D. 1981. *Subjective confidence in forecasts.* Tech. Rep. PTR-1092-81-12. Woodland Hills, Calif: Perceptronics

Fitter, M. 1979. Towards more "natural" interactive systems. *Int. J. Man-Machine Stud.* 11:339–50

Fitter, M. J., Cruickshank, P. J. 1983. Doctors using computers: A case study. See Sime & Coombs 1983, pp. 239–60

Fitter, M. J., Green, T. R. G. 1979. When do diagrams make good computer language? *Int. J. Man-Machine Stud.* 11:235–61

Fitts, P., Jones, R. E. 1961. Analysis of factors contributing to 460 "pilot error" experiences in operating aircraft controls. In *Selected Papers on Human Factors in the Design and Use of Control Systems*, ed. W. Sinaiko, pp. 332–58. New York: Dover

Fournier, B. A., Stager, P. 1976. Concurrent validation of a dual-task selection test. *J. Appl. Psychol.* 61:589–95

Fowler, F. D. 1980. Air traffic control problems: A pilot's view. *Hum. Factors* 22:645–54

Freidman, A., Polson, M. C. 1981. The hemispheres as independent resource systems: Limited capacity processing and cerebral specialization. *J. Exp. Psychol: Hum. Percept. Perform.* 7:1031–58

Gai, E., Curry, R. 1976. A model of the human observer in failure detection tasks. *IEEE Trans. Syst. Man Cybern.* 6:85

Gai, E., Curry, R. 1978. Perseveration effects in detection tasks with correlated decision intervals. *IEEE Trans. Syst. Man Cybern.* 8:93–100

Geiselman, R. E., Samet, M. 1982. Personalized vs. fixed formats for computer-displayed intelligence messages. *IEEE Trans. Syst. Man Cybern.* 12:490–95

Gentner, D., Stevens, A. L. 1983. *Mental Models.* Hillsdale, NJ: Erlbaum

Getty, D. J. 1982. Three-D displays: Perceptual research and applications to military systems. *Proc. Natl. Acad. Sci. Symp. 3-D Displays.* Washington DC: Off. Naval Res. Rep.

Gettys, C. F., Fisher, S. D. 1978. Hypothesis plausibility and hypothesis generation.

Organ. Behav. Hum. Perform. 24:93–110

Gibson, R., Liaos, L. 1978. The presentation of information to the job scheduler. *Hum. Factors* 20:725–32

Goldin, S. C., Thorndyke, P. W. 1982. Simulating navigation for spatial knowledge acquisition. *Hum. Factors* 24:457–72

Gomez, L. M., Egan, D. E., Wheeler, E. A., Sharma, D. K., Gruchacz, A. M. 1983. Learning to use a text editor. See Janda 1983, pp. 176–81

Gonzalez, R. C., Howington, L. C. 1977. Machine recognition of abnormal behavior in nuclear reactors. *IEEE Trans. Syst. Man Cybern.* 7:717–28

Goodstein, L. P. 1981. Discriminative display support for process operators. See Rasmussen & Rouse 1981, pp. 433–50

Goodwin, N. C. 1975. Cursor positioning on an electronic display using lightpen, lightgun or keyboard for three basic tasks. *Hum. Factors* 17:289–95

Gopher, D. 1982. A selective attention test as a prediction of success in flight training. *Hum. Factors* 24:173–84

Gopher, D. 1985. On the contribution of vision based imagery to the acquisition and operation of a transcription skill. In *Cognitive and Motor Processes*, ed. A. Sanders, W. Prinz. New York: Springer-Verlag

Gopher, D., Koenig, W. 1983. Hand coordination in data entry with a two-hand chord typewriter. *Proc. 19th Ann. Conf. Manual Control, MIT, Cambridge, Mass*, pp. 140–49

Gopher, D., North, R. 1977. The conditions of training in time-sharing performance. *Hum. Factors* 19:583–94

Gorenstein, G. W., Ellsworth, P. C. 1980. Effect of choosing an incorrect photograph on later identification by an eyewitness. *J. Appl. Psychol.* 65:616–22

Gould, J. D. 1975. Some psychological evidence on how people debug computer programs. *Int. J. Man-Machine Stud.* 7:151–82

Gould, J. D., Boies, S. J. 1978. How authors think about writing, speaking, and dictating. *Hum. Factors* 22:495–512

Gould, J. D., Drongowski, P. 1974. An exploratory study of computer program debugging. *Hum. Factors* 16:258–77

Govinderaj, T., Rouse, W. 1981. Modelling the human controller in environments that include continuous and discrete tasks. *IEEE Trans. Syst. Man Cybern.* 11:410–17

Green, T. R. G., Sime, M. E., Fitter, M. J. 1980. The problems the programmer faces. *Ergonomics* 23:893–907

Greening, C. P. 1976. Mathematical models of air to ground target acquisition. *Hum. Factors* 18:111–48

Grunwald, A. J., Merhav, S. J. 1978. Effectiveness of basic display augmentation in vehicular control by visual field cues. *IEEE Trans. Syst. Man Cybern.* 8:679–90

Hammerton, M. 1975. The use of same or different sensory modalities for information and instructions. *Ergonomics* 18:683–86

Harris, L. R. 1977. User oriented database query with ROBOT natural language query system. *Int. J. Man-Machine Stud.* 9:697–713

Harris, L. R. 1983. The advantages of natural language programming. See Sime & Coombs 1983, pp. 73–86

Hart, S. G. 1975. Time estimation as a secondary task to measure workload. *Proc. 11th Ann. Conf. on Man Control, NASA-AMES. Moffett Field, CA*

Hart, S. G., Sheridan, T. B. 1984. Pilot workload, performance, and aircraft control automation. *Proc. NATO/AGARD Symp. High Performance Aircraft, Williamsburg, VA.*

Hendler, J. A., Michaelis, P. R. 1983. The effects of limited grammar on interactive natural language. *Proc. Hum. Factors in Computing Systems, Boston*, pp. 190–92

Hess, R. 1981a. Aircraft control-display analysis and design using the optimal control model of the human pilot. *IEEE Trans. Syst. Man Cybern.* 11:465–80

Hess, R. 1981b. Pursuit tracking and higher levels of skill development in the human pilot. *IEEE Trans. Syst. Man Cybern.* 11:465–80

Hicks, T. G., Wierwille, W. W. 1979. Comparison of five mental workload assessment procedures in a moving base driving simulator. *Hum. Factors* 21:129–43

Hill, I. D. 1983. Natural language versus computer language. See Sime & Coombs 1983, pp. 55–72

Holding, D. H. 1981. *Human Skills*. New York: Wiley

Hopkins, C. D., Synder, H., Price, H. E., Hornick, R., Mackie, R., et al. 1982. Critical human factors issues in nuclear power regulation. NUREG/CE-2833, Vols. 1–3. Washington DC: GPO

Howard, J. H., Kerst, R. C. 1981. Memory and perception of cartographic information for familiar and unfamiliar environments. *Hum. Factors* 23:495–504

Hunt, R. M., Rouse, W. B. 1981. Problem-solving skills of maintenance trainees in diagnosing faults in simulated power plants. *Hum. Factors* 23:317–28

Hurst, R. 1976. *Pilot Error*. London: Granada

Hurst, M. W., Rose, R. M. 1978. Objective workload and behavioral response in airport radar control rooms. *Ergonomics* 21:559–65

Isreal, J. B., Chesney, G. L., Wickens, C. D., Donchin, E. 1980a. P300 and tracking difficulty: Evidence for multiple resources in dual-task performance. *Psychophysiology* 17:259–73

Isreal, J. B., Wickens, C. D., Chesney, G. L.,

Donchin, E. 1980b. The event-related brain potential as an index of display monitoring workload. *Hum. Factors* 22:211–24

Jacob, R. J. K., Egeth, H. E., Bevon, W. 1976. The face as a data display. *Hum. Factors* 18:189–200

Jagacinski, R. J., Miller, D. 1978. Describing the human operator's internal model of a dynamic system. *Hum. Factors* 20:425–34

Jagodzinski, A. P. 1983. A theoretical basis for the representation of online computer systems to naive users. *Int. J. Man-Machine Stud.* 18:215–52

Janda, A. 1983. *Proc. Human Factors in Computing Systems.* Sponsored by ACM Special Interest Group on Computer and Human Interaction (SIGCHI) and Human Factors Society, Boston

Jennings, A. E., Chiles, W. D. 1977. An investigation of time-sharing ability as a factor in complex performance. *Hum. Factors* 19: 535–47

Jensen, R. J. 1981. Prediction and quickening in prospective flight displays for curved landing and approaches. *Hum. Factors* 23: 333–64

Jensen, R. 1982. Pilot judgment: Training and evaluation. *Hum. Factors* 24:61–74

Jex, H. R., Clement, W. F. 1979. Defining and measuring perceptual-motor workload in manual control tasks. See Moray 1979, pp. 125–78

Johannsen, G., Moray, N., Pew, R., Rasmussen, J., Sanders, A., Wickens, C. D. 1979. Final report of the Experimental Psychology group. See Moray 1979, pp. 101–16

Johannsen, G., Rouse, W. 1979. Mathematical concepts for modelling human behavior in complex man-machine systems. *Hum. Factors* 21:733–47

Johannsen, G., Rouse, W. B. 1983. Studies of planning behavior of aircraft pilots in normal, abnormal, and emergency situations. *IEEE Trans. Syst. Man Cybern.* 13:267–78

Johnson, R. D., Bershader, D., Leiffer, L. 1983. *Autonomy and the human element in space: Executive summary.* Rep. 1983 NASA/ASEE summer faculty workshop, Stanford Univ.

Johnson, W. B., Rouse, W. B. 1982a. Analysis and classification of human errors in troubleshooting live aircraft power plants. *IEEE Trans. Syst. Man Cybern.* 12:389–93

Johnson, W. B., Rouse, W. B. 1982b. Training maintenance technicians for troubleshooting: Two experiments with computer simulations. *Hum. Factors* 24:271–76

Kahneman, D., Slovic, P., Tversky, A., eds. 1982. *Judgment Under Uncertainty: Heuristics and Biases.* New York: Cambridge Univ. Press

Kamman, R. 1975. The comprehensibility of printed instructions and the flowchart alternative. *Hum. Factors* 17:183–91

Kantowitz, B. H., Sorkin, R. D. 1983. *Human Factors: Understanding People-System Relationships.* New York: Wiley

Keeney, R. L. 1977. The art of assessing multiattribute utility functions. *Organ. Behav. Hum. Perform.* 19:267–310

Kelly, M. J., Chapanis, A. 1977. Limited vocabulary natural language dialog. *Int. J. Man-Machine Stud.* 9:477–501

Kiguchi, T., Sheridan, T. B. 1979. Criteria for selecting measures of plant information with applications to nuclear reactors. *IEEE Trans. Syst. Man Cybern.* 9:165–75

Kinsbourne, M., Hicks, R. 1978. Functional cerebral space. In *Attention and Performance VII*, ed. J. Requin, pp. 345–62. Hillsdale, NJ: Erlbaum

Kleinman, D., Pattipati, K. R., Ephrath, A. 1980. Quantifying an internal model of target motion on a manual tracking task. *IEEE Trans. Syst. Man Cybern.* 10:624–36

Kragt, H., Landeweerd, J. A. 1974. Mental skills in process control. See Edwards & Lees 1974, pp. 149–62

Kramer, A., Wickens, C. D., Donchin, E. 1983. An analysis of the processing demands of a complex perceptual-motor task. *Hum. Factors* 25:597–621

Krohn, G. S. 1983. Flowcharts used for procedural instructions. *Hum. Factors* 25:573–81

Lachman, R., Lachman, J. R., Butterfield, E. C. 1979. *Cognitive Psychology and Information Processing.* Hillsdale, NJ: Erlbaum

Landeweerd, J. A. 1979. Internal representation of a process fault diagnosis and fault correction. *Ergonomics* 22:1343–51

Landeweerd, J. A., Seegers, H. J., Praageman, J. 1981. Effects of instruction, visual imagery, and educational background on process control performance. *Ergonomics* 24:133–41

Lea, W., ed. 1980. *Trends in Speech Recognition.* Englewood Cliffs, NJ: Prentice Hall

Lees, F. P. 1981. Computer support for diagnostic tasks in the process industries. See Rasmussen & Rouse 1981, pp. 369–88

Lees, F. P., Sayers, B. 1976. The behavior of process operators under emergency conditions. See Sheridan & Johannsen 1976, pp. 331–42

Leippe, M. R., Wells, G. L., Ostrom, T. 1978. Crime seriousness as a determinant of accuracy in eyewitness identification. *J. Appl. Psychol.* 63:345–51

LePlat, J. 1978. Factors determining workload. *Ergonomics* 21:143–49

LePlat, J., Hoc, J. 1981. Subsequent verbalization in the study of cognitive processes. *Ergonomics* 24:743–56

Levin, H., Lord, W. 1975. Speech pitch frequency as an emotional state indicator. *IEEE Trans. Syst. Man Cybern.* 5:259–73

Liaos, L. 1978. Predictive aids for discrete tasks with input uncertainty. *IEEE Trans. Syst. Man Cybern.* 8:19–29

Lindsay, R. C., Wells, G. L., Rumpel, C. M. 1981. Can people detect eyewitness identification accuracy within and across situations? *J. Appl. Psychol.* 67:79–89

Lintern, G., Gopher, D. 1978. Adaptive training: Issues, results, and future directions. *Int. J. Man-Machine Stud.* 10:521–51

Liuzzo, S. G., Drury, C. 1980. An evaluation of blink inspection. *Hum. Factors* 22:201–10

Lochovsky, F. 1978. *Database management system user performance.* PhD thesis. Univ. Toronto, Canada

Loftus, E. F. 1979. *Eyewitness Testimony.* Cambridge, Mass: Harvard Univ. Press

Loftus, E. 1980. Impact of expert psychological testimony on the unreliability of eyewitness identification. *J. Appl. Psychol.* 65:9–15

Logan, G. D. 1979. On the use of concurrent memory load to measure attention and automaticity. *J. Exp. Psychol: Hum. Percept. Perform.* 5:198–207

Long, C. M., Waag, W. L. 1981. Limitations, practical applicability of d' and beta as measures. *Hum. Factors* 23:283–90

Luce, P. A., Feustel, T. C., Pisoni, D. B. 1983. Capacity demands in short term memory for synthetic and natural speech. *Hum. Factors* 25:17–32

Lusted, L. B. 1976. Clinical decision making. In *Decision Making and Medical Care,* ed. F. DeDombal, J. Grevy. Amsterdam: North Holland

Mackie, R. R. 1977. *Vigilance: Relationships Among Theories, Physiological Correlates and Operational Performance.* New York: Plenum

Madni, A., Samet, M., Freedy, A. 1982. A trainable on-line model of the human operator in information acquisition tasks. *IEEE Trans. Syst. Man Cybern.* 12:504–11

Malpass, R. S., Devine, P. G. 1981. Guiding memory in eyewitness identification. *J. Appl. Psychol.* 67:343–50

Marshall, E. C., Duncan, K. D., Baker, S. M. 1981. Role of withheld information in process fault diagnosis training. *Ergonomics* 24:711–24

Mayer, R. E. 1975. Different problem solving competencies established in learning computer programming with and without meaningful models. *J. Educ. Psychol.* 67:725–34

Mayer, R. E. 1981. The psychology of how novices learn computer programming. *Comput. Surv.* 13:122–41

McCauley, M. A. 1984. Human factors in voice technology. In *Human Factors Review,* ed. F. Muckler, Santa Monica, CA: Human Factors

McCormick, E. J., Sanders, M. S. 1982. *Human Factors in Engineering and Design.* New York: McGraw-Hill

McLeod, P. D. 1977. A dual task response modality effect: Support for multiprocessor models of attention. *Q. J. Exp. Psychol.* 30:83–90

McLeod, P. D. 1978. Does probe RT measure central processing demand? *Q. J. Exp. Psychol.* 30:83–90

McLeod, P. D., McCallum, I. R. 1975. Control strategies with experienced and novice controllers with a 0 energy reactor. *Ergonomics* 18:547–54

McRuer, D. T. 1980. Human dynamics in man-machine systems. *Automatica* 16:237–53

McRuer, D., Clement, W. F., Allen, W. 1981. A theory of human error. *Proc. 17th Ann. Conf. on Manual Control,* Pasadena, CA, pp. 241–58

McRuer, D., Weir, D., Jex, H., Magdeleno, R., Allen, W. 1975. Measurement of driver-vehicle multiloop response properties with a single disturbance input. *IEEE Trans. Syst. Man Cybern.* 5:490–97

Mehle, T. 1982. Hypothesis generation in an automobile malfunction inference task. *Acta Psychol.* 52:87–116

Merhav, S. J., Ben Ya'acov, O. 1976. Control augmentation and workload reduction by kinesthetic information from the manipulator. *IEEE Trans. Syst. Man, Cybern.* 6:825–35

Merhav, S. J., Gabay, E. A. 1975. A method for unbiased parameter estimation. *IEEE Trans. Auto. Cont.* 20:372–78

Miller, D. P. 1981. The depth-breadth tradeoff in hierarchial computer menus. See Sugarman 1981, pp. 296–300

Mitchell, C., Miller, R. 1983. Design strategies for computer-based information displays in real time control systems. *Hum. Factors* 25:353–70

Moran, T. P. 1981a. An applied psychology of the user. *Comput. Surv.* 13:1–12

Moran, T. P. 1981b. The comand language grammar: A representation for the user interface of interactive computer systems. *Int. J. Man-Machine Stud.* 15:3–50

Moray, N. ed. 1979. *Mental Workload: Its Theory and Measurement.* New York: Plenum

Moray, N. 1981. The role of attention in the detection of errors and the diagnosis of errors in man-machine systems. See Rasmussen & Rouse 1981, pp. 185–98

Moray, N. 1982. Subjective mental workload. *Hum. Factors* 24:25–40

Moray, N. 1984. Attention to dynamic visual displays in man-machine systems. See Parasuraman & Davies 1984

Morowski, T., Drury, C., Karwan, M. H. 1980. Predicting search performance for multiple targets. *Hum. Factors* 22:707–18

Morris, N. 1982. The human operator in process control. Georgia Inst. Technol. Sch. Indust. Eng. Cent. Man-Machine Syst. Res. Rep. No. 82-1

Morris, N., Rouse, W. 1983. The effects of level of knowledge upon human problemsolving in a process control task. See Pope & Haugh 1983, pp. 690–99

Mulder, G., Mulder, L. J. 1981. Information processing and cardiovascular control. *Psychophysiology* 18:392–401

Murphy, A. H., Winkler, R. L. 1974. Subjective probability forecasting experiments in meteorology: Some preliminary results. *Bull. Am. Meteorol. Soc.* 55:1206–16

Murrell, G. 1977. Calibration of evidence in a probabilistic visual search and detection task. *Organ. Behav. Hum. Perform.* 18:3–18

Nakatani, L. H., O'Connor, K. D. 1980. Speech feedback and touch keying. *Ergonomics* 23:643–54

Natani, K., Gomer, F. E. 1981. Electrocortical activity and operator workload: A comparison of changes in the electroencephalogram and in event-related potentials. MDC E2424, McDonnell Douglas Corp., St. Louis

National Research Council. 1984. Applications of automatic speech recognition in severe environments. Washington DC: Natl. Acad. Press

Navon, D., Gopher, D. 1979. On the economy of the human processing system. *Psychol. Rev.* 86:254–85

Neal, A. S. 1977. Time intervals between keystrokes, records and fields in data entry with skilled operators. *Hum. Factors* 19:163–70

Nickerson, R. S. 1981. Why interactive computer systems are sometimes not used by people who might benefit from them. *Int. J. Man-Machine Stud.* 15:469–83

Norman, D. A. 1981a. Categorization of action slips. *Psychol. Rev.* 88:1–15

Norman, D. A. 1981b. *Steps towards a cognitive engineering: Systems images, system friendliness, mental models.* Presented at Symp. Models of Human Perform., ONR Contractors Meet., La Jolla, Calif.

Norman, D. A., Fisher, D. 1982. Why alphabetic keyboards are not easy to use: Keyboard layout doesn't much matter. *Hum. Factors* 24:509–20

Noro, K., Okada, Y. 1983. Robotization and human factors. *Ergonomics* 26:1001–16

North, R. A., Gopher, D. 1976. Measurements of attention as a predictor of flight performance. *Hum. Factors* 18:1–14

Noyes, L. 1980. The positioning of type on maps. *Hum. Factors* 22:353–60

Noyes, J. 1983. The QWERTY keyboard: a review. *Int. J. Man-Machine Stud.* 18:265–81

Ogden, W. C., Brooks, S. R. 1983. Query languages for the casual user: Exploring the middle ground between formal and natural languages. See Janda 1983, pp. 161–65

Ogden, G. D., Levine, J. W., Eisner, E. J. 1979. Measurement of workload by secondary tasks. *Hum. Factors* 21:529–48

Osborne, P. D., Barsam, H. F., Burgy, D. C. 1981. Human factors considerations for implementation of a "green board" concept in an existing "red/green" power plant control room. See Sugarman 1981, pp. 14–18

Pachella, R. 1974. The use of reaction time measures in information processing research. In *Human Information Processing,* ed. B. H. Kantowitz, pp. 41–82. Hillsdale, NJ: Erlbaum

Parasuraman, R. 1979. Memory load and event rate control sensitivity decrements in sustained attention. *Science* 205:924–27

Parasuraman, R., Davies, R. 1984. *Varieties of Attention.* San Diego: Academic

Parsons, H. M., Kearsley, G. P. 1982. Robotics and human factors: Current status and future prospects. *Hum. Factors* 24:535–52

Patternote, P. H., Verhagen, L. H. M. J. 1979. Human operator research with a simulated distillation process. *Ergonomics* 22:19

Pattipati, K. R., Kleinman, D., Ephrath, A. 1982. A dynamic decisional model of human task selectional performance. *IEEE Trans. Syst. Man Cybern.* 12:145–66

Payne, J. W. 1980. Information processing theory: Some concepts and methods applied to decision research. See Wallsten 1980, pp. 95–116

Petrick, S. R. 1976. On natural language based computer systems. *IBM J. Res. Dev.* 20:314–25

Pew, R. W. 1974. Human perceptual-motor performance. See Kantowitz 1974, pp. 1–40

Pew, R. W. 1979. Secondary tasks and workload measurement. See Moray 1979, pp. 23–28

Pew, R. W., Baron, S. 1978. The components of an information processing theory of skilled performance based on an optimal control perspective. In *Information Processing in Motor Control and Learning,* ed. G. E. Stelmach, pp. 71–78. New York: Academic

Pew, R. W., Miller, D. C., Feehrer, C. E. 1981. Evaluating nuclear control room improvements through analysis of critical operator decision. See Sugarman 1981, pp. 100–9

Pitz, G., Heerboth, J., Sachs, N. 1980. Assessing the utility of multiattribute utility assessments. *Organ. Behav. Hum. Perform.* 26:65–80

Pope, A., Haugh, L., eds. 1983. *Proc. 27th*

Ann. Meet. Human Factors Soc. Santa Monica, Calif: Human Factors

Potash, L. M. 1977. Maps and map-related research. *Hum. Factors* 19:139–50

Poulton, E. C. 1974. *Tracking Skills and Manual Control.* New York: Academic

Price, L. A., Cordova, C. A. 1983. Use of mouse buttons. See Janda 1985, pp. 262–66

Rabbitt, A. M. A. 1978. Detection of errors by skilled typists. *Ergonomics* 21:945–58

Ramsey, H. R., Atwood, M. E., Kirshbaum, P. J. 1978. *A critically annotated bibliography of the literature of human factors in computer systems.* Englewood, Colo: Science Applications

Rasmussen, J. 1981. Models of mental strategies in process control. See Rasmussen & Rouse 1981, pp. 241–48

Rasmussen, J. 1983. Skills, rules, and knowledge: Signals, signs, and symbols, and other distinction in human performance models. *IEEE Trans. Syst. Man Cybern.* 13:257–66

Rasmussen, J., Jensen, A. 1974. Mental procedures in real life tasks: A case study of electronic troubleshooting. *Ergonomics* 17:193–207

Rasmussen, J., Lind, M. 1981. Coping with complexity. In *First European Annual Conference on Human Decision Making and Manual Control,* ed. H. G. Stassen. New York: Plenum

Rasmussen, J., Rouse, W. B., eds. 1981. *Human Detection and Diagnosis of System Failures.* New York: Plenum

Reason, J. T. 1984. Lapses of attention in everyday life. See Parasuraman & Davies 1984

Reid, G. B., Shingledecker, C. A., Eggemeier, F. T. 1981a. Application of conjoint measurement to workload scale development. See Sugarman 1981, pp. 522–26

Reid, L. D., Solowka, E. N., Billing, A. M. 1981b. A systematic study of driver steering behavior. *Ergonomics* 24:447–62

Reisner, P. 1981. Human factors studies of database query languages: A survey and assessment. *Comput. Surv.* 13:121–41

Roberts, J., Golder, T., Chick, G. 1980. Judgment, oversight, and skill: A cultural analysis of P-3 pilot error. *Hum. Organ.* 39:5–21

Robertson, S. P., Black, J. B. 1983. Planning units in text editing behavior. See Janda 1983, pp. 217–21

Rolfe, J. M. 1971. The secondary task as a measure of mental load. In *Measurement of Man at Work,* ed. W. T. Singleton, J. G. Fox, D. Witfield, pp. 135–48. London: Taylor, Francis

Roscoe, S. N. 1968. Airborne displays for flight and navigation. *Hum. Factors* 10:321–32

Roscoe, A. H. 1978. *Assessing pilot workload.* AGARD-A6-233

Roscoe, S. N. 1981. *Aviation Psychology.* Iowa City: Univ. Iowa Press

Roscoe, S. N., Corl, L., Jensen, R. S. 1981. Flight display dynamics revisited. *Hum. Factors* 23:341–53

Rouse, W. B. 1977. Human-computer interactions in multitask situations. *IEEE Trans. Syst. Man Cybern.* 7:384–92

Rouse, W. B. 1979a. Problem-solving performance of maintenance trainees in a fault diagnosis task. *Hum. Factors* 21:195–203

Rouse, W. B. 1979b. A model of human decision making in fault diagnosis tasks that include feedback and redundancy. *IEEE Trans. Syst. Man, Cybern.* 9:237–41

Rouse, W. B. 1981a. Experimental studies and mathematical models of problem-solving in fault diagnosis tasks. See Rasmussen & Rouse 1981, pp. 199–216

Rouse, W. B. 1981b. Human-computer interactions in the control of dynamic systems. *Comput. Surv.* 13:71–99

Rouse, W. B., Hunt, R. M. 1984. Human problem-solving in fault and diagnosis tasks. In *Advances in Man-Machine System Research.* ed. R. Rouse. Greenwich, CT: JAI Press

Rouse, W. B., Rouse, S. H. 1979. Measures of complexity of fault diagnosis tasks. *IEEE Trans. Syst. Man Cybern.* 9:720–27

Rouse, W. B., Rouse, S. H. 1983a. Analysis and classification of human error. *IEEE Trans. Syst. Man Cybern.* 13:539–49

Rouse, W. B., Rouse, S. H. 1983b. A framework for research on adaptive decision aids. Air Force Aerospace Med. Res. Lab. Tech. Rep. AFAMRL-TR-83-082

Rouse, W. B., Rouse, S. H., Hamner, J. 1982. Design and evaluation of an on-board computer-based information system for aircraft. *IEEE Trans. Syst. Man Cybern.* 12:451–63

Rubenstein, T., Mason, A. F. 1979. The accident that shouldn't have happened: An analysis of Three Mile Island. *IEEE Spectrum,* Nov., pp. 33–57

Ruffle-Smith, H. P. 1979. A simulator study of the interaction of pilot workload with errors, vigilance, and decision. NASA Tech. Memo. 78482. Washington DC: NASA Tech. Inf. Off.

Sage, A. 1981. Behavioral and organizational considerations in the design of information systems and processes for planning and decision support. *IEEE Trans. Syst. Man Cybern.* 11:640–78

Salvendy, G. 1983. Review and reappraisal of human aspects in planning robotic systems. *Behav. Inf. Technol.* 2:263–87

Salvendy, G., LeBold, W., Shodja, S., Lange, T. 1983. *Correlates of computer programming performance.* Presented at the 7th Ann. Conf. Prod. Res., Windsor, Canada

Savage, R. E., Wierwille, W. W., Cordes, R.

E. 1978. Evaluating the sensitivity of various measures of operator workload using random digits as a secondary task. *Hum. Factors* 20:649–54

Schank, R. C., Abelson, R. P. 1977. *Scripts, Plans, Goals and Understanding.* Hillsdale, NJ: Erlbaum

Schiflett, S. G. 1980. *Evaluation of pilot workload assessment device to test alternative display formats and control handling qualities.* Tech. Rep. SY-33R-80. Patuxent River, Md: Naval Air Test Center

Schum, D. 1975. The weighing of testimony of judicial proceedings from sources having reduced credibility. *Hum. Factors* 17:172–203

Schum, D. A. 1980. Sorting out the effects of witness sensitivity and beta placement on the inferential value of testimonial evidence. *Organ. Behav. Hum. Perform.* 27:153–96

Schustack, M. W., Sternberg, R. J. 1981. Evaluation of evidence in causal inference. *J. Exp. Psychol. Gen.* 110:101–20

Shackel, B. 1976. Process control—simple and sophisticated display devices as decision aids. See Sheridan & Johannsen 1976, pp. 429–44

Sharit, J., Salvendy, G. 1982. External and internal attentional environments. II. Reconsideration of the relationship between sinus arrhythmia and information load. *Ergonomics* 25:121–32

Sheil, B. A. 1981. The psychological study of programming. *Comput. Surv.* 13:101–20

Shepherd, A., Marshall, E., Turner, A., Duncan, K. 1977. Diagnosing plant failures from a control panel: A comparison of three training methods. *Ergonomics* 20:347–61

Sheridan, T. B. 1980. Mental workload—What is it? Why bother with it? *Hum. Factors Soc. Bull.* 23:1–2

Sheridan, T. B. 1981. Understanding human error and aiding human diagnostic behavior in nuclear power plants. See Rasmussen & Rouse 1981, pp. 19–36

Sheridan, T. B. 1982. *Supervisory control: Problems, theory, and experiment in application to undersea remote control systems.* MIT Man-Machine Syst. Lab. Rep., Feb.

Sheridan, T. B., Ferrell, L. 1974. *Man-Machine Systems.* Cambridge, Mass: MIT press

Sheridan, T. B., Johannsen, G., eds. 1976. *Monitoring Behavior and Supervisory Control.* New York: Plenum

Sheridan, T. B., Simpson, R. W. 1979. *Toward the definition and measurement of the mental workload of transport pilots.* FTR Rep. R-79-4. Cambridge, MA: MIT Flight Transp. Lab.

Shneiderman, B. 1977. Measuring computer program quality and comprehension. *Int. J. Man-Machine Stud.* 9:465–78

Shneiderman, B. 1980. *Software Psychology: Human Factors in Computer and Information Systems.* Cambridge, Mass: Winthrop

Shneiderman, B., Mayer, R. 1979. Syntatic/semantic interactions in programmer behavior: a model and experimental results. *Int. J. Comput. Inf. Sci.* 8:2219–38

Shneiderman, B., Mayer, R., McKay, D., Heller, P. 1977. Experimental investigations of the utility of detailed flowcharts in programming. *ACM Commun.* 20:378–81

Sime, M. E., Coombs, M. J., eds. 1983. *Designing for Human-Computer Interaction.* New York: Academic

Simpson, C., Williams, D. H. 1980. Response time effects of alerting tone and semantic context for synthesized voice cockpit warnings. *Hum. Factors* 22:319–30

Simpson, H. A. 1982. A human factors style guide for programming design: taking the user into account in the design of software. *BYTE* 7:108–32

Slovic, P., Fischoff, B., Lichtenstein, S. 1977. Behavioral decision theory. *Ann. Rev. Psychol.* 28:1–39

Small, D. W., Weldon, L. J. 1983. An experimental comparison of natural and structured query languages. *Hum. Factors* 25:253–63

Smith, H. T., Crabtree, R. 1975. Interactive planning. *Int. J. Man-Machine Stud.* 7:213

Smith, J., Mitchell, T. R., Beach, L. R. 1982. A cost-benefit mechanism for selecting problem-solving strategies. *Organ. Behav. Hum. Perform.* 29:370–96

Smith, S. L. 1981. Design guidelines for user-system interface of on-line computer systems: A survey report. See Sugarman 1981, pp. 509–14

Smith, S., Aucella, A. 1982. *Design Guidelines for the User Interface to Computer-Based Information systems.* Bedford, Mass: MITRE Corp.

Snowberry, K., Parkinson, S. R., Sisson, N. 1983. Computer display menus. *Ergonomics* 26:699–712

Sperandio, J. C. 1978. The regulation of working methods as a function of workload among air traffic controllers. *Ergonomics* 21:195–202

Steeb, R. 1980. Automated management of communications with remote systems: A decision analysis appraisal. *Int. J. Man-Machine Stud.* 13:437–53

Steeb, R., Johnston, S. 1981. A computer based interactive system for group decision making. *IEEE Trans. Syst. Man Cybern.* 11:544–52

Steeb, R., Weltman, G., Freedy, A. 1976. *Man/machine interaction in adaptive computer-aided control: Human factors guidelines.* Tech. Rep. PTR-1008-76-1/31. Woodland Hills, Calif: Perceptronics

Stengel, R. F., Broussard, J. R. 1978. Predictions of pilot-aircraft stability boundaries and performance contours. *IEEE Trans. Syst. Man Cybern.* 8:349–56

Stillwell, W. G., Barron, F. H., Edwards, W. 1983. Evaluating credit applications: A validation of multiattribute utility weight elicitation techniques. *Organ. Behav. Hum. Perform.* 32:87–108

Sugarman, R. C., ed. 1981. *Proc. 25th Ann. Meet. Hum. Factors Soc.* Santa Monica, Calif: Human Factors

Sverko, B., Jereik, Z., Kalenovic, A. 1983. A contribution to the investigation of time-sharing ability. *Ergonomics* 26:151–60

Swain, A. D. 1977. Error and reliability in human engineering. In *International Encyclopedia of Psychiatry, Psychoanalysis and Neurology,* ed. B. Wolman, 4:371–73. New York: Van Nostrand Reinhold

Swain, A. D., Guttman, H. E. 1980. *Handbook of human reliability analysis with emphasis on nuclear power plant application.* NUREG/CR-1278. Washington, DC: GPO

Swennsen, R. G., Hessel, S. J., Herman, P. G. 1977. Omissions in radiology: Faulty search or stringent reporting criteria? *Radiology* 123:563–67

Swets, J. A., Pickett, R. M. 1982. *The Evaluation of Diagnostic Systems.* New York: Wiley

Teichner, W. H., Mocharnuk, J. B. 1979. Visual search for complex targets. *Hum. Factors* 21:259–76

Tennant, H. R., Ross, K. M., Thompson, C. W. 1983. Usable natural language interfaces through menu based natural language understanding. See Janda 1983, pp. 154–60

Thorndyke, P., Hayes-Roth, B. 1982. Differences in spatial knowledge acquired through maps and navigation. *Cognit. Psychol.* 14:560–89

Tickner, A. H., Poulton, E. C. 1975. Watching people and actions. *Ergonomics* 18:35–51

Towne, D. M. 1981. A general purpose system for simulating and training complex diagnosis and trouble-shooting tasks. See Rasmussen & Rouse 1981, pp. 621–36

Towstopiat, O. 1983. Human factors guidelines for computer software design. See Pope & Haugh 1983, pp. 1035–39

Tulga, M. K., Sheridan, T. B. 1980. Dynamic decision and workload in multitask supervisory control. *IEEE Trans. Syst. Man Cybern.* 10:217–32

Tversky, A., Kahneman, D. 1974. Judgment under uncertainty: Heuristics and biases. *Science* 185:1124–31

Tversky, B. 1981. Distortion of memory for maps. *Cognit. Psychol.* 13:407–33

Umbers, I. G. 1979a. A study of the control skills of gas grid control engineers. *Ergonomics* 22:557–72

Umbers, I. G. 1979b. Models of the process operator. *Int. J. Man-Machine Stud.* 11:263–84

Umbers, I. G. 1981. A study of control skills in an industrial task and in a simulation using the verbal protocol technique. *Ergonomics* 24:1057–80

Underwood, G. 1978. *Human Information Processing.* New York: Academic

Van Es, F. L. 1976. Analysis of keying errors. *Ergonomics* 19:165–74

Veldhuyzen, W., Stassen, H. G. 1977. The internal model concept: An application to modelling human control of large ships. *Hum. Factors* 19:367–80

Walden, R., Rouse, W. 1978. A queing model of pilot decision making in multitask flight management situations. *IEEE Trans. Syst. Man Cybern.* 8:867–75

Wallsten, T. S., ed. 1980. *Cognitive Processes in Choice and Decision Behavior.* Hillsdale, NJ: Erlbaum

Waltz, D. 1978. An English language question answering system for a large relational database. *ACM Commun.* 21:526–39

Warshaw, P. R. 1978. Application of selective attention theory to television advertising displays. *J. Appl. Psychol.* 63:366–72

Weinberg, G. M. 1971. *The Psychology of Computer Programming.* New York: Van Nostrand Reinhold

Weisbroad, R. L., Davis, K. B., Freedy, A. 1977. Adaptive utility assessment in dynamic decision processes: An experimental evaluation of decision aiding. *IEEE Trans. Syst. Man Cybern.* 7:377–83

Weizenbaum, J. 1976. *Computer Power and Human Reasoning.* San Francisco: Freeman

Welford, A. T. 1976. *Skilled Performance.* Glenview, Ill: Scott Foresman

Welford, A. T. 1978. Mental workload as a function of demand, capacity, strategy, and skill. *Ergonomics* 21:151–67

Wells, G. L., Leippe, M. R. 1981. How do triers of fact infer the accuracy of eyewitness identification? *J. Appl. Psychol.* 67:682–87

West, B., Clark, J. A. 1974. Operator interaction with a computer controlled distillation column. See Edwards & Lees 1974, pp. 206–21

Whitfield, D., Ball, R. G., Bird, J. M. 1983. Some comparisons of on-display and off-display touch input devices for interaction with computer generated displays. *Ergonomics* 26:1033–53

Whitfield, D., Ball, R. G., Ord, G. 1980. Some human factors aspects of computer-aiding concepts for air traffic controllers. *Hum. Factors* 22:569–80

Wickelgren, W. 1977. Speed-accuracy tradeoff and information processing dynamics. *Acta Psychol.* 41:67–85

Wickens, C. D. 1979. Human workload measurement. See Moray 1979, pp. 77–100

Wickens, C. D. 1980. The structure of attentional resources. In *Attention and Performance*, ed. R. Nickerson, 8:239–58. Hillsdale, NJ: Erlbaum

Wickens, C. D. 1984. *Engineering Psychology and Human Performance.* Columbus, Ohio: Merrill

Wickens, C. D., Gopher, D. 1977. Control theory measurement of tracking as indices of attention allocation strategies. *Hum. Factors* 19:349–65

Wickens, C. D., Kessel, C. 1979. The effects of participatory mode and task workload on the detection of dynamic system failures. *IEEE Trans. Syst. Man Cybern.* 9:24–34

Wickens, C. D., Kessel, C. 1981. Failure detection in dynamic systems. See Rasmussen & Rouse 1981, pp. 155–70

Wickens, C. D., Kramer, A., Vanasse, L., Donchin, E. 1983a. Performance of concurrent tasks: A psychophysiological analysis of the reciprocity of information processing resources. *Science* 221:1080–82

Wickens, C. D., Mountford, S. J., Schreiner, W. 1981. Multiple resources, task-hemispheric integrity, and individual differences in time-sharing. *Hum. Factors* 23:211–29

Wickens, C. D., Sandry, D., Vidulich, M. 1983b. Compatibility and resource competition between modalities of input, central processing, and output: Testing a model of complex performance. *Hum. Factors* 25:227–48

Wickens, C. D., Vidulich, M., Sandry, D. 1984. Principles of S-C-R compatibility with spatial and verbal codes: Implications for voice display and physical location. *Hum. Factors* 26: In press

Wickens, C. D., Yeh, Y. 1983. The dissociation between subjective workload and performance: A multiple resource approach. See Pope & Haugh 1983, pp. 244–47

Wiener, E. 1977. Controlled flight into terrain accidents: System induced errors. *Hum. Factors* 19:171–87

Wiener, E., Curry, R. 1980. Flight deck automation: Promises and problems. *Ergonomics* 23:995–1012

Wierwille, W. W. 1979. Physiological measures of aircrew mental workload. *Hum. Factors* 21:575–94

Wierwille, W. W., Casali, J. G. 1983. A validated rating scale for global mental workload measurement applications. See Pope & Haugh 1983, pp. 129–33

Wierwille, W. W., Connor, S. A. 1983. Evaluation of 20 workload measures using a psychomotor task in a moving-base aircraft simulator. *Hum. Factors* 25:1–16

Wierwille, W. W., Gutmann, J. C. 1978. Comparison of primary and secondary task measures as a function of simulated vehicle dynamics and driving conditions. *Hum. Factors* 20:233–44

Williges, R. C., Wierwille, W. W. 1979. Behavioral measures of aircrew mental workload. *Hum. Factors* 21:549–74

Wohl, J. 1981. Force management decision requirements for Air Force tactical C systems. *IEEE Trans. Syst. Man Cybern.* 11:618–39

Wohl, J. 1982. Maintainability, prediction revisited: Diagnostic behavior, system complexity, and repair time. *IEEE Trans. Syst. Man Cybern.* 12:240–50

Wohl, J. 1983. Cognitive capability versus system complexity in electronic maintenance. *IEEE Trans. Syst. Man Cybern.* 13:624–26

Woods, D., Wise, J., Hanes, L. 1981. An evaluation of nuclear power plant safety parameter display systems. See Sugarman 1981, pp. 110–14

Young, R. M. 1981. The machine inside the machine: User's models of pocket calculators. *Int. J. Man-Machine Stud.* 15:51–86

Zeitlin, L. R., Finkelman, J. M. 1975. Research note: Subsidiary task techniques of digit generation and digit recall as indirect measures of operator loading. *Hum. Factors* 17:218–20

Ann. Rev. Psychol. 1985. 36:349–83

HEALTH PSYCHOLOGY[1]

David S. Krantz, Neil E. Grunberg, and Andrew Baum

Department of Medical Psychology, Uniformed Services University of the Health Sciences, Bethesda, Maryland 20814–4799

CONTENTS

INTRODUCTION AND HISTORICAL BACKGROUND

In recent years, the contact between psychology and the health sciences has expanded beyond mental health to a far broader area concerned with behavioral factors affecting physical health and illness. This new field has contributed to the health-care disciplines and the understanding of disease. Conversely, research on health and behavior already has enriched the general body of psychological knowledge. Since its inception in the late 1970s, health psychology has taken steps toward becoming a generic area of psychology by establishing its own division within APA, its own journal, and a set of training guidelines (Stone 1983). In addition, this problem-oriented field has brought together researchers and practitioners from a wide variety of psychological subspecialties.

Several scientific and health-care developments contributed to the formal emergence of health psychology. Many of these factors are intertwined with the growth of behavioral medicine and are reviewed in Neal Miller's (1983) *Annual Review* chapter, in papers by Matarazzo (1980, 1982), and in recent reports on health and behavior prepared by the Institute of Medicine (Hamburg et al 1982) and the National Research Council (Krantz et al 1982). While "behavioral medicine" is considered to be an interdisciplinary field bringing together biomedical and behavioral knowledge relevant to health and disease (Schwartz & Weiss 1978, Miller 1983), "health psychology" refers to psychology's role in this domain (e.g. Matarazzo 1980).

In this chapter, we describe some of the major scientific and health-care developments which have fostered a broadened role for psychologists in issues of physical health. We highlight mechanisms linking behavior to health and illness and key issues and research areas at the forefront of study in health psychology.

Role of Behavior in Major Health Problems: Shortcomings of the Biomedical Model

At the turn of the century, the greatest contributors to morbidity and mortality in the United States were infectious diseases such as pneumonia and tuberculosis. Today, the leading causes of mortality are chronic diseases, including cardiovascular disorders and cancers. These disease states are caused by a confluence of social, environmental, behavioral, and biological factors (Institute of Medicine 1978, USDHEW 1979a). Cardiovascular diseases, for example, are not an inevitable consequence of aging and genetic make-up (Kannel 1979). Environmental and behavioral variables such as cigarette smoking, diet, obesity, and stress are involved in the etiology and pathogenesis of these disorders. The most important risk factors for cancers are also behavioral variables, namely, cigarette smoking and diet. Thus, the importance of behavioral and psychosocial variables in major health problems sets the stage for psychologists to study these issues and also provides them with a role in developing techniques of disease prevention.

Behavioral factors also are crucial ingredients in the effective treatment and management of disease. High blood pressure, a symptomless chronic disorder with potentially serious consequences, can be pharmacologically controlled (HDFP 1979). However, the success of drug therapies requires that patients comply with medication prescription, and many cases are treated with dietary and habit changes rather than with drugs. Behavioral techniques also have been applied to rehabilitation and to reduce postsurgical pain and complications.

The role of behavior in today's most pressing health problems challenges the traditional medical model, which views disease as a purely biological phenomenon, that is, the product of specific agents or pathogens and bodily dysfunction. As a result, from both behavioral and biomedical communities there has been renewed interest in a broader model of health and illness encompassing psychological and social variables and their interaction with biological processes (Engel 1977, Matarazzo 1980, Miller 1983).

The interplay of psychology and the health sciences only begins with documenting the important associations between psychosocial variables and health outcomes. In addition, a "biobehavioral paradigm" has emerged in an effort to advance scientific understanding beyond the descriptive level. In contrast to a purely correlational approach, biobehavioral research in health psychology explores *mechanisms* linking behavioral processes to health and disease. An example is provided by recent evidence linking psychosocial factors (e.g. emotional stress) to the development of cardiovascular disease. Behavioral scientists working in this area are devoting increasing attention to the physiological processes (e.g. neuroendocrine activity) implicated in the development of coronary heart disease in order to determine how these processes are influenced by behavioral events. By considering mechanisms, it becomes possible to translate historical and epidemiological descriptors such as age, personality, genetics, or nutritional history into psychophysiological processes that can be modified or altered. For psychosocial processes as well, such as why adolescents begin to smoke cigarettes, the understanding of basic mechanisms (modeling, attitude change) has resulted in effective preventive interventions (Evans et al 1981).

In a chapter of this length, it is impossible to represent fully the broad

spectrum of research in health psychology, which spans the range of orientations from social to physiological. Instead, we focus on a selected number of
areas which have been actively studied or which promise to be at the cutting
edge of future work. No doubt there are important areas of study that will not be
described here. Our review is organized around three mechanisms by which
behavior can affect physical health.

MECHANISMS LINKING BEHAVIOR TO PHYSICAL DISEASE

The processes by which behavior can influence health and disease may be
grouped into three broad categories: direct psychophysiological effects, health-
impairing habits and life styles, and reactions to illness and the sick role. The
diverse effects of behavior on aspects of health and illness (ranging from
etiology and prevention to rehabilitation) may be considered within this
framework.

Direct Psychophysiological Effects

Psychophysiological effects involve alterations in tissue function via physiological responses to psychosocial stimuli. This mechanism encompasses bodily
changes (e.g. stress-induced) without the intervention of external agents such
as cigarette smoking or dietary risk factors, although the two sets of variables
may produce interactive effects (e.g. stress and smoking might increase,
synergistically, the risk of coronary heart disease).

Central to this process is the concept of stress popularized by Hans Selye,
who described it as a nonspecific (i.e. general) response of the body to external
demands (Selye 1976). Current views and definitions of stress have become
increasingly sophisticated as the focus of research has changed from responses
by specific organ systems to an integrated, "whole body" response. Early work
maintained strict disciplinary perspectives, concentrating on either the biological responses of one or two systems or the person's psychological evaluation
of and response to particular situations. More recently, as we will describe in a
later section, efforts have been made to join these approaches, suggesting that
stress is a complex, multilevel process that considers interaction with the
external world as a series of integrated responses with implications for health
(e.g. Kasl 1984).

Health-Impairing Habits and Behaviors

A second means by which behavior leads to physical illness occurs when
individuals engage in habits and styles of life that are damaging to health, as
amply documented by recent Surgeon General's reports on smoking and health
and on health promotion and disease prevention (USDHEW 1979a,b).

Cigarette smoking is probably the most salient behavior in this category, for it has been implicated as a risk factor for the leading causes of death in the United States. Poor diet, lack of exercise, excessive alcohol consumption, and poor hygienic practices also have been linked to disease outcomes (USDHEW 1979a, Institute of Medicine 1978). These habits may be deeply rooted in cultural practices or initiated by social influences (e.g. smoking to obtain peer group approval). Many are often maintained as part of an achievement-oriented life style as well as by the interaction of biological and behavioral mechanisms of addiction. Therefore, a major focus of research in health psychology has been on the role of individual belief systems, life styles, and social-psychological processes as they affect the development of chronic diseases. Considerable attention by psychologists also has been directed toward the development of techniques to modify behaviors that constitute risk factors for illnesses, and, increasingly, to promote healthy behaviors (cf Matarazzo et al 1984).

Reactions to Illness and the Sick Role

A third process through which behavior leads to physical illness occurs when individuals minimize the significance of symptoms, delay in seeking medical care, or fail to comply with treatment and rehabilitation regimens. One prominent example is the sizeable number of heart attack patients who procrastinate in seeking help, thereby diminishing their chances of survival. These actions are representative of a larger area of study (illness behavior) concerned with the way people react to the experience of organ dysfunction as well as to the experience of being in the role of a sick person (Kasl & Cobb 1966). To succeed, medical therapies require that the patient follow the physician's advice and directions, but an extensive literature reports disturbingly low rates of compliance with health and medical care regimens (Sackett & Haynes 1976, Haynes et al 1979). Accordingly, there has been considerable research on social and psychological processes involved in patients' reactions to pain and illness, perceptions of symptoms, and compliance with medical regimens. This research has led to the development of interventions that have been applied in treatment and rehabilitation settings, and to increasing attention by health psychologists toward understanding mechanisms of symptom perception and compliance in health settings (Pennebaker 1982, Leventhal et al 1984), as well as processes involved in coping with chronic disease (Burish & Bradley 1983).

STRESS AND ITS EFFECTS ON HEALTH

Stress is a process central to the relationship between behavior and health because it helps to explain how psychologically relevant events translate into health-impairing physiological changes and illness. Although definitions of stress are often imprecise (Kasl 1984), research has identified a number of direct physiological effects of stressors (e.g. immunosuppression, increased blood pressure) that may influence susceptibility to disease. Indirect effects of stress involving behavioral changes that are harmful (e.g. cigarette smoking, alcohol or drug abuse) also have been noted, and together these influences provide mechanisms by which psychosocial events may affect health (see Elliott & Eisdorfer 1982).

Walter Cannon's (e.g. 1929) description of the "fight or flight response" was an important early contribution to stress research. Cannon argued that arousal of the sympathetic branch of the autonomic nervous system (SNS), mediated by the secretion of adrenaline, was a basic expression of stress. Increased heart rate, respiration, and other SNS-related changes prepare an organism to act upon a challenge or danger, either by fight or by flight. Psychological dangers or emotional distress also could trigger this system.

Hans Selye (1976) defined stress as a syndrome of bodily responses to noxious agents. His model focused on responses of the pituitary-adrenal-cortical axis, and he described a pattern of pathological physiologic reactions that seemed to result from almost any noxious agent he applied (e.g. heat, cold, chemical insults). He argued that all stressors caused the same sequence of responses called the General Adaptation Syndrome. Its early stages were alarm, during which the organism prepared to deal with a stressor, and resistance, during which coping and adaptation occurred. Selye believed that most organisms could resist effectively, but that there were limits to this ability. After depletion of resources by repetitive or prolonged stressors, exhaustion occurred and the organism was at risk for illness (so-called "diseases of adaptation"). Although aspects of Selye's model have been criticized (Mason 1975), the model served to explain how noxious environmental events might influence the development of disease.

The term "stress" is also used in a *psychological* sense by investigators (e.g. Lazarus 1966) to refer to an internal state of the individual who perceives threats to physical and/or psychic well-being. This use of the term emphasizes the organism's perception and evaluation of potentially harmful stimuli, and considers the perception of threat to arise from a comparison between the demands imposed upon the individual and the individual's ability to cope with these demands. A perceived imbalance in this mechanism gives rise to the experience of stress and to the stress response, which may be physiological and/or behavioral.

Physiological responses to stress include neural and endocrine activity which, in turn, can influence bodily processes including metabolic rate, cardiovascular and autonomic nervous system functioning, and immune reactions (Mason 1971, Baum et al 1982). Short-term stress responses include hormonal and cardiovascular reactions (e.g. increased heart rate and blood pressure) which may precipitate clinical disorders (e.g. stroke, cardiac instabilities and pain syndromes, psychosomatic symptoms) in predisposed individuals. If stimulation becomes pronounced, prolonged, or repetitive, the result may be chronic dysfunction in one or more systems (e.g. gastrointestinal, cardiovascular).

Psychological or behavioral responses to stress also may produce health-relevant affects. For example, stress has been shown to increase the perception or reporting of symptoms (Mechanic 1968, Pennebaker 1982) and increased absenteeism and health care utilization (House 1975).

Mediators of Response to Stress

Whereas early stress research emphasized the generality or nonspecificity of responses to a wide variety of stimuli, subsequent research has recognized that the link between stress and disease is not simple. It depends upon the context in which the stressful agent occurs, how individuals appraise it, and the social supports and personal resources available (Lazarus 1966, Mason 1971, Cohen et al 1982). These are wide individual differences in physiological responses to stressors, which depend on biological predispositions and on the individual's perceived ability to cope with or master conditions of harm, threat, or challenge. Although stressful events (e.g. failure, loss of loved ones, divorce) are inevitable, only a minority of individuals suffers lasting adverse effects. A variety of social and psychological factors (e.g. styles of coping and social supports provided by others) modify or buffer the impact of stressful events on illness (Cohen et al 1982).

One important mediator of response to stressors, social support, is defined in terms of benefits obtained from interpersonal relationships. Emotional support, instrumental aid, opportunities for social comparison, and self-esteem come from membership in a group in which one feels as if he or she "belongs" (Cobb 1976, Cohen & McKay 1984). Having social support seems to have general beneficial effects on health; e.g. people who have social support are less likely to die prematurely than are those who lack it (Berkman & Syme 1979, Cohen & Syme 1985). It is not clear whether its effect results from the stressful nature of not having social support or to the buffering effects of support when stress occurs independently (Cohen & McKay 1984). Nevertheless, social support reduces negative outcomes during stressful episodes such as unemployment, surgery, or bereavement, but different aspects of stress responding may be differentially influenced by support (Fleming et al 1982, Cohen & Syme 1985).

Coping styles also appear to affect stress response, but in a situation-specific fashion. For example, denial seems to be effective in reducing stress only under certain conditions. Acute stress may be successfully avoided, but evidence suggests that denial is not effective in coping with chronic stress (Mullin & Suls 1982, Collins et al 1983). Similarly, coping styles are differentially affected by the amount of information available to an individual and fear-inducing properties of the setting (Janis 1958, Johnson & Leventhal 1974). Overall hardiness, specific attitudes and perceptions of the world, and physiological predispositions also appear to increase or decrease vulnerability to stress-related health consequences (Kobasa 1979, Weiner 1979, Krantz & Glass 1984).

Perceived control is another powerful mediator of response to stressful settings. The belief that one could exert control over a noxious event is an important determinant of stress-related catecholamine levels, and several studies have shown that perceived or actual control in occupational settings reduces physiological and psychological symptoms of stress (Frankenhaeuser 1983). Mason (1975) also suggested that having control affects one's response to stress, and research by Glass & Singer (1972) showed that the perception of control reduces aftereffects of stress exposure. Similarly, providing adequate information to alter responses to threat can have stress-reducing effects. For example, cognitive techniques involving instructions in coping and the provision of adequate information have been shown to reduce distress in medical settings and facilitate recovery from surgery (Johnson & Leventhal 1974, Leventhal et al 1984).

The Life Event Approach

Identifying and quantifying events that lead to negative appraisals and adverse responses has been an important issue in stress research. Characterizations of these events has ranged from unpleasant stimuli to cataclysmic events such as natural disaster or war (Lazarus & Cohen 1977). It has become increasingly clear that no event is universally stressful; the ultimate impact of an event is determined by factors that go far beyond the precipitating agent. Nevertheless, some occurrences seem to be more likely than others to have a negative impact on health and behavior, and research has sought to identify these events.

Holmes & Rahe (1967) developed a life events scale to determine whether the effects of repeated adjustments required by life changes deplete adaptive resources during coping and increase vulnerability to stress-related illness. Events such as imprisonment, injury, pregnancy, and loss of a job were included in the scale, and respondents indicated those that had been experienced during specified time periods. These events were summed or weighted by their judged impact, and an index of life change computed. An increase in this index, or a clustering of life changes, tends to occur prior to the onset of illness (Holmes & Masuda 1974, Garrity & Marx 1979). Life changes also are associated with stress-related endocrine changes that may underlie enhanced vulnerability to illness (Mason et al 1979).

The Holmes-Rahe approach has been criticized on methodological and conceptual grounds (Rabkin & Streuning 1976, Dohrenwend & Dohrenwend 1978). Unique interactions between specific events may be missed if the frequency of all events is considered alone, and the relatively low rate of occurrence of major life events may limit the usefulness of this approach (DeLongis et al 1982). Negative results also have been reported, showing little reliable relationship between life events and subsequent illness (e.g. Hinkle 1974). In addition, many of the items in the life-change lists are symptomatic of health changes; as a result, one simply may be using health change to predict other health outcomes (Costa & Schroeder 1984).

To remedy some of these shortcomings, alternate forms of life change assessment require respondents to rate the perceived valence and impact of each life change, thereby incorporating the individual's appraisal into the assessments. Another approach is to measure everyday events of lesser magnitude (so-called "hassles and uplifts") which may affect the individual to an equal or greater extent than more major or externally visible life changes (e.g. DeLongis et al 1982). The direct measurement of "perceived stress" is also being explored for its effects on health (Cohen et al 1983).

Intensive Study of Single Events

Considerable research has examined intensively the responses to a single life stressor that may be acute or chronic in nature. However, there is some evidence that single episodes of acute exposure to stressors produce a temporary response, but that repeated exposure to brief encounters with stress may produce more serious problems (DeLongis et al 1982). Chronic stressors, including job stress, long-term unemployment, uncertainty, and imprisonment, appear to be more likely to cause long-term psychological and physiological problems (Kasl & Cobb 1970, Baum et al 1983). In some cases, these problems persist long after the stressful event has ended (Gleser et al 1981). In addition, the process of coping with chronic disease has received considerable attention, with illness itself viewed as a stressor (Burish & Bradley 1983).

PSYCHONEUROIMMUNOLOGY

The immune system is a surveillance mechanism responsible for combating disease-causing microorganisms and other foreign agents in the body. Research in the last decade suggests that rather than being an autonomous defense agency, this system is integrated with other physiologic processes and is sensitive to changes in central nervous system and endocrine functioning, such as those which accompany psychological stress. Accordingly, a new interdisciplinary area called "psychoneuroimmunology" (Ader 1981) studies interactions between psychological and immunological processes and holds promise of explaining many of the psychophysiological links between behavior and disease. Research in this field is particularly relevant to the study of psychological influences on infectious diseases and cancers.

Effects of Stress on Immune Function

Laboratory stressors can suppress the responsiveness of the immune system in animals, and stress-responsive hormones, including corticosteroids, can directly and indirectly alter components of the immune response (Ader 1981, Riley 1981). Animal and human studies demonstrate that laboratory and naturalistic stressors can reduce the number of lymphocytes (cells important in the immune process), lower the level of interferon (a substance which may prevent the spread of cancer), and cause damage in immunologically related tissue (Ader 1981, Sklar & Anisman 1981). Of particular relevance to cancers are animal studies demonstrating that stress can inhibit defenses against malignancy and lead to enhanced tumor growth (Riley 1981). However, some studies find the opposite, reporting that stress reduces tumor growth (see Sklar & Anisman 1981). Attempts to understand this finding have focused on the relationship between immune function and "stress hormones" such as corticosteroids. Administration of these hormones shortly before implantation of a tumor appears to increase resistance to the tumor, but administration after implantation caused the familiar pattern of immunosuppression and enhanced tumor growth (see Riley 1981, Sklar & Anisman 1981).

Studies of humans also show evidence of stress-linked changes in immunocompetence. Conditions such as bereavement, surgery, and sleep deprivation are associated with decreases in responsiveness of the immune system, usually followed by eventual return to normal levels (Schleifer et al 1980, Jemmott & Locke 1984). These effects have been inferred from observed relationships between stress and incidence of infectious illnesses (e.g. Jemmott & Locke 1984). However, more direct evidence of stress-related changes in lymphocyte number or responsiveness also has been reported (Schleifer et al 1980, Dorian et al 1982).

The mechanisms by which these effects are generated are presently of great interest. Evidence points to the adrenal hormones, including epinephrine, norepinephrine, and cortisol, as primary agents of immunosuppression (see Stein 1983). Research also has found that increases in these hormones often precede episodes of infectious disease (Jemmott & Locke 1984). However, the activity of adrenal hormones does not appear to be sufficient to explain stress-induced immunosuppression, and the mechanisms by which this effect is achieved remain to be clarified (Stein 1983).

Conditioning Effects on Immunity

Stress is not the sole avenue of psychological influence of immune function. Research by Ader and Cohen (e.g. 1984) has shown that pairing of a neutral stimulus with immunosuppressive drugs leads to conditioning of an immunosuppressive response to the neutral stimulus. When consumption of saccharin was paired with an injection of a drug that suppresses immune function, reexposure to saccharin alone was associated with decreases in antibody response. Subsequent studies have found similar results under different conditions, and using a variety of indices of immune function (Ader & Cohen 1984).

Conditioning is also suggested by reports of links between exposure to uncontrollable stress ("learned helplessness"; Seligman 1975) and lowered immunocompetence. In yoked designs in which animals receive aversive stimulation (i.e. shock), those with the ability to terminate the stimuli or escape show less tumor growth than do animals with no option for control (e.g. Sklar & Anisman 1981, Visintainer et al 1983). This effect may be due to the modulation of experienced stress by levels of control rather than to helplessness per se, but these findings suggest other instances of psychological influence of the immune system.

Stress and Human Cancers

It has been suggested that stress may play a role in the early development or appearance of cancers in humans (see Fox 1978, Sklar & Anisman 1981). Several studies have found that stressful events, such as loss of a loved one, have been linked to cancer. Similarly, emotional states such as helplessness or hopelessness and psychological traits such as depression have been correlated to the appearance of this disorder. Most of these studies are retrospective and are open to several very compelling criticisms: the long recruitment period of neoplastic diseases makes identification of a specific cause difficult; retrospective reports of life events may not be accurate; and perceptions and emotions are affected by the disease itself (see reviews by Fox 1978, Krantz & Glass 1984).

A more promising and ultimately more productive line of study involves the possible relationship of stress and personality to the progression and outcome of diagnosed cancers. In this regard, several studies have examined survival differences as a function of psychological characteristics of patients (see Fox 1978, Barofsky 1981, Krantz & Glass 1984). Results seem to suggest that states such as depression and helplessness are associated with poorer survival rates, whereas psychological responses of anger and hostility are related to more favorable outcomes. While further work is required to assess the reliability of these findings and the mechanisms involved, studying progression of diagnosed disease rather than early etiology overcomes some of the difficulties associated with the long period of development of cancers.

BEHAVIORAL FACTORS IN CARDIOVASCULAR DISORDERS

Despite a decline in cardiovascular mortality in the last ten years (USDHEW 1979c), the major cardiovascular disorders, including coronary heart disease (CHD), essential hypertension (EH), and sudden death, still account for one in two deaths in the United States. Potentially modifiable behavioral variables are important in all phases of cardiovascular disease, ranging from etiology and prevention to treatment and rehabilitation. As a result, the cardiovascular disorders are among the most well-developed research areas in the study of behavioral influences on health. For comprehensive reviews of psychological contributions to this area, see Gentry & Williams (1979), Krantz et al (1983), Ostfeld & Eaker (1984), and Steptoe (1981).

Smoking, diet, exercise, obesity, Type A behavior, and stress all account for variations in disease incidence (Kannel 1979), as do social factors such as occupational status, education, and income (Ostfeld & Eaker 1984). Unfortunately, the predictive value of many of the "risk factors" for clinical coronary heart disease is far from being a settled issue. For example, the role of diet and exercise in the etiology of CHD are quite controversial (e.g. Mann 1977, Froelicher et al 1980), and identifiable biologic risk factors by themselves are poor predictors of sudden death (Verrier et al 1983).

Standard Risk Factors

A risk factor is an attribute of the population of interest, or of the environment, which increases the likelihood of developing one or more cardiovascular diseases. Behavioral research on coronary heart disease was stimulated because many of the standard risk factors include behavioral components. For example, cigarette smoking is a preventable behavior caused and supported by psychosocial forces. Enhanced risk due to sex and age also may derive from nonbiological correlates of these variables, such as occupational pressures, stressful life events, and behavior patterns (Elliott & Eisdorfer 1982, Hamburg et al 1982). High salt intake may be associated with high blood pressure levels in some cultures and population groups. However, the relationship between salt intake and EH is complex, and salt intake may result in sustained blood pressure levels only in genetically predisposed individuals (e.g. Dahl et al 1962). Obesity is another behaviorally relevant phenomenon that plays an important role in hypertension, although the precise reasons for the higher prevalence of EH in obese patients have not been determined (Shapiro 1983).

Psychosocial Risk Factors

Biobehavioral research on the etiology and pathogenesis of cardiovascular disease has received further impetus from limitations in the ability of the standard biologic risk factors to identify most new cases of coronary disease (Jenkins 1976). A broadened search for mechanisms and influences contributing to risk of cardiovascular disorders has examined social indicators (e.g. socioeconomic status) and psychological factors (e.g. anxiety, psychological stress, and overt patterns of behavior). These results have been encouraging, but not definitive (see Jenkins 1976, Ostfeld & Eaker 1984). The two most promising psychosocial risk factors for CHD and hypertension to emerge in recent years are psychological stress and the Type A "coronary-prone" behavior pattern for coronary heart disease.

Certain conditions, such as excessive workload, job responsibility and dissatisfactions, may enhance coronary risk (House 1975). However, the relationship of psychosocial factors (e.g. occupational status) to CHD seems to depend on the way individuals perceive their life situations. For example, the Framingham Heart Study showed that working women in general were not at significantly higher risk of subsequent CHD than housewives (Haynes & Feinleib 1980). However, clerical workers and working women with children were more likely to develop subsequent CHD, as were individuals with nonsupportive employers. It appears that psychological factors, such as perceived demands and nonsupport from one's boss, determine whether objectively defined socioeconomic indicators increase risk of heart disease.

Stress from psychosocial causes also is a factor which has been implicated in the etiology and maintenance of high blood pressure, although results are equivocal (see Gutmann & Benson 1971, Syme & Torfs 1978). Chronic exposure to environmental stresses, such as high intensity occupational or community noise, also might be linked to cardiovascular problems (Cohen et al 1981, Peterson et al 1981). Possibly, psychological stimuli that threaten the organism result in cardiovascular and endocrine responses that play an important role in the development of high blood pressure (Julius & Esler 1975, Obrist 1981, Steptoe 1981).

Type A Behavior

The Type A or "coronary-prone" behavior pattern has been widely studied as a risk factor for CHD. First identified by cardiologists Friedman & Rosenman (1959), Type A is characterized by excessive competitive drive, impatience, hostility, and rapid speech and motor movements. A contrasting behavior pattern, called Type B, consists of the relative absence of these characteristics and a somewhat different style of coping. Several epidemiologic studies have found a relationship between Type A behavior and risk of subsequent CHD in men and women, comparable to the effect of risk factors such as smoking and hypertension (Rosenman et al 1975, Haynes et al 1980, Review Panel 1981). However, several recent studies have reported a weakened relationship between Type A and coronary disease, particularly among high risk subjects (see Matthews 1984). This change might reflect modifications in the method of assessing Type A behavior or changes in the prevalence of CHD risk factors. However, Type A components such as hostility, anger, and vigorous speech still remain related to CHD in recent studies (Matthews 1984, Dembroski et al 1985).

The extensive involvement of psychologists with research on Type A began with psychometric work (Jenkins et al 1971) and experimental work (Glass 1977). Currently, one active research area is to examine differences between Type A and Type B subjects in physiological responses to psychological stressors. The aim of this research is to understand the psychophysiological mechanisms linking Type A to CHD, and the nature of situations which elicit increased responding in Type A subjects (cf Matthews 1982). Physiological (especially sympathetic nervous system) reactivity in response to stress is measured as distinct from the observation of basal or resting levels of physiological variables. These changes in functioning, not detected by basal risk-factor measurement, may yield a better index of the pathogenic processes involved in coronary heart disease (see Krantz & Manuck 1984).

Another research direction has been the examination of particular components of Type A behavior, especially anger and speech stylistics, as they relate to disease endpoints and psychophysiological responses (Matthews 1984, Dembroski et al 1985). A third area actively being studied is the examination of Type A behavior in various age, sex, and cultural groups. Of particular interest has been the study of origins (both psychological and biological) as well as developmental antecedents of Type A behavior which appear to be identifiable in children as early as preschool age (see Matthews 1982, Krantz & Durel 1983).

In addition, researchers are examining the feasibility of modifying the Type A pattern (Suinn 1982). From a public health perspective, this is perhaps the most important area in the Type A field. Unfortunately, it is the least developed and most exploratory, partly because Type A refers to a heterogeneous set of behavioral characteristics that are difficult to target clinically, and partly because these behaviors are of instrumental and social value in our society. Several clinical techniques have been employed to modify Type A in both healthy volunteers and CHD patients. These include relaxation training, cognitive restructuring, guided practice, aerobic physical exercise, and psychodynamic and behavioral group therapies (see Suinn 1982). By and large, results of these studies suggest that brief psychological interventions promote changes in certain Type A behaviors at posttesting.

The most ambitious Type A intervention study to date is the Recurrent Coronary Prevention Project. Its major purpose is to determine whether Type A behavior can be modified in cardiac patients by using cognitive restructuring, relaxation training, and guided practice, and whether such modification will lower subsequent recurrence rates of coronary events. Results of this study reported to date have been encouraging (Thoresen et al 1982).

Biobehavioral Antecedents of Essential Hypertension

Essential hypertension is a heterogeneous disorder. Several pathogenic mechanisms may bring about blood pressure elevations, and different physiological and/or behavioral mechanisms are implicated at various stages of the disorder (Weiner 1979, Kaplan 1982). Psychological stimuli such as emotionally stressful events correlate highly with the exacerbation of hypertensive episodes in patients with established hypertension (Weiner 1979). Recent research on behavioral influences has focused increasingly on earlier rather than later stages of the disease. Despite many findings suggesting characteristics of suppressed hostility, anxiety, and/or social insecurity among patients with EH, the notion of a "hypertensive personality" has not received consistent support in the epidemiologic literature (see Krantz & Glass 1984).

Experimental work has sought to identify those individuals who are at risk of developing EH and the types of situations that might activate genetic predispositions to high blood pressure. Given that borderline EH is characterized by heightened responsiveness of the cardiovascular and sympathetic nervous system to mental stress (Julius & Esler 1975), recent research has examined the role of increased cardiovascular responsiveness as a marker in the development of the disorder. In this regard, reactivity to stress appears to be a stable and persistently evoked response that can be measured reliably. Heightened cardiovascular responsiveness and increased sodium retention by the kidneys caused by certain psychological stimuli also are positively related to family history of EH (a hypertension risk factor), even among individuals who have normal resting blood pressure levels and display no overt signs of the disorder (Obrist 1981, Light et al 1983, Krantz & Manuck 1984).

Nonpharmacologic Approaches to Treatment

A variety of nonpharmacologic approaches are considered to be effective adjuncts to drug therapy, or in the case of mild hypertension, potential alternatives to drug treatments. The three major modalities of such therapy include diet (restriction of sodium intake and weight control), physical exercise, and behavior modification/stress reduction (Shapiro 1983). Markedly decreasing salt intake in the diet can have a measurable effect on blood pressure in hypertensives (Parjis et al 1973). Similarly, weight loss—even without sodium restriction—can result in significant blood pressure reductions, as can long-term participation in a program of aerobic exercise (Shapiro 1983).

Another set of behavioral methods proposed in the management of hypertension involves techniques of relaxation training and biofeedback to reduce stress. These techniques produce small blood pressure reductions, but they are most effective when used as adjunctives to drug therapies (Shapiro 1983). These techniques may be useful in reducing the dosages of medications necessary or in enabling patients to maintain lower blood pressures once drugs are withdrawn (Fahrion 1981, Patel et al 1981). Another area under current investigation is in the application of behavior-modification techniques toward reducing reactivity to stress (e.g. English & Baker 1983).

In cardiac rehabilitation, health psychologists have made several recent contributions (see reviews in Blumenthal et al 1983, Krantz 1985). Behavioral strategies such as exercise, dietary changes, smoking cessation, Type A modification, and interventions for psychosocial problems of the cardiac patient (e.g. return to work and sexual functioning) are necessary components of successful rehabilitation (Razin 1982, Blumenthal et al 1983). The activities of psychologists in this area are particularly promising because increasing numbers of patients are surviving initial heart attacks, and because these individuals are highly motivated to change their behavior (Institute of Medicine 1978).

CIGARETTE SMOKING AND TOBACCO USE

Cigarette smoking is the single most preventable cause of mortality and morbidity in the United States (USDHEW 1979a). Most medical problems, disorders, and illnesses affect 1/100,000, 1/10,000 or, at the most, 1/100 people; by contrast, smoking (not including passive smoking) and its resulting health hazards directly affect one out of every three people.

Increased awareness by the public and medical community of the health hazards of smoking (largely because of the Surgeon Generals' reports beginning in 1964) has resulted in a decrease in the *percentage* of the population who are habitual smokers (USDHHS 1983). However, the *number* of habitual smokers has increased over the years and now includes roughly 54 million people in this country alone.

Premature mortality from cigarette smoking results from increased death rates from several diseases, but primarily from coronary heart disease, cancers of the respiratory tract, emphysema, and bronchitis. The likelihood of premature mortality increases with the amount smoked and the duration of smoking; the health risk drops with time since quitting. Despite the extensive health hazards of smoking, many smokers either cannot quit or they drift back to the old habit (Bernstein & Glasgow 1979, Leventhal & Cleary 1980). In light of the impressive and frightening list of hazards associated with cigarettes, considerable research has sought to determine the reasons why people smoke.

Initiation of Smoking

The initiation of smoking involves social, psychological, and perhaps psychobiological factors. People begin smoking in response to social pressure, to imitate peers of family members, and to imitate role models (including actors, athletes, and adults in general). Some youths begin smoking as an expression of adolescent rebellion or antisocial tendencies. Misconceptions concerning the risks of smoking (including lack of understanding or admission of the health risks and of dependence processes) may contribute to the likelihood of initiation (Pomerleau 1979). Also, there is some evidence that personality factors (especially extraversion) are moderately associated with the likelihood of initiation (Kozlowski 1979). Recently it has been proposed that biological factors that affect the quality of initial experiences with cigarette smoking affect the likelihood of initiation; for example, if early experiences include intense nausea, one is less likely to begin smoking habitually (Silverstein et al 1982).

Initiation of smoking behavior has been explained by several psychological and sociological theories. The psychoanalytic approach emphasizes the importance of oral fixation. Erikson's (1963) theory of psychosocial development maintains that two of the eight stages of psychosocial crises are most relevant to initiation of smoking: struggle to overcome inferiority (ages 6–11) and effort to establish an identity (ages 12–18). Bandura's (1977) social learning theory emphasizes the immediate social reinforcing consequences of smoking (e.g. imitation of models and media stereotypes, peer influence, and support), compared to the delayed aversive consequences. Within this context any psychologist has to be impressed with the effective and alluring images of beauty, strength, athletic prowess, and social desirability that the advertising industry associates with cigarette smoking. Eysenck's (1973) arousal model argues that people smoke to become biologically aroused and that people who find arousal more rewarding (e.g. extraverts) are more likely to become habitual smokers. Based on a longitudinal study of high school students followed through college, Jessor & Jessor (1977) proposed that adolescent deviant behavior (including smoking initiation) is determined by a multivariate network of personality and environmental factors. These determining factors include individual personality traits (including alienation or closeness to societal values and attitudes toward deviant behavior of peers); current perception of the social environment (including influence on beliefs of parents and friends); and history of other deviant behaviors (e.g. alcohol use, lying, and stealing).

Figure 1 presents some of the positive and negative factors that influence the development of smoking behavior, from initiation through maintenance of a habitual behavior. This diagram is designed to provide some indication of the chronology of contributing factors and to indicate whether they generally act to increase (+) or decrease (−) the likelihood of the behavior.

Maintenance of Smoking

The same psychological and social factors that influence initiation of smoking act to maintain this behavior. In addition, biological and psychobiological factors relating to addictive mechanisms are extremely important. Kozlowski & Herman (1984) have proposed a "boundary model" that includes psychological and pharmacological factors and distinguishes when each class of factors is particularly important.

Some investigators argue that habitual smokers self-administer tobacco to obtain physiological effects of nicotine that result in psychological rewards

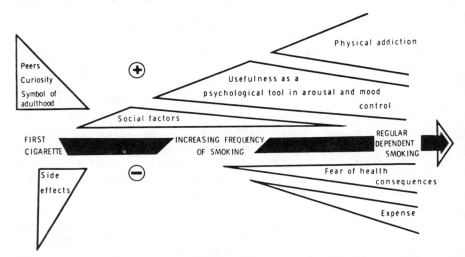

Figure 1   Factors affecting different stages in the development of smoking. Reproduced with permission of *British Journal of Diseases of the Chest* (Stepney 1980).

such as increased attention or decreased stress (cf Ashton & Stepney 1982). This explanation is known as the "psychological tool model." A more commonly held biological explanation for smoking maintenance is that repeated administration of some component of tobacco (probably nicotine or one of its metabolites) results in physical dependence (Jarvik 1979). Support for this view derives from evidence that human smokers smoke more low nicotine than high nicotine cigarettes, that human smokers smoke less when given nicotine chewing gum or intraveneous nicotine administration, and that rats will self-administer nicotine. After physical dependence has been established, a smoker must continue to smoke to avoid the unpleasantness of withdrawal (Schachter 1978, Russell 1979).

Maintenance of smoking involves the intertwining of learning mechanisms with the physiological and biochemical effects of smoking (Hunt & Matarazzo 1970, Dunn 1973). The physical effects of smoking may be linked through conditioning to social and environmental events, and environmental variables affect the nature of the reinforcing properties involved in maintenance of smoking (e.g. Barrett 1983). An argument for the importance of negative reinforcement in the maintenance of smoking behavior was offered by Schachter and colleagues in what has been termed the "nicotine titration model," based on the notion that smokers smoke to maintain a certain level of nicotine (Schachter et al 1977, Schachter 1978). Recently this model has been modified to consider other pharmacodynamic factors and behavioral effects of nicotine (Grunberg et al 1983). In contrast, Pomerleau has argued that positive reinforcement via nicotine-induced biochemical mechanisms is important in maintaining smoking behavior (Pomerleau 1981). Regardless of which theoretical view is correct, it is now unquestionable that maintenance of smoking involves the interplay of psychological, social, and biological factors.

Smoking Cessation

Techniques employed in smoking cessation include public health educational efforts, individual and medical counseling, persuasive communications with phone-call campaigns, drug treatments, hypnotherapy, behavior modification approaches, cognitive therapy, group support, and multicomponent interventions that include a number of these techniques (Pechacek 1979). The success of these approaches is difficult to assess for several reasons. Follow-ups—when done—are usually incomplete, self-reports of maintenance of smoking cessation have limited validity, and participants in these programs are self-selected (e.g. only about one in three smokers report that they are interested in these programs).

The high recidivism rates (50–75%) among smokers who initially abstain at the end of a program have discouraged many smokers and therapists. However, most smokers who successfully kick the habit do so on their own. Also, the recidivism rates can be misleading because the "hard core addicts" may be the subjects in most cessation studies and because it may simply take multiple attempts before cessation is successful (Schachter 1981).

Although it is not clear which treatment is best, it is clear that different treatments work for individual smokers. Public health campaigns can reduce tobacco use, as shown by the effects of the U.S. Government's intensive antismoking campaign circa 1970 (USDEW 1979a). In addition, the Stanford Heart Disease Prevention Project in the United States and a nationwide multiple-component program in Finland demonstrated that smoking behavior can be somewhat affected by public health campaigns when the health risks of smoking are made salient and techniques and support to change smoking behavior are provided (see the section below on health promotion and disease prevention) (Pomerleau 1979, Roskies 1983).

Prevention Approaches

Prevention approaches have considered and applied some of the same psychological principles discussed for initiation (Evans et al 1981). Success has been modest but encouraging. Prevention studies and trials are currently receiving a marked increase in effort by researchers and clinicians, particularly social learning approaches using peer role models (e.g. Evans et al 1981) and approaches that use peers to teach specific skills to resist social pressures and to emphasize short-term physiological consequences of smoking (e.g. Murray et al 1984).

Effects of Smoking Cessation and Relapse

Because of the risks of cigarette smoking, research has concentrated on the effects of this behavior rather than on the effects of cessation. However, it is important to note that in 1980 roughly 30% of the men and 16% of the women in this country were former smokers, compared to 20% of the men and 8% of the women in 1965 (USDHHS 1983). Clearly, a sizable and increasing number of Americans belong to this group. These exsmokers may experience irritability, sleep disturbances, inability to concentrate, and other psychological and physical problems (Schachter 1978, Grunberg & Bowen 1985). In addition, many exsmokers gain weight—a situation that discourages some people from trying to quit and that results in new health hazards for those who quit and gain large amounts of weight (Grunberg 1982a, Wack & Rodin 1982). All of these effects of cessation, their duration, frequency, and how to deal with them, deserve increased research and clinical attention.

Our discussion of cigarette smoking has focused on smoking as only one example of a health-impairing habit. Smoking also is a prime exemplar of an *addictive behavior* and may be studied to try to understand substance abuse. Clearly, both reasons for studying this behavior are cogent and important. Unfortunately, many psychopharmacologists and neuroscientists work and publish separately from those who identify themselves as health psychologists; historical roots and circumstances are probably responsible for this artificial separation. Space limitations do not permit a broader consideration of other types of substance abuse in this chapter. However, we hope that advances in biobehavioral research on common mechanisms and treatment of abused substances (cf Istvan & Matarazzo 1984, Shiffman & Wills 1985) will promote an even closer relationship between health psychology and other disciplines.

OBESITY AND EATING DISORDERS

Etiology and Treatment of Obesity

Obesity and weight reduction have become important areas of study in health psychology for at least two reasons. First, obesity is a highly prevalent, chronic medical condition that is directly or indirectly associated with medical disorders such as diabetes, hypertension, and certain cancers (Powers 1980). Although the relationship between obesity and certain health risks are not simple linear functions (Andres 1980), it is clear that being overweight is a socially stigmatized condition. Many people want to lose weight, and many who are overweight feel badly about themselves. A second reason for the widespread interest of health psychologists in this problem is that the behavioral treatment of obesity has become one of the most common paradigms for generic research on behavior therapies. As Stunkard (1979) has recently noted, more people have been receiving behavioral treatment for obesity than for all other conditions combined.

Obesity is a complex phenomenon with biological, behavioral, and social variables involved in its causes and consequences (Rodin 1981, Grunberg 1982b). Despite extensive research, there are major gaps in knowledge concerning the biological and psychological factors which cause obesity, and relatively little of this etiological work has been directly translated into treatment techniques. Investigations of biological causes of obesity have considered the role of particular brain centers (e.g. ventromedial and ventrolateral hypothalamus), the neurochemical pathways through these areas, and neurotransmitters and other hormones which are involved in eating behavior and hunger regulation (Powley 1977, Rodin 1981). Explanations for obesity based on "set point"—the notion that the body regulates weight to maintain a certain amount of body fat—also have been studied (Nisbett 1972). In addition, programmatic research has considered that weight regulation is based on the number and size of adipocytes or fat cells, determined by genetics or early nutritional experience (Hirsch & Knittle 1970, Faust 1980).

Environmental and social-psychological factors such as cultural norms and attitudes toward thinness also affect body weight. The Midtown Manhattan Study found inverse relationships between obesity and socioeconomic status and between generation in the United States and obesity (Stunkard 1975). Studies of eating behavior also have reported that obese individuals are particularly sensitive to external cues while normal weight individuals are relatively more sensitive to internal, physiological hunger cues (Schachter & Rodin 1974). However, recent studies suggest that "external responsiveness" may be more a function of dieting than of obesity per se (Herman & Mack 1975, Rodin 1981).

Treatments for obesity include diet and fasting, surgery, pharmacologic agents, exercise, psychotherapy, behavioral treatment, and a host of additional therapies (see Powers 1980, Stuart et al 1981, Grunberg 1982b). Of these approaches, behavioral treatment is probably the safest and most effective way to lose weight. Components of behavior modification programs for obesity include describing the behavior to be changed by record-keeping, identifying stimuli that precede eating, employing techniques to control eating, and modifying the consequences of eating to reward the performance of desired behaviors (Stunkard 1979).

As with maintenance of abstinence from cigarette smoking, maintenance of weight loss also appears to be a major problem; people can lose weight, but they can't keep it off. Recently it has been argued that individuals who participate in these programs are those who have the most difficulty losing weight on their own. Regardless of whether this interpretation is correct, systematic approaches involving behavioral-modification techniques (including diet and exercise) are probably the best, safest ways to maintain weight loss. Social support, positive reinforcement of weight loss, and changes in life style also seem to help maintain decreased body weight (Stunkard 1979).

Other Eating Disorders: Anorexia and Cachexia

Recently there has been a dramatic increase in the prevalence and media attention directed to other eating disorders: specifically, anorexia and cachexia. "Anorexia" refers to a decreased appetite; "cachexia" involves malnourishment and decreased body weight. These disorders are important to study because they are diagnostic of other medical conditions, may disturb quality of life (e.g. in cancer patients), and can result in premature mortality. Despite these dangers, these disorders are not yet well understood.

The term "anorexia nervosa" is misleading, i.e. it implies a nervous disorder. Therefore, the more descriptive term "starvation-amenorrhea" has been proposed (Van DeWiele 1980). The syndrome classically involves an adolescent girl from a well-to-do family who is an excellent student and who initiates weight loss by dieting, pursuing lower and lower weights while denying her thinness. Premature mortality for this syndrome is in the range of 10–15% (Van DeWiele 1980).

Some writers argue that anorexia nervosa results from psychological causes (e.g. desire to escape postpubertal development, high expectations from family, etc), whereas others discuss biological causes (e.g. hypothalamic dysfunction, blunted feedback responses to hormones). Treatments include family and individual psychotherapy, behavior therapy, and drugs (Vigersky 1977). The causes and treatments of this disorder are badly in need of further study and have begun to attract the attention of health psychologists.

Anorexia and cachexia also accompany cancer and cancer treatments, thereby affecting quality of life and responsiveness to cancer therapies. Again, these conditions seem to involve interactions of biological, metabolic, and psychological factors (e.g. depression, changes in eating behavior). In part, the study of cachexia represents one aspect of the growing interest of health psychologists in behavioral aspects of cancer and cancer treatment. This research has examined behavioral phenomena related to cancer chemotherapy such as conditioned nausea, taste aversions, and management of these conditions (see Burish et al 1984).

Thus far we have considered instances in which behavioral factors contribute to illness and unhealthy habits and conditions. However, as noted at the outset, behavior is also important in the treatment process as well as in preventing illness and maintaining health. Space does not allow a full review of research in these areas. As examples, we will consider research on compliance with medical regimens and discuss several prevention efforts.

COMPLIANCE WITH HEALTH CARE REGIMENS

The failure of patients to follow medical advice or prescription reduces the effectiveness of preventive and palliative health care and increases the overall cost of illness (Sackett & Haynes 1976). Prevalence estimates of noncompliance vary, but up to 50% of patients may fail to adhere to medicine-taking regimens (Ley 1977). Compliance with preventive or long-term regimens such as diet or life-style change is even poorer, and chronic regimens for asymptomatic illnesses such as hypertension have proved particularly problematic (Haynes et al 1979).

Causes of Noncompliance

The causes of noncompliance include psychological factors (e.g. attitudes, feelings), environmental conditions (e.g. time, cost), and the interaction between patient and physician (DiMatteo & DiNicola 1982). Psychological factors have been described as resistance to authority (Appelbaum 1977) and as an outcome of dissonance reduction or cognitive evaluation of health beliefs (e.g. Kasl & Cobb 1966, Mechanic 1968, Becker & Maiman 1975). Demographic variables seem to exert little influence on compliance (Haynes et al 1979). Cultural factors and social norms appear to be more relevant (Stone et al 1979, DiMatteo & DiNicola 1982). Compliance can be predicted by considering beliefs about severity, susceptibility, and consequences of an illness as well as costs of a regimen and its likelihood of success (Becker & Maiman 1975).

The Health Belief Model holds that specific conditions must be met before people will seek medical care or comply with prescribed regimens (Rosenstock 1966). Adherence to medical recommendations is enhanced if the individual believes that he/she is vulnerable to an illness, that the consequences of the illness are severe, and that the prescribed regimen is efficacious. Becker & Maiman (1975) have focused this model on compliance, expanding it to include exogenous factors such as the nature of health care, costs involved, and so on.

Disruption of daily routine caused by a regimen and complexity of the prescription can affect adherence (Haynes et al 1979). Practical considerations ranging from the patient's financial resources to the fit between ongoing behavior patterns and the nature of the regimen also must be considered. These variables only appear to be good predictors of compliance in combination with other factors such as the nature of the doctor-patient communication.

The crux of problems with compliance appears to be poor communication between physician and patient. Although some patient variables and physician variables are independently related to adherence, outcomes of this interaction appear to be strong predictors of compliance (Stone et al 1979). These outcomes include satisfaction with health care and the quality of information exchange between doctor and patient (Korsch & Negrete 1972, Ley 1977).

Several aspects of the doctor-patient relationship determine patient satisfaction, including the physician's manner, the physician's ability to communicate understanding, the degree to which patients' expectations are met, and the clarity of the diagnosis. For example, Korsch & Negrete (1972) found that mothers' satisfaction with pediatric clinic care of their children was largely determined by these variables. More than 80% who felt that their physician had tried to understand their concerns were satisfied compared with only 32% of those who did not feel that their doctor had been understanding. Less than half of the mothers whose expectations were not met reported being satisfied with the care received.

The quality of communication of information also affects feelings of involvement in decision making, alienation of patients from care providers, and understanding and recall of the prescribed regimen (Ley 1977, Rodin & Janis 1979, Stone et al 1979). Much of the failure to follow a doctor's advice may be attributable to problems in understanding and remembering what was told. Patients often have misconceptions about illness and may lack the basic physiological knowledge necessary to understand a regimen. Leventhal et al (1984) have suggested that naive theories about illness that people derive for themselves can affect compliance; e.g. an individual on an antihypertensive regimen who believes that blood pressure increases are accompanied by headaches may only follow the regimen when a headache is experienced rather than as per prescription.

Intervention Techniques

Methods of improving compliance have been developed, many of which are derived from the findings already discussed. For example, improving patient understanding and recall of information has been shown to increase compliance (Ley 1977). Training physicians to have better communication skills and to address patient concerns more sensitively has also been accomplished (DiMatteo & DiNicola 1982). The most successful approaches have been programs that individually tailor attention to each patient and those that increase supervision. The application of operant learning principles and the use of self-monitoring techniques also appear to increase compliance (Masur 1981).

PREVENTION OF DISEASE AND PROMOTION OF HEALTH

The substantial associations between major chronic diseases and seemingly modifiable behavioral factors have fostered the application of behavioral principles to health promotion and the prevention of disease. Theories and techniques of attitude and behavior change are relevant to the prevention area, as are beliefs and motives concerning health threats and the ways to cope with them. For reviews of research on applications of psychology to health promotion, see Davidson & Davidson (1980), Kirscht (1983), Leventhal & Hirschman (1982), Matarazzo (1982), and Matarazzo et al (1984).

The Relapse Problem and Barriers to Behavior Change

Although health habits can be altered, it is often difficult to maintain these changes over long periods of time. Figure 2 illustrates a characteristic pattern of relapse identified by Hunt and colleagues (e.g. Hunt et al 1971). These relapse curves seem to apply not only to the treatment of smoking, alcohol abuse, and heroin addiction but also to behaviors such as exercise habits (Dishman 1982), diet modifications (Foreyt et al 1979, Carmody et al 1982), and preventive dental care (Lund & Kegeles 1982).

The refractory problem of relapse directs attention to barriers to behavior change. In this regard, two broad sets of factors are considered to be major obstacles to lifestyle modification. The first is the learning theory notion that immediate rewards and punishments are much more effective than delayed ones (Stuart 1980, Miller 1983). The health threats posed by smoking, poor diet, overweight, and not exercising seem remote compared to the immediate pleasures of indulgence, and the inconvenience and effort involved in adopting

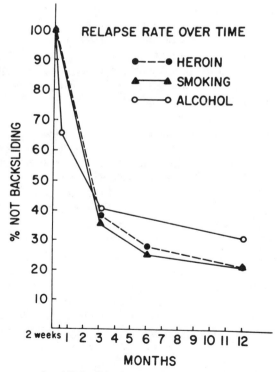

Figure 2   Relapse rates for addictive behaviors following treatment. Reproduced with permission of *Journal of Clinical Psychology* (Hunt et al 1971).

more healthful preventive behaviors act as further deterrents to behavior change. A second major set of barriers to lifestyle modification are forces in the social environment; that is, health habits are developed and maintained by social and cultural influences deriving from the family and society (Syme 1978). Americans have made significant progress in the changing societal attitudes toward exercise and proper nutrition, and have become increasingly informed about the modifiable risk factors for cancers and cardiovascular disorders. However, there are still potent social and economic pressures which lead teenagers to smoke and physicians and other health-care providers to resist putting needed effort into prevention (Leventhal & Hirschman 1982, Stachnik et al 1983). Moreover, further economic and structural barriers are found in the financial cost and lower availability of healthier foods and in the lack of time and opportunity for exercise at many worksites (Grunberg 1982b).

Intervention Research on Preventive Behavior

Studies of preventive health behavior vary in approach and size from large-scale efforts to change multiple habits via media communication (see Farquhar et al 1977, Lau et al 1980) to smaller studies aimed at single risk factors and involving face-to-face instruction (e.g. Foreyt et al 1979). Most of these studies have attempted to achieve behavior change and risk-reduction by using multiple available methods; fewer studies have examined in detail the psychological processes responsible for the efficacy or nonefficacy of single interventions.

Early laboratory studies examined the role of fear in motivating health attitude and behavior change (see Leventhal & Hirschman 1982). These studies generally found that moderate levels of fear about negative consequences of poor hygiene were optimal in changing health attitudes, but these studies emphasized negative reasons for changing behavior and suffered from lack of external validity. Later studies in clinic settings used combinations of social learning, educational, and behavior modification techniques to induce changes in health habits. For example, Foreyt et al (1979) compared several strategies to induce dietary change: an educational intervention involving a diet booklet, nutrition counseling alone, and counseling plus a behavioral intervention involving group discussion. They found initial reductions in dietary cholesterol; however, considerable relapse occurred after a period of six months.

Preventive studies in schools designed to deter smoking in adolescents by using peer modeling and a variety of other social learning and social-psychological techniques have been employed with some success (see section on smoking). Comprehensive reviews of preventive studies involving exercise, smoking, stress reduction, weight control, alcohol consumption, and diet may be found in Dishman (1982), Leventhal & Cleary (1980), Leventhal & Hirschman (1982), Matarazzo et al (1984), and Roskies (1983).

A particularly ambitious project is the Stanford Heart Disease Prevention Project (Farquhar et al 1977, Meyer et al 1980). This project was designed to address a broad range of risk factors including smoking, dietary fat intake, exercise, and blood pressure. Three communities were studied: one served as a control; a second was exposed to a mass media campaign on heart disease risk factors; and a third received the mass media campaign and face-to-face behavioral therapy for selected high-risk persons. The media campaign alone produced some reductions in smoking at three-year follow-up, but more substantial reductions occurred when the media campaign was supplemented by face-to-face therapeutic instruction. These encouraging findings must be evaluated cautiously because of several methodological problems—namely, the high drop-out rate and/or other difficulties encountered when subjects do not adhere to the randomly assigned interventions involving lifestyle changes (Kasl 1980). In addition, the study has been criticized for not yielding information regarding the social and psychological processes responsible for producing changes in health practices (Leventhal & Hirschman 1982). Currently, the Stanford group is conducting a five-city study designed to examine some of the mechanisms of changes in risk factors and also to obtain measures of cardiovascular morbidity and mortality.

Other large-scale community studies using either media approaches or clinic-based approaches have been or are being conducted in Finland, Belgium, Pennsylvania, Minnesota, and Rhode Island (see Roskies 1983, Matarazzo et al 1984). These studies should contribute further to the understanding of health behavior change processes and techniques, as well as offering further insight into whether health-promotion efforts can produce long-lasting and cost-effective effects of reducing morbidity and mortality.

No discussion of cardiovascular risk-reduction studies is complete without consideration of the recently completed Multiple Risk Factor Intervention Trial (MRFIT 1982). This project involved the selection of nearly 13,000 high-risk individuals, half of whom were randomly assigned to a clinic-based Special Intervention (SI) to reduce cholesterol, smoking, and blood pressure. This SI program involved health education, behavior modification, group support approaches, and a maintenance program to prevent recidivism. The remainder of the subjects received the Usual Care (UC) accorded them by their health care providers. Results of the MRFIT project have spurred controversy and confusion in the prevention community. The Special Intervention group showed a decrease in cardiovascular risk factors over the six-year span of the study, but so did the Usual Care group. This change in risk factors in the UC group was consistent with general cardiovascular risk factor reductions in the United States population in the last decade (USDHEW 1979c); however, this trend was not anticipated at the time the study was designed. In addition, pharmacologic treatment of hypertension in certain subsets of patients was associated with higher-than-expected mortality. Needless to say, a study of this scale has drawn considerable attention. It lends support to the effectiveness of some types of lifestyle changes (since the control group showed lower than expected mortality), and suggests the need for reassessment of other interventions. As results of other preventive trials are available, further light will be shed on the various explanations offered for the MRFIT findings.

Worksite Interventions

The occupational setting is a convenient place for health behavior modification. This is so because of the considerable time spent at work and because employees stand to benefit from healthier employees. In addition, the work site is a natural environment where behavior can be observed and where organizational and social structures can be utilized in the design of interventions (Chesney 1984).

Worksite programs include hypertension screening and treatment, smoking cessation, weight loss, stress management, and supervised aerobic physical exercise (Fielding 1984). Evaluation research concerning these programs has been of uneven quality, and the scientific basis for the efficacy of these programs remains unclear. However, such programs do appear to be feasible. More systematic evaluation of existing worksite programs and development of effective, convenient, and cost-effective strategies will no doubt receive increasing attention from health psychologists in the future.

SUMMARY AND CONCLUDING COMMENTS

A review of this length can only begin to convey some of the richness and breadth of current research in health psychology. Important areas that were omitted or underrepresented here include biofeedback and behavior modification applications to treatment and rehabilitation (Dworkin 1982, Miller 1983), special applications to pediatric and aging populations (Baum & Singer 1982), pain and pain control, symptom perception and health care attitudes (Krantz et al 1980, Pennebaker 1982), health policy and clinical practice issues, and psychological interventions in the prevention and treatment of other specific diseases (e.g. diabetes, cancers) (Burish & Bradley 1983).

The role of psychologists in disease prevention is rapidly increasing, and work in this area promises to expand further as we learn more about mechanisms of behavioral influences on health and processes that motivate healthy behavior. In addition, several methodological advances will likely influence further developments in health psychology research. For example, it is now possible to measure behavioral and endocrinological responses simultaneously and to assess physiological measures in naturalistic settings such as home or workplace (Frankenhaeuser 1975, Baum et al 1982). These techniques allow for multilevel assessments of responses to stimulus situations and multilevel evaluations of the effectiveness of treatment interventions. Also, recent studies have used portable electronic devices to provide biofeedback to assist in the rehabilitation of paralyzed patients (Dworkin 1982). Other research has employed portable blood withdrawal pumps and blood pressure monitors to measure responses during daily periods of stress and exercise (see Krantz & Manuck 1984). Moreover, research in health psychology increasingly includes longitudinal designs with relatively long-term followups or evaluations to examine health status over periods of time (e.g. in studies of chronic stress or in evaluations of prevention programs).

Health psychology provides an interface for the concerns and interests of researchers and practitioners. Indeed, recent graduate training recommendations include programs which emphasize aspects of practice and research (Stone 1983). Health psychologists must be broadly trained in psychology and in elements of the biomedical sciences necessary to understand the clinical symptoms, pathophysiology, and underlying biology of the disorders they study or treat. Also, knowledge of public health and the health care system is a requisite for research on prevention. These interdisciplinary elements are important constituents of the body of theory and knowledge in health psychology.

ACKNOWLEDGMENTS

Preparation of this chapter was assisted by NIH grant HL31514 and grants from USUHS. Opinions expressed reflect those of the authors and do not imply official endorsement of the Uniformed Services University of the Health Sciences. We thank Sophia Demchyshyn and Marguerite Perikles for their aid in the preparation of this chapter.

Literature Cited

Ader, R., ed. 1981. *Psychoneuroimmunology.* New York: Academic

Ader, R., Cohen, N. 1984. Behavior and the immune system. In *Handbook of Behavioral Medicine,* ed. W. D. Gentry, pp. 117–73. New York: Guilford

Andres, R. 1980. Effect of obesity on total mortality. *Int. J. Obesity* 4:381–86

Appelbaum, S. A. 1977. The refusal to take one's medicine. *Bull. Menninger Clin.* 41:511–21

Ashton, H., Stepney, R. 1982. *Smoking: Psychology and Pharmacology.* New York: Tavistock

Bandura, A. 1977. *Social Learning Theory,* Englewood Cliffs, NJ: Prentice-Hall

Barofsky, I. 1981. Issues and approaches to the psychosocial assessment of the cancer patient. In *Medical Psychology: Contributions to Behavioral Medicine,* ed. C. K. Prokop, L. A. Bradley, pp. 57–64. New York: Academic

Barrett, J. E. 1983. Interrelationships between behavior and pharmacology as factors determining the effects of nicotine. *Pharm. Biochem. Behav.* 19:1027–29

Baum, A., Gatchel, R. J., Schaeffer, M. A. 1983. Emotional, behavioral, and physiological effects of chronic stress at Three Mile Island. *J. Consult. Clin. Psychol.* 51:565–72

Baum, A., Grunberg, N. E., Singer, J. E. 1982. The use of psychological and neuroendocrinological measurements in the study of stress. *Health Psychol.* 1:217–36

Baum, A., Singer, J. E., eds. 1982. *Handbook of Psychology and Health,* Vol. 2: *Issues in Child Health and Adolescent Health.* Hillsdale, NJ: Erlbaum

Becker, M. H., Maiman, L. A. 1975. Sociobehavioral determinants of compliance with health and medical care recommendations. *Med. Care* 13:10–24

Berkman, L. F., Syme, S. L. 1979. Social networks, host resistance, and mortality: A nine-year follow-up study of Alameda County residents. *Am. J. Epidemiol.* 109:186–204

Bernstein, D. A., Glasgow, R. E. 1979. Smoking. See Pomerleau & Brady 1979, pp. 233–54

Blumenthal, J. A., Califf, R., Williams, R. S., Hindman, M. 1983. Cardiac rehabilitation: A new frontier for behavioral medicine. *J. Cardiac Rehabil.* 3:637–56

Burish, T. G., Bradley, L. A., eds. 1983. *Coping with Chronic Disease: Research and Applications.* New York: Academic

Burish, T. G., Levy, S. M., Meyerowitz, B. E. 1984. *Nutrition, Taste Aversion, and Cancer: A Biobehavioral Perspective.* Hillsdale, NJ: Erlbaum. In press

Cannon, W. B. 1929. *Bodily Changes in Pain, Hunger, Fear, and Rage.* New York: Appleton-Century-Crofts

Carmody, T. P., Fey, S. C., Pierce, D. K., Cannor, W. E., Matarazzo, J. D. 1982. Behavioral treatment of hyperlipidemia: Techniques, results, and future directions. *J. Behav. Med.* 5:91–116

Chesney, M. A. 1984. Behavior modification and health enhancement. See Matarazzo et al 1984

Cobb, S. 1976. Social support as a moderator of life stress. *Psychosom. Med.* 38:300–14

Cohen, F., Horowitz, M. J., Lazarus, R. S., Moos, R. H., Robins, L. N., et al. 1982. Panel report on psychosocial assets and modifiers of stress. See Elliott & Eisdorfer 1982, pp. 147–88

Cohen, S., Kamarck, T., Mermelstein, R. 1983. A global measure of perceived stress. *J. Health Soc. Behav.* 24:385–96

Cohen, S., Krantz, D. S., Evans, G. W., Stokols, D. 1981. Cardiovascular and behavioral effects of community noise. *Am. Sci.* 69:528–35

Cohen, S., McKay, G. 1984. Social support, stress, and the buffering hypothesis: A theoretical analysis. In *Handbook of Psychology and Health,* Vol. 4: *Social Psychological Aspects of Health,* ed. A. Baum, J. E. Singer, S. E. Taylor. Hillsdale, NJ: Erlbaum

Cohen, S., Syme, S. L., eds. 1985. *Social Support and Health.* New York: Academic. In press

Collins, D. L., Baum, A., Singer, J. E. 1983. Coping with chronic stress at Three Mile Island: Psychological and biochemical evidence. *Health Psychol.* 2:149–66

Costa, P. T., Schroeder, D. H. 1984. Influence of life event stress on physical illness: Substantive effects or methodological flaw. *J. Pers. Soc. Psychol.* 46:853–63

Dahl, L. K., Heine, M., Tassinari, L. 1962. Role of genetic factors in susceptibility to experimental hypertension due to chronic excess salt ingestion. *Nature* 194:480–82

Davidson, P. O., Davidson, S. M., eds. 1980.

Behavioral Medicine: Changing Health Life Styles. New York: Brunner/Mazel

DeLongis, A., Coyne, J. C., Dakof, G., Folkman, S., Lazarus, R. S. 1982. Relationship of daily hassles, uplifts, and major life events to health status. *Health Psychol.* 1:119–36

Dembroski, T. M., MacDougall, J. M., Williams, B., Haney, T. L. 1985. Components of Type A, hostility, and anger-in: Relationship to angiographic findings. *Psychosom. Med.* In press

DiMatteo, M. R., DiNicola, D. D. 1982. *Achieving Patient Compliance: The Psychology of the Medical Practitioner's Role.* New York: Pergamon

Dishman, R. K. 1982. Compliance/adherence in health related exercise. *Health Psychol.* 1:237–67

Dohrenwend, B. S., Dohrenwend, B. P. 1978. Some issues in research on stressful life events. *J. Nerv. Ment. Dis.* 166:7–15

Dorian, B. J., Keystone, E., Garfinkel, P. E., Brown, G. M. 1982. Aberrations in lymphocyte subpopulations and functions during psychological stress. *Clin. Exp. Immunol.* 50:132–38

Dunn, W. L., ed. 1973. *Smoking Behavior: Motives and Incentives.* New York: Wiley

Dworkin, B. R. 1982. Instrumental learning for the treatment of disease. *Health Psychol.* 1:45–59

Elliott, G. R., Eisdorfer, C. 1982. *Stress and Human Health: Analysis and Implications of Research.* New York: Springer

Engel, G. L. 1977. The need for a new medical model: A challenge for biomedicine. *Science* 196:129–36

English, E. H., Baker, T. B. 1983. Relaxation training and cardiovascular response to experimental stressors. *Health Psychol.* 2:239–59

Erikson, E. H. 1963. *Childhood and Society.* New York: Norton

Evans, R. I., Rozelle, R. M., Maxwell, S. E., Raines, B. E., Dill, C. A., et al. 1981. Social modeling films to deter smoking in adolescents: Results of a three year field investigation. *J. Appl. Psychol.* 66:399–414

Eysenck, H. J. 1973. Personality and the maintenance of the smoking habit. See Dunn 1973, pp. 113–46

Fahrion, S. L. 1981. *Etiology and Intervention in Essential Hypertension: A Biobehavioral Approach.* Topeka Kans: Menninger Found. Unpublished manuscript

Farquhar, J. W., Breitrose, H., Haskell, W. L., Meyer, A. J., Maccoby, N., et al. 1977. Community education for cardiovascular health. *Lancet* 1:1192–95

Faust, I. M. 1980. Nutrition and the fat cell. *Int. J. Obesity* 4:314–21

Fielding, J. D. 1984. Health promotion and

disease prevention at the worksite. *Ann. Rev. Public Health* 5:237–66

Fleming, R., Baum, A., Gisriel, M. M., Gatchel, R. J. 1982. Mediating influences of social support on stress at Three Mile Island. *J. Hum. Stress* 8:14–22

Foreyt, J. P., Scott, L. W., Mitchell, R. E., Gotto, A. M. 1979. Plasma lipid changes in the normal population following behavioral treatment. *J. Consult. Clin. Psychol.* 47:440–52

Fox, B. H. 1978. Premorbid psychological factors as related to cancer incidence. *J. Behav. Med.* 1:45–133

Frankenhaeuser, M. 1975. Experimental approaches to the study of catecholamines and emotion. In *Emotion: Their Parameters and Measurement*, ed. L. Levi, pp. 209–34. New York: Raven

Frankenhaeuser, M. 1983. The sympathetic-adrenal and pituitary-adrenal response to challenge: Comparison between the sexes. In *Biobehavioral Bases of Coronary Heart Disease*, ed. T. M. Dembroski, T. H. Schmidt, G. Blumchen, pp. 91–105. Basel: Karger

Friedman, M., Rosenman, R. H. 1959. Association of specific overt behavior pattern with blood and cardiovascular findings—blood cholesterol level, blood clotting time, incidence of arcus senilis, and clinical coronary artery disease. *J. Am. Med. Assoc.* 162:1286–96

Froelicher, V., Battler, A., McKirnan, M. D. 1980. Physical activity and coronary heart disease. *Cardiology* 65:153–90

Garrity, T. F., Marx, M. B. 1979. Critical life events and coronary disease. See Gentry & Williams 1979, pp. 31–49

Gentry, W. D., Williams, R. B., eds. 1979. *Psychological Aspects of Myocardial Infarction and Coronary Care*. St. Louis: Mosby. 2nd ed.

Glass, D. C. 1977. *Behavior Patterns, Stress, and Coronary Heart Disease*. Hillsdale, NJ: Erlbaum

Glass, D. C., Singer, J. E. 1972. *Urban Stress: Experiments on Noise and Social Stressors*. New York: Academic

Gleser, G. C., Green, B. L., Winget, C. 1981. *Prolonged Psychosocial Effects of Disaster*. New York: Academic

Grunberg, N. E. 1982a. The effects of nicotine and cigarette smoking on food consumption and taste preferences. *Addict. Behav.* 7:317–31

Grunberg, N. E. 1982b. Obesity: Etiology, hazards, and treatment. In *Handbook of Psychology and Health*, Vol. 1: *Clinical Psychology and Behavioral Medicine: Overlapping Disciplines*, ed. R. J. Gatchel, A. Baum, J. E. Singer, pp. 103–20. Hillsdale, NJ: Erlbaum

Grunberg, N. E., Bowen, D. 1985. Coping with sequelae of smoking cessation. *J. Cardiac Rehabil.* In press

Grunberg, N. E., Morse, D., Barrett, J. E. 1983. Effects of urinary pH on the behavioral responses of squirrel monkeys to nicotine. *Pharm. Biochem. Behav.* 19:553–57

Gutmann, M. C., Benson, H. 1971. Interaction of environmental factors and systemic arterial pressure. *Medicine* 50:543

Hamburg, D. A., Elliott, G. R., Parron, D. L., eds. 1982. *Health and Behavior: Frontiers of Research in the Biobehavioral Sciences*. Washington DC: Natl. Acad. Press

Haynes, R. B., Taylor, D. W., Sackett, D. L. 1979. *Compliance in Health Care*. Baltimore: Johns Hopkins Univ. Press

Haynes, S. G., Feinleib, M. 1980. Women, work, and coronary heart disease: Prospective findings from the Framingham Heart Study. *Am. J. Public Health* 70:133–41

Haynes, S. G., Feinleib, M., Kannel, W. B. 1980. The relationships of psychosocial factors to coronary disease in the Framingham Study. III. Eight-year incidence of coronary heart disease. *Am. J. Epidemiol.* 111:37–58

HDFP Cooperative Group. 1979. Five year findings of the hypertension detection and follow-up program. *J. Am. Med. Assoc.* 242:2562–71

Herman, C. P., Mack, D. 1975. Restrained and unrestrained eating. *J. Pers.* 43:647–60

Hinkle, L. E. 1974. The effect of exposure to culture change, social change, and changes in interpersonal relations on health. In *Stressful Life Events: Their Nature and Effects*, ed. B. S. Dohrenwend, B. P. Dohrenwend, pp. 9–34. New York: Wiley

Hirsch, J., Knittle, J. L. 1970. Cellularity of obese and nonobese human adipose tissue. *Fed. Proc.* 29:1516–21

Holmes, T. H., Masuda, M. 1974. Life change and illness susceptibility. In *Stressful Life Events: Their Nature and Effects*, ed. B. S. Dohrenwend, B. P. Dohrenwend, pp. 45–72. New York: Wiley

Holmes, T. H., Rahe, R. H. 1967. The social readjustment rating scale. *J. Psychosom. Res.* 11:213–18

House, J. S. 1975. Occupational stress as a precursor to coronary disease. In *Psychological Aspects of Myocardial Infarction and Coronary Care*, ed. W. D. Gentry, R. B. Williams, pp. 24–36. St. Louis: Mosby. 1st ed.

Hunt, W. A., Barnett, L. W., Ranch, L. G. 1971. Relapse rates in addiction programs. *J. Clin. Psychol.* 27:455–56

Hunt, W. A., Matarazzo, J. D. 1970. Habit mechanisms in smoking. In *Learning Mechanisms in Smoking*, ed. W. A. Hunt. Chicago: Aldine

Institute of Medicine. 1978. *Perspectives on Health Promotion and Disease Prevention in* the United States. Washington DC: Natl. Acad. Sci.

Istvan, J., Matarazzo, J. D. 1984. Tobacco, alcohol, and caffeine use: A review of their interrelationships. Psychol. Bull. 95:301–26

Janis, I. L. 1958. Psychological Stress. New York: Wiley

Jarvik, M. D. 1979. Biological influences on cigarette smoking. In Surgeon General's Report, Smoking and Health, pp. (15-5)–(15-32). DHEW Publ. No. 79-50066. Washington DC: GPO

Jemmott, J. B., Locke, S. E. 1984. Psychosocial factors, immunologic mediation, and human susceptibility to infectious diseases: How much do we know? Psychol. Bull. 95:52–77

Jenkins, C. D. 1976. Recent evidence supporting psychologic and social risk factors for coronary disease. N. Engl. J. Med. 294:987–94, 1033–38

Jenkins, C. D., Zyzanski, S. J., Rosenman, R. H. 1971. Progress toward validation of a computer-scored test for the Type A coronary-prone behavior pattern. Psychosom. Med. 33:193–202

Jessor, R., Jessor, S. L. 1977. Problem Behavior and Psychosocial Development: A Longitudinal Study of Youth. New York: Academic

Johnson, J., Leventhal, H. 1974. The effects of accurate expectations and behavioral instructions on reactions during a noxious medical examination. J. Pers. Soc. Psychol. 29:710–18

Julius, S., Esler, M. 1975. Autonomic nervous cardiovascular regulation in borderline hypertension. Am. J. Cardiol. 36:685–996

Kannel, W. B. 1979. Cardiovascular disease: A multifactorial problem (Insights from the Framingham Study). In Heart Disease and Rehabilitation, ed. M. L. Pollock, D. H. Schmidt, pp. 15–31. New York: Wiley

Kaplan, N. M. 1982. Clinical Hypertension. Baltimore: Williams & Wilkins. 3rd ed.

Kasl, S. V. 1980. Cardiovascular risk reduction in a community setting: Some comments. J. Consult. Clin. Psychol. 48:143–49

Kasl, S. V. 1984. Stress and Health. Ann. Rev. Public Health 5:319–42

Kasl, S. V., Cobb, S. 1966. Health behavior, illness behavior, and sick role behavior. Arch. Environ. Health 12:246–66, 531–41

Kasl, S. V., Cobb, S. 1970. Blood pressure changes in men undergoing job loss: A preliminary report. Psychosom. Med. 32:19–38

Kirscht, J. P. 1983. Preventive health behavior: A review of research and issues. Health Psychol. 2:277–302

Kobasa, S. C. 1979. Stressful life events, personality, and health: An inquiry into hardiness. J. Pers. Soc. Psychol. 37:1–11

Korsch, B., Negrete, V. 1972. Doctor-patient communication. Sci. Am. 227:66–78

Kozlowski, L. T. 1979. Psychosocial influences on cigarette smoking. In Smoking and Health: A Report of the Surgeon General. DHEW Publ. No. 79-50066. Washington DC: GPO

Kozlowski, L. T., Herman, C. P. 1984. The interaction of psychosocial and biological determinants of tobacco use: More on the boundary model. J. Appl. Soc. Psychol. 14: In press

Krantz, D. S., ed. 1985. Special issue on stress management in health and rehabilitation. J. Cardiac Rehabil. In press

Krantz, D. S., Baum, A., Singer, J. E., eds. 1983. Handbook of Psychology and Health. Vol. 3: Cardiovascular Disorders and Behavior. Hillsdale, NJ: Erlbaum

Krantz, D. S., Baum, A., Wideman, M. V. 1980. Assessment of preferences for self-treatment and information in health care. J. Pers. Soc. Psychol. 39:977–90

Krantz, D. S., Durel, L. A. 1983. Psychobiological substrates of the type A behavior pattern. Health Psychol. 2:393–411

Krantz, D. S., Glass, D. C. 1984. Personality, behavior patterns, and physical illness: Conceptual and methodological issues. See Ader & Cohen, pp. 38–86

Krantz, D. S., Glass, D. C., Contrada, R., Miller, N. E. 1982. Behavior and health: The biobehavioral paradigm. In Behavioral and Social Science Research: A National Resource (Part II) (Rep. Natl. Res. Council), ed. R. McC. Adams, N. J. Smelser, D. J. Treiman, pp. 76–145. Washington DC: Natl. Acad. Press

Krantz, D. S., Manuck, S. B. 1984. Acute psychophysiologic reactivity and risk of cardiovascular disease: A review and methodologic critique. Psychol. Bull. 96:435–64

Lau, R., Kane, R., Berry, S., Ware, J., Roy, D. 1980. Channeling health campaigns. Health Educ. Q. 7:56–89

Lazarus, R. S. 1966. Psychological Stress and the Coping Process. New York: McGraw-Hill

Lazarus, R. S., Cohen, J. B. 1977. Environmental stress. In Human Behavior and the Environment: Current Theory and Research, ed. I. Altmann, J. F. Wohlwill, pp. 89–127. New York: Plenum

Leventhal, H., Cleary, P. D. 1980. The smoking problem: A review of research and theory in behavioral risk modification. Psychol. Bull. 88:370–405

Leventhal, H., Hirschman, R. S. 1982. Social psychology and prevention. In Social Psychology of Health and Illness, ed. G. S. Sanders, J. Suls, pp. 183–226. Hillsdale, NJ: Erlbaum

Leventhal, H., Zimmerman, R., Gutmann, M.

1984. Compliance: A self-regulatory perspective. See Ader & Cohen, pp. 369–423

Ley, P. 1977. Psychological studies of doctor-patient communication. In *Contributions to Medical Psychology*, Vol. 1, ed. S. Rachman. Oxford: Pergamon

Light, K. C., Koepke, J. P., Obrist, P. A., Willis, P. W. 1983. Psychological stress induces sodium and fluid retention in men at high risk for hypertension. *Science* 220:429–31

Lund, A. K., Kegeles, S. 1982. Increasing adolescents' acceptance of long-term personal health behavior. *Health Psychol.* 1:27–43

Mann, G. V. 1977. Diet-heart: End of an era. *N. Engl. J. Med.* 297:644–50

Mason, J. W. 1971. A re-evaluation of the concept of "non-specificity" in stress theory. *J. Psychiatr. Res.* 8:323–33

Mason, J. W. 1975. A historical view of the stress field: Part II. *J. Hum. Stress* 1:22–36

Mason, J. W., Buescher, W. L., Belfer, M. L., Artenstein, M. S., Mougey, E. H. 1979. A prospective study of corticosteroid and catecholamine levels in relation to viral respiratory illness. *J. Hum. Stress* 5:18–27

Masur, F. T. 1981. Adherence to health care regimens. In *Medical Psychology: Contributions to Behavioral Medicine*, ed. C. K. Prokop, L. A. Bradley, pp. 442–70. New York: Academic

Matarazzo, J. D. 1980. Behavioral health and behavioral medicine: Frontiers for a new health psychology. *Am. Psychol.* 35:807–17

Matarazzo, J. D. 1982. Behavioral health's challenge to academic, scientific and professional psychology. *Am. Psychol.* 37:1–14

Matarazzo, J. D., Weiss, S. M., Herd, J. A., Miller, N. E., Weiss, S., eds. 1984. *Behavioral Health: A Handbook of Health Enhancement and Disease Prevention*. New York: Wiley

Matthews, K. A. 1982. Psychological perspectives on the type A behavior pattern. *Psychol. Bull.* 91:293–323

Matthews, K. A. 1984. Assessment of type A, anger, and hostility in epidemiological studies of cardiovascular disease. See Ostfeld & Eaker 1984

Mechanic, D. 1968. *Medical Sociology*. New York: Free Press

Meyer, A. J., Nash, J. D., McAlister, A. L., Maccoby, N., Farquhar, J. W. 1980. Skills training in a cardiovascular education campaign. *J. Consult. Clin. Psychol.* 48:129–42

Miller, N. E. 1983. Behavioral medicine: Symbiosis between laboratory and clinic. *Ann. Rev. Psychol.* 34:1–31

Mullin, B., Suls, J. 1982. The effectiveness of attention and rejection as coping styles. *J. Psychosom. Res.* 26:43–49

Multiple Risk Factor Intervention Trial Research Group (MRFIT). 1982. Multiple risk factor intervention trial: Risk factor changes and mortality results. *J. Am. Med. Assoc.* 248:1465–77

Murray, D. M., Johnson, C. A., Luepker, R. V., Mittelmark, M. B. 1984. The prevention of cigarette smoking in children: A comparison of four strategies. *J. Appl. Soc. Psychol.* 14: In press

Nisbett, R. E. 1972. Hunger, obesity, and the ventromedial hypothalamus. *Psychol. Rev.* 79:433–53

Obrist, P. A. 1981. *Cardiovascular Psychophysiology: A Perspective*. New York: Plenum

Ostfeld, A., Eaker, E. 1984. *Measuring Psychosocial Variables in Epidemiologic Studies of Cardiovascular Disease*. Bethesda: NIH. In press

Parjis, J., Joussens, J. V., Vander Linden, L., Verstreken, G., Amer, A. K. 1973. Moderate sodium restriction and diuretic in the treatment of hypertension. *Am. Heart J.* 85:22–25

Patel, C. H., Marmot, M. G., Terry, D. J. 1981. Controlled trial of biofeedback-aided behavioral methods in reducing mild hypertension. *Br. Med. J.* 282:2005–8

Pechacek, T. F. 1979. Modification of smoking behavior. In *Smoking and Health: A Report of the Surgeon General*, pp. (19-5)–(19-63). DHEW Publ. (PHS) 79-50065. Washington DC: GPO

Pennebaker, J. W. 1982. *The Psychology of Physical Symptoms*. New York: Springer-Verlag

Peterson, E. A., Augenstein, J. S., Tanis, D. C., Augenstein, D. G. 1981. Noise raises blood pressure without impairing auditory sensitivity. *Science* 211:1450–52

Pomerleau, O. F. 1979. Behavioral factors in the establishment, maintenance, and cessation of smoking. In *Smoking and Health: A Report of the Surgeon General*, pp. (16-31)–(16-23). DHEW Publ. (PHS) 79-50066. Washington DC: GPO

Pomerleau, O. F. 1981. Underlying mechanisms in substance abuse: Examples from research on smoking. *Addict. Behav.* 6:187–96

Pomerleau, O. F., Brady, J. P. 1979. *Behavioral Medicine: Theory and Practice*. Baltimore: Williams & Wilkins

Powers, P. S. 1980. *Obesity, The Regulation of Weight*. Baltimore: Williams & Wilkins

Powley, T. 1977. The ventromedial hypothalmic syndrome, satiety, and a cephalic phase hypothesis. *Psychol. Rev.* 84:89

Rabkin, J. G., Streuning, E. L. 1976. Life events, stress, and illness. *Science* 194:1013–20

Razin, A. M. 1982. Psychosocial intervention in coronary artery disease: A review. *Psychosom. Med.* 44:363–87

Review Panel. 1981. Coronary-prone behavior and coronary heart disease: A critical review. *Circulation* 673:1199–1215

Riley, V. 1981. Psychoneuroendocrine influences on immunocompetence and neoplasia. *Science* 212:1100–9

Rodin, J. 1981. Current status of the internal-external hypothesis for obesity: What went wrong? *Am. Psychol.* 36:361–72

Rodin, J., Janis, I. L. 1979. The social power of health-care practitioners as agents of change. *J. Soc. Issues* 35:60–81

Rosenman, R. H., Brand, R. J., Jenkins, C. D., Friedman, M., Straus, R., et al. 1975. Coronary heart disease in the Western Collaborative Group Study: Final follow-up experience of 8½ years. *J. Am. Med. Assoc.* 223:872–77

Rosenstock, I. M. 1966. Why people use health services. *Milbank Mem. Fund Q.* 44:94–124

Roskies, E. 1983. Modification of coronary-risk behavior. See Krantz et al 1983, pp. 231–76

Russell, M. A. H. 1979. Tobacco dependence: Is nicotine rewarding or aversive? In *Cigarette Smoking as a Dependence Process*, ed. N. A. Krasnegor, pp. 100–21. NIDA Res. Monogr. 23. USDHEW, DHEW Publ. (ADM) 79-800. Washington DC: GPO

Sackett, D. L., Haynes, R. B. 1976. *Compliance with Therapeutic Regimens*. Baltimore: Johns Hopkins Univ. Press

Schachter, S. 1978. Pharmacological and psychological determinants of smoking. *Ann. Int. Med.* 88:104–14

Schachter, S. 1981. Recidivism and self-cure of smoking and obesity. *Am. Psychol.* 31: 436–44

Schachter, S., Rodin, J. 1974. *Obese Humans and Rats*. Hillsdale, NJ: Erlbaum

Schachter, S., Silverstein, B., Kozlowski, L. T., Perlick, D., Herman, C. P., Liebling, B. 1977. Studies of the interaction of psychological and pharmacological determinants of smoking. *J. Exp. Psychol: Gen.* 106:3–40

Schleifer, S., Keller, S., McKegney, F., Stein, M. 1980. *Bereavement and Lymphocyte Function*. Presented to Am. Psychiatr. Assoc. Ann. Meet., Montreal

Schwartz, G. E., Weiss, S. M. 1978. Behavioral medicine revisited: An amended definition. *J. Behav. Med.* 1:249–51

Seligman, M. E. 1975. *Helplessness: On Depression, Development, and Death*. San Francisco: Freeman

Selye, H. 1976. *The Stress of Life*. New York: McGraw-Hill. 2nd ed.

Shapiro, A. P. 1983. The non-pharmacologic treatment of hypertension. See Krantz et al 1983, pp. 277–94

Shiffman, S., Wills, T. A., eds. 1985. *Coping and Substance Abuse*. New York: Academic. In press

Silverstein, B., Kelley, E., Swan, J., Kozlowski, L. 1982. Physiological predisposition towards becoming a cigarette smoker: Experimental evidence for sex differences. *Addict. Behav.* 7:83–86

Sklar, L. S., Anisman, H. 1981. Stress and cancer. *Psychol. Bull.* 89:369–406

Stachnick, T., Stoffelmayr, B., Hoppe, R. B. 1983. Prevention, behavior change, and chronic disease. See Burish & Bradley 1983, pp. 475–82

Stein, M. 1983. *Psychosocial Perspectives on Aging and the Immune Response*. Presented at Ann. Meet. Acad. Behav. Med. Res., Reston, Va.

Stepney, R. 1980. Smoking behavior: A psychology of the cigarette habit. *Br. J. Dis. Chest* 74:325–44

Steptoe, A. 1981. *Psychological Factors in Cardiovascular Disorders*. New York: Academic

Stone, G. C., ed. 1983. Proceedings of the National Working Conference on education and training in health psychology. *Health Psychol.* (Suppl.) 2:1–153

Stone, G. C., Cohen, F., Adler, N. E., eds. 1979. *Health Psychology: A Handbook*. Washington DC: Jossey-Bass

Stuart, R. B. 1980. Weight loss and beyond: Are they taking it off and keeping it off? See Davidson & Davidson 1980, pp. 151–94

Stuart, R. B., Mitchell, C., Jensen, J. A. 1981. Therapeutic options in the management of obesity. In *Medical Psychology: Contributions to Behavioral Medicine*, ed. C. K. Prokop, L. A. Bradley, pp. 321–54. New York: Academic

Stunkard, A. J. 1975. From explanation to action in psychosomatic medicine: The case of obesity. *Psychosom. Med.* 37:195–236

Stunkard, A. J. 1979. Behavioral medicine and beyond: The example of obesity. See Pomerleau & Brady 1979, pp. 279–98

Suinn, R. M. 1982. Intervention with Type A behaviors. *J. Consult. Clin. Psychol.* 50: 797–803

Syme, S. L. 1978. Life style intervention in clinic-based trials. *Am. J. Epidemiol.* 108: 87–91

Syme, S. L., Torfs, M. S. 1978. Epidemiological research in hypertension: A critical appraisal. *J. Hum. Stress* 4:43–48

Thoresen, C. E., Friedman, M., Gill, J. K., Ulmer, D. 1982. Recurrent coronary prevention project: Some preliminary findings. *Acta Med. Scand. Suppl.* 660:172–92

United States Department of Health and Human Services. 1983. *The Health Consequences of Smoking: Cardiovascular Disease*. Rockville, Md: Public Health Serv. Publ. (PHS) 84-50204

United States Department of Health, Education, and Welfare. 1979a. *Healthy People: A*

Report of the Surgeon General on Health Promotion and Disease Prevention. Washington DC: GPO DHEW Publ. (PHS) 79-55071

United States Department of Health, Education, and Welfare. 1979b. *Smoking and Health: A Report of the Surgeon General.* Washington DC: GPO DHEW Publ. (PHS) 79-50066

United States Department of Health, Education, and Welfare. 1979c. *Proceedings of the Conference on the Decline in Coronary Heart Disease Mortality.* Bethesda, Md: NIH Publ. 79-1610

Van DeWeile, R. L. 1980. Anorexia nervosa and the hypothalamus. In *Neuroendocrinology,* ed. D. T. Krieger, J. C. Hughes. Sunderlura, Mass: Sinauer

Verrier, R. L., DeSilva, R. A., Lown, B. 1983. Psychological factors in cardiac arrhythmias and sudden death. See Krantz et al 1983, pp. 125–54

Vigersky, R. A., ed. 1977. *Anorexia Nervosa: A Monograph of the National Institute of Child Health and Human Development.* New York: Raven

Visintainer, M. A., Seligman, M. E. P., Volpicelli, J. 1983. Helplessness, chronic stress, and tumor development. *Psychosom. Med.* 301:1249–54

Wack, J. T., Rodin, J. 1982. Smoking and its effects on body weight and the systems of caloric regulation. *Am. J. Clin. Nutr.* 35: 366–80

Weiner, H. 1979. *Psychobiology of Essential Hypertension.* New York: Elsevier

Ann. Rev. Psychol. 1985. 36:385–418

HYPNOSIS

John F. Kihlstrom

Department of Psychology, University of Wisconsin, Madison, Wisconsin 53706

CONTENTS

"I have been hypnotizing, on a large scale, the students, and have hit one or two rather pretty unpublished things of which I hope someday I may send you an account."

William James—Letter to Carl Stumpf, January 1, 1886

Hypnosis may be defined as a social interaction in which one person, designated the subject, responds to suggestions offered by another person, designated the hypnotist, for experiences involving alterations in perception, memory, and voluntary action. In the classic case, these experiences and their

0066-4308/85/0201-0385$02.00

accompanying behaviors are associated with subjective conviction bordering on delusion, and involuntariness bordering on compulsion.

ASSESSMENT OF HYPNOTIZABILITY

The signal event in the revival of hypnosis research in the late 1950s and early 1960s was the introduction of the Stanford Hypnotic Susceptibility Scales (SHSS) by Weitzenhoffer and Hilgard (E. R. Hilgard 1965; for recent reviews, see E. R. Hilgard 1978–1979). These scales consist of an induction of hypnosis accompanied by suggestions for a set of representative hypnotic experiences; response to each suggestion is scored in terms of objective behavioral criteria. The Stanford scales are available in a graded series: SHSS:A and SHSS:B are parallel forms emphasizing motor items, which makes test-retest studies possible; SHSS:C emphasizes cognitive alterations of various sorts and has come to serve as the standard against which all other scales are compared. At about the same time, the Harvard Group Scale of Hypnotic Susceptibility, Form A (HGSHS:A) was developed. Based on SHSS:A, it permits the economies of group testing. A "tailored" version of SHSS:C permits an individual suggestion of special interest to be substituted for one of the items in the published version without any sacrifice in terms of psychometric properties (E. R. Hilgard et al 1979). In addition, the Stanford Profile Scales of Hypnotic Susceptibility (SPSHS), available in two parallel forms (I and II), permit assessment of individual strengths and weaknesses within the general domain of hypnosis, somewhat in the manner of the profiles derived from subscales of the WAIS or MMPI.

Alternatives

While such a rigorous, systematic assessment program is desirable in principle, many clinicians (and some experimentalists) balk at it on the grounds that it takes a minimum of three hours to complete just HGSHS:A and SHSS:C. Accordingly, the Stanford laboratory recently introduced the Stanford Hypnotic Clinical Scale (SHCS) in two forms suitable for use with adults and children (Morgan & Hilgard 1978–1979a,b). These scales correlate highly with SHSS (r = .72 and .67 for the adult and child forms, respectively), require only 20 minutes for administration, and appear to be the procedure of choice for purposes of rapid clinical assessment.

Even 20 minutes seems to be too long for some clinicians and patients, and so there is a continuing interest in the development of even more rapid techniques for assessing hypnotizability. In particular, Spiegel (1977, Stern et al 1979) developed the Hypnotic Induction Profile (HIP), consisting of an eye-roll sign, accompanied by a very brief hypnotic induction and test, as a measure of hypnotizability. The eye-roll sign itself, independent of the hypnotic induction, does not appear to correlate substantially with hypnotizability as measured by standardized laboratory procedures (Eliseo 1974, Orne et al 1979, Sheehan et al 1979, Switras 1974, Wheeler et al 1974). The correlation between the results of the brief induction and standardized scale scores also appears to be too low to serve the purposes of individual assessment and prediction. Orne et al (1979) found a correlation of .19 in the better of their two studies. However, a correlation of .63 has been reported between induction scores and SHSS:C (Frischholz et al 1980), so the actual relationship between the two scales remains somewhat controversial (Hilgard & Hilgard 1979, Hilgard 1981a,b, 1982, Frischholz et al 1981, Spiegel et al 1982). Even granting that the induction score is a valid measure of hypnotizability, the eye-roll score is not; and the induction component, for its part, contains too few items to provide a representative assessment of the individual's response to hypnotic suggestions.

A characteristic of the Stanford-type scales is that hypnotizability is typically measured in terms of objectively observable behavioral response. A radical departure from this practice is represented by the Creative Imagination Scale (CIS; Barber & Wilson 1977). This scale consists of 10 suggestions similar to those offered on the Stanford scales, with the exception that response is scored only in terms of the subjective reality of the suggested imagery. Two studies found correlations between CIS and HGSHS:A of .28 (McConkey et al 1979) and .55 (E. R. Hilgard et al 1981), and factor analyses found that the items of the two scales tend to load on different factors. The CIS may serve as an alternate measure of mental imagery ability, but probably not as an alternate measure of hypnotizability. Shor (1979b) has proposed a phenomenological method for assessing hypnotic response, which combines both objective and subjective indices.

Recently, Spanos and his associates introduced the Carleton University Responsiveness to Suggestion Scale (CURSS; Spanos et al 1983c,d). The CURSS consists of an induction and suggestions for seven representative experiences. When scored in terms of objective behavioral response, it has adequate psychometric properties of internal consistency and reliability, and a factor structure and score distributions roughly comparable to SHSS. The correlation between behavioral scores on CURSS and SHSS:C is .65. While the CURSS clearly taps the domain of hypnosis to some degree, it also tends to define hypnosis in terms of the subject's willingness to cooperate with the procedures rather than in terms of subjective experience, as is characteristic of the Stanford scales.

The Classic Suggestion Effect

Although hypnotizability is usually measured in terms of behavioral response to suggestions, hypnosis may be distinguished from voluntary or coerced behavioral compliance by the classic suggestion effect, in which hypnotic responses are experienced as occurring involuntarily (Weitzenhoffer 1974). The effect may be related to the inability of some subjects to resist hypnotic suggestions (Zamansky 1977, Lynn et al 1983), and to the posthypnotic persistence of uncancelled suggestions (Duncan & Perry 1977, Perry 1977b). Recently, Weitzenhoffer (1980) criticized the Stanford scales because they measure only overt behavioral response and not involuntariness (for a convincing reply to these and other complaints, see E. R. Hilgard 1981c).

The problem of the classic suggestion effect was raised in a different way in the standardization of the CURSS by Spanos et al (1983d). In addition to objective behavioral scoring, the CURSS items are also evaluated in terms of the degree of subjective conviction and involuntariness associated with them. Thus, CURSS directly addresses the occurrence of the classic suggestion effect. However, the distribution of involuntariness scores yields a reverse-J rather than a more bell-like shape, which suggests that the behavioral response of most subjects to its items reflects overt compliance rather than the classic suggestion effect. (Unfortunately, Spanos et al do not report the correlation between CURSS behavioral and involuntariness scores.)

Spanos et al suggest, in apparent agreement with Weitzenhoffer (1980), that the Stanford scales are also highly contaminated with compliance, although neither Weitzenhoffer nor Spanos provide any empirical support for the claim. In fact, the available data suggest that this is not the case. Bowers (1981a), for example, scored the items of SHSS:A in terms of both overt behavior and experienced involuntariness. Within SHSS:A, the total behavioral score correlated .77 with the behavioral score of SHSS:C; and SHSS:A involuntariness correlated .85 with SHSS:C behavior (no involuntariness score was collected for SHSS:C). Similar findings were obtained with HGSHS:A (Farthing et al 1983). Thus, while the behavioral scores on CURSS may, as Spanos et al (1983d) suggest, be contaminated with overt behavioral compliance, this is not the case with the Stanford scales. Response to the Stanford scales seems to tap the classic suggestion effect and the experience of involuntariness that is central to hypnosis as it has been understood historically. Further support for this conclusion comes from an earlier study comparing the Stanford scales with the Barber Suggestibility Scale on which the CURSS is based (Ruch et al 1974).

Hypnotic Susceptibility vs Hypnotic Depth

Although the hypnotizability scales have achieved a position of dominance in the measurement of hypnosis, scales of hypnotic depth continue to be employed as an index of the individual's involvement in the hypnotic experience. A large number of such scales have been produced, and these were reviewed by Tart (1979). Subjective ratings of hypnotic depth typically correlate highly with objective measures of hypnotic susceptibility. In a recent study by Perry & Laurence (1980), for example, the correlations were .85 and .88 in two samples. When collected under relatively neutral circumstances, depth reports may serve as useful correctives for overt behavioral compliance, in the same manner as the subjective scores collected on the CURSS and other hypnotizability scales.

An emerging question concerns the determinants of these subjective depth reports. Radtke & Spanos (1981b) offered an attributional interpretation of these reports, based on self-perception theory. They argue that subjects' experiences during hypnosis are typically ambiguous, forcing them to rely on contextual factors to make inferences concerning their internal states. Radtke & Spanos (1981b) note that self-reports of depth are influenced by the definition of the situation as hypnosis (as opposed to relaxation or imagination, for example), preexperimental and manipulated expectations concerning hypnosis, the expressed opinion of the hypnotist, and the wording of the scales on which subjects make their ratings. The attributional account is also consistent with the correlation between depth ratings and hypnotizability scores, given the assumption that subjects base their depth ratings in part on self-observations of their response to specific suggestions administered during hypnotizability scales—including those suggestions that are tested before hypnosis is induced or after it is terminated (Perry & Laurence 1980).

Correlates of Hypnotizability

The finding of stable individual differences in hypnotizability over intervals as long as two years (Morgan et al 1974) led to research designed to uncover personality and cognitive characteristics that might be related to this capacity. Unfortunately, hypnotizability has not been found to correlate with the sorts of "traits" measured by the common multidimensional personality inventories such as the MMPI and CPI. The strongest finding in all of this research is that hypnotizable individuals have a high capacity for involvement in imaginative activities outside hypnosis (e.g. J. R. Hilgard 1974, Tellegen & Atkinson 1974; for a review, see J. R. Hilgard 1979). Tellegen & Atkinson (1974) also performed a factor analysis showing that absorption was not represented on the two major factors of the MMPI. These findings suggest that the earlier attempts failed to discover significant personality correlates of hypnosis principally because the instruments used simply did not sample the kinds of cognitive skills and dispositions that are relevant to the experience.

More recent work yielded an interesting set of results. For example, the induction of hypnosis typically emphasizes the focusing of attention, and a number of studies found differences in attentional deployment between hypnotizable and insusceptible subjects (Graham & Evans 1977, Karlin 1979). Furthermore, many hypnotic phenomena involve the production of vivid mental images or other fantasies, and significant correlations are consistently obtained between hypnotizability and questionnaire measures of vividness of mental imagery (Sheehan 1979, 1982); more mixed results are obtained with various measures of creativity (Bowers & Bowers 1979). P. Bowers (1978, 1979, 1982) gave a new perspective on these kinds of findings by showing that the degree to which involvements, images, or creative ideas occur effortlessly correlates more highly with hypnotizability than the simple level of absorption, vividness, or creativity.

In a series of papers, Crawford (1981, 1982a,b, 1983) argues that the common denominator of all these correlations is synthetic or holistic thinking. In one set of studies, she reported a number of significant correlations between hypnotizability and performance on Gestalt closure tasks (Crawford 1981). Converging evidence was obtained in another series of studies where the induction of hypnosis, in subjects known to be hypnotizable, facilitated performance on a successive visual discrimination task requiring the use of mental imagery, but not on a simultaneous discrimination task that did not require imagery (Crawford & Allen 1983). Moreover, on the successive discrimination task the hypnotizable subjects reported a strong shift to holistic as opposed to analytic strategies following the induction of hypnosis.

Other evidence in this regard comes from studies of hemispheric specialization. Thus, Gur & Gur (1974) reported that hypnotizable subjects are more likely to show reflective eye movement shifts to the left than insusceptible subjects; Graham (1977) found that the induction of hypnosis led to increases in autokinetic movement to the left, compared to the normal waking state. Sackeim et al (1979) reported that hypnotizable individuals tend to sit on the right side of classrooms. All three results seem to reveal a preference for processing information in the right hemisphere that is related to hypnotizability and/or hypnosis. More directly, MacLeod-Morgan & Lack (1982) found an apparent shift in cortical activation (as measured by EEG alpha density) from the left to the right hemisphere when hypnotizable individuals enter hypnosis. Similarly, Graham & Pernicano (1979) found that hypnotized individuals showed more autokinetic shifts to the left than their unhypnotized counterparts.

Modification of Hypnotizability

A number of investigators have taken the "skill" metaphor to mean that the ability to enter hypnosis is learned, and thus subject to improvement by means of training procedures. This position was expressed most forcefully by Diamond (1974, 1977), who lists a number of ostensibly effective modification procedures. However, Perry (1977a) offers a number of compelling criticisms of this position. In fact, very few studies of the modification of hypnotic susceptibility have met rudimentary conceptual and methodological requirements. In the one study that approaches all the standards, Gur (1974) observed persistent, generalized gains that were very small in magnitude and strongly correlated with baseline levels of hypnotic susceptibility.

Self-Hypnosis

Highly hypnotizable subjects show a tendency to have hypnotic-like experiences in the normal waking state, and there is some evidence that they may not always require a formal induction in order to experience hypnotic suggestions. These facts raise the question of self-hypnosis, and its comparison to more conventional hypnotic procedures (Johnson 1981, Orne & McConkey 1981). One line of research compared the two forms of hypnosis along phenomenological lines. Fromm and her colleagues (Fromm et al 1981) selected subjects on the basis of high scores on HGSHS:A and SHSS:C, familiarized them further with SPSHS:I, and then introduced them to hypnosis by having them complete the Inventory of Self Hypnosis (ISH), an adaptation of HGSHS:A. Thereafter, the subjects were asked to practice self-hypnosis one hour per day for four weeks, and to complete a questionnaire after each session in which they described their subjective experiences and compared them to heterohypnosis. Practiced in this manner, self-hypnosis apparently emphasized relaxation and reverie instead of the usual sorts of hypnotic suggestions, effectively precluding behavioral comparisons. Experientially, heterohypnosis was reported to involve steadier, more focused attention and diminished distraction.

Other investigators have reported behavioral comparisons between self-hypnosis and heterohypnosis. Self- and heterohypnosis commonly yield roughly equivalent sample means and variances on such scales and the order of item difficulties is roughly the same, but it is not clear that the experiences are equivalent in other respects. For example, Shor & Easton (1973) obtained correlations of only .33–.39 between HGSHS:A and two forms of the ISH; and Johnson (1979; reported also in Johnson & Weight 1976) obtained a correlation of .47 between those same scales. A later study obtained correlations of .51 and .62 (Johnson et al 1983). In all these studies, the subjects administered both the induction procedure and the test suggestions to themselves. In an experiment involving self-administration of the induction but tape-recorded administration of the test suggestions, Ruch (1975) obtained correlations of .61 between self-hypnotic and heterohypnotic versions of HGSHS:A, and .62 between corresponding versions of SHSS:C. Although self- and heterohypnosis have something in common, it also appears that the two experiences draw on somewhat different underlying processes.

INVESTIGATIONS OF SPECIFIC PHENOMENA

From the late 1950s to 1965, research on hypnosis was dominated by individual differences in hypnotizability, their measurement, correlates, and modification; the primary topic of the next decade was analgesia. Experimental investigation in the period under review has expanded to include other classic hypnotic phenomena, as well as newly discovered ones.

Analgesia

Numerous case reports of major and minor surgery and other medical procedures performed with hypnosis as the sole analgesic agent leave no doubt as to the effectiveness of the technique under certain circumstances (for a review, see Hilgard & Hilgard 1983). Experimental investigations have contributed detailed analyses of the parameters of the effect and its underlying mechanisms. Just how effective and dependable hypnosis can be was illustrated in an extraordinarily spartan laboratory study in which subjects were exposed to both ischemic and cold-pressor pain (Stern et al 1977). Overall, hypnosis proved to be more effective than any other challenging agent, including (among others) morphine, diazepam, and acupuncture. The results with hypnosis were especially favorable for those who were highly hypnotizable, although hypnotizability did not mediate response to any of the other procedures. Highly hypnotizable subjects respond differently to analgesia suggestions than insusceptible subjects who are simulating hypnosis (Hilgard et al 1978b). Other research confirms the superiority of hypnosis to acupuncture, and the lack of correlation between response to acupuncture and hypnotizability (Knox & Shum 1977, Knox et al 1978, 1979, 1981). In a careful clinical study, J. Hilgard & LeBaron (1982, 1984) found that hypnotizable children undergoing chemotherapy for cancer showed significantly more pain reduction during bone-marrow aspirations than did their insusceptible counterparts.

Laboratory research on the psychophysics of pain reveals that the experience has two components: (*a*) sensory pain, which informs the person of the location and extent of insult, injury, or disease, and (*b*) suffering, which has to do with the meaning of the pain to the person. An experiment with highly hypnotizable subjects showed equal and dramatic reductions in both sensory pain and emotional suffering (Knox et al 1974). Similarly, the discovery of endorphins prompted the speculation that the effect of hypnotic suggestion is somehow mediated by the release of endogenous opiates. However, naloxone, a morphine antagonist, does not affect hypnotic analgesia (Goldstein & Hilgard 1975).

A great deal of research in the past decade addressed the role of individual differences in the perception of pain, coping strategies, and response to hypnotic suggestions for analgesia (Chaves & Barber 1974, Spanos et al 1974, 1975, 1979b, 1981a,c). These studies show that successful response to hypnotic suggestions is often accompanied by the deliberate use of cognitive strategies such as distraction or pleasant imagery. Similarly, a dimension of coping vs catastrophizing style appears to be related in part to individual differences in pain perception in both hypnosis and the normal waking state. Hypnotic analgesia is not wholly mediated by such strategies, but the fact that coping can be taught leaves open the possibility for successful cognitive control of pain even in subjects who are insusceptible to hypnosis.

Amnesia

In the hypnotic context, amnesia refers to the subject's failure, following an appropriate suggestion, to remember events that occurred during the hypnotic session. A series of papers describe amnesia as it occurs on the standardized scales of hypnotic susceptibility (Evans et al 1973, Nace et al 1974, Kihlstrom & Evans 1976, 1977, 1978, Cooper 1979, McConkey 1980). The most salient property of hypnotic amnesia is that the target memories can be recovered following administration of a prearranged signal. Reversibility marks amnesia as a phenomenon of retrieval, rather than of encoding or storage. Among investigators of hypnosis, there is agreement on the basic observations, but considerable disagreement as to how to account for them (Coe 1978, Kihlstrom 1977, 1978, 1983, Spanos & Radtke 1982). From a cognitive point of view, amnesia is held to be a genuine disorder of memory retrieval analogous to ordinary forgetting and certain clinical amnesias. From an interpersonal point of view, amnesia is held to be a phenomenon of strategic social behavior analogous to the keeping of secrets.

Evidence bearing on the cognitive point of view is provided by studies employing concepts, principles, and methods familiar in memory research. For example, it appears that standard suggestions for amnesia affect episodic memory, as represented by recall of a wordlist memorized during hypnosis, but not semantic memory, as represented by the use of the same wordlist items as responses on word association and similar tasks (Evans 1979, Kihlstrom 1980, Spanos et al 1982b). As another example, it appears that free recall is much more affected by amnesia suggestions than either recognition (Kihlstrom & Shor 1978, McConkey & Sheehan 1981, McConkey et al 1980, St. Jean & Coe 1981) or retroactive inhibition (Coe et al 1973, 1976).

During the period under review, a great deal of research attempted to understand the role of organizational processes in the retrieval deficits observed during amnesia. Among subjects who recall at least some of their experiences despite a suggestion for complete amnesia, for example, hypnotizable subjects tended not to organize their output according to the temporal sequence in which the events occurred (Evans & Kihlstrom 1973, Kihlstrom & Evans 1979). This disorganization did not appear to be a state-dependent effect of hypnosis alone, or a product of some cognitive style correlated with hypnotizability (Kihlstrom & Evans 1979; but see Schwartz 1978, 1980). Similar disorganization effects are observed in conceptual replications involving category clustering in more conventional verbal-learning procedures (Radtke-Bodorik et al 1979, Spanos & Bodorik 1977, Spanos et al 1980a). One study failed to show a decline in clustering during amnesia (Coe et al 1973), but this was probably due to poor initial acquisition (Radtke-Bodorik et al 1980). The clustering effect is not consistently found in unhypnotized subjects who are strongly motivated to forget the critical material (Spanos & Bodorik 1977, Radtke-Bodorik et al

1979, 1980, Spanos et al 1980b); nor does it occur in subjects who have been instructed to simulate hypnosis and amnesia (Spanos et al 1980b). Somewhat paradoxically, two investigations largely failed to replicate the original temporal disorganization effect on which the clustering replications were based (Radtke & Spanos 1981, St. Jean & Coe 1981), but the effect was reconfirmed in studies employing both hypnotizability scales (Geiselman et al 1983) and wordlists (Kihlstrom & Wilson 1984).

Evidence bearing on the social-psychological point of view comes from a variety of experiments. For example, simulators typically present different patterns of performance on tests of source amnesia (Evans 1979), disorganized recall (Spanos et al 1980b), and recognition (McConkey et al 1980) compared to hypnotized subjects, which indicates that these effects are not due to the demand characateristics of the hypnotic situation. Furthermore, subjects' preexisting expectations concerning their hypnotic behavior are not particularly powerful determinants of their actual response to amnesia suggestions (Young & Cooper 1972, Ashford & Hammer 1978, Shor et al 1984). Although the deliberate suppression of memory reports is rather rare, hypnotic subjects often report engaging in cognitive strategies that might impair the retrieval of the critical material. However, the relationship between strategic helping of this sort and actual amnesia is weak (Kihlstrom 1977, Spanos & Bodorik 1977, Spanos et al 1980a,b Kihlstrom et al 1983,)

Additional relevant evidence is provided by experiments that vary the instructional demands placed on subjects during the time the amnesia suggestion is tested. In one experiment, subjects of moderate and high hypnotizability who met a criterion for initial amnesia did not respond differentially to the various instructions for effort, honesty, organization, or repeated recall. All conditions showed an increase in memory from the first to the second test of amnesia, however, an effect that may reflect the dissipation of the amnesic process over time (Kihlstrom et al 1983). Subsequent research by Coe and his colleagues found that insertion of a putative lie detector test or strong honesty demands could affect the memory reports of hypnotizable, amnesic subjects (Howard & Coe 1980, Schuyler & Coe 1981). However, these effects were found in those subjects who reported that their amnesic behavior was under voluntary control. In the absence of strong honesty demands, the amount of spontaneous recovery observed during amnesia is unrelated to reports of either subjective conviction or stragetic helping (Kihlstrom et al 1983).

In contrast to the selective disruption in episodic memory observed in amnesia, hypnotic suggestions can also disrupt the functioning of the semantic memory system, as represented by a disruption in word-association performance as well, resulting in a kind of *agnosia* instead of amnesia (Spanos et al 1982b). Hypnotic agnosia has often been observed in the standardized scales of hypnotic susceptibility as an inadvertent consequence of suggestions for nominal aphasia (E. R. Hilgard 1965, 1977a), but it has not yet been explored systematically.

Hypnotic suggestions can also alter memory performance in the absence of specific suggestions for amnesia. For example, Blum and his associates found that distinctive mental contexts suggested to subjects during an encoding phase served as effective memory cues during a retrieval phase, much in the manner of state-dependent retrieval (Blum 1967, Blum et al 1968b, 1971). More recently, Bower and his colleagues (Bower 1981, Bower et al 1978, 1981) found that hypnotically suggested mood states could, under some conditions, induce similar state-dependent effects on retrieval.

Hypermnesia

Many experienced clinicians contend that hypnosis can improve a person's memory for events experienced in the past, outside hypnosis. This effect has been employed to refresh the memories of witnesses, victims, and occasionally even suspects and defendants. Laboratory studies of hypnotic hypermnesia have a history extending back to the beginnings of the modern period of hypnosis research (Diamond 1980, Kihlstrom 1982, Orne 1979, Orne et al 1984, Smith 1983). The current burst of research on hypnotic hypermnesia began with a report confirming earlier observations that hypnotic suggestions facilitated the recall of linguistically meaningful material (in this case, prose) but not nonsense syllables (Dhanens & Lundy 1975). However, some earlier research indicated that any increases in valid memory obtained through hypnosis may be accompanied by corresponding increases in inaccurate recollection or confabulation. Dywan & Bowers (1983) found that hypnotic testing led to substantial increases in recall for pictorial material, even after the subjects reached a plateau in waking recall, and that this increase was correlated with hypnotizability. However, hypnosis also led to an increase in false recollection that was also correlated with hypnotizability, and the ratio of false to accurate memory was roughly 2:1.

The likelihood of memory distortion may be increased if leading questions are delivered while the subject is hypnotized (as compared to biased interrogation in the normal waking state) (Putnam 1979, Zelig & Beidelman 1981, Sanders & Simmons 1983; Sheehan & Tilden 1983), and confabulated memories produced through hypnotic means can be unshakable when subsequently cross-examined and contradicted in the normal waking state (Laurence & Perry 1983). In contrast to the situation in normal waking memory, there is not a positive relationship between accuracy and confidence in hypnotically elicited memory (Dywan & Bowers 1983, Sanders & Simmons 1983, Sheehan & Tilden 1983). Given these findings, it seems difficult to maintain the position that hypnosis yields meaningful increases in memory.

These laboratory reports are, of course, discrepant with the claims from the field. For example, one report (Reiser & Nielson 1980) covering approximately 400 consecutive cases interviewed at the Los Angeles Police Department (LAPD) states that new information was elicited in 80% of the hypnotic interviews, and that for the 50% of these where independent corroboration was possible, the new information was at least "somewhat accurate" 91% of the time. However, the criterion for accuracy was not specified, so the results are difficult to evaluate objectively. Moreover, terms such as "somewhat accurate" suggest that the product of hypnosis was typically a mix of accurate and inaccurate memory reports, in a manner reminiscent of the Dywan–Bowers study. Recently, a remarkable and more definitive field study was reported, based on a consecutive sample of 44 cases seen at the LAPD just after the Reiser–Nielson study was concluded (Sloane 1981). Actual witnesses and victims were interviewed in the normal waking state, and then randomly assigned to one of four treatment conditions for a second interview. Half of these were conducted in hypnosis, and half in the normal waking state; within each of these conditions, half employed a conventional interrogation format, while the remainder employed special instructions for visual imagery (the "television technique"; Reiser & Nielson 1980). All interviews were conducted by police investigators specially trained in forensic hypnosis. The information obtained in both interviews was objectively recorded, and the police were given 60 days to verify each item. Contrary to the earlier report, and the enthusiastic claims of individual case studies, there were no effects of hypnosis on memory—overall productivity, accurate recollection, or error—either as a main effect or in interaction with interview technique.

Age Regression

In age regression a subject appears to relive an experience that occurred at an earlier point in his or her life; in the classic case of an adult regressed to childhood, the individual typically takes on a childlike demeanor. Upon superficial examination, the phenomenon appears to involve a constellation of ablation (the functional loss, similar to amnesia, of knowledge acquired after the age targeted by the suggestion), reinstatement (the return to developmentally previous modes of psychological functioning), and revivification (a recovery, similar to hypermnesia, of previously inaccessible memories). Past research has addressed all three facets of the phenomenon (Kihlstrom 1982, Orne et al 1984).

Little formal research has been done on revivification: while age regression is occasionally used in forensic hypnosis, the laboratory studies of hypnotic hypermnesia have all involved direct suggestions for enhanced memory instead of age regression. Experiments bearing on ablation often reveal apparent contradictions in behavior, as when a subject claiming to be young continues to draw upon knowledge and other resources available to him or her only as an adult (Perry & Walsh 1978). Historically, most effort has been devoted to reinstatement. Wallace and his colleagues (Wallace 1978, Walker et al 1976) reported that age-regressed adults showed levels of eidetic imagery tasks characteristic of children, but Spanos et al (1979a) were not able to replicate this finding. In another study (Nash et al 1979), age-regressed subjects asked to imagine themselves in a moderately frightening situation behaved in a manner appropriate to the suggested age, whereas simulating subjects did not. To date, this is the only study that provides compelling evidence of reinstatement during age regression; all the others either could not be replicated, or the effects were manifested by simulating as well as hypnotic subjects.

Perceptual Effects

A variety of perceptual effects have been reported in hypnosis, especially in the context of suggestions for positive and negative hallucinations. In the former case, the subject claims to perceive an object that is not objectively present; in the latter, no perception is claimed for a stimulus that is present in the perceptual field. There are also occasional claims for increases in sensory acuity in hypnosis. The typical experiment attempts to assess the "reality" of the suggested effect by determining whether perceptual functions change in a manner appropriate to the claim. Thus, it was found that hypnotic suggestions led to improvements in visual acuity in myopic subjects that could not be accounted for by peripheral changes (Graham & Leibowitz 1972, E. P. Sheehan et al 1982), and that suggestions for color-blindness reduce (but do not eliminate) interference on the Stroop color-word test (Harvey & Sipprelle 1978). On the other hand, subjects administered suggestions for unilateral deafness continue to show intrusions from the affected ear in a dichotic listening task (Spanos et al 1982a), and those who receive suggestions for color-blindness do not mimic the performance of the congenitally color-blind on the Farnsworth-Munsell 100-hues test (Cunningham & Blum 1982).

The most popular modality in which the perceptual effects of hypnosis are studied is vision. For example, hypnotizability was reported to be positively correlated with susceptibility to the autokinetic effect (Wallace et al 1974), the Ponzo illusion (Miller 1975), and reversible figures such as the Necker cube and the Schroeder staircase (Wallace et al 1976). Other studies examined the effects of specific visual alterations suggested in hypnosis. For example, Leibowitz and his colleagues examined the effects of hypnotic ablation of background on the perception of the Ponzo illusion (Miller & Leibowitz 1976), and suggestions for tubular vision on size constancy (Leibowitz et al 1980, 1981, Miller et al 1973). Sheehan & Dolby (1975, Dolby & Sheehan 1977) found that the hypnotized subjects countered the effect of recency on the perception of the wife/mother-in-law ambiguous figure, behaving instead in accordance with the expectations of the hypnotist.

A wealth of studies has been generated on visual effects of various sorts by Blum (1979) and his associates. In a case study, hypnotic suggestions for tubular vision led to restrictions in the visual field that remained constant over varying viewing distances, much in the manner of hysterical amblyopia (Blum 1975). Other studies have explored the effects of negative hallucinations for selected objects of the visual field, as opposed to simple suggestions for hypnotic blindness or reduced overall visual acuity (Blum et al 1978). For example, suggested blurring of form or color impaired the identification of these properties in tachistoscopically presented letters (Blum & Porter 1973). Other experiments have examined the effects of ablating the background on the magnitude of the Titchener-Ebbinghaus circles illusion (Blum et al 1981). Jansen, Blum & Loomis (1982) found that suggested ablation of slanted lines surrounding a slanted target line did not reliably alter the perception of slant in the target, but that *positive* hallucinations for slanted outer lines did so. Finally, MacCracken et al (1980) employed a combination of positive and negative hallucinations, altering the perceived distance between the subject and a point of light. Such suggestions altered estimated distance in the appropriate direction, but not the apparent motion of the target when the subject's head was moved from side to side.

In addition to these findings, Blum and his associates have used hypnosis as a technique for controlling cognitive arousal, as documented by EEG measures (Blum & Nash 1982). Hypnotically induced arousal can affect visual discrimination (Blum et al 1967b), reaction time in tachistoscopic identification (Blum & Graef 1971), selective attention (Blum & Porter 1973), and the "reverberation" of stimulus input in the cognitive system (Blum 1968, Blum et al 1967a, 1968a,c, Blum & Porter 1972). Yet other studies have explored the effects of specific hypnotically induced emotional states, such as anxiety and arousal, on perceptual identification (Blum & Barbour 1979) and cognitive reverberation (Blum & Green 1978, Blum & Wohl 1971).

Psychophysical studies employing the method of magnitude estimation show clear changes in auditory sensitivity following suggestions for partial hypnotic deafness (Crawford et al 1979), and suggestions for deafness reduce auditory interference on visual choice-reaction time (Blum & Porter 1974). One study reported changes in sensory acuity rather than response bias using a signal-detection paradigm (Graham & Schwartz 1973), but a more extensive study failed to confirm these findings (Jones & Spanos 1982). Suggestions for increased acuity had no effect on sensitivity, but did increase the tendency to report the signal in the presence of noise. On the other hand, suggestions for diminished acuity had no effect on either sensitivity or response bias. Assuming the subjects reported the changes that were suggested to them, this finding implies that signal detection may not be the procedure of choice for tapping the mechanism underlying hypnotic deafness.

While hypnotic analgesia represents the diminished perception of pain, hypnotic anesthesia represents the loss of touch and kinesthesis in the body part targeted by the suggestion. In an interesting series of studies, Wallace and his colleagues tested this effect with a number of different procedures derived from classical work in perception. They found, for example, that anesthesia disrupted perceptual adaptation to errors in visual location induced by distorting prisms (e.g. Wallace & Garrett 1973, 1975, Garrett & Wallace 1975). Other studies revealed that anesthesia disrupted the subjects' ability to touch their noses with their eyes closed (Wallace & Hoyenga 1980), and to perform a variety of other coordinated motor tasks requiring central processing of proprioceptive feedback (Wallace & Hoyenga 1981). All the results of these experiments appear to fit together nicely, but Spanos et al (1981b) reported a failure to replicate the adaptation effect. Although Wallace & Fisher (1982) suggested that this was due to procedural differences, Spanos et al (1983a) reported another failure to replicate even with an appropriately modified procedure.

Time perception has been studied in a variety of ways. Krauss et al (1974) reported that suggestions for distorted subjective time sense improved memory for a list of words studied during that time interval, which suggested that effective study time had been increased. These findings were not replicated by Johnson (1976) or St. Jean (1980), although subjects in the latter study reported high subjective conviction that the passage of time had changed. Bowers & Brenneman (1979) reported that subjects generally underestimated the duration of a standardized test of hypnotic susceptibility, a finding confirmed by others (Bowers 1979, St. Jean et al 1982). In these studies, the effect was not clearly related either to hypnotic susceptibility or to the occurrence of posthypnotic amnesia. St. Jean & MacLeod (1983), however, found significant underestimations of the duration of an absorbing prose passage read during hypnosis, but only among hypnotizable subjects.

A phenomenon related to hypnosis and suggestion is the Chevreul pendulum illusion, in which a weight suspended from the hand moves in the direction of imagined motion, without any perception of motor control. In an elegant series of studies, Easton & Shor (1975, 1976, 1977) showed that the effect reflects skilled cognitive activity, and is mediated by visual capture.

Trance Logic

Many of the effects of hypnosis on perception and memory are characterized by a peculiar pattern of inconsistency and anomaly in the subject's response. In the case of the double hallucination, for example, the subject will see, and interact with, a confederate sitting in an empty chair. In a classic paper, Orne (1959) found that many hypnotic subjects reported that they could see through the (hallucinated) confederate to the back of the chair. Moreover, when their attention was drawn to the real confederate, sitting quietly in a chair outside their field of vision, the subjects were typically able to maintain both the hallucination and the veridical perception, and reported confusion as to which was which. Simulating subjects typically failed to show these behaviors. Orne dubbed this response "trance logic," which he described as a form of thought that permits two mutually contradictory states of affairs to be represented simultaneously in awareness.

Orne's original report was impressionistic in nature, and later investigators tried to study the effect in a more quantitative fashion. An early study failed to confirm Orne's observations (Johnson et al 1972), but a critique and reanalysis by E. R. Hilgard (1972) showed that the findings were actually indeterminate (for a reply, see Johnson 1972). Later studies often found trends toward real-simulator differences on single indices of trance logic (usually the double hallucination), but these do not always reach statistical significance (McDonald & Smith 1975, Obstoj & Sheehan 1977, Perry & Walsh 1978, Peters 1973, Sheehan 1977, Sheehan et al 1976). Although the appearance of trance logic in hypnosis is not always apparent at the level of individual test items, it is clear when differences are assessed in terms of aggregate scores on a battery of tests relevant to trance logic. Peters (1973) showed a significant difference between real and simulating subjects with a battery of six such tests, although few of these discriminated between the groups at the level of the individual item. Even so, there is wide variability in aggregate trance logic scores among highly hypnotizable subjects, and trance logic is shown by hypnotizable individuals under circumstances other than hypnosis (Obstoj & Sheehan 1977). The nature of trance logic remains to be clarified by a definitive experiment.

The Hidden Observer

Along with trance logic, the most controversial hypnotic phenomenon is the "hidden observer." For example, after hypnotic analgesia has been successfully established, it may be suggested to the subject that there is a "hidden part" of the person that may have registered, and can report, the true level of pain stimulation. Under these circumstances, some (but not all) hypnotic subjects give pain reports that are comparable to those collected under normal waking conditions. The hidden observer is a metaphor for this continuing cognitive (but subconscious) representation of pain, and the method by which it may be accessed. First demonstrated in the context of hypnotic analgesia (Hilgard 1973a, Hilgard et al 1975, 1978a, Knox et al 1974), the effect has also been observed in hypnotic deafness (Crawford et al 1979).

Although the hidden observer effect has been replicated in other laboratories (Spanos & Hewitt 1980, Laurence & Perry 1981, Nogrady et al 1983, Spanos et al 1983b), its interpretation is controversial. Hilgard (1973a, 1977a,b, 1979) prefers a cognitive interpretation, in terms of an amnesia-like dissociative process that prevents percepts and memories from being accessible to conscious awareness and control. From a social-psychological point of view, Coe & Sarbin (1977, Sarbin & Coe 1979) suggest that the hidden observer instructions give the subjects permission to report pain that they actually have felt all along. Similarly, Spanos and his colleagues (Spanos & Hewitt 1980, Spanos et al 1983b) reported studies in which the direction of the "hidden" pain reports can be influenced by the wording of instructions. These experiments, however, have been criticized on both conceptual and methodological grounds (Laurence et al 1983; but see Spanos 1983).

There are several reasons for thinking that the hidden observer effect is not entirely a product of social influence. For example, the effect is typically obtained in only about 50% of hypnotic subjects tested, despite the fact that all have been preselected on the basis of their very high level of response to other hypnotic suggestions. Moreover, the occurrence of the effect is not strongly correlated with subjects' expectations following administration of the hidden observer instructions (Hilgard et al 1978a). Perhaps most telling in this respect is the comparison of hypnotized and simulating subjects. Under the usual instructional conditions, which contain strong demands for the hidden observer, Hilgard et al (1978a) obtained such reports in 50% of reals and 75% of simulators; however, a later study employing a weaker form of the suggestion obtained an incidence of 42% in reals and 0% in simulators (Nogrady et al 1983). In other words, the hidden observer reports of simulators, but not of reals, are affected by the demand characteristics of the testing situation.

Some added indications that the hidden observer phenomenon is lawful have been provided by recent successes in predicting which of a selected group of highly hypnotizable subjects will show the effect. The two studies yielding the highest incidence of hidden observers (both 87.5%) employed selection criteria of amnesia and/or automatic writing or talking in addition to high hypnotizability (Knox et al 1974, Spanos & Hewitt 1980; see also Spanos 1983); the remaining published studies employed hypnotizability as the sole selection criterion, yielding an average incidence of 45%. In less stringently selected samples, however, the occurrence of the hidden observer can be predicted almost perfectly by the occurrence of duality response to age regression, in which subjects experience themselves simultaneously as child participants and adult observers (Laurence & Perry 1981, Nogrady et al 1983). Apparently, subjects capable of manifesting the hidden observer have a general capacity for simultaneously representing two contradictory states of affairs in conscious awareness.

CLINICAL APPLICATIONS

The earliest therapeutic use of hypnosis involved direct suggestions for symptom relief or attitude change, and this technique continues to find favor among some therapists of a cognitive-behavioral persuasion. Despite Freud's early rejection of hypnosis on the ground that not all patients were hypnotizable, hypnosis continues to hold a place as an adjunct to psychoanalysis and other forms of psychodynamic psychotherapy. In the period under review, a number of texts appeared that deal with various uses of hypnosis in medical, dental, and psychotherapeutic applications (Crasilneck & Hall 1975, Frankel 1976, Spiegel & Spiegel 1978).

The Relevance of Hypnotizability

The apparent stability of hypnotic susceptibility in the face of efforts to modify it has at least two implications for the clinical use of hypnosis: (*a*) Hypnotizability should be assessed in patients who are candidates for hypnotherapy; and (*b*) Claims that hypnosis is an active ingredient in therapy should be supported by a significant correlation between hypnotizability and outcome. If a person proves to be insusceptible, it would seem better for the clinician to try a nonhypnotic approach to the problem. Clinicians may try to capitalize on what might be called the placebo component of hypnosis, but this practice should be conceptually distinguished from the claim that something occurs beyond the social influence attendant on the hypnotic ritual.

To date there have been very few studies of the hypnotizability of patients in various diagnostic categories, and these yielded conflicting results. Chronic schizophrenics appear to be relatively insusceptible to hypnosis (Lavoie & Sabourin 1980). Acute schizophrenics, depressives, alcoholics, and anorectics seem to show the normal distribution of hypnotizability scores (Pettinati 1982). Phobic patients appear to be relatively highly hypnotizable (Frankel & Orne 1976, John et al 1983), although a study employing the HIP, as opposed to scales of the Stanford type, failed to confirm this finding (Frischholz et al 1982).

The relationship between hypnotizability and treatment outcome is equally confusing at present, not least because of the reluctance of most clinicians to measure hypnotizability in their patients using standard procedures. Fears that poor performance on the scales will reduce the motivation of patients for therapeutic regimes involving hypnosis appear to be unfounded, however (Frankel 1978–1979, 1982, Frankel et al 1979). A relationship with hypnotizability has been definitively established in studies of clinical pain employing both standardized measurements and clinical assessment procedures that possess at least face validity (for a review, see Hilgard & Hilgard 1983). For other symptoms and syndromes, the relationships are complex and poorly understood. Positive correlations are reported between hypnotizability and outcome of hypnotherapy for asthma, migraine headache, headache and vertigo secondary to skull injury, a variety of psychosomatic conditions, and myopia (for reviews, see Bowers & Kelly 1979, Perry et al 1979). However, no correlation is obtained between hypnotizability and outcome for smoking (Perry & Mullen 1975, Perry et al 1979, Holroyd 1980). In those syndromes yielding positive correlations, the hypnotic treatment typically makes use of characteristically hypnotic suggestions for dissociative alterations in experience, thought, and action. By contrast, those treatments yielding null correlations seem to capitalize on the placebo effects of the hypnotic ritual.

Perhaps most intriguing are reports of correlations between hypnotizability and response to nonhypnotic treatment modalities (Benson et al 1975, Nace et al 1982). Such a relationship would suggest that either the syndrome, or the treatment, or both have hypnotic components.

The Utilization of Hypnotic Phenomena

Frankel (1976) noted two principal ways in which hypnosis has traditionally been used in clinical practice: (a) symptom relief by means of direct suggestion; and (b) adjunctive use to aid the exploration and uncovering of clinically relevant material. The paradigm example of the former strategy is hypnotic analgesia, and its success should strongly urge practitioners to adopt analogous techniques in other domains. For example, negative hallucinations for craving and other interoceptive events might be an effective hypnotic treatment for smoking and other addictions. The paradigm example of the latter strategy is hypnotic hypermnesia, and its ambiguous status should encourage caution in assuming the truth value of hypnotic productions. Still, the relationships among hypnosis, hypnotizability, holistic thinking, and creative problem-solving, etc, as described in the work of P. Bowers (Bowers & Bowers 1979), J. R. Hilgard (1979), and Crawford (1982b), suggest that hypnosis may be of service where fantasy and role-taking play an important part in the therapeutic process.

There is some tendency among practitioners to view hypnosis as a kind of placebo therapy, yielding no specific therapeutic effect aside from the "magic" associated with it in popular culture, and the shared belief of clinician and patient that hypnosis will work. Accordingly, there have been relatively few attempts to employ the potential of hypnosis for controlling experience, thought, and action—including cognition and emotion—in the service of treatment (Kihlstrom 1979). The success of hypnotherapy and the correlation between treatment outcome and hypnotizability may both improve where the hypnotic treatment capitalizes on the absorptive and dissociative processes that are central to hypnosis.

Along these lines, Frankel (1976) suggested that, for patients who happen to be hypnotizable, the difficulties that bring them to the clinic may have their origins in naturally occurring states similar to hypnosis. Thus, when the spontaneous, perhaps stress-induced, state terminates, a pathological syndrome—irrational fear, obsessive thought, compulsive behavior, automatism, amnesia—may persist much in the manner of a posthypnotic suggestion.

Frankel found that in such cases the patient's propensity for entering hypnotic-like states may be parlayed from a liability into an asset through a kind of attribution therapy. By producing and cancelling artificial "symptoms" at will through hypnosis, the patients may come to understand that their pathological symptoms are controllable, and that they can cope with future occasions when similar symptoms arise or threaten to do so. Although offered from an eclectic psychodynamic viewpoint, Frankel's ideas mesh quite well with current concepts in cognitive-behavioral therapy such as self-efficacy, and they open up the possibility for a third, radically different approach to hypnotherapy.

THEORETICAL DEVELOPMENTS

Throughout its history, research on hypnosis has been characterized by general consensus on the basic observations, but considerable controversy over their interpretation. Edmonston (1981) revived Braid's argument that hypnosis is fundamentally similar to relaxation, but this seems to apply only to "neutral" hypnosis, in the absence of suggestions for alterations in experience, thought, and action. Banyai & Hilgard (1976) found equivalent responsiveness to test suggestions in subjects who received an induction procedure in which relaxation instructions were omitted and those who pedalled on a bicycle ergometer throughout the testing procedure. Response to suggestions is central to hypnosis, and most theoretical controversy revolves around them. Sheehan & Perry (1977) provided a critical summary of the theoretical paradigms that have dominated hypnosis research in the period since its revival: those of Barber, Hilgard, London & Fuhrer, Orne, Sarbin, and Sutcliffe.

Shor (1979a) placed current theoretical conflicts in historical perspective, identifying the fundamental problem in hypnosis research as the conflict between insufficient skepticism on the one hand, and a failure on the other hand to recognize that hypnotic phenomena offer something new to be learned about the mind. Indeed, in hypnosis it has often been popular to classify individual theories into the "credulous" and the "skeptical." As described by Sutcliffe, the credulous point of view asserts that the psychological processes invoked by hypnotic suggestion are identical with those that would be invoked by actual stimulus conditions; the skeptical account, by contrast, holds that the subject acts in accordance with the suggestions while maintaining conscious awareness of the actual state of affairs. While some approaches clearly fall into each category, many others—including Sutcliffe's own (Sheehan & Perry 1977)—do not. Moreover, some investigators commonly identified by skeptics as credulous have themselves been the most skeptical of certain claims made for hypnosis, as in the case of hypermnesia.

The Controversy over State

Much theoretical heat has been generated over the question of whether hypnosis is a "special" or "altered" state of consciousness. Hilgard (1969, 1978b) identified two versions of the state concept. The strong view asserts that certain phenomena are unique to hypnosis. From this point of view, all hypnotic phenomena, or all hypnotized individuals, share some set of psychological attributes in common. The consistent failure to find any phenomenon of hypnosis (amensia, trance logic, the hidden observer, etc) that occurs consistently in all subjects who have been hypnotized, and which cannot be observed in any state other than hypnosis, is often interpreted as casting doubt on the status of hypnosis as a special state of consciousness (Sarbin & Coe 1972, Barber et al 1974). This is a problem, of course, only if hypnosis is considered to be a proper set defined by singly necessary and jointly sufficient attributes. However, recent work in philosophy and psychology suggests that natural categories are best regarded as fuzzy sets whose instances are related by family resemblance, and that they are represented by a prototype whose features are only probabilistically associated with category membership. From this point of view, trance logic or any other phenomenon may be considered to be more or less characteristic of hypnosis, with some phenomena possessing more cue validity than others but all contributing in some degree to the diagnosis of the state (Orne 1977, Sheehan 1977, Kihlstrom 1984).

Hilgard also identified a weak version of the state view, in which hypnosis serves only as a label representing some domain of characteristic phenomena, including suggested behaviors and self-reports of experience. But, as he notes, this version has difficulty dealing with the fact that all the characteristic phenomena of hypnosis can also be observed posthypnotically, when hypnosis has been formally terminated and subjects no longer indicate that they "feel" hypnotized. If the term "state" is construed only as a kind of shorthand, with no causal properties or defining features associated with it, the question of whether hypnosis is a special state of consciousness disappears as a substantive issue, and investigators can proceed to analyze hypnotic phenomena, and individual differences in hypnotic susceptibility, in terms of their underlying mechanisms.

The Neodissociation Theory of Divided Consciousness

E. R. Hilgard (1973a, 1977a, 1979) offered a dissociative interpretation of hypnosis as an alternative to "state" conceptualizations. Dissociation involves, first, a division of consciousness into multiple, simultaneous streams of mental activity; dissociation proper occurs when one or more of these streams influences experience, thought, and action outside phenomenal awareness and voluntary control. Many of the classic hypnotic phenomena, including motor automatisms, analgesia, blindness, deafness, and amnesia, seem to invite a concept of dissociation. Loss of awareness is exemplified by analgesia and amnesia; that the critical percepts and memories have been registered is indicated by the hidden observer technique in the former case, and reversibility in the latter. Loss of voluntary control is exemplified by motor automatisms such as automatic writing or posthypnotic suggestion (these are often associated with a lack of awareness of the dissociated activity). The concept of dissociation dates back at least to the work of James, Janet, and Prince (E. R. Hilgard 1977a); the new theory is called "neodissociation" to set it apart from the excesses of the older versions. Dissociation, with its emphasis on divided consciousness and amnesic barriers between streams of perceptual-cognitive activity, provides a basis for linking hypnosis to existing theories of attention and memory (Hilgard 1977a, Kihlstrom 1984).

The concept of dissociation has often been criticized on the grounds that ostensibly dissociated percepts, memories, and actions continue to interact with other ongoing cognitive and behavioral events, which results in the anomalies of hypnotic behavior described earlier. In fact, the available evidence suggests that *more* interference occurs when one of the tasks is subconscious. Stevenson (1976) compared conscious color naming with two conscious or subconscious written arithmetic tasks differing in difficulty (counting and serial addition). Simultaneous task performance created mutual interference, the more so when one task was subconscious. Similar results were obtained by Knox et al (1975) comparing color naming with rhythmic key pressing. In the one apparent exception, Bowers & Brenneman (1981) found less interference between shadowing and subconscious nose-touching in response to a signal presented over an unattended channel, although some degree of interference still occurred.

Hilgard (1973a, 1977a,b) argued that the criterion of noninterference is a later importation into the concept of dissociation, and that the only essential properties of the phenomenon are lack of awareness and the experience of involuntariness. The results of the interference experiments, in fact, may be ordered along a continuum representing the attentional demands of the simultaneous tasks, with serial addition arguably the hardest and nose-touching clearly the easiest. Given the assumption that attention is a resource that can be divided according to prevailing task demands (which is what the concept of divided consciousness is all about), the results are approximately as they should be (Kihlstrom 1984). The increase in interference that occurs when one task is performed subconsciously may reflect the need to maintain two streams of thought pertaining to the subconscious task, increasing the draw on the common attentional resource.

Hypnosis as Strategic Social Behavior

While neodissociation theory focuses on the cognitive changes that occur following hypnotic suggestion, another group of theories focuses on the social context in which hypnosis takes place. One approach was developed within sociological role theory by Sarbin & Coe (1972, 1979, Coe & Sarbin 1977, Coe 1978). The theory begins with the proposition that hypnotized individuals do not behave as they do because they have undergone a change in internal state, but because they are striving to enact the role of hypnotized subject as it is defined by the hypnotist and wider sociocultural institutions. In an earlier analysis, they described a number of variables that are important to the success of this role enactment, including the location of individual participants in their proper roles, perceived congruence between self and role, accuracy of role expectations and sensitivity to role demands, possession of role-relevant skills, and the influence of the audience. To the extent that these factors are favorable, the subject can give a performance convincing to both others and oneself. Later analyses made use of concepts of secret-keeping and deception to account for such phenomena as analgesia, amnesia, and the hidden observer.

Another approach within social-psychological theory has been offered as an extension of Barber's task-motivation account of hypnosis (Barber et al 1974, Barber 1979, Spanos 1982a,b). Continuing a line of debunking initiated by Barber, some of the research associated with this position demonstrates that certain claims sometimes made for hypnosis, such as the assertion that suggested deafness or amnesia are identical to corresponding symptoms of organic illness, are incorrect. Another line of research shows that the behavioral effects of hypnosis can often be duplicated by nonhypnotic interventions, which leads to the conclusion, described above, that the concept of hypnotic state is superfluous and unnecessary. While Barber's earlier theory was presented as a behaviorist input-output analysis that eschewed reference to internal states, the more recent version emphasizes the cognitive strategies deployed by subjects in response to explicit and implicit situational demands, in order to produce analgesia, amnesia, and other suggested effects.

The social-psychological approach to hypnosis derives its intuitive plausibility from the fact that the major phenomena occur as a result of suggestion, thus inviting analysis in terms of social influence. Evidence in support of the approach comes from demonstrations that response to hypnotic suggestions is affected by the context in which they are given, which indicates that the underlying processes are not wholly autonomous and involuntary (as might be the case with organically based dysfunctions), and by self-reports of strategies designed to facilitate response to hypnotic suggestions. Just as the cognitive theories of hypnosis must take into account these facts, so must the interpersonal theories take into account the fact that some aspects of hypnosis are not implied by the demand characteristics contained in the hypnotic situation, and that some subjects do not respond to contextual changes. In the social-influence theories, such instances are attributed to degrees of role-involvement in which self and role are merged, or contextual factors that encourage subjects to deceive themselves about the origins and nature of their behaviors. A major disadvantage of allowing these considerations to enter the theory, however, is that they can account for any evidence that would contradict straightforward versions of the theory; this renders them unidentifiable with respect to cognitive theories and thus untestable.

Cognition, Social Influence, and a Possible Rapprochement

Of course, it is not necessary to choose between cognitive and interpersonal theories of hypnosis in an either-or fashion. Many earlier theorists identified with the "state" position, especially Hilgard, Orne, and Shor, explicitly acknowledged the role of interpersonal and sociocultural factors in shaping hypnotic behavior and experience. And among the newer generation of theorists, Sheehan has discussed the role of imagery on the cognitive side of hypnosis and at the same time has underscored the importance of the transference-like interpersonal relationship between the subject and the hypnotist (Sheehan 1979, 1980, 1982, Sheehan & Dolby 1979). More recently, Sheehan & McConkey (1982) emphasized both cognitive and social factors that shape the subjective experiences central to the domain of hypnosis.

Hypnotic phenomena such as paralyses, anesthesias, and amnesias can be genuine even though they do not parallel the symptoms of insult, injury, or disease to the nervous system, and disciplined inquiry can attempt to determine the psychological processes involved in them. From this perspective, a comprehensive analysis of hypnotic phenomena must take into account both the mechanisms underlying cognitive changes and the sociocultural context in which these cognitive changes take place. What might be required is a kind of psychological titration, determining what proportion of variance in response to some suggestion is accounted for by involuntary cognitive changes, and what proportion is due to implicit and explicit social demands.

A somewhat different approach appears implicit in recent trends in role theory, as represented by Coe (1978, Howard & Coe 1980, Schuyler & Coe 1981). Coe distinguishes between two types of responses to hypnotic suggestions: "doings" and "happenings." In the former, the person is an active participant *who makes things happen;* in the latter, the person is a passive participant *to whom things happen.* Roughly half of posthypnotically amnesic subjects modify their memory reports in response to changing contextual demands, which suggests that their amnesia is a "doing"; the remainder do not, which suggests that their amnesia is a "happening." While Coe, like Spanos, prefers to account for the experience of involuntariness in terms of self-deception and attributional processes, he also offers the hypothesis that the cognitive and interpersonal approaches may be equally valid but applicable to different subgroups of hypnotized subjects. For example, the behavior of hypnotic "virtuosos," who make extreme scores on the scales of hypnotic susceptibility, may best be analyzed in terms of underlying dissociative changes in the cognitive system. For the remainder (arguably the greater portion of the population at large), it may be more profitable to focus on the cognitive strategies that they deploy to construct responses to hypnotic suggestions, and the situational factors that lead them to do so.

At the beginning of the period under review, it was suggested that a rapprochement between the cognitive and interpersonal views of hypnosis already existed (Spanos & Barber 1974). However, Hilgard (1973b) had already cautioned that the promised convergence of views was premature, and obscured problems as well as solved them. A decade later, rapprochement appears as distant as ever. Some debunking serves a useful purpose, as in the case of hypermnesia and forensic hypnosis, but scientific progress depends on positive as well as negative findings. It is clear that boundaries must be placed around both the cognitive and interpersonal views of hypnosis, and that the proper investigative stance is not one of "fact or fiction" or "either-or," but rather one of open inquiry or "both-and" in which the laws of hypnotic behavior and experience may be discovered rather than enforced.

NOTES AND ACKNOWLEDGMENTS

This survey covers the period January 1974 through December 1983, with the addition of such articles appearing earlier, or still in press, as is needed to clarify the issues at stake and the findings of current research. Previous reviews of this topic by E. R. Hilgard appeared in the 1965 and 1975 volumes of this series. Preparation of this review was supported in part by Grant #MH-35856 from the National Institute of Mental Health, and in part by an H. I. Romnes Faculty Fellowship from the University of Wisconsin. I thank Kenneth S. Bowers, William C. Heindel, Ernest R. Hilgard, Irene P. Hoyt, Rebecca A. Laird, Campbell Perry, Patricia A. Register, Jeanne Sumi, and Leanne Wilson for their helpful comments.

During the period under review, a number of anthologies have appeared collecting original papers dealing with various aspects of experimental and clinical hypnosis (Edmonston 1977, Frankel & Zamansky 1978, Fromm & Shor 1979, Burrows & Dennerstein 1980), as well as special issues of the *Journal of Abnormal Psychology* (1979, Vol. 88, No. 5) and *Research Communications in Psychology, Psychiatry, and Behavior* (1982, Vol. 7, No. 2). In addition, Bowers (1976) has provided a summary of hypnosis research suitable for use with undergraduates.

Literature Cited

Ashford, B., Hammer, A. G. 1978. The role of expectancies in the occurrence of posthypnotic amnesia. *Int. J. Clin. Exp. Hypn.* 26:281–91

Banyai, E., Hilgard, E. R. 1976. A comparison of active-alert hypnotic induction with traditional hypnotic induction. *J. Abnorm. Psychol.* 85:218–24

Barber, T. X. 1979. Suggested ("hypnotic") behavior: The trance paradigm versus an alternative paradigm. See Fromm & Shor 1979, pp. 217–74

Barber, T. X., Spanos, N. P., Chaves, J. F. 1974. *Hypnosis, Imagination, and Human Potentialities.* New York: Pergamon

Barber, T. X., Wilson, S. C. 1977. Hypnosis, suggestion, and altered states of consciousness: Experimental evaluation of the new cognitive-behavioral theory and the traditional trance-state theory of "hypnosis." See Edmonston 1977, pp. 34–47

Benson, H., Greenwood, M. M., Klemchuck, H. 1975. The relaxation response: Psychophysiologic aspects and clinical applications. *Int. J. Psychiatry Med.* 6:87–97

Blum, G. S. 1967. Experimental observations on the contextual nature of hypnosis. *Int. J. Clin. Exp. Hypn.* 15:160–71

Blum, G. S. 1968. Effects of hypnotically controlled strength of registration vs. rehearsal. *Psychon. Sci.* 10:351–52

Blum, G. S. 1975. A case study of hypnotically induced tubular vision. *Int. J. Clin. Exp. Hypn.* 23:111–19

Blum, G. S. 1979. Hypnotic programming techniques in psychological experiments. See Fromm & Shor 1979, pp. 457–81

Blum, G. S., Barbour, J. S. 1979. Selective inattention to anxiety-linked stimuli. *J. Exp. Psych.: Gen.* 108:182–224

Blum, G. S., Geiwitz, P. J., Hauenstein, L. S. 1967a. Principles of cognitive reverberation. *Behav. Sci.* 12:275–88

Blum, G. S., Geiwitz, P. J., Stewart, C. G. 1967b. Cognitive arousal: The evolution of a model. *J. Pers. Soc. Psychol.* 5:138–51

Blum, G. S., Graef, J. R. 1971. The detection over time of subjects simulating hypnosis. *Int. J. Clin. Exp. Hypn.* 19:211–24

Blum, G. S., Graef, J. R., Hauenstein, L. S. 1968a. Effects of interference and cognitive arousal upon the processing of organized thought. *J. Abnorm. Psychol.* 73:610–14

Blum, G. S., Graef, J. R., Hauenstein, L. S. 1968b. Overcoming interference in short-term memory through distinctive mental contexts. *Psychon. Sci.* 11:73–74

Blum, G. S., Graef, J. R., Hauenstein, L. S., Passini, F. T. 1971. Distinctive mental contexts in long-term memory. *Int. J. Clin. Exp. Hypn.* 19:117–33

Blum, G. S., Green, M. 1978. The effects of mood upon imaginal thought. *J. Pers. Assess.* 42:227–32

Blum, G. S., Hauenstein, L. S., Graef, J. R. 1968c. Studies in cognitive reverberation: Replications and extensions. *Behav. Sci.* 13:171–77

Blum, G. S., Nash, J. K. 1982. EEG correlates of posthypnotically controlled degrees of cognitive arousal. *Mem. Cognit.* 10:475–78

Blum, G. S., Nash, J. K., Jansen, R. D., Barbour, J. S. 1981. Posthypnotic attenuation of a visual illusion as reflected in perceptual reports and cortical event-related potentials. *Acad. Psychol. Bull.* 3:251–71

Blum, G. S., Porter, M. L. 1972. The capacity for rapid shifts in level of mental concentration. *Q. J. Exp. Psychol.* 24:431–38

Blum, G. S., Porter, M. L. 1973. The capacity for selective concentration on color versus form of consonants. *Cogn. Psychol.* 5:47–70

Blum, G. S., Porter, M. L. 1974. Effects of the restriction of conscious awareness in a reaction-time task. *Int. J. Clin. Exp. Hypn.* 22:335–45

Blum, G. S., Porter, M. L., Geiwitz, P. J. 1978. Temporal parameters of negative visual hallucination. *Int. J. Clin. Exp. Hypn.* 26:30–44

Blum, G. S., Wohl, B. M. 1971. An experimental analysis of the nature and operation of anxiety. *J. Abnorm. Psychol.* 78:1–8

Bower, G. H. 1981. Mood and memory. *Am. Psychol.* 36:129–48

Bower, G. H., Gilligan, S. G., Monteiro, K. P. 1981. Selectivity of learning caused by affective state. *J. Exp. Psychol: Gen.* 110:451–73

Bower, G. H., Monteiro, K. P., Gilligan, S. G. 1978. Emotional mood as a context for learning and recall. *J. Verb. Learn. Verb. Behav.* 17:573–85

Bowers, K. S. 1976. *Hypnosis for the Seriously Curious.* Monterey, Calif: Brooks/Cole

Bowers, K. S. 1979. Time distortion and hypnotic ability: Underestimating the duration of hypnosis. *J. Abnorm. Psychol.* 88:435–539

Bowers, K. S. 1981a. Do the Stanford scales tap the "classic suggestion effect"? *Int. J. Clin. Exp. Hypn.* 29:42–53

Bowers, K. S. 1981b. Has the sun set on the Stanford scales? *Am. J. Clin. Hypn.* 24:79–88

Bowers, K. S., Brenneman, H. A. 1979. Hypnosis and the perception of time. *Int. J. Clin. Exp. Hypn.* 27:29–41

Bowers, K. S., Brenneman, H. A. 1981. Hypnotic dissociation, dichotic listening, and active versus passive modes of attention. *J. Abnorm. Psychol.* 90:55–67

Bowers, K. S., Kelly, P. 1979. Stress, disease, psychotherapy, and hypnosis. *J. Abnorm. Psychol.* 88:490–505

Bowers, P. G. 1978. Hypnotizability, creativity and the role of effortless experiencing. *Int. J. Clin. Exp. Hypn.* 26:184–202

Bowers, P. G. 1979. Hypnosis and creativity: The search for the missing link. *J. Abnorm. Psychol.* 88:564–72

Bowers, P. G. 1982. The classic suggestion effect: Relationships with scales of hypnotizability, effortless experiencing, and imagery vividness. *Int. J. Clin. Exp. Hypn.* 30:270–79

Bowers, P. G., Bowers, K. S. 1979. Hypnosis and creativity: A theoretical and empirical rapprochement. See Fromm & Shor 1979, pp. 351–80

Burrows, G., Dennerstein, L., eds. 1980. *Handbook of Hypnosis and Psychosomatic Medicine.* Amsterdam: Elsevier/North Holland

Chaves, J. F., Barber, T. X. 1974. Cognitive strategies, experimenter modelling, and expectation in the attenuation of pain. *J. Abnorm. Psychol.* 83:356–63

Coe, W. C. 1978. The credibility of posthypnotic amnesia: A contextualist's view. *Int. J. Clin. Exp. Hypn.* 26:218–45

Coe, W. C., Sarbin, T. R. 1977. Hypnosis from the standpoint of a contextualist. See Edmonston 1977, pp. 2–13

Coe, W. C., Basden, B., Basden, D., Graham, C. 1976. Posthypnotic amnesia: Suggestions of an active process in dissociative phenomena. *J. Abnorm. Psychol.* 85:455–58

Coe, W. C., Taul, J. H., Basden, D., Basden, B. 1973. Investigation of the dissociation hypothesis and disorganized retrieval in posthypnotic amnesia with retroactive inhibition in free-recall learning. *Proc. 81st Ann. Conv. Am. Psychol. Assoc.* 8:1081–82

Cooper, L. M. 1979. Hypnotic amnesia. See Fromm & Shor 1979, pp. 305–49

Crasilneck, H. B., Hall, J. A. 1975. *Clinical Hypnosis: Principles and Applications.* New York: Grune Stratton

Crawford, H. J. 1981. Hypnotic susceptibility as related to gestalt closure tasks. *J. Pers. Soc. Psychol.* 40:376–83

Crawford, H. J. 1982a. Cognitive processing during hypnosis: Much unfinished business. *Res. Commun. Psychol. Psychiatry Behav.* 7:169–79

Crawford, H. J. 1982b. Hypnotizability, daydreaming style, imagery vividness, and absorption: A multidimensional study. *J. Pers. Soc. Psychol.* 42:915–26

Crawford, H. J., Allen, S. N. 1983. Enhanced visual memory during hypnosis as mediated by hypnotic responsiveness and cognitive strategies. *J. Exp. Psychol: Gen.* 112:662–85

Crawford, H. J., Macdonald, H., Hilgard, E. R. 1979. Hypnotic deafness: A psychophysical study of responses to tone intensity as modified by hypnosis. *Am. J. Psychol.* 92:193–214

Cunningham, P. V., Blum, G. S. 1982. Further evidence that hypnotically induced color blindness does not mimic congenital defects. *J. Abnorm. Psychol.* 91:139–43

Dhanens, T. P., Lundy, R. M. 1975. Hypnotic and waking suggestions and recall. *Int. J. Clin. Exp. Hypn.* 23:68–79

Diamond, B. L. 1980. Inherent problems in the use of pretrial hypnosis on a prospective witness. *Calif. Law Rev.* 68:313–49

Diamond, M. J. 1974. Modification of hypnotizability: A review. *Psychol. Bull.* 81:180–98

Diamond, M. J. 1977. Hypnotizability is modifiable: An alternative approach. *Int. J. Clin. Exp. Hypn.* 25:147–66

Dolby, R. M., Sheehan, P. W. 1977. Cognitive processing and expectancy behavior in hypnosis. *J. Abnorm. Psychol.* 86:334–45

Duncan, B., Perry, C. 1977. Uncancelled suggestion: Initial studies. *Am. J. Clin. Hypn.* 19:166–76

Dywan, J., Bowers, K. S. 1983. The use of hypnosis to enhance recall. *Science* 222:184–85

Easton, R. D., Shor, R. E. 1975. Information-processing analysis of the Chevreul pendulum illusion. *J. Exp. Psychol: Hum. Percept. Perform.* 1:231–36

Easton, R. D., Shor, R. E. 1976. An experimental analysis of the Chevreul pendulum illusion. *J. Gen. Psychol.* 95:111–25

Easton, R. D., Shor, R. E. 1977. Augmented and delayed feedback in the Chevreul pendulum illusion. *J. Gen. Psychol.* 97:167–77

Edmonston, W. E. 1977. Conceptual and investigative approaches to hypnosis and hypnotic phenomena. *Ann. NY Acad. Sci.* 296:1

Edmonston, W. E. 1981. *Hypnosis and Relaxation: Modern Verification of an Old Equation.* New York: Wiley-Interscience

Eliseo, T. S. 1974. The Hypnotic Induction Profile and hypnotic susceptibility. *Int. J. Clin. Exp. Hypn.* 22:320–26

Evans, F. J. 1979. Contextual forgetting: Posthypnotic source amnesia. *J. Abnorm. Psychol.* 88:556–63

Evans, F. J., Kihlstrom, J. F. 1973. Posthypnotic amnesia as disrupted retrieval. *J. Abnorm. Psychol.* 82:317–23

Evans, F. J., Kihlstrom, J. F., Orne, E. C. 1973. Quantifying subjective reports during posthypnotic amnesia. *Proc. 81st Ann. Conv. Am. Psychol. Assoc.* 8:1077–78

Farthing, G. W., Brown, S. W., Venturino, M. 1983. Involuntariness of response on the

Harvard Group Scale of Hypnotic Susceptibility. *Int. J. Clin. Exp. Hypn.* 31:170–81

Frankel, F. H. 1976. *Hypnosis: Trance as a Coping Mechanism.* New York: Plenum

Frankel, F. H. 1978–1979. Scales measuring hypnotic responsivity: A clinical perspective. *Am. J. Clin. Hypn.* 21:208–18

Frankel, F. H. 1982. Hypnosis and hypnotizability scales: A reply. *Int. J. Clin. Exp. Hypn.* 30:377–92

Frankel, F. H., Apfel, R. J., Kelly, S. F., Benson, H., Quinn, T., et al. 1979. The use of hypnotizability scales in the clinic: A review after six years. *Int. J. Clin. Exp. Hypn.* 27:63–73

Frankel, F. J., Orne, M. T. 1976. Hypnotizability and phobic behavior. *Arch. Gen. Psychiatry* 33:1259–61

Frankel, F. H., Zamansky, H. S. 1978. *Hypnosis at its Bicentennial: Selected Papers.* New York: Plenum

Frischholz, E. J., Spiegel, D., Spiegel, H., Balma, D. L., Markell, C. S. 1982. Differential hypnotic responsivity of smokers, phobics, and chronic-pain control patients: A failure to confirm. *J. Abnorm. Psychol.* 91:269–72

Frischholz, E. J., Spiegel, H., Tryon, W. W., Fisher, S. 1981. The relationship between the Hypnotic Induction Profile and the Stanford Hypnotic Susceptibility Scale, Form C: Revisited. *Am. J. Clin. Hypn.* 24:98–105

Frischholz, E. J., Tryon, W. W., Vellios, A. T., Fisher, S., Maruffi, B. L., Spiegel, H. 1980. The relationship between the Hypnotic Induction Profile and the Stanford Hypnotic Susceptibility Scale, Form C: A replication. *Am. J. Clin. Hypn.* 22:185–96

Fromm, E., Brown, D. P., Hurt, S. W., Oberlander, J. Z., Boxer, A. M., Pfeifer, G. 1981. The phenomena and characteristics of self-hypnosis. *Int. J. Clin. Exp. Hypn.* 29:189–246

Fromm, E., Shor, R. E. 1979. *Hypnosis: Developments in Research and New Perspectives.* Chicago: Aldine

Garrett, J. B., Wallace, B. 1975. A novel test of hypnotic anesthesia. *Int. J. Clin. Exp. Hypn.* 23:139–47

Geiselman, R. E., Fishman, D. L., Jaenicke, C., Larner, B. R., MacKinnon, D. P., et al. 1983. Mechanisms of hypnotic and nonhypnotic forgetting. *J. Exp. Psychol. Learn. Mem. Cognit.* 9:626–18

Goldstein, A., Hilgard, E. R. 1975. Lack of influence of the morphine antagonist naloxone on hypnotic analgesia. *Proc. Natl. Acad. Sci. USA* 72:2041–43

Graham, C., Evans, F. J. 1977. Hypnotizability and the development of waking attention. *J. Abnorm. Psychol.* 86:631–38

Graham, C., Leibowitz, H. W. 1972. The effect of suggestion on visual acuity. *Int. J. Clin. Exp. Hypn.* 20:169–86

Graham, K. R. 1977. Perceptual processes and hypnosis: Support for a cognitive-state theory based on laterality. See Edmonston 1977, pp. 274–83

Graham, K. R., Pernicano, K. 1979. Laterality, hypnosis, and the autokinetic effect. *Am. J. Clin. Hypn.* 22:79–84

Graham, K. R., Schwartz, L. M. 1973. Suggested deafness and auditory signal detectability. *Proc. 81st Ann. Conv. Am. Psychol. Assoc.* 8:1091–92

Gur, R. C. 1974. An attention-controlled operant procedure for enhancing hypnotic susceptibility. *J. Abnorm. Psychol.* 83:644–50

Gur, R. C., Gur, R. E. 1974. Handedness, sex, and eyedness as moderating variables in the relation between hypnotic susceptibility and functional brain asymmetry. *J. Abnorm. Psychol.* 83:635–43

Harvey, M. A., Sipprelle, C. N. 1978. Color blindness, perceptual interference, and hypnosis. *Am. J. Clin. Hypn.* 20:189–93

Hilgard, E. R. 1965. *Hypnotic Susceptibility.* New York: Harcourt, Brace, World

Hilgard, E. R. 1969. Altered states of awareness. *J. Nerv. Ment. Dis.* 149:68–79

Hilgard, E. R. 1972. A critique of Johnson, Maher, and Barber's "Artifact in the 'essence of hypnosis': An evaluation of trance logic," with a recomputation of their findings. *J. Abnorm. Psychol.* 79:221–33

Hilgard, E. R. 1973a. A neodissociation interpretation of pain reduction in hypnosis. *Psychol. Rev.* 80:396–411

Hilgard, E. R. 1973b. The domain of hypnosis, with some comments on alternative paradigms. *Am. Psychol.* 28:972–82

Hilgard, E. R. 1977a. *Divided Consciousness: Multiple Controls in Human Thought and Action.* New York: Wiley-Interscience

Hilgard, E. R. 1977b. The problem of divided consciousness: A neodissociation interpretation. See Edmonston 1977, pp. 48–59

Hilgard, E. R. 1978. States of consciousness in hypnosis: Divisions or levels? See Frankel & Zamansky 1978, pp. 15–36

Hilgard, E. R. 1978–1979. The Stanford Hypnotic Susceptibility Scales as related to other measures of hypnotic responsiveness. *Am. J. Clin. Hypn.* 21:68–83

Hilgard, E. R. 1979. Divided consciousness in hypnosis: The implications of the hidden observer. See Fromm & Shor 1979, pp. 45–80

Hilgard, E. R. 1981a. The eye roll sign and other scores of the Hypnotic Induction Profile (HIP) as related to the Stanford Hypnotic Susceptibility Scale, Form C (SHSS:C): A critical discussion of a study by Frischholz, Spiegel, Tryon, and Fisher. *Am. J. Clin. Hypn.* 24:89–97

Hilgard, E. R. 1981b. Further discussion of the HIP and the Stanford Form C: A reply to a reply by Frischholz, Spiegel, Tryon, and Fisher. *Am. J. Clin. Hypn.* 26:106–8

Hilgard, E. R. 1981c. Hypnotic susceptibility scales under attack: An examination of Weitzenhoffer's criticisms. *Int. J. Clin. Exp. Hypn.* 29:24–41

Hilgard, E. R. 1982. Hypnotic susceptibility and implications for measurement. *Int. J. Clin. Exp. Hypn.* 30:394–403

Hilgard, E. R., Crawford, H. J., Bowers, P. G., Kihlstrom, J. F. 1979. A tailored SHSS:C, permitting user modification for special purposes. *Int. J. Clin. Exp. Hypn.* 27:125–33

Hilgard, E. R., Hilgard, J. R. 1983. *Hypnosis in the Relief of Pain.* Los Altos, Calif: Kaufmann. New ed.

Hilgard, E. R., Hilgard, J. R., Macdonald, H., Morgan, A. H., Johnson, L. S. 1978a. Covert pain in hypnotic analgesia: Its reality as tested by the real-simulator design. *J. Abnorm. Psychol.* 87:655–63

Hilgard, E. R., Macdonald, H., Morgan, A. H., Johnson, L. S. 1978b. The reality of hypnotic analgesia: A comparison of highly hypnotizables with simulators. *J. Abnorm. Psychol.* 87:239–46

Hilgard, E. R., Morgan, A. H., Macdonald, H. 1975. Pain and dissociation in the cold pressor test: A study of hypnotic analgesia with "hidden reports" through automatic keypressing and automatic talking. *J. Abnorm. Psychol.* 84:280–89

Hilgard, E. R., Sheehan, P. W., Monteiro, K. P., Macdonald, H. 1981. Factorial structure of the Creative imagination scale as a measure of hypnotic responsiveness: An international comparative study. *Int. J. Clin. Exp. Hypn.* 29:66–76

Hilgard, J. R. 1974. Imaginative involvement: Some characteristics of the highly hypnotizable and the non-hypnotizable. *Int. J. Clin. Exp. Hypn.* 22:138–56

Hilgard, J. R. 1979. *Personality and Hypnosis: A Study of Imaginative Involvement.* Chicago: Univ. Chicago Press. 2nd ed.

Hilgard, J. R., Hilgard, E. R. 1979. Assessing hypnotic responsiveness in a clinical setting: A multi-time clinical scale and its advantages over single-item scales. *Int. J. Clin. Exp. Hypn.* 27:134–50

Hilgard, J. R., LeBaron, S. 1982. Relief of anxiety and pain in children and adolescents with cancer: Quantitative measures and clinical observations. *Int. J. Clin. Exp. Hypn.* 30:417–42

Hilgard, J. R., LeBaron, S. 1984. *Hypnosis in the Treatment of Pain and Anxiety in Children with Cancer: A Clinical and Quantitative Investigation.* Los Altos, Calif: Kaufmann

Holroyd, J. 1980. Hypnosis treatment for smoking: An evaluative review. *Int. J. Clin. Exp. Hypn.* 28:341–57

Howard, M. L., Coe, W. C. 1980. The effect of context and subjects' perceived control in breaching posthypnotic amnesia. *J. Pers.* 48:342–59

Jansen, R. D., Blum, G. S., Loomis, J. M. 1982. Attentional alterations of slant-specific interference between line segments in eccentric vision. *Perception* 11:535–40

John, R., Hollander, B., Perry, C. 1983. Hypnotizability and phobic behavior: Further supporting data. *J. Abnorm. Psychol.* 92:390–92

Johnson, L. S. 1979. Self-hypnosis: Behavioral and phenomenological comparisons with heterohypnosis. *Int. J. Clin. Exp. Hypn.* 27:240–64

Johnson, L. S. 1981. Current research in self-hypnotic phenomenology: The Chicago paradigm. *Int. J. Clin. Exp. Hypn.* 29:247–58

Johnson, L. S., Dawson, S. L., Clark, J. L., Sikorsky, C. 1983. Self-hypnosis versus hetero-hypnosis: Order effects and sex differences in behavioral and experiential impact. *Int. J. Clin. Exp. Hypn.* 31:170–81

Johnson, L. S., Weight, D. G. 1976. Self-hypnosis versus heterohypnosis: Experiential and behavioral comparisons. *J. Abnorm. Psychol.* 85:523–26

Johnson, R. F. Q. 1972. Trance logic revisited: A reply to Hilgard's critique. *J. Abnorm. Psychol.* 79:234–38

Johnson, R. F. Q. 1976. Hypnotic time distortion and the enhancement of learning: New data pertinent to the Krauss-Katzell-Krauss experiment. *Am. J. Clin. Hypn.* 19:98–102

Johnson, R. F. Q., Maher, B. A., Barber, T. X. 1972. Artifact in the "essence of hypnosis": An evaluation of trance logic. *J. Abnorm. Psychol.* 79:104–12

Jones, B., Spanos, N. P. 1982. Suggestions for altered auditory sensitivity, the negative subject effect and hypnotic susceptibility: A signal detection analysis. *J. Pers. Soc. Psychol.* 43:637–47

Karlin, R. A. 1979. Hypnotizability and attention. *J. Abnorm. Psychol.* 88:92–95

Kihlstrom, J. F. 1977. Models of posthypnotic amnesia. See Edmonston 1977, pp. 284–301

Kihlstrom, J. F. 1978. Context and cognition in posthypnotic amnesia. *Int. J. Clin. Exp. Hypn.* 26:246–67

Kihlstrom, J. F. 1979. Hypnosis and psychopathology: Retrospect and prospect. *J. Abnorm. Psychol.* 88:459–73

Kihlstrom, J. F. 1980. Posthypnotic amnesia for recently learned material: Interactions with "episodic" and "semantic" memory. *Cognit. Psychol.* 12:227–51

Kihlstrom, J. F. 1982. Hypnosis and the dissociation of memory, with special reference to posthypnotic amnesia. *Res. Commun. Psychol. Psychiatry Behav.* 7:181–97

Kihlstrom, J. F. 1983. Instructed forgetting: Hypnotic and nonhypnotic. *J. Exp. Psychol. Gen.* 112:73–79

Kihlstrom, J. F. 1984. Conscious, subconscious, unconscious: A cognitive view. In *The Unconscious: Reconsidered,* ed. K. S. Bowers, D. Meichenbaum, pp. 149–211. New York: Wiley

Kihlstrom, J. F., Easton, R. D., Shor, R. E. 1983. Spontaneous recovery of memory during posthypnotic amnesia. *Int. J. Clin. Exp. Hypn.* 31:309–23

Kihlstrom, J. F., Evans, F. J. 1976. Recovery of memory after posthypnotic amnesia. *J. Abnorm. Psychol.* 85:564–69

Kihlstrom, J. F., Evans, F. J. 1977. Residual effect of suggestions for posthypnotic amnesia: A reexamination. *J. Abnorm. Psychol.* 86:327–33

Kihlstrom, J. F., Evans, F. J. 1978. Generic recall during posthypnotic amnesia. *Bull. Psychon. Soc.* 12:57–60

Kihlstrom, J. F., Evans, F. J. 1979. Memory retrieval processes during posthypnotic amnesia. In *Functional Disorders of Memory,* ed. J. F. Kihlstrom, F. J. Evans, pp. 179–218. Hillsdale, NJ: Erlbaum

Kihlstrom, J. F., Evans, F. J., Orne, E. C., Orne, M. T. 1980. Attempting to breach posthypnotic amnesia. *J. Abnorm. Psychol.* 89:603–16

Kihlstrom, J. F., Shor, R. E. 1978. Recall and recognition during posthypnotic amnesia. *Int. J. Clin. Exp. Hypn.* 26:330–49

Kihlstrom, J. F., Wilson, L. 1984. Temporal organization of recall during posthypnotic amnesia. *J. Abnorm. Psychol.* 93:200–6

Knox, V. J., Crutchfield, L., Hilgard, E. R. 1975. The nature of task interference in hypnotic dissociation: An investigation of hypnotic behavior. *Int. J. Clin. Exp. Hypn.* 23:305–23

Knox, V. J., Gekoski, W. L., Shum, K., McLaughlin, D. M. 1981. Analgesia for experimentally induced pain: Multiple sessions of acupuncture compared to hypnosis in high- and low-susceptible subjects. *J. Abnorm. Psychol.* 90:28–34

Knox, V. J., Handfield-Jones, C. E., Shum, K. 1979. Subject expectancy and the reduction of cold pressor pain with acupuncture and placebo acupuncture. *Psychosom. Med.* 41:471–86

Knox, V. J., Morgan, A. H., Hilgard, E. R. 1974. Pain and suffering in ischemia: The paradox of hypnotically suggested anesthesia as contradicted by reports from the "hidden observer." *Arch. Gen. Psychiatry* 30:840–47

Knox, V. J., Shum, K. 1977. Reduction of cold-pressor pain with acupuncture analgesia in high- and low-hypnotic subjects. *J. Abnorm. Psychol.* 86:639–43

Knox, V. J., Shum, K., McLaughlin, D. M. 1978. Hypnotic analgesia versus acupuncture analgesia in high and low susceptible subjects. See Frankel & Zamansky 1978, pp. 101–8

Krauss, H. H., Katzell, R., Krauss, B. J. 1974. Effect of hypnotic time distortion upon free-recall learning. *J. Abnorm. Psychol.* 83:140–44

Laurence, J.-R., Perry, C. 1981. The "hidden observer" phenomenon in hypnosis: Some additional findings. *J. Abnorm. Psychol.* 90:334–44

Laurence, J.-R., Perry, C. 1983. Hypnotically created memory among highly hypnotizable subjects. *Science* 222:523–24

Laurence, J.-R., Perry, C., Kihlstrom, J. F. 1983. "Hidden observer" phenomena in hypnosis: An experimental creation? *J. Pers. Soc. Psychol.* 44:163–69

Lavoie, G., Sabourin, M. 1980. Hypnosis and schizophrenia: A review of experimental and clinical studies. See Burrows & Dennerstein 1980, pp. 377–419

Leibowitz, H. W., Lundy, R. M., Guez, J. R. 1980. The effect of testing distance on suggestion-induced visual field narrowing. *Int. J. Clin. Exp. Hypn.* 28:409–20

Leibowitz, H. W., Post, R. B., Shupert Rodemer, C., Wadlington, W. L., Lundy, R. M. 1981. Roll vection analysis in hypnotically induced visual field narrowing. *Percept. Psychophys.* 28:173–76

Lynn, S. J., Nash, M. R., Rhue, J. W., Frauman, D., Stanley, S. 1983. Hypnosis and the experience of nonvolition. *Int. J. Clin. Exp. Hypn.* 31:293–308

McConkey, K. M. 1980. Creatively imagined "amnesia." *Am. J. Clin. Hypn.* 22:197–205

McConkey, K. M., Sheehan, P. W. 1981. The impact of videotape playback of hypnotic events on posthypnotic amnesia. *J. Abnorm. Psychol.* 90:46–54

McConkey, K. M., Sheehan, P. W., Cross, D. G. 1980. Posthypnotic amnesia: Seeing is not remembering. *Br. J. Soc. Clin. Psychol.* 19:99–107

McConkey, K. M., Sheehan, P. W., White, K. D. 1979. Comparison of the Creative Imagination Scale and the Harvard Group Scale of Hypnotic Susceptibility, Form A. *Int. J. Clin. Exp. Hypn.* 27:265–77

McDonald, R. D., Smith, J. R. 1975. Trance logic in traceable and simulating subjects. *Int. J. Clin. Exp. Hypn.* 23:80–89

MacCracken, P. J., Gogel, W. C., Blum, G. S. 1980. Effects of posthypnotic suggestion on perceived egocentric distance. *Perception* 9:561–68

MacLeod-Morgan, C., Lack, L. 1982. Hemispheric specificity: A physiological concomitant of hypnotizability. *Psychophysiology* 19:687–90

Miller, R. J. 1975. Response to the Ponzo illusion as a reflection of hypnotic susceptibility. *Int. J. Clin. Exp. Hypn.* 23:148–57

Miller, R. J., Hennessy, R. T., Leibowitz, H. W. 1973. The effect of hypnotic ablation of the background on the magnitude of the Ponzo perspective illusion. *Int. J. Clin. Exp. Hypn.* 21:180–91

Miller, R. J., Leibowitz, H. W. 1976. A signal detection analysis of hypnotically induced narrowing of the peripheral visual field. *J. Abnorm. Psychol.* 85:446–54

Morgan, A. H., Hilgard, J. R. 1978–1979a. The Stanford Hypnotic Clinical Scale for Adults. *Am. J. Clin. Hypn.* 21:134–47

Morgan, A. H., Hilgard, J. R. 1978–1979b. The Stanford Hypnotic Clinical Scale for Children. *Am. J. Clin. Hypn.* 21:148–69

Morgan, A. H., Johnson, D. L., Hilgard, E. R. 1974. The stability of hypnotic susceptibility: A longitudinal study. *Int. J. Clin. Exp. Hypn.* 22:249–57

Nace, E. P., Orne, M. T., Hammer, A. G. 1974. Posthypnotic amnesia as an active psychic process: The reversibility of amnesia. *Arch. Gen. Psychiatry* 31:257–60

Nace, E. P., Warwick, A. M., Kelley, R. L., Evans, F. J. 1982. Hypnotizability and outcome in brief psychotherapy. *J. Clin. Psychiatry* 43:129–33

Nash, M. R., Johnson, L. S., Tipton, R. D. 1979. Hypnotic age regression and the occurrence of transitional object relationships. *J. Abnorm. Psychol.* 88:547–55

Nogrady, H., McConkey, K. M., Laurence, J.-R., Perry, C. 1983. Dissociation, duality, and demand characteristics in hypnosis. *J. Abnorm. Psychol.* 92:223–35

Obstoj, I., Sheehan, P. W. 1977. Aptitude for trance, task generalizability, and incongruity response in hypnosis. *J. Abnorm. Psychol.* 86:543–52

Orne, M. T. 1959. The nature of hypnosis: Artifact and essence. *J. Abnorm. Soc. Psychol.* 58:277–99

Orne, M. T. 1977. The construct of hypnosis: Implications of the definition for research and practice. See Edmonston 1977, pp. 14–33

Orne, M. T. 1979. The use and misuse of hypnosis in court. *Int. J. Clin. Exp. Hypn.* 27:311–41

Orne, M. T., Hilgard, E. R., Spiegel, H., Spiegel, D., Crawford, H. J., et al. 1979. The relation between the Hypnotic Induction Profile and the Stanford Hypnotic Susceptibility Scales, Forms A and C. *Int. J. Clin. Exp. Hypn.* 27:85–102

Orne, M. T., McConkey, K. M. 1981. Toward convergent inquiry into self-hypnosis. *Int. J. Clin. Exp. Hypn.* 29:313–23

Orne, M. T., Soskis, D. A., Dinges, D. F., Orne, E. C. 1984. Hypnotically induced testimony. In *Eyewitness Testimony: Psychological Perspectives*, ed. G. L. Wells, E. F. Loftus. Cambridge: Cambridge Univ. Press

Perry, C. 1977a. Is hypnotizability modifiable? *Int. J. Clin. Exp. Hypn.* 25:125–46

Perry, C. 1977b. Uncancelled hypnotic suggestions: The effects of hypnotic depth and hypnotic skill on their posthypnotic persistence. *J. Abnorm. Psychol.* 86:570–74

Perry, C., Gelfand, R., Marcovitch, P. 1979. The relevance of hypnotic susceptibility in the clinical context. *J. Abnorm. Psychol.* 88:592–603

Perry, C., Laurence, J.-R. 1980. Hypnotic depth and hypnotic susceptibility: A replicated finding. *Int. J. Clin. Exp. Hypn.* 28:272–80

Perry, C., Mullen, G. 1975. The effects of hypnotic susceptibility on reducing smoking behavior treated by an hypnotic technique. *J. Clin. Psychol.* 31:498–505

Perry, C., Walsh, B. 1978. Inconsistencies and anomalies of response as a defining characteristic of hypnosis. *J. Abnorm. Psychol.* 87:574–77

Peters, J. 1973. *Trance logic: Artifact or essence of hypnosis?* PhD thesis. Pennsylvania State Univ., Univ. Park

Pettinati, H. M. 1982. Measuring hypnotizability in psychotic patients. *Int. J. Clin. Exp. Hypn.* 30:404–16

Putnam, W. H. 1979. Hypnosis and distortions in eyewitness memory. *Int. J. Clin. Exp. Hypn.* 27:437–48

Radtke, H. L., Spanos, N. P. 1981a. Temporal sequencing during posthypnotic amnesia: A methodological critique. *J. Abnorm. Psychol.* 90:476–85

Radtke, H. L., Spanos, N. P. 1981b. Was I hypnotized? A social-psychological analysis of hypnotic depth reports. *Psychiatry* 44:359–76

Radtke-Bodorik, H. L., Planas, M., Spanos, N. P. 1980. Suggested amnesia, verbal inhibition, and disorganized recall for a long word list. *Can. J. Behav. Sci.* 12:87–97

Radtke-Bodorik, H. L., Spanos, N. P., Haddad, M. 1979. The effects of spoken versus written recall on suggested amnesia in hypnotic and task-motivated subjects. *Am. J. Clin. Hypn.* 22:8–16

Reiser, M., Nielson, M. 1980. Investigative hypnosis: A developing specialty. *Am. J. Clin. Hypn.* 23:75–83

Ruch, J. C. 1975. Self-hypnosis: The result of heterohypnosis or vice-versa? *Int. J. Clin. Exp. Hypn.* 23:282–304

Ruch, J. C., Morgan, A. H., Hilgard, E. R.

1974. Measuring hypnotic responsiveness: A comparison of the Barber Suggestibility Scale and the Stanford Hypnotic Susceptibility Scale, Form A. *Int. J. Clin. Exp. Hypn.* 30:404–16

Sackeim, H. A., Paulus, D., Weiman, A. L. 1979. Classroom seating and hypnotic susceptibility. *J. Abnorm. Psychol.* 88:81–84

Sanders, G. S., Simmons, W. L. 1983. Use of hypnosis to enhance eyewitness accuracy: Does it work? *J. Appl. Psychol.* 68:70–77

Sarbin, T. R., Coe, W. C. 1972. *Hypnosis: A Social Psychological Analysis of Influence Communication.* New York: Holt, Rinehart, Winston

Sarbin, T. R., Coe, W. C. 1979. Hypnosis and psychopathology: Replacing old myths with fresh metaphors. *J. Abnorm. Psychol.* 88:506–26

Schuyler, B. A., Coe, W. C. 1981. A physiological investigation of volitional and nonvolitional experience during posthypnotic amnesia. *J. Pers. Soc. Psychol.* 40:1160–69

Schwartz, W. S. 1978. Time and context during hypnotic involvement. *Int. J. Clin. Exp. Hypn.* 26:307–16

Schwartz, W. S. 1980. Hypnosis and episodic memory. *Int. J. Clin. Exp. Hypn.* 28:375–85

Sheehan, D. V., Latta, W. D., Regina, E. G., Smith, G. M. 1979. Empirical assessment of Spiegel's Hypnotic Induction Profile and eye-roll hypothesis. *Int. J. Clin. Exp. Hypn.* 27:103–10

Sheehan, E. P., Smith, H. V., Forrest, D. W. 1982. A signal detection study of the effects of suggested improvement on the monocular visual acuity of myopes. *Int. J. Clin. Exp. Hypn.* 30:138–46

Sheehan, P. W. 1977. Incongruity in trance behavior: A defining property of hypnosis? See Edmonston 1977, pp. 194–207

Sheehan, P. W. 1979. Hypnosis and the process of imagination. See Fromm & Shor 1979, pp. 381–411

Sheehan, P. W. 1980. Factors influencing rapport in hypnosis. *J. Abnorm. Psychol.* 89:263–81

Sheehan, P. W. 1982. Imagery and hypnosis—Forging a link, at least in part. *Res. Commun. Psychol. Psychiatry Behav.* 7:257–72

Sheehan, P. W., Dolby, R. M. 1975. Hypnosis and the influence of most recently perceived events. *J. Abnorm. Psychol.* 84:331–45

Sheehan, P. W., Dolby, R. M. 1979. Motivated involvement in hypnosis: The illustration of clinical rapport through hypnotic dreams. *J. Abnorm. Psychol.* 88:573–83

Sheehan, P. W., McConkey, K. M. 1982. *Hypnosis and Experience: The Exploration of Phenomena and Process.* Hillsdale, NJ: Erlbaum

Sheehan, P. W., Obstoj, I., McConkey, K. M. 1976. Trance logic and cue structure as supplied by the hypnotist. *J. Abnorm. Psychol.* 85:459–72

Sheehan, P. W., Perry, C. W. 1977. *Methodologies of Hypnosis: A Critical Appraisal of Contemporary Paradigms of Hypnosis.* Hillsdale, NJ: Erlbaum

Sheehan, P. W., Tilden, J. 1983. Effects of suggestibility and hypnosis on accurate and distorted retrieval from memory. *J. Exp. Psychol. Learn. Mem. Cognit.* 9:283–93

Shor, R. E. 1979a. The fundamental problem in hypnosis as viewed from historic perspectives. See Fromm & Shor 1979, pp. 15–41

Shor, R. E. 1979b. A phenomenological method for the measurement of variables important to an understanding of the nature of hypnosis. See Fromm & Shor 1979, pp. 105–35

Shor, R. E., Easton, R. D. 1973. A preliminary report on research comparing self- and hetero-hypnosis. *Am. J. Clin. Hypn.* 16:37–44

Shor, R. E., Pistole, D. D., Easton, R. D., Kihlstrom, J. F. 1984. Relation of predicted to actual hypnotic responsiveness, with special reference to posthypnotic amnesia. *Int. J. Clin. Exp. Hypn.* 32: In press

Sloane, M. C. 1981. *A comparison of hypnosis vs. waking state and visual vs. non-visual recall instructions for witness/victim memory retrieval in actual major crimes.* PhD thesis. Florida State Univ., Tallahassee. *Diss. Abstr. Int.* University Microfilms No. 8125873

Smith, M. C. 1983. Hypnotic memory enhancement of witnesses: Does it work? *Psychol. Bull.* 94:387–407

Spanos, N. P. 1982a. A social psychological approach to hypnotic behavior. In *Integrations of Clinical and Social Psychology,* ed. G. Weary, H. L. Mirels. New York: Oxford

Spanos, N. P. 1982b. Hypnotic behavior: A cognitive social psychological perspective. *Res. Commun. Psychol. Psychiatry Behav.* 7:199–213

Spanos, N. P. 1983. The hidden observer as an experimental creation. *J. Pers. Soc. Psychol.* 44:170–76

Spanos, N. P., Ansari, F., Stam, H. J. 1979a. Hypnotic age regression and eidetic imagery: A failure to replicate. *J. Abnorm. Psychol.* 88:88–91

Spanos, N. P., Barber, T. X. 1974. Toward a convergence in hypnosis research. *Am. Psychol.* 29:500–11

Spanos, N. P., Barber, T. X., Lang, G. 1974. Cognition and self-control: Cognitive control of painful sensory input. In *Thought and Feeling: Cognitive Alteration of Feeling States,* ed. H. London, R. E. Nisbett. Chicago: Aldine

Spanos, N. P., Bodorik, H. L. 1977. Suggested

amnesia and disorganized recall in hypnotic and task-motivated subjects. *J. Abnorm. Psychol.* 86:295–305

Spanos, N. P., Brown, J. M., Jones, B., Horner, D. 1981a. Cognitive activity and suggestions for analgesia in the reduction of reported pain. *J. Abnorm. Psychol.* 90:554–61

Spanos, N. P., Dubreuil, D., Saad, C. L., Gorassini, D. 1983a. Hypnotic elimination of prism-induced aftereffects: Perceptual effect or response to experimental demands? *J. Abnorm. Psychol.* 92:216–22

Spanos, N. P., Gorassini, D. R., Petrusic, W. 1981b. Hypnotically induced limb anesthesia and adaptation to displacing prisms: A failure to confirm. *J. Abnorm. Psychol.* 90:329–33

Spanos, N. P., Gwynn, M. I., Stam, H. J. 1983b. Instructional demands and ratings of overt and hidden pain during hypnotic analgesia. *J. Abnorm. Psychol.* 92:479–88

Spanos, N. P., Hewitt, E. C. 1980. The hidden observer in hypnotic analgesia: Discovery or experimental creation? *J. Pers. Soc. Psychol.* 39:1201–14

Spanos, N. P., Horton, C., Chaves, J. F. 1975. The effects of two cognitive strategies on pain. *J. Abnorm. Psychol.* 84:677–81

Spanos, N. P., Jones, B., Malfara, A. 1982a. Hypnotic deafness: Now you hear it—Now you still hear it. *J. Abnorm. Psychol.* 91:75–77

Spanos, N. P., Radtke, H. L. 1982. Hypnotic amnesia as a strategic enactment: A cognitive, social-psychological perspective. *Res. Commun. Psychol., Psychiatry, Behav.* 7:215–31

Spanos, N. P., Radtke, H. L., Dubreuil, D. L. 1982b. Episodic and semantic memory in posthypnotic amnesia: A reevaluation. *J. Pers. Soc. Psychol.* 43:565–73

Spanos, N. P., Radtke, H. L., Hodgins, D. C., Bertrand, L., Stam, H. J., Dubreuil, D. L. 1983c. The Carleton University Responsiveness to Suggestion Scale: Stability, reliability, and relationships with expectancy and hypnotic experience. *Psychol. Rep.* 53:555–63

Spanos, N. P., Radtke, H. L., Hodgins, D. C., Stam, H. J., Bertrand, L. 1983d. The Carleton University Responsiveness to Suggestion Scale: Normative data and psychometric properties. *Psychol. Rep.* 53:523–35

Spanos, N. P., Radtke, H. L., Hodgins, D. C., Stam, H. J., Noretti, P. 1983e. The Carleton University Responsiveness to Suggestion Scale: Relationships with other measures of susceptibility, expectancies, and absorption. *Psychol. Rep.* 53:723–34

Spanos, N. P., Radtke-Bodorik, H. L., Ferguson, J. D., Jones, B. 1979b. The effects of hypnotic susceptibility, suggestions for analgesia, and the utilization of cognitive strategies on the reduction of pain. *J. Abnorm. Psychol.* 88:282–92

Spanos, N. P., Radtke-Bodorik, H. L., Stam, H. J. 1980a. Disorganized recall during suggested amnesia: Fact not artifact. *J. Abnorm. Psychol.* 89:1–19

Spanos, N. P., Stam, H. J., Brazil, K. 1981c. The effects of suggestion and distraction on coping ideation and reported pain. *J. Ment. Imagery* 5:75–90

Spanos, N. P., Stam, H. J., D'Eon, J. L., Pawlak, A. E., Radtke-Bodorik, H. L. 1980b. The effects of social psychological variables on hypnotic amnesia. *J. Pers. Soc. Psychol.* 39:737–50

Spiegel, D., Tryon, W. W., Frischholz, E. J., Spiegel, H. 1982. Hilgard's illusion. *Arch. Gen. Psychiatry* 39:972–74

Spiegel, H. 1977. The Hypnotic Induction Profile (HIP): A review of its development. See Edmonston 1977, pp. 129–42

Spiegel, H., Spiegel, D. 1978. *Trance and Treatment: Clinical Uses of Hypnosis.* New York: Basic Books

St. Jean, R. 1980. Hypnotic time distortion and learning: Another look. *J. Abnorm. Psychol.* 89:20–24

St. Jean, R., Coe, W. C. 1981. Recall and recognition memory during posthypnotic amnesia: A failure to confirm the disrupted-search hypothesis and the memory disorganization hypothesis. *J. Abnorm. Psychol.* 90:231–41

St. Jean, R., MacLeod, C., 1983. Hypnosis, absorption, and time perception. *J. Abnorm. Psychol.*

St. Jean, R., MacLeod, C., Coe, W. C., Howard, M. 1982. Amnesia and hypnotic time distortion. *Int. J. Clin. Exp. Hypn.* 30:127–37

Stern, D. B., Spiegel, H., Nee, J. C. 1979. The Hypnotic Induction Profile: Normative observations, reliability, and validity. *Am. J. Clin. Hypn.* 21:109–33

Stern, J. A., Brown, M., Ulett, G. A., Sletten, I. 1977. A comparison of hypnosis, acupuncture, morphine, valium, aspirin, and placebo in the management of experimentally induced pain. See Edmonston 1977, pp. 175–93

Stevenson, J. A. 1976. Effect of posthypnotic dissociation on the performance of interfering tasks. *J. Abnorm. Psychol.* 85:398–407

Switras, J. E. 1974. A comparison of the eye-roll test for hypnotizability and the Stanford Hypnotic Susceptibility Scale: Form A. *Am. J. Clin. Hypn.* 17:54–55

Tart, C. T. 1979. Measuring the depth of an altered state of consciousness, with particular reference to self-report scales of hypnotic depth. See Fromm & Shor 1979, 567–601

Tellegen, A., Atkinson, G. 1974. Openness to absorbing and self-altering experiences ("absorption"), a trait related to hypnotic susceptibility. *J. Abnorm. Psychol.* 83:268–77

Walker, N. S., Garrett, J. B., Wallace, B. 1976. Restoration of eidetic imagery via hypnotic age regression: A preliminary report. *J. Abnorm. Psychol.* 85:335–37

Wallace, B. 1978. Restoration of eidetic imagery via hypnotic age regression: More evidence. *J. Abnorm. Psychol.* 87:673–75

Wallace, B., Fisher, L. E. 1982. Hypnotically induced limb anesthesia and adaptation to displacing prisms: Replication requires adherence to critical procedures. *J. Abnorm. Psychol.* 91:390–91

Wallace, B., Garrett, J. B. 1973. Reduced felt arm sensation effects on visual adaptation. *Percept. Psychophys.* 14:597–600

Wallace, B., Garrett, J. B. 1975. Perceptual adaptation with selective reductions of felt sensation. *Perception* 4:437–45

Wallace, B., Garrett, J. B., Anstadt, S. P. 1974. Hypnotic susceptibility, suggestion, and reports of autokinetic movement. *Int. J. Clin. Exp. Hypn.* 87:117–23

Wallace, B., Hoyenga, K. B. 1980. Reduction of proprioceptive errors with induced hypnotic anesthesia. *Int. J. Clin. Exp. Hypn.* 28:140–47

Wallace, B., Hoyenga, K. B. 1981. Performance of fine motor coordination activities with an hypnotically anesthetized limb. *Int. J. Clin. Exp. Hypn.* 29:54–65

Wallace, B., Knight, T. A., Garrett, J. B. 1976. Hypnotic susceptibility and frequency reports to illusory stimuli. *J. Abnorm. Psychol.* 85:558–63

Weitzenhoffer, A. M. 1974. When is an "instruction" an instruction? *Int. J. Clin. Exp. Hypn.* 22:258–69

Weitzenhoffer, A. M. 1980. Hypnotic susceptibility revisited. *Am. J. Clin. Hypn.* 22:130–46

Wheeler, L., Reis, T., Wolff, E., Grupsmith, E., Mordkoff, A. M. 1974. Eye-roll and hypnotic susceptibility. *Int. J. Clin. Exp. Hypn.* 22:327–34

Young, J., Cooper, L. M. 1972. Hypnotic recall amnesia as a function of manipulated expectancy. *Proc. 80th Ann. Conv. Am. Psychol. Assoc.* 7:857–58

Zamansky, H. S. 1977. Suggestion and countersuggestion in hypnotic behavior. *J. Abnorm. Psychol.* 86:346–51

Zelig, M., Beidelman, W. B. 1981. The investigative use of hypnosis: A word of caution. *Int. J. Clin. Exp. Hypn.* 29:401–12

Ann. Rev. Psychol. 1985. 36:419–94

CELLULAR MECHANISMS OF LEARNING, MEMORY, AND INFORMATION STORAGE

Joseph Farley

Department of Psychology, Program in Neuroscience and Behavior, Princeton University, Princeton, New Jersey 08544

Daniel L. Alkon

Section on Neural Systems, Laboratory of Biophysics, NIH-NINCDS, Marine Biological Laboratories, Woods Hole, Massachusetts 02543

CONTENTS

INTRODUCTION

Until recently, serious discussion of the cellular mechanisms underlying learning and memory was limited to speculation as to what was possible and

419

0066-4308/85/0201-0419$02.00

plausible. Indeed, the gap between the characteristics of the learned behavior of intact animals and cellular neurophysiology seemed nearly unbridgable two decades ago. Two of the most salient features of learned behavior—its persistence over time and resistance to disruption—seemed to be contradicted by the current understanding of neuronal excitability and synaptic transmission. Persistent changes in either, as initiated by normal, physiological stimulation, were rare. Fortunately, the situation is no longer as paradoxical as it once seemed. The last few years have witnessed a tremendous explosion of interest in "neural plasticity" and cellular mechanisms of learning, and a modest amount of success in localizing sites within nervous systems that demonstrably play a causal role in mediating learning and memory. In a few cases it has also been possible to outline plausible biophysical and biochemical accounts of neuronal excitability changes underlying learning for which some direct evidence exists.

We emphasize at the outset, however, that even in these most favorable of circumstances, considerable uncertainty still exists as to the exact mechanisms of long-term information storage. The details are still very unclear. Moreover, the generality of these accounts for the learned behavior of intact vertebrates— let alone humans—is also unknown.

Having dispensed with the necessary caveats, we draw attention to the following themes running throughout much of the recent literature. First, memory can be localized. Learning-correlated changes in neural activity have been reported for each model system we review. Demonstrations of sites of neural change that are causally related to the long-term behavioral modifications of intact animals are restricted, so far, to the invertebrates *Hermissenda* and *Aplysia*. Secondly, persistent changes in neuronal excitability and synaptic transmission were shown to correlate directly with learned behavior. Regulation of a family of K^+ conductances has been implicated in a number of preparations as a mechanism accounting for some of the observed electrophysiological correlates of learning. Third, changes in the levels of the intracellular second messenger molecules calcium, cAMP, or cGMP were suggested in many cases as the initial event that triggers long-term neural change. Fourth, protein phosphorylation is being considered as a general mechanism by which a host of neural functions, relevant to an understanding of cellular plasticity, learning, and memory, can be regulated.

In this review, our primary emphasis is placed upon those invertebrate and vertebrate model system preparations that have explicitly attempted to relate cellular plasticity to the learned behavior of intact animals. In discussing each preparation, we pay particular attention to the following issues. What are the characteristics of the learned behavior under study, and how well do these characteristics agree with the contemporary understanding of animal and human learning and conditioning? Which crucial features remain to be demonstrated for the various preparations, before one can accept the model as a reasonable one for learning? How completely have the neural circuits underlying the behavior been delineated? Have sites of plastic change been convincingly demonstrated? Are such sites causal for learning, or are they mere correlates? What is the current understanding of the biophysical and biochemical steps involved in acquisition of learning and long-term storage of information?

Secondary emphasis is placed upon various neuromodulatory phenomena proposed as "models" for memory. Since these examples of neural plasticity occur on time scales longer than that of impulse activity, but have not yet been closely tied to the learned behavior of intact organisms, a discussion of the cellular mechanisms underlying these phenomena serves to define what is possible and plausible in the intact brain. The relevance of such mechanisms for the learned behavior of intact animals has not yet been established, however.

With the exception of those few cases that suggest a mechanism of explicit relevance for the learning of normal adult animals, we exclude the following topics from our review: (a) the developmental neurobiology literature on synapse formation (e.g. Purves & Lichtman 1983); (b) the effects of experience that departs from the animal colony norm (both deprivation and enrichment) upon nervous system development, learning (Rosenzweig & Bennett 1977, 1978), and vision (Movshon & Van Sluyters 1981); (c) the vast literatures concerning recovery of function following injury or trauma (Stricker & Zigmond 1976, Spear 1979, Brown et al 1981, Cotman & Nieto-Sampedro 1982, Marshall 1984); (d) the genetics of learning and memory; and (e) modulation of spinal reflexes (see Mendell 1984 for review). No doubt many mechanisms discussed within each of these areas will subsequently be shown to be relevant for an understanding of learning and memory in the normal adult animal. Our problem at present is that each of these areas offers an embarrassment of potential riches. Hence, we constrain our selection somewhat arbitrarily by requiring a demonstrable link to learned behavior and to electrophysiology.

INVERTEBRATE MODEL SYSTEMS

Nonassociative learning

HABITUATION AND SENSITIZATION OF GILL- AND SIPHON-WITHDRAWAL BEHAVIOR IN APLYSIA   In *Aplysia californica,* an ambitious and intensive attempt to analyze the processes of habituation and sensitization in biophysical and biochemical terms has been made by Byrne, Carew, Castellucci, Hawkins, Klein, Kandel, Pinsker, Schwartz, and colleagues. As originally reported by Pinsker et al (1970), restrained but otherwise intact *Aplysia* exhibit progressive response declines in gill withdrawal when circumscribed receptive fields on the siphon and mantle shelf are repeatedly stimulated tactilely. For example, when a moderately intense tactile stimulus was repeatedly delivered to the siphon 80 times, profound response decrements were observed within 10–15 stimulus presentations. The gill-withdrawal response fully and spontaneously recovered to its original amplitude following a 122-min rest period. With the exception of a failure for habituation of one receptive field to generalize to others, eight of the nine defining characteristics of habituation in vetebrate model systems (Thompson & Spencer 1966) have been found to apply to short-term habituation of these reflexes.

Long-term retention of habituation has also been demonstrated (Carew et al 1972). Siphon-withdrawal response decrements of unrestrained animals were reported for up to 21 days following original training. Similar experiments assessing retention of memory for gill-withdrawal habituation were also reported, with decrements observed for retention intervals of a week. As was the case for the short-term habituation effects, delivery of a single sensitizing stimulus was sufficient to counteract the long-term response decrement (Castelluci et al 1978, Carew et al 1979a).

NEURAL CONTROL OF GILL- AND SIPHON-WITHDRAWAL REFLEXES   Both reflexes are mediated by central (abdominal ganglion) as well as peripheral components of the nervous system. Under conditions of moderately intense stimulation, innervation of gill musculature has been asserted by some to occur virtually exclusively through abdominal ganglion pathways. Attempts to evoke gill withdrawal after removal of the abdominal ganglion are generally unsuccessful, and the abdominal ganglion may contribute to about 95% of the gill-withdrawal response (see Kandel 1976). Stronger stimuli evidently activate additional extra-abdominal pathways, which have not yet been fully analyzed (Kupfermann et al 1971, 1974, Carew et al 1979b).

Others have obtained evidence for greater involvement of the peripheral nervous system. Peretz (1970) found that habituation, dishabituation, and spontaneous recovery could all be observed in the absence of the abdominal ganglion, in the excised mantel preparation. Under these conditions, the gill response is mediated by the peripheral branchial ganglion and an associated neural plexus. When Peretz et al (1976) removed the abdominal ganglion, after first measuring the amplitude of the gill response in the intact situation, no net effect upon response amplitude was seen. A subsequent study by Carew et al (1979b) compared the methods of Peretz—a tapper stimulus and the lack of a minimal response criteria for selecting animals—with the mechanical probe stimulus customarily used by the Columbia group. They found that removal of the ganglion enhanced the response elicited by the tapper, but abolished the response elicited by the mechanical probe. However, this occurred only when the initial amplitude of the gill response was small. Carew et al (1979b) summarize their results by noting that when stimulus parameters and response criteria are appropriately selected one can examine a reflex that is at least 90% dependent upon the abdominal ganglion. The siphon-withdrawal reflex appears to be under considerably less central control than the gill-withdrawal reflex (Peretz 1970, Lukowiak & Jacklet 1972). The abdomial ganglion's contribution to this reflex of behavior is estimated to be 55% (Perlman 1979).

SYNAPTIC DEPRESSION AND FACILITATION: CORRELATES OF HABITUATION AND SENSITIZATION   Motoneurons that innervate the gill and siphon musculature receive both monosynaptic and polysynaptic input from sensory neurons. Castellucci et al (1970) first reported, in a reduced preparation, that repetitive mechanical or electrical stimulation of the skin resulted in progressive decrements in the complex excitatory postsynaptic potentials (EPSPs) in a gill motor neuron (L7), while input resistance of L7 remained unchanged. Upon cessation of stimulation, the complex EPSP recovered. Further experiments indicated that the monosynaptic component of the complex EPSP also decreased with repeated tactile stimulation. As in the case of the complex EPSP, the unitary synaptic potential recovered with rest, was facilitated by a dishabituating stimulus (connective stimulation), and exhibited greater decrements with short vs long interstimulus intervals (ISI).

Castellucci & Kandel (1974) next applied a quantal analysis (Katz & Miledi 1967, Kuno 1971) to this synapse to analyze further the mechanisms of synaptic depression. In the isolated abdominal ganglion preparation, conditions of low release were produced by bathing the preparation in high divalent cation solutions. Sensory neurons were repeatedly stimulated intracellulary to elicit action potentials, while postsynaptic potentials (PSPs) were recorded in 11 separate follower cells (L7s). Estimates of M (mean quantum content, an index of efficiency of presynaptic factors) and q (mean size of transmitter quantum) indicated that q remained unchanged during the course of declines in PSP amplitude, while M decreased by a factor of $\sim 50\%$. These results were interpreted as indicating that a decrease in the probability of transmitter release was responsible for the decline in synaptic transmission.

Some caution should be exercised in the interpretation of these results. Since the postsynaptic cell (L7) received multiple synaptic inputs, it was presumably difficult to resolve miniature synaptic potentials, and hence to identify unambiguously a single sensory neuron as their source. More importantly, in this particular *Aplysia* synapse, it has not proved possible to either voltage-clamp the presynaptic terminal, or to obtain focal extracellular recordings from the synapse (Katz & Miledi 1965a,b) and thereby examine directly the dependence of quantal events upon terminal depolarization, independent of impulse activity in the presynaptic neuron. Thus, it is not possible to conclude with any certainty whether decrements in transmitter release accompanying behavioral habituation reflect invasion of the presynaptic terminal by smaller amplitude action potentials, less Ca^{2+} influx with an action potential of normal amplitude, normal Ca^{2+} influx but refractoriness of release sites, etc.

Klein & Kandel (1980) proposed that the homosynaptic depression presumed to underly habituation in *Aplysia* results from a usage-dependent decrease in a Ca^{2+} current, in the presynaptic terminals at these synapses. Repeated stimulation of sensory neurons reduced the duration and amplitude of the sensory neuron action potential in a solution containing tetraethylammonium (TEA) ions, which block some of the delayed K^+ currents. This was paralleled by declines in the PSP recorded from follower motor neurons. When treated with TEA, the sensory neuron action potential is largely a Ca^{2+} spike (Klein & Kandel 1978, 1980). This parallel change in the duration of the TEA spike and the amplitude of the PSP is the evidence to date that habituation results from changes in synaptic Ca^{2+} currents. Exactly how the presumed change in the Ca^{2+} current is supposed to occur has not yet been described.

Carew & Kandel (1973) also studied relatively long-term retention of habituation in the isolated ganglion preparation. Subsequent studies have assessed long-term synaptic changes by recording from freshly dissected preparations at various retention intervals following long-term training. Castellucci et al (1978) exposed animals to a minimum of five days of habituation training, and then assessed synaptic transmission 24 hr, 8–10, or 24–32 days later. Their results indicated significantly less incidence of detectable sensory neuron–L7 synaptic connections for experimental vs untrained control animals at all retention intervals. This depressed transmission for many weeks following training is an impressive result. In a similar study, with controls for extended husbandry, Carew et al (1979a) found that a single sensitizing stimulus effectively reversed both the habituation-induced synaptic transmission decrement and the decline in behavior. As these authors noted, the finding of rapid reactivation tends to preclude gross structural changes (synapse retraction, disconnection, etc) as underlying long-term habituation. The long-term habituation effect has not yet been correlated with changes in the Ca^{2+} current.

Castellucci et al (1970) found that the presumed monosynaptic component of L7's EPSP, which decreased with repeated direct intracellular stimulation of a sensory neuron, could be restored when a separate pathway (left connective) was stimulated. While the decrement was not accompanied by measurable conductance changes in L7, no comparable data were reported for the effects of the sensitizing stimulus and there is no compelling evidence that restricts the effects of the sensitizing stimulus to the presynaptic terminal. Castellucci & Kandel's (1976) quantal analysis at this synapse suggested that connective stimulation produced heterosynaptic facilitation through an action upon the presynaptic terminal. With the preparation bathed in high Mg^{2+}–high Ca^{2+}

solution, connective stimulation increased the average amplitude of the sensory neuron PSP for as long as 50 min. Significant increases in M values followed connective stimulation, but no change in q was found. Given the necessity of a high divalent-cation solution to increase the monosynaptic contribution to the L7 PSP (in order to undertake the quantal analysis at this synapse), it was not possible to determine whether or not comparable changes in M occurred in solutions with physiological Ca^{2+} levels. This is a potentially important point because if increased extracellular Ca^{2+} results in a greater Ca^{2+} current in the sensory neuron terminal, then the increased EPSP may depend upon the conditions used to detect its presence. Whether or not comparable changes occur under normal physiological conditions is difficult to say.

MECHANISMS OF FACILITATION   Brunelli et al (1976) reported that many of the effects of connective stimulation could be simulated be exposing the ganglion to serotonin (5-HT), or adenosine 3',5'-monophosphate (cyclic AMP), thought to be involved in the modulation of synaptic transmission (Greengard 1976, 1978). In an elevated Mg^{2+}–Ca^{2+} solution, decremented PSPs in L7 were enhanced following exposure of the isolated abdominal ganglion to 5-HT, but not to octopamine or dopamine. These effects of 5-HT could be blocked by cinanserin, but not other known serotonin antagonists (LSD and curare). The effects of 5-HT could be mimicked by bath application of cAMP, and even more effectively by injecting cAMP directly into the sensory neuron soma. These effects of cAMP were relatively specific since neither vehicle, 5'-AMP nor cGMP, produced comparable effects. They also occurred rapidly, within 30 sec.

Brunelli et al (1976) suggested that connective stimulation resulted in: (a) stimulation of abdominal interneurons, with processes near the sensory neuron presynaptic terminals; (b) release of serotonin, or a similar substance from these interneuron processes; and (c) modulation of transmitter release at the sensory neuron–L7 synapse mediated by increased cAMP within the terminal. Brunelli et al (1976) noted the following features of their account for which direct evidence was not yet available: (a) The presumed facilitatory inter-neurons had yet to be identified and characterized as serotonergic; and (b) That 5-HT actually increased endogenous cAMP levels in the sensory neurons, had not been demonstrated. Although recent experiments support the latter expecta-ton (Bernier et al 1982), immunocytochemical studies indicate that 5-HT does not appear to be contained within the presumed facilitatory interneurons (Kist-ler et al 1983). Whether it is in fact the neuromodulator used, and if so where it comes from, has not been determined.

Klein & Kandel (1978, 1980) attempted to characterize further the bio-physical bases of presynaptic facilitation. They proposed that 5-HT induced long-term increases in the transmembrane Ca^{2+} flux, and would thus result in greater transmitter release. They further supposed that the long-term changes in Ca^{2+} current were accomplished through serotonin's stimulation of a membrane-bound adenyl cyclase, a resulting increase in intracellular cAMP, and a further series of biochemical steps involving protein phosphorylation with eventual modification of channel proteins. Initially, serotonin was thought to directly enhance a Ca^{2+} current. Subsequently it has been asserted that the Ca^{2+}-current enhancement is an indirect result of K^+-current suppression.

The evidence for the proposed model is as follows. Simultaneous recordings from sensory and motor neurons, following stimulation of the pleuroabdominal connective (sensitizing pathway), reveal a very slight decrease in the rate of decay of the soma action potential in normal seawater. This prolongation of the plateau phase of the action potential following connective stimulation was magnified in high Ca^{2+}-Mg^{2+} solution, was further exaggerated when TEA ion (a K^+-current blocker) was added to the bath, occurred in the absence of extracellular) Na^+, and was reversibly blocked by the addition of Co^{2+}, a calcium-channel blocker. The addition of 5-HT to normal artificial sea water (ASW) mimicked the action potential and PSP changes produced by connective stimulation. These changes were relatively specific to 5-HT. The amplitude of the plateau phase increased with increasing extracellular Ca^{2+} concentrations. Collectively, the results indicate that a substantial portion of the inward current for the sensory neuron's action potential is in fact carried by Ca^{2+} under these conditions. The reported correlation of changes in action potential duration with PSP amplitude in follower cells further encourages the view that changes in action potential wave form and kinetics parallel, to some degree, changes occurring in synaptic terminals. However, the stronger claim that the changes observed in the soma are isomorphic to those occurring in the terminal is seriously compromised by the inability to examine directly presynaptic conductances. Conclusions as to what is occurring in the terminal are necessarily based upon indirect evidence in this situation. This type of evidence is particularly questionable given the abundant evidence for both quantitative and qualitative differences in ionic channels for different areas of excitable membrane.

Klein & Kandel (1980) voltage-clamped the sensory neuron somata, and reported that presynaptic facilitation produced by connective stimulation, or serotonin, results from a decrease in a voltage-dependent outward K^+ current. In normal seawater, stimulation of the pleuroabdominal connective resulted in a sustained inward current and a conductance decrease. This corresponds to a depolarizing EPSP in the unclamped sensory neuron, which is occasionally seen (Klein & Kandel 1978). Reversal potentials obtained for the serotonin-evoked current are generally consistent with those for K^+ currents in other molluscan neurons.

Recent studies (Klein et al 1982) indicate that the K^+ current suppressed by serotonin (S current) is unlike any other that has been reported previously in molluscan neurons (Adams et al 1980), or since. Among its unusual features is its failure to inactivate with sustained depolarization. Single-channel measurements of the S channel (Siegelbaum et al 1982) reveal the following similarities to the macroscopic current measurements under voltage clamp: (*a*) S channels are open at the resting potential of the cell, (*b*) S channels (in the cell-attached patch) are reversibly closed by 5-HT and cAMP, (*c*) S channels (in the isolated patch) are relatively unaffected by Ca^{2+}. It is still somewhat unclear, however, as to whether the single-channel data and the macroscopic current measurements reflect the same class of channel. Single S-channel data from patch clamp recordings (isolated patch) indicate that channel activation is, at best, only weakly voltage dependent (Camardo et al 1984), whereas the TEA, Ba, and 4-AP resistant macroscopic current exhibits a moderate degree of voltage dependency.

A tentative molecular model links presynaptic facilitation with protein phosphorylation in the sensory neurons. Direct injection of the catalytic subunit of cAMP-dependent protein kinase transiently broadened the action potential in the TEA-treated cell, increased the input resistance in 5 of 10 cases, and increased the PSP in a follower neuron (Castellucci et al 1980). The duration of the effect was limited to several minutes; the proteins that were presumably phosphorylated were not identified. More recently, Castellucci et al (1982) determined that injection of the Walsh inhibitor, which is specific to cAMP-dependent protein kinase, prevented presynaptic facilitation caused by serotonin or connective stimulation. Further, Castellucci et al report that injection of the inhibitor after presynaptic facilitation has already been produced by serotonin will quickly reverse it. They concluded that the persistence of presynaptic facilitation must reside in persistent activation of kinase activity. Evidently, once phosphorylated, the K^+-channel protein can be rapidly dephosphorylated. The mechanism seems to be quite transient (minutes). Bernier et al (1982) showed that cAMP levels are elevated for 10 min in sensory neurons, following treatment with either serotonin or connective stimulation. Castellucci et al (1983) have since reported that serotonin's elevation of cAMP levels appears to be due to persistent activity of adenylate cyclase. A cyclase inhibitor ($GDP_\beta S$) reversed the facilitation; a cyclase stimulant (forskolin) could partially reverse the $GDP_\beta S$ inhibition.

EVALUATION   The attempts by Kandel and colleagues to analyze habituation and sensitization in *Aplysia* at the biophysical and molecular levels is one of the most comprehensive and thorough model system attempts to date. Because of its potential importance, their account merits close scrutiny.

It is still unclear as to whether the primary sites at which sensitization occurs are the sensory-to-motor-neuron synapses, and further whether this occurs exclusively at the presynaptic terminals. As was the case for habituation, analysis of the circuits responsible for producing the behavior is still unfinished. In the case of siphon withdrawal, substantial dishabituatory effects can be produced in the isolated siphon preparation (Lukowiak & Jacklet 1972) without the presence of the abdominal ganglion. New networks within the abdominal ganglion have also been described that facilitate with aversive stimulation of the animal, and may therefore be expected to contribute substantially to sensitization effects under many circumstances (Kanz et al 1979).

The purported identification of facilitatory interneurons is not convincing. Hawkins et al (1981a,b) report that L22, L28, and L29 interneurons facilitated the sensory neuron-PSP in motor neurons, yet examination of the data reveals that brisk stimulation of L29 enhanced the PSP only 27% of the time (59 of 219 cases). The evidence that L29's occasional enhancement of the PSP in L7 is due to heterosynaptic facilitation of the PSP from the sensory neuron, as opposed to its own direct (or indirect) addition to the L7 PSP, stems from only one successful experiment. Moreover, the records from this experiment seem to indicate that the sensory neuron-PSP results in a complex—rather than a unitary—PSP in L7. The presumed facilitatory role of the L22 and L28 cells is even less secure.

Even if one provisionally grants the occurrence of heterosynaptic PSP enhancement at the sensory-motor-neuron synapse, conclusion as to the mechanism of change is still largely speculative. As already noted, it is unclear as to whether serotonin is the neuromodulator released in response to a sensitizing stimulus under normal physiological conditions (Kistler et al 1983), and if so, where it is released from.

The presumed role of the neuromodulator 5-HT also raises other questions. For example, how does a neuromodulator that is released in the sensitizing pathway and that is then proposed to interact with receptor sites near the sensory neuron presynaptic terminals, quite a distance away from the soma, decrease the conductance in the soma just a few seconds after the onset of the sensitizing stimulus? One possibility is that the soma possesses receptors for the transmitter, and connective stimulation results in a general and diffuse extracellular increase in a transmitter/neuromodulatory substance throughout the ganglion. Cedar et al (1972) and Cedar & Schwartz (1972) reported that connective stimulation resulted in increased cAMP levels within the whole abdominal ganglion. Bailey et al (1981) interpreted their results as indicative of axosomatic contacts, from facilitatory interneurons upon sensory neurons. Thus, the possiblity remains that the sensitizing neurotransmitter is acting directly upon the soma. If this were indeed the case, however, it would substantially complicate the interpretation of the voltage-clamp data reported so far.

Two other possibilities should be mentioned. First, the primary site of action for the transmitter may be the presynaptic terminal, but the changes are reflected electrotonically, many centimeters away in the soma. The small depolarization often recorded in the soma following connective stimulation in later studies (Klein & Kandel 1978, 1980) but not earlier ones (e.g. Carew et al 1971) might be plausibly interpreted in this way; but the decreased conductance of the soma is much more difficult to interpret as a consequence of remote changes in membrane potential.

The evidence presented to date concerning the presumed heterosynaptic facilitation underlying sensitization-produced increases in the PSP recorded from motor neurons is indirect and incomplete. It has not proved possible to voltage-clamp the presynaptic terminals of the sensory neurons and hence to examine the basis of changes in synaptic transmission directly. Why is it necessary to eliminate K^+ currents with TEA in order to see robust differences in sensory neuron action potentials and S-current changes produced by serotonin or connective stimulation? Are the effects of serotonin in the sensory neuron exclusively mediated by S-current suppression? In other *Aplysia* neurons, for example, Pellmar (1984) reported that serotonin enhances a voltage-dependent inward Ca^{2+} current. Farley and Wu & Farley (1984) found in *Hermissenda* B photoreceptors that 5-HT also enhances an inward Ca^{2+} current (I_{Ca}), but in addition reduces the fast, rapidly inactivating K^+ current (I_A) as well as the Ca^{2+}-activated K^+ current (I_C).

Finally, and perhaps most importantly, it should be noted that the duration of the biophysical changes hypothesized to underlie sensitization are relatively short-lived. The enhancement of PSPs in the motor neuron, as well as the conductance changes observed in the soma, last for minutes—perhaps an hour at most. They are, in fact, no longer than those that have been reported at many other synapses.

Associative Learning

CHEMOSENSORY AVERSION LEARNING IN *PLEUROBRANCHAEA*   The first report of robust behavioral changes produced by an associative training procedure in a gastropod involved the classical conditioning of a feeding response to tactile stimulation (Mpitsos & Davis 1973). Normally, naive *Pleurobranchaea* withdraw from tactile stimulation of the oral veil (CS) and show feeding responses to food chemicals (UCS). Parings of touch and food evoked feeding responses to touch. CS-alone controls showed little behavioral change. A second control procedure, in which CS-alone trials were followed 3–4 hr later by food, resulted in considerable response acquisition, which after a week of continued training was, however, significantly less than that of the paired animals. Subsequent research (Mpitsos & Collins 1975, Mpitsos et al 1978) used a chemosensory aversion paradigm with *Pleurobranchaea*. Initial experiments involved the exposure of intact animals to repeated pairings of a food extract with electric shock, or one of a number of control procedures to exclude possible nonassociative sources of feeding suppression. More recently, discriminative chemosensory learning was reported with this preparation (Davis et al 1980), which indicates that the suppression of feeding is to some degree specific to the particular food extract paired with shock.

The difference between the associative training group and controls in these experiments is relatively pairing specific. However, some caution must be urged in interpreting the greater suppression of feeding for "paired" animals as indicative of associative learning. First, there are the problems concerning the "nonblind" application of shock and possible differences in shock severity for experimental vs control animals, as initially noted by Lee (1976).

Second, there are the interpretative problems surrounding the use of the "yoked control" procedures in these experiments. The application of electric shock for "paired" animals in these studies involves an instrumental contingency whereby an animal is "punished" if it strikes at, or fails to withdraw from, the CS^+. A yoked control animal (explicitly unpaired) received the same shock presented in an unpaired fashion with the CS. Thus, the "paired" animal's withdrawal threshold to shock determines the severity, frequency, and schedule of shock for the unpaired animal. As initially noted by Church (1964), the use of such a design may introduce a systematic bias in favor of greater nonassociative suppressive effects for "paired" animals. If, for example, a paired animal happens to have a relatively high shock-withdrawal threshold, the yoked unpaired animal receiving the same nominal shock schedule will experience a functionally more aversive shock schedule, since on the average its threshold is likely to be less than the paired animal. Thus, any significant difference in the behavior of paired and yoked control animals may simply be due to individual differences in the degree of sensitization, pseudoconditioning, etc.

Third, there remains the problem of whether the reduced feeding for animals exposed to food-shock pairings is a primary or secondary consequence of those pairings. Does the reduced feeding represent associative learning, or instead reflect feeding motivation differences between training groups that arise from different patterns of ingestion on training days? In many of these experiments, the interval between the application of shock on one trial, and subsequent exposure to food on the ensuing food-shock trial was one hour for paired animals. For unpaired animals, this same interval was one half hour. The question arises as to whether the two groups feed equally in these two cases, and whether subsequent differences in feeding reflect differences in satiation. Reduced feeding upon a chemosensory cue that was previously paired with shock may reflect differing degrees of ingestion, or chemosensory experience, arising as secondary consequences of training procedures. Unpaired animals may, for example, simply eat less during the conditioning day (because they were shocked before being exposed to the food extract on each trial). Thus they may be hungrier and more receptive to feeding on the substance when tested later. This possibility also must be considered in assessing the neural correlates reported for *Pleurobranchaea*.

Another interpretative problem concerns the degree to which reduced feeding reflects de novo acquisition of new behavior, as opposed to nonassociative amplification of neophobic reactions. It is interesting to consider the recent demonstrations of differential chemosensory aversion learning (Davis et al 1980) from this perspective, since this data provides the best evidence for the associative nature of aversion learning in this paradigm.

To test for the specificity of the conditioned aversion to the training stimulus, hungry *Pleurobranchaea* were exposed to either pairings of squid extract with electric shock, or unpaired presentations of these stimuli. Animals were then tested for changes in two behavioral categories reflecting feeding, or the interaction of feeding with defensive withdrawal behavior. Threshold measurements of the amount of concentrated squid extract required for the elicitation of proboscis extension and bite-strike reponses (and their latencies) were first assessed. The percentage of animals that actively withdrew from application of squid extract to the oral veil was also assessed for the two groups. Identical tests were then conducted with a novel food substance (*Corynactic* homogenate).

Davis et al (1980) report the following results for animals exposed to squid-shock pairings: (*a*) Significantly more animals withdrew from squid, 1 and 2 days following training, when compared with unpaired control animals. (*b*) Proboscis extension and bite-strike latencies were significantly greater than those of unpaired animals for concentrated squid extract 1, 2, and 8 days after training. Similar differences were apparent for threshold data for feeding responses. These multiple behavioral measures provide impressive evidence for differences in the feeding behavior of animals exposed to the associative vs the nonassociative training procedure.

The data also provide ample evidence that the aversion to squid was not entirely specific. Tests with *Corynactis* extract revealed: (*a*) Both paired and unpaired animals withdrew from *Corynactis,* 1 and 2 days post-training. (*b*) Proboscis extension and bite-strike latencies were increased (paired and unpaired), relative to baseline, 1 and 2 days following training. (*c*) The concentration required to elicit bite-strike and extension thresholds increased. In each of the above cases, the changes appear to represent substantial divergences from baseline, pretraining behavioral levels, though the statistical significance of these changes was not assessed.

A set of comparisons relevant to the issue of stimulus specificity were not explicitly discussed by Davis et al (1980). This involves asking whether the suppressed feeding response to the CS$^+$ (e.g. squid) was significantly different from that to the CS$^-$ (*Corynactis*), and whether the two training procedures affected these differences equally. When the results are examined from this perspective, the evidence for selective associative learning appears considerably weaker.

The appropriate interpretation of this relative lack of specificity is not entirely clear. On the one hand, as Davis et al correctly note, the responses of paired vs unpaired animals to CS$^-$ *(Corynactis)*—while clearly different than baseline levels—were significantly different in only two of fifteen cases. Since paired vs unpaired animals' responses to squid were generally significant, Davis et al interpreted their results as indicating an associatively acquired aversion, specific to squid, for animals exposed to squid-shock pairings. An alternative interpretation is that shock exposure resulted in a nonassociative aversion to the relatively novel chemosensory cue *(Corynactis)*, which was approximately equivalent for paired vs unpaired animals, and a nonassociative aversion to squid, which was greater for paired than for unpaired animals.

When a chemosensory cue is paired with shock, it may produce a selective suppression of appetitive behavior directed to that cue that is greater than when these two events are unpaired. It may nevertheless still reflect *nonassociative* behavioral processes. A consequence of exposure to strong electric shock may be suppression of feeding to any and all food substances. But, since pairing a novel chemosensory cue with shock might well constitute a functionally greater aversive experience for a sensitized animal (since novel chemosensory cues may well elicit avoidance reactions in sensitized animals irrespective of previous pairings with an aversive event), differences between aversive motivational states would be expected between paired vs unpaired training conditions. Thus, the nonassociative consequences of food-shock pairings may include greater suppression of intake of this food for paired vs unpaired control animals.

In addition, since unpaired presentations of food and shock potentially allow for greater habituation to the aversive aspects of both shock and (especially) the chemosensory cue, greater suppression of food intake for paired animals might be expected for this reason as well. Thus, the presumably greater sensitization effect on paired animals, and the correspondingly greater opportunity for attenuation (habituation) of neophobic chemosensory reactions for unpaired animals, would both be expected to lead to the reduced intake of a chemosensory cue paired with shock. Without belaboring the point, this same analysis applied in principle to the reports by Davis et al (1980) of differential conditioning within the same animal.

In *Pleurobranchaea*, a neural correlate of the associative chemosensory aversion paradigm occurs at the level of the 10–12 paracerebral command neurons (PCNs) in the cerebropleural ganglion of the animal (Davis & Gillette 1978). Whole-animal preparations, previously exposed to either paired or unpaired presentations of squid homogenate and shock, and naive untrained animals (either hungry or food satiated) were exposed to infusions of squid over the oral veil, while intracellular recordings were obtained. These recordings were made using blind procedures at retention intervals ranging from half an hour to two days following conditioning for paired and unpaired animals, and 2–6 hours after satiation for untrained animals.

Application of squid homogente to the oral veil of naive, hungry animals evoked synaptic depolarization and bursting of the PCNs. This pattern of activity was previously shown to be correlated with ingestion of palatable substances in the intact and whole-animal preparations, as well as with feeding motor program activity as recorded from the nerve in the isolated nervous system (Gillette et al 1982). In contrast, recordings from PCN cells in preparations previously exposed to squid-shock pairings revealed the presence of pronounced inhibitory synaptic input, sufficient in many cases to suppress the rhythmic bursting activity of these cells. The response of the PCN cells from untrained, satiated animals was indistinguishable from that of the conditioned (paired CS-UCS) animals. The PCN response of cells from the unpaired control procedure was highly similar to that of the untrained, hungry animals.

The quantitative treatment of the data indicated that 64% of the 14 "conditioned" PCNs exhibited responses to squid judged as inhibitory, as compared to 37% of the 16 cells for naive animals and 0% (of 10 cells) for unpaired controls. Satiated animals, in turn, exhibited inhibitory responses in 83% of the 12 cells examined. While the differences between paired and unpaired animals were clear, the differences between paired and untrained, hungry animals and between unpaired and untrained animals were not. No statistical evaluations were reported to indicate whether the observed differences were any greater than would be expected by chance. Pronounced inhibition of the PCNs following associative training was also recently reported for the isolated nervous system preparation.

While Davis & Gillette (1978) identified a correlate of associative training, by their own admission the PCNs do not appear to be sites of neuronal change causally related to the learning. The differences in PCN activity were attributed to changes in the nature of the synaptic input to these cells. Recent work has concerned itself with further specification of the neuronal circuits that comprise the feeding motor program and with identification and characterization of those cells that are involved in these circuits (Gillette et al 1982). Recently, interneurons responsible for PCN inhibition and training-correlated differences in these cells were reported (London & Gillette 1983).

The finding that the synaptic input to the PCNs is indistinguishable for associatively trained and food-satiated animals warrants two comments. In our previous discussion of the pattern of behavioral results reported with this preparation, we noted that the procedures used in the associative training of animals may not simply produce effects within the nervous system that share common mechanisms with food satiation, but may in fact actually permit greater ingestion of food. Insofar as the neural correlate of learning is concerned, it is critical to demonstrate that the presumed learning effect is *not* the motivational one. In other words, it is important to show that the increased cyclic inhibition of the PCNs is not, in fact, a by-product of training-induced differences in satiation.

CHEMOSENSORY AVERSION LEARNING IN *LIMAX*   Gelperin and colleagues used a chemosensory aversion-learning paradigm with the slug *Limax*. In the early work (Gelperin 1975), the animal was allowed to feed upon a relatively novel food (such as carrot) and was then exposed to CO_2 toxicosis. Rejection of the food for many days following training was observed. More recent work utilizing a one-trial odor-aversion (Sahley et al 1981a) paradigm (e.g. carrot odor paired with Quinidine) provides evidence that the learning is, to some degree, both pairing and stimulus specific. Moreover, Sahley et al (1981b) also demonstrated blocking, second-order conditioning, and UCS pre-exposure effects with this paradigm, which suggests that the phenomenology of learning in the slug is potentially as rich as that in vertebrates.

As in the case of *Pleurobranchaea,* however, the occurrence of pairing- and stimulus-specific changes does not unambiguously implicate an associative learning process (cf Farley & Alkon 1984a). It is possible that much of the aversion to a relatively novel odor, after its pairing with an aversive chemical, reflects an amplification of innate neophobic reactions to the odor. Hungry slugs that have been sensitized by quinidine may avoid any relatively novel odor if an alternative "safe" source of gustatory stimulation is present. Exposure to the novel odor alone, in the absence of aversive chemosensory stimulation (as in a CS-alone or explicitly unpaired CS-UCS procedures) might be expected to render the novel odor familar (habituation of neophobia). This might well produce a general, pairing- and stimulus-nonspecific amplification of a neophobic reaction to novel gustatory stimulation, as well as a pairing- and stimulus-specific failure of habituation of neophobia. In principle, such an analysis could apply to those demonstrations of higher-order features of learning also.

Neural correlates of the chemosensory aversion-learning paradigm have been reported for "acquisition" of learning in the isolated nervous systems of initially untrained animals (in vitro conditioning; Chang & Gelperin 1980) as well as on retention days following training of intact animals (Gelperin & Culligan 1982). The correlate of learning in these studies is a change in chemically triggered feeding motor program (FMP), as inferred from extracellular recordings from buccal nerves that innervate feeding muscles (Gelperin et al 1978). Feeding is not measured in the more recent odor-aversion choice paradigm; hence the behavioral paradigm most analogous is the earlier one in which food was ingested (Gelperin 1975).

The in vitro conditioning studies (Chang & Gelperin 1980) that applied a palatable food extract (such as those derived from potato, mushroom, or carrot) initially resulted in activation of FMP. When the chemosensory stimulus was followed by a 20-min application of the aversive chemical (colchicine, nicotine, or tannic acid) FMP was not exhibited to the same food substance, subsequently applied after a 30-min wait. If FMP continued, additional pairings were administered until it ceased to be elicited by the training chemosensory stimulus (an upper limit of six trials was used). Selectivity for the suppression of FMP was tested by infusing a second, presumably novel chemosensory stimulus (CS_2), following training.

The results of this experiment were expressed in terms of a composite ratio score, which compared three aspects of the FMP response to CS_1 vs CS_2. The three components were: (a) ratio of the number of FMP cycles for CS_2 vs CS_1 (numbers greater than $+1.0$ indicate selective suppression to CS_1); (b) number of tests with the positive CS_1 that elicited no response; and (c) number of training trials required to establish a difference in the response of CS_2 vs CS_1. Thus, positive values indicate selective suppression of FMP for CS_1 vs CS_2; $\pm$ values indicate lack of a selective effect (either FMP responses to both CS_1 and CS_2, or lack of a response to both).

In initial experiments, 11 of 29 preparations ($\sim 38\%$) exhibited selective FMP suppression. In a second series of experiments, using better conditions, 12 of 16 (75%) of the preparations exhibited selective suppression of FMP to CS_1. While the data for the best ($+4$) preparations were quite impressive, it is not clear that a statistical analysis of the results from the latter experiment would reveal the pattern, as a whole, to be significantly different from that expected by chance alone. Statistical tests of one of the component measures of this composite ratio score, the ratio of FMP cycles for CS_2 vs CS_1, were statistically significant.

Experiments that delimit, to some degree, the possible sites of neuronal plasticity in *Limax* were recently reported by Gelperin et al (1981). Delivery of CS_1 to the left lip, followed by exposure to a bitter taste, and testing of both lips revealed suppression of FMP when CS_1 was presented to the trained (left) as well as the untrained (right) lip. This seems to indicate that learning is occurring within the central nervous system and not in the periphery.

INSTRUMENTAL MOTOR LEARNING IN THE LOCUST   Hoyle and colleagues (Tosney & Hoyle 1977, Woollacott & Hoyle 1977, Forman 1984) used a leg-position learning procedure in the locust to study the cellular mechanisms underlying instrumental learning. This paradigm is a considerably refined adaptation of one initially developed by Horridge (1962) for the cockroach. A variety of reinforcers and punishers were examined, and it is possible to arrange contingencies so that the animal will either raise or lower its leg (see Hoyle 1982 for summary). Thus, the changes are quite general and bidirectional.

In the most current implementation of this paradigm (Tosney & Hoyle 1977), the "response" of the animal is the mean frequency of impulse activity in an identified motor neuron (AAdC), which innervates the principal muscle involved in the adjustment of leg position, the anterior adductor of the coxa. Mean frequency is assessed by computer measurement of the frequency of the excitatory junction potentials (EJPs) recorded intracellularly from the AAdc muscle. If some predetermined criteria is not met, a brief train of shocks is delivered to the leg. In the most common form of training (the "up training" mode), AAdC activity must exceed a predetermined tonic level to avoid the shock. A computer continually samples AAdC activity until the desired tonic change in activity is achieved. Typically, a further increase in AAdC activity is then required, and training continues until no further increments in AAdC activity appear likely.

Tosney & Hoyle (1977) reported that 68% of the 189 preparations exposed to the "up training" procedure showed statistically significant increases in AAdC activity. For successful learners, AAdC activity increased from a mean level of 13.7 to 30.2 Hz (average 141% increase). The mean time taken to achieve stable learning was a relatively rapid 27.6 min. The issue of how specific the changes in AAdC activity were to the experimentally arranged associative contingency between AAdC activity and shock avoidance was evaluated by comparing results for "up learning" animals with those of yoked-control animals. This revealed statistically significant increases in AAdC activity for "up learning" vs control animals, and significantly greater declines in AAdC activity for "down learning" vs controls.

These reported changes in AAdC activity are impressive. They were the first documented example of a short-term (min) neural correlate of an associative behavioral change, which was potentially causally related to the behavior in question.

The assertion that the observed learning-correlated differences in AAdC activity reflect intrinsic changes in pacemaker activity, as opposed to differences in synaptic input to this cell, rests upon the finding of residual training-correlated differences in AAdC activity under conditions of synaptic blockade. Woollacott & Hoyle (1977) reported results for nine preparations exposed to the "up learning" procedure, which indicated an average 53% increase in AAdC activity, approximately 30 min after training and exposure of the dendritic area of the cell to high Mg^{2+}–low Ca^{2+} solution. A comparable decrease of 57% was reported for preparations exposed to the "down training" procedure. All of these "% change" scores were determined by comparing impulse activity before and after training (both times under synaptic blockade). Training was conducted with synaptic input to the cell relatively intact. Examination of the reliability in the nine "up training" cases revealed that an increase occurred in each case. It is important to note that the changes in AAdC activity reported to date are relatively transient ones. While the change can be prolonged indefinitely (from 20 hours to 3 days) with continued training, cessation of training evidently leads to a relatively rapid decline in AAdC changes.

As Woollacott & Hoyle (1977) note, it is unlikely that the changes intrinsic to the AAdC cell provide a complete explanation for even the short-term changes due to learning, Their data provided evidence for learning-correlated changes in synaptic input to the AAdC cell. This was most apparent from the comparison of the "% changes in AAdC" activity scores obtained with and without synaptic blockade. The latter were typically much higher than the former (average of 149% vs 53% for "up learning" animals).

Woollacott & Hoyle attribute the increased pacemaker activity in the AAdC cell to a learning-induced decrease in a voltage-dependent K^+ conductance (g_k), but the evidence for this mechanism is quite indirect (see Hoyle 1982). What has been reported is that as AAdC activity increases (in "naive" preparations), the shape of the action potential (as recorded from the nonspiking soma) changes in ways that are consistent with decreased g_k. The spike duration increases as AAdC frequency increases from 5 to 20 Hz. With low frequencies (5 Hz), there is a marked undershoot in the action potential (1.5–3 mV) and an increase in the steepness of the depolarizing ramp potential that precedes the action potential. These changes are observed when AAdC activity increases spontaneously, or through direct depolarization from the injection of positive current. In the naive preparation, it has also been reported (unpublished data; Hoyle (1982) that the input resistance of the AAdC cell increases as impulse activity frequency does; and appropriate changes in impulse activity and input resistance occur during both "up" and "down" training. The undershoot of the slowly firing cell was reported to be immediately abolished by both intracellular TEA, and extracellular 4-AP, treatments that block different K^+ currents. Direct evidence to support the suggestion that associative training is accompanied by g_k decreases requires the ability to voltage-clamp the AAdC cell, something that has not been accomplished so far.

ALPHA-CONDITIONING IN *APLYSIA*   Carew et al (1981) found a pairing-specific enhancement of the defensive gill- and siphon-withdrawal reflexes in *Aplysia* when weak tactile stimulation is paired with a strong sensitizing stimulus. Hawkins et al (1983) and Walters & Byrne (1983) proposed that classical conditioning in their systems reflects "activity-dependent amplification of presynaptic facilitation."

Conditioning of the siphon reflex in the Carew et al (1981) study was accomplished by pairing tactile stimulation of the siphon funnel (CS), and electrical stimulation of the tail (UCS). Successful conditioning evidently depends upon shock delivery to the tail region, since pairing-specific effects have not been reported for the customary means of sensitizing the intact animal: strong aversive stimulation of the head. This change in the nature of the UCS is important to bear in mind when assessing the claim that classical conditioning reflects an amplification of an already well-characterized sensitization process. In fact, the circuitry mediating the effects of tail shock has only begun to be characterized (Walters et al 1982).

In the first of three experiments reported, the mean duration of CS-evoked siphon withdrawal was transiently increased for animals exposed to 15 CS-UCS pairings, relative to an explicitly unpaired CS-UCS control. Next, six different groups of animals were exposed to 31 training trials, with testing occurring every 5 trials throughout acquisition, and for ten CS-alone trials following the conclusion of training. Animals were also retested 24 hr later. The conditions examined were paired CS-UCS, explicitly unpaired CS-UCS, a random control, UCS alone, CS alone, and untrained animals. During and immediately following training, paired CS-UCS animals, but no others, exhibited a progressive increase in CS-evoked siphon-withdrawal duration. Declines to near the original baseline levels were also observed for the paired CS-UCS animals. This was interpreted as reflecting an extinction effect; however, it may simply have reflected the passage of time.

One conspicuously anomalous result was addressed by Carew et al (1981): UCS-alone, explicitly unpaired CS-UCS, and random CS-UCS animals failed to show any short-term enhancement of siphon withdrawal, though previous research—as well as the theoretical interpretation that classical conditioning grows out of sensitization—would seem to require that they should. Carew et al noted that 24-hr retention tests resulted in the appearance of a moderate "delayed sensitization" effect for UCS-alone animals, as well as significant retention for paired CS-US animals. Another experiment demonstrated that delivery of either a single UCS to some animals, or 15 UCSs to others, resulted in the subsequent appearance of enhanced siphon-withdrawal durations 30 and 60 min following the last UCS delivery. This was attributed to the delayed onset of sensitization, though neither tests for unstimulated control animals nor tests for the generality of the sensitization effect were reported. Another study examined retention of the CS-evoked enhanced siphon-withdrawal response and found that 30 CS-UCS pairings produced significantly greater enhancement for paired vs unpaired and UCS-alone groups, up to and including retention days 2 and 3, respectively. A second anomaly was not addressed by Carew et al (1981): the lack of any evidence for habituation to the CS-alone and explicitly unpaired groups.

Finally, Carew et al (1981) also reported classical conditioning of the gill-withdrawal reflex in *Aplysia,* potentially a very important demonstration since it is the circuitry of this reflex (not the siphon-withdrawal) that has been most extensively analyzed and that has formed the basis for the neurophysiological and biochemical analyses of habituation and sensitization. They reported that 15 pairings of electrical stimulation of siphon (CS) with electrical stimulation of the tail (UCS) resulted in no significant enhancement of CS-evoked gill withdrawal, relative to preconditioning baseline levels, for animals tested 5 min after the conclusions of training. Nevertheless, a randomly selected subset ($n = 5$) of these same animals subsequently exhibited significantly enhanced gill withdrawal, in response to siphon stimulation, when retested an hour or more after the conclusion of training.

Unfortunately, however, the retention data reported for paired training condition animals was collected an hour or so after a surgical procedure (sham operation). Paired and explicitly unpaired animals were exposed to either deganglionation or a sham operation, in order to assess the contribution of central vs peripheral neural control of changes in gill withdrawal. Thus, the effects of prior conditioning treatment (paired vs unpaired CS-UCS presentations) upon gill-withdrawal changes were confounded with those of surgical intervention. In the absence of one-hour retention data for paired animals *not* exposed to the potentially sensitizing effects of surgery, the increases in gill withdrawal in this experiment cannot be attributed unambiguously to the animal's previous experience with CS-UCS pairings.

How might the sham operation have occasioned an increase in gill withdrawal for paired animals? Carew et al (1981) argue that the enhanced postsurgical gill-withdrawal responses for the sham-operated animals were *not* attributable to sensitization, since sham-operated unpaired control animals failed to exhibit these same responses. While paired and unpaired animals might be plausibly assumed to be equated for sensitization effects arising from surgery per se, it seems inconsistent to assume that the two groups would be equivalent in terms of prior sensitization and habituation accruing from exposure to the paired vs unpaired treatment conditions.

As Carew et al (1981) acknowledge, animals exposed to the explicitly unpaired control procedure may be partially habituated to the CS, because of their repeated experience with funnel stimulation in the absence of strong noxious tail stimulation. Presumably they are more habituated than paired animals, since the latter always receive a dishabituating/sensitizing stimulus (the UCS) shortly after each CS. Given the neural circuit previously proposed to mediate sensitization effects for gillwithdrawal, it does not seem unreasonable to expect differential sensitization effects for the two conditions as well. Siphon (CS) and tail (UCS) pathways both converge upon facilitatory interneurons (the L29 group), which may mediate sensitization (Hawkins et al 1981b, Walters et al 1982). Thus, one would expect greater activation of the L29 group during the course of training for paired vs unpaired animals, and presumably even further enhancement for paired animals following exposure to the sham operation. Indeed, the likelihood of greater habituation of siphon sensory neurons for the unpaired animals also raises the possibility of unequal sensitization effects due to surgery per se, for the two training conditions.

Carew et al (1983) further report that the siphon-withdrawal reflex can be differentially conditioned. In this study, within-animal comparisons of siphon withdrawal to two CSs (siphon- or mantle-tactile stimulation) were conducted. One stimulus (CS^+) was paired 15 times with tail-shock UCS; the other (CS^-) was explicitly unpaired. The results indicated significantly longer siphon-withdrawal times to CS^+ vs CS^-, 30 minutes post-training, for both within-animal and between-group comparisons. Pooled results (across siphon and mantle CS^+ groups) indicated significant increases to both CS^+ and CS^-, relative to initial baseline values, but significantly greater increases to CS^+. Whether these differences were significant for each of the CS^+ and CS^- subgroups was not reported.

These results clearly indicate that pairing-specific increases in siphon-withdrawal duration can be produced. No such demonstration for the gill-withdrawal reflex has yet been provided, and it was the circuitry for the latter reflex that was analyzed in the sensitization studies. Moreover, it is still unclear as to whether the CS^+ vs CS^- differences represent an associative-learning process, or a combination of nonassociative ones. This is a problem in any study of alpha-conditioning and/or pseudoconditioning where the CS elicits the CR prior to training. For example, CS-UCS pairings may produce a general sensitization effect within both CS^+ and CS^- pathways, but allow for greater habituation to occur within the CS^- pathway, as Carew et al (1981) previously argued. Since the CS^+-evoked increases produced by five CS-UCS pairings were equalled by the CS^--evoked increases resulting from 15 unpaired CS/UCS presentations, it remains to be demonstrated that a uniquely associative-learning process is operative in these studies.

In companion papers, Hawkins et al (1983) and Walters & Byrne (1983) report the results of electrophysiological studies that are cellular analogues of the conditioning in the intact animal. In these studies, which involved the isolated ganglion attached to the tail, intracellular stimulation of sensory neurons was used as the CS, and tail or posterior pedal nerve shock was the UCS. Five paired and unpaired presentations of CS and UCS were administered to each preparation; the magnitude and duration of the sensory-motoneuron PSP were measured. EPSP amplitudes increased with training and were significantly greater for CS^+ vs CS^-, 5–15 minutes following training. It was not reported in this study how reliable these findings were. It is unclear whether the summary statistics were based upon all preparations examined, or only those showing some minimal degree of facilitation. Spike broadening in the sensory neuron was also reported in TEA solutions, and the fact that cobalt abolished the training-produced difference was argued to indicate that the Ca^{2+}-component had changed. For the Walters & Byrne (1983) study, it is important to note that no corresponding behavioral changes in the intact animal have been demonstrated. Finally, the following point should be underscored: In none of the studies of associative learning to date with *Aplysia* have associative neural changes been reported for animals initially trained as intact with the natural stimuli. What has been reported to date are, strictly speaking, cellular analogues of conditioning. Similar reports of in vitro associative conditioning of the gill-withdrawal reflex to a different sensory CS (light) were reported by Lukowiak and colleagues (Lukowiak 1982, 1983, Lukowiak & Sahley 1981). Although no long-term behavioral correlates of training for the intact animal have yet been reported, the in vitro results that have been described are notable since the CS (light) used in these studies evidently does not elicit the reflex prior to conditioning.

CONDITIONED SUPPRESSION OF PHOTOTAXIC BEHAVIOR IN *HERMISSEN-DA* Analysis of associative learning in the nudibranch mollusc *Hermissenda* has focused upon the conditioned suppression of phototaxic behavior that results from repeated pairings of light and rotation. In brief, the neuronal organization of the animal's visual and vestibular systems is such that repeated pairings of light and rotation produce a cumulative depolarization and consequent rise in intracellular Ca^{2+} within Type B photoreceptors. This, in turn, is thought to result in a long-lasting (days) suppression of at least two distinct K^+ currents (I_A and I_C) in the B cell. Suppression of these currents results in a post-training enhancement of the B cells' light-induced depolarizing generator potential and impulse activity. For associatively trained animals, this greater light response of the Type B cell is, in part, responsible for a pairing-specific decrease in the light response of a second class of photoreceptor, the Type A cell. After associative training, Type A cells are less effective in their capacity to excite interneurons and motoneurons that mediate photoaxis.

Behavior At a strictly behavioral level, associative suppression of photoaxis is relatively well characterized. Short-term (~ 1 hr), nonassociative suppression of phototaxis was initially described (Alkon 1974b) for animals exposed to prolonged paired or unpaired presentations of light and turbulence. Subsequently, Crow & Alkon (1978) demonstrated pairing-specific decreases in phototaxis persisting for >3 days after training.

More recent research confirmed and extended these findings of long-duration pairing-specific reductions in phototaxic behavior (Farley & Alkon 1980a,b, 1982a, Farley et al 1983a,b, Farley 1984a,b, Richards et al 1983, 1984), and also demonstrated a number of additional commonalities with the behavioral conditioning of vertebrates. For example, the pairing-specific suppression of phototaxic behavior in *Hermissenda* is stimulus specific. The decreased movement toward light does not reflect generalized decreases in arousal, or a diminished capacity for evoked locomotion of any sort, since light-rotation pairings do not reduce the animal's negative geotaxic response (Farley & Alkon 1982a). Post-training tests of phototaxic behavior with light intensities substantially different from those used in training generally fail to reveal significant effects of pairings (Farley 1984a).

Associative learning in *Hermissenda* occupies an apparently unique position within invertebrate—particularly gastropod—learning: nonassociative-learning processes, such as habituation, sensitization, and pseudoconditioning, simply fail to play an appreciable role in the basic conditioning effect (see Richards et al 1983, 1984, Farley 1984a). Attempts to produce a persistent suppression of phototaxis by maximizing any nonassociative effects of light and/or rotation have been singularly unsuccessful. Distributing extra light- or rotation-alone presentations throughout a sequence of pairings fails to enhance the associative suppression and instead attenuates it (Farley 1984a,b, Farley & Kern 1984). Pre-exposure of animals to large numbers of light- or rotation-alone presentations prior to pairings, which might be expected to either retard (latent inhibition) or alternatively enhance acquisition (latent facilitation), fails to affect subsequent conditioning (Farley 1984a). Increased intensities of light and rotation produce no suppression for longer than an hour or so, when efforts to simulate the associative effects of the customary stimulus intensities through nonassociative training protocols are undertaken (Farley 1984a). Insofar as modifications of phototaxic behavior by prior experience with light and rotation is concerned, there seems to be primarily one way in which to produce suppressed phototaxis: by pairing light and rotation. These results imply that those cellular mechanisms that mediate phototaxic suppression are specialized for associative learning. They in no sense represent an elaboration upon a more primitive nonassociative process, such as sensitization, as has been argued for alpha-conditioning of the gill- and siphon-withdrawal reflexes of *Aplysia*.

Contingency experiments with *Hermissenda* indicate that these animals behave in much the same fashion as vertebrates. A behavioral demonstration (Farley 1984b) of contingency sensitivity was first arranged by comparing the extent of phototaxic suppression produced by consistent pairings of light and rotation with that resulting from a degraded contingency treatments in which either extra rotation-alone or light-alone presentations were delivered between pairings of light and rotation. Animals receiving only pairings of light and rotation exhibited pronounced suppression of phototaxis during retention, while animals experiencing a degraded contingency exhibited little conditioning at all. These results demonstrate that the behavior in *Hermissenda* is sensitive not only to the number of light-rotation pairings but also the degree to which light is a valid and reliable predictor of rotation. In general, the conditions under which the added light- and rotation-alone presentations will attenuate conditioning can be predicted from our understanding of the neuronal organization of the visual and vestibular systems, and support the following conclusions: The cellular machinery that provides for simple associative learning in *Hermissenda* also provides for contingency learning.

These contingency experiments also underscore the unique degree to which the behavioral changes resulting from the associative training procedure can be attributed to associative-learning mechanisms in *Hermissenda*. Indeed, contigency experiments provide a general analytic means of establishing whether associative or nonassociative processes account for the pairing-specific behavioral changes observed within other invertebrate conditioning paradigms (cf Farley & Alkon 1984a, Farley 1984a for further discussion). If the greater behavioral change seen for paired vs unpaired training paradigms reflects a differential nonassociative-learning process (such as greater sensitization of the gill and siphon withdrawal in *Aplysia*), then adding additional UCS-alone presentations would further enhance the effects of pairings, rather than attenuate it. On the other hand, if the pairing-specific behavioral changes genuinely reflect an associative process, analogous to that of vertebrate conditioning, then the added UCS-alone presentations should attenuate conditioning due to pairings in these preparations as they do in *Hermissenda*.

Hermissenda's conditioned suppression of phototaxic behavior is also subject to "extinction": it disappears after repeated post-training exposures to nonreinforced light presentations (Richards et al 1983, 1984). Aside from the criterion of reversibility exemplified in this demonstration, extinction in *Hermissenda* is interesting for another reason. It occurs in the absence of any demonstrable habituation to light and fails to exhibit the features of spontaneous recovery and disinhibition (Pavlov 1927). All three characteristics generally accompany extinction of Pavlovian conditioning in vertebrate species. Historically these features have prompted some to suggest that extinction is little more than the process of habituation to the CS, and, correspondingly, spontaneous recovery and disinhibition are little more than reflections of dishabituation or sensitization. However, their absence in *Hermissenda* implies that a major portion of the decline of phototaxic suppression following extinction is attributable to a reversal of the original process of acquisition, rather than to a simple masking of the original learning due to habituation. Intracellular recordings from cells known to play a causal role in acquisition and retention confirm this notion.

For *Hermissenda*, the temporal order relation most commonly used in training is a "simultaneous" one, in which both the onsets and offsets of light and rotation occur together. However, this designation of the temporal arrangement as "simultaneous" is only approximately correct. Owing to the inertia of the turntable motor used to deliver rotational stimulation, maximum g is reached with a delay of 500–1000 msec. Hence, the arrangement more closely approximates a forward sequential arrangement. Grover & Farley (1983) explicitly compared the relative effectiveness of forward, simultaneous, and backward pairings and found the nominal simultaneous procedure to be superior to both backward conditioning and to a forward delayed-conditioning procedure in which 30 sec intervened between light and rotation onsets. Whether phototaxic suppression in *Hermissenda* exhibits the steep ISI functions characteristic of many vertebrate preparations remains to be determined.

More recent experiments (Lederhendler et al 1983) indicate that light actually acquires the capacity to produce motor behavior ("clinging") normally triggered by rotation. Animals exposed to paired, but not random, presentations of light and rotation exhibit a light-triggered contraction of the foot following training.

In summary, the associative suppression of phototaxic behavior in *Hermissenda* is characterized by many of the critical and defining features of associative learning for vertebrates. These features include pairing and stimulus specificity, well-behaved acquisition and retention functions, and a virtual absence of nonassociative-learning processes. In addition, *Hermissenda's* learning also shares some of the more interesting and complex characteristics of associative learning and causal detection for more evolved animals: namely, contingency learning, extinction, superior conditioning for distributed vs massed training procedures, and sensitivity to the temporal order of light and rotation.

Localization of sites of learning: Type B and A photoreceptors   Three lines of evidence converge to imply that two of the three Type B photoreceptors in a *Hermissenda* eye are primary sites of neural change that mediate acquisition and retention of the learned suppression of phototaxis. This evidence includes demonstrations of correlations between long-term training-produced electrophysiological characteristics of Type B cells and the associative training paradigm (West et al 1982), as well as correlations with the behavior of intact animals: (*a*) during acquisition (Alkon 1980, Farley & Alkon 1980b, 1982b, 1984b); (*b*) during short- (Crow & Alkon 1980) as well as long-term retention intervals (Farley & Alkon 1982a, 1983, 1984c, Farley 1984a,b, Alkon et al 1984); (*c*) following extinction (Richards et al 1983, 1984), partial reinforcement (Farley 1984a), and degraded contingency training (Farley 1984a); (*d*) for comparisons of massed vs distributed training trials (Farley 1984a); and (*e*) for a variety of light-rotation ISI conditions (Grover & Farley 1983). Second, these training-produced changes are intrinsic to the Type B cells; they are not secondary consequences of changes elsewhere (Crow & Alkon 1980, West et al 1982, Alkon et al 1982a, Farley 1984b). These changes are well-correlated with and predict some of the training-produced light-evoked differences in phototaxic interneurons and motorneurons (Goh & Alkon 1982, Lederhendler et al 1982). Finally, artificial induction of membrane changes in the Type B cells of previously untrained, semi-intact, behaving animals is sufficient to produce long-term changes in phototaxic behavior (Farley et al 1982, 1983b).

Crow & Alkon (1980) first reported that immediately following three days of training, Type B photoreceptors from paired animals exhibited significantly more depolarized membrane potentials and enhanced input resistances than did random controls.

Similar correlations between long-term electrophysiological changes in Type B cells and associative modifications of phototaxis also obtain (Farley & Alkon 1981, 1982a, 1983, 1984c; Farley et al 1982, 1983a, West et al 1982, Richards et al 1983, Alkon et al 1984). Increased input resistances and enhanced peak, steady-state, and LLD responses are apparent for paired vs random conditioning treatments, one and two days following training. In addition, impulse frequency during light steps is also greater for B cells from the paired training condition (Farley & Alkon 1982a). Unlike the recordings obtained immediately after training, no difference in cells' resting potentials for paired vs random treatment conditions is apparent (Farley & Alkon 1981, 1982a, 1983, 1984a,b, West et al 1982, Richards et al 1983). Pairing-specific depolarization of B cells seems to be a relatively transient expression of the membrane changes undergone by B cells, confined to the first hour or so following training (Farley & Alkon 1982a,b, 1984b, Grover & Farley 1983).

In addition to playing a major role in mediating the effects of simple associative learning, a wealth of data suggests that these same cells also play a crucial role in mediating some of the more complex phenomenology of associative learning as well. Following extinction training (Richards et al 1983, 1984), the light responses and input resistances of Type B cells are indistinguishable from those of naive or random control animals, apparently reverting to an untrained state when light, no longer followed by rotation, is repeatedly presented. Similarly, recordings obtained from animals exposed to degraded contingency conditions indicate that conditions failing to produce substantial learning also fail to produce persistent changes in Type B cells. Simply put, over a wide range of training conditions, the behavior of intact animals and the properties of the Type B cells parallel one another (see Farley 1984a for review).

Recent evidence (Richards et al 1983, Farley 1984a, Richards & Farley 1984) indicates that the Type A cells are also changed by light-rotation pairings. Interestingly enough, whereas the B cell's light response is enhanced by light-rotation pairings, that of the A cell is diminished. This complementary intrinsic change of the A cell combines with the increased synaptic inhibition from B cells following training (Farley & Alkon 1982a) to reduce phototaxic behavior still further. The complementary nature of the Type B and A cell changes also underscores the point that learning is the response of a neural *system,* in this case one selected by evolution to detect consistent regularities in the temporal conjunction of light and rotation.

The correlations between B cell electrophysiology and behavior arise, at least in part, through well-characterized synaptic interactions involving Type B and A photoreceptors (Alkon & Fuortes 1972), interneurons (Alkon 1974a), and motoneurons (Goh & Alkon 1982) involved in phototaxis. Type B cells exert greater inhibition upon A cells following associative training (Farley & Alkon 1982a), which in turn are less effective in their excitation of identified interneurons and motoneurons that innervate the pedal musculature (Goh & Alkon 1982, Lederhendler et al 1982).

Acquisition mechanisms: Cumulative depolarization of Type B cells   A major factor in the production of Type B cell changes during acquisition may be a cumulative depolarization of the Type B cell, which occurs during the course of associative training and which derives from a pairing-specific synaptic facilitation of the B cells' long-lasting depolarizing (LLD) response to light (Alkon 1980, Farley & Alkon 1980b, 1982b, 1984b). As a consequence of cumulative depolarization, intracellular levels of Ca^{2+} rise (Connor & Alkon 1984) and are thought to produce persistent changes in B cell ionic conductances and hence excitability of B cells by light.

The pairing-specific cumulative depolarization of Type B cells arises largely from two sources. First, both light and vestibular (caudal hair cell) stimulation inhibit the S/E optic ganglion cell (Tabata & Alkon 1982, Farley & Alkon 1982b, 1984b), which responds to the termination of inhibition with a rebound-increase in depolarization and impulse activity. Second, there is a pairing-specific disinhibition of Type B cells that results from post-stimulation hyperpolarization of caudal hair cells (Farley & Alkon 1982b, 1984b).

The causal role of both these sources of synaptic facilitation was documented through in vitro conditioning techniques for the isolated nervous-system of *Hermissenda* (Farley & Alkon 1982b, 1984b, Farley 1984a,b, Grover & Farley 1983). This stimulation of the training received by intact animals entails intracellular stimulation and recording from three classes of neurons: the Type B photoreceptor, the S/E optic ganglion cell, and a caudal hair cell in the statocyst. Exposure of the isolated nervous system to five pairings of light and current-induced impulse activity of the caudal hair cell results in an average 10-mV depolarization of Type B cells, which is significantly greater than that produced by five random presentations of these two stimuli (Farley & Alkon 1982c, 1984a). Cumulative depolarization of the B cell is substantially reduced when the S/E cell is hyperpolarized throughout the course of pairings of light and caudal hair cell stimulation. Similarly, light paired with depolarizing current injections to the S/E cell is sufficient to produce large and prolonged cumulative depolarization in B cells. Thus, the S/E optic ganglion cell, which is a critical convergence point for visual and vestibular (statocyst hair cell) information, appears to be both necessary and sufficient to mediate the pairing effects of light and rotation upon the Type B photoreceptor (Farley & Alkon 1982b, 1984b).

Cumulative depolarization of Type B cells represents the initial step in the production of long-term associative neural and behavioral changes in *Hermissenda*. Depolarization of B cells results in an initially transient suppression of K^+ currents in Type B cells [I_A: the fast, rapidly inactivating K^+ current (Connor & Stevens 1971); I_k: the delayed rectifier (Hodgkin & Huxley 1952a)] through a conventional voltage-dependent inactivation mechanism (Hodgkin & Huxley 1952b). Suppression of I_A and I_K in turn leads to sustained depolarization of the B cell and would be expected to increase intracellular Ca^{2+} levels throughout training (Connor & Alkon 1982). Increased levels of intracellular Ca^{2+} arise, in part from a voltage-dependent Ca^{2+} current during activation of and following light steps paired with rotation (Alkon et al 1983, 1984). Increased intracellular Ca^{2+} levels are thought to produce more persistent reductions (days) in I_A and the calcium-activated K^+ current (I_C) (Meech 1974).

The previously described results implicate cumulative depolarization and increased intracellular Ca^{2+} levels as major contributors to the persistent changes in Type B cell ionic conductances that occur with training, but other mechanisms may play a role as well. For example, accumulating evidence suggests a role for training-induced pharmacological modulation of B cell ionic currents, by neuromodulators within the optic ganglion (McElearney & Farley 1983). Serotonin (5-HT) mimics many of the effects of training (Wu & Farley 1984) and may play a role in the initiation and maintenance of long-term membrane changes. Norepinephrine may also be involved (Sakakibara et al 1984).

Type B cells also exhibit contingency-sensitive modifications during both acquisition and retention of learning (Farley 1984a,b). In vitro simulation of the training procedures used with intact animals (by exposing preparations to five pairings of light and hair cell stimulation plus extra light or hair cell stimulation) significantly attenuates the cumulative depolarization in Type B cells, relative to that occurring from just pairings alone. The extra light stimuli are disruptive primarily because they introduce temporary, nonassociative, light adaptation effects in B cells. The light-adapted B cell during such a treatment responds with less of a depolarizing generator potential than normally, and consequently the post-pairing depolarization is less. Although each light-alone step results in some depolarization, this is insufficiently compensated for by its proactive intereference with pairing-produced depolarization. A major role in the reduction of the light-induced generator potential is inactivation of the transient light-induced Na^+ current (Farley 1984a), mediated in part by intracellular Ca^{2+} (Alkon et al 1982b) and activation of the Ca^{2+}-

activated K^+ current (Alkon 1979), which is due to prior intracellular release of Ca^{2+} by light (Farley 1984a, Alkon & Sakakibara 1984).

Cumulative depolarization by the extra steps of unpaired caudal hair cell stimulation is attenuated for a different reason. Caudal hair cell impulse trains synaptically hyperpolarize Type B cells, thus reversing the depolarization produced by prior pairings. Unlike light-alone presentation, the effects of the added hair cell stimulation are primarily retroactive. In the absence of prior pairings, they exert little lasting effect upon the neural response of the B cell (or behavior of the intact animal). Once the cumulative depolarization of B cells has been initiated by the pairings of light and rotation, however, the added hair cell stimulation acts to restore the original membrane potential of the cell.

Cumulative depolarization of the B cell is also unique to vestibular stimulation of the *caudal* hair cells in the statocyst, since it is these that synaptically inhibit both the S/E cell and the Type B photoreceptor. Pairing light with *cephalad* hair cell stimulation fails to produce cumulative depolarization of B cells (Alkon 1980, Farley & Alkon 1980a), and training conditions that maximize this manner of vestibular stimulation also fail to produce persistent behavioral suppression (Farley & Alkon 1980b).

Despite the strength of these correlations between neural changes in B cells and the behavior of intact animals, it is nonetheless important to recognize that they are only that: correlations. Indeed, it is important to realize that correlated neural changes, which occur with learning, are all that have been previously demonstrated for any simple system preparation. Recently, we demonstrated a direct causal relationship between membrane changes, as they occur during acquisition, and long-term behavioral changes in phototaxis (Farley et al 1982, 1983b).

The strategy in these experiments was to produce, through electrophysiological means, the acquisition-correlated membrane changes (cumulative depolarization and increased input resistance) in a single Type B cell in intact animals, and then to assess long-term changes in phototaxis. The experimental treatment designed to simulate the associative training procedure with natural stimuli involved exposing animals to five pairings of 30 sec of light and depolarizing current into Type B cells. These stimulation parameters were directly derived from our previous experience (Farley & Alkon 1982b, 1984b) with in vitro conditioning of the isolated nervous system. We also examined two control conditions. One condition involved exposing animals to five unpaired presentations of light and depolarizing current, the general parameters of light and current being identical to those of the paired condition. The second simply involved microelectrode impalement of Type B cells, without administering any training stimulation. Animals were allowed to recover and were then tested, using "blind" observational procedures, for changes in phototaxic behavior.

Pairings of light and positive current produced a cumulative depolarization in Type B cells significantly greater than the negligible change that occurred for cells exposed to the unpaired treatment. The paired treatment cells also exhibited a significant increase in input resistance, whereas the unpaired treatment yielded no change in this measure of cell conductance. In short, we successfully produced the membrane changes in Type B cells of intact animals that we had previously observed in the conditioning of isolated nervous systems.

One and two days following training, all animals exhibited longer phototaxic latencies (compared to initial baseline levels), but animals receiving paired presentations of light and depolarizing current exhibited significantly greater suppression of phototaxic behavior than either control group. Thus, pairings of light and membrane depolarization of Type B cells were sufficient to produce retained suppression of phototaxis.

Biophysical mechanisms for retention: Reduction of K^+ conductances   Alkon et al (1982a) reported a 30% reduction in the peak amplitude, and a more rapid inactivation, of the fast, rapidly inactivating A current (Connor & Stevens 1971) for associatively trained animals, one and two days following training. This is consistent with the likelihood that increased input resistances and enhanced light-induced depolarizing generator potentials of Type B cells from associatively trained animals reflects a decrease in one or more outward K^+ currents. Subsequent research demonstrated that the A current could be suppressed for intermediate lengths of time (~ 10–15 min) following introduction of Ca^{2+} loads into the cell (Alkon et al 1982b). Efforts to develop a Hodgkin-Huxley model of the voltage- and light-dependent currents in the B photoreceptor indicate that a 30% reduction in the A current can enhance the magnitude of the peak and steady-state components of the generator potential by 10 to 20% (Shoukimas & Alkon 1983) in a manner approximating the effects of training.

The question naturally arises as to whether the A current is the only current changed by associative training; if not, which other(s) change? A number of studies indicate that neither the transient inward light-induced Na^+ current (West et al 1982, Forman et al 1984) nor the delayed rectifier (I_K) (Alkon et al 1982a) are affected by training. More recent results (Farley et al 1983a, 1984, Farley & Alkon 1983) suggested changes in the calcium-activated potassium current (I_C). Reduction of training-produced differences in the contribution of I_A to Type B photoreceptor light responses enhances, rather than attenuates, the associative differences (Farley et al 1983a, Farley & Alkon 1983). Recent results demonstrate long-term pairing-specific reductions in I_C following training of intact animals (Forman et al 1984, Farley et al 1984). Pairing-specific increases in I_{Ca} (Farley et al 1984) may occur as well.

The biochemical mechanisms by which long-term reductions in I_A and I_C occur are not known for certain, but a variety of studies implicate Ca^{2+}-calmodulin-mediated phosphorylation as a mechanism. The selective suppression of I_A (Alkon et al 1982b) and I_C (Alkon et al 1983) by the introduction of Ca^{2+} loads has already been described. Acosta-Urquidi et al (1984) showed that injection of phosphorylase kinase into B cells, and its subsequent activation by light-induced increases in intracellular Ca^{2+}, simulates some of the membrane changes that occur with associative training. Neary et al (1981) reported learning-correlated changes in low-molecular-weight (20–25K) phosphoprotein bands, which also appear to be calcium dependent. Thus, the opportunity presents itself to identify more specific biochemical regulation mechanisms involved in the control of ionic fluxes as these are responsible for long-term expressions of associative learning.

VERTEBRATE MODEL SYSTEMS

Cerebellar Cortex and Plasticity of the Horizontal Vestibular Ocular Reflex

Ito and colleagues (1970, 1982) provided direct evidence that adaptive changes occurring within the rabbit's horizontal vestibulo-ocular reflex (HVOR) reflect neural changes occurring within the cerebellar flocculus. The development of this preparation was heavily influenced by the models of Marr (1969) and Albus (1971) concerning the synaptic organization of cerebellar cortex and its plastic capacities.

The HVOR consists of horizontal eye movements, initiated by rotation-induced vestibular signals, which occur in a direction opposite to head movement, presumably to stabilize retinal images. This allows vertebrates to see and move at the same time. In the laboratory, the HVOR is conventionally measured by securing the experimental subject to a turntable, and, with its head fixed, exposing it to sinusoidal whole-body rotation. The reflexive eye movements are then measured.

The HVOR is remarkably plastic. Both increases and decreases in VOR gain (defined as the magnitude of smooth compensatory eye velocity divided by imposed head velocity) have been described for cats, primates, humans, and rabbits, in experiments that introduce the need for recalibration of the reflex. For example, appropriate changes in VOR gain can be produced by fitting primates, humans, or cats with magnifying or miniaturizing goggles. Alternatively, dove prisms, which reverse left and right visual space and therefore introduce large "retinal error" signals, also result in the eventual compensation of eye movements to the artificial disruption of visual space (Miles & Fuller 1974, Gonshor & Melville-Jones 1976a,b, Robinson 1976, Miles et al 1980, Miles & Braitman 1980). For example, if fitted with 2× magnifying goggles—

which thus required an eye/head velocity gain ratio of 2.0 for stabilzation of visual images—monkeys gradually converged upon VOR gains of 1.6–1.8 over the course of several days (Miles & Fuller 1974).

The type of adaptive VOR change most closely approximating the types of behavioral modifications that psychologists attributed to "associative" learning processes involves the progressive changes in VOR gain produced by conjoint visual-vestibular stimulation. Sustained (12 hr) pairing of sinusoidal rotation with stationary whole-field illumination typically induces a persistent gain increase (140% of control levels) in the VOR, and a decreased phase shift, measured in either dark or light (Ito et al 1974, Ito et al 1979a). Neither sustained rotation-alone nor sustained visual stimulation in the absence of rotation effected such a change. In another instance of plasticity, conjoint turntable rotation and *moving* light (in phase with the turntable-produced vestibular stimulation, but with an amplitude twice that of the turntable) produced a progressive decrease in VOR gain, but no phase shift (Baarsma & Collewijn 1974, Ito et al 1979a).

These gain changes are relatively persistent, lasting for hours to days depending upon the conditions of measurement. Moreover, they are pairing specfic, to some degree. No long-term HVOR changes have been observed for sustained visual-alone or vestibular-alone stimulation, and the effects of random or explicitly unpaired stimulation sequences have not been described; nor have timing and temporal order sequences been investigated. In terms of stimulus specificity, the HVOR changes are rather general. Neither the gain increases nor decreases are specific to the frequency of rotational stimulation used to elicit the HVOR (Ito et al 1979a). In terms of response specificity, the changes are quite restricted. Measurements of the optokinetic response (OKR), a reflex that shares some common circuitry with the HVOR, indicate that this reflex is largely unchanged by training.

The neural pathways mediating the HVOR are classically divided into direct and indirect (Lorente de No 1933). The direct pathway is a three-neuronal arc consisting of primary vestibular neurons, secondary vestibulo-ocular neurons, and ocular motoneurons, with no provision for feedback. Indirect pathway(s) are formed by a number of polysynaptic routes through the reticular formation, as well as the cerebellum (summarized by Precht 1979). These indirect pathways have been postulated to be the repositories of sites underlying the plastic gain and phase changes.

A considerably oversimplified view of the direct pathway is as follows. Rotation of the head (e.g. to the left) results in vestibular stimulation, proportional to angular acceleration, of both horizontal semicircular ducts. Because of the hydraulics of the canals, primary vestibular fibers then convey a head velocity signal to medial and superior vestibular nuclei. In the hemisphere toward which head movement is directed (in this example, the left), increased firing frequency of the primary afferents produces greater excitation of the contralateral (right) vestibular neurons. This, in turn, enhances excitation of ipsilateral (left III) and contralateral (right VI) cranial nerve nuclei, which cause contraction of the ipsilateral (left) medial and contralateral (right) lateral rectii muscles. This excitatory component of the reflex is abetted by a complementary inhibitory component. Vestibular hair cells in the right (contralateral) semicircular canal diminish in activity, hence there is less excitation of contralateral (left) vestibular neurons projecting to the antagonistic ocular muscles (left eye—lateral rectus; right eye—medial rectus). Thus, if the head is moved to the left, the eyes move toward the right, and vice versa. The direct pathway functions as an open-loop reflex, with no apparent feedback signal of eye position converging upon the primary vestibular neurons.

Feedback signals were assumed by Ito (1977; but see Robinson 1976) to indicate retinal error and to enter the direct VOR pathway exclusively at the level of the vestibular-ocular relay cells. In Ito's view, the pathway through the cerebellar flocculus conveys this information, and also harbors the site of plastic gain changes. Excitatory vestibular inputs arrive at cortical Purkinje cells via mossy fiber/parallel fiber inputs (Brodal & Hoivik 1964). Visual information, presumably reflecting retinal error information during VOR, also converges upon Purkinje cells, through visual climbing fiber pathways (Ito 1972, Maekawa & Simpson 1973), coursing through the dorsal cap of the contralateral inferior olive (Haddad et al 1980). Purkinje cell outputs are exclusively inhibitory and in the case of the flocculus, project to the vestibular-ocular relay nucleii (Ito et al 1970, Baker et al 1972, Fukuda et al 1972).

The evidence that flocculus mediates these gain changes derives from lesion and recording studies, and recent demonstrations of the depression of parallel-fiber-to-Purkinje cell synaptic transmission when mossy fiber activity (simulating vestibular information) is paired with climbing fiber stimulation (simulating visual information) (Ito et al 1982a). Flocculus lesions abolish or severely disrupt the capacity for plastic gain changes, without substantially affecting the baseline characteristics of the reflex. For example, chronic ablations depress the rapid modification of VOR by visual input (i.e. the instantaneous gain increases) (Ito et al 1974, Takemori & Cohen 1974) as well as the capacity for long-term changes (Robinson 1976, Ito et al 1982b). In the albino rabbit, this effect is specific to the flocculus. Lesions of other cerebellar regions (nodulus, uvula, lobules VI and VII, and paraflocculus) do not compromise the capacity for plastic gain changes. The importance of intact olivary projections in mediating the visual feedback signal was also demonstrated (Maekewa & Simpson 1973, Ito & Miyashita 1975, Ito et al 1978, 1979b). Electrical stimulation studies of cerebellar microzones in rabbit flocculus further reveal that microstimulation of those Purkinje cell areas (H-zones), projecting to the vestibulo-ocular relay nuclei (as revealed by HRP labeling) evokes horizontal movement (abduction) of the ipsilateral eye (Dufosse et al 1977). These results are consistent with flocculus Purkinje cell inhibition of the HVOR.

Recordings from H-zone Purkinje cells in rabbit flocculus during sinusoidal rotation of the animal reveal that a high percentage (90%) of the cells examined exhibit significant modulation of spontaneous *simple spike* frequency (which is a unique consequence of mossy fiber synaptic stimulation) by rotational stimulation. The preponderance of cells fired close to 180° out-of-phase with head velocity (Ghelarducci et al 1975). In other words, flocculus output during the normal operation of the VOR (gain = 1.0) is predominantly out-of-phase with the discharge of the primary afferents, and thus serves to disinhibit firing of the relay cells. Changes in the efficacy of flocculus transmission would be expected to cause predictable changes in VOR gain. Thus, one would expect to observe the following correlations between VOR gain changes and flocculus simple spike frequency: gain increases should be accompanied by greater out-of-phase discharge of Purkinje cells; conversely, gain decreases should be accompanied by decreased out-of-phase discharge (more in-phase). These predictions were elegantly confirmed for the rabbit (Dufosse et al 1978a).

It should be mentioned, however, that other investigators question the species generality of the flocculus as the site of VOR gain changes. Keller & Precht (1979), for example, find in cat that total cerebellectomy does not abolish the instantaneous effects of visual input upon VOR, which clearly indicates extracerebellar visual inputs to VOR for this animal. Lisberger, Fuchs, and Miles (Lisberger & Fuchs 1978, Lisberger & Miles 1980, Miles & Lisberger 1981) raised similar questions concerning the role of flocculus in primates. Whereas the results of flocculus lesions in the monkey (Robinson 1976) agree with those in rabbit, the results of electrophysiological recordings in monkey are unexpected given the rabbit data. Lisberger & Fuchs (1978) for example, correlated Purkinje cell discharges with three distinct types of eye movement: (a) VORs elicited by rotation in the dark; (b) smooth pursuit movements in the absence of imposed head movement; and (c) suppression of VOR by visual fixation in light. These investigators observed that rotation in darkness was *not* accompanied by any appreciable modulation of firing, and modulations opposite to those expected were observed during smooth pursuit or during VOR suppression (cf Miles & Fuller 1974).

Miles & Lisberger (1981) suggested a reinterpretation of the role of the flocculus in mediating gain changes in VOR. They note that the lesion data do not uniquely support Ito's model. Changes may be occurring prior to flocculus Purkinje cells, which are then routed through this portion of the cerebellum. Alternatively, the flocculus may be an important part of a pathway that transmits information to other sites, where the plasticity occurs. Miles & Lisberger (1981) further suggest a tentative model of signal processing in the

VOR and flocculus, a model that would in principle allow for the modulation of discharge frequencies of Purkinje cells and correlated VOR gain changes that occur under Ito's hypothesis, although the site of plasticity (unspecified) is proposed to lie outside the flocculus proper. They conclude that, at least in the monkey, flocculus receives an eye *velocity* signal from brain stem regions, which in turn are the sites of plasticity. It is the changed eye velocity signal (rather than retinal eror signal) that is fed to flocculus Purkinje cells, and is thus responsible for the VOR-correlated changes in discharge frequency. Ito, in turn, notes the following: (*a*) The microzones in the flocculus have not yet been mapped for the monkey, and the discrepant electrophysiology may be due to the fact that recordings were not obtained from monkey flocculus cells specifically involved in the VOR. (*b*) Miles & Lisberger (1981) have as yet failed to specify the location of their extrafloccular site of plasticity. (*c*) For the rabbit, there is no evidence that H-zone Purkinje cells receive an eye velocity input signal.

Perhaps the strongest evidence that flocculus Purkinje cells are causal sites is this: electrophysiological protocols that simulate the pairing-specific convergence of visual and vestibular stimulation produce synaptic depression of the Purkinje cells (Ito et al 1982a). Pairing 25 sec of vestibular nerve stimulation (ipsilateral mossy fiber afferents to Purkinje cells) with 25 sec of contralateral inferior olive stimulation (climbing fiber input) produced a depression of simple spike discharge (recorded extracellularly) in Purkinje cells, evoked by vestibular nerve stimulation. Early excitation (3–6 msec range) was depressed and delayed by an average of $47 \pm 21\%$ (ten different cells) when animals were exposed to conjunctive vestibular-olivary stimulation. With a single pairing, the depression lasts for about ten minutes. The depression can be cumulative, however. Repetitive conjunctive stimulation trials led to greater and more prolonged depression, an hour or two at most. It was specific to the test input; impulse activity evoked by contralateral vestibular nerve stimulation was not depressed in five preparations.

Depression must specifically be occurring at the parallel fiber Purkinje cell synapse, because it was not observed at adjacent basket cell synapses. Hence granule cells, which project to the basket cells and by implication all other elements along the vestibular nerve–Purkinje cell pathway, did not appear to change.

Three comments are warranted. First, it is unclear to what extent the effect is exclusively pairing specific. While sustained vestibular nerve stimulation, or olivary stimulation, in isolation produced no appreciable change, unpaired or random stimulation protocols were evidently not examined. Moreover, high-frequency olivary stimulation (in the absence of vestibular stimulation) was found (Ito et al 1982a, Rawson & Tilokskulchai 1982) to produce a persistent (minutes) general depression of Purkinje cell simple spike activity, thereby obscuring the depression due to any specific synaptic input. Second, it is unclear whether cells in which conjoint stimulation depression occurs are representative of Purkinje cells in general. In one experiment, only three of 15 sampled Purkinje cells (from two rabbits) showed the early excitation. The majority (ten cells) showed a depression. Third, only the early excitation was suppressed in the conjoint stimulation experiments. The later excitation— presumably representing secondary volleys from vestibulo-cerebellar nuclei cells—actually appeared to be enhanced. The implications of a transitory reduction in simple spike output are not clear, especially if their reduction is compensated for by delayed increases.

A similar experimental protocol also demonstrated depressed glutamate sensitivity in flocculus Purkinje cells, induced by conjunctive iontophoresis of glutamate and olivary (climbing fiber) stimulation. Glutamate is the putative transmitter used by the mossy-parallel fibers (Sandoval & Cotman 1978). Pairing iontophoresis of glutamate (to cells with high glutamate sensitivity) with olivary stimulation produced a marked depression (50–100%) in glutamate's excitatory response in some (7 of 21) Purkinje cells. The response to aspartate was not depressed despite comparable initial sensitivity. The depression of glutamate response lasted about an hour, but this was somewhat variable. Many Purkinje cells (14 of 21) did not show a depression by conjunctive glutamate-olivary stimulation. Cells that showed initially strong glutamate sensitivity were the ones that changed (7 of 10).

At present, the mechanisms by which depression occurs are not known. Ito (1982) suggested two promising possibilities: (a) Climbing fibers are known to activate a dendritic voltage-dependent Ca^{2+} current (Llinas & Sugimori 1980), and increased intracellular Ca^{2+} may desensitize Purkinje cell dendritic glutamate receptors. (b) Climbing fibers may liberate a chemical that renders the postsynaptic receptors at parallel fiber-to-Purkinje cell synapses insensitive. This is analogous to the purported reduction of glutamate sensitivity in cerebral pyramidal cells caused by TRH (Renaud et al 1979), and is the converse of dopamine's enhancement of muscarinic-cholinergic receptor sensitivity in rabbit sympathetic ganglion cells (Libet 1984). How these proposed mechanisms would depend upon conjoint parallel fiber stimulation is unclear. No direct evidence has yet been presented to indicate that the changes are in fact restricted to postsynaptic membrane (i.e. changes in presynaptic release might as easily be invoked) or that the specific mechanism of receptor desensitization is involved.

In summary, the precise role of the flocculus in VOR plasticity—whether it is in fact a primary site of plasticity and one that is causal for the VOR gain changes, or whether it simply reflects changes that have occurred elsewhere— has not yet been resolved, though the evidence for the rabbit is extremely suggestive.

Cerebellum and Conditioning of Rabbit Nictitating Membrane Response (NMR)

Classical aversive conditioning of the rabbit's nictitating membrane response (NMR) is quite useful for delimiting the possible sites of plasticity underlying one simple form of mammalian associative learning (see Thompson et al 1983, 1984, Moore 1984). The combined results of lesion, neuroanatomical, and unit recording studies implicate ipsilateral cerebellar deep nuclei (medial dentate/ lateral interpositus) and perhaps restricted areas of cerebellar cortex as critical sites for the acquisition and retention of associative learning. Anterior interpositus may also be important.

The NMR response is one of a family of defensive eyelid responses that develop in humans (Prokasy 1972), cats (Woody 1982), and rabbits (Gormezano 1972) following exposure to an aversive Pavlovian conditioning procedure. In a typical experiment, a CS (most commonly whole-field illumination or tone) is repeatedly paired with corneal airpuff or paraorbital shock (UCSs). Such stimulation reflexively elicits eyeball retraction and some contraction of the facial musculature. With continued training, the animal learns to blink during the CS, in apparent anticipation of the impending UCS. The closure of the animal's third eyelid is in fact a passive consequence of eyeball retraction and is measured largely for reasons of convenience. Gormezano and colleagues' (see Gormezano et al 1983) extensive empirical characterization of NMR conditioning revealed numerous features of this example of learning that are particularly advantageous for neurobiological studies of associative learning. Four of these are recapitulated here: (a) The associative CR is largely free from artifacts produced by nonassociative -learning processes such as habituation and sensitization. (b) Both the UCR (~ 13 msec) and the CR (50 msec under optimal ISI conditions) are relatively fast responses in the well-trained animal. This implies that the essential component of the CR involves a pathway with relatively few synapses, and hence may be amenable to detailed circuit analysis. (c) The development of the CR is under strict temporal control, with decreased conditioning occurring as the CS-UCS onset interval is increased from 70 to 3000 msec, for the standard forward-delay procedure. (d) The rabbit NMR is prototypical of Pavlovian conditioned, discrete, adaptive, striated muscle responses. It figures prominently in contemporary attempts to bridge the domains of animal and human cognition with those of animal learning and conditioning (Moore 1979, Wagner 1981).

Systematic series of lesion studies, by several laboratories, implicate brain stem/cerebellar regions as critical for the learned NMR response. What is perhaps clearest from these studies is the degree to which tissue above the level of the thalamus is *not* involved. Bilateral decortication of rabbits (Oakley & Russell 1972) and cats (Norman et al 1974) prior to conditioning interferes little, if at all, with the subsequent establishment of a normal CR. It may even enhance discrimination reversal (Oakley & Russell 1972), and decortication of rabbits after a CR is initially established results in little retention loss of the CR, if the animal was initially trained with its cortex intact (Oakley & Russell 1977). Thus, it would appear that NMR conditioning in the intact mammalian brain is essentially a subcortical event. However, if animals are initially trained as hemi-decorticates, subsequent removal of the remaining tissue abolishes the retained CR (Oakley & Russell 1977). Half a cortex appears to be worse than none at all. A satisfactory account of this latter result has not yet been provided.

Bilateral hippocampectomy fails to prevent subsequent acquisition or to abolish previously acquired CRs (Solomon & Moore 1975) in the simple, standard, NMR conditioning paradigm (that of forward delay). However, it reportedly disrupted CRs acquired in a trace conditioning paradigm in which an appreciable interval of time intervened between CS offset and UCS onset (Weisz et al 1980). It also appears to play a crucial role in the mediation of other more complex phenomenological features of Pavlovian conditioning, such as latent inhibition and blocking (Solomon 1980) and reversal learning (Berger & Orr 1982). Thus, many pyramidal neurons in CA3-CA1 regions of dorsal hippocampus develop an impressive neuronal template of the learned CR (but not UCR) (Berger & Thompson 1978a,b), which is quite interesting given the possible relevance of the mechanisms uncovered by studies of hippocampal LTP. Nevertheless, the hippocampus does *not* appear to be a primary, causal site of information storage. A number of authors suggest that the hippocampus subserves memorial phenomena that are best characterized as extremely dependent upon information presented in the recent past, and which are of utility for a comparably delimited future (Olton et al 1979, Weiskrantz & Warrington 1979, Kesner 1982). Thus, to the degree that performance in any particular classical conditioning paradigm is heavily dependent upon memory for events in the recent past (which intuitively seems to be the case for phenomena such as discrimination reversal, trace conditioning, blocking, etc), it would likely be disrupted by hippocampal lesions.

Recent concerted efforts to delineate CR and UCR pathways, and their possible sites of interaction, indicate that the most peripheral sites in these pathways (primary auditory relay nuclei, and abducens and accesory abducens motor neurons, respectively) are unlikely to be causal sites. Although learning-correlated changes in acoustically evoked unit activity were reported at a number of sites within the auditory system in some studies [e.g. cochlear nucleus (Oleson et al 1975), inferior colliculus (Disterhoft & Stuart 1976), auditory (Disterhoft & Stuart 1976), and association cortex (Disterhoft et al 1982)], they have not been detected in other experiments (Lonsbury-Martin et al 1976, Kettner & Thompson 1982). Furthermore, the recent results of a signal-detection paradigm reveal a clear dissociation between the occurrence of the CR and acoustically evoked unit activity in anteroventral cochlear nucleus, inferior colliculus, and the medial geniculate body (Kettner & Thompson 1982).

Berthier & Moore (1983) characterized motoneurons that innervate the retractor bulbi muscles (Gray et al 1980, 1981). The expected training-correlated differences in unit recordings from abducens motoneurons, which constitute one final common pathway for both CR and UCR, were reported by Cegvaske et al (1979). Nonetheless, for a number of reasons it is unlikely that these cells are primary storage sites. During conditioning of the left NMR, bilateral conditioned eyelid responses develop, and, although all three responses are highly correlated, they can occur independently of one another. This implies that their respective motor nuclei are not strongly coupled, so the correlation must derive from a common source of synaptic input to these distinct nuclei (McCormick et al 1982a), a source that is changed by associative training. The occurrence of lesions that are selective for the CR, but spare the UCR, also may indicate that the changes cannot be occurring in the motor neurons. But both arguments are valid only if motoneuron changes are hypothesized to be general postsynaptic changes in excitability, an assumption not easily justified. In any event, it is clear that a host of neural correlates of the CR can be detected at considerably more central sites. Since these would indicate changes occurring much earlier in the pathway(s), attention has understandably been focused on these sites.

Which areas are involved? Discrete, unilateral lesions of cerebellum (McCormick et al 1982b, Yeo et al 1982, Glickstein et al 1983) and regions of the pons (Lavond et al 1981, Desmond & Moore 1982) completely eliminate previously learned, ipsilateral CRs, without affecting contralateral CRs or UCRs. Red nucleus lesions also selectively disrupt contralateral CRs (Rosenfeld & Moore 1983). The initial report of brainstem/cerebellar lesions selectively disrupting ipsilateral CRs (Desmond & Moore 1982) included damage to dorsolateral pontine, superior cerebellar peduncle, and reticular system regions (supratrigeminal). Subsequent results indicated the damage to cerebellar peduncle (McCormick et al 1982c) and supratrigeminal areas (Desmond & Moore 1983) to have been particularly important. Quite interestingly, lesions that abolish retained ipsilateral CRs, or prevent their acquisition in the naive animal, do not interfere with the positive transfer that occurs to the contralateral eye (Desmond & Moore 1982).

While the importance of these general areas is well documented, which specific sites within some of these areas are important is still unclear. For example, some disagreement exists as to which areas of the cerebellum are critical. Lincoln et al (1982) and McCormick & Thompson (1983), as well as Yeo et al (1982), report that lesions of dentate and interpositus nuclei abolish the learned eyeblink. Axons from these deep cerebellar nuclei project to red nuclei via superior cerebellar peduncle, and, as previously noted, lesions of either site disrupt CRs. However, McCormick & Thompson (1983) further report that massive aspirations of cerebellar cortex as well as other deep nuclear regions fail to abolish CRs. Yet Yeo et al (unpublished results cited in Moore 1984) evidently described a small portion of hemisphere lobus simplex of cerebellar cortex that is necessary for the CR.

The dentate-interpositus (D-I) lesion results were only partially confirmed in McCormick & Thompson's (1983) report that 20 of 54 neurons within D-I nuclei, recorded chronically over the course of long-term training, showed activity related to performance of the CR. The neuronal correlates are evidently not as tightly tied to the CR as CA1-CA3 hippocampal correlates are. While some units responded well in advance (~40–60 msec) of the initiation of the CR, others responded after its initiation. Further, the degree to which the training correlates in unit activity were pairing specific was not reported.

Thompson and colleagues proposed that the dentate-interpositus nuclei play causal roles in acquisition and storage of information involved in the conditioned eyeblink response. This information is thought to be relayed through branchium conjunctivum to red nucleus and ultimately to abducens and accessory abducens neurons. The issue is by no means resolved, however. Desmond et al (1983) note the possibility that primary sites of change might lie within a supratrigeminal region, which then projects to cerebellum. As McCormick & Thompson (1983) also point out, the changes observed in D-I may be postsynaptic to those occurring elsewhere: possible sites include inferior olive, and lobus simplex in the cerebellar cortex. As yet no experiment directly discriminates among these possibilities.

Conditioned Facial Movements and Motor Cortex Plasticity

In the cat, three different facial movements can be conditioned to auditory CSs such as a click or hiss. Woody and colleagues (see Woody 1982, 1984 for review) recorded long-term excitability changes in sensorimotor cortical neurons following Pavlovian conditioning (Brons & Woody 1980). These neurons project polysynaptically to the facial musculature, and presumably play an important role in mediating the conditioned responses.

In the short latency (20–50 ms) eyeblink CR, mediated primarily by orbicularis oculi muscles and produced by pairing a click with a glabella tap (Woody & Engel 1972, Woody & Black-Cleworth 1973), successful conditioning depends upon a functional rostral cortex. KCl-produced spreading depression reversibly eliminates the CR, but spares the UCR to glabella tap (Woody & Brozek 1969a) in the previously trained animal. Lesions of cortex in naive animals prevent CR development but have little effect upon the UCR (Woody et al 1974). It is the short latency eyeblink CR that is selectively abolished; long latency CRs can still occur (Norman et al 1977).

Increases in the incidence and excitability of cortical neurons, which project to facial nuclei, correlate with conditioning (Woody & Engel 1972, Woody & Black-Cleworth 1973). Auditory-evoked unit activity, recorded from pyramidal tract neurons projecting to the target facial musculature (Woody et al 1970), is enhanced following conditioning (Woody et al 1976a, Brons & Woody 1980). In the original report of this effect (Woody et al 1976a), it was somewhat unclear whether the increases were pairing specific. Although click-evoked activity was greater for paired vs untreated control animals, it did not appear that evoked activity was greater for paired vs random control animals. This resulted, in large part, from a significant enhancement of baseline activity for the random control animals. Subsequently, a thorough and painstaking survey of conditioning-correlated changes in cortical neurons (Brons & Woody 1980) clarified matters. Cortical neurons that project to CR musculature from conditioned (CS-UCS pairings) cats exhibited significantly lower thresholds, for activation by intracellular current injections, than did those of animals receiving CS-alone (habituation) training. Threshold current values were also significantly lower for conditioned animals, when compared against the pooled results of animals currently receiving UCS-alone presentations and animals previously (3–28 days ago) exposed to UCS-alone trials. However, the comparison of paired vs UCS-alone animals was not significant, partly because recordings of neural excitability were conducted at relatively short retention intervals, during the time that the UCS exerted its most profound and transient effect upon excitability. When long-term retention (2–38 days post-training) results were compared, cells from CS-UCS animals were significantly more excitable than those from UCS-alone animals. Finally, excitability changes were not different for conditioned vs extinction animals, which implies that the excitability changes in the latter persisted after the CR disappeared.

It is clear from these results that the major differences between CS-UCS and UCS-alone treatments emerged during retention. Neurons from conditioned animals were more excitable, and these changes persisted for a longer time (weeks), than those from animals exposed to UCS-alone presentations. However, UCS-alone presentations exerted a profound effect and accounted for ~60% of the CS-UCS vs CS-alone difference.

Woody (1984) argued that both the pairing-specific and the UCS-alone induced changes in excitability arise from changes in membrane conductances intrinsic to the cortical neurons. Attempts were made to simulate the presumed pattern of convergent activity upon the cortical neurons that would occur during training and these attempts revealed conditioning-like changes in input resistance. In one such study (Woody et al 1976b), cortical neurons were exposed to one of five treatments: (a) ACh and current-induced discharge, (b) ACh and weak depolarization (insufficient to discharge the cell), (c) ACh alone, (d) saline and discharge, (e) discharge alone. ACh alone caused a transient (~3 min) decrease of g_m. Pairing ACh with weak depolarization prolonged the effect somewhat (~8 min). However, pairing ACh with strong depolarization resulted in a cumulative and persistent (~10 min) decrease in g_m. Similar changes could also be produced by substituting intracellular injection of cGMP for extracellular iontophoresis of ACh (Woody et al 1978). Cells exposed to strong depolarization and cGMP exhibited a persistent (~9 min) decrease in g_m, while cells exposed to cGMP alone exhibited only a transient decrease in g_m. Cells exposed to depolarization alone, or 5'-GMP were essentially unchanged. Once established, the decreased g_m resulting from cGMP and depolarization was very resistent to disruption. In more recent work (Woody et al 1983), the effects of depolarization and cGMP could be simulated (namely, decreased g_m) by substituting calcium calmodulin-dependent protein kinase b for cGMP. Presumably, the large depolarization induced Ca^{2+} influx, thus activating the kinase. Exactly which conductances are changed by any of these treatments is not known, though Krnjevic et al (1971) presented evidence that ACh/cGMP reduces a late outward K^+ current in other pyramidal tract cortical neurons.

Red Nucleus and Paw-Flexion Conditioning in Cat

Tsukahara (1978, 1982) and colleagues capitalized upon the remarkable synaptic plasticity of the red nucleus in their attempts to reconstruct classical conditioning of cats' paw-flexion response to shock. This line of research is exceptionally interesting given the demonstration that red nucleus (RN) afferents sprout in response to nervous system damage (denervation) (Tsukahara et al 1975, Murakami et al 1977a,b)—by definition an unlikely stimulus to occasion cellular plasticity in normal, adult brain—as well as in response to cross-innervation of forelimb flexor and extensor nerves, a less drastic physiological intervention (Tsukahara & Fujito 1976, Fujito et al 1982, Tsukahara et al 1982).

Red nucleus plays a key role in motor control. Morphological studies reveal two major subdivisions in mammals, the rostral parvocellular portion and the caudal magnocellular portion, both of which give rise to the rubrospinal tract. The synaptic organization of RN (see Allen & Tsukahara 1974 for review) has also been well characterized. Two important sources of input are afferents from contralateral cerebellar interpositus nucleus (IP), which synapse on the somas of RN neurons, and impulses arising from ipsilateral sensorimotor cortex, which synapse on the apical dendrites of the RN cells via the collaterals of pyramidal tract fibers. Parvocellular RN neurons, in turn, send axons to inferior olive, which provides feedback to cerebellum. Collaterals also project to the spinal cord via the rubrospinal tract. Intracellular recordings from RN neurons in the anesthetized cat reveal relatively large, fast EPSPs following stimulation of IP (which reflects the close electrotonic distance of synapses to the recording site) and small, slow EPSPs arising from stimulation of cortical fibers at the level of the cerebral peduncle (CP) (which reflects the considerably greater electronic distance between distal dendrite synapses and the recording site).

In the kitten, considerable reorganization of input to RN is occasioned by ipsilateral cortical lesions, as evidenced by electrophysiological recordings of enhanced EPSPs from contralateral sensory motor cortex, contralateral IP, and ipsilateral IP (see Tsukahara 1981). For example, ipsilateral cortical lesions give rise to distinct slow-rising components, superimposed upon the fast EPSP, which are evoked by contralateral IP stimulation. Latency measurements and a lack of strong voltage sensitivity for the slow component led Tsukahara and colleagues to infer the sprouting of contralateral IP synapses upon newly vacated regions of distal dendrites. Conversely, contralateral IP lesions lead to the appearance of large, fast EPSPs evoked by ipsilateral CP stimulation, which implies sprouting of CP terminals upon somatic and/or more proximal dendritic areas of membrane. Electron microscopic studies corroborate to some extent the inferences drawn from the electrophysiology (Nakamura et al 1974).

Similar experiments conducted in the adult cat indicate that, although plasticity is considerably reduced relative to young animals, lesion-induced changes in the time course of EPSPs can be detected (Tsukahara et al 1975). The major experimental finding in the adult cat has been the observation of a decrease in the peak rise time of EPSPs induced by cortical (or corticorubral pathway) stimulation, following lesion of contralateral IP. This was attributed to the sprouting of corticorubral synapses upon more proximal somatic/dendritic membrane areas. To assess the alternative possibility, that general changes in the cable properties of the dendritic tree might account for the decreased rise time, electrotonic time constants for denervated and intact preparations were compared (Fujito et al 1982). The small, nonsignificant difference observed was incapable of accounting for more than approximately 5% of the decrease in rise time (Fujito et al 1982). The possibility of denervation-induced supersensitivity for remaining afferent transmitters was unlikely since, although such a mechanism would predict the observed amplitude increases, it would not easily predict the decreased rise time. Changes in presynaptic release mechanisms might, however; this possibility has not yet been addressed.

Sprouting can occur in the adult cat by considerably less drastic intervention, as demonstrated by enhanced rise times of CP-produced EPSPs in RN cells from cats exposed to peripheral cross-innervation surgery, some 2–6 months previously (Fujito et al 1982, Tsukahara et al 1982). Forelimb muscles were cross-innervated by (a) severing the musculocutaneous, median, radial, and ulnar nerves; (b) suturing central radial nerve stumps to peripheral stumps of the other nerves (extensor nerve-to-flexor muscle); and (c) complementarily suturing peripheral radial nerve stumps to central stumps of median, radial, and ulnar nerves (flexor nerves-to-extensor muscle). Successful cross-innervation was subsequently verified. Successful compensation was apparent for some behaviors (e.g. "food catching") but not others (locomotion), presumably indicative of the fact that not all sources of central innervation are equally plastic.

Two to six months after surgery, the rise time of cortical-rubral EPSPs evoked by cerebral penduncle (CP) stimulation was significantly shorter (1.0 ± 0.9 msec, $n=160$ vs 3.6 ± 1.4 msec, $n=100$) than that of normal cats. RN cells from cats measured less than two months after surgery showed a slight, though nonsignificant, decrease in rise time (2.7 ± 1.0 msec, $n=53$). The decreased rise time for cross-innervated cats was attributed to the proportionately greater contribution of a fast component to the PSP, presumably because remote (CP) synapses sprouted into more proximal areas of membrane. Consistent with this speculation was the observation of substantial differences in the voltage sensitivity of fast vs slow components of the EPSP. The fast-rising component increased in size, with electrotonic hyperpolarization, while the slow component remains unchanged. This presumably reflected a shorter electrical distance for fast-component synapses.

The potential relevance of red nucleus in general and sprouting in particular as specific mechanisms underlying learning is enhanced by the recent attempts of Tsukahara and colleagues to link RN plasticity to classical conditioning of the paw-flexion response (Tsukahara et al 1981). Note here should also be made of Smith's (1970) earlier demonstration that rubral lesions abolish tone-conditioned forelimb-flexion responses in the cat. In current work, the paradigm involves the use of central CP electrical stimulation as the CS, and cutaneous paw shock as the UCS. Restriction of stimulation to the cerebral peduncle—red nucleus distal synapses was maximized by severing the CP caudal to the RN. It is not clear which modality of sensory information in the intact animal CP stimulation was supposed to have simulated; presumably somatosensory, perhaps auditory. Future demonstrations of paw-flexion conditioning with intact cats may clarify the nature of the signal conveyed by CS pathways to RN. Flexion responses were measured by potentiometric measures of joint movement, as well as by EMG recordings from biceps and triceps brachii muscles.

Repeated forward CS-UCS pairings (120 per day; ITI = 30 sec; ISI = 100 msec) gradually increased the probability of a flexion response occurring to the CP (CS) stimulation. Comparable decreases in threshold current values of CP stimulation, which were required to elicit a response 100% of the time, were also observed to occur in parallel with training. Average results from ten cats indicated that conditioning peaked on the ninth day. At this time the behavioral measures and threshold current values were significantly different from day 1 of training. Repeated CS-alone trials, delivered on subsequent days, eliminated these changes. The results of a small number of control animals revealed no changes in a random CS-UCS protocol ($n = 2$), or a UCS-alone procedure ($n=1$). This preliminary demonstration of pairing specificity was interpreted as indicative of successful classical conditioning. Further, the fact that current values decreased for CP stimulation, in the expected manner, but did not change for contralateral interpositus stimulation was taken as evidence for localization of changes to the corticorubral (CP-RN synapses) pathways.

Subsequent experiments involving extracellular unit recordings from RN neurons in awake cats during classical conditioning (Oda et al 1981) revealed significantly greater CS-evoked activity for paired vs control cells (1 extinguished, 1 untreated, 1 random control animal). Similar experiments conducted after successful classical conditioning (Tsukahara et al 1981) revealed the appearance of a fast-rising component superimposed upon the corticorubral dendritic EPSPs. Intracellular recordings from anesthetized cats, on the eighth day of training, indicated a modal rise time of 1–2 msec for RN cells from paired animals in response to CP (CS) stimulation, while that for cells from untreated animals was 2.5–3.5 msec. The means were significantly different; no results were reported for other more exacting control conditions. The most straightforward interpretation of these results is to assume, as Tsukahara and colleagues have, that as a result of conditioning, the corticorubral fibers sprouted to form new functional synapses on the proximal portion of the soma. Other possibilities remain, however, and Tsukahara and colleagues are careful to draw attention to them. Changes in dendritic spine morphology at the distal cortical-rubral synpases cannot be excluded, and spine shortening might be expected to decrease the electrotonic length constant. Many of the same mechanisms proposed to underly hippocampal LTP are plausible candidates here as well (see the section on hippocampal LTP). Indeed, Katsumaru et al (1982) report the presence of actin in dendritic spines of RN neurons, raising the possibility of spine morphology changes. The definitive experiment demonstrating, by means of ultrastructural techniques, sprouting induced by classical conditioning has not yet been reported. Thus the evidence that sprouting occurs is still indirect. Nonetheless, careful and painstaking research will no doubt continue to clarify the mechanisms underlying RN plasticity.

As previously noted, with the exception of the EM observations confirming the presence of cortical-rubral synapses upon somatic membrane following IP lesions in the kitten (Nakamura et al 1974), the evidence for sprouting derives exclusively from intracellularly recorded changes in EPSP amplitude and rise time, bolstered by an impressive mathematical model of the cable properties of the dendritic tree (Sato & Tsukahara 1976). Whether such evidence should be regarded as definitive depends to a large degree upon the plausibility of the alternative hypotheses. Generalized increases in somatic excitability (g_m decreases, depolarization, etc) have been shown to be very unlikely, as has denervation-induced supersensitivity. Changes in presynaptic release have not been addressed. This is potentially important since partial denervation can induce compensatory release from synapses in some systems (e.g. Stricker & Zigmond 1976). Localized and remote changes in postsynaptic membrane conductances are exceedingly difficult either to confirm or deny with present techniques. Measurements of electrotonic length based upon somatic injection of current would not be expected to be a sensitive index of remote changes, especially if these are restricted to relatively small and/or specific areas of dendritic membrane (spines). Such measurements reflect the lumped RC properties of the entire soma and dendritic tree, and changes in a relatively small proportion of that area might well be swamped by the lack of change in the relatively greater area. However, such changes, for example a decreased K^+ conductance, if they did occur, might produce detectable differences in voltage recordings obtained from the soma, if the soma comprised a low resistance pathway for synaptic currents relative to the remaining dendritic area.

Cardiac Conditioning in the Pigeon: Changes in Geniculate Neurons

Visually cued cardiac conditioning in the pigeon (Cohen 1982, 1984), which involves the emergence of conditioned tachycardia to a light paired with foot shock, illustrates the interaction of associative- and nonassociative-learning processes well. Prior to light-shock pairings, light presentations evoke heart rate increases, which thereafter decline within 10 trials or so if light-shock pairings do not occur. Systematic pairings of light and shock increase the probability of heart rate change (Cohen 1974). Recordings from vagal and sympathetic cardiac motoneurons during conditioning reveal that the light-evoked discharge frequency of the postganglionic sympathetics increases in probability and magnitude, while that of the vagal's is a complementary reduction in discharge rates. The latency of the post ganglionic sympathetic response is 100 msec, and the duration of their phasic response is 300–400 msec (Cohen 1980). Thus, the sympathetic response to light is finished about 500–600 msec after light onset. Interestingly enough, conditioned tachycardia does not appear until ~1 sec after light onset, and persists for 4–5 sec. Evidently, considerable delay and duration enhancement occur at the periphery, the mechanisms of which are unclear. It is worth noting that, while conditioning enhances the frequency of sympathetics' discharge evoked by light, the latency of the response (~100 msec) is unchanged. Thus, this component of the conditioned behavioral change appears to fall into the category of "alpha-conditioning." It reflects an enhancement of the unconditioned response to light.

Although training-correlated differences exist at the level of the motoneurons, it is difficult to know whether such differences reflect training-induced changes local to this area, or changes occurring considerably earlier in the visual pathways. The combined results of lesion experiments and unit recording data indicate that visual information from the retinal ganglionic cells diverges along three pathways: thalamofugal, tectofugal, and pretectofugal. Lesions of any single pathway are insufficient to produce any persistent conditioned response deficit, although combined lesions of all three pathways abolish the CR (Cohen 1982).

Additional experiments indicate that training-produced changes can be detected during the course of conditioning in certain classes of neurons in at least two relatively peripheral nuclei within the visual system: the principal optic nucleus and the nucleus rotundus. Principal optic nucleus neurons are especially interesting. Prior to training, approximately 70% of these cells show an initial increased phasic discharge triggered by light (Type I), while the remaining 30% show a decrease (Type II). Associative training progressively enhances the light-evoked discharge in Type I cells, whose response latencies make them good candidates for eventual projection to the cardiac sympathetics. Type II neurons, on the other hand, fail to "habituate" with associative training; that is, their response is primarily one of maintained light-evoked decreases in discharge frequency.

Further categorization of geniculate neurons on the basis of their response to the UCS indicates that only neurons whose initial response to shock is inhibitory (and whose response to light is excitatory) show increased light-evoked discharges that are pairing specific (Gibbs et al 1981). At least one source of UCS input to geniculate neurons may be the locus coeruleus (Cohen et al 1982), and the input may be either excitatory (Type I), inhibitory (Type II), or possibly both. Assessing the precise causal role of the geniculate neurons is difficult, however. Bilateral lesions of locus coeruleus fail to abolish establishment of the conditioned response, which indicates that (a) locus coeruleus is not necessary for mediating the shocks' effects, (b) geniculate neurons are not necessary, or (c) possilbly both of the above. Similarly, pairing light with electrical stimulation of the locus coeruleus (Gibbs et al 1983) is sufficient to produce enhanced light-evoked discharges in geniculate neurons but is insufficient to support a behavioral change. The relative contribution of geniculate Type I/Type II neurons to light-evoked synaptic input in either the vagal or sympathetic cardiac motoneurons is unknown, making it difficult to determine whether changes in the geniculate neurons—by themselves—could substantially affect the motoneurons' responses to light. Indeed, the working model favored by Cohen and associates is that conditioning-induced changes are distributed among the three central visual pathways, and further that within any single pathway a serial amplification may be occurring.

NEURAL MODELS AND ANALOGS OF CONDITIONING, LEARNING, AND MEMORY

Hippocampal LTP

Long-term potentiation (LTP) of synaptic transmission in the hippocampus was first demonstrated in vivo by Bliss and colleagues (Bliss & Lomo 1973, Bliss & Gardner-Medwin 1971, 1973) and in vitro in hippocampal slices by Schwartz-kroin & Wester (1975) and Alger & Teyler (1976). Space limitations and the tremendous explosion of research on LTP mechanisms precludes any comprehensive treatment of the topic. The interested reader is referred to a number of excellent reviews of this work (Andersen et al 1980, Swanson et al 1982, Eccles 1983). Following a brief characterization of the properties of LTP, we summarize research implicating the site of LTP and the essential involvement of intracellular Ca^{2+} accumulation within the dendrites and soma of the postsynaptic cell.

Prolonged tetanization of the major synaptic afferents to the dentate gyrus, CA1, or CA3 cell regions of hippocampus is generally sufficient to produce an extraordinarily persistent synaptic facilitation, which is initiated in about 10–20 sec, peaks in a few minutes, and in some cases may persist for many days (cf Swanson et al 1982, Bliss & Lomo 1973, McNaughton 1983 for summaries). Synaptic facilitation is typically measured in vivo, and commonly in vitro as well, by recording extracellularly the population EPSP generated by stimulation of the presynaptic pathway. Additionally, extracellular recordings of the population spike, and more recently intracellular recording of PSPs in the in vitro preparations, have also been used.

As initially summarized by Bliss & Lomo (1973), and Andersen et al (1980), LTP might arise from (a) an increase in the afferent volley; (b) enhanced release of transmitter (i.e. glutamate); (c) other changes in synaptic input from local circuit neurons; (d) general increases in postsynaptic membrane excitability (decreased g_m in soma, changes in cable properties of dendrites, etc); and (e) more restricted changes in the postsynaptic membrane, such as greater receptor density, sensitivity, cooperativity, or changes in the integrative properties of the dendrites. Although the issue is by no means entirely settled, and there is no reason to assume that these mechanisms are mutually exclusive, the bulk of the available evidence indicates that changes in presynaptic release or more restricted changes in postsynaptic excitability are the most likely mechanisms (see also Teyler et al 1982).

The hypothesis that increased afferent volleys account for LTP has great difficulty explaining the failure to find enhanced field potentials from presynaptic regions during LTP (Andersen et al 1977), as well as the failure of LTP to occur under conditions that reduce synaptic release (Dunwiddie & Lynch 1979, Andersen et al 1980) or disrupt transmission by a block of glutamate postsynaptic receptors, presumably without affecting release (Dunwiddie et al 1978). Similar difficulties are encountered by the suggestion that LTP reflects general changes in soma excitability. Antidromic stimulation of axons of the postsynaptic cells fails to reveal the expected increases in field potentials recorded in the soma region during LTP (Bliss & Lomo 1973), and no pronounced changes in g_m or resting potential have been found (Dudek et al 1976, Andersen et al 1977). However, it should be noted that recent evidence indicates two distinguishable components of LTP, which do not co-vary perfectly and which therefore may reflect different sites of localization and perhaps underlying mechanisms. Population EPSP indices of LTP can occur in the absence of a population spike increase (Bliss & Lomo 1973), and vice versa (Bliss et al 1982). There exist some data consistent with the hypothesis that paralleling the development of LTP is a depression of inhibitory synaptic input, from other nonstimulated pathways (Yamamato & Chujo 1978).

A number of investigators consider LTP to reflect primarily postsynaptic changes, initiated by increased intracellular Ca^{2+} levels (Eccles 1983, Lynch & Baudry 1984). Lynch et al (1983a) proposed that tetanizing stimulation increases intracellular Ca^{2+}, primarily though intracellular release (Browning et al 1982). Calcium is hypothesized to activate a membrane-associated proteinase (Calpain I; Murachi 1983), which in turn is responsible for proteolysis of a membrane protein (fodrin), unmasking glutamate receptors. Eccles (1983) presents a similar hypothesis, but views Ca^{2+} levels as arising primarily from transmembrane flux, and the initial biochemical step as involving the complexing of Ca^{2+} and calmodulin (rather than αPDH). Eccles further supposes that, in addition to activating or exposing glutamate receptors (Baudry & Lynch 1979, 1980), Ca^{2+} may have other more persistent effects: (a) Ca^{2+}-calmodulin (CaM) mediated enhancement of protein (receptor?) transport into dendrites, via a microtubule system; (b) Ca^{2+}-CaM mediated protein synthesis in dendritic polyribosomes, which Steward and colleagues (Steward & Levy 1982, Steward & Fass 1983, Steward 1984) suggest may underlie the ultrastructural changes observed at potentiated synapses (van Harreveld & Fifkova 1975, Fifkova & van Harreveld 1977, Desmond & Levy 1983); and (c) changes in protein metabolism (e.g. Duffy et al 1981; see also Shashoua & Teyler 1982).

There are four major lines of evidence strongly arguing that LTP arises from postsynaptic changes. Glutamate-binding blockade by a glutamate receptor antagonist (AFB) prevents LTP, which indicates that ligand interaction with the postsynaptic receptors is crucial (Dunwiddie et al 1978). Small, but reliable, changes in postsynaptic spine density morphology occur during stimulation conditions that would be expected to (Fifkova & van Harreveld 1977, Fifkova et al 1982), or that demonstrably do (Desmond & Levy 1983), induce LTP. Increased glutamate binding follows LTP induction (Baudry et al 1980).

Injection of a calcium chelator (EGTA) into postsynaptic membrane prevents LTP (Lynch et al 1983b).

Interpretation of the AFB results depends critically upon how specific AFB's actions are to postsynaptic membrane. If autoreceptors exist upon presynaptic elements—a speculation for which there is no evidence but one not entirely unlikely—glutamate-initiated changes in presynaptic elements would also be blocked. A similar ambiguity arises in the interpretation of increased glutamate-receptor binding, since it is difficult to know for sure that the increased numbers reflect the postsynaptic spine density pool. The EGTA results are also somewhat difficult to interpret. It is unclear where EGTA's calcium buffering actions occur: at the dendrites, soma, or perhaps even outside the cell (as a result of leakage). Secondly, it is unclear whether EGTA's block of LTP was accomplished by interference with Ca^{2+}-mediated processes *specific* for LTP. EGTA's effects may have been quite widespread and interfered with a host of Ca^{2+}-mediated functions necessary for normal physiological functioning, independent of LTP. Another line of evidence that is, at first glance, inconsistent with the LTP-induced increase in glutamate binding involves the failure to find enhanced responses to iontophoretically applied glutamate during the time that hippocampal cells exhibit LTP, using electrical stimulation of the afferents as the test assay (Turner et al 1982, Taube & Schwartzkroin 1983). It is possible, however, that these results are to be explained by the preferential activation of extrasynaptic glutamate receptors by iontophoresis. Baudry & Lynch (1983a) have, in fact, distinguished between extrasynaptic amino acid receptors that undergo a depression in response to applied glutamate, and a class that do not, which would presumably be those at synapses exhibiting potentiation.

Another unresolved issue is worth noting. It has been reported that postsynaptic discharge is not a necessary condition for LTP. Reducing or blocking the population spike, through inhibition mediated by pathways other than the primary one, does not prevent LTP (McNaughton et al 1978, Douglas et al 1982). Wigstrom et al (1982) also obtained LTP in CA1 cells that had been hyperpolarized sufficiently to prevent discharge and also to increase the subsynaptic membrane potential, as indicated by enhancement of EPSP amplitude. By analogy with the known voltage dependency of Ca^{2+} channels in other systems (Hagiwara & Byerly 1981), one might expect the latter treatment to have sufficiently precluded activation of voltage-dependent Ca^{2+} channels. Thus, if one chooses to explain the previous results in terms of stimulation-induced increases in intracellular Ca^{2+}, due to activation of a voltage-dependent Ca^{2+} flux, it remains to be demonstrated that Ca^{2+} channels are indeed activated at those levels of membrane potential.

The number of glutamate-binding sites in purified hippocampal membranes (Baudry & Lynch 1979) increases in response to low (10 μM) levels of Ca^{2+}.

This evidence is consistent with the role of Ca^{2+} in cytoskeletal and transmitter-binding changes accompanying LTP. In the isolated tissue studies, these effects persist long after Ca^{2+} has been washed from the incubation medium. This is not the case for receptor-binding studies from potentiated slices, however, in which the enhanced binding persists for ~30 min following potentiation induction and is reversible (Baudry et al 1980). The evidence that these effects are mediated by the calcium-activated proteinase Calpain is that inhibitors of this proteinase block the Ca^{2+}-induced increase in glutamate binding. In the case of leupeptin, the block is specific to Ca^{2+}-stimulated increases in glutamate binding and without effect upon basal levels. Interestingly, calmodulin has been reported in relatively high concentrations in postsynaptic densities (Grab et al 1980).

The major alternative to the hypothesis that the LTP changes occur in the dendrites is that they occur at the presynaptic terminals. This hypothesis is supported by the finding of increased resting and evoked release of glutamate following LTP (Skrede & Malthe-Sorenssen 1981, Dolphin et al 1982). However, as was the case for the receptor-binding studies taken as evidence for postsynaptic changes, it is not known from which synapses the enhanced levels of transmitter arise. Voronin (1983) and colleagues performed a quantal analysis upon LTP septo-hippocampal synapses. They concluded that the results are best explained by assuming an increase in the number of quanta released per presynaptic spike. This interpretation is not the only one, however, as Voronin notes.

Any decisive resolution of the these issues would appear to rest upon the ability to assay directly and manipulate—by electrophysiological or biochemical means—local Ca^{2+} concentrations at the putative sites of synaptic plasticity, a formidable technical problem in the case of spines.

Finally, mention should be made of the quite interesting recent demonstrations of associative LTP (Levy & Steward 1979, 1983, Barrionuevo & Brown 1984). It has always been rather unclear as to what kinds of information storage and what kinds of behavioral change might best be subserved by homosynaptic LTP. These recent demonstrations confer considerably greater credibility upon the suggestion that hippocampal LTP may be a quite general mechanism by which associative learning occurs. So too does the recent demonstration by Berger (1984) that induction of LTP facilitates the acquisition of conditioned NMR in the rabbit.

Long-lasting Excitability Changes and Heterosynaptic Interactions in Sympathetic Ganglia

PERSISTENT HOMOSYNAPTIC SLOW POSTSYNAPTIC POTENTIALS   Mammalian and amphibian ganglia provide interesting systems in which three distinct varieties of persistent neuronal responses, induced by homosynaptic inputs, have been described (Kuba & Koketsu 1978a, Libet 1979a, 1984, Weight 1983). In addition, a novel form of heterosynaptic interaction has been described for the mammalian preparations, in which dopamine—acting through the D1 dopaminergic receptor—selectively potentiates the muscarinic-cholinergic EPSP (Libet et al 1975, Libet & Tosaka 1970). These slow PSPs occur on time scales of seconds to minutes, and the DA modulation may persist for hours. Both are amenable to analysis with intracellular recording and voltage-clamp techniques.

The first class of long-lasting, slow synaptic response in the mammalian preparations is a slow cholinergic EPSP, mediated by a muscarinic receptor and blocked by atropine and QNB; it occurs with a synaptic delay of 100–300 msec and persists for up to 100 sec. A slow IPSP, thought to be mediated by dopaminergic interneurons (Eccles & Libet 1961, Libet 1970), has similar temporal characteristics. More persistent examples of synaptically induced changes in neuronal excitability are provided by the "extremely slow" (ss) EPSP (Nishi & Koketsu 1968a), thought to be mediated by a peptide related to substance P in the mammalian preparations or by luteinizing-hormone-releasing (LHRH) in amphibians (Jan et al 1980, Jan & Jan 1982). Synaptic delays for this response are on the order of 1 sec, durations are 20–30 min, if not longer, and the ssEPSP may reach a peak amplitude of 25–50% of the size of the cell's action potential. Current evidence appears to indicate that all three responses occur in the same class of postganglionic cells in the mammalian preparations (Libet & Tosaka 1969) and indirect evidence indicates the ssEPSP may converge as well (Ashe & Libet 1981a). In bullfrog ganglia, greater functional separation has been documented. The ssEPSP is elicited in all cells, B and C. The sEPSP is found in B cells (innervated by the fast B fibers); while C cells (innervated by slow C fibers) exhibit the sIPSP (Tosaka et al 1968).

The functional significance of the first two slow synaptic responses (sEPSP and sIPSP) presumably lies in the extended temporal domain for synaptic integration that they confer upon the postganglionics, chiefly through their effect upon membrane potential. Indeed, it has been repeatedly asserted that under normal physiological conditions, for the mammalian preparations, these two slow PSPs are not accompanied by any detectable changes in membrane conductance (g_m) (Kobayashi & Libet 1968, 1970, Hashiguchi et al 1978, 1982). This implies that the slow PSPs are not generated in a conventional pharmacological manner: opening or closing of ionic channels induced by the receptor-ligand complex. Instead, it has been suggested that the slow PSPs in mammalian ganglia arise from electrogenic pump fluxes (Libet 1984).

As previously noted, neither the sEPSP nor the sIPSP seem to be accompanied by consistent or large changes in g_m under normal physiological conditions. In the case of the sEPSP, the change in membrane potential may arise from the coupling of the muscarinic receptor to cyclic GMP levels (McAfee &

Greengard 1972, Greengard 1976). Consistent with this are the observations that cGMP levels rise in sympathetic ganglia when exposed to ACh or the muscarinic agonist MCh (Kebabian et al 1975). Moreover, bath application of the membrane-soluble (dibutyryl ester) forms of cGMP mimic the steady depolarization induced by ACh, MCh, or preganglionic stimulation (Hashiguchi et al 1978), and, at least for 100-μM concentrations or less, fail to produce detectable conductance changes. These concentrations (25–100 μM) can increase g_m, but only if the membrane is allowed to depolarize and thereby secondarily induce an increase in g_k. Ten-fold higher concentrations regularly produce an increase in g_m, regarded as a nonspecific effect of the nucleotide, since it is also produced by cAMP.

On the other hand, a decrease in g_m is observed during the response to ACh, or during the sEPSP, when membrane potentials are depolarized to less than -60 mV. The decrease in g_m was initially explained as a muscarinic-cholinergic suppression of the increased g_k in depolarized cells (Hashiguchi et al 1978). The class of voltage-dependent K^+ channels closed by muscarine was subsequently characterized by Brown & Adams (1980), who termed it the "M" channel. Thus, while depolarization of the cell may itself increase g_m, which may interact with muscarinic agonists to decrease g_m, the primary effect of depolarization of the cell by cGMP (or ACh) does not appear to arise from closure of the M channels, since these are normally already closed at the resting potential of the cell. Exactly how cGMP levels are supposed to effect changes in membrane potential and by which species of electrogenic pump is still unclear.

The available evidence points rather conclusively to a major role for dopamine in the mediation of the mammalian sIPSP (see Kuba & Koketsu 1978a, Libet 1979b, Ashe & Libet 1982 for reviews). Dopamine (DA) is present in interneurons (SIF cells) presynaptic to the principal sympathetic neurons, and is released from these cells by preganglionic stimulation (Libet & Owman 1974). Application of DA to the postsynaptic neurons mimics the hyperpolarization and general absence of g_m changes accompanying the orthodromically evoked sIPSP (Kobayashi & Libet 1970, Libet 1970). Under suitable conditions, antagonists for the α_2-adrenergic receptor [phenoxybenzamine (PBX) and Yohimbine], which is stimulated by DA, selectively depress or abolish the sIPSP (Ashe & Libet 1982). It should be noted, however, that Cole & Shinnick-Gallagher (1984) report that the sIPSP in rabbit derives from ACh's monosynaptic activation of muscarinic receptors, mediated by an increased potassium conductance. Iontophoretically applied ACh hyperpolarized the sympathetics, at a time when a zero Ca^{2+}/EGTA medium had abolished the orthodromically evoked sIPSP. With continued exposure to the medium, the response to ACh also diminished, however, which these investigators interpreted as implicating a calcium-activated K^+ current (I_C). Other evidence suggesting that the ionic basis of the sIPSP involves increases in a K^+ conductance is reviewed in Weight (1983), and a similar case was made for amphibian sympathetic sIPSPs (Horn & Dodd 1981, Dodd & Horn 1983).

That cAMP is involved in the production of the dopamine-induced sIPSP in mammalian sympathetic ganglion was initially suggested by Greengard (1976) and McAfee & Greengard (1972) for amphibian preparations. Consistent with this suggestion were the observations, in a host of mammalian superior cervical ganglion preparations (see Libet 1979b for review), that cAMP levels were increased by bath application of dopamine and, further, that stimulation of the preganglionics also led to cAMP increases in rabbit, rat, and cat. To be sure, the increases occasioned by bath-applied dopamine were small (15%) in rabbit (Kalix et al 1974) and cat, perhaps because these preparations have greater diffusion barriers to exogenous dopamine. More recent experiments (Mochida 1982, Mochida et al 1981) in the rabbit with the COMT blocker U-0521 produced larger and more consistent cAMP increases. Similar interpretative ambiguities concern those instances in which the "expected" hyperpolarizing effects of dopamine were observed, but no detectable changes in cAMP content were found (Lindl & Cramer 1975). The electrophysiological results and the biochemistry rely upon different cell samples, so there is no necessary inconsistency in their failure to co-vary (Ashe & Libet 1982).

However, while cAMP levels rise in response to synaptic release or bath-application of dopamine, it would appear that cAMP does not mediate the sIPSP. Weight et al (1978), reporting an extensive series of experiments involving intracellular injection of cAMP in bullfrog neurons, failed to find consistent effects of the nucleotide. Kuba & Nishi (1976) and Akasu & Koketsu (1977) similarly failed to find reliable hyperpolarizations produced by the dibutyryl forms. For the mammalian preparations it has been argued that the raised cAMP is involved in another action of dopamine, to induce the persistent modification of the sEPSP (Libet 1979b). Bath application or intracellular injection of cAMP has consistently failed to produce a hyperpolarizing response in the rabbit (Gallagher & Shinnick-Gallagher 1977, Dun et al 1977, Libet 1979b). Similarly, suppression of enzymatic breakdown of cAMP by treatment with the phosphodiesterase inhibitors Ro-20-1724 and IBMX fails to enhance the sIPSP or DA-evoked hyperpolarization (Libet 1979a). An initial finding that the phosphodiesterase inhibitor theophylline augmented the sIPSP (McAfee & Greengard 1972) now seems best explained by supposing that its effect is independent of its action upon cAMP. Libet (1979b) concluded that DA mediates the slow IPSP not via a specific DA receptor for stimulating adenyl cyclase but by acting through an adrenergic receptor (α_2).

Although comparable studies of amphibian sympathetic ganglia (cf Weight 1983 for review) reveal the same complement of fast, slow, and extremely slow PSPs present in mammalian ganglia, there are a disconcertingly large number of apparent discrepancies. Differences exist in the transmitter-receptor complexes that precipitate the responses, their ionic bases, and the degree to which cyclic nucleotides participate in their regulation. The fast cholinergic EPSP, mediated by a nicotinic receptor, results from a net increase in membrane conductance (Nishi & Koketsu 1968b). Recent voltage-clamp experiments (Kuba & Nishi 1979) indicate the synaptic currents underlying the fEPSP to be essentially identical to those present at frog neuromuscular junction (Steinbach & Stevens 1976), and presumed to be those present at vertebrate sympathetic ganglia synapses. The ionic basis of the fEPSP appears to be increased Na^+ and K^+ permeabilities in all three cases.

As in the mammalian preparations, repetitive stimulation of preganglionic (B) fibers in the frog produces a sEPSP, reaching its peak in several seconds and persisting for as long as a minute. ACh is the transmitter; and its effect is mediated by a muscarinic receptor (Nishi & Koketsu 1968a, Tosaka et al 1968, Koketsu 1969, Libet & Tosaka 1969). Under some conditions, the sEPSP is associated with a decreased conductance (Kobayashi & Libet 1968, 1970, Weight & Votava 1970, 1971), which may mean that it arises from a decreased K^+ conductance (Weight & Votava 1970). Subsequent voltage-clamp analyses suggest that suppression of a specific muscarine-sensitive K^+ current (M current), distinct from I_A, I_c, and I_k, is responsible for both the decreased conductance and depolarization induced by ACh (Brown & Adams 1980, Constanti et al 1981). Uncertainty remains, however, as to the exact relation of this decreased conductance—and by implication M-current inactivation—to the sEPSP under normal physiological conditions in both frog and mammalian preparations. Indeed, it is still rather unclear whether or not the sEPSP can occur in amphibian cells under normal physiological conditions, namely, conditions in which the cells are not strongly depolarized by an injury potential arising from intracellular penetration.

As previously noted, Kobayashi, Hashiguchi, Libet, and colleagues observe the mammalian sEPSP in the absence of detectable changes in input resistance (Hashiguchi et al 1978, 1982). Moreover, the M current in both the frog and mammalian preparations does not appear to be appreciably activated at potentials greater than -60 mV (i.e. the normal range of resting potentials in the amphibian cells), yet the sEPSP is detectable at potentials as negative as -70 mV or more (Hashiguchi et al 1982). Muscarine's most important effect in the mammalian—but not amphibian—preparations may be independent of M-current suppression and may be mediated by cGMP, which mimics the effects of muscarine at membrane potentials as negative as -90 mV (Hashiguchi et al 1978) in the rabbit but which is without effect in the bullfrog (Busis et al 1978).

The slow IPSP evoked in C neurons by stimulation of preganglionic C fibers reaches its peak amplitude in 1–2 sec and persists for up to 20 sec. In the bullfrog, the slow IPSP does not appear to originate from a disynaptic pathway involving ACh's stimulation of an adrenergic interneuron, as is argued for the mammalian preparations (Eccles & Libet 1961, Libet 1970, Ashe & Libet 1982). Instead, it most likely arises from a direct effect of ACh upon a muscarinic receptor in C cells (Weight & Padjen 1973b, Weight & Smith 1980, Horn & Dodd 1981, Dodd & Horn 1983). Iontophoretic application of ACh induces a hyperpolarization of C cells, with kinetics and pharmacological sensitivity very similar to the physiologically evoked sIPSP. ACh-induced hyperpolarization also occurs under conditions expected to reduce (low Ca^{2+}), if not abolish, synaptic release (Weight & Padjen 1973b, Horn & Dodd 1981, Dodd & Horn 1983). These results, obtained with intracellular recording techniques and iontophoretic application of ACh, are relatively unambiguous. They clearly indicate that ACh can directly produce a sIPSP in C cell.

Whether the direct muscarinic action of ACh completely accounts for the sIPSP in the frog is still unclear. It may still be argued that the synaptically evoked sIPSP involves the release of a second transmitter. Using the sucrose-gap perfusion chamber (extracellular vs intracellular recording; perfusion vs iontophoresis) and nicotine to block the fast EPSP, Libet & Kobayashi (1974) reported that ACh/MCh hyperpolarization persists under conditions of low release. They attributed the hyperpolarization, however, to an interaction of nicotine with the DA-adrenergic receptor in these studies. When the fEPSP was blocked with curare, instead of nicotine, the ACh/MCh hyperpolarization was abolished. Weight and colleagues have failed to confirm this observation with the sucrose-gap perfusion method and report that pronounced muscarinic-agonist-induced hyperpolarization is still apparent under curarization (Weight & Smith 1980, Smith & Weight 1981).

The conditions under which low Ca^{2+} abolishes ACh/MCh-induced hyper-polarization appear to be complex, however, for the sucrose-gap perfusion experiments. Weight & Smith (1980, Figure 7) actually obtained evidence for abolition of ACh hyperpolarization 30 min after switching to a low-Ca^{2+} medium; with more prolonged application the response returned. Similar uncertainty still surrounds the correct interpretation of the two lines of evidence that apparently support the disynaptic DA hypothesis: (a) the effects of the catechol O-methyltransferase (COMT) inhibitor, U0521, presumed by Libet and colleagues to inhibit enzymatic destruction of catecholamines and observed to potentiate the sIPSP (Libet & Kobayashi 1974); and (b) the diminished sIPSP produced by various adrenergic antagonists (Libet & Kobayashi 1974). Weight (1983), Libet (1979a), Ashe & Libet (1982), and Dun & Karczmar (1980) should be consulted for discussions of these issues.

The electrogenic nature of the slow IPSP also remains controversial. For both frog and mammalian preparations, at least three hypotheses have been proposed. First is the view of Weight & Padjen (1973a) that the sIPSP arises from a decreased Na$^+$ conductance. Evidence consistent with this view includes the observation of membrane conductance decrease during the sIPSP, the reduction of the sIPSP by Na$^+$ removal, and amplitude changes in the sIPSP consistent with membrane potential manipulations of Na$^+$-ion driving force.

Second is the proposal of Nishi & Koketsu (1967, 1968b) and Libet and colleagues (Libet 1984) that the sIPSP arises from synaptic activation of an electrogenic pump; though it is not believed to be the well-known Na$^+$ pump (Hodgkins & Keynes 1955, Thomas 1972). The primary evidence for the pump hypothesis consists of the observation that the sIPSP is abolished by selective inhibitors of the electrogenic Na$^+$ pump, such as ouabain, and the observation of no detectable changes in membrane conductance during the sISPS in nicotinized preparations (Koketsu 1969). As noted by Weight (1983), however, the former line of evidence is equally well explained by the changes in Na$^+$-ion driving force that would be produced by ouabain-produced pump inhibition, but that would not necessarily occur by synaptic stimulation. Na$^+$ should accumulate within the cell; this would lead to reduced resting Na$^+$ flux and a reduced IPSP when the remaining conductance was suppressed. The results of direct tests of the pump hypothesis are less than encouraging. Low (μM) concentrations of ouabain, which effectively inhibit the Na$^+$ pump, fail to abolish the sIPSP (Smith & Weight 1977). In addition, the slow IPSP shows a dependence upon K$^+$-ion driving force, which suggests a contribution of an increased K$^+$ conductance (Akasu et al 1978).

There are, however, problems with the suggestion that the sIPSP arises entirely from decreased Na$^+$ conductance. The most severe difficulty is that the reversal potential for the sIPSP is extremely negative, not positive, as would be predicted by E_{Na^+}. This led Weight & Smith (1981) to a third proposal that the sIPSP arises from a combined decrease in Na$^+$ conductance and an increase in K$^+$ conductance. Qualitatively, at least, such a mechanism could in principle produce an IPSP with a reversal potential more negative than E_k (Brown et al 1971) and little detectable change in net g_m. Separation and characterization of the decreased Na$^+$ conductance and increased K$^+$ conductance using voltage-clamp techniques has not yet been reported.

PERSISTENT HETEROSYNAPTIC FACILITATION EFFECTS   Perhaps the most interesting phenomenon in sympathetic ganglia, from the standpoint of a cellular mechanism that might be involved in associative information storage, is the long-term enhancement (LTE) of the muscarine-cholinergic sEPSP by DA (Libet & Tosaka 1970). In the mammalian preparations, DA's modulatory action is specific to the sEPSP (the fEPSP and ssEPSP are unaffected), develops more slowly but persists longer than the DA-induced sIPSP, and is apparently mediated by increased adenylate cyclase activity and in turn greater cAMP levels. Adenylate cyclase elevation appears to be coupled to both the D2- and D1-DA receptor types (Creese et al 1983), but only the D1 receptor-linked cAMP production is believed to play a prominent physiological role in the sympathetic ganglia (Libet 1984). The D1 receptor agonists apomorphine (Libet et al 1975) and ADTN (Mochida 1982) mimic, in key respects, the long-term enhancement of the sEPSP produced by DA, without appreciable hyperpolarization of the cell. In contrast, β-adrenergic receptor stimulation, which couples DA and the sIPSP (Ashe & Libet 1982), fails to produce the enhancement effect. D1 receptor antagonists (butaclamol, spiroperidol, and flupenthixol) block the LTE produced by D1 agonists, as well as cyclase elevation. The only anomalous result concerns the effects of DA stimulation of cAMP. DA stimulates a greater level of cAMP than does the more specific D1 agonist ADTN. The additional cAMP appears to arise from DA's action upon a β-adrenergic receptor, which can be blocked by the β-receptor antagonist propranolol (Mochida et al 1981, Mochida 1982). However, β-adrenergic agonists fail to produce an LTE effect. One resolution of this discrepancy may be that β-adrenergic receptors are primarily located in non-neural tissue within the ganglia, and that the "extra" cAMP measured reflects a pool not arising in excitable cells.

An interesting analogy has been drawn between the stages of memory induction, consolidation, and retention—terms originally derived from and descriptive of behavioral phenomena—and the temporal characteristics of LTE (Libet 1984). The onset of LTE appears to occur many tens of seconds after the arrival of DA at the postganglionics. Moreover, LTE persists in a relatively labile form for ~4–5 min following its onset. During this time it can be reversed by relatively low levels of cGMP, but not if it is applied (20–50 μm) more than 15 min or so following the onset of LTE (Libet et al 1975). Additional experiments indicate that cGMP's reversal of the LTE does not preclude a subsequent LTE effect, and that cGMP by itself does not enhance subsequent sEPSPs (Libet 1984). Future research will no doubt help to clarify the molecular mechanisms by which DA enhances the sEPSP, and by which the reversal of LTE by cGMP is confined to a relatively brief temporal window following LTE induction.

Before ending our discussion of the sympathetic ganglia, it is appropriate to consider the types of information storage for which these slow PSPs and particularly the heterosynaptic LTE are well suited. Like hippocampal LTP, the slow PSPs are relatively long-lived responses, occurring on a time scale of many minutes; LTE can last for hours. Thus, they are persistent. Unlike most cases of LTP, the LTE potentiation found is not specific to the original synaptic input responsible for it production (DA). However, a necessary condition for its occurrence does not appear to be temporal convergence of the "test" (MCh or muscarinic agonist) and "induction" (DA) synaptic inputs. Indeed, there is nothing at the moment to indicate that the muscarinic-cholinergic input is at all important for the production of LTE; presumably, only DA-D1-stimulated increases in cAMP are. Moreover, one might suppose that under some conditions of paired muscarinic/cholinergic-dopaminergic stimulation, that muscarinic/cholinergic stimulation might even mitigate the LTE effect since it raises cGMP levels, which reverse LTE.

Since no evidence for a requirement of temporal convergence exists, there is little reason to suppose that specific temporal orders would make much of a difference either. Thus, LTE in the sympathetics seems best suited as a mechanism for the persistent modification of a single class of synaptic input, and one which does not require temporally convergent input. This in no way diminishes its potential importance for an understanding of some interesting forms of nonassociative plasticity in the mammalian brain, especially given the increasing evidence that dopaminergic systems are involved (in what way is by no means clear) in a variety of learning and memory phenomena, especially those likely to involve a strong motor component (Beninger 1983).

SUMMARY

In Table 1, we summarize what is convincingly demonstrated to date for the major vertebrate and invertebrate model systems attempting to elucidate cellular mechanisms of associative learning. Two major concerns are the adequacy of the behavioral demonstrations and the completeness and extent of the accompanying neurophysiology.

In addressing the issue of behavior, it is important to define clearly which criteria are both necessary and sufficient to infer the involvement of an associative-learning process. Similarly, it is also important to distinguish among those primary characteristics of associative learning in general, and those secondary or tertiary features that serve to define various subclasses. In our view, it would be unreasonable to require that any given preparation exhibit all the defining features of classical conditioning, for example, in order to qualify as a "legitimate" instance of associative learning. This is especially true if the goal is to understand the more general, rather than the specific, mechanisms involved in associative learning. Hence, we emphasize the following as primary features of learned behavior: (a) pairing specificity, (b) stimulus specificity, (c) long-term retention (arbitrarily defined as lasting for at least 24 hr), (d) a moderate degree of reversibility by subsequent experience (e.g. extinction), and (e) demonstrations that nonassociative-learning processes cannot account for features a–c. Where appropriate, we also identified other interesting features of the learned behavior.

It is apparent from the table that a major unresolved issue for most of the preparations is the extent to which the behavioral changes are exclusively associative. This is no less true for the vertebrate preparations than it is for the invertebrates. The clearest example of an exclusively associative behavioral change is the rabbit NMR. The learning-produced changes in the invertebrate preparations were all shown, to varying degrees, to be pairing specific. Yet a major unresolved issue is the degree to which *apparent* examples of associative-learning reflect complex interactions among basically nonassociative-learning processes. The core issue is really quite simple: Does the associative training procedure result in the acquisition of new or qualitatively different behavior; and is there a strict requirement for an associative relation?

In addressing the adequacy of the neurophysiological analyses, the major issue is that of localization. Logically, there are two components to this. The first is that of circuit analysis, which entails careful mapping of the flow of neural information in the sensory, motor, and interneuronal pathways mediating behavior. The best examples of this among the vertebrates are the VOR pathways in Ito's work, and cardiac conditioning in the pigeon. Electrophysiological identification of areas exhibiting learning-correlated changes is a necessary, though not sufficient, step in assessing the potential causal relevance of a portion of the nervous system. Here it should be noted the vertebrate preparations have on the whole been more successful than the invertebrates, perhaps because plastic capabilities are more widely distributed in the vertebrate brain. With a multitude of plastic sites, it is not so surprising that a convincing demonstration has yet to be provided of a site of long-term information storage in mammalian brain, which is both necessary and sufficient (in the absence of changes that might occur elsewhere) to explain the learned behavioral changes. Indeed long-term cellular changes at sites known to play a causal role in associative behavioral change have only been documented for *Hermissenda*.

What have been established in other cases are relatively short-term, pairing-specific changes in cells involved in the mediation of learned behavior, the durations of which are usually measured on a scale of minutes to an hour. Cat pericruciate cortical cells and rabbit flocculus Purkinje cells are exceptions. Here, long-term changes have been measured, but the causal significance and pairing specificity are unclear.

ACKNOWLEDGMENTS

We thank the following people for their helpful comments and criticisms of earlier versions of this manuscript: Neil Berthier, John Desmond, Lawrence Grover, Benjamin Libet, John Moore, William Richards, and Jed Rose. The responsibility for any errors of fact or interpretation rests solely with the authors. Special thanks to Lynda Holmak for her patience and diligence in preparation of this manuscript. Preparation of this review was supported, in part, by NSF grant BNS-8316707 to J. F.

Table 1 Summary of behavioral and neurophysiological characteristics of various model system approaches to associative learning

	Behavior					Neurophysiological correlates						
	1. Pairing—specific	2. Stimulus—specific	3. Long-term (≥ 24 hr.)	4. Reversible (extinction)	5. Not explained by non-associative factors	1. Adequacy of analysis of circuits underlying behavior	2. Adequacy of analysis of circuits responsible for production of neural correlates	3. Identification of neural correlates	a. pairing—specific	b. simulated training in semi-intact preparations (short-term: < 12 hr.)	c. long-term correlates recorded from previously trained animals	4. Identification of sites of neural change causally related to long-term retention
Invertebrates												
Aplysia (gill withdrawal)	*											
Hermissenda (phototaxic suppression)	*	*	*	*	*	*	*	*	*	*	*	*
Limax (chemosensory aversion learning)	*	*	*		*		*	*	*	*	*	
Locust (instrumental leg-position learning)	*	NR		*	*	*		*	*	*	*	
Pleurobranchaea (chemosensory aversion learning)	*	*	*			*		*		*		
Vertebrates												
Paw-flexion conditioning in cat	*	*	*	*		*		*	*	*		
Conditioned facial movements in cat	*	*	*	*	*	*		*	*	*	*	
Associative modifications of HVOR in rabbit					*	*	*	*	*	*		
NMR conditioning in rabbit	*	*	*	*		*		*	*	*	*	
Cardiac conditioning in pigeons	*	*	*	*				*	*	*		

NR = not relevant in case of instrumental conditioning paradigms

Literature Cited

Acosta-Urquidi, J., Alkon, D. L., Neary, J. T. 1984. Intrasomatic injection of a Ca^{2+} calmodulin dependent protein kinase simulates biophysical effects of associative learning in a *Hermissenda* photoreceptor. *Science.* 224:1254–57

Adams, D. J., Smith, S. J., Thompson, S. H. 1980. Ionic currents in molluscan soma. *Ann. Rev. Neurosci.* 3:141–68

Akasu, T., Koketsu, K. 1977. Effects of dibutyryl cyclic adenosine 3'-,5'-monophosphate and theophylline on the bullfrog sympathetic ganglion cells. *Br. J. Pharmacol.* 60:331–36

Akasu, T., Omura, H., Koketsu, K. 1978. Roles of electrogenic Na^+ pump and K^+ conductance in the slow inhibitory postsynaptic potential of bullfrog sympathetic ganglion cells. *Life Sci.* 23:2405–10

Albus, J. S. 1971. A theory of cerebellar function. *Math Biosci.* 10:25–61

Alger, B. E., Teyler, T. J. 1976. Long-term and short-term plasticity in CA1, CA3 and dentate regions of the rat hippocampal slice. *Brain Res.* 110:463–80

Alkon, D. L. 1974a. Sensory interactions in the nudibranch mollusk *Hermissenda crassicornis*. *Fed. Proc.* 33:1083–90

Alkon, D. L. 1974b. Associative training in *Hermissenda*. *J. Gen. Physiol.* 64:70–84

Alkon, D. L. 1979. Voltage-dependent calcium and potassium ion conductances; a contingency mechanism for an associative learning model. *Science* 205:810–16

Alkon, D. L. 1980. Membrane depolarization accumulates during acquisition of an associative behavioral change. *Science* 210:1375–76

Alkon, D. L., Fuortes, M. G. F. 1972. Responses of photoreceptors in *Hermissenda*. *J. Gen. Physiol.* 60:631–49

Alkon, D. L., Lederhendler, I., Shoukimas, J. J. 1982a. Primary changes of membrane currents during retention of associative learning. *Science* 215:693–95

Alkon, D. L., Shoukimas, J. J., Heldman, E. 1982b. Calcium-mediated decrease of a voltage-dependent potassium current. *Biophys. J.* 40:245–50

Alkon, D. L., Farley, J., Hay, B., Shoukimas, J. J. 1983. Inactivation of a Ca^{2+}-dependent K^+ current can occur without significant Ca^{2+}-current inactivation. *Soc. Neurosci. Abst.* 9:1188

Alkon, D. L., Farley, J., Sakakibara, M., Hay, B. 1984. Voltage-dependent calcium and calcium-activated potassium currents of a molluscan photoreceptor. *Biophys. J.* 46:605–14

Allen, G. I., Tsukahara, N. 1974. Cerebellar communication systems. *Physiol. Rev.* 54:957–1006

Andersen, P., Sundberg, S. H., Sveen, O., Wigstrom, H. 1977. Specific long-lasting potentiation of synaptic transmission in hippocampal slices. *Nature* 266:736–37

Andersen, P., Sundberg, S. H., Sveen, O., Swann, J. W., Wigstrom, H. 1980. Possible mechanisms for long-lasting potentiation of synaptic transmission in hippocampal slices from guinea-pigs. *J. Physiol.* 302:463–82

Ashe, J. H., Libet, B. 1981a. Orthodromic production of non-cholinergic slow depolarizing response in the superior cervical ganglion of the rabbit. *J. Physiol.* 320:333–46

Ashe, J. H., Libet, B. 1981b. Modulation of slow postsynaptic potentials by dopamine in rabbit sympathetic ganglion. *Brain Res.* 217:93–106

Ashe, J. H., Libet, B. 1982. Pharmacological properties and monoaminergic mediation of the slow IPSP, in mammalian sympathetic ganglion. *Brain Res.* 242:345–49

Baarsma, E. A., Collewijn, H. 1974. Vestibulo-ocular and optokinetic reactions to rotation and their interaction in the rabbit. *J. Physiol.* 238:603–25

Bailey, C. H., Hawkins, R. D., Chen, M. D., Kandel, E. R. 1981. Interneurons involved in mediation and modulation of the gill-withdrawal reflex in Aplysia. IV. Morphological basis of presynaptic facilitation. *J. Neurophysiol.* 45:340–60

Baimbridge, K. G., Miller, J. J. 1981. Calcium uptake and retention during long-term potentiation of neuronal activity in the rat hippocampal slice preparation. *Brain Res.* 221:229–305

Baker, R. G., Precht, W., Llinas, R. 1972. Cerebellar modulatory action on the vestibulo-trochlear pathway in the cat. *Exp. Brain Res.* 15:364–85

Barrionuevo, G., Brown, T. H. 1984. Associative long-term potentiation in hippocampal slices. *Proc. Natl. Acad. Sci. USA* 80:7347–51

Baudry, M., Lynch, G., 1979. Regulation of glutamate receptors by cations. *Nature* 282:748–50

Baudry, M., Lynch, G. 1980. Regulation of hippocampal glutamate receptors: evidence for the involvement of a calcium-activated protease. *Proc. Natl. Acad. Sci. USA* 77:2298–2302

Baudry, M., Lynch, G. 1981a. High-affinity binding sites for ^3H-glutamate in hippocampal membranes: The search for a glutamate receptor. *Adv. Biochem. Psychopharmacol.* 29:397–403

Baudry, M., Lynch, G. 1982. Possible mechanisms of LTP: Role of glutamate receptors; In *Hippocampal Long-Term Potentiation: Mechanisms and Implications for Memory,* ed. L. W. Swanson, T. J. Teyler,

R. F. Thompson. *Neurosci. Res. Program Bull.* 20:663–71

Baudry, M., Lynch, G. 1983a. Classification and properties of acidic amino acid receptors in hippocampus. *J. Neurosci.* 3(8):1538–46

Baudry, M., Lynch, G. 1983b. A specific hypothesis concerning the biochemical substrates of memory. *Soc. Neurosci. Abstr.* 9:480

Baudry, M., Oliver, M., Creager, R., Wieraszko, A., Lynch, G. 1980. Increase in glutamate receptors following repetitive electrical stimulation in hippocampal slices. *Life Sci.* 27:325–30

Beninger, R. J. 1983. The role of dopamine in locomotor activity and learning. *Brain Res. Rev.* 6:173–96

Berger, T. W. 1984. Long-term potentiation of hippocampal synaptic transmission affects rate of behavioral learning. *Science* 224:627–29

Berger, T. W., Orr, W. B. 1982. Role of hippocampus in reversal learning of the rabbit nictitating membrane response. See Woody, 1982, pp. 1–12

Berger, T. W., Thompson, R. F. 1978a. Neuronal plasticity in the limbic system during classical conditioning of the rabbit nictitating membrane response. I. The hippocampus. *Brain Res.* 145:323–46

Berger, T. W., Thompson, R. F. 1978b. Identification of pyramidal cells as the critical elements in hippocampal neuronal plasticity during learning. *Proc. Natl. Acad. Sci. USA* 75:1572–76

Bernier, L., Castellucci, V. F., Kandel, E. R., Schwartz, J. H. 1982. Facilitatory transmitter causes a selective and prolonged increase in adenosine 3':5'-monophosphate in sensory neurons mediating the gill and siphon withdrawal reflex in *Aplysia. J. Neurosci.* 2:1682–91

Bertheir, N. E., Moore, J. W. 1983. The nictitating membrane response: An electrophysiological study of the abducens nerve and nucleus and the accessory abducens nucleus in rabbit. *Brain Res.* 258:201–10

Bliss, T. V. P., Goddard, G. V., Riives, M. 1982. Reduction of long-term potentiation in the dentate gyrus of the rat following selective depletion of monoamines. *J. Physiol.* 334:475–91

Bliss, T. V. P., Gardner-Medwin, A. R. 1971. Long-lasting increases of synaptic influence in the unanesthetized hippocampus. *J. Physiol.* 216:32–33

Bliss, T. V. P., Gardner-Medwin, A. R. 1973. Long-lasting potentiation of synaptic transmission in the dentate area of the unanesthetized rabbit following stimulation of the perforant path. *J. Physiol.* 232:357–74

Bliss, T. V. P., Lomo, T. 1973. Long-lasting potentiation of synaptic transmission in the dentate area of the anesthetized rabbit fol-

lowing stimulation of the perforant path. *J. Physiol.* 232:331–56

Brodal, A., Hoivik, B. 1964. Site and mode of termination of primary vestibulo-cerebellar fibres in the cat. *Arch. Ital. Biol.* 102:1–21

Brons, J. F., Woody, C. D. 1980. Long-term changes in excitability of cortical neurons after Pavlovian conditioning and extinction. *J. Neurophysiol.* 44:605–15

Brown, D. A., Adams, P. R. 1980. Muscarinic suppression of a novel voltage-sensitive K^+ current in a vertebrate neurone. *Nature* 283:673–76

Brown, M. C., Holland, R. L., Hopkins, W. C. 1981. Motor nerve sprouting. *Ann. Rev. Neurosci.* 4:17–42

Brown, J. E., Muller, K. J., Murray, G. 1971. Reversal potential for an electrophysiological event generated by conductance changes: mathematical analysis. *Science* 174:318

Browning, M., Baudry, M., Lynch, G. 1982. Evidence that high frequency stimulation influences the phosphorylation of pyruvate dehydrogenase, and that the activity of this enzyme is linked to mitochondrial calcium sequestration. *Prog. Brain Res.* 56:317–37

Brunelli, M., Castellucci, V., Kandel, E. R. 1976. Synaptic facilitation and behavioral sensitization in *Aplysia:* Possible role of serotonin and cyclic AMP. *Science* 194:1178–81

Busis, N. A., Weight, F. F., Smith, P. A. 1978. Synaptic potentials in sympathetic ganglia: are they mediated by cyclic nucleotides? *Science* 200:1079–81

Camardo, J. S., Siegelbaum, S., Kandel, E. R. 1984. Cellular and molecular correlates of sensitization in *Aplysia* and their implications for associative learning. In *Primary Neural Substrates of Learning and Behavioral Change,* ed. D. Alkon, J. Farley, pp. 185–203. New York: Cambridge.

Carew, T. J., Castellucci, V. F., Kandel, E. R. 1971. An analysis of dishabituation and sensitization of the gill-withdrawal reflex in *Aplysia. Int. J. Neurosci.* 2:79–98

Carew, T. J., Pinsker, H., Kandel, E. R. 1972. Long-term habituation of a defensive withdrawal reflex in *Aplysia. Science* 175:451–54

Carew, T. J., Kandel, E. R. 1973. Acquisition and retention of long-term habituation in *Aplysia:* correlation of behavioral and cellular processes. *Science* 182:1158–60

Carew, T. J., Castellucci, V. F., Kandel, E. R. 1979a. Sensitization in *Aplysia:* Rapid restoration of transmission in synapses inactivated by long-term habituation. *Science* 205:417–19

Carew, T. J., Castellucci, V. F., Byrne, J. H., Kandel, E. R. 1979b. A quantitative analysis of the relative contribution of central and peripheral neurons to the gill-withdrawal reflex in *Aplysia*. *J. Neurophysiol.* 42:497–509

Carew, T. J., Walters, E. T., Kandel, E. R. 1981. Classical conditioning in a simple withdrawal reflex in *Aplysia californica*. *J. Neurosci.* 1:1426–37

Carew, T. J., Hawkins, R. D., Kandel, E. R. 1983. Differential classical conditioning of a defensive withdrawal reflex in *Aplysia californica*. *Science* 219:397–400

Castellucci, V., Pinsker, H., Kupfermann, I., Kandel, E. R. 1970. Neuronal mechanisms of habituation and dishabituation of the gill-withdrawal reflex in *Aplysia*. *Science* 167:1745–48

Castellucci, V. F., Kandel, E. R. 1974. A quantal analysis of the synaptic depression underlying habituation of the gill-withdrawal reflex in *Aplysia*. *Proc. Natl. Acad. Sci. USA* 71:5004–8

Castellucci, V. F., Kandel, E. R. 1976. Presynaptic facilitation as a mechanism for behavioral sensitization in *Aplysia*. *Science* 194:1176–78

Castellucci, V. F., Carew, T. J., Kandel, E. R. 1978. Cellular analysis of long-term habituation of the gill-withdrawal reflex of *Aplysia californica*. *Science* 202:1306–8

Castellucci, V. F., Kandel, E. R., Schwartz, J. H., Wilson, F. D., Nairn, A. L., Greengard, P. 1980. Intracellular injection of the catalytic subunit of cyclic-AMP dependent protein kinase simulates facilitation of transmitter release underlying behavioral sensitization in *Aplysia*. *Proc. Natl. Acad. Sci. USA* 77:7492–96

Castellucci, V. F., Nairn, A., Greengard, P., Schwartz, J. H., Kandel, E. R. 1982. Inhibitor of adenosine 3':5'-monophosphate-dependent protein kinase blocks presynaptic facilitation in *Aplysia*. *J. Neurosci.* 12:1673–81

Castellucci, V. F., Bernier, L. F., Schwartz, J. H., Kandel, E. R. 1983. Persistent activation of adenylate cyclase underlies the time course of short-term sensitization in *Aplysia*. *Soc. Neurosci. Abstr.* 9:169

Cedar, H., Schwartz, J. H. 1972. Cyclic adenosine monophosphate in the nervous system of *Aplysia californica*. II. Effect of serotonin and dopamine. *J. Gen. Physiol.* 60:570–87

Cedar, H., Kandel, E. R., Schwartz, J. H. 1972. Cyclic adenosine monophosphate in the nervous system of *Aplysia californica*. I. Increased synthesis in response to synaptic stimulation. *J. Gen. Physiol.* 60:558–69

Cegvaske, C. F., Patterson, M. M., Thompson, R. F. 1979. Neuronal unit activity in the abducens nucleus during classical conditioning of the nictitating membrane response in the rabbit *Oryctolagus cyniculus*. *J. Comp. Physiol. Psychol.* 93:595–609

Chang, J. J., Gelperin, A. 1980. Rapid taste

aversion learning by an isolated molluscan central nervous system. *Proc. Natl. Acad. Sci. USA* 77:6204–6

Church, R. M. 1964. Systematic effects of random error in the yoked control design. *Psychol. Bull.* 62:122–32

Cohen, D. H. 1974. The neural pathways and informational flow mediating a conditioned autonomic response. In *Limbic and Autonomic Nervous System Research*, ed. L. V. DiCara, pp. 223–75. New York: Plenum

Cohen, D. H. 1980. The functional neuroanatomy of a conditioned response. In *Neural Mechanisms of Goal-Directed Behavior and Learning*, ed. R. F. Thompson, L. H., Hicks, V. B. Shvyrkov, pp. 283–302. New York: Academic

Cohen, D. H. 1982. Central processing time for a conditioned response in a vertebrate model system. See Woody 1982, pp. 517–34

Cohen, D. H. 1984. Identification of vertebrate neurons modified during learning: Analysis of sensory pathways. See Camardo et al 1984 pp. 129–54

Cohen, D. H., Gibbs, C. M., Siegelman, J., Gamlin, P., Broyles, J. 1982. Is locus coeruleus involved in plasticity of lateral geniculate neurons during learning? *Soc. Neurosci. Abstr.* 8:666

Cole, A. E., Shinnick-Gallagher, P. 1984. Muscarinic inhibitory transmission in mammalian sympathetic ganglia mediated by increased potassium conductance. *Nature* 307:270–72

Connor, J., Stevens, C. F. 1971. Voltage-clamp studies of a transient outward current in gastropod neural somata. *J. Physiol.* 213:21–30

Connor, J., Alkon, D. L. 1982. Light-induced changes of intracellular Ca^{2+} in *Hermissenda* photoreceptors measured with Arsenazo III. *Soc. Neurosci. Abstr.* 8:944

Constanti, A., Adams, P. R., Brown, D. A. 1981. Why do barium ions imitate acetylcholine? *Brain Res.* 206:244–50

Cotman, C. W., Nieto-Sampedro, M. 1982. Brain function, synapse renewal, and plasticity. *Ann. Rev. Psychol.* 33:371–401

Creese, I., Sibley, D. R., Hamblin, M. W., Leff, S. E. 1983. The classification of dopamine receptors: Relationship to radioligand binding. *Ann. Rev. Neurosci.* 6:43–72

Crow, T. J., Alkon, D. L. 1978. Retention of an associative behavioral change in *Hermissenda*. *Science* 201:1239–41

Crow, T. J., Alkon, D. L. 1980. Associative behavioral modification in *Hermissenda*: cellular correlates. *Science* 209:412–14

Davis, W. J., Villet, J., Lee, D., Rigler, M., Gillette, R., Prince, E. 1980. Selective and differential avoidance learning in the feeding and withdrawal behavior of *Pleurobranchaea californica*. *J. Comp. Physiol.* 138:157–65

Davis, W. J., Gillette, R. 1978. Neural correlate of behavioral plasticity in command neurons of *Pleurobranchaea*. *Science* 199:801–4

Desmond, N. L., Levy, W. B. 1983. Synaptic correlates of associative potentiation/depression: An ultrastructural study in the hippocampus. *Brain Res.* 265:21–30

Desmond, J. E., Moore, J. W. 1982. A brain stem region essential for the classically conditioned but not unconditioned nictitating membrane response. *Physiol. Behav.* 28:1029–33

Desmond, J. E., Moore, J. W. 1983. A supratrigeminal region implicated in the classically conditioned nictating membrane response. *Brain Res. Bull.* 10:765–73

Desmond, J. E., Rosenfeld, M. E., Moore, J. W. 1983. An HRP study of the brainstem afferents to the accessory abducens region and dorsolateral pons in rabbit: Implications for the conditioned nictitating membrane response. *Brain Res. Bull.* 10:747–63

Disterhoft, J. F., Stuart, D. K. 1976. The trial sequence of changed unit activity in auditory system of alert rat during conditioned response acquisition and extinction. *J. Neurophysiol.* 39:266–81

Disterhoft, J. F., Shipley, M. T., Kraus, N. 1982. Analyzing the rabbit NM conditioned reflex arc. See Woody, 1982, pp. 433–50

Dodd, J., Horn, J. P. 1983. A reclassification of B and C neurones in the ninth and tenth paravertebral sympathetic ganglia of the bullfrog. *J. Physiol.* 334:255–91

Dolphin, A. C., Errington, M. L., Bliss, T. V. P. 1982. Long-term potentiation of the perforant path in vivo is associated with increased glutamate release. *Nature* 297:496–98

Douglas, R. M., McNaughton, B. L., Goddard, G. V. 1982. Commissural inhibition and facilitation of granule cell discharge in fascia dentata. *J. Comp. Neurol.* 219:285–94

Dudek, F. E., Deadwyler, S. A., Cotman, C. W., Lynch, G. 1976. Intracellular responses from granule cell layer in slices of rat hippocampus: Perforant path synapses. *J. Neurophysiol.* 29:384–93

Duffy, C., Teyler, T. J., Shashoua, V. E. 1981. Long-term potentiation in the hippocampal slice: evidence for stimulated secretion of newly synthesized proteins. *Science* 212:1148–51

Dufosse, M., Ito, M., Miyashita, Y. 1977. Functional localization in the rabbits' cerebellar flocculus determined in relationship with eye movements. *Neurosci. Lett.* 5:273–77

Dufosse, M., Ito, M., Jastreboff, P. J., Miyashita, Y. 1978a. A neuronal correlate in rabbit's cerebellum to adaptive modification of the vestibulo-ocular reflex. *Brain Res.* 150:611–16

Dufosse, M., Ito, M., Miyashita, Y. 1978b. Diminution and reversal of eye movements induced by local stimulation of rabbit cerebellar flocculus after partial destruction of the inferior olive. *Exp. Brain Res.* 33:139–41

Dun, N. J., Karczmar, A. G. 1980. A comparative study of the pharmacological properties of the positive potential recorded from the superior cervical ganglia. *J. Pharmacol. Exp. Ther.* 215:455–60

Dun, N. J., Kaibara, K., Karczmar, A. G. 1977. Direct postsynaptic membrane effects of dibutyryl cyclic GMP on mammalian sympathetic neurons. *Neuropharmacology* 16:715–17

Dunwiddie, T., Lynch, G. 1978. Long-term potentiation and depression of synaptic responses in the rat hippocampus: localization and frequency dependency. *J. Physiol.* 276:353–67

Dunwiddie, T. V., Lynch, G. 1979. The relationship between extracellular calcium concentrations and the induction of hippocampal long-term potentiation. *Brain Res.* 169:103–10

Dunwiddie, T. V., Madison, D., Lynch, G. 1978. Synaptic transmission is required for initiation of long-term potentiation. *Brain Res.* 150:413–17

Eccles, J. C. 1983. Calcium in long-term potentiation as a model for memory. *Neuroscience* 10:1071–81

Eccles, R. M., Libet, B. 1961. Origin and blockade of the synaptic responses of curarized sympathetic ganglia. *J. Physiol.* 157:484–503

Farley, J. 1984a. Cellular mechanisms for causal detection in a mollusc. In *Neural mechanisms of conditioning*, ed. D. L. Alkon, C. Woody. New York: Plenum. In press

Farley, J. 1984b. Cellular mechanisms of contingency learning in the mollusc *Hermissenda J. Neurophysiol.* In press

Farley, J., Alkon, D. L. 1980a. Neural organization predicts stimulus specificity for a retained associative behavioral change. *Science* 210:1373–75

Farley, J., Alkon, D. L. 1980b. Neural organization predicts stimulus specificity for a retained associative behavioral change. *Soc. Neurosci. Abstr.* 6:786

Farley, J., Alkon, D. 1981. Associative neural and behavioral change in *Hermissenda*: Consequences of nervous system orientation for light- and pairing-specificity. *Soc. Neurosci. Abstr.* 7:325

Farley, J., Alkon, D. 1982a. Associative and behavioral change in *Hermissenda*: Consequences of nervous system orientation for light- and pairing-specificity. *J. Neurophysiol.* 48:785–807

Farley, J., Alkon, D. L. 1982b. Cumulative cellular depolarization and short-term associative conditioning in *Hermissenda*. *Soc. Neurosci. Abstr.* 8:825

Farley, J., Alkon, D. L. 1983. Changes in *Hermissenda* Type B photoreceptors involving a voltage-dependent Ca^{2+} current and a Ca^{2+}-dependent K^+ current during retention of associative learning. *Soc. Neurosci. Abstr.* 9:167

Farley, J., Alkon, D. 1984a. Cellular analysis of gastropod learning. In *Cell Receptors and Cell Communication in Invertebrates*, ed. A. J. Greenberg, New York: Marcel-Dekker. In press

Farley, J., Alkon, D. L. 1984b. *In vitro* associative conditioning of *Hermissenda:* cumulative depolarization of Type B photoreceptors and short-term associative behavioral changes, *J. Neurophysiol.* In press

Farley, J., Sakakibara, M., Alkon, D. L. 1984. Associative-training correlated changes in I_C and I_{Ca} in *Hermissenda* Type B photoreceptor. *Soc. Neurosci. Abstr.* 10:270

Farley, J., Kern, G. 1984. Contingency-sensitive phototaxic behavioral changes in *Hermissenda:* temporally-specific attenuation of conditioning. *Animal Learn. Behav.* In press

Farley, J., Richards, W. G., Ling, L. J., Liman, E., Alkon, D. L. 1982. Membrane changes in a single photoreceptor cause retained associative behavioral changes in *Hermissenda*. *Biol. Bull.* 163:383

Farley, J., Richards, W., Alkon, D. L. 1983a. Evidence for an increased voltage-dependent Ca^{2+} current in *Hermissenda* B photoreceptors during retention of associative learning. *Biophys. J.* 41:294a

Farley, J., Richards, W. G., Ling, L., Liman, E., Alkon, D. L. 1983b. Membrane changes in a single photoreceptor during acquisition cause associative learning in *Hermissenda*. *Science* 221:1201–3

Fifkova, E., Anderson, C. L., Young, S. J., Van Harreveld, A. 1982. Effect of anisomycin on stimulation-induced changes in dendritic spines of the dentate granule cells. *J. Neurocytol.* 11:183–210

Fifkova, E., van Harreveld, A. 1977. Long-lasting morphological changes in dendritic spines of dentate granular cells following stimulation of the entorhinal area. *J. Neurocytol.* 6:211–30

Forman, R. 1984. Leg position learning by an insect. I. A heat avoidance learning paradigm. *J. Neurobiol.* 15:127–40

Forman, R., Alkon, D. L., Sakakibara, M., Harrigan, J., Lederhendler, I., Farley, J. 1984. Changes in I_A and I_C but not I_{Na} accompany retention of conditioned behavior in *Hermissenda*. *Soc. Neurosci. Abstr.* 10:121

Fujito, Y., Tsukahara, N., Oda, Y., Yoshida, M. 1982. Formation of functional synapses in the adult cat red nucleus from the cerebrum following cross-innervation of forelimb flexor and extensor nerves. II. Analysis of newly appeared synaptic potentials. *Exp. Brain. Res.* 45:13–18

Fukuda, J., Highstein, S. M., Ito, M. 1972. Cerebellar inhibitory control of the vestibulo-ocular reflex investigated in rabbit IIIrd nucleus. *Exp. Brain Res.* 14:511–26

Gallagher, J. P., Shinnick-Gallagher, P. 1977. Cyclic nucleotides injected intracellularly into rat superior cervical ganglion cells. *Science* 198:851–52

Gallagher, J. P., Shinnick-Gallagher, P., Cole, A. E., Griffith, W. H. III, Williams, B. J. 1980. Current hypotheses for the slow inhibitory postsynaptic potential in sympathetic ganglia. *Fed. Proc.* 39:3009–15

Gelperin, A. 1975. Rapid food-aversion learning by a terrestrial mollusk. *Science* 189:567–70

Gelperin, A., Chang, J. J., Reingold, S. C. 1978. Feeding motor program in *Limax*. I. Neuromuscular correlates and control by chemosensory input. *J. Neurobiol.* 9:285–300

Gelperin, A., Culligan, N., Wieland, S. 1981. Associative learning by the isolated CNS of a terrestrial mollusk, *Limax maximus*, occurs centrally. *Soc. Neurosci. Abstr.* 7:353

Gelperin, A., Culligan, N. 1982. *In vitro* expression of *in vivo* learning by the cerebral ganglia of the terrestrial mollusc *Limax maximus*. *Soc. Neurosci. Abstr.* 8:823

Ghelarducci, B., Ito, M., Yagi, N. 1975. Impulse discharges from flocculus Purkinje cells of alert rabbits during visual stimulation combined with horizontal head rotation. *Brain Res.* 87:66–72

Gibbs, C. M., Cohen, D. H., Broyles, J., Solin, A. 1981. Conditioned modification of avian dorsal geniculate neurons is a function of their response to the unconditioned stimulus. *Soc. Neurosci. Abstr.* 7:752

Gibbs, C. M., Broyles, J. L., Cohen, D. H. 1983. Further studies of the involvement of locus coeruleus in plasticity of avian lateral geniculate neurons during learning. *Soc. Neurosci. Abstr.* 9:641

Gillette, R. M., Kovac, M. P., Davis, W. J. 1982. Control of feeding motor output by paracerebral neurons in the brain of *Pleurobranchaea californica*. *J. Neurophysiol.* 47:855–908

Glickstein, M., Hardiman, M. J., Yeo, C. H. 1983. The effects of cerebellar lesions on the conditioned nictitating membrane response of the rabbit. *J. Physiol.* 341:30–31P

Goh, Y., Alkon, D. L. 1982. Convergence of

visual and statocyst inputs on interneurons and motoneurons of *Hermissenda:* A network design for associative conditioning. *Soc. Neurosci. Abstr.* 8:825

Gonshor, A., Melvill-Jones, G. 1976a. Short-term adaptive changes in the human vestibulo-ocular reflex arc. *J. Physiol.* 256:361–79

Gonshor, A., Melvill-Jones, G. 1976b. Extreme vestibulo-ocular reversal of vision. *J. Physiol.* 256:381–414

Gormezano, D. 1972. Investigations of defense and reward conditioning in the rabbit. In *Classical Conditioning II: Current Research and Theory,* ed. A. H. Black, W. F. Prokasy, pp. 151–181. New York: Appleton-Century-Crofts

Gormezano, I., Kehoe, E. J., Marshall, B. S. 1983. Twenty years of classical conditioning research with the rabbit, In *Progress in Psychobiology and Physiological Psychology,* ed. J. M. Sprague, A. N. Epstein, 10:197–275. New York: Academic

Grab, D. J., Carlin, R. K., Siekevitz, P. 1980. The presence and functions of calmodulin in the post-synaptic density. *Ann. N. Acad. Sci.* 356:55–72

Gray, T. S., McMaster, S. E., Harvey, J. A., Gormezano, I. 1980. Localization of the motoneurons which innervate the retractor bulbi muscle in the rabbit. *Soc. Neurosci. Abstr.* 6:16

Gray, T. S., McMaster, S. E., Harvey, J. A., Gormezano, I. 1981. Localization of retractor bulbi motoneurons in the rabbit. *Brain Res.* 226:93–106

Greengard, P. 1976. Possible role for cyclic nucleotides and phosphorylated membrane proteins in postsynaptic actions of neurotransmitters. *Nature* 260:101–8

Greengard, P. 1978. *Cyclic Nucleotides, Phosphorylated Proteins and Neuronal Function.* New York: Raven

Grover, L., Farley, J. 1983. Temporal order sensitivity of associative learning in *Hermissenda. Soc. Neurosci. Abstr.* 9:915

Grover, L., Farley, J. 1984. Cumulative depolarization of *Hermissenda* Type B photoreceptors: Ionic basis and the role of calcium. *Soc. Neurosci. Abstr.* 10:621

Haddad, G. M., Demer, J. L., Robinson, D. A. 1980. The effect of lesions of the dorsal cap of the inferior olive on the vestibulo-ocular and optokinetic systems of the cat. *Brain Res.* 185:265–75

Hagiwara, S., Byerly, L. 1981. Calcium channel. *Ann. Rev. Neurosci.* 4:69–125

Hashiguchi, T., Ushiyama, N., Kobayashi, H., Libet, B. 1978. Does cyclic GMP mediate the slow excitatory postsynaptic potential: comparison of changes in membrane potential and conductance. *Nature* 271:267–68

Hashiguchi, T., Kobayashi, H., Tosaka, T.,

Libet, B. 1982. Two muscarinic depolarizing mechanisms in mammalian sympathetic neurons. *Brain Res.* 242:378–83

Hawkins, R. D., Castellucci, V. F., Kandel, E. R. 1981a. Interneurons involved in mediation and modulation of the gill-withdrawal reflex in *Aplysia.* I. Identification and characterization. *J. Neurophysiol.* 45:304–14

Hawkins, R. D., Castellucci, V. F., Kandel, E. R. 1981b. Interneurons involved in mediation and modulation of the gill-withdrawal reflex in *Aplysia.* II. Identified neurons produce heterosynaptic facilitation contributing to behavioral sensitization. *J. Neurophysiol.* 45:315–26

Hawkins, R. D., Abrams, T. W., Carew, T. J., Kandel, E. R. 1983. A cellular mechanism of classical conditioning in *Aplysia:* Activity-dependent amplification of presynaptic facilitation. *Science* 219:400–5

Hodgkin, G., Huxley, A. F. 1952a. Currents carried by sodium and potassium ions through the membrane of the giant axon of *Loligo. J. Physiol.* 116:449–72

Hodgkin, G., Huxley, A. F. 1952b. The dual effects of membrane potential on sodium conductance in the giant axon of *Loligo. J. Physiol.* 116:496–506

Hodgkin, A. L., Keynes, R. D. 1955. Active transport of cations in giant axons from *Sepia* and *Loligo. J. Physiol.* 128:28–60

Horn, J. P., Dodd, J. 1981. Monosynaptic muscarinic activation of K^+ conductance underlies the slow inhibitory postsynaptic potential in sympathetic ganglia. *Nature* 292:625–27

Horridge, G. A. 1962. Learning leg position by the ventral nerve cord of headless insects. *Proc. R. Soc. London, Ser. B* 157:33–52

Hoyle, G. 1980a. Learning, using natural reinforcements, in insect preparations that permit cellular neuronal analysis. *J. Neurobiol.* 11:323–54

Hoyle, G. 1982. Pacemaker change in a learning paradigm. In *Cellular Pacemakers,* ed. D. O. Carpenter, pp. 3–25. New York: Wiley

Ito, M. 1970. Neurophysiological aspects of the cerebellar motor control system. *Int. J. Neurol.* 7:162–76

Ito, M. 1972. Neural design of the cerebellar motor control system. *Brain Res.* 40:81–84

Ito, M. 1977. Neuronal events in the cerebellar flocculus associated with an adaptive modification of the vestibulo-ocular reflex of the rabbit. In *Control of Brain Stem Neurons, Developments in Neuroscience,* ed. R. Baker, A. Berthoz, 1:391–98. Amsterdam: Elsevier

Ito, M. 1982. Experimental verification of Marr-Albus' plasticity assumption for the cerebellum. *Acta Biol. Acad. Sci. Hung.* 33:(2–3)189–99

Ito, M., Highstein, S. M., Fukuda, J. 1970. Cerebellar inhibition of the vestibulo-ocular reflex in rabbit and cat and its blockage by picrotoxin. *Brain Res.* 17:524–26

Ito, M., Shiida, T., Yagi, N., Yamamoto, M. 1974. The cerebellar modification of rabbit's horizontal vestibulo-ocular reflex induced by sustained head rotation combined with visual stimulation. *Proc. Jpn. Acad.* 50:85–89

Ito, M., Miyashita, Y. 1975. The effects of chronic destruction of the inferior olive upon visual modification of the horizontal vestibulo-ocular reflex of rabbits. *Proc. Jpn. Acad.* 50:716–20

Ito, M., Orlov, I., Shimoyama, I. 1978. Reduction of the cerebellar stimulus effect of rat Deiters neurons after chemical destruction of the inferior olive. *Exp. Brain Res.* 33:143–45

Ito, M., Jastreboff, P. J., Miyashita, Y. 1979a. Adaptive modification of the rabbit's horizontal vestibulo-ocular reflex during sustained vestibular and optokinetic stimulation. *Exp. Brain Res.* 37:17–30

Ito, M., Nisimaru, N. M., Shibuki, K. 1979b. Destruction of inferior olive induces rapid depression in synaptic action of cerebellar Purkinje cells. *Nature* 277:568–69

Ito, M., Sakurai, M., Tongroach, P. 1982a. Climbing fibre induced depression of both mossy fibre responsiveness and glutamate sensitivity of cerebellar Purkinje cells. *J. Physiol.* 324:113–34

Ito, M., Jastreboff, P. J., Miyashita, Y. 1982b. Specific effects of unilateral lesions in the flocculus upon eye movements of albino rabbits. *Exp. Brain Res.* 45:233–42

Jan, L. Y., Jan, Y. N. 1982. Peptidergic transmission in sympathetic ganglia of the frog. *J. Physiol.* 327:219–46

Jan, Y. N., Jan, L. Y., Kuffler, S. W. 1980. Further evidence for peptidergic transmission in sympathetic ganglia. *Proc. Natl. Acad. Sci. USA* 77:5008–12

Kalix, P., McAfee, D. A., Schorderet, M., Greengard, P. 1974. Pharmacological analysis of synaptically-mediated increase in cyclic adenosine monophosphate in rabbit superior cervical ganglion. *J. Pharmacol. Exp. Ther.* 188:676–87

Kandel, E. R. 1976. *Cellular Basis of Behavior: An Introduction to Behavioral Neurobiology.* San Francisco: Freeman

Kanz, J. E., Eberly, L. B., Cobbs, J. S., Pinsker, H. M. 1979. Neuronal correlates of siphon withdrawal in freely behaving *Aplysia. J. Neurophysiol.* 42:1538–56

Katsumaru, H., Maurakami, F., Tsukahara, N. 1982. Actin filaments in dendritic spines of red nucleus neurons demonstrated by immunoferritin localization and heavy meromyosin binding. *Biomed. Res.* 3:337–40

Katz, B., Miledi, R. 1965a. Propogation of electric activity in motor nerve terminals. *Proc. R. Soc. London, Ser. B* 161:453–83

Katz, B., Miledi, R. 1965b. The measurement of synpatic delay and the time course of acetylcholine release at the neuromuscular junction. *Proc. R. Soc. London, Ser. B* 161:483–502

Katz, B., Miledi, R. 1967. A study of synaptic transmission in the absence of nerve impulses. *J. Physiol.* 192:407–36

Kebabian, J. W., Bloom, F. E., Steiner, A. L., Greengard, P. 1975. Neurutransmitters increase cyclic nucleotides in postganglionic neurons: immunocytochemical demonstration. *Science* 190:157–59

Keller, E. L., Precht, W. 1979. Adaptive modification of central vestibular neurons in response to visual stimulation through reversing prisms. *J. Neurophysiol.* 42:896–911

Kesner, R. P. 1982. Mnemonic function of the hippocampus: Correspondence between animals and humans. See Woody 1982, pp. 75–84

Kettner, R. E., Thompson, R. F. 1982. Auditory signal detection and decision processes in the nervous system. *J. Comp. Physiol. Psychol.* 96:328–31

Kistler, H. B., Hawkins, R. D., Koester, J., Kandel, E. R., Schwartz, J. H. 1983. Immunocytochemical studies of neurons producing presynaptic facilitation in the abdominal ganglion of *Aplysia californica. Soc. Neurosci. Abstr.* 9:915

Klein, M., Kandel, E. R. 1978. Presynaptic modulation of voltage-dependent Ca^{++} current: Mechanism for behavioral sensitization in *Aplysia californica. Proc. Natl. Acad. Sci. USA* 75:3512–16

Klein, M., Kandel, E. R. 1980. Mechanism of calcium current modulation underlying presynaptic facilitation and behavioral sensitization in *Aplysia. Proc. Natl. Acad. Sci. USA* 77:6912–16

Klein, M., Camardo, J., Kandel, E. R. 1982. Serotonin modulates a new potassium current in the sensory neurons that show presynaptic facilitation in *Aplysia. Proc. Natl. Acad. Sci. USA* 79:5713–17

Kobayashi, H., Hashiguchi, T., Ushiyama, N. 1978. Postsynaptic modulation by cyclic AMP, intra- or extra-cellularly applied, or by stimulation of preganglionic nerve, in mammalian sympathetic ganglion cells. *Nature* 271:268–70

Kobayashi, H., Libet, B. 1968. Generation of slow postsynaptic potentials without increases in ionic conductance. *Proc. Natl. Acad. Sci. USA* 60:1304–11

Kobayashi, H., Libet, B. 1970. Action of noradrenaline and acetylcholine on sympathetic ganglion cells. *J. Physiol.* 208:353–72

Koketsu, K. 1969. Cholinergic synaptic potentials and the underlying ionic mechanisms. *Fed. Proc.* 28:101–31

Krnjevic, K., Rumain, R., Renaud, L. 1971. The mechanism of excitation by acetycholine in the cerebral cortex. *J. Physiol.* 215:247–68

Kuba, K., Koketsu, K. 1978b. Intracellular injection of calcium ions and chelating agents into the bullfrog sympathetic ganglion cells and effects of caffeine. In *Iontophoresis and Transmitter Mechanisms in the Mammalian Central Nervous System*, ed. R. W. Ryall, J. S. Kelly, pp. 158–60. Amsterdam: Elsevier

Kuba, K., Nishi, S. 1976. Rhythmic hyperpolarizations and depolarization of sympathetic ganglion cells induced by caffeine. *J. Neurophysiol.* 39:547–63

Kuba, K., Nishi, S. 1979. Characteristics of fast excitatory postsynaptic current in bullfrog sympathetic ganglion cells. *Pfluegers Arch.* 378:205–12

Kuba, K., Koketsu, K. 1978a. Synaptic events in sympathetic ganglia. *Prog. Neurobiol.* 11:77–169

Kuno, M. 1971. Quantum aspects of central and ganglionic synaptic transmission in vertebrates. *Physiol. Rev.* 51:647–78

Kupfermann, I., Pinsker, H., Castellucci, V. F., Kandel, E. R. 1971. Central and peripheral control of gill movements in *Aplysia*. *Science* 174:1252–56

Kupfermann, I., Carew, T. J., Kandel, E. R. 1974. Local, reflexive and central commands controlling gill and siphon movements in *Aplysia californica*. *J. Neurophysiol.* 37:990–1019

Lavond, D. G., McCormick, D. A., Clark, G. A., Holmes, D. T., Thompson, R. K. 1981. Effects of ipsilateral rostral pontine reticular lesions on retention of classically conditioned nicitating membrane and eyelid responses. *Physiol. Psychol.* 9:335–39

Lederhendler, I., Goh, Y., Alkon, D. L. 1982. Type B photoreceptor changes predict modification of motoneuron responses to light during retention of *Hermissenda* associative conditioning, *Soc. Neurosci. Abstr.* 8:825

Lederhendler, I., Gart, S., Alkon, D. L. 1983. Associative learning in *Hermissenda crassicornis* (gastropoda): Evidence that light (the CS) takes on characteristics of rotation (the UCS). *Biol. Bull.* 165:529

Lee, R. M. 1976. Conditioning of *Pleurobranchaea*. *Science* 193:72–73

Levy, W. B., Steward, O. 1979. Synapses as associative memory elements in the hippocampal formation. *Brain Res.* 175:233–45

Levy, W. B., Steward, O. 1983. Temporal contiguity requirements for long-term associative potentiation/depression in the hippocampus. *Neuroscience* 8:791–97

Libet, B. 1970. Generation of slow inhibitory and excitatory postsynaptic potentials. *Fed. Proc.* 29:1945–56

Libet, B. 1984. Heterosynaptic interaction at a sympathetic neuron as a model for induction and storage of a postsynaptic memory trace. In *Neurobiology of Memory and Learning*, ed. G. Lynch, J. McGaugh, N. Weinberger. New York: Guilford. In press

Libet, B. 1979a. Slow synaptic actions in ganglionic functions. In *Integrative Functions of the Autonomic Nervous System*, ed. C. McBrooks, K. Koizumi, A. Sata. Tokyo and Amsterdam: Tokyo Univ. Press and Elsevier/North Holland Biomed.

Libet, B. 1979b. Which postsynaptic action of dopamine is mediated by cyclic AMP? *Life Sci.* 24:1043–58

Libet, B., Kobayashi, H. 1974. Adrenergic mediation of slow inhibitory postsynaptic potential in sympathetic ganglia of the frog. *J. Neurophysiol.* 37:805–14

Libet, B., Kobayashi, H., Tanaka, T. 1975. Synaptic coupling into the production and storage of a neuronal memory trace. *Nature* 258:155–57

Libet, B., Owman, Ch. 1974. Concomitant changes in formaldehyde-induced fluorescence of dopamine interneurones and in slow inhibitory postsynaptic potentials of rabbit superior cervical ganglion, induced by stimulation of preganglionic nerve or by a muscarinic agent. *J. Physiol.* 237:635–62

Libet, B., Tosaka, T. 1969. Slow inhibitory and excitatory postsynaptic responses in single cells of mammalian sympathetic ganglia. *J. Neurophysiol.* 32:43–50

Libet, B., Tosaka, T. 1970. Dopamine as a synaptic transmitter and modulator in sympathetic ganglia; a different mode of synaptic action. *Proc. Natl. Acad. Sci. USA* 67:667–73

Lincoln, J. S., McCormick, D. A., Thompson, R. F. 1982. Ipsilateral cerebellar lesions prevent learning of the classically conditioned nictitating membrane/eyelid response. *Brain Res.* 242:190–93

Lindl, T., Cramer, H. 1975. Evidence against dopamine as a mediator of the rise of cyclic AMP in the superior cervical ganglion of the rat. *Biochem. Biophys. Res. Commun.* 65:731–39

Lisberger, S. G., Fuchs, A. F. 1978. Role of primate flocculus during rapid behavioral modification of vestibuloocular reflex. I. Purkinje cell activity during visually guided horizontal smooth-pursuit eye movements and passive head rotation. *J. Neurophysiol.* 41:733–63

Lisberger, S. G., Miles, F. A. 1980. Role of primate medial vestibular nucleus in long-term adaptive plasticity of vestibuloocular reflex. *J. Neurophysiol.* 43:1725–45

Llinas, R., Sugimori, M. 1980. Electrophysiological properties of in vitro Purkinje cell dendrites in mammalian cerebellar slices. *J. Physiol.* 305:197–213

London, J. A., Gillette, R. 1983. Changes in specific interneurons presynaptic to command neurons underlying associative learning in *Pleurobranchaea. Soc. Neurosci. Abstr.* 9:914

Lonsbury-Martin, B. L., Martin, G. K., Schwartz, S. M., Thompson, R. F. 1976. Neural correlates of auditory plasticity during classical conditioning in the rabbit. *J. Acoust. Soc. Am.* 60:582

Lorente de No, R. 1933. Vestibulo-ocular reflex arc. *Arch. Neurol. Psychiatry* 30:245–91

Lukowiak, K., Jacklet, J. W. 1972. Habituation and dishabituation: Interactions between peripheral and central nervous systems in *Aplysia. Science* 178:1306–8

Lukowiak, K., Sahley, C. 1981. The in vitro classical conditioning of the gill withdrawal reflex of *Aplysia californica. Science* 212:1516–18

Lukowiak, K. 1982. Associative learning in the isolated siphon, mantle, gill and abdominal ganglion preparation of *Aplysia:* a new paradigm. *Soc. Neurosci. Abstr.* 8:385

Lukowiak, K. 1983. Associative learning in an *in vitro Aplysia* preparation: Facilitation at a sensory motor neuron synapse. *Soc. Neurosci. Abstr.* 9:169

Lynch, G., Baudry, M. 1984. The biochemistry of memory: A new and specific hypothesis. *Science* 224:1057–63

Lynch, G., Halpain, S., Baudry, M. 1983a. Structural and biochemical effects of high frequency stimulation in the hippocampus. In *Neurobiology of the Hippocampus,* ed. W. Seifert, pp. 253–64. New York: Academic

Lynch, G., Larson, J., Kelso, S., Barrionuevo, G., Schottler, F. 1983b. Intracellular injections of EGTA block induction of hippocampal long-term potentiation. *Nature* 305:719–21

Maekawa, K., Simpson, J. I. 1973. Climbing fiber responses evoked in vestibulocerebellum of rabbit from visual system. *J. Physiol.* 36:649–66

Marr, D. 1969. A theory of cerebellar cortex. *J. Neurophysiol.* 36:649–66

Marshall, J. F. 1984. Brain function: Neural adaptations and recovery from injury. *Ann. Rev. Psychol.* 35:277–308

McAfee, D. A., Greengard, P. 1972. Adenosine 3',5'-monophosphate: electrophysiological evidence for a role in synaptic transmission. *Science* 178:310–12

McCormick, D. A., Lavond, D. G., Thompson, R. F. 1982a. Concomitant classical conditioning of the rabbit nictitating membrane

and eyelid responses: correlations and implications. *Physiol. Behav.* 28:769–75

McCormick, D. A., Guyer, P. E., Thompson, R. F. 1982b. Superior cerebellar lesions selectively abolish the ipsilateral classically conditioned nictitating membrane/eyelid response of the rabbit. *Brain Res.* 244:347–50

McCormick, D. A., Clark, G. A., Lavond, D. G., Thompson, R. F. 1982c. Initial localization of the memory trace for a basic form of learning. *Proc. Natl. Acad. Sci. USA* 79:2731–35

McCormick, D. A., Thompson, R. F. 1983. Cerebellum: Essential involvement in the classically conditioned eyelid response. *Science* 223:296–99

McElearney, A., Farley, J. 1983. Persistent changes in *Hermissenda* B photoreceptor membrane properties with associative training: A role for pharmacological modulation. *Soc. Neurosci. Abstr.* 9:915

McNaughton, B. L., Douglas, R. M., Goddard, G. V. 1978. Synaptic enhancement in fascia dentata: Cooperativity among coactive afferents. *Brain Res.* 157:277–93

McNaughton, B. L. 1983. Activity dependent modulation of hippocampal synaptic efficacy: Some implications for memory processes. See Lynch et al 1983a, pp. 233–52

Meech, R. W. 1974. The sensitivity of *Helix aspersa* neurons to injected calcium ions. *J. Physiol.* 237:259–77

Mendell, L. M. 1984. Modifiability of spinal synapses. *Physiol. Rev.* 64:260–324

Miles, F. A., Braitman, D. J. 1980. Long-term adaptive changes in primate vestibuloocular reflex. II. Electrophysiological observations on semicircular canal primary afferents. *J. Neurophysiol.* 43:1426–36

Miles, F. A., Braitman, D. J., Dow, B. M. 1980a. Long-term adaptive changes in primte vestibulooocular reflex. IV. Electrophysiological observations in flocculus of adapted monkeys. *J. Neurophysiol.* 43:1477–93

Miles, F. A., Fuller, J. H. 1974. Adaptive plasticity in the vestibulo-ocular responses of the rhesus monkey. *Brain Res.* 80:512–16

Miles, F. A., Lisberger, S. G. 1981. Plasticity in the vestibulo-ocular reflex: A new hypothesis. *Ann. Rev. Neurosci.* 4:273–300

Miles, F. A., Fuller, J. H., Braitman, D. J., Dow, B. M. 1980. Long-term adaptive changes in primate vestibuloocular reflex. III. Electrophysiological observations in flocculus of normal monkeys. *J. Neurophysiol.* 43:1437–76

Mochida, S. 1982. Physiological characterization of two dopamine receptors in the superior cervical ganglion of rabbits. *J. Tokyo Med. Coll.* 40:201–13

Mochida, S., Kobayashi, H., Tosaka, T., Ito, J., Libet, B. 1981. Specific dopamine receptor mediates the production of cyclic AMP in the rabbit sympathetic ganglia and thereby modulates the muscarinic postsynaptic responses. *Adv. Cyclic Nucleotide Res.* 14:685

Moore, J. W. 1979. Brain processes and conditioning, In *Mechanisms of Learning and Motivation: A Memorial Volume to Jerzy Konorski*, ed. A. Dickinson, R. A. Boakes, pp. 111–42. Hillsdale, NJ: Erlbaum

Moore, J. W. 1984. Two model systems. In *Neural Mechanisms of Conditioning*. ed. D. L. Alkon, C. D. Woody, New York: Plenum. In press

Movshon, J. A., Van Sluyters, R. C. 1981. Visual neural development. *Ann. Rev. Psychol.* 32:477–522

Mpitsos, G. J., Davis, W. J. 1973. Learning: Classical and avoidance conditioning in the mollusc *Pleurobranchaea*. *Science* 180:317–20

Mpitsos, G. J., Collins, S. D. 1975. Learning: Rapid aversion conditioning in the gastropod mollusc *Pleurobranchaea*. *Science* 188:954–57

Mpitsos, G. J., Collins, S. D., McClellan, A. D. 1978. Learning: Model system for physiological studies. *Science* 199:497–506

Murachi, T. 1983. Calpain and calpastatin, *Trends Biochem. Sci.* 167–69

Murakami, F., Tsukahara, N., Fujito, Y. 1977a. Analysis of unitary EPSPs mediated by the newly-formed corticorubral synapses after lesion of the interpositus nucleus. *Exp. Brain Res.* 30:233–43

Murakami, F., Tsukahara, N., Fujito, Y. 1977b. Properties of synaptic transmission of the newly formed corticorubral synapses after lesion of the nucleus interpositus of the cerebellum. *Exp. Brain Res.* 30:245–58

Nakamura, Y., Mizuno, N., Konishi, A., Sato, M. 1974. Synaptic re-organization of the red nucleus after chronic deafferentation from cerebellorubral fibers. An electron-microscope study in the cat. *Brain Res.* 82:298–301

Neary, J. T., Crow, T., Alkon, D. L. 1981. Change in a specific phosphoprotein band following associative learning in *Hermissenda*. *Nature* 293:658–70

Nishi, S., Koketsu, K. 1967. Origin of ganglionic inhibitory postsynaptic potential. *Life Sci.* 6:2049–55

Nishi, S., Koketsu, K. 1968a. Early and late after-discharges of amphibian sympathetic ganglion cells. *J. Neurophysiol.* 31:109–30

Nishi, S., Koketsu, K. 1968b. Analysis of slow inhibitory postsynaptic potential of bullfrog sympathetic ganglion. *J. Neurophysiol.* 31:717–28

Norman, R. J., Villablanca, J., Brown, K. A., Schwafel, J. A., Buchwald, J. S. 1974. Classical eyeblink conditioning of the bi-

laterally hemispherectomized cat. *Exp. Neurol.* 44:363–80

Norman, R. J., Buchwald, J. S., Villablanca, J. R. 1977. Classical conditioning with auditory discrimination of the eyeblink in decerebrate cats. *Science* 196:551–54

Oakley, D. A., Russell, I. S. 1972. Neocortical lesions and Pavlovian conditioning. *Physiol. Behav.* 8:915–26

Oakley, D. A., Russell, I. S. 1977. Subcortical storage of Pavlovian conditioning in the rabbit. *Physiol. Behav.* 18:931

Oda, Y., Kuwa, K., Miyasaka, S., Tsukahara, N. 1981. Modification of rubral unit activities during classical conditioning in the cat. *Proc. Jpn. Acad.* 57:402–5

Oleson, T. D., Ashe, J. H., Weinberger, N. M. 1975. Modification of auditory and somatosensory system activity during pupillary conditioning in the paralyzed cat. *J. Neurophysiol.* 38:1114–39

Olton, D. S., Becker, J. T., Handelman, G. E. 1979. Hippocampus, space, and memory. *Behav. Brain Sci.* 2:313–22

Pavlov, I. P. 1927. *Conditioned Reflexes.* Transl. G. V. Anrep. London: Oxford

Pellmar, T. C. 1984. Enhancement of inward current by serotonin in neurons of *Aplysia*. *J. Neurobiol.* 15:13–26

Peretz, B. 1970. Habituation and dishabituation in the absence of the central nervous system. *Science* 169:379–81

Peretz, B., Jacklet, W., Lukowiak, K. 1976. Habituation of reflexes in *Aplysia*: Contribution of the peripheral and central nervous systems. *Science* 191:1740–42

Perlman, A. 1979. Central and peripheral control of siphon-withdrawal reflex in *Aplysia californica*. *J. Neurophysiol.* 42:510–29

Pinsker, H., Kupfermann, I., Castellucci, V. F., Kandel, E. R. 1970. Habituation and dishabituation of the gill-withdrawal reflex in *Aplysia. Science* 167:1740–42

Pinsker, H. M., Hening, W. A., Carew, T. J., Kandel, E. R. 1973. Long-term sensitization of a defensive withdrawal reflex in *Aplysia. Science* 182:1039–42

Precht, W. 1979. Vestibular mechanisms. *Ann. Rev. Neurosci.* 2:265–89

Prokasy, W. F. 1972. Developments with the two-phase model applied to human eyelid conditioning. In *Classical Conditioning II: Current Research and Theory*, ed. A. H. Black, W. F. Prokasy, pp. 119–47. New York: Appleton-Century-Crofts

Purves, D., Lichtman, J. W. 1983. Specific connections between nerve cells. *Ann. Rev. Physiol.* 45:553–65

Rawson, J. A., Tilokskulchai, K. 1982. Climbing fiber modification of cerebellar Purkinje cell responses to parallel fiber inputs. *Brain Res.* 237:492–97

Renaud, L. P., Blume, H. W., Pittman, Q. J.,

Lamour, Y., Tan, A. T. 1979. Thyrotropin-releasing hormone selectively depresses glutamate excitation of cerebral cortical neurons. *Science* 205:1275–77

Richards, W., Farley, J. 1984. Associative-learning changes intrinsic to *Hermissenda* Type A photoreceptors *Soc. Neurosci. Abstr.* 10:623

Richards, W., Farley, J., Alkon, D. L. 1983. Extinction of associative learning in *Hermissenda:* Behavior and neural correlates. *Soc. Neurosci. Abstr.* 9:916

Richards, W., Farley, J., Alkon, D. L. 1984. Extinction of associative learning in *Hermissenda:* Behavior and neural correlates. *Behav. Brain Res.* In press

Robinson, D. A. 1976. Adaptive gain control of vestibuloocular reflex by the cerebellum. *J. Neurophysiol.* 39:954–69

Rosenfeld, M. E., Moore, J. W. 1983. Red nucleus lesions disrupt the classically conditioned nictitating membrane response in rabbits. *Behav. Brain Res.* 10:393–98

Rosenzweig, M. R., Bennett, E. L. 1977. Effects of environmental enrichment or impoverishment on learning and on brain values in rodents. In *Genetics, Environment, and Intelligence,* ed. A. Oliverio. pp. 163–95. Amsterdam: Elsevier/North Holland

Rosenzweig, M. R., Bennett, E. L. 1978. Experiential influences on brain anatomy and brain chemistry in rodents. In *Studies on the Development of Behavior and the Nervous System.* Vol. 4, *Early influence,* ed. G. Gottleib, pp. 289–327. New York: Academic

Sahley, C., Gelperin, A., Rudy, J. W. 1981a. One-trial associative learning modifies food odor preferences of a terrestrial mollusc. *Proc. Natl. Acad. Sci. USA* 78:640–42

Sahley, C., Rudy, J. W., Gelperin, A. 1981b. An analysis of associative learning in a terrestrial mollusc. I. Higher-order conditioning, blocking, and a transient US preexposure effect. *J. Comp. Physiol.* 144:1–8

Sandoval, M. E., Cotman, C. W. 1978. Evaluation of glutamate as a neurotransmitter of cerebellar fibers. *Neuroscience* 3:199–206

Sato, S., Tsukahara, N. 1976. Some properties of the theoretical membrane transients in Rall's neuron model. *J. Theor. Biol.* 63:151–63

Schwartzkroin, P., Wester, L. 1975. Long-lasting facilitation of a synaptic potential following tetanization in the in vitro hippocampal slice. *Brain Res.* 89:107–19

Shashoua, V. E., Teyler, T. J. 1982. Possible mechanisms of LTP: Role of secreted proteins. In *Hippocampal long-term potentiation: mechanisms and implications for memory,* ed. L. W. Swanson, T. J. Teyler, R. F. Thompson. *Neurosci. Res. Program Bull.* 20(5):671–76

Shoukimas, J. J., Alkon, D. L. 1980. Voltage-dependent, early outward current in a photo-receptor of *Hermissenda crassicornis, Soc. Neurosci. Abstr.* 6:17

Shoukimas, J. J., Alkon, D. L. 1983. Effect of voltage-dependent K⁺ conductances upon initial generator response in β-photoreceptors of *H. Crassicornis. Biophys. J.* 41:37a

Siegelbaum, S., Camardo, J., Kandel, E. R. 1982. Serotonin and cyclic AMP close single potassium channels in *Aplysia* sensory neurons. *Nature* 299:413–17

Skrede, D. D., Malthe-Sorenssen, D. 1981. Increased resting and evoked release of transmitter following repetitive electrical tetanization in hippocampus: a biochemical correlate to long-lasting synaptic potentiation. *Brain Res.* 208:436–41

Siman, R., Baudry, M., Lynch, G. 1983. A possible mechanism for modification of dendritic spine shape. *Soc. Neurosci. Abstr.* 9:103.13

Smith, A. M. 1970. The effects of rubral lesions and stimulation on conditioned fore-limb flexion responses in the cat. *Physiol. Behav.* 5:1121–26

Smith, P. A., Weight, F. F. 1977. Role of electrogenic sodium pump in slow synaptic inhibition is re-evaluated. *Nature* 267:68–70

Smith, P. A., Weight, F. F. 1981. Evidence for generation of the slow IPSP by the direct muscarinic hyperpolarizing action of acetylcholine in bullfrog sympathetic ganglia. *Soc. Neurosci Abstr.* 7:807

Solomon, P. R. 1980. A time and place for everything? Temporal processing views of hippocampal function with special reference to attention. *Physiol. Psychol.* 8:254–61

Solomon, P. R., Moore, J. W. 1975. Latent inhibition and stimulus generalization of the classically conditioned nictitating membrane response in rabbits *(Oryctolagus cuniculus)* following dorsal hippocampal ablations. *J. Comp. Physiol. Psychol.* 89:1192–1203

Spear, P. D. 1979. Behavioral and neurophysiological consequences of visual cortex damage: mechanisms of recovery. *Prog. Psychobiol. Physiol. Psychol.* 8:45–90

Steinbach, J. H., Stevens, C. F. 1976. Neuromuscular transmission, In *Frog Neurobiology,* ed. R. Llinas, W. Precht, pp. 330–92. Berlin, Heidelberg, New York: Springer-Verlag

Steward, O. 1984. Polyribosomes at the base of dendritic spines of CNS neuron; their possible role in synapse construction and modification *Cold Spring Harbor Symp.* In press

Steward, O., Levy, W. B. 1982. Preferential localization of poly-ribosomes under the base of dendritic spines in granule cells of dentate gyrus. *J. Neurosci.* 2:284–91

Steward, O., Fass, B. 1983. Polyribosomes associated with dendritic spines in the denervated dentate syrus: Evidence for local regulation of protein synthesis during reinnervation. *Prog. Brain Res.* 58:131–36

Stricker, E. M., Zigmond, M. J. 1976. Recovery of function after damage to central catecholamine-containing neurons: A neurochemical model for the lateral hypothalamic syndrome. *Prog. Psychobiol. Physiol. Psychol.* 6:121–88

Swanson, L. W., Teyler, T. J., Thompson, R. F. 1982. Mechanisms and functional implications of hippocampal LTP. *Neurosci. Res. Program Bull.* 20:613–769

Tabata, M., Alkon, D. L. 1982. Positive synaptic feedback in visual system of nudibranch mollusk *Hermissenda crassicornis*. *J. Neurophysiol.* 48:174–91

Takemori, S., Cohen, B. 1974. Loss of visual suppression of vestibular nystagmus after flocculus lesions. *Brain Res.* 72:213–24

Taube, J. S., Schwartzkroin, P. A. 1983. Intracellular tests of possible LTP mechanisms. *Soc. Neurosci. Abstr.* 9:30.9

Teyler, T. J., Goddard, G. V., Lynch, G., Andersen, P. 1982. Properties and mechanisms of LTP. In Swanson, L. W., Teyler, T. J., Thompson, R. F., eds. Hippocampal long-term potentiation: mechanisms and implications for memory. *Neurosci. Res. Program Bull.* 20(5):644–63

Thomas, R. C. 1972. Electrogenic sodium pump in nerve and muscle cells. *Physiol. Rev.* 52:563–94

Thompson, R. F., Spencer, W. A. 1966. Habituation: a model phenomenon for the study of neuronal stubstrates of behavior. *Phsycol. Rev.* 173:16–43

Thompson, R. F., McCormick, D. A., Lavond, D. G., Clark, G. C., Kettner, R. E., Mauk, M. K. 1983. The Engram found? Initial localization of the memory trace for a basic form of associative learning. *Prog. Psychobiol. Physiol. Psychol.* 10:167–196

Thompson, R. F., Barchas, J. D., Clark, G. A., Donegan, N., Kettner, R. E., et al. 1984. Neuronal substrates of associative learning in the mammalian brain. See Camardo et al 1984

Tosaka, T., Chichibu, S., Libet, B. 1968. Intracellular analysis of slow inhibitory and excitatory postsynaptic potentials in sympathetic ganglia of the frog. *J. Neurophysiol.* 31:396–409

Tosney, T., Hoyle, G. 1977. Computer-controlled learning in a simple system. *Proc. R. Soc. London, Ser. B.* 195:365–93

Tsukahara, N. 1978. Synaptic plasticity in the red nucleus. In *Neuronal Plasticity,* ed. C. W. Cotman, pp. 113–30. New York: Raven

Tsukahara, N. 1981. Synaptic plasticity in the central nervous system. *Ann. Rev. Neurosci.* 4:351–79

Tsukahara, N. 1982. Brain plasticity: the themes and case studies of neuro-biophysics. *Adv. Biophys.* 15:131–72

Tsukahara, N., Fujito, Y. 1976. Physiological evidence of formation of new synapses from cerebrum in the red nucleus neurons following cross-union of forelimb nerves. *Brain Res.* 106:184–88

Tsukahara, N., Hultborn, H., Murakami, F. 1974. Sprouting of cortico-rubral synapses in red nucleus neurons after destruction of the nucleus interpositus of the cerebellum. *Experimentia* 30:57–58

Tsukahara, N., Hultborn, H., Murakami, F., Fujito, Y. 1975. Electrophysioloical study of formation of new synapses and collateral sprouting in red nucleus neurons after partial denervation. *J. Neurophysiol.* 38:1359–72

Tsukahara, N., Oda, Y., Notsu, T. 1981. Classical conditioning mediated by the red nucleus in the cat. *J. Neurosci.* 1:72–79

Tsukahara, N., Fujito, Y., Oda, Y., Maeda, J. 1982. Formation of functional synapses in the adult cat red nucleus from the cerebrum following cross-innervation of the forelimb flexor and extensor nerves. I. Appearance of new synaptic potentials *Exp. Brain Res.* 45:1–12

Turner, R. W., Baimbridge, K. G., Miller, J. J. 1982. Calcium-induced long-term potentiation in the hippocampus. *Neuroscience* 7:1411–16

van Harreveld, A., Fifkova, E. 1975. Swelling of dendritic spines in the fascia dentata after stimulation of the perforant fibers as a mechanism of post-tetanic potentiation. *Exp. Neurol.* 49:736–49

Voronin, L. L. 1983. Long-term potentiation in the hippocampus. *Neuroscience* 10:1051–69

Wagner, A. R. 1981. SOP: A model of automatic memory processing in animal behavior. In *Information Processing in Animals: Memory Mechanisms,* ed. N. E. Spear, R. R. Miller, pp. 5–47. Hillsdale, NJ: Erlbaum

Walters, E. T., Carew, T. J., Hawkins, R. D., Kandel, E. R. 1982. Classical conditioning in *Aplysia:* Neuronal circuits involved in associative learning. See Woody 1982, pp. 677–96

Walters, E. T., Byrne, J. H. 1983. Associative conditioning of single sensory neurons suggests a cellular mechanism for learning. *Science* 219:405–8

Weight, F. F., Padjen, A. 1973a. Slow synaptic inhibition: evidence for synaptic inactivation of sodium conductance in sympathetic ganglion cells. *Brain Res.* 55:219–24

Weight, F. F., Padjen, A. 1973b. Acetylcholine and slow synaptic inhibition in frog sympathetic ganglion cells. *Brain Res.* 55:225–28

Weight, F. F., Smith, P. A. 1980. Small intensely fluorescent (SIF) cells and the generation of slow postsynaptic inhibition in sympathetic ganglia. In *Histochemistry and Cell Biology of Autonomic Neurons, SIF Cells, and Paraneurons, Advances in Biochemical Psychopharamacology*, ed. O. Eranko, S. Soinila, H. Paivarinta, 25:159–71. New York: Raven

Weight, F. F., Smith, P. A. 1981. IPSP reversal: evidence for increased potassium conductance combined with decreased sodium conductance. *Adv. Physiol. Sci.* 4:351–54

Weight, F. F., Votava, J. 1970. Slow synaptic excitation in sympathetic ganglion cells; evidence for synaptic inactivation of potassium conductance. *Science* 170:755–57

Weight, F. F., Votava, J. 1971. Inactivation of potassium conductance in slow postsynaptic excitation. *Science* 172:504

Weight, F. F., Smith, P. A., Schulman, J. A. 1978. Postsynaptic potential generation appears independent of synaptic elevation of cyclic nucleotides in sympathetic neurons. *Brain Res.* 158:197–202

Weight, F. F. 1983. Synaptic mechanisms in amphibian sympathetic ganglia. In *Autonomic Ganglia*, ed. L.-G. Elfvin, 11:309–44. New York: Wiley

Weiskrantz, L., Warrington, E. K. 1979. Conditioning in amnesic patients. *Neuropsychology* 17:187–94

Weisz, D. J., Solomon, P. R., Thompson, R. F. 1980. The hippocampus appears necessary for trace conditioning. *Bull. Psychon. Soc. Abstr.* 193:244

West, A., Barnes, E., Alkon, D. L. 1982. Primary changes of voltage responses during retention of associative learning, *J. Neurophysiol.* 48:1243–55

Wigstrom, H., McNaughton, B. L., Barnes, C. A. 1982. Long-term synaptic enhancement in hippocampus is not regulated by postsynaptic membrane potential. *Brain Res.* 233:195–99

Woody, C. D. 1982. Neurophysiologic correlates of latent facilitation. In *Conditioning: Representation of Involved Neural Function*, ed. C. D. Woody, pp. 233–48. New York: Plenum

Woody, C. D. 1984. The electrical excitability of nerve cells as an index of learned behavior. See Camardo et al 1984

Woody, C. D., Black-Cleworth, P. 1973. Differences in excitability of cortical neurons as a function of motor projection in conditioned cats. *J. Neurophysiol.* 36:1116

Woody, C. D., Brozek, G. 1969a. Conditioned eye blink in the cat: evoked responses of short latency. *Brain Res.* 12:257–60

Woody, C. D., Brozek, G. 1969b. Gross potential from facial nucleus of cat as an index of neural activity in response to glabella tap. *J. Neurophysiol.* 32:704–16

Woody, C. D., Engel, J. Jr. 1972. Changes in unit activity and thresholds to electrical microstimulation at coronal-pericruciate cortex of cat with classical conditioning of different facial movements. *J. Neurophysiol.* 35:230–41

Woody, C. D., Vassilevsky, N. N., Engel, J. Jr. 1970. Conditioned eye blink: unit activity at coronal-precruciate cortex of the cat. *J. Neurophysiol.* 33:851–64

Woody, C., Yarowsky, P., Owens, J., Black-Cleworth, P., Crow, T. 1974. Effect of lesions of cortical motor areas on acquisition of conditioned eye blink of the cat. *J. Neurophysiol.* 37:385–94

Woody, C. D., Knispel, J. D., Crow, T. J., Black-Cleworth, P. A. 1976a. Activity and excitability to electrical current of cortical auditory receptive neurons of awake cats as affected by stimulus association. *J. Neurophysiol.* 39:1045

Woody, C. D., Carpenter, D. O., Gruen, E., Knispel, J. D., Crow, T. J., Black-Cleworth, P. 1976b. Persistent increases in membrane resistance of neurons in cat motor cortex *Armed Forces Radiobiol. Res. Inst. Sci. Rep.* SR76:1–31

Woody, C. D., Swartz, B. E., Gruen, E. 1978. Effects of acetycholine and cyclic GMP on input resistance of cortical neurons in awake cats. *Brain Res.* 158:373–95

Woody, C. D., Alkon, D. L., Hay, B. 1983. Depolarization-induced effects of intracellularly applied calcium-calmodulin dependent protein kinase in neurons of the motor cortex of cats. *Soc. Neurosci. Abstr.* 9:602

Woollacott, M., Hoyle, G. 1977. Neural events underlying learning: Changes in pacemaker. *Proc. R. Soc. London, Ser. B* 195:395–415

Wu, R., Farley, J. 1984. Serotonin reduces K currents and enhances a Ca^{2+} current in *Hermissenda* Type B photoreceptors. *Soc. Neurosci. Abstr.* 10:620

Yamamoto, C., Chujo, T. 1978. Long-term potentiation in thin hippocampal sections studied by intracellular and extra-cellular recordings. *Exp. Neurol.* 58:242–50

Yeo, C. H., Hardiman, M. J., Glickstein, M., Steele Russel, I. 1982. Lesions of cerebellar nucleii abolish the classically conditioned nictitating membrane response. *Soc. Neurosci. Abstr.* 8:22

Added in proof . . .

Alkon, D. L., Sakakibara, M. 1984. Prolonged inactivation of a calcium-dependent K^+ current but not Ca^{++} current by light-activated release of intracellular calcium. *Soc. Neurosci. Abstr.* 10:10

Connor, J. A., Alkon, D. L. 1984. Light- and voltage-dependent increases of calcium ion concentration in molluscan photoreceptors. *J. Neurophysiol.* 51:745–52

Sakakibara, M., Alkon, D. L., Lederhendler, I., Heldman, E. 1984. α_2-receptor control of Ca^{++}-mediated reduction of voltage-dependent K^+ currents. *Soc. Neurosci. Abstr.* 10:950

Ann. Rev. Psychol. 1985. 36:495–529
Copyright © 1985 by Annual Reviews Inc. All rights reserved

CONTROLLABILITY AND PREDICTABILITY IN ACQUIRED MOTIVATION

Susan Mineka

Psychology Department, University of Wisconsin, Madison, Wisconsin 53706

Robert W. Hendersen

Psychology Department, University of Illinois, Champaign, Illinois 61820

CONTENTS

0066-4308/85/0201-0495$02.00

INTRODUCTION

The phenomena of acquired motivation can be viewed through a variety of different lenses. In this overview we use a particularly wide-angle lens to draw together an array of empirical phenomena that superficially might seem so disparate as to be unrelated. Nevertheless, we believe that the motivational consequences of prediction and control, no matter how diverse, are so intimately related to one another that full appreciation and true understanding of these effects requires examining them together, at all levels of analysis. To achieve the scope of coverage essential to such an overview, we have had to sacrifice focused evaluation and exhaustive coverage; accordingly, we rely heavily on other reviews of subcomponents of this field.

The phenomena reviewed here all reflect the role of prediction and control in determining motivation. That is, we examine how exposure to various kinds of orderly relationships affects processes that instigate, energize, select, and organize action. A central theme of our review is that the effects of control and of prediction are so closely intertwined, both operationally and functionally, that it can be seriously misleading to try to examine one in isolation from the other. For organizational purposes we separate the effects of control, of prediction, and of the interactions of the two, but this separation is necessarily somewhat arbitrary. Indeed, we are concerned throughout this review with how the individually analyzed effects of prediction and control combine, synergize, compete, and interfere with one another as they fit together to form a complicated pattern of motivational effects.

CONTROLLABILITY AND UNCONTROLLABILITY

Overview

Psychology has long been concerned with the importance of control over consequential outcomes (e.g. White 1959, Rotter 1966), but interest in the topic has expanded enormously in the past two decades, partly because of the development of experimental methodologies that allow direct manipulation of the amount of control that people and animals have over events in their environment. Two major categories of effects emerge from the myriad experiments using the standard triadic design (i.e. pretreatment with controllable stimulation, with yoked-uncontrollable stimulation, or with no stimulation). First and best known are the deleterious consequences of exposure to uncontrollable events, in comparison to exposure to controllable events or to no stimulation. These have often been labeled "learned helplessness" effects because of the theory developed to explain some of the early experiments in this area (Overmier & Seligman 1967, Seligman & Maier 1967). Our discussion of these effects is brief, because they are well known and are reviewed extensively elsewhere. The second category, often known as mastery effects, includes beneficial consequences of exposure to controllable events in comparison to exposure to uncontrollable events, or to no stimulation. These effects receive more detailed coverage here because they are less familiar but nonetheless important. Theories of the mechanisms underlying the effects of exposure to controllable and uncontrollable stimulation are discussed in a separate section.

Exposure to Uncontrollable Events

Exposure to uncontrollable aversive events (such as electric shocks, loud noise, or cold water) can result in major behavioral and physiological changes in a wide range of species. The initial finding was that exposure to inescapable shocks results in severe retardation of subsequent learning to escape or avoid shock in a different situation. This proactive interference, or "learned helplessness," effect was hypothesized to stem from both an associative and a motivational deficit. That is, when an organism learns it has no control over important events, there is an impaired ability to detect response-outcome contingencies in later situations and a response-initiation deficit caused by a belief that responses will be ineffective in producing relief (Overmier & Seligman 1967, Maier et al 1969).

It is difficult to establish the existence of these two deficits independently of one another. A major consequence of exposing animals to uncontrollable shock is an activity deficit (Glazer & Weiss 1976a,b, Anisman et al 1978, Jackson et al 1978, Maier & Jackson 1979, Irwin et al 1980). However, experiments in animals also demonstrate an associative deficit that appears to be independent of this activity or motivational deficit (Alloy & Seligman 1979, Jackson et al 1978, 1980; although see Anisman et al 1984 for a failure to replicate some of these effects with mice). In humans exposed to uncontrollable events the existence of an associative deficit that is independent of a motivational deficit is less well established (Alloy & Seligman 1979, Alloy & Abramson 1982).

In addition to activity deficits and possible associative deficits, many other generally adverse consequences follow exposure to uncontrollable events. In animals, uncontrollable shock, compared to controllable shock, results in (a) lowered aggressiveness and competitiveness in a variety of situations (e.g. Rapaport & Maier 1978, Williams 1982); (b) conditioning of higher levels of fear to neutral stimuli paired with the shock (Desiderato & Newman 1971, Mineka et al 1984); (c) increased stress-induced ulceration (Weiss 1971, 1977; but see Murison 1980 for an exception); (d) alterations in levels of cortisol and in a number of important neurotransmitters (Weiss et al 1976, 1981, Anisman & Sklar 1979, Anisman et al 1981, Dess et al 1983); (e) an opiate-mediated analgesia that dissipates fairly rapidly but is reinstatable 24 hours later by exposure to several shocks (Maier et al 1982, 1983a,b); (f) increased susceptibility to the growth of certain kinds of cancer (Sklar & Anisman 1981,

Visintainer et al 1983); and (g) suppression of lymphocyte proliferation (Laudenslager et al 1983; see also Jemmott & Locke 1984).

There are proactive effects of exposing animals to uncontrollable *appetitive,* as well as *aversive,* events. Rats and pigeons exposed to noncontingent "free" food are later retarded at learning to work for their food. Furthermore, prior exposure to noncontingent food impairs learning of escape-avoidance responses, which indicates that learning about lack of control has cross-reinforcer generality (see Overmier et al 1980 for a review).

Exposure to uncontrollable events has myriad effects in humans, although a substantial proportion of these studies have yielded null effects (e.g. *J. Abnorm. Psychol.* 1978, Special Issue: Learned helplessness as a model of depression). In addition to impaired problem-solving and increased passivity (Seligman 1975), there are also (*a*) mood changes such as increased anxiety, hostility and/or depression (e.g. Gatchel et al 1975, Miller & Seligman 1975); (*b*) increased subjective and psychophysiological indices of pain and distress, both in anticipation of painful stimulation, and possibly on impact as well (see Miller 1979, Thompson 1981 for reviews); and (*c*) increased susceptibility to disease and unhappiness in the elderly (Rodin 1980, Rodin & Langer 1980, Schulz 1980, Schulz & Hanusa 1980). (See Garber & Seligman 1980 and Baum & Singer 1980 for reviews of the human helplessness literature.) Furthermore, the effects of *potential* or *perceived* control are similar to effects that occur when subjects have actual control. Thus, the expectation that one *could* exercise control may be sufficient to reduce the stress experienced during exposure to uncontrollable events (see Miller 1979 and Gatchel 1980 for reviews). Finally, individual differences in the effects of perceived uncontrollability have been studied, with variables such as Type A or Type B personality and locus of control interacting with the effects of control on a range of dependent variables (see Gatchel 1980, Glass & Carver 1980 for reviews).

Exposure to Controllable Stimulation

In the great majority of the studies cited above, subjects exposed to noncontingent stimulation differed from those exposed to contingent stimulation or to no stimulation; the latter two groups generally did not differ. However, exposure to contingent stimulation may have beneficial effects. For example, zoo researchers noted that captive animals allowed to work for food and other reinforcers are physically and psychologically healthier than animals maintained under standard "uncontrollable" (but unfortunately not strictly yoked) zoo conditions (e.g. Markowitz & Woodworth 1978, Myers 1978). The beneficial consequences of control may have something to do with why, at least under some circumstances, animals and human children prefer to "work" for reinforcers such as food and water rather than receiving the reinforcers noncontingently, even when a net loss of reinforcement results (see Overmier et al 1980 for a review). There are also some results suggesting a preference for control over lack of control in the case of aversive stimulation (see Miller 1979 for a review).

Regarding mastery effects per se, Goodkin (1976) reported that giving rats operant control of food or shock enhanced subsequent learning in a shock avoidance task. This enhancement occurred relative to the performance of nonpretreated animals, who in turn showed superior learning compared to subjects given pretreatment with inescapable shocks or free food. These results demonstrate mastery and helplessness effects within the same experiment, each with cross-reinforcer generality.

Most studies looking at controllability-uncontrollability effects used test tasks that require the subject to learn an operant response to escape or avoid shock, or to obtain food. Volpicelli et al (1983) instead examined the effects of prior exposure to controllable and uncontrollable shock on the persistence of responding in the face of inescapable shock. Rats that had received an inescapable shock pretreatment were less active than nonpreshocked controls. However, rats that received prior exposure to controllable shocks were much more active than nonpretreated subjects and they also showed more rapid acquisition of a response that, with a short delay, turned off shock. This suggests that prior experience with controlling shock may produce a mastery effect and the animal persists in attempting to find a way to control shock in future situations where it is uncontrollable. Again, in one experiment both mastery and helplessness effects were demonstrated.

Early experience with controllable appetitive events reduces emotionality in novel and threatening situations later in life. Joffe et al (1973) found that rats reared in environments where they could control access to food, water, and visual stimulation were subsequently less emotional and showed more exploratory behavior in an open-field situation than were rats reared in yoked uncontrollable environments. More recently Mineka et al (1984b) found related effects in infant monkeys. Twenty peer-reared rhesus monkeys were reared from 6 weeks of age in one of three environments: one where they had control over access to food, water, and treats (Master groups), or in an identical environment with inoperative manipulanda where they received yoked noncontingent access to the reinforcers (Yoked groups), or in a standard laboratory cage where they had no access to the reinforcers received by the Master and Yoked groups (No Stimulation group). When tested between 6 and 10 months of age the Master groups, relative to Yoked and No Stimulation control groups, were bolder in the presence of a fear-provoking toy monster, showed more eagerness to enter a novel and somewhat frightening playroom situation, explored more in the playroom situation, and adapted somewhat better to stressful separations from peers.

Mastery effects may also occur in human development. Gunnar's (1980a) review indicates there is a facilitation of learning in infants who have received prior experience with contingent stimulation. Dweck & Licht (1980) reviewed work suggesting that school-aged children tend to have either a mastery or helpless orientation to success and failure experiences that is quite independent of their ability. Mastery-oriented children persist longer in the face of failure, and they tend to attribute failures to bad luck, insufficient effort, or increased task difficulty. By contrast, children with a helpless orientation tend to give up faster and to attribute their failures to lack or loss of ability. In addition, helpless-oriented children tend to forget or ignore the relevance of their successes, whereas mastery-oriented children tend to remember their successes and use them to help maintain their belief in their ability to be successful again. These different orientations to success and failure probably derive from a combination of early childhood experiences and from experiences with teachers at school. For example, Dweck and Licht suggested that teachers' differential treatment of girls and boys may help explain why a helpless orientation is more common in girls and a mastery orientation is more common in boys. Teachers attributed boys' failures to a lack of motivation eight times more often than they did girls' failures and girls viewed negative feedback as a more valid measure of their intellectual abilities than did boys. Consequently girls were less likely to persist on difficult problems or in the face of failure.

Recently Dweck & Elliott (1983) also discussed how mastery and helpless orientations interact with two different views of intelligence that have been identified in children—an entity theory and an instrumental-incremental theory. For example, mastery-oriented children with an entity theory (i.e. that intelligence is a rather stable, global trait) tend to adopt goals that will result in positive judgments of their intelligence and forego goals that are risky and might lead to negative judgments of their intelligence. By contrast mastery-oriented children with an instrumental-incremental theory (i.e. that intelligence consists of an ever-expanding repetoire of skills and knowledge) tend to choose what may be more risky goals that involve learning and the acquisition of competence.

At the other end of the developmental spectrum lies the work of Rodin, Langer, and Schulz on the importance of perceived control in the elderly, especially those who are institutionalized, who may perceive that they have lost control over many aspects of their lives. This perception may then adversely affect their physical and psychological well-being. This research has not generally involved the use of a triadic design, which is necessary to draw strong conclusions about the presence of helplessness vs mastery effects, but attempts to reverse these deleterious effects by reinstilling a sense of control or mastery had positive effects on the subjects' psychological and physical well-being (see Rodin & Langer 1980, Rodin 1980, Schulz 1980, Schulz & Hanusa 1980). Moreover, the effects can be long-lasting if the manipulations produce attributions that the source of control is stable (e.g. Langer & Rodin 1976, Rodin & Langer 1977); conversely, the effects can be temporary if the manipulations are not designed to produce stable attributions for control (Schulz 1980, Schulz & Hanusa 1980; see also Krantz & Schulz 1980 for a review of research implicating the importance of instilling a sense of control in cardiac patients during their rehabilitation).

The effects of instilling a sense of control in the elderly parallel the effects of "therapy" for learned helplessness effects, wherein animals and humans that have been exposed to uncontrollable stimulation are given experience with "easy" tasks in order to reinstill a sense of control. Typically, such "therapy" removes the effects of the earlier pretreatment on subsequent learning of a difficult task (e.g. Seligman et al 1975, Klein & Seligman 1976, Williams & Maier 1977, Nation & Massad 1978).

Theories of the Effects of Control

Theories of how control and lack of control mediate the myriad effects discussed above have emerged at many levels of analysis, and the evidence suggests that many levels are necessary for a complete understanding of the effects. Working at a physiological level of analysis, Weiss and his coworkers and Anisman and his coworkers (e.g. Weiss et al 1976, Anisman et al 1981, Anisman & Zacharko 1982) demonstrated that animals exposed to uncontrollable shock show a depletion of catecholamine levels, which in turn results in a motor activation deficit. Such a mechanism can account for many of the short-term effects observed following exposure to very intense shocks, but Maier and Seligman argue it cannot account for all helplessness effects (see Maier & Seligman 1976, Seligman et al 1980). Recently Maier and his colleagues (e.g. Maier et al 1982, 1983a,b) documented that a major effect of exposure to prolonged inescapable shock is an opiate-mediated analgesia, which in turn lowers activity levels in the face of future shocks. Such analgesia effects may well underlie a good number of the so-called helplessness effects that occur in animals following exposure to uncontrollable shock (see the section on analgesia below).

At a behavioral level of analysis, there are a number of competing motor response or learned inactivity hypotheses to account for so-called helplessness effects (e.g. Levis 1976, Glazer & Weiss 1976a,b, Anderson et al 1979). These theories share the basic idea that animals exposed to inescapable shock *learn* to freeze in response to shock during the pretreatment phase, and that they continue to do so on the test task. It is well documented that inactivity occurs following exposure to uncontrollable shocks, but the occurrence of inactivity or freezing is also consistent with theories that assign importance to effects such as analgesia, reduced motivation to respond, motor activation deficit, etc.

Weiss et al (1981) proposed a theory that integrates the physiological and behavioral levels of analysis. They argue that during uncontrollable shock norepinephrine (NE) is depleted and fear is conditioned to apparatus cues. Exposure to apparatus cues that elicit fear results in rapid utilization of NE, which, if the stores of NE are still depleted, results in a motor activation deficit. Several days later, however, noradrenergic neurons have recovered and the fear that comes from exposure to apparatus cues is no longer sufficient to deplete NE to such an extent as to produce lower activity levels. Minor & LoLordo (1984) recently reported data consistent with this theory. They found helplessness effects only when rats were exposed to the same odor during testing as they had been during the inescapable shock pretreatment, thus strongly implicating the role of at least one kind of apparatus cue in mediating helplessness effects.

Another theory that implicates the importance of the generation of fear or anxiety during the *induction* phase is that of Drugan et al (1984). They found that Librium (an anti-anxiety drug) administered during the inescapable shock pretreatment phase prevented the development of a helplessness effect. However, Librium administered during the test phase was ineffective in breaking up a helplessness effect. Therefore, unlike Weiss et al (1981), they suggest that anxiety may be necessary for the induction of helplessness, but that conditioned fear or anxiety does not appear to mediate the effects. Resolution of this controversy awaits further experimentation designed explicitly to assess the role of fear in the various phases of helplessness experiments.

On a more cognitive level of analysis is the influential learned helplessness theory to explain the effects of control and lack of control (Overmier & Seligman 1967, Seligman & Maier 1967, Seligman 1975, Maier & Seligman 1976). According to this theory, when exposed to uncontrollable stimulation the organism learns to expect it has no control, which in turn results in three deficits: (*a*) a cognitive or associative deficit, which makes it very difficult for the organism subsequently to learn that it does have control; (*b*) a motivational deficit, in which the organism has less incentive to initiate active coping responses because it believes that responding will not bring relief; and (*c*) an emotional deficit characterized by sadness or depression, which stems from the feelings of helplessness. The greatest controversy in evaluating this theory concerns whether or not there is an associative deficit that can be demonstrated independent of a motivational deficit. Several experiments with animals appear to have shown such a deficit (see Alloy & Seligman 1979, Maier & Jackson 1979, Jackson et al 1980 for reviews), but there does not appear to be any convincing evidence in humans (see Alloy & Seligman 1979, Alloy & Abramson 1982).

Also at a cognitive level of analysis stands the attributional reformulation of helplessness theory first proposed by Abramson et al (1978; see Miller & Norman 1979 for a similar, independent formulation). These authors proposed that the effects of perceived uncontrollability are determined largely by why people think they lack control. The three orthogonal dimensions on which such attributions may be made are (*a*) internal vs external; (*b*) stable vs unstable; (*c*) global vs specific. Internal, stable, global attributions for lack of control (helplessness) are, according to this theory, most likely to lead to long-lasting, generalized helplessness effects, including performance deficits, depression, and lowered self-esteem. By contrast, individuals who make external, unstable, specific attributions for lack of control or failure are likely to show less generalized and less persistent performance deficits and to be less likely to experience major mood changes. In support of this theory depressed individuals tend to have an attributional style that makes them prone to blame failure and lack of control on internal, stable, and global causes (Seligman et al 1979, Raps et al 1982). Other evidence supporting this model was reviewed in several places (Abramson et al 1980, Metalsky et al 1982, Alloy et al 1984; but see also Wortman & Dintzer 1978 and Silver & Wortman 1980 for critiques of this theory). Peterson et al (1983) and Peterson & Seligman (1984) also argued that one can assess attributions with predictive validity from verbatim transcripts of verbal material as well as from the Attributional Style Questionnaire. Peterson & Seligman suggest that this may allow assessment of the attributional style of groups, which in turn may allow prediction of the outcomes of various group competitions.

In contrast to theories that view passivity, withdrawal, and submissiveness as symptoms of relinquished perceived control or helplessness, Rothbaum et al (1982) argued that helplessness theorists have only focussed on the first of two kinds of perceived control: primary control, which involves bringing the environment into line with an individual's wishes. Rothbaum et al suggest that many of the inward behaviors taken as evidence of helplessness, or relinquished perceived control, actually reflect a process of secondary control, in which individuals attempt to bring themselves in line with environmental forces. They argue that many instances of "helplessness" behaviors do not reflect amotivational states, but rather provide the organism a different kind of perceived control such as predictive control, illusory control, vicarious control, or interpretive control. Only when attempts at secondary control also fail does the organism completely lose motivation for, or perception of, control.

Taylor (1983) proposed a related theory of cognitive adaptation to threatening events. She argued that when a person is faced with an "uncontrollable" naturalistic event, such as the diagnosis of cancer, a tri-faceted readjustment process occurs. (See also Taylor et al 1984 for results supporting this theory). The person attempts to search for meaning in the experience and develops causal attributions for why the event happened. Second, the person attempts to gain a sense of mastery over the event and/or over other aspects of life. Third, the person makes efforts to enhance self-esteem; often this involves making social comparisons to other people facing similar crises who are not coping as well or who have more serious problems. Taylor argues that many of these attempts at finding meaning, mastery, and self-enhancement are based on illusions, but that such illusions pervade normal functioning and healthy adjustment (see Abramson & Alloy 1980, Alloy & Tabachnik 1984 for reviews). Furthermore, contrary to helplessness theory, Taylor et al (1984) found that when people's illusions are shattered or their plans and attempts at mastery are thwarted (e.g. cancer recurs), alternative plans and/or goals are substituted. Thus Taylor, like Rothbaum et al (1982), found humans in real-life situations to be far more adaptable and prone to engage in a variety of cognitive coping strategies before giving up than is the case in the accounts offered by Seligman (1975) and Abramson et al (1978). She argues that some of the limitations of helplessness theory stem from its heavy reliance on experimental paradigms in which a limited range of responses is related to a limited range outcomes. In the real world when uncontrollable events are encountered there are generally a wider range of alternative responses and outcomes available. Or, in the terms of helplessness theory, the persistence characteristic of mastery effects may be far more common than has previously been recognized. (See also Silver & Wortman 1980 for a review of other theories of how people cope with threatening naturalistic events.)

There are fewer theories of mastery effects than there are theories of helplessness effects. With appropriate modifications most of the theories of helplessness effects discussed above could probably account for mastery effects. However, at present the only theories that explicitly address the issue of mastery are the cognitive helplessness theories. In the terms of the original learned helplessness theory, prior experience with controllable stimulation could be expected to produce future expectancies of control that could transfer across time and situations and mediate the superior learning or persistence characteristic of mastery effects. For the attributional reformulation of helplessness theory (Abramson et al 1978), it might be expected that mastery experiences would affect attributional style. If individuals come to develop internal, stable, and potentially global attributions for success, this should mediate persistent coping attempts in other situations. In a related vein, Bandura's (1977) self-efficacy theory proposes that expectations of personal self-efficacy stem from performance accomplishments, verbal persuasion, vicarious experience, and physiological states, and that these expectations determine whether coping behavior will be sustained and how long it will persist in the face of obstacles.

Frustration, Persistence, and Loss of Control

Beneficial consequences of a history of control can accrue either through immunization against the deleterious consequences of later exposure to uncontrollable stimulation, or through learned mastery. However, the consequences of experience with control may not always be beneficial. For example, when the response required to exert control is very difficult, control may be as stressful as lack of control (e.g. Solomon et al 1980). Furthermore, Rodin et al (1980) reviewed evidence suggesting that there may not be an intrinsic need to control the environment per se as suggested by theories such as that of White (1959). Rather, their evidence suggests that the motivation for control stems from the belief that control ensures positive outcomes. Under some circumstances the exertion of control may reduce rather than enhance self-esteem (see Rodin et al 1980 for a review).

Several experiments have examined whether losing control is more or less stressful (because of immunization or mastery effects) than never having had control. For example, Stroebel (1969) found that rhesus monkeys became intensely disturbed and showed a variety of stress symptoms when a lever that had previously controlled several noxious stimuli was removed, even though no further noxious stimuli were presented. Some monkeys also showed depressive-like symptoms that persisted for many weeks. In another study that (unlike the Stroebel study) used a strictly yoked design, Hanson et al (1976) found that when a lever that had previously controlled loud noise was removed from rhesus monkeys, they showed greater elevations in cortisol levels than monkeys who never had control over the noise. (See Mineka 1982 for a further discussion of the effects of loss of control.)

One approach to loss of control stems from an integration of helplessness theory and reactance theory proposed by Wortman & Brehm (1975). They argued that when a person initially loses control, he/she senses that behavioral freedom is being threatened and becomes motivationally aroused, for a time, to restore freedom (reactance). With extended exposure to uncontrollable outcomes, a person becomes convinced that she/he cannot control her or his outcomes and gives up trying. For example, Roth & Kubal (1975) found small amounts of exposure to uncontrollable outcomes resulted in reactance (facilitation of performance) whereas more prolonged exposure resulted in helplessness (interference with performance). The Wortman & Brehm model receives its strongest support when subjects attribute their failures to internal rather than external factors (e.g. Tennen & Eller 1977, Dyck et al 1979, Pittman & Pittman 1979). Internal attributions for failure may result in the subjects attaching greater "psychological significance" to the failure; in their model, the greater the importance of the uncontrollable events or failures, the greater the reactance or helplessness. Brockner et al (1983) demonstrated the importance of individual differences in self-esteem and in self-consciousness in determining the magnitude of reactance and helplessness effects. Subjects who were highly self-focussed and who were low in self-esteem showed the largest reactance effects following small amounts of failure, and low self-esteem subjects were most susceptible to helplessness effects in an extended failure condition.

Finally, Glass & Carver (1980) reviewed evidence suggesting that, relative to individuals with Type B personalities, individuals with Type A personalities become more energized by initial perceived threats of loss of control (reactance), and more withdrawn or helpless with prolonged exposure to uncontrollable stimulation.

In sum, the effects of exposure to uncontrollable outcomes or failure experiences may be reactance or motivational arousal rather than helplessness or reduced motivation. Unfortunately, the boundary conditions that determine whether reactance or helplessness emerges are unknown. Furthermore, the extent to which reactance effects are similar to learned mastery is also unknown. For example, the Volpicelli et al (1983) results discussed above could as well be construed as reflecting reactance as mastery.

A third area of research that more specifically examines reactions to mixed experiences with control and lack of control is the frustration/persistence work of Amsel and his colleagues. According to Amsel (1972, 1979, Amsel & Stanton 1980) when an animal expects that a response will be followed by reward, and the reward is not forthcoming, the animal experiences a primary frustration reaction that is aversive and arousing. If an organism with little or no prior experience with partial (as opposed to continuous) reinforcement repeatedly experiences frustration, it will quickly stop responding (extinction), because of the avoidance tendencies created by frustration. By contrast, if the organism has had a prior history of partial reinforcement (a mixed history of control and lack of control), Amsel argues that the avoidance tendencies innately associated with frustration become counterconditioned to approach tendencies. Such counterconditioning builds the basis for future persistence. This theory of the partial reinforcement extinction effect is thus a theory of the effects of intermittent experience with control of reinforcement on the response to later loss of control (extinction), and the results consistently show an increased persistence in responding (PRE). Amsel and his colleagues' recent work examined the ontogeny of such frustration and persistence reactions. They demonstrated that a very strong PRE can occur in preweanling rats as young as 11–12 days of age (Chen & Amsel 1980) and the duration over which such effects are maintained is comparable to that seen in much older rats (Amsel & Chen 1976). Furthermore, Chen & Amsel (1982) showed that habituation to shock in preweanling and juvenile rats can produce long-lasting persistence effects in the extinction of appetitive responses. This corroborates earlier arguments about the commonality of the motivational states of frustration and punishment (Mowrer 1960, Brown & Wagner 1964).

Nation and Massad developed the implications of frustration theory for immunization and therapy for human helplessness effects. Jones, Nation & Massad (1977) showed that an immunization procedure involving partial success training prevented the development of learned helplessness, whereas total or continuous success training did not. Nation & Massad (1978) then showed that a partial reinforcement procedure was as effective as a continuous reinforcement in reversing learned helplessness deficits. However, only the partial success therapy produced persistent escape responding in extinction. Finally, Nation et al (1979) found that subjects who had received partial success therapy showed persistence during extinction even following interpolated experiences of continuous reinforcement; subjects who had received continuous success therapy did not show such durable persistence.

Such results relating frustration and helplessness theories are of interest for several reasons. First, they demonstrate the relevance of frustration theory to the persistence of aversively motivated (escape) responses, as well as to appetitively motivated responses. Second, they challenge learned helplessness theory, which predicts continuous success to be more effective than discontinuous success as either an immunization or a therapy procedure. Finally, such results suggest that cognitive or behavior therapies for depression or helplessness effects should aim for partial, as opposed to continuous successes if the therapy is going to have long-lasting effects.

Control in Attachment Relationships

The role of control in early social and emotional development has received a good deal of attention. Indeed Levine (1980), Seligman (1975), and Watson (1972, 1979) argue that experience with contingent, controllable stimulation forms the basis for the development of early attachment relationships. These theories stem from several different lines of investigation. First, using correlational techniques researchers have examined the importance of a partner's social responsiveness in stimulating social interaction and have generally found that more positive social responses are elicited by interactive or contingent "social" partners such as mothers or peers (e.g. Clark-Stewart 1973, Levitt 1979, Suomi 1980). Unfortunately, because most of the studies supporting these conclusions are correlational, there are other factors confounded with control that would also be expected to promote positive developmental outcomes (see also Mineka et al 1984b).

Second, Levine (1980) discussed evidence from the primate literature suggesting that in the absence of a contingent relationship between the mother and the infant, true attachments are not formed. For example, although infant monkeys spend a good deal of time with inanimate surrogate mothers (who are not capable of responding to the infant's signals), the relationship of the infant to the surrogate is better described as one of emotional dependence rather than one of specific attachment. Indeed Levine concludes "that the function of attachment is to provide the infant with response contingent relationships which ultimately provide the infant with primary coping responses which permit the organism to behave adaptively and respond appropriately to its environment throughout the rest of its life" (p. 97).

Third, maternal responsiveness or sensitivity to an infant's signals apparently affects the security of attachment relationships. Researchers such as Bowlby (1969, 1973) and Ainsworth (Ainsworth et al 1978, Ainsworth 1982) argue that the infant's capacity to use the mother as a secure base from which to explore the environment is based in part on the history of control the infant has had over the mother's behavior, as reflected in measures of maternal responsiveness to the infant's signals. Ainsworth (1982) and Main & Weston (1982) reviewed evidence suggesting that the behavior of infants in the Ainsworth Strange Situation test is strongly related to the mother's degree of sensitivity in the home situation in responding to infant signals relevant to feeding, to pacing in face-to-face interaction, and to close bodily contact. Infants with responsive mothers are presumed to gain a sense of control in their interactions, which in turn is thought to promote secure attachments. Such infants show distress when their mothers leave them in the strange situation but respond positively to their mothers upon reunion. By contrast, infants who in the Ainsworth Strange Situation test show avoidant or ambivalent behavior toward their mothers upon reunion, tend to have mothers who are much less sensitive to their signals in the home situation. The mothers' insensitivity manifests itself in one or more of three ways: rejection, interference, or ignoring. Rejecting behavior on the part of the mother is most closely associated with avoidant behavior in the infants, and other forms of insensitivity on the part of the mother are more closely associated with ambivalent behavior in the infants. Such infants are thought not to gain a sense of control in their interactions, which in turn is thought to promote their sense of insecure attachment. Main & Weston (1982) even argued that the infant's avoidant behavior functions to maintain a sense of "control, flexibility, and organization" (p. 52) at a time when the infant may be threatened by loss of control and behavioral disorganization. (See also Sroufe 1979, Sroufe & Waters 1982.) Although there is evidence suggesting that an infant's behavior in the Strange Situation predicts behavior even several years later, a recent review by Lamb et al (1984) suggests that the stability and predictive validity of Strange Situation behavior is largely a function of the stability of the family circumstances and caretaking arrangements. Thus if the mother-infant or parent-infant interaction changes substantially, so may the nature of the attachment relationship.

Overlap between Controllability and Predictability

Just as environmental events vary in the degree to which we can or cannot control them, so do they vary in the degree to which we have information about their occurrence. Controllability was discussed extensively above; predictability is discussed below. However, first a brief discussion of the overlap between the two dimensions is necessary because many attempts have been made to reduce the effects of control to the effects of added predictability, and vice versa.

Operationally, the onset of either a controllable or an uncontrollable event may or may not be predictable (signaled). However, an organism that has control over the offset of an event *ipso facto* has predictability about when that event will terminate. Indeed some theorists such as Averill (1973) argue that it is this added predictability inherent in control that produces all of the beneficial consequences of having control, and conversely that it is the unpredictability inherent in not having control that produces all the negative consequences reviewed above. On the other side, predictable events are not necessarily controllable in any obvious or overt way, as for example in a classical conditioning paradigm where a CS predicts the occurrence of the US, but where the organism nominally has no control over either the CS or the US. Nevertheless some theorists argue that a signal that provides predictability allows the organism to "prepare" for the upcoming events and thereby modify their impact (Perkins 1968, 1971; see Cantor 1981 and Dinsmoor 1983 for related discussions); in other words, these theorists reduce the effects of predictability to the effects of added control. Because of these complexities and interactions between control and predictability, the two topics are discussed in conjunction when necessary below.

PREDICTABILITY AND UNPREDICTABILITY

Preference for Predictability

When subjects are given the opportunity to determine behaviorally whether shocks delivered to them will be signaled or unsignaled, they typically respond so as to increase the time they spend in the signaled condition, a phenomenon reviewed by Badia, et al (1979). Behavior that results in differential outcomes can occur for any number of reasons other than preference for one of those outcomes over the other (Irwin 1971), and it is possible to criticize many studies of preference for predictable shock on grounds that they failed to rule out other possible interpretations (Biederman and Furedy 1979). Consequently, debate over proper methodology in this field remains active (e.g. Furedy & Biederman 1981, Abbott & Badia 1984).

Historically, much of the theoretical debate about apparent preference for signaled shock revolved around the question of whether a signal that precedes shock enables an animal to prepare (cf Perkins 1968) for shock delivery in such a way that the impact of the shock is somehow reduced. By accomplishing successfully a *tour de force* of discrimination training with rats, Miller et al (1983) showed that when animals are asked to judge, via an operant discrimination paradigm, the intensity of a signaled or an unsignaled shock, they judge the signaled shock as more intense than the unsignaled one. Despite this effect of the signal, the animals showed an apparent preference (reversible when the contingency was shifted) for the signaled shock. That is, the rats appeared to prefer the signaled shock, even though it was reported to be more intense.

One possible resolution of this paradox comes from Fanselow's (1980) contextual-fear hypothesis. Fanselow found that rats spend more time on the side of a shuttle-box where shocks, but no signals, occur than on a side where *both* shocks and signals that indicate shock-free periods occur. Basing his analysis on an application of the Rescorla & Wagner (1972) model, Fanselow suggested that safety signals exert an inhibitory effect that attentuates extinction of fear to contextual cues, thereby making context more aversive on the side where safety signals occurred than on the side where they did not. Danger signals, on the other hand, should compete for associative strength with contextual cues, thereby reducing the aversiveness of the context wherein shock is signaled. Preference for signaled shock is, in this view, really a preference for the context in which shock is signaled, rather than for the signaled shock per se. Thus, even if signaled shock feels more intense than unsignalled shock, as the Miller et al (1983) results indicate, the benefits of being in a place with lower contextual fear may sufficiently outweigh the costs of a perceptually more severe shock.

The role that Fanselow's theory assigns to safety signals differs from the role they are given in Seligman's (1968, Seligman & Binik 1977) safety-signal theory, which suggests that many of the beneficial consequences of making aversive events predictable derive from the fact that periods when the signal is absent (e.g. the intertrial interval) are safe. Signals let subjects predict not only when aversive events like shock will occur, but also when they will not. The Fanselow data obviously cause problems for the safety-signal account, because animals preferred a setting that lacked safety signals over one where they were present.

Another effect that may sustain preference for signaled shock is reduction of uncertainty (see Imada & Nageishi 1982 for a review of relevant experiments). Important support for this hypothesis was provided by D'Amato & Safarjan (1979), who offered rats a choice between two conditions, one in which signals preceding shocks could be used to predict whether a shock would be of a short or long duration, and one in which the two signals were uncorrelated with the shock duration. In both conditions shocks were signaled, so the conditions were equivalent in terms of reliability of safety signaling. The rats spent a majority of their time in the correlated condition; that is, they preferred the condition that provided information about shock duration. Although this result is a straightforward prediction of the information hypothesis, D'Amato and Safarjan note that it can be derived in more convoluted ways from the safety-signal and preparatory-response theories.

The hypothesis that predictability is valued because it reduces uncertainty has proved difficult to untwine from other hypotheses, not only in the case of signaled aversive events, but also with signaled positive reinforcers. Virtually any theory of the effects of predictability can offer a plausible account of preference for signaled positive reinforcers over unsignaled ones. Therefore, attention has focused on preference for cues that signal the *non*occurrence of reinforcement, because such preference seems to indicate that animals (Lieberman 1972, Schrier et al 1980) and people (Perone & Baron 1980) will seek signals that simply reduce uncertainty. However, whether or not uncertainty reduction is reinforcing remains controversial.

Predictability, Kind of Information, and Coping Style

Giving people information about impending pain often alleviates distress (e.g. Johnson & Leventhal 1974, Johnson 1973), but the extent of this alleviation may depend on the *kind* of information provided. Telling people who were about to undergo cold pressor stimulation about the distinctive sensory properties of the noxious stimulus reduced distress, but the reduction was blocked if the people were also given information about the painfulness of the stimulation (Leventhal et al 1979). Objective stimulus information and emotional, evaluative information about a threat may therefore serve different functions (Leventhal 1982).

The effects of providing people with information that enables them to predict what will happen in a stressful situation may also differ depending on the individual's characteristic way of coping with stress. Miller (1980) reviewed the effects of providing people information about forthcoming stressful experiences, and she suggests that the utility of predictability may depend upon whether an individual characteristically copes by monitoring the details of the situation, or by blunting the effect of stressors by selectively attending to distracting information. Such effects of coping style may be absent in laboratory studies of the effects of predictability, because laboratory investigations usually involve highly constrained circumstances, wherein few distractors compete with the pattern of stimulation imposed by the experimenter. In more naturalistic settings, individual differences in the effects of predictability may become more pronounced.

Such individual differences are reported in a study of the effects of providing extensive predictive information to patients prior to their undergoing a stressful medical procedure (Miller & Mangan 1983). Patients were classified as "monitors" or "blunters" according to a scale that assesses self-reported preferences for information or distraction in stressful situations. Coping style, so assessed, interacted with the level of information provided to the patients in determining the effects of the stressful procedure on pulse rate and on subjective distress. Giving much predictive information may seriously impede the coping ability of subjects whose self-reports indicate they use a distraction-based, "blunting" style.

Effects of Unpredictability on Stress

Painful stimuli disrupt ongoing instrumental and consummatory responding and can cause physiological stress effects such as ulceration. The degree of the disruption and the stress-induced ulceration depend on whether the stimuli were signaled, and therefore predictable, or unsignaled. The directions of these effects, however, vary from experiment to experiment; sometimes predictability seems to reduce stress, while at other times it seems to enhance it. In the cases where predictability does reduce stress, either by causing less response suppression or by causing less stress-induced ulceration, safety-signal theory (Seligman & Binik 1977) appears to explain many of the data. Hymowitz (1979) reviewed the response suppression results and found them generally supportive of the safety-signal account, but he noted that a more detailed analysis of the effects of predictability on response suppression will almost certainly have to examine how safety and danger interact with other variables, including the motivational state of the subject, the particular response under study, and the past history of the animal.

Effects of Control in Mediating the Effects of Predictability

In reviewing the effects of predictability, Weinberg & Levine (1980) concluded that one source of the seeming inconsistency may be that many studies of predictability have included features that vary opportunities for control and for feedback, so many effects attributed to predictability may in fact more correctly be attributed to controllability and information about when a successful coping response has been completed. This theme has long pervaded discussions of preference for signaled shock, but it may prove relevant to other effects of predictability as well. For example, Weiss (1977) concluded that whether predictability reduces shock-induced ulceration depends on whether the situation in which the shocks occur is one in which the animals make unsuccessful attempts to control the shock; that is, the effects of attempting but failing to control the shocks can outweigh the benefits of predictability.

In addition, Davis & Levine (1982) reported results suggesting that control must be present before predictability will affect the plasma corticosterone response in rats exposed to signaled versus unsignaled shocks. Rats that received their shocks while performing a food-reinforced, operant bar-press response showed differences in the temporal pattern of plasma corticosterone response as a function of the predictability of the shock. When a similar experiment was performed with animals who were not simultaneously involved in the food-reinforced operant task, no difference in steroid response was apparent between the signaled-shock and unsignaled-shock groups. Davis &

Levine suggest that the operant task introduced an element of controllability that somehow interacted with the predictability variable to alter the temporal patterning of steroid response. Unfortunately, the animals in the two experiments, with and without the operant baseline, differed in training experience as well as in the availability of control at the time of shock exposure. Thus, resolution of what the critical factor is in determining the difference in corticosterone patterning will require experiments that control for training experience.

Role of Unpredictability in the Proactive Effects of Uncontrollability

Overmier et al (1980) argue that unpredictability may produce associative deficits that are independent of motivational deficits caused by uncontrollability. Overmier & Wielkiewicz (1983) even argued that these proactive associative deficits produced by unpredictability may be an important source of the interference effects seen in many experiments on uncontrollability. In support of the first of these two points, Dess et al (1983) reasoned that if the principal effect of unpredictability is a proactive interference effect, then variations in predictability that yield little or no difference in response patterns at the time they are imposed may nevertheless have important consequences when subjects are subsequently exposed to stressors. This dissociation between the immediate effects and the proactive effects of unpredictability was seen in their experiment examining plasma cortisol responses to shocks in dogs. Both predictability and controllability of shock were manipulated in a factorial design that made it possible to determine their effects independently. Controllability reduced cortisol response during the stress induction procedure; predictability did not. However, predictability had an important proactive effect: Animals that had received predictable shock showed a smaller cortisol response when they were subsequently tested with novel test shocks than did dogs that had previously received unpredictable shock. Thus predictability had effects on stress that were different from those of controllability and that were proactive in nature.

In another domain, the proactive effect of unpredictability on subsequent sensitivity to predictive relationships is familiar as the phenomenon of "learned irrelevance" (Mackintosh 1973, Baker 1976). Attempts to unconfound effects of unpredictability and uncontrollability suggest that learned irrelevance may play a crucial role. Overmier & Wielkiewicz (1983) found that exposing animals to tones and inescapable shocks presented randomly and independently interfered with the learning of a subsequent shock-motivated visual discrimination. This generalization of learned irrelevance from auditory to visual cues suggests that this mechanism may be an important source of the interference effects seen in experiments that nominally manipulate controllability, but also use unpredictable shocks.

Role of Unpredictability in Mediating Other Effects of Uncontrollability

Because of the predictive relationships inherent in situations that permit control, it is possible to ask if other putative consequences of uncontrollability, besides the proactive effects discussed in the preceding section, are fundamentally caused by unpredictability. Averill (1973) argued that the effects of control can be reduced to the added predictability associated with control. Consistent with this argument Burger & Arkin (1980) found that predictability without control over aversive stimulation was just as effective in reducing stress as was control without predictability over the onset of the stimulation. Schulz (1980, Schulz & Hanusa 1980) also found that for the elderly in old age homes, visits on a predictable schedule were just as beneficial as were visits on a predictable and controllable schedule. Nevertheless the results of Dess et al (1983) discussed above suggest that under at least some conditions the effects of predictability over onset and controllability are different and separable. Miller (1979) and Gatchel (1980) also review studies where predictability-over-onset appears not to be as beneficial as perceived control.

To what extent are the effects of control related to the added predictability and feedback about the *termination* of aversive events? Starr & Mineka (1977), Mineka et al (1984a), and Cook et al (1984) examined the dynamics of fear conditioning with master-yoked designs in which one group of yoked subjects received a feedback stimulus when its master made an escape or avoidance response, and in which another group of yoked subjects received no feedback stimulus. (Both yoked groups received identical amounts of shock to their masters.) Using both escape and avoidance paradigms, and several different indices of fear, yoked subjects without feedback showed higher levels of fear than the master subjects, whereas yoked subjects with feedback showed the lower level of fear characteristic of the master subjects with control. Furthermore, feedback and control appeared to be exerting their effects through similar mechanisms. Similarly, Volpicelli et al (1984) showed that standard learned helplessness effects in rats can be eliminated if the yoked subjects receive feedback stimuli when the master subjects make their response in the pretreatment phase. Thus, many effects ascribed to control may be a function of the added feedback or predictability inherent in control.

Predictability and Tolerance

That exposure to addictive drugs can be the source of very strong acquired motives is obvious, but the nature of this motivation remains controversial. While many accounts of addiction emphasize the driving force of the aversive state of drug withdrawal as the primary motivation for continual drug use (e.g. Solomon & Corbit 1974), others emphasize the positive incentive effects of the drug (Stewart et al 1984). Regardless of whether the motivation for self-administration is a positive incentive effect or an effect of escape or avoidance of withdrawal symptoms, predictive relationships appear to modulate the motivational states involved. The modulation most studied in recent years is that involved in drug tolerance. Initial reports indicated that tolerance development is most apparent when the drug exposure that induces tolerance is administered in the same environment as that in which the testing for drug effectiveness is performed. Siegel then performed a series of experiments that pointed to the role of Pavlovian signaling relationships in tolerance development (see Siegel 1983 for a review). These studies suggested the importance of contextual cues as determinants of tolerance, and they provided a variety of evidence that effects of context on tolerance largely follow patterns familiar from studies of conditioning (e.g. Siegel 1977, Siegel et al 1980, Walter & Riccio 1983). Indeed, the consequences of contextual control of tolerance are so profound as to even affect the dose that is sufficient to cause "overdose" death (Siegel et al 1982).

What is the mechanism through which context-specific tolerance effects occur? There are four major theories.

CONDITIONED COMPENSATORY RESPONSE   If tolerance development follows patterns characteristic of Pavlovian conditioning, then tolerance itself may reflect the operation of a conditioned response. In particular, Siegel argues that tolerance is mediated by the development of conditioned compensatory reactions that counteract the effects of the drug itself. This hypothesis has aroused heated debate, partly because several attempts to find such compensatory responses yielded negative results (e.g. Abbott et al 1982, Fanselow & German 1982). That such effects indeed occur now seems inescapable (at least in Siegel's laboratory; compare Sherman 1979 and Siegel et al 1980). What remains an issue is the degree to which conditioned compensatory responses contribute to tolerance. Does the difficulty some investigators have had in obtaining evidence of compensatory responses imply that such effects are too small to account for significant amounts of tolerance, or do such negative results simply reflect a phenomenon whose controlling variables have yet to be identified fully? Consider, for example, the failure of Tiffany et al (1983) to find evidence of a conditioned compensatory response (hyperalgesia), in spite of clear evidence of contextual control of morphine tolerance. Such negative results raise questions about the generality and importance of compensatory responses, but they may not ring a death knell for conditioned compensatory response theory; perhaps the measures simply were not sensitive enough to reveal a subtle compensatory response, or perhaps the form the compensatory response takes is something other than a deflection of the response measure in a direction opposite that caused by the drug. The ultimate status of compensatory response theory will depend on how well it competes with alternative theories in predicting the patterns of change characteristic of tolerance development.

OPPONENT-PROCESS THEORY   Compensatory, opposing processes are also central to Solomon's opponent-process theory (see Solomon 1980 for a review of the theory and relevant research). In this formulation, in contrast to Siegel's, the opposing state is triggered by the response to the drug itself, rather than by contextual cues associated with the drug. The strength and durability of the opponent process grow the more it is activated. According to opponent-process theory, tolerance should develop even if there are no distinctive environmental cues associated with drug administration, as long as the interdose intervals are not too widely spaced. This prediction has been tested by Seaman (1985), who administered morphine through indwelling jugular catheters to eliminate the cues normally inherent in the injection procedure, and who did not expose drugged animals to the test apparatus during the tolerance development sequence. Tolerance developed despite such careful elimination of contextual cues.

Such results do not necessarily rule out the possibility that habituation to an affect-inducing unconditioned stimulus (US) is associatively based; Schull (1979) noted that in the absence of reliable environmental signals, the US and its consequences may provide the cue information necessary to support conditioning of opponent processes. A general problem with opponent-process theory is its inability to predict whether a conditioning procedure will yield conditioned responses that support or oppose the effects of a US (Solomon 1980).

ACTION-SITE ANALYSIS   In an interesting attempt to develop a priori predictions about whether drug-associated cues will produced agonistic or compensatory responses, Eikelboom & Stewart (1982) argued that it is essential to distinguish among the several actions drugs may have. They argue that those drug actions operating through the afferent arm of a regulatory feedback system will serve as USs that support the conditioning of responses agonistic to the drug effects. On the other hand, drug actions that influence effectors through the efferent arm of the regulatory system will support the conditioning of responses that are compensatory to the drug effects. Thus, the role of conditioning in the development of tolerance will depend on the site of a drug's action, and, in the case of drugs with multiple actions, may prove enormously complex but nevertheless predictable.

HABITUATION   A theory that incorporates both associative and nonassociative forms of tolerance (see Kesner & Baker 1981), by viewing both as operating through a common mechanism, was developed by Tiffany & Baker (1984). They emphasize the importance of priming effects, which are central to

Wagner's (1976) theory of habituation. A key feature of the account is that the priming that attenuates drug reactions can be induced either by administering the drug itself (self-generated priming) or by presenting a cue that has signaled drug-exposure (associative priming). Because both kinds of priming are assumed to operate through a common channel, the model successfully predicts trade-offs between manipulations that should affect the efficacy of self-generated priming (e.g. dose, interdose interval) and manipulations that should affect associative priming (e.g. availability of cues, conditioning contingencies).

INTERACTIONS OF PREDICTION AND CONTROL

Transfer of Control

Although we have discussed theories that attempt to reduce the effects of control to predictability and vice versa, another area of research attempts to explore explicitly interactions between the two, with an assumption that operationally they are separable. At the core of the analysis of interactions between prediction and control stands an elegant experimental paradigm known as "transfer of control." In the most basic form of this type of experiment, cues are given signaling power, usually through Pavlovian conditioning, in one situation, then they are superimposed on instrumental learning or performance in a different situation. Thus, the training of control and the conditioning of prediction are operationally separated, allowing a partial unconfounding of processes that are, in most learning situations, intricately intertwined.

A central question is the mechanism by which predictive cues modulate instrumental action. At a motivational level of analysis, transfer effects may depend on the extent to which appetitive and aversive motivational systems reciprocally inhibit one another. Some theorists argue that when the appetitive motivational system is activated it should inhibit activity in the aversive motivational system and vice versa (Konorski 1967, Rescorla & Solomon 1967). If this is so, an excitor for one motivational system should be functionally equivalent to an inhibitor for the opposite motivational system. Empirical tests of this theory of reciprocal inhibition have often been less than clear-cut. In particular, it is difficult to assess the role of peripheral response competition relative to that of competition between central motive states. For example, Bouton & Bolles (1980) report that rats characteristically freeze when faced with a stimulus that signals shock, and this freezing correlates with suppression of food-reinforced operant behavior and of a consummatory lick response. Other problems have arisen from the failure of many investigators to include all the appropriate control groups and different tests for inhibition necessary to draw firm conclusions (see Dickinson & Pearce 1977, Krank 1984, for reviews of the relevant studies and the various interpretive difficulties).

Nevertheless some tentative conclusions are warranted. In an extensive review of the relevant evidence, Dickinson & Pearce (1977) concluded aversive stimuli do indeed have central inhibitory effects on appetitive motivational systems. Experiments by Krank (1984) also support this conclusion, with paradigms that ruled out peripheral response interactions. However, Krank's results also demonstrate that previous work indicating that inhibitory aversive CSs may be functionally equivalent to excitatory appetitive CSs did not include adequate controls and that such conclusions are therefore unwarranted. Regarding the inhibition of the aversive motivational system by the appetitive motivational system, Dickinson & Pearce (1977) argued that the results were not as conclusive as for the inhibitory effects of aversive stimuli on appetitive motivation. They concluded that the strongest evidence for this proposition comes from studies that have counter-conditioned the reinforcing and punishing properties of aversive stimuli. Unfortunately, there does not appear to be any conclusive evidence at the present time regarding whether or not inhibitory appetitive CSs are functionally equivalent to excitatory aversive CSs.

Nowhere does the power of the transfer-of-control paradigm become more evident than in the series of experiments reviewed by Overmier & Lawry (1979). Of the several important theoretical arguments Overmier and Lawry make, two are especially important. First, links between predictive stimuli and mediational states (expectations), and the links between mediational states and action, are sequential and independent of one another. Second, mediational states or expectations have cuing functions that are very important in response selection, perhaps even more important than the energizing functions that have traditionally been attributed to mediators. Thus, the specific expectations activated by signals are key determinants of the effects of those signals on instrumental action. According to this view, drive-summation theories of transfer (e.g. Rescorla & Solomon 1967) are inadequate to explain the degree of control exercised by mediators.

If the stimulus properties of mediators are important determinants of their effects, then it is essential to determine what those stimulus properties are. Accordingly, much of the recent work on transfer-of-control has addressed the question of the specificity of the stimulus control exerted by mediators. For example, studies of transfer from appetitive Pavlovian conditioning to appetitive instrumental responding indicate that the anticipation of a reinforcer has a different effect on instrumental action than the presentation of the reinforcer itself (Lovibond 1983). Furthermore, appetitive transfer effects appear to be reinforcer specific (Baxter & Zamble 1982), and this specificity becomes especially evident when a baseline of instrumental choice behavior is used to assess the specificity (Kruse et al 1983). A related specificity occurs in aversively based transfer-of-control. For example, the capacity of a stimulus signaling one kind of aversive event (airblast) to facilitate behavior directed at avoiding a second, qualitatively different aversive event (shock) varies both with the amount of exposure to the signaling relationship and with the retention interval separating that exposure from the transfer test (Hendersen et al 1980). Thus, the degree of reinforcer specificity of the cuing functions of mediators appears to be fluid, changing systematically with variables that might reasonably be expected to influence the amount of information contained in the learned expectation.

Psychogenic Modification of Pain Reactions

The motivational character of pain has been increasingly recognized (e.g. Bolles & Fanselow 1980), and the discovery of endogenous opiates has given new life to the question of whether some of the effects of controllability and predictability might be mediated by changes in responsiveness to pain. It has also brought to attention an important channel through which motivational effects of prediction and control may interact. Since Bolles & Fanselow (1982) reviewed the role of endogenous opiates, it has become increasingly clear that there are several different processes whereby reactivity to painful stimulation can be modified, and not all of these are blocked by opiate antagonists. Rather than attempting to review this entire area, we focus here on the role of controllability and predictability in psychogenic amelioration of pain reactions. Controllability and predictability may be involved in qualitatively different kinds of psychogenic analgesia.

CONTROLLABILITY AND ANALGESIA   There appear to be different varieties of psychogenic analgesia, some opioid in nature, others not. Lewis et al (1980) showed that different amounts of inescapable shock yield apparently different varieties of analgesia. Three minutes of continuous shock produced an apparent analgesia, but it was insensitive to the opiate antagonist naloxone; however, a longer period of intermittent inescapable shock produced analgesia that was reversed by naloxone and that was cross-tolerant with morphine. These two different kinds of apparent analgesia were further dissociated by Grau et al (1981), who varied the number of inescapable shocks their rats received. They found a U-shaped function relating number of shocks to subsequent decreased responsiveness to pain, with analgesia appearing early in the shock sequence, then disappearing, and finally reappearing. The late-occurring analgesia was blocked by an opiate antagonist, but the early-occurring effect was not, suggesting that only the late-occurring analgesia is opioid-mediated; the analgesia is also cross-tolerant with morphine (Drugan et al 1981). Furthermore, in order for the long sequence of shocks to yield an analgesia that is blocked by an opiate antagonist, it appears essential that the shocks be uncontrollable (Hyson et al 1982).

The importance of controllability in determining these analgesia effects is underscored by the discovery that prior treatment with escapable shock can immunize animals against the analgesic response to subsequent inescapable shock (Moye et al 1981). This immunization effect also occurred when an injection of morphine (see Grau et al 1981), rather than a series of inescapable tail shocks, was used to potentiate the analgesic reaction (Moye et al 1983). It thus appears that the effects of administering morphine are determined, in part, by prior experience with controllability, because prior experience with controllability can block one of the effects of a morphine injection.

Just as experience with controllability may be an important factor in determining the effects of opiates, so may opiates prove to be an important source of the various consequences of exposure to uncontrollability. Administering an opiate antagonist prior to exposing rats to an inescapable shock treatment reduces the deficit seen subsequently in shock escape performance, and it prevents the unconditioned activity deficit (Drugan & Maier 1983). It would be tempting to interpret deficits in shuttle-box escape performance following inescapable shock exposure as representing an opiate-mediated change in the animal's reaction to shock, but if this were correct, then administering morphine should also interfere with shuttle-box escape performance, which is not the case (Mah et al 1980).

PREDICTABILITY AND PAIN REACTIVITY   The importance of predictive signalling relationships in triggering modifications of pain reactivity (see the Bolles & Fanselow 1982 review) is confirmed by the discovery that morphine analgesia is enhanced by shock-associated environmental cues (Sherman et al 1984), and by additional demonstrations of cue-specific effects on pain reactivity (Fanselow & Baakes 1982, Fanselow 1984a). Shock-predictive relationships are clearly important, so to what extent are controllability and prediction confounded in studies of psychogenic analgesia? That is, are the modifications in pain reactivity produced by inescapable shock and those produced by cues that signal shock fundamentally the same? One way the two may differ is in their time course. Maier et al (1979) showed that the effects of the inescapable shock treatment largely disappear within 48 hours of the treatment, even when reinduction shocks are given immediately prior to the test of pain reactivity. This contrasts sharply with the effect of a fear signal on reactivity to shock, which is fully retained over a 90-day retention interval (Davis & Hendersen 1984), and the contrast implies that the two forms of amelioration of pain reactivity are not fundamentally identical.

Different measures of psychogenic analgesia are often discordant, and may in fact reflect different underlying neural systems (Abbott et al 1982). Davis & Hendersen (1984) report that the same fear-conditioning treatment that attentuates freezing in response to shock, suggesting possible analgesia, also produces a hyperalgesic response in the tail-flick test. Resolution of such paradoxical data will almost certainly require a deeper understanding of the behavioral complexities of measures of pain reactivity. Even if pain amelioration proves to be the fundamental process involved in many of these effects (and this has yet to be firmly established), it is important to consider broader interpretations of the behavioral measures, including patterns of motivational organization (Bolles & Fanselow 1980) and patterns of memorial activation (Davis & Hendersen 1984). Careful analysis of the particulars of measures such as freezing in response to shock (Fanselow 1984b, Grau 1984), the tail-flick test, and the formalin test (Fanselow 1984a) are essential to determining how pain reactivity is modified.

It thus appears that many of the motivational effects of prediction and control with aversive events may involve mechanisms that change reactivity to pain, and that some, but not all, of these mechanisms involve endogenous opiates. Much remains to be discovered about the conditions under which such effects occur, the nature of the change in reactivity they produce, and the consequences of such changes for the motivation of action.

CONCLUSIONS

Interest in the motivational consequences of prediction and control has a long and honorable history in experimental psychology. For example, in his classic statement of two-process theory, Mowrer (1947) argued that a "problem-posing" process combines with a "problem-solving" process to yield directed action, and this general perspective can be applied to much of the contemporary interest in motivation as well. However, many of the early theoretical developments regarding prediction and control presumed that their motivational consequences were, at core, relatively simple, perhaps reducible to one or two elementary principles of learning and activation. Recent work, including that reviewed here, forces the conclusion that the effects of prediction and control, while orderly, are extraordinarily complicated, requiring analysis at many different levels before they can properly be understood. Furthermore, the effects do not occur independently of one another, so it is essential that psychologists interested in, for example, the affective consequences of coping style be alert to, for example, the role of predictability in determining, for example, drug tolerance, because of the interrelationships among the various effects of prediction and control. Finally, there is a growing literature not even touched on here that shows that perceptions of prediction and control are often not accurate. These biases may serve to maintain illusions of control, which in turn may help to maintain self-esteem (see Alloy & Tabachnik 1984 and Abramson & Alloy 1980 for reviews).

Prediction and control have long been perceived as important goals of scientific research. One of the things that struck us in reviewing this field is how few of its recent developments could have been anticipated even as recently as a decade ago. That is, the instrumental actions of researchers have produced effects that have, in turn, altered predictions virtually beyond recognition. The motivational consequences of these developments will profoundly shape future discoveries. In what directions we cannot predict, much less control.

ACKNOWLEDGMENTS

Preparation of this chapter was supported in part by Grants BNS-8119041 and BNS-8216141 from the National Science Foundation to the first author, and by a Biomedical Research Support Grant (RR07030) award to the second. During the preparation of the chapter the first author was supported by a NIMH clinical internship stipend at Michael Reese Hospital, Chicago, Illinois, and by a Faculty Development Award from the University of Wisconsin.

Requests for reprints may be sent to either author.

Literature Cited

Abbott, B. B., Badia, P. 1984. Preference for signaled over unsignaled shock schedules: Ruling out asymmetry and response fixation as factors. *J. Exp. Anal. Behav.* 41:45–52

Abbott, F. V., Melzack, R., Leber, B. F. 1982. Morphine analgesia and tolerance in the tail-flick and formalin tests: Dose-response relationships. *Pharmacol. Biochem. Behav.* 17:1213–19

Abbott, F. V., Melzack, R., Samuel, C. 1982. Morphine analgesia in the tail-flick and formalin pain tests is mediated by different neural systems. *Exp. Neurol.* 75:644–51

Abramson, L. Y., Alloy, L. B. 1980. Judgment of contingency: Errors and their implications. See Baum & Singer 1980

Abramson, L. Y., Garber, J., Seligman, M. E. P. 1980. Learned helplessness in humans: An attributional analysis. See Garber & Seligman 1980

Abramson, L. Y., Seligman, M. E. P., Teasdale, J. D. 1978. Learned helplessness in humans: Critique and reformulation. *J. Abnorm. Psychol.* 87:49–74

Ainsworth, M. D. 1982. Attachment: Retrospect and prospect. In *The Place of Attachment in Human Behavior*, ed. C. M. Parkes, J. Stevenson-Hinde. New York: Basic Books

Ainsworth, M. D., Blehar, M. C., Waters, E., Wall, S. 1978. *Patterns of Attachment: A Psychological Study of the Strange Situation*. Hillsdale, NJ: Erlbaum

Alloy, L. B., Abramson, L. Y. 1982. Learned helplessness, depression, and the illusion of control. *J. Pers. Soc. Psychol.* 42:1114–26

Alloy, L. B., Peterson, C., Abramson, L. Y., Seligman, M. E. P. 1984. Attributional style and the generality of learned helplessness. *J. Pers. Soc. Psychol.* 46:681–87

Alloy, L. B., Seligman, M. E. P. 1979. On the cognitive component of learned helplessness and depression. In *The Psychology of Learning and Motivation*, Vol. 13, *Advances in Theory and Research*, ed. G. Bower. New York: Academic

Alloy, L. B., Tabachnik, N. 1984. Assessment of covariation by humans and animals: The joint influence of prior expectations and current situational information. *Psychol. Rev.* 91:112–49

Amsel, A. 1972. Behavioral habituation, counter-conditioning, and a general theory of persistence. In *Classical Conditioning II: Current Research and Theory*, ed. A. H. Black, W. F. Prokasy. New York: Appleton-Century-Crofts

Amsel, A. 1979. The ontogeny of appetitive learning and persistence in the rat. In *Ontogeny of Learning and Memory*, ed. N. E. Spear, B. A. Campbell. Hillsdale, NJ: Erlbaum

Amsel, A., Chen, J. S. 1976. Ontogeny of persistence: Immediate and long-term persistence in rats varying in training age between 17 and 65 days. *J. Comp. Physiol. Psychol.* 90:808–20

Amsel, A., Stanton, M. 1980. The ontogeny and phylogeny of the paradoxical reward effects. In *Advances in the Study of Behavior*, ed. J. S. Rosenblatt, R. A. Hinde, C. Beer, M. Busnel. New York: Academic

Anderson, D. C., Crowell, C. R., Cunningham, C. L., Lupo, J. V. 1979. Behavior during shock exposure as a determinant of subsequent interference with shuttle box escape—avoidance learning in the rat. *J. Exp. Psychol: Anim. Behav. Proc.* 5:243–57

Anisman, H., deCatanzaro, D., Remington, G. 1978. Escape performance following exposure to inescapable shock: Deficits in motor response maintenance. *J. Exp. Psychol: Anim. Behav. Proc.* 4:197–218

Anisman, H., Hamilton, M., Zacharko, R. 1984. Cue and response—choice acquisition and reversal after exposure to uncontrollable shock: Induction of response perseveration. *J. Exp. Psychol: Anim. Behav. Proc.* 10:229–43

Anisman, H., Kokinidis, L., Sklar, L. S. 1981. Contribution of neurochemical change to stress induced behavioral deficits. In *Theory in Psychopharmacology,* ed. S. J. Cooper, Vol. 1. London: Academic

Anisman, H., Sklar, L. S. 1979. Catecholamine depletion in mice upon reexposure to stress: Mediation of the escape deficits produced by inescapable shock. *J. Comp. Physiol. Psychol.* 93:610–25

Anisman, H., Zacharko, R. M. 1982. Depression: The predisposing influence of stress. *Behav. Brain Sci.* 5:89–137

Averill, J. R. 1973. Personal control over aversive stimuli and its relationship to stress. *Psychol. Bull.* 80:286–303

Badia, P., Harsh, J., Abbott, B. 1979. Choosing between predictable and unpredictable shock conditions: Data and theory. *Psychol. Bull.* 86:1107–31

Baker, A. G. 1976. Learned irrelevance and learned helplessness: Rats learn that stimuli, reinforcers, and responses are uncorrelated. *J. Exp. Psychol: Anim. Behav. Proc.* 2:130–41

Bandura, A. 1977. Self-efficacy: Toward a unifying theory of behavioral change. *Psychol. Rev.* 84:191–215

Baum, A., Singer, J. E., eds. 1980. *Advances in Environmental Psychology.* Vol. 2: *Applications of Personal Control.* Hillsdale, NJ: Erlbaum

Baxter, D. J., Zamble, E. 1982. Reinforcer and response specificity in appetitive transfer of control. *Anim. Learn. Behav.* 10:201–10

Biederman, G. B., Furedy, J. J. 1979. A history of rat preference for signalled shock: From paradox to paradigm. *Aust. J. Psychol.* 31:101–18

Bolles, R. C., Fanselow, M. S. 1980. A perceptual-defensive-recuperative model of fear and pain. *Behav. Brain Sci.* 3:121–31

Bolles, R. C., Fanselow, M. S. 1982. Endorphins and behavior. *Ann. Rev. Psychol.* 33:87–101

Bouton, M. E., Bolles, R. C. 1980. Conditioned fear assessed by freezing and by the suppression of three different baselines. *Anim. Learn. Behav.* 8:429–34

Bowlby, J. 1969. *Attachment.* New York: Basic Books

Bowlby, J. 1973. *Separation: Anxiety and Anger.* New York: Basic Books

Brockner, J., Gardner, M., Bierman, J., Mahan, T., Thomas, B., et al. 1983. The roles of self-esteem and self-consciousness in the Wortman–Brehm model of reactance and learned helplessness. *J. Pers. Soc. Psychol.* 45:199–209

Brown, R. T., Wagner, A. R. 1964. Resistance to punishment and extinction following training with shock or nonreinforcement. *J. Exp. Psychol.* 68:503–7

Burger, J. M., Arkin, R. M. 1980. Prediction, control, and learned helplessness. *J. Pers. Soc. Psychol.* 38:482–91

Cantor, M. 1981. Information theory: A solution to two big problems in the analysis of behavior. In *Predictability, Correlation, and Contiguity,* ed. P. Harzem, M. Zeiler, pp. 286–320. New York: Wiley

Chen, J. S., Amsel, A. 1980. Learned persistence at 11–12 but not at 10–11 days in infant rats. *Dev. Psychobiol.* 13:481–92

Chen, J. S., Amsel, A. 1982. Habituation to shock and learned persistence in preweanling, juvenile and adult rats. *J. Exp. Psychol: Anim. Behav. Proc.* 8:113–30

Clark-Stewart, A. 1973. Interactions between mothers and their young children: Characteristics and consequences. *Soc. Res. Child Dev. Monogr.* 38 (6, #153)

Cook, M., Mineka, S., Trumble, D. 1984. The role of control and feedback in the attenuation of fear over the course of avoidance learning. Submitted to *J. Exp. Psychol: Anim. Behav. Proc.*

D'Amato, M. R., Safarjan, W. R. 1979. Preference for information about shock duration. *Anim. Learn. Behav.* 7:89–94

Davis, H. D., Hendersen, R. W. 1984. Effects of conditioned fear on responsiveness to pain: Long-term retention and reversibility by naloxone. *Behav. Neurosci.* In press

Davis, H., Levine, S. 1982. Predictability, control, and the pituitary-adrenal response in rats. *J. Comp. Physiol. Psychol.* 96:393–404

Desiderato, O., Newman, A. 1971. Conditioned suppression produced in rats by tones paired with escapable or inescapable shock. *J. Comp. Physiol. Psychol.* 77:427–31

Dess, N. K., Linwick, D., Patterson, J., Overmier, J. B., Levine, S. 1983. Immediate and proactive effects of controllability and predictability on plasma cortisol responses to shocks in dogs. *Behav. Neurosci.* 97:1005–16

Dickinson, A., Pearce, J. M. 1977. Inhibitory interactions between appetitive and aversive stimuli. *Psychol. Bull.* 84:690–711

Dinsmoor, J. A. 1983. Observing and conditioned reinforcement. *Behav. Brain Sci.* 6:693–728

Drugan, R. C., Grau, J. W., Maier, S. F., Madden, J., Barchas, J. D. 1981. Cross-tolerance between morphine and the long-term analgesic reaction to inescapable shock. *Pharmacol. Biochem. Behav.* 14:677–82

Drugan, R. C., Maier, S. F. 1983. Analgesia and opioid involvement in the shock-elicited activity and escape deficits produced by inescapable shock. *Learn. Motiv.* 14:30–47

Drugan, R. C., Minor, T. R., Maier, S. F. 1984. Librium prevents the analgesia and shuttlebox escape deficit typically observed following inescapable shock. *Pharmacol. Biochem. Behav.* In press

Dweck, C. S., Elliott, E. S. 1983. Achievement motivation. In *Carmichael's Manual of Child Psychology: Social and Personality Development*, ed. P. Mussen, E. M. Hetherington. New York: Wiley

Dweck, C. S., Licht, B. G. 1980. Learned helplessness and intellectual achievement. See Garber & Seligman 1980, pp. 197–221

Dyck, O. G., Vallentyne, S., Breen, L. J. 1979. Duration of failure, causal attributions for failure, and subsequent reactions. *J. Exp. Soc. Psychol.* 15:122–32

Eikelboom, R., Stewart, J. 1982. Conditioning of drug-induced physiological responses. *Psychol. Rev.* 89:507–28

Fanselow, M. S. 1980. Signaled shock-free periods and preference for signaled shock. *J. Exp. Psychol: Anim. Behav. Proc.*, 6:65–80

Fanselow, M. S. 1984a. Shock-induced analgesia on the formalin test: Effects of shock severity, naloxone, hypophysectomy, and associative variables. *Behav. Neurosci.* 98:79–95

Fanselow, M. 1984b. Opiate modulation of the active and inactive components of the post-shock reaction: Parallels between naloxone pretreatment and shock intensity. *Behav. Neurosci.* 98:269–77

Fanselow, M. S., Baakes, M. P. 1982. Conditioned fear-induced opiate analgesia on the formalin test: Evidence for two aversive motivational systems. *Learn. Motiv.* 13:200–21

Fanselow, M. S., German, C. 1982. Explicitly unpaired delivery of morphine and the test situation: Extinction and retardation of tolerance to the suppressing effects of morphine on locomotor activity. *Behav. Neurol. Biol.* 35:231–41

Furedy, J. J., Biederman, G. B. 1981. The asymmetrical changeover procedure in the preference-for-signaled-shock literature: The penultimate word? *Psychol. Rec.* 31:371–76

Garber, J., Seligman, M. E. P. 1980. *Human Helplessness: Theory and Applications.* New York: Academic

Gatchel, R. J. 1980. Perceived control: A review and evaluation of therapeutic implications. See Baum & Singer 1980

Gatchel, R. J., Paulus, P. B., Maples, C. W. 1975. Learned helplessness and self-reported affect. *J. Abnorm. Psychol.* 84:732–34

Glass, D. C., Carver, C. S. 1980. Environmental stress and the type A response. See Baum & Singer 1980

Glazer, H. I., Weiss, J. M. 1976a. Long-term and transitory interference effects. *J. Exp. Psychol: Anim. Behav. Proc.* 2:191–201

Glazer, H. I., Weiss, J. M. 1976b. Long-term interference effect: An alternative to "learned helplessness." *J. Exp. Psychol: Anim. Behav. Proc.* 2:202–13

Goodkin, F. 1976. Rats learn the relationship between responding and environmental events: An expansion of the learned helplessness hypothesis. *Learn. Motiv.* 7:382–93

Grau, J. W. 1984. Influence of naloxone on shock-induced freezing and analgesia. *Behav. Neurosci.* 98:278–92

Grau, J. W., Hyson, R. L., Maier, S. F., Madden, J., Barchas, J. D. 1981. Long-term stress-induced analgesia and activation of the opiate system. *Science* 213:1409–11

Gunnar, M. 1980a. Contingent stimulation: A review of its role in early development. In *Coping and Health*, ed. S. Levine, H. Ursin. New York: Plenum

Gunnar, M. 1980b. Control, warning signals, and distress in infancy. *Dev. Psychol.* 16:281–89

Hanson, J. P., Larsen, M. E., Snowdon, C. T. 1976. The effects of control over high intensity noise on plasma cortisol levels in rhesus monkeys. *Behav. Biol.* 16:333–40

Hendersen, R. W., Patterson, J. M., Jackson, R. L. 1980. Acquisition and retention of control of instrumental behavior by a cue signaling airblast: How specific are conditioned anticipations? *Learn. Motiv.* 11:407–26

Hymowitz, N. 1979. Suppression of responding during signaled and unsignaled shock. *Psychol. Bull.* 86:175–90

Hyson, R. L., Ashcraft, L. J., Drugan, R. C., Grau, J. W., Maier, S. F. 1982. Extent and control of shock affects naltrexone sensitivity of stress-induced analgesia and reactivity to morphine. *Pharmacol. Biochem. Behav.* 17:1019–25

Imada, H., Nageishi, Y. 1982. The concept of uncertainty in animal experiments using aversive stimulation. *Psychol. Bull.* 91:573–88

Irwin, F. 1971. *Intentional Behavior and Motivation: A Cognitive Theory.* New York: Lippincott

Irwin, J., Suissa, A., Anisman, H. 1980. Differential effects of inescapable shock on escape performance and discrimination learning in a water escape task. *J. Exp. Psychol: Anim. Behav. Proc.* 6:21–40

Jackson, R. L., Alexander, J. H., Maier, S. F. 1980. Learned helplessness, inactivity and associative deficits: Effects of inescapable shock on response choice escape learning. *J. Exp. Psychol: Anim. Behav. Proc.* 6:1–20

Jackson, R. L., Maier, S. F., Rapaport, P. M. 1978. Exposure to inescapable shock produces both activity and associative deficits in the rat. *Learn. Motiv.* 9:69–98

Jemmott, J. B. III, Locke, S. E. 1984. Psychosocial factors, immunologic mediation, and human susceptibility to infectious disease: How much do we know? *Psychol. Bull.* 95:78–108

Joffe, J., Rawson, R., Mulick, J. 1973. Control of their environment reduces emotionality in rats. *Science* 180:1383–84

Johnson, J. E. 1973. Effects of accurate expectations about sensations on the sensory and distress components of pain. *J. Pers. Soc. Psychol.* 27:261–75

Johnson, J. E., Leventhal, H. 1974. Effects of accurate expectations and behavioral instructions on reactions during a noxious medical examination. *J. Pers. Soc. Psychol.* 29:710–18

Jones, S. L., Nation, J. R., Massad, P. 1977. Immunization against learned helplessness in man. *J. Abnorm. Psychol.* 86:75–83

Journal of Abnormal Psychology. 1978. *Special Issue: Learned Helplessness as a Model of Depression* 87:1–198

Kesner, R. P., Baker, T. B. 1981. A two-process model of opiate tolerance. In *Endogenous Peptides and Learning and Memory Processes*, ed. J. L. Martinez, R. A. Jensen, R. B. Messing, H. Rigter, J. L. McGaugh. New York: Academic

Klein, D. E., Seligman, M. E. P. 1976. Reversal of performance deficits in learned helplessness and depression. *J. Abnorm. Psychol.* 85:11–26

Konorski, J. 1967. *Integrative Activity of the Brain: An Interdisciplinary Approach.* Chicago: Univ. Chicago Press

Krank, M. D. 1984. Asymmetrical effects of Pavlovian excitatory and inhibitory aversive transfer on Pavlovian appetitive responding and acquisition. *Learn. Motiv.* In press

Krantz, D. S., Schulz, R. 1980. A model of life crisis, control, and health outcomes: Cardiac rehabilitation and relocation of the elderly. See Baum & Singer 1980

Kruse, J. M., Overmier, J. B., Konz, W. A., Rokke, E. 1983. Pavlovian conditioned stimulus effects upon instrumental choice behavior are reinforcer specific. *Learn Motiv.* 14:165–81

Lamb, M. E., Thompson, R. A., Gardner, W. P., Charnou, E. L., Estes, D. 1984. Security

of infantile attachment as assessed in the "strange situation." *Behav. Brain Sci.* 7:127–71

Langer, E. J., Rodin, J. 1976. The effects of choice and enhanced personal responsibility for the aged: A field experiment in an institutional setting. *J. Pers. Soc. Psychol.* 34:191–98

Laudenslager, M. L., Ryan, S. M., Drugan, R. C., Hyson, R. L., Maier, S. F. 1983. Coping and immunosuppression: Inescapable but not escapable shock suppresses lymphocyte proliferation. *Science* 221:568–70

Leventhal, H. 1982. The integration of emotion and cognition: A view from the perceptual-motor theory of emotion. In *Affect and Cognition: The Seventeenth Annual Carnegie Symposium on Cognition*, ed. M. S. Clark, S. T. Fiske. Hillsdale, NJ: Erlbaum

Leventhal, H., Brown, D., Shacham, S., Engquist, G. 1979. Effects of preparatory information about sensations, threat of pain, and attention on cold pressor distress. *J. Pers. Soc. Psychol.* 37:688–714

Levine, S. 1980. A coping model of mother-infant relationships. See Gunnar 1980a, pp. 87–99

Levis, D. J. 1976. Learned helplessness: Reply and an alternative S-R interpretation. *J. Exp. Psychol: Gen.* 105:47–65

Levitt, M. 1979. *Contingent feedback, familiarization and infant affect: How a stranger becomes a friend.* Presented at Soc. Res. Child Dev., San Francisco

Lewis, J. W., Cannon, J. T., Liebeskind, J. C. 1980. Opioid and nonopioid mechanisms of stress analgesia. *Science* 208:623–25

Lieberman, D. A. 1972. Secondary reinforcement and information as determinants of observing behavior in monkeys (*Macaca mulatta*). *Learn. Motiv.* 3:341–58

Lovibond, P. F. 1983. Facilitation of instrumental behavior by a Pavlovian appetitive conditioned stimulus. *J. Exp. Psychol: Anim. Behav. Proc.* 9:225–47

Mackintosh, N. J. 1973. Stimulus selection: Learning to ignore stimuli that predict no change in reinforcement. In *Constraints on Learning*, ed. R. A. Hinde, J. Stevenson-Hinde, pp. 75–96. London/New York: Academic

Mah, C., Suissa, A., Anisman, H. 1980. Dissociation of antinociception and escape deficits induced by stress in mice. *J. Comp. Physiol. Psychol.* 94:1160–71

Maier, S. F., Coon, D. J., McDaniel, M. A., Jackson, R. L., Grau, J. W. 1979. The time course of learned helplessness, inactivity, and nociceptive deficits in rats. *Learn. Motiv.* 10:467–87

Maier, S. F., Drugan, R. C., Grau, J. W. 1982. Controllability, coping behavior, and stress-induced analgesia in the rat. *Pain* 12:47–56

Maier, S. F., Jackson, R. L. 1979. Learned helplessness: All of us were right (and wrong): Inescapable shock has multiple effects. See Alloy & Seligman 1979

Maier, S. F., Jackson, R. L., Grau, J., Hyson, R., MacLennan, A. J., Moye, T. 1983a. Learned helplessness, pain inhibition, and the endogenous opiates. In *Advances in Analysis of Behavior*, Vol. 3. New York: Wiley

Maier, S. F., Seligman, M. E. P. 1976. Learned helplessness: Theory and evidence. *J. Exp. Psychol: Gen.* 105:3–46

Maier, S. F., Seligman, M. E. P., Solomon, R. L. 1969. Pavlovian fear conditioning and learned helplessness. In *Punishment and Aversive Behavior*, ed. B. Campbell, R. Church. New York: Appleton-Century-Crofts

Maier, S. F., Sherman, J., Lewis, J., Terman, G., Liebeskind, J. 1983b. The opioid/nonopioid nature of stress-induced analgesia and learned helplessness. *J. Exp. Psychol: Anim. Behav. Proc.* 9:80–90

Main, M., Weston, D. R. 1982. Avoidance of the attachment figure in infancy: Descriptions and interpretations. See Ainsworth 1982

Markowitz, H., Woodworth, G. 1978. Experimental analysis and control of group behavior. In *Behavior of Captive Wild Animals*, ed. H. Markowitz, V. J. Stevens. Chicago: Nelson Hall

Metalsky, G. I., Abramson, L. Y., Seligman, M. E. P., Semmel, A., Peterson, C. 1982. Attributional styles and life events in the classroom: Vulnerability and invulnerability to depressive and mood reactions. *J. Pers. Soc. Psychol.* 43:612–17

Miller, I. W., Norman, W. H. 1979. Learned helplessness in humans: A review and attribution theory model. *Psychol. Bull.* 86:93–118

Miller, R. R., Greco, C., Vigorito, M., Marlin, N. A. 1983. Signaled tailshock is perceived as similar to a stronger unsignaled tailshock: Implications for a functional analysis of classical conditioning. *J. Exp. Psychol: Anim. Behav. Proc.* 9:105–31

Miller, S. M. 1979. Controllability and human stress: Method, evidence, and theory. *Behav. Res. Ther.* 17:287–304

Miller, S. M. 1980. When is a little information a dangerous thing?: Coping with stressful life-events by monitoring vs. blunting. See Gunnar 1980a, pp. 145–69

Miller, S. M., Mangan, C. E. 1983. Interacting effects of information and coping style in adapting to gynecologic stress: Should the doctor tell all? *J. Pers. Soc. Psychol.* 45:223–36

Miller, W. R., Seligman, M. E. P. 1975. Depression and learned helplessness in man. *J. Abnorm. Psychol.* 84:228–38

Mineka, S. 1982. Depression and helplessness in primates. In *Child Nurturance Series: Vol. 3: Studies of Development in Nonhuman Primates*, ed. H. E. Fitzgerald, J. A. Mullins, P. Gage. New York: Plenum

Mineka, S., Cook, M., Miller, S. 1984a. Fear conditioned with escapable and inescapable shock: The effects of a feedback stimulus. *J. Exp. Psychol: Anim. Behav. Proc.* 10:307–23

Mineka, S., Gunnar, M., Champoux, M. 1984b. The effects of control in the early social and emotional development of rhesus monkeys. Submitted to *Child Dev.*

Minor, T., LoLordo, V. 1984. Escape deficits following inescapable shock: The role of contextual odor. *J. Exp. Psychol: Anim. Behav. Proc.* 10:168–81

Mowrer, O. H. 1947. On the dual nature of learning—A reinterpretation of "conditioning" and "problem-solving." *Harvard Educ. Rev.* 17:102–48

Mowrer, O. H. 1960. *Learning Theory and Behavior*. New York: Wiley

Moye, T. B., Coon, D. J., Grau, J. W., Maier, S. F. 1981. Therapy and immunization of long-term analgesia in rats. *Learn. Motiv.* 12:133–48

Moye, T. B., Hyson, R. L., Grau, J. W., Maier, S. F. 1983. Immunization of opioid analgesia: Effects of prior escapable shock on subsequent shock-induced and morphine-induced antinociception. *Learn. Motiv.* 14:238–51

Murison, R. 1980. Experimentally induced gastric ulceration: A model for psychosomatic research. See Gunnar 1980a, pp. 281–93

Myers, W. A. 1978. Applying behavioral knowledge to the display of captive animals. See Markowitz & Woodworth 1978

Nation, J. R., Cooney, J. B., Gartrell, K. E. 1979. Durability and generalizability of persistence training. *J. Abnorm. Psychol.* 88:121–36

Nation, J. R., Massad, P. 1978. Persistence training: A partial reinforcement procedure for reversing learned helplessness and depression. *J. Exp. Psychol: Gen.* 107:436–51

Overmier, J. B., Lawry, J. A. 1979. Pavlovian conditioning and the mediation of behavior. See Alloy & Seligman, 13:1–55

Overmier, J. B., Patterson, J., Wielkiewicz, R. M. 1980. Environmental contingencies as sources of stress in animals. See Gunnar 1980a, pp. 1–38

Overmier, J. B., Seligman, M. E. P. 1967. Effects of inescapable shock upon subsequent escape and avoidance responding. *J. Comp. Physiol. Psychol.* 63:28–33

Overmier, J. B., Wielkiewicz, R. M. 1983. On unpredictability as a causal factor in "learned helplessness." *Learn. Motiv.* 14:324–37

Perkins, C. C. 1968. An analysis of the concept of reinforcement. *Psychol. Rev.* 75:155–72

Perkins, C. C. 1971. Reinforcement in classical conditioning. In *Essays in Neobehaviorism: A memorial volume to Kenneth W. Spence,* ed. H. H. Kendler, J. T. Spence, pp. 113–36. New York: Appleton-Century-Crofts

Perone, M., Baron, A. 1980. Reinforcement of human observing behavior by a stimulus correlated with extinction or increased effort. *J. Exp. Anal. Behav.* 34:239–61

Peterson, C., Luborsky, L., Seligman, M. E. P. 1983. Attributions and depressive mood shifts: A case study using the symptom-context method. *J. Abnorm. Psychol.* 92:96–103

Peterson, C., Seligman, M. E. P. 1984. Causal explanations as a risk factor for depression: Theory and evidence. *Psychol. Rev.* 91:347–74

Pittman, N. L., Pittman, T. S. 1979. Effect of amount of helplessness training and internal-external locus of control on mood performance. *J. Pers. Soc. Psychol.* 37:39–47

Rapaport, P. M., Maier, S. F. 1978. Inescapable shock and food-competition dominance in rats. *Anim. Learn. Behav.* 6:160–65

Raps, C. S., Peterson, C., Reinhard, K. E., Abramson, L. Y., Seligman, M. E. P. 1982. Attributional style among depressed patients. *J. Abnorm. Psychol.* 91:102–8

Rescorla, R. A., Solomon, R. L. 1967. Two-process learning theory: Relationships between Pavlovian conditioning and instrumental learning. *Psychol. Rev.* 74:151–82

Rescorla, R. A., Wagner, A. R. 1972. A theory of Pavlovian conditioning: Variations in the effectiveness of reinforcement and nonreinforcement. See Amsel 1972

Rodin, J. 1980. Managing the stress of aging: The role of control and coping. See Gunnar 1980a

Rodin, J., Langer, E. J. 1977. Long-term effects of a control-relevant intervention with the institutionalized aged. *J. Pers. Soc. Psychol.* 35:897–902

Rodin, J., Langer, E. J. 1980. The effects of labeling and control on self-concept in the aged. *J. Soc. Issues* 36:12–29

Rodin, J., Rennert, K., Solomon, S. K. 1980. Intrinsic motivation for control: Fact or fiction. See Baum & Singer 1980

Roth, S., Kubal, L. 1975. The effects of noncontingent reinforcement on tasks of differing importance: Facilitation and learned helplessness effects. *J. Pers. Soc. Psychol.* 32:680–91

Rothbaum, F., Weisz, J. R., Snyder, S. 1982. Changing the world and changing the self: A two-process model of perceived control. *J. Pers. Soc. Psychol.* 42:5–37

Rotter, J. B. 1966. Generalized expectancies for internal versus external control of reinforcement. *Psychol. Monogr.* 80 (1, Whole No. 609)

Schrier, A. M., Thompson, C. R., Spector, N. R. 1980. Observing behavior in monkeys *(Macaca arctoides). Learn. Motiv.* 11:355–65

Schull, J. 1979. A conditioned opponent theory of Pavlovian conditioning and habituation. See Alloy & Seligman, 13:57–90

Schulz, R. 1980. Aging and control. See Abramson et al 1980

Schulz, R., Hanusa, B. H. 1980. Experimental social gerontology: A social psychological perspective. *J. Soc. Issues* 36:30–46

Seaman, S. F. 1985. Morphine tolerance growth, the effect of dose size and interval between doses. In *Affect, Conditioning, and Cognition: Essays on the Determinants of Behavior,* ed. F. R. Brush, J. B. Overmier. Hillsdale, NJ: Erlbaum. In press

Seligman, M. E. P. 1968. Chronic fear produced by unpredictable shock. *J. Comp. Physiol. Psychol.* 66:402–11

Seligman, M. E. P. 1975. *Helplessness: On Depression, Development, and Death.* San Francisco: Freeman

Seligman, M. E. P., Abramson, L. Y., Semmel, A., von Baeyer, C. 1979. Depressive attributional style. *J. Abnorm. Psychol.* 88:242–47

Seligman, M. E. P., Binik, Y. 1977. The safety-signal hypothesis. In *Operant-Pavlovian Interactions,* ed. H. Davis, H. M. B. Hurwitz, pp. 165–80. Hillsdale, NJ: Erlbaum

Seligman, M. E. P., Maier, S. F. 1967. Failure to escape traumatic shock. *J. Exp. Psychol.* 74:1–9

Seligman, M. E. P., Rossellini, R. A., Kozak, M. 1975. Learned helplessness in the rat: Reversibility, time course, and immunization. *J. Comp. Physiol. Psychol.* 88:542–47

Seligman, M. E. P., Weiss, J. M., Weinraub, M., Schulman, A. 1980. Coping behavior: Learned helplessness, physiological change and learned inactivity. *Behav. Res. Ther.* 18:459–512

Sherman, J. E. 1979. The effects of conditioning and novelty on the rat's analgesic and pyretic responses to morphine. *Learn. Motiv.* 10:383–418

Sherman, J. E., Strub, H., Lewis, J. W. 1984. Morphine analgesia: Enhancement by shock-associated cues. *Behav. Neurosci.* 98:293–309

Siegel, S. 1977. Morphine tolerance as an associative process. *J. Exp. Psychol: Anim. Behav. Proc.* 3:1–13

Siegel, S. 1983. Classical conditioning, drug tolerance, and drug dependence. In *Research Advances in Alcohol and Drug Problems,* Vol. 7, ed. Y. Israel et al. New York: Plenum

Siegel, S., Hinson, R. E., Krank, M. D., McCully, J. 1982. Heroin "overdose" death:

The contribution of drug-associated environmental cues. *Science* 216:436–37

Siegel, S., Sherman, J. E., Mitchell, D. 1980. Extinction of morphine analgesic tolerance. *Learn. Motiv.* 11:289–301

Silver, R. L., Wortman, C. B. 1980. Coping with undesirable life events. See Abramson et al 1980, pp. 279–375

Sklar, L. S., Anisman, H. 1981. Stress and cancer. *Psychol. Bull.* 89:369–406

Solomon, R. L. 1980. The opponent-process theory of acquired motivation: The cost of pleasure and the benefits of pain. *Am. Psychol.* 35:691–712

Solomon, R. L., Corbit, J. D. 1974. An opponent-process theory of motivation. I. Temporal dynamics of affect. *Psychol. Rev.* 81:119–45

Solomon, S., Holmes, D. S., McCaul, K. D. 1980. Behavioral control over aversive events: Does control that requires effort reduce anxiety and physiological arousal. *J. Pers. Soc. Psychol.* 39:729–36

Sroufe, L. A. 1979. Individual patterns of adaptation from infancy to preschool. *Minn. Symp. Child Psychol.*, Vol. 16

Sroufe, L. A., Waters, E. 1982. Issues of temperment and attachment. *Am. J. Orthopsychiatry* 52:743–46

Starr, M. D., Mineka, S. 1977. Determinants of fear over the course of avoidance learning. *Learn. Motiv.* 8:332–50

Stewart, J., deWit, H., Eikelboom, R. 1984. Role of unconditioned and conditioned drug effects in the self-administration of opiates and stimulants. *Psychol. Rev.* 91:251–68

Stroebel, C. 1969. Biologic rhythm correlates of disturbed behavior in the monkey. *Biblio. Primatol.* 9:91–105

Suomi, S. J. 1980. Contingency, perception and social development. In *Infant Social Cognition: Empirical and Theoretical Considerations*, ed. L. R. Sherrod, M. E. Lamb. Hillsdale, NJ: Erlbaum

Taylor, S. 1983. Adjustment to threatening events: A theory of cognitive adaptation. *Am. Psychol.* 38:1161–73

Taylor, S. E., Lichtman, R. R., Wood, J. V. 1984. Attributions, beliefs about control, and adjustment to breast cancer. *J. Pers. Soc. Psychol.* 46:489–502

Tennen, H., Eller, S. J. 1977. Attributional components of learned helplessness and facilitation. *J. Pers. Soc. Psychol.* 35:265–71

Thompson, S. C. 1981. Will it hurt less if I can control it? A complex answer to a simple question. *Psychol. Bull.* 90:89–101

Tiffany, S. T., Baker, T. B. 1984. Morphine tolerance as habituation. *Psychol. Rev.* In press

Tiffany, S. T., Petrie, E. C., Baker, T. B., Dahl, J. L. 1983. Conditioned morphine tolerance in the rat: Absence of a compensatory response and cross-tolerance with stress. *Behav. Neurosci.* 97:335–53

Visintainer, M. A., Seligman, M. E. P., Volpicelli, J. R. 1983. Helplessness, chronic stress, and tumor development. *Psychosom. Med.* 45:75

Volpicelli, J. R., Ulm, R. R., Altenor, A. 1984. Feedback during exposure to inescapable shocks and subsequent shock-escape performance. *Learn. Motiv.* In press

Volpicelli, J. R., Ulm, R. R., Altenor, A., Seligman, M. E. P. 1983. Learned mastery in the rat. *Learn. Motiv.* 14:204–22

Wagner, A. R. 1976. Priming in STM: An information processing mechanism for self-generated or retrieval-generated depression in performance. In *Habituation: Perspectives from Child Development, Animal Behavior, and Neurophysiology*, ed. T. J. Tighe, R. N. Leaton. Hillsdale, NJ: Erlbaum

Walter, T. A., Riccio, D. C. 1983. Overshadowing effects in the stimulus control of morphine analgesic tolerance. *Behav. Neurosci.* 97:658–62

Watson, J. S. 1972. Smiling, cooing, and the "game." *Merrill-Palmer Q.* 18:322–39

Watson, J. S. 1979. Perception of contingency as a determinant of social responsiveness. In *Origins of Infant's Social Responsiveness*, ed. E. Thoman. New York: Erlbaum

Weinberg, J., Levine, S. 1980. Psychobiology of coping in animals: The effects of predictability. See Gunnar 1980a

Weiss, J., Glazer, H., Pohorecky, L. 1976. Coping behavior and neurochemical changes in rats: An alternative explanation for the original "learned helplessness" experiments. In *Animal Models in Human Psychobiology*, ed. G. Serban, A. Kling, pp. 141–73. New York: Plenum

Weiss, J., Goodman, P., Losito, B., Corrigan, S., Charry, J., Bailey, W. 1981. Behavioral depression produced by an uncontrollable stressor: Relationship to norepinephrine, dopamine, and seratonin levels in various regions of rat brain. *Brain Res. Rev.* 3:167–205

Weiss, J. M. 1971. Effects of coping behavior in different warning-signal conditions on stress pathology in rats. *J. Comp. Physiol. Psychol.* 77:1–13

Weiss, J. M. 1977. Psychological and behavioral influences on gastrointestinal lesions in animal models. In *Psychopathology: Experimental Models*, ed. J. Maser, M. E. P. Seligman, pp. 232–69. San Francisco: Freeman

White, R. 1959. Motivation reconsidered: The concept of competence. *Psychol. Bull.* 66:317–30

Williams, J. L. 1982. Influence of shock controllability by dominant rats on subsequent attack and defensive behaviors toward colony intruders. *Anim. Learn. Behav.* 10:305–13

Williams, J. L., Maier, S. F. 1977. Trans-situational immunization and therapy of learned helplessness in the rat. *J. Exp. Psychol: Anim. Behav. Proc.*, 3:240–52

Wortman, C. B., Brehm, J. W. 1975. Responses to uncontrollable outcomes: An integration of reactance theory and the learned helplessness model. *Adv. Exp. Soc. Psychol.* Vol. 8

Wortman, C. B., Dintzer, L. 1978. Is an attributional analysis of learned helplessness phenomenon viable? A critique of the Abramson-Seligman-Teasdale Reformulation. *J. Abnorm. Psychol.* 87:75–90

Ann. Rev. Psychol. 1985. 36:531–72

SOCIAL FACTORS IN PSYCHOPATHOLOGY:
Stress, Social Support, and Coping Processes

Ronald C. Kessler, Richard H. Price, and Camille B. Wortman[*]

The University of Michigan Institute for Social Research, Ann Arbor, Michigan 48106

CONTENTS

    The first chapter on social and cultural influences on psychopathology was written for the *Annual Review of Psychology* by Dohrenwend & Dohrenwend (1974). In the intervening decade, three updates on this topic have appeared (King 1978, Strauss 1979, Eron & Peterson 1982). In these reviews, one can chart the progression of research in this area from an early interest in case finding and demographic description, through a period of debate between the contending "social causation" and "social selection" interpretations, to a more contemporary focus on theory testing and experimental intervention.

    Over the past decade, research on the influences of social and cultural factors on psychopathology has been dominated by an interest in stress and factors that

---

[*]Order of authorship is alphabetical.

0066-4308/85/0201-0531$02.00

modify its influence. Our review reflects this interest. In the first section of this paper, we examine attempts to conceptualize and measure stress and to estimate its impact on emotional functioning. Both acute and chronic stresses are considered. As we describe in more detail below, however, it has become increasingly clear that the vast majority of people who are exposed to stressful life events do not develop emotional disorder. In recent years, investigators have attempted to identify variables—so-called vulnerability or resistance factors—that may influence individual reactivity to stressful life experiences. In the second section of this review, we focus on two vulnerability factors that have generated intense interest over the past decade: social support and coping strategies.

This focus on factors that may modify the impact of stress on mental health departs from previous *Annual Review* chapters, which have focused primarily on group differences in psychopathology. In the past, considerable research effort has been devoted to documenting differences in the stress experienced by different racial or socioeconomic groups. Investigators are now beginning to consider the possibility that race, sex, and class differences in psychopathology may reflect differences in vulnerability to stress (Kessler 1979). In the final section of the chapter, we discuss how recent developments in research on stress, social support, and coping have influenced current work in the group differences area.

LIFE STRESS

For the past two decades, nonexperimental research on the relationship between stress and mental health has been based primarily on the study of life events. More recently, there has been increasing research interest in chronic stresses. Both types of research are discussed in this section. There are two different life events literatures, one grounded in epidemiology and the other in clinical practice. The first is based on large-scale survey research or on case-control studies of ill populations and well controls (e.g. Myers et al 1974, Brown & Harris 1978). In this work, investigators have focused primarily on the association between recent life events and some measure of mental distress. The Holmes & Rahe (1967) Social Adjustment Rating Scale was highly influential in refining this line of research. This life event inventory combines information about many different types of events into one overall measure of recent stress exposure. In its first decade of existence, the scale was used in over 1000 publications, many of them concerned with the mental health effects of life events (Holmes 1979). Variants on the Holmes-Rahe scale have been even more widely used in subsequent research (Thoits 1983).

In large-scale surveys of the general population, the assessment of psychopathology is usually made with a screening scale of nonspecific psychological distress, such as the Langner Scale (Langner 1962) or the Hopkins Symptom Checklist (Derogatis et al 1974). This type of scale is sensitive to both clinically significant mood disorders and to subclinical levels of distress or "demoralization: (Link & Dohrenwend 1980). In case-control studies, a sample of carefully diagnosed psychiatric patients is usually compared with a separate sample of general population control subjects (e.g. Brown & Harris 1978).

The second type of life event research is based on small samples of people who have been victimized by one particular life crisis such as widowhood, rape, or job loss (see Gore 1978, Burgess & Holmstrom 1979, Vachon et al 1982a,b). Matched control samples are sometimes used as well. Most of these studies have been designed and implemented by researchers with a practical interest in the populations in question. For the most part, these studies have not been guided by or designed to test particular theories (Silver & Wortman 1980). Researchers are usually interested in assessing the impact of the life crisis on general emotional well-being and functioning. For this reason, they typically cast a wide net in the mental health outcomes that are assessed. Screening scales of nonspecific psychological distress, measures of role impairment, and assessments of general life satisfaction are all commonly employed. The small samples typically used in life crisis research make it difficult to estimate rates of clinically significant psychiatric impairment. As a result, careful psychiatric diagnoses are seldom made of respondents in research of this sort. Each of these research traditions is considered in more detail below.

Normal Population and Case-Control Research on Life Events

Much of the research on life event effects has been based on the pioneering work of Cannon (1939) and Selye (1956). According to these theorists, life change creates a disequilibrium which imposes a period of readjustment. The readjustment period can leave the person more vulnerable to stress and its consequences. Until the mid-1970s, most research on life events focused on the task of demonstrating through epidemiological evidence that exposure to such events can, in fact, lead to illness (Rabkin & Struening 1976).

It is difficult to demonstrate that the stress typically assessed in life event inventories, like widowhood, divorce, or job loss, leads to mental health problems, although case studies of people who have lived through wars or natural disasters show that catastrophic crises can provoke significant distress (Dohrenwend & Dohrenwend 1981). The main issue in documenting the impact of more common stressors is that prior emotional difficulties can bring about some events, such as divorce or job loss, thus leading to ambiguity in the causal meaning of associations between events and disorder. This possibility is a very real one. Indeed, a substantial percentage of the events in standard life event inventories have been judged by a sample of clinicians to be symptoms of emotional disorder (Dohrenwend et al 1984).

Although sensitivity to this problem has increased over the past decade, no final resolution to this difficulty has yet been devised. Some recent studies have gone so far as to limit analysis to events that were judged unlikely to have resulted from prior psychopathology (e.g. Brown & Harris 1978). Although there is debate in the literature (cf Tennant 1983), the weight of evidence suggests that stressful events are causally implicated in some types of acute depressive disorders as well as in the elevation of dysphoric mood and demoralization (Thoits 1983, Brown & Harris 1984).

Yet the relations that have been documented are extremely small. Rabkin & Struening (1976) estimated that no more than 9% of the variance in health outcomes is explained by life events. The same predictive power is found when mental health outcomes are the focus of analysis (Thoits 1983). Early attempts to account for the disappointingly weak relationship between life events and disturbance focused on methodological shortcomings of the research (Dohrenwend & Dohrenwend 1974). Several methodological improvements were introduced in the measurement of life events, such as specifying ambiguously worded items with respect to their desirability, and eliminating events, such as minor illnesses, that may be indicative of symptomatology (Dohrenwend & Dohrenwend 1981). However, these and other refinements have not appreciably increased predictive power. Consequently, researchers have attempted to conduct a more careful analysis of the specific kinds of events that are associated with particular kinds of disorder. Some improvement results from discriminating events in terms of their desirability, controllability, predictability, seriousness, and time-clustering (Thoits 1983). Nonetheless, even with these improvements, the relationship between life changes and emotional disorder is modest. This small association may stem from the fact that a substantial percentage of the distress detected in screening scales of nonspecific psychological distress is chronic and not a result of acute life stress (Depue & Monroe 1984). Yet even in research on acute onset of clinically significant disorders, life events alone do not strongly predict outcomes (Brown & Harris 1978).

Current work is under way to extend our understanding of life events in a manner that might help account for this weak association. One important direction of this work is to improve measurement by obtaining contextually specific information about events (Brown & Harris 1978, Link et al 1983). The emotional effects of a job loss, for example, will probably differ considerably depending on the financial resources that are available to cushion the income loss, and the meaning work had for the person during the time of employment. There is general agreement that contextual information is critical for a full appreciation of life event effects (Brown 1974). However, there is controversy about how to obtain this information. Some researchers advocate asking respondents to rate the stressfulness of events directly without obtaining objective information about contexts (Sarason et al 1978). At the other extreme, some advocate a complex scheme where an interviewer presents information about the objective circumstances under which the events occurred to a panel of raters who then score the events on a variety of contextual dimensions such as forewarning (Brown & Harris 1978).

Neither of these approaches is ideal. When respondents' ratings of perceived stressfulness are used as measures of contextual importance, estimates of buffering or modifier effects are biased downward and therefore more difficult to detect. This is because some modifiers of life event effects, such as social support or coping strategies, may operate by reducing subjective perceptions of stress (Dohrenwend & Dohrenwend 1981). Subjective judgments of a particular event as stressful may also reflect underlying psychopathology, thus confounding any attempt to make a causal interpretation. Moreover, studies relying solely on ratings of perceived stressfulness provide no opportunity to illuminate the conditions under which particular events are appraised as stressful. The panel rating scheme sidesteps one part of this problem by elaborating several different dimensions of the objective context that might be consequential for health outcomes. However, if the researcher relies on information about context provided by the respondent—information that may be influenced to some degree by the respondent's vulnerability to stress or underlying psychopathology—this approach may lend itself to the same distortion of modifier effects as the subjective rating procedure (Tennant et al 1981). Some researchers are experimenting with new approaches to obtain objective information, such as using the spouse as an informant (e.g. Stone & Neale 1984). Others have maintained that the confounding between stressors and appraisal is inevitable because these variables will be fused together in nature (Lazarus et al 1984).

A two-pronged approach is needed for advancement here. First, theoretical work is necessary to develop a more complete perspective about the features of life events that are stress-provoking and the process through which events may exert noxious influence. In an excellent discussion of these issues, Thoits (1983) has concluded that the features documented as most important for the development of psychopathology are undesirability, magnitude, and time clustering, although uncontrollability is quite important with respect to depression. These characteristics may provide important clues about the processes through which exposure to events influences the development of psychopathology (Thoits 1983, Wortman 1983). For example, people who are exposed to events that are undesirable and uncontrollable may draw inferences about themselves or the world that impair their subsequent coping responses (Pearlin et al 1981, Wheaton 1982). If a woman takes many precautions to protect herself, yet is raped by an intruder who breaks into her locked apartment, she may conclude that there is no point in initiating coping efforts, since uncontrollable factors can always smash into one's life and wreak havoc (Scheppele & Bart 1983). The various mechanisms through which events may have pernicious influence have also been discussed by Kaplan et al (1983). These investigators have suggested that exposure to life events can undermine feelings of self-esteem by disrupting the person's repertoire of coping responses, or by increasing demands upon the individual and thus increasing the probability of failing to meet these demands. Investigators have also suggested that life events may exert noxious influence by increasing the number of chronic stressors to which one is exposed (e.g. see Pearlin et al 1981). Because few studies have examined the impact of life events on self-esteem, coping strategies, social support, or the number of chronic stressors experienced, it is difficult to evaluate the validity of these alternative mechanisms (Menaghan 1983).

Second, operational procedures must be developed to obtain data that are sufficiently rich to study the contextual features of life events. Preliminary work on this problem continues (Link et al 1983), but much more work is necessary to advance understanding on the empirical front. In particular, an effort must be made to take context into account rather than treating events in aggregate fashion. Such an approach could be extremely useful in clarifying the process through which life events may lead to emotional disorder.

Research on Life Crises

There is a long history of research on how people react to specific life crises such as bereavement, chronic illness, or rape. In the past, these studies have not been designed to examine whether exposure to life crises leads to psychopathology. For the most part, they were conducted by practitioners who were primarily interested in developing an understanding that could guide clinical practice. For this reason, research on exposure to specific life crises has consisted of relatively small, descriptive studies focusing on how people react to crises and how such reactions change over time. Most of the research findings have centered on emotional reactions. We know, for example, that these reactions are characterized by extreme variability (see Silver & Wortman 1980 for a more complete discussion). For example, depression is a very common reaction to bereavement, but relatively rare among rape victims, at least during the initial period following the attack. There is also evidence for variability of responses within a given type of crisis (e.g. Burgess & Holmstrom 1974). At present, there is no basis for predicting the conditions under which a particular emotional reaction is likely to occur. In addition, little is known about the relationship between initial emotional distress and long-term adjustment. Although it is widely believed that emotional distress must be expressed in order to resolve the crisis, research does not support this claim. In most studies (e.g. Vachon et al 1982a,b), those who show little distress soon after a crisis continue to score low in distress at subsequent times.

A review of the life crisis literature also suggests that there is no support for the widely held view that people go through stages of emotional reaction as they attempt to deal with a crisis. A variety of different stage models have been advocated, some postulating that individuals will go through an anger-depression sequence (e.g. Wortman & Brehm 1975, Klinger 1977) and others suggesting passage through such stages as shock, denial, anger, depression, and acceptance (see Silver & Wortman 1980 for a review). The few studies that have assessed emotional reactions longitudinally provide no support for any of these views. However, these models are particularly difficult to test or discon-firm, since some theorists have contended that people may experience more than one stage simultaneously, may move back and forth among the stages, and may skip certain stages completely (e.g. see Kubler-Ross 1969, Klinger 1977). Nonetheless, there is a pervasive belief among caregivers and helping profes-sionals that such stages exist, and they are often used as a yardstick by which to assess the patient's progress.

In the studies on reactions to life crises, is there any evidence that exposure to particular life crises is associated with the development of psychopathology? Taken together, the literature on reactions to life crises demonstrates that a substantial minority of respondents—between 20 and 40 percent—do not recover fully from the crisis despite the passage of time (see Silver & Wortman 1980 for a review). Among the bereaved, for example, Parkes (1975) found that 30% were judged as showing "bad outcomes" on a combined assessment of psychological distress, social functioning, and physical health measured two to four years after the loss (see also Parkes & Weiss 1983). It is difficult to interpret results of this sort, since the assessment of adjustment is not always made rigorously and control groups are seldom included. Nonetheless, the few studies that have included control groups and validated measures of emotional functioning reinforce the conclusion that a sizable minority of individuals suffer long-term psychiatric impairment as a result of experiencing a life crisis. For example, Maguire et al (1978) have reported that 39% of the breast cancer patients they studied were still experiencing levels of anxiety or depression "serious enough . . . to warrant psychiatric help" (p. 963) one year after their mastectomy. These problems were significantly more prevalent that those in a matched control group of women with benign breast disease. Similarly, Leh-man et al (1984) studied individuals who had lost a spouse or child in a motor vehicle accident four to seven years ago. These individuals showed significant-ly more psychopathology, particularly depression, than matched control re-spondents who did not suffer such a loss.

Most of the theoretical accounts advanced regarding how people react to life crises provide no basis for making predictions about the conditions under which a particular person will recover (cf Silver & Wortman 1980). As in the research on life events, there has been increasing interest in identifying variables that will help explain why some people show long-term distress while others recover fairly quickly. In recent years, investigators have begun to examine the role of social support and coping strategies in moderating the impact of particular life crises. These findings are discussed in a later section of the chapter.

As life event researchers become more interested in studies of reactions to specific life crises, more sophisticated research on the impact of particular events is likely to appear in the literature. There are a number of ways in which the methods developed by life events researchers can be profitably applied to the study of life crises. For example, life crisis researchers have, for the most part, devoted little attention to providing an objective characterization of the stressful experience. Clearly, a life crisis such as losing a job or becoming ill can vary enormously in the objective stress or coping challenge that is presented. Because life crisis researchers have not concerned themselves with this problem, it is not clear from most studies whether variations in outcome represent variations in exposure to stress or variations in response.

Although the empirical evidence is not yet sufficient to warrant it, another area of probable development will be the comparative analysis of different life crises. To date, most life crisis research has focused on specific events like widowhood or job loss. There have been few serious attempts to abstract from these particular events to develop a more general understanding of how the predictors of adjustment vary from one stressful situation to another. However, enough research is now in progress on specific crises that a comparative analysis will be feasible and is likely to be enlightening.

Some beginning efforts to develop a broad-based comparative perspective of this sort have recently emerged from researchers in the epidemiologic tradition. To approximate the finer texture available in crisis studies, these researchers have disaggregated their life event inventories into a series of event types including financial, health, work, death, and interpersonal events (Eckenrode & Gore 1981, Kessler et al 1984). Despite the fact that diverse events were combined in these clusters, results were far more theoretically rich than those produced in standard analyses of life event inventories. For example, while aggregate analyses document that women are more emotionally vulnerable than men to the effects of life events, they do not indicate whether this vulnerability is pervasive or confined to a special subset of events. Kessler et al (1984) were able to show on the basis of a disaggregated analysis that only a small subset of events—consisting mostly of network crises that have the capacity to provoke distress primarily through the creation of empathic concern—are involved in this sex difference in vulnerability. Future research will almost surely find it profitable to search for additional specifications of this sort.

Research on Chronic Stress

Research on the relation between chronic stress and emotional disorder is much less well developed than work on life events. It is easier to determine whether or not an event has occurred than to measure objectively the existence of an ongoing stressful situation. If we discovered, for instance, a relationship between death of a loved one and depression, we would probably interpret this as evidence that the death precipitated the depression. But what of the relationship between marital stress and depression? Typical measures of marital stress rely heavily on subjective reports from the marital partners themselves (Pearlin & Schooler 1978). On the basis of such data, it is difficult to determine whether actual or perceived marital stress has produced depression or whether depression has produced a distorted perception of the marriage or an increase in marital stress. Because of these difficulties, researchers have favored life event measures over chronic stress measures in their studies.

These reasons for focusing on life events do not argue that life events are more important than chronic stresses in explaining the distribution of mental illness in society; rather, they are methodological expedients. Recent research, in fact, has presented suggestive evidence that chronic role-related stresses (Pearlin & Schooler 1978, Kanner et al 1981, Pearlin et al 1981, Eckenrode 1984) are more strongly associated with nonspecific distress in community surveys than are life event inventories. However, there is ambiguity in these results, since the chronic stress measures are based on subjective assessment. Indeed, some chronic stresses might even be symptomatic of psychiatric impairment (Monroe 1983). Dohrenwend et al (1984) have claimed that measures of chronic stress, such as the Kanner et al (1981) Daily Hassles scale, are more confounded with measures of psychological distress than the Holmes and Rahe Scale of Life Events (see Lazarus et all 1984). Nonetheless, available evidence suggests that chronic stressors are worthy of further investigation.

Pearlin et al (1981) and Brown & Harris (1978) have done the most important work to date on the relationship between chronic stress and mental illness. As noted earlier, Pearlin and his colleagues found that chronic role-related stresses mediate the relationship between life events and depressed mood in a general population sample. They found that income loss events affected well-being largely by exacerbating already existing financial difficulties. Drawing from this research, some investigators have emphasized that in most cases life events bring about chronic stressors (Thoits 1983). Loss of a spouse, for example, may force a widow to contend with a variety of daily stressors such as relocation, financial problems, and single parenting. Brown and Harris suggest another interplay between events and chronic difficulties. They argue that continuing stresses can exacerbate the effects of life events. This can occur by creating stress overload, as when a person whose current life circumstances are straining his or her coping capacities is confronted with an additional difficulty created by an unanticipated life event. Brown and Harris also suggest that an event can "trigger" an onset of psychiatric impairment by forcing an individual to see his or her life situation in a new and more negative light. Events of this sort can be trivial in and of themselves, but they take on a new meaning in the context of chronic difficulties. For example, one woman in the Brown and Harris study became severely depressed shortly after her daughter went on vacation. In her words, the daughter's temporary departure led her to "realize then for the first time that one of these days I would lose both of the children. It made me realize just how lonely I was and how I depended on their ways" (Brown & Harris 1978, p. 145).

If the effects of life events are modified by chronic stresses in these ways, then this may explain why research on life events has failed to document large influences of events on mental illness. Clearly, explicit consideration of chronic stresses is necessary. As noted above, this is difficult to do. One difficulty with the use of perceptual measures of chronic stress is that feelings of distress can cause people to distort these perceptions and so create an inflated estimate of the relationship between strain and distress. However, instrumental variable strategies that separate subjective and objective stress components might well help resolve this problem. These techniques permit the investigator to adjust for this bias by explicitly estimating the reciproval influences of distress on perceived strain and strain on distress. Although they have not yet been applied to the analysis of chronic strain, models including instrumental variables are plausible for situations of this sort (Kessler 1982, 1983). As research on chronic strain advances, this approach will surely become more widely known among researchers on social factors in psychiatric disorder.

A second development is the creation of chronic strain inventories that are objective in the same sense as are life event inventories. Several inventories of this sort have been developed (see Stone & Neale 1982 for a review). They are alike in using the life event inventory as a model, but assess "small" events that occur in a variety of daily role activities (e.g. child becoming ill; see Zautra & Dohrenwend 1983). Because small events of this sort are more commonly experienced than serious events, it is necessary to ask respondents about their occurrence over the past week or month rather than over the last year, the most common time frame in life events research. These inventories can also be used to ask respondents about a "typical week," in which case the results can be interpreted as a measure of characteristic chronic stress. Although the possibility of reciprocal causation must be considered when using these inventories, just as in the case of previous life event research, the construction of a chronic stress profile from a list of small events may improve the quality over that obtained through subjective assessment procedures.

THE STUDY OF VULNERABILITY FACTORS

As described above, the evidence is clear in suggesting that the majority of people who are exposed to stressful life experiences do not develop emotional disorder. In fact, there is emerging evidence that stressful encounters can sometimes promote coping capacity (see Haan 1982 for a review). For these reasons, the major thrust of current research on life events involves the identification of variables—so-called vulnerability or resistance factors—that may explain differences in stress responsiveness. Several different types of factors have been examined in the literature. Some investigators have focused on the role of predispositions, or enduring physiological or psychological characteristics that may influence the impact of stressful life experiences. A variety of factors have been explored in the literature, including biogenic constitution and various aspects of personality such as hardiness (e.g. see Kobasa et al 1982), learned resourcefulness (e.g. Rosenbaum & Palmon 1984), neuroticism (e.g. Depue & Monroe 1984), and dispositional optimism (see Haan 1982 or Moos & Billings 1982 for reviews).

Investigators have also examined the role of several different psychosocial resources in influencing vulnerability to stressful life experiences. Psychosocial resources are attitudes, skills, or assets that are advantageous in coping with stress across many situations (Menaghan 1983). Resources that have been conceptualized as influencing vulnerability to stress include intellectual capacities such as cognitive flexibility and effective problem-solving behaviors; interpersonal skills, such as social competence and communication skills; financial assets; coping strategies; and social support (see Haan 1982, Moos & Billings 1982, and Menaghan 1983 for reviews).

Research on vulnerability factors represents an important new direction in work on the relationship between social factors and psychopathology. Because full consideration of all of these vulnerability factors is beyond the scope of this chapter, we have decided to focus our discussion on two variables that have generated intense interest among investigators in recent years: social support and coping strategies.

Social Support

During the past decade, there has been a great deal of interest in social support, a term that has been widely used to refer to the mechanisms by which interpersonal relationships presumably protect people from the deleterious effects of stress. This interest was triggered by a series of influential review papers published in the mid-1970s (Caplan 1974, Cassel 1974, 1976, Cobb 1976). These studies reviewed literature demonstrating associations between psychiatric disorder and such factors as marital status, geographic mobility, and social disintegration. They argued that a theme present in all of these associations is the absence of adequate social ties or supports or the disruption of social networks. Although highly inferential in their arguments, and not always clear about their definition of the concept, these early reviews generated a great deal of scientific interest in the possibility that social support can protect health.

In recent years, this initial enthusiasm has been replaced by a more critical examination of the issues (see Heller 1979, House 1981, Thoits 1982, Broadhead et al 1983, Heller & Swindle 1983, Cohen & McKay 1984, House & Kahn 1984, Wortman & Conway 1984). Although the nature, meaning, and measurement of social support are still being debated intensely in the literature, investigators have come to appreciate the need for more systematic and precise conceptualizations of the construct. Toward this end, attempts have been made to identify several distinct types or components of support. Some of these concern the structural aspects of relationships, such as living arrangements (e.g. living alone or with others), frequency of social contact, participation in social activities, or involvement in a social network (i.e. group of people who may have varying degrees of contact with one another). Investigators have also identified several different functions that support may provide, such as the expression of positive affect or emotional support; expression of agreement with a person's beliefs or feelings; encouraging the expression or "ventilation" of feelings; provision of advice or information; and the provision of material aid (see House 1981 or Wortman 1984 for a more detailed discussion).

In addition to providing greater specificity in the conceptualization and measurement of the construct, researchers have become increasingly sensitive to the methodologic problems inherent in many of the early studies, which employed cross-sectional, retrospective, or case-control designs. As several investigators have noted, the majority of these early studies are flawed by their inability to address the issue of causality (Heller 1979, House 1981, Thoits 1982, Broadhead et al 1983). In the past few years, a number of well-controlled, prospective longitudinal studies have appeared in the literature, as have an increasing number of randomized experiments involving supportive interventions (for reviews see Broadhead et al 1983, Gottlieb 1984, and Kessler & McLeod 1984).

The question of whether social relationships are associated with vulnerability to psychiatric disorder has been addressed in a variety of ways. Some studies have focused on the social relationships or support networks of clinical populations in comparison to normal populations. Others have examined the relationship between life stress, social support, and mental distress in normal population surveys or in case-control studies. Still others have examined the part social support may play in adjustment to a particular life crisis. Finally, a number of recent studies have involved the experimental manipulation of support. Each of these will be considered briefly in turn.

STUDIES IN CLINICAL SAMPLES   Research comparing the social networks of psychiatric patients and normals has been reviewed by Mueller (1980) and Levy (1983). Clear differences among these networks have been reported, with psychotics having very tight kin-based networks and neurotics having quite loose and sparse networks when compared to normals, but it is not clear how to interpret these data. It might be that these network structures are causally implicated in the disorders, but it is equally likely that they are the result of the disorders.

This causal ambiguity has been resolved to some degree in a related line of research in which the supportiveness of psychiatric patients' networks at the time of onset is assessed and used to predict subsequent relapse. There is evidence in this literature that the supportiveness of family members is related to the probability of relapse among schizophrenics. The pioneering work of Brown and his colleagues in London (e.g. Brown et al 1962) has been elaborated by Vaughn & Leff (1976), Goldstein (1983, Goldstein & Doane 1982). The master concept here is that of "expressed emotion," a constellation typically characerized by hostile feelings and intrusiveness on the part of the patient's family, which is predictive of poor prognosis among patients who return home to these families at the end of a hospitalization. There is also evidence to suggest that intervening with families of schizophrenics to reduce their high expressed emotion can reduce the patient relapse rate (Boyd et al 1981). Research on relapse for depression has begun (Surtees 1980), but lags far behind the research that has been done on schizophrenics (Coyne et al 1984).

NORMAL POPULATION AND CASE-CONTROL STUDIES   Research on the relationship between support and course of illness has been somewhat uncharacteristic in focusing on the direct effects of social support. Most recent research has concentrated instead on "buffering" effects, or the ability of support to ameliorate the impact of stress on health (see Heller & Swindle 1983 or Thoits 1982 for reviews). For example, in an influential program of research, Brown & Harris (1978) demonstrated that among a sample of urban women who experienced significant life stress, the presence of an intimate, confiding relationship with a boyfriend or husband seemed to protect women from depression. Almost 40% of the stressed women without a confidant developed depression, whereas only 4% of those with access to a confidant became depressed. This result has been replicated in epidemiologic community surveys of depressed mood and in case-control studies of recent onset psychiatric cases and normal population comparison groups (e.g. Miller & Ingham 1976, Slater & Depue 1981).

Although these studies provide suggestive evidence that social support ameliorates the impact of life stress, serious methodological problems make such results difficult to interpret. In many cases, life events involve the disruption of social relationships (Mueller 1980), and this fact confounds any attempt to estimate the effect of support on the stress-illness relationship. Furthermore, in many cases it is not possible to determine whether the support deficits associated with vulnerability to stress represent a cause or consequence of the psychiatric disorder. Abnormal behavior may impede the development of close, mutually rewarding relationships. An association between impaired social relationships and psychopathology might also reflect a tendency of disturbed people to judge their social relationships harshly.

As investigators have come to recognize these methodological problems, a number of panel studies have been initiated. In these studies, a normal population sample is interviewed at two points in time (e.g. see Henderson et al 1981, Turner & Noh 1982, Lin & Ensel 1984). An inventory measuring life events that occurred between the two time points is generally used to predict changes in symptoms between the two observations. Kessler & McLeod (1984) have recently completed a comprehensive review of these studies. Although the evidence for a stress-buffering effect of support is far from uniform, the methodologically strongest of these studies indicate that certain types of support—especially emotional support and perceiving that one has access to broad-based support that could be mobilized if needed—diminish the impact of life stress on mental distress. The data suggest that emotional support may play a more important role in protecting individuals from the deleterious effects of stress than structural measures of support, such as social involvement or activity (see Kessler & McLeod, 1984, for a more detailed discussion).

STUDIES ON REACTIONS TO LIFE CRISES   In the past decade, numerous studies have been conducted to assess the impact of social support on adjustment to specific life events such as widowhood (e.g. Vachon et al 1982a,b), unemployment (Gore 1978), and criminal victimization (Burgess & Holmstrom 1979; see Silver & Wortman 1980 for a review). Such studies are often longitudinal, and most have found support to be an important predictor of subsequent emotional adjustment. For example, Vachon and associates (1982b) have found that among individuals who lost a spouse, low satisfaction with social support at one month was a significant predictor of general distress at two years. Moreover, these studies are beginning to provide more specific information about the impact of particular types of supportive ties on particular problems. For example, it has been found that when life events necessitate obtaining new information or adopting new roles, low density networks characterized by weak ties can aid adaptive striving more than high density networks (see Hirsch 1979, 1980, Wellman 1979).

Life crisis studies allow investigation of support in a way that is impossible in general population studies, which are based on aggregated data from a large number of people experiencing different events at different times. Studies of reactions to specific crises enable the investigator to examine short-term and long-term reactions to the crisis and to monitor changes in the support system as the individual attempts to cope with the crisis. Such studies also provide an opportunity to examine social support in relation to other aspects of the stress process—such as cognitions, feelings about the self, and coping strategies—

and thus create an opportunity to clarify the mechanisms through which support may protect mental health in high stress situations.

A major difficulty in studying support processes among victims of life crises is that successful adjustment to the crisis is the outcome of major interest. There is no consensus on how to define successful adjustment (see Haan 1982 or Wortman 1983 for a more detailed discussion). One approach is to identify characteristics thought to reflect mastery of a crisis situation, such as keeping one's distress within manageable bounds, maintaining a realistic appraisal of the situation, and being able to function adequately in major life roles (Friedman et al 1963, Hamburg & Adams 1967, Haan 1977). However, closer examination suggests that this approach may not always be satisfactory. In one study, for example, spinal cord injured patients who were most distressed about their disability were subsequently rated as making the most progress in rehabilitation (Goldsmith 1955). This observation suggests that emotional distress may play a part in motivating effective coping efforts. Those facing life crises may also experience intense emotional distress if they attempt to meet a variety of role obligations despite the crisis. For these reasons, it would clearly be a mistake to treat emotional distress as a sign of poor adjustment in all cases.

Another problem in assessing effective adjustment is that some people cope with a life crisis in ways that reduce their own distress or maintain their own self-concept at someone else's expense. Conventional measures of distress or psychopathology do not reveal this transactional aspect of adaptation and so are likely to overlook serious social costs associated with certain types of coping strategies (Coyne et al 1984). In our judgment, these and other conceptual problems in providing a clear definition of effective adjustment have hindered potential advancement in this field.

To date, studies of specific life crises have not realized their potential, either as a means of increasing our basic understanding of fundamental support processes or as a foundation on which interventions can be built. Most studies of this sort have simply attempted to show that support is associated with subsequent adjustment without linking support to other variables that might help elucidate causal processes. For progress to be made, the advantages of this research design will have to be more fully exploited in the future.

EXPERIMENTAL SUPPORT INTERVENTIONS   As noted above, longitudinal studies have become increasingly common in the literature on social support, as researchers have come to recognize the methodological shortcomings of retrospective and cross-sectional designs. By demonstrating that social support is associated with subsequent mental health or resilience to the psychological effects of stress, longitudinal studies rule out the possibility that low levels of support are merely a consequence of prior disorder. Yet causal interpretation is to some degree clouded even in longitudinal studies. This is true because unmeasured common causes of social support and subsequent disorder might produce a spurious association. Personality dispositions, coping resources, and personal or social competence have all been proposed as common causes of this sort (Henderson et al 1981, Burns & Farina 1984, Wortman & Conway 1984). Few studies have attempted to measure these variables explicitly and control for their impact, perhaps because of the difficulties inherent in operationalizing constructs like competence or coping skill. Thus, such "third variables" remain a plausible alternative explanation for virtually all longitudinal studies showing a relationship between social support and subsequent disorder or resilience to stress.

In the face of this ambiguity, experimental support interventions have become increasingly popular (see DiMatteo & Hays 1981, Mumford et al 1982, Broadhead et al 1983, Levy 1983, Wallston et al 1983, Gottlieb 1984, Wortman & Conway 1984 for reviews). Most intervention studies have been designed and implemented in hospital settings and have examined the impact of support on such variables as preoperative anxiety, recovery from surgery (see Mumford et al 1982 for a review), or compliance with medical regimens to control chronic health problems (see Levy 1983 for a review). There have also been several intervention studies to facilitate coping with life transitions such as the transition to college or parenthood (see Leavy 1983 for a review). These studies have investigated the role of social support in facilitating adjustment to life crises such as widowhood (e.g. Raphael 1977, Vachon et al 1980), serious injury (e.g. Bordow & Porritt 1979), the development of cancer (e.g. Spiegel et al 1981), and heart disease (e.g. Gruen 1975).

These intervention studies have operationalized support in many different ways, although almost all of the interventions have involved both emotional and informational support. Some interventions have included opportunities to express feelings and/or tangible help as well (e.g. Vachon et al 1980). A few studies have compared the impact of different types of support, but the vast majority have not. In addition, almost all of the studies to date have involved interventions delivered by health care professionals, although a few have examined interventions provided by support groups (e.g. Barrett 1978, Spiegel et al 1981) or lay persons with similar problems (e.g. Spiegel et al 1981). Surprisingly, few supportive interventions have been designed to enhance the support available from naturally occurring support networks. For the most part, the support interventions involved in these studies have been modest in scope. They have generally involved limited resources and a small number of sessions, and most have not been individually tailored to meet the particular support needs of the respondent. Nonetheless, in the vast majority of these studies, the manipulations have been effective in fostering adjustment to life crises.

These intervention studies strongly suggest that social support may protect individuals at risk from subsequent mental disorder. However, these studies were not designed to illuminate the mechanisms through which this influence occurs. Furthermore, as most of the interventions were multifaceted, it is impossible to determine what aspects of support produced the impact. Finally, the investigators have not assessed constructs such as coping effectiveness, self-esteem, or compliance that might help to elucidate the processes through which social support may protect individuals from subsequent impairment.

FUTURE DIRECTIONS IN RESEARCH ON SOCIAL SUPPORT   Taken as a whole, the evidence reviewed above suggests that lack of social support may play an important part in the development and course of psychopathology. A clearer understanding of this influence will require research advances in several areas. A central problem concerns how social support should be conceptualized and measured (see House & Kahn 1984, and Wortman 1984 for reviews). There is general consensus that an attempt should be made to assess several different types or components of support, since there is evidence that different components have varying effects on different outcomes (see Cohen & McKay 1984, House & Kahn 1984 or Wortman 1984 for reviews). There is converging evidence as well that the supportiveness of particular behaviors may well depend on who provides them. For example, women with breast cancer may be more likely to accept emotional support from someone else who previously went through the same experience than from a well-meaning, but uninformed, friend (Dunkel-Schetter & Wortman 1982, Wortman & Lehman 1984).

It would also be useful to balance information about support with parallel information about negative regard and disaffection. The literature clearly suggests that interactions between psychiatrically impaired individuals and those in their social network are characterized by tension, conflict, and hostility (see Coyne et al 1984 for a review). It would be illuminating to assess negative social exchanges among individuals at risk for disorder, since such exchanges may play an important role in provoking disorder. In the few studies that have compared positive and negative elements of social interaction, the negative elements have been more strongly related to mental health outcomes (Fiore et al 1983, Rook 1984a).

A particularly serious measurement problem involves the potential contamination of support measures with disorder (Dohrenwend et al 1984). People who are experiencing distress may also judge their social relationships more negatively, and this can contaminate self-report measures of stress. A number of correctives have been suggested to this problem, including the use of more objective behavioral measures of support and the use of network informants (House & Kahn 1984). There is as yet no consensus on the best way to deal with this potential problem.

Beyond problems of measurement, there are several important issues of research focus that have not been addressed empirically. Past research has for the most part focused on the recipient of support, to the neglect of the provider of support. We believe that the complex causal web that links support and psychopathology can only be unraveled if we focus attention equally on providers and, even more importantly, on support transactions (Coyne et al 1984).

Some beginning efforts along this line have been made in studies of the psychiatrically impaired. Attention has focused on the part played by family environments in maintaining disorder and influencing the likelihood of relapse. There is evidence to suggest that the family relationships of disordered persons are far more conflictual than those of normal individuals, and that the level of family conflict is associated with relapse (Goldstein & Doane 1982, Goldstein 1983, Coyne et al 1984). At this point, however, very little is known about precisely what behaviors of the disordered person tend to provoke nonsupportive responses from family members. In addition, it would be desirable to have a more complete understanding of the behavioral responses that are common among family members of the disordered (e.g. displaying anger, becoming overly solicitous, or withdrawing emotionally from the disordered person) and the potential role these may play in provoking relapse.

A related issue is whether attempts to provide support are sometimes experienced as unhelpful by the recipients (Fisher et al 1983). There is some evidence to suggest that family members may have little insight concerning the impact of their behavior on the disordered person. For example, McLean et al (1973) report that spouses tend to regard their communications with the depressed person as "constructive criticism," although these communications are judged by observers as simple hostility. There also is some evidence that unintended negative consequences of this sort are fairly common among victims of life crises (see Wortman & Lehman 1984 for a review). By enjoining a crisis victim to look on the bright side, for example, the supporter may lead the victim to feel that his feelings and behaviors are inappropriate. By offering advice or tangible aid, supporters may convey to recipients that they are incapable of handling their own problems (Brickman et al 1982). More systematic research is needed to determine whether certain classes of behaviors presumed to be supportive are likely to contribute to subsequent disorder.

Interestingly, when asked in the abstract how they would support a person in crisis, many people appear to know what to do (Wortman & Lehman 1984). Yet in actual encounters with crisis victims, support attempts are often ineffective. It is not clear why this is so. It appears that support providers find it very difficult to tolerate the distress caused by encounters with crisis victims. For this reason, they often engage in behaviors such as minimizing the victim's problems or attempting to be cheerful, behaviors that reduce their own distress but only make the victims feel more isolated (Dunkel-Schetter & Wortman

1982, Wortman & Lehman 1984). Studies of interactions between supporters and recipients would help to clarify this issue.

Thus far, the majority of studies on social support have focused on the effects of various kinds of support. We need more information about characteristics of the recipient, provider, and the setting that may determine whether effective support is provided. The recipient's skills in eliciting support from others may be one such determinant. Such qualities as sociability, assertiveness, ability to empathize with others, positive attitudes toward others, and social problem-solving skills may be directly relevant to obtaining support (Heller & Swindle 1983, Hansson et al 1984). In the past, there has been a surprising lack of discussion of the role people play in influencing the quality of their support networks, and in mobilizing support in specific instances (Mitchell & Trickett 1980, Eckenrode 1983, Gottlieb 1983, Carpenter et al 1984, Jones 1984). Researchers interested in this issue may benefit from current work on loneliness, which has explored various individual differences that are related to the maintenance of social bonds (e.g. see Jones 1982, Peplau & Perlman 1982, Hansson et al 1984, Rook 1984b,c).

The severity of the recipient's problems, as well as his or her ability to cope with those problems, may also determine the amount of support received. There is evidence from the social psychological literature that people are often threatened and made uncomfortable by those who have experienced a life crisis, particularly if they feel vulnerable to a similar fate (see Wortman 1976 for a review). For this reason, the more severe the victim's problems, the more threatened, and therefore unsupportive, others may become. Among cancer patients, there is some evidence that those with the worst prognosis are less likely to receive support than those in better physical health (Peters-Golden 1982). Moreover, those who indicate that they are coping well with life crises are less likely to be judged negatively and avoided by others than those who indicate that they are having some difficulties in coping (Coates et al 1979). Taken together, these results suggest that those in greatest need of social support may be least likely to get it. In subsequent research, it would be worthwhile to identify additional characteristics of the recipient that may influence support provision. For example, do some types of emotional expression (e.g. anger, bitterness) impede empathic responding on the part of support providers more than other types (e.g. sorrow; cf Wortman 1983)?

To date, most research on support has focused on the consequences of receiving support; considerably less attention has been paid to the consequences of providing it. The deleterious consequences of support provision may be substantial. In many such cases, those close to the recipient may become emotionally drained from the long-term provision of support which the recipient may be unable or unwilling to reciprocate (Belle 1982). There is some recent evidence to suggest that women are at particular risk here, because they are more likely to be called upon as caregivers (Belle 1982), and to become emotionally involved in the problems of others (Kessler et al 1984). Before intervention programs that enlist the cooperation of family members as supporters are disseminated on a wider basis, it is important to assess these risks and develop mechanisms for reducing them to the extent possible.

The research agenda sketched above requires experimental interventions that manipulate well-defined and measured aspects of support. It is important that interactions between providers and recipients be monitored to determine whether and how manipulations are carried out (Heller et al 1980, Price & Smith 1984). There is also a need for more research on support transactions in natural settings. We need to learn more about what is actually done when people attempt to provide support and how these actions are perceived by the recipient (Glidewell et al 1982, Fisher et al 1983). For example, when are support providers' calming, minimizing appraisals of a crisis effective in reducing the recipient's distress, and when do they increase distress because they make the recipient feel that his or her concerns are not being heard? Finally, we need more and better naturalistic prospective studies of crisis victims to monitor the part played by support in the unfolding process of adjustment. Studies of this sort are the foundation on which preventive interventions are constructed (Price et al 1980), and without them it will be difficult to develop innovative support interventions in high risk populations.

Coping Processes

During the past several years, there has been increasing interest in the concept of coping, which is generally defined as the cognitive and behavioral effort made to master, tolerate, or reduce demands that tax or exceed a person's resources (Pearlin & Schooler 1978, Cohen & Lazarus 1979). Historically, work on coping processes has been shaped by psychoanalytic conceptions (Freud 1946, Haan 1977) which viewed coping and defense as largely unconscious responses to internal conflicts. As investigators became increasingly interested in the impact of life events, attention has shifted to the process of coping with external stressors. This shift in emphasis has been largely influenced by the work of Lazarus (e.g. Lazarus & Launier 1978), who focused on the role of cognitive appraisal in shaping responses to stress and guiding coping efforts. Current conceptualizations of coping have also been shaped by social learning theorists (e.g. Bandura 1977, Mischel 1977), who have emphasized the process of reciprocal interaction between the person and the environment, as well as by cognitive behavior therapists (e.g. Meichenbaum 1977), who have stressed the role that cognitive processes play in therapeutic change. All of these formulations emphasize the active role that the individual plays in construing his or her psychological world and in utilizing resources to manage stress or to modify problematic aspects of the environment.

There is considerable controversy about how coping should be conceptualized and measured (see Haan 1982, and Moos & Billings 1982 for reviews).
Some investigators have conceptualized coping primarily as a dispositional
trait or a typical, habitual preference to approach problems in particular ways,
such as denial. Others have questioned the assumption that coping behavior is
consistent across situations and have chosen to study the particular coping
efforts, or specific actions that an individual employs to deal with different
problems (Pearlin & Schooler 1978, Folkman & Lazarus 1980). The question
of cross-situational consistency is difficult to evaluate, since relatively few
studies have examined the issue. Gorzynski et al (1980) report striking stability
of dispositional coping style, as assessed by a psychiatrist among women
awaiting breast biopsy, and again ten years later. Stone & Neale (1985) and
Pearlin & Schooler (1978) have reported that people are relatively consistent in
the coping strategies that they use to deal with the same problem or role domain
on different occasions. However, people show little consistency across life
situations (Folkman & Lazarus 1980) or across different role domains such as
coping with work stress or marital dissatisfaction (Pearlin & Schooler 1978).

A second area of disagreement concerns the extent to which people are aware
of their coping efforts. Many current conceptualizations of coping are based on
the assumption that people can accurately report the coping strategies they use
(e.g. Folkman & Lazarus 1980, Billings & Moos 1981). In recent years,
several self-report instruments have been used to assess coping. Perhaps the
most widely used of these is Lazarus's Ways of Coping Checklist (see Folkman
& Lazarus 1980), which requires individuals to endorse any of 68 specific
coping strategies that reflect how they dealt with a particular stressor. However, the assumption that respondents are capable of reporting their coping efforts
has been criticized (e.g. Horowitz & Wilner 1980, Haan 1982, Ray et al 1982).
These investigators believe that coping efforts are not always deliberate or
conscious and that indirect assessments of coping are therefore necessary. Few
attempts have been made, however, to compare self-reports about coping with
more indirect projective assessments or with clinical observations (Haan 1982,
Stone & Neale 1982). Therefore, there is little empirical evidence with which
to adjudicate between these contending positions.

A large number of coping strategies have been identified and explored in the
literature, such as active problem-solving, information-seeking, distraction,
tension reduction, and the use of humor. Many attempts have been made to
classify these strategies into conceptual domains (see Moos & Billings 1982 for
a review and an integrative scheme). Although no typology is generally agreed
upon, three dimensions of coping common to most of them include altering the
problem directly, changing one's way of viewing the problem, and managing
emotional distress aroused by the problem (Pearlin & Schooler 1978). These
different modes of coping are generally not regarded as mutually exclusive;
they can be applied simultaneously or sequentially to a given problem. In fact,

one of these coping functions may be achieved at the expense of another (Lazarus & Launier 1978). For example, a woman with breast cancer may minimize her distress by denying initial symptoms, thus delaying treatment and reducing her chances for a favorable outcome.

Coping researchers have paid relatively little attention to the conceptual and empirical overlap that may exist between coping strategies and symptoms of psychological disorder (Dohrenwend et al 1984). A number of investigators have argued that it is important to separate the coping process, or the specific strategies that are used to deal with a stressful event, from the coping outcome, or impact of these strategies on subsequent symptomology (Horowitz 1979). Yet in many studies it is difficult to make a clear conceptual distinction between coping processes and symptoms. At what point does heavy drinking change from a coping strategy for tension reduction to a symptom? In our judgment, theoretical advancement in the field has been hampered by the failure of researchers to address this problem.

For the purposes of this chapter, the central substantive question in coping research is whether, among individuals exposed to a particular stressful experience, variation in coping strategies is associated with variation in emotional adjustment. As in the social support literature, this issue has been explored in a variety of ways. Some investigators have examined coping strategies employed by psychiatrically impaired individuals to deal with stress. Others have studied whether coping strategies ameliorate the impact of stress among normal populations. Still others have examined this issue among respondents faced with a particular life crisis such as bereavement. Each of these will be considered in turn. We then turn our attention to conceptual and methodological issues that have hampered research on the coping process, and suggest some possible approaches for subsequent empirical work.

STUDIES IN CLINICAL SAMPLES   While there have been numerous studies of the social relationships and networks of the psychiatrically impaired (see Mueller 1980 and Leavy 1983 for reviews), only a few studies have focused specifically on how disordered individuals cope with the stressful events that they encounter (Coyne et al 1981, Doerfler & Richards 1981). For example, Coyne et al (1981) found that depressed individuals were more likely to appraise situations as requiring more information in order to act, more likely to seek emotional or informational support, and more likely to engage in wishful thinking (i.e. endorsing such items as wishing they were stronger persons). These studies suggest that the coping strategies of depressed people are characterized by negative self-preoccupations that may hamper their ability to deal decisively and effectively with their problems.

As in the case of social support, it is difficult to know whether a causal interpretation of these data is appropriate. It is not clear from data of this sort whether coping strategies play a role in the development of disorder, are an aspect or a result of the disorder itself, or play a part in perpetuating and maintaining disorders. Nonetheless, the studies conducted to date suggest that coping strategies may be important predictors of the course of psychiatric illness, and may be an appropriate focus of intervention efforts among the psychiatrically impaired (Meichenbaum & Jaremko 1983).

STUDIES WITH NORMAL POPULATIONS   The relationship between coping and responsiveness to life stress has only been studied in a handful of normal population studies. The measurement of coping has varied considerably across studies, which could account for the inconsistent evidence of an influence of coping strategies on adjustment to life stress (Andrews et al 1978, Billings & Moos 1981). Causal interpretation is hampered further by the fact that all the studies reported to date have been based on cross-sectional data. A few prospective studies of coping have been conducted (Folkman & Lazarus 1980, Stone & Neale 1984), but results on the relationship between the use of particular strategies and subsequent adjustment to stress have not yet been reported.

In general population studies of coping with life events, the relationship between life stress, coping, and psychopathology has been explored in two different ways. Some investigators have asked individuals to respond to highly aggregated lists of life events and then to indicate how they cope, in general, or how they coped with a specific event that happened during the past few months (e.g. Andrews et al 1978). Other investigators (e.g. Folkman & Lazarus 1980, Billings & Moos 1981, Stone & Neale 1984) have asked respondents to identify the most stressful event that happened to them in the recent past, and to provide information about the coping strategies they utilized to deal with the event. Unfortunately, there are major problems with both of these approaches. Studies using aggregated life events lists are forced to rely on retrospective data that are likely to be distorted by recall bias as well as by the nonspecific focus of the question. A more specific referent may be necessary to elicit accurate information about coping strategies.

Studies that ask respondents to identify the most stressful episode from the past day, week, or month (e.g. Folkman & Lazarus 1980, Stone & Neale 1984) reduce this problem somewhat, but it is difficult to make judgments about the coping process in studies that rely on events that are identified as stressful by respondents. The appraisal of an event as stressful may be indicative of prior coping failures with similar sorts of events or of underlying psychopathology. Moreover, if emotional distress is associated with differences in stress appraisal, it is unclear whether this reflects differences in coping strategies or differences in the nature of the stress that was encountered. In future studies of coping, some of the techniques that were identified above for obtaining objective information about chronic stress could be employed to help resolve this problem.

It now seems clear that chronic stresses may constitute the specific components of life events that make them problematic. If this is so, then the analysis of coping with chronic stress would seem to be a promising area in which to study the relationship between coping and psychopathology. The most influential work of this sort to date has been done by Leonard Pearlin and his associates (Pearlin & Schooler 1978, Pearlin et al 1981), who measured role-related difficulties among a representative community sample in four broad problem areas (work, economic life, marriage, and parenting) as well as respondents' characteristic coping responses to problems in these domains. Since all respondents were asked about the same life domains, it was possible to make comparisons between respondents who reported similar difficulties but coped with them differently. It was also possible to examine whether there is consistency in coping responses across domains and whether the effectiveness of particular responses depends on the domain in which they are employed.

A number of important findings have emerged from this work. Pearlin & Schooler (1978) provided clear evidence that coping efforts which are successful in one domain might have no effect, or be detrimental, in others. Further, the more varied an individual's coping repertoire, the more protected he or she is from distress. There was little evidence for consistency across domains; those who use direct action in the parental domain, for example, might not do so in dealing with marital problems. Finally, the most effective coping strategies are more likely to be employed by men, by the educated, and by the affluent members of society, which suggests that "the groups most exposed to hardship are also least equipped to deal with it" (Pearlin & Schooler 1978, p. 18).

The analysis of coping with life events in general population surveys probably requires the disaggregation of life events into their constituent chronic stresses and the analysis of coping strategies directed at each of these stress domains. We know of no study that has used this approach. In the work we have reviewed here, however, the groundwork for such an effort can be seen clearly. It remains for future research to build on it.

COPING WITH SPECIFIC LIFE CRISES   Studies on reactions to specific life crises provide the opportunity to follow the respondent longitudinally from the onset of the crisis, and thus study the coping process as it unfolds. Unlike the general population surveys described above, life crisis studies provide some basis for comparing subjects' reactions to the same stressful experience. Few studies have taken advantage of these opportunities to explore the relationship between coping processes and adjustment. The vast majority of studies of coping with specific life crises have focused on the process of coping with physical health problems or with major surgery (see Lazarus & Cohen 1977 for a review). In almost all cases, the studies have focused on the impact of denial on recovery (see Cohen & Lazarus 1979 or Mullen & Suls 1982 for reviews) and have utilized outcome measures indicative of physical health status.

Only a handful of studies have examined the role of coping strategies in facilitating adjustment to such life crises as loss of a child (Videka-Sherman 1982); rape (Burgess & Holmstrom 1979); permanent paralysis (Rosenthal & Roth 1981); divorce (Berman & Turk 1981); and the accident at Three Mile Island (Collins et al 1983, Cleary & Houts 1984). For the most part, these studies are characterized by methodological shortcomings such as small and unrepresentative samples. Many of these studies have simply identified a group of respondents who experienced a crisis at some point in the past, rather than following respondents longitudinally after the onset of the crisis. Moreover, almost none of these studies have included adequate measures of psychopathology. Taken together, however, these studies provide suggestive evidence that coping processes may play a role in ameliorating the impact of life stressors. For example, Collins et al (1983) found that in coping with the chronic stress of living near the site of a nuclear accident, reappraisal of the situation was more effective in ameliorating the consequences of stress than problem-oriented modes of coping, or than attempts to deny the stress. In many of these studies, however, the impact of coping strategies on subsequent adjustment has been rather modest (e.g. Cleary & Houts 1984, Felton & Revenson 1984, Felton et al 1984).

One advantage in studies of coping with life crises is that unlike normal population surveys, all respondents are faced with a stressor that is similar in many ways. A factor that life crisis researchers have tended to ignore, however, is that there are likely to be important differences between respondents in the amount and type of stress that is experienced from a particular crisis. More work is necessary to describe various objective features of life crises so that the impact of coping strategies and other variables such as social support can be assessed more adequately.

Another issue that has received relatively little attention among life crisis researchers concerns the appropriate focus for questions about coping. In studies on bereavement, for example, should individuals be asked to identify those strategies that they are using to cope with the experience of loss in general, or should they be asked to indicate how they are coping with the variety of problems that accompany the loss, such as loneliness, financial matters, or household tasks? Most investigators have restricted their focus of inquiry to coping with the crisis as a whole. If life crises have their impact through the chronic strains that accompany them, it may be important to assess coping with these associated stressors.

EXPERIMENTAL INTERVENTIONS   Randomized experiments designed to facilitate the use of appropriate coping strategies could provide persuasive evidence that coping is consequential for mental health outcomes. A number of treatments designed to alleviate depression, such as various forms of cognitive-behavioral therapy (Meichenbaum & Cameron 1983), can be conceptualized as interventions of this sort. Furthermore, several studies have been designed to evaluate the effectiveness of various coping strategies for dealing with laboratory-induced stress. A few studies have evaluated the impact of interventions designed to teach coping skills to patients experiencing pain (Turk et al 1983) or undergoing various surgical procedures (e.g. see Langer et al 1975, Leventhal & Everhart 1979). With few exceptions (e.g. Roskin 1982), however, controlled experimental interventions designed to enhance coping effectiveness have not been attempted among populations who have experienced stressful life events. This is perhaps not surprising considering the lack of basic research findings on which such intervention efforts might be based. The development of interventions may also have been hampered by the belief that it may be harmful to tamper with an individual's characteristic coping style. For example, some people believe that if an individual is coping with life-threatening illness with minimization or denial, experimental treatments that expose respondents to information, or encourage active coping efforts, may be detrimental.

Nonetheless, there are some reasons why it may be desirable to develop interventions to facilitate effective coping among those experiencing life stress. Left to their own devices, people often employ coping mechanisms that exacerbate the very problems that they are designed to solve. For example, Pearlin & Schooler (1978) found that more than 40% of the strategies employed to deal with chronic role strains were actually related to greater role stress (see also Menaghan 1983). There is evidence available from several sources (e.g. Weiss et al 1976, Herrmann & Wortman 1984) that those who attempt to cope with their problems but are unsuccessful may suffer more deleterious consequences than those who do not even attempt to cope with their problems. Moreover, such coping failures might initiate a "malignant spiral" in which poor coping results in greater role strain, which results in still more ineffective coping (Menaghan 1983). It is worth considering whether intervention efforts could short-circuit this process.

A major impediment to the implementation of such interventions is our lack of knowledge about how coping strategies are best imparted to others. Some investigators have delineated various guidelines to enhance coping skills in therapeutic situations (Meichenbaum & Jaremko 1983). Yet the evidence is clear that in the majority of cases, those who experience life crises rarely turn to professionals for help. Victims of life crises are much more likely to turn to informal support systems, such as family, friends, and neighbors (Veroff et al 1981). This obviously represents a point of intersection between the literatures on social support and coping. There is growing consensus that we need to devote more attention to the relationship between coping and support processes. Thoits (1983) has suggested that social support can be conceptualized as "coping assistance." In attempting to support crisis victims, for example, others may provide advice about how to behave, or suggest new ways of interpreting the crisis. Yet there is emerging evidence that some suggestions for coping are regarded by the victims as annoying and unhelpful (Wortman & Lehman 1984). For example, Maddison & Walker (1967) have reported that "conversations that aroused interest in new activities, development of new friendships, [or the] resumption of old hobbies or occupations" during the first three months after the death of a spouse were greeted with hostility. Similarly, there is evidence that individuals who find some meaning in stressful life experiences are able to cope more effectively with the event than those who are not (Silver et al 1983). However, others' well-intentioned attempts to impart meaning (for example, by suggesting that the death of one's spouse was "God's will") often do not have beneficial effects. Clearly, the issue of how effective coping strategies are best imparted to people who experience of life crises is an important topic for subsequent research.

FUTURE RESEARCH ON COPING   Numerous conceptual and methodological difficulties have hampered research efforts on coping processes. One problem is that although many investigators have emphasized the importance of conceptualizing coping as a dynamic process (e.g. Lazarus & Launier 1978), few studies have been designed to permit an assessment of the process. In most studies, respondents are asked to complete an inventory identifying all of the coping strategies that they have used to deal with a particular problem over the past several weeks or months. Clearly, such a paradigm provides no information about how the situation was appraised, what coping strategy was initiated first, whether this strategy was appropriate under the circumstances, or whether it proved effective in alleviating the problem and/or the respondent's emotional distress. Such designs also fail to clarify whether the person was able to alter or modify the strategy depending on the situation. Capturing the coping process represents a difficult challenge. It may require a much more frequent monitoring of coping behavior than is possible in most surveys. One such approach has been developed by Stone & Neale (1984), who have used daily diaries to collect information about daily events, mood, and methods of coping. But even studies as detailed as these provide no means of assessing such important issues as the accuracy of the person's appraisal of the situation, the appropriateness of coping efforts that were employed, and the ability of the person to be responsive to feedback from the environment.

A second problem with much of the past research on coping is that investigators have typically focused on a single, isolated event, such as breast cancer, widowhood, or the birth of a child. By examining how people cope with a variety of different problems, it would be possible to address a number of important issues. Such research would provide valuable information about cross-situational consistency in coping. It would also help to clarify whether those who shift from one strategy to another, depending on the requirements of the situation, cope more effectively than those who rely on certain strategies extensively regardless of the problem area. It would augment our knowledge about the contexts in which particular strategies are likely to be effective. Finally, it may help to clarify whether coping with one problem imparts insights or skills that can be useful in dealing with other problems. There are some intriguing hints in the literature regarding this issue. For example, Burgess & Holmstrom (1979) found that women who had experienced the loss of a parent, spouse, or child through death, divorce, or separation recovered significantly more rapidly from rape than women who had not been through such an experience. However, women who had experienced a criminal assault prior to the rape took significantly longer to recover than individuals who had not experienced such victimization. Clearly, it would be desirable to have a fuller understanding of the conditions under which subsequent coping would be facilitated or hindered by prior coping efforts.

Even in those few studies that have examined how individuals cope with more than one problem or role domain (e.g. Pearlin & Schooler 1978, Folkman & Lazarus 1980, Stone & Neale 1984), respondents typically are asked to provide a separate assessment of how they coped with each problem or role stress in question. Unfortunately, we know very little about how individuals integrate, organize, and balance various problems and activities simultaneously. This issue is likely to be important even in crisis coping, when an individual may be faced with a variety of specific problems, all requiring immediate attention. How does an individual decide which problem should be approached first? Some individuals may appeal to higher-level principles or values when attempting to balance multiple demands; others may simply respond to whatever is more urgent. At present, we know very little about effective strategies for coping with multiple problems, stresses, or role demands.

One important reason for studying how people balance multiple roles and problems in their lives is that those who are able to do this successfully may be able to minimize the likelihood of subsequent stressful events. At present, the majority of studies on coping have focused on how people cope with a problem or stressor once it has occurred. We know less about the role that people play in creating or avoiding the stressful experiences that confront them. In the past, coping research has also focused almost exclusively on the strategies that people use to deal with negative events or experiences. The ability to initiate positive experiences may be just as important to one's long-term mental health as the ability to deal with negative ones. To date, however, coping researchers have devoted little attention to the processes through which positive experiences are initiated or sustained.

Finally, there is a need to know more about the determinants of coping efforts. It seems clear that the choice of coping strategies is influenced importantly by the person's appraisal of the situation (Lazarus & Launier 1978). At present we know little about the factors, either personal or situational, that lead to errors in the appraisal process and the deployment of coping strategies that are therefore inappropriate or ineffective. An important development in this area has been the renewed interest in underlying personality dispositions that may channel appraisals and coping efforts (e.g. Kohn 1977, Husaini et al 1982, Wheaton 1982). While a review of such literature is beyond the scope of this chapter, it is important to note that relatively stable clusters of coping dispositions have been isolated empirically (e.g. Kobasa et al 1981, Rosenbaum 1984). Prospective evidence shows that these dispositions influence the choice and success of coping efforts in particular stress situations. It is important that subsequent research refine our knowledge about how these dispositions develop and about the processes through which they influence coping efforts.

In summary, despite the enthusiasm and interest that have been shown for the construct of coping, we have just barely begun to scratch the surface. There is debate about how coping strategies should be conceptualized, and little progress has been made in developing objective, reliable, and valid ways of capturing the coping process. Although it is widely assumed that choice of coping strategies can ameliorate the impact of stressful experiences, there is surprisingly little sound, empirical research bearing on this assumption. Hopefully, subsequent research will augment current knowledge about the determinants of particular coping strategies and the conditions under which they are likely to be effective. It would also be desirable to enhance our understanding of how coping strategies are acquired or how maladaptive strategies can be changed.

GROUP DIFFERENCES IN PSYCHOLOGICAL DISORDER

A good part of the research on social factors in psychopathology concerns itself with structural correlates of psychiatric illness: social class, sex, race, and other group differences that define broad sectors of the population. Early work on group differences focused on the simple hypothesis that differential exposure to stress could account for group differences in psychiatric impairment. Much of the early research on this issue examined the relationship between social class and mental illness, stimulated by the seminal work of Faris & Dunham (1939), Hollingshead & Redlich (1958), and Langner & Michael (1963). This work showed convincingly that differential exposure to stress cannot account for the relationship between class and mental illness (Kessler & Cleary 1980).

Vulnerability factors subsequently have taken the center stage in research on group differences. Research here has attempted to do two things: to document group differences in vulnerability factors such as social support and coping resources, and to estimate the influence of vulnerabiltiy factors in accounting for group differences in psychiatric impairment. In the next section we briefly review current research on several group differences. In each case we point to recent findings, lingering issues, and directions for future research.

Social Class Differences

One of the oldest and most firmly established associations in psychiatric epidemiology is the one between social class and mental illness. People in socially disadvantaged positions have been shown to have higher rates of psychiatric disorder than their more advantaged counterparts (Schwab & Schwab 1978). This difference has been reflected both in treatment statistics (Rosen 1977) and in higher rates of nonspecific distress in community surveys (Kessler & Cleary 1980).

Until the early 1970s the dominant line of thinking in the literature on class and mental illness was that lower class people were exposed to more stressful life experiences than those in more advantaged social statuses, and that this differential exposure accounted for the negative relationship between class and mental illness. This view was challenged for the first time in the Midtown Manhattan Study (Langner & Michael 1963). These investigators attempted to demonstrate empirically that the lower class excess of mental health problems could be accounted for by greater exposure to stressful life experiences. Although this attempt was unsuccessful, a more complex association was documented: that stressful life experiences have a greater capacity to provoke mental health problems in the lower class than in the middle class. Subsequent work has shown that this class-linked vulnerability to stress accounts for the major part of the association between social class and depression (Brown & Harris 1978) as well as between social class and nonspecific distress (Kessler & Cleary 1980).

There are several ways that this vulnerability might come about. One of the most plausible is that some type of selection or "drift" of incompetent copers to the lower classes might lead to the relationship between class and vulnerability. Another is that one's experience as a member of a particular class leads to the development of individual differences in coping capacity as well as to differences in access to interpersonal coping resources.

There is evidence consistent with both of these hypotheses. Most of the evidence for the drift hypothesis comes from studies of major mental illnesses, primarily schizophrenia (Turner & Gartrell 1978). These studies show that early onset of a disorder can reduce one's chances of subsequent socioeconomic achievement. This seems to be true primarily for people who become ill prior to establishing themselves in a career. At the same time, less severe disorders do not seem to interfere with socioeconomic achievement (Wheaton 1978).

Evidence for vulnerability factors tied to one's class position is widespread. Liem & Liem (1978) reviewed the literature and provided evidence from a variety of sources that lower class people are disadvantaged in their access to supportive social relationships. There is also some evidence that personality characteristics associated with vulnerability to stress, such as low self-esteem, fatalism, and intellectual inflexibility, are more common among lower class people (Kohn 1977, Wheaton 1980). To date, the major efforts to see if these vulnerability factors actually account for the greater impact of life events on lower class people have been confined to the study of social support. The most influential work here has been that of Brown and his associates (e.g. Brown & Harris 1978), who documented that lower class people have fewer confidants than those in the middle class, and that this importantly contributes to their vulnerability to undesirable life events. This work has been replicated in several subsequent investigations (Brown & Harris 1984). More work needs to be done to investigate in parallel fashion the importance of coping strategies and personality characteristics. At the same time, as most investigations of class and stress have focused on life events, a more serious investigation of ongoing stressful situations may help us to develop a more complete understanding of the relationship between class and psychopathology.

Sex Differences

Community surveys show that adult women are twice as likely as men to report extreme levels of psychiatric distress (Kessler & McRae 1981). In community surveys of psychiatric cases, women are between two and three times as likely as men to report a history of affective disorder (Al-Issa 1982). There are other types of psychopathology that are as common among men as women and others still that are more prevalent among men than women (Dohrenwend & Dohrenwend 1976). Most research to date, however, has focused on affective disorders and nonspecific distress in community samples.

Much research on sex differences in nonspecific distress has been done over the last decade. Two lines of research can be discriminated. The first is based on indirect assessment of role-related stresses. For the past decade, the dominant perspective has held that women are disadvantaged relative to men because their roles expose them to more chronic stress (Gove 1978). Given the difficulties in measuring chronic stress objectively, empirical analysis has used indirect assessments based on measures of objectively defined role characteristics or constellations of multiple roles to document this relationship.

Gove (1972) popularized this style of argument in a demonstration that the relationship between sex and first admission to psychiatric hospitals was stronger among the married than the never married or previously married. On the basis of this observation he argued that female role stresses are particularly pronounced in traditional role situations. This conclusion is not the only plausible one, though. An interpretation that emphasizes selection into roles is equally consistent with the data (Kessler & McRae 1984). The major impediment to a more direct analysis has been that no objective measures of role-related stresses exist.

The second line of research on sex differences has examined stressful events. This work has shown that there is a significant interaction between sex and undesirable events in predicting distress (Kessler 1979), with women appearing more vulnerable than men to the effects of stressful events. Several different hypotheses have been advanced to account for female vulnerability to stress. These have included arguments that females are disadvantaged in access to social support (Belle 1982), in the use of effective coping strategies (Pearlin & Schooler 1978), and in personality characteristics (Radloff & Monroe 1978).

Although aggregate analyses of life event inventories show that women are, on the average, more vulnerable than men, there are some events for which this is not true. Research on widows, for example, shows that women adjust better than men (Stroebe & Stroebe 1983). Women also adjust as well or better than men to divorce (Wallerstein & Kelly 1980), and financial difficulties do not affect women as much as men (Kessler 1982).

A challenge for future research will be to reconcile the discrepancy between these studies of particular life events and aggregate life event surveys. To date, only one attempt has been made to do this (Kessler et al 1984). This was a meta-analysis of several different large-scale community surveys in which the effects of different types of events were assessed separately. This analysis found no evidence that women are more distressed than men by such major life crises as job loss, divorce, or widowhood. Their greater vulnerability is primarily associated with events that occur to people close to them—death of a loved one other than a spouse being the most commonly reported event.

There are several ways to interpret the greater impact of network events on women than men. It is likely that one component of this difference is linked to the fact that women provide more support than men and that this creates stresses and demands that can lead to psychological impairment (Belle 1982). Another is that women might be more empathic than men, or might extend their concern to a wider range of people. These and other possibilities need to be investigated in the future, since the part played by network events appears to account for a very substantial part of the overall sex-distress relationship.

Race Differences

Much of the research on race differences in psychopathology has focused on black-white differences. A growing body of research has also been done on the comparison of Americans of Mexican heritage with Anglos. These two bodies of research are reviewed briefly below.

BLACK-WHITE DIFFERENCES   Some authors who have examined treatment statistics argue that blacks have higher rates of treatment for psychosis than whites (Fried 1975). However, studies that focus on a broader array of disorders are more ambiguous. Most careful reviews state that no black-white difference exists in overall treatment rates (Fischer 1969, Kramer et al 1973). Community surveys paint a much more consistent picture, with blacks clearly evidencing higher average levels of distress than whites. However, statistical control for the fact that blacks generally have lower socioeconomic levels than whites accounts entirely for this race difference in nonspecific distress (Kessler & Neighbors 1983).

This demonstration implies that minority status and the life experiences associated with it are not themselves instrumental in creating mental health problems once socioeconomic factors are controlled. There are several different ways to understand this observation. The most actively pursued in the literature is that minority status, although related to experiences of prejudice and discrimination, is also related to structural resources that can help protect against the adverse mental health effect of these stresses (Kessler & Neighbors 1983).

There is a long tradition that emphasizes the stress-buffering effect of group solidarity among members of deprived groups. Theoretically, this effect stems from two sources: 1. the group provides cognitions that identify responsibility for their deprivation with structural conditions, thus removing any self-blame for their lack of financial achievement (Gurin et al 1978); 2. the group provides emotional support that can buffer the effects of life stress in a variety of ways (Turner 1983).

Some beginning attempts have been made to investigate this counterbalancing effect of group solidarity on the mental health of blacks (e.g. see Myers 1982). However, this work has been hampered by the fact that the stresses of minority status have not been measured explicitly. In particular, only one study of race differences in exposure and response to life events has been reported in the literature (Kessler 1979), and this study found both greater exposure and vulnerability to undesirable events among nonwhites. Other work has inferred that blacks are exposed to more stresses than whites, by virtue of their disadvantaged social status, but there have been no attempts to measure stress explicitly.

Evidence has been presented that indirectly supports the view that blacks develop cognitions that shield them from the self-esteem assaults that can come with some types of stress. Specifically, the relationship between personal efficacy and self-esteem is much weaker among blacks than whites (Jackson et al 1981). Perhaps a group ideology that explains low personal efficacy as a result of discrimination negates the damaging effects that feelings of low efficacy would otherwise have. More work is needed on this possibility, and on extensions that would take into consideration vulnerabilities to particular types of stress situations.

HISPANIC-ANGLO DIFFERENCES   There is consistent evidence that Americans of Mexican heritage are underrepresented in treatment statistics relative to their proportions in the population (Keefe 1979). Furthermore, community surveys of Anglo-Hispanic differences in nonspecific psychological distress report mixed results, with no consistent evidence for a difference in the levels of distress experienced by members of the two groups (see Kessler & Neighbors 1983 for a review).

The underrepresentation of persons of Mexican origin in treatment groups and the inconclusiveness of normal population surveys have been the source of much speculation. There is a general view among minority scholars that Mexican Americans have much greater mental health needs than these statistics show and that further research should measure that need accurately and study the determinants of underutilization (Arce et al 1976). There has also been considerable research on the possibility that minority communities and family structures provide protective resources that bolster the mental health of Hispanics. Most of this work focuses on the relationship between group identification and mental health. The general view is that acculturation leads to heightened psychological distress by exposing the individual to conflicting values and pulling him or her away from the traditionally supportive environment that buffered him from the effects of life stress (Gurin & Hatchett 1982). The most provocative work on this point has been done by Fabrega & Wallace (1968). They demonstrated that Mexican American mental patients were more often in a conflicted position between traditional Mexican values and the more mainstream values of American society than were nonpatients. To date this finding has not been subjected to replication or extension.

Systematic evidence is lacking about how minority families foster identities and create nurturant environments. Personal identity is created in the context of an early childhood environment where most significant interactions take place with people of the same race or ethnicity as the child. Group identity, in comparison, takes place later as a result of contacts with the larger society. There is currently a great deal of interest in the parallel developments of these two identities and the conditions under which they are tied to each other (e.g. see Porter & Washington 1979). Our ability to develop a deeper understanding of minority mental health hinges centrally on unraveling these developmental processes and their implications for self attributions, supports, and coping efforts.

SUMMARY

Our review has focused centrally on the etiologic significance of social factors in the development of psychopathology. Our implicit assumption has been that social factors in general, and stressors in particular, may play a causal role in the development of psychopathology. Yet the evidence is clear that the vast majority of people who are exposed to stressful life events or to chronic stress situations do not develop significant psychiatric impairments. For this reason, research interest over the past decade has shifted to factors like social support and coping strategies that may ameliorate the impact of stress.

We have examined some of the important empirical results from recent studies of stress, support, and coping, and we have discussed ways in which these new understandings have informed long-standing attempts to explain group differences in emotional functioning. In each section of the review we have attempted not only to summarize existing results but also to provide some evaluation of the literature and suggestions for future research.

It is important to recognize that the contributors to the work reviewed here do not all share a common research agenda. Some of them are primarily committed to unraveling the psychosocial determinants of a particular clinical disorder. Others are mainly concerned with the effects of a particular stressor. Still others are interested in the processes that link stress to health across a broad array of stress situations and health outcomes. In the face of these diverse interests, it is little wonder that our understanding of social factors in psychopathology is uneven.

There is good reason to believe, however that these diverse strands of research are beginning to converge on a common conception of the stress process and on a common research design. The conception at present is only in rough form, but its outlines are nonetheless capable of description. At its center is the notion that stress exposure sets off a *process of adaptation*. It recognizes that this process unfolds over time, and it acknowledges that this process is modified by structural factors as well as by personal dispositions and vulnerabilities. There is growing recognition that the analysis of this process requires longitudinal methods. Also, it is becoming increasingly clear that experimental interventions are required to unravel the parts of this process that link stress and health.

It is too early to know if this nascent convergence will lead to an integrative theory of adaptation, yet it is almost certain to promote methodological and conceptual rigor and facilitate replication and cumulation of findings. These developments should make the next decade an exciting one for research on social and cultural influences on psychopathology.

ACKNOWLEDGMENTS

Work on this paper was supported by Research Scientist Developmental Award IK0a MH00707 and by grants 1R01MH37706, 1P50MH38330, 1R01DA03272, and MCJ260470. The authors thank Anita DeLongis, Christine Dunkel-Schetter, David Ihilevich, Nancy Kline, Darrin R. Lehman, Jay Schlegel, Roxane L. Silver, Peggy Thoits, and Joanne Turnbull for critical comments on an earlier version of this paper.

Literature Cited

Al-Issa, I. 1982. Gender and adult psychopathology. In *Gender and Psychopathology*, ed. I. Al-Issa, pp. 83–101. New York: Academic

Andrews, G., Tennant, C., Hewson, D. M., Vaillant, G. E. 1978. Life event stress, social support, coping style, and risk of psychological impairment. *J. Nerv. Ment. Dis.* 166(5):307–16

Arce, C., Gurin, P., Gurin, G., Estrada, L. 1976. *National study of Chicano identity and mental health: A proposal for research.* Unpublished research proposal

Bandura, A. 1977. *Social Learning Theory.* Englewood Cliffs, NJ: Prentice-Hall

Barrett, C. 1978. Effectiveness of widows' group in facilitating change. *J. Consult. Clin. Psychol.* 46:20–31

Belle, D. 1982. The stress of caring: Women as providers of social support. In *Handbook of Stress: Theoretical and Clinical Aspects,* ed. L. Goldberger, S. Breznitz, pp. 496–505. New York: Free Press

Berman, W. E., Turk, D. C. 1981. Adaptation to divorce: Problems and coping strategies. *J. Marriage Fam.* Feb:179–89

Billings, A. G., Moos, R. H. 1981. The role of coping responses and social resources in attenuating the stress of life events. *J. Behav. Med.* 4:139–57

Bordow, S., Porritt, D. 1979. An experimental evaluation of crisis intervention. *Soc. Sci. Med.* 13A:251–56

Boyd, J. L., McGill, C. W., Falloon, I. R. H. 1981. Family participation in the community rehabilitation of schizophrenics. *Hosp. Community Psychiatry* 32(9)629–32

Brickman, P., Rabinowitz, B. C., Karuza, J. Jr., Cohn, E., Kidder, L. 1982. Models of helping and coping. *Am. Psychol.* 37(4):368–84

Broadhead, W. E., Kaplan, B. H., James, S. A., Wagner, E. H., Schoenbach, V. J., et al. 1983. The epidemiologic evidence for a relationship between social support and health. *Am. J. Epidemiol.* 117:521–37

Brown, G. W. 1974. Meaning, measurement, and stress of life events. In *Stressful Life Events: Their Nature and Effects,* ed. B. S. Dohrenwend, B. P. Dohrenwend, pp. 217–44. New York: Wiley

Brown, G. W., Harris, T. O., 1978. *Social Origins of Depression: A Study of Psychiatric Disorder in Women.* Free Press

Brown, G. W., Harris, T. O. 1984. *Establishing causal links: The Bedford College studies of depression.* Unpublished manuscript

Brown, G. W., Monck, E. M., Carstairs, G. M., Wing, J. K. 1962. The influence of family life on the course of schizophrenia illness. *Br. J. Prev. Soc. Med.* 16:55–68

Burgess, A. W., Holmstrom, L. L. 1974. Rape trauma syndrome. *Am. J. Psychiatry* 131:981–86

Burgess, A. W., Holmstrom, L. L. 1979. Adaptive strategies and recovery from rape. *Am. J. Psychiatry* 136:1278–82

Burns, G. L., Farina, A. 1984. Social competence and adjustment. *J. Soc. Pers. Relat.* 1:99–113

Cannon, W. B. 1939. *The Wisdom of the Body.* New York: Norton

Caplan, G. 1974. *Support Systems and Community Mental Health.* New York: Behavioral Publ.

Carpenter, B. N., Hansson, R. O., Rountree, R., Jones, W. H. 1984. Relational competence and adjustment in diabetic patients. *J. Soc. Clin. Psychol.* In press

Cassel, J. 1974. Psychosocial processes and "stress": Theoretical formulations. *Int. J. Health Serv.* 4:471–82

Cassel, J. 1976. The contribution of the social environment to host resistance. *Am. J. Epidemiol.* 104:107–23

Cleary, P. D., Houts, P. S. 1984. The psychological impact of the Three Mile Island incident. *J. Hum. Stress.* In press

Coates, D., Wortman, C. B., Abbey, A. 1979. Reactions to victims. In *New Approaches to Social Problems,* ed. I. H. Frieze, D. Bar-tal, J. S. Carroll, pp. 21–52. San Francisco: Jossey-Bass

Cobb, S. 1976. Social support as a moderator of life stress. *Psychosom. Med.* 38(5):300–14

Cohen, F., Lazarus, R. S., 1979. Coping with the stresses of illness. In *Health Psychology*, ed. G. C. Stone, F. Cohen, N. E. Adler, pp. 217–54. San Francisco: Jossey-Bass

Cohen, S., McKay, G. 1984. Social support, stress and the buffering hypothesis: A theoretical analysis. In *Handbook of Psychology and Health*, ed. A. Baum, J. E. Singer, S. E. Taylor, 4:253–63. Hillsdale, NJ: Erlbaum

Collins, D. L., Baum, A., Singer, J. E. 1983. Coping with chronic stress at Three Mile Island: Psychological and biochemical evidence. *Health Psychol.* 2:149–66

Coyne, J. C., Aldwin, C., Lazarus, R. S. 1981. Depression and coping in stressful episodes. *J. Abnorm. Psychol.* 90(5):439–47

Coyne, J. C., Kahn, J., Gotlib, I. H. 1984. Depression. In *Family Interaction and Psychopathology*, ed. T. Jacob. New York: Plenum. In press

Depue, R. A., Monroe, S. M. 1984. *Life stress and human disorder: Conceptualization and measurement of the disordered group*. Univ. Pittsburgh. Unpublished paper

Derogatis, L. R., Lipman, R. S., Rickels, K., Uhlenhuth, E. H., Covi, L. 1974. The Hopkins Symptom Checklist (HSCL): A self-report symptom inventory. *Behav. Sci.* 19:1–15

DiMatteo, M., Hays, R. 1981. Social support and serious illness. In *Social Networks and Social Support*, ed. B. Gottlieb, pp. 117–48. Beverly Hills, Calif: Sage

Doerfler, L. A., Richards, C. S. 1981. Self initiated attempts to cope with depression. *Cognit. Ther. Res.* 5(4):367–71

Dohrenwend, B. P., Dohrenwend, B. S. 1974. Social and cultural influences on psychopathology. *Ann. Rev. Psychol.* 25:417–52

Dohrenwend, B. P., Dohrenwend, B. S. 1976. Sex differences and psychiatric disorders. *Am. J. Sociol.* 81(1):1447–54

Dohrenwend, B. S., Dohrenwend, B. P. 1981. Life stress and illness: Formulation of the issues. In *Stressful Life Events and Their Contexts*, ed. B. S. Dohrenwend, B. P. Dohrenwend, pp. 1–27. New York: Prodist

Dohrenwend, B. S., Dohrenwend, B. P., Dodson, M., Shrout, P. E. 1984. Symptoms, hassles, social supports, and life events: Problem of confounding measures. *J. Abnorm. Psychol.* 93:222–30

Dunkel-Schetter, C., Wortman, C. B. 1982. The interpersonal dynamics of cancer: Problems in social relationships and their impact on the patient. In *Interpersonal Issues in Health Care*, ed. H. S. Friedman, M.

R. DiMatteo, pp. 69–100. New York: Academic

Eckenrode, J. 1983. The mobilization of social supports: Some individual constraints. *Am. J. Community Psychol.* 2:509–28

Eckenrode, J. 1984. The impact of chronic and acute stressors on daily reports of mood. *J. Pers. Soc. Psychol.* In press

Eckenrode, J., Gore, S. 1981. Stressful events and social supports: The significance of context. In *Social Networks and Social Support*, ed. B. H. Gottlieb, pp. 43–68. Beverly Hills, Calif: Sage

Eron, L. D., Peterson, R. A. 1982. Abnormal behavior: Social approaches. *Ann. Rev. Psychol.* 33:231–36

Fabrega, H., Wallace, C. 1968. Value identification and psychiatric disability: An analysis involving Americans of Mexican descent. *Behav. Sci.* 13:362–71

Faris, R., Dunham, H. W. 1939. *Mental Disorders in Urban Areas*. New York: Hafner

Felton, B. J., Revenson, T. A. 1984. Coping with chronic illness: A study of illness controllability and the influence of coping strategies on psychological adjustment. *J. Consult. Clin. Psychol.* 52:343–53

Felton, B. J., Revenson, T. A., Hinrichsen, G. A. 1984. Stress and coping in the explanation of psychological adjustment among chronically ill adults. *Soc. Sci. Medi.* 18:889–98

Fiore, J., Becker, J., Coppel, D. 1983. Social network interactions: A buffer or a stress? *Am. J. Community Psychol.* 11:423–39

Fischer, J. D. 1969. Negroes and whites and rates of mental illness: Reconsideration of a myth. *Psychiatry* 32:428–46

Fisher, J. D., Nadler, A., DePaulo, B. 1983. *New Directions in Helping*: Vol. 1, *Recipient Reactions to Aid*. New York: Academic

Folkman, S., Lazarus, R. S. 1980. An analysis of coping in a middle-aged community sample. *J. Health Soc. Behav.* 21:219–39

Freud, A. 1946. *The Ego and the Mechanisms of Defense*. New York: Int. Univ. Press

Fried, M. 1975. Social differences in mental health. In *Poverty and Health: A Sociological Analysis*, ed. J. Kosa, I. Zola, pp. 113–67. Cambridge, Mass: Harvard Univ. Press

Friedman, S. B., Chodoff, P., Mason, T. W., Hamburg, D. A. 1963. Behavioral observations on parents anticipating the death of a child. *Pediatrics* 32:610–25

Glidewell, J. C., Tucker, S., Todt, M., Cox, S. 1982. Professional support systems: The teaching profession. In *Applied Research in Help-Seeking and Reactions to Aid*, ed. A. Nadler, J. Fisher, B. M. DePaulo. New York: Academic

Goldsmith, H. 1955. *A contribution of certain personality characteristics of male paraplegics to the degree of improvement in reha-*

bilitation. PhD thesis. New York Univ., New York, NY

Goldstein, M. J. 1983. Family interaction: Patterns predictive of the onset and course of schizophrenia. In *Psychosocial Interventions in Schizophrenia,* ed. H. Stierlin, L. C. Wynne, M. Wirsching, pp. 5–19. New York: Springer–Verlag

Goldstein, M. J., Doane, J. A. 1982. Family factors in the onset, course, and treatment of schizophrenia spectrum disorders: An update on current research. *J. Nerv. Ment. Dis.* 170:692–700

Gottlieb, B. H. 1983. Social support as a focus for integrative research in psychology. *Am. Psychol.* March: 278–87

Gottlieb, B. H. 1984. *Social support and the study of personal relationships.* Presented at 2nd Int. Conf. Personal Relationships, Madison, Wis.

Gore, S. 1978. The effect of social support in moderating the health consequences of unemployment. *J. Health Soc. Behav.* 19:157–65

Gorzynski, J. G., Holland, J., Katz, J. L., Weiner, H., Zumoff, B., et al. 1980. Stability of ego defenses and endocrine responses in women prior to breast biopsy and ten years later. *Psychosom. Med.* May: 42(3):323–28

Gove, W. R. 1972. The relationship between sex roles, marital status, and mental illness. *Soc. Forces* 51:34–44

Gove, W. R. 1978. Sex differences in mental illness among adult men and women: An evaluation of four questions raised regarding the evidence on the higher rates of women. *Soc. Sci. Med. B* 12:187–98

Gruen, W. 1975. Effects of brief psychotherapy during the hospitalization period on the recovery process in heart attacks. *J. Consult. Clin. Psychol.* 43:223–32

Gurin, P., Gurin, G., Morrison, B. 1978. Personal and ideological aspects of internal and external control. *Soc. Psychol.* 41:275–96

Gurin, P., Hatchett, S. 1982. *Group identity and subjective mental health.* Unpublished research proposal

Haan, N. 1977. *Coping and Defending: Processes of Self-Environment Organization.* New York: Academic

Haan, N. 1982. The assessment of coping, defense and stress. In *Handbook of Stress: Theoretical and Clinical Aspects,* ed. L. Goldberger, S. Breznitz, pp. 254–69. New York: Free Press

Hamburg, D. A., Adams, T. E. 1967. A perspective on coping behavior: Screening and utilizing information in major transitions. *Arch. Gen. Psychiatry* 17:277–84

Hansson, R. O., Jones, W. H., Carpenter, B. N. 1984. Relational competence and social support. In *Review of Personality and Social Psychology,* Vol. 5, ed. P. Shaver. Beverly Hills, Calif: Sage. In Press

Heller, K. 1979. The effects of social support: Prevention and treatment implications. In *Maximizing Treatment Gains: Transfer Enhancement in Psychotherapy,* ed. A. P. Goldstein, F. H. Kanfer, pp. 353–82. New York: Academic

Heller, K., Price, R. H., Sher, K. J. 1980. Research and evaluation in primary prevention: Issues and guidelines. See Price et al 1980. pp. 285–313

Heller, K., Swindle, R. 1983. Social networks, perceived social support and coping with stress. In *Prevention Psychology: Theory, Research and Practice in Community Intervention,* ed. R. D. Felner, L. A. Jason, J. Moritsugu, S. S. Farber, pp. 87–103. New York: Pergamon

Henderson, S., Byrne, D. G., Duncan-Jones, P. 1981. *Neurosis and the Social Environment.* New York: Academic

Herrmann, C., Wortman, C. B. 1984. Action control and the coping process. In *Action Control: From Cognition to Behavior,* ed. J. Kuhl, J. Beckmann. New York: Springer

Hirsch, B. J. 1979. Social networks and the coping process. In *Social Networks and Social Support,* ed. B. Gottlieb, pp. 149–70. Beverly Hills, Calif: Sage

Hirsch, B. J. 1980. Natural support systems and coping with major life change. *Am. J. Community Psychol.* 8:159–72

Hollingshead, A. B., Redlich, F. C. 1958. *Social Class and Mental Illness.* New York: Wiley

Holmes, T. H. 1979. Development and application of a quantitative measure of life change magnitude. In *Stress and Mental Disorder,* ed. J. E. Barrett, pp. 37–54. New York: Raven

Holmes, T. H., Rahe, R. H. 1967. The social readjustment rating scale. *J. Psychosom. Res.* 11:213–18

Horowitz, A. 1979. Models, muddles, and mental illness labeling. *J. Health Soc. Behav.* 20:296–300

Horowitz, M. J., Wilner, N. 1980. Life events, stress, and coping. In *Aging in the 1980's: Psychological Issues,* ed. L. W. Poon. Washington DC: Am. Psychol. Assoc.

House, J. S. 1981. *Work, Stress, and Social Support.* Reading, Mass: Addison–Wesley

House, J. S., Kahn, R. 1984. Measuring social support. In *Social Support and Health,* ed. S. Cohen, L. Syme. New York: Academic

Husaini, B. A., Neff, J. A., Newbrough, J. R., Moore, M. C. 1982. The stress-buffering role of social support and personal competence among the rural married. *J. Community Psychol.* 10:409–26

Jackson, J., McCullough, W., Gurin, G. 1981. Group identity development within black families. In *Black Families*, ed. H. McAdoo. Beverly Hills, Calif: Sage

Jones, W. H. 1982. Loneliness and social behavior. See Peplau & Perlman 1982

Jones, W. H. 1984. The psychology of loneliness: Some personality issues in the study of social support. In *Social Support: Theory, Research and Application*, ed. I. G. Sarason, B. R. Sarason. The Hague: Martinus Nijhof. In press

Kanner, A. D., Coyne, J. C., Schaefer, C., Lazarus, R. S. 1981. Comparison of two modes of stress measurement: Daily hassles and uplifts versus major life events. *J. Behav. Med.* 14:1–39

Kaplan, H. B., Robbins, C., Martin, S. S. 1983. Antecedents of psychological distress in young adults: Self-rejection, deprivation of social support, and life events. *J. Health Soc. Behav.* 24:230–44

Keefe, S. 1979. Mexican Americans' underutilization of mental health clinics: An evaluation of suggested explanations. *Hisp. J. Behav. Sci.* 1:93–115

Kessler, R. C. 1979. Stress, social status, and psychological distress. *J. Health Soc. Behav.* 20:259–72

Kessler, R. C. 1982. Life events, social supports and mental illness. In *Deviance and Mental Illness*, ed. W. R. Gove, pp. 247–71. Beverly Hills, Calif; Sage

Kessler, R. C. 1983. Methodological issues in the study of psychosocial stress: Measurement, design, and analysis. In *Psychosocial Stress: Recent Developments in Theory and Research*, ed. H. B. Kaplan, pp. 267–341. New York: Academic

Kessler, R. C., Cleary, P. D. 1980. Social class and psychological distress. *Am. Sociol. Rev.* 45:63–78

Kessler, R. C., McLeod, J. 1984. Social support and psychological distress in community surveys. In *Social Support and Health*, ed. S. Cohen, L. Syme. New York: Academic. In press

Kessler, R. C., McLeod, J. D., Wethington, E. 1984. The costs of caring: A perspective on the relationship between sex and psychological distress. In *Social Support: Theory, Research and Applications*, ed. I. G. Sarason, B. R. Sarason. The Hague: Martinus Nijhof. In press.

Kessler, R. C., McRae, J. A. Jr. 1981. Trends in the relationship between sex and psychological distress: 1957–1976. *Am. Sociol. Rev.* 46:443–52

Kessler, R. C., McRae, J. A. Jr. 1984. A note on the relationships of sex and marital status to psychological distress. In *Research in Community and Mental Health*, Vol. 4, ed. J. R. Greenley. Greenwich, Conn: JAI Press. In press.

Kessler, R. C., Neighbors, H. W. 1983. Special issues related to racial and ethnic minorities in the U.S. Inst. Soc. Res., Univ. Mich. Unpublished paper

King, L. M. 1978. Social and cultural influences on psychopathology. *Ann. Rev. Psychol.* 29:405–33

Klinger, E. 1977. *Meaning and Void: Inner Experience and the Incentives in People's Lives.* Minneapolis: Univ. Minn. Press

Kobasa, S. C., Maddi, S. R., Courington, S. 1981. Personality and constitution as mediators in the stress-illness relationship. *J. Health Soc. Behav.* 22:368–78

Kobasa, S. C., Maddi, S. R., Kahn, S. 1982. Hardiness and health: A prospective study. *J. Pers. Soc. Psychol.* 52(2):244–52

Kohn, M. L. 1977. *Class and Conformity: A Study in Values* Chicago: Univ. Chicago Press. 2nd ed.

Kohn, M. L., Schooler, C. 1983. *Work and Personality: An Inquiry into the Impact of Social Stratification.* Norwood, NJ: Ablex

Kramer, M., Rosen, B., Willis, E. 1973. Definitions and distributions of mental disorders in a racist society. In *Racism and Mental Health*, ed. C. Willie, M. Kramer, B. Brown, pp. 353–459. Univ. Pittsburgh Press

Kubler-Ross, E. 1969. *On Death and Dying.* New York: Macmillan

Langer, E., Janis, I. L., Wolfer, J. A. 1975. Reduction of psychological stress in surgical patients. *J. Exp. Soc. Psychol.* 11:155–65

Langner, T. S. 1962. A twenty-two item screening score of psychiatric symptoms indicating impariment. *J. Health Soc. Behav.* 3:269–76

Langner, T. S., Michael, S. T. 1963. *Life Stress and Mental Health: The Midtown Manhattan Study.* New York: Free Press

Lazarus, R. S., Cohen, J. B. 1977. Environmental stress. In *Human Behavior and the Environment: Current Theory and Research*, ed. I. Altman, J. F. Wohlwill. New York: Plenum

Lazarus, R. S., DeLongis, A., Folkman, S., Gruen, R. 1984. Stress and adaptational outcomes: The problem of confounded measures. *Am Psychol.* In press

Lazarus, R. S., Launier, R. 1978. Stress-related transactions between person and environment. In *Perspectives in International Psychology*, ed. L. A. Pervin, M. Lewis. New York: Plenum

Leavy, R. L. 1983. Social support and psychological disorder: A review. *J. Community Psychol.* 11:3–21

Lehman, D. R., Wortman, C. B., Williams, A. F. 1984. Long-term effects of losing a spouse or child in a motor vehicle crash. Under review

Leventhal, H., Everhart, D. 1979. Emotion, pain and physical illness. In *Emotions and*

Psychopathology, ed. C. Izard. New York: Plenum

Levy, R. L. 1983. Social support and compliance: A selective review and critique of treatment integrity and outcome measurement. *Soc. Sci. Med.* 17(8):1329–38

Liem, R., Liem, J. 1978. Social class and mental illness reconsidered: The role of economic stress and social support. *J. Health Soc. Behav.* 19(2):139–56

Lin, N., Ensel, W. M. 1984. Depression-mobility and its social etiology: The role of life events and social support. *J. Health Soc. Behav.* 25:176–88

Link, B. G., Dohrenwend, B. P. 1980. Formulation of hypotheses about the true prevalence of demoralization in the United States. In *Mental Illness in the United States: Epidemiological Estimates,* ed. B. P. Dohrenwend, B. S. Dohrenwend, M. S. Gould, B. Link, R. Neugebauer, R. Wunsch-Hitzig, pp. 114–32. Praeger

Link, B. G., et al. 1983. *Measuring life events: The problem of variability within life event categories.* Soc. Psychiatry Res. Unit, Columbia Univ. Unpublished manuscript

Maddison, D., Walker, W. L. 1967. Factors affecting the outcome of conjugal bereavement. *Br. J. Psychiatry* 113:1057–67

Maguire, G. P., Lee, E. G., Bevington, D. J., Kuchemann, C. S., Crabtree, R. J., Cornell, C. E. 1978. Psychiatric problems in the first year after mastectomy. *Br. Med. J.* 1:963–65

McLean, P. D., Ogston, K., Grauer, L. 1973. A behavioral approach to the treatment of depression. *J. Behav. Res. Exp. Psychiatry* 134:140–52

Meichenbaum, D. 1977. *Cognitive-Behavior Modification: An Integrative Approach.* New York: Plenum

Meichenbaum, D., Cameron, R. 1983. Stress inoculation training: Toward a general paradigm for training coping skills. See Meichenbaum & Jaremko 1983, pp. 115–57

Meichenbaum, D., Jaremko, M. E., eds. 1983. *Stress Reduction and Prevention.* New York: Plenum

Menaghen, E. G. 1983. Individual coping efforts: Moderators of the relationship between life stress and mental health outcomes. In *Psychosocial Stress: Trends in Theory and Research,* ed. H. B. Kaplan, pp. 157–91. New York: Academic

Miller, P., Ingham, J. G. 1976. Friends, confidants and symptoms. *Soc. Psychiatry* 11:51–58

Mischel, W. 1977. Self-control and the self. In *The Self: Psychological and Philosophical issues,* ed. T. Mischel. Totowa, NJ: Rowman & Littlefield

Mitchell, R. E., Trickett, E. J. 1980. Task force report: Social networks as mediators of social support (an analysis of the effects and determinants of social networks). *Community Ment. Health J.* 16:27–44

Monroe, S. M. 1983. Major and minor life events as predictors of psychological distress: Further issues and findings. *J. Behav. Med.* 6:189–205

Moos, R. H., Billings, A. G. 1982. Conceptualizing and measuring coping resources and processes. In *Handbook of Stress: Theoretical and Clinical Aspects,* ed. L. Goldberger, S. Breznitz, pp. 212–30. Free Press

Mueller, D. P. 1980. Social networks: A promising direction for research on the relationship of the social environment to psychiatric disorder. *Soc. Sci. Med.* 14A:147–61

Mullen, B., Suls, J. 1982. The effectiveness of attention and rejection as coping styles: A meta-analysis of temporal differences. *J. Psychosom. Res.* 26(1):43–49

Mumford, E., Schlesinger, H. J., Glass, G. V. 1982. The effects of psychological intervention on recovery from surgery and heart attacks: An analysis of the literature. *Am. J. Public Health* 72(2):141–51

Myers, H. F. 1982. Stress, ethnicity, and social class: A model for research with black populations. In *Minority Mental Health,* ed. E. Jones, S. Korchin, pp. 123–37. New York: Holt, Rinehart & Winston

Myers, J. K., Lindenthal, J. J., Pepper, M. P., Ostrander, D. R. 1974. Social class, life events and psychiatric symptoms: A longitudinal study. In *Stressful Life Events: Their Nature and Effects,* ed. B. S. Dohrenwend, B. P. Dohrenwend, pp. 191–206. New York: Wiley

Parkes, C. M. 1975. Unexpected and untimely bereavement: A statistical study of young Boston widows and widowers. In *Bereavement: Its Psychosocial Aspects,* ed. B. Schoenberg, I. Gerber, A. Wiener, A. H. Kutscher, D. Peretz, A. C. Carr, pp. 119–38. New York: Columbia Univ. Press

Parkes, C. M., Weiss, R. S. 1983. *Recovery from Bereavement.* New York: Basic Books

Pearlin, L. I., Lieberman, M. A., Meneghan, E. G., Mullen, J. T. 1981. The stress process. *J. Health Soc. Behav.* 22:337–56

Pearlin, L. I., Schooler, C. 1978. The structure of coping. *J. Health Soc. Behav.* 19:2–21

Peplau, L. A., Perlman, D. 1982. Perspectives on loneliness. In *Loneliness: A Sourcebook of Current Theory, Research and Therapy,* ed. L. A. Peplau, D. Perlman, pp. 1–18. New York: Wiley-Interscience

Peters-Golden, M. 1982. Breast cancer: Varied perceptions of social support in the illness experience. *Soc. Sci. Med.* 16:483–91

Porter, J. R., Washington, R. E. 1979. Black identity and self-esteem: A review of studies of black self-concept. *Ann. Rev. Sociol.* 5:53–74

Price, R. H., Ketterer, R. F., Bader, B. C., Monahan, J., eds. 1980. *Prevention in Community Mental Health: Research, Policy and Practice.* Beverly Hills, Calif: Sage

Price, R. H., Smith, S. S. 1984. *Evaluating Prevention Programs in Mental Health.* Rockville, Md: Nat. Inst. Ment. Health Monogr. In press

Rabkin, J. G., Struening, E. L. 1976. Life events, stress and illness. *Science* 194:1013–20

Radloff, L. S., Monroe, M. K. 1978. Sex differences in helplessness—with implications for depression. In *Career Development and Counselling of Women*, ed. L. S. Hansen, R. S. Rapoza, pp. 137–52. Springfield, Ill: Thomas

Raphael, B. 1977. Preventive intervention with the recently bereaved. *Arch. Gen. Psychiatry* 34:1450–54

Ray, C., Lindop, J., Gibson, S. 1982. The concept of coping. *Psychol. Med.* 12:385–95

Rook, K. S. 1984a. The negative side of social interaction: Impact on psychological well-being. *J. Pers. Soc. Psychol.* In press

Rook, K. S. 1984b. The functions of social bonds: Perspectives from research on social support, loneliness and social isolation. In *Social Support: Theory, Research and Application*, ed. I. G. Sarason, B. R. Sarason. The Hague: Martinus-Nijhof. In press

Rook, K. S. 1984c. Promoting social bonding: Strategies for helping the lonely and socially isolated. *Am. Psychol.* In press

Rosen, B. M. 1977. Mental health and the poor: Have the gaps between the poor and the 'nonpoor' narrowed in the last decade? *Med. Care* 15:647–61

Rosenbaum, M. 1984. A model for research on self-regulation: Reducing the schism between behaviorism and general psychology. In *Paradigmatic Behavior Therapy: Critical Perspectives on Applied Social Behaviorism*, ed. I. M. Evans. New York: Springer

Rosenbaum, M., Palmon, N. 1984. Helplessness and resourcefulness in coping with epilepsy. *J. Consult. Clin. Psychol.* 52 (2):244–52

Rosenthal, A. K., Roth, S. 1981. Relationship between cognitive activity and adjustment in four spinal-cord-injured individuals: A longitudinal investigation. *J. Hum. Stress* 7:35–43

Roskin, M. 1982. Coping with life changes: A preventative social work approach. *Am. J. Community Psychol.* 10:331–40

Sarason, I. G., Johnson, J. H., Siegel, J. M. 1978. Assessing the impact of life changes: Development of the life experiences survey. *J. Consult. Clin. Psychol.* 46:932–46

Scheppele, K. L., Bart, P. B. 1983. Through women's eyes: Defining danger in the wake of sexual assault. *J. Soc. Issues* 39(2):63–80

Schwab, J. J., Schwab, M. E. 1978. *Sociocultural Roots of Mental Illness: An Epidemiologic Survey.* New York: Plenum

Selye, H. 1956. *The Stress of Life.* New York: McGraw-Hill

Silver, R. L., Boon, C., Stones, M. H. 1983. Searching for meaning in misfortune: Making sense of incest. *J. Soc. Issues* 39(2):81–102

Silver, R. L., Wortman, C. B. 1980. Coping with undesirable life events. In *Human Helplessness: Theory and Applications*, ed. J. Garber, M. E. P. Seligman, pp. 279–375. New York: Academic

Slater, J., Depue, R. A. 1981. The contributions of environmental events and social support to serious suicide attempts in primary depressive disorder. *J. Abnorm. Psychol.* 90:275–85

Spiegel, D., Bloom, J., Yalom, I. 1981. Group support for patients with metastatic cancer. *Arch. Gen. Psychiatry* 38:527–33

Stone, A. A., Neale, J. M. 1982. Development of a methodology for assessing daily experiences. In *Advances in Environmental Psychology: Environment and Health*, ed. A. Baum, J. Singer, 4:49–89. New York: Erlbaum

Stone, A. A., Neale, J. M. 1984. Effects of severe daily events on mood. *J. Pers. Soc. Psychol.* 46:137–44

Stone, A. A., Neale, J. M. 1985. A new measure of daily coping: Development and preliminary results. *J. Pers. Soc. Psychol.* In press

Strauss, J. S. 1979. Social and cultural influences on psychopathology. *Ann. Rev. Psychol.* 30:397–415

Stroebe, M., Stroebe, W. 1983. Who suffers more? Sex differences in health risks of the widowed. *Psychol. Bull.* 93:279–301

Surtees, P. G. 1980. Social support, residual adversity, and depressive outcome. *Soc. Psychol.* 15:71–80

Tennant, C. 1983. Life events and psychological morbidity: The evidence from prospective studies. *Psychol. Med.* 3:483–86

Tennant, C., Bebbington, P., Hurry, J. 1981. The short-term outcome of neurotic disorders in the community: The relation of remission to clinical factors and to "neutralizing" life events. *Br. J. Psychiatry* 139:213–20

Thoits, P. A. 1982. Conceptual, methodological and theoretical problems in studying social support as a buffer against life stress. *J. Health Soc. Behav.* 23:145–59

Thoits, P. A. 1983. Dimensions of life events that influence psychological distress: An evaluation and synthesis of the literature. In

Psychosocial Stress: Trends in Theory and Research, ed. H. B. Kaplan, pp. 33–103. New York: Academic

Turk, D. C., Meichenbaum, D., Genest, M. 1983. *Pain and Behavioral Medicine: A Cognitive Behavioral Perspective*. New York: Guilford

Turner, R. J. 1983. Direct, indirect, and moderating effects of social support on psychological distress and associated conditions. In *Psychosocial stress: Trends in Theory and Research*, ed. H. B. Kaplan, pp. 105–56. New York: Academic

Turner, R. J., Gartrell, J. W. 1978. Social factors in psychiatric outcome: Toward the resolution of interpretive controversies. *Am. Sociol. Rev.* 43:368–82

Turner, R. J., Noh, S. 1982. *Social support, life events and psychological distress: A three way panel analysis*. Presented at Ann. Meet. Am. Sociol. Assoc., San Francisco

Vachon, M. L. S., Lyall, W. A. L., Rogers, J., Freedman-Letofsky, K., Freeman, S. J. J. 1980. Controlled study of self-help intervention for widows. *Am. J. Psychiatry* 137:1380–84

Vachon, M. L. S., Rogers, J., Lyall, W. A. L., Lancee, W. J., Sheldon, A. R., Freeman, S. J. J. 1982b. Predictors and correlates of adaptation to conjugal bereavement. *Am. J. Psychiatry* 139(8):998–1002

Vachon, M. L. S., Sheldon, A. R., Lancee, W. J., Lyall, W. A. L., Rogers, J., Freeman, S. J. J. 1982a. Correlates of enduring distress patterns following bereavement: Social network, life situation and personality. *Psychol. Med.* 12:783–88

Vaughn, C. E., Leff, J. P. 1976. The influence of family and social factors on the course of psychiatric illness: A comparison of schizophrenic and depressed neurotic patients. *Br. J. Psychiatry* 129:125–37

Veroff, J., Douvan, E., Kulka, R. A. 1981. *The Inner American: A Self Portrait from 1957–1976*. New York: Basic Books

Videka-Sherman, L. 1982. Coping with the death of a child: A study over time. *Am. J. Orthopsychiatry* 52(4):688–98

Wallerstein, J. S., Kelly, J. B. 1980. *Surviving the Breakup: How Children and Parents Cope with Divorce*. New York: Basic Books

Wallston, B. S., Alagna, S. W., DeVellis, B. M., DeVellis, R. F. 1983. Social support and physical health. *Health Psychol.* 2(4):367–91

Weiss, J. M., Glazer, H. I., Pohorecky, L. A. 1976. Coping behavior and neurochemical changes in rats: An alternative explanation for the original "learned helplessness" experiments. In *Animal Models in Human Psychobiology*, ed. G. Serban, A. King, pp. 141–73. New York: Plenum

Wellman, B. 1979. The community question: The intimate networks of East Yorkers. *Am. J. Sociol.* 84:1201–31

Wheaton, B. 1978. The sociogenesis of psychological disorder: Reexamining the causal issues with longitudinal data. *Am. Sociol. Rev.* 43:383–403

Wheaton, B. 1980. The sociogenesis of psychological disorder: An attributional theory. *J. Health Soc. Behav.* 21:100–23

Wheaton, B. 1982. A comparison of the moderating effects of personal coping resources on the impact of exposure to stress in two groups. *J. Community Psychol.* 10:293–311

Wortman, C. B. 1976. Causal attributions and personal control. In *New Directions in Attributional Research*, ed. J. Harvey, W. Ickes, R. F. Kidd, pp. 23–52. Hillsdale, NJ: Erlbaum

Wortman, C. B. 1983. Coping with victimization: Conclusions and implications for future research. *J. Soc. Issues* 39(2):195–221

Wortman, C. B. 1984. Social support and the cancer patient: Conceptual and methodologic issues. *Cancer* 53(10):2339–60

Wortman, C. B., Brehm, J. W. 1975. Responses to uncontrollable outcomes: An integration of reactance theory and the learned helplessness model. *Adv. Exp. Soc. Psychology* 8:277–36

Wortman, C. B., Conway, T. 1984. The role of social support in adaptation and recovery from physical illness. In *Social Support and Health*, ed. S. Cohen, L. Syme. New York: Academic. In press

Wortman, C. B., Lehman, D. R. 1984. Reactions to victims of life crises: Support efforts that fail. In *Social Support: Theory, Research and Application*, ed. I. B. Sarason, B. R. Sarason. The Hague: Martinus Nijhof. In press

Zautra, A. J., Dohrenwend, B. P. 1983. *The measurement of small events*. Presented at Ann. Meet. Am. Psychol. Assoc., Los Angeles

Ann. Rev. Psychol. 1985. 36:573–611

ORGANIZATIONAL BEHAVIOR

Benjamin Schneider

Department of Psychology and Center for Innovation, University of Maryland, College Park, Maryland 20742

CONTENTS

INTRODUCTION

This is the fourth review of Organizational Behavior (OB) in six years. The first was published by Mitchell in 1979, followed by Cummings (1982) and Staw (1984). Four reviews in a relatively brief time period have allowed authors to take a broad perspective on this growing field because they have not had to summarize many years of work in one review.

This review will use the historical works of the field as a framework for interpretation. Within that framework, the journal literature in OB that appeared in 1983 will be highlighted. In addition, a recurring methodological theme, the level of analysis issue, will be presented. Finally, a strong argument

0066-4308/85/0201-0573$02.00

will be made for adopting utility (cost-benefit) analyses as a way (but not the only way) of documenting the practical significance of OB.

What is OB?

OB is the confluence of individual, group, and organizational studies flowing from industrial-organizational (I/O) psychology and organization and management theory (OMT) with headwaters in psychology (social, psychometrics), sociology (organizational, work, and occupational), and management (scientific, human relations). The field is bounded by concern for behavior primarily in profit-making work organizations, so the study of public, educational, and civic institutions is not usual even though many people work there.

Most OB researchers and theoreticians are currently located in American business schools, but impressive theoretical and practical contributions have also come from England (e.g. Pugh 1981, Trist 1981). Also worthwhile is an examination of Japanese management and organizational design (e.g. Ouchi 1981, Pascale & Athos 1981), as well as more discipline-oriented programs in I/O psychology and sociology (work and occupations).

Because of this mixed heritage, the range of issues addressed by OB scholars is very broad indeed, ranging from "micro OB" studies of individual employee motivation to "macro OB" studies of organizational structural arrangements (size, span of control, technology) as a function of environmental turbulence. Unfortunately, micro and macro issues have rarely been theoretically integrated much less concurrently studied (Roberts et al 1978), although recently this has been changing.

OB is fundamentally, and perhaps logically, schizophrenic with respect to a focus on organizational survival and effectiveness versus concern for the human element in the organization. The management lineage, concerned with strategies focused on survival, remained relatively uninfluenced by psychology and sociology until the early 1960s. Since then, however, management has certainly taken on a more humanistic tone (Perrow 1973, Schein 1980). Industrial-organizational (I/O) psychologists, in particular, were attracted by schools of business, and by 1971 OB was strong enough to have its own division of the Academy of Management. While the tension between the disciplines of general management and OB is now seldom found in business and industry, the tension in business schools between OB and other business disciplines can be felt. Marketers, finance/accountants, management scientists (those in management who did not "go behavioral"), and especially economists share the common language of dollars while OB speaks the foreign language of motivation, leadership, job satisfaction, environmental turbulence, and so on. In a business school, OB (including personnel management and organization theory) is a definite and different field.

In summary, OB is a field which experiences numerous healthy tensions yielding differences in foci for theory and research, some of which lead to different perspectives on conducting research, and some of which result in a "we-they" tension in business schools. Perhaps this tension might be somewhat alleviated if OB researchers paid more attention to the economic benefits of OB (Cascio 1982).

Chapter Organization

The reason why OB encompasses such a wide variety of perspectives is that employee, organizational, and environmental issues are continually in reciprocation (McGuire 1973, Weick 1979). Because reciprocal rather than unidirectional cause and effect relationships predominate, the OB researcher must make judgments about the proper focus for theory and/or research. The two major foci of choice are the individual and his/her group and the organizational work context. However, because these foci are in reciprocal relationship, a concentration on any one level frequently makes it appear that the other levels are irrelevant.

For example, an absenteeism problem in an organization cannot be understood as an environmental problem unless the context of the organization is considered (Clegg 1983). The usual approach in OB to understanding absenteeism would be to conduct an individually focused study by perhaps correlating individual attitudes with absenteeism. This kind of study would make the implicit assumption that individual attitudes is the issue of interest and that individual variance in attitudes is the major correlate of absenteeism.

An alternative perspective would be that there is something unique about the organization that provides a milieu in which the absenteeism rate is likely to be high (e.g. Smith 1977) and, within that milieu, who will be absent is predictable based on assessments of individual attitudes. By only assessing individual attitudes, the absenteeism problem is thus an individual behavioral problem. By having an interorganizational perspective, absenteeism is an organizational behavior problem. Almost no research in OB concurrently focuses on individual and organizational variance in behavior in an attempt to explain both who does what and in what contexts particular behavior rates occur.

This extended introduction to the organization of the review was necessary because the reviewer's dilemma is both to capture the multilevel nature of problems studied in OB and to develop each of the major topics in the field. Resolution of the dilemma resulted in a presentation of separate topics, but with continual reminders of the reciprocity across levels of concern.

The three major topics to be covered are individual (motivation, job attitudes), group and organization (groups, leadership, climate and culture), and productivity and utility. A number of topics are not explicitly covered: organization structure (including technology, organization-environment relationships), decision making (by individuals, groups, management), personnel management (selection, appraisal, wage and salary administration), industrial relations (unions), research methodology, and organization development and change. Research methodology and change are referenced throughout the chapter but only particular issues (ones that fit the writer's biases in both areas?) are mentioned.

INDIVIDUAL FOCI

Worker Motivation

Worker motivation is at the very foundation of OB. The earliest theory and research in what has come to be OB was concerned with understanding why workers failed to behave the way management said it wanted them to behave. Argyris (1957), Herzberg (Herzberg et al 1959), McGregor (1960), and Likert (1961) all made important early statements about worker motivation, generally supporting the thesis that management frustrates rather than facilitates the display of employee energy toward the accomplishment of organizational goals.

The early theories tended to be proposed by organizational diagnosticians (Argyris, Likert), organizational researchers (Herzberg et al), or ex-managers (McGregor). The organizational frame of reference yielded works that ascribed common motives to employees. Unfortunately, the well-trained researchers in the early days of OB translated the theories into individual differences models. This resulted in tests of Argyris's and McGregor's formulations being conducted on many individuals in one setting instead of across many settings. These efforts generally failed to find support for such formulations, thus disillusioning psychologists with the more universally focused portraits of employee motivation (Campbell & Pritchard 1976).

In contrast, Vroom's (1964) individually oriented expectancy theory and its early variants (Porter & Lawler 1968) were enthusiastically adopted, resulting in a flood of research papers. Although only moderately supported by research, this perspective on motivation was consistent with the training of researchers. Because of the necessity to test various nuances in the theory, expectancy theory articles persisted in the literature through the middle 1970s and recently have begun to appear again. The more recent papers focus on some older issues such as within- versus between-subjects designs (Kennedy et al 1983, Wanous et al 1983), but some newer efforts have also appeared. These include the novel long-term prediction of job satisfaction by Pulakos & Schmitt (1983) and of stress by Cooke & Rousseau (1983), a potential integration of expectancy theory and goal-setting theory that employs both effort level and direction of effort to predict performance (Katerberg & Blau 1983), and the role of expectancies of success in the decision to pursue job alternatives (Rynes & Lawler 1983).

Paradoxically, the more universal formulations about human motivation that were found inappropriate by researchers were more readily adopted by management, while expectancy theory never really was accepted (except in the crude form of incentive pay). The reason for this appears to be that managers know they must do things that affect large numbers of workers rather than one individual at a time. Where worker motivation is concerned, then, workers as a group are the target of interest.

One topic that replaced expectancy theory for researchers was goal-setting theory, a work motivation theory unconcerned with individual differences in needs, desires, or instrumentality perceptions. The theory is also nonspecific with respect to management philosophy about workers, but it does seem useful in improving worker productivity (Locke et al 1981). At present, this motivation theory is receiving the most research attention. It is fairly well established now that specific, difficult goals accompanied by feedback result in performance superior to general "do your best" goals and the absence of feedback. Boundary conditions on the general propositions just noted are a focus for study, especially contrasting the effects of participation and goal setting on performance (Latham & Steele 1983; goal setting is superior again), explicating the role of self-regulation regarding goal acceptance in the model and research (Erez & Kanfer 1983), and concern for the nature (Matsui et al 1983) and role (Ashford & Cummings 1983) of feedback in performance. This last paper is particularly intriguing when viewed as a vehicle for introducing some individual differences in internal states into the goal-setting paradigm—the variable is called feedback-seeking behavior (FSB).

A second topic that received attention by researchers interested in motivation was what has come to be called job characteristics research (JCR; Hackman & Oldham 1980). JCR represented a contemporary integration of the Herzberg/ McGregor/Argyris perspectives on the relative centrality of the work itself as a motivator of performance with a consistent trend concerned with the role of tasks in the design of organizations (Turner & Lawrence 1965, Hackman & Lawler 1971, Miller 1976). JCR was very prominent during the middle to late 1970s, but by 1983 essentially no new work was being published. The relatively negative review of the topic by Roberts & Glick (1981) may have merely signaled an already existing decline of interest in JCR.

That review, essentially a critique of perceptions as "real" data and as distinct from job satisfaction, argued for abandoning JCR as a viable approach to explicating work as a central role in motivation. Perhaps most damaging was Roberts & Glick's idea that perceptions of task characteristics are just perceptions and do not represent the attributes of tasks. Griffin (1983) and Jenkins et al (1983) convincingly show that this is *not* true, that perceptions are a useful source of data about jobs. Given the long history of successful job analysis work in I/O psychology, this comes as no surprise (McCormick 1979).

A work motivation theory that never became as popular as expectancy theory, goal setting, or JCR, but continues to generate research, is equity theory (Adams 1963). A reformulation of equity theory by Cosier & Dalton (1983) presents the idea that the equity theory formulation most familiar to researchers is ahistorical and that in laboratory tests the theory did not take history into account. Cosier & Dalton argue that an important consideration for people in judging equity is the *past* inequities that have been experienced, that past inequities lead to the "straw that breaks the camel's back."

Equity theory, of course, has provided a useful framework for research on pay in organizations (Lawler 1981). On the one hand it is unfortunate that the theory typically has been applied only to pay (for an exception see Telly et al 1971), but we should be thankful that pay research has at least been able to find a contemporary home (Birnbaum 1983).

Some other research on pay has been accomplished recently, especially work having to do with comparable worth issues at hiring (Rynes et al 1983) or the setting of market wages (Schwab & Wichern 1983). Two interesting studies, one of participatively set wages for engineers (Bullock 1983) and the other of tipping in a luxury hotel (Shamir 1983), revealed that when wages are participatively set, workers perceive equity and a performance-pay relationship. In the hotel study, the comparison was between those who receive tips and those who receive only wages. What continues to amaze this reviewer is how little is known about pay and how little it is studied.

In summary, the universalistic motivation theories of Argyris and McGregor are not thought of as motivation theories any longer; now they are theories of organization design, perhaps included under the Quality of Work Life (QWL) rubric (Seashore 1981). This is unfortunate because it removes motivation from the arena of comparative organization studies and fails to entertain the idea that people with different motivations are attracted to different kinds of organizations (Holland 1973, Schein 1978, Schneider 1983a). Without a macro motivation construct, comparative organization behavior becomes person-less, a study of the anatomy of organizations.

At the other extreme, contemporary motivation theory is relatively devoid of good new testable frameworks depicting internal states. Essentially there is no research on the older need-based formulations or expectancy theory, and gratuitous inclusion of "individual differences" in a piece of research does not make it a motivation study (for an exception see Kohn & Schooler's 1983 book on work and personality). Only in the later discussion of research on turnover will internal states return as important for understanding human behavior at work. One could ask "What happened to motivation research?"

Job Satisfaction and Related Attitudes and Behavior

There is far more contemporary research on attitudes, specifically job satisfaction, than on motivation. The distinction between the two is that attitudes are evaluations/feelings *about* objects/conditions/outcomes while motivation refers to the energizing and directing of effort toward the *attainment* of objects/conditions/outcomes. The idea in job satisfaction research in particular is that people are motivated to attain objects/conditions/outcomes and that when attainment is achieved they will feel good.

JOB SATISFACTION   One aim of all management and motivation theories is to have a satisfied work force; the differences exist over what management and motivation theorists believe is satisfying. Taylor (1911) believed incentive pay would be satisfying, Herzberg et al (1959) that "motivators" would be satisfying (talk about confusion!), and Alderfer (1972) that attaining desires would be satisfying. The problem is that we have no comprehensive theories of what leads to job satisfaction except perhaps for equity theory which specifies quite precisely the conditions for dissatisfaction.

One hypothesis for the importance accorded job satisfaction in OB research is relative ease of study of important issues. For example, what is the relationship between flexitime (Krausz & Freiback 1983), unions (Berger et al 1983), or status (Golding et al 1983) and job satisfaction?

An alternative hypothesis is that satisfaction is an important human outcome of organizational life. As such it deserves study because the satisfaction people experience in organizations is as much a part of the organization as anything else. This perspective would maintain that meaningful differences in satisfaction exist for members of different organizations and that these differences are worthy of study. A few earlier studies supported this perspective (Herman et al 1975, Sutton & Rousseau 1979) as do some recent efforts. For example, Green et al (1983) showed that the market characteristics of branch banks (obtained from archival data) were related to differences in employee satisfaction. More multiunit and/or multiorganization studies investigating job satisfaction of organizational members as a correlate of larger environmental forces might enhance our knowledge of the human side of organizations, especially if those studies are lodged in a meaningful conceptual framework.

A third hypothesis, sometimes supported by the literature, is that satisfaction is a useful predictor of important behaviors like absenteeism (the literature on this is not clear according to Clegg 1983) and turnover (fairly consistent findings according to Youngblood et al 1983); turnover will receive additional attention later.

These three hypotheses as a group suggest the necessity for useful conceptual models of satisfaction itself. As noted earlier, a major inhibition to the development of such a framework has been the continual confounding of motivation and satisfaction (Miner & Dachler 1973). A second problem is the wide variety of individual and organizational variables that have been shown to be related to job satisfaction (Locke 1976). The combination of poor theory and a wide variety of variables has led to a proliferation of measures making any comparison of findings from different studies difficult.

Perhaps the simplest, most useful model of the determinant of global job satisfaction is congruence or fit of the person to the setting, because this conceptualization underlies all attempts to study satisfaction (Locke 1976, Tziner 1983). The element to note here is the focus on global job satisfaction because from a basic research standpoint this is what theories need to predict. They need to predict this because (a) the variety of facets that are potentially predictable is great, and (b) the sum of the facets does not appear to be the same as the results obtained from global measures (Scarpello & Campbell 1983). Given a global measure of job satisfaction as a criterion in studies of the antecedents of satisfaction, and the same global measure as a predictor in studies of other criteria of interest, perhaps a grounded theory would emerge that captures the role of satisfaction in organizational studies.

A focus on the fit of people to work settings would, in turn, tend to eliminate studies in which raw personal attributes like age, sex, or race are examined. These physiognomic variables are not very interesting, even when they correlate with something (and frequently they do not; e.g. Golding et al 1983). It is the psychology or sociology or organizational behavior associated with these variables (e.g. self-esteem, family situation, or supervisory behavior) that is relevant, not the demographics per se. This issue will be discussed again under the section on intergroup theory.

Because no accepted taxonomy exists for specifying the kinds of issues to assess in conducting studies on person-environment fit (cf Pervin & Lewis 1978), each researcher specifies the variables of interest. As such studies accumulate, the person and environment variables important for the study of job satisfaction will become evident, as summarized by Locke (1976), for example. Personality-organization fit (Sterns et al 1983, Wiggins et al 1983) and the fit of personal values with job and organizational characteristics (Butler 1983, Greenhaus et al 1983) are only two examples of the kinds of interesting research that can be accomplished.

ROLE STRESS   Obviously, job satisfaction is not the only job attitude of interest in organizational behavior; role stress (ambiguity and conflict) and organizational commitment have also been foci of study. As with job satisfaction research, theoretical formulations have lagged behind the proliferation of measures (House et al 1983) and bivariate studies. Because the hard conceptual work has not preceded data collection (Roberts et al 1978), not only are the results of any one study difficult to interpret, but how a study of commitment differs from one on satisfaction and from organizational identification and from role stress is also frequently not clear. For example, in a meta-analytic study, Fisher & Gitelson (1983) showed that role conflict and role ambiguity consistently correlate about .20–.35 with organizational commitment, job involvement, and various kinds of facet satisfaction—facts that are difficult to interpret in the absence of a nomological net (Morrow 1983). The point is that correlations of .50, .60, or even .70 certainly do not reflect redundancy; they only do so in the absence of reasonable explanations for why they are *not* redundant. This is a case where redundancy is presumed in the absence of competing hypotheses for observed data.

The simple bivariate studies of the past on role conflict and role ambiguity appear to have stopped, and more complex formulations for these variables in particular and stress in general have appeared. For example, Nicholson & Goh (1983) explored how different kinds of work environments might moderate role stress-satisfaction relationships. Their findings were mixed, as are most moderator variable studies in field settings, but the effort represents the desirable goal of understanding linkages between organizations and member reactions to them.

Jackson (1983) also proposed and tested a more complex formulation of the role of experienced conflict and ambiguity in organizations. She studied nurses' and hospital clericals' participation in decision making as an antecedent to role conflict/ambiguity and then role conflict/ambiguity as antecedents to job satisfaction. The implied hypotheses were supported utilizing a modified Solomon four-group design permitting some more-than-usual causal ordering. Similarly permitting causal inferences, Bateman & Strasser (1983) studied nurse satisfaction in reciprocal causal relationship with job tension in a cross-lagged regression design. Apparently nurses are a good and available sample for research on stress; Vredenburgh & Trinkhaus (1983) also studied them, as did Murphy (1983) and Sheridan & Abelson (1983).

Murphy's (1983) study is particularly interesting because he studied the utility of three stress reduction techniques for nurses (biofeedback, progressive muscle relaxation, and the control condition—self-relaxation). Not only were daily sessions for one hour over two weeks effective in reducing tension for the biofeedback and progressive muscle relation groups, but at the end of three months these groups reported significantly higher levels of job satisfaction. It may be useful to note that Murphy's study was found in *Human Factors* (see 1983), an excellent source for research on stress. It also must be noted that stress reduction experiments are not being reported in the usual OB outlets.

The fact that nurses were available for stress studies suggests a caution regarding drawing conclusions from research efforts on any one occupational group, from any single organization study, or indeed from any *set* of organizational studies where self-selection or volunteerism could be an important factor (Pfeffer 1981). Such caution is obvious when one considers the empirical documentation of differences in person types in different careers (e.g. Holland 1973) and organizations (e.g. Wanous et al 1983). The caution is further substantiated by the finding that behavior-based job analysis information itself [Position Analysis Questionnaire (PAQ)] correlates with job stress (Shaw & Riskind 1983), suggesting that people who enter particular jobs are likely to experience high levels of stress.

Shaw & Riskind used archival data for both PAQ data and stress scores for jobs, thus eliminating any R-R contamination; their results are thus for jobs and not for individuals. Shaw & Riskind's results were quite strong, with some astounding relationships found between PAQ dimension and job stress indicants. Some multiple correlations of PAQ dimensions against stress were frequently about $R = .60$ (suicides = .61; role conflict = .65; role ambiguity = .77; cardiovascular problems = .71; respiratory problems = .79). These results suggest that correlations within a job class (like nurses) may be constrained by range restrictions and, perhaps more importantly, that job and organizational (e.g. Gaines & Jermier 1983, Parker & DeCotiis 1983) differences in stress may only be symptomatic of other important job differences in, for example, satisfaction (Yukl 1981), information-privacy values (Stone et al 1983), and motivation (Litwin & Stringer 1968). These are differences that warrant more attention.

A major category of newer studies of job stress became clear in 1983: namely, research on life-job relationships. While this relationship has had a long history in studies of satisfaction, it is relatively new for job stress, except for some earlier studies of dual career women (Hall & Gordon 1973). Bhagat (1983) and Martin & Schermerhorn (1983), for example, developed frameworks for studying how life events and work factors jointly determine satisfaction and then both physical and mental health (stress for Bhagat).

OB researchers seem not to be crossing over into the more physiological assessment of stress, depending essentially on self-reports of coping, tension, and conflict/ambiguity. It could be argued that failure to tie experienced job stress to individual physiological health and/or organizational economic health will prevent OB from influencing major decision making with both the medical and business establishments (Brief et al 1981).

COMMITMENT   A major contribution to the commitment literature was presented by Morrow (1983), who summarized research on the five major forms of work commitment: value focus (e.g. Protestant work ethic), career focus (career salience), job focus (job involvement), organizational focus (organizational commitment and identification), and union focus (attitudes toward unions). In addition to summarizing work accomplished under each focus, Morrow revealed that much of the literature on work commitment cuts across these various foci. She concluded that (1983, p. 486): ". . . these concepts are partially redundant and insufficiently distinct to warrant continued separation."

Perhaps one reason for this state of redundancy is the use of existing measures as a source of items for new measures. In studies of job involvement, for example, the Lodahl & Kejner (1965) measure in original or modified form dominated the early literature on work commitment; more recently, the Organization Commitment Questionnaire (OCQ; Mowday et al 1982) has been the measure of choice. Examination of the items in the OCQ reveal most of them tap into the feelings of attachment, and intentions to remain attached through effort and physical presence, that have appeared in the literature on job satisfaction and the various foci of work commitment as outlined by Morrow (1983). It is not surprising, then, that when OCQ results are related to other surveys and attachment intentions the results are substantial (Ferris & Aranya 1983).

A few authors have been promoting some new ideas about commitment. Organ and his colleagues (Bateman & Organ 1983, Smith et al 1983), following on the works of Katz & Kahn (1978), present the idea that it is behaviors that go beyond the job description—cooperativeness, performance in a crisis—that define commitment. They call these behaviors organizational citizenship behaviors and show two forms these behaviors take: altruism (helping other persons) and generalized compliance. Conceptualized this way, commitment behaviors can be rated by observers (supervisors) as performance and, when this is done, job satisfaction is found to be quite strongly related to performance ($r = .40$) and, apparently, reciprocally so (Bateman & Organ 1983).

A novel and relevant question regarding commitment was asked by Jackson et al (1983): What happens to people who are committed to working when they experience forced unemployment? In a 3-year longitudinal study, Jackson et al showed: (*a*) psychological distress is higher for the unemployed than for the employed, and (*b*) this is particularly true for those whose employment commitment was high. The Jackson et al study was conducted in England; in the U.S. an entire issue of *Human Resource Management* (1983) was devoted to individual and organizational coping under conditions of retrenchment and decline. While the articles are provocative, the reports of research are more directed to practicing human resources consultants and professionals than researchers.

SOCIALIZATION   Some interesting new directions were noted in studies of socialization to work. Socialization can be conceptualized as an organization's formal and informal attempts to influence employees' future attitudes (and behavior, but attitudes has been the focus). Past research has tended to be concerned almost exclusively with what organizations do to people (Van Maanen 1976) and how people experience and cope with these attempts to help the newcomer learn the ropes (Louis 1980). More recent work has introduced the idea that people approach new jobs from different experiential backgrounds so the outcomes of the "same" socialization processes may differ across people (Jones 1983a). In a similar paper, Louis et al (1983) showed that socialization practices are differentially available to newcomers and that some practices are more helpful than others. Finally, Feldman & Brett (1983) showed that people are proactive in their own socialization in that they seek social support and help from others. Feldman & Brett's paper is one of very few examples to include the role of the person in socialization research (Schneider 1983b).

Putting these three papers together suggests an interesting framework for research on socialization: availability of various formal and informal organizational practices × prior experience of newcomer × level of proactive behavior of newcomer = job attitudes and behavior. Perhaps explicating the variety of ways by which people can become socialized to work can explain some of the differences found in research on the realistic job preview (RJP; Breaugh 1983). That is, the RJP has been researched as a process equally applicable to all newcomers, but the proposed framework suggests at least two individually based sources of variability in effects: level of prior work experience and level of proactive behavior. Individual differences have not received attention in either the RJP or socialization research literatures (Schneider 1983b), but these recent writings suggest some possible projects.

TURNOVER   Turnover and absenteeism are the criteria most often used in studies concerned with the job attitudes reviewed above. In fact, studies in OB so frequently focus on these withdrawal behaviors that Staw (1984) made them a focus of his review; as such, the background of the study of turnover is not presented here and, because research on absenteeism was rare, that topic is not addressed at all.

The 1983 literature on turnover continues to focus on the early participation model of March & Simon (1958), the more elaborate "intermediate linkages" version presented by Mobley et al (1979), or a matching model patterned after the work adjustment theory of Lofquist & Dawes (1969) and Wanous (1980). Jackofsky & Peters (1983a), for example, tested the March & Simon proposition that a combination of perceived ease of movement and the perceived desirability of one's present job predicts actual movement. A twist in their study was the criterion: internal movement vs movement to another organization. Their results supported the hypothesis that the desirability of a job helps predict job (internal) movement better than it predicts movement to another organization. Incidentally, in another paper they (1983b) suggest that people with higher levels of ability may experience greater perceived ease of movement, but that model has not yet been tested.

In another twist on March & Simon, Motowidlo (1983) deduced that pay was a critical issue in turnover, specifically current pay satisfaction and future pay expectations. He showed in a 19-month study that pay satisfaction, but not pay expectations, was a stronger correlate of turnover than general satisfaction but that turnover intentions were the strongest correlate of turnover (Mobley 1982).

Mobley's (1982) model in fact attempts to explicate what leads to turnover intentions precisely because intentions are the immediate cause of turnover. Spencer et al (1983) and Youngblood et al (1983) both showed the value of various linkages in understanding this cognitive model of the individual turnover process. The Youngblood et al study is an important effort because of the unusual care taken to (a) explicate and operationalize the model, (b) obtain multiple (three or four years) time-period assessments, and (c) obtain a sufficiently large sample for testing multiple linkages (N = 1445). This care responds to many of the criticisms of turnover research raised in an excellent methodological and conceptual critique of turnover and absenteeism research by Clegg (1983).

Another noteworthy longitudinal, multiphase effort was conducted by Rusbult & Farrell (1983), who tested an investment model of turnover. Their approach was to monitor how various costs and benefits change for individuals over time and to examine how these changes are reflected in turnover. They showed that those who left experienced a decline in job commitment over time that was associated with a decline in rewards, an increase in costs, and a decrease in investment size, with costs and investments increasing in importance over time. Such results provide support for the ideas that turnover is a process and that the process can be monitored.

Sheridan & Abelson (1983) explicitly tested a dynamic decision process model using job tension and organizational commitment as key variables. Employing a catastrophe (discontinuous) framework, they were able to show that the turnover process is characterized by discontinuity (abrupt shifts followed by relative stability), and that when this characteristic of the process is considered, more accurate predictions of leavers is possible. In support of Rusbult & Farrell, Sheridan & Abelson also showed that changes in commitment over time are important for understanding differences between stayers and leavers. In addition, as proposed by Zedeck et al (1983), tension was also an important issue.

The Sheridan & Abelson and Rusbult & Farrell papers address one of Clegg's (1983) major conclusions, that the major conceptual correlate of turnover is failure to have individuals "pulled in" rather than them being "pushed out" of organizations. Conceptually, then, commitment to the organization should be superior to satisfaction as predictors of turnover. In his own work, Clegg shows this to be so, and Mowday et al (1982) support the conclusion as well. These results also suggest the potential importance of socialization to the work setting as a determinant of turnover.

These are exciting developments in the prediction and understanding of individual turnover. However, it is not time to be sanguine, for it is clear that

586   SCHNEIDER

understanding the cognitive processes of individuals as they consider their futures yields relatively little direct insight into what interested organizations can do to improve retention rates. That is, it may be one problem to be able to predict which of a group of people is more likely to leave but another problem to change the rates at which people, collectively, leave. The issue here is one of emphasizing the slope of the regression line rather than its intercept, of asking whether we can predict and understand individual differences in turnover versus whether we can change our turnover rate.

As an example of the latter issue, consider the Katz & Tushman (1983) study which asks: how does a supervisor's behavior at t_1 relate to his subordinates' eventual turnover at t_2? In other words, are the rates of turnover different for different supervisors? In fact, Katz & Tushman showed that young R & D engineers who worked for gatekeeper supervisors (really those with high external liaison activity) at t_1 were far more likely to still be employed at t_2 (5 years later).

Of course, across a number of supervisors, their gatekeeper behavior could be used as a direct correlate of *individual* subordinate behavior by assigning to each subordinate his or her supervisor's behavior. However, as noted earlier, there exist precious few examples of this kind of analysis (see Bowers 1983 for an exception) and, except in productivity intervention efforts to be described later, there are essentially no OB studies of turnover rates for organizations.

SUMMARY   The literature on job satisfaction and other job attitudes is characterized by a focus on the assessment of postorganization entry experiences (job satisfaction, role stress, commitment) as correlates of other organizational attributes (flexitime, participation in decision making, socialization), and outcomes (turnover, absenteeism). A problem noted with the literature was one concerning redundancy of measures across attitude constructs because of insufficient conceptual clarity. Even so, some encouraging conceptual and empirical work on commitment and socialization were noted.

Contrary to this reviewer's expectations, the "social construction of reality" (SCR) movement (Salancik & Pfeffer 1978) does not seem to have received recent research attention. When it did, little or equivocal support for it was found (Griffin 1983, Jenkins et al 1983). That SCR receives little support is not surprising to the present author for, as noted elsewhere (Schneider 1983b), much of the conceptual support for the SCR construct was derived from one-shot laboratory studies devoid of meaningful frames of reference in which laboratory subjects could interpret their experiences.

Finally, a brief survey of the turnover research conducted in 1983 revealed some excellent conceptual and methodological efforts. Collectively they extend our knowledge about the turnover process and clearly show a capability to make useful predictions.

GROUP AND ORGANIZATIONAL FOCI

There has always been a certain tension between OB researchers who take a more micro focus (on motivation and job attitudes) and those who study other units of analysis. The issue here is more than one of just letting each party "do its own thing," because the differences in foci lead to different levels of conceptualization and thus the use of different levels of analysis (Mossholder & Bedeian 1983a,b). Clarity about the level or unit of analysis problem is central to avoiding the ecological fallacy. The ecological fallacy is the OB researchers' equivalent of anthropomorphizing in biology—attributing characteristics to a unit of analysis different from the one studied (what Mossholder & Bedeian call cross-level inferences). Simply stated, if groups or organizations are studied, one can only say something about the *rates* of behavior in a group or organization because predictions about particular individuals are not possible.

Group and organizational research looks loose and sloppy to individually oriented researchers because, of necessity, more macro/inclusive variables (management philosophy, intergroup competition) are assessed. Fine-grained micro data on individuals are not useful, much less required, when attempting to predict competitiveness in a particular market or industry. Focus, or the criterion of interest, pushes the level at which the research will be conceptualized. The question of concern in evaluating research should not be "does the research meet some arbitrary micro standards?" but "does the research achieve prediction and understanding of the criterion of interest?" When research is thought of this way, good research allows for prediction and understanding only for criteria of interest, not for all criteria. This is why anthropologists can be accurate in the generalizations they make about norms surrounding male-female relationships, food-gathering, or warfare that characterize a culture, but they might be inaccurate when predicting the behavior of a particular person in that culture.

This long introduction to the group and organization topics was intended to highlight a problem many psychologists ponder, namely how does one study a whole organization when we have enough difficulty studying individuals? The answer is: we change what we look at and how we look at it. We look at planets not atoms with a telescope; we follow Thorngate's (1976) rule that because it is not possible to be specific, accurate, and general at the same time, no one piece of research can be expected to answer all relevant questions at all relevant levels of analysis.

Leadership and Management

Leadership and management are topics that, on the surface, one would suspect would be researched concurrently, but this is not true (Campbell et al 1970, Filley et al 1976). It follows from the introductory notes to the section on group and organization studies that if micro OB researchers study leadership, they will focus on the attributes and behaviors of leaders of clearly defined groups. Conversely, if macro OB people study management, they will concentrate on the attributes and behaviors of people who manage in larger systems where *what* and *who* is being managed is not easily defined. In the early history of leadership studies, researchers were primarily psychologists untrained in business but well versed in trait and group studies. These researchers studied the traits, either personality (Stogdill 1948) or behavior (Fleishman 1953a), of leaders in interpersonal interaction with each other. These studies tended to ignore the noninterpersonal facets of managing (financial, informational, political); in fact, Stogdill's (1974) *Handbook of Leadership* failed to index the word management.

Because numerous recent and excellent reviews of leadership and management have appeared recently (Bass 1981, Yukl 1981), none of the major frameworks are presented here in detail. Suffice it to say that, as with motivation, 1983 was not a good year for more traditional topics of research: no papers appeared on behavior trait approaches (consideration and initiating structure); Fiedler's (1967) contingency theory, especially the use of the Least-Preferred Coworker (LPC) measure, was still controversial (see Vecchio's 1983 reply to Strube & Garcia's 1981 meta-analytic data supporting Fiedler); other contingency theoretical approaches (e.g. House 1971) received little attention (see Wofford & Srinivasan 1983 for an exception); Vertical Dyadic Linkage (VDL) theory (Dansereau et al 1975) received one extensive test (Rosse & Kraut 1983) with moderate support, and Vroom & Yetton's (1973) decision-based theory received no attention.

On the management side, a similarly bleak picture exists with almost no research on what managers do (a la Mintzberg 1973) nor what they do that makes them effective. Campbell et al (1970) would be saddened by the failure to develop the kinds of behavior taxonomies of managerial work that would build on the early job analyses performed by Hemphill (1959).

Apparently only Lau and his associates (Lau et al 1980, Lau & Pavett 1980, Pavett & Lau 1983) and McCall and his colleagues (McCall et al 1978) have recently pursued the development of measures of managerial activities that pattern the classical management functions (e.g. planning, organizing) as supplemented by Mintzberg's (1973) data on what chief executive officers do. Lau and his coworkers have not only developed a set of managerial behaviors based on job analysis, but have shown how different kinds of management jobs (functional specialty, e.g. sales/marketing, production/engineering) require different patterns of behaviors for effectiveness. This line of research, building on job analysis methodology (cf McCormick 1979) and supplemented by a focus on effectiveness, could prove useful if used as a basis for the design of additional techniques to assess and predict managerial effectiveness. The word "additional" is used because, contrary to some textbook treatment of the role of individual differences in the prediction of management effectiveness, the trait approach (especially via the assessment center method) is alive and well (Schmitt & Schneider 1983).

In fact, a development in leadership and management has been a renewed focus on traits as correlates of effectiveness. The newer efforts focus on cognitive complexity or cognitive style (Robey & Taggart 1981) defined as the way people process and evaluate information. Exactly what is new here is not clear because some of the measures being employed are quite old (e.g. Embedded Figures Test, Myers-Briggs Type Indicator) and are suspect in terms of traditional psychometric standards (Schweiger 1983). Especially the MBTI seems to enjoy popularity with consultants despite, as Schweiger notes, negative reviews of its psychometric properties.

It is questionable whether particular traditional personality tests can be used effectively to predict leadership and/or management behavior across various situations. Note that the question is not whether particular personality tests (or other relevant measures of individuals) can predict but which particular ones can predict for which jobs in which situations (Yukl 1981, Schneider 1983b).

Perhaps what is required is a new way of thinking about leader or manager attributes if the goal is to make predictions based on one or more universal measures of some inidividual difference or differences. In interactional psychology, the concept of coherence is used to describe a person for whom behavioral differences from setting to setting is characteristic (Magnusson & Endler 1977). Thus, consistency in behavior for a coherent person would be change, but similar change when confronting the same or similar situations. A considerable amount of evidence exists to support situational specificity of behavior in general (Mischel 1968) and for managers in particular (James & White 1983). Some have concluded from these findings that people do not have stable predispositions that guide their behavior, and therefore behavior is not predictable based on the assessment of predispositions. This is an incorrect conclusion for two reasons: (*a*) behavior in work organizations, as noted earlier, is predictable, and (*b*) people can behave coherently (flexibly), changing in ways that are characteristic for them as they move from one situation to another (Bowers 1973, Mischel 1973).

A major contribution to this line of thinking was published by Kenny & Zaccaro (1983). Using as data a reanalysis of a rotation design study (each person is confronted by different situations, both members and tasks, that provide an opportunity for leadership), Kenny & Zaccaro showed that between 49% and 82% of leadership variance can be accounted for by some "stable" characteristic. Perhaps the stable characteristic is flexibility or, as it is known in the assessment center literature, "behavior flex." While numerous writings address a personality characteristic such as flexibility (e.g. Mischel 1973), paper and pencil measures focused on behavior flex appear to be nonexistent. Some measures, like Miner's (1978) Sentence Completion Blank, might be adapted for future use in this area.

In summary, research studies of leadership and management appear to be in a somewhat similar position as motivation; there is a dearth of new activity. One possible explanation for this is the absence of a link between leadership and management and organizational effectiveness. Thus, while studies of OD interventions targeted on management and supervision tend to result in positive improvements for various hard criteria (Katzell & Guzzo 1983, Nicholas 1982), the correlational studies of the past have not yielded the kinds of systems-oriented results desired; this probably is a result of the focus on narrow micro criteria (Yukl 1981) to the exclusion of macro indices of systems effectiveness. Again, as with motivation theory, the initial focus on the enterprise somehow yielded research at the individual level of analysis.

Perhaps it is time to return to a macro level integration of motivation and leadership/management theory. It is sometimes difficult to remember that early OB scholars viewed motivation and management as essentially two faces of the same coin: management's role was to create conditions for subordinate motivation and commitment (Argyris 1957, McGregor 1960). In those early treatises, the relatively sloppy criteria of organizational functioning and organizational health were the outcomes of interest. Recent excellent work by Nicholas (1982) in summarizing the importance of systems-wide interventions that necessarily involve management, and which focus explicitly on improving general levels of staff motivation through OD, show just how much we really can affect organizational effectiveness positively.

More general, systems-like perspectives on leadership and management could move us closer to capturing the complex, multipressured, juggling, hip-shooting but planful nature of management jobs and the crucial role even (especially?) the lowest level supervisor plays in organizational growth and survival. Perhaps when it is recognized that managers are the real cause of efficient organizational subsystem functioning (Katz & Kahn 1978) and design (Van de Ven & Joyce 1981), then the research that is needed will be accomplished at the unit or organizational level of analysis required (Roberts et al 1978) and over the time periods necessary for the observation of real growth (Kimberly & Miles 1980). The use of a simulation of managers at work, a kind of group assessment center called Looking Glass, Inc. (Lombardo et al 1983), might facilitate this kind of work.

Groups

One level of analysis not yet addressed is the group. It is interesting to realize that an entire section on leadership and management never required the mention of groups. Leavitt (1975) argues that it is possible to ignore groups because

American industry and American psychologists have implicitly subscribed to an individualistic design for organizations making individuals rather than groups the focus of interest. Given an American value system that emphasizes the individual, it could be expected that both management and management's psychologists would focus on the role individuals play in organizational effectiveness. Leavitt argues that if we took groups seriously, then groups not individuals would be the building block of organizations. Then we would select, train, pay, promote, design jobs for, or fire groups rather than individuals. Only when organizations are literally designed around the group, says Leavitt, will groups be an important focus of study.

Likert's (1961) framework for describing organizations emphasized groups, and the sociotechnical systems literature also reflects this emphasis (Pasmore & Sherwood 1978, Trist 1981), but for the most part, OB researchers have yielded the study of groups to OD. In fact, previous OB chapters in the *Annual Review of Psychology* have not discussed groups, leaving the topic to social psychology (McGrath & Kravitz 1982) or as a component of Organization Development (OD; Alderfer 1977).

There are a few critical exceptions to the abandonment of the study of work groups to vehicles for intervention and change in organizations. One exception is the intergroup conceptualization, a multifaceted way of viewing group memberships as a source of knowing and behaving (Alderfer 1983). A second exception, in some ways quite similar to intergroup theory, is called social systems or organizational demography. This theory emphasizes the role of intergenerational differences that arise from regeneration processes in organizations (Pfeffer 1983). A third theme concerns the continued attempt to describe various facets of group structure as correlates of group or team performance (Bass 1980). Parenthetically, it is worth noting that of these three contemporary foci on groups only the team performance issue summarized by Bass (1980) received attention in the last *Annual Review of Psychology* chapter on groups (McGrath & Kravitz 1982).

INTERGROUP THEORY   Intergroup theory (Alderfer 1983, Brown 1983, Smith 1983) is an emerging set of constructs for conceptualizing not only groups but individuals, organizations, and nations. The logic of intergroup theory is that interactions between people *at any level of analysis* (individuals, groups, etc) represent the effects of group memberships. In its most reductionist form this perspective is a view of individuals as a composite of group memberships (sex, race, management, generation, school and so on), and in its most expanded form it emphasizes the embedded nature of groups, i.e. every group is always embedded in other groups (units in an organization in an industry in a market in a society, and so on), and thus behavior is a product of multilevel embeddedness. For example, two work groups composed of the "same" people but functioning in different departments (sales vs engineering) would not be the "same" people.

There are two major kinds of groups according to intergroup theory: identity groups (e.g. gender, ethnicity, and family) and organizational groups (e.g. tasks and hierarchy; Smith 1983). Generally speaking intergroup theorists deny the relevance of single identity group characteristics like sex or ethnicity, arguing that it is the psychological component of identity attributes, not the attributes themselves, that is important. Thus research in 1983 on sex correlates of leadership (Garland et al 1983) or commitment (Bruning & Snyder 1983, Graddick & Farr 1983, Lacy et al 1983) all failed to support the idea that sex was an important variable (for a counterargument see Heilman 1983). The point in intergroup theory is that constellations of identity and organizational group characteristics are meaningful ways of characterizing people and that a single attribute would probably not be useful.

Alderfer (1983) has presented a very clear and thorough review of the history and current thinking on intergroup theory, including applications of the theory to understanding issues as diverse as group composition, organizational culture, and the teaching of OB in schools of management. The review is an excellent source of insight into group processes in general because it asks the reader to think about groups from a new perspective.

DEMOGRAPHICS   Pfeffer (1983) has proposed that an overlooked issue in understanding OB concerns the nature of cohorts inside organizations. He argues that the presence of clearly defined demographic cohorts may lead to conflict between cohorts over various resource issues and that within cohorts, group solidarity and a "we-they" mode of thinking might emerge.

The presence of generational differences in organizations has been noted before (e.g. Alderfer 1971), and they are included explicitly in intergroup theory. What is unique about the demographic approach is its exclusive emphasis on generational cohort differences to the exclusion of other group or individual characteristics. Perhaps more interesting is the apparent power of this focus on generational differences in an organization to account for important differences in organizationally relevant outcomes.

For example, McCain et al (1983) presented results showing that a significant portion of the variance in the turnover rates of faculty in 32 academic departments could be accounted for by demographic indices over and above the variance accounted for by such department attributes as size or budget per faculty.

Pfeffer suggests that intergenerational differences may help account for conflict between groups, including power struggles over scarce resources. Research to support such an hypothesis is presented by him as well as by

Alderfer, suggesting the utility of a group focus in attempting to understand various organizational phenomena.

GROUP STRUCTURE AND TEAM PERFORMANCE   Group structure here refers to what Bass (1980) means by the interaction (more technically the intersection) of member characteristics (demographics, abilities), task characteristics, and group design (interpersonal relationships, group training and experience). In his review of team or group performance Bass showed that, other things being equal, interaction processes within a group are the determinant of effectiveness. Unfortunately, actual interaction processes in groups have not been a focus of contemporary research, so little is known about the micro facets of interaction that are critical for effectiveness (Hackman 1983).

Some thinking exists, however, about the idea that training a group to be cooperative/interactive may not be as important as previously imagined; that the conditions in which the group must function (the "climate" of the situation) is the major determinant of cooperativeness (Boss 1983, Hackman 1983). For example, Hughes et al (1983) showed that, following team development, long-term changes in both team climate and performance were observed but probably only because the situations to which the teams returned were ones that supported and expected the changes.

In a wide-reaching paper on group structure, performance and organizational context, Pearce & David (1983) reached a similar conclusion. They developed the argument that previous research on the relationship between organizational design and group performance has yielded conflicting results because different group structures emerge under different organization design properties. Thus, in a mechanistic vs organic organization, they note that different patterns of connectedness, centrality, differentiation, evaluation formation, and so on can be expected. It follows that different performance outcomes should also emerge. The framework developed by Pearce & David yields a number of testable hypotheses and suggests possibilities for integrating group and organization design foci in OB. Schneider (1983a) has presented a similar argument. He notes that particular kinds of people are attracted to and selected by organizations and leave if they do not fit. The result of what he calls the attraction-selection-attrition cycle is a relatively homogenous group of similar people. In his framework, then, the people are both the group and the context.

Boss (1983), in another paper, showed how group functioning can be attributed to the group's context. He attempted to counter the team building regression effect noted by Beer (1980) and others (Berney 1983). This effect, similar to one documented in the training of foremen more than 30 years ago (Fleishman 1953b), is revealed when immediate post-training assessments fail to be transferred to the work setting (Goldstein 1980). To enhance the support of team building, Boss had the Chief Executive Officer (CEO) meet (usually biweekly) with unit supervisors to facilitate their mutual support of the process. Results across some 23 groups in both the public and private sector suggest the benefits of such personal management interviews (PMI) as vehicles for reducing regression effects.

In the traditional social psychological literature the context in which the group must function is a generally unresearched area, yet both the intergroup and team development perspectives on work groups suggest its potential importance for any understanding of the role of groups at work. Perhaps a failure to focus on the embedded nature of groups in organizations has resulted in so much inconsistency in field study findings that it drives much of the fine-grained research into the laboratory. In addition, a contextual orientation drives most of the field efforts to having groups be only one component of systems-wide OD efforts (Hackman 1983). Summaries of OD efforts suggest that this is the case (Katzell et al 1977, Nicholas 1982), that groups are only one of many foci in OD efforts. Teasing out the effects of group-based interventions in larger OD efforts will be very difficult. This is especially true if findings like those presented by Scarpello (1983) continue to emerge. His results suggest the possibility that OD interventions may have systems effects without being reflected in group or individual changes. The interpretation of his results is difficult because of some methodological problems Scarpello faced, but they serve to caution against the assumption that a change at one level will necessarily be reflected in change at another level.

Hackman (1983) integrated much of the early literature on small groups with the OD perspective on groups in his pursuit of a normative model of group effectiveness. He also shows how work group context is strategically important in understanding team effectiveness. This is especially true with respect to information about the goals of the group and access to such data as the consequences of adopting different group strategies and achieving different outcomes. In addition to context, Hackman emphasizes the critical nature of group design (structure of task, composition of groups, establishment of norms) and group synergy (actual follow-through on planning and implementing). Hackman's normative model not only specifies what should exist for effective team functioning but points out the role of management in facilitating those conditions. This model is a call for action at the organizational level and an assignment of responsibility for making groups *a* focus, not *the* focus of attempts to improve organizations.

SUMMARY   The three foci of this section, intergroup theory, demography theory, and teams, represent a dramatic change from the more traditional groups literature. That literature was characterized by single laboratory studies of communication patterns, cohesiveness, coalition formation, or interpersonal attraction (McGrath & Kravitz 1982). The change suggests rich theoretical and normative frameworks for achieving Leavitt's (1975) plea to take groups in the work context seriously.

Organizational Climate and Culture

The review of the work group literatures makes the embedded nature of behavior in work settings quite clear from a holistic conceptual perspective. The idea that groups and organizations have cultures or climates has been acknowledged since Lewin et al's (1939) research on creating social climates (authoritarian, democratic, laissez-faire). Climate, in particular, has a relatively rich history in OB, probably because the definition and measurement problems have generated some interesting research efforts both in the laboratory (Litwin & Stringer 1968) and the field (Jones & James 1979), as well as critical commentary (Guion 1973, Woodman & King 1978). While there have been only a few active researchers of climate itself, the term is used by almost everyone who studies quality of work life (QWL), OD, or innovation (the group researchers retain the more neutral "context").

Most people who use the term climate are referring to interpersonal practices (the social climate). When used this way it refers to both formal and informal policies and activities that are typical of the way peers relate to each other ("open") and/or the "style" that characterizes superior-subordinate relationships ("trusting"). But climate has also been used as a shorthand for describing other sets of formal and informal policies and activities that reward, support, and expect service (Schneider et al 1980), safety (Zohar 1980), and innovation (Abbey & Dickson 1983), among others (Schneider & Reichers 1983).

Climate research, which came out of the Gestalt psychology tradition after Lewin (Schneider 1975), like Gestalt psychology seems to have died from acceptance. Although there are certainly conceptual and methodological advances still to be made in climate research (Mossholder & Bedeian 1983a, Schnake 1983), it now seems clear that multiple dimensions of policies and activities relevant to a particular issue (interpersonal relationships, service) can be assessed reliably and validly.

Although used interchangeably for years (e.g. Katz & Kahn 1966, 1978), the climate and the culture constructs are apparently in opposite patterns of descendance and ascendance. Culture is not only academically prominent (entire issues of *Administrative Science Quarterly* and *Organizational Dynamics* were devoted to the subject in 1983) but prominent in business and industry as well. For example, *In Search of Excellence* (Peters & Waterman 1982) has been a number one best seller for many months (see Carroll 1983 for an insightful critique of this book as research).

Recent writers on culture, like writers on climate before them (Guion 1973), have generally failed to reference earlier works going by a different name. So almost no reference is made to climate research in the *Administrative Science Quarterly* issue (e.g. Smircich 1983) despite some overlapping theory (Schneider & Reichers 1983). There also appears to be essentially no overlap in research methods. Culture researchers favor more qualitative and/or case study methodologies (Gregory 1983) compared to the survey methods most often used in climate research (Schneider 1975). At one level, one hopes that culture researchers will pay as much attention to the collection of data and to the nuances of their ethnomethodology (Van Maanen 1976, Morgan 1984) as climate researchers tended to adhere to the psychometric tradition. At another level, one agrees with Daft (1983) that perhaps the choice is not between ethnomethod (qualitative) and psychometric (quantitative); researchers should capitalize on ways to profit from application of the whole of the research craft, not just parts of it.

Culture is thought to be a deeper construct than climate has been. Whereas climate researchers have been concerned with the dimensions or facets of policies and activities that characterize particular organizational phenomena (service, innovation), culture scholars want to understand (*a*) the norms and value systems that give rise to the policies and activities (Jones 1983b, Sathe 1983) and (*b*) the modes by which the norms and values are communicated and transmitted (Schall 1983).

In pursuit of these goals, research focuses on meaning—the meaning people attach to policies and activities and the mechanisms by which meaning is transmitted and shared (Barley 1983, Mitroff 1983) and becomes part of the ego of organizational members (Broms & Gahmberg 1983). Of special interest to researchers of culture is the role myths and stories play as vehicles for transmitting meaning (Koprowski 1983, Smith & Simmons 1983, Wilkins 1983), thus providing the "glue" for the sharing of meaning. Joyce & Slocum (1982, 1984) found a novel technique for revealing how organization members share meaning. They administered climate questionnaires to employees, converted item responses into profiles, and cluster analyzed the resultant individual profiles. The resultant clusters represented groups of employees who literally shared meaning. In fact, the clusters reproduced known groupings (functions, jobs) of employees.

Some other interesting findings are emerging from the energy being focused on the culture construct, especially when the research has a comparative focus. For example, Martin et al (1983) argue that seven kinds of stories seem to occur in diverse kinds of organizations. Through script and content analysis of stories, the following types emerged (some names are mine): rule-breaking, founder, rags to riches, reductions in force (rif), relocation of employees, reactions to mistakes, and organizational coping. Of course, although these are common story types, their frequency profile from organization to organization could be a useful diagnostic.

Wilkins & Ouchi (1983) present data to show, however, that every organization does not have a distinct culture—distinct meaning different from others and/or different from the larger environment of which it is a part. Conversely, Riley (1983) and Martin & Siehl (1983) find that organizations frequently have subcultures and countercultures, respectively! It seems obvious that, depending on one's focus (level of analysis), both findings are possible.

Climate and, more recently, culture seem to have taken OB full circle to the idea that organizations are a viable behavioral unit of analysis; that organizations themselves can be described in terms of patterns of activities (Argyris 1957), philosophies (McGregor 1960), and unit relationships (Likert 1961).

One thing that has been learned in the interim, mostly implicitly, is that to describe organizations requires macro level research methods and foci that fit the descriptive terminology of organizations; that to conduct research on individuals *as individuals* as the unit of analysis is important and interesting but not when trying to understand and predict an organization's behavior (Mossholder & Bedeian 1983a). A second principle has been that at each level of analysis at which important and interesting research can be conducted, the next larger unit in which the behavior of interest is embedded will also have an impact (Alderfer 1983). This principle has both practical and methodological implications. On the practical side it says that when changing anything to achieve a goal, the context of the change also needs to be at least considered and probably also changed.

Methodologically the implication is that a study that includes data derived from a focus on only one unit of analysis will yield relatively weak relationships because phenomena exist at multiple levels of analysis and need to be assessed at multiple levels (Wallace 1983). Thus, individually based motivation studies of performance or turnover on the one hand, or group-based studies of group output on the other hand, cannot be expected to yield strong findings because the unit of analysis being studied is embedded in, *and affected by,* at least the next level of analysis.

It is very important here to differentiate "affected by" from "moderated by." All of the research that is called contingency (or "it depends") research is of the "moderated by" form. These efforts have yielded an infinite regress to more dependencies and few significant findings (Schneider 1983b). The argument being presented here is that different levels of analysis have direct (linear) effects on behavior. For example, the linear logic suggests that individual motivation and group structure correlate with individual behavior, not that group structure moderates the relationship between individual motivation and individual behavior. Also, the logic implies that group effectiveness would be a linear function not only of group characteristics but of the larger context of the group itself.

This view of the behavior in and of organizations takes a holistic perspective (Astley & Van de Ven 1983, Wallace 1983) similar to the one implicitly used in

OD (Asplind et al 1983, Bartunek 1983) and organization design (Van de Ven & Joyce 1981). This perspective will be useful in the discussion of productivity that follows.

PRODUCTIVITY

In the past few years a number of researchers have addressed the potential for behavioral science approaches to resolve organizational problems, especially productivity problems. These scholars have searched the research literature and cataloged the kinds of interventions that have proved effective; these will be summarized below.

There are three major reasons for summarizing these findings. First, it is very important for the science that inferences about the real world of organizations be tested in that world. Because most of OB research is at best quasi-experimental in method, and more likely is merely one-shot correlational, any relationships that are established and any inferences that are made about what can be changed to yield a desired effect must be tested. The question is: is there validity to the inferences that have been made?

A second reason to summarize these findings is to encourage more of an integration of the OB and organization change literatures. Past chapters on OB have failed to address intervention successes, while chapters on change (Friedlander & Brown 1974, Alderfer 1977, Faucheux et al 1982) have tended to focus on change processes rather than on the variables being changed or the dependent variables being studied (see Staw 1984 for a review of dependent variables in OB). Here the focus will be on the latter topics, and no claim whatever is made that this is a review of the organizational change literature.

Third, it will become clear that the literature on productivity interventions suggests that theories of behavior in and of organizations appear to have considerable validity for achieving productivity improvements. Given this success, it will be argued that OB researchers should address the potential economic benefits of their findings as a vehicle for (a) bringing about a rapproachement with other areas of business study and, (b) more importantly, educating business, industry, and government to the very large (e.g. Hunter & Schmidt 1983) potential benefits of research and intervention in OB.

Literature Summarizing Productivity and OB

Katzell & Guzzo (1983) summarized the more extensive works by Katzell et al (1977) and Guzzo & Bondy (1983), each of whom reviewed worker productivity experiments in the U.S. for five-year periods. Thus, the Katzell & Guzzo data cover the period 1971–1981.

Katzell & Guzzo reviewed only studies in which an independent variable was actually manipulated and which had at least one concrete measure of productivity as a dependent variable. Their content analysis of 107 experiments revealed 11 types of interventions: recruitment and selection, training and instruction, appraisal and feedback, goal setting, financial compensation, work redesign, supervisory methods, organization structure/design, decision-making techniques, work schedules, and sociotechnical systems redesign.

The effects of these interventions were evaluated against three major criteria, worker output (quantity, quality, or cost effectiveness), withdrawal behaviors (turnover, absenteeism), and work disruptions (accidents). Most of the studies used worker output (57%), then withdrawal behaviors (34%), then disruptions.

Eighty-six percent of the studies against output, 75% of those against withdrawal behaviors, and 77% against disruptions revealed significant effects. Goal setting, appraisal and feedback, sociotechnical systems redesign, and supervisory methods seem to be particularly effective in increasing output, with better than 92% of such reported attempts yielding the desired increases. In addition to productivity increases, when quality of work life data were also collected in the experiment, across all studies 75% reported favorable changes; for changes in supervisory methods and sociotechnical systems redesign the figures were both 100%.

Nicholas (1982) summarized the effects of 65 OD interventions against 10 hard criteria: turnover, absenteeism, grievances, costs, profits, sales, efficiency (e.g. input-output ratio), production quantity (units per hour), effectiveness (locally defined critical indices such as downtime, accidents), and production quality.

Nicholas only included OD interventions that met the same experimental criteria as used by Katzell & Guzzo. He described three classes of OD interventions, human processual (T-Groups, team building, survey feedback), technostructural (job redesign and enrichment, sociotechnical systems), and multifaceted (the use of multiple behavioral techniques). The extent of overlap between Nicholas and Katzell & Guzzo is unknown since Nicholas does not cite Katzell et al (1977) and the Guzzo & Boudy (1983) book was probably "in press" when Nicholas's paper was prepared.

Nicholas's findings were less encouraging than those reported by Katzell & Guzzo; about 50% of the studies revealed positive effects. There were no differences in overall success rate as a function of the general class of intervention, but uniformly positive effects (about 70%) across criteria were associated with sociotechnical system and participative job enlargement (workers participate in the design) interventions.

A particularly interesting facet of Nicholas's findings, especially given the earlier concerns noted with units of analysis, was his subgrouping of interventions by group and organizational levels of analysis. This breakdown revealed that the human process and multifaceted interventions may have the most success at the organizational level whereas the technostructural approaches work best at the group level.

It is difficult to know why Nicholas's findings were less positive than Katzell & Guzzo's. One possibility is that because Nicholas included only studies that were in the OD tradition, more micro individual-level interventions were excluded, the focus being more on unit/organizational productivity. A second and related possibility concerns the criterion problems associated wih large unit interventions, especially the opportunities for confounding of effects.

In any case, the Katzell & Guzzo and Nicholas summaries suggest that at least one-half, and more likely 90 percent, of the interventions that are published report a significant effect. While there probably are intervention failures that were not published (see Mirvis & Berg 1977 for some of these), there are undoubtedly successes that also fail to become published for proprietary reasons and because of the interventionist's lack of interest/time/expertise to publish.

Although reference to technical reports was explicitly excluded from this review because of the abundance of the existing published literature, an attempt was made to ascertain the extent of successes that have not been published by exploring some Department of Defense (DOD) productivity programs. Oliver et al (1983) report, for example, that in the Army such programs as productivity gainsharing (improvements in time to complete a task), quality circles (solution to production problems by workers meeting at the work place), and sociotechnical interventions have all been shown to be effective. An idea of the magnitude of these efforts in the Army can be appreciated by considering the following: at eight sites with a total of 853 employees, gain sharing resulted in a savings of 74,000 personhours and payments of $376,000 to employees; at the many hundreds of quality circles, when careful documentation is maintained, a return on investment in productivity of about 2 to 1 is not unusual (there appear to be no changes in attitudes). Sociotechnical interventions in many sites are currently under way, including formative as well as summative evaluation plans.

For the Navy, two sources of data were available. Crawford (1983) summarized efforts at the Navy Personnel Research and Development Center (NPRDC) where research on productivity has been under way since 1975. As in the Army, gainsharing and quality circles appear to have significant effects. Crawford notes that these are particularly useful when the larger context is receptive and supportive. Incidentally, Crawford also reported no changes in attitudes for the QC program.

More broadly, Broedling & Huff (1983) summarized *all* Navy productivity enhancement programs using Katzell & Guzzo's (1983) classification scheme (primarily). Twenty technical reports not published elsewhere are referenced in their report, with essentially all of them reporting significant effects. Organizational appraisal and feedback (survey feedback as an OD effort), financial compensation (mostly gainsharing and other monetary incentives), and supervisory methods (especially the implementation of traditional management practices) were the most frequently used methods. Some of the projects described by Broedling & Huff were "in process," but the wide variety of completed (fully evaluated) efforts and the apparent positive benefits were impressive.

Ginnett (1983) summarized similar efforts in the Air Force. In contrast to the Army and Navy interventions that have been accomplished under a centrally controlled authority (and most frequently on *civilians*), Air Force productivity improvement efforts are decentralized and most frequent with military rather than civilian personnel. Decentralization of the effort made it difficult for Ginnett to track down productivity improvement programs, and some programs appeared to be relatively undocumented. Nonetheless, work in all of Katzell & Guzzo's (1983) categories existed.

Finally, an overview of productivity programs throughout the federal sector was presented by King et al (1983). This report is a sampling of more extensive talks presented at a workshop on productivity in the federal sector sponsored by the Office of Naval Research. Information from such diverse agencies as NASA, NSF, and DOE, as well as DOD, are presented.

Pfeffer (1981, p. 415) has noted (with tongue in cheek?) that ". . . in the field of organizational behavior, there is frequently very little that is either organizational or behavioral. Rather much of the research is a study of individual attitudes." The brief review of productivity enhancement efforts just presented suggests that considerable progress has been made on the behavioral and on the organizational level of analysis.

Given the enormous criterion problems that have been documented so well in so many places (e.g. Tuttle 1983), it is a tribute to researcher ingenuity (Daft 1983) that this large number of programmatic research efforts has been accomplished and documented.

Some themes emerging from the literature on productivity and productivity improvement follow:

1. Productivity is a term used to describe various organizationally relevant outcomes (quantity, quality, turnover) at all levels of analysis (individual, group, organizational).
2. Behavioral approaches to productivity improvement are effective far more often than not, but they constitute only one kind of improvement efforts and should not be expected to accomplish everything (Hambrick & Schechter 1983, Tuttle 1983).
3. Productivity interventions are enhanced by systems-wide commitment to improvement and to the possibility that the intervention might yield im-

provement (Reilly & Fuhr 1983). This kind of commitment also facilitates the durability of the change (Goodman 1982).

4. Essentially all productivity improvement efforts are attempts at changing the group and/or organizational context in the hopes of enhancing worker motivation. This comment does not apply to interventions of a personnel selection sort (Hunter & Schmidt 1983) but to all other interventions listed by Katzell & Guzzo (1983) and Nicholas (1982).

5. Productivity interventions rarely contribute to refinements of theory; they are attempts to capitalize on existing theory and data. As such, they most frequently have confounded micro variables in order to achieve an effect. In some sense, then, they follow the "burn the pig house down to get cooked pork" rule for action rather than trying to isolate *precisely* what needs to be done to achieve the desired result. But *effect,* not *precision,* is the goal of action.

6. When converted into cost-benefit terminology (as in the Army and Navy reports in particular), the productivity improvements are very dramatic indeed in terms of dollars saved; this point will be addressed again below.

Utility

For at least 45 years (Taylor & Russell 1939), methods for calculating the dollar benefits of using personnel selection procedures for making decisions have been known. For 35 years (Brogden & Taylor 1950) techniques applicable to this calculation for any intervention have been known, and for 20 years (Cronbach & Gleser 1965) application has been urged. Recently, Cascio (1982) has presented a wonderfully clear book filled with examples for calculating the utility of changes in organizations.

At its most basic level, the question of utility is: what is the dollar payoff? That is, taking into account the costs associated with an intervention (for example, improved selection, training, job design, job satisfaction, or sociotechnical system to achieve increased individual, unit, or organizational productivity or decreased turnover), what are the benefits?

In the past, the major stumbling block to the calculation of utility was the standard deviation in dollar terms (Brogden & Taylor 1950) of the criterion variable—the degree of variability on the index of productivity. Schmidt et al (1979) have apparently resolved this problem through a straightforward estimation procedure (for which good interrater reliability was obtained). In fact, once the relationship between a predictor and criterion is known (say the relative presence or absence of a sociotechnical systems organization design and production quality), and the standard deviation in productivity (here production quality) is known in dollar terms, the benefits of changing an organization more toward a sociotechnical systems, say one-quarter standard deviation more toward sociotechnical systems, can be calculated. From that calculation, of course, one subtracts the costs (e.g. of consultants, lost production time, and so on) to estimate return-on-investment (ROI).

Personnel selection researchers and researchers in the Department of Defense have been doing these calculations now for a number of years; it is time for OB researchers in general and change agents in particular to also begin presenting them (Feldman 1983). Such data will be very impressive because the benefits add up very quickly and the costs of OB interventions are relatively negligible. Anyone doubting the potential payoff and the speed at which benefits accumulate should see Cascio (1982).

Toward an Integrated View of OB

OB exists at many levels of analysis, all of which are correct and appropriate foci for understanding the behavior, and the outcomes of behavior, in and out of organizations. Indeed, it seems likely that larger units of analysis than are typically studied by OB researchers (e.g. industries) are amenable to study with behavioral variables (Hage 1980). What allows these multiple levels of research to form a gestalt, to all be under the OB umbrella, is a focus on human attributes. Assumptions about humans are tested, not simply stated (as for example in economics), and they are tested with respect to important human outcomes regarding work and work organizations.

It would be an error to conclude that micro studies of the relationship between individual commitment or work motivation and turnover or performance will yield many valid insights into improved organizational functioning. Conversely, it would be similarly inappropriate to attempt to predict an individual's performance or turnover based on whether his/her organization functions in a dynamic or static environment. These are inappropriate and unreasonable because the predictors and criteria of interest exist at different levels of analysis.

This review has noted numerous instances of problems related to the level of analysis issue from misinterpretations about the level of analysis of early OB theoreticians to the interpretation of intervention efforts. It appears that neither researchers nor change agents have been careful in specifying the level of analysis of their efforts, and such carelessness has yielded a failure to substantiate hypotheses and/or to produce the desired change.

From a contemporary perspective on research and practice, the level of analysis issue cautions against the tendency to want to infer across levels. For example, if it is known that individual incentive systems produce higher rates of individual productivity, it does not necessarily follow that an organization that puts all of its workers on individual incentive systems will be more productive. Similarly, it does not follow that an individual worker who works in an organization characterized by the sociotechnical systems perspective will be less likely to leave. The traditional incentive system example is calibrated to handle only individual prediction and understanding, while the sociotechnical system example is calibrated to predict *rates* of individual behavior at the group or organizational level of analysis. The motto is to pick your levels carefully.

In addition to cautions against making the ecological fallacy, the level of analysis issue suggests some potentially very interesting research. For example, what are the effects of individual incentive systems on unit and organizational productivity (Lawler 1981)? Or, what does working in a unit characterized by a sociotechnical systems perspective do to suppress/enhance individual differences in individual productivity? The point here is not that some of these between-levels kinds of studies have not been proposed before (see Van de Ven & Joyce 1981 for an excellent example), but that in doing these studies it must be clear why one would expect a variable at one level of analysis to be related to another variable at another level of analysis. The literature seems to be able to handle the first issue but it has lacked clarity on the second (Roberts et al 1978). Clarity on this second issue might permit more of an integration in OB now that it is clearly possible to bring about change at many levels of analysis through the manipulation of numerous theoretically relevant variables.

CONCLUSIONS

Older perspectives of OB are being used as bases for effective intervention, and new questions are being raised about individual, group, and organizational issues. More specifically, goal setting is the dominant motivation perspective, and commitment and stress seem to have replaced satisfaction as major thrusts in individual motivation and attitude theory and research. At the group level, leadership research appears to be languishing, but group research may yet have a resurgence based on either or both intergroup theory and a normative framework that considers the emotional life of group members. At the organizational level of analysis, organizational culture has arrived as a vehicle for attempting to understand why some organizations seem to have characteristic thrusts and/or modes of functioning. Of special interest to culture researchers are the processes by which culture is transmitted in organizations.

It has been stated that culture theory and research emerging about 25 years after the real start of OB was noteworthy, especially because both the conceptual framework and the level of analysis (the organization) are similar to earlier theories. Reviews of OB productivity enhancement interventions based on the theory and research in the field yielded encouraging data regarding effectiveness, especially for non-OD based interventions. Finally, an argument was made for the conversion of OB findings into dollar utility estimates.

Throughout this review, a major methodological/conceptual theme concerned the issue of level of analysis. It was noted that research needs to be carried out (*a*) at the level of analysis compatible with the original conceptualization and (*b*) in which the levels of analysis of predictor and criterion are conceptually congruent (though not at all necessarily the same). In conclusion, it is clear that OB is alive and well and living on many levels.

ACKNOWLEDGMENTS

Preparation of this review was partially supported by the Organizational Effectiveness Research Group, Psychological Sciences Division, Office of Naval Research under Contract No. N00014-83-K-0551, Contract Authority Identification Number NR270-958. Without the help of Liz Berney, Nancy Moeller, and Dan Schechter this review would never have been completed. They as well as Irv Goldstein, Joe Schneider, Dave Schoorman, and Cindy Staehle made very helpful suggestions on an earlier draft.

Literature Cited

Abbey, A., Dickson, J. W. 1983. R & D work climate and innovation in semiconductors. *Acad. Manage. J.* 26:362–68

Adams, J. S. 1963. Toward an understanding of inequity. *J. Abnorm. Soc. Psychol.* 67:422–36

Administrative Science Quarterly 1983. 28:331–495

Alderfer, C. P. 1971. Effects of individual, group and intergroup relations on attitudes towards a management development program. *J. Appl. Psychol.* 55:302–11

Alderfer, C. P. 1972. *Human Needs in Organizational Settings.* New York: Free Press

Alderfer, C. P. 1977. Organization development. *Ann. Rev. Psychol.* 28:197–223

Alderfer, C. P. 1983. An intergroup perspective on group dynamics. In *Handbook of Organizational Behavior,* ed. J. Lorsch. Englewood Cliffs, NJ: Prentice-Hall

Argyris, C. 1957. *Personality and Organization.* New York: Harper

Ashford, S. J., Cummings, L. L. 1983. Feedback as an individual resource: Personal strategies of creating information. *Organ. Behav. Hum. Perform.* 32:370–98

Asplind, J., Behrendtz, H., Jernberg, F. 1983. The Norwegian savings bank case: Implementaton and consequences of a broadly scoped, long-term, system-driven program for management development. *J. Appl. Behav. Sci.* 19:381–94

Astley, W. G., Van de Ven, A. H. 1983. Central perspectives and debates in organization theory. *Adm. Sci. Q.* 28:245–73

Barley, S. R. 1983. Semiotics and the study of occupational and organizational cultures. *Adm. Sci. Q.* 28:393–413

Bartunek, J. M. 1983. How organization development can develop organizational theory. *Group Organ. Stud.* 8:303–18

Bass, B. M. 1980. Individual capability, team performance, and team productivity. In *Human Performance and Productivity,* ed. E. A. Fleishman, M. D. Dunnette. Hillsdale, NJ: Erlbaum

Bass, B. M. 1981. *Stogdill's Handbook of Leadership.* New York: Free Press

Bateman, T. S., Organ, D. W. 1983. Job satisfaction and the good soldier: The relationship between affect and employee "citizenship". *Acad. Manage. J.* 26:887–95

Bateman, T. S., Strasser, S. 1983. A cross-lagged regression test of the relationships between job tension and employee satisfaction. *J. Appl. Psychol.* 68:439–45

Beer, M. 1980. *Organization Change and Development: A Systems View.* Santa Monica, Calif: Goodyear

Berger, C. J., Olson, C. A., Boudreau, J. W. 1983. Effects of unions on job satisfaction: The role of work-related values and perceived rewards. *Organ. Behav. Hum. Perform.* 32:289–324

Berney, E. J. 1983. Here and now trainer action to make experiential learning applicable. *Group Organ. Stud.* 8:154–56

Bhagat, R. S. 1983. Effects of life events on individual performance effectiveness and work adjustment processes within organizational settings: A research model. *Acad. Manage. Rev.* 8:660–71

Birnbaum, M. H. 1983. Perceived equity of salary policies. *J. Appl. Psychol.* 68:49–59

Boss, W. R. 1983. Team building and the problem of regression: The personal management interview as an intervention. *J. Appl. Behav. Sci.* 19:67–83

Bowers, D. G. 1983. What would make 11,500 people quit their jobs? *Organ. Dyn.* 12:4–19

Bowers, K. S. 1973. Situationism in psychology: An analysis and critique. *Psychol. Rev.* 80:307–36

Breaugh, J. A. 1983. Realistic job previews: A critical appraisal and future research directions. *Acad. Manage. Rev.* 8:612–19

Brief, A. P., Schuler, R. S., Van Sell, M. 1981. *Managing Job Stress.* Boston: Little, Brown

Broedling, L. A., Huff, K. H. 1983. *Productivity enhancement in the Navy using behavioral science approaches.* Presented at Ann. Meet. Am. Psychol. Assoc., Anaheim

Brogden, H. E., Taylor, E. K. 1950. The dollar criterion: Applying the cost accounting concept to criterion construction. *Personnel Psychol.* 3:133–54

Broms, H., Gahmberg, H. 1983. Communication to self in organizations and cultures. *Adm. Sci. Q.* 28:482–95

Brown, L. D. 1983. *Managing Conflict at Organizational Interfaces.* Reading, Mass: Addison-Wesley

Bruning, N. S., Snyder, R. A. 1983. Sex and position as predictors of organizational commitment. *Acad. Manage. J.* 26:485–91

Bullock, R. J. 1983. Participation and pay. *Group Organ. Stud.* 8:127–36

Butler, J. K. Jr. 1983. Value importance as a moderator of the value fulfillment-job satisfaction relationship: Group differences. *J. Appl. Psychol.* 68:420–28

Campbell, J. P., Dunnette, M. D., Lawler, E. E. III, Weick, K. E. Jr. 1970. *Managerial Behavior, Performance, and Effectiveness.* New York: McGraw-Hill

Campbell, J. P., Pritchard, R. D. 1976. Motivation theory in industrial and organizational psychology. In *Handbook of Industrial and Organizational Psychology,* ed. M. D. Dunnette. Chicago: Rand McNally

Carroll, D. T. 1983. A disappointing search for excellence. *Harvard Bus. Rev.* Nov.–Dec: 78–88

Cascio, W. F. 1982. *Costing Human Resources: The Financial Impact of Behavior in Organizations.* Boston: Kent

Clegg, C. W. 1983. Psychology of employee lateness, absence, and turnover: A methodological critique and an empirical study. *J. Appl. Psychol.* 68:88–101

Cooke, R. A., Rousseau, D. M. 1983. Relationship of life events and personal orientations to symptoms of strain. *J. Appl. Psychol.* 68:446–58

Cosier, R. A., Dalton, D. R. 1983. Equity theory and time: A reformulation. *Acad. Manage. Rev.* 8:311–19

Crawford, K. 1983. *Productivity research at the Navy Personnel Research and Development Center (NPRDC).* Presented at AFHRL Prod. Conf., Brooks Air Force Base, Texas

Cronbach, L. J., Gleser, G. C. 1965. *Psychological Tests and Personnel Decisions.* Urbana: Univ. Ill. Press

Cummings, L. L. 1982. Organizational behavior. *Ann. Rev. Psychol.* 33:541–79

Daft, R. L. 1983. Learning the craft of organizational research. *Acad. Manage. Rev.* 8: 539–46

Dansereau, F. Jr., Graen, G., Haga, W. J. 1975. A vertical dyad linkage approach to leadership within formal organizations: A longitudinal investigation of the role making process. *Organ. Behav. Hum. Perform.* 13:46–78

Erez, M., Kanfer, F. H. 1983. The role of goal acceptance in goal setting and task performance. *Acad. Manage. Rev.* 8:454–63

Faucheux, C., Amado, G., Laurent, A. 1982. Organizational development and change. *Ann. Rev. Psychol.* 33:343–70

Feldman, D. C., Brett, J. M. 1983. Coping with new jobs: A comparative study of new hires and job changers. *Acad. Manage. J.* 26:258–72

Feldman, J. M. 1983. Problems and prospects of organizational interventions. In *Research in Personnel and Human Resources Management,* Vol. 1, ed. K. M. Rowland, G. R. Ferris. Greenwich, Conn: JAI

Ferris, K. R., Aranya, N. 1983. A comparison of two organizational commitment scales. *Personnel Psychol.* 36:87–98

Fiedler, F. E. 1967. *A Theory of Leadership Effectiveness.* New York: McGraw-Hill

Filley, A. C., House, R. J., Kerr, S. 1976. *Managerial Process and Organizational Behavior.* Glenview, Ill: Scott, Foresman. 2nd ed.

Fisher, C. D., Gitelson, R. 1983. A meta-analysis of the correlates of role conflict and ambiguity. *J. Appl. Psychol.* 68:320–33

Fleishman, E. A. 1953a. The description of supervisory behavior. *J. Appl. Psychol.* 37: 1–6

Fleishman, E. A. 1953b. Leadership climate, human relations training, and supervisory behavior. *Personnel Psychol.* 6:205–22

Friedlander, F., Brown, L. D. 1974. Organization development. *Ann. Rev. Psychol.* 25: 313–41

Gaines, J., Jermier, J. M. 1983. Emotional exhaustion in a high stress organization. *Acad. Manage. J.* 26:567–86

Garland, H., Hale, K. F., Burnson, M. 1983. Attributions for the success and failure of female managers: A replication and extension. *Psychol. Women Q.* 7:155–61

Ginnett, R. C. 1983. *Productivity enhancement in the Air Force using behavioral science techniques.* Presented at Ann. Meet. Am. Psychol. Assoc., Anaheim

Golding, J., Resnick, A., Crosby, F. 1983. Work satisfaction as a function of gender and job status. *Psychol. Women Q.* 7:286–92

Goldstein, I. L. 1980. Training in work organizations. *Ann. Rev. Psychol.* 31:229–72

Goodman, P. S., ed. 1982. *Change in Organizations.* San Francisco: Jossey-Bass

Graddick, M. M., Farr, J. L. 1983. Professionals in scientific disciplines: Sex-related differences in working life commitments. *J. Appl. Psychol.* 68:641–45

Green, S. G., Blank, W., Liden, R. C. 1983. Market and organizational influences on bank employees' work attitudes and behaviors. *J. Appl. Psychol.* 68:298–306

Greenhaus, J. H., Seidel, C., Marinis, M. 1983. The impact of expectations and values on job attitudes. *Organ. Behav. Hum. Perform.* 31:394–417

Gregory, K. L. 1983. Native-view paradigms: Multiple cultures and culture conflicts in organizations. *Adm. Sci. Q.* 28:359–76

Griffin, R. W. 1983. Objective and social sources of information in task redesign: A field experiment. *Adm. Sci. Q.* 28:184–200

Guion, R. M. 1973. A note on organizational climate. *Organ. Behav. Hum. Perform.* 9:120–25

Guzzo, R. A., Bondy, J. 1983. *A Guide to Worker Productivity Experiments in the United States 1976–81.* New York: Pergamon

Hackman, J. R. 1983. The design of work teams. In *Handbook of Organizational Behavior,* ed. J. Lorsch. Englewood Cliffs, NJ: Prentice-Hall

Hackman, J. R., Lawler, E. E. III 1971. Employee reactions to job characteristics. *J. Appl. Psychol.* 55:259–86

Hackman, J. R., Oldham, G. R. 1980. *Work Redesign.* Reading, Mass: Addison-Wesley

Hage, J. 1980. *Theories of Organization: Form, Process, and Transformation.* New York: Wiley

Hall, D. T., Gordon, F. E. 1973. The career choices of married women: Effects on conflict, role behavior and satisfaction. *J. Appl. Psychol.* 58:42–48

Hambrick, D. C., Schecter, S. M. 1983. Turnaround strategies for mature industrial-product business units. *Acad. Manage. J.* 26:231–48

Heilman, M. E. 1983. Sex bias in work settings: The lack of fit model. In *Research in Organizational Behavior,* Vol. 5, ed. L. L. Cummings, B. M. Staw. Greenwich, Conn: JAI Press

Hemphill, J. K. 1959. Job descriptions for executives. *Harvard Bus. Rev.* 37:55–67

Herman, J. B., Dunham, R. B., Hulin, C. L. 1975. Organizational structure, demographics, and employee responses. *Organ. Behav. Hum. Perform.* 13:206–32

Herzberg, F., Mausner, B., Snyderman, B. 1959. *The Motivation to Work.* New York: Wiley. 2nd ed.

Holland, J. L. 1973. *The Psychology of Vocational Choice.* Waltham, Mass: Blaisdell. Revised ed.

House, R. J. 1971. A path goal theory of leader effectiveness. *Adm. Sci. Q.* 16:321–39

House, R. J., Schuler, R. S., Levanoni, E. 1983. Role conflict and ambiguity scales: Reality or artifacts? *J. Appl. Psychol.* 68: 334–37

Hughes, R. L., Rosenback, W. E., Clover, W. H. 1983. Team development in an intact, ongoing work group: A quasi-field experiment. *Group Organ. Stud.* 8:161–86

Human Resource Management 1983. 22:335–489

Hunter, J. E., Schmidt, F. L. 1983. Quantifying the effects of psychological interventions on employee job performance and workforce productivity. *Am. Psychol.* 38:473–78

Jackofsky, E. F., Peters, L. H. 1983a. Job turnover versus company turnover: Reassessment of the March and Simon participation hypothesis. *J. Appl. Psychol.* 68:490–95

Jackofsky, E. F., Peters, L. H. 1983b. The hypothesized effects of ability in the turnover process. *Acad. Manage. Rev.* 8:46–49

Jackson, P. R., Stafford, E. M., Banks, M. H., Warr, P. B. 1983. Unemployment and psychological distress in young people: The moderating role of employment commitment. *J. Appl. Psychol.* 68:525–35

Jackson, S. E. 1983. Participation in decision-making as a strategy for reducing job-related strain. *J. Appl. Psychol.* 68:3–19

James, L. R., White, J. F. III. 1983. Cross-situational specificity in managers' perceptions of subordinate performance, attributions, and leader behaviors. *Personnel Psychol.* 36:809–56

Jenkins, G. D., Glick, W. H., Gupta, N. 1983. Job characteristics and employee responses. In *Proceedings of the Academy of Management,* ed. K. H. Chung, Wichita, Kans: Wichita State Univ.

Jones, A. P., James, L. R. 1979. Psychological climate: Dimensions and relationships of individual and aggregated work environment perceptions. *Organ. Behav. Hum. Perform.* 23:201–50

Jones, G. R. 1983a. Psychological orientation and the process of organizational socialization: An interactionist perspective. *Acad. Manage. Rev.* 8:464–74

Jones, G. R. 1983b. Transaction costs, property rights, and organizational culture: An exchange perspective. *Adm. Sci. Q.* 28:454–67

Joyce, W. F., Slocum, J. W. 1982. Climate discrepancy: Refining the concept of psychological and organizational climate. *Hum. Relat.* 35:951–72

Joyce, W. F., Slocum, J. W. 1984. Collective climate: Agreement as a basis for defining aggregate climates in organizations. *Acad. Manage. J.* In press

Katerberg, R., Blau, G. J. 1983. An examination of level and direction of effort and job performance. *Acad. Manage. J.* 26:249–57

Katz, D., Kahn, R. L. 1966. *The Social Psychology of Organizations.* New York: Wiley

Katz, D., Kahn, R. L. 1978. *The Social Psychology of Organizations.* New York: Wiley. 2nd ed.

Katz, R., Tushman, M. L. 1983. A longitudinal study of the effects of boundary spanning on turnover and promotion in research and development. *Acad. Manage. J.* 26:437–56

Katzell, R. A., Bienstock, P., Faerstein, P. F. 1977. *A Guide to Worker Productivity Experiments in the United States 1971–75.* New York: New York Univ. Press

Katzell, R. A., Guzzo, R. A. 1983. Psychological approaches to productivity improvement. *Am. Psychol.* 38:468–72

Kennedy, C. W., Fossum, J. A., White, B. J. 1983. An empirical comparison of within-subjects and between-subjects expectancy theory models. *Organ. Behav. Hum. Perform.* 32:124–43

Kenny, D. A., Zaccaro, S. J. 1983. An estimate of variance due to traits in leadership. *J. Appl. Psychol.* 68:678–85

Kimberly, J. R., Miles, R. H., eds. 1980. *The Organizational Life Cycle.* San Francisco: Jossey-Bass

King, B. T., Lau, A. W., Sinaiko, H. W., eds. 1983. *Productivity Programs and Research in U. S. Government Agencies.* Washington DC: Smithsonian Inst.

Kohn, M. L., Schooler, C., eds. 1983. *Work and Personality.* Norwood, NJ: Ablex

Koprowski, E. J. 1983. Cultural myths: Clues to effective management. *Organ. Dyn.* 12:39–51

Krausz, M., Freiback, N. 1983. Effects of flexible working time for employed women upon satisfaction, strains, and absenteeism. *J. Occup. Psychol.* 56:155–59

Lacy, W. B., Bokemeier, J. L., Shepard, J. M. 1983. Job attribute preferences and work commitment of men and women in the United States. *Personnel Psychol.* 36:315–30

Latham, G. P., Steele, T. P. 1983. The motivational effects of participation versus goal setting on performance. *Acad. Manage. J.* 26:406–17

Lau, A. W., Newman, A., Broedling, L. A. 1980. The nature of managerial work in the public sector. *Public Adm. Rev.* 40:513–20

Lau, A. W., Pavett, C. M. 1980. The nature of managerial work: A comparison of public and private sector managers. *Group Organ. Stud.* 5:453–66

Lawler, E. E. III. 1981. *Pay and Organization Developement.* Reading, Mass: Addison-Wesley

Leavitt, H. J. 1975. Suppose we took groups seriously. In *Man and Work in Society,* ed. E. L. Cass, F. G. Zimmer. New York: Van Nostrand

Lewin, K., Lippitt, R., White, R. K. 1939. Patterns of aggressive behavior in experimentally created "social climates". *J. Soc. Psychol.* 10:271–99

Likert, R. 1961. *New Patterns in Management.* New York: McGraw-Hill

Litwin, G. H., Stringer, R. A. 1968. *Motivation and Organization Climate.* Boston: Harvard Bus. Sch. Div. Res.

Locke, E. A. 1976. The nature and causes of job satisfaction. In *Handbook of Industrial and Organizational Psychology,* ed. M. D. Dunnette. Chicago: Rand McNally

Locke, E. A., Shaw, K. N., Saari, L. M., Latham, G. P. 1981. Goal setting and task performance: 1969–1980. *Psychol. Bull.* 90: 125–52

Lodahl, T. M., Kejner, M. 1965. The definition and measurement of job involvement. *J. Appl. Psychol.* 49:24–33

Lofquist, L. H., Dawes, R. V. 1969. *Adjustment to Work.* New York: Appleton-Century

Lombardo, M. M., McCall, M. W. Jr., De-Vries, D. L. 1983. *Looking Glass.* Glenview, Ill: Scott, Foresman

Louis, M. R. 1980. Surprise and sense making: What newcomers experience in entering unfamiliar organizational settings. *Adm. Sci. Q.* 25:226–51

Louis, M. R., Posner, B. Z., Powell, G. N. 1983. The availability and helpfulness of socialization practices. *Personnel Psychol.* 36:857–81

Magnusson, D., Endler, N. S. 1977. Interactional psychology: Present status and future prospects. In *Personality at the Crossroads: Current Issues in Interactional Psychology,* ed. D. Magnusson, N. S. Endler. Hillsdale, NJ: Erlbaum

March, J. G., Simon, H. A. 1958. *Organizations.* New York: Wiley

Martin, J., Feldman, M. S., Hatch, M. J., Sitkin, S. B. 1983. The uniqueness paradox in organizational stories. *Adm. Sci. Q.* 28: 438–53

Martin, J., Siehl, C. 1983. Organizational culture and counterculture: An uneasy symbiosis. *Organ. Dyn.* 12:52–64

Martin, T. N., Schermerhorn, J. R. Jr. 1983. Work and nonwork influences on health: A research agenda using inability to leave as a critical variable. *Acad. Manage. Rev.* 8: 650–59

Matsui, T., Okada, A., Inoshita, O. 1983. Mechanism of feedback affecting task performance. *Organ. Behav. Hum. Perform.* 31:114–22

McCain, B. E., O'Reilly, C., Pfeffer, J. 1983. The effects of departmental demography on turnover: The case of a university. *Acad. Manage. J.* 26:626–41

McCall, M. W. Jr., Morrison, A. M., Hannan, R. L. 1978. *Studies of Managerial Work: Results and Methods.* Greensboro, NC: Center for Creative Leadership

McCormick, E. J. 1979. *Job Analysis: Methods and Applications.* New York: Amacom

McGrath, J. E., Kravitz, D. A. 1982. Group research. *Ann. Rev. Psychol.* 33:195–230

McGregor, D. M. 1960. *The Human Side of Enterprise.* New York: McGraw-Hill

McGuire, W. J. 1973. The yin and yang of progress in social psychology: Seven Koan. *J. Pers. Soc. Psychol.* 26:466–56

Miller, E. J., ed. 1976. *Task and Organization.* New York: Wiley

Miner, J. B. 1978. Twenty years of research on role motivation theory of managerial effectiveness. *Personnel Psychol.* 31:739–60

Miner, J. B., Dachler, H. P. 1973. Personnel attitudes and motivation. *Ann. Rev. Psychol.* 24:379–402

Mintzberg, H. 1973. *The Nature of Managerial Work.* New York: Harper & Row

Mirvis, P. H., Berg, D. N., eds. 1977. *Failures in Organization Development and Change.* New York: Wiley

Mischel, W. 1968. *Personality and Assessment.* New York: Wiley

Mischel, W. 1973. Toward a cognitive social learning reconceptualization of personality. *Psychol. Rev.* 80:252–83

Mitchell, T. R. 1979. Organizational behavior. *Ann. Rev. Psychol.* 30:243–81

Mitroff, I. I. 1983. Archetypal social systems analysis: On the deeper structure of human systems. *Acad. Manage. Rev.* 8:387–97

Mobley, W. H., 1982. *Employee Turnover in Organizations.* Reading, Mass: Addison-Wesley

Mobley, W. H., Griffeth, R. W., Hand, H. H., Meglino, B. M. 1979. Review and conceptual analysis of the employee turnover process. *Psychol. Bull.* 86:493–522

Morgan, G., ed. 1984. *Beyond Method: Strategies for Social Research.* Beverly Hills, Calif: Sage

Morrow, P. C. 1983. Concept redundancy in organizational research: The case of work commitment. *Acad. Manage. Rev.* 8:486–500

Mossholder, K. W., Bedeian, A. G. 1983a. Cross-level inference and organizational research: Perspectives on interpretation and application. *Acad. Manage. Rev.* 8:547–58

Mossholder, K. W., Bedeian, A. G. 1983b. Group interaction processes: Individual and group effects. *Group Organ. Stud.* 8:187–202

Motowidlo, S. J. 1983. Predicting sales turnover from pay satisfaction and expectation. *J. Appl. Psychol.* 68:484–89

Mowday, R. T., Porter, L. W., Steers, R. M. 1982. *Employee Organization Linkages: The Psychology of Commitment, Absenteeism, and Turnover.* New York: Academic

Murphy, L. R. 1983. A comparison of relaxation methods for reducing stress in nursing personnel. *Hum. Factors* 25:431–40

Nicholas, J. M. 1982. The comparative impact of organization development interventions on hard criteria measures. *Acad. Manage. Rev.* 7:531–42

Nicholson, P. J. Jr., Goh, S. C. 1983. The relationship of organization structure and interpersonal attitudes to role conflict and ambiguity in different work environments. *Acad. Manage. J.* 26:148–55

Oliver, L. W., van Rijn, P., Babin, N. 1983. *Productivity improvement efforts in Army organizations.* Presented at Ann. Meet. Am. Psychol. Assoc., Anaheim

Organizational Dynamics. 1983. 12:4–80

Ouchi, W. 1981. *Theory Z.* Reading, Mass: Addison-Wesley

Parker, D. F., DeCotiis, T. A. 1983. Organizational determinants of job stress. *Organ. Behav. Hum. Perform.* 32:160–77

Pascale, R. T., Athos, A. G. 1981. *The Art of Japanese Management.* New York: Simon & Schuster

Pasmore, W. A., Sherwood, J. J., eds. 1978. *Sociotechnical Systems: A Sourcebook* LaJolla, Calif: Univ. Assoc.

Pavett, C. M., Lau, A. W. 1983. Managerial work: The influence of hierarchical level and functional specialty. *Acad. Manage. J.* 26: 170–77

Pearce, J. A. II, David, F. R. 1983. A social network approach to organizational design-performance. *Acad. Manage. Rev.* 8:436–44

Perrow, C. 1973. The short and glorious history of organizational theory. *Organ. Dyn.* 2:4–17

Pervin, L. A., Lewis, M., eds. 1978. *Perspectives in Interactional Psychology.* New York: Plenum

Peters, T. J., Waterman, R. H. 1982. *In Search of Excellence.* New York: Harper & Row

Pfeffer, J. 1981. Four laws of organizational research. See Van de Ven & Joyce 1981

Pfeffer, J. 1983. Organizational demography. See Heilman 1983

Porter, L. W., Lawler, E. E. III. 1968. *Managerial Attitudes and Performance.* Homewood, Ill: Irwin-Dorsey

Pugh, D. S. 1981. The Aston program perspective. See Van de Ven & Joyce 1981

Pulakos, E. D., Schmitt, N. 1983. A longitudinal study of a valence model approach for the prediction of job satisfaction of new employees. *J. Appl. Psychol.* 68:307–12

Reilly, B. J., Fuhr, J. P. Jr. 1983. Productivity: An economic and management analysis with a direction towards a new synthesis. *Acad. Manage. Rev.* 8:108–17

Riley, P. 1983. A structurationist account of political culture. *Adm. Sci. Q.* 28:414–37

Roberts, K. H., Glick, W. 1981. The job characteristics approach to task design: A critical review. *J. Appl. Psychol.* 66:193–217

Roberts, K. H., Hulin, C. L., Rousseau, D. M. 1978. *Developing an Interdisciplinary Science of Organizations.* San Francisco: Jossey-Bass

Robey, D., Taggart, W. 1981. Measuring managers' minds: The assessment of style in human information processing. *Acad. Manage. Rev.* 6:375–83

Rosse, J. G., Kraut, A. I. 1983. Reconsidering the vertical dyad linkage model of leadership. *J. Occup. Psychol.* 56:63–71

Rusbult, C. E., Farrell, D. 1983. A longitudinal test of the investment model: The impact on job satisfaction, job commitment, and turnover of variations in rewards, costs, alternatives, and investments. *J. Appl. Psychol.* 68:429–38

Rynes, S. L., Lawler, J. 1983. A policy-capturing investigation of the role of expectancies in decisions to pursue job alternatives. *J. Appl. Psychol.* 68:620–31

Rynes, S. L., Schwab, D. P., Heneman, H. G. III. 1983. The role of pay and market pay variability in job application decisions. *Organ. Behav. Hum. Perform.* 31:353–64

Salancik, G. R., Pfeffer, J. 1978. A social information processing approach to job attitudes and task design. *Adm. Sci. Q.* 23:224–53

Sathe, V. 1983. Some action implications of corporate culture: A manager's guide to action. *Organ. Dyn.* 12:4–23

Scarpello, V. 1983. Who benefits from participation in long-term human process interventions? *Group Organ. Stud.* 8:21–44

Scarpello, V., Campbell, J. P. 1983. Job satisfaction: Are all the parts there? *Personnel Psychol.* 36:577–600

Schall, M. S. 1983. A communication-rules approach to organizational culture. *Adm. Sci. Q.* 28:557–81

Schein, E. H. 1978. *Career Dynamics: Matching Individual and Organizational Needs.* Reading, Mass: Addison-Wesley

Schein, E. H. 1980. *Organizational Psychology.* Englewood Cliffs, NJ: Prentice-Hall. 3rd ed.

Schmidt, F. L., Hunter, J. E., McKenzie, R. C., Muldrow, T. W. 1979. Impact of valid selection procedures on work-force productivity. *J. Appl. Psychol.* 64:609–26

Schmitt, N., Schneider, B. 1983. Current issues in personnel selection. In *Research in Personnel and Human Resource Management,* ed. K. Rowland, R. Ferris. Greenwich, Conn: JAI Press

Schnake, M. E. 1983. An empirical assessment of the effects of affective response in the measurement of organizational climate. *Personnel Psychol.* 36:791–807

Schneider, B. 1975. Organizational climates: An essay. *Personnel Psychol.* 28:447–79

Schneider, B. 1983a. An interactionist perspective on organizational effectiveness. In *Organizational Effectiveness,* ed. K. S. Cameron, D. A. Whetten. New York: Academic

Schneider, B. 1983b. Interactional psychology and organizational behavior. See Heilman 1983

Schneider, B., Parkington, J. J., Buxton, V. M. 1980. Employee and customer perceptions of service in banks. *Adm. Sci. Q.* 25:252–67

Schneider, B., Reichers, A. E. 1983. On the etiology of climates. *Personnel Psychol.* 36:19–40

Schwab, D. P., Wichern, D. M. 1983. Systematic bias in job evaluation and market wages: Implications for the comparable worth debate. *J. Appl. Psychol.* 68:60–69

Schweiger, D. M. 1983. Measuring managers' minds: A critical reply to Robey and Taggart. *Acad. Manage. Rev.* 8:143–51

Seashore, S. E. 1981. Quality of working life perspective. See Van de Ven & Joyce 1981

Shamir, B. 1983. A note on tipping and employee perceptions and attitudes. *J. Occup. Psychol.* 56:255–59

Shaw, J. B., Riskind, J. H. 1983. Predicting job stress using data from the Position Analysis Questionnaire. *J. Appl. Psychol.* 68:253–61

Sheridan, J. E., Abelson, M. A. 1983. Cusp catastrophe model of employee turnover. *Acad. Manage. J.* 26:418–36

Smircich, L. 1983. Concepts of culture and organizational analysis. *Adm. Sci. Q.* 28:339–58

Smith, C. A., Organ, D. W., Near, J. P. 1983. Organizational citizenship behavior: Its nature and antecedents. *J. Appl. Psychol.* 68:653–63

Smith, F. J. 1977. Work attitudes as predictors of attendance on a specific day. *J. Appl. Psychol.* 62:16–19

Smith, K. K. 1983. Social comparison processes and dynamic conservatism in intergroup relations. See Heilman 1983

Smith, K. K., Simmons, V. M. 1983. A Rumpelstiltskin organization: Metaphors on metaphors in field research. *Adm. Sci. Q.* 28:377–92

Spencer, D. G., Steers, R. M., Mowday, R. T. 1983. An empirical test of the inclusion of job search linkages into Mobley's model of the turnover decision process. *J. Occup. Psychol.* 56:137–44

Staw, B. M. 1984. Organizational behavior: A review and reformulation of the field's outcome variables. *Ann. Rev. Psychol.* 35:627–66

Sterns, L., Alexander, R. A., Barrett, G. V., Dambrot, F. H. 1983. The relationship of extraversion and neuroticism with job preferences and job satisfaction for clerical employees. *J. Occup. Psychol.* 56:145–53

Stogdill, R. M. 1948. Personal factors associated with leadership: A survey of the literature. *J. Psychol.* 25:35–71

Stogdill, R. M. 1974. *Handbook of Leadership: A Survey of Theory and Research.* New York: Free Press

Stone, E. F., Gueutal, H. G., Gardner, D. G., McClure, S. 1983. A field experiment comparing information-privacy values, beliefs, and attitudes across several types of organizations. *J. Appl. Psychol.* 68:459–68

Strube, J. J., Garcia, J. E. 1981. A metaanalytic investigation of Fiedler's model of leadership effectiveness. *Psychol. Bull.* 90:307–21

Sutton, R. I., Rousseau, D. M. 1979. Structure, technology, and dependence on a parent organization: Organizational and environmental correlates of individual responses. *J. Appl. Psychol.* 64:675–87

Taylor, F. W. 1911. *The Principles of Scientific Management.* New York: Harper

Taylor, H. C., Russell, J. T. 1939. The relationship of validity coefficients to the practical effectiveness of tests in selection: Discussion of tables. *J. Appl. Psychol.* 23:565–78

Telly, C. S., French, W. L., Scott, W. G. 1971. The relationship of inequity to turnover among hourly workers. *Adm. Sci. Q.* 16:164–72

Thorngate, W. 1976. "In general" vs. "it depends": Some comments on the Gergen-Schlenker debate. *Pers. Soc. Psychol. Bull.* 2:404–10

Trist, E. L. 1981. The sociotechnical perspective. See Van de Ven & Joyce 1981

Turner, A. M., Lawrence, P. 1965. *Industrial Jobs and the Worker: An Investigation of Response to Task Attributes.* Boston, Mass: Harvard Univ. Press

Tuttle, T. C. 1983. Organizational productivity: A challenge for psychologists. *Am. Psychol.* 38:479–86

Tziner, A. 1983. Correspondence between occupational rewards and occupational needs and work satisfaction: A canonical redundancy analysis. *J. Occup. Psychol.* 56:49–56

Van de Ven, A. H., Joyce, W. F., eds. 1981. *Perspectives on Organization Design and Behavior.* New York: Wiley

Van Maanen, J. 1976. Breaking in: Socialization at work. In *Handbook of Work, Organization, and Society,* ed. R. Dubin. Chicago: Rand McNally

Vecchio, R. P. 1983. Assessing the validity of Fiedler's contingency model of leadership effectiveness: A closer look at Strube and Garcia. *Psychol. Bull.* 93:404–8

Vredenburgh, D. J., Trinkhaus, R. J. 1983. An analysis of role stress among hospital nurses. *J. Vocat. Behav.* 23:82–95

Vroom, V. H. 1964. *Work and Motivation.* New York: Wiley

Vroom, V. H., Yetton, P. W. 1973. *Leadership and Decision-Making.* Pittsburgh: Univ. Pittsburgh Press

Wallace, M. J. Jr. 1983. Methodology, research practice, and progress in personnel and industrial relations. *Acad. Manage. Rev.* 8:6–13

Wanous, J. P. 1980. *Organizational Entry: Recruitment, Selection and Socialization of Newcomers.* Reading, Mass: Addison-Wesley

Wanous, J. P., Keon, T. L., Latack, J. C. 1983. Expectancy theory and occupational/organizational choices: A review and test. *Organ. Behav. Hum. Perform.* 32:66–86

Weick, K. E. 1979. *The Social Psychology of Organizing.* Reading, Mass: Addison-Wesley. 2nd ed.

Wiggins, J. D., Lederer, D. A., Salkowe, A., Rys, G. S. 1983. Job satisfaction related to testing congruence and differentiation. *J. Vocat. Behav.* 23:112–21

Wilkins, A. L. 1983. The culture audit: A tool for understanding organizations. *Organ. Dyn.* 12:24–38

Wilkins, A. L., Ouchi, W. G. 1983. Efficient culturers: Exploring the relationship between culture and organizational performance. *Adm. Sci. Q.* 28:468–81

Wofford, J. C., Srinivasan, T. N. 1983. Experimental tests of the leader-environment-follower interaction theory of leadership. *Organ. Behav. Hum. Perform.* 32:35–54

Woodman, R. W., King, D.C. 1978. Organizational climate: Science or folklore. *Acad. Manage. Rev.* 3:816–26

Youngblood, S. A., Mobley, W. H., Meglino, B. M. 1983. A longitudinal analysis of the turnover process. *J. Appl. Psychol.* 68:507–16

Yukl, G. A. 1981. *Leadership in Organizations.* Englewood Cliffs, NJ: Prentice-Hall

Zedeck, S., Jackson, S. E., Summers, E. 1983. Shiftwork schedules and their relationship to health, adaptation, satisfaction and turnover intention. *Acad. Manage. J.* 26:297–310

Zohar, D. 1980. Safety climate in industrial organizations: Theoretical and applied implications. *J. Appl. Psychol.* 65:96–102

Ann. Rev. Psychol. 1985. 36:613–48
Copyright © 1985 by Annual Reviews Inc. All rights reserved

STAGES AND INDIVIDUAL DIFFERENCES IN COGNITIVE DEVELOPMENT

Kurt W. Fischer

Department of Psychology, University of Denver, Denver, Colorado 80208

Louise Silvern

Department of Psychology, University of Colorado, Boulder, Colorado 80302

CONTENTS

A dilemma that has obstructed the pursuit of satisfactory explanations of human behavior is that, on the one hand, there appears to be sufficient constancy of behavior across variable environmental conditions to warrant the inference that explanation requires the introduction of dispositional concepts (e.g. schemes, operations, structures, rules); on the other hand,

613

0066-4308/85/0201-0613$02.00

behavior is also variable among individuals to the point that explanation requires the specification of environmental determinants. Frequently, investigators have sought to re-solve the dilemma by denying or trivializing one or the other of its components (Overton & Newman 1982, p. 217).

INTRODUCTION

Does cognitive development occur in universal, discontinuous stages, structur-al reorganizations that are common to all people everywhere and that character-ize all domains of development? Or is cognitive development continuous and discrete, with all people showing different developmental patterns as a function of their learning histories and with no uniform sequence of stages across domains? Unfortunately, the debate about stages and individual differences in cognitive development is typically cast in dichotomous terms similar to these. We have phrased the arguments baldly, of course, but many of the debates in the literature fit this characterization. Hundreds of studies have been designed to demonstrate stages, with little or no attempt to assess individual differences or environmental effects. Hundreds have been designed to demonstrate en-vironmental effects or to examine individual differences without any assess-ment of stages. Of course, there have always been a few exceptions to the isolation of research on stages from that on individual differences and environ-mental effects, but it has generally held.

Developmental scientists have begun to express dissatisfaction with this traditional dichotomization and with the concomitant isolation of research traditions (e.g. Baltes et al 1980, Feldman 1980, McCall 1981, Block 1982, Higgins & Eccles 1983, Kessen & Scott 1983, Rest 1983, Cole et al 1984, Fischer & Bullock 1984, Gollin 1984a, Silvern 1984; R. J. Lerner & M. B. Kauffman, unpublished manuscript).

The data demonstrate that both positions are valid. Cognitive development shows evidence of stage-like change and of consistency across domains; at the same time, environmental effects and individual differences abound. A framework is needed that explains how both types of developmental patterns can occur. Because the evidence is strong for both arguments, the fault must lie in the dichotomous nature of the arguments.

Several intellectual threads in present-day life sciences virtually necessitate abandonment of such dichotomous ways of thinking. These threads are particu-larly evident in the biology of developmental plasticity and in the psychology of lifespan development, and so those will be reviewed briefly. Transcending the dichotomization of stages and individual differences also requires understand-ing its foundations in certain basic assumptions about the nature of develop-ment, as encapsulated in organismic and mechanistic models, and these too will be reviewed briefly.

With this background, presentation of the findings on the nature of cognitive development will be straightforward. What is the evidence for stages? What is the evidence for variability in stage as a result of environmental or organismic influences? What is the evidence for individual differences in cognitive development?

Resolution of the controversy, we argue, requires a framework that conjoins organism and environment by building transactional or collaborational models of stages and individual differences. That is, the child's development is seen as arising from a combination of organismic and environmental variables, and major explanatory constructs are recast in these explicitly conjoint terms.

Finally, a word is necessary about the scope of this chapter. We have chosen to review stages and individual differences in cognitive development, not cognitive development more generally. Still our topic is broad, and we have had to omit many appropriate research areas, theories, and articles. Apologies to our colleagues whom we have been unable to cite.

CONTEXT FOR RESOLUTION OF THE CONTROVERSY

Developmental plasticity and lifespan development provide particularly clear examples of the sources of current dissatisfaction with the traditional dichotomy. In these areas, scholars have concluded that development both occurs in stages and shows great individual diversity, and so they have frequently appealed for integration of stages and individual differences.

Developmental Plasticity

Definitions of developmental plasticity all share a theme: that development varies in response to environmental variation (Gollin 1984b, Lerner 1984). The phenomena of what is often called "maturation" show remarkable diversity, and at the same time, the diversity is constrained by the organization of developmental stages. Consequently, the concept of maturation itself is being recast to reflect findings that stages and individual differences occur together.

The roots of the concept of developmental plasticity lie in behavioral biology, ethology, and embryology (Gottlieb 1973, 1983, Gould 1977, Movshon & Van Sluyters 1981). Those literatures illustrate that members of the same species developing in different contexts may vary dramatically not only in such strongly canalized behaviors as those of aggression and sex (Harding & Strum 1976, Moore 1984) but also in gross morphology and physiology (Gould 1977). Human beings who develop at very high elevations, for example, develop physiologically in ways that would cause death in other settings (Gould & Lewontin 1979).

Such enormous variability in developmental course and outcome brings into question the very meaning of "species typical" developmental path. Maturational status does constrain the possible effects of the environment on further development (Gollin 1981, Lerner 1984), but the concept of organic maturation itself has changed. A useful construct for maturation is *probabilistic epigenesis* (Gottlieb 1973, 1983). Developmental norms reflect not what must happen in development but what is typical (i.e. probable) under the usual environmental and organismic conditions. Inevitably there will be variations.

In probabilistic epigenesis, individuals function differently in different contexts, and that functioning influences subsequent structures, which in turn influence subsequent functioning, and so on. Thus, given differing contexts, the same initial structural conditions will produce different developmental sequences and outcomes.

So many factors at so many different levels jointly affect an organism's condition (e.g. genetics, neuroanatomy, physiology, behavior, environmental context, social group organization, and for people, cultural organization). The nature of the factors and the relations among them change during development. Variations at each level condition the impact of any one variant upon further development (Gollin 1981, Scarr & McCartney 1983). The sheer number of variable factors and relations among factors determines that within a species the course of development will be probabilistic.

Species differ in the plasticity of their development, and human beings are presumed to be unusually plastic (Gould 1977). It is not surprising, then, that arguments from the developmental plasticity literature have begun to appear in discussions of human development (e.g. Kagan 1982, Thomas 1982, Chess & Thomas 1983, Silvern 1984).

The remainder of this review rests not on an analogy with other biobehavioral processes but on analyses of cognitive developmental data and theories. The point of discussing the plasticity literature is that contemporary conceptions of maturation strongly support the effort to eliminate dichotomous thinking about stages and individual differences. The literature on the biology of developmental plasticity calls into question the root metaphor (Reese & Overton 1970) used in traditional structural models of stage development—that the organism unfolds along a predetermined course (Overton 1984) or through a predetermined epigenesis (Gottlieb 1973, 1983). Developmentalists should not assume that predetermined epigenesis is based upon good biological evidence. If, for example, the functions and morphology of sexual reproduction manifest dramatically different developmental courses in differing contexts (Gould 1977), then human cognitive development may also show such individual differences. *At every stage, maturing structure provides opportunities for individual differences as well as constraints upon them* (Gollin 1981, Scarr & McCartney 1983).

Lifespan Study

The portrait of development in the biological literature is similar to that in the literature on psychological development across the lifespan. Maturation shows a common overall pattern and at the same time progresses in importantly different ways for different individuals in different contexts (Chess & Thomas 1983, Lerner 1984). Within the lifespan orientation, the psychological differences between widely different age groups highlight the stage-like aspects of development. On the other hand, the consistent differences in the development of individuals over long periods and the relations of those differences to personal and societal history accentuate the importance of individual diversity.

In general, research on development over long periods in children and adults demonstrates big differences between age groups as well as substantial differences between individuals within age groups (Horn 1976, McCall et al 1977, Vaillant 1977, Mussen et al 1980). Both sets of differences are significant. It is misleading to speak in terms of stages without also noting the wide range of individual differences in development, and it is misleading to speak in terms of individual differences without noting the commonalities that occur across individuals.

Scholars taking a lifespan perspective have often objected to the emphasis in traditional stage theories on a uniform developmental sequence. Their observations seem to demand a view that development proceeds through diverse sequences (Lerner 1984). Factors that affect the diversity they observe in cognition include not only age-related abilities but also cohort differences (Baltes et al 1980), domains of interest and expertise (Crosson & Robertson-Tchabo 1983), and other historical and experiential differences. Furthermore, the lifespan literature suggests that the salience of individual differences generally waxes with age after early childhood, while that of stage-related uniformities wanes (Cairns et al 1980, McCall 1981, Chess & Thomas 1983, Scarr & McCartney 1983, Lerner 1984). After early childhood, individuals function in ever more diverse contexts, and they also show increasing diversity in how they select and manage those contexts.

CONCEPTUAL OBSTACLES IN BASIC ASSUMPTIONS

"Development does not lurk directly in the population(s) studied but resides fundamentally in the perspective used" (Kaplan 1983, p. 196).

"Observation of phenomena that look coherent, similar, or unitary to one observer may look differential, unrelated, or specific to another, largely because of what each means by same or different. . . ." (Selman 1980, p. 19).

The research literatures on developmental plasticity and lifespan development both hold that diversity in developmental sequences coexists with a maturational course that conditions the possibilities for that diversity. What is still needed, however, is a formal analytic model of this coexistence—a conceptual integration of stages and individual differences.

A crucial barrier to such an integration is that traditional frameworks for studying development have effectively defined either stages or individual differences as irrelevant (Toulmin 1981, Kaplan 1983, Overton 1984; R. J. Lerner & M. B. Kauffman, unpublished manuscript). Inevitably, a priori assumptions and definitions have influenced the methods of study and the types of evidence taken as bearing upon questions of universality or diversity. Consequently, researchers in one tradition have found evidence for universal stages, with individual differences occurring only in the rate of progress through the stages. Researchers in the other tradition have found a plethora of environmental influences and individual differences, with no stages in evidence except for limited developmental orderings within particular task domains.

Two models have engendered these incompatible approaches to development (Reese & Overton 1970): the organism model, emphasizing structure, and the mechanism model, focusing on function (Fischer & Bullock 1984). Scholars working in the organismic-structural tradition find that development occurs in universal stages, which reflect the structure of thought that lies behind the diversity of manifest behavior. Scholars working in the mechanistic-functional tradition find development (or more commonly, learning) in manifest behavior, which varies widely across diverse environments and functions. Observations made by the methods of the one approach are easily discounted as irrelevant by proponents of the other.

An integration of stages and individual differences requires a conceptual liberation of the observations from the two sets of incompatible and exclusionary a priori assumptions about the nature of development. What is needed is a view fully grounded in the fact that cognitive development appears diverse under some observational conditions and universal under others. We argue here that all cognitive assessments depend on both a context and a particular stage-related cognitive structure. The methods prescribed by organismic and mechanistic approaches simply hold constant the context or structure, respectively, or they ignore it. With a framework that integrates stages and individual differences, it will be possible to specify (*a*) conditions that will produce stage-like development with few individual differences and (*b*) conditions that will produce diverse behaviors with no evidence of stages. Before we can elaborate an alternative, however, we must consider more fully recent discussions of the two approaches.

Organismic-Structural Approaches and Universal Stages

The organismic approach takes the growing biological organism as its root metaphor (Reese & Overton 1970). Growth unfolds toward its species-specific adult form, and development is the necessary sequence from initial to adult form. Identifying a developmental sequence therefore requires an initial determination of an end point for the sequence and then a rational analysis of the changes that are necessary for development from the beginning to the end point (Kaplan 1983, R. Kitchener 1983, Kohlberg et al 1983).

Within this tradition, end points are defined broadly, with observed variations treated as developmentally equivalent. By analogy, an acorn normally develops into an oak tree; differences in the shape of the branches, the distribution of the leaves, or the brittleness of the wood are unimportant. Any oak-like form is taken to be the end point, and any developmental sequences that result in that form are considered equivalent. The goal is the explanation of species-wide progression, which is thought to require a level of analysis different from the explanation of diversity among individuals.

Typically, organismic approaches have taken as their end point the structure of adult thought, such as Piaget's (1970) formal operations. According to Overton (1984), a structure is a relatively stable, organized configuration of principles or rules revealed by rational analysis to account for relatively stable ways of functioning. To be useful, a structural analysis must account for a wide diversity of behaviors with relatively few rules. Consequently, the end point is defined in terms of similarity across overtly diverse behaviors, and the diversity is usually not analyzed.

A developmental sequence involves a series of progressive structures culminating in the structure of the end point, as in Piaget's sequence of sensorimotor, preoperational, concrete operational, and formal operational stages. The structural sequence, it is argued, is logically necessary for the specified end point, just as it is necessary that an oak grow in sequence from acorn to sapling to adult tree, and not the reverse. An earlier developmental state constitutes a prior stage only when it must precede some later stage. When alternative states can occur at a given point in the sequence, they are considered equivalent variants of the same stage. Such manifest alternatives are not considered true changes in the stage sequence itself. Indeed, Kaplan (1983) warned against seeking confirmation for universal stage models in empirical observation, because, he said, sequences are ideal, rational constructions based upon the definition of the end point.

When Piaget (1957) hypothesized that each stage is a structured whole *(structure d'ensemble)*, he took to its extreme the assumption that uniform structures underlie manifest diversity. According to his hypothesis, the structure that characterizes a stage has a gestalt-like quality that rapidly takes over the mind, as if it were a pervasive catalyst producing change in diverse schemes throughout the mind (Fischer & Bullock 1981). Consequently, differences in the domain or context of a behavior should be irrelevant to assessment of structured wholes. The child should show what Kohlberg and his colleagues (1983) call "hard stages."

Furthermore, potential sources of differences between or within individuals cannot count as causes of developmental sequence or structure. Material causes such as physiological variation and efficient causes such as context and task influences cannot induce the characteristics of a developmental sequence but can only affect the speed of development through the sequence (Gollin 1981, Lerner 1984, Overton 1984).

Within this framework, the only accepted cause of cognitive stages is the form or structure of thought. As part of the dismissal of varying material and efficient causes in favor of universal structural (formal) causes, Piaget (1952 [1936]) distinguished between development and learning. Development involved the structuring of true knowledge, and learning involved behavioral change arising from material or efficient causes. Learning, he concluded, was equivalent to the acquisition of circus tricks by animals or children: Children are not altered developmentally when they are trained to recite the Declaration of Independence. Broughton (1981) concluded that Piaget's theory is logically compelled to disallow any impact of organismic or environmental variations, as is any other theory that explains thought by its structure. Variable factors, such as mother-infant attachment, defensive style, and motive, are consigned to explaining only nondevelopmental variations, including individual differences. Piaget (1971, 1975) himself eventually came close to acknowledging the limitations of this position when he said that his theory only dealt with the epistemic subject, the ideal philosopher-child who was not influenced by factors such as context or motive. The psychological subject remained for others to explain.

According to this approach, then, the possibility of diverse sequences is ruled out a priori. The observations that most cogently argue for individual differences in kind of developmental sequence (rather than merely in rate of progress or stage of fixation) are considered irrelevant. The possibility of diverse end points is ruled out by the a priori stipulation of a single end point, which is described sufficiently abstractly to subsume diversity. Diverse sequences are ruled out by the structured-whole formulation and the proposition that the sequence itself is logically necessary. These assumptions, which are often implicit, inform research designs and methods that effectively preclude the detection of individual differences or environmental influences. For example, measures are used that assess only one developmental sequence and consequently cannot uncover any diversity in sequence; or the ages of the children tested are varied, but there are no variations in the testing conditions.

In the face of the need to explain development only in terms of universal structures, context-sensitive variations have often been acknowledged by identifying *performance* as the site of individual differences and contrasting it with *competence,* which is presumed to develop through structural stages (Chomsky 1965, Flavell & Wohlwill 1969, Overton & Newman 1982). Despite the enormous variations evident in performance, competence does not vary. True development is maintained as a closed structure within the organism. One of the origins of this approach is the literature on intelligence testing, where competence is defined as the best score a child can obtain, whereas performance involves variations below that score arising from motivational and contextual factors. In the competence/performance models, however, the distinction is no longer merely practical but theoretical. Competence is identified with structure, and it is competence alone that shows true stage-like development. A person's competence at a single point on the developmental scale defines a stage. Apparent variations in stage are said to be produced by performance factors, which do not involve structures. For competence to be evident in performance, it must somehow be activated or primed. The concept of activation is necessary because of the conceptual isolation of structures from variable performance and must be taken on faith. Indeed, a general criticism of performance-competence models is that, like the organismic and mechanistic approaches combined in them, they ultimately maintain the conceptual isolation of universally developing structures from immediate organismic and environmental variations (Bullock 1981).

Scholars recently have expressed dissatisfaction with stage theory's ultimate neglect of almost all interesting developmental differences among individuals or cultures (Baltes et al 1980, Feldman 1980, Toulmin 1981, Gilligan 1982, Thomas 1982, Higgins & Eccles 1983, Snarey et al 1983, Cole et al 1984, Fischer & Bullock 1984, Gollin 1984a, Lerner 1984, Silvern 1984). The central complaints boil down to two: (a) The approach rules out consideration of too much observable developmental variation. (b) The approach is too greatly constrained by the values inherent in a specified, out-of-context developmental end point. When outcomes that are effective in their own contexts do not fit the specific end point, their effectiveness is ignored and they are categorized as immature. In general, intelligence is presented as a virtually closed system that can be assessed without consideration of contextual influences.

On the other hand, the payoffs of the approach are the converse of the complaints. A universal developmental sequence provides a criterion for finding similarities and a basis for comparing development across contexts and cultures (Edwards 1983, Silvern 1984). It also preserves a meaningful criterion for development amid the diversity of behavior (Kaplan 1983). Most fundamentally, the organismic-structural approach emphasizes that not all things are possible in development, that certain cognitive changes must precede others, and that only some environmental variables are capable of affecting cognition at a particular point in development.

Mechanistic-Functional Approaches and Individual Differences

The root metaphor of the mechanistic perspective is the machine (Reese & Overton 1970). Developmental change cannot occur without impact from the environment—i.e. from efficient causes. Development is caused and variably shaped by environmental factors. Lawfulness resides in the principles that associate independent variables (efficient causes, primarily) with dependent variables, not in the internal structural consistency of the organism (Catania 1973, Kessen & Scott 1983). With its emphasis on the variable nature of environmental influences, the mechanistic approach readily explains individual differences.

In contrast to the organismic definition of development in terms of structure, mechanistic approaches are concerned primarily with learning or problem solving, not with development. The principles of conditioning provide one of the central mechanistic explanations for changes in behavior (Skinner 1969). All such principles explain behavioral change in terms of particular functions that are served by the change, such as the achievement of specific events or states sought by the organism. A number of information processing theories fit the mechanistic-functional framework, specifying, for example, how a child builds a production system to achieve a particular goal—e.g. to solve a problem or obtain a desired object (Klahr & Wallace 1976).

Individual differences are a central focus of mechanistic-functional approaches. Such perspectives hold that context affects behavior via the principles of learning or problem solving and that behavioral change (i.e. development) is as variable as its context. Development is assessed in terms of manifest behavior in particular tasks within specific contexts. Few organismic constraints on development are acknowledged explicitly, although researchers have come to recognize that species characteristics do constrain what can be learned (Schwartz 1983).

According to this perspective, there is no structural end point that defines the course of development, and there is no straightforward criterion by which to judge developmental status as more or less mature (Kaplan 1983, Snarey et al 1983). Instead, the primary criterion for learning or development is achievement of a specific function or purpose in a particular context. For example, does the 2-year-old boy succeed in feeding himself? Does the 8-year-old girl obtain sufficient peer recognition for her accomplishments at school? If the specified function is effectively served by the behavior, then learning or development has been successful.

Investigators using this framework do not search for developmental change as construed by the structuralists. Children are not described as moving through general stages across domains. The closest thing to development is the description of a sequence of skills within a domain (Gagne 1970); but such a sequence is considered a relatively arbitrary consequence of the particular environmental circumstances experienced by the child, including the nature of the task and the pattern of environmental contingencies. A sequence of steps in learning to count, for example, is a result of such environmental factors as the specific problems encountered and the teaching methods used. Consequently, developmental sequences are specific to domains and experiences, potentially infinite in their diversity.

Behaviors can become more complex over time, and certain behaviors are prerequisites to others. Children must learn to count before they can add, and they must be able to add before they can do algebra. These orderings are called habit-family hierarchies or production-system hierarchies and are held to be entirely specific to particular domains (Keil 1981).

According to the mechanistic view, different children seem to develop certain skills at the same age primarily because (a) complex behaviors take longer to learn than simple ones do and (b) the social environment teaches skills at certain ages (Higgins & Eccles 1983). Similarly, developmental synchrony across domains can be explained in nonstructural terms (Flavell 1982). Just as Piaget could analyze learning as analogous to the mastery of circus tricks, Skinner (1969) or Klahr & Wallace (1976) can treat development as an illusion based on cumulative learning.

Mechanistic methodologies presume the importance of observing learning or problem solving in various contexts and among people with various histories. The resulting research designs and methods can readily detect environmental effects and individual differences in performance but cannot uncover stage-like uniformities. For example, tasks or testing conditions are manipulated to demonstrate the variability of behavior in different contexts, or problem-solving strategies are assessed to demonstrate the variability of behavior across individuals. However, no analyses are done to detect consistencies in behavior across tasks for a particular age group or consistent differences between age groups.

In order to acknowledge the relevance of cognitive structures to intelligence, a few investigators have developed a mechanistic-functional version of the competence/performance approach (Chomsky 1965, Gelman & Baillargeon 1983). They posit that at birth (or some other early point in development) infants have the competence for all human cognition—i.e. they possess a set of universal logical structures. Behavioral change occurs not in this competence but in performance, which is affected by diverse environmental and organismic factors. This approach denies a progression of general stages but accepts logical structures present early in life. As with the organismic-structural models of competence and performance, the structures are isolated from behavior and from immediate environmental and organismic influences (Bullock 1981).

The mechanistic-functional approach is strong exactly where the organismic-structural one is weak. Cognitive differences across cultures and individuals can be compared in terms of their context-specific functions; their maturity in other terms need not be ranked (Snarey et al 1983, Silvern 1984).

Developmental differences can be attributed to the observed influence of environmental variations (Fischer 1980, Biggs & Collis 1982). The plentiful evidence of individual differences and unevenness in development [what Piaget (1971) called *décalage*] can be taken seriously.

On the other hand, the mechanistic perspective provides no basis for identifying developmental universals or constraints upon the nature of environmental impact at a particular age (R. J. Lerner & M. B. Kauffman, unpublished manuscript; Silvern 1984). The fundamental commitment to diversity discourages consideration of the suggestion that context is effective only when an organism can understand and respond. The search for consistency and universals is effectively ruled out by the prescribed level of analysis and the methods of observation.

Overcoming the Conceptual Dichotomy

The attempt to integrate hypotheses involving stages with those involving individual differences is an effort to incorporate the advantages of both organismic and mechanistic approaches. Finding a point of integration requires obviating the profound separation between organism and environment presumed by the two approaches. Both frameworks have isolated the organism theoretically from the environment (Chandler 1977). The organismic-structural framework has located the impetus for knowledge in structures inside the person, separable from context and function. The mechanistic-functional framework has located the impetus for knowledge in environments that affect the individual (Fischer & Bullock 1984). Competence/performance models have attempted to reconcile the opposing frameworks by giving each one responsibility for a different aspect of behavior. Competence reflects the structure of the organism's mind; performance derives from the variability in function arising from environmental and organismic influences.

In contrast, many scholars have recently attempted to describe development as residing in a relation between organism and environment—in a transaction (Gollin 1981, 1984b, Sameroff et al 1982), collaboration (Fischer & Bullock 1984), fit (Chess & Thomas 1983, Lerner 1984, Silvern 1984), interaction (Cole & Traupman 1981), or convergence (Bullock 1983). These contemporary efforts to introduce a level of analysis that conjoins organismic structure and environmental variation differ from traditional studies of the interaction between two discrete factors. In the conjoint analyses, the factors are not independent; instead, the relevance of each for development involves that of the other (Fischer 1980, Silvern 1984). Characteristics of the individual, such as structures, are said to have meaning only in particular contexts, while variable contexts have meaning for development only in light of the individual's developmental status.

Instead of identifying a closed developmental sequence of structures, the investigator seeks to specify how structures show stabilities and changes in different contexts for people of different ages. Instead of identifying the regularity of environmental impacts, the investigator seeks to specify how environments have similar and differing effects as a function of human structures and motivations. No cognitive assessment can ever be free of context or free of the effect of age-related changes in cognitive organization. Thus the findings of both the organismic and the mechanistic viewpoints remain relevant, and the prescription for new research is to combine the methods of the two viewpoints.

Cole & Traupman (1981) provided a memorable illustration of the benefits of viewing cognition as a person-environment collaboration. They presented the cases of two boys, one of whom had a serious learning disability. In standard intelligence testing, the disabled boy showed his disability, and the other boy tested as normal; but for the activity of baking bread in a class setting, the outcome was reversed, even though this activity required reading and other skills assessed in the intelligence test. In this setting, the disabled boy actively worked to get around his deficits, using the skills he had; the relative lack of constraint in the class facilitated his construction of the situation to fit his abilities. The normal boy responded to the lack of constraint by becoming distractable and disorganized—characteristics not evident in the more constrained situation of intelligence testing. Intellectual adequacy was a function of the fit between person and context.

Efforts to build a conjoint framework require concepts for characterizing the collaboration of person and environment. Vygotsky's (1978) work has proved a fertile source of such concepts. Adequate cognitive progression requires a process of scaffolding, in which adults provide children with the specific environmental support they need for acccomplishing a task that would otherwise be beyond them (Wood 1980, Bruner 1982, Kaye 1982). The children provide whatever components they can for the task and with the adults' guidance gradually reinvent the solution that the adults already know (Fischer & Bullock 1984). Adequate scaffolding requires that the adults carefully monitor each child's current structure, interest, and goal (Westerman & Fischman-Havstad 1982). In interactions between adults, similar scaffolding processes occur, with each adult supporting certain kinds of behaviors in the other.

This framework is not only a description of how the social environment contributes to the person's cognitive structure. It also has implications for how this structure in context is evaluated. A person's cognitive status cannot be identified independently of the degree of scaffolding or other environmental support he or she is experiencing during the assessment. A person has no single ability but a "zone of proximal development" that is accessed differently under different support conditions (Vygotsky 1978). At the same time, the influence of context on cognition cannot be assessed independently from the responsiveness of the particular person to that context. Person and environment always collaborate to produce any behavior.

With concepts like environmental support and zone of proximal development, the issues of stages and individual differences can be integrated. Indeed, under certain conditions of observation and degrees of abstraction, universal stages of cognitive organization can be observed; under others, important individual differences in developmental sequences occur.

EVIDENCE FOR STAGES

The concept of stage has long been a center of controversy in developmental psychology (Wohlwill 1973). Part of the basis for the controversy lies in the fundamental differences between the priori assumptions of the organismic and mechanistic approaches. In addition, organismic-structural investigators have frequently been vague about the empirical criteria that define a stage.

What patterns of developmental data can be used to index a stage? A number of criteria have been proposed or implied by stage theorists, and data are available to test them all. When the strongest empirical criteria for stage are used, the evidence for stages is notably weak. But with a less stringent set of criteria, there is good evidence that development shows stages under some conditions.

Empirical Criteria

Piaget (1957, 1975), Kohlberg and colleagues (1983), and others have proposed a long list of characteristics that stages must have to be consistent with the structural framework. For example, each stage must be a structured whole, and all later stages must subsume the structures of earlier ones. As part of our effort to move beyond the definitional restrictions of the organismic-structural framework, however, we focus on empirical criteria—the patterns of data required or implied by structural hypotheses.

Fischer & Bullock (1981) argue that all proposed characteristics of stages involve three general patterns of data: developmental sequences, synchronies in developmental steps across sequences, and constraints on the possible sequences and synchronies that are predicted to occur. Developmental sequences have been the only one of these three patterns of data to be routinely observed and replicated (Wohlwill 1973, Flavell 1982); and sequences alone do not evidence stages, because a sequence may, for example, characterize only a particular domain and show no synchronies or other relations across domains. Unless synchronies or constraints also obtain, developmental stages cannot be demonstrated.

STRUCTURED WHOLE: UNIVERSALITY AND SYNCHRONY   Piaget's (1957) structured-whole hypothesis specifies at least two patterns of sequence, synchrony, and constraint (Broughton 1981, Fischer & Bullock 1981, Flavell 1982). First, knowledge should develop through one universal developmental sequence in diverse domains, the same sequence for all people in all cultures (Kohlberg et al 1983). Second, each child should demonstrate high synchrony in the sequence across domains, at least at each age when a new structured whole emerges. The most important structured wholes are (*a*) sensorimotor and representational groups, which are achieved at the end of the sensorimotor period; (*b*) concrete operations; and (*c*) formal operations (Piaget 1970). Preoperational thought does not manifest a structured whole (Piaget et al 1968).

For example, according to the synchrony criterion, when individual children develop concrete operations in one type of conservation (e.g. amount of water) they should simultaneously develop concrete operations in others (e.g. length of a string). Strictly speaking, the structured-whole should even induce concrete-operational structures simultaneously in tasks involving schemes other than conservation, such as classification, seriation, and number (Inhelder & Piaget 1964 [1959]). According to the most literal interpretation of the structured-whole hypothesis, children should develop concrete operations in all domains at virtually the same point in time, thereby showing what is called point synchrony (Fischer & Bullock 1981). However, point synchrony across domains has never been found. To the contrary, children manifest high unevenness or décalage (Feldman 1980, Biggs & Collis 1982, Flavell 1982). Piaget acknowledged this unevenness but never explained it; late in his life he asserted that it could not be explained (Piaget 1971). Within the structuralist tradition, it is difficult if not impossible to explain such variation (Broughton 1981).

In the same way, research has not confirmed any strong form of the universal-sequence hypothesis. Although the data suggest that virtually all children show the sensorimotor and preoperational stages (Dasen et al 1978), many adolescents and adults in non-Western cultures do not demonstrate Piagetian formal operations or even concrete operations (Dasen 1977, Cole et al 1984). However, this apparent failure of the hypothesis may be due to the fact that tests for universality have used Piaget's tasks, which were devised for Western European children. A few studies have used tasks devised for a specific non-Western culture, such as navigation tasks for a culture where people regularly navigate boats between distant islands (Gladwin 1970). With such culturally appropriate, familiar tasks, all people do seem to show concrete and formal operations (Greenfield 1976, Super 1980, Cole et al 1984).

These cross-cultural findings illustrate a general pattern that holds for synchrony, universality, and virtually every other criterion for stage: When environmental factors are disregarded, the data do not support stage theory; when environmental factors are taken into account, the evidence for stages becomes much stronger. Only under certain environmental conditions do people develop in a stage-like manner. This pattern supports a perspective that conjoins organism and environment.

RELATION OF PERFORMANCE WITH AGE   Although synchronous onset and universal sequence have been the stated criteria for stages, most research conducted by Piaget and others within the organismic-structural tradition has been designed to test a weaker criterion: On tasks designed to assess a given stage, success should be age-dependent.

By this criterion, the concept of stage has received overwhelming support. In scores of studies using the tasks originally designed to assess conservation, most children in industrialized countries have demonstrated concrete operations between 6 and 10 years of age, and the same is true for concrete operational tasks in other domains (Inhelder & Piaget 1964 [1959], Wohlwill 1973, Halford 1982, Case 1984).

For all of Piaget's four main stages, most children in industrialized cultures have succeeded at his tasks at about the ages he described (Dasen 1977, McCall et al 1977, Dasen et al 1978). With the original tasks and testing conditions, Piaget's findings are highly replicable. Indeed, on a host of tasks devised by other investigators (e.g. Watson 1981, Case 1984), age is the most potent, easily measurable predictor of stage of performance. The form of cognitive growth seems to be highly similar on the average for children from industrialized cultures. Of course, when tasks or testing conditions are changed, or when children are tested on tasks never encountered in their culture, the age predictions do not hold (Feldman 1980, Fischer 1980, Biggs & Collis 1982, Flavell 1982). Few studies have used tasks appropriate to nonindustrial cultures.

A common criticism from mechanistic-functional investigators is that these findings can be explained away by environmental factors that are correlated with age (Higgins & Eccles 1983). However, while environmental factors do correlate with age, it is not clear that they produce the cognitive changes in children. Adults gear a child's social environment to the level of the child's developing capacities (Vygotsky 1978, Cairns et al 1980, Kaye 1982). The criticism thus provides no alternative explanation. Teasing apart contributions intrinsic to the child from those of the social environment will require the construction of specific models of the collaboration between child and environment.

Although the relation between average performance and age is a highly replicable result, it remains an unsatisfactory criterion for stage. First, the relation is imprecise, with the data showing substantial divergences from the average age for certain tasks, testing conditions, and children. Second, the age results alone provide no criteria for demarcating transitions between stages or specifying how developmental progressions are stage-like. Upon what basis can we assert that a certain accomplishment marks a new stage?

QUALITATIVE CHANGE   Some investigators have focused on qualitative change as a more specific criterion for stage transition. In general, qualitative changes involve the organization rather than the amount of a behavior or capacity. For example, consider a 5-year-old boy who can understand variations in the height of the water in two containers (correctly specifying which container has higher water) but cannot deal with variations in the total quantity of water (conservation). A year or two later, when that boy comes to understand the relation of height and width and so constructs an understanding of conservation, he will have demonstrated a qualitative change in his knowledge. Consequently, he will be said to have entered a new stage. The qualitative-change criterion has been used explicitly in a number of neo-structural theories (McCall et al 1977, Bickhard 1978, Biggs & Collis 1982, Halford 1982, Commons et al 1984) and implicitly by many other researchers in the Piagetian tradition.

Research on cognitive development demonstrates a large number of qualitative changes associated with Piagetian stages, but which of these changes signals transition to a new stage? When a girl learns to button her shirt or a woman learns to walk on showshoes, her behavior has undergone a qualitative change. With qualitative change as the criterion, every increment of learning would mark a new stage (Fischer et al 1984).

In practice, most researchers have sidestepped this problem by using an intuitive sense of what counts as an important qualitative change. For general theories of cognitive development, such as those of Biggs & Collis (1982), Case (1984), Halford (1982), and of course Piaget (1970), structural definitions such as that for conservation have been provided to specify important changes.

Within a given theory, such definitions indicate which qualitative changes mark transitions to new stages or levels, but problems arise when theories are compared. Biggs & Collis (1982), for example, define one level on the basis of an adolescent's ability to construct a number of independent, abstract concepts about a topic (e.g. to suggest several reasons why it is rainy on the coastal side of a mountain range). Fischer (1980) and Case (1984) describe a level at about the same age but define it as involving the construction of a relation between two abstract concepts. Inhelder & Piaget (1958 [1955]) specify no major stage at the same point but only a substage elaborating formal operations. Which of the several posited qualitative changes provides the better evidence for a stage? A criterion is needed that allows determination of which qualitative changes merit designation as a stage.

In summary, the criterion of age can be measured precisely and reliably, but it lacks specificity in that by itself (without a theoretical framework) it provides no definition of what age-related changes are sufficient to define stage transitions. The criterion of qualitative change provides ways of defining a stage, but as it has been used, it has not been possible to bring data to bear upon alternative claims about the qualitative changes that count as stages.

DISCONTINUITY   One of the traditional criteria for stage transitions, discontinuity, has been generally neglected in cognitive developmental research (Werner 1948, Globerson 1985): When a new stage emerges, the change in behavior in a given domain should be large and rapid. Of course, the term "discontinuity" has many other meanings as well, including qualitative change; but large, rapid change seems to be the most straightforward.

With any continuous or approximately continuous developmental scale, it is possible to detect discontinuities by using procedures that independently assess each important step, such as scalogram techniques and longitudinal assessments (Uzgiris & Hunt 1975, Seibert et al 1984). A discontinuity occurs whenever development along this scale changes abruptly (spurts or drops). The question of whether a specific qualitative change is important enough to count as a new stage is not an issue; the magnitude of the discontinuity with respect to the rest of the developmental curve speaks for itself. Several methods are available for finding and analyzing this kind of discontinuity (Fischer et al 1984). In general, most of them provide ways of detecting either (a) that large numbers of subjects cluster at certain points on a developmental scale or (b) that individual subjects spend long periods at certain points on a scale before they develop to higher points.

The discontinuity criterion has not often been used in developmental research. However, several investigators who have used it in studies of development in the first two years of life have found a cluster of spurts and other rapid developmental changes at specific ages (Emde et al 1976, Kagan 1982, Corrigan 1983, Zelazo & Leonard 1983, Seibert et al 1984). In one of the most elegant studies, McCall and his colleagues (1977) found a series of four rapid drops in the stability of the first unrotated factor on infant intelligence tests, along with major changes in the kinds of items that loaded on that factor. A number of recent studies of stages in infancy have found four similar stages or levels (Fischer 1982).

For childhood and adolescence, the few investigators who have used the discontinuity criterion have also obtained promising findings (Jaques et al 1978, Tabor & Kendler 1981, Kenny 1983). Only one such set of results is widely known, however, and its significance has been misinterpreted. Epstein (1974, 1980) found evidence of several growth spurts in head circumference and brain-wave patterns in childhood and adolescence. The ages of the spurts correlated generally with the ages of emergence of Piagetian stages as described in Piaget's original research. However, the few behavioral data in

Epstein's reports left these correlations unconvincing. Despite the limitations of these data, major conclusions were drawn about learning capacities, including claims that children can learn new skills only at the ages when they show brain-growth spurts (Epstein 1978). Recent direct tests of this learning hypothesis have not supported it (McCall et al 1983; A. C. Petersen & S. M. Kavrell, unpublished data). In addition, it seems that some of the data analyses of the physical-growth variables were done carelessly (McQueen 1982).

From these several studies, the discontinuity criterion seems particularly promising as a straightforward index of stage. We suspect, however, that unless investigators adopt a collaborational perspective, they will encounter serious problems in using this criterion, just as they have with others. Discontinuities will come and go as a function of not only the child but also the environment, they will be evident in some tasks and under some testing conditions (Fischer & Bullock 1984).

UPPER LIMIT   Another traditional criterion for stage that has been neglected to some degree is stage-specific learning capacity. If a stage is characterized by an upper limit on cognitive capacity, then what can be learned at that stage should be predictable from that capacity: Children at that stage should (*a*) be able to learn tasks requiring the characteristic capacity, and (*b*) be unable to learn tasks that require the capacity of later stages, even when adults provide learning procedures that are successful for children at those next stages. Several studies have demonstrated both stage-specific learning capacity and stage-specific failure to learn (Jaques et al 1978, O'Brien & Overton 1982, Case 1984, Fischer et al 1984).

Many mechanistic-functional studies have demonstrated that changes in tasks or testing conditions can alter the child's performance on some class of tasks (Gelman 1978, Flavell 1982). These results have often been taken to mean that children do not show stage-specific learning capacity or stage-specific failure to learn. For example, on Piaget's tasks children cannot usually demonstrate conservation of number until the kindergarten or elementary-school years, but with simplified tasks they can show something like conservation as early as 2 or 3 years of age. Although such results do create problems for the organismic-structural conception of stage, they do not preclude a less extreme conception. Indeed, they are expected within a collaborationist perspective, because its adherents hold that environmental conditions such as task complexity contribute to stage of performance. Learning capacities will come and go as a function of both the condition of the child and the condition of the environment. If stages exist, the coming and going will not be disorderly. It will follow specific collaborational principles that can be used to predict when children will and will not demonstrate task-specific learning capacity and task-specific failure to learn.

PUTTING THE CRITERIA IN A COLLABORATIONAL FRAMEWORK   For each criterion for stage, the portrait painted by research is similar. Under some circumstances, the data support the existence of stages, but under other circumstances they do not. The only exception to this generalization seems to be the structured-whole hypothesis, which the data do not support for any testing circumstances. Yet even the structured-whole hypothesis can be decomposed into its principal empirical criteria, universality and synchrony, which, when considered separately from the hypothesis, share the fate of the others. As already mentioned, people develop through something like Piaget's sequence of four universal stages so long as the assessments of their development use culturally appropriate, familiar tasks (Greenfield 1976, Dasen 1977, Super 1980, Cole et al 1984).

The sequence of stages is therefore neither a characteristic of the entire human mind unaffected by context, as structuralists would have it, nor the product of context-bound performance on particular tasks, as functionalists would have it. Instead, the sequence reflects the development of certain intellectual functions under a limited class of environmental conditions. The specific tasks mastered are not universal. Individual and cultural differences occur routinely in the specifics of sequences. Predicting which tasks will reflect the universal stages for given cultures or individuals requires intimate knowledge of both the contexts familiar to those people and the goals they are pursuing (Cole et al 1984). *The sequence holds only when performance and assessment conditions are described in highly abstract terms, not when particular behaviors, tasks, or procedures are specified.*

Similarly for synchrony, environmental conditions must be introduced into the analysis. Many studies have found some degree of synchrony across a number of tasks designed to measure the same stage (Feldman 1980, McCall et al 1983, Case 1984, Seibert et al 1984); many others have found little or no such synchrony (Rubin 1973, Biggs & Collis 1982, Flavell 1982, Rest 1983, Sternberg & Powell 1983). The studies finding evidence for synchrony typically have employed modest criteria—general statistical relations requiring only moderate degrees of synchrony in large samples of children performing many different tasks.

Using a research design in which familiarity, practice, priming, and so forth combined to provide environmental support for high-level functioning, a few studies have demonstrated high synchrony with fewer tasks and smaller samples (Corrigan 1983, Kenny 1983). These results suggest a collaborational hypothesis: High synchrony will occur when the environment, providing strong support for high-level functioning, enables the subject to operate at his or her highest level in the several assessed domains (Fischer et al 1984).

Because the data do not support the traditional concept of stage while they do provide evidence for some weaker form of stage-like change, many developmental scholars now avoid "stage" in favor of some more modest term. One of the most common replacement terms is "level," which we shall use for the rest of this chapter to refer to neo-Piagetian concepts of stage.

Consensus on Levels

The collaborational approach may eventually produce a workable framework for predicting when behavior shows stage-like change. In the meantime, however, guidelines are needed about where to look for developmental levels. Happily, a consensus is developing about the main levels (or transitions or reorganizations) that occur in infancy and childhood. In general, neostructural theorists searching for developmental changes in the organization of behavior have inferred similar levels at similar ages. Of course, any particular theorist does not necessarily posit all the levels suggested by other theorists.

In this chapter, we consider a level to exist when (a) neostructural theories show substantial consensus about it and (b) evidence supports at least four of the six empirical criteria discussed above. By these criteria, at least eight developmental levels mark the period between birth and early adulthood (see Table 1).

Table 1   Eight developmental levels supported by research and by theoretical consensus

Level	Documented characteristics	Modal age of emergence[a]
Sensorimotor actions	Single actions and perceptions, first social responsiveness	2–4 months
Sensorimotor relations of a few actions	Differentiation and coordination of means and end, attachment relation to caretaker	7–8 months
Sensorimotor systems of several actions	Location of characteristics in objects and people, single words	11–13 months
Representations	Symbolization of people and objects, vocabulary spurt, multiword utterances	18–24 months
Relations of a few representations	Coordination of categories in a simple relation, solution of simplified concrete operations tasks	4–5 years
Concrete operations	Coordination of several complex categories, solution of Piagetian concrete operations tasks	6–8 years
Beginning formal operations	Abstractions, hypothetical ideas, solution of easiest Piagetian formal operations tasks, concepts of personality traits	10–12 years
Relations of abstract generalizations	Coordination of abstractions, solution of most Piagetian formal operations tasks, concepts of personality dynamics	14–16 years

[a] These ages indicate the period when a level first appears according to research on middle-class Western children.

In every case, the evidence for these levels extends beyond traditional cognitive tasks. Along with the cognitive changes come changes in personality and social behavior (Sroufe 1979, Selman 1980, Harter 1983, Seibert et al 1984, Fischer & Elmendorf 1985), changes in perceptual abilities (Vurpillot 1976 [1972], Fischer 1982, Strauss & Curtis 1984), and changes in biological or physical variables such as brain waves or sleep cycles (White 1970, Epstein 1974, 1980, Emde et al 1976, Kagan 1982, Fischer & Bullock 1984).

The extent of consensus about infancy is remarkable. Repeatedly, investigators have hypothesized four major levels or reorganizations of sensorimotor intelligence during the first two years of life, in contrast to the six stages that Piaget (1952 [1936]) described. The emergence of each of these levels appears to be closely associated with age, at least for middle-class children in Western cultures. It is beyond the scope of this chapter to cite the many relevant articles, but several general reviews have been published (Uzgiris 1976, Sroufe 1979, Fischer 1982, Harris 1983, Case 1984). Below we cite only additional articles especially central to each developmental level.

The first sensorimotor level, which emerges between 2 and 4 months of age, involves the capacity for intelligent adaptation of a single action, such as looking at a face or grasping a rattle. Following Piaget (1952[1936]), this level is often hypothesized to mark the beginning of intelligent, voluntary adaptation of actions. The second sensorimotor level, which begins at 7 to 8 months of age, produces the capacity to construct a simple relation of actions. For example, infants can differentiate a means from an end, as when they use what they see to guide how they crawl across a platform (Campos et al 1978). At the third sensorimotor level, appearing between 11 and 13 months, infants can construct a complex relation of actions that includes multiple sensorimotor components in a single cognitive system (Zelazo & Leonard 1983). One hallmark of such a system is that children can understand that an object, event, or person has some constant property, such as that a rattle makes a certain type of sound no matter what action is used to shake it.

An especially significant change appears to occur in the second year with the emergence of the fourth level, representation—the symbolization of objects, events, or people independently of any particular action of the child. [Note that the term "representation" here follows Piaget's (1952 [1936]) usage, which differs from that common in mechanistic-functional information-processing models (Klahr & Wallace 1976).] Speech surges forward, with a burst of new vocabulary and the beginning of multiword utterances; and pretend play changes dramatically, increasing in frequency and showing the onset of symbolization of people and objects as acting on their own (Corrigan 1983). Virtually all neostructural theories agree that the emergence of a new cognitive unit, representation, marks an especially large change (Piaget 1952 [1936]). The representations that emerge at this fourth level lay the basis for the understanding of increasingly complex relations among representations at the next several levels.

For childhood and adolescence, the consensus among neostructural theorists is also remarkable, though here a few more disagreements are evident than among infancy researchers. In general, at least four major levels or reorganizations are posited beyond the levels of infancy (Jaques et al 1978, Fischer 1980, Biggs & Collis 1982, Halford 1982, Case 1984, Commons et al 1984).

Virtually every neostructural theorist has hypothesized a level developing at approximately 4 years of age, even though Piaget (Piaget et al 1968) did not postulate a structured whole at this point (theories cited above plus Pascual-Leone 1970, Wallon 1970, Bickhard 1978, Siegler 1981). Children develop the capacity to build a simple relation of representations, coordinating two or more ideas in a single skill. For example, they can do simple perspective-taking tasks in which they relate their own perspective to that of someone else in order to understand how the two differ; they can also perform simplified versions of many of Piaget's concrete operations tasks, such as conservation and transitivity (Gelman 1978).

The sixth level, concrete operations, emerges at 6 or 7 years. There is strong research evidence to indicate a major change in capacity at this age that fits all six empirical criteria (Inhelder & Piaget 1964 [1959], White 1970, Siegler 1981, Tabor & Kendler 1981, Watson 1981). Children become able to combine multiple representations to form a complex construct, so that they can understand many of the complexities of characteristics of concrete objects and events. In conservation, for example, they can relate the height and width of water in one container to the height and width of water in another container. Despite the consensus about this level among most neostructural theorists, a few hypothesize that concrete operations is not a separate level but a continuation and elaboration of the level of relations of representations (Pascual-Leone 1970, Case 1984).

The seventh level, formal operations (Inhelder & Piaget 1958 [1955]), marks another especially significant transformation: At 10 to 12 years, children develop the capacity to generalize across concrete instances so as to construct abstract generalizations or hypothetical ideas, such as conformity, justice, possibility, and personality (Gruber & Vonéche 1976, Selman 1980, Harter 1983). Neostructuralists agree that this level is not the endpoint of cognitive development but the beginning of a new type of understanding, involving abstract ideas. This new capability underlies further developmental levels, much as the fourth level, representation, lays the basis for the fifth and sixth levels.

The number of levels beyond formal operations is not yet clear, but theory and research suggest at least one additional level emerging at approximately 14 to 16 years. Adolescents become able to relate abstractions or hypothetical ideas, so that they can deal with relational concepts such as liberal and conservative, generate new hypotheses instead of merely testing old ones, and solve the majority of Piaget's formal operations tasks (Martarano 1977, Commons et al 1984). Cognitive growth clearly continues beyond 16 years of age, as individuals become able to deal with complex relations among abstractions (K. Kitchener 1982), but we do not yet know whether these changes meet the criteria of further developmental levels.

Besides the additional levels hypothesized for adolescence and early adulthood, several theorists have hypothesized additional levels at two other points in development. Fischer (1980) has suggested that three levels occur in rapid succession in the first four months of life, before the first sensorimotor level of single actions. Case (1984) and Biggs & Collis (1982) have postulated three additional levels in the early preschool years, between the levels of representations and simple relations of representations.

In summary, under some conditions behavioral development fits all the main empirical criteria for stage. Neostructural theories agree that humans move through at least eight levels between birth and 18 years of age. The six empirical criteria and the eight levels provide guidelines for how and where to look for levels in doing research within a collaborationist framework. Another central need is for guidelines about how and where to investigate variations in stage or level arising from environmental and organismic factors.

EVIDENCE FOR ENVIRONMENTAL AND ORGANISMIC FACTORS AFFECTING LEVELS

One of the best documented facts in developmental research is that people show wide variations in level as a function of both environmental and organismic factors (Feldman 1980, Fischer 1980, Biggs & Collis 1982, Flavell 1982). Unevenness in level, or décalage, is clearly the norm in development. Much of the research documenting unevenness has derived from the mechanistic-functional tradition and has been designed to demonstrate that stages do not exist.

Developmental unevenness, however, does not demonstrate that levels do not exist. Instead, it demonstrates that level varies as a function of many factors besides a stable competence in the organismic-structural sense. A fruitful approach is to seek order in the variation: what factors affect level, and how can they be characterized?

Environment

All the factors traditionally studied within the mechanistic-functional orientation influence developmental level: practice, stimulus, testing procedure, task, and so forth (Gelman 1978, Odom 1978, Fischer & Bullock 1981, Sternberg &

Powell 1983). For example, Jackson and colleagues (1978) used traditional object-permanence tasks to assess the ability of 8–to 12-month-old infants to find a hidden object. The researchers varied practice, type of task, and nature of the object being hidden. All three factors produced significant changes along the developmental scale; for practice and task, the variation amounted to one full sensorimotor level (from the second to the third level in Table 1).

Task difficulty affects performance in a straightforward way. Simplification of tasks on which age norms were initially established allows success at younger ages (Gelman 1978, Flavell 1982). Although claims have sometimes been made that such findings disprove stage theories, they fit easily within a neostructural framework. It can be argued, for example, that variations in the difficulty of a task change the complexity of the skills it requires and therefore change the developmental level it indexes. A simple task for conservation of number can be performed earlier than a more complex one because the two tasks assess different steps in a developmental sequence for conservation of number. Developmental levels arise from the collaboration of the child with the task.

Differences in task content also affect cognitive level. Even when tasks have been designed to assess the same structural accomplishment (e.g. perspective-taking), tasks with different content frequently produce different levels of performance (Ford 1979, Rubin 1973, Higgins & Eccles 1983). For example, a task that assesses how well a subject understands the perspective of someone looking at one side of a complex display is likely to produce a different developmental pattern from one that assesses understanding the perspective of someone in the midst of a social interaction. What seem to be minor differences in content can even influence the order of steps in a developmental sequence. In one study, a task involving circular motion revealed one developmental sequence, while for a task involving linear motion the sequence was reversed (Levin 1985).

There is order in the variations arising from different types of tasks. The individual's particular abilities collaborate with the content and complexity of the task to produce performance. Within the psychometric testing tradition, many models of intelligence represent this collaboration in terms of classes of tasks that produce similar patterns of individual differences (Horn 1976, Sternberg & Powell 1983). In fact, some scholars have argued that different classes of tasks may tap entirely different types of intelligence, which show distinct and independent developmental patterns (Turiel 1977, Keil 1981, Gardner 1983).

Seemingly minor variations in procedure can also substantially affect determination of level. Many of these variations concern the degree of environmental support for high-level performance (Vygotsky 1978, Gollin & Garrison 1980, Fischer & Pipp 1984). For example, in several studies assessing children's understanding of social interaction in pretend play, two slightly different procedures produced vastly different levels of performance (Watson & Fischer 1980, Hand 1981). The procedures differed in degree of support but not in task or content. Under the high-support procedure, children heard a sample story for each step assessed in the developmental sequence. Under the low-support procedure, they were asked to make up stories of their own similar to the ones they had acted out under the high-support procedure.

Elementary-school children were typically able to act out a concrete-operational story in the high-support condition. That is, they could make two dolls simultaneously occupy two intersecting social categories, such as nice and mean. In the low-support procedure, they acted out much less advanced stories. Nine-year-olds typically dropped from the level of concrete operations to the level of simple relations of representations—their performance comparable to that of 4- or 5-year-olds under the high-support procedure.

The potent effect of environmental support on developmental level does not mean that there are no maturational constraints on children's performance. To the contrary, these studies found consistent age differences for each of the two support conditions and for the degree of discrepancy between the two conditions. In another series of studies, Gollin and his colleagues (Gollin & Garrison 1980, and unpublished manuscripts) have found predictable age differences in the effects of environmental supports on preschool children, with specific types of support having an effect only at a specific age. The characteristics of the child collaborate with those of the environment to produce level of performance.

Most of the studies illustrating the effects of task difficulty, content, and environmental support used a developmental scale to represent the variations in level. When studies are designed to include assessment of the variations along a developmental scale, different conditions often move performance forward or backward on the scale (Wolff 1966, Feldman 1980, Prechtl & O'Brien 1982). Such scales are important tools for research within a collaborational framework, because they provide a common means of ordering the effects of both organismic and environmental variations.

Organism

Although environmental influences have received much of the attention in discussions of developmental unevenness, organismic influences appear to be equally important. Factors that characterize individuals have potent effects on developmental level, moving performance up or down a developmental scale in the same way that environmental factors do. Some such individual characteristics, such as arousal state, vary over short periods, while others, such as internalization, ability, and attribution bias, are relatively stable.

In general, organismic and environmental factors interact to produce behavior. Virtually any factor that is classified as organismic from one perspective can be classified as environmental from another, and vice versa. Arousal state, for example, is typically classified as an organismic factor, but arousal is not understandable aside from an arousing context, and the arousing aspects of a context cannot be identified independently of knowledge about the individual. When children encounter a situation that affects them emotionally, their arousal level changes. The arousal level is actually a characteristic of the child-in-a-context. In turn, arousal has an effect on the child's cognitive level in that context, and the cognitive adequacy of his or her understanding influences the experienced nature of the context. In a developmental version of the Yerkes-Dodson law, degree of arousal appears to have a curvilinear relation to developmental level. Children manifest their highest level at an intermediate degree of arousal and lower levels as arousal increases or decreases from that point (Fischer & Elmendorf 1985). This phenomenon has been thoroughly documented for young infants (Wolff 1966, Prechtl & O'Brien 1982), but further investigation is required for children of other ages.

Individual characteristics that are relatively stable also function in collaboration with the environment. In internalization, for example, people subsume information from the environment into their own skills. Mechanistic-functional analyses of internalization often emphasize the environmental information and forget that internalization is a characteristic of a person. People provide environmental support or scaffolding for themselves. Individuals differ both in the degree to which they have internalized a particular task and the degree to which they are skilled at internalization in general (Vygotsky 1978). With greater internalization, people show a smaller gap in level of performance between high- and low-support situations (Belsky et al 1984, Fischer & Pipp 1984).

Skill at internalization is an instance of a more general class of organismic factors that affect development—ability. IQ as measured by standardized tests was originally intended to index the rate of an individual's intellectual development in relation to age-group norms. Much of the variation in ability, then, involves variation along a developmental scale. The extensive research on intelligence tests indicates that individuals vary enormously in both their general facility for test problems and their specific facilities for particular problem types, such as spatial puzzles or verbal analogies (Horn 1976, Sternberg & Powell 1983). Once again, characteristics of the individual work together with characteristics of the environment to produce performance.

A wide range of personality factors influence cognitive level—e.g. motives, anxiety, defenses, emotions, and interpersonal attributions. These factors appear to influence level in contexts such as moral reasoning (Rest 1983), interpersonal understanding (Selman 1980, Fischer & Pipp 1984), and general intellectual functioning (Block 1982). As an example of the importance of a personality variable, children are differently affected by negative evaluations of their intellectual performance. Children in one category called "helpless" by analogy to learned helplessness, do worse after negative evaluations; their effort, expectation of success, and maturity of problem solving all decline (Dweck & Goetz 1978, Boggiano & Ruble 1984). Other children do not manifest this pattern. This difference between children seems to arise from the helpless children's attributions of the failure to their own supposedly poor ability. Thus evaluation, an environmental variable, influences cognitive level more for some children than for others, while helplessness, a personal characteristic, is influential in some situations (those of negative evaluation) but not in others. The fit between child and situation is crucial. Moreover, the nature of this fit can extend beyond immediate effects to produce long-term domain-specific individual differences in cognitive achievement (Dweck & Goetz 1978).

Organismic variables, however, do more than raise or lower cognitive level. Both theory and data force consideration of the possibility that organismic factors, especially emotion and motivation, have potent, differential effects on developmental patterns. By affecting how individuals characteristically think, these factors organize the sequences through which those individuals develop.

INDIVIDUAL DIFFERENCES IN DEVELOPMENTAL SEQUENCES AND OUTCOMES

A direct implication of the evidence for variations in developmental level is that different individuals should show different developmental patterns. If a host of environmental factors produce cognitive variations, then individuals must differ developmentally whenever they encounter systematically diverse environments. Likewise, if a host of organismic factors produce variations, then individuals must differ developmentally whenever they manifest systematic diversity in their organismic characteristics. Environmental and organismic factors are not merely the conditions of performance (as opposed to competence); they are the conditions of development itself.

However, most stage-based research on individual differences asks only two questions, both dictated by organismic-structural epistemology: (a) Do individuals differ in maturity, i.e. do they occupy different stages along a single developmental sequence? (b) Do they differ in the speed of their passage through that sequence? In practice, most studies concern only the first of these questions; manifest differences in cognitive functioning are categorized into prescribed higher or lower stages. The sequence itself is seldom directly tested to determine if the stages indeed develop in the predicted order. Consequently, it is not possible to determine whether individuals move through the sequence at different speeds, or indeed whether they move through it at all (Wohlwill 1973, Feldman 1980, Fischer & Bullock 1981). In a few studies, the sequence is directly tested with methods that provide independent assessments of the various stages or levels (Fischer et al 1984). These methods allow direct measurement of variation in the rate of stage progression. Nevertheless, even then the organismic-structural perspective simply rules out the possibility that manifest differences reflect movement along alternative sequences, and so methods are used that preclude detection of such alternatives.

A framework that conjoins organism and environment holds that people move through different developmental sequences, different series of specific skills. There is neither a fixed organism nor a fixed environment to produce a single, fixed developmental sequence.

It is important to recognize that the concepts of individual differences and universality in developmental sequences are not mutually exclusive (Fischer & Bullock 1984). When behavior is analyzed in highly abstract terms, such as the criteria outlined above for the eight developmental levels, all people may be seen to develop through the same sequence. On the other hand, when behavior is analyzed in terms concrete enough to subsume environmental context and organismic state (without being limited to particular behaviors), then people can be seen to differ in both the content and the number of steps in their developmental sequences.

Few studies have assessed development in a way that allows the direct detection of individual differences. Nevertheless, there is some clear evidence of individual differences in sequences. In the study in which McCall and his colleagues (1977) demonstrated four developmental levels in infant test performance, they also found individual differences in more specific sequences. For example, if a 12-month-old girl was obedient, cooperative, and not highly active, she would most likely show high verbal skills at 24 months; this sequence was not prominent in boys. Individual differences in developmental sequences have also been found repeatedly in language development (Bloom et al 1975). For instance, some children seem to develop their first single words and global sentences at the same time, whereas others develop sentences only after single words (Peters 1977).

The study of such differences requires methods that enable the detection of different sequences. In one of the most powerful and straightforward methods, children are assessed on multiple tasks that can be ordered in different ways. Then scalogram analyses are used to determine empirically what sequences obtain (Krus 1977). To demonstrate a scalogram sequence, children's performances on a series of tasks must fall in an order such that all tasks are passed to a certain point and all are failed beyond that point. One study using this method to assess the development of early reading skills found that a child could show any of three different sequences (Knight 1982). Children who manifested the most common sequence had no serious reading difficulties, but in the other two sequences children demonstrated difficulties in spelling or rhyming.

Literature concerning the roles of emotion and motivation in development provides powerful evidence that development can proceed along diverse paths (Vaillant 1977, Selman 1980, Block 1982, Silvern 1984). A large body of research indicates, for example, that the patterns of emotion in interactions between parent and infant can have potent effects on the course of the child's cognitive development (Sroufe 1979). Abuse of the child by the parents may have an especially potent effect, as suggested by recent research on the rare syndrome of multiple personality, in which the person constructs distinct, mutually incompatible personalities that control consciousness at different times (Bliss 1980, Fischer & Pipp 1984; F. Putnam et al, unpublished data). It seems that most individuals with multiple personality suffered especially severe abuse at an early age. As a result, they developed along a sequence for constructing the self that was very different from the normal self sequence, even though it seems to fit the same developmental levels in the highly abstract terms of neostructural theories.

Studies of psychopathology provide many illustrations that emotional and motivational influences induce important differences in developmental sequences. Sometimes these differences involve variations in relative maturity along a single dimension, as in retardation; but in many cases pathology involves developing differently rather than failing to develop (Block 1982, Fischer & Pipp 1984, Silvern 1984). For example, one popular hypothesis has been that childhood psychopathology, and particularly aggressiveness, arises from general structural immaturities in social perspective-taking or problem-solving. In contrast, collaborational formulations have emphasized that apparent immaturities are specific to contexts in which aggressive or socially isolated children have unusual emotional reactions or atypical goals, or in which they make unusual hostile attributions about others' intentions (Selman 1980, Waterman et al 1981, Dodge 1984). These disturbed children frequently manifest age-appropriate social cognition in situations that do not provoke their peculiar context sensitivity. The crucial developmental questions about these children cannot be answered with a traditional structural analysis that rules out individual differences in context sensitivity.

CONCLUSIONS: BUILDING AN INTEGRATED APPROACH

The research evidence is clear: Many studies have documented that cognitive development demonstrates some stage-like properties and some consistency across domains. Human beings seem to move through at least eight developmental levels between birth and 18 years of age. At the same time, research also shows that environmental and organismic factors have powerful effects on levels, and individual differences in development seem to be common. Different children show different developmental patterns as a function of both environmental and organismic factors. Our conclusion is that both stages and individual differences exist.

Any incompatibility between stages and individual differences arises not from nature but from two incompatible viewpoints—the organismic-structural approach and the mechanistic-functional approach. These approaches place the primary locus of explanation of behavioral change either in the organism or in the environment, although there is some acknowledgment of the importance of both. The major theoretical constructs and the most common research designs focus on variation in either the organism or the environment, not in both.

Many scholars have recognized the difficulty with these incompatible approaches. One of the main attempts to resolve the incompatibility has been to distinguish competence from performance and to hypothesize that stages are associated with the former and individual differences with the latter. While clearly a helpful step toward integrating organism and environment, competence/performance approaches in general suffer from a common shortcoming: They continue to isolate the stages of organismic structure (competence) from directly observable and variable ordinary functioning (performance).

An approach is needed that conjoins organism and environment in its central methods and explanatory constructs. Our favorite metaphors for that conjoining are transaction and collaboration. People transact with their environment or collaborate with it; they work with and affect it, and it works with and affects them.

To move toward such an approach, research designs should routinely incorporate variations in both important organismic variables, such as age, ability, and emotional state, and important environmental variables, such as task, practice, and environmental support. Only such comparative research can reveal the full range of plasticity and constraint arising from cognitive levels and environmental contexts. Also, assessment techniques should be used that allow the detection of individual differences in developmental sequences. Assessment must be sensitive to the possibility that people reason differently, not just more or less maturely.

Theories should build explanatory constructs that simultaneously incorporate organismic and environmental factors. For example, the evidence suggests that behavior in a domain varies along a developmental scale as a result not only of developing capacities but also of other factors, such as environmental support and arousal state. Competence does not seem to be a point but a range or zone on a developmental scale, with both environmental and organismic influences affecting movement within that zone.

With the construction of a collaborational approach, we predict that researchers will finally be able to prove both the organismic-structural approach and the mechanistic-functional one. Under one specified set of assessment conditions, all people will develop through the same set of distinct levels and show high synchrony in the level they manifest across domains. Under another set of assessment conditions, people will develop separate skills in different domains, showing high unevenness across domains, substantial individual differences in their developmental patterns, and no evidence of stage-like change. Of course, the approach that specifies the conditions for these patterns of data will also treat them as merely two patterns from a wide range that includes both levels and individual differences in cognitive development.

ACKNOWLEDGMENTS

We would like to thank Carol Bach, Ann Boggiano, Daniel Bullock, Richard Canfield, and Michael Westerman for their contributions to this article. Preparation of the article was supported by grants from the Carnegie Corporation of New York, the Spencer Foundation, and the University of Colorado Council on Research and Creative Work. The statements made and views expressed are solely the responsibility of the authors.

Literature Cited

Baltes, P. B., Reese, H. W., Lipsitt, L. P. 1980. Life-span developmental psychology. *Ann Rev. Psychol.* 31:65–110

Belsky, J., Rovine, M., Taylor, D. G. 1984. The Pennsylvania Infant and Family Development Project III. The origins of individual differences in infant-mother attachment: Maternal and infant contributions. *Child Dev.* 55:718–28

Bickhard, M. H. 1978. The nature of developmental stages. *Hum. Dev.* 21:217–233

Biggs, J. B., Collis, K. F. 1982. *Evaluating the Quality of Learning.* New York: Academic

Bliss, E. L. 1980. Multiple personalities. *Arch. Gen. Psychiatry* 37:1388–97

Block, J. 1982. Assimilation, accommodation, and the dynamics of personality development. *Child Dev.* 53:281–95

Bloom, L., Lightbown, P., Hood, L. 1975. Structure and variation in child language. *Monogr. Soc. Res. Child Dev.* 40(2, Ser. No. 160). 97 pp.

Boggiano, A. K., Ruble, D. N. 1984. Children's reactions to evaluative feedback. In *The Self in Anxiety, Stress, and Depression,* ed. R. Schwarzer. Hillsdale, NJ: Erlbaum. In press

Broughton, J. M. 1981. Piaget's structural developmental psychology. V. Ideology-critique and the possibility of a critical developmental theory. *Hum. Dev.* 24:382–411

Bruner, J. S. 1982. The organization of action and the nature of adult-infant transaction. In *The Analysis of Action,* ed. M. Cranach, R. Harre, pp. 313–27. New York: Cambridge Univ. Press

Bullock, D. 1981. On the current and potential scope of generative theories of cognitive development. *New Dir. Child Dev.* 12:93–109

Bullock, D. 1983. Seeking relations between cognitive and social-interactive transitions. *New Dir. Child Dev.* 21:97–108

Cairns, R. B., Green, J. A., MacCombie, D. J. 1980. The dynamics of social development. In *Early Experiences and Early Behavior,* ed. E. C. Simmel, pp. 79–106. New York: Academic

Campos, J. J., Hiatt, S., Ramsay, D., Henderson, C., Svejda, M. 1978. The emergence of fear on the visual cliff. In *The Origins of Affect,* ed. M. Lewis, L. Rosenblum, pp. 149–82. New York: Wiley

Case, R. 1984. *Intellectual Development: A Systematic Reinterpretation.* New York: Academic. In press

Catania, A. C. 1973. The psychologies of structure, function, and development. *Am. Psychol.* 28:434–43

Chandler, M. J. 1977. Social cognition: A selective review of current research. In *Knowledge and Development,* ed. W. F.

Overton, J. M. Gallagher, 1:93–147. New York: Plenum

Chess, S., Thomas, A. 1983. Dynamics of individual behavioral development. See Levine et al 1983, pp. 158–75

Chomsky, N. 1965. *Aspects of the Theory of Syntax*. Cambridge, Mass: MIT Press

Cole, M., Hood, L., McDermott, R. 1984. *Ecological Invalidity as an Axiom of Experimental Cognitive Psychology*. Cambridge, Mass: Harvard Univ. Press. In press

Cole, M., Traupman, K. 1981. Comparative cognitive research: Learning from a learning disabled child. *Minn. Symp. Child Psychol.* 14:125–54

Commons, M. L., Richards, F. A., Armon, C. eds. 1984. *Beyond Formal Operations*. New York: Praeger

Corrigan, R. 1983. The development of representational skills. *New Dir. Child Dev.* 21:51–64

Crosson, C. W., Robertson-Tchabo, E. A. 1983. Age and preference for complexity among manifestly creative women. *Hum. Dev.* 26:149–55

Dasen, P. ed. 1977. *Piagetian Psychology: Cross-cultural contributions*. New York: Gardner

Dasen, P., Inhelder, B., Lavallee, M., Retschitzki, J. 1978. *Naissance de l'Intelligence chez l'Enfant Baoulé de Côte d'Ivoire*. Berne: Hans Huber

Dodge, K. A. 1984. Attributional bias in aggressive children. In *Advances in Cognitive-Behavioral Research and Therapy*, ed. P. Kendall, Vol. 4. New York: Academic. In press

Dweck, C., Goetz, T. E. 1978. Attributions and learned helplessness. In *New Directions in Attribution Research*, ed. J. H. Harvey, W. Ickes, R. F. Kidd, pp. 157–79. Hillsdale, NJ: Erlbaum

Edwards, C. P. 1983. Moral development in comparative cultural perspective. In *Cultural Perspectives on Child Development*, ed. D. A. Wagner, H. W. Stevenson, pp. 248–79. San Francisco: Freeman

Emde, R., Gaensbauer, T., Harmon, R. 1976. Emotional expression in infancy: A biobehavioral study. *Psychol. Issues* 10(37). 198 pp.

Epstein, H. T. 1974. Phrenoblysis: Special brain and mind growth periods. *Dev. Psychobiol.* 7:207–24

Epstein, H. T. 1978. Growth spurts during brain development: Implications for educational policy and practice. In *Education and the Brain*, ed. J. S. Chall, A. F. Mirsky, pp. 343–70. Chicago: Univ. Chicago Press

Epstein, H. T. 1980. EEG developmental stages. *Dev. Psychobiol.* 13:629–31

Feldman, D. H. 1980. *Beyond Universals in Cognitive Development*. Norwood, NJ: Ablex

Fischer, K. W. 1980. A theory of cognitive development: The control and construction of hierarchies of skills. *Psychol. Rev.* 87:477–531

Fischer, K. W. 1982. Human cognitive development in the first four years. *Behav. Brain Sci.* 5:282–83

Fischer, K. W., Bullock, D. 1981. Patterns of data: Sequence, synchrony, and constraint in cognitive development. *New Dir. Child Dev.* 12:1–20

Fischer, K. W., Bullock, D. 1984. Cognitive development in school-age children: Conclusions and new directions. In *The Elementary School Years: Understanding Development during Middle Childhood*, ed. W. A. Collins, pp. 70–146. Washington DC: Natl. Acad. Press

Fischer, K. W., Elmendorf, D. M. 1985. Becoming a different person: Transformations in personality and social behavior. *Minn. Symp. Child Dev.* 18:In press

Fischer, K. W., Pipp, S. L. 1984. Development of the structures of unconscious thought. In *The Unconscious Reconsidered*, ed. K. Bowers, D. Meichenbaum, pp. 88–148. New York: Wiley

Fischer, K. W., Pipp, S. L., Bullock, D. 1984. Detecting discontinuities in development: Method and measurement. In *Continuities and Discontinuities in Development*, ed. R. N. Emde, R. Harmon, pp. 95–121. Norwood, NJ: Ablex

Flavell, J. H. 1982. On cognitive development. *Child Dev.* 53:1–10

Flavell, J. H., Markman, E. M., eds. 1983. *Cognitive Development*, Vol. 3, *Handbook of Child Psychology*, ed. P. H. Mussen. New York: Wiley

Flavell, J. H., Wohlwill, J. F. 1969. Formal and functional aspects of cognitive development. In *Studies in Cognitive Development*, ed. D. Elkind, J. H. Flavell, pp. 67–120. London: Oxford Univ. Press

Ford, M. E. 1979. The construct validity of egocentrism. *Psychol. Bull.* 86:1169–88

Gagne, R. M. 1970. *The Conditions of Learning*. New York: Holt, Rinehart & Winston

Gardner, H. 1983. *Frames of Mind: The Theory of Multiple Intelligences*. New York: Basic

Gelman, R. 1978. Cognitive development. *Ann. Rev. Psychol.* 29:297–332

Gelman, R., Baillargeon, R. 1983. A review of some Piagetian concepts. See Flavell & Markman 1983, pp. 167–230

Gilligan, C. 1982. New maps of development: New visions of maturity. *Am. J. Orthopsychiatry* 52:199–212

Gladwin, T. 1970. *East Is a Big Bird: Navigation and Logic in Puluwat Atoll*. Cambridge, Mass: Harvard Univ. Press

Globerson, T. 1985. When do structural

changes underlie stage changes: The case of mental-capacity growth. See I. Levin, In press

Gollin, E. S., ed. 1981a. *Developmental Plasticity: Behavioral and Biological Aspects of Variations in Development.* New York: Academic

Gollin, E. S. 1981b. Development and plasticity. See Gollin 1981a, pp. 231–51

Gollin, E. S. 1984a. Developmental malfunctions: Issues and problems. See Gollin 1984c, pp. 1–25

Gollin, E. S. 1984b. Early experience and developmental plasticity. *Ann. Child Dev.* 1:239–61

Gollin, E. S., ed. 1984c. *Malformations of Development.* New York: Academic

Gollin, E. S., Garrison, A. 1980. Relationships between perceptual and conceptual mediational systems in young children. *J. Exp. Child Psychol.* 30:325–35

Gottlieb, G. 1973. The roles of experience in the development of behavior and the nervous system. In *Neuronal and Behavioral Specificity,* ed. G. Gottlieb. New York: Academic

Gottlieb, G. 1983. The psychobiological approach to developmental issues. See Haith & Campos 1983, pp. 1–26

Gould, S. J. 1977. *Ontogeny and Phylogeny.* Cambridge, Mass: Harvard Univ. Press

Gould, S. J., Lewontin, R. C. 1979. The spandrels of San Marco and the Panglossian paradigm: A critique of the adaptationist programme. In *The Evolution of Adaptation by Natural Selection,* ed. J. Maynard Smith, R. Halliday, pp. 581–98. London: Roy. Soc. London

Greenfield, P. M. 1976. Cross-cultural research and Piagetian theory: Paradox and progress. In *The Developing Individual in a Changing World,* ed. K. F. Riegel, J. A. Meacham, 1:322–33. The Hague: Mouton

Gruber, H., Voneche, J. 1976. Réflexions sur les opérations formelles de la pensée. *Arch. Psychol.* 64(171):45–56

Haith, M. M., Campos, J. J., eds. 1983. *Handbook of Child Psychology,* Vol. 2, *Biology and Infancy,* ed. P. H. Mussen. New York: Wiley

Halford, G. S. 1982. *The Development of Thought.* Hillsdale, NJ: Erlbaum

Hand, H. H. 1981. *The development of concepts of social interaction: Children's understanding of nice and mean.* PhD thesis. Univ. Denver, Denver, Colo. 208 pp.

Harding, R. S., Strum, S. C. 1976. The predatory baboons of Kekosey. *Nat. Hist.* 85(3):46–53

Harris, P. L. 1983. Infant cognition. See Haith & Campos 1983, pp. 689–782

Harter, S. 1983. Developmental perspectives

on the self-system. In *Handbook of Child Psychology,* ed. P. H. Mussen. Vol. 4, *Socialization, Personality, and Social Development.* ed. E. M. Hetherington, pp. 275–385. New York: Wiley

Higgins, E. T., Eccles, J. E. 1983. Social cognition and the social life of the child: Stages in subcultures. In *Social Cognition and Social Behavior,* ed. E. T. Higgins, D. N. Ruble, W. W. Hartup, pp. 15–62. New York: Cambridge Univ. Press

Horn, J. L. 1976. Human abilities: A review of research and theory in the early 1970s. *Ann. Rev. Psychol.* 27:437–86

Inhelder, B., Piaget, J. 1958 [1955]. *The Growth of Logical Thinking from Childhood to Adolescence,* transl. A. Parsons, S. Seagrim. New York: Basic Books

Inhelder, B., Piaget, J. 1964 [1959]. *The Early Growth of Logic in the Child,* transl. G. A. Lunzer, D. Papert. New York: Harper & Row

Jackson, E., Campos, J. J., Fischer, K. W. 1978. The question of decalage between object permanence and person permanence. *Dev. Psychol.* 14:1–10

Jaques, E., Gibson, R. O., Issac, D. J. 1978. *Levels of Abstraction in Logic and Human Action.* London: Heinemann

Kagan, J. 1982. *Psychological Research on the Human Infant: An Evaluative Summary.* New York: Grant Found.

Kaplan, B. 1983. A trio of trials. In *Developmental Psychology: Historical and Philosophical Perspectives,* ed. R. J. Lerner, pp. 185–227. Hillsdale, NJ: Erlbaum

Kaye, K. 1982. *The Social and Mental Life of Babies.* Chicago: Univ. Chicago Press

Keil, F. 1981. Constraints on knowledge and cognitive development. *Psychol. Rev.* 88:197–227

Kenny, S. L. 1983. Developmental discontinuities in childhood and adolescence. *New Dir. Child Dev.* 21:81–96

Kessen, W., Scott, D. 1983. The development of behavior: Problems, theories, and findings. See Levine et al 1983, pp. 27–49

Kitchener, K. S. 1983. Human development and the college campus: Sequences and tasks. *New Dir. Stud. Serv.* 20:17–45

Kitchener, R. 1982. Developmental explanations. *Rev. Metaphys.* 36:791–817

Klahr, D., Wallace, J. G. 1976. *Cognitive Development: An Information Processing View.* Hillsdale, NJ: Erlbaum

Knight, C. C. 1982. *Hierarchical relationships among components of reading abilities of beginning readers.* PhD thesis. Arizona State Univ., Tempe. 192 pp.

Kohlberg, L., Levine, C., Hewer, A. 1983. *Moral Stages: A Current Formulation and a Response to Critics.* New York: Karger

Krus, D. J. 1977. Order analysis: An inferential

model of dimensional analysis and scaling. *Educ. Psychol. Meas.* 37:587–601

Lerner, R. M. 1984. *On the Nature of Human Plasticity.* New York: Cambridge Univ. Press

Levin, I., ed. 1985. *Stage and Structure in Cognitive Development.* Norwood, NJ: Ablex. In press

Martarano, S. C. 1977. A developmental analysis of performance on Piaget's formal operations tasks. *Dev. Psychol.* 13:666–72

McCall, R. 1981. Nature-nurture and the two realms of development. *Child Dev.* 52:1–12

McCall, R. B., Eichorn, D. H., Hogarty, P. S. 1977. Transitions in early mental development. *Monogr. Soc. Res. Child Dev.* 42(3, Ser. No. 171). 108 pp.

McCall, R. B., Meyers, E. D. Jr., Hartman, J., Roche, A. F. 1983. Developmental changes in head-circumference and mental-performance growth rates: A test of Epstein's phrenoblysis hypothesis. *Dev. Psychobiol.* 16:457–68

McQueen, R. 1982. *Brain Growth Periodization: Analysis of the Epstein Spurt-Plateau Findings.* Portland, Ore: Multnomah County Educ. Serv. Dist. Educ. Assoc.

Moore, C. L. 1984. Development of mammalian sexuality. In *The Comparative Development of Adaptive Skills: Evolutionary Implications,* ed. E. S. Gollin. New York: Academic. In press

Movshon, J. A., Van Sluyters, R. C. 1981. Visual neural development. *Ann. Rev. Psychol.* 32:477–522

Mussen, P. H., Eichorn, D. H., Honzik, M. P., Bieber, S. L., Meredith, W. H. 1980. Continuity and change in women's characteristics over four decades. *Int. J. Behav. Dev.* 3:333–48

O'Brien, D. P., Overton, W. F. 1982. Conditional reasoning and the competence-performance issue: A developmental analysis of a training task. *J. Exp. Child Psychol.* 34:274–90

Odom, R. D. 1978. A perceptual-salience account of decalage relations and developmental change. In *Alternatives to Piaget,* ed. L. S. Siegel, C. J. Brainerd, pp. 111–30. New York: Academic

Overton, W. F. 1984. World views and their influence on psychological theory and research: Kuhn-Lakatos-Laudan. In *Advances in Child Development and Behavior,* ed. H. W. Reese. New York: Academic. In press

Overton, W. F., Newman, J. L. 1982. Cognitive development: A competence-activation/utilization approach. In *Review of Human Development,* ed. T. M. Field, A. Huston, J. C. Quay, L. Troll, G. E. Finley, pp. 217–41. New York: Wiley

Pascual-Leone, J. 1970. A mathematical model

for the transition rule in Piaget's developmental stages. *Acta Psychol.* 32:301–45

Peters, A. M. 1977. Language learning strategies: Does the whole equal the sum of the parts? *Language* 53:560–73

Piaget, J. 1952 [1936]. *The Origins of Intelligence in Children,* transl. M. Cook. New York: Int. Univ. Press

Piaget, J. 1957. Logique et équilibre dans les comportements du sujet. *Étud. Épist. Gén.* 2:27–118

Piaget, J. 1970. Piaget's theory. In *Carmichael's Manual of Child Psychology,* ed. P. H. Mussen, 1:703–32. New York: Wiley

Piaget, J. 1971. The theory of stages in cognitive development. In *Measurement and Piaget,* ed. D. R. Green, M. P. Ford, G. B. Flamer, pp. 1–11. New York: McGraw-Hill

Piaget, J. 1975. L'équilibration des structures cognitives: Problème central du développement. *Étud. Épist. Gén.* 33. 188 pp.

Piaget, J., Grize, J. B., Szeminska, A., Vinh Bang. 1968. Epistemologie et psychologie de la fonction. *Étud. Épist. Gén.* 23. 238 pp.

Prechtl, H. F. R., O'Brien, M. J. 1982. Behavioral states of the full-term newborn: The emergence of a concept. In *Psychobiology of the Human Newborn,* ed. P. Stratton, pp. 53–73. New York: Wiley

Reese, H. W., Overton, W. F. 1970. Models of development and theories of development. In *Life-span Developmental Psychology: Research and Theory,* ed. L. R. Goulet, P. B. Baltes, pp. 115–45. New York: Academic

Rest, J. R. 1983. Morality. See Flavell & Markman 1983, pp. 556–629

Rubin, K. H. 1973. Egocentrism in childhood: A unitary construct? *Child Dev.* 44:102–10

Sameroff, A. J., Seifer, R., Zax, M. 1982. Early development of children at risk for emotional disorder. *Monogr. Soc. Res. Child Dev.* 47(7, Ser. No. 199). 82 pp.

Scarr, S., McCartney, K. 1983. How people make their own environments: A theory of genotype–environment effects. *Child Dev.* 54:424–35

Schwartz, B. 1983. *Psychology of Learning and Behavior.* New York: Norton

Seibert, J. M., Hogan, A. E., Mundy, P. C. 1984. Mental age and cognitive stage in young handicapped and at-risk children. *Intelligence* 8:11–29

Selman, R. L. 1980. *The Growth of Interpersonal Understanding.* New York: Academic

Siegler, R. S. 1981. Developmental sequences within and between concepts. *Monogr. Soc. Res. Child Dev.* 46(2, Ser. No. 189). 84 pp.

Silvern, L. E. 1984. Emotional-behavioral disorders: A failure of system functions. See Gollin 1984c, pp. 95–152

Skinner, B. F. 1969. *Contingencies of Reinforcement.* New York: Appleton-Century-Croft

Snarey, J., Kohlberg, L., Noam, G. 1983. Ego development in perspective: Structural stage, functional phase, and cultural age-period models. *Dev. Rev.* 3:303–38

Sroufe, L. A. 1979. Socioemotional development. In *Handbook of Infant Development*, ed. J. D. Osofsky, pp. 462–516. New York: Wiley

Sternberg, R. J., Powell, J. S. 1983. The development of intelligence. See Flavell & Markman 1983, pp. 341–419

Strauss, M. S., Curtis, L. E. 1984. Development of numerical concepts in infancy. In *The Origins of Cognitive Skills,* ed. C. Sophian, pp. 131–55. Hillsdale, NJ: Erlbaum

Super, C. M. 1980. Cognitive development: Looking across at growing up. *New Dir. Child Dev.* 8:59–69

Tabor, L. E., Kendler, T. S. 1981. Testing for developmental continuity or discontinuity: Class inclusion and reversal shifts. *Dev. Rev.* 1:330–43

Thomas, A. 1982. Current trends of developmental theory. *Ann. Prog. Child Psychiatry Child Dev. 1982:*7–45

Toulmin, S. 1981. Epistemology and developmental psychology. See Gollin 1981a, pp. 253–67

Turiel, E. 1977. Distinct conceptual and developmental domains: Social convention and morality. *Neb. Symp. Motiv.* 25:77–116

Uzgiris, I. C. 1976. Organization of sensorimotor intelligence. In *Origins of Intelligence: Infancy and Early Childhood,* ed. M. Lewis, pp. 123–64. New York: Plenum

Uzgiris, I. C., Hunt, J. McV. 1975. *Assessment in Infancy: Ordinal Scales of Psychological Development.* Urbana: Univ. Ill. Press

Vaillant, G. E. 1977. *Adaptation to Life.* Boston: Little, Brown

Vurpillot, E. 1976 [1972]. *The Visual World of the Child,* transl. W. E. C. Gillham. New York: Int. Univ. Press

Vygotsky, L. S. 1978. *Mind in Society: The Development of Higher Psychological Processes.* Cambridge, Mass: Harvard Univ. Press

Wallon, H. 1970. *De l'Acte a la Pensée.* Paris: Flammarion

Waterman, J., Sobesky, W., Silvern, L., Aoki, B., McCauley, M. 1981. Social perspective taking in emotionally disturbed, learning disabled, and normal children. *J. Abnorm. Child Psychol.* 9:133–48

Watson, M. W. 1981. The development of social roles: A sequence of social-cognitive development. *New Dir. Child Dev.* 12:33–42

Watson, M. W., Fischer, K. W. 1980. Development of social roles in elicited and spontaneous behavior during the preschool years. *Dev. Psychol.* 16:483–94

Werner, H. 1948. *Comparative Psychology of Mental Development.* New York: Science Editions

Westerman, M. A., Fischman-Havstad, L. 1982. A pattern-oriented model of caretaker-child interaction, psychopathology, and control. In *Children's Language,* ed. K. E. Nelson, 3:204–46. Hillsdale, NJ: Erlbaum

White, S. H. 1970. Some general outlines of the matrix of developmental changes between five and seven years. *Bull. Orton Soc.* 20:41–57

Wohlwill, J. F. 1973. *The Study of Behavioral Development.* New York: Academic

Wolff, P. H. 1966. The causes, controls, and organization of behavior in the neonate. *Psychol. Issues* 5(17)

Wood, D. J. 1980. Teaching the young child: Some relationships between social interaction, language, and thought. In *The Social Foundations of Language and Thought,* ed. D. R. Olson, pp. 280–96. New York: Norton

Zelazo, P. R., Leonard, E. L. 1983. The dawn of active thought. *New Dir. Child Dev.* 21:37–50

AUTHOR INDEX

(Names appearing in capital letters indicate authors of chapters in this volume.)

SUBJECT INDEX

A

Absenteeism
  and organizational behavior, 575
  and satisfaction, 579
  and stress, 355
Accomplishment
  and sex differences, 73
Accuracy
  relation to confidence
    engineering psychology, 322
Achievement
  and motivation
    studies, 57
  orientation
    and integration, 121
Acoustical axis
  and tone frequency
    in sound localization, 260
Acoustic modality
  and contralateral spatial representation, 270
Acoustic stimuli
  and neural coding
    in sound localization, 258
  upper sound field
    sound localization, 262
Acupuncture
  and hypnosis, 392
Acute depressive disorder
  and stressful events, 534
Adaptation
  and acquisition of familiarity, 9
  effect
    and hypnosis, 399
Adaptiveness
  and motivated strategies, 295
Adaptive systems
  and automation, 336
Adaptive training
  in engineering psychology, 336
Adjustment
  and life crisis studies, 544
Adolescence
  and acquisition of familiarity, 5
  and smoking
    preventive studies, 374
Aerobic exercise
  relation to cardiovascular disease, 363
Affect
  in personality theory, 95-96
Affective response
  control in
    and motivated strategies, 288

Affirmative action programs
  effects of
    and intergroup relations, 229
Age regression
  and hypnosis, 396-97
Aggregation
  and personality theory, 99-100
  principle of
    and trait theory, 86
Aggression
  and animal behavior genetics, 197-99
Aging
  and animal behavior genetics, 186
  and cardiovascular disease, 351
Alarm indicators
  nature of
    and engineering psychology, 326-27
Alcohol consumption
  excessive
    and disease outcomes, 353
Alcoholism
  and animal behavior genetics, 182-83
Allocation
  biases
    intergroup relations, 226
Amnesia
  and hypnosis, 393
Analgesia
  and hypnosis, 392
Androgeny
  as psychological concept, 52
Anger
  in response to frustration
    motivated strategies, 288
  and sex differences
    in social behavior, 60
  in Type A behavior
    relation to disease endpoints, 362
Anorexia
  and eating disorders, 370
Antidromic stimulation
  and postsynaptic cells
    in learning, 468
Anti-poverty movement
  and the educational movement, 116
Anti-Vietnam movement
  and the educational system, 116
Anxiety
  and controllability in acquired motivation, 498
  preoperative
    impact of support on, 546

social
  motivated strategies, 285
  the test-anxious person, 287
Aplysia
  alpha-conditioning in, 437
  and associative learning, 441
  and cellular mechanisms of learning, 420
  gill- and siphon-withdrawal behavior in, 421-22
Appetitive responses
  extinction of
    in acquired motivation, 506
Appraisal
  and organizational behavior, 599
Arbitration
  case studies
    in studies, 132-33
Arousal
  and acquisition of familiarity, 9
  and frustration
    in acquired motivation, 506
Arousal level
  and mental workload, 316
Arousal state
  as environmental influence
    in cognitive development, 638-39
Arrival-time disparity
  and sound localization, 255
Artificial intelligence
  and trait theory, 92
Aspartate
  and cellular mechanisms of learning, 455
Assessment
  personality
    state of the art, 84
  practices in public schools, 129
  techniques
    for physiological workload, 318
Associative learning
  cellular mechanisms in, 429-50
  mechanisms involved in, 478
Associative training
  in cellular mechanisms in learning, 466
  inhibition of PCNs following, 466
Asymptomatic illness
  and motivated strategies, 292
Athletic prowess
  and advertising imaging
    in cigarette smoking, 365
Attachment
  and acquistion of familiarity, 10

CUMULATIVE INDEXES

CONTRIBUTING AUTHORS, VOLUMES 32–36

697

CHAPTER TITLES, VOLUMES 32–36

ORDER FORM

Annual Reviews Inc.

A NONPROFIT SCIENTIFIC PUBLISHER

4139 EL CAMINO WAY • PALO ALTO, CA 94306-9981 • (415) 493-4400

rders for Annual Reviews Inc. publications may be placed through your bookstore; subscription agent; participating professional societies; or directly from Annual Reviews Inc. by mail or telephone (paid by credit card or purchase order). Prices subject to change without notice.

Individuals: Prepayment required in U.S. funds or charged to American Express, MasterCard, or Visa.
Institutional Buyers: Please include purchase order.
Students: Special rates are available to qualified students. Refer to Annual Reviews *Prospectus* or contact Annual Reviews Inc. office for information.
Professional Society Members: Members whose professional societies have a contractural arrangement with Annual Reviews may order books through their society at a special discount. Check with your society for information.

Regular orders: When ordering current or back volumes, please list the volumes you wish by volume number.
Standing orders: (New volume in the series will be sent to you automatically each year upon publication. Cancellation may be made at any time.) Please indicate volume number to begin standing order.
Prepublication orders: Volumes not yet published will be shipped in month and year indicated.
California orders: Add applicable sales tax.
Postage paid (4th class bookrate /surface mail) by Annual Reviews Inc.

ANNUAL REVIEWS SERIES		Prices Postpaid per volume USA/elsewhere	Regular Order Please send:	Standing Order Begin with:
			Vol. number	Vol. number
Annual Review of ANTHROPOLOGY				
Vols. 1-10	(1972-1981)	$20.00/$21.00		
Vol. 11	(1982)	$22.00/$25.00		
Vols. 12-13	(1983-1984)	$27.00/$30.00		
Vol. 14	(avail. Oct. 1985)	$27.00/$30.00	Vol(s). _____	Vol. _____
Annual Review of ASTRONOMY AND ASTROPHYSICS				
Vols. 1-19	(1963-1981)	$20.00/$21.00		
Vol. 20	(1982)	$22.00/$25.00		
Vols. 21-22	(1983-1984)	$44.00/$47.00		
Vol. 23	(avail. Sept. 1985)	$44.00/$47.00	Vol(s). _____	Vol. _____
Annual Review of BIOCHEMISTRY				
Vols. 29-34, 36-50	(1960-1965; 1967-1981)	$21.00/$22.00		
Vol. 51	(1982)	$23.00/$26.00		
Vols. 52-53	(1983-1984)	$29.00/$32.00		
Vol. 54	(avail. July 1985)	$29.00/$32.00	Vol(s). _____	Vol. _____
Annual Review of BIOPHYSICS				
Vols. 1-10	(1972-1981)	$20.00/$21.00		
Vol. 11	(1982)	$22.00/$25.00		
Vols. 12-13	(1983-1984)	$47.00/$50.00		
Vol. 14	(avail. June 1985)	$47.00/$50.00	Vol(s). _____	Vol. _____
Annual Review of CELL BIOLOGY				
Vol. 1	(avail. Nov. 1985)	est. $27.00/$30.00	Vol. _____	Vol. _____
Annual Review of EARTH AND PLANETARY SCIENCES				
Vols. 1-9	(1973-1981)	$20.00/$21.00		
Vol. 10	(1982)	$22.00/$25.00		
Vols. 11-12	(1983-1984)	$44.00/$47.00		
Vol. 13	(avail. May 1985)	$44.00/$47.00	Vol(s). _____	Vol. _____
Annual Review of ECOLOGY AND SYSTEMATICS				
Vols. 1-12	(1970-1981)	$20.00/$21.00		
Vol. 13	(1982)	$22.00/$25.00		
Vols. 14-15	(1983-1984)	$27.00/$30.00		
Vol. 16	(avail. Nov. 1985)	$27.00/$30.00	Vol(s). _____	Vol. _____

1

Annual Review of ENERGY

Vols. 1-6	(1976-1981)	$20.00/$21.00		
Vol. 7	(1982)	$22.00/$25.00		
Vols. 8-9	(1983-1984)	$56.00/$59.00		
Vol. 10	(avail. Oct. 1985)	$56.00/$59.00	Vol(s). _____	Vol. _____

Annual Review of ENTOMOLOGY

Vols. 8-16, 18-26	(1963-1971; 1973-1981)	$20.00/$21.00		
Vol. 27	(1982)	$22.00/$25.00		
Vols. 28-29	(1983-1984)	$27.00/$30.00		
Vol. 30	(avail. Jan. 1985)	$27.00/$30.00	Vol(s). _____	Vol. _____

Annual Review of FLUID MECHANICS

Vols. 1-5, 7-13	(1969-1973; 1975-1981)	$20.00/$21.00		
Vol. 14	(1982)	$22.00/$25.00		
Vols. 15-16	(1983-1984)	$28.00/$31.00		
Vol. 17	(avail. Jan. 1985)	$28.00/$31.00	Vol(s). _____	Vol. _____

Annual Review of GENETICS

Vols. 1-15	(1967-1981)	$20.00/$21.00		
Vol. 16	(1982)	$22.00/$25.00		
Vols. 17-18	(1983-1984)	$27.00/$30.00		
Vol. 19	(avail. Dec. 1985)	$27.00/$30.00	Vol(s). _____	Vol. _____

Annual Review of IMMUNOLOGY

Vols. 1-2	(1983-1984)	$27.00/$30.00		
Vol. 3	(avail. April 1985)	$27.00/$30.00	Vol(s). _____	Vol. _____

Annual Review of MATERIALS SCIENCE

Vols. 1-11	(1971-1981)	$20.00/$21.00		
Vol. 12	(1982)	$22.00/$25.00		
Vols. 13-14	(1983-1984)	$64.00/$67.00		
Vol. 15	(avail. Aug. 1985)	$64.00/$67.00	Vol(s). _____	Vol. _____

Annual Review of MEDICINE: Selected Topics in the Clinical Sciences

Vols. 1-3, 5-15	(1950-1952; 1954-1964)	$20.00/$21.00		
Vols. 17-32	(1966-1981)	$20.00/$21.00		
Vol. 33	(1982)	$22.00/$25.00		
Vols. 34-35	(1983-1984)	$27.00/$30.00		
Vol. 36	(avail. April 1985)	$27.00/$30.00	Vol(s). _____	Vol. _____

Annual Review of MICROBIOLOGY

Vols. 17-35	(1963-1981)	$20.00/$21.00		
Vol. 36	(1982)	$22.00/$25.00		
Vols. 37-38	(1983-1984)	$27.00/$30.00		
Vol. 39	(avail. Oct. 1985)	$27.00/$30.00	Vol(s). _____	Vol. _____

Annual Review of NEUROSCIENCE

Vols. 1-4	(1978-1981)	$20.00/$21.00		
Vol. 5	(1982)	$22.00/$25.00		
Vols. 6-7	(1983-1984)	$27.00/$30.00		
Vol. 8	(avail. March 1985)	$27.00/$30.00	Vol(s). _____	Vol. _____

Annual Review of NUCLEAR AND PARTICLE SCIENCE

Vols. 12-31	(1962-1981)	$22.50/$23.50		
Vol. 32	(1982)	$25.00/$28.00		
Vols. 33-34	(1983-1984)	$30.00/$33.00		
Vol. 35	(avail. Dec. 1985)	$30.00/$33.00	Vol(s). _____	Vol. _____

SEE ORDERING INFORMATION ON PAGE 4